THE COLUMBIA
DOCUMENTARY HISTORY
OF RACE AND ETHNICITY
IN AMERICA

# THE COLUMBIA DOCUMENTARY HISTORY OF RACE AND ETHNICITY IN AMERICA

*Edited by*
RONALD H. BAYOR

COLUMBIA UNIVERSITY PRESS
*New York*

COLUMBIA UNIVERSITY PRESS

Publishers Since 1893

New York   Chichester, West Sussex

Copyright © 2004 Columbia University Press
All rights reserved

Library of Congress Cataloging-in-Publication
Data

The Columbia documentary history of race and
ethnicity in America / edited by Ronald H.
Bayor.

   p.   cm.

  Includes bibliographical references (p.) and
index.

  ISBN 0-231-11994-1 (alk. paper)

   1. United States—Race relations—
History—Sources   2. United States—Ethnic
relations—History—Sources.   I. Bayor,
Ronald H., 1944–

E184.A1C57 2004

305.8′00973—dc22

2003067412

♾

Columbia University Press books are printed on
permanent and durable acid-free paper.

Printed in the United States of America

c 10 9 8 7 6 5 4 3 2 1

Columbia University Press gratefully
acknowledges permission to reprint from the
following previously printed material:

Molefi Kete Asante, excerpts from *The Afrocentric
Idea*. Copyright © 1987 by Temple University.
Reprinted with the permission of Temple Uni-
versity Press. All rights reserved.

Excerpt from *Travels by His Highness Duke Bernard
of Saxe-Weimar-Eisenach Through North America in
the Years 1825 and 1826*, translated by William
Jeronimus, edited by C. J. Jeronimus. Copyright © 2001. Reprinted with the permission
of University Press of America.

Black Panther Party, "Platform and Program of
the Black Panther Party" (October 1966). Reprinted with the permission of Frederika Newton and the Dr. Huey P. Newton Foundation.

Franz Boas, excerpts from "The Question of Racial Purity" from *The American Mercury* (October
1924): 163–169. Reprinted with the permission of Dr. Norman F. Boas.

Patrick J. Buchanan, "West's Doors Closing?"
(Speech, June 7, 1993), from http://www.
buchanan.org/pa-93-0607.html. Copyright ©
1993 by Patrick J. Buchanan. Reprinted with
the permission of the author.

Stokely Carmichael and Charles V. Hamilton, excerpt from *Blackpower: The Politics of Liberation in
America*. Copyright © 1965 by Stokely Carmichael and Charles V. Hamilton. Reprinted with
the permission of Random House, Inc.

Stephanie Chavez, "Touched by Fire; A Legacy of
Pain and Hope" from *Los Angeles Times* (Novem-
ber 16, 1992). Copyright © 1992 The Times
Mirror Company. Reprinted with permission.

Nicolas Collin, "Extract of the Most Noteworthy
Transactions during My Incumbency as Rector
at the Raccoon and Pensneck Congregations,
from September 30, 1773" from *The Journal and
Biography of Nicholas Collin, 1746–1831*, translated by Amandus Johnson. Copyright 1936 by
Amandus Johnson. Reprinted with permission.

*(Continued on page 993)*

*In Loving Memory of my wife, Leslie*

# CONTENTS

CHAPTER 2.
ETHNICITY IN EIGHTEENTH-
CENTURY NORTH AMERICA,
1701–1788
GRAHAM RUSSELL HODGES
89

DOCUMENTS

## CHAPTER 4.
## RACIAL AND ETHNIC IDENTITY IN THE UNITED STATES, 1837–1877
### MICHAEL MILLER TOPP

## DOCUMENTS

CHAPTER 5.
RACE, NATION, AND
CITIZENSHIP IN LATE
NINETEENTH-CENTURY
AMERICA, 1878–1900
MAE M. NGAI

CHAPTER 6.
THE CRITICAL PERIOD:
ETHNIC EMERGENCE AND
REACTION, 1901–1929
ANDREW R. HEINZE
413

CHAPTER 7.
CHANGING RACIAL MEANINGS: RACE AND ETHNICITY IN THE UNITED STATES, 1930–1964
THOMAS A. GUGLIELMO AND EARL LEWIS
599

DOCUMENTS

CHAPTER 8.
RACIAL AND ETHNIC
RELATIONS IN AMERICA,
1965–2000
TIMOTHY J. MEAGHER
667


DOCUMENTS

# INTRODUCTION

"I THOUGHT TO WRITE A HISTORY of the immigrants in America. Then I discovered that the immigrants were American history." Historian Oscar Handlin's words convey some of the inspiration behind this book. To understand the development and complexity of contemporary American society, it is important to know the history of immigration, race, and ethnicity. Voluntary and involuntary immigrants; different races, religions, and linguistic groups; conflicting nationalities; the development of a sense of ethnicity; initial interaction with Native Americans; the emergence of a dominant culture all shaped an American identity and society.

This book, then, seeks to explore that shaping, to get a sense of how the peopling of America took place. Written as a general history using race and ethnicity as its primary focus, this study is also intended as a primary research resource for students of this subject. It is divided into eight chronological chapters covering the following periods: 1600–1700, 1701–1788, 1789–1836, 1837–1877, 1878–1900, 1901–1929, 1930–1964, 1965–2000. Although any chronological division would present some problems in regard to overlap for some group histories, these dates were chosen with the intention of highlighting certain events and issues that are pertinent to an ethnic and racial history while avoiding repetition as much as possible. For example, 1965 marks the passage of a new immigration act that reversed earlier laws based on national-origins quotas; 1901–1929 covers the period of large-scale Eastern and Southern European migration, the main immigration restriction laws, southern African American migration north, and the rise of the Ku Klux Klan; 1837–1877 is the time of substantial Irish and German migration, expansion into Mexican territory, Civil War and Reconstruction, and the removal of the Cherokees on their "Trail of Tears."

Authors in these chapters were asked to write essays that would bring together the history of racial and ethnic groups and discuss the variety of experiences with migration, intergroup relations, nativism and racism, identity formation, etc., among a number of groups in different locales. Another focus of each essay was American society's views on immigration, race, and ethnicity during that period and what changes were evident. Each author was also asked to provide a number of primary source documents that further illuminate the topics and era under study. These documents form a crucial part of the book, for they allow students to read firsthand the formative written historical record. Documents are drawn from a variety of sources and include, for example, the 1655 petition of Jewish merchants to the West India Company regarding the admission of Jews to the colony of New Netherlands; an 1819 play that illustrates

the discussion over Indian assimilation; an 1855 letter from a German immigrant to his relatives in the Old World; an 1897 court case regarding the "whiteness" of Mexicans in the United States; W. E. B. DuBois's 1903 essay challenging Booker T. Washington's accommodationist approach; an excerpt from Italian-American educator Leonard Covello's 1958 memoir on educating immigrant children; letters form the 1909 *Jewish Daily Forward*; an interview with a Chinese American worker regarding a 1938 strike in San Francisco; the 1966 platform of the Black Panther party; excerpts from the 1978 Supreme Court decision in *Bakke* v. *California* regarding affirmative action; and excerpts from a 1997 town meeting for the Commission on Race.

The authors of this volume ably wrote the essays, selected the documents, and thereby provided a comprehensive effort to merge immigration and racial and ethnic history into one narrative. They were given some leeway on what they chose to emphasize in their narratives, but each provided an effective analysis of the main immigration, racial, and ethnic events and issues of their period. As with any book that encompasses the work of multiple authors, the emphasis and writing style in each is slightly different, depending on the focus of the author. The essays range from a narrative to a more theory-based work, and some stress foreign policy or culture more than others. However, certain themes stand out in all that together define American society: diversity, Americanization, ethnicization, the predominance of race as a national obsession, and the development of a sense of whiteness among European Americans. This last point is particularly revealing, since the people in each group came with their own national or regional identities. Many of these people were vilified for their old-world traits yet eventually found commonality and protection in their whiteness. How this transpired and what it says about the development of American life is one of the important concerns of this book.

The essays that follow weave together the various strands of the American story. Carol Berkin (1600–1700) relates the contact between colonists and Indians and the effect each had on the other; intra-European rivalries for land and power; the multiculturalism evident early on in places such as New Amsterdam as English, Dutch, Danes, Norwegians, Africans, French, Germans, Jews, and Muslims intermingled; and the beginning of slavery. In the next essay, Graham Hodges (1701–1788) continues the themes raised in the earlier essay, discussing the relations between Indians, the English, and the French as well as interethnic/religious rivalries, but he extends his narrative to include Spanish colonists in New Spain in the present-day western United States. Slavery was by then a secure fixture in the colonies, although slave revolts occurred. Virginia's slave population soared from approximately 26,000 in 1730 to about 100,000 in 1750 and to more than 287,000 in 1790. The American Revolution's impact on ethnicity and race relations is noted as well.

Marion Casey's chapter (1789–1836) carries the story through the Jackson administration and thus deals with America's expansion westward, the Alien and Sedition acts, anti-Catholicism and nativism, attitudes toward slavery and African Americans, ethnic colonization efforts, and Indian removal and reservation policies.

The absorption of new groups through expansion (Mexicans) and large-scale immigration (Irish, Germans, and Chinese), as well as the topics of slavery, abolitionism, the Civil War, Reconstruction, and the Indian Wars are the hallmarks of Michael Topp's chapter (1837–1877). In this era, nativism reached a high point and focused its wrath on the Irish and Chinese. The 1875 Page Law set the precedent for the soon-to-be-passed Chinese Exclusion Act. Who the excluded or included groups were took on sharper focus as nativist and racist activities increased.

Mae Ngai (1878–1900) takes us into the beginnings of Southern and Eastern European immigration as hundreds of thousands of Jews, Italians, and others left their *shtetl*, village, and city to come to America. A mass migration to America from small towns in Galicia and Sicily and from such cities as Bialystok and Naples occurred. Jim Crow laws, designed to institutionalize segregation, were passed throughout the South, and the *Plessy* v. *Ferguson* case established the separate but equal doctrine. Assimilation, cultural subordination, and the acceptance of "scientific" race theories affected the treatment of all minorities, whether black, Mexican, Indian, Chinese, or Southern and Eastern European. This factor was especially evident as the United States dealt with the territories gained after the Spanish-American War.

During Andrew Heinze's period

(1901–1929) the foreign-born population increased to the highest level in the history of the country, representing 14.7 percent of the American people in 1910. U.S. cities reflected what was happening nationally: by 1910, New York's inhabitants were 41 percent foreign born; Chicago, 36 percent; San Francisco, 34 percent. Furthermore, a large migration of southern blacks to the North occurred. Reaction to the immigrant increase took the form of immigration-restriction laws, which culminated in the National Origins Act of 1924. During these decades there was considerable discussion of maintaining the country's racial balance and preventing the newer groups from controlling America's future. A sense of superior and inferior races continued to dominate the public consciousness. In addition to immigration-restriction laws, race riots revealed the public's hostile reaction to the changing demographics. In these riots, whites attacked blacks throughout a city, in black and white neighborhoods alike. Atlanta's 1906 riot reflected continued hostility toward southern African Americans, but riots became a national, not just a southern event, taking place in Springfield, Illinois (1908); Chicago (1919); and elsewhere in the nation. The revival of the Ku Klux Klan in 1915, with its attacks on blacks, Jews, Catholics, and the foreign-born, further illustrated the tensions during this period. This was also the era of Sacco-Vanzetti, Henry Ford's anti-Semitic publications, and the anti-Catholicism evoked by Al Smith's campaign for president.

Thomas Guglielmo and Earl Lewis focus their chapter (1930–1964) on the issue of racial identity and whiteness. Picking up on discussions in earlier chapters of scientific race theories, and continuing on to look at changing racial identities as well, the authors analyze how various Americans came to terms with shifting racial definitions. While the immigrants of European origin and their descendants began to coalesce within the white racial category and thereby benefited from America's color line, blacks and others fought the social and political implications of their designations. World War II and the struggle against Nazism's racist hatred was an important factor in eventually helping to transform America's racial structure, although during the war the incarceration of Japanese Americans revealed the extent to which excluded groups could be mistreated. Following the war, African Americans took the lead in confronting racial discrimination and pushed southern governments, through various court cases and mass on-the-street protests, to dismantle the segregation system. The end of this era brought the Civil Rights Act of 1964 and the soon-to-be-passed (1965) Voting Rights Act and Immigration Act.

In the concluding chapter (1965–2000), Timothy Meagher takes the story to the end of the twentieth century. He notes that during these thirty-five years "a new structure of thinking about ethnicity and race . . . emerged." Meagher moves us through the civil rights movement, Malcolm X's influence, Black Power, and the urban race riots of the 1960s. Largely inspired by the movement for black equality, Native Americans, Latinos, and Asian Americans responded with similar efforts to transform the American racial and ethnic political and cultural landscape.

"Red Power" protests led to recognition from the federal government in the form of favorable legislation such as the Indian Child Welfare Act of 1978. It also increased pride in Indian culture. "Brown Power" reflected the Latino efforts in regard to politics, cultural pride, and self-assertion. Mexican Americans, Puerto Ricans, Cuban Americans, and other Spanish-speaking groups pushed for their political and civil rights and for a pan-Hispanic identity. Asian Americans came together in a new pan-Asian movement during this time as well. As with the other groups, Asian Americans sought their civil rights, political empowerment, and cultural identity. "Yellow Power" became their slogan. Even white ethnics were drawn into the new focus and became part of an ethnic revival.

Changes in the immigration laws in 1965 and after resulted in an increasing number of immigrants from Asian and Latino nations as well as black Caribbean countries. This migration, and the ethnic movements triggered by the African American struggle for equality, began changing not only U.S. demographics but the power structure and conceptions of race and ethnicity. Meagher concludes by analyzing the significance of a "white ethnic" identity, multiculturalism, ongoing conflicts involving minorities, and the continued racial divide.

Readers will come away from this book with a clearer sense of the important role that immigration, race, and ethnicity have played in national events and development. The essays and documents can help clarify who the American people are and what has shaped their identity and society. This is an ongoing story as the country continues to receive immigrants, discusses the incorporation of newcomers, debates the continuing role of race, and watches as ethnicization ebbs and flows. The complexity of this story is reflected in the differing opinions of the authors in regard to, for example, when a sense of whiteness began to develop, how persistent the ethnic divisions among European immigrant groups were, and whether those divisions are still relevant.

Readers are urged to go beyond the essays—to consider the documents and suggested publications in order to reach their own conclusions about these and other questions related to America's ethnic and racial history.

# ACKNOWLEDGMENTS

My thanks go first and foremost to James Warren, executive editor of Columbia University Press. He initially proposed this project to me and has offered consistent encouragement throughout its development.

The contributing authors deserve special thanks as well for their good work. They were amenable to revisions and considerate of time constraints and generally made my job as editor much easier.

LaDonna Bowen provided her usual excellent help in preparing the manuscript for the press, and I thank her for the close and valuable attention she paid to the project. Enid Pearsons as copyeditor improved the book considerably, and I appreciate her effort. My thanks go as well to Ronald Harris of the press, who supervised the publication of this documents book, and to Susan Heath, who carefully read over the documents for errors.

My thanks go also to Jill, Robin, David, Ellie, and Logan for lifting my spirits and thereby helping me to finish this work during a particularly difficult time for all of us.

THE COLUMBIA

DOCUMENTARY HISTORY

OF RACE AND ETHNICITY

IN AMERICA

# CHAPTER 1
# ETHNICITY IN
# SEVENTEENTH-CENTURY
# ENGLISH AMERICA,
# 1600–1700

## CAROL BERKIN

THE ENGLISH COLONIES OF THE seventeenth century were notable for their diversity of population, religious institutions, and government structures, a diversity arising in large part from the variety of purposes and methods that spurred their creation. Unlike the Spanish and French governments, the English Crown steadfastly refused to finance colonization, relying instead on private citizens to take the risks involved in establishing outposts in the Americas. The Crown was willing to grant charters to companies and bestow huge tracts of land on favorites in the Court, but it was not willing to deplete the royal treasury or provide military support for colonization. Few private citizens rose to the challenge in the sixteenth century, for the dismal failure of Sir Walter Raleigh's efforts at Roanoke Island, and Raleigh's resulting bankruptcy dampened even the most patriotic zeal.

Dreams of an American empire did not entirely vanish, however. Indeed, they were enthusiastically revived in the early seventeenth century as English entrepreneurs learned to employ the principles of the joint-stock company to diminish individual risks. The Virginia Company's success in planting the

Jamestown settlement in 1607, coupled with the Stuart kings' largesse in land grants, resulted in the creation of proprietary colonies, such as Maryland, Carolina, and Pennsylvania, and colonies chartered to joint-stock companies, such as Massachusetts. But what the Crown saved in expenses it lost in the ability to establish uniformity. Each proprietor or joint-stock company could declare its own purposes and goals and establish its own institutions and regulations as long as they did not run contrary to the laws, trade regulations, and diplomatic policies of England. By the end of the century, the crescent of colonies that hugged the Atlantic Ocean on the North American mainland reflected the variety of motives and methods of their founders: some colonies had been established by religious sects seeking refuge, others came into existence for profit, and still others emerged as offshoots from older communities, created by land-hungry settlers or exiled religious deviants.

The State's refusal to be responsible for the founding of the colonies also meant that key institutions were weak, or absent, in the formal and informal development of these communities. For example, the absence of Anglican church control or organized missionary activity contrasted sharply with the role the Catholic church played in both the French and Spanish colonial world. There was a noticeable lack of uniformity of religious practices, governmental structures, or Indian and land policies, and clearly there was no grand design for settlement. When, late in the century, the king attempted to rationalize and centralize the mainland empire,

his efforts met with considerable resistance. The Dominion of New England, which united the colonies of New England, New York, and New Jersey under one governor, was the first American casualty of the Glorious Revolution. Before the debacle of the Dominion—and for several decades after—the English colonies continued to evolve in highly individualistic ways.

Regional distinctions did emerge, however, not only in economies and labor systems, but in patterns of ethnic and racial diversity. All regions were biracial in the early seventeenth century, for Indian populations remained within the borders of each colony. By the end of the century, small concentrations of African servants and slaves suggested a new pattern of triracial colonies, especially in the Chesapeake and Lower South. Throughout the century, the New England colonies remained ethnically more homogeneous than other regions. Massachusetts, for example, openly discouraged and even outlawed non-Puritan settlers, although by the end of the century, its transformation into a royal colony opened up settlement to Anglicans as well. The shortage of available land in New England, already a problem by the end of the century, would discourage the waves of immigrants from Ireland and Germany that would fill the backcountries of the middle and southern colonies in the next century. To the south, the Chesapeake was largely an English society, but one marked by the presence of Catholics as well as Protestants and by small communities of radical dissenting sects. The Lower South, still in its early phases of settlement in 1700, would not see its influx of Scots-Irish, Irish, and German settlers until the middle decades of the eighteenth century. The Middle Colonies of New York, New Jersey, Delaware, and Pennsylvania were, by comparison, notably heterogeneous, in part because of the non-English origins of the first three and in part because of liberal immigration or land policies that did not discriminate based on religion or national origins. Thus, in the seventeenth century, the ethnic diversity of the middle colonies was the most striking regional anomaly.

## ENGLISH COLONISTS AND INDIANS

Conquest, conflict, migration, and acculturation were historical realities among the peoples East of the Mississippi long before the arrival of European and English colonists. Indeed, the social and political map of Native American societies was no more static or stable than the map of Europe in the sixteenth and seventeenth centuries. In the Northeast, two massive alliances had, for centuries, shaped the realities of political and cultural life among local communities, pitting the Hurons, Algonquins, Abenakis, Micmacs, Ottawas, and several smaller tribes against the powerful Iroquois Confederacy that was based in New York. In what the English would call Virginia, a confederation of Algonquian-speaking tribes known as the Powhatans dominated local cultures, commanding tribute and military loyalties from a widening circle of villages. By the time John Smith arrived in Jamestown, the Pow-

hatan had forced into its political sphere of control some thirty different Indian peoples. To the south, descendants of Siouan-speaking migrants, who had journeyed over the mountains centuries before Columbus journeyed to the Americas, created communities linked by a common culture but politically independent of one another. Like the Hurons to the north or the subjects of the Powhatans in the Chesapeake, these Siouan descendants had long experience with the aggression of would be conquerors, for Mississippians, intent on seizing territory and compelling political submission, had followed the Siouan groups eastward. Viewed from a global perspective, Europe and North America seemed to be experiencing similar patterns in the sixteenth and seventeenth centuries: shifting boundaries, migration prompted by aggression or by flight from aggression, refugee societies regrouping, and acculturation to the communities that gave them safe haven or to those who conquered them. For the Finns, for the Walloons, for the Irish, the tales of cultural conflict told by the Huron, the Mannahoacs, and the Stuckanocks would be familiar ones.

Many decades before English adventurers and their servants came to Jamestown or Separatist pilgrims arrived at Plymouth, Native Americans had felt the devastation that contact with Europeans would bring to their world. Not the sword, but disease proved the most effective weapon of destruction: an epidemiological disaster of immeasurable proportions swept away Native populations, as smallpox, measles, and other illnesses to which Indians enjoyed no immunities traveled rapidly throughout the Americas following contact with the Europeans. Historians now estimate that millions of Indians died in the centuries before English settlement began.

This catastrophic "exchange" between Europeans and Indians might best be personalized in the life of Squanto, the Wampanoag Indian who befriended the radical Separatist sect known as the Pilgrims and negotiated the treaty with his tribe that insured the survival of their refugee English community at Plymouth in the 1620s. Several years before the Pilgrims set sail for America aboard the *Mayflower,* Squanto had been taken prisoner by English fishermen sailing the coast of Massachusetts. He remained in English society, learning the language and absorbing the culture, for some three years before returning to his homeland. Here he discovered that his exile had protected him from an epidemic that destroyed his entire village at Patuxet. This outbreak had reached far beyond Patuxet, of course; of the twenty thousand Wampanoag Indians of Massachusetts, fewer than 10 percent remained when Squanto returned to America. Ironically, the Pilgrims' settlement of Plymouth was built upon the remains of Squanto's Patuxet.

Despite the devastation wrought by disease, the Indian societies of the Eastern coast did not immediately fall under the control of the European colonizers. Indeed, as historians now understand, negotiation and compromise marked the earliest years of contact between French, Dutch, and English authorities and the local Indians. A "middle ground," a cul-

tural space contributed to by both Indian and white colonists, emerged, allowing the two worlds some possibility of understanding and cooperation. Although each society was interpreted through the prism of the observing culture, some genuine communication was nevertheless made possible; on the middle ground, a compromise of language, belief systems, political structures, and patterns of physical and emotional intimacy evolved. If the French were more flexible than the English or Dutch, even these more ethnocentric nationals made efforts to engage in commercial exchange, political alliance, and social interaction throughout the century.

The English brought to the "middle ground" a firm sense of their cultural superiority. Their assumptions about Indians varied greatly, with some seventeenth-century observers recording glowing accounts of the nobility and simplicity of tribal life and others detailing the heathen savagery of the indigenous population. The romantic notion of the "Noble Savage" thus existed side by side with the contemptuous judgment that Indians were uncivilized, without religion or culture. The assumed character of the Indian often depended on the English colonists' vision of themselves. Thus, among the Puritan colonists, who saw the hand of God directing their settlement, Indians appeared as Satanic obstacles to their mission rather than as proper objects for missionary zeal. The Quaker founders of Pennsylvania, committed to a belief that all people shared God's grace, demonstrated their religious convictions by efforts to treat Native Americans in an egalitarian fashion. In both cases, the prism through which the Indian was seen was self-referential.

No matter what their assumptions or stereotypes, most of the early settlers recognized that their survival depended upon a basic exchange of supplies and knowledge with local Indians. In Jamestown to the south and Plymouth to the north, the willingness of Native Americans to share corn and other foodstuffs as well as information on how to grow these crops made the difference between starvation and sustenance in the early years. In New Netherland, and later in New York, a thriving trade in beaver pelts and other furs secured most of the profits that Europeans wrested from their Hudson River colony. And, in alliances formed with Indian tribes, the English and Dutch found the safety from hostile attack by European rivals and their Indian allies critical to their communities' survival. To varying degrees, Indians who negotiated the "middle ground" acquired the fruits of European technology: weapons, iron and copper utensils, and woolens. Exchanges of a less concrete or tangible nature altered both white and Indian life as new theologies, modes of production, notions of property, and ideas of social organization passed between colonists and natives.

The creation of the middle ground did not, however, insure peace between Native Americans and European colonists. In the English colonies in particular, the settlers' relentless expansionist impulse eventually brought them into conflict with local Indians. As English populations grew, the willingness to negotiate and compromise diminished. Even when disputes arose between English communities, nearby Indians were likely to suffer the consequences. For example, in New England in the late 1630s, an intense rivalry between Massachusetts land developers and the expanding Connecticut settlements proved harmful to the nearby Pequots. Rather than initiating a damaging intra-Puritan conflict, the Massachusetts and Connecticut leadership agreed to turn their aggression outward. They decided to settle their differences by a contest, a winner take all for the colony that managed to conquer the Pequots first. By 1637, Pequot leader Sassacus and his men faced attack from two armies. The Pequot situation worsened when Massachusetts governor John Winthrop ordered Captain John Underhill to attack civilian rather than military targets. The resulting massacre at Mystic Village was recorded in all its gruesome details by Underhill, who noted with satisfaction that "Many [Pequots] were burnt in the fort, both men, women, and children." Villagers who attempted to surrender were brutally murdered. Soon afterward Indian resistance crumbled, and Massachusetts claimed victory over Connecticut in a contest that virtually eliminated the Pequots from New England. The few Indian survivors were rounded up and sold into slavery. The accounts, both private and public, of this brutal war of elimination waged against the Pequots reveal the Puritan certitude that God approved the destruction of heathen obstacles in the path of the faithful.

Thirty-eight years later, the long

reign of peace enjoyed between Wampanoag Indians and the Plymouth colonists also came to an end, eroded by the land-hunger of the Pilgrim community. In 1675, Wampanoag leader, Metacomet, mounted a guerilla war against the English, raiding white settlements. Forging an alliance with other regional tribes, Metacomet (or King Philip, as the English called him) expanded the war. The English struck back, aided by Iroquois mercenaries sent by the governor of New York. King Philip's War ended in Metacomet's death and the total elimination of several of the tribes who had come to his aid. Those few who escaped death or enslavement scattered, seeking refuge with Indians to the north and the west. The English victory came at great cost to the colonists as well: over two thousand men, women, and children lost their lives in this short but brutal war.

To the south, a similar pattern could be detected. Alliances formed by struggling English colonists and native Powhatan Indians began to show strains before a decade of settlement had ended. In 1609, war broke out, marked by atrocities such as decapitation and torture on both sides. As the colony prospered and the desire for additional tobacco lands grew, aggressive policies replaced compromise and cooperation between the two races. In 1622, Powhatan leader Opechancanough mounted a surprise attack on Jamestown, killing one-fourth of the settlers in one day. Virginians retaliated, and the war continued sporadically for a decade. The Powhatan population was devastated; of forty thousand people, only five hundred remained by the 1630s.

Despite the steady collapse of cooperation between most English colonies and local Indians, the two races remained a presence in one another's lives. Accounts of predawn Indian raids on New England villages run like a leitmotif through the diaries of Puritan fathers and mothers and the sermons of their ministers. Captivity narratives, written by those who were ransomed from French-allied Indians or from French Canadian officials, recount grueling forced marches through snow and storm, injuries, unaccustomed work, and—in some cases—proselytizing efforts by Catholic priests or nuns. Yet these narratives also reveal the diversity of views on Indian life and culture: while some denounce their captors as heathen and savage, others show a growing respect for, and understanding of, a culture strikingly different from their own. Among those differences is the willingness of the Indian communities to accept white captives into their midst, to adopt them into their families fully and without any debilitating traces of racism. English colonists did not reciprocate: the limited efforts by Puritan ministers to convert Indians to Christianity, for example, never resulted in the integration of these "praying Indians" into the colonial community.

## MAKING FOREIGN COLONIES INTO ENGLISH COLONIES

The contests for land and resources that erupted between Native Americans and the English were not the only conflicts in these early decades of settlement. Intra-European rivalries emerged as well, for the English did not initially monopolize the territory along the Atlantic coast from present-day Maine to Georgia. The Dutch, basing their claims upon Henry Hudson's 1609 voyage, created trading posts at Albany and Manhattan as early as 1614. Although Hudson had praised the area as a land of "Grasse & flowers," New Netherland attracted few settlers. Throughout the seventeenth century, Holland's Caribbean possessions held out the promise of quicker, and more extensive, riches. In 1621, a newly formed trading company, the Dutch West India Company, took over the task of colonizing. To encourage settlement, the Company devised a *patroon* system, creating subcolonies within New Netherland made up of vast estates whose proprietors enjoyed manorial rights in law and were allowed to collect rents from their tenant farmers. Only one patroonship, Rensselaerwyck, proved successful. Using a sample taken from 1630–1644, historian Oliver Rink drew a portrait of the colonists who settled on Kiliaen van Rensselaer's million-acre holding. Most were single young men in their teens and twenties, drawn from the economically depressed area around Utrecht—immigrants similar in age and circumstances to the English indentured servants who flocked to the Chesapeake in the seventeenth century. Only 18 percent of the Rensselaerwyck tenants were married and had three or more children. Although most of van Rensselaer's tenants were farmers, a sizeable number were artisans—masons, carpenters, millwrights, and wheelwrights, along with cobblers, tailors, a baker, and a blacksmith.

Despite its efforts, the colony boasted only three hundred settlers in 1629, most of them Protestant Walloon refugees from the southernmost areas of the Spanish Netherlands. Slowly, because of the West India Company's liberal admission standards, a heterogeneous collection of adventurous, profit-hungry colonists trickled in. By 1673, there were somewhere between six thousand and nine thousand colonists in New Netherland, although few of them were Dutch. Nearly 40 percent were German, mostly from Aachen, Cleves, East Friesland, Westphalia, Bremen, Hamburg, and Oldenburg. This German emigration had been prompted by the devastation of war in southwest Germany, an experience of displacement they shared, although without acknowledgement or sympathy, with many of the Indian communities in the Hudson Valley. New Englanders accounted for much of the population on Long Island, while the multicultural atmosphere in New Amsterdam was intensified by the arrival of Danes and Norwegians, free and enslaved Africans, French Huguenots, a sprinkling of Muslims, and a small community of Jews.

The Jewish influx illustrates well the impact of the trading company's openness to diversity—and the resulting tensions within the colony. In 1654, twenty-three Jews had arrived from South America, most of them Iberians seeking asylum after Dutch rule ended in Brazil. Peter Stuyvesant, then governor of New Netherland, was outraged, and sought to banish these refugees from his colony. Writing to the directors of the Dutch West India Company, Stuyvesant insisted that they should not tolerate members of a "deceitful race—such hateful enemies and blasphemers of the name of Christ" who would "infect and trouble this colony." The directors ignored his advice and Stuyvesant had to be content with passing measures that restricted Jewish participation in the life of the larger community, limited their trading rights, and imposed special taxes upon them. Nevertheless, the Jewish population increased, and by the turn of the century, Jews constituted about 2.5 percent of Manhattan's population. While a small Jewish community also appeared in 1658 in Newport, Rhode Island, and four Jewish colonists settled in Charleston, South Carolina, in 1697, the Manhattan community remained the largest in mainland America.

Meanwhile, the Dutch faced what they considered to be Swedish interlopers along the Delaware River. Although the Netherlands claimed this area, in March 1638, two Swedish ships sailed up the river to present-day Wilmington. The Swedes and Finns aboard these ships—citizens of a single kingdom in the seventeenth century—named the site Paradise Point. Ironically, one of the moving forces behind this colonizing venture was a Dutchman familiar to residents of Manhattan: Peter Minuit. In 1626, Minuit had purchased Manhattan island from local Indians; now, in 1638, he repeated the process, this time buying lands for the New Sweden Company, the brainchild of the Finnish admiral Klas Fleming and Minuit himself.

Only a few hundred people ever settled in the colony, most of them Finns. By midcentury, these settlers lived in a half-dozen fortified areas—from Fort Christina in the south, to Fort New Korsholm on the Schuylkill in the north, to Fort Elfsborg on the eastern shore of the Delaware in New Jersey. Despite the meager size of this Swedish colony, the Dutch always viewed it as an incursion into their domain. In 1638, William Kieft, governor of New Netherland, warned Peter Minuit that the Netherlands considered the colony to be illegitimate, adding that he considered Minuit a traitor for accepting the post of governor of New Sweden. Insisting that Minuit had no authority to construct forts along the river, Kieft declared, "We do, therefore protest against all injury to property, and all the evil consequences of bloodshed, uproar, and wrong which our Trading Company may thus suffer." The letter ended with the threat that New Netherland would "protect our rights in such manner as we may find most advisable." Military action followed. By 1656, Dutch forces had seized the Swedish forts, meeting little resistance from the colonists. In 1664, however, control of the area again changed hands, as New Netherland fell, also without resistance, to the naval assault of the English Duke of York. Surprisingly, the Duke of York pursued a liberal policy toward the Dutch citizens of what was now the colony of New York. The Dutch Reform Church was allowed to continue to serve the largely Calvinist population, Dutch property holdings were honored, and Dutch inheritance patterns, strikingly different from the English, remained legal. The Dutch tolerance of diversity within the colony also seemed to be acceptable to the new English proprietor. Indeed, between 1665 and 1685, the colony became a religious refuge for Scottish Presbyterians, English Quakers, and French Huguenots. By the time James ascended to the throne of England in 1685, New York was a thriving colony of fifteen thousand, representing the greatest variety of faiths, races, and ethnic backgrounds the English colonial world had yet seen.

If New York was multicultural, its colonists did not always live in harmony. English, Dutch, and German merchants engaged in sometimes ruthless competition over control of the City's trade. The three ethnic groups were equally fierce in their rivalry to dominate the cultural life of the City. A similar struggle for dominance characterized life in Albany. The only thing that could possibly have united these quarreling factions was a shared threat to their prosperity and autonomy. That threat came in 1685, when James II decided to reorganize the northern mainland colonies, abolishing the separate governments of New England and New York and creating a single administrative unit called the Dominion of New England. New Englanders no less than New Yorkers chafed at the merger, and all came to loathe the profiteering by the Dominion's leadership.

In 1689, news reached New York of the Glorious Revolution in England and the consequent end to James's rule. Four years of burning resentment burst into flame and revolts broke out in Boston, Long Island, and New York City. While Bostonians imprisoned Edmund Andros, the hated governor of the Dominion, Jacob Leisler, a German merchant, led the uprising against Dominion

authorities in New York City. Leisler had personal reasons to resent Andros, whose favoritism toward English colonists had dealt a blow to the German immigrant's social and political ambitions. Thus when several towns on Long Island revolted against the Dominion, Leisler extended the revolt to New York City. He seized control of the fort, imprisoned Andros's representatives—and then, for good measure, jailed some of his local non-German business rivals.

By the end of the summer, Leisler had declared himself commander in chief of the entire colony. Acting as head of a ten-man "committee of safety," he proceeded to imprison more opponents and drive others into exile. Insisting that he was the legitimate head of a constitutional government under William and Mary, Leisler looked for, and received, support from many of the less Anglicized Dutch colonists. Not all the Dutch citizens of the colony backed him, however. In fact, the Dutch community in Albany strongly opposed him, fearing his policies would do their city more damage than those of Andros. In the end, Leisler's Rebellion seemed to be an uprising of two distinct groups: New York City merchants and shopkeepers who were disadvantaged by the Dominion and Long Island communities of Puritan background

Despite Albany's refusal to acknowledge his authority, Leisler proceeded to establish a colonial government, create courts, and raise taxes. He believed he had initiated an era of home rule, but to his surprise, William and Mary did not support his efforts or reward them. Instead they sent a new governor from England. When Jacob Leisler refused to turn over the reins of power, the coalition that supported him dissolved, and he was eventually arrested, convicted of treason, and executed. Hanged, disemboweled while still alive, and then drawn and quartered, Leisler and his son-in-law now became local martyrs to the German community. For many years to come, New York's political life was marked by conflict between Leislerites and supporters of the royal governor and the Crown.

## SERVANTS AND SLAVES IN THE CHESAPEAKE

While colonies like New York and Pennsylvania opened their doors to a wide variety of Protestant sects and European settlers, the colonies to the south were not without some pockets of diversity. Seventeenth-century Virginia's eastern shore contained immigrants from the Netherlands, Sweden, Portugal, Spain, Germany, and even Turkey. Maryland, founded as a Catholic refuge by the Calvert family, never attracted a majority of Catholic colonists. Settled largely by Protestants, the colony was frequently torn apart by its religious divisions. Protestants and Catholics were often as antagonistic as Dutch and English or Puritan and Indian, and over the course of the seventeenth century, despite the efforts of the Calverts to enforce and encourage religious toleration, violence erupted. When Oliver Cromwell's Puritan government repealed Cecil Calvert, Lord Baltimore's Act of Toleration

and took the colony from its proprietor, civil war broke out in Maryland. The Protestants triumphed, but Cromwell's government crumbled and, with the Restoration, the Calvert family became Maryland's proprietors once more. Anti-Catholic sentiment did not vanish, however; rebellions were attempted in 1659, 1676, and again in 1681. When William and Mary ascended the throne in 1688, Maryland's Protestants saw their chance. Led by Anglican minister John Coode, the Protestant Association defeated the Catholics and persuaded the new monarchs to make Maryland a royal colony. Coode was no hero, however, to many Maryland Protestants, and his abrasive personality, like Jacob Leisler's, soon generated strong opposition. When the Calverts converted to Anglicanism in the early eighteenth century, Maryland was returned to their keeping, much to the relief of many of the colonists.

Despite Maryland's origins as a Catholic haven, the majority of the immigrants to both Chesapeake colonies were young, single Englishmen, driven from their family farms by the economic dislocation of the era. Traveling from depressed areas of the English countryside into local market towns, then on to major port cities such as Bristol or London, these increasingly desperate young men agreed to bind, or indenture, themselves to ship captains or Chesapeake, contracting to work from 3 to 7 years in exchange for passage to America, meager sustenance during their term of servitude, and the promise of land ownership when their term of service ended. Even Maryland, originally conceived of as a Catholic refuge by its proprietors, the Calverts, was largely populated by young, impoverished English Protestants.

Tobacco was the magnet that drew both independent settlers and tens of thousands of indentured servants to the Chesapeake. Cultivation of this crop was time-consuming, tedious, and exhausting; more important, it was labor-intensive, for tools and machinery were in short supply in the colonial world. There seemed to be an insatiable need for field hands, as planters expanded their production to increase profits in boom times and to cover costs when prices fell. Most planters believed that indentured servitude was the most economical labor system, given the realities of the region. The disease-ridden environment of the Chesapeake resulted in high mortality rates, and only the small purchase cost for a bound servant compensated the planter for the loss of labor when malaria or dysentery claimed the worker's life. Few tobacco planters considered the preferred labor force of the Caribbean, the African slave, for supplies were limited on the mainland, prices were high, and the initial investment of capital would be lost if the slave fell victim to disease.

A shift to slave labor did begin by century's end, however. Several factors came into play: mortality rates dropped as colonists learned how to protect themselves within the disease environment; the supply of English indentured servants dried up as economic conditions—and employment possibilities—improved at home; and finally, the monopoly on the slave trade, once enjoyed by the Dutch, was wrested away by the English, thus increasing the supply of African workers to all English colonies and lowering the purchase price. The mass importation of enslaved workers and the rise of a slave society in the Chesapeake was still decades away, in the eighteenth century, but the process had begun before the close of the seventeenth century.

Before midcentury, most slaves in the mainland colonies came from Angola, a region that stretched along the Central African coast of the Atlantic from Cape Lopez to Benguela. While some of the wealthiest residents of Virginia's eastern shore could afford to purchase slaves directly from Africa from the Dutch shipmasters, most of the blacks transported to Virginia had, as historian Douglas Deal notes, endured years of service on the sugar plantations of British, Spanish, or Dutch Caribbean islands. Many of these "seasoned" servants could speak English well and were accustomed to English cultural patterns. But however these black colonists were acquired, they remained a rarity in the colonial tobacco world until the 1680s.

Laws and regulations based on race developed slowly and unevenly in the counties and parishes of the Chesapeake. In the early decades, white and black servants cooperated, feeling they had more in common with one another than with their masters. English servant James Revel, who left behind a remarkable poem recounting his arduous and dreary life in the tobacco fields, attested to the camaraderie felt among all servants, black and white. Court records demonstrate that blacks and whites drank, caroused, and fornicated together. More important, they occasionally plotted their escape from servitude together. In 1640, for example, seven African and English servants stole weapons and a small boat and attempted to reach Dutch-held territory by water. White men were willing to put their faith in black ones whose skill or daring might insure the success of an escape plan.

Although African workers did not sign indenture contracts, they were not always deemed servants for life before the eighteenth century. Records remain of black landowners who enjoyed most of the rights their white neighbors enjoyed, including legal recognition of their marriages, ownership of property, and the right to distribute that property in their wills. Marriages between free black men and free white women continued to occur throughout the 1650s and 1660s on the eastern shore, and African landowners purchased white indentured servants to help them work their lands.

By 1662, however, racial barriers began to be erected and the outlines of enslavement for life were drawn. In that year, for example, Virginia's legislature declared that a child's condition followed that of the mother rather than that of the father, thus condemning all children born to slave women to a lifetime of servitude. This law stood in stark contrast to the English assumptions that paternal rather than maternal status defined the status of offspring. Nonmarital sex between the races was punished more severely than fornication or adultery between whites, and by 1691, any white colonist who married an African,

an Indian, or a mulatto was banished from Virginia forever.

The regulation of interracial contact and the distinctions between white and black conditions of service were, in part, the result of the slow increase in the number of African field hands. But other factors contributed to the growing number of distinctions based on race. In 1676, the violent and protracted revolt known as Bacon's Rebellion, pitting backcountry planters against the tidewater or coastal planter elite, proved to have deleterious consequences for black Virginians.

Nathaniel Bacon was a gentleman, not a former servant, but like many would-be planters after midcentury, he found the best of the coastal lands already claimed by a local elite. These tidewater planters dominated the tobacco economy and the legislature as well. Struggling to find prosperity on lands that bordered Indian territories, men like Bacon were caught between hostile enemies to the west and self-interested enemies in the House of Burgesses. Tidewater planters were willing to tax the backcountry colonists, but they were rarely willing to use that tax money to mount the military protection these western farmers believed was needed. When a new round of violence erupted between Indians and colonists in 1676, Nathaniel Bacon took the lead in demanding that the royal governor and his Tidewater supporters send military assistance. The governor refused—and Bacon and his followers took their revolt to the colonial capital. Along the way, the ranks of the rebellion swelled; servants rallied to Bacon's side, including roughly 10 percent of the black male population of the colony. Although the revolt was eventually suppressed, Virginia's political and economic elite feared the possibility of further cooperation between lower class whites and blacks. Many historians feel that Bacon's Rebellion marked a turning point in racial history in the colony, propelling the planter elite to a conscious policy of racial divisiveness.

By the late seventeenth century almost three-quarters of the Africans imported into the Chesapeake came primarily from two regions: Senegambia, at the mouth of the Gambia River, and the Bight of Biafra. Their numbers grew steadily: between 1670 and 1700, six thousand slaves arrived directly from Africa. The nature of the black population in the Chesapeake was thus changing: the new arrivals rarely spoke English and were unfamiliar with English customs, work patterns, or religion. In addition, although the sex ratio among the "seasoned" blacks had been equal, the slaves imported directly from Africa were almost exclusively young men and boys. Thus by the end of the century, the Chesapeake faced an influx of genuinely foreign colonists, Africans who had come not by choice but by force.

## FIRST SETTLEMENTS IN THE LOWER SOUTH

To the south of the tobacco region lay Carolina, a vast area that included swamps and lowlands that King Charles had granted to eight of his wealthy supporters. Although these proprietors drafted an elaborate scheme for a feudal

society in Carolina, the colony actually developed much as Virginia had by offering land to anyone willing to emigrate. After experimenting with several cash crops, including tobacco, sugar cane, and even olives, the Carolina planters soon focused their efforts on rice cultivation. Although the significant development of the Lower South, as the Carolinas and Georgia were called, would lie in the eighteenth century, the biracial outlines of that society were already evident in the seventeenth. The Barbadian planters who were among the earliest settlers of the Carolinas brought slaves with them to the mainland; unlike the Chesapeake tobacco farmers, these West Indian émigrés did not need to evolve a rationale or a legal structure for racial slavery.

## IMPERIAL CONFLICTS IN THE SEVENTEENTH CENTURY

The colonies were separated from their mother country by three thousand miles of ocean, but they did not escape the consequences of England's aggressive foreign policy. England's slow rise to power during the seventeenth century made that nation a central player in the competition to control North America and its resources and to dominate the Atlantic trade. This competition influenced key aspects of colonial life, from settlement patterns to Indian alliances to militia activity and its funding. The mainland colonies, situated between the French North American empire to the north and the Spanish territories to the south and southwest, were quickly drawn into the four wars for empire among Spain, France, and England—and their allies and satellites—that began in earnest in the 1680s.

The succession to the throne of William and Mary in 1688 sparked the first major conflict between France and England. English allies included Holland, Sweden, and Spain, but for the colonists, the alliance between the French and the powerful Hurons was more important. Like their European counterparts, Indians of the Great Lakes and Northern New York regions were divided into competing camps of Huron and Iroquois. Their struggle for control of the richest fur regions was now joined to the European struggle known in America as King William's War as Hurons allied themselves with the French and the Iroquois with the English.

Few British or French military forces took part in the American theater of war. Instead, Canadian militias battled New England militia companies while Iroquois and Huron troops staged raids and incursions on enemy territories. New England colonies rushed to enforce militia laws that required service by all but ministers, magistrates, doctors, schoolmasters, fishermen, and students. In Massachusetts, each town was required to raise a band or company of militiamen, amateur soldiers led by elected officers. Canadians organized in a similar fashion, calling on tenants to do military service as a duty to their landlords. The first serious blow had been dealt even before war was officially declared, when Iroquois warriors attacked the French outpost at Lachine in July of 1689, killing somewhere between sixty

and two hundred inhabitants and taking more than a hundred prisoners. The French Canadians were quick to retaliate. Well-planned raids in Maine and New Hampshire destroyed garrison houses and cost the lives of local militia leaders. The violence spread quickly from Canadian border towns like Dover, New Hampshire, to upstate New York. In February 1690, a force of Indians and French troops struck the village of Schenectady, leveling the town in only a few hours, and killing sixty residents.

Accounts of atrocities began to spread early in the war—many of them true: children's heads dashed against staircases or apple trees; women hacked to death by hatchets. When these murders were perpetrated by the Indian allies of the French, the colonists decried them as savagery, but when Hannah Duston, a matron from Haverhill, Massachusetts, killed ten of her captors while they slept, scalping them in the bargain, she was hailed as a Christian heroine, honored in sermons by such distinguished divines as Cotton Mather. When the war finally ended in 1697, at least 650 English colonists were dead, killed in battle, in raids, or in captivity. The Iroquois death toll was far greater, reaching somewhere between six hundred and thirteen hundred.

England's rivalry with France would grow even more intense in the next century, and colonists would draw upon their memories, real and imagined, of what they called Indian savagery. But the French were the true objects of their hatred, and a fierce anti-Catholicism, synonymous for many with anti-French sentiments, became the rallying cry until this old enemy became the colonists' new ally during the American Revolution.

## CONCLUSION

By 1700, a clear ethnic and racial map of the mainland English colonies had emerged. To the north, New England remained the most homogeneous of the regions, populated primarily by English Calvinists in the countryside but with a growing urban population of Anglicans once Massachusetts became a royal colony in 1692. Few Indians remained in the area, for the wars against Pequot, Narragansett, and Wampanoag had ended the era of cooperation and co-existence between the races. The black population was small, concentrated in the slave-trading towns of Rhode Island and on the docks of Boston. The shortage of available land, already a problem by the end of the century, would discourage the waves of immigrants from Ireland and Germany that would fill the backcountries of the middle and southern colonies in the next century.

South of New England, Pennsylvania was just beginning to attract European settlers, drawn to the colony by its liberal land policies and religious tolerance. New York, and particularly New York City, remained the most cosmopolitan, heterogeneous spot on the English mainland, with the Dutch, German, and English in lively competition for cultural hegemony, and with Jews, French Huguenots, and Africans adding to the city's tradition of diversity.

The transition of the Chesapeake and the Lower South from a society with slaves to a slave society, defined by the presence of a social caste based on race, had begun by 1700. Despite the arrival of Scotch-Irish, Irish, and German immigrants in the next century, race rather than ethnicity would be the defining characteristic of this southern culture.

## ANNOTATED BIBLIOGRAPHY

Acrelius, Israel. *A History of New Sweden, or The Settlements on the River Delaware.* New York: Arno Press, 1972.

One of the few attempts to narrate the history of this small seventeenth-century colony of Swedes and Finns. The volume focuses on political origins of the settlement and the background of the immigrants themselves.

Axtell, James. *Natives and Newcomers: The Cultural Origins of North America.* New York: Oxford University Press, 2000.

Axtell describes the major encounters between Indians and Europeans and analyzes how they ultimately shaped a unique American character. He explores both the short- and long-term consequences of these encounters on the two cultures.

Bailyn, Bernard *The Peopling of British North America: An Introduction.* New York: Vintage, 1988.

In this introduction to Bailyn's multi-volume work, *The Peopling of British North America,* one of the leading scholars in early American history identifies central themes relating to the transatlantic transfer of people from the Old World to the North American continent.

Bailyn, Bernard, and Philip D. Morgan. *Strangers within the Realm: The Cultural Margins of the First British Empire.* Chapel Hill: University of North Carolina Press, 1991.

This collection of essays, dealing with British expansion in the seventeenth and eighteenth centuries, addresses the processes of Anglicization on the peripheries of the British Empire.

Calloway, Colin. *New Worlds for All: Indians, Europeans, and the Remaking of Early America.* Baltimore: Johns Hopkins University Press, 1997.

This study, which encompasses continental America for a span of three hundred years, explores the various ways in which Indians and Europeans forged alliances in early America and sufficiently comingled to create a unique American identity and culture.

Games, Alison. *Migration and the Origins of the English Atlantic World.* Harvard Historical Studies. Cambridge: Harvard University Press, 1999.

This in-depth analysis of the seventy-five hundred people who traveled from London to the New World in 1635 explores the attempt and ultimate failure of the travelers to re-create English society in their overseas outposts.

Goodfriend, Joyce D. *Before the Melting Pot: Society and Culture in Colonial New York City, 1664–1730.* Princeton: Princeton University Press, 1991.

Exploring the vast ethnic diversity of New York City that was present from its earliest days, Goodfriend seeks to discover the meaning of ethnicity in early America. Arguing against the prevailing notion of rapid Anglicization, she suggests that ethnicity proved to be a persistent force into the eighteenth century.

Jaffee, David. *People of the Wachusett: Greater New England in History and Memory, 1630–1860.* Ithaca: Cornell University Press, 1999.

Through the lens of one New England town, Jaffee paints a portrait of the cultural history of America's original frontier. Firsthand narratives of founding citizens are explored to provide a personal account of the founding of America, town by town.

Kupperman, Karen O. *Indians and English: Facing Off in Early America.* Ithaca: Cornell University Press, 2000.

Kupperman explores the complex interactions between colonists and Native Americans between 1580 and 1640. In examining the sources of precolonial stereotypes, she discovers the interconnectedness of the two cultures.

Lepore, Jill. *The Name of War: King Philip's War and the Origins of American Identity.* New York: Random House, 1999.

An exploration of King Philip's War, not only as a historical event but as a literary event. Lepore stresses the advantage the English enjoyed as a literate culture in controlling the accounts of this war, its motives, and the nature of its participants.

Merwick, Donna. *Possessing Albany, 1620–1710: The Dutch and English Experiences.* New York: Cambridge University Press, 1990.

This is a study of the role of the Dutch in shaping the political and cultural life of seventeenth-century New York. Merwick narrates early New York history from a Dutch rather than an Anglo perspective.

Morgan, Edmund. *American Slavery, American*

*Freedom: The Ordeal of Colonial Virginia.* New York: Norton, 1975.

This award-winning examination of the roots of slavery in colonial Virginia traces its development to Bacon's Rebellion and the effort to ameliorate class tensions among English colonists by creating a caste system based on race.

Morgan, Philip. *Slave Counterpoint: Black Culture in the Eighteenth-Century Chesapeake and Lowcountry.* Chapel Hill: University of North Carolina Press, 1998.

This prize-winning book provides a richly textured comparison of African American life in eighteenth-century Chesapeake and Low-Country society, addressing such issues as work patterns, family organization, and black-white relationships in the two regions.

Rink, Oliver A. *Holland on the Hudson: An Economic and Social History of Dutch New York.* Ithaca: Cornell University Press, 1973

Instead of focusing on the failures of the Dutch West India Company, Rink explores the successes of private Amsterdam merchants in creating the Dutch colony on the Hudson. Rink paints a portrait of a thriving Dutch society, rather than a faltering one, on the eve of conquest by the British.

Shuffelton, Frank, ed. *A Mixed Race: Ethnicity in Early America.* New York: Oxford University Press, 1993.

This collection of essays suggests that American society was inescapably multicultural from its inception and that cultural differences fundamentally defined American culture. This topically and chronologically broad collection, which focuses on the eighteenth century, addresses issues such as the representation of cultural differences between European immigrants and Native Americans and the circumstances in which the first African American autobiographical narratives arose.

White, Richard. *The Middle Ground: Indians, Empires, and Republics in the Great Lakes Region, 1650–1815.* New York: Cambridge University Press, 1991.

This compelling study of relations between Indians and Europeans in the Great Lakes concentrates on the necessity for the creation of a "middle ground" between two alien cultures. This middle ground allowed communication, alliances, and trade as well as the transference of cultural values and behaviors for almost three hundred years.

Wood, Betty. *The Origins of American Slavery: Freedom and Bondage in the English Colonies.* New York: Hill and Wang, 1997.

Wood examines the role of the English in the development of slavery in this synthesis of the scholarly debate on the origins of slavery in America.

# DOCUMENTS

## A Letter from a Gentleman of the City of New-York to Another, Concerning the Troubles which happen'd in That Province in the Time of the late Happy Revolution, 1698

*Attacks and justification of the revolt led by Jacob Leisler continued for over a decade after Leisler was arrested, tried, found guilty of treason, and publicly executed. The divisions*

*between Leislerites and Anti-Leislerites sur-*
*vived in New York City politics into the eigh-*
*teenth century.*

*Source:* Charles M. Andrews, ed., *The Narra-*
*tives of the Insurrections, 1675–1690* (New York: Barnes and Noble, 1915), pp. 361–371.

*Sir;*

I cannot but admire to hear that some Gentlemen still have a good Opinion of the late Disorders committed by Capt. Jacob Leysler, and his Accomplices, in New-York, as if they had been for His Majesties Service, and the Security of that Province; and that such Monstrous Falshoods do find Credit, That the Persons before in Commission, and did labour to oppose and prevent those Disorders, were Jacobites, or Persons ill affected to the Happy Revolution in England. But it has been often the Calamity of all Ages to palliate Vice with false Glosses, and to criminate the best Actions of the most Virtuous and most Pious Men. So that Truth and Innocency, without some Defence, has not proved at all times a sufficient Bullwork against malitious Falshoods and Calumnies. Wherefore I shall endeavour to give you a true and brief Account of that matter, as I my self have been a Personal Witness to most of them.

It was about the beginning of April, 1689, when the first Reports arrived at New-York, that the Prince of Orange, now his present Majesty, was arrived in England with considerable Forces, and that the late King James was fled into France, and that it was expected War would be soon proclaimed between England and France.

The Leiut. Governour, Francis Nicholson, and the Council, being Protestants, resolved thereupon to suspend all Roman Catholicks from Command and Places of Trust in the Government, and accordingly suspended Major Baxter from being a Member of Council and Captain of a Company at Albany, and Bartholomew Russel from being Ensign in the Fort at New-York, they both being Papists, who forth-with left their Command, and departed the Province.

And because but three Members of the Council were residing in New-York, *viz.* Mr. Frederick Phillips, Coll. Stephanus Cortlandt, and Coll. Nicholas Bayard, all of Dutch Birth, all Members, and the two last, for the space of near thirty Years past, Elders and Deacons of the Dutch Protestant Church in New-York, and most affectionate to the Royal House of Orange, It was Resolved by the said Lieut. Governor and Council, to call and conveen to their Assistance all the Justices of the Peace, and other civil Magistrates, and the Commission Officers in the Province, for to consult and advise with them what might be proper for the Preservation of the Peace, and the Safety of said Province in that Conjuncture, till Orders should arrive from England.

Whereupon the said Justices, Magistrates and Officers were accordingly convened, and stiled by the Name of The General Convention for the Province of New-York; and all matters of Government were carried on and managed by the major Vote of that Convention.

And in the first place it was by them

agreed and ordered, Forth-with to for-tifie the City of New-York.

And that for the better Security of the Fort (since the Garrison was weak, and to prevent all manner of Doubts and Jealousies) a competent Number of the City Militia should keep Guard in said Fort, and Nicholas Bayard, Coll. of said Militia, recommended to give suitable Orders accordingly.

And that the Revenue should be con-tinued and received by some Gentlemen appointed by that Convention, for Re-pairing the Fort, and Fortifying of the City; but against this Order Capt. Leys-ler (who as a Captain was a Member of that Convention) did enter his dissent, with some few others.

It was also recommended to said Coll. Bayard to hasten to fortifie the City with all possible speed, who upon the Credit of the Revenue did advance what Money was needful for Materials, And by the Assistance of the Militia Officers, and daily Labour of the Inhabitants, had the same finish't before the end of May, excepting Capt. Leysler's Quota.

About the middle of May the Ship *Beaver*, John Corbit Master, being ready to sail for England, the Lieut. Gover-nour and Council sent in her by Mr. John Riggs, and in several other Ships that soon followed, Letters to the Earl, now Duke, of Shrewsbury, then Principal Secretary of State, and to the Lords of the Committee for Trade and Planta-tions, wherein they signified their re-joycing at the News of his Royal High-ness the Prince of Orange, now his present Majesties, arrival in England, in order to Redress the Grievances of the Nation, and giving a particular Account

of the state of Affairs of this Province, and that they would endeavour to pre-serve its Peace and Security till Orders should arrive from England, which they humbly prayed might be hastened with all possible speed. Which said Letters were most graciously received, and an-swered by his Majesties Letter, bearing date the 30th of July, 1689.

But against Expectation it soon hap-pened, that on the last day of said Moneth of May, Capt. Leysler having a Vessel with some Wines in the Road, for which he re-fused to pay the Duty, did in a Seditious manner stir up the meanest sort of the In-habitants (affirming, That King James be-ing fled the Kingdom, all manner of Gov-ernment was fallen in this Province) to rise up in arms, and forcibly possess themselves of the Fort and Stores, which accordingly was effected whilest the Lieut. Governour and Council, with the Convention, were met at the City Hall to consult what might be proper for the common Good and Safety; where a party of Armed Men came from the Fort, and forced the Lieut. Governour to deliver them the Keys; and seized also in his Chamber a Chest with Seven Hundred Seventy Three Pounds, Twelve Shillings, in Money of the Government. And though Coll. Bayard, with some others appointed by the Convention, used all endeavours to prevent those Disorders, all proved vain; for most of those that ap-peared in Arms were Drunk, and cryed out, They disown'd all manner of Gov-ernment. Whereupon, by Capt. Leysler's perswasion, they proclaimed him to be their Commander, there being then no other Commission Officer amongst them.

Capt. Leysler being in this manner

possest of the Fort, took some Persons to his Assistance, which he call'd, The Committee of Safety. And the Lieut. Governour, Francis Nicollson, being in this manner forced out of his Command, for the safety of his Person, which was daily threatned, withdrew out of the Province.

About a week after, Reports came from Boston, That their Royal Highnesses, the Prince and Princes of Orange were proclaimed King and Queen of England. Whereupon the Council and Convention were very desirous to get that Proclamation, and not only wrote for it, but some of them hearing that two Gentlemen were coming from Connecticut with a Copy of said Proclamation, went out two days to meet them, in expectation of having the Happiness to proclaim it; but Major Gold and Mr. Fitz, missing them, having put the Proclamation into Capt. Leysler's hands, he, without taking any Notice of the Council or Convention, did proclaim the same, though very disorderly, after which he went with his Accomplices to the Fort, and the Gentlemen of the Council and Magistrates, and most of the principal Inhabitants and Merchants, went to Coll. Bayards House and drank the Health and Prosperity of King William and Queen Mary with great Expressions of Joy.

Two days after, a printed Proclamation was procured by some of the Council, dated the 14th of February, 1688, whereby their Majesties confirmed all Sheriffs, Justices of the Peace, Collectors and Receivers of the Revenues, etc., being Protestants; which was forth-with published at the City Hall by the Mayor and Alder-men, accompanyed with the Council, and most of the chief Citizens and Merchants. And pursuant thereunto the Collector, Mat. Plowman, being a Papist, was forth-with suspended by the Convention; and Coll. Bayard, Alderman, Paul Richards, Capt. Thomas Winham, and Lieut. John Haynes, Merchants, were by them commissionated and appointed to collect the Revenue until Orders should arrive from England. Whereupon those Gentlemen were sworn by Coll. Cortland, then Major of the City, they being the first in this Province that took the Oathes to their Majesties appointed by Act of Parliament, instead of the Oathes of Allegiance and Supreamacy.

But as soon as those Gentlemen entered upon the Office, Capt. Leysler with a party of his Men in Arms, and Drink, fell upon them at the Custom-House, and with Naked Swords beat them thence, endeavouring to Massacree some of them, which were Rescued by Providence. Whereupon said Leysler beat an Alarm, crying about the City, "Treason, Treason," and made a strict search to seize Coll. Bayard, who made his escape, and departed for Albany, where he staid all Summer, in hopes that Orders might arrive from England to settle those Disorders.

The said Capt. Leysler, finding almost every man of Sence, Reputation, or Estate in the place to oppose and discourage his Irregularities, caused frequent false Alarms to be made, and sent several parties of his armed Men out of the Fort, drag'd into nasty Goals within said Fort several of the principal Magistrates, Officers and Gentlemen, and others, that would not own his Power to be lawful, which he kept in close Prison during Will and Pleasure, without any Process, or allowing them to Bail. And he further publish't several times, by beat of Drums, That all those who would not come into the Fort and sign their hands, and so thereby to own his Power to be lawful, should be deemed and esteemed as Enemies to his Majesty and the Country, and be by him treated accordingly. By which means many of the Inhabitants, tho' they abhor'd his Actions, only to escape a nasty Goal and to secure their Estates were by fear and compulsion drove to comply, submit and sign to whatever he commanded.

And though Capt. Leysler had at first so violently opposed the collecting of the Revenue, alledging it unlawful, as soon as his Wines were landed, and that he got into some Power, he forth-with set up for himself the collecting of said Revenue by Peter d' Lanoy, allowing him a great Sallary, and all the Perquisits of that Office.

Upon the 10th of December following returned the said Mr. John Riggs from England, with Letters from his Majesty and the Lords, in answer to the Letters sent by the Lieut. Governour and Council above recited, Directed, "To Our Trusty and Well-beloved Francis Nicholson, Esq; Our Lieutenant Governour and Commander in chief of Our Province of New-York in America, and in his absence To such as for the time being, take care for the Preservation of the Peace, and administring the Laws in Our said Province." Whereby his Majesty approved of the Proceedings and Care that had been taken by said Lieut.

Governour and Council for the Peace and Safety of the Province, with further Power and Directions to continue therein till further Orders. Which said Letters the said Mr. Riggs designed to deliver on the following Morning to the Gentlemen of the Council, to whom they properly did belong, being an answer to their said Letter; but was obstructed therein by said Leysler, who sent a party of his Men in Arms, and brought said Riggs to the Fort, where he forced said Letters from him, though some Gentlemen of the Council, that went the same time to the Fort, protested against it, but he drove them out of the Fort, calling them Rogues, Papists, and other opprobious Names.

Soon after the Receipt of said Letters, said Capt. Leysler stiled himself Lieutenant Governour, appointed a Council, and presumed further to call a select Number of his own Party, who called themselves The General Assembly of the Province, and by their advice and assistance raised several Taxes and great Sums of Money from their Majesties good Subjects within this Province. Which Taxes, together with that 773£. 12s. in Money, which he had seized from the Government, and the whole Revenue, he applyed to his own use, and to maintain said Disorders, allowing his private men 18d. per Day, and to others proportionably.

On the 20th of January following Coll. Bayard and Mr. Nicolls had the ill fortune to fall into his hands, and were in a barbarous manner, by a party in Arms, drag'd into the Fort, and there put into a Nasty place, without any manner of Process, or being allowed to bayl, though the same was offered for said Coll. Bayard, by some of the ablest and richest Inhabitants, to the Sum of Twenty Thousand Pounds, either for his appearance to answer, or depart the Province, or to go for England; but without any Cause given, or Reasons assigned, laid said Coll. Bayard in Irons, and kept him and Mr. Nicolls close Prisoners for the space of fourteen Moneths, where they, with several others, that had been long detained Prisoners, were set at Liberty by Governour Slaughter.

And whilest he kept those Gentlemen in Prison, he quartered his armed Men in their Houses, where they committed all manner of Outrages; And to give one Instance of many others, A Party of twelve Men were quartered at the House of Coll. Bayard, with directions to pillage and plunder at discretion, which was bought off with Money and plentiful Entertainment. But the same day, when that party had received their Money, another party came in with Naked Swords, opened several Chambers and Chests in said House, and did Rob and carry away what Money and other Goods they found.

At the same time Coll. Bayard and Mr. Nicolls were taken, strict search was made for Coll. Cortlandt, but he, with several other Gentlemen, having made their escape, were forced to leave their Families and Concerns, and remain in Exile, till relieved by the arrival of Governour Slaughter.

It is hardly to be exprest what Cruelties Capt. Leysler and his Accomplices imposed upon the said Prisoners, and all others that would not own his Power to be lawful. Neither could the Protestant Ministers in the Province escape their Malice and Cruelty; for Mr. Selyns, Minister of New-York, was most grosly abused by Leysler himself in the Church at the time of Divine Service, and threatned to be silenced, etc. Mr. Dellius, Minister at Albany, to escape a nasty Goal, was forced to leave his Flock, and fly for shelter into New-England. Mr. Varick, Minister of the Dutch Towns on Nassaw-Island, was by armed men drag'd out of his House to the Fort, then imprisoned without bayl, for speaking (as was pretended) Treasonable words against Capt. Leysler and the Fort; then prosecuted, and decreed by Peter d' Lanoy, pretended Judge, without any Commission or Authority, To be deprived from his Ministerial Function, amerced in a Fine of 80£. and to remain in close Prison till that Fine should be paid; yea, he was so tormented, that in all likelyhood it occasioned and hastened the suddain Death of that most Reverend and Religious Man. The French Ministers, Mr. Perret and Mr. Dellie, had some better Quarters, but were often threatned to be prosecuted in like manner, because they would not approve of his Power and disorderly proceedings.

None in the Province, but those of his Faction, had any safety in their Estates; for said Capt. Leysler, at will and pleasure, sent to those who disapproved of his Actions, to furnish him with Money, Provisions, and what else he wanted, and upon denial sent armed men out of the Fort, and forcibly broke open several Houses, Shops, Cellars, Vessels, and other places where they expected to be supplied, and without any the least payment or satisfaction, carried their Plunder to the Fort; all which was extreamly approved of by those poor Fellows which he had about him, and was forced to feed and maintain; and so he stiled those his Robberies with the gilded Name and Pretence, That it was for their Majesties King William and Queen Mary's special Service, though it was after found out, that whole Cargo's of those stolen goods were sold to his Friends in the City, and Shipt off for the West Indies and else where.

In this manner he the said Leysler, with his Accomplices, did force, pillage, rob and steal from their Majesties good Subjects within this Province, almost to their utter Ruin, vast Sums of Money, and other Effects, the estimation of the Damages done only within this City of New-York amounting, as by Account may appear, to the Sum of Thirteen Thousand Nine Hundred and Fifty Nine Pounds, besides the Rapines, Spoils and Violences done at Coll. Willets on Nassaw-Island, and to many others in several parts of the Province.

And thus you may see how he used and exercised an Exorbitant, Arbitrary and Unlawful Power over the Persons and Estates of his Majesties good Subjects here, against the known and Fundamental Laws of the Land, and in subvertion of the same, to the great Oppression of his Majesties Subjects, and to the apparent decay of Trade and Commerce.

In this Calamity, Misery and Confusion was this Province, by those Disorders, enthrawled near the space of two years, until the arrival of his Majesties Forces, under the command of Major Ingoldsby, who, with several Gentlemen of the Council, arrived about the last day of Jan-

uary, 1690/1, which said Gentlemen of the Council, for the Preservation of the Peace, sent and offered to said Leysler, That he might stay and continue his Command in the Fort, only desiring for themselves and the Kings Forces quietly to quarter and refresh themselves in the City, till Governour Slaughter should arrive; but the said Leysler, instead of complying, asked Mr. Brooke, one of his Majesties Council, Who were appointed of the Council in this Province? and Mr. Brooke having named Mr. Phillips, Coll. Cortland and Coll. Bayard, he fell into a Passion and cry'd, "What! those Papist Dogs, Rogues! Sacrament! if the King should send Three Thousand such I would cut them all off"; And without any cause given, he proclaimed open War against them. Whereupon they, for Self-preservation, protection of the Kings Forces and Stores, and the safety of the City, were necessitated to perswade to their assistance several of their Majesties good Subjects then in Opposition against the said Leysler, with no other intent, as they signified to him by several Letters and Messages, but only for self-security and Defence; yet notwithstanding, the said Leysler proceeded to make War against them and the Kings Forces, and fired a vast Number of great and small Shot in the City, whereby several of his Majesties Subjects were killed and wounded as they passed in the streets upon their lawful Occasions, tho' no Opposition was made on the other side.

At this height of Extremity was it when Governour Slaughter arrived on the 19th of March, 1691, who having publish't his Commission from the City Hall, with great signs of Joy, by firing all the Artillary within and round the City, sent thrice to demand the surrender of the Fort from Capt. Leysler and his Accomplices, which was thrice denied, but upon great Threatnings, the following Day surrendered to Governor Slaughter, who forth-with caused the said Capt. Leysler, with some of the chief Malefactors, to be bound over to answer their Crimes at the next Supream Court of Judicature, where the said Leysler and his pretended Secretary Millborn did appear, but refused to plead to the Indictment of the grand Jury, or to own the Jurisdiction of that Court; and so after several hearings, as Mutes, were found guilty of High Treason and Murder, and executed accordingly.

Several of the other Malefactors that pleaded were also found Guilty, and particularly one Abraham Governeer for Murdering of an Old Man peaceably passing along the Street, but were Reprieved by Governour Slaughter, and upon Coll. Fletcher's arrival by him set at liberty, upon their Submission and promise of good Behaviour.

*Sir*, All what is here set down is True, and can be proved and justified by the Men of greatest Probity and best Figure amongst us. If I were to give a particular Narrative of all the Cruelties and Robberies perpetrated upon their Majesties most affectionate Subjects in this Province, they would fill a Volumn: There was no need of any Revolution here; there were not ten Jacobites in the whole; they were all well known, and the strictest Protestants, and men of best Figure, Reputation and Estates were at the Helm, it may plainly be perceived by the several steps and measures were fol-

lowed at that time, and by their Letters to the then Earl, now Duke of Shrewsbury, and to the Lords, and the Kings Answer thereunto. The Copy of which Answer, and some other Papers worthy of your perusal, are inclosed.

So soon as Governour Sloughter arrived, an Assembly was called, which upon the 18th of April, 1691, did present an Address to his Excellency, signed by their Speaker, together with the Resolves of that House, which when you are pleased to read, gives the Conclusive Opinion and Judgment of the General Assembly of this Province, of all those disorderly Proceedings, for which those two have suffered Death, and their Sentence was since approved by Her Majesty, of ever blessed Memory, in Council.

Many worthy Protestants in England, and other parts of the world, being sincerely devoted to his Majesties Interest, have yet notwithstanding (unacquainted with our Circumstances, and not duely apprized of the truth) been more easily induced to give credit to the false Glosses and Calumnies of byassed and disaffected Persons from this Province. But in my Observation, most Gentlemen that have come hither so prepossessed, after some time spent here have been thorowly convinced of their Mistake, and that those men who suffered Death, did not from pure zeal for their Majesties Interest, and the Protestant Religion, but being of desperate Fortune, thrust themselves into Power, of purpose to make up their wants by the Ruin and Plunder of his Majesties Loyal Subjects, and were so far engaged in their repeated Crimes, that they were driven to that height of Desperation, had not the Providence of Almighty God prevented it, the whole Province had been Ruined and Destroyed.

I have put this in writing at your Request, to assist your Memory, and leave it to his Excellency Coll. Fletcher, and your own Observations, to enlarge upon the Characters of those Persons who have been the greatest Sufferers in the time of those Disorders, and of their Patience and Moderation since your arrival; also, of the Disaffected, and the Causes which you have frequently observed to hold this Province in Disquiet and Trouble. Notwithstanding all which, and the frequent Attachs of the French and Indians upon our Fronteers, this Province has not lost one foot of ground during the War, but have had considerable Advantages upon the Enemy, which, under God, is due to the prudent and steady Conduct and great Care and Diligence of Coll. Fletcher, our present Governour.

You have been an Eye Witness, and have had Time and Experience enough to enable you to inform others in England, which if you will please to do, I doubt not but it will gain Credit, and be an extraordinary piece of Service to this Province. I am,

*Sir,*
*Your Most Humble Servant.*
*New-York, December 31, 1697*

# The Beginning, Progress, and Conclusion of Bacon's Rebellion in Virginia, in the Years 1675 and 1676

*Although this document is dated 1705, it is an account of the most famous uprising in Virginia in the seventeenth century, Bacon's Rebellion.*

*Source:* First printed in the *Richmond Enquirer,* *September 1, 5, 8, 1804;* reprinted by editor Peter Force, 1835. The original was written by an anonymous author, "T.M.," to Robert Harley, Esq., member of the Privy Council, on July 13, 1705.

*To the right hono'ble Robert Harley*
*esq'e. Her Maj ties Principal Secretary of*
*State, and one of her most Hono'ble*
*Privy Council*
*S'r.*

The great honour of your command obliging my pen to step aside from it's habituall element of ffigures into this little treatise of history ; which having never before experienced, I am like Sutor ultra crepidam and therefore dare pretend no more than (nakedly) to recount matters of ffact.

Beseeching yo'r hono'r will vouchsafe to allow, that in 30 years, divers occurrences are laps'd out of mind, and others imperfectly retained.

So as the most solemn obedience can be now paid, is to pursue the track of bare-fac'd truths, as close as my memory can recollect, to have seen, or believed, from credible ffriends, with concurring circumstances.

And whatsoever yo'r celebrated wisdom shall finde amisse in the composure, my intire dependence is upon yo'r candour favourably to accept these most sincere endeavo'rs of . . .

*Yo'r Hono'rs Most devoted humble ser't*
*the 13 July 1705 . . . T.M.*

This About the year 1675, appear'd three prodigies in that country which, from th' attending disasters, were look'd upon as ominous presages.

The one was a large comet, every evening for a week or more, at southwest, thirty-five degrees high, streaming like a horse's taile, westwards, untill it reach'd (almost) the horrison, and setting toward the northwest.

Another was, fflights of pigeons, in breadth nigh a quarter of the midhemisphere, and of their length there was no visible end; whose weight brake down the limbs of large trees whereon these rested at night, of which the ffowlers shot abundance and eat 'em; this sight put the old planters under the more portentous apprehensions, because the like was seen as they said) in 1640 when th' Indians committed the last massacre, but not after, until that present year 1675.

The third strange appearance was swarms of fflyes about an inch long, and as big as the top of a man's little finger, rising out of spigot holes in the earth, which would eat the new sprouted leaves from the tops of the trees without other harm, and in a month left us.

My dwelling was in Northumberland, the lowest county on the Potomack river, Stafford being the upmost, where, having also a plantation, servants, cattle, &c., my overseer there had agreed with one Robert Hen to come thither and be my herdsman, who then lived ten miles above it ; but on a Sabbath day morning in the summer anno 1675, people in their way to church, saw this Hen lying thwart his threshold, and an Indian without the door, both chopt on their heads, arms, and other parts, as if done with Indian hatchets, th' Indian was dead, but Hen when ask'd who did that? answered: Doegs, Doegs, and soon died, then a boy came out from under a bed, where he had hid himself, and told them, Indians had come at break of day and done those murders.

From this Englishman's bloud did (by degrees) arise Bacon's rebellion with the following mischiefs which overspread all Virginia and twice endangered Maryland, as by the ensuing account is evident.

Of this horrid action, Colonel Mason, who commanded the militia regiment of ffoot, and Capt. Brent, the troop of horse of that county (both dwelling six or eight miles downwards), having speedy notice, raised 30, or more men, and pursu'd those Indians 20 miles up and 4 miles over that river into Maryland, where, landing at dawn of day they found two small paths each leader with this party took a separate path and in less than a furlong, either found a cabin, which they (silently) surrounded. Capt. Brent went to the Doegs' cabin (as it proved to be) who speaking the Indian tongue called to have a "matchacomicha, weewhio," i.e. a councill called presently such being the usuall manner with Indians) the king came trembling forth, and wou'd have fled, when Capt. Brent, catching hold of his twisted lock (which was all the hair he wore) told him he was come for the murderer of Robert Hen, the king pleaded ignorance and slipt loos, whom Brent shot dead with his pistoll, th' Indians shot two or three guns out of the cabin, th' English shot into it, th' Indians throng'd out at the door and fled, the English shot as many as they cou'd, so that they killed ten, as Capt. Brent told me, and brought away the king's son of about 8 years old, concerning whom is an observable passage, at the end of this expedition; the noise of this shooting awaken'd the Indians in the cabin, which Coll. Mason had encompassed, who likewise rush'd out and fled, of whom his company (supposing from that noise of shooting Brent's party to be engaged) shott (as the Coll. informed me) ffourteen before an Indian came, who with both hands shook him (friendly) by one arm saying Susquehanoughs netoughs i.e. Susquehanough friends and fled, whereupon he ran amongst his men, crying out "ffor the Lords sake shoot no more, these are our friends the Susquehanoughs.

This unhappy scene ended; Collo. Mason took the king of the Doegs son home with him, who lay ten dayes in bed, as one dead, with eyes and mouth shutt, no breath discern'd, but his body continuing warm, they believed him yett alive; th' aforenamed Capt. Brent (a papist) coming thither on a visit, and seeing his little prisoner thus languishing said "perhaps he is pawewawd i. e. bewitch'd, and that he had heard baptism was an effectuall remedy against witchcraft wherefore advis'd to baptize him Collo. Mason answered, no minister cou'd be had in many miles; Brent replied yo'r clerk Mr. Dobson may do that office, which was done by the church of England liturgy; Coll. Mason with Capt. Brent godfather and Mrs. Mason godmother, my overseer Mr. Pimet being present, from whom I first heard it, and which all th' other persons (afterwards) affirm'd to me; the ffour men return'd

to drinking punch, but Mrs. Mason staying and looking on the child, it open'd the eyes and breath'd, whereat she ran for a cordial, which he took from a spoon, gaping for more and so (by degrees) recovered, tho' before his baptism, they had often tryed the same meanes but could not by no endeavours wrench open his teeth.

This was taken for a convincing proofe against infidelity.

But to return from this digression, the Susquehanoughs were newly driven from their habitations, at the head of Chesepiack bay, by the Cineca Indians, down to the head of Potomack, where they sought protection under the Pascataway Indians, who had a fort near the head of that river, and also were our ffriends.

After this unfortunate exploit of Mason and Brent, one or two being kill'd in Stafford, boats of war were equipt to prevent excursions over the river, and at the same time murders being (likewise) committed in Maryland, by whom not known, on either side the river, both countrys raised their quota's of a thousand men, upon whose coming before the ffort, th' Indians sent out 4 of their great men, who ask'd the reason of that hostile appearance, what they said more or offered, I do not remember to have heard; but our two comanders caused them to be (instantly) slaine, after which the Indians made an obstinate resistance shooting many of our men, and making frequent, fierce and bloody sallyes, and when they were call'd to, or offered parley, gave no other answer, than "where are our four cockarouses, i.e. great men?

At the end of six weeks, march'd out

seventy five Indians with their women children &c. who (by moonlight past our guards hallowing and firing att them without opposition, leaving 3 or 4 decrepits in the ffort.

The next morning th' English followed, but could not, or (for fear of ambuscades) would not overtake these desperate fugitives the number we lost in that siege I did not here was published.

The walls of this fort were high banks of earth, with fflankers having many loop-holes, and a ditch round all, and without this a row of tall trees fastned 3 foot deep in the earth, their bodies from 5 to 8 inches diameter, watled 6 inches apart to shoot through with the tops twisted together, and also artificially wrought, as our men could make no breach to storm it nor (being low land) coud they undermind it by reason of water neither had they cannon to batter itt, so that 'twas not taken, untill ffamine drive the Indians out of it.

They escap'd Indians (forsaking Maryland) took their rout over the head of that river, and thence over the heads of Rapahanock and York rivers, killing whom they found of th' upmost plantations untill they came to the head of James river, where (with Bacon and others) they slew Mr. Bacon's overseer, whom he much loved, and one of his servants, whose bloud hee vowed to revenge if possible.

In these frightfull times the most exposed small families withdrew into our houses of better numbers, which we fortified with pallisadoes and redoubts, neighbours in bodies joined their labours from each plantation to others alternately, taking their arms into the ffields,

and setting centinels; no man stirr'd out of door unarm'd, Indians were (ever and anon) espied, three 4. 5. 6 in a party lurking throughout the whole land, yet (what was remarkable) I rarely heard of any houses burnt, though abundance was forsaken, nor ever, of any corn or tobacco cut up, or other injury done, besides murders, except the killing a very few cattle and swine.

Frequent complaints of bloodshed were sent to S'r Wm. Berkeley (then Govern'r) from the heads of the rivers, which were as often answered with promises of assistance.

These at the heads of James and York rivers (having now most people destroyed by the Indians fflight thither from Potomack) grew impatient at the many slaughters of their neighbours and rose for their own defence, who chusing Mr. Bacon for their leader sent oftentimes to the Govern'r, humbly beseeching a comission to go against those Indians at their own charge which his hono'r as often promisd but did not send; the misteryes of these delays, were wondred at and which I ne're heard any coud into, other than the effects of his passion, and a new (not to be mentioned) occasion of avarice, to both which, he was (by the comon vogue) more than a little addicted: whatever were the popular surmizes and murmurings, vizt.

"that no bullets would pierce bever skins.

"rebbells forfeitures would be loyall inheritances &c.

During these protractions and people often slaine, most or all the officers, civill and military with as many dwellers next the heads of the rivers as made up

300 men taking Mr. Bacon for their co-man'r, met, and concerted together, the danger of going without a comiss'n on the one part, and the continuall murders of their neighbors on th' other part (not knowing whose or how many of their own turns might be next) and came to this resolution vizt. to prepare themselves with necessaries for a march, but interim to send again for a comission, which if could or could not be obteyned by a certaine day, they woud proceed comission or no comission.

This day lapsing and no com'n come, they march'd into the wilderness in quest of these Indians after whom the Govern'r sent his proclamacon, denouncing all rebells, who shoud not return within a limited day, whereupon those of estates obey'd; but Mr. Bacon with 57 men proceded untill their provisions were near spent, without finding enemy's when coming nigh a ffort of ffriend Indians, on the' other side a branch of James river, they desired reliefe offering paym't. which these Indians kindly promised to help them with on the morrow, but put them off with promises untill the third day, so as having then eaten their last morsells they could not return, but must have starved in the way homeward and now 'twas suspected, these Indians had received private messages from the Governo'r. and those to be the causes of these delusive procrastinations; whereupon the English waded shoulder deep thro' that branch to the ffort pallisado's still intreating and tendering pay, for victuals ; but that evening a shot from the place they left on the other side of that branch kill'd one of Mr. Bacon's men, which made them believe, those in the ffort had sent for other Indians to come behind 'em and cut 'em off.

Hereupon they fired the palisado's, storm'd & burnt the ffort and cabins, and (with the losse of three English) slew 150 Indians.

The circumstances of this expedicn Mr. Bacon entertain'd me with, at his own chamber, at a visit I made him, the occasion whereof is hereafter menconed.

Ffom hence they return'd home where writts were come up to elect members for an assembly, when Mr. Bacon was unanimously chosen for one, who coming down the river was comanded by a ship with guns to come on board, where waited Major Hone the high sheriff of Jamestown ready to seize him, by whom he was carried down to the Govern's and by him receiv'd with a surprizing civillity in the following words "Mr. Bacon have you forgot to be a gentleman. No, may it please yo'r hon'r answer'd Mr. Bacon; then replyed the Gover'r I'll take yo'r parol, and gave him his liberty in March 1675–76 writts came up to Stafford to choose their two members for an assembly to meet in May; when Collo. Mason Capt. Brent and other gentlemen of that county, invited me to stand a candidate; a matter I little dreamt of, having never had inclinacons to tamper in the precarious intrigues of govern't. and my hands being full of my own business; they preas't severall cogent argum'ts. and I having considerable debts in that county, besides my plantation concerns, where (in one and th' other) I had much more severely suffered, than any of themselves by th' Indians disturbances in the sumer and winter foregoing. I held it not (then) discreet to disoblige the rules of it, so Coll. Mason with myself were elected without objection, he at time convenient went on horseback ; I took my sloop and the morning I arriv'd to James town after a weeks voyage, was welcomed with the strange acclamations of All's over Bacon is taken, having not heard at home of the southern comotons, other than rumours like idle tales, of one Bacon risen up in rebellion, no body knew for what, concerning the Indians.

The next forenoon, th' assembly being met in a chamber over the generall court & our speaker chosen, the govern'r sent for us down, where his hono'r with a pathetic emphasis made a short abrupt speech wherein were these words.

"If they had killed my grandfather and grandmother, my father and mother and all my friends, yet if they come to treat of peace, they ought to have gone in peace and sat down.

The two chief comanders at the forementioned siege, who slew the ffour Indian great men, being present and part of our assembly.

The govern'r stood up againe and said "if there be joy in the presence of the angels over one sinner that repenteth, there is joy now, for we have a penitent sinner come before us, call Mr. Bacon; then did Mr. Bacon upon one knee at the bar deliver a sheet of paper confessing his crimes, and begging pardon of God the king and the govern'r. Whereto (after a short pause) he answered "God forgive you, I forgive you, thrice repeating the same words ; when Collo. Cole (one

of the councill) said, "and all that were with him, Yea, said the govern'r and all that were with him, twenty or more persons being then in irons who were taking coming down in the same and other vessels with Mr. Bacon.

About a minute after this the govern'r starting up from his chair a third time said "Mr. Bacon! if you will live civilly but till next quarter court (doubling the words) but till next quarter court, Ile promise to restore you againe to yo'r place there pointing with his hand to Mr. Bacons seat, he having been of the council before these troubles, tho' he had been a very short time in Virginia but was deposed by the foresaid proclamacon, and in th' afternoon passing by the court door, in my way up to our chamber, I saw Mr. Bacon on this quondam seat with the govern'r and councill, which seemed a marveilous indulgence to one whom he had so lately proscribed as a rebell.

The govern'r had directed us to consider of meanes for security from th' Indian insults and to defray the charge &c. advising us to beware of two rogues amongst us, naming Laurence and Drumond both dwelling at Jamestown and who were not at the Pascataway siege.

But at our entrance upon businesse, some gentlemen took this opportunity to endeavor the redressing several grievances the country then labour'd under, motions were made for inspecting the publick revenues, the collectors accompts &c. and so far was proceeded as to name part of a committee whereof Mr. Bristol (now in London) was and myself another, when we were interrupted by pressing messages from the govern'r to medle with nothing, until the Indian business was dispatch't.

This debate rose high, but was over-ruled and I have not heard that those inspections have since then been insisted upon, tho' such of that indigent people as had no benefits from the taxes groand under our being thus overborn.

The next thing was a committee for the Indian affaires, whereof in appointing the members, myself was unwillingly nominated having no knowledge in mar-tiall preparations, and after our names were taken, some of the house moved for sending 2 of our members to intreat the govern'r wou'd please to assign two of his councill to sit with, and assist us in our debates, as had been usuall.

When seeing all silent looking each at other with many discontented faces, I adventur'd to offer my humble opinion to the speaker "for the committee to form methods as agreeable to the sense of the house as we could, and report 'em whereby they would more clearly see, on what points to give the govern'r and council that trouble if perhaps it might bee needful.

These few words rais'd an uproar, one party urging hard "it had been cus-tomary and ought not to be omitted; whereto Mr. Presly my neighbour an old assembly man, sitting next me, rose up, and (in a blundering manner replied) "tis true, it has been customary, but if we have any bad customes amongst us, we are come here to mend 'em which set the house in a laughter.

This was huddl'd off without coming to a vote, and so the committee must submit to be overaw'd, and have every carpt at expression carried streight to the governor.

Our commitee being sat, the Quenn of Pamunkey (descended from Oppe-chankenough a former Emperor of Vir-ginia) was introduced, who entred the chamber with a comportment gracefull to admiration, bringing on her right hand an Englishman interpreter, and on the left her son a stripling twenty years of age, she having round her head a plat of black and white wampum peague three inches broad in imitation of a crown, and was cloathed in a mantle of dress't deer skins with the hair outwards and the edge cut round 6 inches deep which made strings resembling twisted frenge from the shoulders to the feet; thus with grave courtlike gestures and a majestick air in her face, she walk'd up our long room to the lower end of the table, where after a few intreaties she sat down; th' interpreter and her son stand-ing by her on either side as they walked up, our chairman asked her what men she woud lend us for guides in the wil-derness and to assist us against our en-emy Indians, she spake to th' interpreter to inform her what the chairman said, (tho' we believed she understood him) he told us she bid him ask her son to whom the English tongue was familiar, and who was reputed the son of an En-glish colonel, yet neither woud he speak to or seem to understand the chairman but th' interpreter told us, he referred all to his mother, who being againe urged she after a little musing with an earnest passionate countenance as if tears were ready to gush out and a fervent sort of expression made a harangue about a quarter of an hour often, interlacing (with a high shrill voice and vehement passion) these words "Tatapatamoi Chepiack, i.e. Tatapamoi dead Coll. Hill being next me, shook his head, I ask'd him what was the matter, he told me all she said was too true to our shame, and that his father was generall in that battle, where diverse years before Tatapatamoi her husband had led a hundred of his Indians in help to th' English against our former enemy Indians, and was there slaine with most of his men; for which no compensation (at all) had been to that day rendered to her wherewith she now upbraided us.

Her discourse ending and our morose chairman not advancing one cold word toward asswaging the anger and grief her speech and demeanor manifested under her oppression, nor taking any notice of all she had said, neither considering that we (then) were in our great exigency; supplicants to her for a favour of the same kind as the former, for which we did not deny the having been so ingrate, he rudely push'd againe the same question "what Indians will you now contribute, &c.? of this disregard she signified her resentment by a disdainfull aspect, and turning her head half aside, sate mute till that same question being press'd, a third time, she not returning her face to the board, answered with a low slighting voice in her own language "twelve, tho' she then had a hundred and fifty Indian men, in her town, and so rose up and gravely walked away, as not pleased with her treatment.

Whilst some daies passed in setling the quota's of men arms and amunicon pro-

visions &c. each county was to furnish, one morning early a bruit ran about the town Bacon is fled, Bacon is fled, whereupon I went straight to Mr. Lawrence, who (formerly) was of Oxford university, and for wit learning and sobriety was equall'd there by few, and who some years before (as Col. Lee tho' one of the councill and a friend of the govern'rs inform'd me) had been partially treated at law, for a considerable estate on behalf of a corrupt favourite; which Lawrence complaining loudly of, the govern'r bore him a grudge and now shaking his head, said, "old treacherous villain, and that his house was scarcht that morning, at day break, but Bacon was escaped into the country, having intimation that the governor's generosity in pardoning him, and his followers and restoring him to his seat in councill, were no other than previous weadles to amuse him and his adherents and to circumvent them by stratagem, forasmuch as the taking Mr. Bacon again into the councill was first to keep him out of assembly, and in the next place the govern'r knew the country people were hastning down with dreadfull threatnings to double revenge all wrongs shoud be done to Mr. Bacon or his men, or who-ever shou'd have had the least hand in 'em.

And so much was true that this Mr. Young Nathaniel Bacon (not yet arrived to 30 yeares) had a nigh relation namely Col. Nathaniel Bacon of long standing in the councill a very rich politick man, and childless, designing this kinsman for his heir, who (not without much paines) had prevailed with his uneasy cusin to deliver the forementioned written recantation at the bar, having compiled it ready to his hand and by whose means 'twas supposed that timely intimation was conveyed to the young gentleman to flee for his life, and also in 3 or 4 daies after Mr. Bacon was first seiz'd I saw abundance of men in town come thither from the heads of the rivers, who finding him restor'd and his men at liberty, return'd home satisfied; a few daies after which the govern'r seeing all quiet, gave out private warrants to take him againe, intending as was thought to raise the militia, and so to dispose things as to prevent his friends from gathering any more into a like numerous body and coming down a second time to save him.

In three of ffour daies after this escape, upon news that Mr. Bacon was 30 miles up the river, at the head of four hundred men, the govern'r sent to the parts adjacent, on both sides James river for the militia and all the men could be gotten to come and defend the town, espress's came almost hourly of th' army's approaches, who in less than 4 daies after the first account of 'em att 2 of the clock entered the town, without being withstood, and form'd a body upon a green, not a flight shot from the end of the state house of horse and ffoot, as well regular as veteran troops, who forthwith possest themselves of all the avenues, disarming all in town, and coming thither in boats or by land.

In half an hour after this the drum beat for the house to meet, and in less than an hour more Mr. Bacon came with a file of ffusileers on either hand near the corner of the state house where the govern'r and councill went forth to him; we saw from the window the govern'r open his breast, and Bacon strutting betwixt his two files of men with his left arm on Kenbow flinging his right arm every way both like men distracted; and if in this moment of fury, that enraged multitude had faln upon the govern'r and council we of the assembly expected the same imediate fate; I stept down and amongst the crowd of spectators found the seamen of my sloop, who pray'd me not to stir from them, when in two minutes, the govern'r walk'd towards his private apartm't. A coits cast distant at th' other end of the state house, the gentlemen of the council following him, and after them walked Mr. Bacon with outragious postures of his head arms body, and leggs, often tossing his hand from his sword to his hat and after him came a detachment of ffusileers (musketts not being there in use) who with their cocks bent presented their ffusils at a window of the assembly chamber filled with faces, repeating with menacing voices "we will have it, we will have itt, half a minute when as one of our house a person known to many of them, shook his handkercher out at the window, saying you shall have it, you shall have itt, 3 or 4 times; at these words they sate down their fusils unbent their locks and stood still untill Bacon coming back, followed him to their main body; in this hubub a servant of mine got so nigh as to hear the govern'rs words, and also followed Mr. Bacon, and heard what he said, who came and told me, that when the govern'r opened his breast he said "here! shoot me, foregod fair mark shoot, often rehearsing the same, without any other words; whereto Mr. Bacon answer'd "no may it please yo'r hono'r we will not hurt a hair of yo'r head, nor of any other mans, we are come for a comission to save our lives from th' Indians, which you have so often promised, and now we will have it before we go.

But when Mr. Bacon followed the govern'r and councill with the forementioned impetuos (like delirious) actions whil'st that party presented their ffusils at the window full of ffaces, he said "Dam my bloud I'le kill govern'r councill assembly and all, and then I'le sheath my sword in my own heart's bloud; and afterwards 'twas said Bacon had given a signall to his men who presented their fusils at those gasing out at the window, that if he shoud draw his sword, they were on sight of it to fire, and slay us, so near was the massacre of us all that very minute, had Bacon in that paroxism of phrentick fury but drawn his sword before the pacifick handkercher was shaken out at the window.

In an hour or more after these violent concussions Mr. Bacon came up to our chamber and desired a comission from us to go against the Indians; our speaker sat silent, when one of Mr. Blayton a neighbor to Mr. Bacon and elected with him a member of assembly for the same county (who therefore durst speak to him) made answer, " 'twas not in our province, or power, nor of any other, save the king's viceregent our govern'r, he press'd hard nigh half an hours harangue on the preserving our lives from the Indians, inspecting the publick revenues, th' exorbitant taxes and redressing the grievances and calamities of that deplorable country, whereto having no other answer, he went away dissatisfied.

Next day there was a rumour the govern'r and councill had agreed Mr. Bacon shou'd have a comission to go generall of the fforces, we then were raising, whereupon I being a member for Stafford, the most northern frontier, and where the war begun, considering that Mr. Bacon dwelling in the most southern ffrontier county, might the less regard the parts I represented, I went to Coll. Cole (an active member of the councill) desiring his advise, if applicacons to Mr. Bacon on that subject were then seasonable and safe, which he approving and earnestly advising I went to Mr. Lawrence who was esteemed Mr. Bacons principall consultant, to whom he took me with him, and there left mewhere I was entertained 2 or 3 hours with the particular relacons of diverse before recited transactions; and as to the matter I spake of, he told me, that th' govern'r had indeed promised him the comand of the forces, and if his hon'r shou'd keep his word (which he doubted) he assured me "the like care shoud be taken of the remotest corners in the land, as of his own dwelling-house, and pray'd me to advise him what persons in those parts were most fit to bear comands I frankly gave him my opinion that the most satisfactory gentlemen to govern'r and people, would be comanders of the militia, wherewith he was well pleased, and himself wrote a list of those nominated.

That evening I made known what had past with Mr. Bacon to my colleague Coll. Mason (whose bottle attendance doubled my task) the matter he liked well, but questioned the govern'rs approbacon of it.

I confess'd the case required sedate thoughts, reasoning, that he and such gentlemen must either comand or be comanded, and if on their denials Mr.

Bacon should take distaste, and be constrained to appoint comanders out of the rabble, the govern'r himself with the persons and estates of all in the land woud be at their dispose, whereby their own ruine might be owing to themselves; in this he agreed and said "If the govern'r woud give his own comission he would be content to serve under generall Bacon (as now he began to be intituled) but first woud consult other gentlemen in the same circumstances; who all concur'd 'twas the most safe barier in view against pernicious designes, if such shoud be put in practice; with this I acquainted Mr. Lawrence who went (rejoicing) to Mr. Bacon with the good tidings, that the militia comanders were inclined to serve under him, as their generall, in case the governor woud please to give them his own comissions.

Wee of the house proceeded to finish the bill for the war, which by the assent of the govern'r and councill being past into an act the govern'r sent us a letter directed to his majesty, wherein were these words "I have above 30 years governed the most flourishing country the sun ever shone over, but am now encompassed with rebellion like waters in every respect like to that of Massanello except their leader, and of like import was the substance of that letter. But we did not believe his hono'r sent us all the wrote to his majesty.

Some judicious gentlemen of our house likewise penn'd a letter or remonstrance to be sent his maj'tie setting forth the gradations of those erupcons, and two or three of them with Mr. Minge our clerk brought it me to compile a few lines forthe conclusion of it, which I did (tho' not without regret in those watchfull times, when every man had eyes on him, but what I wrote was with all possible deference to the govern'r and in the most soft terms my pen cou'd find the case to admit.

Col. Spencer being my neighbor and intimate friend, and a prevalent member in the councill I pray'd him to intreat the govern'r we might be dissolved, for that was my first and shoud be my last going astray from my wonted sphere of merchandize and other my private concernments into the dark and slippery meanders of court embarrassments, he told me the govern'r had not (then) determined his intention, but he wou'd move his hono'r about itt, and in 2 or 3 dayes we were dissolved, which I was most heartily glad of, because of my getting loose againe from being hampered amongst those pernicious entanglem'ts in the labyrinths and snares of state ambiguities, and which untill then I had not seen the practice nor the dangers of, for it was observ'd that several of the members had secret badges of distinction fixt upon 'em, as not docill enough to gallop the future races, that court seem'd dispos'd to lead 'em, whose maximes I had ofte times heard whisper'd before, and then found confirm'd by diverse considerate gentlem'n vizt. "that the wise and the rich were prone to ffaction and sedition but the fools and poor were easy to be governed.

Many members being met one evening nigh sunsett, to take our leaves each of other, in order next day to return homewards, came Genll. Bacon with his hand full of unfolded papers and overlooking us round, walking in the room said "which of these gentlem'n shall I intreat to write a few words for me where every one looking aside as not willing to meddle; Mr. Lawrence pointed at me saying "that gentleman writes very well which I endeavouring to excuse, Mr. Bacon came stooping to the ground and said "pray Sir do me the hon'r to write a line for me.

This surprizing accostm't shockt me into a melancholy consternation, dreading upon one hand, that Stafford county would feel the smart resentment if I should refuse him whose favour I had so lately sought and been generously promis'd on their behalf; and on th' other hand fearing the govern'rs displeasure who I knew woud soon hear of it: what seem'd most prudent at this hazadous dilemma, was to obviate the present impending peril; so Mr. Bacon made me sit the whole night by him filling up those papers, which I then saw were blank comissions sign'd by the govern'r incerting such name and writing other matters as he dictated; which I took to be the happy effects of the consult before mentioned, with the comanders of the militia becausehe gave me the names of very few others to put into these comissions, and in the morning he left me with an hours worke or more to finish, when came to me Capt. Carver, and said he had been to wait on the Generall for a comission, and that he was resolved to adventure his old bones against the Indian rogues with other the like discourse, and at length told me that I was in mighty favor—and he was bid to tell me, that whatever I desired in the general's power, was at my service, I pray'd him humbly to thank his hon'r and to acquaint him I had no other boon to

crave, than his promis'd kindnesse to Stafford county, for beside the not being worthy, I never had been conversant in military matters, and also having lived tenderly, my service cou'd be of no benefit because the hardships and fatigues of a wilderness campaigne would put a speedy period to my daies little expecting to hear of more intestine broiles, I went home to Patomack, where reports were afterwards various: we had account that Generall Bacon was march'd with a thousand men into the fforest to seek the enemy Indians, and in a few daies after our next news was, that the govern'r had sumoned together the militia of Glocester and Middlesex counties to the number of twelve hundred men, and proposed to them to follow and suppress that rebell Bacon; whereupon arose a murmuring before his face "Bacon Bacon Bacon, and all walked out of the field, muttering as they went "Bacon Bacon Bacon, leaving the governor and those that came with him to themselves, who being thus abandon'd wafted over Chesepiacke bay 30 miles to Occomack where are two countres of Virginia.

Mr. Bacon hearing of this came back part of the way, and sent out parties of horse patrolling through every county, carrying away prisoners all whom he distrusted might any more molest his Indian prosecucon yet giving liberty to such as pledg'd him their oaths to return home and live quiet; the copies or contents of which oaths I never saw, but heard were very strict, tho' little observed.

About this time was a spie detected pretending himself a deserter who had twice or thrice come and gone from party to party and was by councill of warr sentenced to death, after which Bacon declared openly to him "that if any one man in the army wou'd speak a word to save him, he shou'd not suffer, which no man appearing to do, he was execeuted, upon this manifestation of clemency Bacon was applauded for a mercifull man, not wiling to spill Christian bloud, nor indeed was it said, that he put any other man to death in cold bloud, or plunder any house; nigh the same time came Maj. Langston with his troop of horseand quarterd two nights at my house who (after high compliments from the generall) told me I was desired "to accept the lieutenancy for preserving the peace in the s. northern counties betwixt Potomack and Rappahannock rivers, I humbly thank'd his hon'r excusing myself; as I had done before on that invitation of the like nature at Jamestown, but did hear he was mightily offended at my evasions and threatened to remember me.

The govern'r made a 2d attempt coming over from Accomack with what men he could procure in sloops and boats forty miles up the river to Jamestown, which Bacon hearing of, came againe down from his fforest persuit, and finding a bank not a flight shot long, cast up thwart the neck of the peninsula there in Jamestown, he stormed it, and took the town, in which attack were 12 men slaine and wounded but the govern'r with most of his followers fled back, down the river in their vessells.

Here resting a few daies they concerted the burning of the town, wherein Mr. Lawrence and Mr. Drumond owning the two best houses save one, set fire each to his own house, which example

the souldiers following laid the whole town (with church and state-house) in ashes, saying, the rogues should harbour no more there.

On these reiterated molestacons Bacon calls a convention at Midle plantation 15 miles from Jamestown in the month of August 1676, where an oath with one or more proclamations were formed, and writts by him issued for an assembly; the oaths or writs I never saw, but one proclamation comanded all men in the land on pain of death to joine him and retire into the wildernesse upon arrival of the forces expected from England, and oppose them untill they shoud propose or accept to treat of an accomodation, which we who lived comfortably could not have undergone, so as the whole land must have become an Aceldama if God's exceeding mercy had not timely removed him.

During these tumults in Virginea a 2d danger menaced Maryland by an insurrection in that province, complaining of their heavy taxes &c. where 2 or 3 of the leading malecontents (men otherwise of laudable characters) were put to death, which stifled the father spreading of that flame, Mr. Bacon (at this time) press't the best ship in James river carrying 20 guns and putting into her his lieutenant generall Mr. Bland (a gentleman newly come thither from England to possesse the estate of his deceased uncle late of the council) and under him the forementioned Capt. Carver formerly a comander of merch'ts ships with men and all necessaries, he sent her to ride before Accomack to curband intercept all smaller vessels of war comission'd by the govern'r coming often over and making depredations on the western shoar, as if we had been fforreign enemies, which gives occasion to his place to digresse a few words.

Att first assembly after the peace came a message to them from the govern'r for some marks of distinction to be sett on his loyal friends of Accomack, who received him in his adversity which when came to be consider'd Col. Warner (then speaker) told the house "ye know that what mark of distinction his hon'r coud have sett on those of Accomack unlesse to give them earmarks or burnt marks for robbing and ravaging honest people, who stay'd at home and preserv'd the estates of those who ran away, when none intended to hurt 'em.

Now returning to Capt. Carver the govern'r sent for him to come on shoar, promising his peacable return, who answer'd, he could not trust his word, but if he woud send his hand and seal, he wou'd adventure to wait upon his hono'r which was done, and Carver went in his sloop well armed and man'd with the most trusty of his men where he was caress'd with wine &c. and large promises, if he would forsake Bacon, resigne his ship or joine with him; to all which he answer'd that "if he served the Devill he woud be true to his trust, but that he was resolved to go home and live quiet.

In the time of this recepcon and parley, an armed boat was prepared with many oars in a creek not far off, but out of sight, which when Carver sail'd, row'd out of the creek, and it being almost calm the boat outwent the sloop whilst all on board the ship were upon the deck, staring at both, thinking the boats company coming on board by Carvers invitation to be civilly entertained in requitall of the kindness (they supposed he had received on shoar, untill coming under the stern, those in the boat slipt nimbly in at the gun room ports with pistols &c. When one couragious gentleman ran up to the deck, and clapt a pistoll to Blands breast, saying you are my prisoner, the boats company suddainly following with pistolls swords &c. And after Capt. Larimore (the comander of the ship before she was prest) having from the highest and hindmost part of the stern interchang'd a signal from the shoar by flirting his handkercher about his nose, his own former crew had laid handspikes ready, which they (at that instant) caught up &c. so as Bland and Carvers men were amazed and yielded.

Carver seeing a hurly burly on the ships deck, would have gone away with his sloop, but having little wind and the ship threatning to sink him, he tamely came on board; where Blandand he with their party were laid in irons and in 3 or 4 daies Carver was hang'd on shoar, which Sir Henry Chicheley the first of the councill then a prisoner, (with diverse other gentlemen) to Mr. Bacon, did afterwards exclaim against as a most rash and wicked act of the govern'r. he (in particular) expecting to have been treated by way of reprizall, as Bacons friend Carver had been by the govern'r. Mr. Bacon now returns from his last expedicon sick of a fflux; without finding any enemy Indians, having not gone far by reason of the vexations behind him, nor had he one dry day in all his marches to and fro in the fforest whilst the plantations (not 50 miles distant) had a sumer so dry as stinted the Indian corn and tobacco &c. Which the people ascribed to the pawawings i.e. the sorceries of the Indians, in a while Bacon dyes and was succeeded by his Lieuten't Genll. Ingram, who had one Wakelet next in comand under him, whereupon hasten'd over the govern'r to York river, and with him they articled for themselves and whom else they could, and so all submitted and were pardoned exempting those nominated and otherwise proscribed, in a proclamation of indempnity, the principall of whom were Lawrence and Drumond.

Mr. Bland was then a prisoner having been taken with Carver, as before noted, and in few daies Mr. Drumond was brought in, when the govern'r being on board a ship came imediately to shore and complimented him with the ironicall sarcasm of a low bend, saying "Mr. Drumond! you are very welcome, I am more glad to see you, than any man in Virginia, Mr. Drumond you shall be hang'd in half an hour; who answered what yo'r hon'r pleases, and as soon as a council of war cou'd meet, his sentence be dispatcht and a gibbet erected (which took up near two houses) he was executed.

This Mr. Drumond was a sober Scotch gentleman of good repute with whome I had not a particular acquaintance, nor do I know the cause of that rancour his hono'r had against him, other than his pretensions in comon for the publick but meeting him by accident the morning I left the town, I advis'd him to be very wary, for he saw the govern'r had put a brand upon him he (gravely expressing my name) answered

"I am in over shoes, I will be over boots, which I was sorry to heare and left him.

The last account of Mr. Lawrence was from an uppermost plantation, whence he and ffour others desperado's with horses pistolls &c. march'd away in a snow ancle deep, who were thought to have cast themselves into a branch of some river, rather than be treated like Drumond.

Bacons body was so made away, as his bones were neverfound to be exposed on a gibbet as was purpos'd, stones being laid in his coffin, supposed to be done by Lawrence.

Near this time arrived a small ffleet with a regiment from England S'r John Berry admirall, Col. Herbert Jefferies comander of the land forces and Collo. Morrison who had one year been a former govern'r there, all three joined in comission with or to S'r William Barclay, soon after when a generall court and also an assembly were held, where some of our former assembly (with so many others) were put to death, diverse whereof were persons of honest reputations and handsome estates, as that the assembly petitioned the governour to spill no more bloud, and Mr. Presley at his coming home told me, he believed the govern'r would have hang'd half the countrey, if they had let him alone. The first was Mr. Bland whose ffriends in England had procured his pardon to be sent over with the ffleet, which he pleaded at his tryall, was in the govern'rs pocket (tho' whether 'twas so, or how it came there, I know not, yet did not hear 'twas openly contradicted,) but he was answered by Coll. Morrison that he pleaded his pardon at swords point, which was look'd upon an odd sort of reply, and he was executed; (as was talked) by private instructions from England the Duke of York having sworn "by God Bacon and Bland shoud dye.

The govern'r went in the ffleet to London (whether by comand from his majesty or spontaneous I did not hear) leaving Col. Jefferyes in his place, and by next shipping came back a person who waited on his hono'r in his voyage, and untill his death, from whom a report was whisper'd about, that the king did say "that old fool has hang'd more men in that naked country, than he had done for the murther of his ffather, whereof the governo'r hearing dyed soon after without having seen his majesty; which shuts up this tragedy.

## APPENDIX

To avoid incumbering the body of the foregoing little discourse, I have not therein mentioned the received opinion in Virginia, which very much attributed the promoting these perturbacons to Mr. Lawrence and Mr. Bacon with his other adherents, were esteemed, as but wheels agitated by the weight of his former and present resentments, after their choler was raised up to a very high pitch, at having been (so long and often) trifled with on their humble supplications to the govern'r for his imediate taking in hand the most speedy meanes towards stopping the continued effusions of so much English bloud, from time to time by the Indians; which comon sentim'ts I have the more reason to believe were not altogether groundlesse, because my-

self have heard him (in his familiar discourse) insinuate as if his fancy gave him prospect of finding (at one time or other) some expedient not only to repaire his great losse, but therewith to see those abuses rectified that the countrey was oppressed with through (as he said) the forwardness advarice and French despotick methods of the govern'r. and likewise I know him to be a thinking man, and tho' nicely honest, affable, and without blemish, in his conversation and dealings, yet did he manifest abundance of uneasiness in the sense of his hard usages, which might prompt him to improve that Indian quarrel to the service of his animosities, and for this the more fair and frequent opportunities offered themselves to him by his dwelling at Jamestown, where was the concourse from all parts to the govern'r. and besides that he had married a wealthy widow who kept a large house of publick entertainm't. unto which resorted those of the best quality, and such others as businesse called to that town, and his parts with his even temper made his converse coveted by persons of all ranks; so that being subtile, and having these advantages he might with lesse difficulty discover mens inclinations, and instill his notions where he found those woud be imbib'd with greatest satisfaction.

As for Mr. Bacon fame did lay to his charge the having run out his patrimony in England except what he brought to Virginia and of that the most part to be exhausted, which together made him suspected of casting an eye to search for retrievment in the troubled waters of popular discontents, wanting patience to wait the death of his oppulent counsin, old Collo. Bacon, whose estate he expected to inherit.

But he was too young, too much a stranger there, and of a disposition too precipitate, to manage things to that length those were carried, had not thoughtful Mr. Lawrence been at the bottom.

## Edward Winslow, "Chapter 7," *Good Newes from New England,* 1624

*In this chapter of* Good Newes, *which is a continuation of Winslow's earlier* Mourt's Relation: A Journal of the Pilgrims at Plymouth *(London, 1624), Winslow provides a detailed description of the religious beliefs, gendered division of labor, political structures, and customs of the Indians he encountered in Massachusetts.*

*Source:* Edward Winslow, *Good Newes from New England* (London, 1624)

Thus have I made a true and full Narration of the state of our Plantation, and such things as were most remarkable therein since December 1621. If I have omitted any thing, it is either through weakness of memory, or because I judged it not material: I confess my stile rude, and unskillfulness in the task I undertook, being urged hereunto by opportunity, which I knew to be wanting in others, and but for which I would not have undertaken the same; yet as it is rude so it is plain, and therefore the eas-ier to be understood; wherein others may see that which we are bound to acknowledge, viz. That if ever any people in these later ages were upheld by the providence of God after a more special manner then others, then we: and therefore are the more bound to celebrate the memory of his goodness, with everlasting thankfulness. For in these forenamed straits, such was our state, as in the morning we had often our food to seek for the day, and yet performed the duties of our Callings, I mean other daily labors, to provide for after time: and though at some times in some seasons at noon I have seen men stagger by reason of faintness for want of food, yet ere night by the good providence and blessing of God, we have enjoyed such plenty as though the windows of heaven had been opened unto us. How few, weak, and raw were we at our first beginning, and there selling, and in the midst of barbarous enemies? yet God wrought our peace for us. How often have we been at the pits brim, and in danger to be swallowed up, yea, not knowing, till afterward that we were in peril? and yet God preserved us: yea, and from how many that we yet know not of, he that knoweth all things can best tell: So that when I seriously consider of things, I cannot but think that God hath a purpose to give that Land as an inheritance to our Nation, and great pity it were that it should long lie in so desolate a state, considering it agreeth so well with the constitution of our bodies, being both fertile, and so temperate for heat and cold, as in that respect one can scarce distinguish New-England from Old.

A few things I thought meet to add hereunto, which I have observed amongst the Indians, both touching their Religion, and sundry other Customs amongst them. And first, whereas my self and others, in former Letters (which came to the Press against my will and knowledge) wrote, that the Indians about us are a people without any Religion, or knowledge of any God, therein I erred, though we could then gather no better: For as they conceive of many divine powers, so of one whom they call Kiehtan, to be the principal and maker of all the rest, and to be made by none: He (they say) created the heavens, earth, sea, and all creatures contained therein. Also that he made one man and one woman, of whom they and we and all mankind came: but how they became so far dispersed that know they not. At first they say, there was no Sachem, or King, but Kiehtan, who dwelleth above in the Heavens, whither all good men go when they die, to see their friends, and have their fill of all things: This his habitation lyeth far West-ward in the heavens, they say; thither the bad men go also, and knock at his door, but he bids them Quatchet, that is to say, Walk abroad, for there is no place for such; so that they wander in restless want and penury: Never man saw this Kiehtan; only old men tell them of him, and bid them tell their children, yea, to charge them to teach their posterities the same, and lay the like charge upon them. This power they acknowledge to be good, and when they would obtain any great matter, meet together, and cry unto him, and so likewise for plenty, victory, etc. sing, dance, feast, give thanks, and hang up Garlands and other things in memory of the same.

Another power they worship, whom they call Hobomok, and to the Northward of us Hobbamoqui; this as far as we can conceive is the Devil, him they call upon to cure their wounds and diseases. When they are curable, he persuades them he sends the same for some conceived anger against them, but upon their calling upon him can and cloth help them: But when they are mortal, and not curable in nature, then he persuades them Kiehtan is angry and sends them, whom none can cure: in so much, as in that respect only they somewhat doubt whether he be simply good, and therefore in sickness never call upon him. This Hobomok appears in sundry forms unto them, as in the shape of a Man, a Deer, a Fawn, an Eagle, etc. but most ordinarily a Snake: He appears not to all but the chiefest and most judicious amongst them, though all of them strive to attain to that hellish height of honor.

He appeareth most ordinary and is most conversant with three sorts of people, one I confess I neither know by name nor office directly of these they have few but esteem highly of them, and think that no weapon can kill them: another they call by the name of Powah, and the third Pniese. The office and duty of the Powah is to be exercised principally in calling upon the Devil, and curing diseases of the sick or wounded. The common people join with him in the exercise of invocation, but do but only assent, or as we term it, say ten to that he saith, yet sometime break out into a short musical note with him. The Powah is eager and free in speech, fierce in countenance, and joineth many antics and laborious gestures with the same over the party diseased. If the party be wounded he will also seem to suck the wound, but if they be curable (as they say) he toucheth it not, but a Skooke, that is the Snake, or Wobsacuck, that is the Eagle, sitteth on his shoulder and licks the same. This none see but the Powah, who tells them he cloth it himself. If the party be otherwise diseased, it is accounted sufficient if in any shape he but come into the house, taking it for an undoubted sign of recovery.

And as in former ages Apollo had his temple at Delphos, and Diana at Ephesus; so have I heard them call upon some as if they had their residence in some certain places, or because they appeared in those forms in the same. In the Powahs speech he promiseth to sacrifice many skins of beasts, kettles, hatchets, beads knives, and other the best things they have to the fiend, if he will come to help the party diseased: But whether they perform it I know not. The other practices I have scene, being necessarily called at some times to be with their sick, and have used the best arguments I could make them understand against the same: They have told me I should see the Devil at those times come to the party, but I assured my self and them of the contrary, which so proved: yea, them selves have confessed they never saw him when any of us were present. In desperate end extraordinary hard travel in childbirth, when the party cannot be delivered by the ordinary meals, they send for this Powah though ordinarily their travel is not so extreme as in our parts of the world, they being of a more hardy nature; for on the third day after child-birth I have scene the mother with the infant upon a small occasion in cold weather in a boat upon the Sea.

Many sacrifices the Indians use, and in some cases kill children. It seemeth they are various in their religious worship in a little distance, and grow more and more cold in their worship to Kiehtan; saying in their memory he was much more called upon. The Narragansetts exceed in their blind devotion, and have a great spacious house wherein only some few (that are as we may term them Priests) come: thither at certain known times resort all their people, and offer almost all the riches they have to their gods, as kettles, skins, hatchets, beads, knives, etc. all which are cast by the Priests into a great fire that they make in the midst of the house, and there consumed to ashes. To this offering every man bringeth freely, and the more he is known to bring, hath the better esteem of all men. This the other Indians about us approve of as good, and wish their Sachems would appoint the like: and because the plague hath not reigned at Narragansetts as at other places about them, they attribute to this custom there used.

The Pnieses are men of great courage and wisdom, and to these also the Devil appeareth more familiarly then to others, and as we conceive maketh covenant with them to preserve them from death, by wounds, with arrows, knives, hatchets, etc. or at least both themselves and especially the people think themselves to be freed from the same. And though against their batters all of them by painting disfigure themselves, yet they are known by their cottage and boldness, by reason whereof one of them will chase almost an hundred men, for they account it death for whomsoever stand in their way. These are highly esteemed of all sorts of people, and are of the Sachems Council, without whom they will not war or undertake any weighty business. In war their Sachems for their more safety go in the midst of them. They are commonly men of the greatest stature and strength, and such as will endure most hardness, and yet are more discreet, courteous, and humane in their carriages then any amongst them scorning theft, lying, and the like base dealings, and stand as much upon their reputation as any men.

And to the end they may have store of these, they train up the most forward and likeliest boys from their childhood in great hardness, and make them abstain from dainty meat, observing divers orders prescribed, to the end that when they are of age the Devil may appear to them, causing to drink the juice of Sentry and other bitter herbs till they cast, which they must disgorge into the platter, and drink again, and again, till at length through extraordinary oppressing of nature it will seem to be all blood, and this the boys will do with eagerness at the first, and so continue till by reason of faintness they can scarce stand on their legs, and then must go forth into the cold: also they beat their shins with sticks, and cause them to run through bushes, stumps, and brambles, to make them hardy and acceptable to the Devil, that in time he may appear unto them.

Their Sachems cannot be all called Kings, but only some few of them, to whom the rest resort for protection, and

pay homage unto them, neither may they war without their knowledge and approbation, yet to be commanded by the greater as occasion serveth. Of this sort is Massasoit our friend, and Conanacus of Narragansett our supposed enemy.

Every Sachem taketh care for the widow and fatherless, also for such as are aged, and any way maimed, if their friends be dead or not able to provide for them.

A Sachem will not take any to wife but such an one as is equal to him in birth, otherwise they say their seed would in time become ignoble, and though they have many other wives, yet are they no other then concubines or servants, and yield a kind of obedience to the principal, who ordereth the family, and them in it. The like their men observe also, and will adhere to the first during their lives; but put away the other at their pleasure.

This government is successive and not by choice. If the father die before the son or daughter be of age, then the child is committed to the protection and tuition of some one amongst them, who ruleth in his stead till he be of age, but when that is I know not.

Every Sachem knoweth how far the bounds and limits of his own Country extendeth, and that is his own proper inheritance, out of that if any of his men desire land to set their come, he giveth them as much as they can use, and sets them their bounds. In this circuit whosoever hunteth, if they kill any venison, bring him his fee, which is the fore parts of the same, if it be killed on the land, but if in the water, then the skin thereof:

The great Sachems or Kings, know their Own bounds or limits of land, as well as the rest.

All travelers or strangers for the most part lodge at the Sachems, when they come they tell them how long they will stay, and to what place they go, during which time they receive entertainment according to their persons, but want not.

Once a year the Pnieses use to provoke the people to bestow much come on the Sachem. To that end they appoint a certain time and place near the Sachems dwelling, where the people bring many baskets of come, and make a great stack thereof. There the Pnieses stand ready to give thanks to the people on the Sachems behalf, and after acquainteth the Sachems therewith, who fetcheth the same, and is no less thankful, bestowing many gifts on them.

When any are visited with sickness, their friends resort unto them for their comfort, and continue with them ofttimes till their death or recovery. If they die they stay a certain time to mourn for them. Night and morning they perform this duty many days after the burial in a most doleful manner, insomuch as though it be ordinary and the note musical, which they take one from another, and all together, yet it will draw tears from their eyes, and almost from ours also. But if they recover then because their sickness was chargeable, they send come and other gifts unto them at a certain appointed time, whereat they feast and dance, which they call Commoco.

When they bury the dead they sow up the corps in a mat and so put it in the earth. If the party be a Sachem they cover him with many curious mats, and bury all his riches with him, and enclose the grave with a pale. If it be a child the father will also put his own most special jewels and ornaments in the earth with it, also will cut his hair and disfigure himself very much in token of sorrow. If it be the man or woman of the house, they will pull down the mattes and leave the frame standing, and bury them in or near the same, and either remove their dwelling or give over house-keeping.

The men employ themselves wholly in hunting, and other exercises of the bow, except at some times they take some pains in fishing.

The women live a most slavish life, they carry all their burdens, set and dress their come, gather it in, seek out for much of their food, beat and make ready the come to eat, and have all household care lying upon them.

The younger sort reverence the elder, and do all mean offices whilst they are together, although they be strangers. Boys and girls may not wear their hair like men and women, but are distinguished thereby. A man is not accounted a man till he do some notable act, or show forth such courage and resolution as becometh his place. The men take much tobacco, but for boys so to do they account it odious.

All their names are significant and variable, for when they come to the state of men and women, they alter them according to their deeds or dispositions.

When a maid taken in marriage sue first cutteth her hair, and after weareth a covering on her head till her hair be grown out. Their women are diversely disposed, some as modest as they will scarce talk one with another in the company of men, being very chaste also; yet other some light, lascivious and wanton.

If a woman have a bad husband, or cannot affect him, and there be war or opposition between that and any other people, she will run away from him to the contrary party and there live, where they never come unwelcome: for where are most women, there is greatest plenty.

When a woman hath her monthly terms she separateth herself from all other company, and liveth certain days in a house alone: after which she washeth her self and all that she hath touched or used, and is again received to her husbands bed or family.

For adultery the husband will beat his wife and put her away, if he please. Some common strumpets there are as well as in other places, but they are such as either never married, or widows, or put away for adultery: for no man will keep such an one to wife.

In matters of unjust and dishonest dealing the Sachem examineth and punisheth the same. In case of thefts, for the first offense he is disgracefully rebuked, for the second beaten by the Sachem with a cudgel on the naked back, for the third he is beaten with many strokes, and hath his nose slit upward, that thereby all men may both know and shun him. If any man kill another, he must likewise die for the same. The Sachem not only passeth the sentence upon male-factors, but executeth the same with his own hands, if the party be then present; if not, sendeth his own knife in case of death, in the hands of others to perform the same. But if the offender be to re-

ceive other punishment, he will not receive the same but from the Sachem himself, before whom being naked he kneeleth, and will not offer to run away though he beat him never so much, it being a greater disparagement for a man to cry during the time of his correction, then is his offense and punishment.

As for their apparel they wear breeches and stockings in one like some Irish, which is made of Deer skins, and have shoes of the same leather. They wear also a Dears skin loose about them like a cloak, which they will turn to the weather side. In this habit they travel, but when they are at home or come to their journeys end, presently they pull off their breeches, stocking, and shoes, wring out the water if they be wet, and dry them, and rub or chafe the same. Though these be off, yet have they another small garment that covereth their secrets. The men wear also when they go abroad in cold weather an Otter or Fox skin on their right arm, but only their bracer on the left. Women and all of that sex wear strings about their legs, which the men never do.

The people are very ingenious and observative, they keep account of time by the moon, and winters or summers; they know diverse of the stars by name, in particular, they know the North-star and call it maske, which is to say the bear. Also they have many names for the winces. They will guess very well at the wince and weather before hand, by observations in the heavens. They report also, that some of them can cause the wince to blow in what part they list, can raise storms and tempests which they usually do when they intend the death or destruction of other people, that by reason of the unseasonable weather they may take advantage of their enemies in their houses. At such times they perform their greatest exploits, and in such seasons when they are at enmity with any, they keep more careful watch then at other times.

As for the language it is very copious, large, and difficult, as yet we cannot attain to any great measure thereof; but can understand them, and explain our selves to their understanding, by the help of those that daily converse with us. And though there be difference in an hundred miles distance of place, both in language and manners, yet not so much but that they very well understand each other. And thus much of their lives and manners.

Instead of Records and Chronicles, they take this course, where any remarkable act is done, in memory of it, either in the place, or by some path-way near adjoining, they make a round hole in the ground about a foot deep, and as much over, which when others passing by behold, they inquire the cause and occasion of the same, which being once known, they are careful to acquaint all men, as occasion serveth therewith. And least such holes should be filled, or grown up by any accident, as men pass by they will oft renew the same: By which means many things of great Antiquity are fresh in memory. So that as a man travelleth, if he can understand his guide, his journey will be the less tedious, by reason of the many historical Discourses will be related unto him.

## Peter Schaghen to the Directors of the West India Company, 1626

*Schaghen was the representative of the States General in the Assembly of the Nineteen of the West India Company. In this report to the directors of the company he announces the purchase of Manhattan Island for sixty guilders. This is the earliest reference to the purchase of Manhattan that scholars have found.*

*Source:* New Netherland Project, New York State Archives; original in Rijksarchief in The Hague.

RCVD. 7 NOVEMBER 1626

*High and Mighty Lords,*
Yesterday the ship the Arms of Amsterdam arrived here. It sailed from New Netherland out of the River Mauritius on the 23d of September. They report that our people are in good spirit and live in peace. The women also have borne some children there. They have purchased the Island Manhattes from the Indians for the value of 60 guilders. It is 11,000 morgens in size [about 22,000 acres]. They had all their grain sowed by the middle of May, and reaped by the middle of August They sent samples of these summer grains: wheat, rye, barley, oats, buckwheat, canary seed, beans and flax. The cargo of the aforesaid ship is:

7246 Beaver skins
178½ Otter skins
675 Otter skins
48 Mink skins
36 Lynx skins

33 Minks

34 Weasel skins

Many oak timbers and nut wood. Herewith, High and Mighty Lords, be commended to the mercy of the Almighty,

*Your High and Mightinesses' obedient,*

*P. Schaghen*

## Richard Frethorne to His Father and Mother, March 20, April 2 and 3, 1623

*The Frethorne letter is the best example of indentured servants' complaints and sufferings in the seventeenth-century Chesapeake.*

Source: Susan Kingsbury, ed., *The Records of the Virginia Company of London* (Washington, D.C.: Government Printing Office, 1935), 4:58–62.

*Loving and Kind Father and Mother*

My most humble duty remembered to you, hoping in god of your good health, as I myself am at the making hereof. This is to let you understand that I you child am in a most heavy case by reason of the country, is such that it causeth much sickness, as the scurvy and the bloody flux and diverse other diseases, which maketh the body very poor and weak. And when we are sick there is nothing to comfort us; for since I came out of the ship I never ate anything but peas, and loblollie. As for deer or venison I never saw any since I came into this land. There is indeed some fowl, but we are not allowed to go and get it, but must work hard both early and late for a mess of water gruel and a mouthful of bread

and beef. A mouthful of bread for a penny loaf must serve for four men which is most pitiful if you did know as much as I, when people cry out day and night, Oh That they were in England without their limbs and would not care to lose any limb to be in England again, yea, though they beg from door to door. For we live in fear of the emeny every hour, yet we have had a combat with them on the Sunday before Shrovetide, and we took two alive, and make slaves of them, but it was by policy, for we are in great danger; for our plantation is very weak by reason of the death and sickness of our company. For we came but twenty for the merchants, and they are half dead just; and we look every hour when two more should go. Yet there came some four other men yet to live with us, of which there is but one alive; and our Lieutenant is dead, and his father, and his brother. And there was some five or six of the last year's twenty, of which there is but three left, so that we are fain to get other men to plant with us; and yet we are but 32 to fight against 3000 if they should come. And the nighest help that we have is ten mile of us, and when the rogues overcame this place last they slew 80 persons. How then shall we do, for we lie even in their teeth? They may easily take us, but that God is merciful and can save with few as well as with many, as he showed to Gilead. And like Gilead's soldiers, if they lapped water, we drink water which is but weak. And I have nothing to comfort me, nor is there nothing to be gotten here but sickness and death, except that one had money to lay out in some things for profit. But I have nothing at all—no, not a shirt to my back but two rags, nor clothes but one poor suit, nor but one pair of shoes, but one pair of stockings, but one cap, but two bands. My cloak is stolen by one of my fellows, and to his dying hour would not tell me what he did with it; but some of my fellows saw him have butter and beef out of a ship, which my cloak, I doubt, paid for. So that I have not a penny, nor a penny worth, to help me too either spice or sugar or strong waters, without the which one cannot live here. For as strong beer in England doth fatten and strengthen them, so water here doth wash and weaken these here only keeps life and soul together. But I am not half a quarter so strong as I was in England, and all is for want of victuals; for I do protest unto you that I have eaten more in day at home than I have allowed me here for a week. You have given more than my day's allowance to a beggar at the door; and if Mr. Jackson had not relieved me, I should be in a poor case. But he like a father and she like a loving mother doth still help me. For when we go to Jamestown that is 10 miles of us, there lie all the ships that come to land, and there they must deliver their goods. And when we went up to town [we would go], as it may be, on Monday at noon, and come there by night, [and] then load the next day by noon, and go home in the afternoon, and unload, and then away again in the night, and be up about midnight. Then if it rained or blowed never so hard, we must lie in the boat on the water and have nothing but a little bread. For when we go into the boat we have a loaf allowed to two men, and it is all if we stayed there two days, which is hard; and must lie all that while in the boat. But that Goodman Jackson pitied me and made me a cabin to lie in always when I come up, and he would give me some poor jacks home with me, which comforted me more than peas or water gruel. Oh, they be very godly folks, and love me very well, and will do anything for me. And he much marvelled that you would send me a servant to the Company; he saith I had been better knocked on the head. And indeed so I find it now, to my great grief and misery; and saith that if you love me you will redeem me suddenly, for which I do entreat and beg. And if you cannot get the merchants to redeem me for some little money, then for God's sake get a gathering or entreat some good folks to lay out some little sum of money in meal and cheese and butter and beef. Any eating meat will yield great profit. Oil and vinegar is very good; but, father, there is great loss in leaking. But for God's sake send beef and cheese and butter, or the more of one sort and none of another. But if you send cheese, it must be very old cheese; and at the cheesemonger's you may buy very good cheese for twopence farthing or halfpenny, that will be liked very well. But if you send cheese, you must have a care how you pack it in barrels; and you must put cooper's chips between every cheese, or else the heat of the hold will rot them. And look whatsoever you send me—be in never so much—look, what[ever] I make of it, I will deal truly with you. I will send it over and beg the profit to redeem me; and if I die before it come, I have entreated Goodman Jackson to send you the worth of it, who hath promised he will. If you send, you must direct your letters to Goodman Jackson, at Jamestown, a gunsmith. You must set down his freight, because there be more of his name there. Good father, do not forget me, but have mercy and pity my miserable case. I know if you did but see me, you would weep to see me; for I have but one suit. But it is a strange one, it is very well guarded. Wherefore, for God's sake, pity me. I pray you to re-member my love to all my friends and kindred. I hope all my brothers and sis-ters are in good health, and as for my part I have set down my resolution that certainly will be; that is, that the answer of this letter will be life or death to me. Therefore, good father, send as soon as you can; and if you send me any thing let this be the mark.

ROT

Richard Freethorne,
Martin's Hundred

## Powhatan [Wahunsonacock] to John Smith, 1609

*John Smith claims to have copied down these words from Wahunsonacock, known to the En-glish as Chief Powhatan, as he addressed the colonists at Jamestown.*

Source: Edward Arber, ed., *Travels and Works of Captain John Smith* (Edinburgh, 1910), 1:132–136.

Captaine Smith, you may understand that I having seene the death of all my people thrice, and not any one living of these three generations but my selfe; I know the difference of Peace and Warre better than any in my Country. But I am now grown old, and must soon die; my brothers, Opitchapan, Opechancanough and Catataugh, and then my two sisters, and their two daughters, are distinctly each others successors. I wish their ex-perience was equal to mine; and that your love to us might not be less than ours to you.

But this bruit from Nandsamund, that you are come to destroy my Country, so much affrighteth all my peopke as they dare not visit you. What will it availe you to take that by force you may quickly have by love, or to destroy them that provide you food. What can you get by warre, when we can hide our provi-sions and fly to the woods? whereby you must famish by wronging us your friends. And why are you thus jealous of our loves seeing us unarmed, and both doe, and are willing stille to feede you, with that you cannot get but by our la-bours? Thinke you I am so simple, not to know it is better to eate good meate, lye well, and sleepe quietly with my women and children, laugh and be merry with you, have copper, hatchets, or what I want being your friend: then be forced to flie from all, to lie cold in the woods, feede upon Acornes, rootes, and such trash, and be so hunted by you, that I can neither rest, eate, nor sleepe; but my tyred men muct watch, and if a twig but breake, every one cryeth there sommeth Captaine Smith: then must I fly I know not whether: and thus with mis-erable feare, end my miserable life, leav-ing my pleasures to such youths as you, which through your rash unadvisednesse may quickly as miserably end, for want of that, you never know where to finde.

Let this threrfore assure you of our loves, and every yeare our friendly trade shall furnish you with Corne; and now also, if you would come in friendly manner to see us, and not thus with your guns and swords as to invade your foes.

I, therefore, exhort you to peaceable councils; and, above all, I insist that the guns and swords, the cause of all our jealousy and uneasiness, be removed and sent away.

## Reverend Samuel Smith to Ichabod Smith, January 1698/99

*Smith's letter is an excellent illustration of the hardships of early settlement and of Puritan attitudes toward Indians.*

*Source:* The original of this letter is lost. The letter is printed in Helen Evertson Smith, *Colonial Days and Ways* (Hartford, 1900), pp. 49–51. N.B:: This version, the only one extant, appears to be missing a final section.

HADLEY, MASSACHUSETTS
COLONY
JAN. THE FIRST 1698/99

*My dear and dutiful son:*
I was at so tender an age at the death of my beloved father that I am possessed of but little of the information for which you seek. My reverend father was an ordained minister of the Gospel, educated at Cambridge in England, and came to the land by reason of the great persecution by which the infamous Archbishop Laud and the Black Tom Tyrant (as Mr. Russell was always wont to call

the Earl of Strafford) did cause the reign of His Majesty Charles the First to lose favor in the sight of the people of England. My father and mother came over in 1636/37, first to Watertown, which is near Boston, and after a year or two to Wethersfield on the great river, where he became the first settled pastor. Concerning of the early days, I can remember but little save hardship. My parents had brought both menservants and maidservants from England, but the maids tarried not but till they got married, which was shortly for there was a great scarcity of women in the colonies. The men did abide better. One of them had married one of my mother's maids, and they did come with us to Wethersfield, to our great comfort for some years, until they had many little ones of their own. I do well remember the face and figure of my honored father. He was 5 foot, 10 inches tall, and spare of build, though not lean. He was as active as the redskinned men and sinewy. His delight was in sports of strength, and with his own hands he did help to rear both our own house and the first meetinghouse of Wethersfield, wherein he preached years too few. He was well-featured and fresh-favored with fair skin and long curling hair (as near all of us have had), with a merry eye and sweet smiling mouth, though he could frown sternly enough when need was.

The first meetinghouse was solidly made to withstand the wicked onslaughts of the redskins. Its foundations was laid in the fear of the Lord, but its walls was truly laid in the fear of the Indians, for many and great was the terrors of them. I do mind me [i.e., remember] that all the ablebodied men did work thereat, and the old and feeble did watch in turns to espy if any savages was in hiding near[by], and every man kept his musket nigh to his hand. I do not myself remember any of the attacks made by large bodies of Indians whilst we did remain in Wethersfield, but did oftimes hear of them. Several families which did live back a ways from the river was either murdered or captivated in my boyhood, and we all did live in constant fear of the like. My father ever declared [that] there would not be so much to fear if the redskins was treated with such mixture of justice and authority as they could understand, but if he was living now he must see that we can do naught but *fight* them and that right heavily.

After the redskins the great terror of our lives at Wethersfield, and for many years after we had moved to Hadley to live, was the wolves. Catamounts were bad enough, and so was the bears, but it was the wolves that was the worst. The noise of their howlings was enough to curdle the blood of the stoutest, and I have never seen the man that did not shiver at the sound of a pack of them. What with the way we hated them and the good money that was offered for their heads, we do not hear them now so much, but when I do I feel again the young hatred rising in my blood, and it is not a sin, because God made them to be hated. My mother and sister did each of them kill more than one of the gray howlers, and once my oldest sister shot a bear that came too near the house. He was a good fat one, and kept us all in meat for a good while. I guess one of her daughters has got the skin.

As most of the Wethersfield settlers did come on foot through the wilderness and brought with them such things only as they did need at the first, the other things was sent round from Boston in vessels to come up the river to us. Some of the ships did come safe to Wethersfield, but many was lost in a great storm. Amongst them was one which held all our best things. A good many years later, long after my father had died of the great fever and my mother had married Mr. Russell and moved to Hadley, it was found that some of our things had been saved and kept in the fort which is by the river mouth, and they was brought to us. Most of them was spoiled with seawater and mold, especially the books and the plate. Of this there was no great store, only the tankard, which I have, and some spoons, divided among my sisters, which was all so black [that] it was long before any could come to its own color again.

## Declaration or Confession of [Roger] Court Crotosse, 1684

*This remarkable document illustrates the co-operation between black and white servants in the early Chesapeake.*

Source: Warren Billings, ed., *The Old Dominion in the Seventeenth Century: A Documentary History of Virginia, 1606–1689* (Chapel Hill: University of North Carolina Press, 1975), pp. 144–146.

1st. Saith that about a year since he went from mary branch to his masters mill [with] John Fisher a Servant to his master alsoe (being miller) to fetch some meale the miller not being within[,] this declarant Saith he went into the mill and there lookinge for meale found in a Caske amongst Some woole and yarne a turkey warme and the feathers pluckt of [f] and the neck twisted about which Turkey this declarant drest and with a negro of his masters Eat it, And about two nights after this declarant goeing from mary branch to Chequonessex with one Sandy Coloured Turkey and one black turkey under his armes John Fisher then had this declarant to say nothing but come to the mill at night and he should eate parte of them which this declarant did and eate parte of one of them but did not See the other

2nd. That at the last Springe the aforesaid John Fisher perswaded this declarant and Thomas Hartly (another of Col. Wests Servants) to kill a Lamb and lent us his knife to kill it which accordingly we did and carried into the Swamp and [illegible] drest it some of it wee then Eat and next morning he went with us and he Eat what he would and Said it was well done

3rd. That about August last the said John Fisher perswaded this declarant and a negro Tony to carry a Sheep from Chequonessex to mary branch and there kill it but if it were not fatt then lett it loose amongst the Sheep there att mary branch And there take one of the best of those Sheep and kill it accordingly wee carry away a Sheep upon the horse Tyger from Chequonessex and killed it att mary branch house but did not Exchange it as he ordered: The next day John Fisher came and Eat Some of it and Carryed some of it with him.

4th. That about the last of August last this declarant and the aforesaid John Fisher and the aforesaid Thomas Hartley (by Fishers perswasions) killed a Sow att Chequonessex house and by the said John Fishers order fleade [flayed] her and tyed up her gutts in the skin and Stones with them and threw them into the pond afterwards wee tooke a Pott and the Sowe and carryed them into the Swamp and there drest halfe of it and the rest wee Eat at the Indian towne.

5th. That about the seaventh day of october last this declarant beinge att breakfast att Chequonessex house heard mr Francis Chambers bid the aforesaid John Fisher Catch two piggs and bring them in afterwards this declarant beinge at plow the said Fisher bade him goe along with him to help him and take his gun with him which he accordingly did And shott one pigg and would have carried that into the house but the said John Fisher would not but had him goe kill another for one would not doe but this declarant could not[.] there upon the said Fisher said he would roast that and golt a Spitt for the purpose and asked this declarant if he Could gett fire who answered he could not thereupon the said Fisher Stopt the touchhole of the Gunn and gott fire and there roasted it and Eat it[.] In the time the pigg was roasting old mr Johnson Came to the fire but the said Fisher seeing him come ran away with the spilt and kept out of sight untill the old man went away

6th. That abought a fortnight or three weeks since this declarant and the aforesaid John Fisher Thomas Hartley and jack A negro at two sever-all times killed four piggs one of them being marked with my masters marke carryed them away and Eate them.

[7th.] That on Tuesday last was a fortnight alt night to this declarant and the said Thomas Hartley sitting by the fire in the middle roome the said John Fisher came to us and bade us goe along with him (which we did) then he went out with us to the henhouse and said jonny Negro had hid a bag of potatoes there and that he would steale them whereupon he put downe a board by the doore and then unlockt the doore And tooke the Potatoes presently after the same night this declarant and Thomas Hartley went to the henhouse againe and tooke a Turkey and a hen and carryed them into the shoomakers shop loft and there pluckt them and boyled them in the shop

8th. That about a week since my master Calling this declarant the said Fisher and Hartley to question for our misdemeanors Afterwards the said Fisher said to us that if he was brought to any damage he would begone and if he could gett there he would send his master a very Loveing Letter that his sheep his hoggs and turkeys were very fat etc.

9th. That what is above written and declared is very true And that this Declarant can depose to the same when Called Dated this 6th day of November anno Domini 1684

10th. also this declarant farther saith that there was another sheep killed by him and John Fisher which he did not remember when he was examined before Col. [Daniel] Jenifer.

The marke of
Roger Court Crotosse
X

## "Whereas Hugh Gwyn . . .," July 9, 1640

*This decision by the Virginia Council and General Court demonstrates the growing distinctions between indenture and enslavement.*

*Source:* Henry R. McIlwaine, ed., *Minutes of the Council and General Court of Colonial Virginia, 1622–1632, 1670–1676. With Notes and Excerpts from Original Council and General Court Records, into 1683, Now Lost* (Richmond: Virginia State Library, 1924), p. 466.

### 9TH OF JULY 1640.

*Whereas Hugh Gwyn* hath by order from this Board Brought back from *Maryland* three servants formerly run away from the said *Gwyn, the court doth therefore order* that the said three servants shall receive the punishment of whipping and to have thirty stripes apiece one called *Victor, a dutchman,* the other a *Scotchman* called *James Gregory,* shall first serve out their times with their master according to their Indentures, and one whole year apiece after the time of their service is Expired. By their said Indentures in recompense of his Loss sustained by their absence and after that service to their said master is Expired to serve the colony for three whole years apiece, and that the third being a negro named *John Punch* shall serve his said master or his assigns for the time of his natural Life here or elsewhere.

# John Rolfe to Sir Thomas Dale, 1614

*A famous document, in which Rolfe explains his motives for marrying Pocahontas, emphasizing the opportunity to Christianize her.*

Source: Lyon G. Tyler, ed. *Narratives of Early Virginia* (New York, 1907), pp. 239–244.

*Honorable Sir, and most worthy Governor:*

When your leisure shall best serve you to peruse these lines, I trust in God the beginning will not strike you into a greater admiration than the end will give you good content. It is a matter of no small moment, concerning my own particular, which here I impart unto you, and which toucheth me so nearly as the tenderness of my salvation. How be it, I freely subject myself to your grave and mature judgement, deliberation, approbation, and determination, assuring myself of your zealous admonitions and godly comforts, either persuading me to desist or encouraging me to persist therein, with a religious fear and godly care—for which (from the very instant that this began to root itself within the secret bosom of my breast) my daily and earnest prayers have been, still are, and ever shall be produced forth with as sincere a godly zeal as I possibly may, to be directed, aided, and governed in all my thoughts, words, and deeds, to the glory of God, and for my eternal consolation. To persevere wherein I never had more need, nor (till now) could [I] ever imagine to have been moved with the like occasion.

But (my case standing as it doth) what better worldly refuge can I here seek than to shelter myself under the safety of your favorable protection? And did not my ease proceed from an unspotted conscience, I should not dare to offer to your view and approved judgement these passions of my troubled soul, so full of fear and trembling is hypocrisy and dissimulation. But knowing my own innocence and godly fervor in the whole prosecution hereof, I doubt not of your benign acceptance and clement construction. As for malicious depravers and turbulent spirits, to whom nothing is tasteful but what pleaseth their unsavory palate, I pass not for them, being well assured in my persuasion (by the often trial and proving of myself, in my holiest meditations and prayers) that I am called hereunto by the spirit of God, and it shall be sufficient for me to be protected by yourself in all virtuous and pious endeavors. And for my more happy proceeding herein, my daily oblations shall ever be addressed to bring to pass so good effects that your self and all the world may truly say: this is the work of God, and it is marvelous in our eyes.

But to avoid tedious preambles and to come nearer the matter: first suffer me, with your patience, to sweep and make clean the way wherein I walk from all suspicions and doubts which may be covered therein, and faithfully to reveal unto you what should move me hereunto.

Let therefore this, my well-advised protestation, which here I make between God and my own conscience, be a sufficient witness at the dreadful Day of

Judgement (when the secret of all men's hearts shall be opened) to condemn me herein, if my chiefest intent and purpose be not to strive with all my power of body and mind in the undertaking of so mighty a matter—[in] no way led (so far forth as man's weakness may permit) with the unbridled desire of carnal affection, but [striving] for the good of this plantation, for the honor of our country, for the glory of God, for my own salvation, and for the converting to the true knowledge of God and Jesus Christ [of] an unbelieving creature, namely Pocahontas, to whom my hearty and best thoughts are, and have [for] a long time been, so entangled, and enthralled in so intricate a labyrinth, that I was even wearied to unwind myself thereout. But Almighty God, who never faileth His [followers] that truly invoke His Holy Name, hath opened the gate and led me by the hand [so] that I might plainly see and discern the safe paths wherein to tread.

To you, therefore, most noble Sir, the patron and father of us in this country, do I utter the effects of this my settled and long-continued affection (which hath made a mighty war in my meditations), and here I do truly relate to what issue this dangerous combat is come unto, wherein I have not only examined but thoroughly tried and pared my thoughts even to the quick, before I could find any fit, wholesome, and apt applications to cure so dangerous an ulcer. I never failed to offer my daily and faithful prayers to God for His sacred and holy assistance. I forgot not to set before mine eyes the frailty of mankind, his proneness to evil, his indulgence of wicked thoughts, with many other imperfections wherein man is daily ensnared and oftentimes overthrown, and them compared to my present estate. Nor was I ignorant of the heavy displeasure which Almighty God conceived against the sons of Levi and Israel for marrying strange wives, nor of the inconveniences which may thereby arise, with other the like good motions which made me look about warily and with good circumspection into the grounds and principal agitations which thus should provoke me to be in love with one whose education hath been rude, her manners barbarous, her generation accursed, and so discrepant in all nurture from myself that oftentimes with fear and trembling I have ended my private controversy with this [thought]: surely these are wicked instigations, hatched by him who seeketh and delighteth in man's destruction. And so, with fervent prayers to be ever preserved from such diabolical assaults (as I took those to be), I have taken some rest.

Thus, when I had thought [that] I had obtained my peace and quietness, behold, another but more gracious temptation hath made breaches into my holiest and strongest meditations, with which I have been put to a new trial in a straighter manner than the former. For besides the many passions and sufferings which I have daily, hourly, yea, and in my sleep endured, even awaking me to astonishment, taxing me with remissness and carelessness, [with] refusing and neglecting to perform the duty of a good Christian, pulling me by the ear and crying, "why dost not thou endeavor to make her a Christian?" (and these have happened, to my greater wonder, even when she hath been furthest separated from me, which in common reason, were it not an undoubted work of God, might breed forgetfulness of a far more worthy creature)—besides, I say, the holy spirit of God hath often demanded of me, why I was created, if not for transitory pleasures and worldly vanities, but to labor in the Lord's vineyard, there to sow and plant, to nourish and increase the fruits thereof, daily adding with the good husband in the gospel somewhat to the talent, [so] that in the end the fruits may be reaped, to the comfort of the laborer in this life and his salvation in the world to come? And if this be, as undoubtedly this is, the service Jesus Christ requireth of His best servant: woe unto him that hath these instruments of piety put into his hands and willfully despiseth to work with them. Likewise, adding hereunto her great appearance of love to me, her desire to be taught and instructed in the knowledge of God, her capableness of understanding, her aptness and willingness to receive any good impression, and also the spiritual, besides her own, incitements stirring me up hereunto.

What should I do? Shall I be of so untoward a disposition as to refuse to lead the blind into the right way? Shall I be so unnatural as not to give bread to the hungry? Or [so] uncharitable as not to cover the naked? Shall I despise to actuate these pious duties of a Christian? Shall the base fear of displeasing the world overpower and withhold me from revealing unto man these spiritual works of the Lord, which in my meditations and prayers I have daily made known to

Him? God forbid. I assuredly trust He hath thus dealt with me for my eternal felicity and for His glory, and I hope so to be guided by His heavenly grace that in the end, by my faithful pains and Christian-like labor, I shall attain to that blessed promise, pronounced by that holy prophet Daniel, unto the righteous that bring many unto the knowledge of God: namely, that they shall shine like the stars forever and ever. A sweeter comfort cannot be to a true Christian, nor a greater encouragement for him to labor all the days of his life in the performance thereof, nor a greater gain of consolation to be desired at the hour of death and in the Day of Judgement.

Again, by my reading and [by] conference with honest and religious persons have I received no small encouragement—besides *serena mea conscientia*, the clearness of my conscience clean from the filth of impurity, *quae est instar muri abenei*, which is unto me as a brazen wall. If I should set down at large the perturbations and godly motions which have stricken within me, I should but make a tedious and unnecessary volume. But I doubt not [that] these shall be sufficient both to certify you of my true intents in [the] discharging of my duty to God and to yourself, to whose gracious providence I humbly submit myself, for His glory, your honor, our country's good, the benefit of this plantation, and for the converting of one unregenerate to regeneration, which I beseech God to grant, for His dear son Christ Jesus, His sake.

Now if the vulgar sort, who square all men's actions by the base rule of their own filthiness, shall tax or taunt me in this my Godly labor, let them know [that] it is not [from] any hungry appetite to gorge myself with incontinency. [To be] sure, (if I would, and were so sensually inclined), I might satisfy such desire–though not without a seared conscience, yet with Christians more pleasing to the eye and less fearful in the offence unlawfully committed. Nor am I in so desperate an estate that I regard not what becometh of me. Nor am I out of hope but one day to see my country, nor so void of friends, nor mean in birth, but there to obtain a match to my great content. Nor have I ignorantly passed over my hopes there, nor [do I] regardlessly seek to lose the love of my friends by taking this course. I know them all, and have not rashly overslipped any.

But shall it please God thus to dispose of me (which I earnestly desire [in order] to fulfill my ends before set down), I will heartily accept of it as a Godly task appointed [for] me. And I will never cease, (God assisting me), until I have accomplished and brought to perfection so holy a work, in which I will daily pray God to bless me, to mine and her eternal happiness. And thus desiring no longer to live, to enjoy the blessings of God, than this my resolution doth tend to such Godly ends as are by me before declared; [and] not doubting of your favorable acceptance, I take my leave, beseeching Almighty God to rain down upon you such plenitude of His heavenly graces as your heart can wish and desire. And so I rest,

at your command, most willing
to be disposed of,
John Rolfe

## Petition of Jewish Merchants, January 1655

*This petition illuminates the debate over the admission of Jews into the colony of New Netherland.*

*Source:* Samuel Oppenheim, *Early History of the Jews in New York* (New York, 1909), pp. 9–11; petition translated here from the Dutch. (In Dutch the title of the document is *Aende Ed: Heeran de Beswinthebberen vand geoctroljeerde Wesjndischle Compé ter Camera der Stad Amstelredamme.*).

*To the Honorable Lords, Directors of the Chartered West India Company, Chamber of the City of Amsterdam.*

The merchants of the Portuguese Nation residing in this City respectfully remonstrate to your Honors that it has come to their knowledge that your Honors raise obstacles to the giving of permits or passports to the Portuguese Jews to travel and to go to reside in New Netherland, which if persisted in will result to the great disadvantage of the Jewish nation. It also can be of no advantage to the general Company but rather damaging.

Granted that they may reside and traffic, provided they shall not become a charge upon the deaconry or the Company.

There are many of the nation who have lost their possessions at Pernambuco and have arrived from there in great poverty, and part of them have been dispersed here and there. So that your petitioners had to expend large sums of money for their necessaries of life, and through lack of opportunity all cannot remain here to live. And as they cannot go to Spain or Portugal because of the Inquisition, a great part of the aforesaid people must in time be obliged to depart for other territories of their High Mightinesses the States-General and their Companies, in order there, through their labor and efforts, to be able to exist under the protection of the administrators of your Honorable Directors, observing and obeying your Honors' orders and commands.

It is well known to your Honors that the Jewish nation in Brazil have at all times been faithful and have striven to guard and maintain that place, risking for that purpose their possessions and their blood.

Yonder land is extensive and spacious. The more of loyal people that go to live there, the better it is in regard to the population of the country as in regard to the payment of various excises and taxes which may be imposed there, and in regard to the increase of trade, and also to the importation of all the necessaries that may be sent there.

Your Honors should also consider that the Honorable Lords, the Burgomasters of the City and the Honorable High Illustrious Mighty Lords, the States-General, have in political matters always protected and considered the Jewish nation as upon the same footing as all the inhabitants and burghers. Also it is conditioned in the treaty of perpetual peace with the King of Spain that the Jewish nation shall also enjoy the same liberty as all other inhabitants of those lands. Your Honors should also please consider that many of the Jewish nation are principal shareholders in the Company. They having always striven their best for the Company, and many of their nation have lost immense and great capital in Its shares and obligations.

The Company has by a general resolution consented that those who wish to populate the Colony shall enjoy certain districts of land gratis. Why should now certain subjects of this State not be allowed to travel thither and live there? The French consent that the Portuguese Jews may traffic and live in Martinique, Christopher and others of their territories, whither also some have gone from here, and your Honors know. The English also consent at the present time that the Portuguese and Jewish nation may go from London and settle at Barbados, whither also some have gone.

As foreign nations consent that the Jewish nation may go to live and trade in their territories, hew can your Honors forbid the same and refuse transportation to this Portuguese nation who reside here and have been settled here well on to about sixty years, many also being born here and confirmed burghers, and this to a land that needs people for its increase?

Therefore the petitioners request, for the reasons given above (as also others which they omit to avoid prolixity), that your Honors be pleased not to exclude but to grant the Jewish nation passage to and residence in that country; otherwise this would result in a great prejudice to their reputation. Also that by an Apostille and Act the Jewish nation be permitted, together with other inhabitants, to travel, live and traffic there, and with them enjoy liberty on condition of contributing like others, &c. Which doing, &c

## The Case of Maria Negro, 1681

*This African American woman was convicted of arson, undoubtedly an act of resistance to enslavement, and rather than being hanged, she was sentenced to a burning at the stake.*

*Source: Publications of the Colonial Society of Massachusetts (1904), 6:321.*

## AT A COURT OF ASSISTANTS HELD AT BOSTON, 6 SEPTEMBER, 1681

Maria Negro, servant to Joshua Lambe of Roxbury in the County of Suffolk in New England, being presented by the Grand Jury, was indicted by the name of Maria Negro for not having the fear of God before her eyes and being instigated by the Devil at or upon the eleventh day of July last in the night did wittingly, willingly and feloniously set on fire the dwelling house of Thomas Swann of said Roxbury by taking a coal from under a sill and carried it into another room and laid it on the floor near the door and presently went and crept into hole at a back door of thy master Lamb's house and set it on fire. Also taking a live coal between two chips and carried it into the chamber by which also it was consumed as by your confession will appear contrary to the peace of our Sovereign Lord the king, his Crown and dignity, the laws of this jurisdiction. The prisoner at the bar pleaded and acknowledged herself to be guilty of this fact. And accordingly, the next day being again brought to the bar, had sentence of death pronounced against her by the Honorable Governor, yet she should go from the bar to the prison whence she came and thence to the place of execution and there be burned.

## Declaration Against the Proceedings of Nathaniel Bacon, 1676

*William Berkeley was governor of Virginia during Bacon's Rebellion. This document, shorter than the anonymous account of the rebellion also included in this collection of documents, is a defense of Berkeley's actions during the rebellion. It might be used instead of, or along with, the anonymous acount.*

*Source: Collections of the Massachusetts Historical Society, 4th series (Boston, 1871), 9:178–181.*

The declaration and remonstrance of Sir William Berkeley, his most sacred Majesty's Governor and Captain-General of Virginia.

Sheweth: that about the year 1660, Col. Mathews the then Governor died, and then in consideration of the service I had done the country, in defending them from, and destroying great numbers of the Indians, without the loss of three men, in all the time that war lasted, and in contemplation of the equal and uncorrupt justice I had distributed to all men, not only the Assembly, but the unanimous votes of all the country, concurred to make me Governor in a time when, if the rebels in England had prevailed, I had certainly died for accepting it. 'Twas, Gentlemen, an unfortunate love shewed to me, for, to shew myself grateful for this, I was willing to accept of this government again, when by my gracious king's favor I might have had other places much more profitable and less toilsome then this hath been. Since that time that I returned into the country, I call the great God, judge of all things in heaven and earth to witness, that I do not know of anything relative to this country, wherein I have acted unjustly, corruptly, or negligently, in distributing equal justice to all men, and taking all possible care to preserve their proprieties, and defend them from their barbarous enemies.

But, for all this, perhaps I have erred in things I know not of. If I have, I am so conscious of human frailty, and my own defects, that I will not only acknowledge them, but repent of, and amend them, and not, like the rebel Bacon, persist in an error, only because I have committed it; and tells me in divers of his letters that it is not for his honor to confess a fault, but I am of opinion that it is only for divels to be incorrigible, and men of principles like the worst of divels; and these he hath, if truth be reported to me, of divers of his expressions of atheism, tending to take away all religion and laws. And now I will state the question betwixt me as a governor and Mr. Bacon, and say that if any enemies should invade England, any counsel—or, justice of peace, or other inferior officer, might raise what forces they could to protect his Majesty's subjects. But I say again, if, after the king's knowledge of this invasion, any the greatest peer of England should raise forces against the king's prohibition, this would be now—and ever was in all ages and nations—accompted treason. Nay, I will go further, that though this peer was truly zealous for the preservation of his king, and subjects, and had better and greater abilities then all the rest of his fellow subjects, to do his king and country service, yet if the king (though by false information) should suspect the contrary, it were treason in this noble peer to proceed after the king's prohibition: and for the truth of this I appeal to all the laws of England, and the laws and constitutions of all other nations in the world. And yet further, it is declared by this Parliament that the taking up arms for the king and Parliament is treason; for the event shewed that whatever the pretense was to seduce ignorant and well-affected people, yet the end was ruinous both to king and people—as this will be if not prevented. I do therefore again declare that Bacon, proceeding against all laws of all nations, modern and ancient, is rebel to his sacred Majesty and this country; nor will I insist upon the swearing of men to live and die together, which is treason by the very words of the law.

Now, my friends, I have lived thirty-four years amongst you, as uncorrupt and diligent as ever Governor was; Bacon is a man of two years amongst you, his person and qualities unknown to most of you, and to all men else, by any virtuous action that ever I heard of. And that very action which he boasts of was sickly and foolishly, and, as I am informed, treacherously carried to the dishonor of the English nation; yet in it he lost more men then I did in three years' war; and by the grace of God will put myself to the same dangers and troubles again when I have brought Bacon to acknowledge the laws are above him, and I doubt not but by God's assistance to have better success then Bacon hath had. The reason of my hopes are, that I will take counsel of wiser men then myself; but Mr. Bacon hath none about him but the lowest of the people.

Yet I must further enlarge, that I cannot without your help, do anything in this but die in defence of my king, his laws, and subjects, which I will cheerfully do, though alone I do it; and considering my poor fortunes, I cannot leave my poor wife and friends a better legacy then by dying for my king and you: for his sacred Majesty will easily distinguish between Mr. Bacon's actions and mine, and kings have long arms, either to reward or punish.

Now, after all this, if Mr. Bacon can shew one precedent or example where such actings in any nation whatever was approved of, I will meditate with the King and you for a pardon, and excuse for him; but I can shew him an hundred examples where brave and great men have been put to death for gaining victories against the command of their superiors.

Lastly, my most assured friends, I would have preserved those Indians that I knew were hourly at our mercy, to have been our spies and intelligence, to find out our bloody enemies; but as soon as I had the least intelligence that they also were treacherous enemies, I gave out commissions to destroy them all, as the commissions themselves will speak it.

To conclude, I have done what was possible both to friend and enemy; have granted Mr. Bacon three pardons, which he hath scornfully rejected, supposing himself stronger to subvert then I and you to maintain the laws, by which only, and God's assisting grace and mercy, all men must hope for peace and safety. I will add no more, though much more is still remaining to justify me and condemn Mr. Bacon, but to desire that this declaration may be read in every county court in the country, and that a court be presently called to do it before the Assembly meet, that your approbation or dissatisfaction of this declaration may be known to all the country, and the King's Council, to whose most revered judgments it is submitted.

Given the 29th day of May, a happy day in the 28th year of his most sacred Majesty's reign, Charles the Second, who God grant long and prosperously to reign, and let all his good subjects say Amen.

*William Berkeley*

## An Act Defining the Status of Mulatto Bastards, December 1662

*This is the law most often cited in discussions of the establishment of racial slavery in the mainland colonies.*

Source: William Hening, ed., *The Statutes at Large, Being a Collection of All the Laws of Virginia, from the First Session of the Legislature in the Year 1619* (Richmond, 1809–1823), 2:170.

[December 1662] Whereas some doubts have arrisen whether children got by an Englishman upon a negro woman should be slave or Free, Be it therefore enacted and declared by this present grand assembly, that all children borne in this country shall be held bond or free only according to the condition of the mother, And that if any christian shall committ Fornication with a negro man or woman, hee or shee soe offending shall pay double the Fines imposed by the former act.

## Petition of Richard Saltonstall, 1645

*This petition of Richard Saltonstall is an early piece of evidence both of the trade in Africans in New England and opposition to it.*

Source: John Winthrop, *History of New England from 1630 to 1645*, ed. James Savage (1826), 2:379–380 (1972; reprinted in Elizabeth Donnan, ed., *Documents Illustrative of the History of the Slave Trade to America*, vol. 3, *New England and the Middle Colonies* (New York: Hippocrene Books, 1965), pp. 6–7.

*To the Honoured General Court,*
The oath I took this yeare att my enterance upon the place of assistante was to this effect: That I would truly endeavour the advancement of the gospell and the good of the people of this plantation (to the best of my skill,) dispencing justice equally and impartially (according to the laws of God and this land) in all cases wherein I act by virtue of my place. I conceive myselfe called by virtue of my

place to act (according to this oath) in the case concerning the Negers taken by captain Smith and Mr. Keser; wherein it is apparent that Mr. Keser upon a sabboth day gave chace to certaine Negers; and upon the same day tooke divers of them; and at another time killed others; and burned one of their townes. Omitting several misdemeinours which accompanied these acts above-mentioned, I conceive the acts themselves to bee directly contrary to these following laws (all which are capitall by the word of God; and 2 of them by the lawes of this jurisdiction.)

The act (or acts) of murder (whether by force or fraude) are expressly contrary both to the law of God, and the law of this country.

The act of stealing Negers, or of taking them by force, (whether it be considered as theft, or robbery) is (as I conceive) expressly contrary, both to the law of God, and the law of this country.

The act of chaceing the Negers (as aforesayde) upon the sabboth day (beeing a servile worke and such as cannot be considered under any other heade) is expressly capitall by the law of God.

These acts and outrages beeing committed where there was noe civill government which might call them to accompt, and the persons by whome they were committed beeing of our jurisdiction, I conceive this court to bee the Ministers of God in this case; and therfore my humble request is that the severall offenders may be imprisoned by the order of this court, and brought unto their deserved censure in convenient time; and this I humbly crave, that soe the sinn they have committed may be upon their owne heads, and not upon ourselves (as otherwise it will).

## The Remonstrance of the Inhabitants of Flushing, Long Island, Against the Law Against Quakers and Subsequent Proceedings, January 1, 1658

*This remonstrance to Governor Peter Stuyvesant demonstrates the religious toleration of the residents of this Long Island community in contrast to Stuyvesant's own efforts to prevent radical sects from settling within his colony.*

Source: "Ecclesiastical Records of the State of New York," published by The State of New York, under the supervision of Hugh Hastings, State Historian (Albany, N.Y., 1901), pp. 412–413.

*Right Honorable.*

You have been pleased to send up unto us a certain Prohibition or Command, that wee shoulde not receive or entertaine any of those people called Quakers, because thay are supposed to bee by some seducers of the people; for our parte wee cannot condem them in this case, neither can wee stretch out our hands against them to punish, bannish or persecute them, for out of Christ, God is a consuming fire, and it is a fearful thing to fall into the handes of the liveing God; wee desire therefore in this case not to judge least wee be judged, neither to Condem least wee bee Condemed, but rather let every man stand and fall to his own. Maister wee are bounde by the Law to doe good unto all men, especially to those of the Household of faith; and though for the present wee seeme to bee unsensible of the law and the Lawgiver; yet when death and the Law assault us; if we have (not) our advocate to seeke, who shall plead for us in this case of Conscience betwixt God and our own soules; the powers of this world can neither attack us neither excuse us, for if God justify who can Condem, and if God Condem there is none can justifye; and for those Jealowsies and suspitions which some haue of them that they are destructive unto Magistracy and Ministry that cannot bee; for the Magistrate hath the Sword in his hand and the Minister hath the Sword in his hand as witnesse those tow great examples which all Maiestrates and Ministers are to follow M(oses) and Christ; whom God raised up Maintained and defended against all the Enemies both flesh and spirit, and therefore that wich is of God will stand, and that which is of Man will (come) to noething: and as the Lord hath taught Moses, or the Civill power, to give an outward libertie in the State by the Law written in the heart designed (for) the good of all and can truly judge who is good and who is evill, who is true and who is false, and can pass definitiue sentence of live or (death) against that man which rises up against the fundamental law of the States Generall, soe (he) hath made his Ministers a savor of life unto (life?), and a savor of death unto death.

The law of loue, peace and libertie in the states extending to Jews, Turks and Egyptians, as they are considered the sonnes of Adam, which is the glory of the outward State of Holland; so loue, peace and libertie extending to all in Christ Jesus, Condems hatred, warre and bondage; and because our Savior saith it is impossible but that offence will come, but woe be unto him by whom they Commeth, our desire is not to offend one of his little ones in whatsoever forme, name or title hee appreares in, whether Presbyterian, Independent, Baptist or Quaker; but shall be glad to see anything of God in any of them: desireing to doe unto all men as wee desire all men should doe unto us, which is the true law both of Church and State; for our Savior saith this is the Law and the Prophets; Therefore if any of these said persons come in loue unto us, wee cannot in Conscience lay violent hands upon them, but give them free Egresse into our Towne and howses as God shall preswade our Consciences; and in this we are true subjects both of the Church and State; for wee are bounde by the law of god and man to do good unto all men, and evill to no man; and this is according to the Pattent and Charter of our Towne given unto us in the name of the States Generall which we are not willing to infringe and violate but shall hold to our pattent and shall remaine your Humble Subjects the inhabitants of Vlishing; written the 27th of December in the Yeare 1657 by mee.

Edward Heart,
Clericus.
Tobias Feake
William Thorne. Sr.
Edward Tarne?
Nathaniel Hefferd
The Marke of William Pidgion

Ellias Doughtie
Richard Stocton
Nathaniel Tue
The Marke M of Micah Tue
Edward Ffarington
Robert Efield, Jr.
Michael Milner
George Wright
Henry Samtell
John Mastine
The Marke of William Noble
The mark of William Thorne,
John Storer
Benjamin Hubbard
The Marke of George Clere
Antonie Feild
Edward Griffine
Nicolas Blackford
The Marke P of Philipp Ud
Robert Efield, Sr.
Nick Colas Parsell
Henry Townsend
John Foard
Edward Heart
John Townesend
First of January, 1658

## William Bradford Describes His Encounter with Samoset, 1621

*Bradford's account of the history of Plymouth cannot be reproduced in full; this excerpt contains Bradford's account of Samoset, Squanto, and the treaty these Indians helped the Pilgrims negotiate with the Wampanoag chief, Massosoit.*

Source: William Bradford, *Of Plymouth Plantation, 1620–1647*, ed. Samuel Eliot Morrison (New York: Alfred A. Knopf, 1953).

All this while the Indians came skulking about them, and would sometimes show themselves aloof off, but when any approached near them, they would run away, and once they stole away their tools where they had been at work and were gone to dinner. But about the 16th of March, a certain Indian came boldly amongst them and spoke to them in broken English, which they could well understand but marveled at it. At length they understood, by discourse with him, that he was not of these parts but belonged to the eastern parts where some English ships came to fish, with whom he was acquainted and could name sundry of them by their names, amongst whom he had got his language. He became profitable to them in acquainting them with many things concerning the state of the country in the east parts where he lived, which was afterward profitable unto them, as also of the people here, of their names, number, and strength, of their situation and distance from this place, and who was chief amongst them. His name was Samoset. He told them also of another Indian whose name was Squanto, a native of this place, who had been in England and could speak better English than himself.

Being, after some time of entertainment and gifts, dismissed, a while after he came again, and five more with him, and they brought again all the tools that were stolen away before, and made way for the coming of their great Sachem [chief], called Massasoit. Who, about four or five days after, came with the chief of his friends and other attendance, with the aforesaid Squanto. With whom, after friendly entertainment and some gifts given him, they made a peace with him (which hath now continued this 24 years) in these terms:

1. That neither he nor any of his should injure or do hurt to any of their people.
2. That if any of his did hurt to any of theirs, he should send the offender, that they might punish him.
3. That if anything were taken away from any of theirs, he should cause it to be restored, and they should do the like to his.
4. If any did unjustly war against him, they would aid him, if any did war against them, he should aid them.
5. He should send to his neighbors confederates to certify them of this, that they might not wrong them, but might be likewise comprised in the conditions of peace.
6. That when their men came to them, they should leave their bows and arrows behind them.

After these things he returned to his place, called Sowams, some 40 miles from this place, but Squanto continued with them and was their interpreter and was a special instrument sent of God for their good beyond their expectation. He directed them how to set their corn, where to take fish and to procure other commodities, and was also their pilot to bring them to unknown places for their profit, and never left them till he died. He was a native of this place, and scarce any left alive besides himself. He was carried away [earlier] with divers others by one Hunt, a master of a ship, who thought to sell them for slaves in Spain. But he got away for England and was entertained by a merchant in London, and employed to Newfoundland and other parts by one Mr. Dermer, a gentlemen employed by Sir Ferdinando Gorges and others for discovery and other design in these parts.

# Rev. Johannes Megapolensis to the Classis of Amsterdam, March 18, 1655

*This document illustrates the anti-Semitism of the residents of New Amsterdam upon the arrival of Jews in the city.*

*Source:* J. Franklin Jameson, *Narratives of New Netherland, 1609–1664* (1909), pp. 392–393.

*Reverendi Domini, Fratres in Christo, Synergi observandi:*

I feel it my duty to answer the letter of your Reverences, dated the 11th of November, [1654].

We have cause to be grateful to the Messrs. Directors and to your Reverences for the care and trouble takent to procure for the Dutch on Long Island a good clergyman, even though it has not yet resulted in anything. Meanwhile, God has led Domine Jannes Polheimus from Brazil, by way of the Caribbean Islands, to this place. He has for the present gon to Long Island, to a village called midwout, which is somewhat the *meditallium* of the other villages, to wit, Breuckelen, Amersfoort and Gravesande. There he has preached for the accommodation of the inhabitants on Sundays during the winter, and has administered the sacraments, to the sat-

isfaction of all, as Director Stuyvesant has undoubtedly informed the Messrs. Directors.

As to William vestiens, who has been schoolmaster and sexton here, I could neigher do much, nor say much, in his favor, to the Council, because for some years past they were not satisfied or pleased with his services. Thereupon when he asked for an increase of salary last year, he received the answer, that if the service did not suit him, he might ask for his discharge. Only lately I have been before the Council on his account, and spoken about it, in consequence of your letter, but they told me that he had fulfilled his duties on so-so and theat he he did little enough for his salary.

Some Jews cam from Holland last summer, in order to trade. Later, some Jews came upon the same ship as D. Polheymius; they were healthy, but poor. It would have been proper, that they should have been supported by their own people, but have been at our charge, so that we have had to spend several hundred guilders for their support. They came several times to my house, weeping and bemoaning their misery. When I dierected them to the Jewish merchant, they said, that he would not lend them a single stiver. Some more have come from Holland this spring. They report that many more of the same lot would follow, and then they would build here a synagogue. This causes among the congregation here a great deal of complaint and murmuring. These people have no othe God than the Mammon of unrighteousness, and no other aim than to get possession of Christian property, and to overcome all other merchants by drawing all trade towards themselves. Therefore we request your Reverences to obtain from the Messrs. Directors, that these godless rascals, who are of no benefit to the country, but look at everything for their own profit, may be sent qway from here. For as we have here Papists; Mennonites and Lutherans among the Dutch; also many Puritans or Indepents, and many atheists and various other servants of Baal among the English under this Government, who conceal themselves under the name of Christians; it would create a still greater confusion, if the obstinate and immovable Jews came to settle here.

In closing I commend your Reverences with your families to the protection of God, who will bless us and all of you in service of the divine word.

*Your obedient*
*Johnan. Megapolensis*
*Amsterdam in New Netherland*
*the 18th of March, 1655.*

## Statement Showing Wherein Capt. Daniel Brodhead Has Exceeded the Instruction Given by the Honorable Richard Nicols, Governor General, April 25, 1667

*This document demonstrates the conflict between Dutch and English citizens of New York City (formerly New Amsterdam) following the seizure of the colony of New Netherland by the English in 1664.*

Source: Nicolls-Lovelace Papers, New York Historical Society; printed in Peter R. Christogh, ed. *Administrative Papers of Governors Richard Ni-* *colls & Francis Lovelace, 1664–1673* (Baltimore: Genealogical Publishing Company, 1980).

Firstly, said Capt. Broodhead in the month of January of the year 1666, new style, came into court when the Bench was in session, and demanded who had authorized the Court to meet without his knowledge, as he said he was Governor of this place and no session should be held without his knowledge and consent, and angrily shoved the papers off the court bench, in violation of the first article of the Instruction accorded to the Schout and Commissioners, which said authority above mentioned is not to be found in Capt. Broodhead's instruction.

2ndly, Regarding the quartering of the soldiers which the honorable Governor General has referred to the Schout and Commissioners; the said Captain has opposed it, contrary to the fifth article of the Instruction, given to the Schout and Commissioners, when at the house of Cornelis Slecht he tore up the billets that were issued, and on the contrary gave others in their stead, and on this account in the presence of the Commissioner Jan Joosten picked a quarrel with the Schout because he continued to do so according to authority; likewise has he presumed to exact from divers burghers, being working people, a schepel of wheat per week for himself on condition of relieving them from having soldiers quartered on them. They are Louis du Bois, Walran du Mont, Albert Jansen, Roeloff Swartwout, Jan Jansen from Amersfort, Albert Gerretsen; and he has on the same condition received from

Pieter Cornelissen two schepels of wheat, and if unwilling he has quartered soldiers on some of them. This authority for billeting is not to be found in Capt. Broodhead's instructions.

3rdly, In violation of the Seventh Article of the Instruction of the Schout and Commissioners Capt. Broodhead has presumed to arrest without prior complaint the following persons: to wit, Schout Willem Beeckman, Court Messenger Albert Jansen van Steenwyck, Cornelis Barentsen Slecht twice, Tjerck Claesen de Wit, Albert Govertsen, Teunis Jacobsen, Walran du Mont, Magdalena Dirricks wife of Harmen Hendricks, Ariaen Huybertsen, in utter violation even of the Instruction to Capt. Broodhead himself.

Done in Wildwyck in the Esopus this 25th April, 1667.

## Petition of Marylanders, November 20, 1690 and the Response to the Petition by John Coode and Kenelm Cheseldine, December 22, 1690

*This petition to Charles II comes from representatives of the Catholic minority in Maryland who feared continued religious persecution in the wake of John Coode's Protestant Association victory in 1690. In their reply John Coode and fellow Protestant leaders refute all charges that they had acted illegally and insist their government ought to be recognized as legitimate.*

*Source: Archives of Maryland, vol. 8, Proceedings of the Council of Maryland, 1687/8–1693, Wil-*liam Hand Browne, ed. (Baltimore: State Archives, 1890), pp. 212–214, 225–228.

The humble Petition of several of your Maties Loyal Protestant Subjects, and ancient Inhabitants of your Province of Maryland, and lately from thence here arrived, in behalf of themselves and most of the Inhabitants of the said Province.

Sheweth

That your Petrs have for many years enjoy'd the blessing of Peace under the mild Government of the Lord Baltemore and his Father and have been equal partakers of their Justice as well as favours with your Majties subjects there of other perswasions, untill of late your Petrs have been by the malicious designs and wicked Practices of one John COODE and his Accomplices disturbed and deprived of their long continued happiness and yor Majties peaceable and Dutifull subjects have been most barbarously and inhumanly treated by them, having not only in a Tumultuous manner wrested the Government into their owne hands, seizing the Publick Records wherein is the security of your Petitioners Estates and reposing them in the hands of unfitt persons that arbitrarily seized and plundered your Petr's estates and imprisoned their Persons to the ruine of themselves and families, and have violently perverted the Laws of the Province having done what their own wicked Wills suggested which they maintain by force seeking to shelter their oppressions from your Majesties Ears by covering their Actions with the pretence of Zeale for your Majties service, not regarding your

Majesties gracious coffiands by your Royal Letter of the first of February in the first year of your Reigne for the preservation of the peace of the said Province; and unjustly stileing those who will not join with them Traytors to your MLs Government Notwithstanding your Petitionrs (as like wise several hundreds of your Majesties Protestant subjects of that your Province and who abhor the Actions of the said Coode and his Complices) no sooner received notice of your Majesties happy Accession to the Crowne but that they shewed themselves with all possible Demonstrations of Joys and only waited your Majesties Orders for your being proclaimed, The Declaration of the said Coode. and eight more persons, which he falsely says to be that of your Majestie's Protestant subjects of Maryland being most notoriously false as were also the subscriptions to the Addresses they presented to your Majtic forged as your Petitioner can make appear; Which persons have also levied Taxes on us illegally. Those and many other grievances and Irregularities which are set forth in several Addresses of your Majties subjects of that your Province (and here ready in all humble manner to be tendred to your Majtie) will inevitably in a short time bring that your Mats flourishing Province into Ruine and Confusion, unless your Majtie shall in your princely wisdom interpose your Royall Authority to put a stop thereto.

Your Petitioners therefore most humbly pray your Majtie That you will graciously be pleased to give your Orders that the said John Coode together with one Kenelm Cheselyn, who is one of his Accomplices and are both now here in London may be sent for before your Majtie to answer the Complaints occasioned by the aforesaid oppressions of your Petitioner, and that your Majtie will be pleased to grant such Redress to your Petr against the said Coode and his Accomplices as upon making appear our said Grievances to your Majtie your Majtie in your Princely Justice and wisdome shall think fit.

    And your Petr (as in duty bound)
        shall ever pray &c:
John Lillingston George Lingan
    Henry Coursey
Thomas Knighton Miles Gibson
    Thomas Tailler
John Hinson. Samuel Chew Richard
    Hill
Abraham Wilde. Edward Dorsey.

(Endorsed)
Maryland
Referr d by Order of 20.
    Nov: 1690.
Read 22. Nov: 1690.

The Answer of John Coode and Kenelm Cheseldine Maryland Agents and Commissioners from the late Convention of their Majesties Province of Maryland on behalfe of the said Convention and themselves to a Paper Exhibitted against them: To the Kings most Excellent Majesty by Richard Hill Henry Coursey George Wells George Lingham, Edward Dorsey &c: The Chief and most of which were the Protestants that opposed their present Majesties Right and Tytle to the Allegiance Obedience and subjection of their said Majesties subjects in the said Province.

Margin: 3 of the Peticrs sd Taylour & Lillingston at the Revolution

As to the first Allegation in the said Paper, that they petition on behalfe of themselves and most of the Inhabitants of the said Province is false For they can produce no power or qualification from any other persons whatsoever. The whole Province (as by Addresses from the severall Counties heretofore delivered in and now ready to be delivered to their Majesties fully manifesting the contrary as well as severall persons (viva voce) to testify the same.

As to the second Allegation That the Province hath in his Lordspp and his Father's time enjoyed a continuall peace and that persons of all perswasions have enjoyed equall favours from the Government is also untrue. Witness the Insurrection at the Clifts occasioned by his Lordspps Writts of Elleccon comanding Four Representatives for each County to be elected as an Assembly out of which Four, his Lordspp afterwards called only two that he thought most fitt for his Interest to be an Assembly who laid the greatest Levy upon the People that ever was laid in that Province. Which they refused to pay as not being laid by their legall Representatives and for which three of them were condemned and two of them executed. Witness also the Comotions in the said Province upon his Lordspps arrivall there in the time of the Popish Plott. As also upon the Indians killing divers English at the Lower end of the Towne (being a place there so called) and ever since have the people beene in continuall feares and jealousies of the French and Northern Indians who often pass by the Confines of the said Province with French Priests who were acquainted with the English and Irish Preists there inhabiting, and as to the equall enjoyment of favours as is pretended. It is well known that of late yeares there have not been any Protestants preferred to Offices were there were Papists fitt to enjoy the same That of all perswasions there, the Church of England have had the least encouragement and respect.

And as to that Clause, in the said Paper wherein they maliciously charge the said John Coode and his Accomplices to be the Disturbers of the Province and changers of the Government These Respondts do deny that either he the said Cood or any by his order or Privity ever unjustly disturbed or changed the same But do say that five moneths after their present Majesties were settled in the Throne and the generality of their dominions had submitted to them and after they were proclaimed in Virginia the adjacent Country and all other their Majesties Colonies in America of which the Popish Government of Maryland were as well assured as they could be of any matter of Fact. The said Deputy Governours (with the Papists and severall of the aforesaid Petitioners their Adherents) disclaiming their Allegiance to their Majesties and politickly disarmeing the Protestants denying to call the Assembly to examine the Confederacy charged on them by Indians by whom they were accused as well as the English useing daily invectives against their Majesties persons and Government and all the Protestant Peers of the Realm conniveing at and encourageing all others to do the same, binding Protestants to their good behaviour endeavouring to imprison others for the least shew of their allegiance sending Warrants for such as but read or heard any of their Majesties Proclamacon or the Parliament Papers termeing them Treason able Papers and those that read or heard them or should but say God Bless the King Traitors daily broaching lyeing news (as they pretended sent to the Preists and Jesuitts from all parts of the French Kings invinceable Army to conquer England and the late King James his Victory in Scotland and Ireland and his great party in England to joyn with them to subdue the Rebells as they termed the Protestants as also the great strength of the French and Canada Indians if occasion served to invade the Province and other their Majesties Protestant Colonies in those Parts praying publickly in their Popish Chappells for the Irish and French success against the English and daily drinking health to the same wishing the arrivall of that golden day as they termed it To the great terrour of the Protestants and encouragement of the Papists The Protestants standing continually upon their guards and some flying for fear into Virginia so enraged the people as that it was not easy to restraine them from riseing tho they had no armes nor amunition to defend themselves and the more thinking men were plunged in their minds what course to take For Armes and Ammunition they had not to defend themselves and to depart the Province was to ruine their Estates and Familyes and stay they could not with safety without owneing their Allegiance to the late King James and

fidelity to that present Popish Government thereby denying their Faith Allegiance Mary land and subjection to their present Majesties which would have been high Treason and adhereing to their Enemies against the conscience and interest of all good Protestants and to involve them into the same crimes of Disloyalty with their Enemies and subject them to the penaltyes of the Law for High Treason. Whereupon the most eminent Protestants in the Province associated themselves with this Resolution That as God Almighty had given their Majesties a just call to the Crown to whom their Faith and Allegiance was due so according to their Duty and the Laws of the land they would with their lives and fortunes mainteyne their Majesties Right and Title to the Faith and Allegiance Obedience and subjection of their subjects in the said Province.

Thus matters stood untill towards the latter part of July 1689 at which time the people of Virginia did often threaten us and were ready (in great numbers) to come over into Maryland to reduce us alleadging wee were Rebells for not Proclaimeing their Majesties in the mean time news being brought to some of the aforesaid Protestants that the Deputy Governors were fortifying the Court house at St Maries and Matapany garrison and raiseing men to keep the same; they sent over to the Magistrates in Virginia desireing them to restrain the proceedings and designes aforesaid of their people. And there upon about two hundred and fifty Protestants tho very badly provided with Armes and Ammunition marched down to the City of St Maries to know the truth of the aforesaid Report and to desire the Deputy Governors to call an Assembly which had been for a long time prorogued against the desires of all honest men. That speedy course might be taken for the satisfaction of both Protestants and Papists untill orders from England. But when they arrived there they found the said Court house full of armed men made a garrison ready to oppose them. Whereupon they sent into the said Fort the Protestant Declaration demanding to have King William and Queen Mary to be proclaimed and submitted To which they refuseing to do the said Protestants marched up resolutely to the said Garrison and haveing gained the Doores and Windows and being ready to enter Those within did surrender takeing with them their private armes and leaveing the publick armes to the Protestants and then they marched to Matapany Fort about eight miles distant where about four hundred men were in Garrison and demanded surrender of the same to the use of King William and Queen Mary the which they refused for sometime to do. But finding the number of the Protestants to encrease and resolveing to attacke the same They surrendered upon Articles and thereupon a convention of the cheife of the Protestants kept all the said Articles inviolable yet notwithstanding the said Deputy Governors endeavoured by all wicked meanes possible to pervert and draw the people from their Allegiance to their Majesties and stirr them up to Rebel lion and obstruct the said Convention from settling the Countrey in Peace and quietness untill order from their Majesties which notwithstanding they proceeded unto. And first

of all pursuant to their Duty they caused their Majesties to be pro claimed and drew up an Address to them and then proceeded to settle the Province untill Orders from them, as first to settle the Military and civill Officers continueing all Protestants in their places and removeing all Papists and putting Protestants in their Rooms pursuant to their Majesties Declaration and continued all the Tempoary Laws in the Province laid the publique Levy which (notwithstanding the great occasion) was the least that had beene in that Province for many yeares tho they also paid the debts of the old Governmt out of the same and then drew all up into an Ordinance of Assembly whereby those matters do more fully appeare, after which the Deputy Governts and severall of the Petitioners their Adherents (being of the Lord Baltemores Comission) did on the behalfe of King James endeavour all they could to raise Rebellion against their Majesties in all the parts of the Province In the opposeing of which if any received Damage it is more then those Re spondts know or ever heard of before there being none done by them or their Order And do verily beleive there was none done by any other But if any such there were lett them prove the same agat those that did it, and the Law is open for their Remedy the Convention never giveing authority thereto.

As to that other part of the charge in the said Paper of acting contrary to their Majesties Letter These Respondts humbly conceive that the Convention hath given sufficient Answer in their last Letter to their Majesties unto which they do in all humility desire to be referred.

As to the generall charge of Forgery in the latter part of the aforesaid Petition to his Majesty These Respondts know not to whom it relates and do therefore look upon it to be a notorious Falsehood forged by themselves

And the Respondts do humbly desire that the Depositions Evidences and Papers relateing to the prmisses ready to bee produced to this Right Honble Board may be read and heard.

*(Endorsed)*
*Mr Coode &c:—*
*Answere to the petition*
*Read the 22d Dee: 1690.*

## Benjamin Tompson, *New England's Crisis,* 1676

*Tompson's epic poem is one of the most vivid accounts of the Anglo-Indian conflict known to the English as King Philip's War.*

*Source:* Original is in the Huntington Library, California; reprinted in Richard Slotkin and James K. Folsom, eds., *So Dreadful a Judgment: Puritan Responses to King Philip's War, 1676–1677* (Middletown, Conn.: Wesleyan University Press, 1978), pp. 215–231.

*To the Reader*
*Courteous Reader:*
I never thought this babe of my weak fantasy worthy of an imprimatur; but being an abortive, it was begged in these perplexing times to be cherished by the charity of others. If its lineaments please not the reader better than the writer, I shall be glad to see it pressed to death:

but if it displease not many and satisfy any, it's to me a glorious reward, who am more willing than able to any service to my country and friend.

*Farewell*

THE PROLOGUE

The times wherein old Pompion was a
   saint,
When men fared hardly yet without
   complaint
On vilest cates; the dainty Indian maize
Was eat with clamshells out of wooden
   trays
Under thatched huts without the cry of
   rent,
And the best sauce to every dish, content.
When flesh was food, & hairy skins made
   coats,
And men as well as birds had chirping
   notes.
When simnels were accounted noble blood
Among the tribes of common herbage
   food.
Of Ceres' bounty formed was many a
   knack
Enough to fill *Poor Robin's Almanac.*
These golden times (too fortunate to hold)
Were quickly signed away for love of gold.
'Twas then among the bushes, not the
   street
If one in place did an inferior meet,
"Good morrow, brother, is there ought you
   want?
Take freely of me, what I have you ha'n't."
Plain Tom and Dick would pass as
   current now,
As ever since "Your servant, Sir," and bow.
Deep-skirted doublets, puritanic capes
Which now would render men like upright
   apes,

Was comelier wear our wiser fathers
    thought
Than the cast fashions from all Europe
    brought.
'Twas in those days an honest grace would
    hold
Til an hot pudding grew at heart a cold.
And men had better stomachs to religion
Than I to capon, turkey cock, or pigeon.
When honest sisters met to pray not prate
About their own and not their neighbors'
    state.
During plain dealing's reign, that worthy
    stud
Of th'ancient planters race before the
    flood.
These times were good, merchants cared
    not a rush
For other fare than jonakin and mush.
Although men fared and lodged very hard
Yet innocence was better than a guard.
'Twas long before spiders & worms had
    drawn
Their dungy webs or hid with cheating
    lawn
New England's beauties, which still
    seemed to me
Illustrious in their own simplicity.
'Twas ere the neighboring virgin land had
    broke
The hogsheads of her worse than hellish
    smoke.
'Twas ere the islands sent their presents in,
Which but to use was counted next to sin.
'Twas ere a barge had made so rich a
    freight
As chocolate, dust gold, and bitts of eight.
Ere wines from France and Muscovado too
Without the which the drink will
    scarcely do,
From western isles, ere fruits and
    delicacies,

Did rot maids' teeth & spoil their
    handsome faces.
Or ere these times did chance the noise
    of war
Was from our towns and hearts
    removed far.
No bugbear comets in the crystal air
To drive our Christian planters to despair.
No sooner pagan malice peeped forth
But valor snibbed it; then were men of
    worth
Who by their prayers slew thousands
    angel-like,
Their weapons are unseen with which they
    strike.
Then had the churches rest, as yet the
    coals
Were covered up in most contentious
    souls.
Freeness in judgment, union in affection,
Dear love, sound truth, they were our
    grand protection.
These were the twins which in our
    counsels sate,
These gave prognostics of our future fate,
If these be longer lived our hopes increase,
These wars will usher in a longer peace:
But if New England's love die in its youth
The grave will open next for blessed truth.
This theme is out of date, the peaceful
    hours
When castles needed not but pleasant
    bowers.
Not ink, but blood and tears now serve
    the turn
To draw the figure of New England's urn.
New England's hour of passion is at hand,
No power except divine can it withstand;
Scarce hath her glass of fifty years run
    out,
But her old prosperous steeds turn heads
    about,

Tracking themselves back to their poor
  beginnings,
To fear and fare upon their fruits of
  sinnings:
So that the mirror of the Christian world
Lies burnt to heaps in part, her streamers
  furled.
Grief reigns, joys flee and dismal fears
  surprise,
Not dastard spirits only but the wise.
Thus have the fairest hopes deceived
  the eye
Of the big swollen expectant standing by.
Thus the proud ship after a little turn
Sinks into Neptune's arms to find its urn.
Thus hath the heir to many thousands born
Been in an instant from the mother torn.
Even thus thine infant cheeks begin to
  pale,
And thy supporters through great losses
  fail.
This is the prologue to thy future woe,
The epilogue no mortal yet can know.

## NEW ENGLAND'S CRISIS

In seventy-five the critic of our years
Commenced our war with Philip and his
  peers.
Whether the sun in Leo had inspired
A feverish heat, and pagan spirits fired?
Whether some Romish agent hatched the
  plot?
Or whether they themselves?
  appeareth not.
Whether our infant thrivings did invite?
Or whether to our lands pretended right?
Is hard to say; but Indian spirits need
No grounds but lust to make a Christian
  bleed.
And here methinks I see this greasy lout
With all his pagan slaves coiled round
  about,

Assuming all the majesty his throne
Of rotten stump, or of the rugged stone
Could yield; casting some bacon-rind-like
  looks,
Enough to fright a student from his books,
Thus treat his peers, & next to them his
  commons,
Kenneled together all without a summons.
"My friends, our fathers were not half so
  wise
As we ourselves who see with younger
  eyes.
They sell our land to Englishmen who
  teach
Our nation all so fast to pray and preach:
Of all our country they enjoy the best,
And quickly they intend to have the
  rest.
This no wunnegin, so big matchit law,
Which our old fathers' fathers never saw.
These English make and we must keep
  them too,
Which is too hard for them or us to do,
We drink we so big whipped, but English
  they
Go sneep, no more, or else a little pay.
Me meddle squaw me hanged, our fathers
  kept
What squaws they would, whether they
  waked or slept.
Now if you'll fight I'll get you English
  coats,
And wine to drink out of their captains'
  throats.
The richest merchants' houses shall be
  ours,
We'll lie no more on mats or dwell in
  bowers.
We'll have their silken wives take they our
  squaws,
They shall be whipped by virtue of our
  laws.

If ere we strike 'tis now before they
    swell
To greater swarms than we know how to
    quell.
This my resolve, let neighboring sachems
    know,
And everyone that hath club, gun, or
    bow."
This was assented to, and for a close
He stroked his smutty beard and cursed his
    foes.
This counsel lightning-like their tribes
    invade,
And something like a muster's quickly
    made,
A ragged regiment, a naked swarm,
Whom hopes of booty doth with
    courage arm,
Set forth with bloody hearts, the first they
    meet
Of men or beasts they butcher at their
    feet.
They round our skirts, they pare, they
    fleece, they kill,
And to our bordering towns do what they
    will.
Poor hovels (better far than Caesar's
    court
In the experience of the meaner sort)
Receive from them their doom next
    execution,
By flames reduced to horror and
    confusion:
Here might be seen the smoking funeral
    piles
Of wildred towns pitched distant many
    miles.
Here might be seen the infant from the
    breast
Snatched by a pagan hand to lasting rest:
The mother, Rachel-like, shrieks out "My
    child."

She wrings her hands and raves as she
    were wild.
The brutish wolves suppress her anxious
    moan
By cruelties more deadly of their own.
Will she or nill the chastest turtle must
Taste of the pangs of their unbridled lust.
From farms to farms, from towns to towns
    they post,
They strip, they bind, they ravish, flay, and
    roast.
The beasts which want their master's crib
    to know,
Over the ashes of their shelters low.
What the inexorable flames do spare
More cruel heathen lug away for fare.
These tidings ebbing from the outward
    parts
Makes tradesmen cast aside their wonted
    arts
And study arms: the craving merchants
    plot
Not to augment but keep what they have
    got.
And every soul which hath but common
    sense
Thinks it the time to make a just
    defense.
Alarums everywhere resound in streets,
From West sad tidings with the Eastern
    meets.
Our common fathers in their counsels
    close
A martial treaty with the pagan foes.
All answers center here that fire and
    sword
Must make their sachem universal lord.
This arms the English with a resolution
To give the vaporing scab a retribution.
Heavens they consult by prayer, the best
    design
A furious foe to quell or undermine.

Resolved that from the Massachusetts
    bands
Be pressed on service some Herculean
    hands
And certainly he well deserved a jerk
That slipped the collar from so good a
    work.
Some volunteers, some by compulsion go
To range the hideous forest for a foe.
The tender mother now's all bowels
    grown,
Clings to her son as if they'd melt in one.
Wives clasp about their husbands as the
    vine
Hugs the fair elm, while tears burst out
    like wine.
The new-sprung love in many a virgin
    heart
Swells to a mountain when the lovers part.
Nephews and kindred turn all springs of
    tears,
Their hearts are so surprised with panic
    fears.
But doleful shrieks of captives summon
    forth
Our walking castles, men of noted worth,
Made all of life, each captain was a Mars,
His name too strong to stand on waterish
    verse:
Due praise I leave to some poetic hand
Whose pen and wits are better at
    command.
Methinks I see the Trojan horse burst ope,
And such rush forth as might with giants
    cope:
These first the natives' treachery felt, too
    fierce
For any but eyewitness to rehearse.
Yet sundry times in places where they
    came
Upon the Indian skins they carved their
    name.

The trees stood sentinels and bullets flew
From every bush (a shelter for their crew).
Hence came our wounds and deaths from
    every side
While skulking enemies squat undescried,
That every stump shot like a musketeer,
And bows with arrows every tree did bear.
The swamps were courts of guard, thither
    retired
The straggling blue-coats when their guns
    were fired,
In dark meanders, and these winding
    groves,
Where bears & panthers with their
    monarch moves
These far more cruel slyly hidden lay,
Expecting Englishmen to move that way.
One party lets them in, the other greets
Them with the next thing to their
    winding-sheets;
Most fall, the rest thus startled back
    return,
And from their bypassed foes receive
    an urn.
Here fell a captain, to be named with
    tears,
Who for his courage left not many peers,
With many more who scarce a number left
To tell how treacherously they were
    bereft.
This flushed the pagan courage, now they
    think
The victory theirs, not lacking meat or
    drink.
The ranging wolves find here and there a
    prey,
And having filled their paunch they run
    away
By their hosts' light, the thanks which they
    return
Is to lead captives and their taverns burn.
Many whose thrift had stored for after use

Sustain their wicked plunder and abuse.
Poor people spying an unwonted light,
Fearing a martyrdom, in sudden fright
Leap to the door to fly, but all in vain,
They are surrounded with a pagan train;
Their first salute is death, which if they
   shun
Some are condemned the gauntelet to run;
Death would a mercy prove to such as
   those
Who feel the rigor of such hellish foes.
Posts daily on their Pegasean steeds
Bring sad reports of worse than Nero's
   deeds,
Such brutish murders as would paper stain
Not to be heard in a Domitian's reign.
The field which nature hid is common laid,
And mothers' bodies ripped for lack
   of aid.
The secret cabinets which nature meant
To hide her masterpiece is open rent,
The half-formed infant there receives a
   death
Before it sees the light or draws its breath,
Many hot welcomes from the natives' arms
Hid in their skulking holes many alarms
Our brethren had, and weary weary trants,
Sometimes in melting heats and pinching
   wants:
Sometimes the clouds with sympathizing
   tears
Ready to burst discharged about their ears:
Sometimes on craggy hills, anon in bogs
And miry swamps better befitting hogs,
And after tedious marches little boast
Is to be heard of stewed or baked or roast,
Their beds are hurdles, open house they
   keep
Through shady boughs the stars upon them
   peep,
Their crystal drink drawn from the
   mother's breast

Disposes not to mirth but sleep and rest.
Thus many days and weeks, some months
   run out
To find and quell the vagabonding rout,
Who like enchanted castles fair appear,
But all is vanished if you come but near,
Just so we might the pagan archers track
With towns and merchandise upon their
   back;
And thousands in the south who settled
   down
To all the points and winds are quickly
   blown.
At many meetings of their fleeting crew,
From whom like hail arrows and bullets
   flew;
The English courage with whole swarms
   dispute,
Hundreds they hack in pieces in pursuit.
*Sed haud impune*, English sides do feel
As well as tawny skins the lead and steel
And some such gallant sparks by bullets
   fell,
As might have cursed the powder back to
   hell:
Had only swords these skirmishes decided
All pagan skulls had been long since
   divided.
The lingering war outlives the
   summer sun,
Who hence departs hoping it might be
   done,
Ere his return at Spring: but, ah!
   he'll find
The sword still drawn, men of unchanged
   mind.
Cold winter now nibbles at hands and toes
And shrewdly pinches both our friends and
   foes.
Fierce Boreas whips the pagan tribe
   together
Advising them to fit for foes and weather:

The axe which late had tasted Christian
  blood
Now sets its steely teeth to feast on wood.
The forests suffer now, by weight
  constrained
To kiss the earth with soldiers lately
  brained.
The lofty oaks and ash do wag the head
To see so many of their neighbors dead;
Their fallen carcasses are carried thence
To stand our enemies in their defense.
Their myrmidons enclosed with clefts of
  trees
Are busy like the ants or nimble bees:
And first they limber poles fix in the
  ground,
In figure of the heavens convex: all round
They draw their arras-mats and skins of
  beasts
And under these the elves to make their
  nests.
Rome took more time to grow than twice
  six hours,
But half that time will serve for Indian
  bowers.
A city shall be reared in one day's space
As shall an hundred Englishmen out-face.
Canonicus' precincts there swarms unite,
Rather to keep a winter guard than fight.
A dern and dismal swamp some scout had
  found
Whose bosom was a spot of rising ground
Hedged up with mighty oaks, maples, and
  ashes,
Nursed up with springs, quick bogs & miry
  plashes,
A place which nature coined on very
  nonce
For tigers not for men to be a sconce.
'Twas here these monsters, shaped and
  faced like men,
Took up their rendezvous and brumal den,

Deeming the depth of snow, hail, frost,
  and ice
Would make our infantry more tame and
  wise
Than by forsaking beds and loving wives,
Merely for Indian skins to hazard lives:
These hopes had something calmed the
  boiling passion
Of this incorrigible warlike nation.
During this short parenthesis of peace
Our forces found, but left him not at
  ease.
Here English valor most illustrious shone,
Finding their numbers ten times ten
  to one.
A shower of leaden hail our captains feel
Which made the bravest blades among us
  reel.
Like to some anthill newly spurned
  abroad,
Where each takes heels and bears away his
  load:
Instead of plate and jewels, Indian trays
With baskets up they snatch and run their
  ways.
Sundry the flames arrest and some the
  blade,
By bullets heaps on heaps of Indians laid.
The flames like lightning in their narrow
  streets
Dart in the face of everyone it meets.
Here might be heard an hideous
  Indian cry,
Of wounded ones who in the
  wigwams fry.
Had we been cannibals here might we feast
On brave Westphalia gammons ready
  dressed.
The tawny hue is Ethiopic made
Of such on whom Vulcan his clutches laid.
Their fate was sudden, our advantage great
To give them once for all a grand defeat;

But tedious travel had so cramped our toes
It was too hard a task to chase the foes.
Distinctness in the numbers of the slain,
Or the account of pagans which remain
Are both uncertain, losses of our own
Are too too sadly felt, too sadly known.
War digs a common grave for friends and
    foes,
Captains in with the common soldier
    throws.
Six of our leaders in the first assault
Crave readmission to their mother's vault
Who had they fell in ancient Homer's days
Had been enrolled with hecatombs of
    praise.
As clouds dispersed, the natives' troops
    divide,
And like the streams along the thickets
    glide.
Some breathing time we had, & short God
    knows
But new alarums from recruited foes
Bounce at our ears, the mounting, clouds
    of smoke
From martyred towns the heavens for aid
    invoke:
Churches, barns, houses with most
    ponderous things
Made volatile fly o'er the land with wings.
Hundreds of cattle now they sacrifice
For airy spirits up to gormandize;
And to the Moloch of their hellish guts,
Which craves the flesh in gross, their ale in
    butts.
Lancaster, Medfield, Mendon, wildred
    Groton,
With many villages by me not thought on
Die in their youth by fire that useful foe,
Which this grand cheat the world will
    overflow.
The wandering priest to everyone he
    meets

Preaches his church's funeral in the streets.
Sheep from their fold are frighted,
    keepers too
Put to their trumps not knowing what
    to do.
This monster war hath hatched a beauteous
    dove
In dogged hearts, of most unfeigned love,
Fraternal love the livery of a saint
Being come in fashion though by sad
    constraint,
Which if it thrive and prosper with us long
Will make New England forty thousand
    strong.
But off the table hand, let this suffice
As the abridgment of our miseries.
If mildew, famine, sword, and fired towns,
If slaughter, captivating, deaths, and
    wounds,
If daily whippings once reform our ways,
These all will issue in our Father's praise;
If otherwise, the sword must never rest
Till all New England's glory it divest.

A SUPPLEMENT
What means this silence of Harvardine
    quills
While Mars triumphant thunders on our
    hills.
Have pagan priests their eloquence
    confined
To no man's use but the mysterious mind?
Have pow-wows charmed that art which
    was so rife
To crouch to every Don that lost his life?
But now whole towns and churches fire
    and die
Without the pity of an elegy.
Nay rather should my quills were they all
    swords
Wear to the hilts in some lamenting
    words.

I dare not style them poetry but truth,
The dwindling products of my crazy
    youth.
If these essays shall raise some quainter
    pens
'Twill to the writer make a rich amends.

## MARLBORO'S FATE

When London's fatal bills were blown
    abroad
And few but specters travelled on the
    road,
Not towns but men in the black bill
    enrolled
Were in gazettes by typographers sold:
But our gazettes without erratas must
Report the plague of towns reduced to
    dust:
And fevers formerly to tenants sent
Arrest the timbers of the tenement.
Ere the late ruins of old Groton's cold,
Of Marlboro's peracute disease we're
    told.
The feet of such who neighboring
    dwellings urned
Unto her ashes, not her doors returned.
And what remained of tears as yet unspent
Are to its final gasps a tribute lent.
If painter overtrack my pen let him
An olive color mix, these elves to trim;
Of such an hue let many thousand thieves
Be drawn like scarecrows clad with oaken
    leaves,
Exhausted of their verdant life and blown
From place to place without an home
    to own.
Draw devils like themselves, upon their
    cheeks
The banks for grease and mud, a place for
    leeks.
Whose locks, Medusa's snakes, do ropes
    resemble,

And ghostly looks would make Achilles
    tremble.
Limn them besmeared with Christian
    blood & oiled
With fat out of white human bodies
    boiled.
Draw them with clubs like mauls & full of
    stains,
Like Vulcan's anvilling New England's
    brains.
Let round be gloomy forests with cragged
    rocks
Where like to castles they may hide their
    flocks,
Till opportunity their cautious friend
shall jog them fiery worship to attend.
Show them like serpents in an avious path
Seeking to sow the firebrands of their
    wrath.
Most like Aeneas in his cloak of mist,
Who undiscovered move wheree'er they
    list
Cupid they tell us hath two sorts of darts,
One sharp and one obtuse, one causing
    wounds,
One piercing deep the other dull
    rebounds,
But we feel none but such as drill our
    hearts.
From Indian sheaves which to their
    shoulders cling,
Upon the word they quickly feel the
    string.
Let earth be made a screen to hide
    our woe
From heaven's monarch and his
    lady's too;
And lest our jealousy think they partake,
For the red stage with clouds a curtain
    make.
Let dogs be gagged and every quickening
    sound

Be charmed to silence, here and there all
   round
The town to suffer, from a thousand holes
Let crawl these fiends with brands and
   fired poles,
Paint here the house & there the barn on
   fire,
With holocausts ascending in a spire.
Here granaries, yonder the churches
   smoke
Which vengeance on the actors doth
   invoke.
Let Morpheus with his leaden keys have
   bound
In featherbeds some, some upon the
   ground,
That none may burst his drowsy shackles
   till
The brutish pagans have obtained their
   will,
And Vulcan files them off; then Zeuxis
   paint
The frenzy glances of the sinking saint.
Draw there the pastor for his bible crying,
The soldier for his sword, the glutton
   frying
With streams of glory fat, the thin-jawed
   miser,
"Oh had I given this I had been wiser."
Let here the mother seem a statue turned
At the sad object of her bowels burned.
Let the unstable weakling in belief
Be mounting Asshur's horses for relief.
Let the half convert seem suspended twixt
The dens of darkness, and the planets
   fixed,
Ready to quit his hold, and yet hold fast
By the great Atlas of the heavens vast.
Paint papists muttering o'er their apish
   beads
Whom the blind follow while the blind
   man leads.

Let Ataxy be mounted on a throne
Imposing her commands on everyone,
A many-headed monster without eyes
To see the ways which want to make men
   wise.
Give her a thousand tongues with wings
   and hands
To be ubiquitary in commands,
But let the concave of her skull appear
Clean washed and empty quite of all but
   fear,
One she bids flee, another stay, a third
She bids betake him to his rusty sword,
This to his treasure, th'other to his
   knees,
Some counsels she to fry and some to
   freeze,
These to the garrison, those to the road,
Some to run empty, some to take their
   load:
Thus while confusion most men's hearts
   divide
Fire doth their small exchequer soon
   decide.
Thus all things seeming ope or secret foes,
An infant may grow old before a close,
But yet my hopes abide in perfect
   strength.

## THE TOWN CALLED PROVIDENCE ITS FATE

Why muse we thus to see the wheels run
   cross
Since Providence itself sustains a loss:
And yet should Providence forget to watch
I fear the enemy would all dispatch;
Celestial lights would soon forget their
   line,
The wandering planets would forget to
   shine,
The stars run all out of their common
   spheres,

And quickly fall together by the ears:
Kingdoms would jostle out their kings
    and set
The poor mechanic up whom next
    they met,
Or rather would whole kingdoms with the
    world
Into a chaos their first egg be hurled.
There's none this providence of the most
    high
Who can survive and write its elegy.
But of a solitary town I write,
A place of darkness yet receiving light
From pagan hands a miscellaneous nest
Of error's hectors, where they sought a
    rest
Out of the reach of laws but not of God,
Since they have felt the smart of
    common rod.
'Twas much I thought they did escape so
    long,
Who gospel truth so manifestly wrong:
For one Lot's sake perhaps, or else I think
Justice did at greatest offenders wink
But now the shot is paid, I hope the dross
Will be cashiered in this common loss.
Houses with substance feel uplifting
    wings,
The earth remains, the last of human
    things:
But know the dismal day draws near
    wherein
The fire shall earth itself dissolve and sin.

## SEEKONK PLAIN ENGAGEMENT

On our Pharsalian Plains, comprising space
For Caesar's host brave Pompey to
    outface,
An handful of our men are walled round
With Indian swarms; anon their pieces
    sound
A madrigal like heaven's artillery

Lightning and thunderbolts their bullets
    fly.
Here's hosts to handfuls, of a few they
    leave
Fewer to tell how many they bereave.
Foolhardy fortitude it had been sure
Fierce storms of shot and arrows to
    endure
Without all hopes of some requital to
So numerous and pestilent a foe.
Some musing a retreat and thence to run,
Have in an instant all their business done,
They sink and all their sorrows' ponderous
    weight
Down at their feet they cast and tumble
    straight.
Such who outlived the fate of others fly
Into the Irish bogs of misery.
Such who might die like men like beasts
    do range
Uncertain whither for a better change,
These natives hunt and chase with currish
    mind,
And plague with cruelties such as they
    find.
When shall this shower of blood be over?
    When?
Quickly we pray, oh, Lord! say thou
    "Amen."

## SEEKONK OR REHOBOTH'S FATE

I once conjectured that those tigers hard
To reverend Newman's bones would have
    regard,
But were all saints they met 'twere all one
    case,
They have no reverence to an angel's face:
But where they fix their griping lion's
    paws
They rend without remorse or heed to
    laws.
Rehoboth here in common English, Rest,

They ransack, Newman's relics to molest.
Here all the town is made a public stage
Whereon these Nimrods act their
    monstrous rage.
All cruelties which paper stained before
Are acted to the life here o'er and o'er.

## CHELMSFORD'S FATE

Ere famous Winthrop's bones are laid to
    rest
The pagans Chelmsford with sad flames
    arrest,
Making an artificial day of night
By that plantation's formidable light.
Here's midnight shrieks and soul-amazing
    moans,
Enough to melt the very marble stones:
Firebrands and bullets, darts and deaths
    and wounds
Confusive outcries everywhere resounds:
The natives shooting with the mixed cries,
With all the cruelties the foes devise
Might fill a volume, but I leave a space
For mercies still successive in their place
Not doubting but the foes have done their
    worst,
And shall by heaven suddenly be cursed.
Let this dear Lord the sad conclusion be
Of poor New England's dismal tragedy.
Let not the glory of thy former work
Blasphemed be by pagan, Jew, or Turk:
But in its funeral ashes write thy name
So fair all nations may expound the same:
Out of her ashes let a Phoenix rise
That may outshine the first and be more
    xwise.

## ON A FORTIFICATION AT BOSTON BEGUN BY WOMEN DUX FEMINA FACTI

A grand attempt some Amazonian
    dames
Contrive whereby to glorify their names,
A ruff for Boston neck of mud and turf,
Reaching from side to side from surf to
    surf,
Their nimble hands spin up like Christmas
    pies,
Their pastry by degrees on high doth
    rise.
The wheel at home counts it an holiday,
Since while the mistress worketh it may
    play.
A tribe of female hands, but manly
    hearts
Forsake at home their pastry-crust and
    tarts
To knead the dirt, the samplers down they
    hurl,
Their undulating silks they closely furl.
The pickaxe one as a commandress
    holds,
While t'other at her awkness gently
    scolds.
One puffs and sweats, the other
    mutters why
Can't you promove your work so fast
    as I?
Some dig, some delve, and others' hands
    do feel
The little wagon's weight with single
    wheel.
And lest some fainting fits the weak
    surprise,
They want no sack nor cakes, they are
    more wise.
These brave essays draw forth male
    stronger hands
More like to daubers than to martial
    bands;
These do the work, and sturdy bulwarks
    raise,
But the beginners well deserve the
    praise.

## Vincent Bigot's Report, "Of the Piety and Devotion of the Christian Iroquois," 1677

*This account, written by Jesuit missionary Vincent Bigot and revised by his superior, Claude Dablon, demonstrates the difference in French and English attitudes and practices regarding the conversion of Indians to Christianity.*

*Source:* Reuben G. Thwaites, ed., *The Jesuit Relations and Allied Documents: Travels and Explorations of the Jesuit Missionaries in New France, 1610–1791*, vol. 61, *1677–1680* (Cleveland, 1900), pp. 208–213.

Since the year 1673, prayer has been offered at gandaouagé,—which is one of the villages of agnié, of which father Bonniface has had charge,—both morning and evening, as steadily as in the best-regulated families of france. There is nothing more Comforting than to witness these good Christians pray together aloud, and finish that holy act with spiritual Canticles. Several little children, also, 7 or 8 years of age, have formed their own little Choir, and do on earth what the angels never cease to do in Heaven. It is a pleasure to see these little innocents marshaling themselves in the Chapel and rendering to God their homage as well as do those most advanced in age.

A little Cradle, prepared at christmas, illuminated with a number of lights and adorned with evergreens, excited to a wonderful degree the devotion of the christians, who in their Hymns bestowed on the infant Jesus tokens of their gratitude and love. There was no way of resisting the Entreaties which came from those who are still infidels, to go in and Gratify their Curiosity by a lengthened Survey of that which rendered the spot pleasing to their eyes. The festival was spent in Singing and praying—for a longer time than usual, notwithstanding the severity of the cold. Their devotion toward this endearing mystery is so tender that, to assist their piety, the father permitted them to Go on with their tunes and christmas carols Until easter. Nothing could be desired more fervent or more touching, in a country which at first seemed inaccessible to the faith.

But would it be readily believed that the Ceremony of the blessed bread takes place every sunday, by turns, at agnié?— that means, among people who have been reputed cannibals; who in former times gorged themselves not only on the Fresh of their enemies, but even of those who announced to them the gospel. They practice this ancient custom of the church with all the more Joy, inasmuch as they are all brethren, and children of God, whose bread they now eat while awaiting the time when he will cause them to taste of eternal delights. She who provides the blessed bread serves a slight repast to all the Christians at her home, at which the prayer before and after meals is said. The Civility that they show to the one who has invited them has about it nothing of the savage, and These gatherings serve wonderfully in fostering fervor and Charity. *Here indeed, it must be said, is the finger of God; and that it pertains only to him to effect such changes, and so to humanize brutal natures as to render wolves worthy of being counted in the flock of the great shepherd of souls.*

I will say nothing of the estimation in

which This new church holds all tokens of our holy religion. Crosses and medals are their most precious jewels; they treasure them so dearly that they carry them round their Necks Even into the conventicles new holland, where the heretics have never succeeded in snatching away a single bead from their Rosaries.

## Testimony of Marmaduke Stevenson, 1659

*Marmaduke Stevenson was one of the "Boston martyrs," a Quaker hanged on October 27, 1659, by the Massachusetts government for entering the colony and attempting to proselytize.*

*Source:* London Yearly Meeting, *Christian Life, Faith, and Thought, Being the First Part of Christian Discipline of the Religious Society of Friends of Great Britain* (London, 1922).

In the beginning of the year 1655, I was at the plough in the east parts of Yorkshire in Old England, near the place where my outward being was; and, as I walked after the plough, I was filled with the love and presence of the living God, which did ravish my heart when I felt it, for it did increase and abound in me like a living stream, so did the life and love of God run through me like precious ointment giving a pleasant smell, which mad me to stand still. And, as I stood a little still, with my heart and mind stayed upon the Lord, the word of the Lord came to me in a still, small voice, which I did hear perfectly, saying to me in the secret of my heart and conscience, "I have ordained thee a prophet unto the nations," and, at the hearing of the word of the Lord, I was put to a stand, seeing that I was but a child for such a weighty matter. So, at the time appointed, Barbados was set before me, unto which I was required of the Lord to go and leave my dear and loving wife and tender children; for the Lord said unto me, immediately by HIs Spirit, that He would be as an husband to my wife and as a father to my children, and they should not want in my absence, for He would provide for them when I was gone. And I believed the Lord would perform what He had spoken, because I was made willing to give up myself to His work and service, to leave all and follow Him, whose presence and life is with me, where I rest in peace and quietness of spirit, with my dear brother [William Robinson] under the shadow of His wings, who hath made us willing to lay down our lives for His name's sake, if unmerciful men be suffered to take them from us. And, if they do, we know we shall have rest and peace with the Lord for ever in His holy habitation, when they shall have torment night and day.

So, in obedience to the living God, I made preparation to pass to Barbados in the Fourth month [June] 1658. So, after some time that I had been on the said island in the service of God, I heard that New England had made a law to put the servants of the living God to death if they returned after they were sentenced away, which did come near me at that time; and, as I considered the thing and pondered it in my heart, immediately came to word of the Lord unto me, saying, "Thou knowest not but that thou mayst go thither."

But I kept this word in my heart and did not declare it to any until the time appointed, so, after that, a vessel was made ready for Rhode Island, which I passed in. so, after a little time that I had been there, visiting the seed which the Lord had blessed, the word of the Lord came to me saying, "Go to Boston with they brother William Robinson," and at His command I was obedient and gave up to His will, that so His work and service may be accomplished. for He had said unto me that He had a great work for me to do, which is now come to pass. And, for yielding obedi-

ence to and for obeying the voice and command of the everlasting God, which created heaven and earth and the foundations of waters, do I, with my dear brother, suffer outward bonds near unto death.

And this is given forth to be upon record, that all people may know who hear it, that we came not in our own will but in the will of God.

Given forth by me, whom am know to men by the name of Marmaduke Stevenson, but have a new name given me, which the world knowns not of, written in the book of life.

# CHAPTER 2
# ETHNICITY IN EIGHTEENTH-CENTURY NORTH AMERICA, 1701–1788

## GRAHAM RUSSELL HODGES

ETHNICITY WAS A DEFINING characteristic for early Americans. Among a plethora of New World societies where, except for Native Americans, few individuals could trace their residence back more than three generations, a person's language, personal habits, and customs often derived directly from roots in old-world cultures. Continuing waves of voluntary and coerced immigration from Europe and Africa between 1700 and 1788, along with religious revivals and celebration of secularized rituals, refreshed old-world cultures among colonial Americans. Two historical views have shaped discussion of ethnicity in early America. One side holds firmly that eighteenth-century Americans soon became acculturated or "Anglicized" into the dominant political English society. Opposing this view is one that contends that ethnicity and race proved strong enough for groups to resist Anglicization and maintain traditional customs and beliefs. A third view, adopted in this essay, is that Anglicization depended heavily upon English demographic dominance in particular regions. The English controlled the Atlantic seaboard but did not dominate demographically, except for New England.

In this essay I contend that although the English controlled the Atlantic Coast politically and militarily, the British Empire held no hegemony, which could have eliminated other cultures. A more nuanced term for the effects of English political and military control on ethnicity is Americanization. In this definition, members of an ethnic group necessarily accepted English rule, but within their culture sustained traditional traits. At the same time, they frequently interacted with other ethnic groups and melded particular cultural practices to their own.

Even though English political and religious authorities pined for immigrants from the British Isles, they often recruited enslaved and bonded peoples from other societies as laborers. At the outset of the eighteenth century, observers often commented on the heterogeneity of the Atlantic Coast colonies. New York City was the best example of this; in this port city lived English, Dutch, Scots, Irish, Germans, Walloons, Portuguese, Africans, and Jews. Such diversity held little appeal to English authorities. Yet their efforts to Anglicize African slaves and European servants often floundered under local pressures. Elsewhere, throughout the eighteenth century, drives to acculturate people to English ways had mixed results. Even in New England, which was dominated by English peoples, by midcentury, more than 30 percent of its inhabitants came from outside of England. As Jon Butler has observed, Africans, Scots, Scotch-Irish, and Irish were numerous enough to have a "critical mass" to support burgeoning group identities. Further south,

African Americans presented a major alternative to English culture along with substantial influence from German arrivals. Westward from the Mississippi and Ohio River Valleys to the Pacific coast, Native American, French, and Spanish power held sway throughout most of the eighteenth century. In this essay, I treat the history of ethnicity in North America by emphasizing time and space. I have divided the essay geographically, and have attempted to cover all the regions that make up contemporary United States.

Although the English language generally served as a lingua franca, there was little commonality between the sections of the Atlantic Coast. These sections include New England, the Mid Atlantic, the Chesapeake or Upper South, and the Lower South. Further into the interior, English power dissipated rapidly. The Iroquois Confederacy controlled much of the land between the Onondaga region to present-day Illinois. The Midwest was a contested middle ground. In the Southeast, Native Americans maintained a precarious grip on traditional homelands, as European Americans with African slaves occupied ports along the Gulf of Mexico. In the Southwest, Spanish Tejanos exerted firm control over the remnants of Native American nations from New Mexico to California while warring against Apache and other guerilla Indians in the intermountain West.

## ENCOUNTERING NATIVE AMERICANS

All nonindigenous settlers coming to North America in the eighteenth century had to interact with Native American societies. Although Native America sustained control over most of the interior land of North America until after the American Revolution, genocidal war practices, forced removal, and disease directly decimated their numbers. It was during the eighteenth century that the balance of power tipped irretrievably away from Native Americans. Part of that loss was demographic. From an estimated population of 5 million persons in 1500, Native American nations dramatically declined to about six hundred thousand by 1800. Tributary groups of Native Americans around New England, New York, Pennsylvania, and down to Virginia were generally extirpated and survivors had to retreat behind a Proclamation Line established in 1676. By 1700, there were few Native Americans left close to the Atlantic Ocean. To stem this slaughter, Native Americans attempted to regroup by assembling new nations out of the remnants of older ones and practiced adoption into the tribe or band on a large scale. They were able to do this in the newer English colonies. The example of South Carolina is instructive. There refugees of the Saponis joined Tutelos or Occaneechees in a desperate effort to survive. They did not accept all comers, however, and rejected other tribal survivors because of language. For a short period, until the Tuscarora War of 1714, they were able to play off competing officials in Virginia and Carolina, but by 1717, the Saponis were restricted to a narrow reservation of six square miles. This method of contraction can be found elsewhere in the mission reserves of New France, praying towns of New England, settlement tribes of southwest New England, and small nations of Louisiana. Over the next few decades, their Native American traditions were swept away by the further impact of European trade. Worsening relations over local issues such as livestock, real estate, and personal conflicts often escalated into full-scale military confrontations, with Native Americans invariably ceding further rights in peace negotiations.

Native Americans experienced a brief respite from the downward cycle during the Long Peace following the imperial wars between European nations between 1689 and 1713. For about thirty years, there were small skirmishes, but most of the invasions of interior America were commercial. As Native Americans, especially the Iroquois, attempted to regroup, relations with Europeans centered on trade goods. Within Native American societies, distinct class lines emerged between those with access to consumer goods and those without. Pan-Indian revival movements led by Neolin in the 1760s and Handsome Lake at the end of the eighteenth century were attempts to exclude European American trade from Native American societies.

The situation was more complex in the interior of the continent. Native American survival techniques of adoption produced a plethora of multiethnic villages. The Iroquois federation was made up of a melting pot of peoples descended from evicted bands from the Northeast. West of Iroquoian lived Wyandots, Ottawas, Miamis, and others, occupying a territory known as the pays d'en haut, which Richard White has fittingly called a "middle ground" and a "world made of fragments." Similar configurations existed among the Cherokees, Muskogees, Chicasaws, and Choctaws of the Southeast. Of all ethnic groups of early America, Native Americans fit most closely the modern ideal of the melting pot.

Trade and warfare were not the only assimilating influences upon Native Americans. Religion was a key force. James Axtell has argued that the "Invasion Within" by Jesuit priests in the late seventeenth century, overcame the demographic superiority of the Iroquois over the French and helped to create New France. In the eighteenth century, as French power gradually dissipated from a long series of wars, English Protestantism grew in influence. Religious enthusiasms connected to the Great Awakening among European Americans in the 1740s were matched by contemporary revivals among Native Americans. The mid-eighteenth century saw continual diplomacy between Native Americans, the French, and the English. The last conflict emanating from this uneasy triangular relationship resulted in Native American alliances with the French, who lost the war and much of their territory. Although the English attempted to reinstate a boundary between white and Indian settlements, American settlers poured across the Appalachian Mountains and into the southeastern Indian homelands. One key theme of revolutionary discourse was Patriot discontent with English attempts to hedge settlements east of the Appalachians.

## SPANISH TERRITORIES

Patriots also lusted for lands controlled by the Spanish since the late sixteenth century. In the southeast, English colonists established colonies in the Carolinas to raid and check Spanish settlements in Florida. The Spanish in turn welcomed runaway slaves from the English colonies; African American refugees were quickly adopted into Creek Indian villages, themselves a product of European rivalries. Around 1700, the Spanish governor estimated that around three hundred mixed-race refugees lived around St. Augustine. Successive wars drove more Creeks into the northern panhandle of Florida. By 1767, there were nearly two thousand Creeks and African Americans in Florida; together they became known as Seminoles, a corruption of the Spanish term *cimmaron,* or runaway. Native Americans and blacks quickly formed new communal systems for land, food distribution, and work. Although slavery was practiced, the slaves were more like prisoners of war than victims of the lifetime bondage evolving in the English colonies. Even after the Spanish ceded Florida to the British under the 1753 Treaty of Paris, the territory continued to be attractive to self-emancipated blacks from the Carolinas and Georgia.

Further west, Spanish influence was larger. New Spain extended from present-day Texas to far up the Pacific Coast. Its center was New Mexico. Demographic data for New Mexico is anecdotal before 1749, and even the census of that year was incomplete. At the close of the seventeenth century, about 3,000 nominally white Spanish people lived in the province, joined by about 9,000 Pueblo Indians. Fifty years later, the Spanish population had grown only slightly to 3,808; growth beyond 8,783 people virtually stalled among Pueblo Indians. Thereafter the Spanish population increased to 9,743 in 1776 and jumped to 16,358 by 1790. The Pueblo Indian population barely maintained itself through the second half of the eighteenth century and in 1790 was at 8,840.

Early in the eighteenth century, Native American ethnicity dominated California. Conjugal couples and their children and aged relatives formed basic units of small villages, which acknowledged a chief. Joined together these local organizations formed a tribe of up to one thousand people. Hierarchies of wealth, status, and power were hereditary. Throughout society, kinship constituted the fundamental social contract; communities were composed of extended residence groups that were linked by formal ties. Household economies were based upon hunting and gathering within a sexual division of labor. These highly traditional traits existed more purely in California than in eastern regions because of the lack of European contact. That changed in 1769, when Spanish settlers arrived. Many Spanish families shared such common traits with Native Americans as sexual hierarchy, dutiful alliances through marriage, and female control over the household economy. Intermarriage between Native Americans, Africans, and Spanish created a mestizo population. Although Roman Catholic missions worked steadily to eradicate Native American cultures, epidemic diseases were the strongest forces in the transition into Spanish rule.

## THE ST. LAWRENCE VALLEY

The survival of the Iroquois Nations in the region from New France to the Midwest can be directly attributed to the weak population growth among the French. In the first two decades of the eighteenth century, after more than one hundred years of settlement, French immigration was concentrated in the cities of Montreal and Quebec City, with about fourteen thousand inhabitants in 1700. Further west, the French presence amounted to less than seventeen hundred people, of whom only 10 percent were females; many of those were celibate members of Catholic religious orders. Over the next twenty years, immigration crept up to only eighteen hundred souls, of whom women accounted for but seventy-five. The second largest group of immigrants came from prisoners. Despite these daunting numbers and the low social status of immigrants, the population grew because of high female fecundity, quick remarriage after spousal death, low general mortality, and large families of seven to eight children. With the sizable jump in immigration after 1740, the French demographic situation was very favorable at the time of the English conquest in 1763. By then the French population had reached seventy thousand along the St. Lawrence, allowing for retention of a staunch Franco-American peasantry well into the future.

## NEW ENGLAND

From a total of 91,100 in 1700, the region's population grew steadily, passing 115,000 in the next ten years, to more than 360,000 by 1750, and then leaping to just less than 700,000 in 1790. Of all the North American colonial regions, New England was the best example of English ways. At the end of the colonial period, over 80 percent of the area's population was of English descent, with the rest largely of such related origins as Welsh, Scotch-Irish, and Scottish. While there were antagonisms among these groups, English language and culture was dominant.

The frontier proved no barrier to New England's growth in the eighteenth century. Population growth in New Hampshire after 1700 came from natural reproduction and from European immigration. The typical couple in New Hampshire produced at least four children who attained adulthood; few of these children left the colony for the West in the early decades of the century. This natural growth was interrupted in the mid-1730s by a "throat distemper," which combined diphtheria and scarlet fever. It killed over fifteen hundred inhabitants, many under sixteen years of age. Wars also hampered internal growth, but by 1750 the population of twenty-five thousand souls was large enough to absorb these losses. Any shortfall was also made up by immigration. English farmers, deserting sailors and soldiers, and arrivals from the British West Indies, who brought several hundred enslaved Africans with them, bolstered the colony's population.

Other Englishmen came from southern New England in search of land. Major growth came from Ulster, from which enough Scottish Presbyterians arrived in New Hampshire to make up 10 percent of the colony's population by 1750.

The population of Massachusetts was overwhelmingly derived from England. The colony did not have its first census until 1764 and 1765, when its population stood at 245,698, making it one of the three largest English colonies in North America. It had been populous long before that; at the beginning of the eighteenth century, Boston was the dominant town in North America. The colony was 97.2 percent white, with the vast majority of English ancestry. Youth was a significant factor in eighteenth-century New England. In a number of urban counties, nearly half the population was under sixteen years of age. Connecticut also did not enumerate its citizens until late in the colonial period. In the first reasonable census of 1756, the colony's population stood at 130,612; it rose to 197,000 in 1774. As in Massachusetts and New Hampshire, whites made up over 96 percent of the population. Rhode Island displayed a bit more diversity, but primarily in the cities of Providence and Newport.

That was the case throughout New England. The continued involvement of New England merchants in the slave trade produced pockets of enslaved Africans in coastal towns. Though often sparsely distributed, there were more than four thousand blacks in Massachusetts in 1750 and three thousand in Connecticut. By 1770 that figure had jumped to more than fifty-seven hundred. Even

New Hampshire was home to 550 African Americans. As many as 18.3 percent of Newport, Rhode Island was black in 1755. William Pierson has described how "Black Yankees" were often fully assimilated. Black New Englanders were spread broadly across the region; nearly every town in the region was home to a few African Americans. Even so, black Yankees were able to re-create African folk customs, such as the mock election of a governor, and sustained an African religious base throughout the colonial period. In addition, Africans intermarried with local Native Americans in rural New England.

Over the course of the seventeenth century, the living standards of whites and blacks in New England diverged sharply. African Americans in New England had significantly higher mortality rates than white servants by every measure. Boston's black infant mortality in the mid-eighteenth century was actually higher than experienced by their counterparts in Virginia. A smallpox epidemic in 1752 hastened the death of black adults in Boston. The living also showed disparities in health. White servants in Boston and in Philadelphia were generally taller and better fed than African Americans.

## THE MID ATLANTIC

This region was the most ethnically diverse of the Atlantic colonies. Even at the end of the colonial period, after a strong wave of English migration just before the American Revolution, the proportion of the populace with English roots was only about 50 percent in New York and New Jersey and only 25 percent in Pennsylvania. In 1700, English military rule insured its political hegemony but could not stamp out ethnic traditions; English political and military power controlled New York, New Jersey, and Pennsylvania at the beginning of the eighteenth century and maintained suzerainty until the American Revolution. Nonetheless, in New York and New Jersey, English power uneasily held sway over a mixture of nations. The Dutch, who, one commentator claimed, would readily extinguish the English, incorporated French Huguenots into their churches and political organizations. Differences between city and countryside were sharp. In New York City, according to Randall Balmer, the Dutch elite gradually accepted English power by using the language of hegemony in church services. Joyce Goodfriend has cogently argued that among poorer urban Dutch, women retained their ancestral language at home and worship. Occupations continued to show ethnic retentions. The Dutch dominated the carting trade in New York City until after the American Revolution, even as they accepted English foremen. The urban Dutch presence was bolstered by internal migration from rural areas.

As persistent as Dutch culture was, arrivals from home slowed dramatically in the eighteenth century. More characteristic immigrants came from parts of the British Isles and the West Indies. From across the social strata came Londoners (the largest contributor to New York's population from abroad), Scotch-Irish, and Irish, adding complexity to the phrase English New Yorker. Merchants and artisans came from London while farmers and their families came from rural England and provincial cities. As the conditions for white laborers worsened in the slave societies of the West Indies, Englishmen migrated up to New York in search of fortunes.

Scots differentiated themselves from the English by religion. Their Presbyterian faith was a strong dissent from the hegemonic Church of England. The controversy over King's College in the 1750s is illustrative. Anglican clerics, longing for a college that could train local priests and eventually establish a bishopric, proposed a new institution for those purposes. *The Independent Reflector,* edited by the Presbyterian Scotsman William Livingston, angrily attacked the plan and referred to the Anglican clergymen's "ghastly juggling, their Pride, and their insatiate Lust for Power." Anglicans were forced to open the tiny college without public support.

After 1730 the number of Irish soared in New York City. At first they remained undifferentiated from other members of the British Isles. Coming as indentured servants, as paying passengers, as soldiers in the British army, and as convicts, most Irishmen soon gained access to New York's occupations. Generally, they affiliated with Scot Presbyterians. During the eighteenth century, Catholicism was generally banned from most Atlantic colonies (except for Pennsylvania and parts of Maryland), but Catholic Irish came to New York as soldiers and sailors. Catholic priests occasionally traveled to private homes to conduct clandestine services. Discrimination against

Catholicism in New York was so great that one unlucky priest was caught up in the repression of the 1741 Slave Conspiracy and condemned to death on flimsy evidence. In contrast to Catholicism, Jewish New Yorkers assimilated with the dominant culture. There were approximately 225 Jews in New York around 1730. Although local Jews opened a synagogue that year, other Jews, primarily Sephardic merchants, intermarried with Anglicans and joined the Church of England.

Recognized in importance only recently, the African presence in New York was critical to labor and social needs. Originally creolized captives taken from Spanish vessels, and later from the Angolan Coast, Africans in eighteenth century New York came increasingly from the West Indies and by direct importation from the West Coast of Africa. Between 1703 and 1775, the black population of New York City soared from 630 to over three thousand. Africans constituted about 15 percent of the city's population during the eighteenth century. Ethnic relations took on a variety of forms. For a privileged few, access to Anglican schools offered literacy and at least an illusion of potential freedom. Among Africans living among poorer Englishmen, the Dutch, and the Huguenots, who decided that their chattel had no souls, little acculturation was possible. Daily necessities demanded comprehension of European languages and some European mores, but African cultural survivals may be found in secularized rituals, among self-proclaimed religious leaders, and in the character of revolt reflected in the conspiracies of 1712 and

1741. In the planning of these two suppressed rebellions, conspirators swore oaths inside chalk circles, sucked blood from each other's self-inflicted wounds, and stated their allegiance to African nationality. A lively debate has recently arisen as to whether the conspirators used African military methods, as John K. Thornton has insisted, or drew from pan-Atlantic Christian forms of allegiance, as recently claimed by Marcus Rediker and Peter Linebaugh. In both cases authorities used brutal methods of torture and execution to quell the conspiracies. Ira Berlin has claimed that the effect of these revolts was to convince white slave traders to purchase human chattel directly from Africa rather than accept Creoles from the West Indies, who held dangerous views of freedom.

In rural New York and East Jersey, slavery was even more critical for the labor-starved farmers, millers, and coastal sea captains. Kings County in New York was more than one-third black in 1738, and about 20 percent of the inhabitants of Bergen County in East Jersey were enslaved Africans. Derived from the slave trade out of New York City, Philadelphia, and, to a small extent, Perth Amboy, New Jersey, Africans in East Jersey were an amalgam of Angolan, West African, and Creole. While high mortality was not a critical issue, the biggest problems for African reproduction in rural New York and Jersey were the gender imbalance of males over females and the small-farm character of slavery, which inhibited any family solidarity. As noted below, English religious hegemony failed outside of New York, and such ethnic groups as the French Hu-

guenots, Dutch, and Lutherans made little attempt to acculturate Africans. The limited acculturation of enslaved Africans was mirrored among other groups and occupations. For mariners on the Hudson River, the Dutch language was the lingua franca among Dutch, English, African, and other sailors. Dutch, German, and French remained the tongues of worshipers in pietist rural congregations. Dutch farmers remote from New York City kept their cultures long into the nineteenth century. Earlier settlements of non-English Europeans were reinforced by migrations from the Palatine in the 1710s. German Lutherans, beckoned by colonial officials seeking settlement of northern New York, initially had a disastrous reception. Many quickly removed to Pennsylvania while the remnants maintained a precarious existence west of Albany, New York. The push into the frontier continued late in the colonial period with the arrival of several thousand immigrants from Britain through the port of New York en route to the northern counties above Albany.

Rural New Jersey proved a fertile ground for maintaining ethnicity. Considered the most diverse colony along the Atlantic coast, New Jersey lacked a dominant ethnic group. Religion was the dividing issue. Anglicans, whose theological authority lessened with each mile away from New York, vied for influence and power with Dutch Reformed in the north, Scotch-Irish Presbyterians in the north-central counties, and Quakers in the middle and southern regions. Monmouth, the largest county, was home to all, although sharp divisions by religion showed in the formation of agricultural townships. Generally, enslaved Africans served as farm laborers and domestics throughout Jersey. Arrivals from the West Coast of Africa and seasoned slaves from the West Indies gradually supplanted earlier forced immigrants from Angola and Congo.

In Pennsylvania, the Society of Friends, a dissident sect with significant ties to the English Crown settled Philadelphia and its immediate hinterland. In order to develop what became known as the "poor man's best country," the Quakers invited other denominations to settle outside of Philadelphia. From the beginning of settlement in the 1680s and into the eighteenth century, there was segregation of national groups. English Quakers controlled the city of Philadelphia and the eastern rural regions.

German Dunkards, Schwenkfelders, and Moravians occupied the north. The German immigration in the second quarter of the eighteenth century was one of the largest mass arrivals of the era. Between 1710 and 1775, more than eighty thousand Germans arrived in America through the port of Philadelphia; the vast majority came before 1756. Many came as redemptioners or as indentured servants. Sharon Salinger has pointed out that the presence of Germans in these key immigrant groups transformed these methods of immigration from paternalist to capitalist ventures. The eighty thousand arrivals accounted for over 72 percent of all Germans coming to America in the colonial period. Germans, Jon Butler has argued, retained much of their cultural solidarity because of their rural isolation, density of population,

and reaction to English prejudice. For example, German women married outside of their culture only occasionally. German insularity, language differences, and communal economics placed them apart from Anglo-Americans. Germans became the first European immigrant group viewed with suspicion and prejudice. Such differences had political consequences. The dominant Society of Friends in Philadelphia refused to allot colonial tax revenues for a militia, which angered Germans living in close proximity to Native Americans who were anxious about white imposition upon their homelands. By the 1760s, acrimony between Friends and Germans became so sharp that rural dwellers nearly marched into Philadelphia to enforce their demands. In following years, Friends largely withdrew from politics.

The Scotch-Irish, who were largely Presbyterian, lived in the west with some overlap in the east. All of these immigrants were European Protestants who shared common agricultural methods and dietary preferences and had common beliefs in bourgeois liberal individualism (which quickly overcame earlier communalism). Despite national differences, these sects shared perfectionist beliefs. Exclusive and self-righteous, and occasionally otherworldly, Pennsylvania's theological communities attained a fairly equal economic status. Tensions arose over the rising power of non-English groups over the course of the eighteenth century. Distinct minorities early in the century, Germans and Scotch-Irish accounted for well over half by 1790. Much of this population was on the frontier, where frequent conflicts with Iroquois nations resulted in demands for stronger defenses, expenditures the pacifist Quakers would not fund. Even so, David Fischer has argued, the Society of Friends was able to construct a polity within which various ethnic groups coexisted. In Delaware, Irish Protestants arrived in a small but steady flow of a few hundred immigrants annually.

## THE UPPER SOUTH

Though often regarded as strongly Anglicized, Maryland, Virginia, and North Carolina were actually quite pluralistic. Sixty percent of Virginia's stock was English, but North Carolina and Maryland were only about 50 percent English. Scotch-Irish settlers accounted for almost sixteen percent of North Carolinians. North Carolina was the goal of several hundred German Lutherans around 1728.

The counterpart to English mores in the Upper South was its African presence. As the tobacco colonies moved from indentured to chattel bondage in the late seventeenth century, farmers large and small became steady customers of the Atlantic slave trade. After a slow start at the beginning of the eighteenth century, the arrival of Africans soared. Between 1720 and 1750, the numbers of enslaved African people in Maryland jumped from 12,500 to more than 43,000. In Virginia, the increase was even more dramatic. From about 26,000 slaves in 1730, the Old Dominion became home to more than 100,000 black people just twenty years later. By 1790, Virginia slave masters owned more than

287,000 enslaved Africans. North Carolina slave owners, who also started slowly, accelerated their purchases so that a populace of 1,000 enslaved people became 100,000 by 1790. These colonies merited the definition of slave societies in which servitude was the principal mode of labor relations. Not all of the ethnic contact in Virginia was conflicted. Mechal Sobel has demonstrated how Africans and European Americans derived culture from each other. Sobel has shown how premodern whites and blacks shared similar perceptions of time, key events, space and the natural world, and death and the afterlife. They also created new people. As recent collections by Martha Hodes and Catherine Clinton have demonstrated, rural areas were the locales for interracial sex among Native Americans and European Americans. Whatever cultural interaction did occur, the general experience of African Americans was servitude. Edmund Morgan's exploration of Virginia's tilt toward human bondage for blacks and freehold promises for whites continues to shape the discussion of race relations. Alan Kulikoff has shown how white migrants to the frontier tried to take enslaved peoples with them. Kathleen Brown has demonstrated how over the course of the eighteenth century, the experiences of white and black women differed. White females, as the plantation economy boomed, became less tied to farm work, owned more consumer items, and became generally wealthier. In contrast, as the slave trade brought increased numbers of Africans to Virginia, the childbearing potential of black women became devalued. As a result, black females were more likely to be field hands in 1790 than at the beginning of the century. The experiences of Virginia were magnified in the lower colonies.

## THE LOWER SOUTH

South Carolina and Georgia were more pluralistic than were the tobacco colonies to the north. Less than 50 percent of South Carolina's population hailed from England; nearly 20 percent were Scotch-Irish and 10 percent were from Scotland. French Huguenots accounted for a sizable number of new arrivals. Whatever ethnic controversies existed between low- and up-county residents in South Carolina, the racial imbalance of the colony congealed ethnicity into whiteness. South Carolina landowners adopted rice as a staple crop late in the seventeenth century and chose West Africans as their principal laborers. In this slave society, the number of Africans rose from about 3,000 in 1700 to 39,000 in 1750 and 107,000 in 1790. It then doubled again by the close of the century. Georgia initially resisted slavery. Only six hundred enslaved Africans lived there in 1750. The colony soon overcame its hesitancy. Masters purchased more than 15,000 enslaved Africans by 1770, a figure dwarfed by the black population of 105,000 at the start of the nineteenth century.

## LOUISIANA

Sparsely settled at the time of its first census in 1726, French Louisiana was home to 1663 whites, 1,385 Africans and Indians, and 570 soldiers in a total population of 3,618. It comprised tiny settlements along the Mississippi River below Red River, a handful of interior clusters in Arkansas and near Natchez, and Gulf Coast settlements. New Orleans was the largest community, with 630 people. Generally, males outnumbered females; in some instances, such as the African population below German Village on the West Bank of the Mississippi, where 210 males lived with four females, family life was impossible. African slaves were far more consolidated than French, German, or Spanish. Over three-quarters of enslaved Africans lived along the lower Mississippi River. Slaves were often channeled into skilled occupations, which caused resentment among some European workers. The answer was for white artisans to purchase skilled slaves, a process that further implanted servitude in this frontier society.

Growth was slow in Louisiana over the course of the century. Shortly after the American Revolution, the total population of the territory had grown only to 30,471. Of these 13,076 were white, 16,248 were black (Louisiana was rapidly becoming a slave society), and 1,147 were Creole or free people of color. The impact of direct importation of enslaved peoples directly from Africa amplified the racial identification of people of color. Although free people of color were becoming the norm in the northern states and had sizable numbers in the Upper South, their presence in Louisiana owed less to abolitionism than to their unique status as people of mixed blood. Creoles in Louisiana, survivors of the intermingling of peoples common in the early seventeenth-century colonies, were virtually stamped out by hardening racial lines along the Atlantic Coast. Soon after this, the introduction of the cotton culture into the region and the arrival of ambitious German farmers would herald the further decline of the Creoles and the triumph of a slave society.

## ETHNICITY AND THE AMERICAN REVOLUTION

The American Revolution was as much a war to determine who should rule at home as it was a war to see who would rule. That dictum, used by Carl Becker early in the twentieth century to describe the class nature of the War for Independence, might also be used to enable us to comprehend the importance of ethnicity at the start of American nationhood. The war was a civil war in many regions, disrupting political economies and folding local animosities into an imperial conflict. So it was that recently arrived Englishmen in upper New York and North Carolina remained loyal to the Crown. So too did the Dutch in New Jersey side with the English against their Patriot enemies. Lord Dunmore, the English governor of Virginia, and several generals made appeals to slaves and indentured servants and offered freedom in exchange for military service. This time-honored method of undercutting a foe by riling up its servants proved highly successful in the revolution as tens of thousands of slaves left their masters in search of freedom behind the British lines. The English specialized so heavily in ethnic appeals that Bishop Henry Muhlenberg condemned the Crown practice of raising regiments of German, Irish, Indians, and blacks to repress the rebellion. The American Revolution churned the black population as enslaved and free people joined marauding armies, sending Afro-Virginians up to New York and New Yorkers to the South Carolina front. Florida remained highly attractive to African American refugees from slavery.

Eventually, more than ten thousand African Americans left with the British from the ports of New York and Savannah. As important as were these hegiras to freedom, the major impact of the American Revolution was the close of the slave trade. Cutting off the supply of new Africans to America and bringing together a congregation of Black Loyalists within the British army should have created a separate African American society. Of such persuasion is the claim of Jon Butler, who contends that African Americans had to accept European theologies because of the holocaust of African beliefs. Yet it is striking that after just a few frustrating years in Nova Scotia, Black Loyalists successfully petitioned for assistance to move their society to Sierra Leone and founded a new nation there. Within a few years, these Black Loyalists formed a leadership cadre yet also resuscitated African cultural traits. For the white population, as much as things changed, they remained the same. The first federal census of the United States, taken in 1790, provided information about ethnicity among white Americans. Overall, 60 percent of

Americans were of English descent, ranging from a high of 82.5 percent in Massachusetts to 35 percent in Pennsylvania and 47 percent in New Jersey. The Mid Atlantic proved to be the most pluralistic region. New York and New Jersey (with 17.5 and 16.6 percent) were the only states with sizable Dutch populations. Pennsylvania was one-third German; only Kentucky, Tennessee, and Maryland also had more than 10 percent (14 and 11.7 percent). Scots lived primarily in the upper and lower southern regions. Eighteen percent of Georgia's residents were Irish. What these figures indicate is that, although the ethnic breakdown of the Atlantic coast states remained much as before the American Revolution, the newer western regions experienced greater diversity. Further west, American claims on Northwest and Spanish territories would include regions in which English residents were a distinct minority. In Louisiana, for example, 65 percent of white residents were French-speaking and only 11.2 percent were English. Nearly as many residents of Louisiana were German. The egalitarian promises of the Declaration of Independence did not apply equally. The egalitarian promises of the Declaration of Independence did not apply equally across ethnic and racial lines. Native American populations continued their tumble into near oblivion anywhere whites encroached upon their territories. Scholars generally agree that the American Revolution was a major setback for Native Americans. The claims of the new nation to lands west of the Appalachian Mountains into the Ohio Valley meant constant white migration

and seizure of Indian homelands. In the South, white farmers moved into Cherokee and Choctaw homelands in Georgia. In upstate New York, Native Americans were quickly pushed far to the north and west. Within twenty years, virtually no Indian nation held land east of the Appalachians. The Euro-American drive across the continent seemed inexorable.

Easily the biggest change in American society was the renewed importance of African Americans. In New England, blacks remained a tiny percentage of the population; nearly all were free by 1790. In the Mid Atlantic, where the institution of slavery survived into the nineteenth century, free blacks formed a new force. In the South and Southwest, after a brief period of self-examination and religious soul-searching over slavery, English, Scots, Germans, and French quickly transformed their states into slave societies. Louisiana had the most striking change, but South Carolina, Georgia, and the newer territories of Kentucky and Tennessee all tightened their embrace with slavery.

The post-Revolutionary movement of white yeoman farmers, going west in search of new lands, created a sense of "whiteness" among settlers. Whether Anglo-Americans from New England, Dutch from the Mid Atlantic, or Scotch-Irish from the Carolinas, postwar settlers—many of them veterans paid by the federal government with promises of western lands—wanted a society free of slavery and of African Americans. Although the northern states passed gradual emancipation laws in the first two decades of the nation's history, African

Americans remained significant portions of these societies well into the nineteenth century. In the Old Northwest (the Ohio Valley), that was not the case. New settlements tended to be entirely white. The Continental Congress had passed a bill in 1707 that promised to end the slave trade twenty years later. The effect differed by region. In the North, state laws gradually eroded the legality of any slave sales. As immigration from Europe resumed, the percentage of African Americans in the populations sharply declined. At the same time, white prejudice toward African Americans increased. Encouraged by the philosophical musings of Thomas Jefferson on race, white Americans viewed blacks as different and biologically inferior. State after state passed legislation insuring that even free blacks would have little or no say politically and that permitted economic isolation and discrimination. In the next century, the chief Euro-American reaction to the growing numbers of free blacks in the north and to the national debate over slavery was to encourage, however fantastic, the mass migration of blacks to Africa, a choice very few African Americans were willing to make. As the stock of Euro-Americans gradually congealed into a white race, African Americans and Native Americans came to be regarded as separate and unequal.

## BIBLIOGRAPHIC ESSAY

The demographic history of the colonial period can be found in John J. McCusker and Russell R. Menard, *The Economy of British America, 1607–1789* (Chapel Hill: University of North Carolina Press for the Institute of Early American History and Culture, 1985) and Michael R. Haines and Richard H. Steckel, eds., *A Population History of North America* (New York: Cambridge University Press, 2000), 99–143. See also Thomas L. Purvis, "The European Ancestry of the United States Population, 1790," *William and Mary Quarterly,* 3rd ser. 41 (1984) and Robert Wells, *The Population of the British Colonies in America Before 1776* (Princeton: Princeton University Press, 1975), 85, 95–103; *Historical Statistics of the United States, Colonial Times to 1970* (Washington, DC: U.S. Government Printing Office for the Department of Commerce, 1976), 2 vols.

A general study on the colonial period that emphasizes English influence is David Hackett Fischer, *Albion's Seed: Four British Folkways in America* (New York: Oxford University Press, 1989). Three books by Jon C. Butler, which combined Anglicization and cultural diversity, are *The Huguenots in America: A Refugee People in New World Society* (Cambridge: Harvard University Press, 1983); *Awash in a Sea of Faith: Christianizing the American People* (Cambridge: Harvard University Press, 1994); and *Becoming America: The Revolution Before 1776* (Cambridge: Harvard University Press, 2000).

The most emphatic study of the continued impact of ethnicity on a colonial society is Joyce Goodfriend, *Before the Melting Pot: Society and Culture in Colonial New York City, 1664–1730* (Princeton: Princeton University Press, 1992). Books that argue for continued African influences are Michael Gomez, *Exchanging Our Country Marks: The Transformation of African Identities in the Colonial and Antebellum South* (Chapel Hill: University of North Carolina Press, 1998) and

Margaret Washington Creel, *A Peculiar People: Slave Community Culture among the Gullahs* (New York: New York University Press, 1988).

For studies of the demography of Native Americans, see Henry F. Dobyns, *Their Number Become Thinned: North American Population Dynamics in Eastern North America* (Knoxville: University of Tennessee Press, 1983). Influential studies of Native American regrouping include James H. Merrill, *The Indians' New World: Catawbas and Their Neighbors from European Contact Through the Era of Removal* (Chapel Hill: University of North Carolina Press for the Institute of Early American History and Culture, 1989) and Daniel K. Richter, "Native American History: Perspectives on the Eighteenth Century," in Michael V. Kennedy and William G. Shade, eds., *The World Turned Upside Down: The State of Eighteenth-Century Studies at the Beginning of the Twenty-first Century*, 268–89 (Bethlehem, Penn.: Lehigh University Press, 2001). The most important study about the intersections of Native Americans, French, English and Americans is Richard White, *The Middle Ground: Indians, Empires, and Republics in the Great Lakes Region, 1650–1815* (Cambridge: Cambridge University Press, 1991). See also Daniel H. Usner, Jr., *Indians, Settlers, and Slaves in a Frontier Exchange Economy: The Lower Mississippi Valley Settlers, and Slaves in a Frontier Exchange Economy: The Lower Mississippi Valley Before 1783* (Chapel Hill: University of North Carolina Press for the Institute of Early American History and Culture, 1992), Gregory Evans Dowd, *A Spirited Resistance: The North American Indian Struggle for Unity, 1745–1815* (Baltimore: Johns Hopkins University Press, 1992); Martha Hodes, ed., *Sex, Love, Race: Crossing Boundaries in North American History* (New York: New York University Press, 1999); and Catherine Clinton and Michele Gillespie, eds., *The Devil's Lane: Sex and Race in the Early South* (New York: Oxford University Press, 1997). For a study that emphasizes ideological influence, see James Axtell, *The Invasion Within: The Contest of Cultures in Colonial North America* (New York: Oxford University Press, 1985). The fullest studies of changes in southwestern Indian cultures are Ramon Guttierez, *When Jesus Came, the Corn Mothers Went Away: Marriage, Sexuality, and Power in New Mexico, 1500–1846* (Stanford: Stanford University Press, 1991) and Albert Hurtado, *Indian Survival on the California Frontier* (New Haven: Yale University Press, 1988). For studies of Native Americans and African Americans together, see Kenneth W. Porter, *The Black Seminoles: History of a Freedom-Seeking People*, Revised Edition (Lexington: University of Kentucky Press, 1996); Kevin Mulroy, *Freedom on the Borders: The Seminole Maroons in Florida, the Indian Territory, Coahuila, and Texas* (College Station: Texas Tech University Press, 1993); Jane Landers, *Black Society in Spanish Florida* (Urbana: University of Illinois Press, 1999).

On black Americans in New England, see William D. Piersen, *Black Yankees: The Development of an Afro-American Subculture in Eighteenth-Century New England* (Amherst: University of Massachusetts Press, 1988) and Ira Berlin, *Many Thousands Gone: The First Two Centuries of Slavery in North America* (Cambridge: Harvard University Press, 1998), 366.

For a good study of the Mid Atlantic, with emphasis on the intersection of politics and diversity, see Gary B. Nash, *The Urban Crucible: Social Change, Political Consciousness, and the Origins of the American Revolution* (Cambridge: Harvard University Press, 1979). Carl L. Becker, *The History of Political*

Practice in the Province of New York, 1760–1776 (Madison: University of Wisconsin Press, 1909). For studies of ethnicity in the Mid Atlantic, see Joyce D. Goodfriend, Before the Melting Pot (Princeton: Princeton University Press, 1992) and Goodfriend, "The Irish in Colonial New York City," in Ronald H. Bayor and Timothy J. Meagher, eds., The New York Irish, 35–48 (Baltimore: Johns Hopkins University Press, 1996).

On blacks in the Mid Atlantic, see Graham Russell Hodges, Root & Branch: African Americans in New York and East Jersey, 1613–1863 (Chapel Hill: University of North Carolina Press, 1999.) and Hodges, Slavery and Freedom in the Rural North: African Americans in Monmouth County, New Jersey, 1660–1865 (Madison, Wisc.: Madison House Publishers, 1997). For a discussion of the role of blacks in the military see John K. Thornton, Warfare in Atlantic Africa, 1500–1800 (London: UCL Press, 2000). On the Pan-Atlantic influences see Peter Linebaugh and Marcus Rediker, The Many Headed Hydra: Sailor, Slave, Commoners and the Hidden History of the Revolutionary Atlantic (Boston: Beacon Press, 2000). On the Dutch, see Randall Balmer, A Perfect Babel of Confusion: Dutch Religion and English Culture in the Middle Colonies (New York: Oxford University Press, 1989) and David Steven Cohen, The Dutch-American Farm (New York: New York University Press, 1992). On Germans, see A. G. Roeber, Palatines, Liberty, and Property: German Lutherans in Colonial British America (Baltimore: Johns Hopkins University Press, 1993) and Marianne S. Wokeck, Trade in Strangers: The Beginnings of Mass Migration to North America (University Park: The Pennsylvania State University Press, 1999). On later English migration, see Bernard Bailyn, Voyagers to the West: A Passage in the Peopling of America on the Eve of the Revolution (New York: Knopf, 1986), 573–80. On ethnicity generally in New Jersey, see Peter Wacker, Land & People: A Cultural Geography of Preindustrial New Jersey: Origins and Settlement Patterns (New Brunswick: Rutgers University Press, 1975). On the Scotch-Irish, see Ned C. Landsman, Scotland and Its First American Colony, 1683–1765 (Princeton: Princeton University Press, 1985). For the story of changing ethnicity in labor relations see Sharon V. Salinger, "To Serve Well and Faithfully": Labor and Indentured Servants in Pennsylvania, 1682–1800 (New York: Cambridge University Press, 1987).

For the complicated story of African and Euro-Americans in the tobacco colonies, see Mechal Sobel, The World They Made Together: Black and White Values in Eighteenth-Century Virginia (Princeton: Princeton University Press, 1987); Woody Holton, Forced Founders: Indians, Debtors, Slaves, and the Making of the American Revolution in Virginia (Chapel Hill: University of North Carolina Press for the Institute of Early American History and Culture, 1999); Edmund S. Morgan, American Slavery, American Freedom: The Ordeal of Colonial Virginia (New York: Norton, 1975); Allan Kulikoff, Tobacco and Slaves: The Development of Southern Cultures in the Chesapeake, 1680–1800 (Chapel Hill: University of North Carolina Press, 1986), and Kathleen M. Brown, Good Wives, Nasty Wenches, and Anxious Patriarchs: Gender, Race, and Power in Colonial Virginia (Chapel Hill: University of North Carolina Press for the Institute of Early American History and Culture, 1996). On the Southeast, see Gwendolyn Midlo Hall, Africans in Colonial Louisiana: The Development of Afro-Creole Culture in the Eighteenth Century (Baton Rouge: Louisiana State University Press, 1992).

# DOCUMENTS

## Indian Women of Cabo San Lucas, c. 1746

*This document tells much about the dress and child-rearing culture among Native American women in northern California and offers an interesting comparison between Christian and non-Christian peoples. Note the changes that occur in dress after conversion.*

Source: Rose Marie Beebe and Robert M. Sen-kewicz, eds., *Lands of Promise and Despair: Chronicles of Early California, 1535–1846* (Santa Clara, Cal.: Heyday Books, 2001), pp. 106–107.

These Indian women of Cabo San Lucas wear their hair long, loose, and hanging on the back. They make some very graceful necklaces from figures cut out of mother-of-pearl and mixed with berries, little reeds, snail shells, and pearls. The front of these neck adornments hangs down to the waist. They also make bracelets similarly and of the same material. Even these barbarians living in that remote corner of the world are inspired to create these inventions, in order to fulfill their wish to present a good appearance. The color of the people of all this Pericú nation is generally less dark and even notably fairer than that of the rest of the Californians.

The dress of the Cochimi women of the north is different and poorer, as it begins at the waist and ends at the knees in some territories, a little lower in others. In front they wear a sort of skirt formed by the small joints of very small reeds which they cut close to the nodes, both above and below. They throw away the reeds themselves, as they are no good for their purpose, and keep only the joints. They bore a hole through these and they string them up in strings or thin cords which they get out of the agave plants, the same way one would string up a rosary. These closely packed strings are then tied by one end to other little cords which are tied to the waist and are hanging loose on the opposite end. They reach down at least to the knees, although in some territories they wear them longer, almost halfway down the leg. In this manner, all together, they constitute a little curtain which protects their modesty, even if not their bodies against inclement weather. They cover the opposite part with a deerskin, or with that of some other animal which the husbands might have killed. From Mission San Borja, at 30 degrees of latitude, northward, the Indians have the custom of covering their bodies with small cloaks made of the pelt of sea otter or hare, rabbits, or some other animals. . . .

The manner in which women of Christian California (and even farther north) carry their children is the following. They put the child in a small net which does not close up as a purse, but remains open on the upper part. They line the bottom of the net with dry plants, particularly using the soft pelts of rabbits, hares, or other animals. This keeps the net open at the top and at the same time it cushions the child from the discomfort of strings and knots. After they became Christians and had some clothes, they added to some of these a piece of cloth to better protect the child.

On both sides of these nets there are long cords from which they form a long handle. They hang the net with the child from anywhere using this handle. When they are moving from one place to another, they carry their children on their backs, the strings of the net being held in a bundle from the mother's forehead. When the child is a little older, they do not usually carry it in the net, but in their arms. And when they are about two or three years old, they have them sit on their mother's shoulders, as if riding horseback, and so that their feet come to the front, resting on the breast of the mother, who will then take one foot of her child in one hand and the other foot with the other hand so that he does not fall down. At the same time, the little boy secures his position by grabbing tightly with his little hands the uncombed and dirty hair of his mother. When the child has learned to hold on tight while sitting this way, one woman alone can carry two children, one sitting on her shoulders and the other one, only a few months old, at her breast or inside the net on her back. Sometimes they may even carry three: two of them as I have just described, and the third one, about four years old, led by the hand as he walks beside his mother. All this does not prevent the woman from taking along with her all her belongings. . . .

## Detailed Reports on the Salzburger Emigrants Who Settled in America, 1749

*This document details the introduction of German servants into Georgia at a time when* the colony's trustees were changing its charter to allow purchase and use of African slaves. The document tells of the farming methods of German immigrants, their religious doubts, and their anger over competition from enslaved Africans.

Source: Samuel Urlsperger, ed., *Detailed Reports on the Salzburger Emigrants Who Settled in America*, vol. 13, *1749*, trans., David Roth, George Fenwick Jones, ed. George Fenwick Jones (Athens: University of Georgia Press, 1989), pp. 110–115.

*Monday, the 16th of October.* Today I heard complaints from two householders about their servants, who acted restless because they had to serve longer than some in Savannah and threatened to run away. Their behavior moved me to call them all to me this afternoon with their masters so that I might speak with them about what was necessary for our and their good. First I let them show me the recommendations they had brought from Germany, from which Mr. Meyer wrote down their baptismal and family names, their homeland, and the place of their birth. Then I told them that an unpleasant report of unrest and evil intentions of some young people had caused me to hold this meeting. I told them that already for some years we had desired servants from Germany who had learned only farming and field work and who, we thought, would fit here best. We had also hoped to receive them. However, because they (our present servants) had offered themselves to the Lord Trustees to be sent to this colony as hired hands and serving girls, then the servants we had actually desired had had to remain behind. For the Lord Trustees had expressly written that Senior Urlsperger should not deal with any others, because it was not in the Trustees' means to do more for us than to send the present servants.

Now, before they were sent here, it had been told them often enough in London in the name of the Trustees that their tradesmen, such as bakers (which most in their transport are), millers, weavers, etc. had no value in this country, rather the most usual and frequent business was agriculture, and those who did not wish it should remain behind. In spite of that, they had chosen to come here. After many of these servants had been taken away from me in Savannah and I had noticed some unrest and disinclination to serve in Ebenezer, I had resolved to take with me only those who were willing to serve and to leave the unwilling ones there, but none of them who are here wished to remain behind, rather they promised to serve loyally. Now they should consider how improperly and unChristianly they were behaving when they were restless and glum about working or even wished to run away. For then they would disgracefully and irresponsibly break the contract that they had solemnly made with the Lord Trustees and now with the Council and of which they had a copy with them. In it they had promised with their mouths and with their signatures and their seals to serve for four years as serving men and women. . . .

## OCTOBER

*Sunday, the first of October.* On this Sunday, the Nineteenth Sunday after Trinity, our merciful God has let us live a new month in rest, health, and blessing; and for this it is mete and right that we give Him humble praise. Last month He did, to be sure, send many kinds of fever and weakness among us after the many rains we had in the summer and the beginning of fall; yet in comparison with others in Carolina, it has still been quite bearable. We are now having a very dry period that is very good for the harvest. It must be the same way among the Indians up in the mountains because the Savannah River has become so low that the ebb and flood can be detected at our place and even up in Ebenezer Creek, and this has seldom happened. The flood tide usually comes up to the milldam unless the water in the main river is so high and strong that it does not allow the flood to come up. The Mill River is very convenient for us for going between here to Savannah by boat, and it is a great blessing.

None of the mills can operate now, but the water needs to rise only a little and then we will be able to use the lower course again. The mills are such a great blessing for us that no one who has a Christian spirit can think of them without praising God.

*Monday, the 2nd of October.* A friend communicated a couple of letters to me which Mr. Zouberbuhler (the Anglican preacher in Savannah) had sent from London to a friend in Savannah, and which give this reliable news: 1) that the Lord Trustees will send a transport of poor German people here to Georgia at their own humble request, with whom he himself (Mr. Zouberbuhler) will return to his former post after having achieved what he wished, a salary of fifty pounds Sterling annually. 2) that the Lord Trustees have received from Parliament for this colony not the £15,000 Sterling (as it was spread around here) but only £5304. This sum will hardly suffice to pay the many debts in this country, therefore we can hardly presume that they will send our inhabitants such loyal and industrious servants as we have requested. Furthermore, the secretary of the Lord Trustees has now written the same thing to the President and Council. When hearing such reports, my heart always says, "May He do with us and this land as it well pleases Him!"

*Tuesday, the 10th of October.* At the beginning of last week I had necessary business with the Council in Savannah; and, because our German servants also arrived there, I had to remain there for eight full days. I will summarize the main events that have occurred during my sojourn in Savannah and most concern our congregation in the following points: 1) God has so blessed my presentations, which were supported by Mr. Habersham (a member of the Council), that the gentlemen of the Council have granted our community all the good land behind Abercorn and up to our cowpen; and this will be surveyed for those who have been provided with no land so far or only with very bad land. It is an excellent stretch of land, of which kind little is to be found. We have also had our glebe land surveyed in the same district, all told 600 acres, and an additional 300 acres for a minister who might come to a future congregation in this area.

Because Negroes or Moorish slaves are permitted now under certain conditions, good land will become scarce. Should the 300 acres for a third minister not be necessary, it can be used for the good of the young people among us when they come of age. On the other hand, the so-called Uchee land near us on the Savannah River will be reserved for some of our older inhabitants and workers, but especially for the loyal servants whom we are now getting and shall get in the future.

2) Sixty-three German people arrived fresh and sound in Savannah on the 3rd and 4th of the monthe, who were very well cared for by a good-natured captain named Peter Bogg. . . .

3) The authorities in Savannah and also other inhabitants there have, to be sure, attested enough that they would rather have Negroes than white people as servants, as the Lord Trustees well enough know. Nevertheless, they have selected twenty-one people from this transport, for some they have paid six pounds Sterling and some they have charged to the Trustees. These are mostly useful craftsmen like carpenters, wheelwrights, cabinetmakers, etc. and the most useful people. I have now brought to our place five families with children, two single little girls whose parents are serving one of the Councilmen, and fifteen single men who are mostly bakers, millers, tailors, and shoemakers. These were distributed in good order today by lot to our dear worn-out inhabitants as far as they would go, but the remainder got none.

Some servants from this transport have the promise from the gentlemen in Savannah that they will not have to serve more than one or two years; and it seems hard on those who were left for us to have to serve three years and five months. Because I was afraid of disorder and annoyance from this at our place, I had all our servants assembled and told them that I did not wish to take any to our place under compulsion. Therefore every man should tell me whether he would rather remain in Savannah and buy himself free in about three months (as the Trustees' permission reads) or go with me to Ebenezer where there were, to be sure, good foodstuffs but no work for them other than farming and cattle raising. They chose the latter and promised to follow their calling loyally. Otherwise I was resolved to follow the example of other people in Savannah and choose the best and to leave the others for the Lord Trustees and their agents in Savannah.

Two large families, who have very small children, could not be sheltered here by any householder; and therefore they fell through necessity to me and my dear colleague. We are engaging a pious Salzburger to instruct them in their work on a piece of land on the Mill River. I hope that the Lord Trustees will allow us something for their maintenance, as they are doing for the minister in Savannah with his big salary, who is receiving £24 Sterling annually to support his two servants. 5) The Lord Trustees have now allowed the introduction of Negroes, and the stipulations for that are not only fitting but pleasing. We will now see whether the colony will flourish from it.

*Wednesday, the 11th of October.* After the arrival of these servants a heavier burden has fallen on me than I have had in previous years. God, who has helped me numerous times in my whole life in miraculous ways, will mercifully help me further in everything and through everything that He lays on me so that I will be able to praise His name here and there.

*Thursday, the 12th of October.* One of our servants drawn by lots, a shoemaker by trade, was redeemed yesterday for £6 Sterling; and by this our honest and sickly Brandner was robbed of his servant, for which he had waited for several years. This anomaly can not be prevented because, according to their contract with the Lord Trustees, all these servants have three months grace to redeem themselves by anyone they wish and however they can. If this disadvantageous point were not in the contract, it would be better for us and for these servants.

## The Life, History, and Unparalleled Sufferings of John Jea, the African Preacher, c. 1800

*Telling of conditions for African Americans living among the Dutch around New York after the American Revolution, this document is remarkable for the writer's description of both his African ancestry and his desperate desire to be saved spiritually by understanding the Bible, the great text of European-American Christianity. Also included are comments on the refusal by Dutch farmers to consider the souls of their chattel.*

Source: Graham Russell Hodges, ed., *Black Itinerants of the Gospel: The Narratives of John Jea and*

*George White* (New York: Palgrave, 2002), pp. 89–92.

I, John Jea, the subject of this narrative, was born in the town of Old Callabar, in Africa, in the year 1773. My father's name was Hambleton Robert Jea, my mother's name Margaret Jea; they were of poor, but industrious parents. At two years and a half old, I and my father, mother, brothers, and sisters, were stolen, and conveyed to North America, and sold for slaves; we were then sent to New York, the man who purchased us was very cruel, and used us in a manner, almost too shocking to relate; my master and mistress's names were Oliver and Angelika Triehuen, they had seven children–three sons and four daughters; he gave us a very little food or raiment, scarcely enough to satisfy us in any measure whatever; our food was what is called Indian corn pounded, or bruised and boiled with water, the same way burgo is made, and about a quart of sour butter-milk poured on it; for one person two quarts of this mixture, and about three ounces of dark bread, per day, the bread was darker than that usually allowed to convicts, and greased over with very indifferent hog's lard; at other times when he was better pleased, he would allow us about half-a-pound of beef for a week, and about half-a-gallon of potatoes; but that was very seldom the case, and yet we esteemed ourselves better used than many of our neighbors.

Our labour was extremely hard, being obliged to work in the summer from about two o'clock in the morning, till about ten or eleven o'clock at night, and in the winter from four in the morning, till ten at night. The horses usually rested about five hours in the day, while we were at work; thus did the beasts enjoy greater privileges than we did. We dared not murmur, for if we did we were corrected with a weapon an inch and-a-half thick, and that without mercy, striking us in the most tender parts, and if we complained of this usage, they then took four large poles, placed them in the ground, tied us up to them, and flogged us in a manner too dreadful to behold; and when taken down, if we offered to lift up our hand or foot against our master or mistress, they used us in a most cruel manner; and often they treated the slaves in such a manner as caused their death, shooting them with a gun, or beating their brains out with some weapon, in order to appease their wrath, and thought no more of it than if they had been brutes: this was the general treatment which slaves experienced. After our master had been treating us in this cruel manner, we were obliged to thank him for the punishment he had been inflicting on us, quoting that Scripture which saith, "Bless the rod, and him that hath appointed it." But, though he was a professor of religion, he forgot *that* passage which saith "God is love, and whoso dwelleth in love dwelleth in God, and God in him." And, again, we are commanded to love our enemies; but it appeared evident that his wretched heart was hardened; which led us to look up unto him as our god, for we did not know him who is able to deliver and save all who call upon him in truth and sincerity. Conscience, that faithful monitor, (which either excuses or accuses) caused us to groan, cry, or sigh, in a manner which cannot be uttered.

We were often led away with the idea that our masters were our gods; and at other times we placed our ideas on the sun, moon, and stars, looking unto them, as if they could save us; at length we found, to our great disappointment, that these were nothing else but the works of the Supreme Being; this caused me to wonder how my master frequently expressed that all his houses, land, cattle, servants, and every thing which he possessed was his own; not considering that it was the Lord of Hosts, who has said that the gold and the silver, the earth, and the fullness thereof, belong to him.

Our master told us, that when we died, we should be like the beasts that perish; not informing us of God, heaven, or eternal punishments, and that God hath promised to bring the secrets of every heart into judgement, and to judge every man according to his works.

From the following instances of the judgements of God, I was taught that he is God, and there is none besides him, neither in the heavens above, nor in the earth beneath, nor in the waters under the earth; for he doth with the armies of heaven and the inhabitants of the earth as seemeth him good; and there is none that can stay his hand, nor say unto him, with a prevailing voice, *what dost thou?*

My master was often disappointed in his attempts to increase the produce of his lands; for oftentimes he would command us to carry out more seed into the field to insure a good crop, but when it sprang up and promised to yield plentifully, the Almighty caused the worms to

eat it at the root, and destroyed nearly the whole produce; God thus showing him his own inability to preserve the fruits of the earth.

At another time he ordered the trees to be pruned, that they might have brought forth more fruit, to have increased his worldly riches, but God, who doth not as man pleaseth, sent the caterpiller, the cankerworm, and the locust, when the trees bore a promising appearance, and his fond hopes were blasted, by the fruits being all destroyed. Thus was he again disappointed, but still remained ignorant of the hand of God being in these judgements.

Notwithstanding he still went on in his wickedness until another calamity befell him; for when the harvest was full ripe, the corn cut down, and standing in shocks ready to be carried into the barn, it pleased God to send a dreadful storm of thunder and lightning, hail and rain, which compelled them to leave it out, till it rotted on the ground. Often were his cattle destroyed by distempers of various kinds; yet he hearkened not unto the voice of the Lord.

At one time, when his barns and storehouses were filled with all sorts of grain, and he rejoiced in the greatness of his harvest, it pleased the Almighty to send a very dreadful storm of thunder and lightning, which consumed a great part of his property; such scenes as these occurred several times, yet he regarded not the power of the Almighty, nor the strength of his arm; for when we poor slaves were visited by the hand of God, and he took us from time to eternity, he thought no more of our poor souls than if we had had none, but lamented greatly the loss of the body; which caused me very much to wonder at his actions, I being very young, not above eight or nine years of age, and seeing the hand of the Almighty, though I did not at that time know it was his works, in burning up the pastures, in permitting the cattle to die for want of water, and in causing the fruits of the earth to be blighted. At the same time a most violent storm of thunder and lightning was experienced, which, in the space of thirty or forty miles, consumed about thirteen houses, barns, and store-houses, which terrified us poor slaves in a terrible manner, not knowing what these things meant. Even my master and mistress were very much terrified, fearful of being destroyed by the violence of the weather.

About two or three days after this awful scene, a day of fasting, prayer, and thanksgiving, was commanded by General Washington, to pray to Almighty God to withdraw his anger from us; which day was observed by all, but us poor slaves, for we were obliged to fast, but were not exempted from work; our masters thinking us not worthy to go to a place of worship; which surprised me a great deal, being very ignorant, and I asked my parents what all this meant, but they could not tell me, but supposed, from what they had heard them say, they were worshipping their god; then I began to enquire how this could be, having heard my master often say, that all he possessed was his own, and he could do as he pleased with it; which, indeed, was the saying of all those who had slaves. My curiosity being thus raised, I made bold to speak to my master's sons, and asked them the reason

they prayed and called upon God, and they told me because of the awful judgements that had happened on the land; then I asked what awful judgements they meant, and they said unto me, have you not seen how the Lord hath destroyed all things from off the face of the earth? and I answered yes; I then asked them who did this, and they told me God; then, said I, ought not God to be feared, seeing that he can build up and he can cast down, he can create and he can destroy, and though we may cultivate our lands and sow our seed, we can never secure the crop without the favour of Him who, is the sovereign disposer of all things? They answered, yes. From this I observed that there were those who feared God when the weather was tempestuous, but feared him not when it was fine.

Seeing them act in such a wicked manner, I was encouraged to go on in my sins, being subject to all manner of iniquity that could be mentioned, not knowing there was a God, for they told us that we poor slaves had no God. As I grew up, my desire to know who their God was increased, but I did not know who to apply to, not being allowed to be taught by any one whatever, which caused me to watch their actions very closely; and in so doing, I, at one time, perceived that something was going forward which I could not comprehend, at last I found out that they were burying a slave master, who was very rich; they appeared to mourn and lament for his death, as though he had been a good man, and I asked them why they let him die; they said they could not help it, for God killed him: I said unto them, what, could you not have taken him away from God? They said, no, for he killed whomever he pleased. I then said he must be a dreadful God, and was led to fear least he should kill me also; although I had never seen death, but at a distance. But this fear did not last long, for seeing others full of mirth, I became so too.

A short time after this, there were great rejoicings on account of a great victory obtained by the Americans over the poor Indians, who had been so unfortunate as to lose their possessions, and they strove against the Americans, but they over-powered and killed thousands of them, and numbers were taken prisoners, and for this cause they greatly rejoiced. They expressed their joy by the ringing of bells, firing of guns, dancing and singing, while we poor slaves were hard at work. When I was informed of the cause of these rejoicings, I thought, *these* people made a great mourning when *God* killed one man, but they rejoice when *they* kill so many. I was thus taught that though they talked much about their God, they did not regard him as they ought. They had forgotten that sermon of our blessed Saviour's on the mount, which you find in St. Matthew's gospel, v. *chap* 43, 44, v.; and I had reason to think their hearts were disobedient, not obeying the truth, though it was read and preached to them; their hearts being carnal, as the Scriptures saith, were at enmity with God, not subject to the law of God, neither indeed could be; for they gave themselves up to the works of the flesh, to fulfil it in the lusts thereof.

My dear reader, consider the great obligations you are under to the Wise Disposer of all events, that you were not born in Africa, and sold for a slave, on whom the most cruel tortures are exercised, but that you were born in Britain, a land of freedom; and above all, be thankful for the opportunities you have of knowing the "true God, and Jesus Christ whom he has sent," and recollect that as you possess much, much will be required; and, unless you improve your advantages, you had better be a slave in any dark part of the world, than a neglecter of of the gospel in this highly favoured land; recollect also that even here you might be a slave of the most awful description:—a slave to your passions—a slave to the world—a slave to sin—a slave to satan—a slave of hell—and, unless you are made free by Christ, through the means of the gospel, you will remain in captivity, tied and bound in the chains of your sin, till at last you will be bound hand and foot, and cast into outer darkness, there shall be weeping and gnashing of teeth for ever.

## Journal of Nicolas Collin, 1746–1831; Extract of the Most Noteworthy Transactions During My Incumbency as Rector at the Raccoon and Pensneck Congregations, from September 30, 1773

*The diary of this early Swedish cleric in the nation's only colony upriver from Philadelphia tells of the difficulties of sustaining the Swedish Lutheran faith, the hardships of remote life, and the Lutherans' gradual affiliation with other denominations and ethnicities.*

*Source:* Amandus Johnson, trans., *The Journal and Biography of Nicholas Collin, 1746–1831* (Philadelphia: The New Jersey Society of Pennsylvania, 1936), pp. 217–219.

These parishes extend a distance of 5 [Swedish] miles in length and two in width, on the east shore of the river Delaware, over a neighborhood full of marshes and woods. The churches are of wood, in very bad repair, two and a half [Swedish] miles away from each other. The vicarage is close to the Raccoon church in a small place intended for a town called Sveaborg (in English Swedesborough), which is laid out on the church property and pays rent for it [to the church]. As the greater part of the congregation lives closer to this church, the pastor lives quite in the center of his activities, but [he] must, however, often travel two and sometimes three [Swedish] miles below Pensneck church.

The people are scattered among other sects, and many families are quite mixed in regard to extraction, some of them also in their religion. During Swedish Divine Service seldom more than 80 or 90 persons are seen, but all those who partly speak and understand the language number about two hundred persons. Some thirty Germans also ally themselves with us, and occasionally get Divine Service. The Swedes in Raccoon, the English there and [in] Pensneck, each have their Sunday. The last mentioned [congregation] is entirely English, and at Raccoon the English congregation is much larger than the Swedish. Swedish Divine Service can therefore not be held oftener than every third Sunday and on all important holidays, especially Christ-

mas Day, New Year's Day and Good Friday. At Raccoon both Swedish and English sermons are often preached on the same day. Frequently after Divine Service has been held there or in Pensneck, I travel to some suitable place located between the churches or in some other well inhabited district in the vicinity in order to hold Divine Service. These congregations were formed at a much later date than the Christina and Wicacoa [congregations], and have suffered through several and long vacancies. The one which occurred after Pastor Tranberg was transferred was very injurious [to the congregation]. The people became indifferent and scattered; several families were drawn to the Moravian sect, and together with other English and German members built a meeting-house about half a mile from the Raccoon church, to which [sect] they have belonged ever since. The last confusion [caused] by Lidenius' faults and misfortunes was also considerable. My esteemed predecessor's zeal and neverceasing work has accomplished much [good], but it is easily understood that much is still lacking. In this country the most able pastor cannot even during his whole life bring even the smallest congregation into a perfect state. The scattered location of the people causes a pastor unbelievable toil; often he must travel four to five [Swedish] miles in one day, especially during those times when fevers, influenza, dysentery and other illnesses rage, which often cause great havoc in these districts. At times in the summer one suffers terribly from a heat which kills both people and animals, and frequently in the winter from piercing rain or a fearful cold, especially as one must travel on horse-back on the miserable roads. Since many of the members are sluggish and indifferent, or in some cases delinquent, they must often be visited in their homes with admonitions and reminders about going to church, about the baptism and training of their children, etc. Frequently it is necessary to ride in great haste day or night a long distance to baptize a dying child. In this province, which is New Jersey, certain magistrates have the [legal] right to marry people, and they are employed by many, if the pastor is not ready to serve them immediately in whatever weather or place it may be; the fees acquired on such occasions make up a large portion of his income, besides which this duty belongs to the office, and the religious sanctity [of the ceremony] is lessened not a little, when laymen take such things upon themselves.

## Life of the Reverend Devereux Jarratt, Written by Himself: Excerpts, 1806

*This document details the family experiences of a young Scottish-Irish minister to the colonies. In this case, he was literate and so was able to retell his story.*

Source: John Demos, ed., *Remarkable Providence* (New York: George Brazilier, 1972), pp. 104–105.

. . . I was born in New Kent, a county in Virginia, about 25 miles below Richmond, on January 6th, 1732–3, O. S. [Old Style]. I was the youngest child of Robert Jarratt and Sarah his wife. My grandfather was an Englishman, born, I believe, in the city of London, in Devereux County, in Essex Street, which is so called from Robert Devereux, Earl of Essex. From this circumstance, perhaps, or from his being a soldier in the army of the Earl of Essex, he named his first son Robert, and his second son Devereux. He had only these two sons and one daughter, who was married to Walter Clopton of new Kent. But from whencesoever the name Devereux was derived, it is certain, as far as I have known or heard, [that] my uncle was the first who had that name in Virginia, or even in America, and it was confined to our family for 50 or 60 years. But after I became a minister of this parish (Bath) a number of people, out of respect to me, called one of their sons after my name.

My grandmother, as I was told, was a native of Ireland. Both she and my grandfather died before I was born, and I have had no account of them, except that they were poor people, but industrious, and rather rough in their manners. They acquired a pretty good tract of land, of near 1200 acres, but they had no slaves—probably they were prejudiced against that kind of property. The family of the Jarratts have been remarkably short-lived, and very few of the name are to be found now living.

My father was brought up to the trade of a carpenter, at which he wrought till the very day before he died. He was a mild, inoffensive man, and much respected among his neighbors. My mother was the daughter of Joseph Bradley, of Charles City, a county bordering on New Kent. None of my ancestors, on either side, were either rich or great, but had the character of honesty and industry, by which they lived in credit among their neighbors, free from real want, and above the frowns of the world. This was also the habit in which my parents were. They always had plenty of plain food and raiment, wholesome and good, suitable to their humble station, and the times in which they lived. Our food was altogether the produce of the farm or plantation, except a little sugar, which was rarely used and our raiment was altogether my mother's manufacture, except our hats and shoes, the latter of which we never put on but in the winter season. We made no use of tea or coffee for breakfast or at any other time, nor did I know a single family that made any use of them. Meat, bread, and milk was the ordinary food of all my acquaintance. I suppose the richer sort might make use of those and other luxuries, but to such people I had no access. We were accustomed to look upon what were called *gentle folks* as being of a superior order. For my part, I was quite shy of them, and kept off at a humble distance. A periwig, in those days, was a distinguishing badge of gentle folk–and when I saw a man riding the road, near our house, with a wig on, it would so alarm my fears, and give me such a disagreeable feeling, that, I dare say, I would run off, as for my life. Such ideas of the difference between *gentle* and *simple* were, I believe, universal among all of my rank and age. . . .

My parents neither sought nor expected any titles, honors, or great things, either for themselves or [their] children. Their highest ambition was to teach their children to read, write, and understand the fundamental rules of arithmetic. I remember also they taught us short prayers, and made us very perfect in repeating the church catechism. They wished us all to be brought up in some honest calling, that we might earn our bread by the sweat of our brow, as they did. Two of their children died in infancy before I was born and only four lived to years of maturity, three sons and a daughter. I was a great favorite, as being the youngest.

When I was between six and seven years of age I had the misfortune to lose my father, by a very sudden stroke. I remember, on the morning in which he died, I saw him go out of the house about his business as usual, and by nine o'clock I saw him expiring in his chamber. His sudden exit was attributed to his taking a dose of *tartar emetic* as he complained of being something unwell. The remembrance of this event has made me cautious of *tartar* all my days. I never knowingly took a grain of it, though I suspected that a physician once gave me some of it in disguise, but it almost put an end to me. It brought on the same symptoms of the cramps and cold sweat, which came on my father just before he expired—but I, being of a stronger constitution than he, survived the attack.

My father, dying so suddenly and unexpectedly, had made no will, the consequence was that my elder brother, Robert, heired all the landed estate. Of the perishable estate an equal division was made, and my part, as well as the rest, amounted to £25 current money of Virginia, which I was to receive at the age of twenty-one. . . .

## Itinerarium of Dr. Alexander Hamilton, 1744

1. *In this excerpt, Hamilton describes a medley of peoples in a tavern by reference to their religion. There are biased references to members of the Society of Friends (Quakers) and later references to the negative effects of a visit by George Whitefield, the famed revivalist.*

2. *In this article, Hamilton describes briefly Presbyterians in East Jersey and, then, more fully, a bilingual landlady, who spoke Dutch and English.*

3. *Hamilton derides the German Moravians of the upper Hudson Valley.*

4. *Here Hamilton gives a full description of Dutch Albany in 1741.*

*Source:* Wendy Johnson, ed., *Colonial American Trade Narratives* (New York: Penguin, 1994), pp. 191–193, 204–205, 218–219, 228–231.

1

*Friday, June 8.* I read Montaign's Essays in the forenoon which is a strange medley of subjects and particularly entertaining.

I dined att a taveren with a very mixed company of different nations and religions. There were Scots, English,

Dutch, Germans, and Irish; there were Roman Catholicks, Church men, Presbyterians, Quakers, Newlightmen, Methodists, Seventh day men, Moravians, Anabaptists, and one Jew. The whole company consisted of 25 planted round an oblong table in a great hall well stoked with flys. The company divided into comittees in conversation; the prevailing topick was politicks and conjectures of a French war. A knott of Quakers there talked only about selling of flower and the low price it bore. The[y] touched a little upon religion, and high words arose among some of the sectaries, but their blood was not hot enough to quarrell, or, to speak in the canting phraze, their zeal wanted fervency. A gentleman that sat next me proposed a number of questions concerning Maryland, understanding I had come from thence. In my replys I was reserved, pretending to know little of the matter as being a person whose business did not lye in the way of history and politicks.

In the afternoon I went to see some ships that lay in the river. Among the rest were three vessels a fitting out for privateers—a ship, a sloop, and a schooner. The ship was a large vessel, very high and full rigged; one Capt. Mackey intended to command her upon the cruise. Att 6 a'clock I went to the coffee house and drank a dish of coffee with Mr. H[asel]l.

After staying there an hour or two, I was introduced by Dr. Phineas Bond into the Governour's Club, a society of gentlemen that met at a taveren every night and converse on various subjects. The Governour gives them his presence once a week, which is generally upon

Wednesday, so that I did not see him there. Our conversation was entertaining; the subject was the English poets and some of the foreign writers, particularly Cervantes, author of Don Quixot, whom we loaded with elogiums due to his character. Att eleven a'clock I left this club and went to my lodging.

*Saturday, June 9th.* This morning there fell a light rain which proved very refreshing, the weather having been very hot and dry for severall days. The heat in this city is excessive, the sun's rays being reflected with such power from the brick houses and from the street pavement which is brick. The people commonly use awnings of painted cloth or duck over their shop doors and windows and, att sun set, throw buckets full of water upon the pavement which gives a sensible cool. They are stocked with plenty of excellent water in this city, there being a pump att almost every 50 paces distance. There are a great number of balconies to their houses where sometimes the men sit in a cool habit and smoke.

The market in this city is perhaps the largest in North-America. It is kept twice a week upon Wednesdays and Saturdays. The street where it stands, called Market Street, is large and spacious, composed of the best houses in the city.

They have but one publick clock here which strikes the hour but has neither index nor dial plate. It is strange they should want such an ornament and conveniency in so large a place, but the chief part of the community consisting of Quakers, they would seem to shun ornament in their publick edifices as well as in their aparrell or dress.

The Quakers here have two large meetings, the Church of England one great church in Second Street, and another built for Whitfield in which one Tennent, a fanatick, now preaches, the Romans one chapell, the Anabaptists one or two meetings, and the Presbyterians two.

The Quakers are the richest and the people of greatest interest in this government; of them their House of Assembly is chiefly composed. They have the character of an obstinate, stiff necked generation and a perpetuall plague to their governors. The present governour, Mr. Thomas, has fallen upon a way to manage them better than any of his predecessors did and, att the same time, keep pritty much in their good graces and share some of their favours. However, the standing or falling of the Quakers in the House of Assembly depends upon their making sure the interest of the Palatines in this province, who of late have turned so numerous that they can sway the votes which way they please.

Here is no publick magazine of arms nor any method of defence, either for city or province, in case of the invasion of an enimy. This is owing to the obstinacy of the Quakers in maintaining their principle of non-resistance. It were a pity but they were put to a sharp triall to see whether they would act as they profess.

I never was in a place so populous where the gout for publick gay diversions prevailed so little. There is no such thing as assemblys of the gentry among them, either for dancing or musick; these they have had an utter aversion to ever since Whitefield preached among them. Their chief employ, indeed, is traffick and mercantile business which turns their thoughts from these levitys. Some Virginia gentlemen that came here with the Commissioners of the Indian Treaty were desirous of having a ball but could find none of the feemale sex in a humour for it. Strange influence of religious enthusiasm upon human nature to excite an aversion at these innocent amusements, for the most part so agreeable and entertaining to the young and gay, and indeed, in the opinion of moderate people, so conducive to the improvement of politeness, good manners, and humanity.

2

## Perth Amboy

At nine in the morning we stoped att the Sign of the King's Arms in Amboy where I breakfasted. As I sat in the porch I observed an antick figure pass by having an old plaid banyan, a pair of thick worsted stockings, ungartered, a greasy worsted nightcap, and no hat. "You see that originall," said the landlord. "He is an old batchellor, and it is his humour to walk the street always in that dress. Tho he makes but a pitifull appearance, yet is he proprietor of most of the houses in town. He is very rich, yet for all that, has no servant but milks his own cow, dresses his own vittles, and feeds his own poultry himself."

Amboy is a small town (it is a very old American city, being older than the city of New York) being a chartered city, much less than our Annapolis, and here frequently the Supream Court and Assembly sit. It has in it one Presbyterian meeting and a pritty large market house, lately built. It is the principall town in New Jersey and appears to be laid out in the shape of a St. George's cross, one main street cutting the other att right angles. 'Tis a sea port, having a good harbour but small trade. They have here the best oysters I have eat in America. It lyes close upon the water, and the best houses in town are ranged along the water side.

In the Jerseys the people are chiefly Presbyterians and Quakers, and there are so many proprietors that share the lands in New Jersey, and so many doubtfull titles and rights that it creates an inexhaustible and profitable pool for the lawers.

## Narrows Ferry

I came to the Narrows att two a'clock and dined att one Corson's that keeps the ferry. The landlady spoke both Dutch and English. I dined upon what I never had eat in my life before—a dish of fryed clams, of which shell fish there is abundance in these parts. As I sat down to dinner I observed a manner of saying grace quite new to me. My landlady and her two daughters put on solemn, devout faces, hanging down their heads and holding up their hands for half a minute. I, who had gracelessly fallen too without remembering that duty according to a wicked custom I had contracted, sat staring att them with my mouth choak full, but after this short meditation was over, we began to lay about us and stuff down the fryed clams with rye-bread and butter. They took such a deal of chawing that we were long att dinner, and the dish began to cool before we had eat enough. The landlady called for the bedpan. I could not guess what she intended to do with it unless it was to warm her bed to go to sleep after dinner, but I found that it was used by way of a chaffing dish to warm our dish of clams. I stared att the novelty for some time, and reaching over for a mug of beer that stood on the opposite side of the table, my bag sleeve catched hold of the handle of the bed pan and unfortunatly overset the clams, at which the landlady was a little ruffled and muttered a scrape of Dutch of which I understood not a word except mynheer, but I suppose she swore, for she uttered her speech with an emphasis.

## 3

### *Poughcapsy*

We anchored att eight o'clock att the entry of that part of the river called Long Reach, the weather being very thick and rainy, and close by us on the starboard side stood a small village called Poughcapsy where the master and hands went ashore and left us to keep the sloop.

*Sunday, June 24th.* At four in the morning Mr. M—s [Milne] and I went ashore to the taveren, and there we met with a justice of the peace and a New Light taylor. The justice seemed to have the greatest half or all the learning of the county in his face, but so soon as he spoke, we found that he was no more learned than other men. The taylor's phizz was screwed up to a santified pitch,

and he seemed to be either under great sorrow for his sins or else a hatching some mischief in his heart, for I have heard that your hipocriticall rogues always put on their most solemn countenance or vizzard when they are contriving how to perpetrate their villanies. We soon discovered that this taylor was a Moravian. The Moravians are a wild, fanatick sect with which both this place and the Jerseys are pestered. They live in common, men and women mixed in a great house or barn where they sometimes eat and drink, sometimes sleep, and sometimes preach and howl, but are quite idle and will employ themselves in no usefull work. They think all things should be in common and say that religion is intirely corrupted by being too much blended with the laws of the country. They call their religion the true religion, or the religion of the Lamb, and they commonly term themselves the followers of the Lamb, which I believe is true in so far as some of them may be wolves in sheep's clothing. This sect was first founded by a German enthusiast, Count Zenzindorff, who used to go about some years agoe and perswade the people to his opinions and drop a certain catechism which he had published upon the high way. They received a considerable strength and addition to their numbers by Whitefield's preaching in these parts but now are upon the decline since there is no opposition made to them. M—ls [Milne] and I anatomized this Moravian taylor in his own hearing, and yet he did not know of it, for we spoke Latin. He asked what language that was. The justice told him he believed it was Latin, att which the cabbager sigh'd and said it was a pagan language. We treated him, however, with a dram and went from the tavern to one Cardevitz's who, having the rheumatism in his arm, asked my advice, which I gave him. The land here is high and woody, and the air very cool.

4

*Oversleigh*

Att seven o'clock we reach the Oversleigh and there run aground again. In the meantime a Dutch gentleman, one Volckert Douw, came on board a passenger, and I flattered myself I should not be quite alone but enjoy some conversation; but I was mistaken, for the devil a word but Dutch was bandied about betwixt the saylors and he, and in general there was such a medley of Dutch and English as would have tired a horse. We heaved out our anchor and got off the shoal att half an hour after seven, so got clear of the Oversleigh, the only troublesom part in the whole voyage. We sailed four miles below it, the wind north east and the night very rainy and dark. We dropt anchor at nine at night and went to bed.

The city of Albany lyes on the west side of Hudson's River upon a rising hill about 30 or 40 miles below where the river comes out of the lake and 160 miles above New York. The hill whereon it stands faces the south east. The city consists of three pritty compact streets, two of which run paralell to the river and are pritty broad, and the third cuts the other two att right angles, running up towards the fort, which is a square stone building about 200 foot square with a bastion att each corner, each bastion mounting eight or ten great guns, most of them 32 pounders. In the fort are two large, brick houses facing each other where there is lodging for the souldiers. There are three market houses in this city and three publick edifices, upon two of which are cupolos or spires, vizt., upon the Town House and the Dutch church. The English church is a great, heavy stone building without any steeple, standing just below the fort. The greatest length of the streets is half a mile. In the fort is kept a garrison of 300 men under the King's pay, who now and then send reinforcements to Oswego, a frontier garrison and trading town lying about 180 miles south [north] and by west of Albany. This city is inclosed by a rampart or wall of wooden palisadoes about 10 foot high and a foot thick, being the trunks of pine trees rammed into the ground, pinned close together, and ending each in a point att top. Here they call them stockadoes. Att each 200 foot distance round this wall is a block house, and from the north gate of the city runs a thick stone wall down into the river, 200 foot long, att each end of which is a block house. In these block houses about 50 of the city militia keep guard every night, and the word all's well walks constantly round all night long from centry to centry and round the fort. There are 5 or 6 gates to this city, the chief of which are the north and the south gates. In the city are about 4,000 inhabitants, mostly Dutch or of Dutch extract.

The Dutch here keep their houses very neat and clean, both without and within. Their chamber floors are generally laid with rough plank which, in time, by constant rubbing and scrubbing becomes as smooth as if it had been plained. Their chambers and rooms are large and handsom. They have their beds generally in alcoves so that you may go thro all the rooms of a great house and see never a bed. They affect pictures much, particularly scripture history, with which they adorn their rooms. They set out their cabinets and bouffetts much with china. Their kitchens are likewise very clean, and there they hang earthen or delft plates and dishes all round the walls in manner of pictures, having a hole drilled thro the edge of the plate or dish and a loop of ribbon put into it to hang it by. But notwithstanding all this nicety and cleanliness in their houses, they are in their persons slovenly and dirty. They live here very frugally and plain, for the chief merit among them seems to be riches, which they spare no pains or trouble to acquire, but are a civil and hospitable people in their way but, att best, rustick and unpolished. I imagined when I first came there that there were some very rich people in the place. They talked of 30, 40, 50 and 100 thousand pounds as of nothing, but I soon found that their riches consisted more in large tracts of land than in cash. They trade pritty much with the Indians and have their manufactorys for wampum, a good Indian commodity. It is of two sorts—the black, which is the most valuable, and the white wampum. The first kind is a bead made out of the bluish black part of a clam shell. It is valued att 6 shillings York money per 100 beads. The white is made of a conch shell from the W. Indies and is not so valuable. They grind the beads to a shape upon a stone, and then with a well tempered needle dipt in wax and tallow, they drill a hole thro' each bead. This trade is apparently triffling but would soon make an estate to a man that could have a monopoly of it, for being in perpetuall demand among the Indians from their custome of burying quantitys of it with their dead, they are very fond of it, and they will give skins or money or any thing for it, having (tho they first taught the art of making it to the Europeans) lost the art of making it themselves.

They live in their houses in Albany as if it were in prisons, all their doors and windows being perpetually shut. But the reason of this may be the little desire they have for conversation and society, their whole thoughts being turned upon profit and gain which necessarily makes them live retired and frugall. Att least this is the common character of the Dutch every where. But indeed the excessive cold winters here obliges them in that season to keep all snug and close, and they have not summer sufficient to revive heat in their veins so as to make them uneasy or put it in their heads to air themselves. They are a healthy, long lived people, many in this city being in age near or above 100 years, and 80 is a common age. They are subject to rotten teeth and scorbutick gumms which, I suppose, is caused by the cold air and their constant diet of salt provisions in the winter, for in that season they are obliged to lay in as for a sea voyage, there being no stirring out of doors then for fear of never stirring again. As to religion they have little of it among them and of enthusiasm not a grain. The bulk of them, if any thing, are of the Lutheran church. Their women in generall, both old and young, are the hardest favoured ever I beheld. Their old women wear a comicall head dress, large pendants, short petticoats, and they stare upon one like witches. They generally eat to their morning's tea raw hung beef sliced down in thin chips in the manner of parmezan, cheese. Their winter here is excessive cold so as to freeze their cattle stiff in one night in the stables.

## List of Different Nations and Tribes of Indians, Early 1700s

*This list details the many nations of Native Americans east of the Mississippi River in the early eighteenth century. It notes the number of "fighting men," and details their hunting grounds. The lengthy number indicates the preservation of Indian ethnicity and territories, even after a century of European-American invasions.*

Source: Reuben Gold Thwaites, ed., *Early Western Travels, 1748–1846*, vol. 1, *Journals of Conrad Weiser (1748), George Croghan (1750–1765), Christian Frederick Post (1758), and Thomas Morris (1764)* (Cleveland, Ohio: Arthur H. Clark, 1904).

## J. Hector St. John Crèvecoeur, "What Is an American?" 1783

*This famous essay, written at the time of the American Revolution, states the effect of decades of interaction between ethnic groups in America. The result, argues Crèvecoeur, is the creation of a "new man," an American. His argument is the earliest and one of the most eloquent statements of the melting pot thesis, which dominated twentieth-century views of ethnicity in the United States.*

Source: J. Hector St. John Crèvecoeur, *Letters from an American Farmer* (1783; reprint with preface by W. P. Trent and introduction by Ludwig Lewisohn, London: Chatto and Windus; New York: Duffield and Company, 1908).

## LETTER 3

### What Is an American?

I wish I could be acquainted with the feelings and thoughts which must agitate the heart and present themselves to the mind of an enlightened Englishman, when he first lands on this continent. He must greatly rejoice that he lived at a time to see this fair country discovered and settled; he must necessarily feel a share of national pride, when he views the chain of settlements which embellishes these extended shores. When he says to himself, this is the work of my countrymen, who, when convulsed by factions, afflicted by a variety of miseries and wants, restless and impatient, took refuge here. They brought along with them their national genius, to which they

# A List of the Different Nations and Tribes of Indians in the Northern District of North America, with the Number of Their Fighting Men

| Names of the Tribes | Nos. | Their Dwelling Ground | Their Hunting Grounds |
| --- | --- | --- | --- |
| Mohocks, a | 160 | Mohock River. | Between that and Lake George. |
| Oneidas, b | 300 | East side of Oneida Lake, & on the head waters of the east branch of Susquehannah. | In the country where they live. |
| Tuscaroras, b | 200 | Between the Oneidas and Onandagoes. | Between Oneida Lake & Lake Ontario. |
| Onandagoes, b | 260 | Near the Onandaga Lake. | Between Onandago L. & mouth of Seneca River, near Oswego. |
| Cayugas, b | 200 | On two small Lakes, called the Cayugas, on the north branch of Susquehannah. | Where they reside. |
| Senecas, b | 1,000 | Seneca Country, on the waters of Susquehannah, the waters of Lake Ontario, and on the heads of Ohio River. | Their chief hunting country thereabouts. |
| Aughquages, c | 150 | East branch of Susquehannah River, and on Aughquaga. | Where they live. |
| Nanticokes, c | 100 | Utsanango, Chagmett, Oswego, and on the east branch of Susquehannah. | Do. |
| Mohickons, c | 100 | | |
| Conoys, c | 30 | | |
| Monsays, c | 150 | At Diahogo, and other villages up the north branch of Susquehannah. | Do. |
| Sapoones, c | 30 | | |
| Delawares, c | 150 | | |

a These are the oldest Tribe of the Confederacy of the Six Nations.
b Connected with New York, part of the Confederacy with New York.
c Connected with, and depending on the Five Nations.

| Names of the Tribes | Nos. | Their Dwelling Ground | Their Hunting Grounds |
|---|---|---|---|
| Delawares, d | 600 | Between the Ohil & Lake Erie, on the branches of Beaver Creek, Muskingum and Guyehugo. | Where they live. |
| Shawness, d | 300 | On Scioto & branch of Muskingum. | Do. |
| Mohickone, d | 300 | In villages near Sandusky. | Do. |
| Goghnawages, d | | On the head banks of Scioto. | |
| Twightwees, e | 250 | Miame River, near Fort Miame. | On the ground where they live. |
| Wayoughtanies, f | 300 | | |
| Pyankeshas, f | 300 | On the branches of Ouabache, near Fort Ouitanon. | Between Ouitanon & the Miames. |
| Shockays, f | 390 | | |
| Huskhuskeys, g | 300 | Near the French settlements, in the Illinois Country. | |
| Illinois, g | 300 | | |
| Wayondotts, h | 250 | | |
| Ottawas, h | 400 | Near Fort Detroit. | About Lake Erie. |
| Putawatimes, h | | | |
| Chipawas, i | 200 | On Sagana Creek, which empties into Lake Huron. | Thereabouts. |
| Ottawas, | | | |
| Chippawas, j | 400 | Near Michilimachinac. | On the north side of Lake Huron. |
| Ottawas, j | 260 | | |

d Dependent on the Six Nations, and connected with Pennsylvania.
e Connected with Pennsylvania.
f Connected with the Twightwees.
g These two Nations the English had never any trade, or connection with.
h Connected formerly with the French.
i Connected with the Indians about Detroit, and dependant on the commanding officer.
j Always connected with the French.

| Names of the Tribes | Nos. | Their Dwelling Ground | Their Hunting Grounds |
|---|---|---|---|
| Chipawas,* k | 400 | Near the entrance of Lake Superior, and not far from Fort St. Mary's. | Thereabouts. |
| Chepawas, k | | | |
| Mynonamies, k | 550 | Near Fort Labay on the Lake Michigan. | Thereabouts. |
| Shockeys, k | | | |
| Putawatimes, k | 150 | Near Fort St. Joseph's. | Thereabouts. |
| Ottawas, k | 150 | | |
| Kicapoos, l | | | |
| Outtagamies, l | | | |
| Musquatans, l | 4,000 | On Lake Michigan and between it and the Mississippi. | Where they respectively reside. |
| Miscotins, l | | | |
| Outtamacks, l | | | |
| Musquaykeys, l | | | |
| Oswegatches, h | 100 | Settled at swagatchy in Canada, on the River St. Lawrence. | Thereabouts. |
| Connesedagoes, k | 300 | | |
| Coghnewagoes, k | | Near Montreal. | |
| Orondocks, k | 100 | | |
| Abonakies, k | 150 | Settled near Trois Rivers. | |
| Alagonkins, k | 100 | | |
| La Suil,* | 10,100 | South-west of Lake Superior. | |

k Connected with the French.

* There are several villages of Chipawas settled along the bank of Lake Superior, but as I have no knowledge of that country, cannot ascertain their numbers.

l Never connected in any trade or otherwise with the English.

* These are a nation of Indians settled south-west of Lake Superior, called by the French La Sue, who, by the best account that I could ever get from the French and Indians, are computed ten thousand fighting men. They spread over a large tract of country, and have forty odd villages; in which country are several other tribes of Indians, who are tributaries to the La Sues, none of whom except a very few, have ever known the use of fire-arms: as yet but two villages. I suppose the French don't choose to risk a trade among such a powerful body of people, at so vast a distance.

principally owe what liberty they enjoy, and what substance they possess. Here he sees the industry of his native country displayed in a new manner, and traces in their works the embrios of all the arts, sciences, and ingenuity which flourish in Europe. Here he beholds fair cities, substantial villages, extensive fields, an immense country filled with decent houses, good roads, orchards, meadows, and bridges, where an hundred years ago all was wild, woody and uncultivated! What a train of pleasing ideas this fair spectacle must suggest; it is a prospect which must inspire a good citizen with the most heartfelt pleasure. The difficulty consists in the manner of viewing so extensive a scene. He is arrived on a new continent; a modern society offers itself to his contemplation, different from what he had hitherto seem. It is not composed, as in Europe, of great lords who possess every thing, and of a herd of people who have nothing. Here are no aristocratical families, no courts, no kings, no bishops, no ecclesiastical dominion, no invisible power giving to a few a very visible one; no great manufacturers employing thousands, no great refinements of luxury. The rich and the poor are not so far removed from each other as they are in Europe. Some few towns excepted, we are all tillers of the earth, from Nova Scotia to West Florida. We are a people of cultivators, scattered over an immense territory, communicating with each other by means of good roads and navigable rivers, united by the silken bands of mild government, all respecting the laws, without dreading their power, because

they are equitable. We are all animated with the spirit of an industry which is unfettered and unrestrained, because each person works for himself. If he travels through our rural districts he views not the hostile castle, and the haughty mansion, contrasted with the clay-built hut and miserable cabbin, where cattle and men help to keep each other warm, and dwell in meanness, smoke, and indigence. A pleasing uniformity of decent competence appears throughout our habitations. The meanest of our log-houses is a dry and, comfortable habitation. Lawyer or merchant are the fairest titles our towns afford; that of a farmer is the only appellation of the rural inhabitants of our country. It must take some time ere he can reconcile himself to our dictionary, which is but short in words of dignity, and names of honour. There, on a Sunday, he sees a congregation of respectable farmers and their wives, all clad in neat homespun, well mounted, or riding in their own humble waggons. There is not among them an esquire, saving the unlettered magistrate. There he sees a parson as simple as his flock, a farmer who does not riot on the labour of others. We have no princes, for whom we toil, starve, and bleed: we are the most perfect society now existing in the world. Here man is free as he ought to be; nor is this pleasing equality so transitory as many others are. Many ages will not see the shores of our great lakes replenished with inland nations, nor the unknown bounds of North America entirely peopled. Who can tell how far it extends? Who can tell the millions of men whom it will feed and contain? for no European foot has as yet travelled half the extent of this mighty continent!

The next wish of this traveller will be to know whence came all these people? they are a mixture of English, Scotch, Irish, French, Dutch, Germans, and Swedes. From this promiscuous breed, that race now called Americans have arisen. The eastern provinces must indeed be excepted, as being the unmixed descendents of Englishmen. I have heard many wish that they had been more intermixed also: for my part, I am no wisher, and think it much better as it has happened. They exhibit a most conspicuous figure in this great and variegated picture; they too enter for a great share in the pleasing perspective displayed in these thirteen provinces. I know it is fashionable to reflect on them, but I respect them for what they have done; for the accuracy and wisdom with which they have settled their territory; for the decency of their manners; for their early love of letters; their ancient college, the first in this hemisphere; for their industry; which to me who am but a farmer, is the criterion of everything. There never was a people, situated as they are, who with so ungrateful a soil have done more in so short a time. Do you think that the monarchical ingredients which are more prevalent in other governments, have purged them from all foul stains? Their histories assert the contrary.

In this great American asylum, the poor of Europe have by some means met together, and in consequence of various causes; to what purpose should they ask one another what countrymen they are?

Alas, two thirds of them had no country. Can a wretch who wanders about, who works and starves, whose life is a continual scene of sore affliction or pinching penury; can that man call England or any other kingdom his country? A country that had no bread for him, whose fields procured him no harvest, who met with nothing but the frowns of the rich, the severity of the laws, with jails and punishments; who owned not a single foot of the extensive surface of this planet? No! urged by a variety of motives, here they came. Every thing has tended to regenerate them; new laws, a new mode of living, a new social system; here they are become men: in Europe they were as so many useless plants, wanting vegitative mould, and refreshing showers; they withered, and were mowed down by want, hunger, and war; but now by the power of transplantation, like all other plants they have taken root and flourished! Formerly they were not numbered in any civil lists of their country, except in those of the poor; here they rank as citizens. By what invisible power has this surprising metamorphosis been performed? By that of the laws and that of their industry. The laws, the indulgent laws, protect them as they arrive, stamping on them the symbol of adoption; they receive ample rewards for their labours; these accumulated rewards procure them lands; those lands confer on them the title of freemen, and to that title every benefit is affixed which men can possibly require. This is the great operation daily performed by our laws. From whence proceed these laws? From our government. Whence the government? It is derived from the original genius and strong desire of the people ratified and confirmed by the crown. This is the great chain which links us all, this is the picture which every province exhibits, Nova Scotia excepted. There the crown has done all; either there were no people who had genius, or it was not much attended to: the consequence is, that the province is very thinly inhabited indeed; the power of the crown in conjunction with the musketos has prevented men from settling there. Yet some parts of it flourished once, and it contained a mild harmless set of people. But for the fault of a few leaders, the whole were banished. The greatest political error the crown ever committed in America, was to cut off men from a country which wanted nothing but men!

What attachment can a poor European emigrant have for a country where he had nothing? The knowledge of the language, the love of a few kindred as poor as himself, were the only cords that tied him: his country is now that which gives him land, bread, protection, and consequence: *Ubi panis ibi patria*, is the motto of all emigrants. What, then is the American, this new man? He is either an European, or the descendant of an European, hence that strange mixture of blood, which you will find in no other country. I could point out to you a family whose grandfather was an Englishman, whose wife was Dutch, whose son married a French woman, and whose present four sons have now four wives of different nations. *He* is an American, Who leaving behind him all his ancient prejudices and manners, receives new ones from the new mode of life he has em-

braced, the new government he obeys, and the new rank he holds. He becomes an American by being received in the broad lap of our great *Alma Mater*. Here individuals of all nations are melted into a new race of men, whose labours and posterity will one day cause great changes in the world. Americans are the western Pilgrims, who are carrying along with them that great mass of arts, sciences, vigour, and industry which began long since in the east; they will finish the great circle. The Americans were once scattered all over Europe; here they are incorporated into one of the finest systems of population which has ever appeared, and which will hereafter become distinct by the power of the different climates they inhabit. The American ought therefore to love this country much better than that wherein either he or his forefathers were born. Here the rewards of his industry follow with equal steps the progress of his labour; his labour is founded on the basis of nature, *self-interest*; can it want a stronger allurement? Wives and children, who before in vain demanded of him a morsel of bread, now, fat and frolicsome, gladly help their father to clear those fields whence exuberant crops are to arise to feed and to clothe them all; without any part being claimed, either by a despotic prince, a rich abbot, or a mighty lord.

## Miami Deaths of 1732, Report of Jean-Charles d'Arnaud, 1732

*This extraordinary firsthand document tells of the tragic consequences of contact between Europeans and Miami Indians, who lacked im-*

munity to the diseases of white people. These epidemics decimated Native American populations from the 1500s until well into the nineteenth century.

Source: Joseph Peyser, "It Was Not Smallpox: The Miami Deaths of 1732 Reexamined," *Indiana Magazine of History* 81 (June 1985): 159–169.

## THE COMMANDANT'S NOSTRUM

What evidence, then, justifies reopening this case to challenge the smallpox theory? The first bit of evidence is the nostrum that d'Arnaud administered to the Miamis he saved.

The day after I had arrived at my post fifteen or sixteen Miami canoes arrived from Oswego loaded with four hundred casks of brandy. Five or six days later they knocked one in, in which there was the complete skin of a man's hand. This news spread through the village and surprised them immensely. However, it did not put a stop to their drunkenness; after three days two individuals who were fine in the evening were buried the next day at eight in the morning. Then for more than three weeks, at least four died each day. My statements to them that they had no decent food whatever in their village, and that by dispersing in the woods they would find meat which would give them strength to fight off the disease combined with the foul air (which the great number of bodies which surrounded them created) persuaded them to go off to their winter quarters from which I have heard that several were dying from time

to time but not in as great numbers as in their village. (The number of dead is presently one hundred fifty persons.)

The first did not astonish me at all; I attributed it to the excessive drinking. But the rest astonished me more. I had the dead stripped and examined, and the conclusion for me was that it was a poison as subtle as it was crafty, only taking effect after a rather considerable time. I wanted to have more certain proof of this: a war chief of this nation who had become particularly attached to me and who deserved to be saved was attacked by the sickness. I gave him a strong dose of orvietan which saved his life. In the same way I saved several with this medicine, but not having any more, those who were deprived of this help all died, and not one of those who used it perished.

The Miamis are not the only victims of this poison. The Ouiatanons came one hundred thirty strong to perform the dance of the peace pipe. The brandy was not held back from them, but after their return home, the same sickness overtook them and several letters from that location informed me that almost all of them had died.

## The Independent Reflector, William Livingston on Kings College, 1753

*Here William Livingston, a Scottish-Irish, Presbyterian intellectual and politician, appeals to various ethnicities through their religious beliefs, in an attempt to convince them that the new college in New York City should be nonsectarian. Though his argument failed to convince New York's authorities, whose goal was to make Kings College a training school for Anglican clergy and bishops, Livingston's argument for separation of church and state was also a plea for a universal education rather than one based upon faith and ethnicity.*

Source: Milton M. Klein, ed., *The Independent Reflector, or Weekly Essays on Sundry Important Subjects More Particularly Adapted to the Province of New-York*, by William Livingston and Others (Cambridge, Mass.: The Belknap Press of Harvard University Press, 1963), pp. 209–212.

## THURSDAY, APRIL 26, 1753

You, Gentlemen of the Church of England, cannot but condemn the unaccountable Assurance of whatever Persuasion, presumes to rob you of an *equal* Share in the Government of what *equally* belongs to all. With what Indignation and Scorn, must you, the most numerous and richest Congregation in this City, regard so insolent an Attempt! You who have the same Discipline, and the same Worship with the Mother Church of the Nation, and whose fundamental Articles are embrac'd by all protestant Christendom,—what Colour of Reason can be offered to deny you your just Proportion in the Management of the College? Methinks a due Respect for the national Church, nay common Decency and good Manners, are sufficient to check the presumptuous Attempt, and redden the Claimant with a guilty Blush. Resent, therefore, so shameless a Pretence, so audacious an Encroachment.

Nor can you Gentlemen of the Dutch Church, retrospect the Zeal of your Ancestors in stipulating for the Enjoyment of their religious Privileges, at the Surrender of the Province, without a becoming Ardor for the same Model of public Worship which they were so anxious in preserving to you in its primitive Purity. Or higher still, to trace the Renown of your Progenitors, recollect their Stand, their glorious and ever memorable Stand against the Yoke of Thraldom, and all the Horrors of ecclesiastic Villainy, its inseparable Concomitants. For their inviolable Attachment to pure unadulterated Protestantism, and the inestimable Blessings of Freedom civil and sacred, History will resound their deathless Praises; and adorned with the precious Memorials of their heroic and insuppressible Struggles against Imposition and Despotism, will shine with eternal and undecaying Splendor. Impell'd by their illustrious Example, disdain the Thoughts of a servile Acquiescence in the usurp'd Dominion of others, who will inevitably swallow up and absorb your Churches, and efface even the Memory of your having once formed so considerable a Distinction. Pity methinks it would be and highly to be deplor'd, that you should, by your own Folly, gradually crumble into Ruin, and at length sink into total and irrecoverable Oblivion.

Remember Gentlemen of the English Presbyterian Church, remember with a sacred Jealousy, the countless Sufferings of your pious Predecessors, for Liberty of Conscience, and the Right of private Judgment. What Afflictions did they not endure, what fiery Trials did they not encounter, before they found in this remote Corner of the Earth, that Sanctuary and Requiem which their native Soil inhumanly deny'd them? And will you endanger that dear-bought Toleration for which they retired into voluntary Banishment, for which they agoniz'd, and for which they bled? What drove your Ancestors to this Country, then a dreary Waste and a barren Desert? What forced them from the Land of their Fathers, the much-lov'd Region where first they drew the vital Air? What compell'd them to open to themselves a Passage into these more fortunate Climes? Was it not the Rage of Persecution and a lawless Intolerance? Did they not seek an Asylum amongst the Huts of Savages more hospitable, more humaniz'd than their merciless Oppressors? Could Oceans stop or Tempests retard their Flight, when Freedom was attack'd and Conscience was the Question? And will you entail on your Posterity that Bondage, to escape which they brav'd the raging Deep, and penetrated the howling Wilderness!

You, my Friends, in Derision called Quakers, have always approv'd yourselves Lovers of civil and religious Liberty; and of universal Benevolence to Mankind. And tho' you have been misrepresented as averse to human Learning, I am confident, convinced as you are of the Advantages of useful Literature, by the Writings of your renown'd *Apologist*, and other celebrated Authors of your Persuasion, you would generously contribute to the Support of a College founded on a free and catholic Bottom. But to give your Substance to the rearing of Bigotry, or the tutoring Youth in the enticing *Words of Man's Vanity*, I know to be repugnant to your candid, your ra-

tional, your manly Way of thinking. Since the first Appearance of the *Friends*, thro' what Persecutions have they not waded? With what Difficulties have they not conflicted, e'er they could procure the unmolested Enjoyment of their Religion? This I mention not to spur you to revenge the Indignities offered to your Brethren, who being now beyond the Reach of Opposition and Violence, you, I am sure will scorn to remember their Tribulations with an unchristian Resentment. But to make their inhuman Treatment a Watch-Tower against the like Insults on your Descendants, is but wise, prudent and rational. At present, as ever you ought, you enjoy a righteous Toleration. But how long you will be able to boast the same Immunity, when the Fountain of Learning is directed, and all the Offices of the Province engrossed by one Sect, God only knows, and yours it is to stand on your Guard.

Equally tremendous will be the Consequences to you, Gentlemen of the French, of the Moravian, of the Lutheran, and of the Anabaptist Congregations, tho' the Limits of my Paper deny me the Honour of a particular Application to your respective Churches.

### Thomas Jefferson, "Notes on the State of Virginia," 1783

*This famous excerpt from "Notes on the State of Virginia," written by Jefferson at the close of the American Revolution, indicates, through his use of pseudoscience, a replacement of ethnicity with race. Jefferson's opinions about African Americans in particular formed the basis for nineteenth-century racism.*

Source: Alan Gallay, ed., *Voices of the Old South: Eyewitness Accounts, 1528–1861* (Athens and London: University of Georgia Press, 1994), pp. 157–161.

To emancipate all slaves born after passing the act. The bill reported by the revisers does not itself contain this proposition; but an amendment containing it was prepared, to be offered to the legislature whenever the bill should be taken up, and farther directing, that they should continue with their parents to a certain age, then to be brought up, at the public expense, to tillage, arts, or sciences, according to their geniuses, till the females should be eighteen, and the males twenty-one years of age, when they should be colonized to such places as the circumstances of the time should render most proper, sending them out with arms, implements of household and of the handicraft arts, seeds, pairs of the useful domestic animals, &c., to declare them a free and independent people, and extend to them our alliance and protection, till they have acquired strength; and to send vessels at the same time to other parts of the world for an equal number of white inhabitants; to induce them to migrate hither, proper encouragements were to be proposed. It will probably be asked, why not retain and incorporate the blacks into the State, and thus save the expense of supplying by importation of white settlers, the vacancies they will leave? Deep-rooted prejudices entertained by the whites; ten thousand recollections, by the blacks, of the injuries they have sustained; new provocations; the real distinctions which

nature has made; and many other circumstances, will divide us into parties, and produce convulsions, which will probably never end but in the extermination of the one or the other race. To these objections, which are political, may be added others, which are physical and moral. The first difference which strikes us is that of color. Whether the black of the negro resides in the reticular membrane between the skin and scarf-skin, or in the scarf-skin itself; whether it proceeds from the color of the blood, the color of the bile, or from that of some other secretion, the difference is fixed in nature, and is as real as if its seat and cause were better know to us. And is this difference of no importance? Is it not the foundation of a greater or less share of beauty in the two races? Are not the fine mixtures of red and white, the expressions of every passion by greater or less suffusions of color in the one, preferable to that eternal monotony, which reigns in the countenances, that immovable veil of black which covers the emotions of the other race? Add to these, flowing hair, a more elegant symmetry of form, their own judgment in favor of the whites, declared by their preference of them, as uniformly as is the preference of the Oranootan [Orang-utan] for the black woman over those of his own species. The circumstance of superior beauty, is thought worthy attention in the propagation of our horses, dogs, and other domestic animals; why not in that of man? Besides those of color, figure, and hair, there are other physical distinctions proving a difference of race. They have less hair on the face and body. They secrete less by the kidneys, and more by the glands of the skin, which gives them a very strong and disagreeable odor. This greater degree of transpiration, renders them more tolerant of heat, and less so of cold than the whites. Perhaps, too, a difference of structure in the pulminary apparatus, which a late ingenious experimentalist has discovered to be the principal regulator of animal heat, may have disabled them from extricating, in the act of inspiration, so much of that fluid from the outer air, or obliged them in expiration, to part with more of it. They seem to require less sleep. A black after hard labor through the day, will be induced by the slightest amusements to sit up till midnight, or later, though knowing he must be out with the first dawn of the morning. They are at least as brave, and more adventuresome. But this may perhaps proceed from a want of forethought, which prevents their seeing a danger till it be present. When present, they do not go through it with more coolness or steadiness than the whites. They are more ardent after their female; but love seems with them to be more an eager desire, than a tender delicate mixture of sentiment and sensation. Their griefs are transient. Those numberless afflictions, which render it doubtful whether heaven has given life to us in mercy or in wrath, are less felt, and sooner forgotten with them. In general, their existence appears to participate more of sensation than reflection. To this must be ascribed their disposition to sleep when abstracted from their diversions, and unemployed in labor. An animal whose body is at rest, and who does not reflect, must be disposed to sleep of

course. Comparing them by their faculties of memory, reason, and imagination, it appears to me that in memory they are equal to the whites; in reason much inferior, as I think one could scarcely be found capable of tracing and comprehending the investigations of Euclid; and that in imagination they are dull, tasteless, and anomalous. It would be unfair to follow them to Africa for this investigation. We will consider them here, on the same stage with the whites, and where the facts are not apochryphal on which a judgment is to be formed. It will be right to make great allowances for the difference of condition, of education, of conversation, of the sphere in which they move. Many millions of them have been brought to, and born in America. Most of them, indeed, have been confined to tillage, to their own homes, and their own society; yet many have been so situated, that they might have availed themselves of the conversation of their masters; many have been brought up to the handicraft arts, and from that circumstance have always been associated with the whites. Some have been liberally educated, and all have lived in countries where the arts and sciences are cultivated to a considerable degree, and all have had before their eyes samples of the best works from abroad. The Indians; with no advantages of this kind, will often carve figures on their pipes not destitute of design and merit. They will crayon out an animal, a plant, or a country, so as to prove the existence of a germ in their minds which only wants cultivation. They astonish you with strokes of the most sublime oratory; such as prove their reason and sentiment strong, their imagination glowing and elevated. But never yet could I find that a black had uttered a thought above the level of plain narration; never saw even an elementary trait of painting or sculpture. In music they are more generally gifted than the whites with accurate ears for tune and time, and they have been found capable of imagining a small catch. Whether they will be equal to the composition of a more extensive run of melody, or of complicated harmony, is yet to be proved. Misery is often the parent of the most affecting touches in poetry. Among the blacks is misery enough, God knows, but no poetry. Love is the peculiar oestrum of the poet. Their love is ardent, but it kindles the senses only, not the imagination. Religion, indeed, has produced a Phyllis Whately; but it could not produce a poet. The compositions published under her name are below the dignity of criticism. . . .

The improvement of the blacks in body and mind, in the first instance of their mixture with the whites, has been observed by every one, and proves that their inferiority is not the effect merely of their condition of life. We know that among the Romans, about the Augustan age especially, the condition of their slaves was much more deplorable than that of the blacks on the continent of America. The two sexes were confined in separate apartments, because to raise a child cost the master more than to buy one. Cato, for a very restricted indulgence to his slaves, in this particular, took from them a certain price. But in this country the slaves multiply as fast as the free inhabitants. Their situation and manners place the commerce between the two sexes almost without restraint. The same Cato, on a principle of economy, always sold his sick and superannuated slaves. He gives it as a standing precept to a master visiting his farm, to sell his old oxen, old wagons, old tools, old and diseased servants, and everything else become useless. . . . The American slaves cannot enumerate this among the injuries and insults they receive. . . . With the Romans, the regular method of taking the evidence of their slaves was under torture. Here it has been thought better never to resort to their evidence. When a master was murdered, all his slaves, in the same house, or within hearing, were condemned to death. Here punishment falls on the guilty only, and as precise proof is required against him as against a freeman. Yet notwithstanding these and other discouraging circumstances among the Romans, their slaves were often their rarest artists. They excelled too in science, insomuch as to be usually employed as tutors to their master's children. Epictetus, Terence, and Phaedrus, were slaves. But they were of the race of whites. It is not their condition then, but nature, which has produced the distinction. Whether further observation will or will not verify the conjecture, that nature has been less bountiful to them in the endowments of the head, I believe that in those of the heart she will be found to have done them justice. That disposition to theft with which they have been branded, must be ascribed to their situation, and not to any depravity of the moral sense. The man in whose favor no laws of property exist, probably feels himself less bound to respect those made in favor of others. When arguing for ourselves, we lay it down as a fundamental, that laws, to be just, must give a reciprocation of right; that, without this, they are mere arbitrary rules of conduct, founded in force, and not in conscience; and it is a problem which I give to the master to solve, whether the religious precepts against the violation of property were not framed for him as well as his slave? And whether the slave may not as justifiably take a little from one who has taken all from him, as he may slay one who would slay him? That a change in the relations in which a man is placed should change his ideas of moral right or wrong, is neither new, nor peculiar to the color of the blacks. . . .

Notwithstanding these considerations which must weaken their respect for the laws of property, we find among them numerous instances of the most rigid integrity, and as many as among their better instructed masters, of benevolence, gratitude, and unshaken fidelity. The opinion that they are inferior in the faculties of reason and imagination, must be hazarded with great diffidence. . . . To our reproach it must be said, that though for a century and a half we have had under our eyes the races of black and of red men, they have never yet been viewed by us as subjects of natural history. I advance it, therefore, as a suspicion only, that the blacks, whether originally a distinct race, or made distinct by time and circumstances, are inferior to the whites in the endowments both of body and mind. It is not against experience to suppose that different species of the same genus, or varieties of the same species, may possess different qualifica-

tions. Will not a lover of natural history then, one who views the gradations in all the races of animals with the eye of philosophy, excuse an effort to keep those in the department of man as distinct as nature has formed them? This unfortunate difference of color, and perhaps of faculty, is a powerful obstacle to the emancipation of these people. Many of their advocates, while they wish to vindicate the liberty of human nature, are anxious also to preserve its dignity and beauty. Some of these, embarrassed by the question, "What further is to be done with them?" join themselves in opposition with those who are actuated by sordid avarice only. Among the Romans emancipation required but one effort. The slave, when made free, might mix with, without staining the blood of his master. But with us a second is necessary, unknown to history. When freed, he is to be removed beyond the reach of mixture.

## "A Gouging Match"; "A Backwoods Ball and Fight," c. 1780s

*This amusing account of a "gouging match" held in Kentucky just after the American Revolution shows a change in ethnic identification from Scot-Irish and English to Virginian and Kentuckian. Later, the narrator gives a good account of drinking, music, and dancing, all done to an amalgam of ethnicities.*

*Source:* Alan Nevins, ed., *American Social History, as Recorded by British Travelers* (New York: Henry Holt, 1923), pp. 58–63.

## A GOUGING MATCH

Yesterday two fellows drinking in a public-house, the conversation turned on the merit of their horses-two wretched animals they had ridden into town that morning, and which had remained fasting at a post. A wager, the consequence of every argument on this side of the mountains, was made, and the poor brutes were galloped off to the race-course. Two thirds of the population followed: blacksmiths, shipwrights, all left work; the town appeared a desert. The stores were shut. I asked a proprietor why the warehouses did not remain open. He told me all good was done for that day: that the people would remain on the ground till night, and many stay till the following morning. I was determined to see this Virginian recreation, which caused such an abandonment of care and business. On my arrival on the ground, the original race had been won, and the price of a saddle was collecting to excite another course, and raise new opponents. This was soon effected; the course was cleared, and six poor devils were started for the saddle, and numerous bets laid by the owners and spectators. The number of persons interested in this affair, and some disputed points which occurred in the adjustment of it, gave rise to a variety of opinion; umpires were called in; their judgment was rejected, and a kind of general battle ensued. This affray over, the quarrel took a smaller circle, confined to two individuals, a Virginian by birth, and a Kentuckian by adoption. A ring was formed, and the mob demanded whether they proposed to *fight fair*, or to *rough and tumble*. The latter mode was preferred. Perhaps you do not exactly understand the distinction of these terms. Fight fair however is much in the English manner; and here, as there, any thing foul requires interference; but when the parties choose to *rough and tumble*, neither the populace nor individuals are to intermeddle or hinder either combatant from tearing or rending the other on the ground, or in any other situation. You startle at the words *tear* and *rend*, and again do not understand me. You have heard these terms I allow applied to beasts of prey, and carnivorous animals; and your humanity cannot conceive them applicable to man: it nevertheless is so, and the fact will not permit me the use of any less expressive term. Let me proceed. Bulk and bone were in favour of the Kentuckian; science and craft in that of the Virginian. The former promised himself victory from his power, the latter from his science. Very few rounds had taken place, or fatal blows given, before the Virginian contracted his whole form, drew up his arms to his face, with his hands nearly closed in a concave, by the fingers being bent to the full extension of the flexors, and summoning up all his energy for one act of desperation, pitched himself into the bosom of his opponent. Before the effect of this could be ascertained, the sky was rent by the shouts of the multitude; and I could learn that the Virginian had expressed as much *beauty* and *skill* in his retraction and bound, as if he had been bred in a menagerie, and practised action and attitude among panthers and wolves. The shock received by the Kentuckian, and the want of breath, brought him instantly to the ground. The Virginian never lost his hold, like those bats of the South who never quit the subject on which they fasten till they taste blood, he kept his knees on his enemy's body; fixing his claws in his hair, and his thumbs on his eyes, gave them an instantaneous start from their sockets. The sufferer roared aloud, but uttered no complaint. The citizens again shouted with joy; and bets of three to one were offered on the Virginian. The Kentuckian not being able to disentangle his adversary from his face, adopted a new mode of warfare; and, in imitation of the serpent which crushes such creatures to death as it proposes for its food, he extended his arms around the Virginian, and hugged him into closer contact with his huge body. The latter disliking this, cast loose the hair and convex eyes of his adversary, when both, folded together like bears in an embrace, rolled several turns over each other. The acclamations increased, and bets run that the Kentuckian *"would give out,"* that is, after being mutilated and deprived of his eyes, ears, and nose, he would cry for mercy and aid. The public were not precisely right. Some daemon interposed for the biggest monster; he got his enemy under him, and in an instant snapped off his nose so close to his face that no manner of projection remained. The little Virginian made one further effort, and fastening on the under lip of his mutilator tore it over the chin. The Kentuckian at length *gave out,* on which the people car-

ried off the victor, and he preferring a triumph to a doctor, who came to cicatrize his face, suffered himself to be chaired round the ground as the champion of the times, and the first *rougher and tumbler.* The poor wretch, whose eyes were started from their spheres, and whose lip refused its office, returned to the town, to hide his impotence and get his countenance repaired.

## A BACKWOODS BALL AND FIGHT

This spectacle ended, and the citizens refreshed with whiskey and biscuit, sold on the ground, the races were renewed, and possibly other editions of the monstrous history I have just recited; but I had had sufficient of the *sports of the day,* and returned to my Quaker friend, with whom I had engaged to take my dinner. He was afflicted, but by no means surprised at the news I brought him, and informed me further, that such doings were common, frequently two or three times a week; and that twice a year, or at the spring and fall races the continued for fourteen days without interruption, aided by the licentious and profligate of all the neighbouring States. As to the savage practise of fighting in the manner of wild beasts, my host entertained no hopes whatever of ever seeing it put down. It might be called a national taste, which the laws appeared afraid to violate; and therefore it reared its head above authority. Few nights elapsed without the exhibition of this new gymnastic; few mornings appeared that did not bring to day a friend or acquaintance with the loss of an eye, or the multilation of half his features. Alarmed at this account, I asked whether this kind of conduct spread down the river. I understood that it did on the left hand side, and that I would do well to land there as little as possible; that many of the small inns on the Virginia and Kentucky shore, were held in solitary situations by persons of infamous character, driven from the interior and the headwaters, by the gradual encroachments made on them by morals, religion and justice. At such taverns there were s persons at no loss for a subject of quarrel. The invariable consequence of which was, the loss of sight, and sometimes of life, and the total confiscation property, by the villains, who, on maiming, or murdering, the inoffensive party, rush out of the house, seize his boat, and descend the river, never more to be heard heard of-the landlord swearing he had never seen them before, or had any knowledge to what place they belonged. All the taverns, however, are not so bad. There was generally to be found one of a better sort in towns and villages where there was some semblance of law, or some apprehension of justice. I again demanded how a stranger was to distinguish a good from a vicious house of entertainment? I was answered, by previous inquiry, or, if that was impracticable, a tolerable judgement could be formed, from observing in the landlord, a *possession, or an absence of ears*; many of the properties of small inns being men who had left those members nailed to certain penintential market crosses in Maryland, Pennsylvania, and the Carolinas, in lien of certain horses

and cattle of which they had from time to time become the illegal owners. Furnished with these useful instructions, I left my kind entertainer, and retired to my inn with a view of passing a peaceable night. It was not so ordained. It seems the storekeepers, and the principal citizens, knowing the people had no intention of returning to their avocations, had resolved to amuse themselves, and associated for the purpose of having a ball and supper at the principal inn. On my arrival the landlord, with much politeness, told me, that my quality of stranger and a gentleman, gave me a title to enter the public room. I benefited by this intimation, yet, notwithstanding the delicacy and hospitality it conveyed, I could not resist casting a glance, *en passant*, at the head of my host, to observe whether it was provided with ears. Pleased on perceiving these ornamental appendages, or, to follow up the Quaker's idea, these indications of character and safety, I entered the ballroom, which was filled with persons at cards, drinking, smoking, dancing, etc. The *music* consisted of two bangies, played by negroes nearly in a state of nudity, and a lute, through which a Chickasaw breathed with much occasional exertion and violent gesticulations. The dancing accorded with the harmony of these instruments. The clamour of the card tables was so great, that it almost drowned every other; and the music of Ethiopia was with difficulty heard. A man should never judge of the principles of the entertainment of others, by his individual conceptions. This ball, considered a violent vulgar uproar by me, afforded the utmost delight to the assembly, and possibly would have concluded with infinite joy and satisfaction at an early hour next day, had not an unlucky wight of a drunken politician, seized a friend by the throat, and threatened to annihilate him, if he did not drink "Damnation to Thomas Jefferson." A bustle and crowd collected about the parties; the ladies and the music made a precipitate retreat, and I quickly followed, and learned from the landlord, who sat by his fireside perfectly composed, that the ball was over-that a row had commenced, which was the signal for the retreat of the graces, and a general breakup. I hinted at the propriety of his interference, when he very coolly told me, that if there were any ruffians in company, it was fit they should be kicked out, and that bad as the place was, there were always gentlemen at his balls who obligingly took that office on themselves. His words were soon verified. A cry of *out, out; whip them all!* issued from the room, immediately after a torrent rushed through the passage, and a noise of sticks and cries, and execrations of every shade, modulation, and sort. The door locked on the whole party, and silence again restored, we visited the theatre of the late effervescence, and found but one person stretched on the ground. I was proceeding to express some apprehension, when my host exclaimed, "O! it is Mr.—, he is only drunk, he will remain here quietly till morning." With that he drew him along the floor to a corner, and having placed a few chairs as a guard, considered that he had done much towards his accommodation.

## Rev. Alexander Stewart to Rev. John Waring, 1764; Rev. Samuel Auchmuty to Rev. John Waring, 1761

1. *This report by a Virginia Anglican cleric details the difficulties he is having convincing planters to allow their enslaved Africans to attend catechism classes. It also requests more textbooks, which the minister will use to instruct the slaves in Anglican catechism. In so doing, he was giving them a step-by-step introduction into English society.*

2. *Another report, this one by Reverend Samuel Auchmuty of the Bray Associates in New York City, detailing his activities among local slaves and listing their owners and names. The slaves' names, which are either biblical or common English names, indicate a large degree of personal acculturation.*

*Source:* John C. Van Horne, ed., *Religious Philanthropy and Colonial Slavery: The American Correspondence of the Associates of Dr. Bray, 1717–1772* (Urbana and Chicago: University of Illinois Press, 1985), pp. 166–167, 207–208.

## REV. ALEXANDER STEWART TO REV. JOHN WARING

BATH N: CAROLINA
MAY THE 1ST. 1764

*Revd. Sir,*

I recd. your favour of the 7th. of April 1763,1 which I shou'd have answered much Sooner; had I not waited to return a more Satisfac- ory one, than that I am at present Obliged for to give.

Upon Shewing your Letters, to some of the Inhabitants, I was fed up with Hopes of erecting three Schools in this & the neighbouring Counties in a Short time; but after I had distributed parts of your Books among the School masters & encourag'd them all I could, I found at length that it was but Labour & Sorrow, owing to the mean, low Prejudices of the People of North America. I made one Short lived Effort, you may see by the Inclosed to erect a School (not altogether on the Societies plan) for the Instruction of ten Indian & Negro Children at Attamuskeet in Hyde County; The Master in the Letter signd Jas: Francis shews you the Objections of the people, & the Expectations we are to have. He instructed six Indian Boys & Girls whom I baptized in October 1763, their ages & names you may see bythe Inclos'd rect. for his Quarters Sallary which I have paid, but Whither He continues or not, I am uncertain of, having not since heard from him, It being above 70 Miles by Water from this place.

The other Letter from Anthony Kinnin who lives about 30 miles to the Westward of this town, I likewise inclose to you, that your So-ciety may see that I have not been regardless of their good & pious Design, and tho' it has not been in my power hitherto to carry it on to any Purpose, yet that my best Wishes attend it, & that I shall always be reddy upon the least dawn of Success, again to renew my endeavours.

The 1st. Box of Books directed to Mr. Palmer I have never had in possession but remains in his Stores unopened; the 2d. Box I almost distributed and am Sorry to no better purpose. The remain-

der may beorderd to any place where they will be more useful but they can be carried to no place where they are more wanted among the poor & Ignorant Whites.

I am Revd. Sir your obedient & humble Servant

*Alexr: Stewart*

It wou'd give me great pleasure to correspond with the Society, & to know whether an Indian School in the Manner I have begun, comes within their Scheme.

Ballance due to me is 33s. 9d. Sterling.

## REV. SAMUEL AUCHMUTY TO REV. JOHN WARING

NEW YORK OCTOBER THE 7TH. 1761.

*Revd. Sir*

Your very obliging favor of the first of last June, is now before me, & affords me a very sensible pleasure; as, it acquaints me that my proceedings, with regard to the Negro School, in this City, have hitherto met with the Approbation of so worthy a set of Gentlemen, as are the Associates of that late truely Christian Divine, Dr. Bray. It certainly is the indispensable Duty of every Clergyman, to use his utmost endeavors to inlarge the Kingdom of our blessed Redeemer, which is the glorious design of the Associates; and, I have the happiness to think, & say, that it is also the Inclination, & hearty desire, of the American Clergy, sincerely to join with their worthy Brethren, on your side the Water, in every Scheme, that can be offered, towards the promoting so laudable, and glorious an Undertaking.

As the Negro's here are more immediately intrusted to my Care, by that very worthy & charitable Body, the Society for the Propagation of the Gospel in foreign parts; so, the Negro School has a right to demand all the Care & Attention that I can spare it; And, I thank God, my Duty happily co-incides with my Inclination, and pleasure. I could indeed wish, that the Duties of this parish, which are very great, and executed by my very worthy Friend, & Brother, Dr. Barclay, and my self, as his Assistant, would allow me more time, to visit the School, than I now have: however, I take care that few Week's pass without My going to the School, & examining the Scholars. And, I now upon a very late Visit, can with pleasure inform you, that the School is quite full; that several have been refused for want of Room; that the mistress appears to be very diligent & Industrious; that the Children are clean, & orderly, & begin to read, sow, say their Catechise & prayers, as well as I could expect for the time.

In your Letter You observe, that the Associates, are inform'd, that "too many both of Masters & Slaves are possessed with a groundless perswasion that Baptism breaks asunder the bonds of Slavery." If the Information extends to this province, I am very confident it is a very wrong one; for, I am very sure there are very few Negro Children born here but what are baptized; & out of the thirty now in the school, only three are unbaptized, & the Owners of these three have requested me to baptize them, which I shall soon do. For some Years

past I have not baptized less than 80, or 90 Negro Children, & often upwards of 100; besides, several Adults. Dr. Barclay has also baptized many, & the Dutch Ministers & the Dissenters dayly do the same, and yet they continue peaceable Slaves.

## Abigail Franks to Naphtali Franks, June 7, 1743

*This letter details the marriage of the daughter of a Jewish merchant in New York to the son of a wealthy Anglican family. The marriage indicates how prosperous Jews assimilated through marriage into the dominant English ethnic group. Although the letter writer is not especially happy about the union, she is clearly prepared to accept it.*

*Source:* Leo Hershkowitz and Isadore S. Meyer, eds., *The Lee Max Friedman Collection of American Jewish Colonial Correspondence, Letters of the Franks Family, Studies in American Jewish History*, no. 5 (Waltham, Mass., American Jewish Historical Society, 1968), pp. 116–122.

FLATT BUSH [TUESDAY]
JUNE 7TH 1743

*Dear HeartSey*

My Wishes for your Felicity Are As great as the Joy I have to hear You Are happyly Married May the Smiles of Providence Waite allways on y[ou]r Inclinations And your Dear Phila's whome I Salute with Tender affections pray[in]g kind Heaven to be propitious to Your wishes in making her a happy mother I Shall think the time Teadious Until I Shall have that happy Information for I dont Expect to hear it by the return of these Ships and therefore must Injoyn Your care in Writting by the first Oppertunity (after the birth of wathever it shall please god to bless you with) Either by Via Carrolina barbadoz or any other. I am now retired from Town and would from my Self (if it Where Possiable to have Some peace of mind) from the Severe Affliction I am Under on the Conduct of that Unhappy Girle Good God Wath a Shock it was when they Acquainted me She had Left the House and Had bin Married Six months I can hardly hold my Pen whilst I am a writting it Itts wath I Never could have Imagined Especialy Affter wath I heard her Soe often Say that noe Consideration in Life should Ever Induce her to Disoblige Such good parents. I had heard the report of her goeing to be married to Oliver delancey but As Such Reports had offten bin of Either off your Sisters I gave noe heed to it further than a Generall Caution of her Conduct wich has allways bin Unblemish[e]d And is Soe Still in the Eye of the Christians whoe allow She has DisObliged Us but has in noe way bin Dishonorable being married to a man of worth and Charector My Spirits Was for Some time Soe Depresst that it was a pain to me to Speak or See Any one I have Over come it Soe far as not to make My Concern Soe Conspicuous but I Shall Never have that Serenity nor Peace within I have Soe happyly had hittherto My house has bin my prisson Ever Since I had not heart Enough to Goe Near the Street door, its a pain to me to think off goeing again to Town And If your Fathers buissness would Premit him to Live out of it I never

would Goe Near it Again I wish it was in my Power to Leave this part of the world I would come away in the first man of war that went to London. Oliver has Sent Many times to beg Leave to See me but I never would tho' now he Sent word that he will come here I dread Seeing him and how to Avoid I know noe way. Neither if he comes can I Use him rudly I May Make him Some reproaches but I know My Self soe well that I Shall at Last be Civill tho' I never will give him Leave to Come to my house in Town And as for his wife I am Determined I never will See nor Lett none of ye Family Goe near her he intends to write to You and My brother Isaac to Endeavour a reconcilation I would have You Answer his Letter. if you dont hers for I must be Soe Ingenious [as] to conffess nature is Very Strong and It would give me a Great Concern if She Should Live Un happy tho' its a Concern she does not Meritt. As to the Other Affair you wrote me Abouth You may be Very Eassy on that head the Person Concern'd will give You All the Sattisfaction you desire Wath you say abouth y[ou]r Sisters comeing to England I shall Very readly agree to it and the Sooner the better if it was only a Means of her not Seeing the Other wich She will hardly be able to avoid Unless She intirely Excludes her Self from all Company wich She has don for this three months past tho' Phila has not bin in Town Since she Left Us but has (wathever I have forbid) found means to Send Messages for as they Lived Very Affectionately it Subsists Still And I am Sure She will find all the means She Can to See Richa. I thank you and your Dear Phila in the behalf of your

Sisters & My Self for the Profussion of Preas[en]ts Sent Uss I Shall make mine Up but cant Tell when I Shall Wear it for in the mind I am in now I have noe Inclination for dress or Visiting ye Girles will Make theres Up as Soon as they goe to Town wich will be ye Latter end of the Summer they was Just in mourning for my aunt Isaacs whoe had bin Just Dead when they receiv[e]d them the reasson why I did not Write to Mr. Aaron Franks was not from [lack of] a Due Sence of Obligations and Gratitude but from an Apprehensiveness of being Trouble Some You may Assure him I am Sensiable of the many kindnesses and Favours rec[eiv]ed from him And it gives me pain to Express my Gratitude because wathever I Can Say falls Short of wath is his due from my Family and my Self, tho' If I can bring my mind into any State of Ease I Shall write him by this I wish I could find Any thing Agreeable to send to my Dear Phila Moses Sends her a pott of Sweet meets and mordechay Gomez's wife has Given me a Small pot for You wich I dare Say is Exceeding Good. And I hope You may Use it with pleassure All Friends Say many kind things to You And wish you a great deall of Joy, I shall take Care and Send Some quaills next faull and secure them better than ye Last. Make my Compliments to Uncle Abraham Franks with thanks for his kind Letters wich I Shall not Answer by this And therefore Desire you would make an Excuse for me Your brother david I hope will doe Very well the Ship is not yet Arrived at Phil[ade]l[phia] as to w[a]th you Say Concerning My brother Nathans Marrying your reassons are perfectly Just but then on the Other

hand it is a great Disadvantage for a man to keep house without a good Mistress Soe that a Wife to him is a Nesscessary Evill my brother mich[a]ell keeps his health And Good Charector wich is to me a great Satisfaction Sol[omon] Hart is absconded in Very Unhappy Circumstance his wife and child is with [about two words made illegible by the fold] wich is all they've got for the honor of being Allyed to M H[ar]t Its Commonly Said the rich man is gods Steward. M H[ar]t is a Very Saveing one whoe will Lett a brother Perish when Such a Triffle as £200 might make him happy the married Sister wrote him She had some Tickets in the Lottery and if She got a good Prise she would Send him a pr[e]s[en]t if the prayers of the poor Prevaill She may have Success if Sol[omon] Hart puts Up prayers for her being he is Realy Poor & Needy

Now Lett me Say Something for the Distress wee are more nearly Concern'd in and that is poor good moses Solomons is that Unhappy Youth to Spend the best part of his Life as it Where in a Goall for Such may be Termed the Confin[e]d Life he is in att pr[e]s[en]t. wee rec[eiv]ed Letters from him Last week wherin he Complains Pittyously of the Ill Treatm[en]t he meets with from his friends whoe he hardly hears from and when he does never Lett him know wath will be the Consequence of his Detention or wich way he may be cleared Its Very Severe that he Must be the Victim of anothers Villiany the manner in wich he Committed his Error was wath a person of Greater penatration in buissness might have fell into, his Letting Mr. [Sam] Levy come off was noe fault because Mr. Levys pretence was to Come here in order to make Up his Own Affairs that he might the better be inable'd to assist in Dischargeing there Joynt Debts: wich I am affraid he has not much in his power to per form Your Father will Give You a farther Acc[oun]t of this Mellancholy affair. wich I wish may in some Meassure be Happly Terminated: My Compliments to Mrs. Compton & Capt[ain] Riggs I beg they will be Soe good to forgive me that I dont Answer there agreeable Favour by this: my Spirets is too Depresst to write It is with reluctancy I doe write to Any one at pr[e]s[en]t therefore whoever I Omit You must Excuse me to them I think I've Spun this to a Considerable Lenght and shall Conclude with the Repetition of my prayers for Your Health and Happyness I am

> My Dear Son
> Your Affectionate Mother
> Abigaill Franks

P.S: Nap[htal]y Hart myers goes on Very well he had noe View but the Discharge of His duty when he Offered his Service to Come over to be with that poor Unhappy Youth whoe I Hartly wish may be Reinstated to his health both of body & mind.

## Daniel Horsmanden, *The New York Conspiracy*, 1741

*This brief excerpt indicates the presence of "Spanish Negroes" in New York. These were free people from Colombia who had been kidnapped by slave traders and brought to New York City and sold into slavery. Their desire for revenge is clear in this excerpt. Also note-worthy are the combinations of names of the conspirators, which show use of English, biblical, and African derivation.*

*Source:* Thomas J. Davis, ed., *The New York Conspiracy* by Daniel Horsmanden (Boston: Beacon Press, 1971), pp. 117–121.

## MONDAY, JUNE 1.

*Examination* of Sandy (Niblet's negro) before one of the judges—No. 3.—He said,

1. "That he heard by captain Lush's house, about six of the Spaniards (about fourteen days before the fort was burnt) say, that if the captain would not send them to their own country, they would ruin all the city; and the first house they would burn should be the captain's, for they did not care what they did: He (Sandy) stood by Arden's door, and they did not (as he thought) see him; and that (pointing to Lush's house) they said, *d—n that son of a b—h, they would make a devil of him:* which was the first time he ever heard of the conspiracy.

2. "That the second time Quack (y) called to him by Coentics Market, and told him he wanted to speak to him; and said, will you help to burn the fort? and answered as he said at the trial, and in his examination before the grand jury; said that Quack told him the first time he met him, he would make an end of him.

3. "That the third time, at Comfort's house, one Sunday, when Comfort's Jack called to him to come to him,

and he went in, Sarah (Burk's negro wench) d——d him, and bid him drink, having before refused.

4. "That there was a great number of negroes present, and about six Spanish negroes among them; but none of them were the same that he saw at Lush's. That he did drink.

5. "That Comfort's Jack brought out about eleven penknives, which were rusty; some complained their knives were dull and would not cut, which they went to sharpen on a stone; Jack (Comfort's) said his knife was so sharp, that if it came a-cross a white man's head, it would cut it off; on which he (Sandy) said, if you want to fight, go to the Spaniards, and not fight with your masters.

6. "That they asked him (and Comfort's Jack in particular) if he would help to burn some houses; he cried: on which Jack (Comfort's) said, d——n you, do you cry? I'll cut your head off in a hurry, and surrounded him; on which Burk's wench said he deserved it, if he would not say yes, on which he consented, and said yes; whereupon they did not threaten him, but bid him say nothing to black or white about it, and every one would do his part, and take a round, and fire the town.

7. "That Jack (Comfort's) said they had not men enough this year, but next year would do it, every one present was to set his master's house on fire first, and then do the rest at once, and set all the houses on fire in the town, which when they had done, they would kill all the white men, and have their wives for themselves.

8. "That Mr. Moore's Cato, Caesar (Pintard's negro), Mr. Jay's Brash, Jack (that is in jail) knows him if he sees; Todd's Dundee, Chambers's Robin, Patrick (English's), Peck's Caesar, a Caromantee, Cowley's Cato, Comfort's Maph alias Cook, Kip's Harry, and three country negroes, who called Comfort's Jack, uncle, and brother, and cousin, burnt) Ben Moore's Tom, Leffert's Pompey, Duane's Prince, Comfort's old Caromantee woman, Vaarck's Caesar (hanged) were there also; the room being quite full.

9. "That Augustine and Wilkins' Fortune were to burn their master's houses, which he heard them say, as they were talking by Frazier's corner, about a week before the fort was burnt.

10. "That at the aforesaid meeting at Comfort's Jack, the old man, and the old woman, and three of the Spaniards were sworn to the effect, that the first thunder that came, might strike them dead, if they did not stand to their words.

11. "That they asked him to come again the next day to be sworn; the rest said they would come to be sworn the next day."

The negroes Tom (Ben Moore's), Prince (Duane's), and Pompey (Leffert's), apprehended and committed.

*Examination* of Fortune, (Wilkins's negro) before one of the judges—No. 3.— He said,

1. "That Quack (z) one Sabbath day afternoon, asked him to walk into the

fields, and pressed him to it: third meeting, told him he should see a great alteration at the fort; and told him that they were going to burn the fort; threatened that some of his mates would poison him if he told.

2. "That Niblet's boy told him that Gomez's negro was to assist in burning the fort.

3. "That he heard Quack talk to Gomez's negro Cuffee on the dock, that he must meet him to burn the house, and if white people came, to shoot them with pistols; which was before the meeting him by Mr. Rickets's.

4. "That when he asked Sandy (Niblet's negro) who was to burn the fort? He answered, Quack, himself, and Gomez's Cuffee; that he asked him (Sandy, Niblet's negro) to be concerned and that he said to Quack, he had no mind to be hanged, he might go to h—ll and be d—d.

5. "That he never talked to any negro but Quack and Niblet's about any conspiracy or design of firing.

6. "Never heard of a house where they met, nor knew Hughson. Cuffee however, has asked him to go down to a house by the north river, and dance with him; but he never did."

*Examination* of Sarah, (Burk's negro wench) before one of the judges, Mr. Chambers, and others—No. 2.—She said,

1. "That one Sunday afternoon, about four or five of the clock, she was at Comfort's house, in the kitchen, about five weeks before the fort was fired; a great many negroes sitting round the table, betwixt twenty and thirty, amongst whom were Dr. Fisher's Harry, Bagley's Jemmy, widow Schuyler's tall slender negro, Abeel's mulatto Tom, Niblet's Sandy. She staid there about an hour, and rum was there; Mrs. Clopper's Betty, Robin (Chamber's negro), Mr. Clarkson's Tom, Old Frank, Philipse's Cuffee, Teller's Sarah, Vaarck's Caesar, Auboyneau's Prince, Comfort's Jack, Comfort's Cook, Comfort's Jenny, Jack a busy man, Patrick (English's boy), Hunt's Warwick (a negro that cut his throat), Todd's Dundee, Brinkerhoff's Tom, Pintard's Caesar, Old Kip's Harry, Teneyck's Bill, Silvester's Sambo, a tall negro living at John Dewit's (a stranger), Kierstead's Braveboy, John Hunt's Jenny, the Long Bridge Boys. Patrick (English's boy) used to say, let us go to Romer's —Alsteyn's Cato, Shurmur's Cato, Leffert's Pompey: Comfort's Jack and others sharpened their knives, and said they would go and set fire along the docks; Comfort's Jack proposed the fort first; Cook said no, they would find them out if they did: every one was to set their master's house on fire; Clopper's Betty carried her there; they swore, and said they wished thunder might strike them to the hearts if they told. Three negroes, viz.—Comfort's two, and old Harry, swore; Cuffee was sworn, and Caesar, Auboyneau's Prince. All that made the right bargain swore, the rest were to come the next day; De Lancey's Anthony there, and Roosevelt's

Quack: Comfort's Jack drew out his knife and threatened the negro of Niblet, on which Sandy consented.

2. "That they whetted their knives on a stone, some complaining that their knives were rusty and blunt, and some said that their knives were sharp enough to cut a white man's head, that they would kill the white men, and have the white women for their wives.

3. "That on a dispute between them, Quack was pitched upon to fire the fort; others having refused, Quack undertook it; Curacoa Dick there, and consented.

4. "Confessed she threatened Niblet's negro, and bid them cut his head off, if he did not drink.

5. "That she believed there were Spanish negroes there, and that Mr. Moore's Cato was there, and consented."

# CHAPTER 3
# THE LIMITS OF EQUALITY: RACIAL AND ETHNIC TENSIONS IN THE NEW REPUBLIC, 1789–1836

## MARION R. CASEY

*There is no place in the world where a man meets so rich a reward for good conduct and industry as in America.* —JOHN DUNLAP, PHILADELPHIA, 12 MAY 1789

IN THE WAKE OF THE RATIFICATION of the Constitution, the United States ventured forth into a democratic experience without any road map and with a wary eye on the French version evolving across the Atlantic. By the time Andrew Jackson's presidency was coming to a close, the republican ideal of equality for all had been put to the test on several fronts. Four overlapping spheres—broadly labeled citizenship, religion, language, and segregation—dominated political and social intercourse during this half-century. An increasingly multiethnic, multiracial population pushed at their interstices, forcing Anglo-Americans to attempt reconciliation between policy and practice.

The Constitution called for uniform rules of naturalization and of representation based on the population of the United States. It allowed for the regulation of commerce with Indian tribes, permitted the migration or importation of "such persons as any of the states now existing shall think proper to admit" until 1808, provided for equal legal jurisdiction in all the states over persons "held to service or labour," and banned religious tests as the basis for holding public office. This appressed form of articulation is, in fact, the document's only commentary on issues related to race and ethnicity. There appears to have been no need to make explicit in the actual Constitution that which its intended audience already understood: in practice there were limits to equality.

Despite its basis in the philosophy of natural rights, the Constitution did not create a polycracy. During the ratification process between November 1789 and December 1791, ten amendments emerged to address personal liberties in more specific language. Even so, the Bill of Rights did not anticipate areas of civil interaction that would require delicate negotiation in a diverse population, save for the proscription on an established religion in the first amendment. In practice, the socially vulnerable and the politically disfranchised—immigrants, indentured servants, redemptioners, Indians, and slaves—often remained marginalized or ineligible for the privileges of natural rights and their political corollary, equality, throughout the New Republic.

Between 1789 and 1836 the profile of the United States changed in fundamental ways. There was a fourfold increase in the total population, from 3.9 to 17 million. The number of square miles within its territorial jurisdiction—stretching from the Atlantic to the Rockies—doubled to 1.8 million, up from 889,000 at the end of the Revolution. This was accompanied by an administrative expansion as a dozen new states were admitted to the Union, encompassing Maine to Louisiana. Even as the majority of the American people were concentrated in rural areas, there was a dramatic increase in the residents of cities. The number of urban places with more than twenty-five hundred people jumped from twenty-four in 1790 to ninety in 1830. New York City's population multiplied by six—easily taking the lead as the country's largest—but Baltimore, Boston, Philadelphia, Charleston, and New Orleans also grew during that period, though in less spectacular demographic proportions. Significantly, much of this was the result of in-migration rather than natural growth.

A federal law mandating an enumeration of the population was passed in 1790, and the census count began on August 1. Once the tally of all fifteen states was in, the population of the United States stood about evenly divided between the North, with 1,968,040, and the South, with 1,961,174. Because of a political compromise, enslaved blacks counted for only three-fifths of a white when determining proportional representation in Congress. The categories developed for the census to calculate this "three-fifths compromise" embodied a classification system in which everyone was measured against "white"—the designation into which 80.7 percent of the 1790 population fell.

While the dominant race of the United States may have been "white," by no means was this homogeneous. The word encompassed much ethnic and linguistic variety—Irish, Scots, Welsh, Germans, Dutch, Swiss, French, Swedes, and Spanish as well as English. The composition of this foreign-stock population was determined by three surname analyses of the 1790 census completed in the twentieth century. Although not without error and controversy, the surname method is a rudimentary measure (in the absence of any better) that serves to document the diversity of the country's Northern European roots. The very broadest generalizations point to the predominance of peoples from the British Isles (including Ireland) and Germany, with settlement patterns that were increasingly non-English the further south and west of New York City one went in the early national period. The regional dispersion of this population was focused on the Middle Atlantic states, partly a reflection of the preeminence of Baltimore, Philadelphia, and New York as ports of arrival. The most ethnic states in 1790 were Pennsylvania, with its large German element, and New York and New Jersey, where colonial Dutch settlement had been concentrated.

By contrast, the most "racial" states were Virginia, Maryland, and the Carolinas. The black population was ten times greater in the South than in the North in 1790. The North-South racial disparity is best illustrated by Massachusetts, which (with a population of 378,787) was almost as dense as North Carolina (with a population of 393,751), although the former had no slaves and the latter had more than one hundred thousand. The census established that 18 percent of the American population was enslaved and 42 percent of all slaves lived in Virginia. In addition, it counted 59,557 free blacks, or 12.7 percent of a total black population of 757,181.

Native Americans, on the other hand, were not considered citizens and therefore were neither taxed nor counted in the 1790 census. Under the Constitution, tribes were classified as foreign nations, and their relationship to the United States was diplomatic. It was 1820 before enumerators broke out figures for the 4,631 Native Americans who paid taxes within the borders of the United States and, by including a question on citizenship, counted some fifty-three thousand resident aliens.

The naturalization of foreign-born whites became one of the key issues to emerge during the era of partisan politics that began in the 1790s. The first Congress required only two years residency for citizenship. This entitled a propertied man to the vote but, in the wake of the French Revolution, it also gave many Americans pause. The European who had simply been a "colonist" before Independence was, in the period of the New Republic, reconceptualized as an "immigrant," a word with increasingly pejorative connotations. It came to symbolize all that was the opposite of the Anglo-American ideal, a convenient scapegoat for any national ill. Restrictionist attitudes appeared, such as that expressed by Federalist Congressman Harrison Gray Otis (1765–1848): "If some means are not adopted to prevent the indiscriminate admission of wild Irishmen and others to the right of suffrage, there will soon be an end to liberty and property."

At the end of February 1794 Albert Gallatin's Swiss birth was used to prevent him from taking his elected seat as a Senator from Pennsylvania on a residency technicality. With bipartisan support, the residency requirement was raised to five years in 1795 during a spate of Gallophobia. By the spring of 1797 attitudes had hardened further. The Federalists proposed a $20 tax on naturalization certificates, arguing that the United States needed to discourage immigration. Harrison Gray Otis declared that America could no longer afford to invite the "turbulent and disorderly of all parts of the world, to come here with a view to disturb our tranquility, after having succeeded in the overthrow of their own Governments." The tax was not passed; nevertheless, the following year Congress enacted four laws to suppress domestic dissent that had implications for those of foreign birth. Thereafter, ethnicity was a factor to a certain extent in determining political alignments: Anglo-Americans were typically Federalist, whereas Irish, Scots, and Germans were Democratic-Republicans.

The most severe of the alien laws was a Naturalization Act that again lengthened the residency requirement for citizenship from five to fourteen years and mandated the registration of all foreigners living in the United States. Combined with the Sedition Act, it effectively blocked those with European sympathies from influencing American elections. The first victim of the speech provisions of the Sedition Act was Irish-born Matthew Lyon, a naturalized citizen serving as a Republican congressman from Vermont. He was fined $1,000 and sentenced to four months' imprisonment for criticizing President John Adams in print. He served his term in the Vergennes jail, which he described in a letter to the *Independent Chronicle* in November 1798 as the "common receptacle for horse-thieves, money-makers, runaway-negroes, or any kind of felons." Indeed there was an element of racism in the selective way in which the sedition law was put into effect. The Federalists called Lyons an "animal who apes a monkey," who "talks and writes a gibberish between Wild Irish and vulgar American."

Likewise, when Dr. James Reynolds of Philadelphia protested the Alien and Sedition Acts, he was actually prosecuted for "seditious riot." Reynolds was a United Irish political refugee. Following a short but bloody uprising in Ireland in 1798 that had had French support, the British government banned these rebels from its territories. Hundreds, like Reynolds, sailed immediately from Belfast for New York or Philadelphia. But the American ambassador in London, the Federalist Rufus King, vigorously protested further banishment to the United States, and the leaders of the United Irishmen were imprisoned in Scotland instead. As he wrote to the American secretary of state, "I cannot persuade myself that the Malcontents of any character or country will ever become useful Citizens of ours." King lived to rue these words. Once Thomas Jefferson took office, draconian anti-immigrant legislation was allowed to expire, restoring the five-year naturalization period and clearing the way for the emigration of the Irish political prisoners. Among them were the able lawyers Thomas Addis Emmet (1764–1827) and William Sampson (1764–1836), who encouraged Irish support for the pro-immigrant party of Jefferson.

Naturalization again surfaced as an issue during the Napoleonic Wars, but this time the United States was forced to defend its foreign-born. The Royal Navy boldly stopped American trading vessels and forcibly impressed former British subjects into service to replenish its ranks under the principle "once an Englishman, always an Englishman." An estimated six to eight thousand citizens were impressed between 1803 and 1812 despite American efforts to protect them through trade sanctions and military force. Thirteen American ships sailing from Ireland were intercepted in 1812, including four still in Irish waters. At the same time, federal restrictions limited the freedom of English immigrants on the mainland who had maritime activities. New York City merchants of English birth, for example, were interned upstate at Fishkill, and a similar relocation occurred in Charleston, South Carolina, to prevent potentially subversive acts.

Suspicion of foreign-born loyalties was perennial. In 1835, in response to a suggestion by the *New York Evening Post* editor that immigrants be naturalized after twelve months in a state and six months in a town or ward, New York University professor Samuel F. B. Morse (1791–1872) wrote:

> he would put the Foreigner, the moment of his landing, on the same footing with native American citizens no matter from what country he may come, no matter what his early habits, his character or condition, whether Hottentot or Turk, or Russian serf, or New-Zealand cannibal; the moment he sets foot on our shores, and simply sig-

nifies a wish to become a citizen, he is to be a citizen. He would in fact give foreigners of all kinds, not merely the protection, and instruction, and other advantages of citizenship, but the privilege also of electing our rulers; yes, and of being themselves preferred and elected over native Americans.

Immigrant entitlement during this period hinged not only on citizenship. While the federal Constitution guaranteed religious expression, some states continued to distinguish it from civil rights. In New York all naturalized citizens seeking political office were required to take an oath of loyalty. Other states, like New Jersey, Delaware, and North Carolina, restricted elective office to Protestants, a policy that excluded Jews as well as Catholics. Catholicism, in particular, presented a challenge to republican ideals. Early Catholic leaders were sensitive to their position as a barely tolerated minority, acutely aware of American Protestant suspicions about any foreign jurisdiction. Their immediate priority following the Revolution was to change the status of the American church from "mission" to "national" in order to remove any dependency on the Propaganda office in Rome. The connection with the Vatican was to be spiritual rather than temporal, given current political prejudices.

At the end of the eighteenth century association with the Pope—a "foreign prince"—was compounded by a rise in the number of foreign-born Catholics. In addition to French speakers who had been inherited from the Diocese of Quebec in the recently acquired territory between the Appalachians and the Mississippi, Irish immigrants had already begun to dilute what had hitherto been an English- and German-stock Catholic population on the eastern seaboard. This caused significant administrative problems because, although the understaffed church needed priests, many itinerant European clergymen refused to take direction from American church leaders. Irish priests in New York, French priests in Boston, and German priests in Philadelphia all caused internal dissent that reflected poorly on Catholicism in general at the very moment that Catholics were struggling to gain civil rights in various states as well as independent jurisdiction from Rome.

A new era of ecclesiastical structure or authority for the Catholic Church in the United States began with the selection of John Carroll (1736–1815) as its first Bishop in 1789. Based in Baltimore, Carroll took charge of an estimated thirty-five thousand Catholics, nearly two-thirds of whom were in Maryland (including approximately three thousand African slaves). The timing of Carroll's appointment coincided not only with these image problems but with political upheaval on the Continent. The American Catholic Church was thus in a unique position to offer refuge to European religious orders, like the Sulpicians, who were threatened by the French Revolution. In the continued absence of a native-born clergy, the public face of Catholicism at the parish level during this period therefore continued to be foreign. Carroll insisted that European priests serving under him in America

learn English as well as American laws and customs. With Carroll's encouragement, a vernacular edition of the Catholic Bible was published by Mathew Carey in 1790. Nevertheless, by 1820 the consequences of a foreign-born clergy were being felt through a more traditional and conservative strand of practice appearing in the American church.

A critical turning point in the acquisition of civil rights for Catholics was the refusal of Fr. Anthony Kohlmann, a Jesuit from Alsace, to divulge the identity of a thief because he had received the information while hearing confession. This 1813 test case became the first free-exercise-of-religion litigation in American constitutional history and, in the words of legal historian Walter J. Walsh, the "jurisgenerative origin of the priest-penitent evidentiary privilege." Arguing in New York's Court of General Sessions, William Sampson, a Protestant lawyer from Ireland, darkly contrasted England's history of Catholic discrimination with the protections promised by the American constitution. He concluded that providence had decreed this land to be "the grave of persecution, and the cradle of tolerance," declaring, "every citizen here is in his own country. To the protestant it is a protestant country; to the catholic, a catholic country; and the jew, if he pleases, may establish in it his New Jerusalem."

Sampson published the trial as *The Catholic Question in America* (1813), but minds and hearts were slower to change than the law. The problem with religious toleration was that by the second decade of the nineteenth century, Catholics from Ireland vastly outnumbered those of any other ethnicity. Their immigration became particularly significant to the rapid expansion of the Catholic Church in America after 1820. "Its growth here appears to me almost impossible," Frances Kemble (1809–1893) noted,

> for if ever there were two things more opposite in their nature than all other things, they are the spirit of the Roman Catholic religion, and the spirit of the American people. It's true, that of the thousands who take refuge from poverty upon this plenteous land, the greater number bring with them that creed, but the very air they inhale here presently gives them a political faith, so utterly incompatible with the spirit of subjection, that I shall think the Catholic priesthood here workers of miracles, to retain anything like the influence over their minds which they possessed in those countries, where all creeds, political and polemical, have but one watch-word—faith and submission.

The United States was still culturally Anglo-Saxon, and soon, inherited racial attitudes toward the Irish surfaced that, combined with anti-Catholicism, resulted in the rise of virulent nativism. In 1827 the Society for the Defence of the Roman Catholic Religion from Calumny and Abuse, in response to what it felt was a libelous attack by the Gideonite Society in Philadelphia, published a fourth edition of Mathew Carey's pamphlet *Letters on Religious Persecution* for free distribution. The parliamentary campaign for Catholic emancipation in Ireland in 1829 no doubt exacerbated nativist conditions in the United States, particularly in cities like New Orleans, where moral and financial support for Daniel O'Connell was very public among Irish immigrants. The backlash included anti-Irish employment ads such as those in New York protested by *The Truth Teller*, a Catholic weekly:

> Wanted.—A woman well-qualified to take charge of the cooking and washing of a family—any one but a Catholic who can come well recommended may call at 57 John Street.
>
> (*Journal of Commerce,* 8 July 1830)

> Wanted.—A Cook or a Chambermaid. They must be American, Scotch, Swiss, or African—no Irish.
>
> (*Evening Post,* 4 September 1830)

Passions were further aroused by the mob burning of St. Mary's in New York City the following year and an Ursuline convent and school in Charlestown, Massachusetts, in 1834, as well as by the publication of sensational tracts like Samuel F. B. Morse's *Imminent Dangers to the Free Institutions of the United States Through Foreign Immigration* (1835) and Maria Monk's *Awful Disclosures of the Hotel Dieu Nunnery of Montreal* (1836).

Not only was Catholicism perceived as "immigrant" in the 1820s and 1830s, it was also seen as urban. The confluence of cities, race, and ethnicity had ramifications when cholera struck the United States in 1832. Lack of understanding about its scientific causes led to an assumption of moral depravity, seemingly confirmed through accepted stereotypes of the urban poor—often African Americans or Irish living in crowded and unsanitary conditions—who were its principal victims. "Whether he was free or slave, Americans believed, the Negro's innate character invited cholera," wrote medical historian Charles Rosenberg in 1962. "He was, with few exceptions, filthy and careless in his personal habits, lazy and ignorant by temperament. A natural fatalist, moreover, he took no steps to protect himself from disease." A similar profile was drawn of Irish immigrants, with the additional onus of supposedly having aided cholera in breaching the Atlantic divide. In September 1832, New Yorker Philip Hone confided to his diary,

> they have brought the cholera this year and they will always bring wretchedness and want. The boast that our country is an asylum for the oppressed in other parts of the world is very philanthropic and sentimental, but I fear that we shall before long derive little comfort from being made the almshouse and refuge for the poor of other countries.

Underpinning relations with (not between) African Americans and Irish lay a widely accepted hierarchy of race that degraded the humanity of both groups. Nevertheless "whiteness" mattered—in the decennial census as we have seen—and in other legislation such as New York State's suffrage extension in 1821 and again in 1826, which removed property qualifications and voting restrictions for

all men except for blacks. This gave the Irish a ballot but little else; from this point until the Emancipation Proclamation in 1863, the relationship of the two groups to northern Protestant Americans diverged considerably in the political arena. The abolitionist movement elevated the African American to a cause célèbre at the same time that Irish were denigrated by Whig elites. During the election of 1834, the *New England Review* called the Irish "the most corrupt, the most debased, and the most brutally ignorant portion of the population of our large cities" while the Journal of Commerce wrote that "Colored Persons" were "attached to our institutions, and are intelligent, and in many respects far better qualified to participate in our elections." Nevertheless, compared to the average American, blacks and the Irish were on a par socially and economically. And, like the Irish, African Americans had developed religious congregations and institutions that set them apart from white Protestants, such as the A.M.E. Zion Church, established in 1796, and the African Methodist Episcopal Church, founded in 1816.

While the moral tensions inherent in perpetuating bondage in a democratic society were part of the new federal political discourse, it was pure economics that kept slavery alive in the United States after 1790. The invention of the cotton gin in 1792 resolved the impending crisis in the southern plantation system by facilitating a shift away from tobacco, rice, and indigo toward a more lucrative cash crop. Growing cotton was labor-intensive and, as it dominated the southern economy, the number of slaves nearly tripled—from more than seven-hundred thousand in 1790 to 2.3 million in 1830. Slavery was increasingly a southern institution, especially after New York (1799) and New Jersey (1804) joined the other northern states that had already outlawed it.

Fear in the aftermath of the 1791 uprising in Haiti led to the passage of legislation regulating slave imports, especially in southern states like the Carolinas, Virginia, and Maryland. Fear was also the genesis of the Fugitive Slave Act of 1793, which gave wide latitude to masters in retrieving their human "property." Under this law, African Americans could be convicted on oral testimony only and were not privy to trial by jury, rights which white ethnics enjoyed under the Bill of Rights. About ninety thousand slaves arrived in the United States between the end of the Revolution and January 1, 1808, the date after which Congress—under abolitionist pressures from Great Britain and New England—expressly banned the overseas slave trade. However, lax enforcement and the domestic sale of slaves to plantations in the new Louisiana Territory—as well as their intentional breeding for sale—allowed the slave trade to flourish during the early national period. As late as 1836, twelve thousand slaves from Virginia were sold further south when prices for prime field hands were nearing $1,200 to $1,300 in Kentucky, Georgia, Alabama, and Louisiana. A profitable adjunct to slave trading was slave hiring, which placed blacks in service and laboring work in cities and factory towns and on railroad and canal projects.

At the same time the number of free blacks in the United States increased, from 108,000 in 1800 to 386,000 in 1840. There was a concomitant drop in the number of white indentured servants in response to British restrictions on the emigration of skilled labor to the United States. Combined with relaxed—even fashionable—attitudes toward manumissions, this facilitated black entry into the northern economy, at least until Nat Turner's slave revolt in 1831 when there was considerable retrenchment:

> The calm, deliberate composure with which he spoke of his late deeds and intentions, the expression of his fiend-like face when excited by enthusiasm, still bearing the stains of the blood of helpless innocence about him; clothed with rags and covered with chains; yet daring to raise his manacled hands to heaven, with a spirit soaring above the attributes of man; I looked on him and my blood curdled in my veins.

This 1832 excerpt from Thomas R. Gray's widely circulated version of Turner's confession increased white fears and the imposition of legal restrictions became inevitable. Fanny Kemble, an English actress turned wife of plantation owner Pierce Butler, was horrified to learn about southern restrictions on basic rights. In December 1832 she recorded in her diary, "To teach a slave to read or write is to incur a penalty of fine or imprisonment. They form the larger proportion of the population, by far; and so great is the dread of insurrection on the part of the white inhabitants, that they are kept in the most brutish ignorance, and too often treated with the most brutal barbarity, in order to insure their subjection."

The enforcement of these "black codes" encouraged freed slaves to move to the north, bringing them into direct competition for jobs with Irish immigrants, especially in the mid-Atlantic cities. There were race riots between the two groups in Philadelphia in 1832 and again in 1842. In addition, both peoples faced employment and housing discrimination; relegated to the lowest service-sector positions—such as cooks, servants, waiters, and day laborers—and to the cheapest-rent districts, Irish and African Americans were the victims of pernicious stereotyping. "I never hear an Irishman called Paddy, a colored person called nigger, or the contemptuous epithet 'old beggar man,' without a pang in my heart for I know that such epithets, inadvertently used, are doing more to form the moral sentiments of the nation, than all the teachings of the schools," wrote Lydia Maria Child in 1841.

Verbal portraits of racial and ethnic groups in antebellum literature published before 1840 commonly focused on their inferior intelligence and moral capabilities rather than on extrinsic characteristics like appearance that would gain popularity at midcentury (the epitome being the simian depictions of Thomas Nast). The relationship of language to perceptions of the ethnic Other was critical, especially as Americans were defining themselves nationally in the first four decades of the nineteenth century. As the new nation rebuilt a commercial base in its port cities, colonial trading links were renewed. The demand for foreign luxury goods increased their quantity and visibility in American households. One of the consequences was a direct cognitive relationship between product and country of origin.

In other words, a product's identification with specific ethnicity or race entered Anglo-American cultural discourse. Gallophobia, for example, did not preclude a taste for French style in dress or dance fashions. The recruitment of skilled workers from England for certain industries in the United States was independent of political Anglophobia. Immigrants from Staffordshire—with an established reputation for ceramic tableware—were the backbone of the emerging American pottery manufactories at Trenton, New Jersey, from 1832. The highly desired textile printing and metalworking techniques of Lancashire and Sheffield were transferred to Massachusetts and Connecticut factories through British immigrants, enabling American-made products to compete favorably with their English counterparts in the marketplace.

But by far the greatest commercial influence on perceptions of ethnicity was the post-war trade with China. The New York firm of William Constable and Company reaped enormous profits from the 1790–1791 voyage of the *Washington*, heralding a new era in American business. Not only did China become the basis of several mercantile fortunes but chinoiserie became pervasive in social circles with disposable income. Chinese silk, tea, porcelain, and opium contributed to Orientalism, especially among the upper classes. Tea became a necessity rather than a luxury, while the practical value of other items—such as china tea sets—was surpassed only by their value as curios. Although the Chinese presence in America was negligible at the turn of the nineteenth century, Chinese goods were already well established when the Siamese twins Chang and Eng first made appearances in Boston and New York in 1829. For the thousands of Americans who paid to see the brothers over the next decade, it was their first contact with Chinese people. The physical attachment of Chang and Eng, while startling, was nevertheless in keeping with exotic perceptions of China and the Chinese that were current in the early national period. Their duplication literally made flesh a much-admired Oriental art, as the following excerpt from the diary of Anne Gorham Everett in 1835 illustrates:

> I read . . . a very curious account of the exactness of the Chinese. A lady wishing to match some beautiful china, which her husband had received from the East India Company, sent a plate to China to have some more made like it. In due time the plates arrived, and were unpacked; but every one looked as if it had a crack in it, and on examining the pattern it was found that there was a crack in the middle of it.

On the other hand, whereas by the late eighteenth century the word "Irish" in the marketplace was descriptive of good-quality, inexpensive linen, as well as salted herring and mackerel, by the early nineteenth century it had become a synonym for "barbarity." Likewise, Fanny

Kemble commented on how the blackness of slaves had been transformed into an even darker concept. Americans, she wrote, had "learned to turn the very name of their race into an insult and a reproach." In 1833 Thomas Hamilton, a Scottish traveler in the United States, remarked, "It has often happened to me, since my arrival in this country, to hear it gravely maintained by men of education and intelligence, that the Negroes were an inferior race, a link as it were between man and the brutes." This went beyond skin tone, as the New York Irish schoolmaster Patrick S. Casserly grimly observed in 1832: "If a swindler, thief, robber, or murderer, no matter what his color or country commit any nefarious or abominable act, throughout the Union, he is instantly set down as a native of Ireland." Descriptions of the Irish as lazy, unreliable, improvident, childlike, and foolish mirrored descriptions of blacks, creating a popular idiom that was deficient in the very virtues deemed necessary to good republicanism. These were familiarly summed up by the rubric "Paddy" or "Sambo," "Bridget" or "Mammy"—the serving class of white America. In New York's Sixth Ward successive mob violence by native-born whites in 1834 and 1835 targeted blacks and Irish equally, sparked by general trepidation over amalgamation (miscegenation) and foreigners.

Indians, on the other hand, were "noble savages" until at least the late 1820s. Rather than an inherently inferior people, Native Americans were perceived as victims of social, political, and economic circumstances who could be civilized. Why? Indian tribes had been defined as sovereign nations in the earliest treaties made by the United States and, unlike blacks and Irish, were not viewed as an exploitable or cheap source of labor. There were federal and religious attempts to transform tribes into yeoman stock by encouraging the adoption of cash agriculture, Anglo-American education, and political institutions. In 1790 Congress appropriated $20,000 for farming supplies for the Cherokees and in 1819 began annually endowing an Indian Civilization Fund with $10,000. The Cherokees, Chickasaws, Choctaws, and Creeks were the first to respond well but their motives were practical: the need to avoid dispossession of their lands and "black" classification in an increasingly biracial southern society. One of the hallmarks of their successful acculturation was the acquisition of the English language. The Cherokee Phoenix, a bilingual newspaper founded in 1828, as well as eighteen Cherokee schools, clearly demonstrated this by the mid-1820s.

All foreign languages suffered in the rising sense of American nationality after 1790. The supremacy of English as the dominant tongue of the United States was settled by 1815. Giovanni Antonio Grassi, an Italian Jesuit serving as president of Georgetown University at that time, observed, "English is the language universally spoken, and it is not corrupted here as in England by a variety of dialects." In fact, the appearance of books emphasizing accent elimination, such as John Walker's *A Critical Pronouncing Dictionary and Expositor of the English Language* (1818), hastened the adoption of an "American" English standard. Yet,

by the early national period, English as spoken in the United States had already absorbed many ethnic words and inflections, particularly from the intermingling of German and Irish immigrants in the backcountry. This was most pronounced in Appalachia, where the one distinct variation of American English was already evident by 1800. Words like "chaw," "ingine," and "picter" were typical of the region's so-called broad speech.

Unlike immigrants from the British Isles—among whom even these linguistic variations were still recognizable as English—communities who spoke a foreign language were marked off as different. There was natural attrition as immigration failed to replenish the supply of native speakers among the Welsh, French, and Swedes. But for others, abandoning their mother tongues was more difficult because its use was reinforced not only in the home and in the marketplace but also in church.

In the Middle Atlantic states commercial interaction with a rapidly expanding economy eroded the language faster, of necessity, so that the pulpit became the bastion of preservation, especially among the Germans of Pennsylvania and the Dutch of New York. As early as 1794 the Dutch Reformed Church of America began to adopt English, making religious services in Dutch obsolete by the late 1830s. In 1800 Lutheran Church authorities in New York favored English as the language of its official business just as fellow Germans on the western and southern frontiers began to adopt it too. Generally, urban congregations were more successful than rural ones in obtaining dispensations regarding language preference. Clergy trained abroad contributed to resistance to change, but compromises were inevitable as American-born generations pressed for religious services, Bibles, hymn books, and catechisms in English. Translation and dissemination were among the principal activities of the American Bible Society, formed in New York City in 1816. The acceptance of English by German and Dutch Protestants directly diluted a sense of ethnic identity and enhanced an American one.

On the other hand, minority religions retained foreign language services—particularly when multiple ethnicities made a common language more critical. Jews had Spanish, Portuguese, and German roots that made Hebrew integral to worship just as Latin took precedence over mother tongues in Catholic rituals. But Jews and Catholics were not immune to the influence of English. In 1824 the Sephardic congregation in Charleston, South Carolina, petitioned for bilingual services, "so as to enable every member of the congregation fully to understand every part of the service." The issue was so volatile that the petition's refusal led to a splinter Reform congregation that lasted for eight years.

Bishop John Carroll mused on the drawbacks of Mass in Latin: "It is an unknown Tongue, and in this Country, still more than in yours [England] either for want of Books or desirability to read, the greatest part of our Congregation must be entirely ignorant of the meaning and Sense of the publick Offices of the church." For German and French Catholics—minorities within a minority re-ligion—the vernacular assumed a great importance as a marker of identity as well as a source of interethnic friction with the increasingly more numerous Irish. National parishes, such as New York's St. Nicholas founded by Germans in 1833, were one solution. Such linguistic independence had its limits as far as the church hierarchy was concerned, and Germans repeatedly had to capitulate on broader administrative matters.

There are always historical exceptions. Father Felix Varela (1788–1853), a Catholic priest and Cuban political exile, ministered in English to his New York Irish parishioners as well as publishing *El Haberno*—in the 1820s one of the first Spanish-language newspapers in America—to advocate for minority rights, religious toleration, and bilingual cooperation. Scholars continue to debate whether African Americans spoke a form of English learned from contact with white immigrants in the United States or a creole version brought from Africa and the Caribbean, such as the distinctive Gullah of coastal South Carolina and Georgia spoken since the mid-eighteenth century. And, in a rare example of the use of an indigenous language to acculturate to white norms, the Rev. Thomas Roberts of North Carolina oversaw a Cherokee translation of the *American Sunday School Spelling Book (Sunalei akvlvgi no 'gwisi alikalvvsga zvlvgi Gesvi)*, that was published in 1824 "for the benefit of those who cannot acquire the English language."

Native American interaction with white settlers increased due to eastern population pressures after the American Revolution. Several treaties attempted to stabilize tribal boundaries, particularly with the Iroquois at Fort Stanwix on the New York–Canadian border (1784), with the Choctaw, Chickasaw, and Cherokee nations at Hopewell, South Carolina (1785–86), and with the Creeks in Georgia (1790). The result was a nearly tenfold increase in the number of Americans west of the Appalachian Mountains and south of the Ohio River during the 1780s. In the old Northwest (Ohio, Indiana, Illinois, and Michigan) there were more than a dozen agreements made with tribes between 1795 and 1809. However, the provisions of Indian treaties were weakly enforced by the federal government and routinely violated by ambitious settlers. Governor William Henry Harrison (1773–1841) reported that many trespassing frontiersmen in Indiana Territory considered "the murdering of the Indians in the highest degree meritorious."

Treaties with France (Louisiana Purchase 1803), Great Britain (1818), and Spain (Adams-Onis 1819) opened up further migratory possibilities to the west of the Appalachian Mountains and reopened the issue of Native American relations along a wide swath of territory from the Canadian border to Florida and Mexico. The migrants included not only New Englanders and southern planters but black slaves and foreign-born laborers, making the frontier the crucible of racial and ethnic interaction in the early nineteenth century. There is considerable anthropologic, folklore, and cultural geographic evidence that frontier settlers learned from each other and creatively adapted to a challenging natural environment. The Irish borrowed the

log cabin from the Germans and, by the time they reached Indiana, had altered its design to suit domestic customs from Ulster. Both groups used Indian methods of hunting and forest pharmacology to survive in the wilderness. African Americans were frequently trappers and interpreters, negotiating the middle ground between white immigrants and Indian tribes. Yet once again, outside perceptions of the frontier inhabitants were colored. In 1801 William Strickland, an English farmer, declared, "none emigrate to the frontiers beyond the mountains, except culprits, or savage backwoodsmen . . . the outcasts of the world, and the disgrace of it."

Like the opposition of "immigrant" to Anglo-American, "frontier" served to highlight the civility of life in the East. Well into the 1830s some Americans remained uncomfortable over the presence of the foreign-born in their midst. After remarking in his diary on the arrival of 15,825 passengers at the port of New York in May 1836, Philip Hone complained, "All Europe is coming across the ocean; all that part at least who cannot make a living at home; and what shall we do with them? They increase our taxes, eat our bread, and encumber our streets, and not one in twenty is competent to keep himself." Throughout the early national period one of the solutions frequently proposed was the creation of colonies, particularly in the West. The impetus for this kind of segregation sometimes came from within an ethnic or racial group, and sometimes it was imposed from without.

One of the earliest colonization efforts was Gallipolis, founded on the

LaBelle River in Ohio by French-Catholic immigrants in 1790. Several were in Pennsylvania: an Irish settlement begun in 1795 at Buffalo Creek and Slippery Rock in Butler County was flourishing fifty years later under the name Sugarcreek; in Cambria County, a mixture of Germans, Swiss, and Irish Catholics gravitated to Loretto after 1799; and at Silver Lake in Susquehanna County, Fr. Jeremiah F. O'Flynn erected a church in 1827 that shortly drew Catholics from rural public works projects to live in its vicinity. In northwestern New York, French, German, and Irish Catholics farmed several of the Black River Settlements. Bishop Fenwick started a Catholic colony at Benedicta in Maine in 1834, toward which he directed many of his Boston Irish parishioners.

Ethnic colonies were not exclusively Catholic. English political radicals founded Jacobin and Quaker communities in Pennsylvania in the 1790s. Wanborough and Albion, prairie colonies established in Illinois in 1818 by immigrants from Surrey and Hertford, were heavily promoted back home in England. In 1824 Mordecai Manuel Noah, the former American consul at Tunis, purchased fifty square miles on Grand Island in the Niagara River from the New York State Legislature. There he proposed a haven for Jews to be called Ararat, until such time as they could return to the Holy Land. Despite an elaborate ceremony in nearby Buffalo in September 1825, this Jewish colony never materialized.

The Irish leaders in New York, Baltimore, and Philadelphia petitioned Congress in 1818 to set aside lands in the Illinois Territory on easy credit for newly arrived immigrants from Ireland. Their argument was essentially a desire to protect the vulnerable and to guide the innocent:

> They have fled from want and oppression—they touch the soil of freedom and abundance; but the manna of the wilderness melts in their sight. Before they can taste the fruits of happy industry, the tempter too often presents to their lips the cup that turns man to brute, and the very energies which would have made the fields to blossom make the cities groan. Individual benevolence cannot reach this evil. Individuals may indeed solicit, but it belongs to the chosen guardians of the public weal to administer the cure.

This appeal by the Irish Emigrant Association was rejected. In contrast, an attempt by the African Colonization Society to repatriate blacks to the west coast of Africa was modestly successful. Between 1817 and 1830, approximately 1,420 were resettled in Liberia. Although the movement was fraught with ideological conflicts—it was all too easy to see it either as deportation or as a method of Christianizing Africa—a total of twelve thousand eventually migrated from the United States under the auspices of the Society. Abolitionists in particular objected to colonization on the grounds that, by siphoning off the free black population, it strengthened the position of American slaveholding interests.

A far less idealistic colonization

scheme was the United States government's Indian reservation policy. Prior to 1815, Native Americans were pressured to yield their eastern lands either through sale or in exchange for land in the West, at the same time that private acculturation programs—typically run by Christian missionaries—were underwritten by Congress. Success had been qualified, as Rachel Lazarus reported to novelist Maria Edgeworth in 1824:

> I lately saw another very sensible and well written letter from an Indian, in reply to one that made some enquiries relative to the situation of his tribe. He says they are fast advancing in civilisation, that exclusive of Missionary schools, they have established several for the education of their youth; that many of them have embraced the Christian Religion, and that there are among them several men of property, who cultivate flourishing farms which exhibit every appearance of neatness and comfort. He nevertheless deprecates the idea which appears to have been suggested of a free intercourse with the whites. He says, "do not force nature; we are improving, but we are not prepared to live among you, or to receive you among us; time has done a great deal, and may do a great deal more for us, if we are left to ourselves."

Thereafter "removal" was added to the strategies used by Washington, D.C., to deal with Native Americans. "He is unwilling to submit to the laws of the States and mingle with their population," President Andrew Jackson argued in 1830 on behalf of the Removal Act, "To save him from this alternative, or perhaps utter annihilation, the General Government kindly offers him a new home, and proposes to pay the whole expense of his removal and settlement." Once formally implemented by Congress, Indians were to be moved west of the Mississippi—either bought out or forcibly relocated—ostensibly to keep them out of harm's way through isolation. John C. Calhoun (1782–1850) reckoned removal would permit a generation of Indians to become civilized enough for reintegration into white society. In reality, the policy was meant to appease the insatiable demands of white frontiersmen for Mississippi Valley land, which had been building ever since the signing of the Pickney Treaty with Spain in 1795.

The Indian Removal Act affected about seventy-three thousand Native Americans during the 1830s. The Cherokees resisted by suing the state of Georgia in two landmark cases that went to the U.S. Supreme Court. In *Cherokee Nation v. Georgia* (1831) and *Worcester v. Georgia* (1832), Justice John Marshall decided in favor of the Indians, describing them as "domestic dependent nations." President Jackson chose to ignore the Court, enforcing a dubious treaty that gave 7 million acres to the United States and removed fifteen thousand Cherokees under duress to Oklahoma in the winter of 1838–1839. Nearly four thousand did not survive the "Trail of Tears." Likewise, Jackson took aggressive action against the Sac, Fox, and Seminoles when they proved uncooperative about removal. The Black Hawk War (1832) in Illinois and the Second Seminole War in Florida, fought between 1835 and 1842 under the leadership of Osceola, ultimately saw the triumph of federal policy.

In some ways Andrew Jackson (1767–1845) is the classic fulfillment of John Dunlap's prediction in the epitaph that opens this essay. On the other hand, he was born and raised in the Southern backcountry, on the border of North and South Carolina, in an area whose native Waxhaw tribe was eradicated by smallpox and wars, then resettled in the 1740s by an influx of Germans and Irish. Its frontier days were waning even though it was still quite isolated from "civilization." Jackson was also the son of immigrant parents from the north of Ireland, who spoke with a foreign accent and espoused Presbyterianism, a nonconforming brand of Protestantism. By the standards of the New Republic, was he truly an ideal American?

As defined by the Constitution of 1789, he was a native-born white citizen with the right to vote and freedom of conscience. But by then he was living in Nashville, beyond the western edge of the United States and outside its jurisdiction. When Tennessee was admitted to statehood in 1796, it drafted a liberal constitution that even extended suffrage to free blacks. Jackson, in his subsequent professional career, manifested the attitudes of (and accommodations commonly made on) the frontier. As a military officer, he fought alongside free African Americans in the battles of Horseshoe Bend and New Orleans, but never lifted a finger to abolish slavery. During the War of 1812, he also fought against the British with companies of Cherokees and Choctaws, the same tribes he would later dispossess while seventh President of the United States. Their clearance permitted a new generation of Irish and German immigrants to grow up on the settled frontier, just as Jackson had more than half a century earlier. Although Jackson was hailed by "the sons of his father's land" at the St. Patrick's Day 1828 banquet of the Friendly Sons of St. Patrick in New York City, his presidency nevertheless marks the emergence of a bitter Scotch-Irish versus Irish rivalry in American ethnic history, mirroring the rural/urban and Protestant/Catholic tensions already rife in the country. Jackson was a kind of new American for the nineteenth century, the complicated and anomalous result of the interplay of citizenship, religion, language, and segregation during the early national period.

## BIBLIOGRAPHIC ESSAY

For general overviews of race and ethnicity in the Early National period, see Leonard Dinnerstein and David M. Reimers, *Ethnic Americans: A History of Immigration*, 3rd ed. (New York: HarperCollins, 1988); Leonard Dinnerstein, Roger L. Nichols, and David M. Reimers, *Natives and Strangers: A Multicultural History of Americans* (New York: Oxford University Press, 1996); and Marcus Lee Hansen, *The Atlantic Migration, 1607–1860* (Cambridge: Harvard University Press, 1951).

On the 1790 census and early republican demographics, see *The Statistical History of the United States from Colonial Times to the Present*

(Stamford, Conn.: Fairfield Publishers, Inc., 1947); Peter D. McClelland and Richard J. Zeckhauser, *Demographic Dimensions of the New Republic: American Interregional Migration, Vital Statistics, and Manumissions, 1800–1860* (New York: Cambridge University Press, 1982); and Margo J. Anderson, ed., *Encyclopedia of the US Census* (Washington, D.C.: CQ Press, 2000). For the twentieth-century surname analyses of the 1790 census, see U.S. Bureau of the Census, *A Century of Population Growth* (Washington, D.C.: Government Printing Office, 1909); American Council of Learned Societies, "Report of Committee on Linguistic and National Stocks in the Population of the United States," American Historical Association, *Annual Report for the Year 1931* (Washington, D.C., 1932); and "The Population of the United States, 1790: A Symposium," *William and Mary Quarterly* 41 (January 1984): 85–135, which includes revised estimates of the ACLS figures by Thomas L. Purvis; see especially Table II, p. 98, although these figures are disputed by Donald Akenson, pp.  102–119. Students should note that despite this lively debate, the U.S. Historical Census Data Browser for 1790 on the Web at http://fisher.lib.virginia.edu/cgi-local/censusbin/census/cen.pl?year=790 is based solely on the controversial *A Century of Population Growth* (1909).

For a good summary of the effects of early restrictionist legislation, see James Morton Smith, *Freedom's Fetters: The Alien and Sedition Laws and American Civil Liberties* (Ithaca: Cornell University Press, 1956).

On the issues of image and language, see Dale T. Knobel, *Paddy and the Republic: Ethnicity and Nationality in Antebellum America* (Middletown, Conn.: Wesleyan University Press, 1986); John Kuo Wei Tchen, *New York*

*Before Chinatown: Orientalism and the Shaping of American Culture, 1776–1882* (Baltimore: Johns Hopkins University Press, 1999); Robert McCrum, William Cran, and Robert MacNeil, *The Story of English* (New York: Viking Penguin, 1986); and John R. Rickford, "The Creole Origins of African American Vernacular English: Evidence from Copula Absence," in Salikoko S. Mufwene, John R. Rickford, Guy Bailey, and John Baugh, eds., *African American English,* (London: Routledge, 1998).

For the history of ethnic and racial Catholics during this period, see John Tracy Ellis, *Catholics in Colonial America* (Baltimore: Helicon Press, 1965); Jay P. Dolan, *The American Catholic Experience: A History from Colonial Times to the Present* (Notre Dame: University of Notre Dame Press, 1992); and Dolan, *The Immigrant Church: New York's Irish and German Catholics, 1815–1865* (Notre Dame: University of Notre Dame Press, 1983; Baltimore: The Johns Hopkins University Press, 1975); and Sister Mary Gilbert Kelly, "Irish Catholic Colonies and Colonization Projects in the United States, 1795–1860," *Studies* (Dublin), Vol. 29 (1940), pp. 95–109.

On turn-of-the-nineteenth-century black history, see John Hope Franklin and Alfred A. Moss, Jr., *From Slavery to Freedom: A History of African Americans,* 7th ed. (New York: McGraw-Hill, 1994). There is an electronic version of *The Confessions of Nat Turner, the Leader of the Late Insurrection in Southampton, VA as fully and voluntarily made to Thomas R. Gray* (Richmond: Thomas R Gray, 1832) on the Web at http://odur.let.rug.nl/_usa/D/1826-1850/slavery/confeso1.htm.

Essays by Theda Perdue and R. David Edmunds in *Indians in American History: An Introduction,* Frederick E. Hoxie, ed. (Arlington Heights, Ill.: Harlan Davidson, 1988) are helpful. See also Angie Debo, *A History of the Indians of the United States* (Norman: University of Oklahoma Press, 1970). Andrew Jackson's Case for the Removal Act, First Annual Message to Congress, 8 December 1830, is reproduced in *A Compilation of the Messages and Papers of the Presidents, 1789–1908*, Volume II, by James D. Richardson, published by the Bureau of National Literature and Art, 1908. The full text of the landmark Supreme Court decisions *Cherokee Nation v. Georgia* (1831) and *Worcester v. Georgia* (1832) are on the Web at http://www.pbs.org/weta/thewest/resources/archives/two/cherokee.htm

For the Irish, see *Essays in Scotch-Irish History,* E. R. R. Green, ed. (London: Routledge & Kegan Paul Ltd, 1969; reprint Ulster Historical Foundation, 1992), especially essays by Maldwyn A. Jones, E. R. R. Green, and E. Estyn Evans; Earl F. Niehaus, *The Irish in New Orleans, 1800–1860* (Baton Rouge: Louisiana State University Press, 1965); Dennis Clark, *The Irish in Philadelphia: Ten Generations of Urban Experience* (Philadelphia: Temple University Press, 1973); and essays by Walter J. Walsh and Graham Hodges in Ronald H. Bayor and Timothy J. Meagher, eds., *The New York Irish* (Baltimore: The Johns Hopkins University Press, 1996). *The Harvard Encyclopedia of American Ethnic Groups,* Stephan Thernstrom, ed. (Cambridge: Belknap Press of Harvard University, 1980) remains an excellent starting place for the early history of the English, Germans, Swedes, Jews, French, and Spanish in the United States.

Quotes from primary documents used in this essay are from the following: "Encouragement to Irish Emigrants," U.S. Senate Doc. No. 449, 15th Congress, 1st Session. 1818; Giovanni Antonio Grassi, *Notizie varie*

*sullo stato presente della repubblica degli Stati Uniti dell'America* ("Observations on the United States"), originally published in 1819, reproduced in *The Annals of America, Vol. 4, 1797–1820, Domestic Expansion and Foreign Entanglements* (Chicago and London: Encyclopedia Britannica, 1968); Thomas Hamilton, *Men and Manners in America* (Edinburgh: W. Blackwood, 1833), quoted in Walter Allen ed., *Transatlantic Crossing* (London: William Heinemann Ltd., 1971); Samuel F. B. Morse, *Imminent Dangers to the Free Institutions of the United States Through Foreign Immigration, and the Present State of the Naturalization Laws* (New York: E. B. Clayton, 1835); Bayard Tuckerman, ed., *The Diary of Philip Hone, 1828–1851* (New York: Dodd, Mead, 1889), as well as Allan Nevins, ed., *The Diary of Philip Hone, 1828–1851* (New York: Dodd, Mead, 1936); *Journal of Frances Anne Butler,* vol. 2 (Philadelphia: Carey, Lea and Blanchard, 1835); and Philippa C. Bush, *Memoir of Anne Gorham Everett, with Extracts from Her Correspondence and Journal* (Boston: privately printed, 1857). There are electronic versions of these last two on the Web at http://www.alexanderstreet2.com/NWLDlive/

# DOCUMENTS

## Sarah Cary to Samuel Cary, July 1792

*From her home in Chelsea, Massachusetts, Sarah Cary wrote to her son, Samuel, in July 1792, casually expressing her thoughts on the subject of converting Native Americans to Christianity. In his address to Congress the previous year, President Washington had out-lined America's policy toward Indians, in-cluding "civilizing" efforts such as education and vocational training. With federal support and sociocultural blessings, much of this latter work continued that which had already been undertaken by missionaries from several Chris-tian denominations. Unlike most of her con-temporaries, however, Sarah Cary gently ad-vocates respect for religious differences rather than proselytizing in the name of civilization. At the same time, she betrays a typical turn-of-the-nineteenth-century attitude toward "inherent" racial characteristics.*

Source: Caroline G. Curtis, *The Cary Letters* (Cambridge, Mass.: Riverside Press, 1891), pp. 97–99; electronic version at http://www.lib.uchicago.edu/efts/asp/NAWLD.

*My Dear Sam, . . .*

I answered fully, I think, your letter of March 27th, excepting only that part mentioning Richard Cary's having at-tempted the conversion of the Indians to the Christian religion. Where, dear Sam, did you get such information? It is new to me. He was aide-decamp to Wash-ington, and conducted with the greatest propriety during the late war. You have often heard me mention him for his pleasing address. There was always since my remembrance a Society for Propa-gating the Gospel among the Indians, with how much success I am not able to tell, but I am rather inclined to believe very little; for I remember, about twenty-two years since, one Indian who was converted, and afterwards brought here by one of our clergy, and really so far civilized as to be introduced into our meeting-houses, where he actually preached several times, but, like poor puss in the fable, he could not disguise his natural propensities, one of which was the immoderate use of strong drink. New England rum, I am told, is a temp-tation the best of those poor creatures can never withstand, and which baffles all the eloquence of those who wish a reform among them. As to their reli-gion, there are various accounts about it. Some say they worship the sun, and at break of day every person upward of twelve years old goes to the waterside until sunrise, then offers tobacco to this planet, and does the same again at sun-set; that they acknowledge one Supreme God, but do not adore him, believing him to be too far exalted above them, and too happy in himself to be con-cerned about the trifling affairs of poor mortals. My dear Sam, is not the partic-ular mode of their worship as acceptable to their Maker as ours? Why are we ar-rogantly to presume to dictate to any sect of people if they have not the ad-vantages of Christianity revealed to them? Neither will the fruits of that holy religion be expected to influence their conduct. For wise purposes, no doubt, have our doctrines been withheld from them. The Judge of all the earth will do right. He is the great Creator of all, and doubtless receives with equal condescen-sion the worship of the Pagan and the Christian. Do these sentiments agree with yours? . . .

*Farewell, my dear boy,*
*and believe me to be*
*Yours most affectionately, S. Cary.*

## Timothy Pickering to Anthony Wayne, April 8, 1795

*One of the earliest problems confronting the new American government was the settlement of its western boundary. There was some ambivalence about the validity of American title to the Northwest Territory under the Treaty of Paris (1783), so post–Revolutionary negotiations with Indian representatives ostensibly permitted white settlement between the Great Lakes and the Ohio River. After the demise of the Iroquois Confederacy, however, this was contested, and warfare erupted again on the frontier. American forces under General Anthony Wayne (1745–1796) eventually defeated Miami, Shawnee, and Delaware resistance to U.S. sovereignty at the Battle of Fallen Timbers (near Toledo) in August 1794. In anticipation of yet another round of negotiations, Secretary of War Timothy Pickering (1745–1829) wrote a long letter to General Wayne in the spring of 1795 with detailed instructions for what eventually became the Treaty of Greenville. His letter contains an implicit respect for the rights and intelligence of Native Americans that is a contrast to the patronizing efforts of subsequent federal and religious policy.*

Source: Richard C. Knopf, ed., *Anthony Wayne, A Name in Arms . . . The Wayne-Knox-Pickering-McHenry Correspondence* (Pittsburgh, 1959), pp. 393–403; reproduced in *The Annals of America*, vol. 3, *1784–1796: Organizing the New Nation* (Chicago and London: Encyclopedia Britannica, Inc., 1968), pp. 583–587.

The overtures for peace which have been made by the Indians northwest of the Ohio bear the appearance of sincerity, and viewed in connection with the events of the last year, it is hardly to be doubted that their overtures have been made in good faith. Taking this for granted, it becomes necessary to communicate to you the ideas of the President of the United States relative to the terms on which peace is now to be negotiated. To gratify the usual expectation of Indians assembling for the purposes of treaty and thereby facilitate the negotiation, it is thought best to provide and forward a quantity of goods. These will amount to at least $25,000, but are to be delivered only in case of a successful treaty: except such small portions of them as humanity may call for pending the negotiation. The residue are to be delivered to them as one of the conditions for their final relinquishment of the lands which the treaty shall comprehend.

Besides the goods, you will stipulate to pay them a sum not exceeding $10,000 annually, as a further and full consideration for all the lands they relinquish.

You will consider how the goods for the treaty should be distributed. Perhaps Indians of several nations will attend, who have no sort of claim to any of the lands we shall retain: yet being present they will expect to participate; and they must participate. In what degree can be adjusted with the chiefs of the tribes who were the true owners of the land. These alone (the true owners), if they can be ascertained or agreed on, are to enjoy the annuity, the share of each nation to be fixed if possible; and it is presumed they will agree on the principles by which your calculation will be governed. They will doubtless, as formerly, manifest their wishes to recover a large part of their best hunting ground as necessary to their subsistence; but the annuity is intended to compensate them for the loss of game, while its amount granted under the present circumstances will evince the liberality of the United States.

With respect to the general boundary line, that described in the treaty made at Fort Harmar January 9, 1789, will still be satisfactory to the United States; and you will urge it accordingly.

The reservations of diverse pieces of land for trading posts, as in the tenth article of the Treaty of Fort Harmar, and the strip six miles wide from the River Rosine to Lake St. Clair in the eleventh article, as a convenient appendage to Detroit, to give room for settlements, it is desirable to have retained for those uses. Some of the military posts which are already established, or which you may judge necessary to have established to preserve or complete a chain of communication from the Ohio to the Miami of the Lake; and from the Miami villages to the head of the Wabash, and down the same to the Ohio and from the Miami villages down to the mouth of the Miami River at Lake Erie, it will also be desirable to secure: but all these cessions are not to be insisted on; for peace and not increase of territory has been the object of this expensive war. Yet, the success of the last campaign authorizes a demand of some indemnification for the blood and treasure expended. Such a boundary line, therefore, as would formerly have been acquiesced in, for the sake of peace, will not now be proposed.

The Treaty of Harmar, as you have announced to the chiefs, is to be the basis of the new treaty. . . . All the lands north and west of this general boundary line to which, by virtue of former treaties with the western Indians, the United States have claims, may be relinquished excepting:

1. The lands which being occupied by the British troops and subjects, and the Indian title to the same being extinguished, were ceded by Great Britain in full right to the United States by the treaty of 1783.

2. Those detached pieces of land on which you have established or shall think proper to establish military posts to form or complete a chain of communication between the Miami of the Ohio and the Miami of Lake Erie, and by the latter from the Lake to Fort Wayne and thence to the Wabash and down the same to the Ohio.

3. The 150,000 acres granted to General Clarke for himself and his warriors near the rapids of the Ohio.

4. The lands in possession of the French people and other white settlers among them, who hold their lands by the consent of the United States.

5. The military posts now occupied by the troops of the United States on the Wabash and the Ohio.

The object of these reservations may be explained to the Indians. They are not destined for their annoyance, or to impose the smallest restraint on their enjoyment of their lands, but to connect the settlements of the people of the United States by rendering a passage from one to the other more practicable and convenient. These posts will also prove convenient to the Indians themselves, as traders may reside at some or all of them to supply them with goods. For these reasons some land about each of these posts, not less than two square miles, should also be reserved, together with a right of passage from one to another.

If the Indians are sincere, and desire to have our friendship, they cannot object to these means of useful intercourse, which will cement that friendship while they will afford a very necessary and important accommodation to the people of the United States, and in the way of trade to the Indians themselves. . . .

The treaties heretofore made with the western Indians have comprised a number of nations; and if there be any truth in their pretensions of late years their interests are blended together. Hence may result the necessity of continuing their former mode of treating. And their uniting in one instrument will save much time and trouble, and prevent tedious and perhaps inconvenient altercations among themselves about their boundaries which are often extremely vague. For instance, the chiefs of the Six Nations last autumn declared that their title to the lands between the Allegany and French Creek on the east and the Muskingum and Cuyahoga on the west was acknowledged by all the western Indians. But when I pressed them on this point to cede that tract to the United States, they confessed that the four most hostile tribes denied their right to it. I am well satisfied that whatever claim the Six Nations might formerly have to the lands westward of the Allegany, they long ago relinquished the same to the Delawares, and others of

the present western Indians. The relinquishment of the country, therefore, to the United States by the Six Nations I consider as affording us but the shadow of a title to it.

The principal reasons given by the western Indians for not adhering to the treaties of Fort McIntonsh, Miami, and Fort Harmar have been these:

1. That the chiefs who treated were not an adequate representation of the nations to whom the lands belonged.
2. That they were compelled by threats to subscribe some of the treaties.
3. That the claim of the United States to the full property of the Indians' lands, under color of the treaty of 1783 with Great Britain, was unfounded and unjust.

To prevent a repetition of such complaints you will use every practicable means to obtain a full representation of all the nations claiming property in the lands in question. And to obviate future doubts it may be expedient to get lists of all the principal and other chiefs of each nation to ascertain who are absent, and whether those present may be fairly considered as an adequate representation of their nation. The explanations and declarations of the chiefs on this point may be noted, and subscribed by them upon each list.

As they will be collected within your power at Greenville, it will highly concern the honor and justice of the United States that strong and decided proofs be given them that they are not under even the shadow of duress. Let them feel that they are at perfect liberty to speak their sentiments, and to sign or refuse to sign such a treat as you are now authorized to negotiate.

The unfortunate construction put by the first commissioners on our treaty of peace with Great Britain and thence continued by General [Arthur] St. Clair in 1789 has since been repeatedly renounced. The commissioners who went to Canada in 1793 were explicit on this head in their messages to the western Indians—copies whereof you will receive. As this construction grasped the whole Indian country southward of the great Lakes and eastward of the Mississippi as the full and absolute property of the United States, a construction as unfounded in itself as it was unintelligible and mysterious to the Indians—a construction which, with the use made of it by the British advisors of those Indians, has probably been the mainspring of the distressing war on our frontiers—it cannot be too explicitly renounced. At the same time you will carefully explain and maintain the preemption right of the United States. Some delicacy, however, will be required to state even this claim without exciting their displeasure. If the land is theirs (and this we acknowledge) they will say "Why shall we not sell it to whom we please?" Perhaps in some such way as the following it may be rendered inoffensive.

The white nations, in their treaties with one another, agree on certain boundaries, beyond which neither is to advance a step. In America, where these boundaries agreed on by the white people pass along the countries of the Indians, the meaning of the treaties is this:

that one white nation shall not purchase or take possession of any Indian land beyond their own boundary so agreed on, even although the Indians should offer to sell or give it to them. The individuals indeed have often attempted to purchase and possess such lands, but being bound by the treaty of their nation, their purchases and possessions have no strength, and the other nation has a right to dispossess and drive them off.

So likewise the individuals of a white nation have not right to purchase and possess Indian lands within the boundaries of their own nations, unless the nation consents. For each white nation makes certain rules about Indian lands, which everyone of the people is obliged to follow. The most important of these rules is that which forbids individuals taking hold of Indian lands without the consent of the nation. When individuals do such things, it is because they wish to cheat not only the Indians but their own nation, which, therefore, has a right to punish them and take away the lands so unlawfully obtained. The United States has made such a rule, the design of which is to protect the Indian lands against such bad men.

. . . One great principle ought to govern all public negotiations—a rigid adherence to truth—a principle that is essential in negotiations with Indians if we would gain their permanent confidence and a useful influence over them. Jealousy is strongest in minds uninformed, so that the utmost purity and candor will hardly escape suspicion. Suspicions occasion delays, and issue in discontents, and these in depredations and war.

## Constitution of The New-York Society for the Information and Assistance of Persons Emigrating from Foreign Countries, 1794

*This constitution was adopted in May 1794 and published in the 1795 edition of the local directory, the* New-York Register. *The society met on the first Thursday of the month, but its seven-member Committee of Conference and Correspondence assembled every Friday evening to address the immediate needs of immigrant applicants looking for work or charity. It was unique in that it did not distinguish between foreigners as did other late-eighteenth-century Irish, English, and Scottish fraternal groups such as the Friendly Sons of St. Patrick, the St. George Society, and the St. Andrew Society.*

Source: "The New-York Society for the Information and Assistance of Persons Emigrating from Foreign Countries," *New-York Register*, 1795; collection of the New-York Historical Society, reprinted in *America Begins in New York: The Peopling of New York City, A Teachers' Resource Manual on Immigration* (A New York City 100 Collaborative Project, 1998), p. 183.

It is certainly a fact, that emigrants from one country to another, are liable to numberless unforeseen disappointments—it is equally true, that change of diet, and confinement on board of vessels, together with difference of climate, often produce diseases, which sometimes prove fatal; nor will it be denied, that in some instances, a little friendly interference might rescue persons from being the victims of misfortune.

To those in affluent circumstances, who may wish for information, the Society can only offer their individual friendship, congratulate them on their safe arrival, and wish them success and happiness.

Those in middling circumstances, who may wish for information, the Society refer to their committee, who will always be ready to shew [sic] them any friendly office in their power.

But to the unfortunate, the sick, the friendless, and the needy, the Society address themselves in a peculiar manner. They request them not to suffer their spirits to droop; and assure them that upon application to either of the committee, their cases will be taken into immediate consideration.

Should any indigent person be so unfortunate as to arrive in a state of sickness, the Society have the happiness to inform them, that their Physician will always be ready to give them every necessary attendance, free of expence [sic].

Those who may wish for immediate employ, have an opportunity of applying to the Register of the Society, who keeps a regular entry of all applications for employ, as well as an account of applications for artificers, labourers, &c.

## The Naturalization of Immigrants, 1795

*The republican tradition carried an implicit distrust of the Old World and old ways that soon put American ideals to the test. In a "new" country dependent for growth upon immigration, citizenship was taken seriously and the power to enact naturalization laws was reserved in the Constitution. The turmoil of the French Revolution increased the number of French émigrés in the United States. There was a concomitant rise in nativist sentiment based on the fear that foreigners, especially those with French sympathies like the Irish, might also be radicals. Congress responded in January 1795 by increasing the residency requirement for naturalization—from the two years mandated under the Act of 1790—to five years. This set a disturbing precedent that would be used again in 1798 to raise the term to fourteen years.*

*Source:* "The Naturalization of Immigrants, 1795," in John P. Sanderson, *The Views and Opinions of American Statesmen on Foreign Immigration* (Philadelphia, 1856), pp. 128–129; reproduced in *The Annals of America*, vol. 3, *1784–1796: Organizing the New Nation* (Chicago and London: Encyclopedia Britannica, Inc., 1968), pp. 581–582.

Any alien, being a free white person, may be admitted to become a citizen of the United States, or any of them, on the following conditions and not otherwise. First, he shall have declared, on oath or affirmation, before the Supreme, Superior, District, or Circuit Court of some one of the states, or of the territories northwest or south of the Ohio River, or a Circuit or District Court of the United States, three years at least before his admission, that it was, bon fide, his intention to become a citizen of the United States, and to renounce forever all allegiance and fidelity to any foreign prince, potentate, state, or sover-eignty whereof such alien may at that time be a citizen or subject.

Second, he shall, at the time of his application to be admitted, declare on oath or affirmation before some one of the courts aforesaid that he has resided within the United States five years at least, and within the state or territory where such court is at the time held, one year at least; that he will support the Constitution of the United States; and that he does absolutely and entirely re-nounce and abjure all allegiance and fi-delity to any foreign prince, potentate, state, or sovereignty whatever, and par-ticularly by name the prince, potentate, state, or sovereignty whereof he was be-fore a citizen or subject; which proceed-ings shall be recorded by the clerk of the court.

Third, the court admitting such alien shall be satisfied that he has resided within the limits and under the jurisdic-tion of the United States five years. It shall further appear to their satisfaction that during that time he has behaved as a man of good moral character, attached to the principles of the Constitution of the United States, and well-disposed to the good order and happiness of the same.

Fourth, in case the alien applying to be admitted to citizenship shall have borne any hereditary title, or been of any of the orders of nobility, in the king-dom or state from which he came, he shall, in addition to the above requisites, make an express renunciation of his title or order of nobility in the court to which his application shall be made; which re-nunciation shall be recorded in said court. . . .

*And be it further enacted*, that the children of persons duly naturalized, dwelling within the United States, and being under the age of twenty-one years at the time of such naturalization, and the children of citizens of the United States born out of the limits and jurisdiction of the United States, shall be considered as citizens of the United States. The right of citizenship shall not descend on persons whose fathers have never been resident of the United States. No person heretofore proscribed by any state, or who has been legally convicted of having joined the army of Great Britain during the late war, shall be admitted as aforesaid, without the consent of the legislature of the state in which such person was proscribed.

## Edward Livingston, "Against the Alien Act," 1798

*America's biggest international relations headache in the 1790s was France, where a new government refused to respect United States delegates or mercantile ships. There was growing consensus that war between the two countries was inevitable, and it was in this climate of fear that, on June 25, 1798, Congress authorized the Alien Act, the second of four restrictive laws passed in as many weeks. This act authorized the president of the United States—at the time John Adams—to deport any foreign-born national suspected of anti-American activities and to imprison anyone who defied such a deportation order for up to three years. In addition, provision was made to provide foreigners with a "license" valid for a certain period of years, subject to good behavior while in the country. Such*

*broad executive powers were not expropriated without protest. Edward Livingston (1764– 1836) of New York spoke out against the Alien Act during the congressional debates on June 21st, but the bill was passed over his objections. Although its implications were quite real for French and Irish immigrants, its provisions were never actually enforced.*

*Source: Edward Livingston, "Against the Alien Act," Debates, 5 Congress, pp. 2006–2015; reproduced in The Annals of America, vol. 4, 1797–1820: Domestic Expansion and Foreign Entanglements (Chicago and London: Encyclopedia Britannica, Inc., 1968), pp. 49–52.*

The state of things, if we are to judge from the complexion of the bill, must be that a number of aliens enjoying the protection of our government, were plotting its destruction; that they are engaged in treasonable machinations against a people who have given them an asylum and support; and that there is no provision to provide for their expulsion and punishment. . . .

We must legislate upon facts, not on surmises; we must have evidence, not vague suspicions, if we meant to legislate with prudence. What facts have been produced? What evidence had been submitted to the House? I have heard, sir, of none; but if evidence of facts could not be procured, at least it might have been expected that reasonable cause of suspicion should be shown. Here again, gentlemen were at fault; they could not show even a suspicion why aliens ought to be suspected. We have, indeed, been told that the fate of Venice, Switzerland, and Batavia was produced by the interference of foreigners. But the instances were unfortunate, because all those powers have been overcome by foreign force, or divided by domestic faction, not by aliens who resided among them; and if any instruction was to be gained from those republics, it would be that we ought to banish not aliens but all those who did not approve of the executive acts. . . . it yet remains to show that any such plots have been detected, or are even reasonably suspected here.

. . . No evidence then being produced, we have a right to say that none exists and yet we are about to sanction a most important act; and on what ground—our individual suspicions, our private fears, our overheated imaginations. Seeing nothing to excite those suspicions, and not feeling those fears, I could not give my assent to the bill, even if I did not feel a superior obligation to reject it on other grounds.

As far as my own observation goes, I have seen nothing like the state of things contemplated by the bill. Most of the aliens I have seen were either triumphant Englishmen or Frenchmen, with dejection in their countenances and grief at their hearts, preparing to quit the country and seek another asylum. But if these plots exist, if this treason is apparent, if there are aliens guilty of the crimes ascribed to them, an effectual remedy presents itself for the evil. We have already wise laws, we have upright judges and vigilant magistrates, and there is no necessity of arming the executive with the destructive power proposed by the bill now on your table. The laws now in force are competent to punish every treasonable or seditious attempt.

But grant, sir—what, however, has not been supported by fact—grant that these fears are not visionary, that the dangers are imminent, and that no existing law is sufficient to avert them, let us examine whether the provisions of the bill are conformable to the principles of the Constitution. If it should be found to contravene them, I trust it will lose many of its present supporters; but if not only contrary to the general spirit and principles of the Constitution, it should also be found diametrically opposite to the most express prohibitions, I cannot doubt that it would be rejected with that indignant decision which our duty to our country and our sacred oath demands.

The 1st Section provides, that it shall be lawful for the president "to order all such aliens as he shall judge dangerous to the peace and safety of the United States, or shall have reasonable grounds to suspect are concerned in any treasonable or secret machinations against the government thereof, to depart out of the United States, in such time as shall be expressed in such order."

Our government, sir, is founded on the establishment of those principles which constitute the difference between a free Constitution and a despotic power; a distribution of the legislative, executive, and judiciary powers into several hands; a distribution strongly marked in the three first and great divisions of the Constitution—by the first, all legislative power is given to Congress; the second vests all legislative functions in the president; and the third declares that the judiciary powers shall be exercised by the Supreme and inferior courts. Here then is a division of the governmental powers strongly marked, decisively pronounced, and every act of one or all of the branches that tends to confound these powers, or alter this arrangement, must be destructive of the Constitution. Examine then, sir, the bill on your able and declare whether the few lines I have repeated from the 1st Section do not confound these fundamental powers of government, vest them all in the more unqualified terms in one hand, and thus subvert the basis on which our liberties rest.

. . . By it the president alone is empowered to make the law, to fix in his mind what acts, what words, what thoughts or looks, shall constitute the crime contemplated by the bill, that is the crime of being "suspected to be dangerous to the peace and safety of the United States." He is not only authorized to make this law for his own conduct but to vary it at pleasure, as every gust of passion, every cloud of suspicion, shall agitate or darken his mind. The same power that formed the law, then, applies it to the guilty or innocent victim, whom his own suspicions, or the secret whisper of a spy, have designated as its object. The president, then, having made the law, the president having construed and applied it, the same president is by the bill authorized to execute his sentence, in case of disobedience, by imprisonment during his pleasure. This, then, comes completely within the definition of despotism—a union of legislative, executive, and judicial powers.

. . . here the law is so closely concealed in the same mind that gave it birth—the crime is "exciting the suspicions of the president," but no man can tell what conduct will avoid that suspicion—a careless word, perhaps misrepresented, or never spoken, may be sufficient evidence; a look may destroy, an idle gesture may insure punishment no innocence can protect, no circumspection can avoid the jealously of suspicion; surrounded by spies, informers, and all that infamous herd which fatten under laws like this, the unfortunate stranger will never know either of the law, of the accusation, or of the judgment until the moment it is put in execution . . .

. . . No indictment; no jury; no trial; no public procedure; no statement of the accusation; no examination of the witnesses in its support; no counsel for defense; all is darkness, silence, mystery, and suspicion.

But, as if this were not enough the unfortunate victims of this law are told in the next section that if they can convince the president that his suspicions are unfounded, he may, if he pleases, give them a license to stay. But, how remove his suspicions when they know not on what act they were founded? Miserable mockery of justice! Appoint an arbitrary judge armed with legislative and executive powers added to his own! Let him condemn the unheard, the uncaused object of his suspicion; and then to cover the injustice of the scene, gravely tell him, you ought not to complain—you need only disprove facts that you have never heard—remove suspicions that have never been communicated to you; it will be easy to convince your judge, whom you shall not approach, that he is tyrannical and unjust; and, having done this, we give him the power he had before, to pardon you if he pleases. . . .

## Red Jacket, "Against White Missions Among the Indians," 1805

*Sagoyewatha (c. 1758–1830), also called Red Jacket, was a Seneca chief among the party of Indians who agreed to discuss Christian proselytizing efforts with Reverend Cram of the Boston Missionary Society at Buffalo Creek in 1805. Red Jacket had fought with the British against the Americans during the Revolution; subsequently, he met with George Washington and urged support for the United States. His tribe, the Senecas, were part of the Iroquois confederation of upstate New York (along with the Mohawks, Oneidas, Onondagas, Cayugas, and Tuscarora), whose tribal organization was matrilineal—a concept that was shocking to Europeans. Their thinking on religion was equally at odds with Western culture, albeit damningly logical, as this excerpt from Red Jacket's speech illustrates.*

Source: Red Jacket, "Against White Missions Among the Indians," in *A Library of American Literature*, Edmund C. Stedman and Ellen M. Hutchinson, eds., vol. 4 (New York, 1889), reproduced in *The Annals of America*, vol. 4, 1797–1820: Domestic Expansion and Foreign Entanglements (Chicago and London: Encyclopedia Britannica, Inc., 1968), pp. 195–196.

You say that you are sent to instruct us how to worship the Great Spirit agreeably to His mind, and, if we do not take hold of the religion which you white people teach, we shall be unhappy hereafter. You say that you are right and we are lost. How do we know this to be true? We understand that your religion is written in a book. If it was intended for us as well as you, why has not the Great Spirit given to us, and not only to us, but why did He not give to our forefathers the knowledge of that book, with the means of understanding it rightly? We only know what you tell us about it. How shall we know when to believe, being so often deceived by the white people?

Brother, you say there is but one way to worship and serve the Great Spirit. If there is but one religion, why do you white people differ so much about it? Why not all agreed, as you can all read the book?

Brother, we do not understand these things. We are told that your religion was given to your forefathers and has been handed down from father to son. We also have a religion which was given to our forefathers and has been handed down to us, their children. We worship in that way. It teaches us to be thankful for all the favors we receive, to love each other, and to be united. We never quarrel about religion.

Brother, the Great Spirit has made us all, but He has made a great difference between His white and red children. He has given us different complexions and different customs. To you He has given the arts. To these He has not opened our eyes. We know these things to be true. Since He has made so great a difference between us in other things, why may we not conclude that He has given us a different religion according to our understanding? The Great Spirit does right. He knows what is best for His children; we are satisfied.

Brother, we do not wish to destroy your religion or take it from you. We only want to enjoy our own.

Brother, you say you have not come to get our land or our money but to enlighten our minds. I will now tell you that I have been at your meetings and saw you collect money from the meeting. I cannot tell what this money was intended for, but suppose that it was for your minister, and if we should conform to your way of thinking, perhaps you may want some from us.

Brother, we are told that you have been preaching to the white people in this place. These people are our neighbors. We are acquainted with them. We will wait a little while and see what effect your preaching has upon them. If we find it does them good, makes them honest and less disposed to cheat Indians, we will then consider again of what you have said.

Brother, you have now heard our answer to your talk, and this is all we have to say at present. As we are going to part, we will come and take you by the hand and hope the Great Spirit will protect you on your journey and return you safe to your friends.

## United German Benefit Society, By-Laws of the United German Benefit Society: Agreed upon at Various Meetings, 1799

*The largest contingent of non–English-speaking people resident in eighteenth-century America were Germans. The language barrier fostered separate communal organization, in-*

*cluding mutual aid associations established in Philadelphia (1764), Charleston (1766), Baltimore (1783), and New York (1784). Most of their membership was drawn from Germans who were craftsmen or merchants. At the turn of the nineteenth century there was a significant downturn in emigration from Germany, and the original mandate of these societies—to protect emigrants from exploitation—lost its impetus. In 1799 the United German Benefit Society of Philadelphia adopted bylaws to which it made a number of subsequent additions before ordering a bilingual printing in 1806. The following translation from the original German indicates that welfare fraud was the new preoccupation, as some members took advantage of the society's full coffers to falsely claim sick benefits, running the risk of social ostracism if caught.*

*Source:* United German Benefit Society, *By-Laws of the United German Benefit Society: Agreed upon at Various Meetings* (Philadelphia: Conrad Zentler, 1806), p. 2.

## 2ND APRIL 1799

With reference to sick members in certain cases

When a member reports sick, and is visited by a supervisor, who however becomes suspicious, or should another member of the Society express doubts, the Presidents or Vice-Presidents should be immediately informed. Some of the Presidents should have the authority to summon an appropriate doctor to visit the patient to determine whether the sickness or indisposition is genuine or not. One of the Presidents, and at least one supervisor, should be present. The doctor should deliver an opinion in writing, and date it. This should remain in the hands of the President until the next scheduled meeting. If the doctor is of the opinion that the patient is malingering, the supervisor should withhold the weekly payment specified in the ninth section of the Constitution. The President shall report the full circumstances to the next meeting of the Society, of which the accused member shall have received notice from the Secretary at least twenty-four hours prior to the meeting. The accused shall he present to defend himself, or be represented by a plenipotentiary. If he fails to appear after receiving the notification, he shall not be entitled to demand another opportunity to defend himself. If two-thirds of the members present agree, he shall be deemed unworthy to remain a member of the Society, and in accordance with the seventh section of the Constitution decreeing the fate of anyone who attempts to defraud the Society, his name shall be struck from the membership list, he shall be declared a cheat, and he shall forfeit everything he has contributed to the funds of the Society Treasury.

## Act to Prohibit the Importation of Slaves, March 2, 1807

*One of the major humanitarian efforts gathering force in the early nineteenth century was the movement to end the slave trade, spearheaded by Quakers on both sides of the Atlantic. In 1807 Great Britain, a longtime beneficiary of the trade's profits, became the* *first country to abolish traffic in human beings. The United States quickly followed suit, enacting legislation to take effect on New Year's Day, 1808. It prohibited the importation of slaves but did not make slavery itself illegal. This is an important distinction. The wording of the act was specific, creating a careful list of prohibitions to cover all conceivable possibilities for circumventing the law. It also indicates the extent to which other economic sectors such as longshore work— employing many white immigrants—would be impacted by the abolition of the slave trade.*

*Source:* "Act to Prohibit the Importation of Slaves, March 2, 1807" (*U.S. Statutes at Large*, vol. 2, p. 426 ff.); reproduced in Henry Steele Commager and Milton Cantor, eds., *Documents of American History*, vol. 1, to 1898 (Englewood Cliffs, N.J.: Prentice Hall, 1988), pp. 197–198.

*An Act to prohibit the importation of Slaves into any port or place within the jurisdiction of the United States, from and after the first day of January, in the year of our Lord one thousand, eight hundred and eight.*

Be it enacted, That from and after the first day of January, one thousand eight hundred and eight, it shall not be lawful to import or bring into the United States or the territories thereof from any foreign kingdom, place, or country, any negro, mulatto, or person of colour, as a slave, or to be held to service or labour.

Sec. 2. That no citizen of the United States, or any other person, shall, from and after the first day of January, in the year of our Lord one thousand eight hundred and eight, for himself, or themselves, or any other person whatsoever, either as master, factor, or owner, build, fit, equip, load or otherwise prepare any ship or vessel, in any port or place within the jurisdiction of the United States, nor shall cause any ship or vessel to sail from any port or place within the same, for the purpose of procuring any negro, mulatto, or person of colour, from any foreign kingdom, place, or country, to be transported to any port or place whatsoever within the jurisdiction of the United States, to be held to service or labour: and if any ship or vessel shall be so fitted out for the purpose aforesaid, every such ship or vessel, her tackle, apparel, and furniture, shall be forfeited to the United States, and shall be liable to be seized, prosecuted, and condemned in any of the circuit courts or district courts, for the district where the said ship or vessel may be found or seized. . . .

Sec. 4. If any citizen or citizens of the United States, or any person resident within the jurisdiction of the same, shall, from and after the first day of January, one thousand eight hundred and eight, take on board, receive or transport from any of the coasts or kingdoms of Africa, or from any other foreign kingdom, place, or country, any negro, mulatto, or person of colour in any ship or vessel, for the purpose of selling them in any port or place within the jurisdiction of the United States as slaves, or to be held to service or labour, or shall be in any ways aiding or abetting therein, such citizen or citizens, or person, shall severally forfeit and pay five thousand dollars, one moiety thereof to the use of any person or persons who shall sue for and prosecute the same to effect. . . .

Sec. 6. That if any person or persons whatsoever, shall, from and after the first day or January, one thousand eight hundred and eight, purchase or sell any negro, mulatto, or person of colour, for a slave, or to be held to service or labour, who shall have been imported, or brought from any foreign kingdom, place, or country, or from the dominions of any foreign state, immediately adjoining to the United States, after the last day of December, one thousand eight hundred and seven, knowing at the time of such purchase or sale, such negro, mulatto, or person of colour, was so brought within the jurisdiction of the United States, as aforesaid, such purchaser and seller shall severally forfeit and pay for every negro, mulatto, or person of colour, so purchased or sold as aforesaid, eight hundred dollars. . . .

Sec. 7. That if any ship or vessel shall be found, from and after the first day of January, one thousand eight hundred and eight, in any river, port, bay, or harbor, or on the high seas, within the jurisdictional limits of the United States, or hovering on the coast thereof, having on board any negro, mulatto, or person of colour, for the purpose of selling them as slaves, or with intent to land the same, in any port or place within the jurisdiction of the United States, contrary to the prohibition of the act, every such ship or vessel, together with her tackle, apparel, and furniture, and the goods or effects which shall be found on board the same, shall be forfeited to the use of the United States, and may be seized, prosecuted, and condemned, in any court of the United States, having jurisdiction thereof. And it shall be lawful for the President of the United States, and he is hereby authorized, should he deem it expedient, to cause any of the armed vessels of the United States to be manned and employed to cruise on any part of the coast of the United States, or territories thereof, where he may judge attempts will be made to violate the provisions of this act, and to instruct and direct the commanders of armed vessels of the United States, to seize, take, and bring into any port of the United States all such ships or vessels, and moreover to seize, take, or bring into any port of the U.S. all ships or vessel of the U.S. wheresoever found on the high seas, contravening the provisions of this act, to be proceeded against according to law. . . .

## Margaret Van Horn Dwight, *A Journey to Ohio in 1810*

*Late in October 1810 Margaret Van Horn Dwight (1790–1834), the niece of the president of Yale University, was en route from New Haven, Connecticut, to Warren, Ohio. In her diary she recorded not only her observations of German immigrants but her very palpable fear of them. To her horror, the Sabbath forced her party to spend two particularly memorable nights at a "Dutch" tavern in Hanover, near Bethlehem in the German heartland of rural Pennsylvania.*

Source: Max Farrand, ed., *A Journey to Ohio in 1810: As Recorded in the Journal of Margaret Van Horn Dwight* (New Haven: Yale University Press, 1912), pp. 16–20; electronic version at http://www.lib.uchicago.edu/efts/asp/NAWLD

I can wait no longer to write you, for I have a great deal to say—I should not have thought it possible to pass a Sabbath in our country among such a dissolute vicious set of wretches as we are now among—I believe at least 50 dutchmen have been here to day to smoke, drink, swear, pitch cents, almost dance, laugh & talk dutch && stare at us—They come in, in droves young & old—black & white—women & children—It is dreadful to see so many people that you cannot speak to or understand—They are all high dutch, but I hope not a true specimen of the Pennsylvanians generally—Just as we set down to tea, in came a dozen or two of women, each with a child in her arms, & stood round the room—I did not know but they had come in a body to claim me as one of their kin, for they all resemble me—but as they said nothing to me, I concluded they came to see us *Yankees*, as they would a learned pig—The women dress in striped linsey woolsey petticoats & short gowns not 6 inches in length—they look very strangely—The men dress much better—they put on their best cloaths on sunday, which I suppose is their only holiday, & "keep it up" as they call it—A stage came on from Bethlehem & stopt here, with 2 girls & a well dress'd *fellow* who sat between them an arm round each—They were probably going to the next town to a dance or a frolic of some kind-for the driver, who was very familiar with them, said he felt just right for a frolic—I suspect more liquor has been sold to day than all the week besides—The children have been calling us Yankees (which is the only english word they can speak) all day long—

Whether it was meant as a term of derision or not, I neither know nor care—of this I am sure, they cannot feel more contempt for me than I do for them;—tho' I most sincerely pity their ignorance & folly—There seems to be no hope of their improvement as they will not attend to any means—After saying so much about the people, I will describe our yesterday's ride—but first I will describe our last nights lodging—Susan & me ask'd to go to bed—& Mrs W spoke to Mr Riker the landlord—(for no woman was visible)—So he took up a candle to light us & we ask'd Mrs W to go up with us, for we did not dare go alone—when we got into a room he went to the bed & open'd it for us, while we were almost dying with laughter, & then stood waiting with the candle for us to get into bed—but Mrs W—as soon as she could speak, told him she would wait & bring down the candle & he then left us—I never laugh'd so heartily in my life—Our bed to sleep on was straw, & then a feather bed for covering—The pillows contain'd nearly a single handful of feathers, & were cover'd with the most curious & dirty patchwork, I ever saw—We had one bedquilt & one sheet—I did not undress at all, for I expected dutchmen in every moment & you may suppose slept very comfortably in that expectation—Mr & Mrs W, & another woman slept in the same room—When the latter came to bed, the man came in & open'd her bed also, after we were all in bed in the middle of the night, I was awaken'd by the entrance of three dutchmen, who were in search of a bed—I was almost frightened to death—but Mr W at length

heard & stopt them before they had quite reach'd our bed—Before we were dress'd the men were at the door—which could not fasten, looking at us—I think *wild Indians* will be less terrible to me, than these creatures—Nothing vexes me more than to see them set & look at us & talk in dutch and laugh—Now for our ride—After we left Mansfield, we cross'd the longest hills, and the worst road, I ever saw—two or three times after riding a little distance on turnpike, we found it fenced across & were oblig'd to turn into a wood where it was almost impossible to proceed—large trees were across, not the road for there was none, but the only place we could possibly ride—It appear'd to me, we had come to an end of the habitable part of the globe—but all these difficulties were at last surmounted, & we reach'd the Delaware—The river where it is cross'd, is much smaller than I suppos'd—The bridge over it is elegant I think—It is covered & has 16 windows each side—As soon as we pass'd the bridge, we enter'd Easton, the first town in Pennsylvania—It is a small but pleasant town—the houses are chiefly small, & built of stone—very near together—The meeting house, Bank, & I think, market, are all of the same description—There are a few very handsome brick houses, & some wooden buildings—From Easton, we came to Bethlehem, which is 12 miles distant from it—Mr W. went a mile out of his way, that we might see the town—It contains almost entirely dutch people—The houses there are nearly all stone—but like Easton it contains some pretty brick houses—It has not half as many stores as Easton—The meeting house is a curious building—it looks like a castle—I suppose it is stone,—the outside is plaister'd—We left our waggon to view the town—we did not know whether the building was a church or the moravian school, so we enquir'd of 2 or 3 men who only answer'd in dutch—Mr & Mrs W were purchasing bread, & Susan & I walk'd on to enquire—we next saw a little boy on horseback, & he could only say "me cannot english" but he I believe, spoke to another, for a very pretty boy came near us & bow'd & expecting us to speak, which we soon did; & he pointed out the school & explained the different buildings to us as well as he was able; but we found it difficult to understand him, for he could but just "english"—We felt very much oblig'd to him, though we neglected to tell him so—He is the only polite dutchman small or great, we have yet seen; & I am unwilling to suppose him a *dutchman*.

## Petition of the Trustees of the Congregation of Shearith Israel, 1811

*Church and state were officially separated by the Constitution, yet, by default, much early national education was denominational. In the absence of a formal school system, "education" was often only available through associations that used religious texts to teach reading and writing. Catholic and Jewish parents were naturally averse to having their children educated from the Protestant Bible and established their own schools as soon as practicable. Nevertheless, government financial aid to schools run by religious groups was* not equitable, as a second petition by Congregation Shearith Israel to the New York State Legislature in 1811 illustrates. New York City was home to most of the country's small American Jewish population before the middle of the nineteenth century. Shearith Israel had been a city institution since 1654, and its Sephardic synagogue on Mill Street was nearly eighty years old at the time this petition was presented. De Witt Clinton (1769–1828) wrote it for Shearith Israel and helped secure its approval in Albany, but success was short-lived. By 1825 New York would cut all public funding for schools.

*Source:* "Petition of the Trustees of the Congregation of Shearith Israel, 1811" in Alexander M. Duskin, ed., *Jewish Education in New York City* (New York, 1918), reproduced in *The Annals of America, vol. 4, 1797–1820: Domestic Expansion and Foreign Entanglements* (Chicago and London: Encyclopedia Britannica, Inc., 1968), p. 282.

The Petition of the Trustees of the Congregation of Shearith Israel in the city of New York most respectfully represent:

That from the year 1793 a school has been supported from the funds of the said congregation for the education of their indigent children. That on the 8th of April, 1801, certain school monies were distributed among seven charity schools of the said city supported by religious societies. That the free school of the Roman Catholic Church and that of your memorialists were overlooked in this benevolent distribution.

That on the 21st of March, 1806, a law was passed placing the school of the former on the same footing as the others. That your memorialists also made application to the legislature, but did not succeed, owing, as they presume, to the pressure of business.

Your memorialists, fully persuaded that the legislature will look with an equal eye upon all occupations of people who conduct themselves as good and faithful citizens, and conscious that nothing has been omitted on their part to deserve the same countenance and encouragement which has been exhibited to others, do most respectfully pray your honorable body to extend the same relief to their charity school which has been granted to all others in this city.

## William Sampson, "The Catholic Question in America, Disclosing the Secrets of Auricular Confession," 1813

*In March of 1813 Fr. Anthony Kohlmann was subpoenaed to testify against two black men and a white immigrant couple accused, respectively, of theft and receiving stolen goods. Kohlmann was an Alsatian Jesuit assigned to New York City's first Catholic parish, St. Peter's, on Barclay Street. One of the thieves had confessed the crime to Fr. Kohlmann, and the priest was the intermediary in the return of the stolen property to its original owner, an Irish coppersmith. Called to the witness stand and sworn in, Fr. Kohlmann asked to be excused from answering questions that might reveal the identity of the confessor. The court had to consider whether he was entitled to such an exemption. The resulting examination was the first legal test of the constitutional right to freedom of religious expression. It was particularly sensitive because it*

*involved Catholic immigrants whose loyalty many Americans already suspected. At a special session, counsellor William Sampson (1764–1836), an Irish Protestant exiled to the United States for political reasons, argued Fr. Kohlmann's case with reference to the harsh penal laws Britain had instituted against Catholics in Ireland. The following is an excerpt from the decision of the court delivered by the presiding judge, De Witt Clinton, Mayor of New York City.*

*Source:* William Sampson, "The Catholic Question in America: Whether a Roman Catholic Clergyman be in any case compellable to disclose the secrets of Auricular Confession" (N.Y.: Edward Gillespy, 1813; facsimile reprint, Cambridge, Mass.: Da Capo Press, 1974), pp. 111–114.

In this country there is no alliance between church and state; no established religion; no tolerated religion—for toleration results from establishment—but religious freedom guaranteed by the constitution, and consecrated by the social compact.

It is essential to the free exercise of a religion, that its ordinances should be administered—that its ceremonies as well as its essentials should be protected. The sacraments of a religion are its most important elements. We have but two in the Protestant Church—Baptism and the Lord's Supper—and they are considered the seals of the covenant of grace. Suppose that a decision of this court, or a law of the state should prevent the administration of one or both of these sacraments, would not the constitution be violated, and the freedom of religion infringed? Every man who hears me will answer in the affirmative. Will not the same result follow, if we deprive the Roman catholic of one of his ordinances? Secrecy is of the essence of penance. The sinner will not confess, nor will the priest receive his confession, if the veil of secrecy is removed: To decide that the minister shall promulgate what he receives in confession, is to declare that there shall be no penance; and this important branch of the Roman catholic religion would be thus annihilated.

It has been contended that the provision of the constitution which speaks of practices inconsistent with the peace or safety of the state, excludes this case from the protection of the constitution, and authorizes the interference of this tribunal to coerce the witness. In order to sustain this position, it must be clearly made out that the concealment observed in the sacrament of penance, is a practice inconsistent with the peace or safety of the state.

The Roman catholic religion has existed from an early period of christianity—at one time it embraced almost all Christendom, and it now covers the greater part. The objections which have been made to penance, have been theological, not political. The apprehensions which have been entertained of this religion, have reference to the supremacy, and dispensing power, attributed to the bishop of Rome, as head of the catholic church—but we are yet to learn, that the confession of sins has ever been considered as of pernicious tendency, in any other respect than its being a theological error—or its having been sometimes in the hands of bad men, perverted to the

purposes of peculation, an abuse inseperable [sic] from all human agencies.

. . . The question is not, whether penance may sometimes communicate the existence of an offence [sic] to a priest, which he is bound by his religion to conceal, and the concealment of which, may be a public injury, but whether the natural tendency of it is to produce practices inconsistent with the public safety or tranquility. There is in fact, no secret known to the priest, which would be communicated otherwise, than by confession—and no evil results from this communication—on the contrary, it may be made the instrument of great good. The sinner may be admonished and converted from the evil of his ways: Whereas if his offence [sic] was locked up in his own bosom, there would be no friendly voice to recal [sic] him from his sins, and no paternal hand to point out to him the road to virtue.

The language of the constitution is emphatic and striking, it speaks of *acts of licentiousness*, of *practices inconsistent* with the *tranquility and safety of the state*; it has reference to something actually, not negatively injurious. To acts committed, not to acts omitted—offences of a deep dye, and of an extensively injurious nature: It would be stretching it on the rack so say, that it can possibly contemplate the forbearance of a Roman catholic priest, to testify what he has received in confession, or that it could ever consider the safety of the community involved in this question. To assert this as the genuine meaning of the constitution, would be to mock the understanding, and to render the exception broader than the rule, to subvert all the principles of sound reasoning, and overthrow all the convictions of common sense.

If a religious sect should rise up and violate the decencies of life, by practicing their religious rites, in a state of nakedness; by following incest, and a community of wives. If the Hindoo should attempt to introduce the burning of widows on the funeral piles of their deceased husbands, or the Mahometan his plurality of wives, or the Pagan his bacchanalian orgies or human sacrifices. If a fanatical sect should spring up, as formerly in the city of Munster, and pull up the pillars of society, or if any attempt should be made to establish the inquisition, then the licentious acts and dangerous practices, contemplated by the constitution, would exist, and the hand of the magistrate would be rightfully raised to chastise the guilty agents.

But until men under pretence of religion, act counter to the fundamental principals of morality, and endanger the well being of the state, they are to be protected in the free exercise of their religion. If they are in error, or if they are wicked, they are to answer to the *Supreme Being*, not to the unhallowed intrusion of frail fallible mortals.

We speak of this question, not in a theological sense, but in its legal and constitutional bearings. Although we differ from the witness and his brethren, in our religious creed, yet we have no reason to question the purity of their motives, or to impeach their good conduct as citizens. They are protected by the laws and constitution of this country, in the full and free exercise of their religion, and this court can never countenance or authorize the application of insult to their faith, or of torture to their consciences.

## Paul Cuffe, Memorial Petition to Congress, 1813

*The disruption of transatlantic trade caused by the War of 1812 was more than a minor inconvenience to Captain Paul Cuffe (1759–1817), a Massachusetts entrepreneur of mixed African and Wampanoag Indian blood. It cut off vital commerce with a fledgling colony of freed slaves on the west coast of Africa. In the summer of 1813 Cuffe sent a petition to the president and Congress asking for permission to trade with Sierra Leone. American Quakers such as Cuffe had been working with London's African Institution for a number of years to effect cultural and economic change in this unique British colony. Their goal was to substitute ivory and spices for human beings in international trade. Cuffe believed his peaceful and benevolent mission warranted an exception to wartime restrictions about trading with the enemy. Despite passing the Senate, his petition failed in the House, and it was 1815 before Cuffe could implement his planned voyage to Africa outlined below.*

*Source:* Rosalind Cobb Wiggins, ed., *Captain Paul Cuffe's Logs and Letters, 1808–1817: A Black Quaker's "Voice from within the Veil"* (Washington, D.C.: Howard University Press, 1996), pp. 252–253.

To the Presedent [sic] Senate and House of Representativess [sic] of the United States of America the memorial petition of Paul Cuffe of Westport state of Massachusetts respectfully showeth that your memorialist actuated by motives which he conceives are dictated by that philanthropy which is the offspring of Christian benevolence he is induced to ask the patronage of the Government of the United States in affording aid in the execution of a plan which he cherishes a hope may ultimately prove beneficial to his bretheren [sic] of the African race within their native climate. In order to give a compleat [sic] view of the object in contemplation it may not be considered trespassing too much upon your time to premiss [sic] some of the leading Circumstances which have led to the present application.

Your memorialist being a decendant [sic] of Africa and early instructed in habits of solicity and industry has gratefully to acknowledge the many favours of bountifully Providence both in preserving him from many of the evils to which people of his colour have too often fallen into, but also by blessing his industry with such a partion [sic] of the comforts of Life as to enable him in some degree not only to communicate but to relieve the sufferings of His fellow creaters [sic]. And having early found implanted in his head the principles of equity and Justice he could not but view the practice of his bretheren [sic] of the African Race in selling their fellow creatures into a state of slavery for life as very inconsistent with that Divine principal, and his mature age having been greatly [instructed or levelled, both crossed out in original] in the abundant Labours of many pious individuals both in this country and in England to pro-

duce a termination of the wrongs of Africa by prohibiting the slave trade and also to improve the condition of the degraded inhabitants of the Land of his ancestors. He conceived it a duty incombent [sic] upon him as a faithful stward [sic] of the mercies he had received to give up a portion of his time and his property in visiting that country and affording such means as might be in his power to promote the improvement to civilization of the Africans. Under these impressions he left his family and with the sacrafice [sic] of both time and money visited Sierra Leone and there gained such information of the country and its inhabitants as enable him to form an opinion of many improvements that appeared to him essential to the well being of that people.

These he had an oppertunity [sic] of personally communicating to several distinguished members of the Royal African Institution in London and he had the satisfaction at that time to find that his recommendations were approved by the celebrated philanthropists the Duke of Gloscester, W. Wilberforce, T. Clarkson, Wm Allen and others and has since Learned that the Institution have also so far acceeded [sic] to his plans as to make some special provisions to carry them into effect. One of these objects was to keep up an intercourse with the People of Coulour [sic] in the United States in the Expectation that some persons of reputation would feel industry sbriety [sic] and frugality amongst the nations of that country. These views having been commincates [sic] by your petition[er] to the People of Coulour [sic] in Baltimore and Philadelphia, New York and Boston they with a Zeal becoming so important a concern have manifested a disposition to promote so laudable an undertaken [sic]. And several family whose characters promise influences have come to a conclusion if proper ways could be open to go to Africa for a Temporary residence in order to give their aid in promoting the objects already adverted to your petitioner still animated with a sincere desire of making the Knowledge he has acquired and the sacrifices he has all ready made more permanently useful in promoting the Civilization of Africa solicits your aid so far as to grant permission that a Vessel may be imployed [sic] if liberty can also be obtained from the British Government between this country and Sierra Leona [sic] to transport such persons and families as may be inclined to go, as also some articles of provisions together with implements of husbandry and machinery for some michanic [sic] arts and to Bring back such of the Natives productions of that country as may be wanted. For Altho pecuniary profit does not enter into calculations in the object in contemplation nor does it afford any very promising prospects yet without a little aid from the trifling [sic] commerce of that country the expenses would fall too heavy upon your petitioner and those of his friends Who feels disposed to patronize the undertaking. Your petitioner therefore craves the attention of Congress to a concern which appears to him Very important to a portion of his fellow creaturs [sic] who have been Long much excluded from the common advantage of Civilized life and prays that they will afford him and his friends such aid as they in their wisdom may think best.

> With much respect
> I am your ashured [sic] friend
> Paul Cuffe
> Westport 6 mo 16 1813

## John Walker, *A Critical Pronouncing Dictionary and Expositor of the English Language*, 1818

*In 1818 John Walker's (1732–1807) A Critical Pronouncing Dictionary and Expositor of the English Language was published, including his "Rules to be Observed by the Natives of Scotland, Ireland and London, for Avoiding their Respective Peculiarities." At nearly eight hundred pages, Walker's dictionary obviously met a popular need among immigrants who were self-conscious about their speech. Its emphasis on accent elimination also supported the supremacy of an accepted standard of English pronunciation, advocated as early as 1789 by Noah Webster. "American" in the new century emphasized uniformity rather than the regional variations of English that distinguished Scots, Irish. and Cockneys, among others. As immigrants interacted in the American crucible, a universal style of deliberately enunciating English words contributed to a common tongue throughout the backcountry and the West.*

*Source:* John Walker, *A Critical Pronouncing Dictionary and Expositor of the English Language* (New York: Collins and Hannay, 1819), p. 9; *Early American Imprints, Second Series,* no. 50015 (New York: Readex Microprint, courtesy of A. A. S., 1981).

## RULES TO BE OBSERVED BY THE NATIVES OF SCOTLAND, FOR ATTAINING A JUST PRONUNCIATION OF ENGLISH

That pronunciation which distinguishes the inhabitants of Scotland is of a very different kind from that of Ireland, and may be divided into the quantity, quality, and accentuation of the vowels. With respect to quantity, it may be observed, that the Scotch pronounce *habit, hay-bit; tepid, tee-pid; sinner, see-ner; conscious, cone-shus;* and *subject, soob-ject*: it is not pretended, however, that every accented vowel is so pronounced, but that such a pronunciation is very general, and particularly of the *i*. This vowel is short in English pronunciation, where the other vowels are long; thus, *evasion, adhesion, emotion, confusion,* have the *a, e, o,* and *u,* long; and in these instances the Scotch would pronounce them like the English; but in *vision, decision,* &c. where the English pronounce the *i* short, the Scotch lengthen this letter by pronouncing it like *ee,* as if the words were written *vee-sion, de-cee-sion,* &c and this peculiarity is universal. The best way, therefore, to correct this, will be to make a collection of the most usual words which have the vowels short, and to pronounce them daily till a habit is formed. See Principles, No. 507.

With respect to the quality of the vowels, it may be observed, that the inhabitants of Scotland are apt to pronounce the *a* like *aw,* where the English give it the slender sound: thus *Satan,* is pronounced *Sawtan,* and *fatal, fawtal.* It may be remarked too, that the Scotch

give this sound to the *a* preceded by the *w,* according to the general rule, without attending to the exceptions, Principles, No. 83; and thus, instead of making *wax, waft,* and *twang,* rhyme with *tax, shaft,* and *hang,* they pronounce them so as to rhyme with *box, soft,* and *song.* The short *e* in *bed, fed, red,* &c. borders too much upon the English sound of *a* in *bad, lad, mad,* &c. and the short *i* in *bid, lid, rid,* too much on the English sounds of *e* in *bed, led, red.* To correct this error, it would be useful to collect the long and short sound of these vowels, and to pronounce the long ones first, and to shorten them by degrees till they are perfectly short; at the same time preserving the radical sound of the vowel in both. . . .

But besides the mispronunciation of single words, there is a tone of voice with which these words are accompanied, that distinguishes a native of Ireland or Scotland, as much as an improper sound of letters. This is vulgarly, and, if it does not mean stress only, but the kind of stress, I think, not improperly called the accent. For though there is an asperity in the Irish dialect and a drawl in the Scotch, independent of the slides and inflections they make use of, yet it may with confidence be affirmed, that much of the peculiarity which distinguishes these dialects may be reduced to a predominant use of one of these slides. Let any one who has sufficiently studied the speaking voice to distinguish the slides, observe the pronunciation of an Irishman and a Scotchman, who have much of the dialect of their country, and he will find that the former abounds with the falling, and the latter with the rising inflection;

and if this is the case, the teacher, if he understands these slides, ought to direct his instruction so as to remedy the imperfection. But as avoiding the wrong, and seizing the right at the same instant, is, perhaps too great a task for human powers, I would advise a native of Ireland, who has much of the accent, to pronounce almost all his words, and end all his sentences, with the rising slide; and a Scotchman in the same manner, to use the falling inflection: this will, in some measure, counteract the natural propensity, and bids fairer for bringing the pupil to that nearly equal mixture of both slides which distinguishes the English speaker, than endeavouring at first to catch the agreeable variety. For this purpose the teacher ought to pronounce all the single words in the lessen with the falling inflection to a Scotchman, and with the rising to an Irishman; and should frequently give the pauses in a sentence the same inflections to each of these pupils, where he would vary them to a native of England.

## John Doyle to His Wife, January 25, 1818

*Most Irish emigrating after the end of the Napoleonic Wars had some skills, and those who traveled directly to the ports of Philadelphia or New York were able to afford the higher passage fares to American rather than Canadian ports. John Doyle had both advantages, as well as entrée via an established network of Irish social and occupational links: he joined his father, who had fled Ireland in the wake of the 1798 rebellion nearly two decades earlier. Thus he was immediately able*

*to find work upon arrival in 1817 and within several months had saved a substantial sum of money. A financial panic in the United States in 1819 would cause a sharp reduction in the number of Irish emigrants crossing the Atlantic, from twenty thousand in 1818 to ten thousand in 1820 and only six thousand in 1821. In this letter written home to his wife in Ireland, Doyle expresses—perhaps with the enthusiasm novelty engenders—the various ways in which an Irishman experienced "freedom" from the oppressiveness of British colonial regulation.*

Source: John Doyle, January 25, 1818, reproduced in William D. Griffin, *The Book of Irish Americans* (New York: Times Book/Random House, 1990), pp. 119–120.

Oh, how long the days, how cheerless and fatiguing the nights since I parted with my Fanny and my little angel. Sea sickness, nor the toils of the ocean, nor the starvation which I suffered, nor the constant apprehension of our crazy old vessel going to the bottom, for ten tedious weeks, could ever wear me to the pitch it has if my mind was easy about you. But when the recollection of you and of my little Ned rushes on my mind with a force irresistible, I am amazed and confounded to think of the coolness with which I used to calculate on parting with my little family even for a day, to come to this *strange* country, which is the grave of the reputations, the morals, and of the lives of so many of our countrymen and countrywomen . . .

We were safely landed in Philadelphia on the 7th of October and I had not so much as would pay my passage in a boat to take me ashore . . . I, however, contrived to get over, and . . . it was not long until I made out my father, whom I instantly knew, and no one could describe our feelings when I made myself known to him, and received his embraces, after an absence of seventeen years. . . . The morning after landing I went to work to the printing . . . I think a journeyman printer's wages might be averaged at 7 ½ dollars a week all the year round . . . I worked in Philadelphia five and one-half weeks and saved 6 pounds, that is counting four dollars to the pound; in the currency of the United States the dollar is worth five shillings Irish . . . I found the printing and bookbinding overpowered with hands in New York. I remained idle for twelve days in consequence; when finding there was many out of employment like myself I determined to turn myself to something else, seeing that there was nothing to be got by idleness . . . I was engaged by a bookseller to hawk maps for him at 7 dollars a week. . . . I now had about 60 dollars of my own saved . . . these I laid out in the purchase of pictures on New Year's Day, which I sell ever since. I am doing astonishingly well, thanks be to God, and was able to make a deposit of 100 dollars in the bank of the United States.

As yet it's only natural I should feel lonesome in this country, ninety-nine out of every hundred who come to it are at first disappointed. . . . Still, it's a fine country and a much better place for a poor man than Ireland . . . and much as they grumble at first, after a while they never think of leaving it . . . One thing I think is certain, that if emigrants knew

beforehand what they have to suffer for about the first six months after leaving home in every respect, they would never come here. However, an enterprising man, desirous of advancing himself in the world, will despise everything for coming to this free country, where a man is allowed to thrive and flourish without having a penny taken out of his pocket by government; no visits from tax gatherers, constables or soldiers, every one at liberty to act and speak as he likes, provided he does not hurt another, to slander and damn government, abuse public men in their office to their faces, wear your hat in court and smoke a cigar while speaking to the judge as familiarly as if he was a common mechanic, hundreds go unpunished for crimes for which they would surely be hung in Ireland; in fact they are so tender of life in this country that a person should have a very great interest to get himself hanged for anything.

## The Shamrock Friendly Association, 1818

*In the early nineteenth century there was a good market for descriptive guides to the various American states. The Picture of New-York and Stranger's Guide through the Commercial Emporium of the United States—all 357 pages plus a map—was published in 1818. In addition to the expected capsule entries on the state's cities and towns, there were sections on the laws governing servants and slaves or public nuisances such as "blowing horns," as well as an annotated list of the various religious and ethnic societies available for membership. It contains a lengthy entry for the Shamrock Friendly Association, a relatively new Irish organization that had just published a helpful pamphlet that was being widely circulated in Europe.*

*Source: The Picture of New-York and Stranger's Guide through the Commercial Emporium of the United States (New York: A. T. Goodrich & Co., 1818), pp. 182–183; Early American Imprints, Second Series, no. 45335 (New York: Readex Microprint, courtesy of A. A. S., 1981).*

*Shamrock Friendly Association*, was formed in 1815, for the purpose of befriending emigrants on their arrival in the United States. This is done by giving them useful information, and procuring them employment. The society is composed chiefly of the natives of Ireland; but their views are not confined to country, politics, or religion. It is enough that the applicant is a *stranger*, to engage their attention. They have already procured employment for upwards of 1,200 individuals in various parts of the country. Having a regular correspondence and connexion with most of the Irish societies in the union, they are enabled to act at a distance with great effect.

During the last year, the society published a useful pamphlet, entitled "Hints to Emigrants from Europe who intend to make a permanent residence in the United States." It has been republished in the United States and in Europe; and contains valuable information, which ought to be known by every stranger on his arrival here:—It considers, "1st, what relates to his *personal* safety in a

new climate; 2d, his interests as a *probationary* resident; and 3d, his future rights and duties as a member of a free state." On the most interesting and important subject to the generality of emigrants, viz. *employment*, it gives the following correct information:

"Industrious men need never lack employment in America. Labourers, carpenters, masons, bricklayers, stonecutters, blacksmiths, weavers, turners, farmers, curriers, tailors and shoemakers, and the useful mechanics generally are always sure of work and wages. Stonecutters now receive in this city (New York) 2 dollars a day, equal to 9 shillings sterling; carpenters 1 dollar and 87½ cents; bricklayers 2 dollars; labourers from 1 dollar to 1 and a quarter; others in proportion. At this time (July, 1817) house carpenters, bricklayers, masons and stonecutters are paid 3 dollars per day in Petersburgh, Virginia. The town was totally consumed by fire about a year since, but it is now rising from its ashes in more elegance than ever Mechanics will find employment there for, perhaps, two years to come."— "There are not many of the laborious classes whom we would advise to reside or even loiter in great towns, because as much will be spent during a long winter as can be made through a toilsome summer, so that a man may be kept a moneyless drudge for life."—"Men of *science*, who can apply their knowledge to useful and practical purposes, may be very advantageously settled; but *mere literary scholars*, who have no profession, or only one which they cannot profitably practice in this country, do not meet with much encouragement; in truth, with little or none, unless they are willing to devote themselves to the education of youth."

This institution is conducted by a president, two vice-presidents, secretary, assistant secretary, treasurer, and a committee of superintendance, consisting of four members, who are elected annually.

## Hezekiah Niles, "Editorial," August 8, 1818

*After Andrew Jackson's defeat of the Creeks in 1814, settlers clamored for land in Alabama, which was officially declared a territory in 1817. That year Congress sold a large tract to the Society for the Olive and the Vine, a group of French immigrants who had persuasively argued the benefits of domestic cultivation of this produce. Likewise, in 1818 the Irish societies in New York, Philadelphia, Baltimore, and Pittsburgh combined to petition Congress to set aside a portion of land in the Illinois Territory. They believed that because the land was remote and uncultivated, it was not prime real estate and therefore poor Irish immigrants might be permitted to settle there on extended credit (a twelve-year mortgage at $2 per acre). The French endeavor was abused, as Hezekial Niles's editorial explains, and led directly to the denial of the Irish petition, even though the reason Congress cited was opposition to the creation of "ethnic political units" rather than concerns about management oversight. Niles went on to offer his opinion of the wisdom of ethnic colonies in general.*

Source: Hezekiah Niles, "Editorial," *Niles' Weekly Register*, August 8, 1818; reproduced in

*The Annals of America*, vol. 4, *1797–1820: Domestic Expansion and Foreign Entanglements* (Chicago and London: Encyclopedia Britannica, Inc., 1968), pp. 495–496.

Among the splendid fooleries which have at times amused a portion of the American people, as well as their representatives in Congress, was that of granting, on most favorable terms to certain emigrants from France, a large tract of land in the Alabama Territory to encourage the cultivation of the vine and olive, passed the 3rd of March 1817.

This tract contains 92,000 acres, and was sold at $2 per acre, payable without interest, in fourteen years—in truth, much better than a mere gratuity of so much land considering the license of selection, and which could not, at this time, probably be purchased of the proprietors for less than $2 million. What was honestly intended as a common benefit to a number of unfortunate persons is understood to have immediately entered, like banking, into the benefit of a few; and I am told that one man's gains by this peculation are estimated at from $500,000 to $1 million.

The act of Congress by which this grant was made contains many provisions to prevent, the public munificence from being converted into a private monopoly. And one of our objects in referring to it is to excite some member of Congress to a rigid inquiry to ascertain if the letter of the law has been satisfied, seeing that its spirit has been violated—in order to a reclamation of the immunities granted, if justice requires it.

So much, indeed, has the beneficence

of Congress been abused, that two or three of the oldest and most respectable members told me, when at Washington last winter, that there was nothing against which they should hereafter be so much upon their guard as those acts called liberal—and one of them observed he never had voted for any law that was intended by him as an advantage to a class of people which he had not sincerely repented of, because the advantages designed for all had uniformly been perverted to the benefit of a few scheming individuals; and he instanced a series of speculations "too tedious to mention." It was the abuse of the Alabama grant that caused the rejection of the petition of the Irish Emigrant Associations for the laying off of a tract of land in the Illinois, though everybody felt satisfied that their design was an honest one.

By the way, however, I very much question the policy of any act of government that has a tendency to introduce and keep up among us a foreign national language or dialect, manners or character, as every large and compact settlement of emigrants from any particular country must necessarily occasion. Though some have seemed almost ready to quarrel with me for the often-repeated assertion, I still assert and will maintain it, that the people of the United States are yet wretchedly deficient of a national character, though it is rapidly forming, and in a short time will be as the vanguard of the national strength. Its progress, however, is retarded by the influx of foreigners, with manners and prejudices favorable to a state of things repugnant to our rules and notions of right, since few enlightened men may be called citizens of the world; but most men's ideas are narrowed to the spot or country, with its habits of thinking and of acting, where they received their education, which it requires at least the mixture of a generation to remove.

These prejudices extend as well to the religious as to the political supremacy of certain poor, weak, and miserable individuals; and considerably prevent an exercise of the right which man has to worship God after the dictates of his own heart, and are at open war with the power that he has, in its liberal sense, to manage all his own concerns in his own way. To lessen the force of prejudices so hostile to our free institutions, it is important that those subject to them should be cast into the common stock of the people; in which, if they do not get more expanded ideas and fall in with the general habits of the nation of which they are members, their scattered condition will measurably forbid them from retarding the growth of a general feeling—or at least, prevent a powerful action against it.

These remarks might be illustrated by many well-known examples; but the case does not require it at present, and would be to travel from the point that is now aimed at. I am notoriously the friend of all persons seeking happiness in this land of liberty, and designing to lay their bones among us; and would afford to them every facility that they may become Americans, indeed—but it is only upon the condition of their becoming so that I wish the presence of any. I most sincerely despise the creature that, rioting in his ease possessed here, adheres to those institutions which drove him from his country. If any love a king better than freedom, let them lick his feet "at home" as long as his majesty will condescend to suffer it—but it is knavery, or folly, in a man who voluntarily takes up his abode in America, this "despicable country," to be always telling us of the roast beef and happiness that he left. And it ought to be resented by advising him to go back again as quickly as possible—adding that we will cheerfully part with him.

## Jesse Torrey, *A Portraiture of Domestic Slavery in the United States,* 1816

*Jesse Torrey (1787–1834), a Pennsylvania junior physician, wrote an essay in late 1816 that advocated the gradual emancipation of slaves and "a colonial asylum for free people of colour." However, unlike most of his contemporaries who were promoting Africa as a haven for former slaves, Torrey's own observations led him to the conclusion that they would prefer to remain in the land of their birth—perhaps in the American West or South—rather than be exiled to a foreign country. He reported that a freed female servant—"a little shaded with a yellowish tint"—told him her fathers did not come from Africa, "and (said she) if they (the Americans) did not want us, they had no need to have brought us away; after they've brought us here, and made us work hard, and disfigured the colour, I don't think it would be fair to send us back again." Torrey's conscience was also sparked by scenes such as one he witnessed in Washington, seven years after the overseas slave trade had been abolished.*

*Source:* Jesse Torrey, *A Portraiture of Domestic Slavery in the United States: Proposing National Measures for the Education and Gradual Emancipation of the Slaves, Without Impairing the Legal Privileges of the Possessor, and a Project of a Colonial Asylum for Free People of Colour: Including Memoirs of Facts on the Interior Traffic in Slaves, and on Kidnapping,* 2d ed. (New York: Ballston Spa, 1818), pp. 63–66, 69–70; *Early American Imprints, Second Series,* no. 45881 (New York: Readex Microprint, courtesy of A. A. S., 1981).

## AMERICAN INTERIOR SLAVE TRAFFIC

On the 4th day of December, 1815, (the day on which the session of congress commenced,) being at the seat of government of the United States, I was preparing to enjoy the first opportunity that had occurred to me, of beholding the assembled representatives of the American Republic. As I was about to proceed to the building where the session was opened, my agreeable reverie was suddenly interrupted by the voice of a stammering boy, who, as he was coming into the house, from the street, exclaimed, "There goes the Ge-Ge-orgy men with a drove o'niggers chain'd together two and two." What's that, said I—I must see, and, going to the door, I just had a distant *glimpse* of a light covered wagon, followed by a procession of men, women and children, resembling that of a funeral. I followed them hastily; and as I approached so near as to discover that they were bound together in pairs, with ropes, and *chains,* (which I had hitherto seen used only for restraining beasts,) the involuntary successive heavings of my bosom became irrepressible. I have since heard an intelligent gentleman, from Scotland, describe a similar affection. He affirmed, that on his arrival upon the coast of the United States, (in Chesapeake Bay,) he first view of the slaves *brought his heart into his throat.* I have also been told by a gentleman, who holds a seat in the senate of the United States, that *"a drove of manacled slaves, was to him, an insupportable spectacle, which he generally endeavored to avoid;"* and by a representative, (since deceased,) from one of the slave states, who was himself a possessor of slaves, *"that he never could bear to see slaves manacled and fettered with bolts and chains, nor families torn asunder and sold to the slave traders, and wondered how any one could be so inhuman as to do such acts."* Overtaking the *caravan,* just opposite to the old Capitol (then in a state of ruins from the conflagration by the British army,) I inquired of one of the *drivers* (of whom there were two) "what part of the country they were taking all these people to?" "To Georgia," he replied. "Have you not, said I, enough such people in that country yet?" "Not quite enough," he answered. I found myself incapable of saying more, and was compelled to avert my eyes immediately from the heart-rending scene! I walked along some distance before them, down Pennsylvania Avenue, and, on turning round, observed that they had left that street, (as if the spirit of PENN had repelled the contact of such a tragedy with his name,) and directed their course towards the Potomac bridge. At the same moment an African passed by, driving a hack; and beholding his brethren,

Trembling, weeping, captive led
[Homer]

extended his arm towards them, and exclaimed, "See there! an't that right down *murder?* Don't you call that right down *murder?*" On uttering to him indistinctly, that I did not know, he renewed his request to be answered and I replied, "I do not know but it is *murder.*"—These expressions instantly reminded me of the frequency of murders and deaths, not only of slaves, but of white and free black men, resulting from despotic slavery, and particularly from the slave traffic. . . .

With these mournful spectra and many more equally shocking, flitting in succession before me, and the black procession still in view, the pleasant anticipations which I had been indulging but fifteen minutes previous, became totally reversed. Returning pensive towards my lodgings, and passing by the Capitol, I thought—Alas! poor Africa—*thy cup* is the *essence* of bitterness! This *solitary magnificent temple, dedicated to liberty*— opens its portals to *all* other nations but *thee,* and bids their sons participate *freely* of the cup of *freedom* and happiness; but when *thy* unoffending, enslaved sons clank their blood-smeared *chains* under its towers, it sneers at their calamity, and mocks their lamentations with the echo of contempt!

## Stockbridge, Maine, 1818

*The Society for Propagating the Gospel among the Indians and Others in North America was established in Boston in 1787,* *with a charter granted by a British association that predated them by a century in the mission of preaching Christianity to the indigenous peoples of New England. The American Society focused on tribes "interspersed among the white inhabitants, or in their neighborhood" rather than on the western frontier. Thus, in the following report accepted in November 1818, the work of the society's missionary, Rev. Mr. Sergeant, at New-Stockbridge, Maine, is described in some detail. Sergeant was paid $50 a month and had been working among this tribe for at least twenty years, encouraging husbandry as a means to Christianizing. As early as 1798 the society had translated the catechism into the language of the Stockbridge Indians and underwritten its printing and distribution.*

*Source: Report of the Select Committee of the Society for Propagating the Gospel Among the Indians and Others in North America (U.S.: 1818), pp. 19–20; Early American Imprints, Second Series, no. 45750a (New York: Readex Microprint, courtesy of A. A. S., 1981).*

## STOCKBRIDGE INDIANS

The Rev. Mr. Sergeant continues to perform the duties of his permanent mission. It must be gratifying to the Society to be presented with examples of intellectual, as well as of moral and religious improvement among the native inhabitants of the wilderness. . . .

After divine service, Mr. S. "catechized the young people in their own language."—A meeting for prayer among the Indian women was, upon invitation, attended by two of our missionary's daughters, who brought the following report to their father. "We found about 20 Christian females collected; a psalm was first sung, after this a prayer by one of their women in their own language, which we did not fully understand; after this we read a chapter out of the Bible; the Bible was then handed to an aged Indian woman, who, putting on her spectacles, looked over the chapter, gave the contents in her own language with much ease and apparent intelligence; a psalm was then sung in their own language. Four prayers were made in all."—"With much pleasure"—observed the visitants—"we contemplated the privilege they enjoyed in making use of their Bible and Psalm books, the gift of the benevolent Societies." They expressed, with sensibility, their impressions on this occasion, particularly that "of the great benefit of reading the Scriptures of truth." "Here was a number of our fellow creatures, apparently in the exercise of a humble Christian spirit, whose hearts were cheered and warmed by meditating on the Word of God and the instructions of the Gospel of Christ. A considerable number have bowed at the foot of the cross, and, as we have reason to hope, understandingly united themselves to the Church of Christ, entirely forsaking their wicked habits of drinking, and becoming industrious. We have reason to believe the Lord has been pleased mercifully to hear and answer the prayers of this feeble band of female persevering sisters in the cause of the glorious Saviour, that he has fulfilled his gracious promise, that the wilderness should blossom as the rose."

At a conference meeting, a female, who by desire had expressed her religious sentiments and views with great seriousness and pertinency, said, in conclusion, "I take the greatest comfort when I am alone, and have no interruption in meditating on the great and glorious things of religion." Our missionary here notes: "The young woman, who delivered the above, has more than common talents, spoke in her own language, but it is correctly translated. She understands better than she can speak in English—has read her Bible through several times." . . . Mr. Sergeant visited the Oneida Indian village, where his children kept a Sunday school; and, though it was a rainy day, found, to his surprise, between 30 and 40 children collected. This village of about 20 families, and upwards of 50 children, has been grossly neglected. "They generally understand and speak a little English, are very industrious, and have made considerable progress in civilization, but there is not one professor of religion among them" They had been "much inclined to work or play on the Sabbath;" our missionary "observes with pleasure, that this Sunday school has put a stop to their profaning the Sabbath."

. . . By communication from him of 11 Sept. last, it appears, that so many of the Indian children have gone from New Stockbridge to White River, that, for this season, a school would be supported in part only from the Society's grant.

The present state of this mission is, on the whole, apparently encouraging; and we may unite our hopes with our prayers, "that a remnant," at least, of this forlorn people, "may be saved."

## By a Lady, *Catherine Brown, the Converted Cherokee*, 1819

*A little twenty-seven-page drama published in 1819 offers an epistemological illustration of the ways in which many Americans viewed Indian assimilation. In it, a Cherokee girl called Catherine Brown is sent by her parents to study at Chickamauga, a Christian missionary school in Brainard, Massachusetts. In scene 4, the headmaster of the school listens while twelve Indian chiefs discuss the importance of white culture and education to their future. The dramatic choices made by the play's anonymous author reveal how historical fact was being massaged in popular culture. "Cherokee," although clearly a southeastern tribe without New England ties, connoted "civilized" because by this time they had made certain accommodations in response to white incursions of their territory. Nevertheless, the Cherokees had proved one of the more difficult tribes to displace. But Catherine Brown's father surrenders when he comes to reclaim his daughter: "We must go as soon as we can—the white people determined to have the country. They steal our cattle, hogs, sheep, they get all they can—we no want to quarrel—rather live in peace—so we go— let them have the land."*

Source: *Catherine Brown, the Converted Cherokee: A Missionary Drama, founded on fact*, written by a lady (New Haven, Conn.: S. Converse, 1819), pp. 16–20; *Early American Imprints, Second Series*, no. 47525 (New York: Readex Microprint, courtesy of A. A. S., 1981).

## SCENE FOURTH

Twelve Chiefs in Council at Mr. Hicks.'
The king is placed on a rug, at one

side of the room, with his back supported with a roll of blankets; Mr. Hicks is by his side, on the same rug. The other Chiefs are placed in chairs in front of the King. They are all deep in thought, when Mr. Hoyt enters. At length Mr. Hoyt is discovered by Mr. Hicks, who beckons to him. Mr. Hoyt advances. Mr. Hicks takes him by the hand, without rising.

MR. HICKS (to the King). This is Mr. Hoyt the Missionary from Chickamauga.

KING. (Takes him by the hand without rising.) Welcome, sir—we are friendly to you—sit in council with us.
(Each Chief in his turn, takes Mr. Hoyt by the hand without rising.)

MR. HICKS. Take a seat with us, our good brother.—
(Sits on a chair and Mr. Hoyt sits down.)
(The Council is then opened by the King.)

KING. My Chiefs—This Council is called for the purpose of talking on the importance of having Missionaries and schools, in our several nations. Let brother speak his mind to brother, and let us see if our sons and our daughters, cannot be made equal to the children of white men.

SECOND CHIEF. My brethren—When I was at the great city of Washington, and had a talk with the President our father, I saw the great men of the land; I heard their talks: They put me in mind of the stately trees, of the forest that look so noble, and whose branches extend far and wide, to shelter the more humble trees, that grow within their reach. I thought, what makes these men so noble? I found it was education. I saw their women: They would appear by the side of our women, like the rose—the honeysuckle—and the ivy—by the side of the cowslip, the daisy, and the snowdrop. I thought, what makes these women so conspicuous? I found it was education. I thought our sons and daughters might be made like them.

THIRD CHIEF. When I have been looking at our young men, and seeing them bounding like the Antelope, over the mountains, and through rivers, in search of prey, and in quest of pleasure; I have thought, why cannot they be tamed? Although their fathers set them the example, we are tired of the chace [sic]—we admire cultivated fields, and our land can be made equal to the gardens of white men. Our daughters are sprightly as the larks—their voices are shrill as the Linnet's—clear as the running brook, and soft as the Nightingale's. I am for schools.

FOURTH CHIEF. Educate bad men and you make them worse. Look at the white traders—how they cheat us. They give our men strong water, that makes them foolish—then they get away their lands and take their cattle. If we have schools, let us have such schools, as will make our children better people.

FIFTH CHIEF. Look at the Senecas—see the Oneidas—there are the Wyandots—yonder is the Stockbridge tribe—all, all, forsaking Indian ways, and learning the religion of the good white men, and for the hunting chase, are making beautiful their cornfields.

SIXTH CHIEF. Many moons ago, several brothers of mine traveled through the country: We went to Washington—to New-York—tarried three days in New-Haven, and thus we went on from city to city, until we arrived at Boston: We saw great men, and beautiful women: We looked at their cotages [sic]: Once in a few miles, they had houses to worship in—to worship the great spirit, who is the giver of all good. It grieved us to think that beautiful country was once ours, and we obliged to wear the name of savage: Let us be savage no longer.

SEVENTH CHIEF. Let us not move to the Arcansas [sic], and sell our lands here—Let us invite schools and Missionaries. Let us build houses for our women and children—Let us work on our lands; and very soon our country will be beautiful, and very soon, at our approach—instead of "there comes the savage," we shall receive the friendly hand, and the great man's bow.

EIGHTH CHIEF. At Chickamauga there is a school—there are Missionaries—the children are happy—they love to work—they read and write—the Missionaries are good to them—they clothe them—they feed them—but they are full—they cannot take more children—we must have schools in our own settlements—we must have them thick.

NINTH CHIEF. My brethren—I would not wish to be considered as an opposer—but let us be considerate—can our young men be tamed? See how they skip like the Rein-Deer, across the plain—See them climb the mountains—Look at our young women—How gay they are, no birds in the forest so gay—They go beyond the Peacock—I wish to be considerate—I am agreed if all are agreed—Let us be considerate.

TENTH CHIEF. My mind is fixed—No girl in our nation is so fine as Catharine Brown—Her father is a great warrior—is rich—allows her as much wampum as

she chooses—He sent her to Chickamauga—She is now modest—pleasant—charming as a bright summer's morning.

ELEVENTH CHIEF. Take a young tree—Place it by your door—Trim it every day—You can make it stand straight as an arrow, or you can make it bend to the north, to the south—to the east, to the west, just as your mind is—It is so with our children. Not long since, some of our young men shook hands, and all agreed not to drink any more—not to be wild—agreed to invite schools—They said they were tired of Indian ways. If fathers, mothers, and young men, walk in the good way—the young women, will soon follow—I am agreed.

MR. HICKS. My brethren—you already know my mind on the subject. Nothing but a conviction of the utility of the proposal, would have made me consent to part with my darling son. Leonard, my beloved son, has gone far away to receive a christian education. Before this time he has reached Cornwal [sic], in Connecticut. There is in that place, a school—which has the charge of youth of many nations, kindred and tongues. There the good men preach—and there the good men pray. There the good women clothe them—young and old are doing what they can to educate Indians and heathen. They are friendly to Indians—let us be friendly to them.

KING. (Arises and makes a bow to Mr. Hoyt.) Brother, will you give us a talk—we are ready and willing to hear your talk. (Sits down.)

MR. HOYT. I perceive, brethren, you are all anxious to have learning and religion introduced in your several nations. This belief affords me much satisfaction. We have long believed you to be men as well as ourselves; that you have minds equally capable of improvement, and souls susceptible of endless felicity. We shall rejoice to see you civilized, and evangelized. There is no enjoyment, nor any privilege, which is in our possession, but that we wish you an equal share: we are willing to do you all the good we can. You have many friends living, at the north, who all wish you happiness here, and hereafter. When your friends have been informed of the cruelty, deceit, and wickedness of the white men that surround your border; when we have been told how these abandoned men would intoxicate and demoralize your people, and steal your cattle; and when your characters have been misrepresented by them, to your disadvantage, we have mourned and wept in compassion to you. And when, by constant and repeated abuse, they make "your poor men wretched, and induce your rich men to move away," still farther from the light of the gospel "our hearts sink within us, and we feel constrained to weep—we seek where to weep; we enter our closets and weep there." Think not, my brothers, that all white men are your enemies. No; many gentlemen and ladies, of the first respectability in the United States, lay your case deeply to heart. They ask themselves where, and what should they have been, had they not been instructed and enlightened—they then say, as we would wish others to do unto us, let us do even so to them; and upon that principle they are making great exertion to promote your welfare, and it will be highly gratifying when they are informed you have so much anxiety on the subject.

(The king then arises, and gives him the friendly hand.)

KING. I give you this friendly hand, and you may tell your people that we are friendly. We thank you for your good talk—we believe all you say. I shall delegate some of my best men to go with brother Hicks, and visit the city of Washington immediately. They must pray the good President, our father, to send us instructors; and you must beseech your good people to send us missionaries.

(Each chief then arises, and advances to Mr. Hoyt and gives him the friend hand.)

(Exit Mr. Hoyt. . . .)

## Anonymous, *Clear and Concise Statement of New-York and the Surrounding Country*, 1819

*False expectations of the promise of America led to many disillusioned immigrants. Vast tracts of land were available for settlement, but that powerful lure often lost its impetus in the face of frontier trials, making even the bleak conditions in the Old World rosy by comparison. A thirty-two-page anonymous pamphlet published in 1819 directly challenged Morris Birkbeck's (1764–1825) account extolling the virtues of an English colony in Illinois that had appeared in two books the previous year. The pamphleteer wrote, "if I only prevent the destruction of one valuable family, or of an individual, it will afford me great consolation." He included a pessimistic multistanza poem, entitled "An Address to the British Before They Leave Their Homes," which satirically advised postponing emigration until the impossible happened: "When fields of corn spontaneous spring From woods and miry bogs, / And emigrants are all content To feed on* snakes and frogs . . . When vile moschetoes [sic] cease to bite And bed-bugs disappear, / When Yankees find good malt and hops, And brew good English beer . . ."

Source: Anonymous, *Clear and Concise statement of New-York and the surrounding country: containing a faithful account of many of those base impositions which are constantly and uniformly practiced upon British emigrants by crafty, designing, and Unprincipled adventurers* (New York: Printed for the author and sold by John Wilson, 1819), pp. 24–26, 28; *Early American Imprints, Second Series,* no. 47640 (New York: Readex Microprint, courtesy of A. A. S., 1981).

If it had been in the power of the legislative authority of England to have kept their mechanics, their farmers and labourers at home, America at this instant would have presented a very different face; but the more distress you have in Great Britain, the more numerous will be the persons desirous of emigrating to some spot where they hope to improve their circumstances; and this they are falsely led to believe will be happily realized when they can accomplish their darling wish of visiting this extensive territory. It is thus that simple men build castles in the air; they figure to themselves the advantages of having a farm of their own; and many of these persons, when they set foot on American soil, become an easy prey to the artifices of speculating knaves, who are prowling about after all new comers, or any other credulous customers who may fall in their way. I wish to put a plain common case which is occurring daily, relative to farms and farmers: this in some measure will elucidate a part of the policy of the American government in their endeavours to bring immense woodlands and other vast barren swamps into a state of some cultivation. In any state, for instance, you may obtain a grant of from one hundred to any number of acres of land, say at a rate of from one to two dollars per acre, paying down a deposit of one third, and entering into bond to pay the remainder in five, six, or seven years: the purchaser then starts full of animation to his wonderful estate, and takes possession of an immense wood, very likely twenty or thirty miles from any turnpike road, and ten or twenty miles from any house or human being. If this gentleman farmer can raise a dog to accompany him to his new freehold, his dog and himself find work enough to employ a regiment of soldiers for seven years, to clear and cultivate a sufficient quantity of land to support a moderate family. Some men, however, have been hardy enough to smile at difficulties, and by a natural determination of character, the sturdy fellow sets to work in real earnest with his axe and spade, and if he can luckily employ labourers who can do without wages for a few years, he may by great exertion and constant, hard, slavish application, get rid of every shilling of his money, and clear or improve a sufficient portion of his farm to produce a few potatoes, some Indian corn, &c. &c. upon which his little establishment entirely subsist; but the time at length arrives when the bond becomes due, and the proper officer serves the panic-struck gentleman with a notice to pay up his arrears for his land and taxes by a certain day: the poor fellow is very likely unable to raise a single dollar; when, behold, a writ is issued, and the estate is advertised for sale, under an execution from the sheriff, and the poor man is totally ruined: all which we see in the New-York papers as common as any other advertisement. These are what we call farmers for the United States; the man seldom gets any thing for his many years slavish and miserable exile. The state merely returns him the money which he paid originally, but all the improvements generally go to the next buyer. It may readily be perceived that if men of large property take a similar course and establish as extensive colony, it is very probable that in the course of thirty or forty years they might form very decent estates and important settlements in some parts of these wild, woody, and unexplored regions, reaching as they do from the very rising to the setting of the sun; and any man, or set of men, who want only to work for posterity, or the American government, and who are disgusted with all social order, let them come to America without loss of time: here they will find the greatest scope to indulge in the rural sport of hunting the rattlesnake, or of getting out of his way; and here also they will find sufficient laborious employment for generation after generation, for ages yet to come. They must leave every thing in the shape of comfort behind them, and bid an eternal farewell to all polished, refined, or even civilized society, to mingle in future with cannibals, wild beasts, or the parchment-skinned, true-blooded Yankee, whom you can distinguish from the rest of the human race, by his meagre jaws, which look like a dried bladder, with small eyes, and remarkable strait hair.

. . . I conclude by stating, that I have seen many of our countrymen who have been thus grossly abused, and who have vainly traversed thousands of miles upon this continent, in search of what they left at home, who after years of comfortless, unsocial existence, have excited the greatest commisseration [sic], and numerous friends have subscribed to enable them to return to the hospitable shores of Britain, which they had left much dissatisfied, in pursuit of those blessings they were obliged to go back to find.

## Pennsylvania General Assembly, *Resolutions Relative to Preventing the Introduction of Slavery into New States*, 1819

*In 1819 Missouri petitioned Congress to be admitted to statehood. Its location caused intense debate over the extension of slavery into the new western territories. That debate was literally in black and white terms: northern states were abolitionist, southern states were slave. Public opinion in the north led to legislative resolutions such as those passed by the Pennsylvania General Assembly that December, strictly instructing their congressional representatives in Washington to vote against the admission of any new state that would permit slavery or indentured servitude. Pennsylvania had been the first state to make slavery illegal (1780), and in 1817 Philadelphia's free black population had expressed its support for abolition by protesting African colonization schemes. The Missouri Compromise in 1820 temporarily settled matters: no restrictions were placed on slavery in Missouri,*

*Maine was admitted as a free state to keep the sectional balance, and slavery was prohibited in all western areas north of 36° 30' latitude.*

Source: Pennsylvania General Assembly, *Resolutions relative to preventing the introduction of slavery into new states* (Harrisburg, Penn.: 1819); *Early American Imprints, Second Series,* no. 49056 (New York: Readex Microprint, courtesy of A. A. S., 1981).

The State and House of Representatives of the commonwealth of Pennsylvania, whilst they cherish the right of the individual states to express their opinions upon all public measures proposed in the congress of the union, are aware that its usefulness must in a great degree depend upon the discretion with which it is exercised. They believe that the right ought not to be resorted to upon trivial subjects or unimportant occasions, but they are also persuaded that there are moments when the neglect to exercise it would be a dereliction of public duty.

Such an occasion as in their judgement demands the frank expression of the sentiments of Pennsylvania, is now presented. A measure was ardently supported in the last congress of the United States, and will probably be earnestly urged during the existing session of that body, which has a palpable tendency to impair the political relations of the several states; which is calculated to mar the social happiness of the present and future generations; which, if adopted, would impede the march of humanity and freedom through the world, and would affix and perpetuate an odious stain upon the present race: a measure, in brief, which proposes to spread the crimes and cruelties of slavery, from the banks of the Mississippi to the shores of the Pacific.

When measures of this character are seriously advocated in the republican congress of America in the nineteenth century, the several states are invoked by the duty which they owe to the Deity, by the veneration which they entertain for the memory of the founders of the republic, and by a tender regard for posterity, to protest against it adoption, to refuse to covenant with crime, and to limit the range of an evil that already hangs in awful boding over so large a portion of the union.

Nor can such a protest be entered by any state with greater propriety than by Pennsylvania. This commonwealth has as sacredly respected the rights of other states, as it has been careful of its own. It has been the invariable aim of the people of Pennsylvania to extend to the universe, by their example, the unadulterated blessings of civil and religious freedom. It is their pride, that they have been at all times the practical advocates of those improvements and charities amongst men, which are so well calculated to enable them to answer the purposes of their Creator; and, above all, they may boast that they were foremost in removing the pollution of slavery from amongst them.

If, indeed, the measure against which Pennsylvania considers it her duty to raise her voice, was calculated to abridge any of the rights guaranteed to the several states; if, odious as slavery is, it was proposed to hasten its extinction by means injurious in the states upon which it was unhappily entailed, Pennsylvania would be amongst the first to insist upon a sacred observance of the constitutional compact. But it cannot be pretended that the rights of any of the states are at all to be affected by refusing to extend the mischiefs of human bondage over the boundless regions of the west, a territory which formed no part of the confederation at the adoption of the constitution; which has been but lately purchased from an European power by the people of the union at large; which may or may not be admitted as a state into the union at the discretion of congress; which must establish a republican form of government, and no other; and whose climate affords none of the pretexts urged for resorting to the labor of natives of the torrid zone. Such a territory has no right, inherent or acquired, such as those states possessed which established the existing constitution. When that constitution was framed in September, seventeen hundred and eighty seven, the concession that three fifths of the slaves in the states then existing should be represented in congress, could not have been intended to embrace regions at that time held by a foreign power. On the contrary, so anxious were the congress of that day to confine human bondage within its ancient home, that on the thirteenth of July, seventeen hundred and eighty seven, that body unanimously declared that slavery or involuntary servitude should not exist in the extensive territories bounded by the Ohio, the Mississippi, Canada and the lakes. And in the ninth section of the first article of the constitution itself, the power of congress to prohibit the migration of servile persons after the year eighteen hundred and eight, is expressly recognized nor is there to be found in the statute book a single instance of the admission of a territory upon the conditions of such admissions.

The Senate and House of Representatives of Pennsylvania, therefore, cannot but deprecate any departure from the humane and enlightened policy, pursued not only by the illustrious congress of 1787, but by their successors, without exception. They are persuaded that to open the fertile regions of the west to a servile race, would tend to increase their numbers beyond all past example, would open a new and steady market for the lawless venders of human flesh, and would render all schemes for obliterating this most foul blot upon the American character, useless and unavailing.

Under these convictions, and in the full persuasion that upon this topic there is but one opinion in Pennsylvania

*Resolved, by the Senate and House of Representatives of the Commonwealth of Pennsylvania,* That the Senators and Representatives of this state in the congress of the United States, be and they are hereby requested, to vote against the admission of another territory as a state into the union, unless "the further introduction of slavery or involuntary servitude, except for punishment of crimes whereof the party shall have been duly convicted, shall be prohibited; and all children born within the said territory, after its admission into the union as a state, shall be free, but may be held to service until the age of twenty-five years."

*Resolved,* That the governor be and he is hereby requested, to cause a copy of the foregoing preamble and resolution to be transmitted to each of the senators and representatives of this state in the congress of the United States.

Joseph Lawrence,
Speaker of the House of Representatives
Isaac Weaver, Speaker of the Senate.
Approved—The twenty-second day of December, one thousand eight hundred and nineteen.
William Findlay
Harrisburg, December 28th, 1819

## Catherine Sedgwick, *Journal*, June 1821

*In late June 1821 Catharine Sedgwick (1789–1867), a Massachusetts novelist and social reformer, was traveling by barge on the western section of the as-yet-unfinished Erie Canal in upstate New York. Not far from Niagara Falls, near the Canadian border, she encountered a group of Irish families and made note of them in her diary. Until the middle of the 1830s, emigrating from Ireland via British North America cost less than half the passage to the United States. While most Protestant Irish from Ulster often settled in Ontario, Catholic Irish walked across the border, to settle in northern New York cities such as Rochester or in towns along the construction path of the 360-mile canal, where foreign-born workers were much in demand. Both groups practiced chain migration, living frugally in order to finance the passage of kin out of Ireland as quickly as possible.*

*Source:* "Diary of Catherine Maria Sedgwick, June 1821," in Mary E. Dewey, ed., *Life and Letters of Catherine M. Sedgwick* (New York: Harper and Row, 1871), p. 130; electronic version at http://www.lib.uchicago.edu/efts/asp/NAWLD

Here, on the margin of the river, were encamped seven families of Irish emigrants, making in all fifty. They had entered the country at Quebec, and expressed great satisfaction at having arrived within our territory. One poor woman, with John Rogers's complement of children, and one sick one in her arms, *hoped* to find her husband in Mercer, in Ohio. In another tent was a poor man with ten children, whose wife had fallen a victim to the hardships of the passage. He looked quite dispirited. I asked him how they liked our country. "Och, ma'am, and we could not miss liking it," said he, "we find the people so free and hospitable." One sweet pretty girl, niece to the woman who had died, had, like Abraham, come out from her country, and kindred, and friends, and without, I believe, the incitement of a special call so to do. I asked her how she could leave them all. "Sure it is, ma'am," said she, "if it thrive well with me, they will all come after." The poor Irishers! they do all come first or last. This pretty girl was a Protestant, so I thought I could not give a better 'God-speed' to her pilgrimage than by bestowing on her my Testament. She received it as if she had some notion of its value.

## *Travels by Duke Bernhard of Saxe-Weimar-Eisenach Through North America, 1825, 1826*

*On a visit to the German areas of Pennsylvania in October 1825, Duke Carl Bernhard*

of Saxe-Weimar-Eisenach (1792–1862) spent several days in Bethlehem. Located about fifty miles north of Philadelphia, he found it "friendly and quiet," a place where the "residents live in great harmony, as in a single family, and who appear to have completely accepted the same conventions, through similar upbringing and constant living together." Education was one of the keys to its stability and ethnic culture. The duke visited two schools in the area and in his diary described circumstances completely opposite to those Margaret Van Horn Dwight had chronicled fifteen years earlier. The perceptions of each were strongly influenced by their ability with the language. Dwight was repulsed by what she could not understand, but Duke Bernhard took "no small delight that I was allowed to converse the entire day in German and that I heard such proper and pure German spoken, which, as a rule, is not often the case in America."

Source: C. J. Jeronimus, ed., William Jeronimus, trans., *Travels by His Highness Duke Bernhard of Saxe-Weimar-Eisenach Through North America in the Years 1825 and 1826*, (New York: University Press of America, 2001), pp. 207–208.

Sixty boys are educated in this [boarding] school [in the village of Schoneck]; forty of these live in this building, the other twenty live with their parents in the village. This school was also established for children of parents who do not belong to the [evangelical Herrnhuter] brotherhood, and is respected by everyone. I immediately noticed the great cleanliness that prevailed throughout the entire building. The school is divided into four classes and accepts children at the age of eight years. The teachers are primarily German or at least speak this language, for it is taught to the boys on the insistence of the parents. The school has a small natural-history collection which was in very good order, and also a collection of eggs from the local area, which had been collected by the students. The students sleep in two large halls; two adults also sleep in each. They eat together, and every afternoon they go on an extended walk, accompanied by their teachers. In addition to the usual school subjects (and the English, German, and French languages), the students learn drawing, music, and double-entry bookkeeping. For music instruction, there was a pianoforte in each class. One chapel is available for the religious services of the school. The boys all appeared very healthy, lively, and open, and were kept very clean. The building also had a seminary for those young people who wished to dedicate themselves to the clergy. This currently numbered five students. The seminarists were required to finish their education in the common theological seminary in Upper-Silesia. . . .

. . . [In Bethlehem] we found about one hundred young girls between the ages of eight and eighteen at this [large girls] school, for the most part very attractive, who receive a very careful education; in addition to the school curriculum, they also receive instruction in art, music, and the preparation for all manner of feminine tasks. They make extremely fine embroidery and tapestry, as well as particularly handsome so-called flower-bands. They are separated into four classes; each class has a pianoforte. I heard that they perform their morning and evening prayers in song. After dinner they have no instruction other than music and female chores; later, they go for a walk in a large garden located in a valley behind the building. They have a pianoforte in the chapel as well, which also serves for a concert hall. They sleep in large halls, attended by their supervisors. There is great cleanliness everywhere, and the girls have a healthy appearance. The convention in European boardinghouses, where all the girls wear the same attire and where the classes are distinguished by different coloured armbands, is not followed here; the girls dress themselves rather the way they see fit. Furthermore, there are students here from all parts of the United States; there are even several from *Alabama*.

## William Lloyd Garrison, *The Liberator*, January 1, 1831

*With the first issue of* The Liberator *on New Year's Day, 1831, William Lloyd Garrison (1805–1879) began what would be more than thirty years' presence in the abolitionist movement. He used the newspaper—which had a circulation of three thousand at its peak—to argue the moral reasons for his opposition to bondage, convinced that they would ultimately prove more effective than either force or the law. A white Bostonian, Garrison's militant tone was not appreciated in the American South, where Georgia put up a $5,000 reward for bringing him to trial there.*

*Source:* William Lloyd Garrison, *The Liberator,* 1:1, January 1, 1831 (reproduced in Henry Steele Commager and Milton Cantor, eds., *Documents of American History, vol. 1, to 1898* (Englewood Cliffs, N.J.: Prentice-Hall, 1988), from *William Lloyd Garrison, 1805–1879: The Story of His Life Told by His Children,* vol. 1 (Boston: Houghton, Mifflin, 1889), pp. 224 ff.

## TO THE PUBLIC

. . . During my recent tour for the purpose of exciting the minds of the people by a series of discourses on the subject of slavery, every place that I visited gave fresh evidence of the fact, that a greater revolution in public sentiment was to be effected in the free states—*and particularly in New England*—than at the south. I found contempt more bitter, opposition more active, detraction more relentless, prejudice more stubborn, and apathy more frozen, than among slave owners themselves. Of course, there were individual exceptions to the contrary. This state of things afflicted, but did not dishearten me. I determined, at every hazard, to lift up the standard of emancipation in the eyes of the nation, *within sight of Bunker Hill and in the birth place of liberty.* That standard is now unfurled; and long may it float, unhurt by the spoilations of time or the missiles of a desperate foe—yea, till every chain be broken, and every bondman set free! Let Southern oppressors tremble—let their secret abettors tremble—let their Northern apologists tremble—let all the enemies of the persecuted blacks tremble.

. . . Assenting to the "self evident truth" maintained in the American Declaration of Independence, "that all men are created equal, and endowed by their

Creator with certain inalienable rights—among which are life, liberty and the pursuit of happiness," I shall strenuously contend for the immediate enfranchisement of our slave population. In Park-Street Church, on the Fourth of July, 1829, in an address on slavery, I unreflectingly assented to the popular but pernicious doctrine of *gradual* abolition. I seize this opportunity to make a full and unequivocal recantation, and thus publicly to ask pardon of my God, of my country, and of my brethren the poor slaves, for having uttered a sentiment so full of timidity, injustice and absurdity. A similar recantation, from my pen, was published in the *Genius of Universal Emancipation* at Baltimore, in September, 1829. My conscience is now satisfied.

I am aware, that many object to the severity of my language; but is there not cause for severity? I *will be* as harsh as truth, and as uncompromising as justice. On this subject, I do not wish to think, or speak, or write, with moderation. No! No! Tell a man whose house is on fire, to give a moderate alarm, tell him to moderately rescue his wife from the hands of the ravisher; tell the mother to gradually extricate her babe from the fire into which it has fallen;—but urge me not to use moderation in a cause like the present. I am in earnest—I will not equivocate—I will not excuse—I will not retreat a single inch—*AND I WILL BE HEARD.* The apathy of the people is enough to make every statue leap from its pedestal, and to hasten the resurrection of the dead.

It is pretended, that I am retarding the cause of emancipation by the coarseness of my invective, and the precipitancy of my measures. *The charge is not true.* On this question my influence,—humble as it is,—is felt at this moment to a considerable extent, and shall be felt in coming years—not perniciously, but beneficially—not as a curse, but as a blessing; and posterity will bear testimony that I was right. I desire to thank God, that he enables me to disregard "the fear of man which bringeth a snare," and to speak his truth in its simplicity and power. . . .

## Mathew Carey, *Letters on the Colonization Society*, 1832

*Emigration to Liberia was still a polarizing issue in the 1830s. To some it was anathema, to others, such as the Philadephia pamphleteer Mathew Carey (1760–1839), it was the most realistic, humane, and practical option under the circumstances. He believed that freedom did not counterbalance immutable white prejudices against black people, declaring, "I speak of things as they are—not as they might or ought to be." In the April 1832 preface to the second edition of his* Letters on the Colonization Society, *Carey appealed specifically to the reason of abolitionists William Lloyd Garrison (1805–1879) and Benjamin Lundy (1789–1839), both opponents of African colonization. He wrote, "such being [the] situation [of freed blacks] in this country, surely they ought to long as eagerly for a settlement in the land of their ancestors, as the captive tribes of Israel hungered for a return to the land of Canaan."*

Source: Mathew Carey, *Letters on the Colonization Society: with a view of its probable results . . . the origin of the Society, increase of the coloured population, manumission of slaves in this country . . . addressed to C. F. Mercer* (Philadelphia, Penn.: Young, 1832, 2d edition), excerpt from the preface.

There are three strong points of view in which this subject may be considered, which must gain for colonization the zealous and efficient support of every man, white or coloured, who is not under the dominion of inveterate and incurable prejudice. I omit other important points which might be mooted.

I. The colony has arrested the progress of the nefarious and accursed slave trade in its neighbourhood; destroyed some slave factories, and liberated a number of slaves who were on the point of being transported across the Atlantic, subject to all the horrors of the passage, and, if they escaped with life, to the horrors of perpetual slavery; and there cannot be a doubt that at no distant day the trade will be annihilated on the whole of the western coast of Africa.

II. It has been the means of securing the emancipation of hundreds of slaves, in various parts of the United States, who are now in a genial climate, enjoying the luxury of freedom with all its attendant blessings; and, from the present disposition of the citizens of some of the slave states, particularly Virginia, there is no doubt that thousands will be emancipated as fast as means of transportation can be procured.

III. It has commenced spreading the blessings of civilization, morals, and religion among the natives in the neighbourhood of the colony, whom it has taught to depend on honest industry in the cultivation of the soil, instead of the demoniac operation of setting fire to towns and villages, for the horrible purpose of seizing the wretched fugitives flying from the flames, which was their former occupation.

Now I freely appeal to Mr. Garrison, and Mr. Lundy, the most formidable opposers of colonization, and to their friends, and beg them to lay their hands on their hearts, and answer in the presence of their Maker, if any one of those objects does not repay tenfold the sacrifice while the whole have cost?

Among the objections—how easy to make plausible objections!—offered to the colonization plan, one is, that considering the immense number of the coloured people in this country, about 2,400,000, it is impossible to make any serious impression on them by emigration, especially as the colony at present, after twelve years existence, contains but 2,000 souls. Let us examine this objection.

The annual increase, as I have shown, is about 60,000. The expense of the government, or the society, will probably be $25 per head for all the emigrants large and small (taking into consideration those who pay, or whose masters will pay their passage), or about $1,500,000 per ann. for that number. This sum, provided the subject were cordially taken up by the state legislatures and congress, would not be attended with the slightest difficulty. Indeed, if encountered with the zeal which its importance demands, twice the sum could be easily raised. But then the objectors emphatically demand, how shall we provide for the transportation of such a number!

It appears from Walsh's Sketches of Brazil that in the year 1828, there were no less than 43,000 slaves received in the single port of Rio de Janeiro—and it is fairly presumable that an equal number were received at the Havanna and other ports—making, with those that died on board, at least 100,000 ravished from their native land in one year. If the wretches engaged in that nefarious traffic could find means of transporting 100,000 human beings in one year across the Atlantic, surely this powerful nation could, to accomplish the great objects in view, and to rescue itself by degrees from the odious stain of slavery, accomplish the conveyance of 60, or even 100,000 to a land where they will be "lords of the soil." 60 or 70,000 persons have emigrated in one year from Great Britain and Ireland.

It has been asked how shall provision be made for such a number in Liberia? they will perish for want of sustenance.

Can there exist any fear on this subject, when the soil of Liberia produces two regular crops a year, with the most imperfect culture?

## Burning of Ursaline Convent, 1834

*In the episodic street violence or "mobocracy" of Jacksonian America, one of the clearest examples of undisguised nativism was the burning of the Ursaline Convent just outside Boston in 1834. The Ursalines were an order of Roman Catholic nuns, predominantly Irish women, who opened a boarding school in Charlestown in 1826. Their presence and purpose were little understood by locals, and on August 11, 1834, a group of vigilantes burned down the nuns' complex of buildings in response to rumors that anticipated the subsequent Maria Monk controversy by two years. Irish workers in nearby Lowell, Worcester, and Providence threatened retaliation but were dissuaded by Bishop Benedict J. Fenwick of Boston. New Yorker Philip Hone (1780–1851), an upper-class Protestant, recorded his take on events in a diary entry that summer. Set beside Irishman Mathew Carey's comments to Bishop John Hughes of New York written four years later, both excerpts force reflection upon the equities of the justice system at the time. A seventeen-year-old—who got caught up in the night's events without premeditation—took the fall for eight others acquitted at the trial.*

*Source:* Bayard Tuckerman, ed., *The Diary of Philip Hone, 1828–1851* (New York: Dodd, Mead and Company, 1889), pp. 110–111; Mathew Carey, *Letters on Irish Immigrants and Irishmen Generally* (Philadelphia, March 12, 1838), p. 3.

## PHILIP HONE, AUGUST 22, 1834

A most disgraceful riot also occurred on the night of Monday, the 11th, at Charlestown, near Boston. The populace having been deceived by ill-designing persons into an erroneous belief that a young lady was confined against her will in the Ursaline Convent, a highly respectable seminary under the charge of the Roman Catholics, made an attack upon the convent, a noble ediface near Charlestown, and the other buildings belonging to the sisterhood, and burned them to the ground with all the valuable furniture, desecrated the cemetery, and committed every species of outrage. This act has caused great excitement in Boston. A meeting was immediately held in Faneuil Hall, at which the most distinguished citizens of all parties attended. Resolutions were adopted reprobating in the strongest terms the unworthy conduct of their neighbors. The Mayor presided, and all the magistrates assisted in the proceedings. Large rewards were offered for the apprehension of the persons concerned in the riot. The venerable Bishop Fenwick of the Catholic Church succeeded in casting the holy oil of his eloquence upon the furious waves which were about rising in his excitable congregation, and the consequences were less serious than at first apprehended. The active and prompt measures which were adopted led to the apprehension of several of the ringleaders, who await their trial.

## MATHEW CAREY, 12 MARCH 1838

I do not mean, except merely en passant, to touch on the fanatical and antichristian hostility which imprinted an indelible stigma on the escutcheon of Massachusetts, by the atrocious destruction of the convent and desecration of the chapel in Charlestown; the cowardly and felonious attack at midnight on a party of highly-interesting and defenceless females, whose sex ought to have been an

Ægis to protect them, and whose pursuits are an honour to human nature; the disgraceful mockery of the trial, and the acquittal of the ruffianly incendiaries; or the no-less-disgraceful result of the abortive attempt to procure the indemnification of their losses, which justice loudly demanded from the legislature of the state. And I shall pass over various minor outrages, resulting from the same spirit of persecution which are highly discreditable, and would amply justify severe castigation. My object is to consider and refute the prejudices, which in a greater or less degree attach to the Irish, merely as Irishmen, wholly independent of the ferocious rancour engendered by fanaticism, the base-begotten progeny of perverted religion.

## Samuel F. B. Morse, *Foreign Conspiracy Against the Liberties of the United States*, 1834

*Samuel F. B. Morse (1791-1872) wrote a series of letters to the* New-York Observer *under the pseudonym of "Brutus" in 1834, which he then collected and published in pamphlet form the following year under the title* Foreign Conspiracy Against the Liberties of the United States. *At the time Morse was Professor of Painting and Sculpture at New York University—where he was experimenting with an electric telegraph system—as well as president of the National Academy of Design. He was politically active with the Native American Democratic Association and his "nativism" is clearly evident in his writings of the period, including* Imminent Dangers to the Free Institutions of the United States through Foreign Immigration, and the Present State of the Naturalization Laws, *which was also published in 1835. Morse saw emigration as a European conspiracy to undermine American democracy, and he was paranoid about Catholicism and Jesuits in particular: "How is it possible that foreign turbulence imported by ship-loads, that riot and ignorance in hundreds of thousands of human priest-controlled machines, should suddenly be thrown into our society, and not produce here turbulence and excess? Can one throw mud into pure water and not disturb its clearness?" Morse unsuccessfully ran for Mayor of New York City in 1836. The following excerpt concludes chapter 5 of* Foreign Conspiracy.

Source: Samuel F. B. Morse, *Foreign Conspiracy Against the Liberties of the United States* (New York: Leavitt, Lord & C., 1835 reprint, New York: Arno Press, 1977), pp. 57–58.

Another weak point in our system is our laws *encouraging immigration,* and affording facilities to *naturalization.* In the early state of the country liberality in these points was thought to be of advantage, as it promoted the cultivation of our wild lands, but the dangers which now threaten our free institutions from this source more than balance all advantages of this character. The great body of emigrants to this country are the hard-working mentally neglected poor of Catholic countries in Europe, who have left a land where they were enslaved, for one of freedom. However well disposed they may be to the country which protects them, and adopts them as citizens, they are not fitted to act with judgement in the political affairs of their new country, like native citizens educated from their infancy in the principles and habits of our institutions. Most of them are too ignorant to act at all for themselves, and expect to be guided wholly by others. These others are of course their priests. Priests have ruled them at home by *divine right;* their ignorant minds cannot ordinarily be emancipated from their habitual subjection, they will not learn nor appreciate their exemption from any such usurpation of priestly power in this country, and they are implicitly at the beck of their spiritual guides. They live surrounded by freedom, yet liberty of conscience, right of private judgement, whether in religion or politics, are as effectually excluded by the priests, as if the code of Austria already ruled the land. They form a body of men whose habits of *action,* (for I cannot say *thought,*) are opposed to the principles of our free institutions, for they are not accessible to the reasonings of the press, they cannot and do not think for themselves.

Every unlettered Catholic emigrant, therefore, that comes into the country, is adding to a mass of ignorance which it will be difficult to reach by any liberal instruction, and however honest, (and I have no doubt most of them are so,) yet from the nature of things they are but obedient instruments in the hands of their more knowing leaders to accomplish the designs of their foreign masters. Republican education, were it allowed freely to come in contact with their minds, would doubtless soon furnish a remedy for an evil for which, in the existing state of things, we have no cure. It is but to continue for a few years the sort of immigration that is now daily pouring its thousands from Europe, and our institutions, for aught that I can see, are at the mercy of a body of foreigners, officered by foreigners, and held completely under the control of a foreign power. We may then have reason to say, that we are the dupes of our own hospitality; we have sheltered in our well provided house a needy body of strangers, who, well filled with our cheer, are encouraged by the unaccustomed familiarity with which they are treated, first to upset the regulations of the houshold [sic], and then to turn their host and his family out of doors.

## Andrew Jackson, "Removal of Southern Indians to Indian Territory," December 7, 1835

*Colonization projects reached an apotheosis in 1836. That year, as dictated by the Treaty of New Echota, the Five Civilized Tribes began to relocate west of the Mississippi under Congressional order and federal supervision. The variety of controversial words that can be used to describe this internal migration of Native Americans ranges from the benevolent concepts of colony or reservation to the more malevolent transplantation and forced removal embodied in the retroactively applied name, "Trail of Tears." All reflect the difficulty Americans still faced in reconciling their legal, moral, and humanitarian responsibilities to the Indians in the face of relentless western expansion. Under President Andrew Jackson (1767–1845), Congress appropriated half a million dollars in 1830 for removal expenses and in 1834 set aside present-day Oklahoma as a special Indian Territory. Despite the Supreme Court's recognition of Native American*

*rights in* The Cherokee Nation v. Georgia *(1831), the final part of this plan to separate Indians from the white population was presented by Jackson to Congress on December 7, 1835.*

Source: Andrew Jackson, "Removal of Southern Indians to Indian Territory," excerpt from his message to Congress, December 7, 1835; reproduced in Henry Steele Commager and Milton Cantor, eds., *Documents of American History,* vol. 1 to 1898, (Englewood Cliffs, N.J.: Prentice Hall, 1988), pp. 259–261.

. . . The plan of removing the aboriginal people who yet remain within the settled portions of the United States to the country west of the Mississippi River approaches its consummation. It was adopted on the most mature consideration of the condition of this race, and ought to be persisted in till the object is accomplished, and prosecuted with as much vigor as a just regard to their circumstances will permit, and as fast as their consent can be obtained. All preceding experiments for the improvement of the Indians have failed. It seems now to be an established fact they can not live in contact with a civilized community and prosper. Ages of fruitless endeavors have at length brought us to a knowledge of this principle of intercommunication with them. The past we can not recall, but the future we can provide for. Independently of the treaty stipulations into which we have entered with the various tribes for the usufructuary rights they have ceded to us, no one can doubt the moral duty of the Government of the United States to protect and if possible to preserve and perpetuate the scattered remnants of this race which are left within our borders. In the discharge of this duty an extensive region in the West has been assigned for their permanent residence. It has been divided into districts and allotted among them. Many have already removed and others are preparing to go, and with the exception of two small bands living in Ohio and Indiana, not exceeding 1,500 persons, and of the Cherokees, all the tribes on the east side of the Mississippi, and extending from Lake Michigan to Florida, have entered into engagements which will lead to their transplantation.

The plan for their removal and reestablishment is founded upon the knowledge we have gained of their character and habits, and has been dictated by a spirit of enlarged liberality. A territory exceeding in extent that relinquished has been granted to each tribe. Of its climate, fertility, and capacity to support an Indian population the representations are highly favorable. To these districts the Indians are removed at the expense of the United States, and with certain supplies of clothing, arms, ammunition, and other indispensable articles; they are also furnished gratuitously with provisions for the period of a year after their arrival at their new homes. In that time, from the nature of the country and of the products raised by them, they can subsist themselves by agricultural labor, if they choose to resort to that mode of life; if they do not they are upon the skirts of the great prairies, where countless herds of buffalo roam, and a short time suffices to adapt their own habits to the changes which a change of the animals destined for their food may require. Ample arrangements have also been made for the support of schools; in some instances council houses and churches are to be erected, dwellings constructed for the chiefs, and mills for common use. Funds have been set apart for the maintenance of the poor; the most necessary mechanical arts have been introduced, and blacksmiths, gunsmiths, wheelwrights, millwrights, etc., are supported among them. Steel and iron, and sometimes salt, are purchased for them, and plows and other farming utensils, domestic animals, looms, spinning wheels, cards, etc., are presented to them. And besides these beneficial arrangements, annuities are in all cases paid, amounting in some instances to more than $30 for each individual of the tribe, and in all cases sufficiently great, if justly divided and prudently expended, to enable them, in addition to their own exertions, to live comfortably. And as a stimulus for exertion, it is now provided by law that "in all cases of the appointment of interpreters or other persons employed for the benefit of the Indians a preference shall be given to persons of Indian descent, if such can be found who are properly qualified for the discharge of the duties."

Such are the arrangements for the physical comfort and for the moral improvement of the Indians. The necessary measures for their political advancement and for their separation from our citizens have not been neglected. The pledge of the United States has been given by Congress that the country destined for the residence of this people shall be forever "secured and guaranteed to them." A country west of Missouri and Arkansas has been assigned to them, into which the white settlements are not to be pushed. No political communities can be formed in that extensive region, except those which are established by the Indians themselves or by the Untied States for them and with their concurrence. A barrier has thus been raised for their protection against the encroachment of our citizens, and guarding the Indians as far as possible from those evils which have brought them to their present condition. Summary authority has been given by law to destroy all ardent spirits found in their country, without waiting the doubtful result and slow process of a legal seizure. I consider the absolute and unconditional interdiction of this article among these people as the first and great step in their melioration. Halfway measures will answer no purpose. These can not successfully contend against the cupidity of the seller and the overpowering appetite of the buyer. And the destructive effects of the traffic are marked in every page of the history of our Indian intercourse. . . .

## George Templeton Strong, "Mass at St. Patrick's," 1836

*George Templeton Strong (1820–1875) was a sixteen-year-old undergraduate at Columbia University when he recorded these observations of Sunday Mass at St. Patrick's Cathedral in New York in December 1836. Earlier that year the Ancient Order of Hibernians had been founded to protect the Church, the priest, and the Mass during a period of anti-Catholicism in the City that had begun with*

*the burning of St. Mary's on Grand Street in 1831. Strong exhibited an odd mixture of fascination and repulsion / curiosity and skepticism about this "foreign" religion that was garnering so much civic attention. On this occasion he heard the preaching of Frenchman John Dubois (1764–1842), Bishop of New York since 1826, who presided over a diocese that included not only Manhattan but all of New York State as well as parts of New Jersey, with a combined total of eight churches, eighteen priests, and 185,000 parishioners. The Shea boy with whom Strong shared a pew that morning was most likely the son of Columbia University English professor James Shea and brother of John Gilmary Shea (1824–1892), later to become the historian of the American Catholic Church.*

*Source:* Allan Nevins and Milton Halsey Thomas, eds., *The Diary of George Templeton Strong,* vol. 1, *Young Man in New York, 1835–1849* (New York: The Macmillan Company, 1952), pp. 43–44.

*December 15, Thursday.* Thanksgiving Day, and no college, of course . . . Having a curiosity today to witness the Catholic services, I determined to go up to St. Patrick's to see High Mass performed by Bishop [John] Dubois. On my way up I met Blatchford; he turned round and we walked to the Cathedral together. After standing for some time near the door, little [Charles Edward] Shea came in and offered us a seat in his pew, which we were very glad to accept. At a little before eleven, the services began. The high altar was very magnificently arrayed with three immense wax candles some six feet high and a great deal of tinsel and frippery besides. At last, in came the bishop, six or seven priests, and as many of the little boys in surplices, one of them with a censer. The bishop was very splendidly arrayed; he had his crosier in his hand, very richly gilt, and his hat— I forget the name—on his head; he is a very venerable looking old man, but was ornamented in rather a ridiculous manner. The priests were very richly dressed also.

The services began by a sort of recitative from the bishop, with responses from the choir. Every time they passed in front of the altar they kneeled or rather performed a sort of genuflexion [sic], not quite kneeling. There was a good deal of incense burning and the whole scene was soon wrapped in *smoke*, very expressive of its real nature. At last Dr. [John] Powers ascended the pulpit and proceeded to give a sermon. He spoke very loud and with a great deal of gesture, and withal rather indistinctly. It was a strange sort of political, metaphysical, doctrinal, begging affair. He talked about the advance of mind and the progress of free principle, the beauties of "our adopted country" and the sweets of liberty, the tender mercies of Mother Church and the lies of the heretics concerning her doctrines. The Roman Church, he said, was not a persecuting church; the heretics advocated destructive principles—and the civil authority condemned them to be burned. Holy Mother Church was very sorry to burn them, but still she was *compelled* to burn them, and so did it, though most reluctantly—such seemed to be the main body of his discourse. He concluded with an appeal to the pockets of his au-

ditors, in behalf of the Orphan Asylum. Then came the ceremonies of Mass—a great deal of chanting, genuflexion [sic], etc. There was a crazy, or tipsy Irishwoman in front of us who created quite a sensation while the bishop was busy with the chalice. She sung out at the top of her voice: "Jest pass the brandy and water along here, will you?"

*December 16* . . . Shea told me today that the collection taken up yesterday at St. Patrick's amounted to $456, which he thought very large. I should think it rather small.

## William L. Stone, *The True History of Maria Monk*, October 8, 1836

*Everyone was talking about Maria Monk in 1836. With the help of the Rev. J. J. Slocum and the New York publisher Howe & Bates, her "memoir" appeared under the provocative title* Awful Disclosures of Maria Monk, as exhibited in a narrative of her sufferings during a residence of five years as a novice, and two years as a black nun, in the Hôtel Dieu at Montreal. *The Hôtel Dieu was a Canadian free hospital for the poor with an attached Roman Catholic cloister. Monk alleged that the cloister was connected by underground passage with the nearby Seminary of St. Sulpice, in order to facilitate nightly sexual visits by the priests with the nuns. The progeny of these illicit encounters were allegedly smothered and their bodies disposed of by a mixture of lime and sulphuric acid. In the nativist climate of the mid-1830s this was sensational "evidence" against Catholic perfidy. William Stone— with a copy of the* Awful Disclosures *in hand, the permission of the Bishop of Mon-*

*treal, and the full cooperation of the nuns—personally conducted a thorough three-hour search of every nook and cranny of the Hôtel Dieu. Stone came to the firm conclusion that Maria Monk was not only an imposter but in fact a prostitute who once resided in Montreal's Magdalen Asylum for fallen women. His report was published in the New York* Commercial Advertiser *(October 8, 1836) as* The True History of Maria Monk.

*Source:* William L. Stone, *The True History of Maria Monk: A Reprint of the Famous Report of Her Charges* (New York: The Paulist Press, 1936), pp. 6–8, 37–39.

Of the verity or falsehood of the truly "Awful Disclosures" of Maria Monk, I had formed no definite opinion previously to entering the province. Indeed, I had not read the book in any other manner than by an occasional and very cursory glance at a few of its pages; still I read much *from* and *of* it, and heard much more; and I am constrained to confess that, although at times a partial believer, and at others a skeptic, as to the truth of her fearful revelations of hypocrisy, lust, and blood, I was rather a believer than otherwise during the earlier part of my Canadian visit . . . my prejudices against the Catholic faith were strong. Its monstrous corruptions in the old world were notorious. The work of Maria Monk I knew to have been written by one of our most estimable citizens, a gentleman of character and approved Christian piety, who had taken every pains, as he supposed, to record the exact truth. I knew, *from his own lips*, that he was a religious believer of all that he

had thus written. I knew that other intelligent and pious gentlemen had, by repeated examinations, endeavored to detect the girl's imposture, if impostor she was, without success. I knew that these men, and multitudes of others, were firm believers in the truth of her revelations. . . . A variety of incidents, moreover, had been communicated to me as facts, while on the way to Montreal, which had materially strengthened the impression upon my mind, arising from this formidable array of circumstances, until I had almost arrived at the belief that, after all, there might be more of truth in the tale than I had been willing at first to admit.

I soon ascertained, however, that such was by no means the opinion of the citizens of Montreal. . . . Such a city of skeptics, in all that pertained to the disclosures of the wronged frail one, was never before seen. Nay, more: so perfectly absurd and ridiculous did the people with one accord consider the whole affair, that they seemed to look upon the intelligent denizens of the United States as laboring under a widely-extended monomania! There was but one voice upon the subject; Protestants and Catholics, those of every and all denominations, born and bred upon the spot; men of intelligence and unquestionable piety; those who had passed the open gates of the Hôtel Dieu; or looked from their casements over its frowning walls every day of their lives—were all stubborn unbelievers. . . .

. . . Again, as to the births and murders of children. In the first place, the whole tale is improbable, both as to the numbers of nuns and infants. Do murderers cluster in numbers to perpetrate their butcheries, and thus purposely furnish the means of conviction? Would they be so foolish and so mad as to keep a written record of their murders? And would so many mothers consent to strangle their own offspring? Can a woman forget her sucking child? It is not so! The voice of indignant nature rises up to proclaim the falsehood. And, moreover, as to the number of novices and infants, Miss Monk states that, on a certain occasion, she discovered a book in the Superior's custody containing the record of the admissions of novices, and of the births of infants who were murdered. About twenty-five of these pages were written over, containing about fifteen entries on a page. "Several of these pages," she says, "were occupied with the records of the murdered infants; and all the records were either of admissions or births." Now we will allow twenty pages for the records of admissions of novices, and five for the births of murdered children. With fifteen entries on a page, twenty pages will give us the number of THREE HUNDRED admissions in two years. Now there are but thirty-six nuns in all, and seldom more than four or five novices or postulants. Again, as to the infants, if we allow five pages to have been devoted to these rec-

ords of births, we have SEVENTY-FIVE births during the same period. Now, as I have already said, there are but thirty-six nuns; more than one-half are "past age." Certainly not more than fifteen of them could, "in the natural course of human events," become mothers. Taking Maria's statements, therefore, as correct data, each of these fifteen nuns—striking the average—must have given birth to two and a half children every year. A most prolific race, truly! What nonsense, and how great the popular credulity to swallow it!

. . . I will, therefore, now close this protracted narrative, by expressing my deliberate and solemn opinion, founded not only upon my own careful examination, but upon the firmest conviction of nearly the entire population of Montreal—embracing the great body of the most intelligent Evangelical Christians—THAT MARIA MONK IS AN ARRANT IMPOSTOR, AND HER BOOK, IN ALL ITS ESSENTIAL FEATURES, A TISSUE OF CALUMNIES. However guilty the Catholics may be in other respects, or in other countries, as a man of honor, and professor of the Protestant faith, I MOST SOLEMNLY BELIEVE THAT THE PRIESTS AND NUNS ARE INNOCENT IN THIS MATTER.

# CHAPTER 4
# RACIAL AND ETHNIC IDENTITY IN THE UNITED STATES, 1837–1877

## MICHAEL MILLER TOPP

IN RECENT YEARS THE SPECTER of identity politics—of people identifying themselves and organizing themselves around their ethnicity or race, for example—has created enormous concerns in American society. Critics, from Michael Kazin and Todd Gitlin on the Left to Arthur Schlesinger, Jr., and Lynne Cheney on the Right, have raised alarms across the political spectrum about the dangers of splintering American reform efforts or American society as a whole. In an age when accusations of reverse discrimination, ethnic and racial separatism, and even Balkanization and tribalism are ubiquitous, we would do well to remember that identity politics—that racial and ethnic identity—have always mattered in the United States.

The period between 1837 and 1877, during which economic and geographic growth thoroughly changed the face of the nation, offers an excellent window on how these aspects of identity defined a person's place in or outside of American society. In these years immigrants began to flood into the United States in unprecedented numbers: the Irish, the Germans, and, on the West Coast, the Chinese foremost among them. American expansionism and industrialization affected each of these populations directly and often dramatically. These forces also touched other populations—Indians, Mexicans, and African Americans—already living in the United States, or in what became the United States, profoundly altering their relationship to American society.

In 1837, American expansionism had tremendous momentum. Texas had just declared its independence from Mexico and was pushing for entry into the United States. Georgians, working with Andrew Jackson's full cooperation, were just completing their successful effort to expand their access to tillable soil by forcing the Five Civilized Tribes westward. The federal government sponsored expeditions into the West throughout this period, scouting out accessible transportation routes and valuable resources; in these years, overland trails were replaced by the transcontinental railroad. Through the Mexican American War, fought between 1846 and 1848, and the Gadsden Purchase in 1853, the United States added California and parts of present-day Arizona, Utah, Nevada, and New Mexico. In the course of these few years, the United States increased in size by more than 70 percent. By 1877, thirteen new states entered the Union, and the rest of what became the continental United States was organized into territories.

Industrialization and economic growth went hand in hand with territorial expansion. The new lands provided raw materials for burgeoning American industries and provided access to new markets for goods. Slave owners in the South mi-

grated west as the nation expanded, leaving tired soil behind them. As cotton production shifted west, it increased its importance to the American textile industry and to the export economy of the country. The new lands spurred the transportation revolution, which produced a transcontinental railroad and the first American corporations by 1869. One clear marker of economic growth was the increase in American production. The goods produced in the United States increased several fold in these decades. The nation produced $483 million in manufactured goods in 1840. In 1870 the gross national product had grown to $7.4 billion, and by 1880 it had climbed to $11.2 billion.

All of this growth and development offered seemingly endless opportunities to people living within the nation's borders. But these opportunities were starkly defined in racial terms. The notion of Manifest Destiny—that American expansion was inevitable because it was the will of God—had obvious racial implications. It indeed offered boundless possibility for those who laid claim to God's blessings, but it had dire consequences for those who stood in the way. Likewise, industrial and geographic expansion opened up new jobs and new acres to farm by the tens of thousands. But as this essay will argue, access to jobs and farms were by and large determined racially as well. Simply stated, those defined as white could opt for inclusion and participation in American society—and access to economic opportunities—while those defined as nonwhite by and large could not. This was, however, no simple binary of exclusion and inclusion.

The reconstitution of the American population during these decades provoked a reassertion—and in many ways a complex reworking—of racial identity and racial hierarchy in the United States.

The Irish were the first white population in the United States to face significant challenges to their racial identity, and to their presence in the country in general. Irish immigrants began to arrive in the United States in the 1820s, and by 1840 they constituted nearly half of all immigrants entering the country. Over the next forty years, more than 2.5 million more Irish immigrated into the United States. So many of them settled in urban areas in the Northeast that immigrant historian Marcus Hansen referred to them as the "second colonization of New England." Though they arrived at an opportune moment in American economic history, they faced serious opposition to their presence in the United States. Not only their racial identity, but also the dire circumstances of their arrival and their Catholicism made them targets of people concerned about their potential impact on the country. These challenges, and their ability to overcome them, determined the extent of Irish access to American society.

Those who came in the 1840s left a country in dire straits. A blight struck potato crops, on which most Irish depended for survival, and between 1845 and 1849 the population of Ireland fell by more than a million. Many left the country, considering themselves involuntary exiles, and many more starved to death. But as Hasia Diner has argued, the famine did not so much create the enormous problems Ireland faced as exacerbate them. English colonialism had created the context for the deadly famine long before it struck, and the downward spiral in population continued well after the blight ended. From 1841 to 1891, Ireland lost almost 50 percent of its population. Marriage rates plummeted as economic conditions grew worse. Family ties nonetheless remained vital to many immigrants; one historian has argued that the Irish were the first to practice chain migration. As often as not, though, it was siblings who traveled together rather than husbands, wives, and children.

The Irish who made their way to the United States were predominantly impoverished and poorly educated, and thus often confined to manual labor. The Irish entered at the bottom of the social and economic scale and took jobs that few others would. Nonetheless, the labor that they provided was vital. Irish men began to arrive just as the United States turned seriously to developing its infrastructure. Irish labor helped build canals in the Northeast, the National Road, and eventually the transcontinental railroad. In general, they eschewed rural life, settling almost exclusively in urban areas. In many northeastern towns and cities, Irish men dominated day labor by the middle of the 1840s.

Unlike any other immigrant group, the majority of the Irish who came to the United States were women. They were not only forced from Ireland by conditions there, but also drawn to this country because of an economic niche open to them—domestic service. This job was always available to Irish immigrant women. By the 1850s they were 80 percent of the domestic servants in New York City. Even decades later their association with this work remained strong. Irish women moved fairly quickly into the textiles industry and into needlework as well. But as late as 1900 over 60 percent of all Irish-born women in the United States still worked as domestics.

Despite the hard labor that Irish immigrants provided, they were routinely maligned by native-born Americans and by those who had immigrated earlier. While there had been Catholics in the United States from its first days, the Irish Catholic population grew enormously in the mid-nineteenth century, reaching 2 million by 1842. This religious difference, and increasing Irish demands for the right to open their own schools, caused alarm among certain Americans. The Irish also gained a reputation for criminality, for pauperism, and for alcohol abuse that increased opposition to their presence.

Opposition to the Irish coalesced into a nativist movement as early as the 1830s. In 1837 New York City elected a nativist mayor and city council. Nativists, who drew on the secretive nature of their organization in calling themselves "Know-Nothings," gained power through the 1840s. Though broadly antiforeign, they focused the majority of their attention on the Irish. By the 1850s, nativists had formed the American Party, which for a time vied with the new Republican Party to replace the defunct Whigs. In 1856, the American Party scored its greatest successes. It elected 7 governors, 8 United States senators, and a staggering 104 members of the United States House of Representatives. Though the North, consumed by the issue of slavery, soon turned to the Republicans, nativist impulses—and racialized threats to Irish presence—still ran deep and strong in American society. In facing challenges to their racial identity as white, the Irish presented one of the most complex reworkings of racial identity and hierarchy in this era. Irish immigrants were often associated—and often associated themselves—with African Americans. Free blacks and Irish often lived in the same neighborhoods and socialized together. They often competed for the same unskilled labor because these were the only jobs open to either; Irish women vied with black women (and with the few Chinese women in the West who had immigrated) for domestic service jobs. Slave owners even occasionally hired Irish day laborers to perform jobs deemed too dangerous for their slaves.

But historians of the construction of whiteness have recognized that as challenged as certain white European immigrant groups might have been, they nonetheless enjoyed access to rights that nonwhites did not. Thomas Guglielmo's analysis of Italian immigrants applies equally to Irish immigrants. He argues that the "whiteness" of these populations was rarely called into serious question; rather the quality of their whiteness was. Thus, for example, unlike immigrants like the Chinese, who were defined as nonwhite, the Irish could naturalize as citizens under the 1790 Naturalization Act, which allowed only whites this access. As Matthew Jacobson has argued, they were "the first to immigrate in huge numbers at once well within the literal language but well outside the deliberate intent of the 'free white persons' clause of 1790." The act's authors may not have intended to include them, but these immigrants were included nonetheless.

Irish immigrants had other ways to separate themselves from their nonwhite counterparts, and they used them to full advantage. Their concentration in urban areas made them the target of scorn and even violence. (The Irish notoriously established the first American "ghettoes," and anti-Catholic riots erupted in Philadelphia and in other cities in the 1840s.) But it also eventually helped them, especially because they arrived just at the outset of American urban development. This not only helped them dominate construction and domestic service jobs in their early years, it also made them critical components of the power base the Democratic Party was trying to build in northeastern cities. As David Roediger has argued, the Irish found in the Democratic Party not only a route to political power, but also a way to assert their whiteness. As the Democrats became outspokenly antiblack (and at times proslavery), Roediger asserts, in northeastern cities, "In areas with virtually no black voters, the Democrats created a 'white vote.'" The Irish were also able to use their ties to political party machines to move into municipal jobs. Irish immigrants used their labor in other ways to gain access to American society. Many Irish women working as domestics had long thought of their jobs as inroads into the American middle class. If they could not join the middle class through their labors, they could at least observe it firsthand. Many Irish men and women also became prominent members of the labor movement that was growing rapidly, if unevenly, in the United States between the 1830s and the 1870s. According to Hasia Diner, "Irish women provided much of the female trade union leadership in the last half of the nineteenth century." Irish men and women became instrumental members of many labor unions in these years, including the newly formed Knights of Labor. Their municipal jobs, their union membership, and the spiritual and institutional strength that the Catholic Church provided them elevated the status of the Irish in American society.

Many, though not all, also used their realization that, as Kerby Miller noted, blacks could be "despised with impunity" to their advantage. Irish attacks on blacks became so common in New York City that bricks were known as "Irish confetti." In 1863 tension in that city over the draft turned violent as many Irish, who saw the war as a battle over slavery, took their frustration at conscription out on the black residents. But if some Irish used attacks on blacks in an attempt to cement their relationship to American society, others used more noble means. General Thomas Meagher's Irish Brigade, for example, suffered losses of two-thirds of its men at Fredericksburg. All told, thousands of Irish Catholics fought for the Union during the Civil War.

Despite these numerous inroads into American society, the status of the Irish in the United States by 1877 in many ways remained insecure. Irish behavior during the 1863 draft riot had horrified many observers; some of them described the Irish, in terms usually reserved for Indian foes, as "savages," "savage mobs," and "demons." At the same time as the riots were taking place, the enigmatic Molly Maguires launched a series of mortal attacks against employers and other officials they deemed unjust in the anthracite region of Pennsylvania. As Kevin Kenny's work makes clear, the Molly Maguires were hardly representative of all Irish immigrants. He notes that ethnic identity is "historical, contingent and contested rather than essential [and] fixed," and many Irish immigrants worked arduously to counter the Molly Maguires' version of Irish ethnic identity. Kenny argued that "in the anthracite region at least, a specific Catholic definition of Irishness emerged victorious in the 1870s." It may have been victorious, but it was not the only one. In June 1877, ten Molly Maguires were hung in a single day, and once more, despite the enormous progress Irish immigrants had made, comparisons with "savage Indians" filled indignant editorials. The Irish by 1877 had taken full advantage of their whiteness; their status in the United States, however, was still being contested.

Germans were, with the Irish, the largest group of white ethnic immigrants to the United States in this period. Unlike the Irish, German immigrants were largely able to avoid vilification and faced far fewer impediments in their efforts to take advantage of American expansionism and industrialization. Highly skilled, well educated, predominantly Protestant, and largely rural (and thus more often able to avoid harmful attention), they were able to make the adjustment to life in the United States with little of the duress experienced by Irish immigrants, much less by those identified as nonwhite. Even the sizable German Jewish population (there were fifty thousand German Jews in New York City by 1860 and as many as ten thousand in smaller cities like Cincinnati in the same year) achieved considerable success in retail industries and in banking. It is little wonder that the metaphor of the United States as a "melting pot" was coined by German immigrant Christian Essellen in 1857, about fifty years before it gained currency in English.

Between 1840 and 1880, almost 3 million Germans arrived in this country; in these decades they were never less than one-fourth of incoming immigrants. Most historians agree that Germans came predominantly for economic reasons—not because of poverty or economic duress, but because changing economic conditions at home made the move across the ocean seem more advantageous. There were, however, some Germans who migrated for religious reasons. For example, some Lutherans made their way here because of the discrimination they faced in their homeland. Still others came for overtly political reasons, like the small but extremely vocal and articulate number of refugees from the failed revolution in 1848.

German immigrants stood out in this period as an unusually skilled and educated population. This was at least true of the men, who were quickly able to exploit their skills in the labor market.

By 1850, for example, almost half of the German immigrants living in Chicago were employed as artisans or skilled workers; almost another 9 percent were small businessmen. German women by and large found work in the service sector, employed in jobs ranging from domestic servant to baker to hotelkeeper to nurse.

German immigrants also distinguished themselves from the Irish by settling predominantly away from northeastern urban areas. Taking full advantage of the United States' push west, and of the benefits it held out to white settlers, a considerable number of these migrants took up farming to earn their livelihood. They settled so broadly in rural areas away from the Atlantic coast that what came to be known as a "German Belt" stretched across eighteen states from the Northeast to the Midwest. As late as 1870, one in four German immigrants was still involved in agricultural pursuits.

Though German immigrants did not endure anything approaching the challenges the Irish faced, German presence in the United States did not go uncontested. Some of their social habits—their unwillingness to give up drinking on Sundays, and certain Germans' willingness to socialize with blacks—created consternation. Many working-class Germans engaged enthusiastically in union activity and in radical politics. They helped establish the Socialist Labor Party, the first socialist party in the United States, in 1877. By that time German anarchists were also organizing Lehr-und-Wehr-Vereins, "Instruction and Protection Societies," which focused on education and military training. The first one, founded in Chicago in 1875, was soon one of the largest workers' militias in the United States. These radical activities caused concern almost immediately. And while German Jews faced little overt discrimination in these decades, Carey McWilliams and John Higham have both argued that religiously and economically based anti-Semitism began to take hold in the United States by 1877.

German immigrants also faced occasional racial challenges. European racial theorist Joseph Arthur Comte de Gobineau, in his 1855 *The Inequality of Human Races,* a book widely read by American scholars, condemned not only Italians and Irish, but also Germans as "the human flotsam of all ages." Germans in the United States—and especially the Catholics among them—were included as well in the objections that nativists raised about immigration.

But these challenges did little to damage Germans' sense of security in their adopted home. They were able to point to a number of lofty cultural achievements and to draw on an organizational life that one historian has described as unrivaled by other immigrant groups. The German press in the United States dated back to the colonial era; German theater productions and music recitals appeared regularly in midwestern and northeastern cities. German immigrants established fraternal organizations, mutual aid societies, and labor associations on neighborhood, urban, and regional levels.

They were able to make inroads into American society in other ways as well.

Like Irish women, German women who worked as domestics could use their proximity to American middle-class women as models for their own patterns of behavior and consumption. Unlike the Irish, whose enthusiasm for the Union during the Civil War was hardly unanimous, Germans established a solid reputation for supporting the Union. German Free-Soilers and members of the German immigrant community in Chicago, for example, were staunch opponents of slavery by the outbreak of the war. During the war, ten German immigrant regiments were raised in New York City alone.

These immigrants withstood challenges to their presence in the United States because of their remarkable level of cultural and racial confidence. Applying many of the same racial theories used to malign other immigrants and races, they were able to argue the equality—at the very least—of Anglo-Saxons and Teutons. During the Mexican American war, when the notion of Manifest Destiny was evoked to justify the conquest of supposedly "inferior" races, one German immigrant was able to assert, "We too, even though we are not Anglo-Saxons, believe in 'manifest destiny' and—we add for the benefit of the nativists—'manifest destiny' also believes in us." In a nation in the process of reformulating its notions of racial hierarchy, German immigrants boldly placed themselves at the top of that hierarchy.

Nevertheless, German immigrants would remain a challenged population in the United States. Their involvement in radical politics and unionizing would make them targets of a Red Scare in 1886. Their insistence on language maintenance—through building their own schools or pushing their local schools to teach German—would make them a highly visible target again in 1917. But before 1877 most problems they faced were internal to their community. There were so many divisions—geographic, religious, and ideological—that historian Kathleen Conzen has questioned whether German immigrants could even be called an ethnic group. Nonetheless, the skills and levels of education many Germans brought with them, their organizational prowess, and especially the confidence that their standing as "superior" whites gave them placed them in a position unrivaled by other immigrant groups in this or any era.

Chinese immigrants did not arrive in nearly the same numbers as German or Irish immigrants, but their concentration on the west coast—itself a product of and a spur to American expansionism and industrialization—and their identity as nonwhites meant that their presence in the United States would be both significant and severely embattled. The first Chinese began to arrive soon after gold was discovered in California in 1848; 325 Chinese were among the first fortune seekers. By 1852, Chinese immigrants numbered more than twenty thousand, most of them still in California. In ensuing decades the Chinese immigrant population continued to climb; the census showed sixty-three thousand Chinese in the United States in 1870, and more than 105,000 in 1880. Almost all of these immigrants were men; for reasons often rooted in cultural traditions, women tended not to travel abroad. They were also discouraged from immigrating by the 1875 Page Law, which in practice treated all Chinese women as potential prostitutes. As late as 1880, Chinese men in the United States still outnumbered women by more than twenty to one. They were drawn not only by the allure of potential riches, but because of the enormous turmoil in China. The first Opium War, fought between the English and the Chinese beginning in 1839, created great unrest and despair in China. Western intervention in the country and internal tensions produced a series of revolts. The Taiping Rebellion, for example, begun in 1850 by a man who claimed he was Jesus' younger brother, would claim 10 million lives across south and central China.

The work that the Chinese did, and the ways in which their work experiences and opportunities evolved, were inseparable from their reception in the United States. For a time they were well received; the Governor of California in 1852 referred to them as "one of the most worthy classes of our newly adopted citizens." In these early years, two-thirds of the Chinese immigrants worked in the gold mines, most of them panning for gold in small placer claims. By 1870 only about one in four were still mining, by then often as company employees, and spread across six states. Two things had happened that caused the numbers of Chinese immigrant miners to drop. First, the most easily accessible gold had been found; companies with capital to purchase extractive equipment now dominated the mines. But even be-

fore this development, white miners had pushed the California state legislature to remove the Chinese from the mines. The 1852 Foreign Miners tax targeted Chinese miners because they were ineligible for citizenship, requiring them to pay $3 a month until the law was overturned in 1870. In 1859, the state legislature passed another law expressly "to protect Free White Labor against competition with Chinese Coolie Labor, and to Discourage the Immigration of the Chinese into the State of California." The law, which misidentified Chinese immigrants as coolies, imposed an additional monthly tax on them (with few exceptions) simply for living in the state.

Chinese immigrants soon found another source of employment helping to build the transcontinental railroad. Once again, racial identity was the definitive issue. The Central Pacific Railroad hired one hundred Chinese workers in 1865, and white workers quickly insisted that they be fired. Leland Stanford, the head of the railroad, weary of labor troubles with white workers, made the decision to hire Chinese workers exclusively for the remainder of the project. By 1869, when the railroad was completed, twelve thousand Chinese were working for the railroad—90 percent of its workforce. They were hired not only to send a warning to unruly white workers, but also because their employers regarded them as an easily exploitable workforce. During the infamous winter of 1866, railroad officials forced their Chinese employees to work despite sixty-foot snowdrifts. They worked in tunnels dug through the snow. A number of Chinese workers were buried when the tunnels gave way; some were not found until the spring thaw. When they struck the next summer, to protest their abusive treatment and the fact that they were paid far less than white workers, their employees cut off their food and starved them into submission.

After the railroad work was completed, Chinese immigrants went in two different directions for employment. Many turned to agriculture, finding jobs as farm laborers throughout California. By the end of the 1870s, they constituted most of the farm labor in four California counties and nearly half of the farm labor force in two others. Many more Chinese moved into urban areas, especially San Francisco. At first they were able to find employment in a variety of burgeoning enterprises—forming almost half of the work force in boot and shoe manufacture, woolen goods, cigars, and sewing. Before long, however, protests from whites drove them almost entirely into self-employment. By the 1860s and 1870s, Chinese restaurants and especially Chinese laundries were ubiquitous. Although self-employment offered certain benefits, external forces confined the Chinese to these economic niches. Their dominance of the laundry business, for example, was entirely a product of immigration. There was no tradition of male launderers in China; laundering was simply one of the only occupations open to them.

Chinese immigrants had faced enormous resistance, and even violence, in California from the first. In 1849, just after they arrived, sixty Chinese miners were chased off their jobs by angry white miners. As Sucheng Chan points out, in 1862 the California State legislature received a list of eighty-eight Chinese miners who had been killed by whites—including eleven killed by collectors of the Foreign Miners tax. Job competition was particularly fierce in San Francisco; by one estimate, in 1870 there were two white workers and one Chinese worker for every job in the city. Especially after the economic depression of 1873 began, anticoolie club members attacked Chinese in the streets, and several were suspected of starting suspicious fires at factories that still hired Chinese workers. In 1877, the local press reported the establishment of the Order of Caucasians, which dedicated itself to driving the Chinese out of the city entirely.

Chinese immigrants sustained themselves in the face of this opposition through a rich organizational life. They quickly formed huiguan, associations of immigrants from the same districts in China, which provided mutual aid and an arena for socializing. By 1862 the leaders of six large huiguan in California organized the Chinese Six Companies, which fought effectively for Chinese immigrants' rights in the United States. Chinese immigrants often formed rotating credit associations, which enabled each member in turn to use the collective resources of the group to found a business or embark on some other economic enterprise. Less wealthy immigrants were often drawn to Tongs, secret societies with revolutionary roots in China, which functioned as "alternative, antiestablishment" institutions in the new land.

But this organizational life, and the contributions that their labor wrought in agriculture, mining, and railroad construction, were not enough to prevent attacks against the Chinese. Even those who recognized the rich and complex history of China dismissed these immigrants as the product of a decaying culture. Opposition to the Chinese had always been strong in California, among both political and working-class leaders. When they were drawn to other regions of the country as prods to uncooperative workers, concern about Chinese immigrants became national.

The first national legislation barring the entry of the Chinese targeted women. The proportion of women among Chinese immigrants had remained very small, and a substantial number of them—as many as 60 percent by 1870—worked as prostitutes. The Page Law, passed in 1875, ostensibly banned Chinese prostitutes from entering the country. But the examinations into their personal lives that Chinese women faced as potential immigrants discouraged most of them from even trying to enter the United States.

By 1877, the Chinese were about to become the first national population to be excluded from entering the United States. This exclusion was rooted solely in their racial identity. President Rutherford B. Hayes asserted that the Chinese "invasion" was "pernicious and should be discouraged." Putting Chinese immigration in the context of "our experience in dealing with the weaker races—the Negroes and the Indians," he argued, "I would consider with favor any suitable means to discourage the Chinese from coming to our shores." The effort to end Chinese immigration almost entirely would succeed a few short years later.

They had made substantial contributions to the American, and especially the Californian, economy, but they found little opportunity to make inroads in this country. Even the 1870 Civil Rights Act, which provided certain protections for Chinese immigrants, gave little solace. Senator Charles Sumner's amendment to strike the word "white" from congressional acts related to naturalization met with widespread opposition. One senator protested, "Mongolians will never lose their identity as a peculiar and separate people." In the ensuing years of the nineteenth century, Chinese immigrants in the United States would become an increasingly secluded—and exoticized—population.

Mexicans—although they are now so commonly associated with immigration, especially by its critics—were not immigrants in this era. They lived on land that became part of the United States through expansionism—through colonial conquest and usurpation justified on racial grounds. Some of the first incursions into Mexican territory came in Texas. Initially invited to settle, Anglos continued to move into the province after the Mexican government banned their migration. A revolt against the Mexican government at first involved both Anglo immigrants and Tejanos (Texas-born Mexicans), some of whose families had lived in Texas for generations. But as Arnoldo de Leon has argued, Texans never experienced enormous hardship under the Mexican government, which was thousands of miles away and wracked by internal dissension. The rebellion quickly became, in the words of historian Reginald Horsman, "a racial clash, not simply a revolt against an unjust government or tyranny."

Relations between Tejanos and Anglos in Texas after the revolt set the tone for the Mexican American War, and for Anglo-Mexican relations after the war. A "peace structure" devised between Anglo immigrants and the Tejano ranch-owning elite, especially in predominantly Mexican areas of south Texas, prevailed for a short time. According to David Montejano, ambitious Anglo men married into Tejano families, often in these early years adopting aspects of Mexican cultural identity as their own. But competition over resources doomed the peace structure. Juan Seguin, a Captain in the Texas army, had fought against Mexico at San Jacinto and would have been at the Alamo, as thirteen Tejanos were, had he not been sent out for reinforcements. In 1840 he was elected mayor of San Antonio. But Sequin's valiant defense of Tejanos against abuses by land-hungry Anglos spelled his ruin. In 1842, he was forced to flee to Mexico, the country against which he had just fought, to protect himself and his family. At least two hundred Tejano families left San Antonio for similar reasons.

The Mexican American War, the United States' first foreign war, was again waged as an explicitly racial conflict. Popular travel journals written by Americans like Richard Henry Dana created lasting stereotypes of sexually accessible Mexican women and slothful, inept Mexican men. Mexicans in general were derided as bestial; one Tennessee soldier described them as "more degraded than the African race among us." Certain Americans compared them unfavorably to Indian populations and predicted that the Mexican "race" would soon become "extinct." Americans fighting against the Mexicans dehumanized them, and acts of brutality against Mexican soldiers and citizens were widespread. In Monterey, for example, Texas Rangers made a sport of shooting Mexicans off rooftops.

The racial ideology that underscored the war did more than justify repeated acts of cruelty. It was at the heart of Americans' sense of self-definition. "Manifest Destiny" was part of a broader assertion of racial superiority by Anglo-Saxons—who, for the first time in this country, defined themselves as a distinct racial group—and of other white ethnics who sought in its guise an explicit acceptance of their ownership of American identity. In this sense, it is not surprising that the phrase was coined by Irish immigrant John O'Sullivan. Those seeking acceptance into American society defined themselves in contrast to those outside its boundaries. For the latter, any manner of treatment was justified. As Horsman described it, "In effect, by mid-century, America's racial theorists were explaining the enslavement of blacks, the disappearance of Indians, and the defeat of Mexicans in a manner that reflected no discredit on the people of the United States."

Once the United States won the war, the 1848 Treaty of Guadalupe Hidalgo brought not only California and much of what is now the American Southwest, but also thousands of Mexicans into the country—by treaty, and as a "defeated race." Nonetheless, Mexicans entered the political framework of this country in the legal sense in complex and not altogether unfavorable ways. On paper, the treaty promised rights that seemed surprising, given the ways that Mexicans had been positioned racially during the war. Described in disparaging terms as a mixed-race population, they were nonetheless granted citizenship rights in the treaty—rights to this point granted to people entering American civic society only if they were white. Acting on these rights, however, and especially on the right to vote, would prove difficult and often impossible.

Moreover, the treaty did little to protect Mexican claims to land ownership. The United States Senate struck a clause from the treaty that would have guaranteed protection of Mexicans' rights to their lands. This had profound implications for the class system that had characterized the preconquest northern Mexican provinces. Tejano and Californio elites had controlled huge tracts of land in Texas and in California. Californios had relied on Indian peonage, establishing a seigneurial system to sustain the comfortable existence that Anglo travelers like Dana (whose uncle had married into a Californio family) had held in such contempt. Tejano ranchers had established a similarly paternalistic attitude toward the mestizo and Indian peones under them. Tied only marginally into the market economy, especially compared to more commercially minded Anglos, they were land rich and cash poor. Over several decades after the war,

most of these rancheros lost their lands through a variety of means. Land claims were difficult and very expensive to establish in American courts, especially without treaty protection. Taxation under the new government forced many rancheros to sell off more and more of their land. Outright theft by unscrupulous Anglos was common.

Less wealthy Mexicans were often deprived of the means to provide for their livelihood. They were also frequent victims of violence. One particularly ironic example was the fate of the Californios who attempted to join the gold rush in California just months after the war. They were obligated, along with Chinese immigrants, to pay the Foreign Miners Tax—in a land in which many of their families had lived for generations. Along with the Chinese, they were also routinely assaulted, and sometimes killed, by Anglo miners who identified them as nonwhite competitors. The combination of the tax and the assaults drove them from the mines. The first Mexican woman known to have been lynched in the United States, a prostitute named Juanita, also met her fate in California in 1851.

Mexicans, in the decades after the war, resisted Anglo incursions and theft, at times informally, at times in more organized fashions. Historian Deena Gonzalez has analyzed how Mexican women in the territory of New Mexico defiantly maintained their cultural practice of unfettered public behavior and their work habits. They also strived through the courts to maintain property and inheritance rights they had enjoyed before the war. Other forms of protest were more violent. In 1859, for example, Juan Cortina, the son of a wealthy Tejano rancher, killed a Brownsville, Texas, sheriff he saw beating one of his father's employees. That incident sparked the "Cortina War." Cortina, who had initially fled, returned to Brownsville with sixty men, freed every Mexican prisoner he found, and executed four Anglos who had killed Mexicans and gone unpunished. Texas Rangers, unable to find him or his followers, retaliated against Mexicans throughout the region. Cortina's brand of informal justice, which some historians have labeled "social banditry," was reproduced throughout the 1860s and 1870s. Mexicans in the 1870s who removed cattle from Anglo ranches, for example, did not consider themselves thieves—they called it reclaiming "Nana's cattle." Anglo ranchers and especially Texas Rangers, whose enmity for Mexicans had only increased after the war, in turn considered killing Mexicans like "killing an enemy in the independence war."

Battles between Mexicans and Anglos continued throughout these years. Mexicans in Texas continued to incur the wrath of ranch owner Richard King, whose ambition at one point had been to own the entire territory between the Nueces and the Rio Grande once disputed by Mexico and the United States. King routinely drew on the Texas Rangers, known by some as the "King Ranch Rangers," to go after Mexican "cattle rustlers." By the end of 1877, battles between them had left more than a dozen Anglos and more than one hundred Mexicans dead. That same year, Anglo officials in El Paso attempted to assume control of salt beds west of the city that had traditionally been used communally by Mexican residents. Judge Charles Howard tried to claim the beds for commercial purposes. When he killed Luis Cardis, who led Mexican opposition to the move, the "El Paso Salt War" began. Angry Mexican residents of El Paso killed Howard and two other Anglos, and defeated a troop of Texas Rangers before being quelled.

By the end of this period Mexicans in the United States were in many ways a subject population. Many Tejano and Californio rancheros had lost their holdings or were in dire financial straits, or both. The process of the proletarianization of this population—its reduction largely to manual, unskilled labor—was well under way. Even vaqueros, Mexican cowboys who had had such enormous pride in their skills and who had taught many incoming Anglos, now had difficulty finding suitable work. The racial hierarchy under which Mexicans lived was clearest on the King Ranch—Mexicans worked as ranch hands, overseen by Anglos, many of whom were former Texas Rangers. Before long, as Arnoldo de Leon has pointed out, Jim Crow signs in south Texas would read "for Mexicans" instead of "for Negroes."

The transition that African Americans made in this era was easily one of the most dramatic. They began the era as an enslaved population (only a fraction of the antebellum population was free). In 1860, the slave population in the South had reached an estimated 4 million. Slave labor sustained all major southern crop production—rice, sugar, tobacco, and especially cotton. Though perhaps in less immediately obvious ways than the other populations discussed in this essay, African Americans too were profoundly affected by the major developments occurring in American society. Expansionism and industrialization in the North and West combined to put the North and South on a collision course that led to civil war. By the end of this era African Americans had been freed, though with the end of Reconstruction the racial challenges they faced remained daunting at best.

The nature of slave labor varied enormously according to where slaves worked. Enslaved African Americans worked not only on various crops throughout the South, but also in both urban and rural settings, on small farms and enormous plantations, in masters' houses and in surrounding fields. Under slavery, everyone worked—men, women, and, as soon as they were able, children. Field hands labored from sunrise to sunset, and even longer during harvest time. House slaves performed a wide range of tasks, including cooking, cleaning, serving as butlers and valets, and providing care for young children. This work was often less physically taxing than field work, and provided access to more and better food. Work in the proximity of whites meant access to valuable information—especially as the war approached. But house servants also were expected to be on twenty-four-hour call, and compelled to live away from family and friends, and from the sustenance of slave culture. The small number of slaves who worked as artisans, or who lived in urban areas, often had increased opportunities. Masters who "hired out" their slaves sometimes let

them keep some of their wages. There were even instances in which masters let them buy their freedom. Urban areas and work with free men and women also provided tremendous access to information—and even chances to escape.

But despite these slim windows of opportunity, slavery as a system was based on coercion and cruelty. Slave owners relied on violence, or the threat of it, to maintain control over the human beings they owned. Whippings were commonplace, and dismemberment of particularly recalcitrant slaves was not unheard of. Enslaved women could face not only these punishments but routine sexual abuse as well. Escaped slave Harriet Jacobs wrote of the horror of having lost her virginity when she was raped by the man who owned her. Rebellious slaves could also be punished through sale away from their loved ones, or by having their spouses or children sold. An estimated one in five slave marriages were broken up by sale; one in three children were sold away from their families.

Nor was sale or forced migration necessarily administered as punishment—it was often a product of American expansionism. Crop production, especially in cotton, shifted westward in the decades before the Civil War. Whereas in 1810, 80 percent of slaves had lived in Virginia, Maryland, and the Carolinas, by 1860 one in three slaves lived in the fabled "black belt" spanning Georgia, Alabama, Mississippi, Louisiana, and further west. An estimated 1.5 million slaves had been forced to migrate west during that half century.

In the face of unrelenting hardship, enslaved African Americans strived to establish space for their own humanity. They relied first and foremost on their families. Slave men and women routinely fought for control over their choices of marriage partner and over the process of childbirth—midwives were valued members of their communities. Slave women formed informal networks—quilting and sewing circles, systems of shared labor away from the fields—that sustained them socially and spiritually. Slave culture was also organized centrally around the church and religious ritual. By 1860, most enslaved African Americans professed some sort of Christianity.

Their relationship to Christianity, however, was a complex one. As scholar Sterling Stuckey has argued, under slavery they created a synthetic religious faith that merged African burial ceremonies, circle rituals, and ring shouts with Christian practices. In Stuckey's words, "Christianity provided a protective exterior beneath which more complex, less familiar [to outsiders] religious principles and practices were operative." These aspects of African religions facilitated the synthesis of diverse African ethnicities into a singular culture—circle rituals, for example, were central to a number of African populations in one form or another. They also enabled people to retain ties to their homeland or, eventually, to the homes of their ancestors, up to and beyond the last days of slavery. When Frederick Law Olmstead traveled through the South in the 1850s, for example, he declared that three-fourths of the slaves on Louisiana and Mississippi plantations were profoundly influenced by African survivals.

The establishment of an African American culture, and the insistence on preserving aspects of African culture, were both survival strategies and implicit forms of resistance. They were by no means the only ones. Although there were few slave rebellions after Nat Turner's 1831 revolt, one important exception was the Seminole Wars in Florida. The Seminole Indian community had been a haven for runaway slaves since the colonial era, and by the 1830s it was in open resistance to the American government. Most resistance occurred on a much more personal level. Occasionally slaves violently attacked their masters, but retribution for these acts was so fierce that resistance was usually much more subtle. Feigning illness, breaking tools, mistreating livestock, destroying crops—all of these were acts of resistance that occurred daily during slavery.

There were also 225,000 free blacks in the North on the eve of the Civil War, and a smaller and shrinking number in the South, whose very existence was an indictment of the implicit assumption that African Americans could not survive, much less prosper, outside of slavery. But they lived very difficult lives, enduring increasing discrimination and segregation in the North, and ever more urgent efforts to expel them or return them to slavery in the South. They had few employment options available to them, and even these began to disappear when European, and especially Irish, immigrants entered the country. As Frederick Douglass noted, "Every hour sees us elbowed out of some employment to make room perhaps for some newly arrived immigrants, whose hunger and color are thought to give them a title to special favor." There were nonetheless instances of resistance to their conditions, and to the conditions endured by African American slaves. Martin Delany, who was able to trace his family roots back to African royalty, called for an early version of African nationalism, and even briefly attempted to organize a collective return to Africa. Free blacks in the North, moreover, were among the first and most enthusiastic participants in the abolitionist movement.

They contributed enormously to growing tensions between anti- and pro-slavery forces in the decades leading up to the Civil War. In the 1830s and 1840s, the abolitionist movement both grew and diversified, as more and more whites and blacks organized to voice their opposition to slavery. By 1840, political, religious, and radical factions had emerged as abolitionists split over the means to attack slavery. These abolitionist forces were countered by increasingly vehement defenses of slavery emerging out of the South. In the decades immediately following the Revolutionary war, many southern slave owners had rationalized slavery as a "necessary evil"—difficult to justify, but absolutely essential to the southern, and the American, economy. By the 1830s, in the face of slave rebellions, economic downturns, and especially the flood of abolitionist literature making its way into the South, southern slave owners began to argue that slavery was, in the words of John Calhoun, a "positive good." Southern politicians and academicians worked in the ensuing decades to defend slavery

and to compare it favorably to capitalist labor relations in the North. They viewed the emergence of the Republican Party in the 1850s with considerable alarm. The new party was staunchly antislavery, though its members were hardly of one mind on racial equality. Some Republicans were abolitionists and upholders of the principle of racial equality. But even more were former Free-Soilers, many of whom wanted neither slavery nor blacks moving into new territories in the West. Disagreement over slavery finally erupted into war in 1861.

The ultimate act of African American rebellion against slavery was their participation in the Civil War. Free blacks from the North and South threw themselves into the war effort. Slaves ran away by the tens of thousands, attaching themselves to Union armies, enduring dismal conditions in "contraband" camps, and offering their services in whatever way possible. Although their assistance was refused early in the war, and they were often relegated to menial labor behind the scenes, blacks organized their first regiment in 1862; the following year, they were fighting on the front lines. By 1865, 186,000 blacks had participated in the war effort.

Postwar Reconstruction represented a seemingly extraordinary opportunity for blacks. Eric Foner described the period as "a massive experiment in interracial democracy." The era held out the promise—though in many ways, only the promise—of freedom. Again in Foner's words, "'freedom' itself became a terrain of conflict." Every aspect of freedom African Americans sought—

personal, institutional, political, and economic—was contested by former slave owners and other southern whites.

Nonetheless, blacks after the war were able to act autonomously in unprecedented ways. They reasserted the centrality of family life; literally thousands left their homes in an effort to find spouses, children, and other loved ones who had been sold away under slavery. They reestablished gender roles within their families; the opportunity for black women not to have to work in the fields was extremely important. African Americans were now free to establish their own churches. By 1877, almost all southern blacks had left white-dominated churches for autonomous institutions like the African Methodist Episcopal Church. They sought not only education but the opportunity to educate themselves; by 1869, black teachers outnumbered white ones in the South. Blacks took advantage of the Fifteenth Amendment not just by voting; they won office in the Reconstruction South in remarkable numbers. All told, African Americans won six hundred legislative seats; between 1868 and 1876, fourteen blacks served as U.S. congressional representatives; two were elected as U.S. Senators; and six served as lieutenant governors.

But the central issue in the minds of many newly freed American citizens was economic. Many blacks fully anticipated that the federal government would provide them the fabled "forty acres and a mule" in return for generations of uncompensated labor. The hope was by no means unfounded. In January 1865, Union General William T. Sherman set aside lands to be distributed to blacks in allotments of forty acres; he later added a proviso enabling the army to loan mules to blacks on these lands. Congress took up a broader land distribution program after the war. But no such program was ever instituted; in fact, lands that had been awarded to blacks to farm and improve were in many instances confiscated. Freed blacks soon found themselves under enormous pressure—often from the Freedman's Bureau, which had been established to oversee their transition to freedom—to sign labor contracts. Their work producing cotton and other crops vital to the southern economy, in some cases on the same plantations they had worked as slaves, soon devolved into a binding system of sharecropping. Working "on shares" offered blacks some semblance of autonomy. But in the cash-poor South, sharecroppers quickly became indebted to exploitive credit merchants. Most ended up in a form of debt peonage, in which the produce women grew became absolutely essential to survival, and from which the only escape was death.

Just as the prospect of economic freedom seemed increasingly remote by the end of Reconstruction, so too did many other freedoms. Most states and localities had passed Black Codes right after the war—oppressive laws that punished blacks severely for a wide range of offenses. After these laws were overturned, whites still sought to control and intimidate blacks at every turn. Even under Reconstruction governments, even having organized themselves into Union League militias, blacks could never be sure of their personal safety. They were killed for petty offenses—for refusal to work, for "insolence," even for being seen as too ambitious. One estimate was that more than two thousand blacks were killed in 1865 alone around Shreveport, Louisiana; another one thousand were reported murdered in Texas between 1865 and 1868. The atmosphere of terror that many southern whites sought to create among newly freed blacks had sexual overtones as well. During Reconstruction, many white southerners still considered black women to be sexually accessible. They acted without fear of punishment. As Deborah Gray White points out, from the end of the Civil War through two-thirds of the twentieth century, no southern white man was convicted of raping a black woman.

Blacks who sought to buy their own land, or who ran for office, became targets of the Ku Klux Klan. Formed in 1869, the KKK served as the armed militia of the Democratic Party in the South, attacking white—but especially black—members of the Republican Party and the Union Leagues. By the time the Ku Klux Klan Acts of 1870 and 1871 were passed, giving the federal government sweeping powers to combat the Klan, it had driven blacks and sympathetic whites from politics in the South.

The Republicans did make one last attempt to assist the efforts of blacks to combat discrimination in the South. The Civil Rights Act of 1875 outlawed discrimination against blacks in public places. But the law ultimately accom-plished little in the eight years before the Supreme Court declared it unconstitutional. A critical clause mandating integrated schools in the South did not pass. The enforcement procedure, moreover, compelled blacks to take their cases to federal court, which was a preventively expensive and cumbersome process. The following year, the Republicans' secretive bargain with the Democrats to resolve disagreement over the election of 1876 signaled the end of the era.

The removal of federal troops in 1877, not from the South entirely, as legend has it, but from the statehouses they had been defending in Louisiana and South Carolina, did not mark the abrupt end of Reconstruction. But it spelled its inevitable demise. The era of promise for blacks ended slowly and unevenly; the South did not begin to pass formal segregation legislation until the early 1880s. But the implications were already clear. Blacks were, in Foner's words, "enmeshed in a seamless web of oppression, whose interwoven economic, political, and social strands all reinforced one another."

American expansionism had dramatic effects on every person living in the United States. But its most profound, and devastating, effect was on American Indians, people who in these years were defined as outside the boundaries of American society. European colonizers, then land-hungry Americans, had been moving into Indian territory and pushing Indians off their lands, either by force or through negotiations, from the first days of contact. Between 1837 and 1877 this process continued with a vengeance, until the fates of Indian populations were all but sealed.

As the era began, one of the most important moments in the history of Indian displacement was just being concluded. In 1837, Cherokees were on the "Trail of Tears," their forced march during which thousands died en route to a newly constructed Indian territory in what became Oklahoma. They had made concerted efforts to assimilate themselves into American society. By the time of the coerced removal they had their own newspaper and a constitution modeled on the American document; some Cherokees even owned African American slaves. But the federal government and anxious American farmers and settlers made it clear that Indians, that "ill-fated race" in the words of Andrew Jackson, had no place in American society. This was the deeper meaning of this removal. As Richard White put it, "Removal made it clear that there was no room for a common world that included independent Indians living with whites." The Jeffersonian notion that assimilated Indians could live among Americans was no longer deemed a possibility.

Their removal was a harbinger of things to come for American Indians. Indian communities already in the Southwest and West faced increasing encroachment on their land, both from other Indians forced into their territories and from Americans seeking land and wealth. Through the middle of the 1840s, federal officials were nonetheless still able to make promises to Indian populations like the Cherokees that they would be undisturbed in their new homes. They constructed an Indian territory on the assumption that American movement west would not prohibit the possibility of a "permanent Indian frontier." This frontier would define the outer boundary of the United States, beyond which Indians could live freely. If the possibility of inclusion of Indian populations within the country no longer existed, at least they could live in relative safety on their own. This possibility too disappeared after the Mexican American War. American victory in the war, and the prospect of settlement on the vast territory it brought into the United States, meant there would be no safe haven for Indian populations between the Atlantic and Pacific Oceans.

The threat to Indian ways of life as Americans engulfed them was already evident in the fates of those who had resisted Jackson's policy of removal. The Choctaw, who had managed to remain in the Southeast rather than moving to the Indian territory that became Oklahoma, fought to keep their cultural traditions alive. They held on to their language, unlike those who had made the move, and they had remained a matrilineal culture. But under increasing pressure from the United States government, their efforts to preserve their culture and traditions faltered. Men who married into the Choctaw community found it impossible to substantiate their wives' land claims in American courts. By the end of the 1850s, the matrilineality of the Choctaws in Mississippi was under serious challenge, and male descent lines were being privileged.

The effort to break down Indian cultural identity became systematic with the formal implementation of the reservation system. There had been reservations east of the Mississippi, but with the end of the prospect of the permanent Indian frontier, reservations became national policy. In theory, their purposes were clear-cut: to remove Indians from travel routes and from areas being settled by Euro-Americans and to attempt, in the words of one federal official, "the great work of regenerating the Indian race." Reservations were supposed to protect Indians by separating them from Euro-American settlers and to facilitate their assimilation—to detribalize and individualize them. In reality, the reservation system was put into place unevenly and even haphazardly. As Richard White has suggested, it "was an improvisation the way survivors of a shipwreck might fashion a raft from the debris of the sunken vessel." Any high-minded ideas about protecting Indians were quickly subsumed under the more pressing effort—in terms of the imperatives of American expansion—to enclose and imprison them. It was an effort that would be successful only after a series of fierce wars fought on the Plains and further west, and one that would leave most Indians either dead or bereft of the cultural and material resources to live their lives on their own terms.

There was only one area of Indian settlement that remained relatively peaceful in the two decades after the Mexican American War—Indian territory in present-day Oklahoma, where many Cherokees and others among the Five Civilized Tribes (the Choctaws, Chickasaws, Creeks, and Seminoles) had been forced to relocate. They spent much of the first decade simply trying to reestablish a sense of unity within the tribes themselves, who had been divided by bitter disagreements over the issue of removal. But within a very short time, they were able to recreate much of their society—still based significantly on the American model—in their new homes. As Robert Utley notes, by the 1850s their public school systems were better than those in Arkansas or Missouri.

But this peace did not prevail elsewhere. Despite the efforts of those like the Five Civilized Tribes who tried to adopt American ways, Indians continued to be seen as savages standing in the way of civilization. In fact, as scholars like Matthew Jacobson and David Roediger have argued in other contexts, the definition of Indians (and various other non-whites) as savages was an essential foundation of the definition of civilization itself. As Roediger pointed out, "'Civilization' continued to define itself as a negation of 'savagery'—indeed, to invent savagery in order to define itself."

During the 1850s and the 1860s, in every corner of the country west of the Mississippi, Indian populations resisted the reservation system, trying to maintain their autonomy and independence, and Americans sought to contain them through negotiation, betrayal, and, ultimately, violence. The United States' effort to turn reservations into national policy was rarely very successful. The reservation system was brutally implemented in Oregon and Washington. It failed terribly in Texas and in California, where Indians were murdered by the thousands by gold rushers. Navajo resistance in New Mexico led to another, if less famous, forced removal. In 1864 the Navajos endured a "Long Walk" to Bosque Redondo, a reservation across the New Mexico territory from their established homeland. Conditions on the reservation were so severe that General William Sherman compared it to Andersonville, the infamous Confederate prisoner of war camp. They would not be permitted to return to a reservation on a reduced section of their homeland until 1868.

Meanwhile, some of the fiercest Indian resistance occurred on the Plains, especially after 1865, when the United States turned its attention from the Civil War back to the West. Warfare between American forces and Plains Indians like the Cheyenne, the Arapahoes, the Lakotas, the Comanches, and the Kiowas became incredibly brutal. Despite the lines between civilization and savagery that they wished to draw so neatly between themselves and Indian populations, white combatants and their supporters often behaved in utterly shocking ways. In one attack on a group of Cheyenne encamped in Sand Creek, Colorado, in 1864—there because their leader, Black Kettle, was attempting to negotiate a peace settlement—Colorado soldiers killed two hundred people, most of them women and children. They scalped and mutilated their bodies and paraded their remains through the streets of Denver. At a local theater, according to one historian, "Theater patrons applauded a display of Cheyenne scalps, some of them of women's pubic hair, strung across the stage at intermission." Though these soldiers were forced

out of the service, they remained heroes to many in Colorado. Despite having legitimized any and all methods of warfare by thoroughly dehumanizing their foes, American soldiers remained unable to secure Indians on reservations through the 1860s.

There were brief moments when the American government attempted to negotiate some sort of peace with resistant Indian populations. A Peace Commission was established after the Civil War, and Ulysses Grant tried to implement a Peace Policy during the first term of his Presidency. Certain Indian leaders were willing to negotiate—Black Kettle had been attempting to do so in Colorado; Oglala Lakota leader Red Cloud visited Washington, D.C., in 1870 on a similar mission. But the end goal of the American government—settlement of all of the land from ocean to ocean—and the perspective most Americans shared of Indians—that they were a race of savages who could not exist within the boundaries of American civilization—made the outcome of these efforts predictable.

By 1877, Indian populations were almost completely enclosed on reservations. Neither battle nor flight proved effective. In June 1876, a collection of Indian tribes killed an overconfident General Custer and all of his men at the Little Bighorn in Montana. Despite the exhilaration the battle evoked, retribution against the victors was swift and fierce. A year later, Chief Joseph and what remained of the Nez Perce raced American troops to Canada. In October 1877 they were caught, just forty miles shy of the border. Sitting Bull and a few

Sioux would not surrender until 1881; Geronimo and a handful of Apaches would hold out until 1886.

Most historians agree that Indians' ultimate confinement on reservations was not the result of a military defeat. In the words of historian Elliott West, they "were not muscled on to reservations because soldiers defeated and sometimes butchered them. They ended up there because they lost command of the resources they needed to live as they wished." What they fought, in other words, were battles not only over territory, but also over the right to maintain control over their identity and their culture. These are battles that in many ways continue to the present day.

This essay has argued the central importance of racial identity in determining the experience of the various racial and ethnic groups who, through various means, came to be included in—or excluded from—American society between 1837 and 1877. American expansionism and industrialization left no population within the United States untouched; distinct experiences of those developments, however, were defined by racial identity and by the racial hierarchy that was reformulated in this era.

It has also sought to provide an overview of Irish, German, Chinese, Mexican, African American, and American Indian experiences in the United States between 1837 and 1877; this is a far more hazardous task than generating a framework within which to understand their particular relations to this country. Inevitably, in a brief summary of the his-

torical experiences of any population, generalizations can hide as much as they reveal. In the hope of suggesting the underlying complexity of each population's history, this essay will sketch out one more issue before closing—how regional distinctions might complicate perceptions of each of these populations.

The experiences of each population varied widely, though to considerably differing degrees, across the regions of the United States. As Matthew Jacobson has argued, Irish immigrants' relationship to whiteness was not the same on the East Coast as it was in California. In New York, when these immigrants rioted against the draft in 1863, they were compared to savage Indians. In California, they merged with and often led other whites united to fight against labor competition from the Chinese. There are other possible complications as well. In Texas, several Anglo ranchers—including the King family, with its enormous holdings—were Irish immigrants or of Irish descent. They ruled over the Mexican population who worked under them with increasingly autocratic power. In New Mexico, on the other hand, many Irish men married Nuevomexicanas and adopted their culture as their own. In Texas and New Mexico, in other words, there were still other possible variations of Irish immigrants' relation to whiteness.

For German immigrants, regional variations were as compelling, if less racially charged. In urban areas in the Northeast and Midwest, the involvement in unions and the radical politics of certain German workers and intellectuals concerned wary Americans. Away from the cities, German immigrants could more easily look like defenders of the American heartland. In western Pennsylvania, for example, German immigrants were prominent on the juries that sat in judgment of the Molly Maguires.

For Chinese immigrants, increasingly maligned nationally as threats to the racial sanctity of the nation, regional variations mattered less but were nonetheless evident. In the late 1860s, after the transcontinental railroad was completed and when Chinese immigrants were increasingly confined to racial economic niches, they were still recruited by employers in the South and the Northeast. Their recruitment was cynical; they were used as strikebreakers in Massachusetts and as prods to ex-slaves in the South. But the fact remains that at this point, away from California, there were certain employers who remained willing to see Chinese immigrants as something other than a threat.

For Mexicans who became Mexican Americans after the war, regional differences reflected profound cultural differences. Californios, Tejanos, and Nuevomexicanos had much in common, but there were also significant differences in their cultural practices. In California, for example, a distinctive Californio culture had emerged by the time of the conquest, centered around ample leisure time and flamboyant ceremonies and celebrations. And although the wealthy among each population suffered the loss of land and prestige, there are historians who argue that Nuevomexicanos were able to hold on to more of their power

and influence than the others. Not only was New Mexico less rich in resources and thus less attractive to incoming Anglos, but some wealthy Mexicans in New Mexico, though by no means all, claimed pure Spanish lineage—claimed, in other words, that they were white descendants of Europeans and had no Indian ancestors. Elite Tejanos and Californios made similar claims, and eventually they all found themselves surrounded by Anglos who rejected these assertions of racial purity. Nonetheless, many Nuevomexicanos continue to make these racial claims in the present day.

Likewise for American Indian populations, regional differences underscored significant cultural differences. Most Indian populations had certain things in common—subsistence economies, the worship of nature, and some sense of collective ownership of property. But Sioux living on the grassy plains, Pueblos living in the arid Southwest, and Yakima living on the plush West Coast, for example, constructed their lives, their cultures, and their traditions very differently. These differences were based on numerous factors, including what their natural environments did or did not provide, and the number, or lack, of foes or allies surrounding them. As with the Mexican population, the region in which various Indians lived also determined the nature of their interaction with Euro-Americans. Although few if any Indians avoided the onus of conquest, the severity of their experience varied considerably. In California, gold rushers engaged in a murderous campaign against the Indian population, whose numbers fell from 150,000 in 1845 to 35,000 in

1860. In the nearby southwest, by stark contrast, certain Indian populations were left relatively free to remain true to their culture and traditions. In the 1860s, for example, the United States government largely ignored Kiowa and Comanche raids against Anglos and Mexicans in Texas. As Utley describes it, the Indian raiders "had always regarded Texans, like Mexicans, as a people distinct from Americans—a view reinforced by the . . . Civil War."

For African Americans, the contrast between regions for much of this period could not have been more stark—the South meant slavery, and the North, freedom. Their hope that change of location—that regional variation—would bring better things remained strong in the face of the disappointments that came with the end of Reconstruction. In 1877, African American "exodusters" founded Nicodemus, Kansas, one of their first communities in the West, hopeful that they had left the angry white South and an increasingly cynical North behind.

## ANNOTATED BIBLIOGRAPHY

Blassingame, John. *The Slave Community.* New York: Oxford University Press, 1972 [rev. 1979].

When first published in 1972, Blassingame's book was one of the first to examine slave culture and slave life systematically. He takes up issues of African heritage, culture and family, plantation life, resistance, and slave personality types.

Chan, Sucheng. *Asian Americans: An Interpretive History.* Boston: Twayne Publishers, 1991.

Chan provides a synthesis of Asian American history with an overt interpretive edge, focusing particularly on placing Asian Americans in a global perspective.

Chen, Jack. *The Chinese of America.* San Francisco: Harper and Row, 1980.

Chen's book is a thorough examination of Chinese American culture, from earliest arrivals through exclusion to the post–World War II era.

Conzen, Kathleen Neils. *Immigrant Milwaukee, 1836–1860: Accommodation and Community in a Frontier City.* Cambridge: Harvard University Press, 1976.

This community study traces the German American presence and involvement in Milwaukee from its earliest days, placing issues of the construction of ethnic identity and eventual accommodation in the context of other immigrant groups and the city's public culture.

De Leon, Arnoldo. *They Called Them Greasers: Anglo Attitudes Toward Mexicans in Texas, 1821–1900.* Austin: University of Texas Press, 1983.

This pointed analysis traces the emergence of Anglo Texans' anti-Mexican attitudes through the Texas revolt and the antebellum and postbellum eras.

Diner, Hasia. *Erin's Daughters in America: Irish Immigrant Women in the Nineteenth Century.* Baltimore: Johns Hopkins University Press, 1983.

Diner analyzes the culture of Irish immigrant women and their relations with American society and culture through their familial connections, work experiences, and associational life.

Foner, Eric. *Reconstruction: America's Unfinished Revolution, 1863–1877.* New York: Harper and Row, 1988.

This masterful book is now the standard

work on Reconstruction. He draws together existing scholarship on the era and creates a new frame for this comprehensive study by emphasizing the experiences, actions, and goals of the newly freed African American population.

Genovese, Eugene. *Roll, Jordan, Roll: The World the Slaves Made.* New York: Pantheon, 1974.

Genovese's classic study examines slave culture in the context of slave-owner paternalism. He explores the possibilities of acquiescence and resistance to slavery, finding in the culture of enslaved African Americans a form of "protonationalism."

Gonzalez, Deena. *Refusing the Favor: The Spanish-Mexican Women of Santa Fe, 1820–1880.* New York: Oxford University Press, 1999.

Gonzalez's work makes effective use of archival sources like wills and trial transcripts to reveal how Spanish-Mexican women faced, and responded to, and resisted Anglo colonizing efforts in New Mexico.

Griswold del Castillo, Richard. *The Treaty of Guadalupe Hidalgo: A Legacy of Conflict.* Norman: University of Oklahoma Press, 1990.

Griswold del Castillo offers a detailed study of the treaty that ended the Mexican American war, focusing on its impact on the new Mexican American population.

Gutman, Herbert. *The Black Family in Slavery and Freedom, 1750–1925.* New York: Random House, 1977.

Gutman asserts the autonomy of the African American family both during and after slavery. He argues that slave families were constituted not only within, but despite slave owners' paternalism. He also counters arguments by sociologists Daniel Moynihan and Nathan Glazer, who argued the dysfunctionality of the African American family.

Horsman, Reginald. *Race and Manifest Destiny: The Origins of American Racial Anglo-Saxonism.* Cambridge: Harvard University Press, 1981.

Reginald Horsman links the development of American racial ideology, and particularly Anglo-Saxons' explicit identification as a distinctive racial group, to American expansionism in the 1840s and 1850s.

Jacobson, Matthew. *Whiteness of a Different Color: European Immigrants and the Alchemy of Race.* Cambridge: Harvard University Press, 1998.

Jacobson's complex and rich work explores a wide variety of historical documents and cultural products in analyzing the construction of whiteness—and the challenges many European immigrants faced in asserting their whiteness—throughout American history.

Johannsen, Robert W. *To the Halls of the Montezumas: The Mexican War in the American Imagination.* New York: Oxford University Press, 1985.

Johannsen argues that the United States' first foreign war produced both assertions of American identity and the demonization and degradation of Mexicans.

Kenny, Kevin. *Making Sense of the Molly Maguires.* New York: Oxford University Press, 1998.

Kenny uses impressive empirical evidence and postmodern methodologies to explore the enigmatic Molly Maguires, and to place them in the broader context of Irish ethnic identity formation.

Limerick, Patricia Nelson. *The Legacy of Conquest: The Unbroken Past of the American West*. New York: Norton, 1987.

One of the first synthetic works to substantially revise American Western history, Limerick's book presents the region in all of its racial complexity.

Miller, Kerby A. *Emigrants and Exiles: Ireland and the Irish Exodus to North America*. New York: Oxford University Press, 1985. This standard work in Irish immigrant history focuses especially on the exile mentality of the Irish.

Montejano, David. *Anglos and Mexicans in the Making of Texas, 1836–1986*. Austin: University of Texas Press, 1987.

Montejano's work analyzes relations between Mexicans and Anglos from the Texas revolt to the very recent past, from the short-lived "peace structure" through land confiscation and anti-Mexican Jim Crow laws to a new period of relative inclusion and equality.

Pitt, Leonard. *The Decline of the Californios: A Social History of the Spanish-Speaking Californians, 1846–1890*. Berkeley: University of California Press, 1966.

Pitt's path-breaking work analyzes the distinctive Californio culture and its demise at the hands of encroaching Anglo Americans.

Roediger, David. *The Wages of Whiteness*. New York: Verso Press, 1991.

Roediger analyzes the implications of whiteness for the construction of working class identity in the decades before and just after the Civil War. He focuses centrally, especially in his last section, on the efforts of Irish immigrants to establish, and to benefit from, their identity as white.

Saxton, Alexander. *The Indispensable Enemy: Labor and the Anti-Chinese Movement in California*. Berkeley: University of California Press, 1971.

Saxton explores the complex reasons for the emergence of anti-Chinese sentiment in California, especially among white workers. He argues that Chinese immigrants were "indispensable," not only for the inexpensive labor they provided but because their presence served to galvanize the white working class as few other issues did.

Stuckey, Sterling. *Slave Culture: Nationalist Theory and the Foundation of Black America*. New York: Oxford University Press, 1987.

Stuckey offers a compelling argument for African survivals in African American slave culture and beyond. He reads emergent black nationalist and liberation thought into the 1940s through this Africanist lens.

Takaki, Ronald. *Strangers from a Different Shore: A History of Asian Americans*. New York: Penguin Books, 1989.

Takaki offers a comprehensive synthetic examination of the history of Asians in the United States.

Trommler, Frank, and Joseph McVeigh, eds. *America and the Germans: An Assessment of a Three-Hundred-Year History*. Philadelphia: University of Pennsylvania Press, 1985. This collection provides a number of useful essays on German American immigration, ethnicity and politics, language, and literature.

Utley, Robert. *The Indian Frontier of the American West, 1846–1890*. Albuquerque: University of New Mexico Press, 1984. Utley explores the last fifty years of open conflict between Indian populations and the expansionist United States, from the 1840s through the "passing of the frontier" in 1890.

West, Elliott. *The Contested Plains: Indians, Goldseekers, and the Rush to Colorado.* Lawrence, Kansas: University of Kansas Press, 1998.

In this provocative book, West argues that the battle between Indians and whites over the Great Plains, specifically Colorado, was a contest over resources that both, in their own ways, were ill-prepared to fight.

White, Deborah Gray. *Ar'n't I a Woman?: Female Slaves in the Plantation South.* New York: Norton, 1985.

In this highly readable study, Deborah Gray White explores the distinctive world of the enslaved African American woman. She examines stereotypical images of women slaves, family and work life, women's networks under slavery, and the particular dangers that enslaved women faced. She closes with a chapter on African American women after slavery.

White, Richard. *"It's Your Misfortune and None of My Own": A History of the American West.* Norman: University of Oklahoma Press, 1991.

This broad revisionist survey of American Western history focuses centrally on the frequently combative and destructive interactions between racial groups in the region.

# DOCUMENTS

## Martin Weitz, Rockville, Connecticut, to His Relatives in Schotten, Vogelsberg, Germany, July 29, 1855

*Weitz, a wool weaver, immigrated to the United States in 1854. His letter speaks to working conditions in his new home, as well as to the associational life that is emerging in the German immigrant community.*

*Source:* Walter D. Kamphoefner, Woflgang Helbich and Ulrike Soommer, eds., *News from the Land of Freedom: German Immigrants Write Home* (Ithaca, N.Y.: Cornell University Press, 1991), pp. 342–342, 346; © C. H. Beck'sche Verlagsbuchhandlunug (Oscar Beck), Munich, 1988; translation © 1991 by Cornell University.

ROCKVILLE, JULY 29TH, 1855

*Dear devoted father, brother, sister-in-law, and children,*

Should my letter reach you in good health, I will be overjoyed. Finally I have fulfilled my longing for you by sending a small gift, I couldn't do it any earlier since I was doing very poorly. Last year from October until March 16th this year I didn't have any work, the factory in Astoria had stopped work. I had to pay 10 dollars training fee. Every newcomer who comes here has to pay, when I had worked it off there was no more work there. From there we went to another factory, a fur factory, there we had rotten jobs where our hands got all swollen up but it didn't last long. Finally we couldn't get any money then I also lost a lot so I made it through the winter splitting wood for a man in Astoria who wasn't able so I could earn some money. But it wasn't enough. I looked around for work in New York and the area, but all for nothing, if I had been able to speak English I could've gotten a job but I can't. I didn't have any money to move on, you can imagine it was terrible. Thousands and thousands were wandering around without work, without money, without food, dying of hunger. They've set up places where they could get lunch but it isn't enough. They poured through the town in great droves demanding that work be found for them, but all for nothing. All over America it was terrible, many hundreds of *Fektori*, that means *Fabricke*, had stopped work, prices went way up and still are, it should not be called America but *Malerika*. It is easy to say you want to go to America but the hard things they never think about. [dangers of ocean voyage] The second point is when you arrive here and don't understand English, you stand there, eyes wide open, like a calf with its throat cut. You have to be careful, they say, there's a greenhorn. How many hundred are lied to and cheated, no one can be careful enough. In Neu Jork every day there's murder, theft, suicide, lies and cheating, and in any large town in America. If you want to come to America you just can't let that scare you off. You have to think the best, the worst comes later. I don't want to advise anyone not to come, whoever wants to come should come. It's best if you have a friend here who gets you a

job in a good state. Dear father and brother, thank God I now have a good job. On March 16th in the newspaper there was a call for 25 weavers in a wool *Fektori* in Rockville in the state of Conecticut to sign up on the 17th at 6 o'clock in the evening. We went there and were accepted. On the 18th we got on the steamboat and went to Hartford, from there to Rockville, first I had to sell my watch otherwise I couldn't have gotten there. When we arrived there in the afternoon they said you have to work nights from 6:30 in the evening till 6:30 in the morning, then we were shocked. I said I didn't care if I only have work, the looms all work by themselves, they are all driven by water, I'd never woven on such a loom. I went to a fellow who taught me during the day, then work started. It didn't go well of course in the beginning, they do difficult patterns. In March and April I didn't earn much, I hardly had enough for *Board*, in July 19½ dollars. Now it's getting better, if you do good work, you earn 18–20 to 24–25 dollars. Dear father, I am now very content with my situation, I'll stay here. Last winter sometimes I just wanted to jump into the water, if you don't have a job in America it's a terrible thing, I can't thank God enough that I have work and am healthy. Here in the *Willischtz* [village], that means *klein Städtgen* or *Dorf* there are almost 250 Germans who work in the *Feckteri*, there are 11 *Feckterie* here. If you don't like it in one you go to another, 3 more are being built. If anyone from Schotten wants to come here, he should come. Springtime is the best, if he has money he can buy land in the state of Wisconsin, it seems to be another Germany, it's healthy there. Where I am in Rockville in the state of Connecticut, 180 miles from Neu Jork, it's also very healthy, the climate seems to me like over there, we had in English 100 degrees of heat, but of course it's not as healthy here in America as over there in Germany. The harvest here in America looks good and there's hope that things will be cheaper than a while ago. There is *Temperes* [temperance] here, that means there's no alcoholic spirits allowed, no beer, no brandy, wine, etc. In many states there's been serious fighting like in the state of Ohio, in Cincinati there was a blood-bath, the Germans won, there were many dead and wounded on both sides. The *Jenkeamerikaner* [Yankees], they call themselves *Nounorthing* [Know-Nothing] yankees, they want to have control, but democracy wins, it looks like there's going to be a revolution. Every Sunday you have to go to church, then the factory bosses like you, you don't learn anything bad there, if you understand English or not, that's fine with me. I can go there. With the singing clubs and music, there the Germans in America are on the rise, they earn a lot of respect for that. Even we in Rockville, we have 2 singing clubs. With our German singing we earn great respect. In Neu Jork there was a big song festival that drew a lot of applause from the Americans. I am here in a German *BoardingHaus*, I have to pay 9 dollars a month which is cheap, you may think it's a lot, but you have to remember that the dollar can't be counted as more than the guilder over there. I can't spend any money except for tobacco, I haven't drunk any *Brenti* [brandy] in three

months. Every noon there's soup, vegetables and meat, every morning and evening meat, cheese and butter. Every morning we get up at 5 o'clock, at 5 thirty the bells ring, we go to the factory till 12 o'clock noon, at 1 o'clock we go in again until half past 6, at 8 o'clock it's already night. At 4 o'clock in the morning it is already daylight. When the sun goes down it gets dark right away. The difference between you and us is when we get up in the morning it's 11 o'clock over there, it's almost 6 hours. Leuning and I are the only ones here from Schotten, Leuning and his family like it very much here too, we work in one *Fektori*. We hardly see each other all day long, it's so big. His son Adam works in our *Fektori*. We live a mile apart, don't see each other often.

## Angela Heck, New York, New York, to Her Relatives in Irrel, Trier, Germany, October 26, 1862

*Heck immigrated to the United States with her husband Nikolaus in 1854. Her eternal optimism is evident in her account of the Civil War and her husband's participation in it— Nikolaus never rose above the rank of private.*

*Source:* Walter D. Kamphoefner, Wolfgang Helbich, and Ulrike Soommer, eds., *News from the Land of Freedom: German Immigrants Write Home* (Ithaca, N.Y.: Cornell University Press, 1991), pp. 373–375; © C. H. Beck'sche Verlagsbuchhandlunug (Oscar Beck), Munich, 1988. Translation © 1991 by Cornell University.

New York, October 26, 1862

*Dearest sister, brother-in-law and all at home,*

I can no longer keep from writing to you, since I have been in America for 8 years and have only received one letter from you, to let you know how I am. I am still hale and hearty. But these are sad times now in America. I imagine you've heard about it, that is the murderous war that we in the North are fighting against the South, in which almost all the average people, most of them German, are involved. The war has already lasted over a whole year and it has already cost a hundred thousand lives and there's no end in sight. My husband, Nikolaus Heck, is also among them. Since October 1st he's been away from the family for a year. But thank the Lord I am well taken care of. He is a first lieutenant in the 52nd Regiment in Company 2. He receives 60 talers a month. Now, though, because of the bravery he showed in 3–4 battles he has become an *Oberst*, that is a colonel. He has command over the entire regiment. The whole regiment is made up of Germans. They were 1000 men strong when they marched away from here. But now with the hardships they have suffered, though, the cold in the winter and in all the many battles, only half that number remain. The decoration that he received over in Berlin helped him to get this high rank here, and also the large number of Prussian officers who are here fighting in the war. For there are 120 regiments, all made up of Germans. Most of the soldiers had never been soldiers in Germany. Almost all of those who had been

soldiers over in Germany have received the rank of colonel. Now as a colonel he earns 100 talers a month, I get my payments every week; that is I get 5 dollars a week. Heck sends me all his money every two months. He gets clothing and food all for free. A common soldier gets 13 talers a month, a *Feldwebel* 30, a sergeant 20 talers a month and the family, every wife gets 5 talers a week until the war is over. They've all enlisted for 3 years. If the war ends earlier than that, they'll all come home. Heck is still in good health. He is now in Washington, the capital of North America. He wrote and told me that I should bring the children and come to see him, he wants to see us so badly. We haven't seen each other for over a year. Now you can well imagine how overjoyed we will be when we see each other again. We will be even happier than we were over there when he returned from Berlin. I receive a letter from him every week, sometimes 2. The state of New York had to supply over 100 regiments. Now though they can't get any new people. Now they're drafting until next week. Then it will hit a lot of people before they have their number. When he comes home safely, every man receives 100 talers. If a man dies or falls in battle, his wife receives a pension for the rest of her life, that is 8 talers a month, as well as the 100 talers.

My dear brother-in-law, I have already saved a lot of money. Should Heck be injured, I will be well taken care of. Should he never return, which I hope will not be the case, it can be that we will see each other again. And if Heck returns safely I want to make him happy by letting him go to Germany, even if a few hundred go to blazes. He wrote to me when I come home safely we should travel to Germany. Then we will give a ball and I will invite all our good friends. So you needn't worry about me. I am doing very well. But the dear Lord should bring him back safely. The 8 years that we have been married we have led a wonderful life together and neither of us has made the other angry in the least. My dear sister, I want to let you know that I still have 2 children, a girl named Evchen and a boy named Nekchen [nickname for Nikolaus]. I lost a five-year-old boy to dropsy. Now it's about a year ago, when my husband left. His whole regiment helped bury him. My daughter is 7 years old and my little boy 2 years and three months old. My dear brother-in-law, everything here is very expensive, all the food. [2 ll.: examples] I believe that you in Germany will feel the effects of the war that's going on here. My dear sister, time doesn't hang heavy here. I'm living among nothing but Germans, and the husbands of all the women here have gone off to war. I don't need to do any work but my housework. [asks about health of the family; postal delivery service in New York; relatives should also write to her husband; greetings; address]

## German Society in Chicago, Annual Report, 1857 –1858

*This report speaks not only to the challenges that even German immigrants faced upon arrival and during recurrent economic depres-* sions in the United States but also to their rich associational life.

*Source:* Frederick Binder and David Reimers, eds. *The Way We Lived: Essays and Documents in American Social History*, vol. 1, *1492–1877*, 4th. ed. (New York: Houghton Mifflin, 2000), pp. 224–226. From "Annual Report of the German Society for April, 1857–1858 " (Chicago: Chg. Sonne, 1858), in Hartmut Keil and John B. Jentz, eds., *German Workers in Chicago: A Documentary History of Working-Class Culture from 1850 to World War I* (Urbana and Chicago: University of Illinois Press, 1988).

Our attention has been focused on preventing the swindling of immigrants by innkeepers and their runners in and around the train stations. We had presented the city council with recommendations for laws to this effect and obtained their passage. One ordinance enacted in June requires that a licensed German innkeeper or runner present a business card when recommending his inn to arriving passengers. The card must give the following information in both English and German: name of the innkeeper, name of the inn and the street where it is located, the cost of meals per day, the cost of a room per night and per week, and whether he transports his guests with or without charge to and from his inn.

In order to see if and how the police were enforcing the new ordinances, the agent and I made an inspection of the various train stations, during which we were insulted by the runners in the most vile manner; the police captain was at a loss and could only suggest that we too be deputized. In this new capacity we brought about the arrests of several transgressors of the above-mentioned ordinance, and this had the desired effect.

Each day, however, we were unpleasantly reminded that our effectiveness would have to remain one-sided and insufficient as long as we did not have access to financial resources. Many families arriving from New York had been forced to ask for advances in Castle Garden using their baggage as collateral, and they subsequently pestered us with requests to retrieve their baggage for them. But this could only be done by paying the freight and the outstanding debt in New York. Similarly, there were people who were still in possession of their baggage and wanted to continue on their way but had no more money to do so; many of them wanted to deposit their bags with us instead of with an immigrant innkeeper. Our means were unfortunately insufficient to aid each person in this manner, and it is possible that this led to frequent and considerable losses at the hands of the innkeepers. . . .

As mentioned above, since last summer, together with the agent, I have taken over the surveillance of the train stations to see that the city ordinances are being enforced. But even if they had sufficient time, two officials would still be too few. I would therefore recommend that the president and agent be assigned to a committee of six to be elected for this purpose and to be called the Train Station Surveillance Committee.

These officials would likewise have to have police authorization. Their duty would not only entail being frequently present at the arrival of immigrant trains, but also at their departure. Here they would ask their departing countrymen whether they were satisfied with the food, living conditions, and treatment at the inn where they stayed; in the case of complaints or accusations, the officials would either take notes or detain the people until the case could be looked into by the proper legal authorities.

After having collected information of this kind for a few months, this committee would be in a position to draw up a list of those immigrant inns which are of good repute in our city. This list would then be sent to those German Societies in eastern port cities which could best make use of it. On the other hand, it would also be the duty of this committee to present the mayor with a list of those inns which have proven detrimental to the interests of immigrants, and to petition for the revocation of their licenses. Here, too, the character of our highest municipal authorities guarantees us the necessary support. . . .

Last winter some honest, upright craftsmen and their families, who were reluctant to ask strangers for help, were forced to bring beds, clothes, and household goods to the pawnbroker. For many, the payment or foreclosure date is at the door, and most of them still have neither work to earn the money nor friends from whom to borrow it. Several such families have turned to me in the past few days to advance them the interest for one or two months in order to put off the due date. They all hope to thus redeem their hard-earned possessions. I would like to recommend lending good families the interest needed to prolong foreclosure, while holding their pawn tickets as security. . . .

I still hear it said that the agent's wages are too high and that he has too little to do, that people would of course like to support the society, but that they don't want their entire contribution going to the preservation of the agent.

I am convinced that these people have not gone to the trouble to investigate what they maintain, and if they had, they would have found that the activities of this official fulfill the most important objectives of the German Society as it has existed to date. These people have not been to the society's office, they haven't seen the throngs—often uninterrupted—of people coming and going. The one asks the agent to find relatives or friends, the agent sees to the relevant notice in the newspapers; the other has lost his baggage on the way from New York to Chicago, the agent writes off to Detroit and Dunkirk; a third would like to send money—safely and without cost—to a relative living somewhere or other, the agent takes care of this, too. Now immigrants come who want advances against their baggage so they can continue their trip; the agent accompanies them to the train station or to the inn, estimates the value of the baggage, pays the advances and has the things brought back to the office. On the way he picks up five letters, all addressed to the same person. The first is not very flattering; "Mr. Agent, I've been waiting so long for my two suitcases, and you said you would see to them immediately. Send the checks back to me so I'll know what's going on!" The good man is of the opinion that the lost things must still be where he last saw them on his trip. His bags, in the meantime, were either pilfered by corrupt railroad officials or have been sent on a grand tour without their owner, but the latter suspects the agent of negligence or even deceit. Next comes an entire family of immigrants, freshly arrived. They have lost one of their suitcases in the train station or have been cheated by an innkeeper; the agent goes along with them so that they, too, will be content. A local citizen wants to bring over a relative from his hometown in Germany. He requests a travel guide with exact directions for getting from his hometown to Chicago, as well as sure means of alerting the cousin of swindlers along the way; the agent, to the best of his ability, also tries to satisfy this request. News is received from an immigrant inn that the proprietor wants to throw out a sick immigrant. The agent goes to see the sick person, gets medical assistance, calms the innkeeper or sees to it that the sick person is brought to a hospital. The agent is once again busy trying to finish a letter to somewhere or other when a man comes in and interrupts him with the words: "Listen, the guy you sent me last time was even worse than the others. I told him to go to the devil! Do you have anyone good today?" Two years ago this same man with the charming manners—always on the lookout for slave labor—was a dues-paying member of the German Society; now, however, he'll not hear of supporting the society because he had the misfortune of having been dissatisfied with the workers referred to him free of charge.

But what the agent has to suffer when he has evoked the righteous anger of a patroness by having secured her a good-for-nothing maid—it would be better if he told you himself. No one, in any case, would envy him this pleasure.

I will not tax your patience any longer. But I would again like to strongly recommend that each member try to introduce at least one of his friends to the society; membership is so easily acquired, as the minimum annual contribution is only $1, and from then on up, absolutely no limits are imposed on generosity.

## August Spies, Autobiography, 1886

*Spies, one of the Haymarket anarchists hung in 1887, was born in Landeckerberg, Germany, in 1855. Although his autobiography deals mostly with his experiences leading up to and during his trial, in this section he discusses his migration to the United States and his early labor and radical activities.*

*Source:* Chicago Historical Society: http://www.chicagohs.org/hadc/manuscripts/M06/M06.htm, pp. 6–9; © 2000, the Chicago Historical Society.

I was educated for a career in the government service (forest branch). As a child I had private tutors and later visited the *Polytechnicum* (and "Forest academy"). At the age of seventeen my father

died suddenly, leaving a large family in moderate circumstances. As I was the eldest one I did not feel justified in continuing my studies, they were expensive, and concluded to go to America, where I had and have now a number of well-to-do relatives. I arrived in New York in 1872 and upon the advise of my friends learned the Furniture Business. The following year I came to Chicago, where I have resided ever since; though I may add that I have been away from the city occasionally for some time. Once, with the intention of settling in the country, I worked on a farm for a year. But seeing that the small farmers and renters were in a worse plight even than the city wage-workers, and that they were equally dependent, I returned to the city. I have also traveled over the southern states to get acquainted with the country and people, and at another time I joined an exploring expedition through upper Canada, which failed.

When I arrived in this country I knew nothing of socialism, except what I had seen in the newspapers—the "public teachers"(?). And from what I'd read I concluded that the socialists were a lot of ignorant and lazy vagabonds "who wanted to divide up everything." Having come but very little in contact with people who earned their living by honest labor in the old country, I was amazed and was shocked when I became acquainted with the condition of the wage-workers in the New World.

The factory: the ignominious regulations, the surveillance, the spy system, the servility and lack of manhood among the workers and the arrogant arbitrary behavior of the boss and mamelukes—

all this made an impression upon me that I have never been able to divest myself of. At first I could not understand why the workers, among them many old men with bent backs, silently and without a sign of protest bore every insult the caprice of the foreman or boss would heap upon them. I was not then aware of the fact that the opportunity to work was a *privilege*, a favor, and that it was in the power of those who were in the possession of the factories and instruments of labor to deny or grant this privilege. I did not then understand how difficult it was to find a purchaser for one's labor, I did not know then that there were thousands and thousands of idle human bodies in the market, ready to hire out upon most any conditions, actually begging for employment. I became conscious of this, very soon, however, and I knew then why these people were so servile, whey suffered the humiliating dictates and capricious whims of their employers. . . . Personally I had no great difficulty in "getting along." I had so many advantages over my co-workers. I would most likely have succeeded in becoming a "respectable business man" myself, if I had been possessed of that unscrupulous egotism which characterizes the "successful business man," and if my aspirations had been that of the avaricious Hamster (the latter belongs to the family of rats and his "pursuit in life" is to steal and accumulate; in some of their depositories the contents of whole granaries have often been found; their greatest delight seems to be possession, for they steal a great deal more than they can consume; in fact they steal, like most

of our respectable citizens, regardless of their capacity of consumption).

My philosophy has always been that the *object* of life can only consist in the *enjoyment of life*; and that the rational application of this principle is *true morality*. I held that asceticism as taught by the church was a crime against nature.

Now observing that the vast mass of the people were wasting their lives in Drudgery, accompanied with want and misery, it was but natural for me to inquire into the causes (I had up to that time never read a book or even an impartial essay on modern Socialism). Was this self-abnegation, this self-crucifixion of the people voluntary, or was it forced upon them, and if so—by whom?

About this time while looking over my books in search of something, my attention was attracted by this passage from Aristotle: ". . . When (at some future age) every tool upon command or by predestination will perform its work, as the artworks of *Daedalus* did, who moved by themselves, or like the three feet of *Hephaestos*, who went to their sacred work spontaneously, when thus the weaver shuttle will weave by themselves, then we will no longer require masters and slaves." (Philosophy of Aristotle)

Had this time, long ago anticipated by the great thinker, not come? Yes, it had. There were the machines . . . but master and slave still existed. The question arose in my mind—is their existence still necessary?

*Antiporas*, a Greek poet, who lived at the time of Cicero, had in a like manner greeted the invention of the watermill (water power) as the emancipator of the male and female slaves.—"Oh, these Heathens!"—writes Karl Marx after quoting the above. "They knew nothing of "Political Economy" and Christendom! They failed to conceive how nicely the machines could be employed to lengthen the hours of toil and to intensify the burdens of the slaves. They (the heathens) excused the slavery of *one* on the ground that it would afford the opportunity of human development to *another*. But to preach the slavery of the masses in order that a few rude and arrogant *parvenus* might become "eminent spinners," "extensive sausage makers" and "influential shoe black dealers"—to do this they lacked that specific Christian organ."

I think it was in 1875, at the time the "Workingmen's Party of Illinois" was organized, when, upon the invitation of a friend, I visited the first meeting in which a lecture on Socialism was delivered. Viewed from a rhetorical standpoint this lecture, delivered by a young mechanic, was not very impressive, but the substance . . . I will simply say that this gave me the *passeparout* to the many interrogation marks which had worried me for a number of years.

I procured every piece of literature I could get on the subject; whether it was adverse or friendly to Socialism made no difference. In the beginning I was a visionary, an enthusiast. I believed as so many righteous people do to-day that the truth only required to be expressed, the argument only to be made to inlist every good man and woman in the good cause, in the cause of humanity. In my youthful

enthusiasm I forgot to apply the experience of historical progress to this particular case. But to my great sorrow, I soon became convinced that the great bulk of humanity were automatons incapable of thinking and reasoning, altogether unconscious of themselves, simply tools of custom.

Then from the sordid is man made,
Usage and custom he doth call his nurse—
    [Goethe]

But nothing could discourage me. The study of French, German and English economists and social scientists soon made me view things differently than I had seen them in my first enthusiasm. Buckle's "History of Civilization," Karl Marx "Kapital" and Morgan's "Ancient History" have probably had the greatest influence over me of any. I now became an attentive observer of the various social phenomena myself. The last ten years have been very favorable for such investigation as I sought. I found my favorite teachers corroborated everywhere. . . .

I think it was in 1877 when I first became a member of the Socialistic Labor Party. The events of that year, the brute force with which the whining and confiding wage-slaves were met on all sides impressed upon me the necessity of *like* resistance. The latter required organization. Shortly afterwards I joined the "Lehr & Wehr Verein," an armed organization of the workingmen, numbering then about 1500 well drilled members. As soon as our Patricians saw that the canaille was arming for defense—to repel such scandalous attacks in the future as had been made upon them in 1877,—they at once commanded their law agents in Springfield to prohibit workingmen from bearing arms. The command was obeyed. . . .

The workingmen also went into politics, independent politics—I served as a nominal candidate myself several times—, but when the noble patricians and the political *augurs* saw that they were successful in electing a number of their candidates, a conspiracy was organized to disfranchise them by fraudulent count and like methods. They workingmen thereupon left the ballot with disgust. . . .

## John O'Sullivan, "Annexation," 1845

*Himself of Irish descent, John O'Sullivan coined the term "manifest destiny" in this article—a catch phrase used to rationalize American expansion and conquest of supposedly inferior races. Though he hails Anglo-Saxonism in this article, O'Sullivan and other Irish immigrant social and political critics remained extremely wary of Anglo-Saxon attitudes toward them.*

*Source:* Hartung Press, http://hartung-press.com/fyi/manifestdestinytexas.htm; © 2001, Robert Hartung—All Rights Reserved.

## JULY, 1845

### Annexation

Texas is now ours. Already, before these words are written, her Convention has undoubtedly ratified the acceptance, by her Congress, of our proffered invitation into the Union; and made the requisite changes in her already republican form of constitution to adapt it to its future federal relations. Her star and her stripe may already be said to have taken their place in the glorious blazon of our common nationality; and the sweep of our eagle's wing already includes within its circuit the wide extent of her fair and fertile land. . . .

Why, were other reasoning wanting, in favor of now elevating this question of the reception of Texas into the Union, out of the lower region of our past party dissensions, up to its proper level of a high and broad nationality, it surely is to be found, found abundantly, in the manner in which other nations have undertaken to intrude themselves into it, between us and the proper parties to the case, in a spirit of hostile interference against us, for the avowed object of thwarting our policy and hampering our power, limiting our greatness and checking the fulfilment of our manifest destiny to overspread the continent allotted by Providence for the free development of our yearly multiplying millions. . . .

It is wholly untrue, and unjust to ourselves, the pretence that the Annexation has been a measure of spoliation, unrightful and unrighteous—of military conquest under forms of peace and law—of territorial aggrandizement at the expense of justice, and justice due by a double sanctity to the weak. This view of the question is wholly unfounded, and has been before so amply refuted in these pages, as well as in a thousand other modes, that we shall not again dwell upon it. The independence of Texas was complete and absolute. It was an independence, not only in fact, but of right No obligation of duty towards Mexico tended in the least degree to restrain our right to effect the desired recovery of the fair province once our own—whatever motives of policy might have prompted a more deferential consideration of her feelings and her pride, as involved in the question. If Texas became peopled with an American population, it was by no contrivance of our government, but on the express invitation of that of Mexico herself; accompanied with such guaranties of State independence, and the maintenance of a federal system analogous to our own, as constituted a compact fully justifying the strongest measures of redress on the part of those afterwards deceived in this guaranty, and sought to be enslaved under the yoke imposed by its violation. She was released, rightfully and absolutely released, from all Mexican allegiance, or duty of cohesion to the Mexican political body, by the acts and fault of Mexico herself, and Mexico alone. There never was a clearer case. It was not revolution; it was resistance to revolution: and resistance under such circumstances as left independence the necessary resulting state, caused by the abandonment of those with whom her former federal association had existed. What then can be more preposterous than all this clamor by Mexico and the Mexican interest, against Annexation, as a violation of any rights of hers, any duties of ours? . . .

Nor is there any just foundation for the charge that Annexation is a great pro-slavery measure—calculated to increase and perpetuate that institution. Slavery had nothing to do with it. Opinions were and are greatly divided, both at the North and South, as to the influence to be exerted by it on Slavery and the Slave States. That it will tend to facilitate and hasten the disappearance of Slavery from all the northern tier of the present Slave States, cannot surely admit of serious question. The greater value in Texas of the slave labor now employed in those States, must soon produce the effect of draining off that labor southwardly, by the same unvarying law that bids water descend the slope that invites it. Every new Slave State in Texas will make at least one Free State from among those in which that institution now exists—to say nothing of those portions of Texas on which slavery cannot spring and grow—to say nothing of the far more rapid growth of new States in the free West and North-west, as these fine regions are overspread by the emigration fast flowing over them from Europe, as well as from the Northern and Eastern States of the Union as it exists. On the other hand, it is undeniably much gained for the cause of the eventual voluntary abolition of slavery, that it should have been thus drained off towards the only outlet which appeared to furnish much probability of the ultimate disappearance of the negro race from our borders. The Spanish-Indian-American populations of Mexico, Centra America and South America, afford the only receptacle capable of absorbing that race whenever we shall be prepared to slough it off—to emancipate it from slavery, and (simultaneously necessary) to remove it from the midst of our own. Themselves already of mixed and confused blood, and free from the "prejudices" which among us so insuperably forbid the social amalgamation which can alone elevate the Negro race out of a virtually servile degradation, even though legally free, the regions occupied by those populations must strongly attract the black race in that direction; and as soon as the destined hour of emancipation shall arrive, will relieve the question of one of its worst difficulties, if not absolutely the greatest. . . .

Texas has been absorbed into the Union in the inevitable fulfilment of the general law which is rolling our population westward; the connexion of which with that ratio of growth in population which is destined within a hundred years to swell our numbers to the enormous population of *two hundred and fifty millions* (if *not* more), is too evident to leave us in doubt of the manifest design of Providence in regard to the occupation of this continent. It was disintegrated from Mexico in the natural course of events, by a process perfectly legitimate on its own part, blameless on ours; and in which all the censures due to wrong, perfidy and folly, rest on Mexico alone. And possessed as it was by a population which was in truth but a colonial detachment from our own, and which was still bound by myriad ties of the very heart-strings to its old relations, domestic and political, their incorporation into the Union was not only inevitable, but the most natural, right and proper thing in the world—and it is only astonishing that there should be any among ourselves to say it nay. . . .

California will, probably, next fall away from the loose adhesion which, in such a country as Mexico, holds a remote province in a slight equivocal kind of dependence on the metropolis. Imbecile and distracted, Mexico never can exert any real governmental authority over such a country. The impotence of the one and the distance of the other, must make the relation one of virtual independence; unless, by stunting the province of all natural growth, and forbidding that immigration which can alone develop its capabilities and fulfill the purposes of its creation, tyranny may retain a military dominion, which is no government in the legitimate sense of the term. In the case of California this is now impossible. The Anglo-Saxon foot is already on its borders. Already the advance guard of the irresistible army of Anglo-Saxon emigration has begun to pour down upon it, armed with the plough and the rifle, and marking its trail with schools and colleges, courts and representative halls, mills and meeting-houses. A population will soon be in actual occupation of California, over which it will be idle for Mexico to dream of dominion. They will necessarily become independent. All this without agency of our government, without responsibility of our people—in the natural flow of events, the spontaneous working of principles, and the adaptation of the tendencies and wants of the human race to the elemental circumstances in the midst of which they find themselves placed. And they will have a right to independence—to self-government—to the possession of the homes conquered from the wilderness by their own labors and dangers, sufferings and sacrifices—a better and a truer right than the artificial title of sovereignty in Mexico, a thousand miles distant, inheriting from Spain a title good only against those who have none better. Their right to independence will be the natural right of self-government belonging to any community strong enough to maintain it—distinct in position, origin and character, and free from any mutual obligations of membership of a common political body, binding it to others by the duty of loyalty and compact of public faith. This will be their title to independence; and by this title, there can be no doubt that the population now fast streaming down upon California will both assert and maintain that independence. Whether they will then attach themselves to our Union or not, is not to be predicted with any certainty. Unless the projected railroad across the continent to the Pacific be carried into effect, perhaps they may not; though even in that case, the day is not distant when the Empires of the Atlantic and Pacific would again flow together into one, as soon as their inland border should approach each other. But that great work, colossal as appears the plan on its first suggestion, cannot remain long unbuilt Its necessity for this very purpose of binding and holding together in its iron clasp our fast-settling Pacific region with that of the Mississippi valley—the natural facility of the route—the ease with which any amount of labor for the construction can be drawn in from the overcrowded populations of Europe, to be paid in the lands made valuable by the progress of the work itself—and its immense utility to the commerce of the world with the whole eastern coast of Asia, alone almost sufficient for the support of such a road—these considerations give assurance that the day cannot be distant which shall witness the conveyance of the representatives from Oregon and California to Washington within less time than a few years ago was devoted to a similar journey by those from Ohio;. . . .

Away, then, with all idle French talk *of balances of power* on the American Continent. There is no growth in Spanish America! Whatever progress of population there may be in the British Canadas, is only for their own early severance of their present colonial relation to the little island three thousand miles across the Atlantic; soon to be followed by Annexation, and destined to swell the still accumulating momentum of our progress. And whosoever may hold the balance, though they should cast into the opposite scale all the bayonets and cannon, not only of France and England, but of Europe entire, how would it kick the beam against the simple, solid weight of the two hundred and fifty, or three hundred millions—and American millions—destined to gather beneath the flutter of the stripes and stars, in the fast hastening year of the Lord 1945!

## Mary Anne Sadlier, *Bessy Conway or, The Irish Girl in America,* 1861

*Over the course of her life, Mary Anne Sadlier, an Irish immigrant, published sixty works of poetry and fiction documenting, among other things, the Famine, migration to the United States, and migration west across this continent. In this passage from* Bessy Conway or, The Irish Girl in America, *the tale of an Irish immigrant domestic, published in 1861, Bessy warns of the perils that potentially await the Irish immigrant woman.*

*Source:* http://www.people.Virginia.EDU/~eas5e/Bessy/, pp. 294–297; hypertext edition taken from the original 1861 edition by D. and J. Sadlier. *Bessy Conway* was originally serialized in the *New York Tablet*. This site is maintained by Liz Szabo at the University of Virginia; e-mail: eas5e@virgina.edu

"Well! I'm not over fond of giving advice," said Bessy, "but as you asked my opinion I'll give it, and then you can't blame me one way or the other. America is a bad place for young girls to go to, unless they have their father, or brothers, or somebody to look after them."

"Humph! who had you to look after yon?"

"Not one but myself and God's good Providence."

"Well! an' wouldn't our girls have the same?" asked the dame sharply.

"I'm not speaking of them, at all," said Bessy, "but I tell you, Mrs. O'Hare, there's many a girl that had as good a mother as ever you were . . . and I'm not saying but you're good enough . . . that leaves home a simple country girl with the fear of God in her heart, and the blush of modesty on her cheek, that turns out very bad and very indifferent in America. If they keep in the state of grace, and go regularly to their duty they're all right, and sure, thanks be to God! there's thousands of them that do, and signs on them and their friends at home . . . but there's just as many . . .

perhaps more . . . that falls in with Protestants and Jews, and everything that way, and in the course of a lithe time forget themselves altogether . . . at least they forget that they have a soul to be saved, or a God to judge them. Dress and finery, and balls and dances is all the God they have then, and you may guess it's not a good end they make of it either for body or soul."

"Well, now, that's curious," put in another neighbor, "an' we hearin' such a different account of it from every one else. Why, there's Jemmy McBride's daughter from beyond the river that got a great match in New York or Philadelphy or some of them place . . . they say she doesn't know the end of her own riches."

Bessy laughed in her own quiet way. "God help your wit, Mrs. Shanaghan! it's little you know here about those great matches.

Now I happen to know something about Ann McBride, for though I never saw her in America, I know them that did, and lived with her, too; she is married to a man in New York that's pretty well off . . . I think he's in the grocery business . . . she lives in a fine house and has very nice furniture and all that, and dresses in the very height of the fashion, but her husband is a Protestant . . . a sort of a one . . . and poor Ann is . . . nothing at all. Himself goes to church of an odd time, but Ann never troubles church or chapel. I was told by a girl that lived with her that when she caught her one night teaching her children their prayers . . . Catholic prayers, of course . . . she was very angry, and told her not to be bothering their brains with them old prayers, they'd have time enough to learn them.' "

Various exclamations of horror and indignation testified the feelings of the listeners Some of them, however, were a little skeptical on the subject.

"Why, then, Bessy ! it's hard to think that girls brought up Catholics could ever come to that!"

"Well! hard or easy, I tell you it's true," said Bessy.

"There's thousands of Irish girls in New York (of course that's the city I know best) that are as good Catholics as any of their people at home, but there's just as many the other way. What would you think of an Irish girl that would tell you she was seven years in America, and had never been to Communion in all that time . . . maybe once or twice to confession?"

"Lord save us, Bessy!" her mother exclaimed, "you're enough to frighten one!"

"I know that, mother, but I'm only telling the truth, and God knows! my heart bleeds to tell it. I knew girls myself that were just as I say, some of them that would laugh at you if you spoke to them of saying their prayers morning or night, and would never think of crossing a Church door if somebody didn't make them go. That all comes, as I told you, of their going out alone to America, without any one to advise or direct them, and them falling into bad places at the very first. Take my advice, Mrs. O'Hare, and keep your girls at home . . . if yon can live here, so can they, and you'll find it better in the long run."

"Well I believe you're about right, Bessy!" replied Mrs. O'Hare; "it's best

keep them under our own eyes. Good night, and God be with you all." The visitors then retired, wondering much at what they had heard.

## John Francis Maguire, *The Irish in America,* 1868

*In these sections of his book on Irish immigrant life in the United States, written in 1868, John Maguire discusses the motivations of the nativist anti-Irish Catholic Know Nothings, as well as the complexities that the Civil War posed for Irish immigrants.*

Source: John Francis Maguire. *The Irish in America* (1868; reprint, New York: Arno Press, 1969), pp. 444, 445, 446, 447–448, 449–450, 452–453, 545–547; © 1969 by Arno Press, Inc.

The Know Nothing movement of 1854 and 1855 troubled the peace of Catholics, and filled the hearts of foreign-born American citizens with sorrow and indignation. They were made the victims of rampant bigotry and furious political partisanship. There was nothing new in this Know Nothingism. It was as old as the time of the Revolution, being Native Americanism under another name. Its animating spirit was hostility to the stranger—insane jealousy of the foreigner. It manifested itself in the Convention which formed the Constitution of the United States, though the right to frame that Constitution had been largely gained through the valour of adopted citizens, born in foreign countries, and through the aid and assistance of a foreign nation. It manifested itself in the year 1796, in laws passed during the Administration of President Adams, a narrow-minded man, much prejudiced against foreigners.

Remembering the history of the last fifty years, during which thousands, hundreds of thousands, nay millions of the population of Europe have been spreading themselves over the vast American continent, building up its cities, penetrating and subduing its forests, reclaiming its wastes, constructing its great works, developing its resources, multiplying its population—in a word, making America what she is at this day—one does not know whether to laugh at the absurdity of those who imagined that, without injury to the future of the States, they might bar their ports to emigrants from foreign countries;

This hostility to the foreigner, intensified by religious prejudice, exhibited itself on various occasions—notably in the disgraceful riots of 1844; but on no occasion was the feeling so universal, or its display so marked, as in the years 1854 and 1855, when the banner of Know Nothingism was made the symbol of political supremacy. Here was every element necessary to a fierce and relentless strife. The Constitution of Know Nothingism was anomalously adopted on the 17th of June, 1854, the anniversary of the Battle of Bunker's Hill. Strange, that a day sacred to the freedom of America should be that on which citizens of a free Republic should plot in the dark against the liberties of their fellow men! But so it was. . . .

Many who joined this organisation had not the excuse, the bad excuse, of

fanaticism for their conduct. Lust of power was their ruling passion; to trample their opponents under foot, and secure everything to themselves, their animating motive. If they could have attained their ends through the Catholic body, they would have employed every art of wile and seduction in the hope of securing their co-operation; but as they deemed it more to their advantage to assail and blacken the Catholics, they accordingly did assail and blacken them to the satisfaction of their dupes. For religion—any form of religion—they did not care a cent; probably they regarded it as so much venerable superstition and priestcraft—a very excellent thing for women and persons of weak mind, but not for men ; at any rate, men of their enlightenment. Members of no congregation, these defenders of the faith never "darkened the door" of a church or meeting-house, and save, like the sailor who did not know of what religion he was, but was "d——d sure he was not a Papist," entertaining a blind prejudice against Catholicity, they were as ignorant of Christian belief as any savage of Central Africa. . . .

It is impossible to describe the frenzy that seemed to possess a certain portion of the American people, whose strongest passions and most cherished prejudices were stimulated by appeals from the press and the platform, the pulpit and the street tub. It seized on communities and individuals as a species of uncontrollable insanity. Bitten by the madness of the moment, acquaintance turned savagely on acquaintance, friend upon friend, even relative upon relative. The kindly feelings which it took years to cement were rudely torn asunder and trampled under foot. The Irish Catholic was the chief object of attack. He was guilty of the double crime of being an Irishman and a Catholic; and, to do him justice, he was as ready to proclaim his faith as to boast of his nativity. His enemies were many, his friends few, his defenders less. Poor Pat had indeed a sad time of it. . . .

Like fever or cholera, this politico-religious epidemic was milder or more virulent in one place than in another. Here it seized hold of the entire community; there it caught but a few individuals. Here it signalised its presence by riots; there by bloodshed. In this city its congenial result was a burning, or a cowardly assassination; in the other, a stand-up fight, in which the Irish Catholic had to encounter enormous odds against him. That comparatively little mischief was done to ecclesiastical property may be accounted for by the manner with which, as by one impulse, the Catholics rallied round churches and convents wherever there was a probability of their being assailed. In New York, Know Nothingism made little external display in mischief and outrage; which fact may be accounted for in two ways—the one, that the Irish population had by this time grown too powerful to be wantonly trifled with; the other, that they listened in an obedient spirit to the advice of the Archbishop, who wisely believed that the madness would speedily die out if left to itself, and if not stimulated by opposition; that it was something similar to a conflagration of flax, violent for the moment, but without any enduring power. The Archbishop was

right in his judgment. It was a frenzy of the hour, artfully inflamed by angry sects, and skilfully directed by unscrupulous politicians—men who would stop at nothing which could in any way further the objects of their selfish ambition. The fury of the madness did die out; but the feelings to which it gave rise, or evoked into new life, did not so readily pass away. . . .

From the very circumstances of their position, it was almost a matter of inevitable necessity that the Irish citizens of America should ally themselves with that political party which, with respect to the foreigner and the stranger, adopted the liberal and enlightened policy of Jefferson and Madison. The Irish, then, being Democrats, naturally sympathised with the prevailing sentiment of the Southern States, which was strongly Democratic. And yet, notwithstanding this sympathy, the result of a general concurrence of opinion with that of the South, the Irish of the Northern States not merely remained faithful to the flag of the Union, but were amongst the foremost and the most enthusiastic of those who rallied in its defence, and the most steadfast in their support of the Federal cause, from the moment that the first gun, fired in Charleston Harbour, echoed through the land, to the hour when Lee surrendered, and the war was at an end. Whatever their opinions or feelings as to the conduct of those who, justly or unjustly, were held responsible for bringing about or precipitating the contest, and deeply as they felt the injury which war was certain to inflict on the country of their adoption, the Irish-born citizens never wavered in their duty.

None more bitterly deplored than they did the sad consequences of civil strife—a conflict which would bring into deadly collision kindred races even of their own people; but once the rupture was irrevocable, they calmly accepted their position. From the first moment to the last, they were animated by a high sense of duty, and an earnest feeling of patriotism. Fortunately for the honour and fame of the Irish. there was in their motives an utter absence of the baneful passions of hatred and revenge, or the least desire to crush or humiliate their opponents. War with all its tremendous consequences they faced as a stern and terrible necessity; but they entered into it with a chivalrous and Christian spirit, which never deserted them throughout the prolonged struggle. They did not stop to argue or split hairs as to the constitutional rights alleged to lie involved; they acted, as they felt, with the community amid whom they lived, and with whom their fortunes were identified. The feeling was the same at both sides of the line. The Irish in the South stood with the State to which, as they believed, they owed their first allegiance, and, as was the case in the North, they caught the spirit of the community of whom they formed part. They also were profoundly grieved at the necessity for war, and would have gladly avoided the calamity of an open rupture. Southern Irishmen have told me that they shed tears of bitter anguish when, in vindication of what they held to be the outraged independence of their State, which to them was the immediate home of their adoption, they first fired on the flag of that glorious country which had been an asylum to millions of their people. The Northern Irishman went into the war for the preservation of the Union—the Southern Irishman for the independence of his State. And each, in his own mind, was as thoroughly justified, both as to right and duty, principle and patriotism, as the other. With the political or constitutional question involved at either side I have no business whatever; and were I competent to disentangle it from the maze into which conflicting opinions and subtle disquisitions have brought it, I should still, from a feeling of delicacy, decline dealing with a subject which may not, as yet, be freely handled without exciting anger and irritation. I have heard the undisguised sentiments of Irishmen at both sides of the line—every man of them loving America with a feeling of profound attachment; and I, who stand, as it were, on neutral ground, have as full faith in the patriotism and purity of motive of the Northern as the Southern, the Confederate as the Federal.

## Dennis Kearney, "History of the American Working Classes," 1878

*Irish-born Dennis Kearney formed the Workingmen's Party in California in 1877 at the age of twenty-three. In this document and in many others, Kearney combined attacks on the wealthy elite of the United States with assaults on Chinese immigrants. If on the East Coast Irish immigrant racial identity was routinely challenged, on the West Coast Irish immigrants could align themselves with other whites to oppose nonwhite immigration.*

Source: http://www.uwm.edu/Course/448-440/misery.com; Dennis Kearney, President, and H. L. Knight, Secretary, "Appeal from California. The Chinese Invasion. Workingmen's Address," *Indianapolis Times*, February 28, 1878.

Our moneyed men have ruled us for the past thirty years. Under the flag of the slaveholder they hoped to destroy our liberty. Failing in that, they have rallied under the banner of the millionaire, the banker and the land monopolist, the railroad king and the false politician, to effect their purpose. We have permitted them to become immensely rich against all sound republican policy, and they have turned upon us to sting us to death. They have seized upon the government by bribery and corruption. They have made speculation and public robbery a science. They have loaded the nation, the state, the county, and the city with debt. They have stolen the public lands. They have grasped all to themselves, and by their unprincipled greed brought a crisis of unparalleled distress on forty millions of people, who have natural resources to feed, clothe and shelter the whole human race.

Such misgovernment, such mismanagement, may challenge the whole world for intense stupidity, and would put to shame the darkest tyranny of the barbarous past. We, here in California, feel it as well as you. We feel that the day and hour has come for the Workingmen of America to depose capital and put Labor in the Presidential chair, in the Senate and Congress, in the State House, and on the Judicial Bench. We are with you in this work. Workingmen must form a party of their own, take charge of the government, dispose gilded fraud, and put honest toil in power.

In our golden state all these evils have been intensified. Land monopoly has seized upon all the best soil in this fair land. A few men own from ten thousand to two hundred thousand acres each. The poor Laborer can find no resting place, save on the barren mountain, or in the trackless desert. Money monopoly has reached its grandest proportions. Here, in San Francisco, the palace of the millionaire looms up above the hovel of the starving poor with as wide a contrast as anywhere on earth. To add to our misery and despair, a bloated aristocracy has sent to China—the greatest and oldest despotism in the world—for a cheap working slave. It rakes the slums of Asia to find the meanest slave on earth—the Chinese coolie—and imports him here to meet the free American in the Labor market, and still further widen the breach between the rich and the poor, still further to degrade white Labor. These cheap slaves fill every place. Their dress is scant and cheap. Their food is rice from China. They hedge twenty in a room, ten by ten. They are wipped curs, abject in docility, mean, contemptible and obedient in all things. They have no wives, children or dependents.

They are imported by companies, controlled as serfs, worked like slaves, and at last go back to China with all their earnings. They are in every place, they seem to have no sex. Boys work, girls work; it is all alike to them. The father of a family is met by them at every turn. Would he get work for himself? Ah! A stout Chinaman does it cheaper. Will he get a place for his oldest boy? He can not. His girl? Why, the Chinaman is in her place too! Every door is closed. He can only go to crime or suicide, his wife and daughter to prostitution, and his boys to hoodlumism and the penitentiary.

Do not believe those who call us savages, rioters, incendiaries, and outlaws. We seek our ends calmly, rationally, at the ballot box. So far good order has marked all our proceedings. But, we know how false, how inhuman, our adversaries are. We know that if gold, if fraud, if force can defeat us, they will all be used. And we have resolved that they shall not defeat us. We shall arm. We shall meet fraud and falsehood with defiance, and force with force, if need be. We are men, and propose to live like men in this free land, without the contamination of slave labor, or die like men, if need be, in asserting the rights of our race, our country, and our families.

California must be all American or all Chinese. We are resolved that it shall be American, and are prepared to make it so. May we not rely upon your sympathy and assistance?

*With great respect for the Workingmen's Party of California.*
*Dennis Kearney, President*
*H. L. Knight, Secretary*

## Act to Protect Free White Labor Against Competition with Chinese Coolie Labor, and to Discourage the Immigration of the Chinese into the State of California, April 26, 1862

*This "Chinese Police Tax," passed in 1862, continued the efforts of California legislators to keep Chinese immigrants out of the mines, and to prevent them from competing with white-owned businesses.*

*Source:* http://www.itp.berkeley.edu/~asam 121/1862htm

The People of the State of California, represented in Senate and Assembly, do enact as follows:

SECTION 1. There is hereby levied on each person, male and female, of the Mongolian race, of the age of eighteen years and upwards, residing in this State, except such as shall, under laws now existing, or which may hereafter be enacted, take out licenses to work in the mines, or to prosecute some kind of business, a monthly capitation tax of two dollars and fifty cents, which tax shall be known as the Chinese Police Tax; provided, That all Mongolians exclusively engaged in the production and manufacture of the following articles shall be exempt from the provisions of this Act, viz: sugar, rice, coffee, tea. . . .

SECTION 4. The Collector shall collect the Chinese police tax, provided for in this Act, from all person refusing to pay such tax, and sell the same at public auction, by giving notice by proclamation one hour previous to such sale; and shall deliver the property, together with a bill of sale thereof, to the person agreeing to pay, and paying, the highest thereof, which delivery and bill of sale shall transfer to such person a good and sufficient title to the property. And after deducing the tax and necessary expenses incurred by reason of such refusal, seizure, and sale of property, the Collector shall return the surplus of the proceeds of the sale, if any, to the person whose property was sold; provided, That should any person, liable to pay the tax imposed in this Act, in any county in this State, escape into any other County, with the intention to evade the payment of such tax, then, and in that event, it shall be lawful for the Collector, when he shall collect Chinese police taxes, as provided for in this section, shall deliver to each of the persons paying such taxes a police tax receipt, with the blanks properly filled; provided, further, That any Mongolian, or Mongolians, may pay the above named tax to the County Treasurer, who is hereby authorized to receipt for the same in the same manner as the Collector. And any Mongolian, so paying said tax to the Treasurer of the County, if paid monthly, shall be entitled to a reduction of twenty percent of said tax. And if paid in advance for the year next ensuing, such Mongolian, or Mongolians, shall be entitled to a reduction of thirty-three and one third percent on said tax. But in all cases where the County Treasurer receipts for said tax yearly in advance, he shall do it by issuing for each month separately; and any Mongolian who shall exhibit a County Treasurer's receipt, as above provided,

to the Collector for the month for which said receipt was given.

SECTION 5. Any person charged with the collection of Chinese police taxes, who shall give any receipt other than the one prescribed in this Act, or receive money for such taxes without giving the necessary receipt therefor, or who shall insert more than one name in any receipt, shall be guilty of a felony, and, upon conviction thereof, shall be fined in a sum not exceeding one thousand dollars, and be imprisoned in the State Prison for a period not exceeding one year.

SECTION 6. Any Tax Collector who shall sell, or cause to be sold, any police tax receipt, with the date of the sale left blank, or which shall not be dated and signed, and blanks filled with ink, by the Controller, Auditor, and Tax Collector, and any person who shall make any alteration, or cause the same to be made, in any police tax receipt, shall be deemed guilty of a felony, and, on conviction thereof, shall be fined in a sum not exceeding one thousand dollars, and imprisoned in the State prison for a period not exceeding 2 years; and the police tax receipt so sold, with blank date, or which shall not be signed and dated, and blanks filled with ink, as aforesaid, or which shall have been altered, shall be received in evidence in any Court of competent jurisdiction.

SECTION 7. Any person or company who shall hire persons liable to pay the Chinese police tax shall be held responsible for the payment of the tax due from each person so hired; and no employer shall be released from this liability on the ground that the employee in indebted to him (the employer), and the Collector may proceed against any such employer in the same manner as he might against the original party owing the taxes. The Collector shall have power to require any person or company believed to be indebted to, or to have any money, gold dust, or property of any kind, belonging to any person liable for police taxes, or in which such person is interested, in his or their possession, or under his or their control, to answer, under oath, as to such indebtedness, or the possession of such money, gold dust, or other property. In case a party is indebted, or has possession or control of any moneys, gold dust, or other property, as aforesaid, of such person liable for police taxes, he may collect from such party the amount of such taxes, and may require the delivery of such money, gold dust, or other property, as aforesaid; and in all cases the receipt of the Collector to said party shall be a complete bar to any demand made against said party, or his legal representatives, for the amounts of money, gold dust, or property, embraced therein.

SECTION 8. The Collector shall receive for his service, in collecting police taxes, twenty percent of all moneys which he shall collect from persons owing such taxes. All of the residue, after deducting the percentage of the Collector, forty percent shall be paid into the County Treasury, for the use of the State, forty percent into the general County Fund, for the use of the County, and the remaining twenty percent into the School Fund, for the benefit of schools within the County; provided, That in counties where the Tax Collector receives a specific salary, he shall not be required to pay the percentage allowed for collecting the police tax into the County Treasury, but shall be allowed to retain the same for his own use and benefit; provided, That where he shall collect the police tax by Deputy, the percentage shall go to the Deputy. . . .

SECTION 10. It is hereby made the duty of the various officers charged with the execution of the provisions of this Act, to carry out said provisions by themselves of Deputies; and for the faithful performance of their said duties in the premises, they shall be liable on their official bonds, respectively. The Treasurer of the respective counties shall make their statements and settlements under this Act with the Controller of State, at the same time and in the same manner they make their settlements under the general Revenue Act.

SECTION 11. This Act shall be take effect and be in force from and after the first day of May, next ensuing.

## Colonel Albert S. Evans, "A Cruise on the Barbary Coast," 1873

*In this voyeuristic view of the Chinese immigrant community in San Francisco, part of a travel narrative titled* A la California: Sketch of Life in the Golden State, *Evans describes the sparse population of women among Chinese immigrants, and especially the prostitute population.*

*Source:* Museum of the City of San Francisco, http://www.sfmuseum.org/hist6/evans.html, pp. 2, 6; Albert S. Evans, *A la California: Sketch of Life in the Golden State*, with an introduction by Col. W. H. L. Barnes and illustrations from original drawings by Ernest Narjot (San Fransciso: A. L. Bancroft, 1873); © 1995–2001, Gladys Cox Hansen.

.

You will see coming forth from the various narrow alleys which intersect the main streets, and are known by the expressive designations of "Murderer's Alley," "China Alley," "Stout's Alley," etc., any number of Chinese females, clad in their loose drawers or pants of blue or black cotton goods, straight-cut sacques of broadcloth, satin, or other costly or cheap material, according to their condition and social rank; shoes of blue satin, richly embroidered with bullion, and with thick soles of white felt and white wood, anklets or bangles, and bracelets of silver, gold, or jade-stone, and lustrous blue-black hair, braided in two strands, hanging down the back from beneath coarse-striped gingham handkerchiefs, thrown over the head, and tied beneath the chin as a badge denoting slavery, and a life of hopeless infamy; or, if the owner happens to be the wife of a laborer, tradesman or gambling-house proprietor, wonderfully gotten up with a species of transparent mucilage, and fashioned into a rudder-like structure sticking out fully a foot behind, supporting a number of skewer-like pins of gold or silver, each six or eight inches in length, and putting to shame by its size and cleanly appearance, the waterfalls of our Caucasian belles— shuffle along in groups of three or four, talking and laughing together like so many little children, or exchanging compliments, which would never bear translation into English, with the male black-guards, loafers and plug-uglies of their race.

These women are intellectually only children, and are more to be pitied and less condemned than the fallen of their sex of any other race. Every second building is occupied as a saloon, in which nobody seems to be stirring, and has a basement, over the door of which is painted the name of the establishment, as "The Roaring Gimlet," "The Bull's Run," "The Cock of the Walk," "Star of the Union," "Every Man is Welcome," etc., etc., but now closed and apparently unoccupied. There are strains of ear-splitting music coming occasionally from the Chinese gambling-houses, and from time to time, as you walk along, you see rows of Chinamen seated at low benches in basements, industriously engaged in making up "every choice brand of Havana and Domestic cigars," as the signs over the doorways inform you.

This is "China Alley," and is occupied solely by Chinese prostitutes. The houses are all small brick affairs, coming flush up to the edge of the alley, and have windows with wickets in them, made by setting one pane of glass in a frame by itself, and hanging it on hinges. There is a front and a rear room to each of these little dens; and, as we walk along, we can see all the arrangements of the outer rooms Each of these places appear to be inhabited by from two to half a dozen Chinese girls, some of whom are dressed in hoops and long dresses "Melican" style, but for the most part are clad in the costume of their own country.

These poor creatures are all slaves,

bought with a price in China, and imported by degraded men of their own race, who, despite our laws, contrive to hold them to a life-long servitude, which is a thousand times more hopeless and terrible than the negro slavery of Louisiana or Cuba could ever be. They have been reared to a life of shame from infancy, and have not a single trace of the native modesty of women left. They are, as we have said, mere children in point of intellect, havIng no education whatever, and no experience of the world outside of the narrow alleys in which they have always lived, and the emigrant ship in which they were brought over to this country. They have their likes and their dislikes, of course, and become attached to each other in a childish way, frequently being seen walking together on the streets, hand in hand, like little Caucasian sisters going home from school. At very long intervals, some of these poor untutored children of the East become imbued with Western notions of liberty and right, and making their escape from the clutches of their masters, become joined in lawful marriage to some laborious washerman, or other countryman, and endeavor to settle down to an honest life; but their chances of escaping kidnapping, and being dragged away to some distant locality, beaten, and reduced again to prostitution and slavery, are very slim indeed. The owner in such cases has always a personal grudge, as well as a pecuniary loss, to urge him on to vindictive measures; and he will willingly spend ten times the value of his escaping chattel to get her back again, and have his revenge. Besides, the safety of this peculiar institution demands that the most rigorous measures should be taken in every case, as an example to deter others from following in the same vicious course.

The girls cost $40 each in Canton, but are valued here at about $400, if passably good-looking, young and healthy, and readily sell at that figure in cash, or approved paper. Each colony of half a dozen girls is under the immediate control of an "old mother," herself a retired prostitute, who jealously watches over each, and receives from them the wages of their shame as fast as earned. From each wicket all the way down the alley a female head may be seen protruding, and there is a constant fire of jokes and repartee going on between the occupants of the dens on each side of the alley, while every passer comes in for his share of personal notice. A girl, with hair carefully braided and decked with artificial flowers, and cheeks and lips cunningly painted so as to resemble those of her frail Caucasian sisters, notices us looking toward her wicket, and instantly raising her hand, taps at the window, but at the moment catches a glimpse of the policeman behind us, and shuts the wicket, and turns away as if she had not seen us at all. The alarm runs down the whole alley in an instant; there is a rattling of wickets, as if a hurricane was sweeping through the place, and in half a minute all is as silent as the grave, and not a head to be seen. It is a special misdemeanor under our city ordinances for a Chinawoman to tap on a window to attract the attention of anybody on the street; and the girls well know what is in store for them if they are caught at it by the police.

## The Chinese—Facts for Atlantic Papers, 1874

*This document makes disparaging comparisons between Chinese immigrants on the one hand, and Irish and German immigrants on the other. Clearly part of the effort to make opposition to Chinese immigration national, it pleads for understanding and support from whites outside of California.*

*Source:* Museum of the City of San Fransico, http://www.sfmuseum.org/hist1/1874.html; *San Francisco Real Estate Circular,* For the Month of September, 1874; © 1995–2001, Gladys Cox Hansen.

All comparisons between Irish and German immigration and that of the Chinese are unjust. The former make their homes here, buy farms and homesteads, are of the same general race, are buried here after death, and take an interest and aid in all things pertaining to the best interests of the country. The Chinese come for a season only; and, while they give their labor, they do not expend the proceeds of such labor in the country. They do not come to settle or make homes, and *not one in fifty of them is married*. Their women are all suffering slaves and prostitutes, for which possession murderous feuds and high-handed cruelty are constantly occurring. To compare the Chinese with even the lowest white laborers is, therefore, absurd.

Our best interests are suffering of these Asiatic slaves; we are trying to make them live decently while here, and to discourage their arrival in such numbers as to drive white laborers out of the country. Nineteen persons out of every twenty here desire and intend that all this shall be done peaceably and without oppression; all that is asked is that motives and acts not entertained or practiced shall not be charged against California by those who discuss this question with but a slight knowledge of the facts, and that knowledge distorted and one sided.

## The Page Law, 1875

*A prelude to the Chinese Exclusion Act of 1882, this act prohibited Asian prostitutes from entering the United States. Its effect was much more far-reaching—because the investigations into the lives of women attempting to immigrate became so deeply personal, the law severely curtailed immigration by any Chinese women.*

*Source:* http://www.itp.berkeley,edu/~asam 121/page.html

### FORTY-THIRD CONGRESS. SESSION II. MARCH 3, 1975

Chapter 141.—An act supplementary to the acts in relation to immigration (only the pertintent sections are included) *Be it enacted by the Senate and House of Representatives of the United States of America in Congress-assembled,* That in determining whether the immigration of any subject of China, Japan, or any Oriental country, to the United States, is free and voluntary, as provided by section two thousand one hundred and sixty two of the Revised Code, title "Immigration," it shall be the duty of the consul-general or consul of the United States residing at the port from which it is proposed to convey such subjects, in any vessels enrolled or licensed in the United States, or any port within the same, before delivering to the masters of any such vessels the permit or certificate provided for in such section, in ascertain for a term of service within the United States, for lewd and immoral purposes; and if there be such contract or agreement, the said consul-general or consul shall not deliver the required permit or certificate.

SEC. 3. That the importation into the United States of women for the purposes of prostitution is hereby forbidden; and all contracts and agreements in relation thereto, made in advance or in pursuance of illegal importation and purposes, are hereby declared void; and whoever shall knowingly and willfully hold, or attempt to hold, any woman to such purposes, in pursuance of such illegal importation and contract or agreement, shalled be deemed guilty of a felony, and, on conviction thereof, shall be imprisoned not exceeding five years and pay a fine not exceeding five thousand dollars.

SEC. 5. That it shall be unlawful for aliens of the following classes to immigrate into the United States, namely, persons who are undergoing sentence for conviction in their own country of felonious crimes other than political or growing out of or the result of such political offenses, and women "imported for the purposes of prostitution." Every vessel arriving in the United States may be inspected under the direction of the collector of the port at which it arrives,

if he shall have reason to believe that such obnoxious persons are on board; and the officer making such inspection shall certify the result thereof to the master or other person in charge of such vessel, designating in such certificate are person or persons, if any there be, ascertained by him to be of either of the classes whose importaion is hereby forbidden. . . .

*Approved, March 3, 1875.*

## Richard Henry Dana, "California and Its Inhabitants," 1840

*Born into a wealthy and influential family in Cambridge, Massachusetts, Richard Henry Dana signed on as a young man as a sailor on the "Pilgrim" for a voyage to the coast of California. His* Two Years Before the Mast, *a classic travel journal, included a dismissive assessment of Californio culture that helped pave the way for American expansion and conquest.*

*Source:* Richard Henry Dana, *Two Years Before the Mast and Twenty Four Years After* (New York: P. F. Collier and Son, 1909), pp. 177–178; © 1909 by P. F. Collier and Son.

In their domestic relations, these people are no better than in their public. The men are thriftless, proud, and extravagant, and very much given to gaming: and the women have but little education, and a good deal of beauty, and their morality, of course, is none of the best: yet the instances of infidelity are much less frequent than one would at first suppose.

In fact, one vice is set over against another: and thus, something like a balance is obtained. The women have but little virtue, but then the jealousy of their husbands is extreme, and their revenge deadly and almost certain. A few inches of cold steel has been the punishment of many an unwary man, who has been guilty, perhaps, of nothing more than indiscretion of manner. The difficulties of the attempt are numerous, and the consequences of discovery fatal. With the unmarried women, too, great watchfulness is used. The main object of the parents is to marry their daughters well, and to this, the slightest slip would be fatal. The sharp eyes of a dueña, and the cold steel of a father or brother, are a protection which the characters of most of them—men and women—render by no means useless; for the very men who would lay down their lives to avenge the dishonor of their own family, would risk the same lives to complete the dishonor of another.

Of the poor Indians, very little care is taken. The priests, indeed, at the missions, are said to keep them very strictly, and some rules are usually made by the alcaldes to punish their misconduct; but it all amounts to but little. Indeed, to show the entire want of any sense of morality or domestic duty among them, I have frequently known an Indian to bring his wife, to whom he was lawfully married in the church, down to the beach, and carry her back again, dividing with her the money which she had got from the sailors. If any of the girls were discovered by the alcalde to be open evil-livers, they were whipped, and kept at work sweeping the square of the presidio, and carrying mud and bricks for the buildings; yet a few reáls would generally buy them off. Intemperance, too, is a common vice among the Indians. The Spaniards, on the contrary, are very abstemious, and I do not remember ever having seen a Spaniard intoxicated.

Such are the people who inhabit a country embracing four or five hundred miles of sea-coast, with several good harbors; with fine forests in the north; the waters filled with fish, and the plains covered with thousands of herds of cattle; blessed with a climate, than which there can be no better in the world; free from all manner of diseases, whether epidemic or endemic: and with a soil in which corn yields from seventy to eighty fold. In the hands of an enterprising people, what a country this might be! we are ready to say. Yet how long would a people remain so, in such a country? The Americans (as those from the United States are called) and Englishmen, who are fast filling up the principal towns, and getting the trade into their hands, are indeed more industrious and effective than the Spaniards; yet their children are brought up Spaniards, in every respect, and if the "California fever" (laziness) spares the first generation, it always attacks the second.

## Antonio María Osio, "The History of Alta California," 1851

*Californio Antonio Osio paints a very different picture of Californio and American interaction in California than Richard Henry Dana. Written just a few years after the Bear Flag Revolt and the Mexican-American war,*

*Osio's account of events reflects the anger of a man whose livelihood and culture are being destroyed. Like many Californios, Osio was unable to retain possession of his land claims—in his case, San Francisco's Point Reyes and Angel Island, where he raised cattle until the war began.*

Source: Antonio María Osio. *The History of Alta California: A Memoir of Mexican California* (Madison: University of Wisconsin Press, 1996), pp. 200–202, 223, 226, 243–244, 246; © 1996 by the Board of Regents of the University of Wisconsin System.

If one were to consider today the veil of schemes which was drawn to hide the uprising by foreigners in 1840, an uprising which finally took place in 1846, one would come to realize that the government of Mexico only slightly attended to or halfway realized what was happening behind the scenes within the capital. The government never considered the advantages to be gained by stimulating development in different parts of this territory, which was so ready for it. That is why today those people with their *considerandos* need to be reminded of a familiar story about two people who inherited vast expanses of adjoining lands. When the landowners met, following the rules of etiquette, they congratulated one another and pledged their friendship. But their habits forced an end to their friendship. The heir to the northern part was a very clever old man and an excellent strategist, especially on economic matters. For example, he would secretly test his servants by paying four reales to a servant who was supposed to earn twenty pesos. He always managed to have excellent servants who would come from everywhere to fill his jobs. Everyone liked him because he would reward deserving individuals well. They agreed with him in large matters and over-looked what was not essential. In this manner he brought progress to them without having to speak of it repeatedly. That inheritance was divided into a number of prosperous *haciendas*. The owner took pleasure in the fact that the workers held him in high esteem. They never referred to him as Master; they called him Uncle Samuel instead.

This old man had a very large telescope, which he used to observe his neighbor from afar as he worked in his usual greedy manner. One day, after admiring the way he had tastefully and symmetrically planted his own fields with choice seeds, sugarcane, wheat, cotton, and other crops, some of which he needed and some of which simply struck his fancy, the old man went to see his neighbor to give him some friendly advice on how to plow his land. He suggested that he first plow his land very superficially, in accordance with the strict style and rules of art in vogue, and then plant the canes, tip down. The rest of the seeds should be selected, preferably, from those found along the seashore. Another time, he saw that his neighbor owned a little pig which he fed only fruit peelings, in the hope that it would grow somewhat so he could sell it to the highest bidder. From afar Señor Clever noticed that the little animal had natural horseshoes which were not made of yellow brass. He immediately went to see his neighbor and offered to buy the pig for fifteen *tlacos,* nine of which were fake, and an agreement was reached. Next he calculated the value of the purchase. After doing so, he was astonished to see how much wealth those fifteen *tlacos* had allowed him to accumulate so quickly. . . .

Those who aspired to possess the territory had their suspicions about what might happen, so they accelerated their plots to acquire it by force or by purchase. They prepared to try the first option, as long as they retained the chance to try the second before trouble began. Colonel Frémont was on an overland expedition and came to the Monterey area on the pretext that he needed to replenish his supplies. His true motive was to convince the inhabitants that they should view his armed intrusion into a foreign territory as a beneficial rather than a hostile act. Don José Castro was somewhat inclined to tolerate this outrage, but at that moment he received a message from his uncle, Don Angel Castro, who stated that three of Colonel Frémont's soldiers had arrived at his ranch (near San Juan Bautista). When they saw that he was alone and unarmed, they had dared try to rape his daughters. Don Angel was one of many people who prided themselves in saying that they had been loyal subjects of His Catholic Majesty. As a veteran presidio soldier, he knew how to protect his honor under any circumstances. When Frémont's soldiers threatened this honorable old man by placing a pistol at his neck so the others could commit the intended crime, the old soldier found energy and courage from the knowledge that his strong fists would not fail him. He told his aggressor that he preferred death to dishonor. Then he grabbed him by the neck, yanked the pistol from his hand, and threw it to the ground. This quick and vigorous action prevented the soldiers from committing their barbaric act. They retreated immediately to Frémont's camp but promised to return again. . . .

When Frémont and Gillespie finally met, they discussed different ways they might initiate hostilities without implicating their government. It was imperative that the United States government not be accused of taking over a defenseless foreign territory solely by force, and it did not want to appear to be acting in bad faith, since both nations were bound by treaties and war had not been declared between them. Therefore, in order to conceal their true intent, or color it so that it would be more in keeping with public opinion, they decided to camouflage the flag of stars and strips with a temporary flag which depicted a brown bear on a white field and a star in the top corner. Captain Montgomery, commander of the corvette *Portsmouth,* which was anchored within the port of San Francisco at Sausalito, sent them supplies. Troops came down from Sacramento and arrived in Sonoma at dawn. They surprised Don Victor Prudón and the brothers Vallejo, Don Guadalupe and Don Salvador, in their beds. After they had seized them and informed them that they were prisoners, they forced them to march to Sacramento. Don Jacobo P. Leese, an American who had arrived in 1833 and was married to a woman from the Vallejo family, wanted to accompany his brothers-in-law to see if he could somehow help them by speaking with his countrymen. When they arrived at Colonel Frémont's camp, they claimed that Leese was not a true descendant of Uncle Samuel and imprisoned him with the others. For more than three months they were fed worse food than the other prisoners in Sonoma, to whom reference has been made, received. Señor Vallejo was being measured with the same yardstick that he used to measure others. Vallejo begged them to allow him to have provisions and his favorite food brought down from his home in Sonoma so he would not go hungry, but they denied his request because they wanted to humiliate him. He was imprisoned for about four months and was released when the war between Mexico and the United States ended, but his health had been shattered. . . .

The Americans had the greatest confidence in the troops commanded by Colonel Frémont, and they were the ones that pursued Don Andrés Pico. Pico, who had ample warning, decided not to avoid combat. He looked for a level area, free of obstacles, where he could lead his young soldiers into battle. They wanted an area where they could spur their horses freely, thrust their lances, and either triumph or die after a brave fight. In a very short time Colonel Frémont found Pico. When the two *jefes* encountered each other, it seems that they both wanted to have a meeting before resorting to weapons. Señor Frémont was recognized for his military expertise, and he correctly esteemed the courage of his opponents. Because he also was a shrewd man, he was convinced that these courageous Mexicans

would be of use to the territory after it became a state. To their dismay, these Mexicans would be viewed as foreigners in their own country, but they would make excellent citizens of the United States. With this in mind, Frémont proposed terms for a surrender to Señor Pico, but he did not accept them. He then suggested other terms to him, and Pico again refused. This negative response almost led to a confrontation; but since Señor Frémont was more experienced, he wisely waited until he could convince Señor Pico with good and benevolent judgment. He explained to Pico that he believed his reasons for not accepting the surrender bordered on fear because he found himself in a very critical situation. He had no support from the Mexican government, and none would be forthcoming, since the enormous distance rendered assistance impossible.

The commanders had lingered too long in their discussion. Since Señor Frémont was needed elsewhere, he wanted to conclude the negotiations for the surrender. Frémont was generous in granting Pico everything that his military honor permitted. The surrender finally was negotiated with the following terms: Señor Pico would march to Los Angeles and enter the city in formation, with drums beating and flag unfurled. After arriving at the *plaza*, he would order his troops to disband. Each soldier would return home, put away his weapons, and live as a peaceful, good, hardworking citizen. The cannon and remaining ammunition, which had been taken from General Kearny, would be surrendered immediately, since they were the property of the United States government. After the terms had been agreed upon and the document was signed, Pico complied with all details of the surrender.

Now that the Americans were in possession of the territory, a number of different naval officers assumed the command in succession until Colonels Mason and Riley were appointed by the government. When they assumed the command, they conducted themselves with the enthusiasm typical of fine military men and the benevolence of excellent citizens. Many other officials and staff people were appointed after the Mexican government sold the territory to the United States and it became a state.

It is evident that this unfortunate country's many riches were hidden from her. A very old legend of unknown origin stated that a number of rivers in the north in both Californias contained sands of gold. Reverend Father Juan Ugarte, who succeeded the distinguished Father Salvatierra in Baja California, said that he had gone to visit the beaches at the mouth of the Colorado River on the first boat that was built in the territory, and he had found nothing.

The Franciscan Fathers from the Colegio de San Fernando in Mexico-took over the administration of those missions when the Jesuit Fathers departed. Later, the Franciscans received orders from their superiors to surrender the missions to the Dominican Fathers. After the Dominicans took possession of and established these missions, they always were occupied with their apostolic work and never endeavored to explore the meadows along the rivers to determine what

was in the sand. Lately, there has been speculation that the Fathers already were aware of the sands of gold. This cannot be true, because, if it is difficult to keep a secret when three people know about it, it would be impossible to do so when more than forty people are involved. Therefore, the most likely if not indisputable scenario is that when a small quantity of gold was discovered in 1844 on land belonging to Mission San Fernando, it became apparent that there was a deposit of gold in this region. Later, in 1848, gold was discovered in abundance at Sutter's establishment in Sacramento.

## The Treaty of Guadalupe Hidalgo, as Ratified by the United States and Mexican Governments, 1848

*The treaty that ended the Mexican-American war not only delineated boundaries between the two nations but also—in the passages included here—dealt with the situation of Mexicans living in what had become part of the United States. Article X, which assured Mexican land rights would be respected, was eliminated from the treaty by the United States Senate. Note too Article XI, which deals with the "savage tribes" of Indians that continued to plague both the United States and Mexican governments in these years.*

*Source:* Richard Griswold del Castillo, *The Treaty of Guadalupe Hidalgo: A Legacy of Conflict* (Norman: University of Oklahoma Press, 1990), pp. 183–184, 189–191, 180–181. Text from pp. 183–184, 189–191 excerpted from Charles I. Bevans, ed., *Treaties and Other International Agreements of the United States of America,*

*1776–1949*, vol. 9 (Washington, D.C.: Department of State, 1972); text from pp. 180–181 excerpted from David Hunter Miller, ed., *Treaties and Other International Acts of the United States of America*, vol. 5 (Washington, D.C.: Government Printing Office, 1937).

In the name of Almighty God:

The United States of America, and the United Mexican States, animated by a sincere desire to put an end to the calamities of the war which unhappily exists between the two Republics, and to establish upon a solid basis relations of peace and friendship, which shall confer reciprocal benefits upon the citizens of both, and assure the concord, harmony and mutual confidence, wherin the two Peoples should live, as good Neighbours, have for that purpose appointed their respective Plenipotentiaries: that is to say, the President of the United States has appointed Nicholas P. Trist, a citizen of the United States, and the President of the Mexican Republic has appointed Don Luis Gonzaga Cuevas, Don Bernardo Couto, and Don Miguel Atristain, citizens of the said Republic; who, after a reciprocal communication of their respective full powers, have, under the protection of Almighty God, the author of Peace, arranged, agreed upon, and signed the following

**Treaty of Peace, Friendship, Limits and Settlement Between the United States of America and the Mexican Republic**

*Article I*
There shall be firm and universal peace between the United States of America and the Mexican Republic, and between their respective Countries, territories, cities, towns and people, without exception of places or persons.

*Article II*
Immediately upon the signature of this Treaty, a convention shall be entered into between a Commissioner or Commissioners appointed by the General in Chief of the forces of the United States, and such as may be appointed by the Mexican Government, to the end that a provisional suspension of hostilities shall take place, and that, in the places occupied by the said forces, constitutional order may be reestablished, as regards the political, administrative and judicial branches, so far as this shall be permitted by the circumstances of military occupation.

*Article VIII*
Mexicans now established in territories previously belonging to Mexico, and which remain for the future within the limits of the United States, as defined by the present Treaty, shall be free to continue where they now reside, or to remove at any time to the Mexican Republic, retaining the property which they possess in the said territories, or disposing thereof and removing the proceeds wherever they please; without their being subjected, on this account, to any contribution, tax or charge whatever.

Those who shall prefer to remain in the said territories, may either retain the title and rights of Mexican citizens, or acquire those of citizens of the United States. But, they shall be under the obligation to make their election within one year from the date of the exchange of ratifications of this treaty: and those who shall remain in the said territories, after the expiration of that year, without having declared their intention to retain the character of Mexicans, shall be considered to have elected to become citizens of the United States.

In the said territories, property of every kind, now belonging to Mexicans not established there, shall be inviolably respected. The present owners, the heirs of these, and all Mexicans who may hereafter acquire said property by contract, shall enjoy with respect to it, guaranties equally ample as if the same belonged to citizens of the United States.

*Article IX*

The Mexicans who, in the territories aforesaid, shall not preserve the character of citizens of the Mexican Republic, conformably with what is stipulated in the preceding article, shall be incorporated into the Union of the United States and be admitted, at the proper time (to be judged of by the Congress of the United States) to the enjoyment of all the rights of citizens of the United States according to the principles of the Constitution; and in the mean time shall be maintained and protected in the free enjoyment of their liberty and property, and secured in the free exercise of their religion without restriction.

*Article X*

Stricken out by U.S. Senate.

*Article XI*

Considering that a great part of the territories which, by the present treaty, are to be comprehended for the future

within the limits of the United States, is now occupied by savage tribes, who will hereafter be under the exclusive control of the Government of the United States, and whose incursions within the territory of Mexico would be prejudicial in the extreme; it is solemnly agreed that all such incursions shall be forcibly restrained by the Government of the United States, whensoever this may be necessary; and that when they cannot be prevented, they shall be punished by the said Government, and satisfaction for the same shall be exacted: all in the same way, and with equal diligence and energy, as if same incursions were meditated or committed within it's own territory against it's own citizens.

It shall not be lawful, under any pretext whatever, for any inhabitant of the United States, to purchase or acquire any Mexican or any foreigner residing in Mexico, who may have been captured by Indians inhabiting the territory of either of the two Republics; nor to purchase or acquire horses, mules, cattle or property of any kind, stolen within Mexican territory by such Indians;

And, in the event of any person or persons, captured within Mexican territory by Indians, being carried into the territory of the United States, the Government of the latter engages and binds itself, in the most solemn manner, so soon as it shall know of such captives being within it's territory, and shall be able so to do, through the faithful exercise of it's influence and power, to rescue them, and return them to their country, or deliver them to the agent or representative of the Mexican Government. The Mexican Authorities will, as far as practicable, give to the Government of the United States notice of such captures; and it's agent shall pay the expenses incurred in the maintenance and transmission of the rescured captives; who, in the mean time, shall he treated with the utmost hospitality by the American Authorities at the place where they may be. But if the Government of the United States, before receiving such notice from Mexico, should obtain intelligence through any other channel, of the existence of Mexican captives within it's territory, it will proceed forthwith to effect their release and delivery to the Mexican agent, as above stipulated.

For the purpose of giving to these stipulations the fullest possible efficacy, thereby affording the security and redress demanded by their true spirit and intent, the Government of the United States will now and hereafter pass, without unnecessary delay, and always vigilantly enforce, such laws as the nature of the subject may require. And finally, the sacredness of this obligation shall never be lost sight of by the said Government, when providing for the removal of the Indians from any portion of the said territories, or for it's being settled by citizens of the United States; but on the contrary, special care shall then be taken not to place it's Indian occupants under the necessity of seeking new homes, by committing those invasions which the United States have solemnly obliged themselves to restrain.

### Article X

All grants of land made by the Mexican Government or by the competent authorities, in territories previously appertaining to Mexico, and remaining for the future within the limits of the United States, shall be respected as valid, to the same extent that the same grants would be valid, if the said territories had remained within the limits of Mexico. But the grantees of lands in Texas, put in possession thereof, who, by reason of the circumstances of the country since the beginning of the troubles between Texas and the Mexican Government, may have been prevented from fulfilling all the conditions of their grants, shall be under the obligation to fulfill the said conditions within the periods limited in the same respectively; such periods to be now counted from the date of the exchange of ratifications of this treaty: in default of which the said grants shall not be obligatory upon the State of Texas, in virtue of the stipulations contained in this Article.

The foregoing stipulation in regard to grantees of land in Texas, is extended to all grantees of land in the territories aforesaid, elsewhere than in Texas, put in possession under such grants; and, in default of the fulfillment of the conditions of any such grant, within the new period, which, as is above stipulated, begins with the day of the exchange of ratifications of this treaty, the same shall be null and void.

## Juan Seguin, "Personal Memoirs," 1858

*Seguin, who fought against Mexico in the Texas Revolt and served as mayor of San Antonio in the early 1840s, came under increasing pressure as he tried to defend fellow Tejanos against land-hungry Anglos. Here he described the circumstances that forced him to leave Texas with his family and flee to Mexico.*

Source: http://seguinfamilyhistory.com/index.html#Personal Memoirs; © 1995 by the Seguin Family Historical Society (Albert Seguin Gonzales, Founder).

Written in the year 1858, the following is from the Personal Memoirs of Colonel Juan N. Seguin. . . . HERO OF THE TEXAS REVOLUTION, ROBBED OF PROPERTY, NAME (One of the most gallant of all heroes of the Texas War for Independence was Juan Nepomuceno Seguin . . . Native born Texan, Statesman, veteran commander of many battles, scholar, namesake for the city of Seguin and victim of the times. Following his legendary career as a leader in the Texas Revolution, Juan Seguin found himself slandered, robbed of property and in peril for his life by his own countrymen—forcing him to flee to a foreign county—Mexico. (The following is his story of that time, as written by his own hand.)

Preface by Juan N. Seguin: "A native of the City of San Antonio de Bexar, I embraced the cause Texas at the report of the first cannon which foretold of her liberty; filled an honorable situation in the ranks of the conquerors of San Jacinto, and was a member of the legislative body of the Republic. I now find myself, in the very land, which in other times bestowed on me such bright and repeated evidences of trust and esteem, exposed to the attacks of scribblers and personal enemies, who, to serve politi-

cal purposes, and engender strife, falsify historical facts, with which they are but imperfectly acquainted. I owe it to myself, my children and friends, to answer them with short, but true exposition of my acts, from the beginning of my public career, to the time of the return of General Woll from the Rio Grande, with the Mexican forces, amongst which I was then serving.

I address myself to the American people; to that people impetuous, as the whirlwind, when aroused by the hypocritical clamors of designing men, but just, impartial and composed, whenever men and facts are submitted to their judgment.

I have been the object of the hatred and passionate attacks of some few disorganisers, who, for a time, ruled, as masters, over the poor and oppressed population of San Antonio. Harpy-like, ready to pounce on everything that attracted the notice of their rapacious avarice, I was an obstacle to the execution of their vile designs.

## Juan Cortina Rebellion in the 1850s

*Juan Cortina organized a rebellion in the 1850s against Anglos in Texas who were mistreating and exploiting Mexican Americans. Here he explains his rationale and urges fellow Mexicans to join him.*

Source: Zaragosa Vargas, *Major Problems in Mexican American History* (Boston: Houghton Mifflin Company, 1999), pp. 154–156; House Executive Documents, 36th Congress, 1st. Session, H. Exec. Doc., no. 52, ser. 1050 (Washington,

D.C.: Thomas H. Ford, Printer, 1860). © 1999 Houghton Mifflin Company.

An event of grave importance, in which it has fallen to my lot to figure as the principal actor since the morning of the twenty-eighth instant, doubtless keeps you in suspense with regard to the progess of its consequences. There is no need of fear. Orderly people and honest citizens are inviolable to us in their persons and interests. Our object, as you have seen, has been to chastise the villainy of our enemies, which heretofore has gone unpunished. These have connived with each other, and form, so to speak, a perfidious inquisitorial lodge to persecute and rob us, without any cause, and for no other crime on our part than that of being of Mexican origin, considering us, doubtless, destitute of those gifts which they themselves do not possess.

To defend ourselves, and making use of the sacred right of self-preservation, we have assembled in a popular meeting with a view of discussing a means by which to put an end to our misfortunes. . . .

Innocent persons shall not suffer—no. But, if necessary, we will lead a wandering life, awaiting our opportunity to purge society of men so base that they degrade it with their opprobrium. Our families have returned as strangers to their old country to beg for an asylum. Our lands, if they are to be sacrificed to the avaricious covetousness of our enemies, will be rather so on account of our own vicissitudes. As to land, Nature will always grant us sufficient to support our

frames, and we accept the consequences that may arise. Further, *our personal enemies shall not possess our lands until they have fattened it with their own gore.* . . . There are, doubtless, persons so overcome by strange prejudices, men without confidence or courage to face danger in an undertaking in sisterhood with the love of liberty, who, examining the merit of acts by a false light, and preferring that of the same opinion contrary to their own, prepare no other reward than that pronounced for the "bandit," for him who, with complete abnegation of self, dedicates himself to constant labor for the happiness of those who, suffering under the weight of misfortunes, eat their bread, mingled with tears, on the earth which they rated.

If, my dear compatriots, I am honored with that name, I am ready for the combat. . . .

Mexicans! When the State of Texas began to receive the new organization which its sovereignty required as an integrant part of the Union, flocks of vampires, in the guise of men, came and scattered themselves in the settlements, without any capital except the corrupt heart and the most perverse intentions. Some, brimful of laws, pledged to us their protection against the attacks of the rest; others assembled in shadowy councils, attempted and excited the robbery and burning of the houses of our relatives on the other side of the river Bravo; while others, to the abusing of our unlimited confidence, when we intrusted them with our titles, which secured the future of our families, refused to return them under false and frivolous pretexts; all, in short, with a smile on their faces, giving the lie to that which their black entrails were meditating. Many of you have been robbed of your property, incarcerated, chased, murdered, and hunted like wild beasts, because your labor was fruitful, and because your industry excited the vile avarice which led them. A voice infernal said, from the bottom of their soul, "kill them; the greater will be our gain!" Ah! this does not finish the sketch of your situation. It would appear that justice had fled from this world, leaving you to the caprice of your oppressors, who become each day more furious toward you; that, through witnesses and false charges, although the grounds may be insufficient, you may be interred in the penitentiaries, if you are not previously deprived of life by some keeper who covers himself from responsibility by the pretence of your flight. There are to be found criminals covered with frightful crimes, but they appear to have impunity until opportunity furnish them a victim; to these monsters indulgence is shown, because they are not of our race, which is unworthy, as they say, to belong to the human species. . . .

Mexicans! Is there no remedy for you? Inviolable laws, yet useless, serve, it is true, certain judges and hypocritical authorities, cemented in evil and injustice, to do whatever suits them, and to satisfy their vile avarice at the cost of your patience and suffering; rising in their frenzy, even to the taking of life, through the treacherous hands of their bailiffs. The wicked way in which many of you have been oftentimes involved in persecution, accompanied by circumstances making it the more bitter, is now well known; these crimes being hid from society under the shadow of a horrid night, those implacable people, with the haughty spirit which suggests impunity for a life of criminality, have pronounced, doubt ye not, your sentence, which is, with accustomed insensibility, as you have seen, on the point of execution.

Mexicans! My part is taken; the voice of revelation whispers to me that to me is entrusted the work of breaking the chains of your slavery, and that the Lord will enable me, with powerful arm, to fight against our enemies, in compliance with the requirements of that Sovereign Majesty, who, from this day forward, will hold us under His protection. On my part, I am ready to offer myself as a sacrifice for your happiness; and counting upon the means necessary for the discharge of my ministry, you may count upon my cooperation, should no cowardly attempt put an end to my days. This undertaking will be sustained on the following bases:

First: A society is organized in the State of Texas, which devotes itself sleeplessly until the work is crowned with success, to the improvement of the unhappy condition of those Mexicans resident therein; exterminating their tyrants, to which end those which compose it are ready to shed their blood and suffer the death of martyrs.

Second: As this society contains within itself the elements necessary to accomplish the great end of its labors, the veil of impenetrable secrecy covers "The Great Book" in which the articles of its constitution are written; while so delicate are the difficulties which must be overcome that no honorable man can have cause for alarm, if imperious exigencies require them to act without reserve.

Third: The Mexicans of Texas repose their lot under the good sentiments of the governor elect of the state, General Houston, and trust that upon his elevation to power he will begin with care to give us legal protection within the limits of his powers.

Mexicans! Peace be with you! Good inhabitants of the State of Texas, look on them as brothers, and keep in mind that which the Holy Spirit saith: "Though shalt not be the friend of the passionate man; nor join thyself to the madman, lest thou learn his mode of work and scandalize thy soul."

## Solomon Northrup, Slave Auction, 1853

*In this passage, Solomon Northup, a free Northern black who was kidnapped and held as a slave for twelve years, provides an eyewitness account of a slave auction held in 1841.*

*Source:* Herbert Aptheker, *A Documentary History of the Negro People in the United States* (1951; reprint, New York: Citadel Press 1969, pp. 206–208, © 1951 by Herbert Aptheker; Solomon Northup, *Twelve Years a Slave* (Auburn, Buffalo, London, 1853).

In the first place we were required to wash thoroughly, and those with beards to shave. We were then furnished with a new suit each, cheap, but clean. The men had hat, coat, shirt, pants and shoes; the women frocks of calico, and handkerchief to bind about their heads. We were now conducted into a a large room in the front part of the building to which the yard was attached, in order to be properly trained, before the admission of customers. The men were arranged on one side of the room, the women at the other. The tallest was placed at the head of the row, then the next tallest, and so on in the order of their respective heights. Emily was at the foot of the line of women. Freeman [Theophilus Freeman, owner of the slave-pen] charged us to remember our places; exhorted us to appear smart and lively,—sometimes threatening, and again, holding out various inducements. During the day he exercised us in the art of "looking smart," and of moving to our places with exact precision.

After being fed, in the afternoon, we were again paraded and made to dance. Bob, a colored boy, who had some time belonged to Freeman, played on the violin. Standing near him, I made bold to inquire if he could play the "Virginia Reel." He answered he could not, and asked me if I could play. Replying in the affirmative, he handed me the violin. I struck up a tune, and finished it. Freeman ordered me to continue playing, and seemed well pleased, telling Bob that I far excelled him—a remark that seemed to grieve my musical companion very much.

Next day many customers called to examine Freeman's "new lot." The latter gentleman was very loquacious, dwelling at much length upon our several good points and qualities. He would make us hold up our heads, walk briskly back and forth, while customers would feel of our hands and arms and bodies, turn us about, ask us what we could do, make us open our mouths and show our teeth, precisely as a jockey examines a horse which he is about to barter for or purchase. Sometimes a man or woman was taken back to the small house in the yard, stripped, and inspected more minutely. Scars upon a slave's back were considered evidence of a rebellious or unruly spirit, and hurt his sale.

An old gentleman, who said he wanted a coachman, appeared to take a fancy to me. From his conversation with Burch [Freeman's business associate], I learned he was a resident in the city. I very much desired that he would buy me, because I conceived it would not be difficult to make my escape from New Orleans on some northern vessel. Freeman asked him fifteen hundred dollars for me. The old gentleman insisted it was too much as times were very hard. Freeman, however, declared that I was sound of health, of a good constitution, and intelligent. He made it a point to enlarge upon my musical attainments. The old gentleman argued quite adroitly that there was nothing extraordinary about the Negro, and finally, to my regret, went out, saying he would call again. During the day, however, a number of sales were made. David and Caroline were purchased together by a Natchez planter. They left us, grinning broadly, and in a most happy state of mind, caused by the fact of their not being separated. Sethe was sold to a planter of Baton Rouge, her eyes flashing with anger as she was led away.

The same man also purchased Rand-all. The little fellow was made to jump, and run across the floor, and perform many other feats, exhibiting his activity and condition. All the time the trade was going on, Eliza was crying aloud, and wringing her hands. She besought the man not to buy him, unless he also bought herself and Emily. She promised, in that case, to be the most faithful slave that ever lived. The man answered that he could not afford it, and then Eliza burst into a paroxysm of grief, weeping plaintively. Freeman turned round to her, savagely, with his whip in his uplifted hand, ordering her to stop her noise, or he would flog her. He would not have such work—such snivelling; and unless she ceased that minute, he would take her to the yard and give her a hundred lashes. Yes, he would take the nonsense out of her pretty quick—if he didn't, might he be d——d. Eliza shrunk before him, and tried to wipe away her tears, but it was all in vain. She wanted to be with her children, she said, the little time she had to live. All the frowns and threats of Freeman, could not wholly silence the afflicted mother. She kept on begging and beseeching them, most piteously, not to separate the three. Over and over again she told them how she loved her boy. A great many times she repeated her former promises—how very faithful and obedient she would be; how hard she would labor day and night, to the last moment of her life, if he would only buy them all together. But it was of no avail; the man could not afford it. The bargain was agreed upon, and Randall must go alone. Then Eliza ran to him; embraced him passionately; kissed him again and again; told him to remember her—all the while her tears falling in the boy's face like rain.

Freeman damned her, calling her a blubbering, bawling wench, and ordered her to go to her place, and behave herself, and be somebody. He swore he wouldn't stand such stuff but a little longer. He would soon give her something to cry about, if she was not mighty careful, and *that* she might depend upon.

The planter from Baton Rouge, with his new purchase, was ready to depart.

"Don't cry, mama. I will be a good boy. Don't cry," said Randall, looking back, as they passed out of the door.

What has become of the lad, God knows. It was a mournful scene indeed. I would have cried myself if I had dared.

## Harriet Jacobs, A Slave's Account, 1861

*Harriet Jacobs's harrowing account of her life under slavery and her eventual escape was published in 1861 with the assistance of Lydia Maria Child. In this section from her narrative, Jacobs discusses the ubiquitous peril that slave women faced—the possibility of sexual assault.*

Source: Harriet A. Jacobs. *Incidents in the Life of a Slave Girl: Written By Herself* (1861; reprint, Cambridge: Harvard University Press, 1987), pp. 27–30.

## THE TRIALS OF GIRLHOOD

During the first years of my service in Dr. Flint's family, I was accustomed to share some indulgences with the chil-
dren of my mistress. Though this seemed to me no more than right, I was grateful for it, and tried to merit the kindness by the faithful discharge of my duties. But I now entered on my fifteenth year—a sad epoch in the life of a slave girl. My master began to whisper foul words in my ear. Young as I was, I could not remain ignorant of their import. I tried to treat them with indifference or contempt. The master's age, my extreme youth, and the fear that his conduct would be reported to my grandmother, made him bear this treatment for many months. He was a crafty man, and resorted to many means to accomplish his purposes. Sometimes he had stormy, terrific ways, that made his victims tremble; sometimes he assumed a gentleness that he thought must surely subdue. Of the two, I preferred his stormy moods, although they left me trembling. He tried his utmost to corrupt the pure principles my grandmother had instilled. He peopled my young mind with unclean images, such as only a vile monster could think of. I turned from him with disgust and hatred. But he was my master. I was compelled to live under the same roof with him—where I saw a man forty years my senior daily violating the most sacred commandments of nature. He told me I was his property; that I must be subject to his will in all things. My soul revolted against the mean tyranny. But where could I turn for protection? No matter whether the slave girl be as black as ebony or as fair as her mistress. In either case, there is no shadow of law to protect her from insult, from violence, or even from death; all these are inflicted by fiends who bear

the shape of men. The mistress, who ought to protect the helpless victim, has no other feelings towards her but those of jealousy and rage. The degradation, the wrongs, the vices, that grow out of slavery, are more than I can describe. They are greater than you would willingly believe. Surely, if you credited one half the truths that are told you concerning the helpless millions suffering in this cruel bondage, you at the north would not help to tighten the yoke. You surely would refuse to do for the master, on your own soil, the mean and cruel work which trained bloodhounds and the lowest class of whites do for him at the south.

Every where the years bring to all enough of sin and sorrow; but in slavery the very dawn of life is darkened by these shadows. Even the little child, who is accustomed to wait on her mistress and her children, will learn, before she is twelve years old, why it is that her mistress hates such and such a one among the slaves. Perhaps the child's own mother is among those hated ones. She listens to violent outbreaks of jealous passion, and cannot help understanding what is the cause. She will become prematurely knowing in evil things. Soon she will learn to tremble when she hears her master's footfall. She will be compelled to realize that she is no longer a child. If God has bestowed beauty upon her, it will prove her greatest curse. That which commands admiration in the white woman only hastens the degradation of the female slave. I know that some are too much brutalized by slavery to feel the humiliation of their position; but many slaves feel it most acutely, and

shrink from the memory of it. I cannot tell how much I suffered in the presence of these wrongs, nor how I am still pained by the retrospect. My master met me at every turn, reminding me that I belonged to him, and swearing by heaven and earth that he would compel me to submit to him. If I went out for a breath of fresh air, after a day of unwearied toil, his footsteps dogged me. If I knelt by my mother's grave, his dark shadow fell on me even there. The light heart which nature had given me became heavy with sad forebodings. The other slaves in my master's house noticed the change. May of them pitied me; but none dared to ask the cause. They had no need to inquire. They knew too well the guilty practices under that roof; and they were aware that to speak of them was an offence that never went unpunished.

I longed for some one to confide in. I would have given the world to have laid my head on my grandmother's faithful bosom, and told her all my troubles. But Dr. Flint swore he would kill me, if I was not as silent as the grave. Then, although my grandmother was all in all to me, I feared her as well as loved her. I had been accustomed to look up to her with a respect bordering upon awe. I was very young, and felt shamefaced about telling her such impure things, especially as I knew her to be very strict on such subjects. Moreover, she was a woman of a high spirit. She was usually very quiet in her demeanor; but if her indignation was once roused, it was not very easily quelled. I had been told that she once chased a white gentleman with a loaded pistol, because he insulted one of her daughters. I dreaded the consequences of a violent outbreak; and both pride and fear kept me silent. But though I did not confide in my grandmother, and even evaded her vigilant watchfulness and inquiry, her presence in the neighborhood was some protection to me. Though she had been a slave, Dr. Flint was afraid of her. He dreaded her scorching rebukes. Moreover, she was known and patronized by many people; and he did not wish to have his villainy made public. It was lucky for me that I did not live on a distant plantation, but in a town not so large that the inhabitants were ignorant of each other's affairs. Bad as are the laws and customs in a slaveholding community, the doctor, as a professional man, deemed it prudent to keep up some outward show of decency.

O, what days and nights of fear and sorrow that man caused me! Reader, it is not to awaken sympathy for myself that I am telling you truthfully what I suffered in slavery. I do it to kindle a flame of compassion in your hearts for my sisters who are still in bondage, suffering as I once suffered.

I once saw two beautiful children playing together. One was a fair white child; the other was her slave, and also her sister. When I saw them embracing each other, and heard their joyous laughter, I turned sadly away from the lovely sight. I foresaw the inevitable blight that would fall on the little slave's heart. I knew how soon her laughter would be changed to sighs. The fair child grew up to be a still fairer woman. From childhood to womanhood her pathway was blooming with flowers, and overarched by a sunny sky. Scarcely one day of her life had been clouded when the sun rose on her happy bridal morning.

How had those years dealt with her slave sister, the little playmate of her childhood? She, also, was very beautiful; but the flowers and sunshine of love were not for her. She drank the cup of sin, and shame, and misery, whereof her persecuted race are compelled to drink.

In view of these things, why are ye silent, ye free men and women of the north? Why do your tongues falter in maintenance of the right? Would that I had more ability! But my heart is so full, and my pen is so weak! There are noble men and women who plead for us, striving to help those who cannot help themselves. God bless them! God give them strength and courage to go on! God bless those, every where, who are laboring to advance the cause of humanity!

## From James Henry Gooding to Abraham Lincoln, September 28, 1863

*James Henry Gooding, a black soldier in the 54th Massachusetts Regiment, wrote this letter to President Lincoln protesting pay inequities for black soldiers in the Union army. Though his regiment was eventually awarded their back pay, Gooding had by that point been wounded and taken prisoner. He died in the infamous prisoner-of-war camp in Andersonville, Georgia, in July 1864.*

Source: Herbert Aptheker, *A Documentary History of the Negro People in the United States* (1951; reprint, New York: Citadel Press, 1969, pp. 482–484; © 1951 by Herbert Aptheker.

*Your Excellency, Abraham Lincoln:*

Your Excellency will pardon the presumption of an humble individual like myself, in addressing you, but the earnest solicitation of my comrades in arms besides the genuine interest felt by myself in the matter is my excuse, for placing before the Executive head of the Nation our Common Grievance.

On the 6th of the last Month, the Paymaster of the Department informed us, that if we would decide to receive the sum of $10 (ten dollars) per month, he would come and pay us that sum, but that, on the sitting of Congress, the Regt. would, in his opinion, be allowed the other 3 (three). He did not give us any guarantee that this would be, as he hoped; certainly he had no authority for making any such guarantee, and we cannot suppose him acting in any way interested.

Now the main question is, are we Soldiers, or are we Laborers? We are fully armed, and equipped, have done all the various duties pertaining to a Soldier's life, have conducted ourselves to the complete satisfaction of General Officers, who were, if anything, prejudiced against us, but who now accord us all the encouragement and honors due us; have shared the perils and labor of reducing the first strong-hold that flaunted a Traitor Flag; and more, Mr. President, to-day the Anglo-Saxon Mother, Wife, or Sister are not alone in tears for departed Sons, Husbands and Brothers. The patient, trusting descendant of Afric's Clime have dyed the ground with blood, in defence of the Union, and Democracy. Men, too, your Excellency, who know in a measure the cruelties of the iron heel of oppression, which in years gone by, the very power their blood is now being spilled to maintain, ever ground them in the dust.

But when the war trumpet sounded o'er the land, when men knew not the Friend from the Traitor, the Black man laid his life at the altar of the Nation,— and he was refused. When the arms of the Union were beaten, in the first year of the war, and the Executive called for more food for its venous maw, again the black man begged the privilege of aiding his country in her need, to be again refused.

And now he is in the War, and how has he conducted himself? Let their dusky forms rise up, out of the mires of James Island, and give the answer. Let the rich mould around Wagner's parapets be upturned, and there will be found an eloquent answer. Obedient and patient and solid as a wall are they. All we lack is a paler hue and a better acquaintance with the alphabet.

Now your Excellency, we have done a Soldier's duty. Why can't we have a Soldier's pay? You caution the Rebel chieftain, that the United States knows no distinction in her soldiers. She insists on having all her soldiers of whatever creed or color, to be treated according to the usages of War. . . . Now if the United States exacts uniformity of treatment of her soldiers from the insurgents, would it not be well and consistent to set the example herself by paying all her soldiers alike?

We of this Regt. were not enlisted under any "contraband" act. But we do not wish to be understood as rating our service of more value to the Government than the service of the ex-slave. Their service is undoubtedly worth much to the Nation, but Congress made express provision touching their case, as slaves freed by military necessity, and assuming the Government to be their temporary Guardian. Not so with us. Freemen by birth and consequently having the advantage of thinking and acting for ourselves so far as the Laws would allow us, we do not consider ourselves fit subjects for the Contraband act.

We appeal to you, Sir, as the Executive of the Nation, to have us justly dealt with. The Regt. do pray that they be assured their service will be fairly appreciated by paying them as American Soldiers, not as menial hirelings. Black men, you may well know, are poor; three dollars per month for a year, will supply their needy wives and little ones with fuel. If you as Chief Magistrate of the Nation, will assure us of our whole pay, we are content. Our Patriotism, our enthusiasm will have a new impetus, to exert our energy more and more to aid our Country. Not that our hearts ever flagged in devotion, spite the evident apathy displayed in our behalf, but we feel as though our Country spurned us, now we are sworn to serve her. Please give this a moment's attention.

## Letter from Hannah Johnson to Abraham Lincoln, July 31, 1863

*Hannah Johnson, whose son is in the 54th Massachusetts Regiment, urges President Lincoln in this letter to retaliate if Confederates sell captured black soldiers into slavery. The day before her letter was written, Lincoln had* *made just such a threat, though he did not carry through with it.*

*Source:* Ira Berlin and Leslie Rowland, eds., *Families and Freedom: A Documentary History of African-American Kinship in the Civil War Era* (New York: New Press, 1997), pp. 81–82; © 1997 by Ira Berlin and Leslie S. Rowland.

BUFFALO [N.Y.] JULY 31 1863

*Excellent Sir*

My good friend says I must write to you and she will send it My son went in the 54th regiment. I am a colored woman and my son was strong and able as any to fight for his country and the colored people have as much to fight for as any. My father was a Slave and escaped from Louisiana before I was born morn forty years agone I have but poor edication but I never went to schol, but I know just as well as any what is right between man and man. Now I know it is right that a colored man should go and fight for his country, and so ought to a white man. I know that a colored man ought to run no greater risques than a white, his pay is no greater his obligation to fight is the same. So why should not our enemies be compelled to treat him the same, Made to do it.

My son fought at Fort Wagoner but thank God he was not taken prisoner, as many were I thought of this thing before I let my boy go but then they said Mr. Lincoln will never let them sell our colored soldiers for slaves, if they do he will get them back quck he will rettallyate and stop it. Now Mr Lincoln dont you think you oght to stop this thing and make them do the same by the colored men they have lived in idleness all their lives on stolen labor and made savages of the colored people, but they now are so furious because they are proving themselves to be men, such as have come away and got some edication. It must not be so. You must put the rebels to work in State prisons to making shoes and things, if they sell our colored soldiers, till they let them all go. And give their wounded the same treatment. it would seem cruel, but their no other way, and a just man must do hard things sometimes, that shew him to be a great man. They tell me some do you will take back the Proclamation, don't do it. When you are dead and in Heaven, in a thousand years that action of yours will make the Angels sing your praises I know it. Ought one man to own another, law for or not, who made the law, surely the poor slave did not. so it is wicked, and a horrible Outrage, there is no sense in it, because a man has lived by robbing all his life and his father before him, should he complain because the stolen things found on him are taken. Robbing the colored people of their labor is but a small part of the robbery their souls are almost taken, they are made bruits of often. You know all about this.

Will you see that the colored men fighting now, are fairly treated. You ought to do this, and do it at once, Not let the thing run along meet it quickly and manfully, and stop this, mean cowardly cruelty. We poor oppressed ones, appeal to you, and ask fair play.

Yours for Christs sake
Hannah Johnson

## Black Code of St. Landry's Parish, Louisiana, 1865

*Soon after the Civil War ended, "black codes" were passed throughout the South in an effort to return African Americans to a state as close to enslavement as possible. This set of codes from St. Landry's parish in Louisiana was typical in its strict policing of African Americans' activity and the severe repercussions it inscribed for minor offenses.*

*Source:* Frederick Binder and David Reimers, eds., *The Way We Lived: Essays and Documents in American Social History*, vol 1, *1492–1877*, 4th ed. (Boston: Houghton Mifflin, 2000), pp. 302–304; from U.S. Congress, Senate Executive Document No. 2 (Washington, D.C., 1865).

Whereas it was formerly made the duty of the police jury to make suitable regulations for the police of slaves within the limits of the parish; and whereas slaves have become emancipated by the action of the ruling powers; and whereas it is necessary for public order, as well as for the comfort and correct deportment of said freedmen, that suitable regulations should be established by their government in the changed condition, the following ordinances are adopted, with the approval of the United States military authorities commanding in said parish, viz:

Section 1. *Be it ordained by the police jury of the parish of St. Landry*, That no negro shall be allowed to pass within the limits of said parish without a special permit in writing from his employer. Whoever shall violate this provision shall pay a fine of two dollars and fifty cents, or in default thereof shall be forced to work four days on the public road, or suffer corporeal punishment as provided hereinafter.

Section 2. *Be it further ordained*, That every negro who shall be found absent from the residence of his employer after 10 o'clock at night, without a written permit from his employer, shall pay a fine of five dollars, or in default thereof, shall be compelled to work five days on the public road, or suffer corporeal punishment as hereinafter provided.

Section 3. *Be it further ordained*, That no negro shall be permitted to rent or keep a house within said parish. Any negro violating this provision shall be immediately ejected and compelled to find an employer; and any person who shall rent, or give the use of any house to any negro, in violation of this section, shall pay a fine of five dollars for each offence.

Section 4. *Be it further ordained*, That every negro is required to be in the regular service of some white person, or former owner, who shall be held responsible for the conduct of said negro. But said employer or former owner may permit said negro to hire his own time by special permission in writing, which permission shall not extend over seven days at any one time. Any negro violating the provisions of this section shall be fined five dollars for each offence, or in default of the payment thereof shall be forced to work five days on the public road, or suffer corporeal punishment as hereinafter provided.

Section 5. *Be it further ordained*, That no public meetings or congregations of negroes shall be allowed within said parish after sunset; but such public meetings and congregations may be held between the hours of sunrise and sunset, by the special permission of writing of the captain of patrol, within whose beat such meetings shall take place. This prohibition, however, is not intended to prevent negroes from attending the usual church services, conducted by white ministers and priests. Every negro violating the provisions of this section shall pay a fine of five dollars, or in default thereof shall be compelled to work five days on the public road, or suffer corporeal punishment as hereinafter provided.

Section 6. *Be it further ordained*, That no negro shall be permitted to preach, exhort, or otherwise declaim to congregations of colored people, without a special permission in writing from the president of the police jury. Any negro violating the provisions of this section shall pay a fine of ten dollars, or in default thereof shall be forced to work ten days on the public road, or suffer corporeal punishment as hereinafter provided.

Section 7. *Be it further ordained*, That no negro who is not in the military service shall be allowed to carry fire-arms, or any kind of weapons, within the parish, without the special written permission of his employers, approved and indorsed by the nearest or most convenient chief of patrol. Any one violating the provisions of this section shall forfeit his weapons and pay a fine of five dollars, or in default of the payment of said fine, shall be forced to work five days on the public road, or suffer corporeal punishment as hereinafter provided.

Section 8. *Be it further ordained*, That no negro shall sell, barter, or exchange any articles of merchandise or traffic within said parish without the special written permission of his employer, specifying the articles of sale, barter or traffic. Any one thus offending shall pay a fine of one dollar for each offence, and suffer the forfeiture of said articles, or in default of the payment of said fine shall work one day on the public road, or suffer corporeal punishment as hereinafter provided.

Section 9. *Be it further ordained*, That any negro found drunk within the said parish shall pay a fine of five dollars, or in default thereof shall work five days on the public road, or suffer corporeal punishment as hereinafter provided.

Section 10. *Be it further ordained*, That all the foregoing provisions shall apply to negroes of both sexes.

Section 11. *Be it further ordained*, That it shall be the duty of every citizen to act as a police officer for the detection of offences and the apprehension of offenders, who shall be immediately handed over to the proper captain or chief of patrol.

Section 12. *Be it further ordained*, That the aforesaid penalties shall be summarily enforced, and that it shall be the duty of the captains and chiefs of patrol to see that the aforesaid ordinances are promptly executed.

Section 13. *Be it further ordained*, That all sums collected from the aforesaid fines shall be immediately handed over to the parish treasurer.

Section 14. *Be it further ordained*, That the corporeal punishment provided for in the foregoing sections shall consist in confining the body of the offender within a barrel placed over his or her shoulders, in the manner practiced in the army, such confinement not to continue longer than twelve hours, and for such time within the aforesaid limit as shall be fixed by the captain or chief of patrol who inflicts the penalty.

Section 15. *Be it further ordained*, That these ordinances shall not interfere with any municipal or military regulations inconsistent with them within the limits of said parish.

Section 16. *Be it further ordained*, That these ordinances shall take effect five days after their publication in the *Opelousas Courier*.

## From Jourdon Anderson to Colonel P. H. Anderson, August 7, 1865

*In this letter, the newly freed Jourdon Anderson attacks with biting humor his former owner's request that he return to work. While some formerly enslaved people continued to work on the plantations they had worked throughout their lives, others, like Anderson, recognized that freedom lay in getting as far away from the site of their previous bondage as possible.*

Source: Lydia Maria Child, *The Freedmen's Book* (1865; reprint, New York: Arno Press, 1968), pp. 265–267; © 1968 by Arno Press, Inc.

DAYTON, OHIO, AUGUST 7, 1865

*To my old Master, Colonel P. H. Anderson, Big Spring, Tennessee.*

Sir: I got your letter, and was glad to find that you had not forgotten Jourdon, and that you wanted me to come back and live with you again, promising to do better for me than anybody else can. I have often felt uneasy about you. I thought the Yankees would have hung you long before this, for harboring Rebs they found at your house. I suppose they never heard about your going to Colonel Martin's to kill the Union soldier that was left by his company in their stable. Although you shot at me twice before I left you, I did not want to hear of your being hurt, and am glad you are still living. It would do me good to go back to the dear old home again, and see Miss Mary and Miss Martha and Allen, Esther, Green, and Lee. Give my love to them all, and tell them I hope we will meet in the better world, if not in this. I would have gone back to see you all when I was working in the Nashville Hospital, but one of the neighbors told me that Henry intended to shoot me if he ever got a chance.

I want to know particularly what the good chance is you propose to give me. I am doing tolerably well here. I get twenty-five dollars a month, with victuals and clothing; have a comfortable home for Mandy,—the folks call her Mrs. Anderson,—and the children— Milly, Jane, and Grundy—go to school and are learning well. The teacher says Grundy has a head for a preacher. They go to Sunday school, and Mandy and me attend church regularly. We are kindly treated. Sometimes we overhear others saying, "Them colored people were slaves" down in Tennessee. The children feel hurt when they hear such remarks;

but I tell them it was no disgrace in Tennessee to belong to Colonel Anderson. Many darkeys would have been proud, as I used to be, to call you master. Now if you will write and say what wages you will give me, I will be better able to decide whether it would be to my advantage to move back again.

As to my freedom, which you say I can have, there is nothing to be gained on that score, as I got my free papers in 1864 from the Provost-Marshal-General of the Department of Nashville. Mandy says she would be afraid to go back without some proof that you were disposed to treat us justly and kindly; and we have concluded to test your sincerity by asking you to send us our wages for the time we served you. This will make us forget and forgive old scores, and rely on your justice and friendship in the future. I served you faithfully for thirty-two years, and Mandy twenty years. At twenty-five dollars a month for me, and two dollars a week for Mandy, our earnings would amount to eleven thousand six hundred and eighty dollars. Add to this the interest for the time our wages have been kept back, and deduct what you paid for our clothing, and three doctor's visits to me, and pulling a tooth for Mandy, and the balance will show what we are in justice entitled to. Please send the money by Adams's Express, in care of V. Winters, Esq., Dayton, Ohio. If you fail to pay us for faithful labors in the past, we can have little faith in your promises in the future. We trust the good Maker has opened your eyes to the wrongs which you and your fathers have done to me and my fathers, in making us toil for you for generations without recompense. Here I draw my wages every Saturday night; but in Tennessee there was never any pay-day for the negroes any more than for the horses and cows. Surely there will be a day of reckoning for those who defraud the laborer of his hire.

In answering this letter, please state if there would be any safety for my Milly and Jane, who are now grown up, and both good-looking girls. You know how it was with poor Matilda and Catherine. I would rather stay here and starve—and die, if it come to that—than have my girls brought to shame by the violence and wickedness of their young masters. You will also please state if there has been any schools opened for the colored children in your neighborhood. The great desire of my life now is to give my children an education, and have them form virtuous habits.

Say howdy to George Carter, and thank him for taking the pistol from you when you were shooting at me.

*From your old servant,*
*Jourdon Anderson.*

## Elias Hill, Testimony Before the Congressional Committee Investigating the Ku Klux Klan, 1871

*Despite the best efforts of Union Leagues and of Reconstruction governments in Southern states, blacks who sought to exercise economic or political power faced increasing threats to their safety. In this document, Elias Hill testifies during congressional hearings about Klan violence.*

Source: Michael P. Johnson, *Reading the American Past: Selected Historical Documents*, vol. 1, to 1877 (Boston: Bedford Books, 1998), pp. 262–265; U.S. Congress, Report of the Joint Select Committee to Inquire into the Condition of Affairs in the Late Insurrectionary States (Washington, D.C., 1872), 1:44–46.

[The committee included a brief description of Hill.] Elias Hill is a remarkable character. He is crippled in both legs and arms, which are shriveled by rheumatism; he cannot walk, cannot help himself, has to be fed and cared for personally by others; was in early life a slave, whose freedom was purchased, his father buying his mother and getting Elias along with her, as a burden of which his master was glad to be rid. Stricken at seven years old with disease, he never was afterward able to walk, and he presents the appearance of a dwarf with the limbs of a child, the body of a man, and a finely developed intellectual head. He learned his letters and to read by calling the school children into the cabin as they passed, and also learned to write. He became a Baptist preacher, and after the war engaged in teaching colored children, and conducted the business correspondence of many of his colored neighbors. He is a man of blameless character, of unusual intelligence, speaks good English, and we put the story of his wrongs in his own language:

On the night of the 5th of last May, after I had heard a great deal of what they had done in that neighborhood, they came. It was between 12 and 1 o'clock at night when I was awakened and heard the dogs barking, and something walking, very much like horses. As I had often laid awake listening for such persons,

for they had been all through the neighborhood, and disturbed all men and
many women, I supposed that it was
them. They came in a very rapid manner, and I could hardly tell whether it
was the sound of horses or men. At last
they came to my brother's door, which
is in the same yard, and broke open the
door and attacked his wife, and I heard
her screaming and mourning. I could not
understand what they said, for they were
talking in an outlandish and unnatural
tone, which I had heard they generally
used at a negro's house. I heard them
knocking around in her house. I was lying in my little cabin in the yard. At last
I heard them have her in the yard. She
was crying and the Ku-Klux were whipping her to make her tell where I lived.
I heard her say, "Yon is his house." She
has told me since that they first asked
who had taken me out of her house.
They said, "Where's Elias?" She said, "He
doesn't stay here; yon is his house."
They were then in the yard, and I had
heard them strike her five or six licks
when I heard her say this. Some one then
hit my door. It flew open. One ran in
the house, and stopping about the middle of the house, which is a small cabin,
he turned around, as it seemed to me as
I lay there awake, and said, "Who's
here?" Then I knew they would take me,
and I answered, "I am here." He shouted
for joy, as it seemed, "Here he is! Here
he is! We have found him!" and he threw
the bedclothes off of me and caught me
by one arm, while another man took me
by the other and they carried me into
the yard between the houses, my
brother's and mine, and put me on the
ground beside a boy. The first thing they

asked me was, "Who did that burning?
Who burned our houses?"—gin-houses,
dwelling houses and such. Some had
been burned in the neighborhood. I told
them it was not me; I could not burn
houses; it was unreasonable to ask me.
Then they hit me with their fists, and
said I did it, I ordered it. They went on
asking me didn't I tell the black men to
ravish all the white women. No, I answered them, They struck me again with
their fists on my breast, and then they
went on, "When did you hold a night-
meeting of the Union League, and who
were the officers? Who was the president?" I told them I had been the president, but that there had been no Union
League meeting held at that place where
they were formerly held since away in
the fall. This was the 5th of May. They
said that Jim Raney, that was hung, had
been at my house since the time I had
said the League was last held, and that
he had made a speech. I told them that
he had not, because I did not know the
man. I said, "Upon honor." They said I
had no honor, and hit me again. They
went on asking me hadn't I been writing
to Mr. A. S. Wallace, in Congress, to
get letters from him. I told them I had.
They asked what I had been writing
about? I told them, "Only tidings." They
said, with an oath, "I know the tidings
were d—d good, and you were writing
something about the Ku-Klux, and haven't you been preaching and praying
about the Ku-Klux?" One asked, "Haven't you been preaching political sermons?" Generally, one asked me all the
questions, but the rest were squatting
over me—some six men I counted as I
lay there, Said one, "Didn't you preach

against the Ku-Klux," and wasn't that what Mr. Wallace was writing to me about? "Not at all," I said. "Let me see the letter," said he; "what was it about?" I said it was on the times. They wanted the letter. I told them if they would take me back into the house, and lay me in the bed, which was close adjoining my books and papers, I would try and get it. They said I would never go back to that bed, for they were going to kill me. "Never expect to go back; tell us where the letters are." I told them they were on the shelf somewhere, and I hoped they would not kill me. Two of them went into the house. . . . They staid in there a good while hunting about and then came out and asked me for a lamp. I told them there was a lamp some-where. They said "Where?" I was so con-fused I said I could not tell exactly. They caught my leg—you see what it is—and pulled me over the yard, and then left me there, knowing I could not walk nor crawl, and all six went into the house. I was chilled with the cold lying in the yard at that time of night, for it was near 1 o'clock, and they had talked and beat me and so on until half an hour had passed since they first approached. After they had staid in the house for a consid-erable time, they came back to where I lay and asked if I wasn't afraid at all. They pointed pistols at me all around my head once or twice, as if they were going to shoot me, telling me they were going to kill me; wasn't I ready to die, and willing to die? Didn't I preach? That they came to kill me—all the time pointing pistols at me. This second time they came out of the house, after plundering the house, searching for letters, they

came at me with these pistols, and asked if I was ready to die. I told them that I was not exactly ready; that I would rather live; that I hoped they would not kill me that time. They said they would; I had better prepare. One caught me by the leg and hurt me, for my leg for forty years has been drawn each year, more and more year by year, and I made moan when it hurt so. One said "G—d d—n it, hush!" He had a horsewhip, and he told me to pull up my shirt, and he hit me. He told me at every lick, "Hold up your shirt." I made a moan every time he cut with the horsewhip. I reckon he struck me eight cuts right on the hip bone; it was almost the only place he could hit my body, my legs are so short—all my limbs. drawn up and withered away with pain. I saw one of them standing over me or by me motion to them to quit. They all had disguises on. I then thought they would not kill me. One of them then took a strap, and buckled it around my neck and said, "Let's take him to the river and drown him." . . . After pulling the strap around my neck, he took it off and gave me a lick on my hip where he had struck me with the horsewhip. One of them said, "Now, you see, I've burned up the d—d letter of Wallace's and all," and he brought out a little book and says, "What's this for?" I told him I did not know; to let me see with a light and I could read it. They brought a lamp and I read it. It was a book in which I had keep an account of the school. I had been licensed to keep a school. I read them some of the names. He said that would do, and asked if I had been paid for those scholars I had put down. I said no. He said I would now have to die. I was somewhat afraid, but one said not to kill me. They said "Look here! Will you put a card in the paper next week like June Moore and Sol Hill?" They had been prevailed on to put a card in the paper to renounce all republicanism and never vote. I said, "If I had the money to pay the expense, I could." They said I could borrow, and gave me another lick. They asked me, "Will you quit preaching?" I told them I did not know. I said that to save my life. They said I must stop that republican paper that was coming to Clay Hill. It has been only a few weeks since it stopped. The republican weekly paper was then coming to me from Charleston. It came to my name. They said I must stop it, quit preaching, and put a card in the newspaper renouncing republicanism, and they would not kill me; but if I did not they would come back the next week and kill me. With that one of them went into the house where my brother and my sister-in-law lived, and brought her to pick me up. As she stooped down to pick me up one of them struck her, and as she was carrying me into the house another struck her with a strap. She carried me into the house and laid me on the bed. Then they gathered around and told me to pray for them. I tried to pray. They said, "Don't you pray against Ku-Klux, but pray that God may forgive Ku-Klux. Don't pray against us. Pray that God may bless and save us." I was so chilled with cold lying out of doors so long and in such pain I could not speak to pray, but I tried to, and they said that would do very well, and all went out of the house.

## Little Bear, "The Sand Creek Massacre," 1864

*This account of the attack on Cheyenne seeking peace at Sand Creek, Colorado, in 1864 points to the fierceness of American efforts to confine Indians to reservations and especially to the brutality of certain American soldiers who saw all Indians—those seeking peace and those engaged in resistance—as foes.*

Source: Colin G. Calloway, ed., *Our Hearts Fell to the Ground: Plains Indian Views of How the West Was Lost* (Boston: Bedford/St. Martin's Press, 1996), pp. 104–105; George E. Hyde, *Life of George Bent: Written from His Letters*, © 1934 by the University of Oklahoma Press.

I got up before daylight to go out to where my brother-in-law Tomahawk had left our pony herd the evening before. He told me where he had left the ponies and said he did not think they would stray far from that place. As soon as I was dressed I went out of the lodge and crossed the creek; but as I was going up on the hill I saw Kingfisher running back toward the camp. He shouted to me that white men were driving off the herds. I looked toward the Fort Lyon Trail and saw a long line of little black objects to the south, moving toward the camp across the bare brown plain. There was some snow on the ground, but only in the hollows. I ran back to the camp as fast as I could, but soldiers had already come up on the other side of the creek and were firing in among the lodges. As I came into camp the people were running up the creek. As I passed Black Kettle's lodge I saw that he had a flag tied to the end of the pole and was standing there holding the pole. I ran to our lodge to get my bow, quiver, shield, and war bonnet. My father, Bear Tongue, had just recently given me these things. I was very young then and had just become a warrior.

By this time the soldiers were shooting into the camp from two sides, and as I put on my war bonnet and took up my shield and weapons, the bullets were hitting the lodge cover with heavy thumps like big hail-stones. When I went out again I ran behind the lodges, so that the troops could not get good shots at me. I jumped over the bank into the creek bed and found Big Head, Crow Neck, Cut-Lip-Bear, and Smoke standing there under the high bank. I joined these young men. The people were all running up the creek; the soldiers sat on their horses, lined up on both banks and firing into the camps, but they soon saw that the lodges were now nearly empty, so they began to advance up the creek, firing on the fleeing people. Our party was at the west end of the camps, not one hundred yards from the lodges. At this point the creek made a bend, coming from the north and turning toward the southeast just at the upper end of the village. As the soldiers began to advance, we ran across to the west side of the creek to get under another high bank over there, but just as we reached this bank another body of cavalry came up and opened fire on us. We hardly knew what way to turn, but Big Head and the rest soon decided to go on. They ran on toward the west, but passing over a hill they ran into another body of troops just

beyond and were surrounded and all killed.

After leaving the others, I started to run up the creek bed in the direction taken by most of the fleeing people, but I had not gone far when a party of about twenty cavalrymen got into the dry bed of the stream behind me. They chased me up the creek for about two miles, very close behind me and firing on me all the time. Nearly all the feathers were shot out of my war bonnet, and some balls passed through my shield; but I was not touched. I passed many women and children, dead and dying, lying in the creek bed. The soldiers had not scalped them yet, as they were busy chasing those that were yet alive. After the fight I came back down the creek and saw these dead bodies all cut up, and even the wounded scalped and slashed. I saw one old woman wandering about; her whole scalp had been taken off and the blood was running down into her eyes so that she could not see where to go.

I ran up the creek about two miles and came to the place where a large party of the people had taken refuge in holes dug in the sand up against the sides of the high banks. I stayed here until the soldiers withdrew. They were on both banks, firing down on us, but not many of us were killed. All who failed to reach these pits in the sand were shot down.

## Herrero, "The Navajo Long Walk," 1860s

*Punished for resisting enclosure on reservations, Navajos were forced to march across*

*New Mexico to Bosque Redondo. There they faced brutal conditions and deprivation, which Navajo leader Herrero discusses here.*

Source: Peter Nabokov, ed., *Native American Testimony: A Chronicle of Indian-White Relations from Prophecy to the Present, 1492–1992* (New York: Penguin Books, 1992), pp. 196–198.

If we had the wool we could make all the clothes for the tribe. All of us know how to cultivate by irrigation. There is plenty of land but somehow the crops do not come out well. Last year the worms destroyed the crops. There is plenty of land and when the ditches are all cut out there will be land enough. There is plenty of water. There is plenty of pasture for all our stock. Some have 25, 30, or 40 [sheep], but more have none. None have a hundred.

We try and keep our sheep for their milk, and only kill them when necessary, when the rations are short or smell bad. We depend on the milk of the sheep to live and to give to our little children. We are honest and do not kill each other's sheep. We own our animals ourselves, and not in common. . . .

Some officers at Fort Canby told us when we got here the government would give us herds of horses, sheep and cattle, and other things we needed, but we have not received them. We had to lose a good deal of our property on account of the war, and the Utahs stole the rest from us. We have been at war with the Utahs nine years, and about the same number of years with the Mexicans. Before the war with the Utahs and Mexicans we had everything we wanted, but now have lost everything. . . .

Some of the soldiers do not treat us well. When at work, if we stop a little they kick us or do something else, but generally they treat us well. We do not mind if an officer punishes us, but do not like to be treated badly by the soldiers. Our women sometimes come to the tents outside the fort and make contracts with the soldiers to stay with them for a night, and give them five dollars or something else. But in the morning they take away what they gave them and kick them off. This happens most every day. In the night they leave the fort and go to the Indian camps. The women are not forced, but consent willingly. A good many of the women have venereal disease. . . .

We would rather prefer to be in our own country, although we have lost everything we want here. We are all of this opinion and would like to have you send us back. And if you have any presents to give us we will distribute them among us. If we are sent back we promise never to commit an act of hostility. . . .

## Wooden Leg, The Battle Against Custer, 1876

*Though the famous battle against General Custer was uncharacteristic in its scale, Indian resistance to American incursions was not. In this account Cheyenne Wooden Leg describes his efforts to ready himself for battle and his response to American soldiers' efforts to escape.*

Source: Colin G. Calloway, ed., *Our Hearts Fell to the Ground: Plains Indian Views of How the West Was Lost* (Boston: Bedford/St. Martin's Press,

1996), pp. 137–140; Thomas B. Marquis, *Wooden Leg: A Warrior Who Fought Custer* (Minneapolis: Midwest, 1931).

In my sleep I dreamed that a great crowd of people were making lots of noise. Something in the noise startled me. I found myself wide awake, sitting up and listening. My brother too awakened, and we both jumped to our feet. A great commotion was going on among the camps. We heard shooting. We hurried out from the trees so we might see as well as hear. The shooting was somewhere at the upper part of the camp circles. It looked as if all of the Indians there were running away toward the hills to the westward or down toward our end of the village. Women were screaming and men were letting out war cries. Through it all we could hear old men calling:

"Soldiers are here! Young men, go out and fight them."

We ran to our camp and to our home lodge. Everybody there was excited. Women were hurriedly making up little packs for flight. Some were going off northward or across the river without any packs. Children were hunting for their mothers. Mothers were anxiously trying to find their children. I got my lariat and my six shooter. I hastened on down toward where had been our horse herd. I came across three of our herder boys. One of them was catching grasshoppers. The other two were cooking fish in the blaze of a little fire. I told them what was going on and asked them where were the horses. They jumped on their picketed ponies and dashed for the camp, without answering me. just then I heard Bald Eagle calling out to hurry with the horses. Two other boys were driving them toward the camp circle. I was utterly winded from the running. I never was much for running. I could walk all day, but I could not run fast nor far. I walked on back to the home lodge.

My father had caught my favorite horse from the herd brought in by the boys and Bald Eagle. I quickly emptied out my war bag and set myself at getting ready to go into battle. I jerked off my ordinary clothing. I jerked on a pair of new breeches that had been given to me by an Uncpapa Sioux. I had a good cloth shirt, and I put it on. My old moccasins were kicked off and a pair of beaded moccasins substituted for them. My father strapped a blanket upon my horse and arranged the rawhide lariat into a bridle. He stood holding my mount.

"Hurry," he urged me.

I was hurrying, but I was not yet ready. I got my paints and my little mirror. The blue-black circle soon appeared around my face. The red and yellow colorings were applied on all of the skin inside the circle. I combed my hair. It properly should have been oiled and braided neatly, but my father again was saying, "Hurry," so I just looped a buckskin thong about it and tied it close up against the back of my head, to float loose from there. My bullets, caps, and powder horn put me into full readiness. In a moment afterward I was on my horse and was going as fast as it could run toward where all of the rest of the young men were going. My brother already, had gone. He got his horse before I got mine, and his dressing was only a long buckskin shirt fringed with Crow Indian hair. The hair had been taken from a Crow at a past battle with them.

The air was so full of dust I could not see where to go. But it was not needful that I see that far. I kept my horse headed in the direction of movement by the crowd of Indians on horseback. I was led out around and far beyond the Uncpapa camp circle. Many hundreds of Indians on horseback were dashing to and fro in front of a body of soldiers. The soldiers were on the level valley ground and were shooting with rifles. Not many bullets were being sent back at them, but thousands of arrows were falling among them. I went on with a throng of Sioux until we got beyond and behind the white men. By this time, though, they had mounted their horses and were hiding themselves in the timber. A band of Indians were with the soldiers. It appeared they were Crows or Shoshones. Most of these Indians had fled back up the valley. Some were across east of the river and were riding away over the hills beyond.

Our Indians crowded down toward the timber where were the soldiers. More and more of our people kept coming. Almost all of them were Sioux. There were only a few Cheyennes. Arrows were showered into the timber. Bullets whistled out toward the Sioux and Cheyennes. But we stayed far back while we extended our curved line farther and farther around the big grove of trees. Some dead soldiers had been left among the grass and sagebrush where first they had fought us. It seemed to me the remainder of them would not live

many hours longer. Sioux were creeping forward to set fire to the timber.

Suddenly the hidden soldiers came tearing out on horseback, from the woods. I was around on that side where they came out. I whirled my horse and lashed it into a dash to escape from them. All others of my companions did the same. But soon we discovered they were not following us.

They were running away from us. They were going as fast as their tired horses could carry them across an open valley space and toward the river. We stopped, looked a moment, and then we whipped our ponies into swift pursuit. A great throng of Sioux also were coming after them. My distant position put me among the leaders in the chase. The soldier horses moved slowly, as if they were very tired. Ours were lively. We gained rapidly on them.

I fired four shots with my six shooter. I do not know whether or not any of my bullets did harm. I saw a Sioux put an arrow into the back of a soldier's head. Another arrow went into his shoulder. He tumbled from his horse to the ground. Others fell dead either from arrows or from stabbings or jabbings or from blows by the stone war clubs of the Sioux. Horses limped or staggered or sprawled out dead or dying. Our war cries and war songs were mingled with many jeering calls, such as:

"You are only boys. You ought not to be fighting. We whipped you on the Rosebud. You should have brought more Crows or Shoshones with you to do your fighting."

Little Bird and I were after one certain soldier. Little Bird was wearing a trailing warbonnet. He was at the right and I was at the left of the fleeing man. We were lashing him and his horse with our pony whips. It seemed not brave to shoot him. Besides. I did not want to waste my bullets. He pointed back his revolver, though, and sent a bullet into Little Bird's thigh. Immediately I whacked the white man fighter on his head with the heavy elk-horn handle of my pony whip. The blow dazed him. I seized the rifle strapped on his back. I wrenched it and dragged the looping strap over his head. As I was getting possession of this weapon he fell to the ground. I did not harm him further. I do not know what became of him. The jam of oncoming Indians swept me on. But I had now a good soldier rifle.

## Old Lady Horse, The Disappearance of the Buffalo, 1882

*Old Lady Horse describes the importance of the buffalo to Kiowa religious life, culture, and sustenance. Americans' slaughter of the buffalo herds they depended on resulted in the end of a way of life and the beginning of a struggle for cultural survival.*

*Source:* Colin G. Calloway, ed., *Our Hearts Fell to the Ground: Plains Indian Views of How the West Was Lost* (Boston: Bedford/St. Martin's Press, 1996), pp. 129–130; from Alice Marriot and Carol K. Rachlin, *American Indian Mythology* (New York: Crowell, 1968) © 1968 by Alice Marriot and Carol K. Rachlin, reprinted with permission of HarperCollins Publishers, Inc.

Everything the Kiowas had came from the buffalo. Their tipis were made of buffalo hides, so were their clothes and moccasins. They ate buffalo meat. Their containers were made of hide, or of bladders or stomachs. The buffalo were the life of the Kiowas.

Most of all, the buffalo was part of the Kiowa religion. A white buffalo calf must be sacrificed in the Sun Dance. The priests used parts of the buffalo to make their prayers when they healed people or when they sang to the powers above.

So, when the white men wanted to build railroads, or when they wanted to farm or raise cattle, the buffalo still protected the Kiowas. They tore up the railroad tracks and the gardens. They chased the cattle off the ranges. The buffalo loved their people as much as the Kiowas loved them.

There was war between the buffalo and the white men. The white men built forts in the Kiowa country, and the woolly-headed buffalo soldiers [the Tenth Cavalry, made up of Negro troops] shot the buffalo as fast as they could, but the buffalo kept coming on, coming on, even into the post cemetery at Fort Sill. Soldiers were not enough to hold them back.

Then the white men hired hunters to do nothing but kill the buffalo. Up and down the plains those men ranged, shooting sometimes as many as a hundred buffalo a day. Behind them came the skinners with their wagons. They piled the hides and bones into the wagons until they were full, and then took their loads to the new railroad stations that were being built, to be shipped east to the market. Sometimes there would be a pile of bones as high as a man, stretching a mile along the railroad track.

The buffalo saw that their day was over. They could protect their people no longer. Sadly, the last remnant of the great herd gathered in council, and decided what they would do.

The Kiowas were camped on the north side of Mount Scott, those of them who were still free to camp. One young woman got up very early in the morning. The dawn mist was still rising from Medicine Creek, and as she looked across the water, peering through the haze, she saw the last buffalo herd appear like a spirit dream.

Straight to Mount Scott the leader of the herd walked. Behind him came the cows and their calves, and the few young males who had survived. As the woman watched, the face of the mountain opened.

Inside Mount Scott the world was green and fresh, as it had been when she was a small girl. The rivers ran clear, not red. The wild plums were in blossom, chasing the red buds up the inside slopes. Into this world of beauty the buffalo walked, never to be seen again.

# CHAPTER 5
# RACE, NATION, AND CITIZENSHIP IN LATE NINETEENTH-CENTURY AMERICA, 1878–1900

## MAE M. NGAI

IN THE SUMMER OF 1893 THE World's Columbian Exposition was held in Chicago, celebrating the four hundredth anniversary of Columbus's arrival in the New World. It was a huge exposition, with gleaming neoclassical buildings that housed triumphant displays of American science, industry, and commerce as well as exhibits from other nations of the world. More than 27.5 million Americans visited the fair. Dubbed the "White City," it was projected as a utopian dream that marked America's progress since 1492 and called the nation to its future.

Myriad symbols and practices of racial exclusion and hierarchy pervaded the ideas of nation and world embodied by the Columbian Exposition, themes that captured and unified the trends of race and nationalism in the late nineteenth century. The fair's governing boards excluded African Americans, prompting black leaders to protest and boycott the event. Of the few African American exhibits, the most popular was the living advertisement of Aunt Jemima, performed by a former slave, for the RT Davis Milling Company's pancake mix. The fair's Department of Anthropology displayed living American Indians from various reservations making and selling handicrafts. The popularity of that exhibit seemed to indicate white Americans' desire to situate Indians in the past as an exotic, backward race.

These representations of African Americans and American Indians underscored their exclusion from the mainstream of American society and from the fair's notions of national progress and achievement. Indeed, the dream of the White City could be understood only as it stood in relation to the exposition's other major feature, the Midway Plaisance, a mile-long row that combined honky-tonk entertainments with an encyclopedic exhibition of the world's races. Living "ethnological villages" set out a racial order from barbarism to civilization—starting at the far end with American Indians, Africans and Dahomeyans, the latter considered by white fair goers as the most savage and threatening, then proceeding to East Asia, West Asia, and the Islamic world (with exotic Orientalist themes) and then, finally, nearest to the gates of the White City, German and Irish villages, representing the Teutonic and Celtic races. Because China boycotted the exposition in protest of the Chinese exclusion laws, the presentation of Chinese civilization was reduced to a Midway display described by the *Chicago Tribune* as "Freaks of Chinese Fancy at the Fair."

The White City and the Midway were designed as an object lesson for the masses in the evolutionary path of humankind, which marked the racial identity and "place" of the world's peoples. The obsession with anthropology and ethnology at the Columbian Exposition reflected the emergence and influence of scientific racism in the last quarter of the nineteenth century. The "scientific" ordering of civilization according to race not only explained cultural difference and Anglo-Saxon superiority, it justified both the extreme economic exploitation and the second-class political status of peoples who had been marked as colored races. Racial segregation in the South, the conquest of American Indian and Mexican lands in the West, Chinese exclusion, and the colonial possession of Hawai'i, the Philippines, and Puerto Rico—these policies were integral to American national development during the last quarter of the nineteenth century. In many ways these policies may be understood as a continuation of old practices. The Old South, of course, haunted the new; and the conquest of the West and the acquisition of new colonies bore a family resemblance to European colonialism in the New World in the seventeenth and eighteenth centuries. But race and colonialism were not simply reproduced; they were constructed anew out of the demands of changing economic and political conditions, out of dynamic processes of national territorial consolidation, rapid industrial development and economic growth, and projections of United States power abroad.

The Columbian Exposition narrated those processes as an inevitable march of scientific and cultural progress, in which material abundance held the key to democracy. Indeed if the Civil War and the expansion of the railroads had established the national market, technological and business innovations in the decades following the war—electrical power, telegraph and telephone, hard steel, precision machine and tool making, and modern corporate management—propelled a vast expansion of the nation's productive capacity. By 1880 American manufacturing output exceeded that of Germany and France combined.

Yet while American economic growth was phenomenal, it was neither linear nor smooth. Between 1873 and 1896 nearly all industrial nations in the world, including the United States, experienced a prolonged economic depression plagued by chronic overproduction and falling prices. In the United States recurrent cycles of boom and bust characterized the economy; the rise to power of the great "robber baron" industrialists like Carnegie, Frick, and Rockefeller took place along with business failures, tightening credit, and the impoverishment of small farmers and workers. The tensions of industrial life were expressed most forcefully in the growing number of labor strikes, involving hundreds of thousands of workers in the peak years of 1877, 1886, and 1892–1893.

The expanding economy had a voracious appetite for labor, especially of the unskilled variety. Immigrants from capitalism's rural peripheries, from Southern and Eastern Europe, Asia, and Mexico, supplied the needed muscle and dramatically diversified the nation's population." Not every foreigner is a workingman," observed a Chicago clergyman in 1887, "but every workingman is a foreigner." The new immigrants confronted both the disdain of elite Anglo-Americans, who welcomed their brawn but questioned their racial fitness for citizenship, and native-born white workers, who often blamed immigrants and blacks for depressing wages or for strikebreaking. The great antimonopolist agrarian movement of the 1880s and 1890s, led by the People's Party (Populists) and militant labor organizations like the Knights of Labor, which fought for the eight-hour day, were inconsistent at multiracial solidarity. They sometimes organized blacks in segregated units and at worst practiced racial exclusion of nonwhites. Thus in this period of national consolidation, economic growth and class conflict, race and ethnicity complicated and cut across the meanings of citizenship and national identity. To understand the patterns of race and racism that emerged in the last quarter of the nineteenth century, we must first turn to the South.

## JIM CROW AND THE NEW SOUTH

The Civil War and the passage of the Thirteenth, Fourteenth, and Fifteenth Amendments to the U.S. Constitution abolished slavery, established national citizenship, and extended the principle of democracy to all Americans. In the South, Reconstruction (1867–1877) brought about profound changes and hopes for African Americans. The former slaves established the autonomy of their personhood and of their families and built churches, schools, and other community institutions. They resisted working on the old plantations as waged gang labor, preferring the semi-autonomous work of sharecropping and tenant farming. And with the vote, they won office—sixteen seats in Congress and more than six hundred in state legislatures.

Reconstruction was not, however, a period of steady advance, but rather one of constant and often bloody conflict. By 1876 most state governments in the South had been "redeemed" by white southern Democrats. Only four states—North Carolina, South Carolina, Louisiana, and Florida—remained under the control of Republicans. Just as important, by the mid-1870s, federal commitment to black equality had foundered. Northern opinion wearied of it, especially after the economic depression of 1873, and Republicans in Congress became increasingly divided over the efficacy of continued federal intervention in the South.

The elections of 1876 assured the reversal of Reconstruction and completed Redemption. As a black southerner sadly stated, "The whole South—every state in the South—had got into the hands of the very men that held us as slaves." Under "home rule," white supremacy retook the South. The Redeemers included both traditional planters and new commercial and industrial interests that championed a "New South." But while politically and socially diverse, Redeemers agreed on a new southern order of racial subordination based on fiscal retrenchment, labor control, and reduced black political power.

In the name of efficiency, Redeemers dismantled the Reconstruction state, slashing state budgets and property taxes. The Mississippi state budget was cut in half between 1875 and 1885. Across the South, public hospitals, asylums, and penitentiaries were closed.

Texas imposed fees for schooling and Alabama abolished state-wide school taxes. The crippling of public education—for both black and poor white southerners—was perhaps the most enduring consequence of fiscal retrenchment. New laws asserted firmer control over black labor. Vagrancy and anti-enticement laws limited black people's mobility. Laws prohibiting the sale of unginned cotton and other farm products after dark cut directly into black farmers' ability to make a living. Most important were the crop lien laws, which, by giving the landowner first rights to the sharecropper's crop, shifted the entire burden of risk to the latter. Black farmers fell into permanent debt and impoverishment as sharecropping turned into debt peonage, which some called a new form of slavery.

Perhaps the cruelest form of coerced labor was convict leasing. During the 1880s southern prisons were filled with young black men, who were incarcerated as a result of new laws that punished blacks severely for crimes against white property. (On the other hand, states repealed Reconstruction laws that had been passed to restrict Klan violence.) Mississippi's notorious "pig law," for example, made theft of any farm animal or any other property valued at ten dollars or more a felony punishable by five years in jail. Convict laborers hired out to private contractors laid three thousand miles of new railroad track across the South; they worked on cotton plantations in Mississippi, on turpentine farms in Florida, and in iron foundries and coal mines in Alabama. Working in shackles and beneath the whip, in water and muck and under the blazing sun, convict laborers were sometimes literally worked to death. During the 1880s not a single leased convict in Mississippi lived long enough to serve out a sentence of ten years.

In Louisiana and South Carolina, where sugar and rice plantations employed waged workers, labor militancy continued from the Reconstruction period, in some areas into the late 1880s. The former slaves in the bayou parishes in Louisiana had a history of worker organization, strikes, and armed defense of the right to vote. In 1886 sugar workers in Terrebonne Parish joined the Knights of Labor, forming an integrated local. Their efforts suggest the possibilities that existed for cross-racial alliances. But a region-wide strike in 1887 was brutally crushed by the planters' use of mass evictions, armed force, and the mobilization of white racism.

Changes in social relations and politics were relatively slower than in the economic sphere. Segregation, which began almost immediately after the Civil War in public schools, proceeded unevenly throughout Reconstruction and into the 1880s and 1890s. During the 1880s blacks and whites increasingly withdrew from each other, but segregation was not absolute and southern race relations were still somewhat flexible. Black people still entered theaters, bars, and some hotels and could get equal seating on streetcars and railway cars.

The process of narrowing black political rights was also uneven and contested. During the 1880s Democratic state governments gerrymandered districts to dilute black voting strength and committed wholesale ballot fraud in counties with black majorities. Yet in other states, where whites had large majorities, such as Arkansas and Texas, black voting continued during Redemption. A few blacks continued to serve in state legislatures and pockets of black political power endured in some plantation counties. It was not until the 1890s that complete racial segregation and legal disfranchisement took place.

Historian C. Van Woodward has argued that while extreme racism had always existed in the South, it had been checked by the conservative paternalism of the old planter class, northern liberal opinion, and southern white radicalism. But in the latter decades of the century, the influence of these elements waned. Northern liberalism had retreated in the 1870s, and the U.S. Supreme Court's ruling in 1883 overturning the Reconstruction civil rights acts sealed federal abandonment of black rights. The Populists' support for a class-based alliance of black and white farmers against monopoly proved to be short-lived. Under pressure of the agricultural depression and bitter political battles with white conservative Democrats, white Populists turned against their black allies in the 1890s.

The policy of strict racial segregation—nicknamed "Jim Crow" after a minstrelsy character—took hold and consolidated during the 1890s as a concession to poor white people, a bid to rebuild a "solid South" unified across class lines by white racism. The Jim Crow laws reached into every nook and cranny of southern life. Their relentless logic created not only separate railroad cars, building entrances, and drinking fountains, but also separate Bibles for swearing witnesses in the courtroom, separate streets for prostitutes, even separate gallows for hanging condemned men.

The chief aim of white supremacy was not so much racial separation, although that was its form, but racial subordination. Jim Crow was a system of countless daily humiliations intended to remind black people of their inferior position. Middle-class blacks were special targets of white resentment, indicating both the progress that black people had made since slavery and the precariousness of lower-class whites' racial confidence. These white southerners resented "uppity," independent-minded Negroes in general and economically successful blacks in particular, described by one white southerner as "that insolent class who desired to force themselves into first-class coaches."

In fact, streetcars and trains were contested public spaces because they were among the very few places in the South where blacks and whites came together on equal footing. An observer explained, "In their homes and in ordinary employment, [whites and blacks] meet as master and servant; but in the street cars they touch as free citizens, each paying for the right to ride; the white not in a place of command, the Negro without an obligation of servitude. Streetcar relationships are, therefore, symbolic of the new conditions."

During the 1880s and 1890s many blacks refused to observe the new rules segregating streetcars and railroad coaches. The transportation companies were also not always keen on assuming the additional expense and responsibility for policing the color line. In 1887 a black newspaper in Georgia encouraged black passengers who purchased first-class tickets to stand their ground. "When a conductor orders a colored passenger from the first-class car it's a bluff, and if the passenger goes to the forward or smoking car, that ends it; should he refuse, it ends it also, for the trainman will reflect seriously before he lays on violent hands."

While some blacks successfully called the trainman's bluff, others were not as fortunate, including a young Ida B. Wells who, while traveling from Memphis in 1884 was dragged from her seat in the first-class ladies car after she refused to move. Wells got off the train at the first stop rather then sit in the smoking car, and then successfully sued the railroad. A few others won similar judgments. But in 1896 Homer Plessy, a light-skinned Negro from Louisiana who sued over his ejection from the first-class car, lost his case before the U.S. Supreme Court. In *Plessy v. Ferguson* the court legitimized racial segregation with the "separate but equal" doctrine. The court ruled that the Fourteenth Amendment protected the rights of black people only in narrow terms of formal political equality. "If one race be inferior to the other socially," it said, "the Constitution of the United States cannot put them upon the same plane."

Many black people made individual decisions to walk rather than ride on segregated cars. Efforts were made at collective action as well, although these were difficult to sustain. Between 1890 and World War I, black people staged boycotts of streetcars in twenty-five cities in every southern state. "Do not trample on our pride by being 'jim crowed'—WALK!" exhorted the Savannah *Tribune*.

The street, too, could be contested terrain. Historian Glenda Gilmore found evidence of street altercations between black and white women in the late 1890s in North Carolina towns where black power had not yet been completely displaced. In Wilmington, where blacks held local office until 1898, a black woman refused to yield the sidewalk to a group of white women. When one of the white women tried to push her aside, the black woman retaliated with her umbrella. "That's right, damn it, give it to her," a black male observer reportedly shouted. Incidents such as these suggest that the generation born in freedom did not easily acquiesce to the reassertion of white supremacy.

But, while it is important to acknowledge resistance to Jim Crow, it should not be overstated. In the main the weight of white supremacy was enormous, and black people lacked political leverage to reverse the trend of racial oppression. Open confrontation invited swift punishment and retribution. Choosing to walk rather than ride segregated cars was an act of indirect resistance; grabbing the opportunity to steal a quick jostle on the street a spontaneous way to assert one's pride; but even such assertions were risky. Indeed, black people were lynched for as much.

Lynching was an old form of extra-legal justice that had been practiced for many years, mainly against whites in the

West and South; but in the 1890s it became both more widespread and increasingly aimed at black people. Between 1890 and 1917 at least two to three black southerners were hanged, burned at the stake, or otherwise murdered every week.

Lynching evolved as a sadistic and public ritual that involved death by prolonged torture, such as mutilation and burning, dismemberment, and the distribution of severed body parts as trophies and souvenirs. It was a gruesome public spectacle, a kind of cathartic blood sport that involved hundreds, even thousands, of cheering witnesses from all strata of southern white society. Mary Church Terrell called modern lynching a "wild and diabolical carnival of blood."

The extremity of the punishment was justified by the nature of the alleged crimes committed, notably the rape of white women by black men. During the era of segregation a climate of sexualized race hysteria engulfed the South, which imagined pure white southern womanhood under siege by the "black beast rapist." In truth, most lynching was not in response to sexual assault. Of nearly three thousand blacks lynched between 1889 and 1918, only 19 percent were accused of rape (and of these, many were falsely accused). Journalist and activist Ida B. Wells, who conducted the first in-depth investigation of lynching, pointed out that sexual liaisons between black men and white women were often consensual and initiated by the latter. If there was rape between the races, she said, it was the age-old practice of white men taking black women. Economic competition and resentment against the black middle class, argued Wells, was the real reason for lynching. White southerners cried the "beast," but lynching revealed more about the savagery of white racism than it did about the character of its victims.

Disfranchisement was the last, but by no means the least, major means of racial oppression to be imposed at the end of the nineteenth century. Enacted throughout the South between 1890 (Mississippi) and 1910 (Tennessee), disfranchisement was achieved mostly by state constitutional amendments that imposed property and literacy qualifications on the vote or by other devices, such as the poll tax.

Concern over widespread corruption in elections was the principal rationale for disfranchisement. Particularly in the black-belt areas, white minorities used myriad tactics to hold power, including vote purchasing, ballot stealing, bribery, intimidation, and violence. These tactics were used not only against black voters but between white factions as well. Many southern political leaders believed cheating at elections disgraced and demoralized southern politics.

Disfranchisement might seem like a paradoxical solution that punished the victims of voting fraud. But its logic was consistent with the view commonly held among white elites that black people were not intelligent enough to hold the franchise responsibly. At another level, some white leaders frankly argued for the economy of disfranchisement. "We are not begging for 'ballot reform'," explained an Alabama Democrat, "but we want to be relieved of purchasing the

Negroes to carry elections. I want cheaper votes."

Conservative Democrats in the South believed that restoring power to the "intelligent and virtuous" propertied classes was also a solution to the expanding democratic vote of poor white people. White power per se was not threatened; at issue, rather, was which whites would have power. Disfranchisement was thus a strategy in diverse political calculations. Conservatives saw it as a solution to Populist challenges; in some states, white majority counties were willing to sacrifice universal manhood suffrage for better advantage against white-controlled black-belt counties.

Disfranchisement virtually eliminated black voting in the South. Although blacks had already been informally disfranchised in most states by intimidation, violence, and the gerrymandering of districts, the institutionalization of disfranchisement set in place a durable legal structure that would last for more than a half-century. In Louisiana, the number of black registered voters dropped from 130,000 in 1896 to 1,342 in 1904. In Alabama only 2 percent of eligible black men were registered to vote by 1906.

Southern lawmakers attempted to exempt poor white people from disfranchisement by creating various loopholes in the law. These included the "understanding clause," which allowed illiterates to vote if they could "understand" any section of the state constitution read to them, and the infamous "grandfather clause," which protected the franchise of all those who had been eligible to vote on January 1, 1867, as well as their sons and their grandsons. Nevertheless, the disfranchisement of whites was significant, owing in large part to the poll tax. In Louisiana, adult white male voter registration dropped from 96.3 percent in 1896 to 52 percent in 1904. Forrest G. Wood has estimated that from 97,000 to 108,000 white voters were disfranchised throughout the South.

For African Americans, Jim Crow was a dark period. An Alabama woman remarked, "There is no wonder that we die. The wonder is that we persist in living." Yet black people persevered and found ways to eke out a living, to school their children, to maintain their self-respect. Many avoided white people wherever possible, in order to avoid humiliation or trouble.

African Americans learned to "wear the mask," to act with deference in the presence of whites while hiding their true thoughts and feelings. As a blues refrain described, "Got one mind for white folks to see, 'nother for what I know is me." Accommodation to white supremacy was necessary for daily survival, but it did not mean submission. Resentment burned inside, especially among the "New Negroes," the generation born in freedom. Black people found ways to subvert the system passively, performed small acts of resistance, and occasionally challenged racism openly. Armed self-defense was rare but not unheard of, and at times even openly advocated in the black press. The Montgomery *Weekly News* advised blacks to "die like men [and] take two or three white devils along."

But in truth, the options were few. While during Reconstruction black people struggled for both political and eco-nomic independence, in the 1890s political action became impossible and the impulse for economic self-sufficiency turned inward, becoming individualized, even conservative. Jim Crow spurred the growth of a black middle class comprising businessmen, professionals, and clergy, who serviced the segregated community and market. In the 1880s and 1890s a conservative leadership that advocated accepting the Negro's subordinate status in the South emerged out of this stratum.

The most forceful and successful spokesman for this approach was Booker T. Washington, who founded the Tuskegee Institute, an agricultural and vocational school, in Alabama. Washington preached racial uplift through economic self-help and vocational education and counseled accepting segregation with "patience, forbearance, and self-control." While during the Reconstruction era, uplift meant the full rights of citizenship, in the 1890s, uplift ideology emphasized winning white people's acceptance by promoting the "better sort" of middle class Negro and blaming the lower classes of black people for their backward condition. Washington's strategy appealed to some African Americans as practical and realistic, even hopeful. But his leadership was also the creation of white society. Washington's message of quiescence and economic self-help resonated with the climate of industry, commerce, and laissez-faire that suffused both North and South and brought him white recognition and financial support.

Not all African Americans subscribed to the strategy of moderation and accommodation. In the early 1890s dissidents such as Ida B. Wells and T. Thomas Fortune, a Florida journalist, formed the Afro-American Council. The council condemned lynching, segregation, and disfranchisement and encouraged economic boycotts. W. E. B. DuBois openly broke with Washington in 1903 because, he said, Washington "apologizes for injustice, . . . does not rightly value the privilege and duty of voting, belittles the emasculating effects of cast distinctions, and opposes the higher training and ambition of our brighter minds."

Yet, while Washington's critics hit at many truths, they too recognized that African Americans had few choices in the South. The Afro-American Council advocated out-migration; Wells herself went into exile in the North after racists burned down her Memphis newspaper, *Free Speech*. In fact, for many black people, leaving the South seemed to be the only alternative. Some sixty thousand black farmers migrated to the West during the 1870s and 1880s, and urban professionals, like Wells, began going north in the 1890s. As much as Du Bois emphasized political and civil rights, the thrust of his work in founding the Niagara Movement and the NAACP appealed to northern conscience to restore the nation's commitment to black political rights.

If southern race policy succeeded in disempowering black people and forcing them into conditions of near servitude, it failed to deliver on its promise to elevate poor whites. A new upper class of white planters, industrialists, and merchants thrived, of course. But for the lower classes of white southerners, the price of racial pride was high, including disfranchisement and the highest rates of illiteracy and poverty in the nation. Small white farmers fell into tenancy and debt, their decline feeding the growth of a low-wage labor force for the burgeoning southern textile industry. Thus while the New South built industries and became integrated into the national market, it remained a backward region based on a colonial economy and repressive labor relations for black and white laborers alike.

The nation's abandonment of racial equality and full citizenship for African Americans had implications beyond the South. The color line cast a long shadow across America, for it also radically foreshortened the possibilities for equality for other nonwhite peoples. Indeed, as white supremacy retook the South, race and racism were also reproduced in the Far West through campaigns of war and assimilation against American Indians and through the dispossession of Mexican-owned land.

## THE WEST: MANIFEST DESTINY REALIZED

### The Last Indian Wars

After the Civil War cheap land offerings by the government and the railroads and opportunities in mining and cattle ranching drew white settlers to the Great Plains. During the 1870s the white population west of the Mississippi grew from 7 million to 11 million. Increasingly, white settlers coveted American

Indian land, both reservations and non-reservation (unceded) lands recognized and protected by treaty with the United States. Indeed, settlement and the integration of the West into the national market rendered impossible the old policy based on the isolation of Indians from whites and their removal to remote storage areas in the West. In the 1870s and 1880s Indian-white armed conflict reached its final and most desperate stage.

In 1874 George Armstrong Custer, a U.S. Army officer, led an illegal military expedition into unceded Sioux lands in the Dakotas that confirmed the presence of gold in the Black Hills. With white miners flocking to the area, the government moved against the Sioux. Although the treaty of Fort Laramie in 1868 had recognized unceded lands in the Powder River area as Sioux hunting grounds, in 1875 the government declared its intention to round up all nonreservation Sioux and bring them in by military force. Three military columns from the Missouri division of the U.S. Army launched a full-scale attack against the Sioux and their Cheyenne allies in the spring of 1876. But the Sioux were a formidable foe. Their most stunning victory took place at Little Big Horn, where four thousand warriors led by Crazy Horse and Sitting Bull annihilated the entire Seventh Cavalry commanded by Custer. The Indians were defeated only after a prolonged U.S. military campaign of pursuit. Crazy Horse surrendered in 1877 and was immediately killed. Sitting Bull, who had gone to Canada with a small band, returned in

1881 and acquiesced, finally, to reservation life. But he, too, was murdered in 1890, as part of the massacre of the Lakota Ghost Dancers at Wounded Knee.

On the southern plains, the Comanche and Kiowas also resisted and lost. Although they had agreed to live on reservations in the Medicine Lodge Treaties, they were unhappy there. They frequently left and conducted raids into Texas and Mexico for livestock. As depredations increased in the 1870s, the government declared all Indians not on the reservations to be hostile. During the Red River War of 1874–1875, five army divisions pursued the Indians until they gave up in exhaustion. In the Southwest, the Apache also went off the reservations for raiding and resisted military control by guerrilla warfare into the 1880s. Geronimo was one of the last American Indian chiefs to accept defeat in 1886.

Historian Richard White has observed that the Indians nearly always won battles with U.S. military forces. They ultimately lost the war, however, because the U.S. Army practiced a kind of reverse guerrilla warfare, in which they pursued the Indians relentlessly, scattering and starving them until they surrendered. In 1877, after the government reduced the size of the Nez Perce reservation in Washington Territory, Chief Joseph attempted to lead his people to Canada, resisting U.S. Army attacks for months along a 1,321-mile-long flight. When he finally surrendered he said, "I am tired of fighting. The old men are all dead. . . . It is cold, and we have no blankets. The little children are freezing to death. My people, some of them, have run away to the hills. From where the sun now stands, I will fight no more forever."

The military campaigns of the 1870s and 1880s were accompanied by legal moves against American Indian sovereignty and tribal lands. In 1871 Congress formally abandoned the treaty system, declaring that the United States would no longer recognize or deal with Indians as sovereign nations. Indian policy shifted to an assimilationist strategy, which would last until 1930. Once the Indians had been militarily defeated, many white Americans pitied their destitute lives on the reservations. These included well-meaning reformers, who believed the Indians were ill served on reservations, which they likened to "pen[s] where a horde of savages are to be fed with flour and beef . . . [and] furnished with paint and gee-gaws by the greed of traders." The reformers believed that the Indians, small in number and widely dispersed, would become extinct unless they "flow[ed] in with the current of the life and ways of the larger [people]." Assimilation would thus "save" the Indians from extinction. But this was inherently a contradictory strategy because assimilation, which required extinguishing the Indians' way of life, was itself a kind of extinction.

One of the central features of assimilation was the cessation of Indian land according to a new federal policy called "allotment by severalty." This policy provided that Indians be "allotted" a fraction of their lands while the government and private interests assumed control of the rest. While the government had previously recognized Indian land as their birthright, it now regarded it as part of the public domain, to be used for the "permanent prosperity" of the West. Allotment was implemented on a tribe-by-tribe basis in the 1880s and in 1887 by the General Allotment Act (the Dawes Act), which committed the government to the allotment of all Indian lands.

The ostensible purpose of allotment was to induce Indians to become farmers on individually owned plots of land. By making Indians into yeoman farmers, allotment aimed to assimilate them into American society. As Secretary of the Interior Carl Schurz explained in 1881, allotment would "fit the Indians for the habits and occupations of civilized life, by work and education, to individualize them in the possession and appreciation of property." Of course, the Anglo-American method of farming required far less land than did the traditional Indian usufruct economies of hunting and casual farming. Anything more than 160 acres per household was surplus.

Assimilation also required the suppression of American Indian religious practices. In 1884 Congress banned the Sioux Sun Dance, and in 1888 it prohibited bundling, a ritual of preserving the spirits of the dead. These prohibitions hurt Indians deeply. A Blackfoot Indian said, "I do not understand why the white men desire to put an end to our religious ceremonials. What harm can they do to our people? If they deprive us of our religion, we will have nothing left. . . . We believe the Sun God is all-powerful, for every spring he makes the trees bud and the grass to grow. We see these things with our own eyes, and, therefore, know that all life comes from him."

Reformers also attempted to convert Indians to traditional Anglo-American gender roles and family structure. They believed the matrilineal kinship structure of many Indian tribes was evidence of sexual promiscuity and the foundation of Indians' supposed savagery. Elevating Indian women to the ideal of white middle-class womanhood, they believed, was central to civilizing the Indians. The Women's National Indian Association was founded by veteran women reformers and modeled on the "women's work for women" of the Protestant women's missions, which emphasized domestic work and Christian values of sexual and moral purity.

Finally, reformers sought to assimilate Indians through education. Between 1879 and 1895 the federal government increased its annual spending for native schooling from $75,000 to $2 million. It built some two hundred day schools on the reservations and twenty boarding schools. The most well-known institution was the Carlisle School in Pennsylvania, a boarding school founded by Henry Pratt in 1878. Pratt had experimented first with a program for American Indian students at the Hampton Institute, the first Negro college established after the Civil War and the alma mater of Booker T. Washington. Pratt's evangelical style, which emphasized instruction in reading, writing, manual skills, and Protestant values, so that the Indians would "rise to civilization," typified the approach to Indian education in the 1870s and 1880s.

If cultural arrogance marked the evangelical approach, it was tempered by an idealistic belief in the humanity—and the ultimate equality—of the Indian. By the 1890s, however, race pessimism had displaced idealism. The boarding school strategy had always been too expensive to be adopted as general policy, and critics questioned its efficacy, observing that the students "regressed" when they returned to the reservations by growing their hair long and wearing native clothing. The critique was part of a general view that doubted the Indians' racial capacity for civilization. Government officials and reformers, influenced by scientific race theories that arose in late nineteenth-century anthropology and ethnology, considered the Indians a hopelessly backward race, frozen in time and space. The American Indian was "an adult child," according to the commissioner of Indian education, Francis Leupp, who might be trained for a life of manual labor, but little more. By the turn of the century vocational schooling was the exclusive focus of Indian education. Indian policy makers invoked Booker T. Washington's model of limited education in the context of racial subordination. Washington, said Leupp in 1902, was successful because "the black man [was] to him a black man, and not merely a white man colored black."

Assimilation thus produced dubious results; just as education policy abandoned the goal of integrating Indians into American society as equal citizens, allotment failed to transform Indians into family farmers. That was a difficult goal to achieve in any event, since by the late 1880s the monopolization of agricultural land was well under way in the West. But the dispossession of the American

Indians proceeded apace. Indian land ownership fell from 155,632,312 acres in 1881 to 77,865,373 acres in 1900. By the turn of the century the premise of the Dawes Act, that tribal land was American Indian private property, and the act's provisions requiring Indians' approval of the sale of their unallotted lands, were rendered moot. In 1900 the Jerome Agreement, a land cession rejected by the Kiowa and Comanche, was approved by Congress and then upheld by the U.S. Supreme Court. In *Lone Wolf v. Hitchcock* (1908) the Court declared that Congress held the "plenary [absolute] power" "to abrogate the provisions of an Indian treaty." All pretenses that recognized Indian sovereignty were gone. The American Indians were no longer nations, not even dependent nations. They were now individual wards of the state.

## Mexicans: Strangers in Their Native Homeland

America's seemingly inexorable expansion to the Pacific Coast involved wresting territory not only from Indians but from Mexico as well. The Treaty of Guadalupe Hidalgo, which negotiated Mexico's defeat in the Mexican American War (1846–1848), gave roughly one half of Mexico—more than a half million square miles—to the United States, a territorial acquisition surpassed only by the Louisiana Purchase.

Yet it took several decades to consolidate American rule over the Southwest. In part this was because not Mexico but American Indians actually controlled

large parts of it. The Mexican population in the Southwest—Californios, Tejanos, and Nuevomexicanos, and others descended from Spanish colonialists and Indians—numbered only about eighty thousand in 1848. Most lived and worked in a subsistence economy as small producers or on ranches characterized by *patron-peon* relations of mutual dependence and obligation. Sixty-one percent of the Californio population were landowners, although only 3 percent owned large *ranchos*.

The process of white settlement to the Southwest was uneven. In some areas white settlers rapidly outnumbered Mexicans. A rate war between rival railroads drove the cost of a ticket from the Missouri Valley to southern California down from $125 in 1886 to $1 in 1887; white migration to southern California skyrocketed, and whites soon outnumbered Mexicans ten to one. In other areas, however, Mexicans continued to dominate the population. Congress delayed statehood for New Mexico and Arizona until 1912 because the white population of those territories remained small through the early 1900s. Mexicans also continued to dominate the South Texas border region, between the Nueces and Rio Grande rivers. Still, racial suspicion and tension, dating to the founding of the Texas Republic and the Mexican American War and stoked by intruding Anglo-dominated market relations, suffused the border area. Historian David Montejano states that the border region remained "untamed" for fifty years after conquest, as local whites and the frontier battalion of the Texas

Rangers, acting as a "military police of occupation," strived to consolidate Anglo power.

On occasion violent conflict erupted, as in the 1877 "salt war" in the El Paso area and the 1871–1876 "skinning wars" in South Texas. Both involved competition over economic resources. In the first instance, Mexicans resorted to arms when Anglos attempted to take over the salt lakes in the foothills of the Guadalupe Mountains, from which locals had developed a salt trade in northern Mexico. The skinning wars grew out of intense competition for cattle, whose hides carried a high market price. For over five years there were organized raids and counterraids on both sides of the Texas-Mexico border and armed conflict between Mexican cattle raiders and Anglo vigilance committees.

The old Spanish and Mexican land grants—some 15 million square miles of land theoretically protected by the Treaty of Guadalupe Hidalgo—posed an obstacle to white American settlers who sought opportunities in ranching and farming in the southwestern territories. From the 1850s to the 1890s, Mexicans were dispossessed of land through myriad strategies, including Anglo marriage into the families of elite Californios and Tejanos, fraud, and theft, as well as through legal means. Both California and Texas required all land titles from the Spanish and Mexican eras to be authenticated according to Anglo-American property law. Many members of the landed elite, whose deeds delineated property according to such markers as "a clump of trees" or whose deeds were long ago misplaced, lost their land. Still others simply could not afford the legal fees required to defend their claims. As a result of the California Land Act of 1851 Californios lost 40 percent of the land they had held in 1846. In Texas, some whites occupied Mexican-owned land and then made legal claim based on their rights as squatters. Tejano-owned land ordered sold by county courts to settle tax arrears went to Anglos for suspiciously low bids. In June 1877, for example, the Hidalgo County sheriff auctioned three thousand acres of the Hinajosa land grant for $15. In New Mexico, a Court of Private Land Claims established in 1891 granted 80 percent of the Mexican land grants to Anglos.

The transfer of the land base to whites and the commercialization of the economy reduced most Mexicans in the Southwest to the status of landless wage labor. No longer could they work as small producers or find sympathetic *patrons* to attach themselves to. But there was plenty of work for Mexican laborers, dirty and difficult work that whites refused to do, such as railroad construction, copper and quicksilver mining, and "grubbing brush," which cleared the way for commercial agriculture. The changes in the nature of the labor market were oppressive to traditional Mexican family and life styles. Among the lower classes, traditional gender roles in the patriarchal household came under pressure, as women often had to do work intended for men. Dangerous and itinerant seasonal work created early widowhood or abandonment; by the 1880s nearly one-third of Mexican American households in California were headed by women.

In the context of conquest and the concomitant shifts in economic and political relations of power, Mexicans in the Southwest underwent a process of ethnic redefinition. Many Mexican Americans, especially among the working classes, withdrew into their own communities, both in towns and in isolated rural areas not yet dominated by Anglo settlers. In these spaces they developed what historian David Gutiérrez describes as a "distinct, if syncretic, variant of Mexican culture in what had become part of the United States." They spoke Spanish and sustained their own cultural and religious practices much in the same ways that they had before conquest. The extended family and the *mutualista,* or mutual aid association, provided networks of support and sustenance. On the other hand, many Californio, Tejano, and Nuevomexicano elites sought to distance themselves from the idea of being "Mexican" because that label carried increasingly negative racial connotations. Denying their mestizo heritage, these elites chose instead to identify as "Spanish" or "Castilian"—that is, white—in order to salvage their social status as the indigenous *gente de razón,* "people of reason." The strategy had limited success, however, for by the turn of the century the old upper classes, dispossessed of land and power, had dwindled in size and influence. But the impulse to claim whiteness remained strong. In part this was a sign of their diminished status. The appeal of whiteness derived also from the bifurcated black-white racial order of American society. Claiming whiteness was believed to be a way of avoiding the degradation of blackness. In fact, Mexicans were perceived in ambiguous racial terms; while some considered them a mixed race of two undesirable elements (Latin and Indian), comparisons to the Negro were also common. The Treaty of Guadalupe Hidalgo granted U.S. citizenship to the inhabitants of the ceded territory, which led a federal court to rule (*In re Rodriguez,* 1897) that Mexicans were "white" for purposes of naturalization, even if ethnologists considered them to be "Indian." Particularly in Texas, positioned geographically where the South and the Southwest intersect, Mexicans came to occupy an ethno-racial space in between white and black.

That trend was augmented when immigration from the Mexico interior to the Southwestern United States began in the 1880s and 1890s. Coincident with a labor shortage in the southwestern United States, the Mexican government of Porfirio Diaz was engaged in an aggressive campaign of modernization. That process opened the country to foreign capital and disrupted the traditional system of land tenure. In 1883 new land laws expropriated the *ejidos* (common lands), which would displace some five million people from their means of subsistence over the next twenty years.

Although the high tide of Mexican immigration would not occur until the 1920s, migration to the United States trebled during the Porfiriato. Anglo growers and employers favored Mexican labor because they seemed more tractable than black labor and because many returned home after one or two seasons of work. As an official of the U.S. Bureau of Labor explained in 1908, Mexican farm workers "do not occupy a position analogous to that of the Negro in the South. They are not permanent, do not acquire land or establish themselves in little cabin homesteads, but remain nomadic and outside of American civilization." Conquest had not only "thrown [Mexicans] among those who were strangers" but made them foreigners in their homeland.

## Chinese Immigration and Asiatic Exclusion

Just as Mexican laborers were perceived as outsiders, so too were the Chinese who came to the Pacific coast during the second half of the nineteenth century. Americans who believed the West was a God-given gift to white civilization loathed sharing it with anyone else. Thus in 1850 California imposed a foreign miner's tax, which was aimed at excluding miners who came from Sonora, Mexico, and China to participate in the gold rush. But the labor needed to develop the West was considerable, and white labor was in short supply, especially for unskilled work that was dirty or dangerous. Employers thus recruited Chinese and Mexicans for railroad construction, for clearing and reclaiming land for agricultural production, and for other work critical to the early development of the West. But white Americans—themselves migrants from the eastern and midwestern U.S. and from Europe—welcomed neither group as permanent settlers or citizens. While Mexicans were tolerated to the extent that they were seasonal workers, Chinese soon earned the dubious distinction of being the only group to

be legally excluded by name from the United States.

Chinese migration to the Pacific Coast was part of a larger exodus of some two million people from southern China in the nineteenth century. The "push" for emigration derived from a combination of factors that included population pressures and natural disasters, domestic political strife, and economic and social dislocations caused by Western intrusions. China's loss to Great Britain in the Opium War (1839–1842) was particularly damaging, as it was forced to open five ports to foreign commerce, to pay a $21 million indemnity, and to grant Westerners immunity from Chinese law.

In the mid-nineteenth century some 150,000 Chinese indentured laborers, or coolies, were recruited to replace African slaves on plantations in South America and the Caribbean after the abolition of slavery. Coolie labor was a form of semislavery. Chinese were often kidnapped or tricked into signing contracts and endured harsh conditions akin to slavery. Coolies who harvested guano off the coast of Peru, for example, did not always live long enough to finish their contracts.

By contrast, Chinese migration to North America and Australia was voluntary. Some half-million Chinese immigrated to these areas in the nineteenth century. With milder climates and waged labor—not to mention the discovery of gold deposits—they were favored destinations for Chinese migrants whose families were of modest or moderate means. Many Chinese laborers came to the United States on the credit ticket system and had to pay back the money advanced for their passage, but they were not bound by contracts and were not coolies. Admittedly, the difference may have seemed slight in practice. For example, the thirty thousand Chinese recruited to build the western portion of the transcontinental railroad from 1867 to 1871 faced arduous conditions and earned wages one-third less than that of white workers building the eastern section. An untold number of Chinese died in the high Sierras, some from working through the freezing winters, others from blasting dynamite while hanging from baskets suspended over the side of the mountain.

Yet, even as Chinese were a highly exploited labor force in the American West, the essentially voluntary nature of their migration had important consequences that encouraged the formation of communities. Because they were not coolies, Chinese more readily entered a range of occupations. As mining gave out, some Chinese became agricultural workers and tenant farmers. Chinese reclaimed the Sacramento-San Joaquin Delta and introduced the production of labor-intensive fruits and vegetables. Others came as or became merchants, who sold provisions and services to their coethnics, or commissioned and sold agricultural products in the general market. Still others became urban artisans and factory workers in San Francisco's nascent manufacturing economy.

Some Chinese started families in America, although relatively few women immigrated. Those who did comprised wives of merchants and, to a lesser extent laborers, servant girls, and prostitutes. As was the case with migrants from Mexico and Europe in the late nineteenth century, Chinese migrants were predominantly men of the laboring classes whose families sent them abroad to work and send money home. Approximately half of the two hundred thousand Chinese who came to the West Coast between 1874 and 1890 returned to China. Among those who stayed in the United States, many continued to maintain households in China. Most *huaqiao* (overseas Chinese) were not, in fact, bachelor sojourners but were members of extended transnational families. Outside of San Francisco, working couples were not uncommon in nineteenth-century fishing, farming, and small western towns. Despite the hardships facing many immigrants, Chinese wives improved their status in America. Free from the domination of their parents-in-law, many worked alongside their husbands and were, in effect, joint heads of household.

By 1870 the Chinese population in California numbered nearly fifty thousand; in San Francisco, Chinese accounted for one-quarter of the city's population in 1870 and 30 percent by 1880. Excluded by white skilled workers from high-wage markets (construction, transportation, metal work), Chinese worked in manufacturing, particularly in sectors where new methods had shifted work from skilled labor to mass production and lowered wages, such as cigar making and shoe making. Economic competition spurred whites' resentment, especially after the depression of the 1870s, but more than jobs and wages were at stake. Race hostility against the Chinese drew from the ideological traditions of Manifest Destiny and free labor. White labor depicted

Chinese as coolies, whom they characterized as representing a racially based condition of servility, as well as disease, moral depravity, and unchecked reproduction. The first federal legislation restricting immigration, the 1875 Page Law excluding prostitutes, was aimed at Chinese. In July 1877 a sandlot rally of the San Francisco Workingmen's Party turned into a three-day rampage against Chinese residents; later that year the party, running on the slogan "the Chinese must go," swept the municipal elections. Anticoolieism became a staple of Democratic Party politics on the Pacific Coast and Chinese exclusion the West's principal demand in Congress. In 1882 Congress suspended Chinese immigration for ten years. Exclusion was renewed in 1892 and 1902 and made permanent in 1904. Although Chinese ineligibility to citizenship was already implicit in the nation's naturalization laws, which provided the right to "free white persons" in 1790 and to "persons of African nativity or descent" in 1870, the exclusion laws explicitly barred Chinese from naturalization.

Exclusion, which legitimated the undesirability of Chinese, encouraged greater violence and discrimination. The worst violence in the 1880s occurred in the Mountain states and in the Pacific northwest, where Chinese miners and railroad workers had settled. In 1885 and 1886 a string of riots and "deportations" took place in Seattle, Tacoma, and Portland, in part in response to the depressed economic conditions that followed the completion of the northern rail lines. In 1885 in Rock Springs, Wyoming territory, a dispute between Chinese and white coal miners led to a full-scale race riot. A mob of whites burned down the Chinese quarter, shot and killed twenty-eight Chinese, wounded fifteen, and drove the rest from town. Chinese were lynched or violently expelled from other towns throughout the West. Few whites ever faced criminal charges for their actions. In California, where the vast majority of Chinese resided, Chinese were pushed to the margins of society. They were driven out of manufacturing and farming and segregated residentially, their children segregated in a separate "Oriental School." Exclusion also gave rise to illegal immigration, through smuggling and through the use of fraudulent documents. Chinatown developed as a segregated and insular community, with surname and place-of-origin associations and other protective societies adapted from China dominating its social organization. In a sense the marginalization of Chinese fulfilled nativist claims about Chinese difference and unassimilability.

Excluded from citizenship and the polity, Chinese challenged racial discrimination in the courts. A number of test cases organized by the Chinese Consolidated Benevolent Association (also known as the Six Companies) went to the U.S. Supreme Court. These cases not only delineated the boundaries of Chinese and Chinese Americans' rights in America but also decided important constitutional questions dealing with immigration and citizenship. These include Congress's plenary (absolute) power over immigration (*Chae Chan Ping v. United States*, 1889) and deportation (*Fong Yue Ting v. United States*, 1893), the applicability of the Fourteenth Amendment to all persons including noncitizens (*Yick Wo v. Hopkins*, 1886), and the universality of birthright citizenship (*United States v. Wong Kim Ark*, 1898).

As Chinese immigration declined in the 1890s, Japanese began coming to the West Coast. Some 118,000 Japanese immigrated between the mid-1880s and 1925. A large number came from Hawai'i, where they had worked as contract laborers on sugar plantations. In California and in other Western states Japanese labor replaced Chinese in farming and in railroad construction. Learning from the experience of the Chinese, some Japanese tried to deflect white hostility by demonstrating a commitment to join American society: they wore Western clothes, bought property, started families, joined Christian churches, and patronized white businesses. Nevertheless, by the turn of the twentieth century, Pacific Coast nativists began agitating for Japanese exclusion, invoking many of the Orientalist tropes that had been used against the Chinese. But anti-Japanese hostility differed in some important respects. Japan was not a backward, semicolonial nation like China but a modern imperialist nation that inspired both respect and anxiety in the West. If the Chinese "yellow peril" was imagined as an endless horde of coolies, the Japanese peril lay in imperialist Japan's alleged designs to take over America. In 1905 Japanese protests over the segregation of their children in San Francisco's Oriental School prompted a diplomatic crisis, which led to the negotiation of the "Gentleman's Agreement" in 1907. In an effort to forestall

statutory exclusion, Japan agreed to restrict the emigration of laborers voluntarily. In a companion piece, President Roosevelt issued an Executive Order in 1908 that effectively barred the migration of Asians from Hawai'i—by then a United States territory—to the mainland. Thus by the first decade of the twentieth century Asiatic exclusion was established as national policy.

## IMMIGRANTS FOR THE INDUSTRIAL AGE

The political and territorial consolidation of the South and West into United States speeded the completion of the country's industrial transformation. The same dynamic growth of capitalism that marked the United States was also evident in Europe, creating conditions there for emigration. As railroads and the capitalist market extended into rural areas, cheaper manufactured goods undercut the livelihoods of local artisans. The demand for agricultural produce in the cities encouraged the growth of large-scale commercial agriculture and the production of cash crops, threatening subsistence farming and small producers. These processes had shaped immigration from Europe to the U.S. since the 1820s, but in the last decades of the nineteenth century, when these dynamics reached deeper into Southern and Eastern Europe, a so-called new immigration began. While older migrant streams continued to flow to the U.S. (Germans were the third largest group of immigrants in this period), most immigrants were as yet unfamiliar to Americans. Italians and Jews from Russia and Eastern Europe were the largest groups, comprising 17 and 14 percent, respectively, of the total immigration from 1880 to World War I. In the decade before the war, the foreign-born comprised nearly 15 percent of the total population, the highest proportion in the nation's history.

Historian John Bodnar has argued against the image of the new immigrants as victimized peasants fleeing poverty. Rather, he describes emigration as a pragmatic choice made by families confronted with rapidly changing economic realities. In Italy, for example, the break up of the feudal land tenure system—which put nearly three hundred thousand parcels of land up for sale between 1861 and 1899—had different regional effects. In areas where farmers competed to buy small properties, as in southern Italy, emigration was a means for generating cash to buy land. In central and northern Italy, where land remained in the hands of large estates and was not for sale, peasant militancy, not emigration, was the strategy for improving one's condition.

In the late nineteenth century Italian migrants maintained strong ties to their home communities. They resisted the idea of permanent settlement in the United States; the annual return migration rate was greater than 45 percent. Few Italians were interested in buying land in America. "This [Italy] is the only true land," explained a Consenzan peasant. "We can live somewhere else for a while. But we can only buy land here."

In central and Eastern Europe, emigration was spurred by economic change as well as by religious persecution and political repression. Throughout the nineteenth century, Tsarist Russia isolated and oppressed Jews, requiring them to live in segregated communities (*shtetls*) within a "Pale of Settlement" along Russia's western border, from the Baltic to the Black Sea, encompassing present-day Byelorussia, Latvia, Lithuania, Moldova, Poland, Russia, and the Ukraine. Barred from owning or renting land outside of towns and cities, Jews worked as merchants and small craftsmen. Yet their occupational positions also came under pressure from increased competition from former serfs, who were emancipated in 1863. In the 1880s and 1890s Jews in Russia faced increased repression. They were expelled from Moscow, St. Petersburg, and Kiev, and faced frequent pogroms, or government-sponsored and inspired mob attacks. From 1880 to 1924, some 2.4 million Jews migrated to the United States.

A diverse population of Slavic peoples also migrated to America at the turn of the century. These included Ukrainians, Poles, Bohemians (Czechs), Slovaks, Slovenians, Croatians, and others who, for the most part, lived under Russian, German, or Austro-Hungarian rule. Most were Eastern Orthodox or Roman Catholic. Emigration became an option for Slavs in areas where landholdings were too small to be successful and alternative employment in industry was lacking. Many also chafed under political and ethnic repression. In the 1870s and 1880s, for example, many Poles left

Prussia in response to chancellor Otto von Bismarck's forced assimilation policies, which included mandatory use of the German language and a state takeover of parochial schools.

The new immigrants were mostly unskilled workers—laborers, farm laborers, and domestic servants—with the exception of Jews, for whom tailoring was the largest occupational group. As with Mexicans and Chinese, a large percentage were unattached males—as many as 90 percent of Bulgarian and Serbian migrants, 87 percent of the Greeks, and 74.5 percent of the Italians. Those groups with a high percentage of males had a correspondingly high rate of return migration. Jews had a more balanced sex ratio and a lower rate of return because their migration tended to be family-based and because political repression in their homelands precluded return.

The many millions of laboring men who poured into the United States in the last decades of the nineteenth century and the first decades of the twentieth fed an explosive growth of urban construction and industrial production. Immigrant laborers erected the modern urban infrastructure: they built roads, dug sewers and subway tunnels, and laid streetcar tracks. They provided unskilled labor in mass production industries, creating and filling a new stratum in the workforce. For example, at the turn of the century the Carnegie steel plants in Pittsburgh employed some fourteen thousand common laborers, of whom more than eleven thousand were from Southern and Eastern Europe. The average wage was $12.50 a week, less than what a family needed for subsistence,

and the accident rate averaged nearly 25 percent a year.

Immigrants' old-world cultures clashed with the requirements of factory discipline. Employers complained that workers frequently missed work for religious occasions and festivals—for example, the Greek Orthodox church had more than eighty festivals a year, and a Polish wedding could last from three to five days. Collective behavior in the workplace and in immigrant communities was often articulated in the language and rituals of premodern village culture like religious oaths, peasant parades, and food riots. Immigrant workers sometimes staged strikes for higher wages, but they were also used to break the strikes of native-born workers, as employers were adept at exploiting ethnic difference. Some labor unions reached out to immigrants, but others, particularly among the craft unions, remained suspicious of them. Among the latter were Irish Americans and German Americans, whose immigrant ancestors had toiled at the bottom rungs of the work force and faced ethnic and religious prejudice in the early and middle nineteenth century. By the late nineteenth century, however, these older immigrant groups had achieved a measure of economic and social incorporation, if not respectability. Irish Americans, for example, were prevalent in some of the skilled trades and in urban political "machines," which emerged in the late nineteenth century, such as New York's Tammany Hall and the Boston organization of Mayor James Curley.

The influx of immigrants in the 1890s and their concentration in poor urban communities elicited a variety of responses among Americans of older immigrant stock. New England elites as well as native-born craft workers considered the new immigrants to be unassimilable backward peasants from the "degraded races" of Europe, lacking the characteristics necessary for economic independence or self-government. The American Protective Association, formed in 1887, was anti-immigration and anti-Catholic, and boasted 2.5 million members at its peak in the mid-1890s. The Immigration Restriction League formed in 1893 with the goal of restricting immigration by means of a literacy test.

Anti-immigrant sentiment was not confined to politics. One of the most brutal anti-immigrant incidents involved the lynching of eleven Italians in New Orleans in 1891. Native-born whites blamed a growing population of Sicilian immigrants and a rumored Italian Mafia for the murder of the New Orleans police chief David Hennessy. After a jury acquitted nine Italians for the crime, a mob that included public officials and businessmen gathered to mete out "justice" on its own terms. Jewish immigrants experienced a growth of anti-Semitism, in Northern cities and in the South. Some of the first anti-Semitic demonstrations in the United States took place in the 1880s in the lower South, against Jewish supply merchants. By 1893 nightriders were burning farmhouses belonging to Jewish landlords. In northern cities, Jewish bankers and immigrants were scapegoated for the 1890s economic depression.

While some native-born Americans expressed hostility toward the new im-migrants, others were more sanguine about the possibilities of assimilation. A new generation of college-educated middle-class Protestant women lobbied for factory reforms, formed settlement houses in immigrant neighborhoods, and promoted Americanization. Yet both the nativists and the social reformers condescended to immigrants and failed to appreciate the richness of their cultures. In fact, immigrant communities were not only sustained by ethnocultural and religious traditions but also comprised diverse political and ideological trends that were part of larger diasporas of exile. Polish immigrants, whose migration was inextricably linked to the division of Poland by its Great-Power neighbors, were keenly nationalist. Among Jews, religious orthodoxy, socialism, and Zionism were all prominent and divergent trends.

At the turn of the century European immigrants occupied an ambivalent and vexatious position in America's racial hierarchy, their place complicated by the demands of other racial categories under construction. While legally defined as "white" for purposes of naturalization, the native-born and older immigrants did not necessarily perceive the newer immigrants as "white," at least not as fully white as the "Anglo-Saxon race." Historians James Barrett and David Roediger have described the new immigrants as "in-between peoples, situated above African and Asian Americans but *below* 'white' people." Many immigrant workers, perceiving the disadvantage of being black in America, embraced whiteness as a strategy for economic and social advancement. But others, having experienced the sting of discrimination and group hostility both in their homelands and in America, identified with non-whites. At the same time, Eastern and Southern European immigrants constructed their identities in ways that were not racial but ethnic, expressing national and religious ties. Over time, however, the process of becoming "American" was inextricably bound up with race.

## THE IMPERIAL REPUBLIC

The racial hierarchies constructed in the last quarter of the nineteenth century were part of the United States' emerging modern national identity, and that identity was defined as much by its projections abroad as by its domestic relations. As the conquest of the West was consolidated and the frontier closed, the United States extended its horizons to the Pacific and to Asia.

Of course, expansion and conquest had been part of the nation's history and identity since its inception. Many of the arguments supporting earlier expansions were reiterated: commerce and trade, an outlet for class tensions, geopolitical considerations with regard to European nations, and providential design. But there were also important differences. Until the late nineteenth century, the nation had expanded into contiguous territory. (The exceptions were Alaska and the Midway islands, both acquired in 1867.) New territories were incorporated into the nation as areas for white settlement and for statehood. But could noncontiguous territories become states? What

would it mean to make their colored inhabitants citizens? Could the United States, a democratic republic born of an anticolonial revolution, have colonies?

### The Colonization of Hawai'i

The colonization of Hawai'i followed the recipe common to eighteenth- and nineteenth-century European colonialism—a succession of traders, Christian missionaries, merchants and planters, and soldiers; a decline of the native population through diseases introduced by Westerners; and the importation of racialized labor to produce cash crops for export.

At the time of contact in the late eighteenth-century, Hawai'ian society, which dated to the second century c.e., comprised highly stratified agricultural chiefdoms. Kinship groups worked the land for subsistence and for tribute to a hierarchy of lords and chiefs (ali'i). The "discovery" of the islands in 1778 by British sea Captain James Cook introduced Hawai'i to a market economy and into the nexus of the Euro-American trade in the Pacific and Asia.

In 1820 the first Christian missionaries arrived from the United States, strict Puritan Protestants from New England. In 1825 they converted Queen Ka'ahumanu and several high-ranking ali'i. The missionaries gained enormous political influence through their close relationship with Hawai'ian royalty. During the 1830s and 1840s American missionaries and lawyers wrote a Hawai'ian constitution and laws (the criminal code was virtually copied from Massachusetts law books) and even administered the state.

The missionaries also pressured the Hawai'ians to change the system of land tenure, as they believed that individual land ownership would civilize the Hawai'ians by promoting industriousness and the nuclear family. The Great *Mahele* (land division) of 1848-1850 divided Hawai'i's land between the crown, the government, and the *ali'i*, and gave commoners the right to hold land in fee simple. By 1852 nonnaturalized foreigners were allowed to buy land.

The Hawai'ian elite has been called naive and passive for seemingly handing control of their sovereign nation over to foreigners. But in the context of rapid economic change and Western economic and military advantage, their actions may be better understood as efforts to stem the erosion of their power. For example, some anthropologists have argued that the *ali'i* may have seen Christianity as a countervailing force against the spread of the merchants' influence. Similarly, the Hawai'ian monarchy acceded to private property interests in the belief that economic prosperity would preserve the kingdom's political independence. The *Mahele* also attempted to keep land under Hawai'ian control, even as it made it alienable. However, few commoners held title to land and many were thrown off the estates, "left to wander in tears on the highway," according to a Hawai'ian contemporary, when *ali'i* leased their land to foreigners.

The passage of land to foreigners was the critical element for developing the plantation sugar industry. The other necessity was labor, which was in short supply because the native Hawai'ian population was dwindling and, more-

over, was averse to the arduous labor of cutting and hauling cane. The planters turned to imported contract labor, first from China and then Japan and Portugal; and, in the early twentieth century, from Korea, Puerto Rico, and the Philippines. By far the greatest number came from Japan in the last decades of the nineteenth century. Between 1875 and 1910, land devoted to sugar cultivation increased from 12,000 to 214,000 acres.

Indeed, sugar made the *haole* (white) elite ever more powerful. In 1876 the planters won a reciprocity agreement between Hawai'i and the United States, which gave their sugar duty-free access to the American market. Increasingly, *haole* leaders pressed for annexation by the United States. Annexation also had support among American military leaders, who coveted Hawai'i's strategic position in the Pacific Ocean and the deep-water port at Pearl Harbor. In 1893 members of the haole elite, including missionary descendents Stanford Dole and Lorrin Thurston, staged a coup, overthrowing Queen Lililuokilani (landing American Marines to face her down), and proclaimed a "Republic of Hawai'i." By any standard of international law it was an illegal takeover of a sovereign kingdom. President Grover Cleveland, however, resisted calls to annex Hawai'i, in large part because he believed it would exacerbate the Asiatic race problem. In 1898, when imperialist sentiment ran high in the United States, Congress approved the annexation of Hawai'i by a simple majority resolution, violating the two-thirds Senate ratification required by the U.S. Constitution. The colonization of Hawai'i may have been obscured by its territorial status, but the process of incorporation resonated with other processes of dispossession and conquest. Recognition by the United States of white territorial government over the sovereign Hawai'ian kingdom was analogous to its ignoring American Indian tribal governments in favor of the white-dominated Oklahoma Territory.

### The Spanish American War and an Empire Without Colonies

Indeed, by 1898 American nationalism had reached a fever pitch. The press clamored for American intervention in Cuba, where Spain had been fighting a nationalist uprising in its colony since 1896. Notwithstanding widespread sympathy in the United States for the Cuban freedom fighters, Americans held significant economic interests in Cuba and Puerto Rico, another Spanish colony.

A proimperialist trend in the United States had grown since the 1880s, suffused with the language of Manifest Destiny and Anglo-Saxonism. The evangelical Reverend Josiah Strong declared expansion to the Pacific was part of the inexorable westward march of Christian civilization. Naval Admiral Alfred Thayer Mahan argued in the language of Social Darwinism, applying the concept of "survival of the fittest" to international competition among nations.

The sinking of the U.S.S. Maine in Havana harbor in February 1898 gave the United States reason to declare war against Spain. In Cuba and Puerto Rico, American troops rather quickly defeated the already weakened Spanish. The "splendid little war" was won nearly too quickly, in fact, as Senator Henry Cabot Lodge instructed Theodore Roosevelt to prolong the fighting until Admiral Dewey's fleet reached the Philippines. In the Treaty of Paris in 1899, Spain ceded its colonial possessions to the United States for $20 million. The transfer of colonies was not so simple, however, because in liberating themselves from Spain, both Cuba and the Philippines had declared themselves independent republics.

Opinion in the United States was deeply divided. A contentious debate over the Senate's ratification of the Treaty of Paris raised questions about America's foundational beliefs. Antiimperialist sentiment involved two lines of thinking. One view was overtly racist. Pointing to the nation's Negro and Asiatic race problems, this view opposed incorporating additional backward colored races into the nation. The other view opposed the acquisition of colonies as antithetical to American principles; as William Jennings Bryan stated, "Our nation must give up any intention of entering upon a colonial policy, such as is now pursued by European countries, or it must abandon the doctrine of consent of the governed." The expansionists argued that the inhabitants of Spain's former colonies were backward races incapable of self-rule, and that the United States had a moral duty to civilize and to protect them from European colonizers. Thus they claimed American interests were noble, unlike old-world colonialism. Alfred Beveridge, Jr., one of the most ardent expansionists in the Senate, declared expansion was "for the Great

Republic, not for Imperialism." Many proimperialists frankly saw no problem, constitutional or moral, in ruling backward races without their consent, citing American Indian policy as precedent. A University of Chicago political scientist argued in 1899 that "uncivilized nations under tribal relations [in the Philippines] would occupy the same status precisely as our own Indians. They are, in fact, 'Indians'-and the fourteenth amendment does not make citizens of Indians."

In the end the expansionists won the day. President McKinley eschewed a formal annexation of Cuba, in part to avoid adding more black people to the nation and in part because the Cuban nationalist movement had gained considerable legitimacy in its fight against Spain. The Platt Amendment, passed by Congress in 1899 and added to the Cuban Constitution, made Cuba a "protectorate," an independent nation under the military protection of the United States.

Puerto Rico and the Philippines were annexed as "unincorporated territories"—that is, territories without the prospect of statehood—and organized as "insular (island) possessions" under the War Department. Puerto Ricans and Filipinos were given the status of "nationals"—that is, they owed allegiance exclusively to the United States but were not U.S. citizens. Each had a junior sort of republican government—for purposes of tutelage—but their affairs were subject entirely to approval by a Governor General appointed jointly by the president and by Congress. The U.S. Supreme Court ruled in the Insular Cases (1901) that the Constitution did not necessarily have to follow the flag. (The

Jones Act of 1917 made Puerto Ricans citizens of the United States, although they had no representation in Congress and their affairs remained under U.S. authority.)

Notwithstanding President McKinley's claims of an American policy of "benevolent assimilation," Filipinos were wary about trading in one colonial oppressor for another. The Philippine revolution had militarily defeated Spain well before the Americans arrived and in 1898 had proclaimed an independent republic. When Spain transferred title to the islands to the United States, they occupied only the city of Manila. Thus, the United States had to impose benevolent rule by means of force. The Philippine American War (1899–1902) was brutal and bloody. The United States committed two-thirds of the Army to a guerrilla war that was led by generals with experience in the American Indian wars of 1870s and 1880s. U.S. troops committed atrocities, including burning villages, killing noncombatants, and torturing prisoners, which shocked Americans when details of the war leaked into the press. The Filipinos fought tenaciously before succumbing to the Americans' superior military force as well as their own internal divisions. Some seven thousand Americans and twenty thousand Filipinos were killed or wounded in the war, and hundreds of thousands of Filipinos—some estimates are as high as 1 million—died of war-related disease or famine.

In both Puerto Rico and the Philippines, the United States combined the use (or threat) of force with a policy of suasion that coopted native elites by giving them economic advantages, including protected access to the American market, political power over their own lower classes, and promises of eventual self-rule. Yet, like Indian assimilation, the strategy of civilizing uplift and self-rule was inherently contradictory, as cultural critic Vicente Rafael has explained, "the 'self' that rules itself can only emerge when the subject has learned to colonize itself."

The policies of subordination and conquest that had developed as solutions to the Negro and Indian questions, America's oldest race problems, provided templates for race policy towards the nation's new immigrants and the inhabitants of its new territorial acquisitions in the late nineteenth century. When congressional leaders and other elites debated taking the Philippines in the aftermath of the Spanish American War, they often made reference to slaves and American Indians to make the argument that democracy was not for everyone. They understood that while various race policies differed in the specifics there were certain important commonalities.

Most significant was the view that the "colored races" lagged far behind whites on civilization's evolutionary scale. The doctrine of "consent of the governed," central to the Declaration of Independence did not apply, it was argued, to "races of people adjudged incompetent for self-government." A journalist asked in 1900, "Were the Negro slaves canvassed and their consent obtained to their condition of slavery? Were the Indians. . . ? For that matter," he added, "has there been, until today, any real opportunity given the . . . 35,000,000 of

the female sex to ascertain their opinion concerning the laws under which they live?" Thus during the last quarter of the nineteenth century, American politics and culture infantilized former slaves, Indian wards, Chinese and Mexican laborers, and Hawai'ian, Puerto Rican, and Filipino colonial subjects in order to justify their exclusion from full citizenship.

At the same time, the Civil War and the Reconstruction amendments to the U.S. Constitution had abolished slavery and established national citizenship and civil rights. Racism had to be squared with these principles. Hence we see the emergence of myriad legal fictions like "separate but equal" and "unincorporated territory" and pronouncements of Congress's "plenary power" over immigration, Indian treaties, and insular policy. America's "colored races" confronted a deep chasm between the formality of equality and the reality of inequality. During the late nineteenth century, policies and practices of race evolved that would ensure, as W. E. B. DuBois observed in 1903, that the most pressing question of the twentieth century would be that of the color line.

## BIBLIOGRAPHIC ESSAY

### Jim Crow South

On the transition from Reconstruction to the "New South," see C. Van Woodward, *Origins of the New South* (Baton Rouge: Louisiana State University Press, 1951). On Jim Crow segregation, see C. Van Woodward, *The Strange Career of Jim Crow* (New York:

Oxford University Press, 1957); Leon Litwack, *Trouble in Mind: Black Southerners in the Age of Jim Crow* (New York: Knopf, 1998); Glenda E. Gilmore, *Gender and Jim Crow* (Chapel Hill: University of North Carolina Press, 1996). On convict labor, see David Oshinsky, *Worse than Slavery: Parchman Farm and the Ordeal of Jim Crow Justice* (New York: Free Press, 1996). On black politics, see Kevin K. Gaines, *Uplifting the Race* (Chapel Hill: University of North Carolina Press, 1996).

## The West

For a general historical overview of the West, see Richard White, *"It's Your Misfortune and None of My Own": A History of the American West* (Norman: University of Oklahoma Press, 1991) and Patricia N. Limerick, *The Legacy of Conquest: The Unbroken Past of the American West* (New York: Norton, 1987).

## American Indians

Frederick Hoxie, *A Final Promise: The Campaign to Assimilate the Indians, 1880–1920* (Norman: University of Oklahoma Press, 1984) and Brian Dippie, *The Vanishing American: White Attitudes and U.S. Indian Policy* (Middletown, Conn.: Wesleyan University Press, 1981) discuss changes in U.S. Indian Policy in the mid- to late-nineteenth century.

## Mexicans

Douglas Monroy, *Thrown Among Strangers* (Berkeley: University of California Press, 1990), discusses the impact of white settlement on Indians and Mexicans in California in the nineteenth century. On Texas, see David Montejano, *Anglos and Mexicans in the Making of Texas* (Austin: University of Texas, 1987).

## Asians

For an overview of Asian American history, see Sucheng Chan, ed., *Entry Denied: Exclusion and the Chinese Community in the U.S.* (Philadelphia: Temple University Press, 1991). On Japanese immigration, see Yuji Ichioka, *The Issei: The World of First Generation Japanese Immigrants 1885–1924* (New York: Free Press, 1988). On exclusion and other discriminatory laws against Chinese, see Charles McClain, *In Search of Equality: The Chinese Struggle against Discrimination in Nineteenth-Century America* (Berkeley: University of California Press, 1994).

## European Immigration

For an overview of late nineteenth-century migration from Europe to the United States, see John Bodnar, *The Transplanted: A History of Immigrants in Urban America* (Bloomington: Indiana University Press, 1985). Matthew Jacobson, *Whiteness of a Different Color: European Immigrants and the Alchemy of Race* (Cambridge: Harvard University Press, 1998), discusses the role of race in the process of immigrant assimilation.

## Imperial Republic

On Hawai'i, see Sally E. Merry, *Colonizing Hawai'i: The Cultural Power of Law* (Princeton: Princeton University Press, 2000) and Rob Wilson, *Reimagining the American Pacific* (Durham: Duke University Press, 2000). On the Philippines, see Stuart Creighton Miller, *Benevolent Assimilation: The American Conquest of* the *Philippines* (New Haven: Yale University Press, 1982) and Vicente Rafael, *White Love and Other Events in Filipino History* (Durham: Duke University Press, 2000). Robert Rydell, *All the World's a Fair* (Chicago: University of Chicago Press, 1984) discusses the imperial self-image of the American nation as expressed at late nineteenth-century world's fairs.

## DOCUMENTS

### "The Life Story of a Negro Peon," 1904

*After the Civil War many African Americans worked on the same plantations, for the same planters. No longer slaves, they worked as free labor for wages or as sharecroppers and tenant farmers. Long-term contracts and constant debt kept many in a state of peonage. State prison officials also contracted black convicts for plantations, railroad construction, and other work. Contemporary critics called these practices a "new slavery."*

Source: "The New Slavery in the South: An Autobiography by a Georgia Negro," *Independent*, February 25, 1904, pp. 409–414, from Hamilton Holt, *Life Stories of Undistinguished Americans as Told by Themselves* (New York: Routledge, 2000).

*The following chapter was obtained from an interview with a Georgia Negro who was a victim of the new slavery of the South.*

I am a negro and was born some time during the war in Elbert County, Ga., and I reckon by this time I must be a little over forty years old. My mother was not married when I was born, and I never knew who my father was or anything about him. Shortly after the war my mother died, and I was left to the care of my uncle. All this happened before I was eight years old, and so I can't remember very much about it. When I was about ten years old my uncle hired me out to Captain ———. I had already learned how to plow, and was also a good hand at picking cotton. I was told that the Captain wanted me for his house-boy, and that later on he was going to train me to be his coachman. To be a coachman in those days was considered a post of honor, and young as I was, I was glad of the chance. But I had not been at the Captain's a month before I was put to work on the farm, with some twenty or thirty other negroes—men, women and children. From the beginning the boys had the same tasks as the men and women. There was no difference. We all worked hard during the week, and would frolic on Saturday nights and often on Sundays. And everybody was happy. The men got $3 a week and the women $2. I don't know what the children got. Every week my uncle collected my money for me, but it was very little of it that I ever saw. My uncle fed and clothed me, gave me a place to sleep, and allowed me 10¢ or 15¢ a week for "spending change," as he called it. I must have been seventeen or eighteen years old before I got tired of that arrangement, and felt that I was man enough to be working for myself and handling my own wages. The other boys about my age and size were "drawing" their own pay, and they used to laugh at me and call me "Baby" because my old uncle was always on hand to "draw" my pay. Worked up by these things, I made a break for liberty. Unknown to my uncle or the Captain I went off to a neighboring plantation and hired myself out to another man. The new landlord agreed to give me 40¢ a day and furnish me one meal. I thought that was doing fine. Bright and early one Monday morning I started for work, still not letting the others know anything about it. But they found it out before sundown. The Captain came over to the new place and brought some kind of officer of the law. The officer pulled out a long piece of paper from his pocket and read it to my new employer. When this was done I heard my new boss say:

"I beg your pardon, Captain. I didn't know this nigger was bound out to you, or I wouldn't have hired him."

"He certainly is bound out to me," said the Captain. "He belongs to me until he is twenty-one, and I'm going to make him know his place."

So I was carried back to the Captain's. That night he made me strip off my clothing down to my waist, had me tied to a tree in his backyard, ordered his foreman to give me thirty lashes with a buggy whip across my bare back, and stood by until it was done. After that experience the Captain made me stay on his place night and day—but my uncle still continued to "draw" my money.

I was a man nearly grown before I knew how to count from one to one hundred. I was a man nearly grown before I ever saw a colored school teacher. I never went to school a day in my life.

To-day I can't write my own name, though I can read a little. I was a man nearly grown before I ever rode on a railroad train, and then I went on an excursion from Elberton to Athens. What was true of me was true of hundreds of other negroes around me—'way off there in the country, fifteen or twenty miles from the nearest town.

When I reached twenty-one the Captain told me I was a free man, but he urged me to stay with him. He said he would treat me right, and pay me as much as anybody else would. The Captain's son and I were about the same age, and the Captain said that, as he had owned my mother and uncle during slavery, and as his son didn't want me to leave them (since I had been with them so long), he wanted me to stay with the old family. And I stayed. I signed a contract—that is, I made my mark—for one year. The Captain was to give me $3.50 a week, and furnish me a little house on the plantation—a one-room log cabin similar to those used by his other laborers.

During that year I married Mandy. For several years Mandy had been the house-servant for the Captain, his wife, his son and his three daughters, and they all seemed to think a good deal of her. As an evidence of their regard they gave us a suit of furniture, which cost about $25, and we set up housekeeping in one of the Captain's two-room shanties. I thought I was the biggest man in Georgia. Mandy still kept her place in the "Big House" after our marriage. We did so well for the first year that I renewed my contract for the second year, and for the third, fourth and fifth year I did the same thing. Before the end of the fifth year the Captain had died, and his son, who had married some two or three years before, took charge of the plantation. Also, for two or three years, this son had been serving at Atlanta in some big office to which he had been elected. I think it was in the Legislature or something of that sort—anyhow, all the people called him Senator. At the end of the fifth year the Senator suggested that I sign up a contract for ten years; then, he said, we wouldn't have to fix up papers every year. I asked my wife about it; she consented; and so I made a ten-year contract.

Not long afterward the Senator had a long, low shanty built on his place. A great big chimney, with a wide, open fireplace, was built at one end of it, and on each side of the house, running lengthwise, there was a row of frames or stalls just large enough to hold a single mattress. The places for these mattresses were fixed one above the other; so that there was a double row of these stalls or pens on each side. They looked for all the world like stalls for horses. Since then I have seen cabooses similarly arranged as sleeping quarters for railroad laborers. Nobody seemed to know what the Senator was fixing for. All doubts were put aside one bright day in April when about forty able-bodied negroes, bound in iron chains, and some of them handcuffed, were brought out to the Senator's farm in three big wagons. They were quartered in the long, low shanty, and it was afterward called the stockade. This was the beginning of the Senator's convict camp. These men were prisoners who had been leased by the Senator from the State of Georgia at about $200 each per year, the State agreeing to pay for guards and physicians, for necessary inspection, for inquests, all rewards for escaped convicts, the cost of litigation and all other incidental camp expenses. When I saw these men in shackles, and the guards with their guns, I was scared nearly to death. I felt like running away, but I didn't know where to go. And if there had been any place to go to, I would have had to leave my wife and child behind. We free laborers held a meeting. We all wanted to quit. We sent a man to tell the Senator about it. Word came back that we were all under contract for ten years and that the Senator would hold us to the letter of the contract, or put us in chains and lock us up—the same as the other prisoners. It was made plain to us by some white people we talked to that in the contracts we had signed we had all agreed to be locked up in a stockade at night or at any, other time that our employer saw fit; further, we learned that we could not lawfully break our contract for any reason and go and hire ourselves to somebody else without the consent of our employer; and, more than that, if we got mad and ran away, we could be run down by bloodhounds, arrested without process of law, and be returned to our employer, who, according to the contract, might beat us brutally or administer any other kind of punishment that he thought proper. In other words, we had sold ourselves into slavery—and what could we do about it? The white folks had all the courts, all the guns, all the hounds, all the railroads, all the telegraph wires, all the newspapers, all the money, and nearly all the land—and we had only our ignorance, our poverty and our empty hands. We decided that the best thing to do was to shut our mouths, say nothing, and go back to work. And most of us worked side by side with those convicts during the remainder of the ten years.

But this first batch of convicts was only the beginning. Within six months another stockade was built, and twenty or thirty other convicts were brought to the plantation, among them six or eight women! The Senator had bought an additional thousand acres of land. and to his already large cotton plantation he added two great big saw-mills and went into the lumber business. Within two years the Senator had in all nearly 200 negroes working on his plantation—about half of them free laborers, so called, and about half of them convicts. The only difference between the free laborers and the others was that the free laborers could come and go as they pleased, at night—that is, they were not locked up at night, and were not, as a general thing, whipped for slight offenses. The troubles of the free laborers began at the close of the ten-year period. To a man, they all wanted to quit when the time was up. To a man, they all refused to sign new contracts—even for one year, not to say anything of ten years. And just when we thought that our bondage was at an end we found that it had really just begun. Two or three years before, or about a year and a half after the Senator had started his camp, he had established a large store, which was called the commissary. All of us free laborers were compelled to buy our sup-

plies—food, clothing, etc.—from that store. We never used any money in our dealings with the commissary, only tickets or orders, and we had a general settlement once each year, in October. In this store we were charged all sorts of high prices for goods, because every year we would come out in debt to our employer. If not that, we seldom had more than $5 or $10 coming to us—and that for a whole year's work. Well, at the close of the tenth year, when we kicked and meant to leave the Senator, he said to some of us with a smile (and I never will forget that smile—I can see it now):

"Boys, I'm sorry you're going to leave me. I hope you will do well in your new places—so well that you will be able to pay me the little balances which most of you owe me."

Word was sent out for all of us to meet him at the commissary at 2 o'clock. There he told us that, after we had signed what he called a written acknowledgment of our debts, we might go and look for new places. The storekeeper took us one by one and read to us statements of our accounts. According to the books there was no man of us who owed the Senator less than $100; some of us were put down for as much as $200. I owed $105, according to the bookkeeper. These debts were not accumulated during one year, but ran back for three and four years, so we were told—in spite of the fact that we understood that we had had a full settlement at the end of each year. But no one of us would have dared to dispute a white man's word—oh, no; not in those days. Besides, we fellows didn't care anything about the amounts—we were after getting away; and we had been told that we might go, if we signed the acknowledgments. We would have signed anything, just to get away. So we stepped up, we did, and made our marks. That same night we were rounded up by a constable and ten or twelve white men, who aided him, and we were locked up, every one of us, in one of the Senator's stockades. The next morning it was explained to us by the two guards appointed to watch us that, in the papers, we had signed the day before, we had not only made acknowledgment of our indebtedness, but that we had also agreed to work for the Senator until the debts were paid by hard labor. And from that day forward we were treated just like convicts. Really we had made ourselves lifetime slaves, or peons, as the laws called us. But, call it slavery, peonage, or what not, the truth is we lived in a hell on earth what time we spent in the Senator's peon camp.

I lived in that camp, as a peon, for nearly three years. My wife fared better than I did, as did the wives of some of the other negroes, because the white men about the camp used these unfortunate creatures as their mistresses. When I was first put in the stockade my wife was still kept for a while in the "Big House," but my little boy, who was only nine years old, was given away to a negro family across the river in South Carolina, and I never saw or heard of him after that. When I left the camp my wife had had two children by some one of the white bosses, and she was living in fairly good shape in a little house off to herself. But the poor negro women who were not in the class with my wife fared about as bad as the helpless negro

men. Most of the time the women who were peons or convicts were compelled to wear men's clothes. Sometimes, when I have seen them dressed like men, and plowing or hoeing or hauling logs or working at the blacksmith's trade, just the same as men, my heart would bleed and my blood would boil, but I was powerless to raise a hand. It would have meant death on the spot to have said a word. Of the first six women brought to the camp, two of them gave birth to children after they had been there more than twelve months—and the babies had white men for their fathers!

The stockades in which we slept were, I believe, the filthiest places in the world. They were cesspools of nastiness. During the thirteen years that I was there I am willing to swear that a mattress was never moved after it had been brought there, except to turn it over once or twice a month. No sheets were used, only dark-colored blankets. Most of the men slept every night in the clothing that they had worked in all day. Some of the worst characters were made to sleep in chains. The doors were locked and barred each night, and tallow candles were the only lights allowed. Really the stockades were but little more than cow sheds, horse stables or hog pens. Strange to say, not a great number of these people died while I was there, though a great many came away maimed and bruised and, in some cases, disabled for life. As far as I remember only about ten died during the last ten years that I was there, two of these being killed outright by the guards for trivial offenses.

It was a hard school that peon camp was, but I learned more there in a few short months by contact with those poor fellows from the outside world than ever I had known before. Most of what I learned was evil, and I now know that I should have been better off without the knowledge, but much of what I learned was helpful to me. Barring two or three severe and brutal whippings which I received, I got along very well, all things considered; but the system is damnable. A favorite way of whipping a man was to strap him down to a log, flat on his back, and spank him fifty or sixty times on his bare feet with a shingle or a huge piece of plank. When the man would get up with sore and blistered feet and an aching body, if he could not then keep up with the other men at work he would be strapped to the log again, this time face downward, and would be lashed with a buggy trace on his bare back. When a woman had to be whipped it was usually done in private, though they would be compelled to fall down across a barrel or something of the kind and receive the licks on their backsides.

The working day on a peon farm begins with sunrise and ends when the sun goes down; or, in other words, the average peon works from ten to twelve hours each day, with one hour (from 12 o'clock to 1 o'clock) for dinner. Hot or cold, sun or rain, this is the rule. As to their meals, the laborers are divided up into squads or companies, just the same as soldiers in a great military camp would be. Two or three men in each stockade are appointed as cooks. From thirty to forty men report to each cook. In the warm months (or eight or nine months out of the year) the cooking is done on the outside, just behind the stockades; in the cold months the cooking is done inside the stockades. Each peon is provided with a great big tin cup, a flat tin pan and two big tin spoons. No knives or forks are ever seen, except those used by the cooks. At meal time the peons pass in single file before the cooks, and hold out their pans and cups to receive their allowances. Cow peas (red or white, which when boiled turn black), fat bacon and old-fashioned Georgia corn bread, baked in pones from one to two and three inches thick, make up the chief articles of food. Black coffee, black molasses and brown sugar are also used abundantly. Once in a great while, on Sundays, biscuits would be made, but they would always be made from the kind of flour called "shorts." As a rule, breakfast consisted of coffee, fried bacon, corn bread, and sometimes molasses—and one "helping" of each was all that was allowed. Peas, boiled with huge hunks of fat bacon, and a hoe-cake, as big as a man's hand, usually answered for dinner. Sometimes this dinner bill of fare gave place to bacon and greens (collard or turnip) and pot liquor. Though we raised corn, potatoes and other vegetables, we never got a chance at such things unless we could steal them and cook them secretly. Supper consisted of coffee, fried bacon and molasses. But, although the food was limited to certain things, I am sure we all got a plenty of the things allowed. As coarse as these things were, we kept, as a rule, fat and sleek and as strong as mules. And that, too, in spite of the fact that we had no special arrangements for taking regular baths. And no very great effort was made to keep us regularly in clean clothes. No tables were used or allowed. In summer we would sit down on the ground and eat our meals, and in winter we would sit around inside the filthy stockades. Each man was his own dish washer—that is to say, each man was responsible for the care of his pan and cup and spoons. My dishes got washed about once a week!

To-day, I am told, there are six or seven of these private camps in Georgia—that is to say, camps where most of the convicts are leased from the State of Georgia. But there are hundreds and hundreds of farms all over the State where negroes, and in some cases poor white folks, are held in bondage on the ground that they are working out debts, or where the contracts which they have made hold them in a kind of perpetual bondage, because, under those contracts, they may not quit one employer and hire out to another except by and with the knowledge and consent of the former employer. One of the usual ways to secure laborers for a large peonage camp is for the proprietor to send out an agent to the little courts in the towns and villages, and where a man charged with some petty offense has no friends or money the agent will urge him to plead guilty, with the understanding that the agent will pay his fine, and in that way save him from the disgrace of being sent to jail or the chain-gang! For this high favor the man must sign beforehand a paper signifying his willingness to go to the farm and work out the amount of the fine imposed. When he reaches the farm he has to be fed and clothed, to be sure, and these things are charged up to his account. By the time he has worked

out his first debt another is hanging over his head, and so on and so on, by a sort of endless chain, for an indefinite period, as in every case the indebtedness is arbitrarily arranged by the employer. In many cases it is very evident that the court officials are in collusion with the proprietors or agents, and that they divide the "graft" among themselves. As an example of this dickering among the whites, every year many convicts were brought to the Senator's camp from a certain county in South Georgia, 'way down in the turpentine district. The majority of these men were charged with adultery, which is an offense against the laws of the great and sovereign State of Georgia! Upon inquiry I learned that down in that county a number of negro lewd women were employed by certain white men to entice negro men into their houses; and then, on a certain night, at a given signal, when all was in readiness, raids would be made by the officers upon these houses, and the men would be arrested and charged with living in adultery. Nine out of ten of these men, so arrested and so charged, would find their way ultimately to some convict camp, and, as I said, many of them found their way every year to the Senator's camp while I was there. The low-down women were never punished in any way. On the contrary, I was told that they always seemed to stand in high favor with the sheriffs, constables and other officers. There can be no room to doubt that they assisted very materially in furnishing laborers for the prison pens of Georgia, and the belief was general among the men that they were regularly paid for their work. I could tell more, but I've said enough to make anybody's heart sick. This great and terrible iniquity is, I know, widespread throughout Georgia and many other Southern States.

But I didn't tell you how I got out. I didn't get out—they put me out. When I had served as a peon for nearly three years—and you remember that they claimed that I owed them only $165—when I had served for nearly three years, one of the bosses came to me and said that my time was up. He happened to be the one who was said to be living with my wife. He gave me a new suit of overalls, which cost about 75¢, took me in a buggy and carried me across the Broad River into South Carolina, set me down and told me to "git." I didn't have a cent of money, and I wasn't feeling well, but somehow I managed to get a move on me. I begged my way to Columbia. In two or three days I ran across a man looking for laborers to carry to Birmingham, and I joined his gang. I have been here in the Birmingham district since they released me, and I reckon I'll die either in a coal mine or an iron furnace. It don't make much difference which. Either is better than a Georgia peon camp. And a Georgia peon camp is hell itself!

## Plessy v. Ferguson, 1896

*In the 1880s and 1890s state and local laws segregated public accommodations throughout the South. The exclusion of black people from first-class railway coaches expressed white southerners' resentment toward economically successful African Americans, as well as their desire to put the Negro in his "place." In*

*1892 Homer Plessy, a light-skinned Negro, sued the East Louisiana Railway for ejecting him from the first-class car. The Supreme Court's ruling, by creating the legal doctrine "separate but equal," upheld that racial segregation was not unconstitutional.*

*Source:* Court records, 163 U.S. 567. Harry Ploski and James Williams, eds., *Reference Library of Black Americans*, vol. 1 (New York: Afro-American Press, 1990), 150–152.

The *Plessy* case was a test of the constitutionality of an 1890 Louisiana law providing for separate railway carriages for whites and blacks.

The information filed in the criminal District Court charged in substance that (Homer) Plessy, being a passenger between two stations within the state of Louisiana, was assigned by officers of the company to the coach used by the race to which he did not belong. Plessy refused to move and was arrested for violation of the law. A suit was filed by Plessy in Louisiana State Court that questioned the constitutionality of the Louisiana law, judge John Ferguson denied the Plessy contention and the case was appealed to the Supreme Court as *Plessy v. Ferguson*.

The lawyer for the defense summed up the case in one sentence. "Instead of being intended to promote the general comfort and moral well being, this act is plainly and evidently intended to promote the happiness of one class by asserting its supremacy and the inferiority of another class."

In the majority opinion of the Court, "separate but equal" accommodations for blacks constituted a "reasonable" use of state police power. Furthermore, it was said that the Fourteenth Amendment "could not have been intended to abolish distinctions based on color, or to enforce social . . . equality, or a co-mingling of the two races upon terms unsatisfactory to either."

Justice John Marshall Harlan delivered a dissenting opinion in this case which proved to be a prophetic one:

"The judgment this day rendered will, in time, prove to be quite as pernicious as the decision made by this tribunal in the Dred Scott case. The thin disguise of equal accommodations for passengers in railroad coaches will not mislead anyone nor atone for the wrong this day done."

In effect, at the time, the Supreme Court had effectively reduced the significance of the Fourteenth and Fifteenth Amendments of the Constitution which were designed to give blacks specific rights and protections. The ruling was termed the *"separate but equal"* doctrine of the Supreme Court and paved the way for segregation of blacks in all walks of life. The decision stood until the *Brown v. Board of Education* decision of 1954.

This case turns upon the constitutionality of an act of the General Assembly of the state of Louisiana, passed in 1890, providing for separate railway carriages for the white and colored races . . .

The constitutionality of this act is attacked upon the ground that it conflicts both with the Thirteenth Amendment of the Constitution, abolishing slavery, and the Fourteenth Amendment, which prohibits certain restrictive legislation on the part of the states.

1. That it does not conflict with the Thirteenth Amendment, which abolished slavery and involuntary servitude, except as a punishment for crime, is too clear for argument. Slavery implies involuntary servitude—a state of bondage; the ownership of mankind as a chattel, or at least the control of the labor and services of one man for the benefit of another, and the absence of a legal right to the disposal of his own person, property, and services. . . .

A statute which implies merely a legal distinction between the white and colored races—a distinction which is founded in the color of the two races, and which must always exist so long as white men are distinguished from the other race by color—has no tendency to destroy the legal equality of the two races, or reestablish a state of involuntary servitude. Indeed, we do not understand that the Thirteenth Amendment is strenuously relied upon by the plaintiff in error in this connection.

2. By the Fourteenth Amendment, all persons born or naturalized in the United States, and subject to the jurisdiction thereof, are made citizens of the United States and of the state wherein they reside; and the states are forbidden from making or enforcing any law which shall abridge the privileges or immunities of citizens of the United States, or shall deprive any person of life, liberty, or property without due process of law, or deny to any person within their jurisdiction the equal protection of the laws. . . .

The object of the amendment was undoubtedly to enforce the absolute equality of the two races before the law, but in the nature of things it could not have been intended to abolish distinctions based upon color, or to enforce social, as distinguished from political, equality, or a commingling of the two races upon terms unsatisfactory to either. Laws permitting, and even requiring, their separation in places where they are liable to be brought into contact do not necessarily imply the inferiority of either race to the other, and have been generally, if not universally, recognized as within the competency of the state legislatures in the exercise of their police power. The most common instance of this is connected with the establishment of separate schools for white and colored children, which has been held to be a valid exercise of the legislative power even by courts of states where the political rights of the colored race have been longest and most earnestly enforced. . . .

So far, then, as a conflict with the Fourteenth Amendment is concerned, the case reduces itself to the question whether the statute of Louisiana is a reasonable regulation, and with respect to this there must necessarily be a large discretion on the part of the legislature. In determining the question of reasonableness it is at liberty to act with reference to the established usages, customs, and traditions of the people, and with a view to the promotion of their comfort, and the preservation of the public peace and good order. Gauged by this standard, we cannot say that a law which authorizes or even requires the separation of the two races in public conveyances is unreasonable or more obnoxious to the Fourteenth Amendment than the acts of Congress requiring separate schools for colored children in the District of Co-

lumbia, the constitutionality of which does not seem to have been questioned, or the corresponding acts of state legislatures.

We consider the underlying fallacy of the plaintiff's argument to consist in the assumption that the enforced separation of the two races stamps the colored race with a badge of inferiority. If this be so, it is not by reason of anything found in the act, but solely because the colored race chooses to put that construction upon it. The argument necessarily assumes that if, as has been more than once the case, and is not unlikely to be so again, the colored race should become the dominant power in the state legislature, and should enact a law in precisely similar terms, it would thereby relegate the white race to an inferior position. We imagine that the white race, at least, would not acquiesce in this assumption. The argument also assumes that social prejudices may be overcome by legislation and that equal rights cannot be secured to the Negro except by an enforced commingling of the two races. We cannot accept this proposition. If the two races are to meet upon terms of social equality, it must be the result of natural affinities, a mutual appreciation of each other's merits, and a voluntary consent of individuals. . . . Legislation is powerless to eradicate racial instincts or to abolish distinctions based upon physical differences, and the attempt to do so can only result in accentuating the difficulties of the present situation. If the civil and political rights of both races be equal, one cannot be inferior to the other civilly or politically. If one race be inferior to the other socially, the Constitution of the United States cannot put them upon the same plane.

It is true that the question of the proportion of colored blood necessary to constitute a colored person, as distinguished from a white person, is one upon which there is a difference of opinion in the different states, some holding that any visible admixture of black blood stamps the person as belonging to the colored race . . . others that it depends upon the preponderance of blood . . . and still others that the predominance of white blood must only be in the proportion of three-fourths . . . But these are questions to be determined under the laws of each state and are not properly put in issue in this case. Under the allegations of his petition it may undoubtedly become a question of importance whether, under the laws of Louisiana, the petitioner belongs to the white or colored race.

The judgment of the court below is therefore, *Affirmed*.

## MR. JUSTICE HARLAN DISSENTING

In respect of civil rights, common to all citizens, the Constitution of the United States does not, I think, permit any public authority to know the race of those entitled to be protected in the enjoyment of such rights. Every true man has pride of race, and under appropriate circumstances when the rights of others, his equals before the law, are not to be affected, it is his privilege to express such pride and to take such action based upon

it as to him seems proper. But I deny that any legislative body or judicial tribunal may have regard to the race of citizens when the civil rights of those citizens are involved. Indeed, such legislation, as that here in question, is inconsistent not only with that equality of rights which pertains to citizenship, national and state, but with the personal liberty enjoyed by everyone within the United States.

The Thirteenth Amendment does not permit the withholding or the deprivation of any right necessarily inhering in freedom. It not only struck down the institution of slavery as previously existing in the United States, but it prevents the imposition of any burdens or disabilities that constitute badges of slavery or servitude. It decreed universal civil freedom in this country. This Court has so adjudged. But that amendment having been found inadequate to the protection of the rights of those who had been in slavery, it was followed by the Fourteenth Amendment, which added greatly to the dignity and glory of the American citizenship, and to the security of personal liberty, by declaring that "all persons born or naturalized in the United States, and subject to the jurisdiction thereof, are citizens of the United States and of the state wherein they reside," and that "no state shall make or enforce any law which shall abridge the privileges or immunities of citizens of the United States; nor shall any state deprive any person of life, liberty, or property without due process of law, nor deny to any person within its jurisdiction the equal protection of the laws." These two amendments, if enforced according to their true intent and meaning, will protect all the civil rights that pertain to freedom and citizenship. Finally, and to the end that no citizen should be denied, on account of his race, the privilege of participating in the political control of his country, it was declared by the Fifteenth Amendment that "the right of citizens of the United States to vote shall not be denied or abridged by the United States or by any state on account of race, color, or previous condition of servitude."

These notable additions to the fundamental law were welcomed by the friends of liberty throughout the world. They removed the race line from our governmental systems.

It was said in argument that the statute of Louisiana does not discriminate against either race but prescribes a rule applicable alike to white and colored citizens. But this argument does not meet the difficulty. Everyone knows that the statute in question had its origin in the purpose, not so much to exclude white persons from railroad cars occupied by blacks, as to exclude colored people from coaches occupied by or assigned to white persons. Railroad corporations of Louisiana did not make discrimination among whites in the matter of accommodation for travelers. The thing to accomplish was, under the guise of giving equal accommodation for whites and blacks, to compel the latter to keep to themselves while traveling in railroad passenger coaches. No one would be so wanting in candor as to assert the contrary. The fundamental objection, therefore, to the statute is that it interferes with the personal freedom of citizens. If a white man and a black man choose to occupy the same public conveyance on a public highway, it is their right to do so, and no government, proceeding alone on grounds of race, can prevent it without infringing the personal liberty of each.

It is one thing for railroad carriers to furnish, or to be required by law to furnish, equal accommodations for all whom they are under a legal duty to carry. It is quite another thing for government to forbid citizens of the white and black races from traveling in the same public conveyance, and to punish officers of railroad companies for permitting persons of the two races to occupy the same passenger coach. If a state can prescribe, as a rule of civil conduct, that whites and blacks shall not travel as passengers in the same railroad coach, why may it not so regulate the use of the streets of its cities and towns as to compel white citizens to keep on one side of a street and black citizens to keep on the other? Why may it not, upon like grounds, punish whites and blacks who ride together in streetcars or in open vehicles on a public road or street? Why may it not require sheriffs to assign whites to one side of a courtroom and blacks to the other? And why may it not also prohibit the commingling of the two races in the galleries of legislative halls or in public assemblages convened for the consideration of the political questions of the day? Further, if this statute of Louisiana is consistent with the personal liberty of citizens, why may not the state require the separation in railroad coaches of native and naturalized citizens of the United States, or of Protestants and Roman Catholics?

The answer given as the argument to

these questions was that regulations of the kind they suggest would be unreasonable and could not, therefore, stand before the law. Is it meant that the determination of questions of legislative power depends upon the inquiry whether the statute whose validity is questioned is, in the judgment of the courts, a reasonable one, taking all the circumstances into consideration? A statute may be unreasonable merely because a sound public policy forbade its enactment. But I do not understand that the courts have anything to do with the policy or expediency of legislation. The white race deems itself to be the dominant race in this country. And so it is, in prestige, in achievements, in education, in wealth, and in power. So, I doubt not, it will continue to be for all time, if it remains true to its great heritage and holds fast to the principles of constitutional liberty. But in view of the Constitution, in the eye of the law, there is in this country no superior, dominant, ruling class of citizens. There is no caste here. Our Constitution is colorblind and neither knows nor tolerates classes among citizens. In respect of civil rights all citizens are equal before the law. The humblest is the peer of the most powerful. The law regards man as man and takes no account of his surroundings or of his color when his civil rights, as guaranteed by the supreme law of the land, are involved. It is, therefore, to be regretted that this high tribunal, the final expositor of the fundamental law of the land, has reached the conclusion that it is competent for a state to regulate the enjoyment by citizens of their civil rights solely upon the basis of race. . . .

The sure guarantee of the peace and security of each race is the clear, distinct, unconditional recognition by our governments, national and state, of every right that inheres in civil freedom, and of the equality before the law of all citizens of the United States without regard to race. State enactments, regulating the enjoyment of civil rights, upon the basis of race, and cunningly devised to defeat legitimate results of the war, under the pretense of recognizing equality of rights, can have no other result than to render permanent peace impossible, and to keep alive a conflict of races, the continuance of which must do harm to all concerned. . . .

The arbitrary separation of citizens, on the basis of race, while they are on a public highway, is a badge of servitude wholly inconsistent with the civil freedom and the equality before the law established by the Constitution. It cannot be justified upon any legal grounds.

If evils will result from the commingling of the two faces upon public highways established for the benefit of all, they will be infinitely less than those that will surely come from state legislation regulating the enjoyment of civil rights upon the basis of race. We boast of the freedom enjoyed by our people above all other peoples. But it is difficult to reconcile that boast with a state of the law which, practically, puts the brand of servitude and degradation upon a large class of our fellow-citizens, our equals before the law. The thin disguise of "equal" accommodations for passengers in railroad coaches will not mislead anyone, nor atone for the wrong this day done. . . .

I am of opinion that the statute of

Louisiana is inconsistent with the personal liberty of citizens, white and black, in that state, and hostile to both the spirit and letter of the Constitution of the United States. If laws of like character should be enacted in the several states of the Union, the effect would be in the highest degree mischievous. Slavery, as an institution tolerated by law, would, it is true, have disappeared from our country, but there would remain a power in the states, by sinister legislation, to interfere with the full enjoyment of the blessings of freedom; to regulate civil rights, common to all citizens, upon the basis of race, and to place in a condition of legal inferiority a large body of American citizens, now constituting a part of the political community called the People of the United States, for whom, and by whom through representatives, our government is administered. Such a system is inconsistent with the guarantee given by the Constitution to each state of a republican form of government, and may be stricken down by congressional action, or by the courts in the discharge of their solemn duty to maintain the supreme law of the land anything in the constitution or laws of any state to the contrary notwithstanding.

For the reasons stated, I am constrained to withhold my assent from the opinion and judgment of the majority. . . .

## Ida B. Wells, "Southern Horrors," 1892

*Responding to the lynching of three friends in 1892, Memphis journalist Ida B. Wells began a crusade against lynching. Wells's investigative reporting exposed as false the charge, commonly made by white southerners to justify lynching, that black men raped white women. She argued that white resentment at the black middle class and the threat of social equality were the real motivations for lynching. The following piece is from Wells's campaign against lynching.*

*Source:* "New York Age Print, 1892," a pamphlet published by *New York Age*, 1892.

The whites of Montgomery, Ala., knew J. C. Duke sounded the keynote of the situation—which they would gladly hide from the world, when he said in his paper, "The Herald," five years ago: "Why is it that white women attract negro men now more than in former days? There was a time when such a thing was unheard of. There is a secret to this thing, and we greatly suspect it is the growing appreciation of white Juliets for colored Romeos." Mr. Duke, like the "Free Speech" proprietors, was forced to leave the city for reflecting on the "honah" of white women and his paper suppressed; but the truth remains that Afro-American men do not always rape (?) white women without their consent.

Mr. Duke, before leaving Montgomery, signed a card disclaiming any intention of slandering Southern white women. The editor of the "Free Speech" has no disclaimer to enter, but asserts instead that there are many white women in the South who would marry colored men if such an act would not place them at once beyond the pale of society and within the clutches of the law. The miscegenation laws of the South only operate against the legitimate union of the races; they leave the white man free to seduce all the colored girls he can, but it is death to the colored man who yields to the force and advances of a similar attraction in white women. White men lynch the offending Afro-American, not because he is a despoiler of virtue, but because he succumbs to the smiles of white women.

## CHAPTER 2: THE BLACK AND WHITE OF IT

The "Cleveland Gazette" of January 16, 1892, publishes a case in point. Mrs. J. S. Underwood, the wife of a minister of Elyria, Ohio, accused an Afro-American of rape. She told her husband that during his absence in 1888, stumping the State for the Prohibition Party, the man came to the kitchen door, forced his way in the house and insulted her. She tried to drive him out with a heavy poker, but he overpowered and chloroformed her, and when she revived her clothing was torn and she was in a horrible condition. She did not know the man but could identify him. She pointed out William Offett, a married man, who was arrested and, being in Ohio, was granted a trial.

The prisoner vehemently denied the charge of rape, but confessed he went to Mrs. Underwood's residence at her invitation and was criminally intimate with her at her request. This availed him nothing against the sworn testimony of a minister's wife, a lady of the highest respectability He was found guilty, and

entered the penitentiary, December 14, 1888, for fifteen years. Some time afterwards the woman's remorse led her to confess to her husband that the man was innocent.

These are her words: "I met Offett at the Post Office. It was raining. He was polite to me, and as I had several bundles in my arms he offered to carry them home for me, which he did. He had a strange fascination for me, and I invited him to call on me. He called, bringing chestnuts and candy for the children. By this means we got them to leave us alone in the room. Then I sat on his lap. He made a proposal to me and I readily consented. Why I did so, I do not know, but that I did is true. He visited me several times after that and each time I was indiscreet. I did not care after the first time. In fact I could not have resisted, and had no desire to resist."

When asked by her husband why she told him she had been outraged, she said: "I had several reasons for telling you. One was the neighbors saw the fellow here, another was, I was afraid I had contracted a loathsome disease, and still another was that I feared I might give birth to a Negro baby. I hoped to save my reputation by telling you a deliberate lie." Her husband horrified by the confession had Offett, who had already served four years, released and secured a divorce.

There are thousands of such cases throughout the South, with the difference that the Southern white men in insatiate fury wreak their vengeance without intervention of law upon the Afro-Americans who consort with their women.

In Natchez, Miss., Mrs. Marshall, one of the *creme de la creme* of the city, created a tremendous sensation several years ago. She has a black coachman who was married, and had been in her employ several years. During this time she gave birth to a child whose color was remarked, but traced to some brunette ancestor, and one of the fashionable dames of the city was its godmother. Mrs. Marshall's social position was unquestioned, and wealth showered every dainty on this child which was idolized with its brothers and sisters by its white papa. In course of time another child appeared on the scene, but it was unmistakably dark. All were alarmed, and "rush of blood, strangulation" were the conjectures, but the doctor, when asked the cause, grimly told them it was a Negro child. There was a family conclave, the coachman heard of it and leaving his own family went West, and has never returned. As soon as Mrs. Marshall was able to travel she was sent away in deep disgrace. Her husband died within the year of a broken heart.

From this exposition of the race issue in lynch law, the whole matter is explained by the well-known opposition growing out of slavery to the progress of the race. This is crystalized in the oft-repeated slogan: "This is a white man's country and the white man must rule." The South resented giving the Afro-American his freedom, the ballot box and the Civil Rights Law. The raids of the Ku-Klux and White Liners to subvert reconstruction government, the Hamburg and Ellerton, S.C., the Copiah County Miss., and the Lafayette Parish, La., massacres were excused as the nat-

ural resentment of intelligence against government by ignorance.

Honest white men practically conceded the necessity of intelligence murdering ignorance to correct the mistake of the general government, and the race was left to the tender mercies of the solid South. Thoughtful Afro-Americans with the strong arm of the government withdrawn and with the hope to stop such wholesale massacres urged the race to sacrifice its political rights for sake of peace. They honestly believed the race should fit itself for government, and when that should be done, the objection to race participation in politics would be removed.

But the sacrifice did not remove the trouble, nor move the South to justice. One by one the Southern States have legally (?) disfranchised the Afro-American, and since the repeal of the Civil Rights Bill nearly every Southern State has passed separate car laws with a penalty against their infringement. The race regardless of advancement is penned into filthy, stifling partitions cut off from smoking cars. All this while, although the political cause has been removed, the butcheries of black men at Barnwell, S.C., Carrolton, Miss., Waycross, Ga., and Memphis, Tenn., have gone on; also the flaying alive of a man in Kentucky, the burning of one in Arkansas, the hanging of a fifteen year old girl in Louisiana, a woman in Jackson, Tenn., and one in Hollendale, Miss., until the dark and bloody record of the South shows 728 Afro-Americans lynched during the past 8 years. Not 50 of these were for political causes; the rest were for all manner of accusations from that of rape of white women, to the case of the boy Will Lewis who was hanged at Tullahoma, Tenn., last year for being drunk and "sassy" to white folks.

## "A Colored Complaint," 1883

*African Americans convened conventions across the South in the decades following the Civil War. By the 1880s, meetings such as this one held in Louisville, Kentucky, struggled to define an agenda that could address the retreats from freedom that had occurred since Reconstruction.*

Source: *Atlanta Constitution*, September 28, 1883, p. 2.

Louisville, September 27.—The national colored convention late last night adopted the following address: The national convention of colored men assembled, respectfully present the following as embracing and presenting their views and sentiments:

1. That we are gratified for and rejoice in the miraculous emancipation that came to our race twenty years ago. The shock of embattled arms was the lullaby of a nation born in a day. We cannot forget the great sacrifice of the women and heroic men who made possible the struggle in which treason and slavery were consigned to a common sepulchre, nor would we be unmindful of the measure of devotion and patriotism that the white and colored soldiers rendered the nation.

2. That we are not insensible to the fact that the congress of the United States has spread the statute books many laws calculated to make us secure in our rights as citizens, nor would we be forgetful of the magnificent amendments to the constitution intended to render for ever impossible the crime of human slavery.

3. We do not ask for any more class legislation. We have had enough of this. But we do believe that many of the laws intended to secure to us our rights as citizens are nothing more than dead letters. In the southern states, almost without exception, colored people are denied justice in the courts, denied the fruit of their honest labor, defrauded of their political rights at the ballot box, shut out from learning the trades, cheated out of their civil rights by innkeepers and common carrier companies and left by the state to an inadequate opportunity for education and general improvement.

4. We regard the labor question, education and sound moral training, paramount to all other questions, We believe that these questions, especialy in the south, need recasting, and that the plantation, credit and mortgage system should be abolished, so that honest labor should be remunerated, so that the landholders of the south should recognize that this question is to be solved by encouraging the negroes to industry, to frugality, and to business habits, by assisting them to acquire an interest in the soil by paying them honest wages for honest work, and by making them content and happy in the land of their nativity. The white men and owners of the soil in the south can settle

the question of labor and capital between white and black.

5. We believe in a broad comprehensive system, looking towards the education of young colored girls, so that they may become intelligent and faithful women, and of young colored boys that they may learn trades and become useful men and good citizens. The religious and moral training of the youth of our race should not be neglected. The hope of every people is in an adherance to sound social logical and ethical principles. The moral element in character is of greater value than wealth or education, and this must be fostered by the family and encouraged by the pulpit.

6. The failure of the freedmans Saving Bank and Trust company, is the marvel of our time. It was established to receive the earnings of persons heretofore held in bondage and the descendents of such persons. It was established by the government, and thought to be solvent. In changing its charter the trustees transcended their authority, and thereby made themselves liable. The government, in appointing the machinery to close the insolvent institution violated the United States statutes in bankruptcy, and should therefore reimburse the creditors of the bank.

7. The distinction made between white and black troops in the regular army is unAmerican, unjust and ungrateful. White men can enter any branch of the service, while colored men are confined to the cavalary and infantry service, and in the appointment of civilians to the regular army all believe it the duty of the president to consider the claims of colored men. This distinction is carried into the navy as well.

8. It is not our province to dictate the policy of the government, or the action of our fellow citizens in the several states. It is a matter that their services, patriotism and needs should shape.

9. As a race struggling and contending for our political and civil rights, we are not unmindful of the efforts of Ireland to gain her rights, and we extend to our Irish friends our profound sympathy and best wishes.

10. We earnestly desire the abolition of the chaingang system, and the admission to trade unions of men of our own race, and to their employment in commercial pursuits.

11. In nearly every state of the union both north and south, our race are not allowed to enter freely into the trades of gain or employment in the higher walks of life. This is unworthy of our institutions and hurtful to the reputation of our country at home and abroad.

After adopting the above address, the convention adjourned and the members dispersed to their homes.

## Booker T. Washington, "Atlanta Compromise," September 18, 1895

*Booker T. Washington was the preeminent black spokesperson in the South in the last decades of the nineteenth century. He was founder and director of the Tuskegee (Alabama) Institute, a vocational and agricultural school for black southerners. While some African Americans despaired at the racism in the South and advocated leaving for the*

*North or elsewhere, Washington believed fervently that the Negro's home was in the South. He counseled accepting and working within the segregated structure of southern society, emphasizing agricultural and vocational education and self-help as strategies for economic advancement. This speech, delivered at the Atlanta Exposition on September 18, 1895, expresses his philosophy.*

Source: *Reference Library of Black America*, vol. 1, Henry Poloski and James Williams, eds. (New York: Gale Research, Afro-American Press, 1990).

Mr. President and Gentlemen of the Board of Directors and Citizens:

One-third of the population of the South is of the Negro race. No enterprise seeking the material, civil, or moral welfare of this section can disregard this element of our population and reach the highest success. I but convey to you, Mr. President and Directors, the sentiment of the masses of my race when I say that in no way have the value and manhood of the American Negro been more fittingly and generously recognized than by the managers of this magnificent Exposition at every stage of its progress. It is a recognition that will do more to cement the friendship of the two races than any occurrence since the dawn of our freedom.

Not only this, but the opportunity here afforded will awaken among us a new era of industrial progress. Ignorant and inexperienced, it is not strange that in the first years of our new life we began at the top instead of at the bottom; that a seat in Congress or the State Legislature was more sought than real estate or industrial skill; that the political convention or stump speaking had more attractions than starting a dairy farm or truck garden.

A ship lost at sea for many days suddenly sighted a friendly vessel. From the mast of the unfortunate vessel was seen a signal: "Water, water; we die of thirst!" The answer from the friendly vessel at once came back: "Cast down your bucket where you are." A second time the signal, "Water, water; send us water!" ran up from the distressed vessel, and was answered: "Cast down your bucket where you are." And a third and fourth signal for water was answered: "Cast down your bucket where you are." The captain of the distressed vessel, at last heeding the injunction, cast down his bucket, and it came up full of fresh, sparkling water from the mouth of the Amazon River. To those of my race who depend on bettering their condition in a foreign land, or who underestimate the importance of cultivating friendly relations with the Southern white man, who is their next door neighbor, I would say: "Cast down your bucket where you are"—cast it down in making friends in every manly way of the people of all races by whom we are surrounded.

Cast it down in agriculture, mechanics, in commerce, in domestic service, and in the professions. And in this connection it is well to bear in mind that whatever other sins the South may be called to bear, when it comes to business, pure and simple, it is in the South that the Negro is given a man's chance in the commercial world, and in nothing is this Exposition more eloquent than in emphasizing this chance. Our greatest danger is, that in the great leap from slavery to freedom we may overlook the fact that the masses of us are to live by the productions of our hands, and fail to keep in mind that we shall prosper in proportion as we learn to dignify and glorify common labor, and put brains and skill into the common occupations of life; shall prosper in proportion as we learn to draw the line between the superficial and the substantial, the ornamental gewgaws of life and the useful. No race can prosper till it learns that there is as much dignity in tilling a field as in writing a poem. It is at the bottom of life we must begin, and not at the top. Nor should we permit our grievances to overshadow our opportunities.

To those of the white race who look to the incoming of those of foreign birth and strange tongue and habits for the prosperity of the South, were I permitted, I would repeat what I say to my own race, "Cast down your bucket where you are." Cast it down among the 8,000,000 Negroes whose habits you know, whose fidelity and love you have tested in days when to have proved treacherous meant the ruin of your firesides. Cast down your bucket among these people who have, without strikes and labor wars, tilled your fields, cleared your forests, builded your railroads and cities, and brought forth treasures from the bowels of the earth, and helped make possible this magnificent representation of the progress of the South. Casting down your bucket among my people, helping and encouraging them as you are doing on these grounds, and, with education of head, hand and heart, you will find that they will buy your surplus land,

make blossom the waste place in your fields, and run your factories. While doing this, you can be sure in the future, as in the past, that you and your families will be surrounded by the most patient, faithful, law-abiding, and unresentful people that the world has seen. As we have proved our loyalty to you in the past, in nursing your children, watching by the sick bed of your mothers and fathers, and often following them with tear-dimmed eyes to their graves, so in the future, in our humble way, we shall stand by you with a devotion that no foreigner can approach, ready to lay down our lives, if need be, in defense of yours, interlacing our industrial, commercial, civil, and religious life with yours in a way that shall make the interests of both races one. In all things that are purely social we can be as separate as the fingers, yet one as the hand in all things essential to mutual progress.

There is no defense or security for any of us except in the highest intelligence and development of all. If anywhere there are efforts tending to curtail the fullest growth of the Negro, let these efforts be turned into stimulating, encouraging, and making him the most useful and intelligent citizen. Effort or means so invested will pay a thousand percent interest. These efforts will be twice blessed—"blessing him that gives and him that takes."

There is no escape through law of man or God from the inevitable:

The laws of changeless justice bind
Oppressor with oppressed;
And close as sin and suffering joined
We march to fate abreast.

Nearly sixteen millions of hands will aid you in pulling the load upwards, or they will pull against you the load downwards. We shall constitute one-third and more of the ignorance and crime of the South, or one-third its intelligence and progress; we shall contribute one-third to the business and industrial prosperity of the South, or we shall prove a veritable body of death, stagnating, depressing, retarding every effort to advance the body politic.

Gentlemen of the Exposition, as we present to you our humble effort at an exhibition of our progress, you must not expect over much. Starting thirty years ago with ownership here and there in a few quilts and pumpkins and chickens (gathered from miscellaneous sources), remember the path that has led from these to the invention and production of agricultural implements, buggies, steam engines, newspapers, books, statuary, carving, paintings, the management of drug stores and banks, has not been trodden without contact with thorns and thistles. While we take pride in what we exhibit as a result of our independent efforts, we do not for a moment forget that our part in this exhibition would fall far short of your expectations but for the constant help that has come to our educational life, not only from the Southern States, but especially from Northern philanthropists, who have made their gifts a constant stream of blessing and encouragement.

The wisest among my race understand that the agitation of questions of social equality is the extremist folly, and that progress in the enjoyment of all the privileges that will come to us must be the result of severe and constant struggle rather than of artificial forcing. No race that has anything to contribute to the markets of the world is long in any degree ostracized. It is important and right that all privileges of the law be ours, but it is vastly more important that we be prepared for the exercise of those privileges. The opportunity to earn a dollar in a factory just now is worth infinitely more than the opportunity to spend a dollar in an opera house.

In conclusion, may I repeat that nothing in thirty years has given us more hope and encouragement, and drawn us so near to you of the white race, as this opportunity offered by the Exposition; and here bending, as it were, over the altar that represents the results of the struggles of your race and mine, both starting practically empty-handed three decades ago. I pledge that, in your effort to work out the great and intricate problem which God has laid at the doors of the South, you shall have at all time the patient, sympathetic help of my race; only let this be constantly in mind that, while from representations in these buildings of the product of field, of forest, of mine, of factory, letters, and art, much good will come, yet far above and beyond material benefits will be that higher good, that let us pray God will come, in a blotting out of sectional differences and racial animosities and suspicions, in a determination to administer absolute justice, in a willing obedience among all classes to the mandates of law. This, coupled with our material prosperity, will bring into our beloved South a new heaven and a new earth.

## W. E. B. Du Bois, "Of Mr. Booker T. Washington and Others," 1903

*W. E. B. Du Bois was a sociologist at Atlanta University when he wrote this essay. Du Bois challenged Washington's accommodationist outlook. He believed Washington's abandonment of African Americans' political and civil rights shifted the burden of the "Negro problem" onto black people. He argued that the degraded condition of black people was caused by slavery and racial subordination, not by the failings of black people. Du Bois supported economic self-help and black uplift but believed these were not possible without the vote, civil rights, or higher education. Du Bois also appealed to other African American leaders who were reluctant to challenge Washington publicly.*

Source: W. E. B. Du Bois, "Of Mr. Booker T. Washington and Others," *The Souls of Black Folk* (Chicago, 1903).

> *From birth till death enslaved; in word, in deed,*
>     *unmanned!*
> *Hereditary bondsmen! Know ye not*
> *Who would be free themselves must strike the*
>     *blow?*
>
>     —Byron

Easily the most striking thing in the history of the American Negro since 1876 is the ascendancy of Mr. Booker T. Washington. It began at the time when war memories and ideals were rapidly passing; a day of astonishing commercial development was dawning; a sense of doubt and hesitation overtook the freedmen's sons—then it was that his leading began. Mr. Washington came, with a single definite programme, at the psychological moment when the nation was a little ashamed of having bestowed so much sentiment on Negroes, and was concentrating its energies on Dollars. His programme of industrial education, conciliation of the South, and submission and silence as to civil and political rights, was not wholly original; the Free Negroes from 1830 up to wartime had striven to build industrial schools, and the American Missionary Association had from the first taught various trades; and Price and others had sought a way of honorable alliance with the best of the Southerners. But Mr. Washington first indissolubly linked these things; he put enthusiasm, unlimited energy, and perfect faith into this programme, and changed it from a by-path into a veritable Way of Life. And the tale of the methods by which he did this is a fascinating study of human life.

It startled the nation to hear a Negro advocating such a programme after many decades of bitter complaint; it startled and won the applause of the South, it interested and won the admiration of the North; and after a confused murmur of protest, it silenced if it did not convert the Negroes themselves.

To gain the sympathy and coöperation of the various elements comprising the white South was Mr. Washington's first task; and this, at the time Tuskegee was founded, seemed, for a black man, well-nigh impossible. And yet ten years later it was done in the word spoken at Atlanta: "In all things purely social we can be as separate as the five fingers, and yet one as the hand in all things essential to mutual progress." This "Atlanta Compromise" is by all odds the most notable thing in Mr. Washington's career. The South interpreted it in different ways: the radicals received it as a complete surrender of the demand for civil and political equality; the conservatives, as a generously conceived working basis for mutual understanding. So both approved it, and to-day its author is certainly the most distinguished Southerner since Jefferson Davis, and the one with the largest personal following.

Next to this achievement comes Mr. Washington's work in gaining place and consideration in the North. Others less shrewd and tactful had formerly essayed to sit on these two stools and had fallen between them; but as Mr. Washington knew the heart of the South from birth and training, so by singular insight he intuitively grasped the spirit of the age which was dominating the North. And so thoroughly did he learn the speech and thought of triumphant commercialism, and the ideals of material prosperity, that the picture of a lone black boy poring over a French grammar amid the weeds and dirt of a neglected home soon seemed to him the acme of absurdities. One wonders what Socrates and St. Francis of Assisi would say to this.

And yet this very singleness of vision and thorough oneness with his age is a mark of the successful man. It is as though Nature must needs make men narrow in order to give them force. So Mr. Washington's cult has gained unquestioning followers, his work has wonderfully prospered, his friends are legion, and his enemies are confounded.

To-day he stands as the one recognized spokesman of his ten million fellows, and one of the most notable figures in a nation of seventy millions. One hesitates, therefore, to criticise a life which, beginning with so little, has done so much. And yet the time is come when one may speak in all sincerity and utter courtesy of the mistakes and shortcomings of Mr. Washington's career, as well as of his triumphs, without being thought captious or envious, and without forgetting that it is easier to do ill than well in the world.

The criticism that has hitherto met Mr. Washington has not always been of this broad character. In the South especially has he had to walk warily to avoid the harsh judgments—and naturally so, for he is dealing with the one subject of deepest sensitiveness to that section. Twice—once when at the Chicago celebration of the Spanish-American War he alluded to the color-prejudice that is "eating away the vitals of the South," and once when he dined with President Roosevelt—has the resulting Southern criticism been violent enough to threaten seriously his popularity. In the North the feeling has several times forced itself into words, that Mr. Washington's counsels of submission overlooked certain elements of true manhood, and that his educational programme was unnecessarily narrow. Usually, however, such criticism has not found open expression, although, too, the spiritual sons of the Abolitionists have not been prepared to acknowledge that the schools founded before Tuskegee, by men of broad ideals and self-sacrificing spirit, were wholly failures or worthy of ridicule. While, then, criticism has not failed to follow

Mr. Washington, yet the prevailing public opinion of the land has been but too willing to deliver the solution of a wearisome problem into his hands, and say, "If that is all you and your race ask, take it."

Among his own people, however, Mr. Washington has encountered the strongest and most lasting opposition, amounting at times to bitterness, and even to-day continuing strong and insistent even though largely silenced in outward expression by the public opinion of the nation. Some of this opposition is, of course, mere envy; the disappointment of displaced demagogues and the spite of narrow minds. But aside from this, there is among educated and thoughtful colored men in all parts of the land a feeling of deep regret, sorrow, and apprehension at the wide currency and ascendancy which some of Mr. Washington's theories have gained. These same men admire his sincerity of purpose, and are willing to forgive much to honest endeavor which is doing something worth the doing. They coöperate with Mr. Washington as far as they conscientiously can; and, indeed, it is no ordinary tribute to this man's tact and power that, steering as he must between so many diverse interests and opinions, he so largely retains the respect of all.

But the hushing of the criticism of honest opponents is a dangerous thing. It leads some of the best of the critics to unfortunate silence and paralysis of effort, and others to burst into speech so passionately and intemperately as to lose listeners. Honest and earnest criticism from those whose interests are most nearly touched—criticism of writers by readers, of government by those governed, of leaders, by those led—this is the soul of democracy and the safeguard of modern society. If the best of the American Negroes receive by outer pressure a leader whom they had not recognized before, manifestly there is here a certain palpable gain. Yet there is also irreparable loss—a loss of that peculiarly valuable education which a group receives when by search and criticism it finds and commissions its own leaders. The way in which this is done is at once the most elementary and the nicest problem of social growth. History is but the record of such group-leadership; and yet how infinitely changeful is its type and character! And of all types and kinds, what can be more instructive than the leadership of a group within a group?—that curious double movement where real progress may be negative and actual advance be relative retrogression. All this is the social student's inspiration and despair.

Now in the past the American Negro has had instructive experience in the choosing of group leaders, founding thus a peculiar dynasty which in the light of present conditions is worth while studying. When sticks and stones and beasts form the sole environment of a people, their attitude is largely one of determined opposition to and conquest of natural forces. But when to earth and brute is added an environment of men and ideas, then the attitude of the imprisoned group may take three main forms—a feeling of revolt and revenge; an attempt to adjust all thought and action to the will of the greater group; or, finally, a determined effort at self-realization and self-development despite environing opinion. The influence of all of these attitudes at various times can be traced in the history of the American Negro, and in the evolution of his successive leaders.

Before 1750, while the fire of African freedom still burned in the veins of the slaves, there was in all leadership or attempted leadership but the one motive of revolt and revenge—typified in the terrible Maroons, the Danish blacks, and Cato of Stono, and veiling all the Americas in fear of insurrection. The liberalizing tendencies of the latter half of the eighteenth century brought, along with kindlier relations between black and white, thoughts of ultimate adjustment and assimilation. Such aspiration was especially voiced in the earnest songs of Phyllis, in the martyrdom of Attucks, the fighting of Salem and Poor, the intellectual accomplishments of Banneker and Derham, and the political demands of the Cuffes.

Stern financial and social stress after the war cooled much of the previous humanitarian ardor. The disappointment and impatience of the Negroes at the persistence of slavery and serfdom voiced itself in two movements. The slaves in the South, aroused undoubtedly by vague rumors of the Haitian revolt, made three fierce attempts at insurrection—in 1800 under Gabriel in Virginia, in 1822 under Vesey in Carolina, and in 1831 again in Virginia under the terrible Nat Turner. In the Free States, on the other hand, a new and curious attempt at self-development was made. In Philadelphia and New York color-prescription led to a withdrawal of Negro commu-

nicants from white churches and the formation of a peculiar socio-religious institution among the Negroes known as the African Church—an organization still living and controlling in its various branches over a million of men.

Walker's wild appeal against the trend of the times showed how the world was changing after the coming of the cotton-gin. By 1830 slavery seemed hopelessly fastened on the South, and the slaves thoroughly cowed into submission. The free Negroes of the North, inspired by the mulatto immigrants from the West Indies, began to change the basis of their demands; they recognized the slavery of slaves, but insisted that they themselves were freemen, and sought assimilation and amalgamation with the nation on the same terms with other men. Thus, Forten and Purvis of Philadelphia, Shad of Wilmington, DuBois of New Haven, Barbadoes of Boston, and others, strove strongly and together as men, they said, not as slaves; as "people of color," not as "Negroes." The trend of the times, however, refused them recognition save in individual and exceptional cases, considered them as one with all the despised blacks, and they soon found themselves striving to keep even the rights they formerly had of voting and working and moving as freemen. Schemers of migration and colonization arose among them; but these they refused to entertain, and they eventually turned to the Abolition movement as a final refuge.

Here, led by Remond, Nell, Wells-Brown, and Douglass, a new period of self-assertion and self-development dawned. To be sure, ultimate freedom and assimilation was the ideal before the leaders, but the assertion of the manhood rights of the Negro by himself was the main reliance, and John Brown's raid was the extreme of its logic. After the war and emancipation, the great form of Frederick Douglass, the greatest of American Negro leaders, still led the host. Self-assertion, especially in political lines, was the main programme, and behind Douglass came Elliot, Bruce, and Langston, and the Reconstruction politicians, and, less conspicuous but of greater social significance, Alexander Crummell and Bishop Daniel Payne.

Then came the Revolution of 1876, the suppression of the Negro votes, the changing and shifting of ideals, and the seeking of new lights in the great night. Douglass, in his old age, still bravely stood for the ideals of his early manhood—ultimate assimilation *through* self-assertion, and on no other terms. For a time Price arose as a new leader, destined, it seemed, not to give up, but to re-state the old ideals in a form less repugnant to the white South. But he passed away in his prime. Then came the new leader. Nearly all the former ones had become leaders by the silent suffrage of their fellows, had sought to lead their own people alone, and were usually, save Douglass, little known outside their race. But Booker T. Washington arose as essentially the leader not of one race but of two—a compromiser between the South, the North, and the Negro. Naturally the Negroes resented, at first bitterly, signs of compromise which surrendered their civil and political rights, even though this was to be exchanged for larger chances of economic development. The rich and dominating North,

however, was not only weary of the race problem, but was investing largely in Southern enterprises, and welcomed any method of peaceful coöperation. Thus, by national opinion, the Negroes began to recognize Mr. Washington's leadership; and the voice of criticism was hushed.

Mr. Washington represents in Negro thought the old attitude of adjustment and submission; but adjustment at such a peculiar time as to make his programme unique. This is an age of unusual economic development, and Mr. Washington's programme naturally takes an economic cast, becoming a gospel of Work and Money to such an extent as apparently almost completely to overshadow the higher aims of life. Moreover, this is an age when the more advanced races are coming in closer contact with the less developed races, and the race-feeling is therefore intensified; and Mr. Washington's programme practically accepts the alleged inferiority of the Negro races. Again, in our own land, the reaction from the sentiment of war time has given impetus to race-prejudice against Negroes, and Mr. Washington withdraws many of the high demands of Negroes as men and American citizens. In other periods of intensified prejudice all the Negro's tendency to self-assertion has been called forth; at this period a policy of submission is advocated. In the history of nearly all other races and peoples the doctrine preached at such crises has been that manly self-respect is worth more than lands and houses, and that a people who voluntarily surrender such respect, or cease striving for it, are not worth civilizing.

In answer to this, it has been claimed that the Negro can survive only through submission. Mr. Washington distinctly asks that black people give up, at least for the present, three things—

First, political power,
Second, insistence on civil rights,
Third, higher education of Negro
  youth—

and concentrate all their energies on industrial education, the accumulation of wealth, and the conciliation of the South. This policy has been courageously and insistently advocated for over fifteen years, and has been triumphant for perhaps ten years. As a result of this tender of the palm-branch, what has been the return? In these years there have occurred:

1. The disfranchisement of the Negro.
2. The legal creation of a distant status of civil inferiority for the Negro.
3. The steady withdrawal of aid from institutions for the higher training of the Negro.

These movements are not, to be sure, direct results of Mr. Washington's teachings; but his propaganda has, without a shadow of doubt, helped their speedier accomplishment. The question then comes: Is it possible, and probable, that nine millions of men can make effective progress in economic lines if they are deprived of political rights, made a servile caste, and allowed only the most meagre chance for developing their exceptional men? If history and reason give any distinct answer to these questions, it

is an emphatic *No.* And Mr. Washington thus faces the triple paradox of his career:

1. He is striving nobly to make Negro artisans business men and property-owners; but it is utterly impossible, under modern competitive methods, for workingmen and property-owners to defend their rights and exist without the right of suffrage.

2. He insists on thrift and self-respect, but at the same time counsels a silent submission to civic inferiority such as is bound to sap the manhood of any race in the long run.

3. He advocates common-school and industrial training, and depreciates institutions of higher learning; but neither the Negro common-schools, nor Tuskegee itself, could remain open a day were it not for teachers trained in Negro colleges, or trained by their graduates.

This triple paradox in Mr. Washington's position is the object of criticism by two classes of colored Americans. One class is spiritually descended from Toussaint the Savior, through Gabriel, Vesey, and Turner, and they represent the attitude of revolt and revenge; they hate the white South blindly and distrust the white race generally, and so far as they agree on definite action, think that the Negro's only hope lies in emigration beyond the borders of the United States. And yet, by the irony of fate, nothing has more effectually made this programme seem hopeless than the recent course of the United States toward weaker and darker peoples in the West

Indies, Hawaii, and the Philippines—for where in the world may we go and be safe from lying and brute force?

The other class of Negroes who cannot agree with Mr. Washington has hitherto said little aloud. They deprecate the sight of scattered counsels, of internal disagreement; and especially they dislike making their just criticism of a useful and earnest man an excuse for a general discharge of venom from small-minded opponents. Nevertheless, the questions involved are so fundamental and serious that it is difficult to see how men like the Grimkes, Kelly Miller, J. W. E. Bowen, and other representatives of this group, can much longer be silent. Such men feel in conscience bound to ask of this nation three things:

1. The right to vote.
2. Civic equality.
3. The education of youth according to ability.

They acknowledge Mr. Washington's invaluable service in counselling patience and courtesy in such demands; they do not ask that ignorant black men vote when ignorant whites are debarred, or that any reasonable restrictions in the suffrage should not be applied; they know that the low social level of the mass of the race is responsible for much discrimination against it, but they also know, and the nation knows, that relentless color-prejudice is more often a cause than a result of the Negro's degradation; they seek the abatement of this relic of barbarism, and not its systematic encouragement and pampering by all agencies of social power from the As-

sociated Press to the Church of Christ. They advocate, with Mr. Washington, a broad system of Negro common schools supplemented by thorough industrial training; but they are surprised that a man of Mr. Washington's insight cannot see that no such educational system ever has rested or can rest on any other basis than that of the well-equipped college and university, and they insist that there is a demand for a few such institutions throughout the South to train the best of the Negro youth as teachers, professional men, and leaders.

This group of men honor Mr. Washington for his attitude of conciliation toward the white South; they accept the "Atlanta Compromise" in its broadest interpretation; they recognize, with him, many signs of promise, many men of high purpose and fair judgment, in this section; they know that no easy task has been laid upon a region already tottering under heavy burdens. But, nevertheless, they insist that the way to truth and right lies in straightforward honesty, not in indiscriminate flattery; in praising those of the South who do well and criticising uncompromisingly those who do ill; in taking advantage of the opportunities at hand and urging their fellows to do the same, but at the same time in remembering that only a firm adherence to their higher ideals and aspirations will ever keep those ideals within the realm of possibility. They do not expect that the free right to vote, to enjoy civic rights, and to be educated, will come in a moment; they do not expect to see the bias and prejudices of years disappear at the blast of a trumpet; but they are absolutely certain that the way for a people to gain their reasonable rights is not by voluntarily throwing them away and insisting that they do not want them; that the way for a people to gain respect is not by continually belittling and ridiculing themselves; that, on the contrary, Negroes must insist continually, in season and out of season, that voting is necessary to modern manhood, that color discrimination is barbarism, and that black boys need education as well as white boys.

In failing thus to state plainly and unequivocally the legitimate demands of their people, even at the cost of opposing an honored leader, the thinking classes of American Negroes would shirk a heavy responsibility—a responsibility to themselves, a responsibility to the struggling masses, a responsibility to the darker races of men whose future depends so largely on this American experiment, but especially a responsibility to this nation—this common Fatherland. It is wrong to encourage a man or a people in evil-doing; it is wrong to aid and abet a national crime simply because it is unpopular not to do so. The growing spirit of kindliness and reconciliation between the North and South after the frightful difference of a generation ago ought to be a source of deep congratulation to all, and especially to those whose mistreatment caused the war; but if that reconciliation is to be marked by the industrial slavery and civic death of those same black men, with permanent legislation into a position of inferiority, then those black men, if they are really men, are called upon by every consideration of patriotism and loyalty to oppose such a course by all civilized

methods, even though such opposition involves disagreement with Mr. Booker T. Washington. We have no right to sit silently by while the inevitable seeds are sown for a harvest of disaster to our children, black and white.

First, it is the duty of black men to judge the South discriminatingly. The present generation of Southerners are not responsible for the past, and they should not be blindly hated or blamed for it. Furthermore, to no class is the indiscriminate endorsement of the recent course of the South toward Negroes more nauseating than to the best thought of the South. The South is not "solid"; it is a land in the ferment of social change, wherein forces of all kinds are fighting for supremacy; and to praise the ill the South is to-day perpetrating is just as wrong as to condemn the good. Discriminating and broad-minded criticism is what the South needs—needs it for the sake of her own white sons and daughters, and for the insurance of robust, healthy mental and moral development.

To-day even the attitude of the Southern whites toward the blacks is not, as so many assume, in all cases the same; the ignorant Southerner hates the Negro, the workingmen fear his competition, the money-makers wish to use him as a laborer, some of the educated see a menace in his upward development, while others—usually the sons of the masters—wish to help him to rise. National opinion has enabled this last class to maintain the Negro common schools, and to protect the Negro partially in property, life, and limb. Through the pressure of the money-makers, the Negro is in danger of being reduced to semi-slavery, especially in the country districts; the workingmen, and those of the educated who fear the Negro, have united to disfranchise him, and some have urged his deportation; while the passions of the ignorant are easily aroused to lynch and abuse any black man. To praise this intricate whirl of thought and prejudice is nonsense; to inveigh indiscriminately against "the South" is unjust; but to use the same breath in praising Governor Aycock, exposing Senator Morgan, arguing with Mr. Thomas Nelson Page, and denouncing Senator Ben Tillman, is not only sane, but the imperative duty of thinking black men.

It would be unjust to Mr. Washington not to acknowledge that in several instances he has opposed movements in the South which were unjust to the Negro; he sent memorials to the Louisiana and Alabama constitutional conventions, he has spoken against lynching, and in other ways has openly or silently set his influence against sinister schemes and unfortunate happenings. Notwithstanding this, it is equally true to assert that on the whole the distinct impression left by Mr. Washington's propaganda is, first, that the South is justified in its present attitude toward the Negro because of the Negro's degradation; secondly, that the prime cause of the Negro's failure to rise more quickly is his wrong education in the past; and, thirdly, that his future rise depends primarily on his own efforts. Each of these propositions is a dangerous half-truth. The supplementary truths must never be lost sight of: first, slavery and race-prejudice are

potent if not sufficient causes of the Negro's position; second, industrial and common-school training were necessarily slow in planting because they had to await the black teachers trained by higher institutions—it being extremely doubtful if any essentially different development was possible, and certainly a Tuskegee was unthinkable before 1880; and, third, while it is a great truth to say that the Negro must strive and strive mightily to help himself, it is equally true that unless his striving be not simply seconded, but rather aroused and encouraged, by the initiative of the richer and wiser environing group, he cannot hope for great success.

In his failure to realize and impress this last point, Mr. Washington is especially to be criticised. His doctrine has tended to make the whites, North and South, shift the burden of the Negro problem to the Negro's shoulders and stand aside as critical and rather pessimistic spectators; when in fact the burden belongs to the nation, and the hands of none of us are clean if we bend not our energies to righting these great wrongs.

The South ought to be led, by candid and honest criticism, to assert her better self and do her full duty to the race she has cruelly wronged and is still wronging. The North—her co-partner in guilt—cannot salve her conscience by plastering it with gold. We cannot settle this problem by diplomacy and suaveness, by "policy" alone. If worse comes to worst, can the moral fibre of this country survive the slow throttling and murder of nine millions of men?

The black men of America have a

duty to perform, a duty stern and delicate—a forward movement to oppose a part of the work of their greatest leader. So far as Mr. Washington preaches Thrift, Patience, and Industrial Training for the masses, we must hold up his hands and strive with him, rejoicing in his honors and glorying in the strength of this Joshua called of God and of man to lead the headless host. But so far as Mr. Washington apologizes for injustice, North or South, does not rightly value the privilege and duty of voting, belittles the emasculating effects of caste distinctions, and opposes the higher training and ambition of our brighter minds—so far as he, the South, or the Nation, does this—we must unceasingly and firmly oppose them. By every civilized and peaceful method we must strive for the right which the world accords to men, clinging unwaveringly to those great words which the sons of the Fathers would fain forget: "We hold these truths to be self-evident: That all men are created equal; that they are endowed by their Creator with certain unalienable rights; that among these are life, liberty, and the pursuit of happiness."

## Standing Bear, Protest, 1879

*After the Civil War, white settlement to the Great Plains and the West grew rapidly, encouraged by railroad construction and the consolidation of a national market, and putting pressure on Indian lands. In 1877 the United States forced the Ponca to leave their lands in Nebraska and to relocate in Indian Territory (Oklahoma). Along the five-hundred-mile long journey, one-third of the*

*Ponca perished. Standing Bear was one of the first Indians to bring the treatment of American Indians to the attention of the American public. The following account is his story as told to the Omaha World-Herald. Letters to Congress led to a Senate investigation of Standing Bear's charges. In a rare move, the government allowed the Ponca to return to Nebraska and compensated them for the property that they lost.*

*Source:* Helen Hunt Jackson, *A Century of Dishonor* (Boston: Roberts Brothers, 1893).

We lived on our land as long as we can remember. No one knows how long ago we came there. The land was owned by our tribe as far back as memory of men goes. We were living quietly on our farms. All of a sudden one white man came. We had no idea what for. This was the inspector. He came to our tribe with Rev. Mr. Hinman. These two, with the agent, James Lawrence, they made our trouble.

They said the President told us to pack up—that we must move to the Indian Territory.

The inspector said to us: "The President says you must sell this land. He will buy it and pay you the money, and give you new land in the Indian Territory."

We said to him: "We do not know your authority. You have no right to move us till we have had council with the President."

We said to him: "When two persons wish to make a bargain, they can talk together and find out what each wants, and then make their agreement."

We said to him: "We do not wish to

go. When a man owns anything, he does not let it go till he has received payment for it."

We said to him: "We will see the President first."

He said to us: "I will take you to see the new land. If you like it, then you can see the President, and tell him so. If not, then you can see him and tell him so." And he took all ten of our chiefs down. I went, and Bright Eyes' uncle went. He took us to look at three different pieces of land. He said we must take one of the three pieces, so the President said. After he took us down there, he said: "No pay for the land you left."

We said to him: "You have forgotten what you said before we started. You said we should have pay for our land. Now you say not. You told us then you were speaking truth."

All these three men took us down there. The man got very angry. He tried to compel us to take one of the three pieces of land. He told us to be brave. He said to us: "If you do not accept these, I will leave you here alone. You are one thousand miles from home. You have no money. You have no interpreter, and you cannot speak the language." And he went out and slammed the door. The man talked to us from long before sundown till it was nine o'clock at night.

We said to him: "We do not like this land. We could not support ourselves. The water is bad. Now send us to Washington, to tell the President, as you promised."

He said to us: "The President did not tell me to take you to Washington; neither did he tell me to take you home."

We said to him: "You have the Indian money you took to bring us down here. That money belongs to us. We would like to have some of it. People do not give away food for nothing. We must have money to buy food on the road."

He said to us: "I will not give you a cent."

We said to him: "We are in a strange country. We cannot find our way home. Give us a pass, that people may show us our way."

He said: "I will not give you any."

We said to him: "This interpreter is ours. We pay him. Let him go with us."

He said: "You shall not have the interpreter. He is mine, and not yours."

We said to him: "Take us at least to the railroad; show us the way to that."

And he would not. He left us right there. It was winter. We started for home on foot. At night we slept in haystacks. We barely lived till morning, it was so cold. We had nothing but our blankets. We took the ears of corn that had dried in the fields; we ate it raw. The soles of our moccasins wore out. We went barefoot in the snow. We were nearly dead when we reached the Otoe Reserve. It had been fifty days. We stayed there ten days to strengthen up, and the Otoes gave each of us a pony. The agent of the Otoes told us he had received a telegram from the inspector, saying that the Indian chiefs had run away; not to give us food or shelter, or help in any way. The agent said: "I would like to understand. Tell me all that has happened. Tell me the truth. . . ."

Then we told our story to the agent and to the Otoe chiefs—how we had been left down there to find our way.

The agent said: "I can hardly believe

it possible that anyone could have treated you so. The inspector was a poor man to have done this. If I had taken chiefs in this way, I would have brought them home: I could not have left them there."

In seven days we reached the Omaha Reservation. Then we sent a telegram to the President; asked him if he had authorized this thing. We waited three days for the answer. No answer came.

In four days we reached our own home. We found the inspector there. While we were gone, he had come to our people and told them to move.

Our people said: "Where are our chiefs? What have you done with them? Why have you not brought them back? We will not move till our chiefs come back."

Then the inspector told them: "To-morrow you must be ready to move. If you are not ready you will be shot." Then the soldiers came to the doors with their bayonets, and ten families were frightened. The soldiers brought wagons, they put their things in and were carried away. The rest of the tribe would not move. . . .

Then, when he found that we would not go, he wrote for more soldiers to come.

Then the soldiers came, and we locked our doors, and the women and children hid in the woods. Then the soldiers drove all the people [to] the other side of the river, all but my brother Big snake and I. We did not go; and the soldiers took us and carried us away to a fort and put us in jail. There were eight officers who held council with us after we got there. The commanding officer

said: "I have received four messages telling me to send my soldiers after you. Now, what have you done?"

Then we told him the whole story. Then the officer said: "You have done no wrong. The land is yours; they had no right to take it from you. Your title is good. I am here to protect the weak, and I have no right to take you; but I am a soldier, and I have to obey orders."

He said: "I will telegraph to the President, and ask him what I shall do. We do not think these three men had any authority to treat you as they have done. When we own a piece of land, it belongs to us till we sell it and pocket the money."

Then he brought a telegram, and said he had received answer from the President. The President said he knew nothing about it.

They kept us in jail ten days. Then they carried us back to our home. The soldiers collected all the women and children together; then they called all the chiefs together in council; and then they took wagons and went round and broke open the houses. When we came back from the council, we found the women and children surrounded by a guard of soldiers.

They took our reapers, mowers. Hay rakes; spades, ploughs, bedsteads, stoves, cupboards, everything we had on our farms, and put them in one large building. Then they put into the wagons such things as they could carry. We told them that we would rather die than leave our lands; but we could not help ourselves. They took us down. Many died on the road. Two of my children died. After we reached the new land, all my horses died. The water was very bad. All our cattle died; not one was left. I stayed till one hundred and fifty-eight of my people had died. Then I ran away with thirty of my people, men and women and children. Some of the children were orphans. We were three months on the road. We were weak and sick and starved. When we reached the Omaha Reserve the Omahas gave us a piece of land, and we were in a hurry to plough it and put in wheat. While we were working, the soldiers came and arrested us. Half of us were sick. We would rather have died than have been carried back; but we could not help ourselves.

## Field Matron's Job Description, 1892

*The movement to assimilate Indians included reformers who believed elevating the Indian woman to the ideal of white middle-class womanhood was key to civilizing the Indians. With the support of the federal government, women reformers and missionaries attempted to teach Indian women in the ways of middle-class domesticity. The following document describes the job of field matron as established by the U.S. Department of Interior's Bureau of Indian Affairs.*

*Source:* Department of Interior, Bureau of Indian Affairs, *Congressional Record*, 43d Congress, 2d session, March 1892, pt. 3:41.

WASHINGTON, D.C., JULY 6, 1892.

*To U.S. Indian Agents:*
The position of field matron has been created in order that Indian women may be influenced in their home life and duties, and may have done for them in their sphere what farmers and mechanics are supposed to do for Indian men in their sphere.

The duties of a field matron, therefore, are to visit Indian women in their homes and to give them counsel, encouragement, and help in the following lines;

1. Care of a house, keeping it clear and in order, ventilated, properly warmed (not over heated), and suitably furnished.
2. Cleanliness and hygienic conditions generally, including disposition of all refuse.
3. Preparation and serving of food and regularity in meals.
4. Sewing, including cutting, making, and mending garments.
5. Laundry work.
6. Adorning the home, both inside and out, with pictures, curtains, homemade rags, flowers, grass plots and trees, construction and repair of walks, fences and drains.

    In this connection there will be opportunity for the matron to give to the male members of the family kindly admonition as to the "chores" and heavier kinds of work about the house which in civilized communities is generally done by men.
7. Keeping and care of domestic animals, such us cows, poultry, and swine; care and use of milk, making of butter, cheese, and curds; and keeping of bees.
8. Care of sick.
9. Care of little children, and introducing among them the games and sports of white children.

10. Proper observance of the Sabbath; organization of societies for promoting literary, religious, moral and social improvement, such as "Lend a Hand" clubs, circles of "King's Daughters," or "Sons," Y.M.C.A, Christian Endeavor and Temperance Societies, etc.

Of course, it is impracticable to enumerate all the directions in which a field matron can lend her aid in ameliorating the condition of Indian women. Her own tact, skill, and interest will suggest manifold ways of instructing them in civilized home life, stimulating their intelligence, ronsing ambition, and cultivating refinement.

Young girls, particularly those who have left school, should find in her a friend and adviser, and her influence should be to them a safeguard against the sore temptations which beset them. She should impress upon families the importance of education and urge upon them to put and keep their children in school.

Besides faithfully visiting Indian homes, the matron should have stated days or parts of days each week when Indian women may come to her home for counsel or for instruction in sewing or other domestic arts which can advantageously be taught to several persons at one time.

The time actually devoted to the above outlined work by the field matron should be not less than eight hours per day for five days in the week, and half a day on Saturday.

The matron shall make reports of her work monthly to the agent and quarterly, through him, to this office upon blank herewith. On August 15th of each year, she shall make an annual report, to be forwarded by the agent to this office for publication.

*Very respectfully,*
*T. J. Morgan,*
*Commissioner.*

## "Omaha Discuss Allotment," 1881

*In the 1880s the federal government began a strategy called "allotment by severalty," by which Indians' tribal lands were divided into individual family-sized plots. Allotment provided Indians a fraction of their land and gave the rest to the government and to private interests. The strategy was meant to civilize Indians by making them into private-property holders and family farmers. The Omaha tribe was divided by the issue; a group called "make believe white men" desired allotment and citizenship, whereas a group known as "those who live in earth lodges" opposed changing their traditional way of life.*

Source: Francis La Flesche and Alice C. Fletcher, *27 Annual Report, 1905–1906, Bureau of American Ethnology* (Washington, D.C.: Smithsonian Institution, 1911).

## A HOUSE OF OUR OWN

XITHA GAXE: I have worked hard on my land so that I should not go round begging. I thought the land was my own, so I went to work and cultivated it. Now I have found out it is not my own, and this makes me stop. I am afraid if I should build a house and spend money on it I would lose it if the Government should move the Indians from this land. Three times I have cut wood to build a house. Each time the agent told me the Government wished to build me a house. Each time my wood has lain and rotted, and now I feel ashamed when I hear an agent telling me such things. . . . I want a title to my land; I want a house that is my own.

WA THISHNADE: Before I began to farm I was just a wild Indian doing as I pleased, going round the country looking for death. . . . We have no government on the reserve. We have trouble which we would not have if we had government and law. We want these. We are right among the white people, and as we have no law we can't get along very well. There are persons living on the reserve who have certificates of allotment; they believe that the land is theirs and that they can always keep it. I know differently. . . . I went on my farm with a certificate. I believed the land was mine. I have found out the land is not mine; that the Government can take it away. We are going to ask for our titles. As long as the Government does not give them, we will ask until the Government gets tired. We won't stop asking until we get our titles.

DU BAMO THI: . . . The road our fathers walked is gone, the game is gone, the white people are all about us. There is no use any Indian thinking of the old ways; he must now go to work as the white man does. We want titles to our lands that the land may be secure to our children. When we die we shall feel easy in our minds if we know the land will belong to our children and that they will

have the benefit of our work. There are some Omahas who do not yet care for titles. We desire the Government to give titles to those who ask for them. . . . We are willing the others should do as they please but we are not willing that they should keep us from getting titles to our lands. Our children would suffer even a greater wrong than would befall us. Give us who ask titles to our lands . . . do not let us be held back and our children be sufferers because of the inaction of those who do not seem to care for our future.

JOSEPH LA FLESCHE: . . . I was born in this country, in Nebraska, and I have always lived among the Indians. There was a time when I used to look only at the Indians and think they were the only people. The Indians must have been long in this country before the white man came. . . . In the spring they would take their seed and farm their 1 or 2 acres. There were no idlers, all worked in the spring. Those who had no hoes worked with pieces of sticks. When they had their seed in, they went on the hunt. They had nothing to worry them; all they thought of was their little garden they had left behind. . . .

Then it was I used to see white men, those who were going around buying furs. Sometimes for two or three years I would not see any white men. At that time the country was empty, only animals to be seen. Then after a while the white men came, just as the blackbirds do, and spread over the country. Some settled down, others scattered on the land, The Indians never thought that any such thing could be, but it matters not where one looks now one sees white people. These things I have been speaking about are in the past and are all gone. We Indians see you now and want to take our steps your way. . . .

It seems as though the Government pushes us back. It makes us think that the Government regards us as unfit to be as white men. The white man looks into the future and sees what is good. That is what the Indian is doing. He looks into the future and sees his only chance is to become as the white man. When a person lives in a place a long time he loves the place. We love our lands and want titles for them. When one has anything he likes to feel it is his own, and belongs to no one else, so we want titles; then we can leave our land to our children. You know, and so do we, that some of us will not live very long; we will soon be gone into the other world. We ask for titles for our children's sakes. For some years we have been trying to get titles but we have never heard from the Government. . . .

We are not strong enough to help ourselves in this matter, so we ask you to help us. In the past we only lived on the animals. We see that it is from the ground that you get all that you possess. The reason you do not look upon us as men is because we have not law, because we are not citizens. We are strangers in the land where we were born. . . . We know that in asking for titles we are asking for that which will bring responsibility. We are ready to accept it and to strive to fulfill its requirements. It seems as though in the past the Government had not listened to the words of the Indians. We know our own needs, and now we speak to you directly.

## Lone Wolf v. Hitchcock, 1903

*The drive by Americans to dispossess Indians of their land during the late nineteenth century collided with the rights that the government had accorded Indians by treaty and by legislation. In* Lone Wolf, *the Supreme Court upheld that the U.S. had no obligation to uphold the treaties it made with American Indians. It declared Indians individual wards of the state and rendered moot the provisions of the Dawes Act, which declared that tribal land was American Indian private property and required Indian approval of the sale of their unallotted lands. Justice Edward Douglas White's opinion suggested that Congress had always exercised plenary authority over the tribal relations of the Indians. He also argued that this power was a political power and was not subject to judiciary control.*

Source: Lone Wolf v. Hitchcock, Supreme Court, 187, U.S. 553; 23 S. Ct. 216, 1903.

## MR. ASSISTANT ATTORNEY GENERAL VAN DEVANTER FOR APPELLEE

Mr. Justice White, after making the foregoing statement, delivered the opinion of the court.

By the sixth article of the first of the two treaties referred to in the preceding statement, proclaimed on August 25, 1868, 15 Stat. 581, it was provided that heads of families of the tribes affected by the treaty might select, within the reservation, a tract of land of not exceeding 320 acres in extent, which should thereafter cease to be held in common, and should be for the exclusive possession of the Indian making the selection, so long as he or his family might continue to cultivate the land. The twelfth article reads as follows:

"Article 12. No treaty for the cession of any portion or part of the reservation herein described, which may be held in common, shall be of any validity or force as against the said Indians, unless executed and signed by at least three fourths of all the adult male Indians occupying the same, and no cession by the tribe shall be understood or construed in such manner as to deprive, without his consent, any individual member of the tribe of his rights to any tract of land selected by him as provided in article III (VI) of this treaty."

The appellants base their right to relief on the proposition that by the effect of the article just quoted the confederated tribes of Kiowas, Comanches and Apaches were vested with an interest in the lands held in common within the reservation, which interest could not be divested by Congress in any other mode than that specified in the said twelfth article, and that as a result of the said stipulation the interest of the Indians in the common lands fell within the protection of the Fifth Amendment to the Constitution of the United States, and such interest—indirectly at least—came under the control of the judicial branch of the government. We are unable to yield our assent to this view.

The contention in effect ignores the status of the contracting Indians and the relation of dependency they bore and continue to bear towards the government of the United States. To uphold the claim would be to adjudge that the in-

direct operation of the treaty was to materially limit and qualify the controlling authority of Congress in respect to the care and protection of the Indians, and to deprive Congress, in a possible emergency, when the necessity might be urgent for a partition and disposal of the tribal lands, of the power to act, if the assent of the Indians could not be obtained.

Now, it is true that in decisions of this court, the Indian right of occupancy of tribal lands, whether declared in a treaty or otherwise created, has been stated to be sacred, or as sometimes expressed, as sacred as the fee of the United States in the same lands. *Johnson* v. *McIntosh*, (1823) 8 Wheat. 543, 574; *Cherokee Nation* v. *Georgia*, (1831) 5 Pet. 1,48; *Worcester* v. *Georgia*, (1832) 6 Pet. 515, 581; *United States* v. *Cook*, (1873) 19 Wall. 591, 592; *Leavenworth &c. R. R. Co.* v. *United States*, (1875) 92 U.S. 733, 755; *Beecher* v. *Wetherby*, (1877) 95 U.S. 517, 525. But in none of these cases was there involved a controversy between Indians and the government respecting the power of Congress to administer the property of the Indians. The questions considered in the cases referred to, which either directly or indirectly had relation to the nature of the property rights of the Indians, concerned the character and extent of such rights as respected States or individuals. In one of the cited cases it was clearly pointed out that Congress possessed a paramount power over the property of the Indians, by reason of its exercise of guardianship over their interests, and that such authority might be implied, even though opposed to the strict letter of a treaty with the Indians. Thus, in *Beecher* v. *Wetherby*, 95 U.S. 517, discussing the claim that there had been a prior reservation of land by treaty to the use of a certain tribe of Indians, the court said (p. 525):

"But the right which the Indians held was only that of occupancy. The fee was in the United States, subject to that right, and could be transferred by them whenever they chose. The grantee, it is true, would take only the naked fee, and could not disturb the occupancy of the Indians; that occupancy could only be interfered with or determined by the United States. It is to be presumed that in this matter the United States would be governed by such considerations of justice as would control a Christian people in their treatment of an ignorant and dependent race. Be that as it may, the propriety or justice of their action towards the Indians with respect to their lands is a question of governmental policy, and is not a matter open to discussion in a controversy between third parties, neither of whom derives title from the Indians."

Plenary authority over the tribal relations of the Indians has been exercised by Congress from the beginning, and the power has always been deemed a political one, not subject to be controlled by the judicial department of the government. Until the year 1871 the policy was pursued of dealing with the Indian tribes by means of treaties, and, of course, a moral obligation rested upon Congress to act in good faith in performing the stipulations entered into on its behalf. But, as with treaties made with foreign nations, *Chinese Exclusion Case*, 130 U.S. 581, 600, the legislative power might pass laws in

conflict with treaties made with the Indians. *Thomas* v. *Gay*, 169 U.S. 264, 270; *Ward* v. *Race Horse*, 163 U.S. 504, 511; *Spalding* v. *Chandler*, 160 U.S. 394, 405; *Missouri, Kansas & Texas Ry. Co.* v. *Roberts*, 152 U.S. 114, 117; The *Cherokee Tobacco*, 11 Wall. 616.

The power exists to abrogate the provisions of an Indian treaty, though presumably such power will be exercised only when circumstances arise which will not only justify the government in disregarding the stipulations of the treaty, but may demand, in the interest of the country and the Indians themselves, that it should do so. When, therefore, treaties were entered into between the United States and a tribe of Indians it was never doubted that the *power* to abrogate existed in Congress, and that in a contingency such power might be availed of from considerations of governmental policy, particularly if consistent with perfect good faith towards the Indians. In *United States* v. *Kagama*, (1885) 118 U.S. 375, speaking of the Indians, the court said (p. 382):

"After an experience of a hundred years of the treaty-making system of government, Congress has determined upon a new departure—to govern them by acts of Congress. This is seen in the act of March 3, 1871, embodied in § 2079 of the Revised Statutes: 'No Indian nation or tribe, within the territory of the United States shall be acknowledged or recognized as an independent nation, tribe, or power, with whom the United States may contract by treaty; but no obligation of any treaty lawfully made and ratified with any such Indian nation or tribe prior to March third, eighteen hundred and seventy-one, shall be hereby invalidated or impaired.' "

In upholding the validity of an act of Congress which conferred jurisdiction upon the courts of the United States for certain crimes committed on an Indian reservation within a State, the court said (p. 383):

"It seems to us that this is within the competency of Congress. These Indian tribes are the wards of the nation. They are communities dependent on the United States. Dependent largely for their daily food. Dependent for their political rights. They owe no allegiance to the States, and receive from them no protection. Because of the local ill feeling, the people of the States where they are found are often their deadliest enemies. From their very weakness and helplessness, so largely due to the course of dealing of the Federal government with them and the treaties in which it has been promised, there arises the duty of protection, and with it the power. This has always been recognized by the Executive and by Congress, and by this court, whenever the question has arisen.

"The power of the general government over these remnants of a race once powerful, now weak and diminished in numbers, is necessary to their protection, as well as to the safety of those among whom they dwell. It must exist in that government, because it never has existed anywhere else, because the theatre of its exercise is within the geographical limits of the United States, because it has never been denied, and because it alone can enforce its laws on all the tribes."

That Indians who had not been fully emancipated from the control and protection of the United States are subject, at least so far as the tribal lands were concerned, to be controlled by direct legislation of Congress, is also declared in *Choctaw Nation* v. *United States*, 119 U.S. 1, 27, and *Stephens* v. *Cherokee Nation*, 174 U.S. 445, 483.

In view of the legislative power possessed by Congress over treaties with the Indians and Indian tribal property, we may not specially consider the contentions pressed upon our notice that the signing by the Indians of the agreement of October 6, 1892, was obtained by fraudulent misrepresentations and concealment, that the requisite three fourths of adult male Indians had not signed, as required by the twelfth article of the treaty of 1867, and that the treaty as signed had been amended by Congress without submitting such amendments to the action of the Indians, since all these matters, in any event, were solely within the domain of the legislative authority and its action is conclusive upon the courts.

The act of June 6, 1900, which is complained of in the bill, was enacted at a time when the tribal relations between the confederated tribes of Kiowas, Comanches and Apaches still existed, and that statute and the statutes supplementary thereto dealt with the disposition of tribal property and purported to give an adequate consideration for the surplus lands not allotted among the Indians or reserved for their benefit. Indeed, the controversy which this case presents is concluded by the decision in *Cherokee Nation* v. *Hitchcock*, 187 U.S. 294, decided at this term, where it was held that full administrative power was possessed by Congress over Indian tribal property. In effect, the action of Congress now complained of was but an exercise of such power, a mere change in the form of investment of Indian tribal property, the property of those who, as we have held, were in substantial effect the wards of the government. We must presume that Congress acted in perfect good faith in the dealings with the Indians of which complaint is made, and that the legislative branch of the government exercised its best judgment in the premises. In any event, as Congress possessed full power in the matter, the judiciary cannot question or inquire into the motives which prompted the enactment of this legislation. If injury was occasioned, which we do not wish to be understood as implying, by the use made by Congress of its power, relief must be sought by an appeal to that body for redress and not to the courts. The legislation in question was constitutional, and the demurrer to the bill was therefore rightly sustained.

The motion to dismiss does not challenge jurisdiction over the subject matter. Without expressly referring to the propositions of fact upon which it proceeds, suffice it to say that we think it need not be further adverted to, since, for the reasons previously given and the nature of the controversy, we think the decree below should be

*Affirmed*.

Concur by: Harlan

Concur:

Mr. Justice Harlan concurs in the result.

## "Kiansis I," c. 1870

*The corrido (ballad) is a traditional Mexican musical form. The following corrido, the earliest one (from the United States) collected in complete form, reflects the involvement of Mexicans in the cattle industry, documenting the cattle drive from Texas to Kansas in the late 1860s and early 1870s. The lyrics indicate some of the intercultural conflict of Anglo-Mexican relations at the time and suggest the Mexican origins of American cowboy culture.*

Source: María Herrera-Sobek, *Northward Bound: The Mexican Immigrant Experience in Ballad and Song* (Bloomington, Ind.: Indiana University Press, 1993). Original in Américo Paredes, *A Texas-Mexican Cancionero: Folksongs of the Lower Border* (Urbana: University of Illinois Press, 1976), pp. 53–54.

| KIANSIS I | KANSAS I |
|---|---|
| Cuando salimos *pa*\* Kiansis | When we left for Kansas |
| con una grande partida, | with a great herd of cattle, |
| ¡ah, qué camino tan largo | Ah, what a long trail it was! |
| no contaba con mi vida! | I was not sure I would survive. |
| | |
| Nos decía el caporal, | The *caporal* would tell us, |
| como queriendo plorar | As if he was going to cry, |
| —allá va la novillada | "Watch out for that bunch of steers |

\*pa' = *para* = for

no me la dejen pasar.
—Don't let them get past you."

¡Ah, qué caballo tan bueno!
Ah, what a good horse I had!
todo se le iba en correr.
He did nothing but gallop.
¡y, ah, qué luerte aguacerazo!
And, ah, what violent cloudbursts!
no contaba yo en volver.
I was not sure I would come back.

Unos pedían cigarro,
Some of us asked for cigarettes,
otros pedían que corner.
Others wanted something to eat;
y el caporal nos decía:
And the *caporal* would tell us,
—Sea por Dios, que hemos de hacer—
"So be it, it can't be helped."

En el charco de Palomas
By the pond at Palomas
se cortó un novillo bragado,
A vicious steer left the herd,
y el caporal lo lazó
And the *caporal* lassoed it
en su caballo melado.
On his honey-colored horse.

Avísenle al caporal
Go tell the *caporal*
que un vaquero se mató,
That a vaquero has been killed.
en las trancas del corral
All he left was his leather jacket
nomás la cuera dejó.
Hanging on the rails of the corral

Llegamos al Río Salado
We got to the Salado River,

y nos tiramos al nado,**
And we swam our horses across;
decía un americano:
An American was saying,
—Estos hombres ya se ahogaron.—
"Those men are as good as drowned

Pues qué pensaría ese hombre
I wonder what the man thought,
que venimos a esp'rimentar,***
That we came to learn, perhaps;
si somos del Río Grande,
Why, we're from the Rio Grande,
de los buenos pa' nadar.
Where the good swimmers are from.

Y le dimos vista a Kiansis,
And then Kansas came in sight,
y nos dice el caporal:
And the *caporal* tells us,
—Ora**** sí somos de vida,
"We have finally made it,
ya vamos a hacer corral.—
We'll soon have them in the corral."

Y de vuelta en San Antonio
Back again in San Antonio,
compramos buenos sombreros,
We all bought ourselves good hats,
y aquí se acaban cantando
And this is the end of the singing
versos de los aventureros.
Of the stanzas about the trail drivers.

### In re Rodriguez, 1897

*Because the Treaty of Guadalupe Hidalgo (1848) granted United States citizenship to*

**al nado = *a nadar* (to swim)
***esp'rimentar = *exprimentar* (to experiment)
**** ora = *ahora* (now)

*inhabitants of the ceded territory, a federal court ruled in this 1897 case that Mexicans were "white" for purposes of naturalization, even if ethnologists considered them "Indian." While the reference to whiteness resulted from the bifurcated nature of racial ordering in the United States, Mexicans often continued to be perceived in ambiguous and mostly negative racial terms, despite the ruling in the Rod-riguez case.*

Source: District Court, W.D. Texas, 81 F. 337; 1897 U.S Dist.

Maxey, District Judge, after stating the case, delivered the following opinion:

Recognizing the delicacy and gravity of the question which the present application involves, it was thought advisable to obtain the views of several members of the bar as to the proper construction of that clause of the naturalization statute which the court is called upon to consider and construe. With that object in view, the court addressed letters to Mr. T. M. Paschal and Mr. Floyd McGown, inclosing therewith copies of the papers and testimony on file. Generously responding to the wish of the court, these gentlemen have submitted able and interesting briefs, which have received, together with those of Mr. Evans and Mr. McMinn, the attentive consideration which the nature of the case and importance of the question demand. And the court now desires to express its acknowledgments to all counsel appearing in the case for the valuable aid thus rendered.

The applicant, a citizen by birth of the republic of Mexico, desires to avail him-self of the inherent right of expatriation, and to invest himself with the rights and privileges pertaining to citizenship of our country. Although 49 years have elapsed since the negotiation of the treaty of Guadalupe-Hidalgo, which greatly increased our territorial area, and incorporated many thousands of Mexicans into our common citizenship, as wilt be hereinafter shown, the question of the individual naturalization of a Mexican citizen is now for the first time, so far as the court is advised, submitted for judicial determination. To the question, why may not he be naturalized under the laws of congress? it is replied that by section 2169 of the Revised Statutes it is provided: "The provisions of this tide shall apply to aliens (being free white persons, and to aliens) of African nativity, and to persons of African descent." The contention is that, by the letter of the statute, a Mexican citizen, answering to the description of the applicant, is, because of his color, denied the right to become a citizen of the United States by naturalization; and, in support of this view, the following authorities are relied upon: In re Ah Yup (decided by Judge Sawyer in 1878)5 Sawy. 155, 1 Fed. Cas. 223; In re Camille (decided by Judge Deady in 1880) 6 Fed. 256; In re Kanaka Nian (decided by the supreme court of Utah in 1889) 21 Pac. 993; In re Saito (decided by Judge Colt in 1894) 62 Fed. 126; and 2 Kent, Comm. 73, whee the learned chancellor expresses a doubt in these words:

"Perhaps there might be difficulties also as to the copper-colored natives of American, or the yellow or tawny races of Asiatics, and it may well be doubted whether any of them are white persons, within the purview of the law."

Of the four cases above cited, In re Ah Yup is the first in point of time, and the leading one. The four applications were denied, Ah Yup being a native of China, Camille a native of British Columbia, and of half Indian and half white blood, Nian a native of the Hawaiian Islands, whose ancestors were Kanakas, and Saito a native of Japan. When the Case of Ah Yup was decided, the Chinese question was flagrant on the Pacific slope, and Judge Sawyer seemed to think, predicating his conclusion upon the debates in congress, that the purpose of the amendment extending the right of naturalization to Africans and persons of African descent was to exclude Chinese from the benefits of naturalization. To quote his own language:

"Many other senators spoke pro and con on the question, this being the point of the contest, and these extracts being fair examples of the opposing opinions. It was finally defeated [the amendment to strike the word "white" from the naturalization laws]; and the amendment cited, extending the right of naturalization to the African only, was adopted. It is clear from these proceedings that congress retained the word 'white' in the naturalization laws for the sole purpose of excluding the Chinese from the right of naturalization. Thus, whatever latitudinarian construction might otherwise have been given to the term 'white person,' it is entirely clear that congress intended by this legislation to exclude Mongolians from the right of naturalization. I am therefore of the opinion that a native of China, of the Mongolian race,

is not a white person, within the meaning of the act of congress. The second question is answered in the discussion of the first. The amendment is intended to limit the operation of the provision as it then stood in the Revised Statutes. It would have been more appropriately inserted in section 2165 than where it is found, in section 2169. But the purpose is clear. It was certainly intended to have some operation, or it would not have been adopted. The purpose undoubtedly was to restore the law to the condition in which it stood before the revision, and to exclude the Chinese. It was intended to exclude some classes, and, as all white aliens and those of the African race are entitled to naturalization under other words, it is difficult to perceive whom it could exclude, unless it be the Chinese."

The opinion of Judge Sawyer is by no means decisive of the present question, as his language may well convey the meaning that the amendment of the naturalization statutes referred to by him was intended solely as a prohibition against the naturalization of members of the Mongolian race. The naturalization of Chinese is, however, no longer an open question, as section 14 of the act of May 6, 1882, expressly provides "that hereafter no state court or court of the United states shall admit Chinese to citizenship; and all laws in conflict with this act are hereby repealed." 22 Stat. 61.

If Chinese were denied the right to become naturalized citizens under laws existing when In re Ah Yup was decided, why did congress subsequently enact the prohibitory statute above quoted? Indeed, it is a debatable question whether the term "free white person," as used in the original act of 1790, was not employed for the sole purpose of withholding the right of citizenship from the black or African race and the Indians then inhabiting this country. But it is not necessary to enter upon a discussion of that question; nor is it deemed material to inquire to what race ethnological writers would assign the present applicant. If the strict scientific classification of the anthropologist should be adopted, he would probably not be classed as white. It is certain he is not an African, nor a person of African descent. According to his own statement, he is a "pure-blooded Mexican," bearing no relation to the Aztecs or original races of Mexico. Being, then, a citizen of Mexico, may he be naturalized pursuant to the laws of congress? If debarred by the strict letter of the law from receiving letters of citizenship, is he embraced within the intent and meaning of the statute? If he falls within the meaning and intent of the law, his application should be granted, notwithstanding the letter of the statute may be against him. . . .

A reference to the constitution of the republic of Texas and the constitution, laws, and treaties of the United States will disclose that both that republic and the United States have freely, during the past 60 years, conferred upon Mexicans the rights and privileges of American citizenship, not individually, it is true, but by various collective acts of naturalization. The first of such acts will be found in the language of section 10 of the general provisions of the constitution of the republic of Texas, adopted in 1836. By that section it is provided:

"All persons (Africans, the descendants of Africans, and the Indians excepted) who were residing in Texas on the day of the declaration of independence [March 2, 1836] shall be considered citizens of the republic, and entitled to all the privileges of such."

Under this provision, Mexicans who resided in Texas on March 2, 1836, become citizens of the republic (Kilpatrick v. Sisneros, 23 Tex. 113; Hardy v. De Leon, 5 Tex. 212; 13 Ops. Attys. Gen. 397, 398); and by the resolutions of March 1, 1845, and December 29, 1845, passed by the national congress, all such citizens, without express authorization, became incorporated into the citizenship of the Union. Thus, it is said by the supreme court, in Boyd v. Nebraska, 143 U.S. 169, 12 Sup. Ct. 385:

"By the annexation of Texas, under a joint resolution of congress of March 1, 1845, and its admission into the Union on an equal footing with the original states, December 29, 1845, all the citizens of the former republic became, without any express declaration, citizens of the United States. 5 Stat. 798; 9 Stat. 108; McKinney v. Saviego, 18 How. 235; Cryer v. Andrews, 11 Tex. 170; Barrett v. Kelly, 31 Tex. 476; Carter v. New Mexico, I N.M. 317."

See, also, Lawr. Wheat. (Append.) 897; Morse, Citizenship, § 94.

The next collective act in chronological order, providing for the naturalization of Mexicans, is the treaty concluded between the United States and Mexico, February 2, 1848, commonly known as the "Treaty of Guadalupe-Hidalgo." The eighth article of that treaty is as follows:

"Art. 8. Mexicans now established in

territories previously belonging to Mexico, and which remain for the future within the limits of the United States, as defined by the present treaty, shall be free to continue where they now reside, or to remove at any time to the Mexican republic, retaining the property which they possess in the said territories, or disposing thereof, and removing the proceeds wherever they please, without their being subjected, on this account, to any contribution, tax, or charge whatever. Those who shall prefer to remain in the said territories may either retain the title and rights of Mexican citizens, or acquire those of citizens of the United States. But they shall be under the obligation to make their election within one year from the date of the exchange of ratifications of this treaty; and those who shall remain in the said territories after the expiration of that year, without having declared their intention to retain the character of Mexicans, shall be considered to have elected to become citizens of the United States. In the said territories, property of every kind, now belonging to Mexicans not established there, shall be inviolably respected. The present owners, the heirs of these, and all Mexicans who may hereafter acquire said property by contract, shall enjoy with respect to it guaranties equally ample as if the same belonged to citizens of the United States."

That Mexicans who remained in the territory ceded by the treaty of 1848, and who failed to declare their intention within the time limited to remain citizens of Mexico, became citizens of the United States, is a fact scarcely open to serious controversy. . . .

It is said by Mr. Justice McLean, in his dissenting opinion in Scott v. Sandford, 19 How. 533, that:

"On the question of citizenship it must be admitted that we have not been very fastidious. Under the late treaty with Mexico, we have made citizens of all grades, combinations, and colors. The same was done in the admission of Louisiana and Florida. No one over doubted, and no court ever held, that the people of these territories did not become citizens under the treaty. They have exercised all the rights of citizens, without being naturalized under the acts of congress.". . .

The next act affecting the question of citizenship to which attention will be directed is the fourteenth amendment of the constitution, declared to be part of the organic law, by resolution of congress, July 21, 1868 (15 Stat. 709, 711). By this amendment, which completely overthrew the last remaining vestige of the doctrine announced in Scott v. Sandford, 19 How. 393, touching the question of citizenship of the African, and invested the native-born negro with the rights of an American citizen (Slaughterhouse Cases, 16 Wall. 36; Elk v. Wilkins, 112 U.S. 101, 5 Sup. Ct. 41; Strauder v. West virginia, 100 U.S. 306–308; In re Look Tin Sing, 21 Fed. 909), it is provided:

"All persons born or naturalized in the United States, and subject to the jurisdiction thereof, are citizens of the United States and of the state wherein they reside."

See, also, Rev. St. § 1992.

While this amendment, as held in the authorities last cited, was intended primarily for the benefit of the negro race, it also confers the right of citizenship upon persons of all other races, white, yellow, or red, born or naturalized in the United States, and "subject to the jurisdiction thereof." The language has been held to embrace even Chinese, to whom the laws of naturalization do not extend. In re Look Tin Sing, supra; Gee Fook Sing v. U.S., 1 C.C.A. 211, 49 Fed. 146; Ex parte Chin King, 35 Fed. 354; In re Yung Sing Hee, 36 Fed. 347; In re Wong Kim Ark, 71 Fed. 382. Mexicans, therefore, born in the United States, and who, at the date of birth, were subject to the jurisdiction of our government— as all were, except children of diplomatic officers, and a few others, not necessary in this connection to notice (In re Look Tin Sing, supra)—are citizens of the United States and of the state wherein they reside. The intimation in some of the briefs of counsel that Elk v. Wilkins, 112 U.S. 94, 5 Sup. Ct. 41, excludes Mexicans from citizenship, is not maintainable. That case refers exclusively to tribal Indians born and residing within the territory forming apart of the United States. . . .

When all the foregoing laws, treaties, and constitutional provisions are considered, which either affirmatively confer the rights of citizenship upon Mexicans, or tacitly recognize in them the right of individual naturalization, the conclusion forces itself upon the mind that citizens of Mexico are eligible to American citizenship, and may be individually naturalized by complying with the provisions of our laws. And this conviction is further strengthened by a consideration of the first section of the act of July 27, 1868, re-enacted as section 1999 of the Revised Statutes. Its language is as follows:

"Whereas the right of expatriation is a natural and inherent right of all people, indispensable to the enjoyment of the rights of life, liberty, and the pursuit of happiness; and whereas in the recognition of this principle this government has freely received emigrants from all nations, and invested them with the rights of citizenship; and whereas it is claimed that such American citizens, with their descendants, are subjects of foreign states, owing allegiance to the governments thereof; and whereas it is necessary to the maintenance of public peace that this claim of foreign allegiance should be promptly and finally disavowed: Therefore any declaration, instruction, opinion, order, or decision of any officer of the United States which denies, restricts, impairs, or questions the right of expatriation, is declared inconsistent with the fundamental principles of the republic."

It will be observed the preamble declares that we have freely received emigrants from all nations, and invested them with the rights of citizens; and the enacting clause denounces, as inconsistent with the fundamental principles of the republic, any opinion, decision, or order of any United States officer which denies, restricts, impairs, or questions the right of expatriation. It may appropriately be said that naturalization is the final step in the process of expatriation, and, literally construed, any order, opinion, or decision of a United States officer denying, restricting, or questioning the right to become a naturalized citizen, save as to Chinese, would come within the denunciation of the statute. It is probable that the statute was not intended to have an effect so far reaching in its consequences, and that the primary purpose was, as the title of the original act asserts, to protect the rights of American citizens in foreign states. But the language of the act is significant as illustrating the policy of the government "to bestow," using the words of vice Chancellor Sandford, "the right of citizenship freely, and with a liberality unknown in the old world." Lynch v. Clarke, 1 Sandf. Ch. 661.

After a careful and patient investigation of the question discussed, the court is of opinion that, whatever may be the status of the applicant viewed solely from the standpoint of the ethnologist, he is embraced within the spirit and intent of our laws upon naturalization, and his application should be granted if he is shown by the testimony to be a man attached to the principles of the constitution, and well disposed to the good order and happiness of the same. It is suggested that the proof fails in this respect; and the objection appears to be based upon the ground, intimated in the briefs, of his inability to understand or explain those principles. That the applicant is lamentably ignorant is conceded, and that he is unable to read and write the testimony clearly discloses. Naturally enough, his untrained mind is found deficient in the power to elucidate or define the principles of the constitution. But the testimony also discloses that he is a very good man, peaceable and industrious, of good moral character, and law abiding "to a remarkable degree." And hence it may be said of him, notwithstanding his inability to undergo an examination on questions of constitutional law, that by his daily walk, during a residence of 10 years in the city of San Antonio, he has practically illustrated and emphasized his attachment to the principles of the constitution. Congress has not seen fit to require of applicants for naturalization an educational qualification, and courts should be careful to avoid judicial legislation. In the judgment of the court, the applicant possesses the requisite qualifications for citizenship, and his application will therefore be granted.

## Leong Shee, Testimony, April 18, 1893

*Chinese immigrants faced rigorous interrogation upon arrival in the United States. Leong Shee's testimony provides an account of female Chinese immigration. While few women actually immigrated, those who did were often wives or daughters of merchants, servant girls, prostitutes, and, to a lesser extent, wives of laborers. Immigration officials believed most Chinese women were prostitutes and interrogated them accordingly.*

Source: Leong Shee, case 12017/37232, Chinese Departure Case Files, San Francisco District Office, Immigration and Naturalization Service, Record Group 85 (National Archives, San Bruno, California), from Judy Yung, *Unbound Voices* (Berkeley: University of California Press, 1999), pp. 21–22.

*San Francisco*, April 18th, 1893.

> *Kind of Certificate, or Paper*, Certificate of Identification *Ticket No.* 388.
> *Name of Passenger*, Leong Yee & Ah Kum, child. *Sex*, Female.
> *Where born?* China.
> *Here in U.S.?* Yes. *Place of former residence in U.S.* San Francisco.
> *Date of departure from U.S.?* Oct. 17/89.
> *Name of Vessel departed on*, Belgic . . .
> *Do you speak English?* No. *Destination*, San Francisco
> *Place of stopping in City*, #808 Sacramento St.
> *Who bought your ticket to China?* My brother-in-law.
> *With whom connected*, Gurm Wo Jan—Jackson St., don't know number.
> *When did you first arrive in U.S.?* 1879.

I was married in San Francisco on Dec. 15, 1885 to Chong [Chin] Lung of the firm of Sang Kee wholesale dealers in tea & rice #808 Sac. St. San Francisco. When I first came to this country I came with my father Leong Hoong Wum and my mother Lee Shee and lived at #613 Dupont St. My father was formerly connected with the firm of Sang Kee #808 Sac. St. My father died in this city Nov. 25, 1887. My mother died in this city 1883 so long ago I have forgotten the date. I went home to China with my brother-in-law Chun Gwun Dai and my daughter Ah Kum who was 4 years of age the time of departure. After I was married I lived on the 2nd floor over the store of Sang Kee #808 Sac. St where my daughter Ah Kum was born on the 28 day of December 1886. My daughter is 8 years old now. My brother-in-law

Chun Gwun Dai returned to S.F. in the later part of year 1891. Lee Moon's wife went home in the same steamer with me. I do not know her name. There was also a woman named Sam Moy and a child Ah Yuck on board. I do not speak English and do not know the city excepting the names of a few streets as I have small feet and never went out.

> H. S. Huff, *Interpreter*
> Leong X [her mark] Yee

## An Agreement Paper by the Person Mee Yung, 1875

*Chinese women were often impressed into prostitution in order to pay their (or their families') debts. The following contract indentured Yut Kum to the mistress Mee Yung according to specific conditions.*

*Source: Congressional Record, 43d Congress, 2d session, March 1875; pt. 3, p. 41, from Judy Yung,* Unbound Voices *(Berkeley: University of California Press, 1999), pp. 141–142.*

### PROSTITUTE'S CONTRACT

At this time there is a prostitute woman, Yut Kum, who has borrowed from Mee Yung $470. It is distinctly understood that there shall be no interest charged on the money and no wages paid for services. Yut Kum consents to prostitute her body to receive company to aid Mee Yung for the full time of four years. When the time is fully served, neither service nor money shall be longer required.

If Yut Kum should be sick fifteen days she shall make up one month. If she conceives, she shall serve one year more. If during the time any man wishes to redeem her body, she shall make satisfactory arrangements with the mistress, Mee Yung. If Yut Kum should herself escape and be recovered, then her time shall never expire. Should the mistress become very wealthy and return to China with glory, then Yut Kum shall fulfill her time, serving another person.

This is a distinct agreement made face to face, both parties willingly consenting. But lest the words of the mouth should be without proof, the agreement-paper is executed and placed in her hands for proof. There are four great sicknesses against which Mee Yung is secured for one hundred days, namely, leprosy, epilepsy, conception, and "stone-woman," i.e., inability to have carnal intercourse with men. For any of these four diseases she may be returned within one hundred days.

Truly with her own hands Mee Yung hands over $470.

Tung Chee 12th year [1874], 8th month, 14th day. The agreement is executed by Mee Yung.

## Chinese in Napa Asylum, 1912

*After Congress passed the Chinese exclusion law in 1882, additional laws required Chinese already residing in the United States to register with the government and to carry certificates of identity (referred to in interviews below as the "chock chee"). These hospital records show Chinese men from the gold rush era, whom the immigration service proposed*

*to deport, languishing decades later in a state institution for the insane. What do the men's silences suggest?*

Source: File 52516/10, Records of INS, RG 85, National Archives.

NOVEMBER 27, 1912.

*Commissioner of Immigration, San Francisco, Calif.*

The Bureau has received your letter of the 18th instant No. 1039–0/1, in which you call attention to the fact that there are about thirty Chinese incarcerated in the California State Asylum at Napa, with respect to whom it is probable that no evidence could be adduced to show a lawful right to be and remain in the United States.

It is believed that this matter should be handled with considerable care and that your office should go slowly in connection with any proposal to institute numerous proceedings against Chinese who have become insane but who have been in the United States more than three years and therefore are not subject to deportation under the provisions of the general immigration law. It would be difficult for an insane Chinese to make any defense if brought into court on a charge of unlawful residence, and there is danger that Chinese lawfully here might be deported unwittingly as the result of this difficulty. The Bureau suggests that as soon as the state of the current work of your office will permit, a thorough inquiry be instituted for the purpose of ascertaining as completely as possible the facts of each case, those facts to be laid before the Bureau before suing out judicial warrants for the arrest of the Chinese.

Commissioner-General.
Daniel J. Keefe

*Napa State Hospital, November 16, 1912.*
   Inspector, D. J. Griffiths.
   Reporter, F. Climn.

## SUPPLEMENTARY HEARING

Q . What is your name?

Q . Yong Fook.

Q . Where were you registered?

A . In 1889, registered Fort Jones, Yreka.

Q . Who were your witnesses?

A . Got letter on money bank at Yreka. Man owns the bank. Only one witness.

Q . Were you a laborer when you were registered?

A . Labored at mining.

Q . Have you got chock chee?

A . Chock chee lost.

Q . How long have you been in this country?

A . About 40 years.

Q . Ever back to China?

A . Never.

Q . When did you register?

A . Fort Jones, Yreka County, 1889.

Q . Were you registered in California?

A . Yes.

*Lee Sing (Admitted Oct. 1899), a public charge in the Napa State Hospital, Napa State Hospital, Napa, Cal. Oct. 19, 1912.*
   Inspector, W. H. Clendenin.
   Reporter, Albert Betz.

Q . How old are you?

(Interpreter states patient does not wish to talk.)

Q . When did you first come to California?

A . No sabe.

Q . You got a Chock Chee? (No answer).

Q . Did you ever have one?

Q . Do you want to go back to China? (No answer to above questions).

Q . Where is your father?

A . No father.

Q . How did you get into the United States? (No answer).

## Robert Ferrari, Autobiography, 1950

*Robert Ferrari's story provides an account of Italian migration to the United States; some of the reasons for leaving one's homeland; the nature of the migration, in which the male head of the family immigrated first; and the details of the actual journey. While Ferrari's father sent for his family after several years, many Italian immigrants resisted the idea of permanent settlement in the United States and chose to return. Jews, on the other hand, had the lowest return rate of the "New" European immigrant groups.*

Source: *American Immigrant Autobiographies*, part 1 (Minneapolis: Immigration History Research Center, University of Minnesota, 1988), microfiche.

And so my story really begins in 1872, in another world, when my father, Vito Salvatore Ferrari, made up his mind to leave my mother, Cecilia, and her child in Rocca Nova until he could make his fortunes in the Argentine and send for them to join him there. Two powerful influences decided him to make the hazardous move that would separate him from his family for an indeterminate time.

My father was born in 1846, twenty-four years before the Unification of Italy, and he had gotten the impress of the Risorgimento, which had fostered a revival of national spirit, of courage to resist foreign opposition, and of hope of a great future for Italy. He had been a follower of Mazzini and Garibaldi, the two champions of Italian liberty and, with Cavour, the fathers of the united Italy. But he had been greatly disappointed when the House of Savoy had come into power after the unification in 1870, for he, with all the Republicans of the country, had hoped for a republic. There was no hope for one now.

That was the political picture. Nor was there any future economically for an ambitious young man in this small mountain village. He did not want to spend the rest of his life tending sheep, wresting vegetables from a small plot of rocky soil, and rearing his family to do precisely the same, as his fathers had done for generations. Conditions in Italy had been unsettled for decades. The time was ripe on all counts for emigration to the Argentine, a new country just opened up and welcoming all comers. Many young men had already gone, spurred on, no doubt, by the knowledge that Garibaldi had lived in South America and for a time had made a name for himself there. The Argentine held promise for the ambitious, and so my parents made the difficult decision to leave Italy for a new world. The father would go first, and send for his family as soon as he was able.

The first problem was, of course, how to get enough money to pay for the very expensive trip. The young couple had been married four years and had one child. They owned their comfortable stone house in Rocca Nova, and my father had gotten along as well as any young man was able to do with the opportunities at hand. They lived in comfort, but there was little money. It would take every lira that they had been able to save to buy one ticket for the long voyage. . . .

It was a long chance for the husband and father to leave the family for so uncertain a future, but perhaps not so long according to the stories that were coming back from those who had already gone to the Argentine. In any case, he took it.

The journey from Rocco Nova to Naples was long and difficult. Everything to be taken was packed in saddle bags on the tiny donkeys, and my father and a companion rode and walked over the mountain roads that led northwest across the Apennines to Naples. When the two hundred miles had been covered and my father arrived at the home of relatives in the city, he learned that the vessel on which he had expected to sail for Buenos Aires was not to go at once. There was, however, a "ship" soon to leave for the United States. Why not New York instead of Buenos Aires? America, too, was a republic and a land of promise where, according to the glamorous advertisements of the steamship companies, there was work and money for all. Garibaldi had been there, too! Now that the final break had been made with Italy, my father was eager to get away, and every day's delay pushed farther into the future his reunion with the wife he had left behind. So without too much disappointment at the change in his destination, he boarded the vessel bound for New York. He had never been in Naples before and the scene from the deck of the vessel as it sailed out of the harbor he was never to forget. Nor was he to see anything as beautiful again. Mt. Vesuvius pushed its summit into an incredibly blue sky. The city itself rose on a series of terraces up high volcanic hills, Down close to the bay, the windows of the imposing thirteenth century *Castel Nuovo* caught the rays of the bright sun. Ascending a long hill, the winding driveway that led from the old city to the new, farther up the heights, divided Naples into two perfect crescents. Could the cities of the New World be as beautiful as this?

The voyage to America on the slow sailing vessel was uneventful, and it was tedious for the impatient and apprehensive group of passengers, who could not hazard a guess as to what might lie ahead of them. They were pitting all they had, physical strength and moral and spiritual courage, against a world completely alien to them.

At the end of three weeks the vessel made its way into New York Harbor, heading for Castle Garden, where the passengers would disembark. The eager group at the rail saw for the first time the modest skyline of the Manhattan of the 1870's. The beautiful spire of a church, which they could not know was historic Trinity, completely dwarfed the smaller buildings around it. No Statue of Liberty greeted them, for this was twelve years before the corner-stone was laid for that structure which later was to welcome to the Western World millions of their countrymen.

New York had no Italian colony of any size at this time. There were only about 2500 Italians in the city, many of them professional musicians and artists. Emigration to America from Italy had not really begun. In the 1880's it was to start in earnest, to increase in the 90's, and become a virtual flood at the turn of the century and the few years following. Many of the villages and small towns of southern Italy were almost depopulated by this later migration. But in 1872 the Italian in New York was very much an alien.

Economically, this country was in bad shape. Grant was President, and the difficult Reconstruction Era to which my father and others of his countrymen were to make their important contribution had just begun. There was corruption in high places of government and business, prices were rocketing, and industrial failures were widespread.

The six years that intervened before my father was able to save enough money to send for his family were marred by pitifully frugal living, stinting, and work of the hardest kind. He was one of thousands of Italians who opened up the West and enriched the East with the work of their hands. Immediately upon their arrival in America, most of these men of Italy secured employment with the railroads and went out to dig tunnels, build roadbeds, and lay tracks across almost every state of the

Union. My father eventually became a foreman of a crew of men who went to Sault Saint Marie to work on the locks of the Soo Canal, but worked for several railroads during these early years. Only a few months after he secured his first railroad job, however, the panic of 1873 occurred, and those companies which did not abandon their building projects altogether, radically reduced wages. But he kept on because he must, going from one railroad to another to obtain work. There was too much at stake to give up.

To this man whose plot of ground back home in Italy had been so small, the American West, through which the railroads were slowly pushing their way, was an almost incredible miracle of nature. So much land waiting to be cultivated, so many wide rivers to be bridged and navigated, such high timber to be cut. His back ached until he could not sleep in his rough bunk at night; his hands blistered and bled and then became as tough as leather; the prairie sun burned his bare shoulders; the dust storms blinded his eyes; Indians and buffaloes made trouble. But this was America. He was helping to build it. And thousands of miles and a many weeks' journey away, his wife was waiting for the word to join him in this land of promise. So, day after day he squared his aching shoulders and dug his pick and shovel with dogged determination into the rock and soil of his adopted country.

Many of this earliest generation of Italians, and thousands who came later, sacrificed their health and even their lives in the building of America, a sacrifice for which most of them received little material reward or appreciation either from the writers of history or from succeeding generations who benefited from their labors. Many of this first generation returned to Italy as poor as they had left it, or remained here to live in the fast-growing slums. The death rate among them, chiefly from tuberculosis, was high.

And much more than physical strength was involved in the early Italians' contribution to America. Everything dear to them was far away, and they were exploited economically, as well as physically. Only their indomitable courage, their high hopes for the future, and their faith in this new country, now their country, kept them going.

After six years of such work, coupled with very frugal living, the day came when he walked to a neighboring post office in downtown Manhattan as casually, to those who passed him on the streets, as if his entire world were not about to change, a fact which he himself could hardly believe. The wait for his family had been so much longer than he had anticipated on the day that he had bade them good-by in Rocca Nova. But now it was here, and in his pocket was all the money he had, a small fortune according to his standards, earned with his pick and shovel. It was the price of his wife's passage to America. And although this left him with nothing in reserve, there were other forms of security for the future of his family. In six years he had travelled thousands of miles across America, most of the time by handcar on newly laid railroad tracks. He knew his country much more intimately now than many more prominent New Yorkers, who lived in beautiful homes around Madison Square, far from the foreign quarters of downtown Manhattan. He had physical strength and the will to work, and the confidence that comes from knowing one's way around and where the jobs are to be found. The nation-wide railroad strikes of the previous year, 1877, were over, and conditions looked brighter to an optimistic youth planning for the future. He was ready, now, to establish his family in America.

Meantime, my mother had waited in Rocca Nova, busy at her loom and with a growing son, but hoping with each letter from America that her husband was sending for her to join him. Of his life there she knew little. Her husband's fingers were less skillful with the pen than with his tools, and the brief notes that accompanied the small sums of money that he sent from time to time were confined to the bare facts of his health and his work. But when the long-awaited message finally came, she was ready. In the small village, where room for expansion was very limited, there was a ready market for her sturdy home, and she sold it immediately. A sister's husband had also gone to America, and now the two young women made plans to go to their husbands together. There was little to pack, for not much could be carried on small donkeys over mountain roads.

On the beautiful summer day of their departure, everybody in the village came to say good-by. Their leaving was an event, for these were the first women to go from Rocca Nova to America. They were, in fact, among the first women to migrate from Italy to other countries.

## Jacob A. Riis, *How the Other Half Lives,* 1890

*Immigrant arrivals in large cities often lived in tenement districts. Jacob Riis was a newspaper photographer who investigated conditions in New York City's Lower East Side. His book* How the Other Half Lives *provided the American public with descriptions and images of slum conditions. Widely read, it stimulated the first significant New York legislation to regulate housing conditions.*

*Source:* Jacob A. Riis, *How the Other Half Lives* (New York: Charles Scribner's Sons, 1890).

### CHAPTER 3

### *The Mixed Crowd*

When once I asked the agent of a notorious Fourth Ward alley how many people might be living in it I was told: One hundred and forty families, one hundred Irish, thirty-eight Italian, and two that spoke the German tongue. Barring the agent herself, there was not a native-born individual in the court. The answer was characteristic of the cosmopolitan character of lower New York, very nearly so of the whole of it, wherever it runs to alleys and courts. One may find for the asking an Italian, a German, a French, African, Spanish, Bohemian, Russian, Scandinavian, Jewish, and Chinese colony. Even the Arab, who peddles "holy earth" from the Battery as a direct importation from Jerusalem, has his exclusive preserves at the lower end of Washington Street. The one thing you shall vainly ask for in the chief city of

America is a distinctively American community. There is none; certainly not among the tenements. Where have they gone to, the old inhabitants? I put the question to one who might fairly be presumed to be of the number, since I had found him sighing for the "good old days" when the legend "no Irish need apply" was familiar in the advertising columns of the newspapers. He looked at me with a puzzled air. "I don't know," he said. "*I wish I did*. Some went to California in '49, some to the war and never came back. The rest, I expect, have gone to heaven, or somewhere. I don't see them 'round here."

Whatever the merit of the good man's conjectures, his eyes did not deceive him. They are not here. In their place has come this queer conglomerate mass of heterogeneous elements, ever striving and working like whiskey and water in one glass, and with the like result: final union and a prevailing taint of whiskey. The once unwelcome Irishman has been followed in his turn by the Italian, the Russian Jew, and the Chinaman, and has himself taken a hand at opposition, quite as bitter and quite as ineffectual, against these later hordes. Wherever these have gone they have crowded him out, possessing the block, the street, the ward with their denser swarms. But the Irishman's revenge is complete. Victorious in defeat over his recent as over his more ancient foe, the one who opposed his coming no less than the one who drove him out, he dictates to both their politics, and, secure in possession of the offices, returns the native his greeting with interest, while collecting the rents of the Italian whose house he

has bought with the profits of his saloon. As a landlord he is picturesquely autocratic. An amusing instance of his methods came under my notice while writing these lines. An inspector of the Health Department found an Italian family paying a man with a Celtic name twenty-five dollars a month for three small rooms in a ramshackle rear tenement— more than twice what they were worth—and expressed his astonishment to the tenant, an ignorant Sicilian laborer. He replied that he had once asked the landlord to reduce the rent, but he would not do it.

"Well! What did he say?" asked the inspector.

"'Damma, man!' he said; 'if you speaka thata way to me, I fira you and your things in the streeta.'" And the frightened Italian paid the rent.

In justice to the Irish landlord it must be said that like an apt pupil he was merely showing forth the result of the schooling he had received, re-enacting, in his own way, the scheme of the tenements. It is only his frankness that shocks. The Irishman does not naturally take kindly to tenement life, though with characteristic versatility he adapts himself to its conditions at once. It does violence, nevertheless, to the best that is in him, and for that very reason of all who come within its sphere soonest corrupts him. The result is a sediment, the product of more than a generation in the city's slums, that, as distinguished from the larger body of his class, justly ranks at the foot of tenement dwellers, the so-called "low Irish."

It is not to be assumed, of course, that the whole body of the population living in the tenements, of which New Yorkers are in the habit of speaking vaguely as "the poor," or even the larger part of it, is to be classed as vicious or as poor in the sense of verging on beggary.

New York's wage-earners have no other place to live, more is the pity. They are truly poor for having no better homes; waxing poorer in purse as the exorbitant rents to which they are tied, as ever was serf to soil, keep rising. The wonder is that they are not all corrupted, and speedily, by their surroundings. If, on the contrary, there be a steady working up, if not out of the slough, the fact is a powerful argument for the optimist's belief that the world is, after all, growing better, not worse, and would go far toward disarming apprehension, were it not for the steadier growth of the sediment of the slums and its constant menace. Such an impulse toward better things there certainly is. The German rag-picker of thirty years ago, quite as low in the scale as his Italian successor, is the thrifty tradesman or prosperous farmer of to-day.

The Italian scavenger of our time is fast graduating into exclusive control of the corner fruit-stands, while his black-eyed boy monopolizes the boot-blacking industry in which a few years ago he was an intruder. The Irish hod-carrier in the second generation has become a bricklayer, if not the Alderman of his ward, while the Chinese coolie is in almost exclusive possession of the laundry business. The reason is obvious. The poorest immigrant comes here with the purpose and ambition to better himself and, given half a chance, might be reasonably expected to make the most of it. To the

false plea that he prefers the squalid houses in which his kind are housed there could be no better answer. The truth is, his half chance has too long been wanting, and for the bad result he has been unjustly blamed.

As emigration from east to west follows the latitude, so does the foreign influx in New York distribute itself along certain well-defined lines that waver and break only under the stronger pressure of a more gregarious race or the encroachments of inexorable business. A feeling of dependence upon mutual effort, natural to strangers in a strange land, unacquainted with its language and customs, sufficiently accounts for this.

The Irishman is the true cosmopolitan immigrant. All-pervading, he shares his lodging with perfect impartiality with the Italian, the Greek, and the "Dutchman," yielding only to sheer force of numbers, and objects equally to them all. A map of the city, colored to designate nationalities, would show more stripes than on the skin of a zebra, and more colors than any rainbow. The city on such a map would fall into two great halves, green for the Irish prevailing in the West Side tenement districts, and blue for the Germans on the East Side. But intermingled with these ground colors would be an odd variety of tints that would give the whole the appearance of an extraordinary crazy-quilt. From down in the Sixth Ward, upon the site of the old Collect Pond that in the days of the fathers drained the hills which are no more, the red of the Italian would be seen forcing its way northward along the line of Mulberry Street to the quarter of the French purple on Bleecker Street and

South Fifth Avenue, to lose itself and reappear, after a lapse of miles, in the "Little Italy" of Harlem, east of Second Avenue. Dashes of red, sharply defined, would be seen strung through the Annexed District, northward to the city line. On the West Side the red would be seen overrunning the old Africa of Thompson Street, pushing the black of the negro rapidly uptown, against querulous but unavailing protests, occupying his home, his church, his trade and all, with merciless impartiality. There is a church in Mulberry Street that has stood for two generations as a sort of milestone of these migrations. Built originally for the worship of staid New Yorkers of the "old stock," it was engulfed by the colored tide, when the draft-riots drove the negroes out of reach of Cherry Street and the Five Points. Within the past decade the advance wave of the Italian onset reached it, and to-day the arms of United Italy adorn its front. The negroes have made a stand at several points along Seventh and Eighth Avenues; but their main body, still pursued by the Italian foe, is on the march yet, and the black mark will be found overshadowing to-day many blocks on the East Side, with One Hundredth Street as the centre, where colonies of them have settled recently.

Hardly less aggressive than the Italian, the Russian and Polish Jew, having over run the district between Rivington and Division Streets, east of the Bowery, to the point of suffocation, is filling the tenements of the old Seventh Ward to the river front, and disputing with the Italian every foot of available space in the back alleys of Mulberry Street. The two races, differing hopelessly in much, have this in common: they carry their slums with them wherever they go, if allowed to do it. Little Italy already rivals its parent, the "Bend," in foulness. Other nationalities that begin at the bottom make a fresh start when crowded up the ladder. Happily both are manageable, the one by rabbinical, the other by the civil law. Between the dull gray of the Jew, his favorite color, and the Italian red, would be seen squeezed in on the map a sharp streak of yellow, marking the narrow boundaries of Chinatown. Dovetailed in with the German population, the poor but thrifty Bohemian might be picked out by the sombre hue of his life as of his philosophy, struggling against heavy odds in the big human bee-hives of the East Side. Colonies of his people extend northward, with long lapses of space, from below the Cooper Institute more than three miles. The Bohemian is the only foreigner with any considerable representation in the city who counts no wealthy man of his race, none who has not to work hard for a living, or has got beyond the reach of the tenement.

Down near the Battery the West Side emerald would be soiled by a dirty stain, spreading rapidly like a splash of ink on a sheet of blotting paper, headquarters of the Arab tribe, that in a single year has swelled from the original dozen to twelve hundred, intent, every mother's son, on trade and barter. Dots and dashes of color here and there would show where the Finnish sailors worship their djumala (God), the Greek pedlars the ancient name of their race, and the Swiss the goddess of thrift. And so on to the end of the long register, all toiling together in the galling fetters of the tenement. Were the question raised who makes the most of life thus mortgaged, who resists most stubbornly its levelling tendency—knows how to drag even the barracks upward a part of the way at least toward the ideal plane of the home—the palm must be unhesitatingly awarded the Teuton. The Italian and the poor Jew rise only by compulsion. The Chinaman does not rise at all; here, as at home, he simply remains stationary. The Irishman's genius runs to public affairs rather than domestic life; wherever he is mustered in force the saloon is the gorgeous centre of political activity. The German struggles vainly to learn his trick; his Teutonic wit is too heavy, and the political ladder he raises from his saloon usually too short or too clumsy to reach the desired goal. The best part of his life is lived at home, and he makes himself a home independent of the surroundings, giving the lie to the saying, unhappily become a maxim of social truth, that pauperism and drunkenness naturally grow in the tenements. He makes the most of his tenement, and it should be added that whenever and as soon as he can save up money enough, he gets out and never crosses the threshold of one again.

## CHAPTER 12

### *The Bohemians: Tenement-House Cigarmaking*

Evil as the part is which the tenement plays in Jewtown as the pretext for circumventing the law that was made to benefit and relieve the tenant, we have not far to go to find it in even a worse role. If the tenement is here continually dragged into the eye of public condemnation and scorn, it is because in one way or another it is found directly responsible for, or intimately associated with, three-fourths of the miseries of the poor. In the Bohemian quarter it is made the vehicle for enforcing upon a proud race a slavery as real as any that ever disgraced the South. Not content with simply robbing the tenant, the owner, in the dual capacity of landlord and employer, reduces him to virtual serfdom by marking his becoming his tenant, on such terms as he sees fit to make, the condition of employment at wages likewise of his own making. It does not help the case that this landlord employer, almost always a Jew, is frequently of the thrifty Polish race just described. . . .

Probably more than half of all the Bohemians in this city are cigarmakers, and it is the herding of these in great numbers in the so-called tenement factories, where the cheapest grade of work is done at the lowest wages, that constitutes at once their greatest hardship and the chief grudge of other workmen against them. The manufacturer who owns, say, from three or four, to a dozen or more tenements contiguous to his shop, fills them up with these people, charging them outrageous rents, and demanding often even a preliminary deposit of five dollars "key money;" deals them out tobacco by the week, and devotes the rest of his energies to the paring down of wages to within a peg or two of the point where the tenant rebels in desperation. . . . When he does rebel, he is given the alternative of submission, or eviction with entire loss of employment. His needs determine the issue. Usually he is not in a position to hesitate long. Unlike the Polish Jew, whose example of untiring industry he emulates, he has seldom much laid up against a rainy day. He is fond of a glass of beer, and likes to live as well as his means will permit. The shop triumphs, and fetters more galling than ever are forged for the tenant. In the opposite case, the newspapers have to record the throwing upon the street of a small army of people, with pitiful cases of destitution and family misery.

Men, women and children work together seven days in the week in these cheerless tenements to make a living for the family, from the break of day till far into the night. Often the wife is the original cigarmaker from the old home, the husband having adopted her trade here as a matter of necessity, because, knowing no word of English, he could get no other work. As they state the cause of the bitter hostility of the trades unions, she was the primary bone of contention in the day of the early Bohemian immigration. The unions refused to admit the women, and, as the support of the family depended upon her to a large extent, such terms as were offered had to be accepted. The manufacturer has ever since industriously fanned the antagonism between the unions and his hands, for his own advantage. The victory rests with him, since the Court of Appeals decided that the law, passed a few years ago, to prohibit cigarmaking in tenements was unconstitutional, and thus put an end to the struggle. While

it lasted, all sorts of frightful stories were told of the shocking conditions under which people lived and worked in these tenements, from a sanitary point of view especially, and a general impression survives to this day that they are particularly desperate. The Board of Health, after a careful canvass, did not find them so then. I am satisfied from personal inspection, at a much later day, guided in a number of instances by the union cigarmakers themselves to the tenements which they considered the worst, that the accounts were greatly exaggerated. Doubtless the people are poor, in many cases very poor; but they are not uncleanly, rather the reverse; they live much better than the clothing-makers in the Tenth Ward, and in spite of their sallow look, that may be due to the all-pervading smell of tobacco, they do not appear to be less healthy than other indoor workers. I found on my tours of investigation several cases of consumption, of which one at least was said by the doctor to be due to the constant inhalation of tobacco fumes. But an examination of the death records in the Health Department does not support the claim that the Bohemian cigarmakers are peculiarly prone to that disease. On the contrary, the Bohemian percentage of deaths from consumption appears quite low. This, however, is a line of scientific inquiry which I leave others to pursue, along with the more involved problem whether the falling off in the number of children, sometimes quite noticeable in the Bohemian settlements, is, as has been suggested, dependent upon the character of the parents' work. The sore grievances I found were the miserable wages and the enormous rents exacted for the minimum of accommodation. And surely these stand for enough of suffering.

## "Immigration Restriction," 1896

*Francis A. Walker, a prominent economist, statistician, and educator who served as the superintendent of the ninth and tenth U.S. Census, was former commissioner of Indian Affairs (1871–72) and president of MIT from 1881 until his death in 1897. He was a central figure in the 1890s immigration restriction movement. Through his service and his writing, he argued that the new immigrants from south and east Europe were unassimilable. In this essay from the* Atlantic Monthly, *Walker presents his case for immigration restriction.*

Source: Atlantic Monthly, June 1896.

Fifty, even thirty years ago, there was a rightful presumption regarding the average immigrant that he was among the most enterprising, thrifty, alert, adventurous, and courageous of the community from which he came. It required no small energy, prudence, forethought, and pains to conduct the inquiries relating to his migration, to accumulate the necessary means, and to find his way across the Atlantic. To-day the presumption is completely reversed. So thoroughly has the continent of Europe been crossed by railways, so effectively has the business of emigration there been exploited, so much have the rates of railroad fares and ocean passage been re-

duced, that it is now among the least thrifty and prosperous members of any European community that the emigration agent finds his best recruiting-ground. The care and pains required have been reduced to a minimum; while the agent of the Red Star Line or the White Star Line is everywhere at hand, to suggest migration to those who are not getting on well at home. The intending emigrants are looked after from the moment they are locked into the cars in their native villages until they stretch themselves upon the floors of the buildings on Ellis Island, in New York. Illustrations of the ease and facility with which this Pipe Line Immigration is now carried on might be given in profusion. So broad and smooth is the channel, there is no reason why every foul and stagnant pool of population in Europe, which no breath of intellectual or industrial life has stirred for ages, should not be decanted upon our soil. Hard times here may momentarily check the flow; but it will not be permanently stopped so long as *any difference of economic level* exists between our population and that of the most degraded communities abroad.

But it is not alone that the presumption regarding the immigrant of to-day is so widely different from that which existed regarding the immigrant of thirty or fifty years ago. The immigrant of the former time came almost exclusively from western and northern Europe. We have now tapped great reservoirs of population then almost unknown to the passenger lists of our arriving vessels. Only a short time ago, the immigrants from southern Italy, Hungary, Austria, and Russia together made up hardly more than one per cent of our immigration. To-day the proportion has risen to something like forty per cent, and threatens soon to become fifty or sixty per cent, or even more. The entrance into our political, social, and industrial life of such vast masses of peasantry, degraded below our utmost conceptions, is a matter which no intelligent patriot can look upon without the gravest apprehension and alarm. These people have no history behind them which is of a nature to give encouragement. They have none of the inherited instincts and tendencies which made it comparatively easy to deal with the immigration of the olden time. They are beaten men from beaten races; representing the worst failures in the struggle for existence. Centuries are against them, as centuries were on the side of those who formerly came to us. They have none of the ideas and aptitudes which fit men to take up readily and easily the problem of self-care and self-government, such as belong to those who are descended from the tribes that met under the oak-trees of old Germany to make laws and choose chieftains.

Their habits of life, again, are of the most revolting kind. Read the description given by Mr. Riis of the police driving from the garbage dumps the miserable beings who try to burrow in those depths of unutterable filth and slime in order that they may eat and sleep there! Was it in cement like this that the foundations of our republic were laid? What effects must be produced upon our social standards, and upon the ambitions and aspirations of our people, by a content

so foul and loathsome? The influence upon the American rate of wages of a competition like this cannot fail to be injurious and even disastrous. Already it has been seriously felt in the tobacco manufacture, in the clothing-trade, and in many forms of mining industry; and unless this access of vast numbers of unskilled workmen of the lowest type, in a market already fully supplied with labor, shall be checked, it cannot fail to go on from bad to worse, in breaking down the standard which has been maintained with so much care and at so much cost. The competition of paupers is far more telling and more killing than the competition of pauper-made goods. Degraded labor in the slums of foreign cities may be prejudicial to intelligent, ambitious, self-respecting labor here; but it does not threaten half so much evil as does degraded labor in the garrets of our native cities. . . .

For it is never to be forgotten that self-defense is the first law of nature and of nations. If that man who careth not for his own household is worse than an infidel, the nation which permits its institutions to be endangered by any cause which can fairly be removed is guilty not less in Christian than in natural law. Charity begins at home; and while the people of the United States have gladly offered an asylum to millions upon millions of the distressed and unfortunate of other lands and climes, they have no right to carry their hospitality one step beyond the line where American institutions, the American rate of wages, the American standard of living, are brought into serious peril. All the good the United States could do by offering indiscriminate hospitality to a few millions more of European peasants, whose places at home will, within another generation, be filled by others as miserable as themselves, would not compensate for any permanent injury done to our republic. Our highest duty to charity and to humanity is to make this great experiment, here, of free laws and educated labor, the most triumphant success that can possibly be attained. In this way we shall do far more for Europe than by allowing its city slums and its vast stagnant reservoirs of degraded peasantry to be drained off upon our soil. Within the decade between 1880 and 1890 five and a quarter millions of foreigners entered our ports! No nation in human history ever undertook to deal with such masses of alien population. That man must be a sentimentalist and an optimist beyond all bounds of reason who believes that we can take such a load upon the national stomach without a failure of assimilation, and without great danger to the health and life of the nation. For one, I believe it is time that we should take a rest, and give our social, political, and industrial system some chance to recuperate. The problems which so sternly confront us to-day are serious enough without being complicated and aggravated by the addition of some millions of Hungarians, Bohemians, Poles, south Italians, and Russian Jews.

## Queen Liliuokalani Defends Her Kingdom, 1893

*The following two statements by Queen Liliuokalani to American minister James H.*

Blount protested the "revolution" of Hawaii by haole (white) sugar interests that desired annexation to the United States. Arriving in Hawaii in 1893, Blount listened to both annexationists and restorationists and concluded that the Hawaiian people sided with the queen. He also concluded that the overthrow of Liliuokalani was illegal and advised President Cleveland to restore the queen. The crown was offered back to the queen on the condition that she pardon those who had dethroned her. Initially refusing to do so, she soon changed her mind and offered clemency, but the delay compromised her political position. In the meantime Congress debated the Hawaiian revolution. On July 4, 1894, the Republic of Hawaii with Sanford B. Dole as president was proclaimed and recognized immediately by the United States government.

Source: "Statement Made by the Queen to Minister Blount," Liliuokalani, *Hawaii's Story by Hawaii's Queen* (Rutland, Vt.: Chas Tuttle, 1964).

I, Liliuokalani, by the grace of God and under the constitution of the Hawaiian kingdom Queen, do hereby solemnly protest against any and all acts done against myself and the constitutional government of the Hawaiian kingdom by certain persons claiming to have established a Provisional Government of and for this kingdom.

That I yield to the superior force of the United States of America, whose Minister Plenipotentiary, His Excellency John L. Stevens, has caused United States troops to be landed at Honolulu, and declared that he would support the said Provisional Government.

Now, to avoid any collision of armed forces, and perhaps the loss of life, I do, under this protest and impelled by said forces, yield my authority until such time as the Government of the United States shall, upon the facts being presented to it, undo (?) the action of its representative, and reinstate me in the authority which I claim as the constitutional sovereign of the Hawaiian Islands.

Done at Honolulu this seventeenth day of January, A.D. 1893.

> (Signed) Liliuokalani R.
> (Signed) Samuel Parker,
> Minister of Foreign Affairs.
> (Signed) Wm. H. Cornwell,
> Minister of Finance.
> (Signed) John F. Colburn,
> Minister of Interior.
> (Signed) A. P. Peterson, Attorney-General.

(Addressed)

To S. B. Dole, Esq., and others composing the Provisional Government of the Hawaiian Islands.

1893

On the 31st of January the Hon. Paul Neumann received his appointment as envoy extraordinary and minister plenipotentiary to the United States of America. On the 1st of February he departed for Washington, with Prince David Kawanauakoa to accompany him on his commission, to negotiate for a withdrawal of the treaty, and to restore to us what had been taken away by the actions of the revolutionists. At my request Mr. E. C. Macfarlane kindly consented to accompany the commission.

Happily Providence ordered otherwise than as was expected by the revolutionists. Man proposes and God disposes. My commissioners arrived in time to stay the progress of the treaty. The members of the Senate became doubtful as to the correctness of the actions of the commissioners of the Provisional Government.

President Harrison's term expired. President Cleveland's first act has been to withdraw that annexation treaty; the second, to send a commissioner to investigate the situation in Hawaii Nei.

Your arrival in this country has brought relief to our people and your presence safety. There is no doubt but that the Provisional Government would have carried out extreme measures toward myself and my people, as you may have already seen ere this, by their unjust actions. If the President had been indifferent to my petitions, I am certain it would have brought serious results to myself and tyranny to my subjects. In this I recognize the high sense of justice and honor in the person who is ruler of the American nation.

In making out this lengthy statement I will present the main points:

(1) That it has been a project of many years on the part of the missionary element that their children might some day be rulers over these Islands, and have the control and power in their own hands, as was the case after the revolution of 1887. Mr. W. W. Hall openly stated that they had planned for this for twelve years. It was a long-thought-of project, a dream of many years. So also said Mr. F. S. Lyman of Hilo, in his speech to the people in the month of January. He said, "Fifteen long years we have prayed for this, and now our prayers are heard."

The disposition of those appointed to positions of authority, to act with the missionary element, tends to make the government unstable; and because they found I could not easily be led by them, they do not like me.

(2) The interference of the American minister, J. L. Stevens, in our local affairs, and conspiring with a few foreign people to overthrow me and annex these Islands to the United States, and by his actions, has placed me and my people in this unhappy position.

(3) My attempt to promulgate a new constitution. It was in answer to the prayers and petitions of my people. They had sent petitions to the late king, and to the legislature ever since 1887.

The legislature is the proper course by which a new constitution or any amendments to the constitution could be made; that is the law. But when members are bribed and the legislature corrupted, how can one depend on any good measure being carried by the House? It is simply impossible. That method was tried and failed. There was only one recourse; and that was, that with the signature of one of the cabinet I could make a new constitution.

There is no clause in the constitution of 1887, to which I took my oath to maintain, stating "that there should be no other constitution but this"; and article 78 reads that

"Wheresoever by this constitution any act is to be done or performed by the king or sovereign it shall, unless otherwise expressed, mean that such act shall be done and performed by the sovereign by and with the advice and consent of the cabinet."

The last clause of the forty-first article of the constitution reads:

"No acts of the king shall have any effect unless it be countersigned by a member of the cabinet, who by that signature makes himself responsible."

My cabinet encouraged me, then afterwards advised me to the contrary. In yielding to their protest I claim I have not committed any unconstitutional or revolutionary act; and having withdrawn, why should the reform party have gone on making preparations for war, as they did?

(4) That on the afternoon of the 16th of January, at five p.m., the United States troops were landed to support the conspirators, by orders of the United States minister, J. L. Stevens.

That on Tuesday, the 17th of January, 1893, at about two thirty o'clock p.m., the Provisional Government was proclaimed, and Minister Stevens assured my cabinet that he recognized that Government; and that at six p.m. of the same day I yielded my authority to the superior force of the United States.

We have been waiting patiently, and will still wait, until such time as the Government of the United States, on the facts presented to it, shall undo the act of its representative.

I hope and pray that the United States and her President will see that justice is done to my people and to myself; that they will not recognize the treaty of annexation, and that it may forever be laid aside; that they will restore to me and my nation all the rights that have been taken away by the action of her minister; that we may be permitted to continue to maintain our independent stand amongst the civilized nations of the world as in years gone by; that your great nation will continue those kind and friendly relations that have always existed for many years past between the two countries. I can assure you that Hawaii and her people have no other sentiment toward America and her President than one of the kindest regard.

The Provisional Government, instead of being under the guidance of the president and cabinet, as the responsible heads of the nation, are virtually led by irresponsible people, who compose the advisory councils and "provisional army," and who set the laws of the land at defiance. A continuation of this state of things I consider dangerous to life and to the community.

I pray, therefore, that this unsatisfactory state of things may not continue, and that we may not suffer further waste, that justice may be speedily granted, and that peace and quiet may once more reign over our land, Hawaii Nei.

*Liliuokalani.*

## Lorrin A. Thurston, *A Handbook on the Annexation of Hawaii,* 1897

*Lorrin Thurston, the son of a Christian missionary, was one of the leaders of the* haole *revolution (1893) that overthrew Queen Liliuokalani. Thurston drafted the constitution for the provisional Hawaiian government and headed the commission to Washington that negotiated annexation. In this excerpt, Thurston lays out arguments in favor of annexation.*

*Source:* Lorrin Thurston, *A Handbook on the Annexation of Hawaii* (St. Joseph, Mich.: A. B. Morse, 1897).

In the whole Pacific Ocean from the Equator on the South, to Alaska on the North; from the Coast of China and Japan on the West, to the American Continent on the East, there is but one spot where a ton of coal, a pound of bread, or a gallon of water can be obtained by a passing vessel and that spot is Hawaii.

The immensity of this area of the earth's surface is comprehended by but few.

The width and size of North Pacific is so great that no naval vessel in existence can carry coal enough to cross the Pacific from any of the existing or possible foreign naval stations, to the Pacific coast of the United States, operate there and return, without recoaling. A modern battleship without coal is like a caged lion—magnificent but harmless.

One of the first principles in naval warfare is, that an operating fleet must have a base of supply and repair.

Any country in possession of Hawaii would possess a base of operations within four or five days steaming distance of any part of the Pacific Coast.

Without the possession of Hawaii, all of the principal countries possessing interest in the Pacific, are so far away that the distance is practically prohibitory of hostile operations against the Pacific Coast.

The United States, in possession and control of Hawaii, will thereby, by simply keeping other nations out, afford almost absolute protection to her Pacific

Coast and commerce from hostile naval attack. On the other hand, Hawaii, in possession of any foreign country, will be a standing menace against, not only the Pacific Coast, but against all of the Ocean-bound commerce to and from that Coast, and, all American commerce on or across the North Pacific.

The Importance of the relation of Hawaii to the commerce of the Pacific is demonstrated by the fact that of the seven trans-Pacific steamship lines plying between the North American Continent and Japan, China and Australia, all but one make Honolulu a way station.

Through causes unnecessary to discuss, the native race has decreased until there are now only thirty odd thousand of them remaining, constituting less than a third of the population of the country, and the decrease is continuing. The day when the aboriginal Hawaiian alone should own and control Hawaii has gone and gone forever. *It is no longer a question of whether Hawaii shall be controlled by the native Hawaiian, or by some foreign people; but the question is, "What foreign people shall control Hawaii."* . . .

The awakening of Japan has introduced a new element into the politics of the world, and more especially of the Pacific. Until within a few years, emigration from Japan was prohibited. Japan has now reversed this policy, and emigration, particularly to Hawaii, is encouraged. So rapidly have the Japanese come to Hawaii that in 1896 they numbered twenty-five thousand; the adult Japanese males outnumbering those of any other nationality.

During the latter part of 1896 and the early part of 1897 they came in at the rate of 2000 a month. If this rate of immigration had continued for a year, they would have numbered one-half of the population of the entire country, and before the end of five years would have outnumbered all of the other inhabitants put together, two to one. The rate at which they were entering Hawaii, is, as compared with the population of the United States, as though a million Japanese a month were entering San Francisco. It has been well said that "this was not immigration but invasion."

Hawaii has attempted to stay this invasion by adopting legislation against contract laborers and paupers, identical with that of the United States, and has thereby become involved in its present controversy with Japan, the latter country refusing to recognize the validity of such legislation and practically claiming the absolute right of emigration, by her people, to Hawaii.

Even though the Hawaiian legislation referred to is sustained, still immigrants who do not come within the terms of the restrictive legislation are free to enter Hawaii, to such an extent as will soon give Japan an overwhelming majority of the inhabitants of the country.

Under the existing constitution of Hawaii, the Japanese are not citizens and are ineligible to citizenship; but it goes without saying, that an energetic, ambitious, warlike, and progressive people like the Japanese can not indefinitely be prevented from participating in the government of a country in which they become dominant in numbers, and the ownership of property.

Already the Japanese in Hawaii are restless under the restrictions imposed upon them, and it needs no gift of prophecy to demonstrate that, with their growing wealth, commerce and numbers, it will be impossible for any local independent government in Hawaii to much longer withhold from them the full privileges which they demand.

Even though political privileges may for some time be with held from them, their commercial men are active and progressive and are rapidly establishing themselves in Hawaii.

Long experience has shown that in Hawaii, as elsewhere blood is thicker than water. . . .

The issue in Hawaii today, is the preliminary skirmish in the great coming struggle between the civilization and the awakening forces of the East and the civilization of the West. The issue is whether, in that inevitable struggle, Asia or America shall have the vantage ground of the control of the naval "Key of the Pacific," the commercial "Crossroads of the Pacific."

All that has held, and that is now holding, Hawaii for the United States, is the indomitable will and pluck of the men in Hawaii, of not only American, but of Hawaiian and European blood, who against heavy odds, are doing and will continue to do all that is within the bounds of possibility to prevent Hawaii from retrograding into an Asiatic outpost, and to hold the country to that destiny which American statesmen have for fifty years, regardless of party, outlined for it. But there is a limit to their strength, and if help from the great Republic is to come in time it must come soon. While the tendency of events in Hawaii is against American interests they

have not progressed so far that they can not be arrested, if the United States will take radical action for its own protection. Annexation will accomplish such a result and nothing else will. A protectorate is suggested by some. The reasons why a protectorate will not meet the requirements of the case are given in full elsewhere herein. It is sufficient to say here that the alternative of "annexation or protectorate" has successively been presented to Presidents Pierce, Harrison, and McKinley, and Secretaries of State Marcy, Foster, and Sherman, in 1854, 1893 and 1897, and has each time been decided in favor of annexation; for the reason that a Protectorate imposes upon the United States responsibility without power to control; while Annexation imposes practically no more responsibility but is accompanied with the full powers of ownership. Under annexetion the United States prohibition of Chinese immigration will apply to Hawaii, and the new treaty with Japan gives the United States full power to control the emigration of laborers.

## Rudyard Kipling, "The White Man's Burden," 1899; Bruce Grit, "Why Talk of the White Man's Burden?" 1899

*Published in* McClure's Magazine *in February of 1899, Rudyard Kipling's poem "The White Man's Burden" appeared at a critical juncture in the imperialism debate after the Spanish American War. Kipling argued that the United States had a moral duty to civilize and protect others from European colonizers. Critics quickly responded to the imperialists' claims of noble duty with parodies of the poem, such as Bruce Grit's "Why Talk of the White Man's Burden?" While Grit's poem focused on racial inequality at home, other responses also examined gender inequality, the "burden" of imperialism on the working people of the United States, and new warfare in the Philippines.*

Sources: *McClure's Magazine,* February 12, 1899; *The Colored American* (D.C.), February 25, 1899.

## THE WHITE MAN'S BURDEN

Take up the White Man's burden—
   Send forth the best ye breed—
Go, bind your sons to exile
   To serve your captives' need;
To wait, in heavy harness,
   On fluttered folk and wild—
Your new-caught sullen peoples,
   Half devil and half child.

Take up the White Man's burden—
   In patience to abide,
To veil the threat of terror
   And check the show of pride;
By open speech and simple,
   An hundred times made plain,
To seek another's profit
   And work another's gain.

Take up the White Man's burden—
   The savage wars of peace—
Fill full the mouth of Famine,
   And bid the sickness cease;
And when your goal is nearest
   (The end for others sought)
Watch sloth and heathen folly
   Bring all your hope to nought.

Take up the White Man's burden—
   No iron rule of kings,
But toil of serf and sweeper—
   The tale of common things.
The ports ye shall not enter,
   The roads ye shall not tread,
Go, make them with your living
   And mark them with your dead.

Take up the White Man's burden,
   And reap his old reward—
The blame of those ye better
   The hate of those ye guard—
The cry of hosts ye humour
   (Ah, slowly!) toward the light:—
"Why brought ye us from bondage,
   Our loved Egyptian night?"

Take up the White Man's burden—
   Ye dare not stoop to less—
Nor call too loud on Freedom
   To cloak your weariness.
By all ye will or whisper,
   By all ye leave or do,
The silent sullen peoples
   Shall weigh your God and you.

Take up the White Man's burden!
   Have done with childish days—
The lightly-proffered laurel,
   The easy ungrudged praise:
Comes now, to search your manhood
   Through all the thankless years,
Cold, edged with dear-bought wisdom,
   The judgment of your peers.

## WHY TALK OF THE WHITE MAN'S BURDEN?

Why talk of the white man's burden;
   What burdens hath he borne
That have not been shared by the black man
   From the day creation dawned?

Why talk of the white man's burden,
   Why boast of the white man's power
When the black man's load is heavier,
   And increasing every hour?

Why taunt us with our weakness,
   Why boast of your brutal strength;
Know ye not that the children of meekness
   Shall inherit the earth—at length?

"Take up the white man's burden!"
   What burdens doth he bear,
That have not been borne with courage
   By brave men everywhere?

Then why the white man's burden?
   What more doth he bear than we—
The victims of his power and greed
   From the great lakes to the sea?

## William Jennings Bryan, Savannah Interview, December 13, 1898

*The popular Democratic leader William Jennings Bryan opposed American acquisition of colonies as antithetical to American principles. But although others took an overtly racist position regarding their anti-imperialist sentiment, Bryan presented a different stance. He had volunteered for military service and urged passage of the treaty annexing the Philippines. In this interview he offers reasons for supporting the treaty and describes how he hopes passage of it will lead to a fruitful discussion on self-government for the Philippines.*

*Source:* William Jennings Bryan, *Bryan on Imperialism* (Chicago: Bentley & Co., 1900). From BoondocksNet.com, ed. Jim Zwick, copyright 1995–2000.

My reason for leaving the army was set forth in my letter to the adjutant-general tendering my resignation. Now that the treaty of peace has been concluded I believe that I can be more useful to my country as a civilian than as a soldier.

I may be in error, but in my judgment our nation is in greater danger just now than Cuba. Our people defended Cuba against foreign arms; now they must defend themselves and their country against a foreign idea—the colonial idea of European nations. Heretofore greed has perverted the government and used its instrumentalities for private gains, but now the very foundation principles of our government are assaulted. Our nation must give up any intention of entering upon a colonial policy, such as is now pursued by European countries, or it must abandon the doctrine that governments derive their just powers from the consent of the governed.

To borrow a Bible quotation, "A house divided against itself cannot stand." Paraphrasing Lincoln's declaration, I may add that this nation cannot endure half republic and half colony— half free and half vassal. Our form of government, our traditions, our present interests and our future welfare, all forbid our entering upon a career of conquest.

Jefferson has been quoted in support of imperialism, but our opponents must distinguish between imperialism and expansion; they must also distinguish between expansion in the western hemisphere and an expansion that involves us in the quarrels of Europe and the Orient. They must still further distinguish between expansion which secures contiguous territory for future settlement, and expansion which secures us alien races for future subjugation.

Jefferson favored the annexation of necessary contiguous territory on the North American continent, but he was opposed to wars of conquest and expressly condemned the acquiring of remote territory.

Some think that the fight should be made against ratification of the treaty, but I would prefer another plan. If the treaty is rejected, negotiations must be renewed and instead of settling the question according to our ideas we must settle it by diplomacy, with the possibility of international complications. It will be easier, I think, to end the war at once by ratifying the treaty and then deal with the subject in our own way. The issue can be presented directly by a resolution of Congress declaring the policy of the nation upon this subject. The President in his message says that our only purpose in taking possession of Cuba is to establish a stable government and then turn that government over to the people of Cuba. Congress could reaffirm this purpose in regard to Cuba and assert the same purpose in regard to the Philippines and Puerto Rico. Such a resolution would make a clear-cut issue between the doctrine of self-government and the doctrine of imperialism. We should reserve a harbor and coaling station in Puerto Rico and the Philippines in return for services rendered and I think we would be justified in asking the same concession from Cuba.

In the case of Puerto Rico, where the people have as yet expressed no desire for an independent government, we might with propriety declare our willingness to annex the island if the citizens desire annexation, but the Philippines are too far away and their people too different from ours to be annexed to the United States, even if they desired it.

## Emilio Aguinaldo, Proclamation to the Philippine People, February 5, 1899

*When the United States declared war on Spain in 1898, Philippine nationalists led by Emilio Aguinaldo had already militarily defeated the Spanish in the Philippines and planned their independence. On January 1, 1899, a constitutional convention proclaimed an independent Philippine Republic with Emilio Aguinaldo its president. But the United States refused to recognize Aguinaldo's authority, and on February 4, 1899, Aguinaldo declared war on U.S. forces in the islands, thus beginning the Philippine American War. After his capture on March 23, 1901, Aguinaldo swore allegiance to the United States and left public life. In the following proclamation of February 5, 1899, Aguinaldo hoped to rally the Philippine people to support fighting a war for independence.*

Source: Major-General E. S. Otis, *Report on Military Operations and Civil Affairs in the Philippine Islands, 1899* (Washington, D.C.: Government Printing Office, 1899), pp. 95–96. From Daniel B. Schirmer and Stephen Rosskamm Shalom, eds., *The Philippines Reader* (Boston: South End Press, 1987), pp. 20–21.

By my proclamation of yesterday I have published the outbreak of hostilities between the Philippine forces and the American forces of occupation in Manila, unjustly and unexpectedly provoked by the latter.

In my manifest of January 8 last I published the grievances suffered by the Philippine forces at the hands of the army of occupation. The constant outrages and taunts, which have caused the misery of the people of Manila, and, finally the useless conferences and the contempt shown the Philippine government prove the premeditated transgression of justice and liberty.

I know that war has always produced great losses; I know that the Philippine people have not yet recovered from past losses and are not in the condition to endure others. But I also know by experience how bitter is slavery, and by experience I know that we should sacrifice all on the altar of our honor and of the national integrity so unjustly attacked.

I have tried to avoid, as far as it has been possible for me to do so, armed conflict, in my endeavors to assure our independence by pacific means and to avoid more costly sacrifices. But all my efforts have been useless against the measureless pride of the American Government and of its representatives in these islands, who have treated me as a rebel because I defend the sacred interests of my country and do not make myself an instrument of their dastardly intentions.

Past campaigns will have convinced you that the people are strong when they wish to be so. Without arms we have driven from our beloved country our ancient masters, and without arms we can repulse the foreign invasion as long as we wish to do so. Providence always has means in reserve and prompt help for the weak in order that they may not be annihilated by the strong; that justice may be done and humanity progress.

Be not discouraged. Our independence has been watered by the generous blood of our martyrs. Blood which may be shed in the future will strengthen it. Nature has never despised generous sacrifices.

But remember that in order that our efforts may not be wasted, that our vows may be listened to, that our ends may be gained, it is indispensable that we adjust our actions to the rules of law and of right, learning to triumph over our enemies and to conquer our own evil passions.

*Emilio Aguinaldo, President of the*
*Philippine Republic Malolos,*
*February 5, 1899*

## "Consent of the Governed," 1900

*Proimperialists had to square colonizing foreign peoples in distant lands with America's founding democratic principles. Some used United States historical relations with American Indians and Negro slaves as evidence that the nation's founders had never intended the principle of consent of the governed to apply to the "backward races," which they deemed were racially unfit for self-government.*

Source: American Monthly Review of Reviews, vol. 21, no. 2 (February 1900): 219–220.

A writer in *Education* for January asks several pertinent questions relative to the application of the phrase "consent of the governed" in American history. It is now charged by the "anti-imperialists" that the present administration at Washington is subverting our form of government in so far as it attempts to administer the Philippines without first obtaining the consent of the inhabitants. This leads the writer in *Education* to ask what was the actual meaning of the fathers when they laid down this famous dictum in the Declaration of Independence.

"In the year 1776 there were probably not exceeding 3,000,000 people inhabiting the thirteen British colonies, now the seaboard Atlantic States. Of these nearly 500,000 were negro slaves; 1,500,000 were of the female sex. Nearly one-third were minors, from the cradle to twenty-one; and several hundred thousand Indians inhabited the Western wilds, afterward brought under the new Government of the United States. How many of these people were referred to in this formula that 'government derives its authority from the consent of the governed'? Were the negro slaves canvassed and their consent obtained to their condition of slavery? Were the Indians, who afterward by relentless war were swept in a body from the Atlantic slope to the unsettled wilderness beyond the Mississippi? Has there been, until today, any real opportunity given the 1,500,000, at present 35,000,000, of the female sex to ascertain their opinion concerning the laws under which they live? Has Young America from the age of fifteen to twenty-one, beyond question more intelligent in all matters pertaining to government than half the people now living in the

world, including the vast majority of the Oriental peoples, been thus canvassed and its consent obtained? There can be no doubt that at the time of the Declaration of Independence a large body—perhaps a fourth, a third, possibly a half—of the men in these colonies were opposed to the revolt against the mother country. Was their 'consent' obtained, either during the war or at the formation of the national Government? What proportion of the mature white men in these colonies, at the time they one by one accepted the Constitution of the United States, were legal voters, and in how many of these new States was there a property or other discriminating qualification for suffrage? The reply to questions like these brings us down to the hard fact that Washington, Jefferson, Adams, Madison, and Monroe, all 'fathers' and participants in the great Declaration, were elected to the Presidency by what would to-day be regarded an insignificant minority of the white men of mature age.

## MINORITY RULE

"Our Government originally made no pretense of obtaining the legal consent of any save a majority of the legal white voters, and that majority to-day is expanded to a plurality. Indeed, no attempt was ever made at national life to carry into practical application this formula of the Declaration, either in regard to races of people adjudged incompetent for self-government or classes like women or minors. The body of people, always the minority, which has decided the vital question of incompetency in our country, like every other, has always been a working majority of the more intelligent, forceful, and generally competent men of the ruling race. The only attempt at a republic founded practically on the consent of the masses was seen during a few months in the French Revolution, when an infuriated populace attempted to secure unanimity and 'consent' by destroying all opponents to 'liberty, equality, and fraternity'; the result being a reaction to the military despotism of Napoleon I.

"There is doubtless a sense in which this Jeffersonian formula has a profound meaning; that it is the moral obligation of every nation to educate the lower orders of mankind in the direction of self-government, and extend full citizenship as fast and as far as the safety of society will permit. In our own country, at home, that limit even as far as the male sex is concerned would seem to be already reached, both in regard to great multitudes of European immigrants in the North and of the freedmen of the South. The proposition that the holding of a colony of people in the condition of millions of the Oriental races, with the ultimate object of their uplift through all the opportunities of modern Christian civilization, is a departure from the

American republican order of society and government or from the American ideal in any way it can he applied in the present condition of mankind, so marked and violent as to threaten a radical change in the national life, when analyzed is so absolutely visionary that it can be only accounted for by the loose habit of thought and indifference to the facts of human nature and life which are in themselves to-day the greatest peril of the republic."

## "Mark Twain's Salutation to the Century," 1900

Source: New York Herald, December 30, 1900. From BoondocksNet.com, ed. Jim Zwick, copyright 1995–2000.

I bring you the stately matron named Christendom, returning bedraggled, besmirched and dishonored from pirate raids in Kiao-Chow, Manchuria, South Africa and the Philippines, with her soul full of meanness, her pocket full of boodle and her mouth full of pious hypocrisies. Give her soap and a towel, but hide the looking-glass.

Mark Twain
New York, Dec. 31, 1900.

# CHAPTER 6
# THE CRITICAL PERIOD:
# ETHNIC EMERGENCE
# AND REACTION,
# 1901–1929

## ANDREW R. HEINZE

THE PRESIDENCY OF THEODORE Roosevelt and the collapse of Wall Street form the most conventional endpoints of the 1901–1929 period. But we may also think of the era in terms of Louis Armstrong and Al Smith. Born in 1901 into a poor African American family in New Orleans, Armstrong emerged in the 1920s as America's most influential musician. Smith hailed from a poor family in New York City, and in 1928 he became the first man of Irish Catholic descent to run for the presidency on the ticket of a major party. Armstrong and Smith symbolized a new era in American life.

It was an era of emergence for ethnic minorities. Between 1900 and 1930, immigrants and their children continued to constitute roughly one-third of the U.S. population, as they had since the late 1800s. But their absolute numbers were impressive. During those three decades the number of people whom the Census Bureau classified as foreign-born white (mostly European and Canadian), or native white with at least one foreign-born parent, climbed from 26 million to 38 million. (America's total population increased from 76 million to 122 million in those decades.) In addition to this large population of immigrants, native-born African Americans increased from 9 million to 12 million between 1900 and 1930. The Native American (Indian) population, after three centuries of demographic catastrophe, stabilized at around 240,000 in 1900 and climbed to 340,000 in 1930. (Population figures are given in round numbers.)

The largest wave of immigrants in this period came from Eastern and Southern Europe: Jews, Slavs, and Italians. Together these three groups produced roughly 10 million immigrants, and more than half of these newcomers remained in the U.S. In addition, nearly 800,000 Mexicans entered the country, at least half of whom settled there. Approximately 350,000 French Canadians, 250,000 Greeks, and 170,000 Japanese came to stay between 1900 and 1930, as did tens of thousands of West Indians, Syrians, and Armenians. Smaller numbers arrived from other parts of Asia, Latin America, and Africa. Though not technically immigrants, Filipinos and Puerto Ricans also came to the mainland U.S. as members of the American commonwealth established in 1898. By 1930 approximately 100,000 Puerto Ricans were living in New York City, and no fewer than 45,000 young Filipino men dwelled in California, Oregon, and Washington. Large populations of Japanese and Filipinos also settled in Hawai'i. (The rates of reemigration varied enormously from group to group. Among Jewish and Irish immigrants, very few returned to the homeland, where they faced extraordinary religious persecution; immigrants from the Balkans, on the other hand, reemigrated at the very high rate of approximately 87 percent. For all immigrants, the median rate of return was probably around 25 percent.)

Immigrants from England, Scotland, Ireland, Germany, Scandinavia, and English-speaking Canada continued to arrive as well; more than 5 million from these lands settled in the U.S. between 1900 and 1930. However, these peoples were culturally much more similar to the American population than were the newcomers from Eastern and Southern Europe, Asia, Latin America and the Caribbean, most of whom were not English-speaking, not Protestant, and not at all familiar with the values and way of life of Americans.

One way of interpreting these statistics of immigration and race is to say that two out of five American residents were in a position of political or social disadvantage as a result of their ethnic or racial background. Who enjoyed which rights and privileges depended on a number of factors, especially skin color, citizenship, religion, and ethnicity.

Whether one was a man or a woman also mattered enormously. Before 1920 women lacked complete voting rights. This limitation circumscribed not only their citizenship but also the political power of the ethnic groups to which many of them belonged. In addition, immigrant women and black migrant women carried special burdens. The prejudicially low wages received by black men obligated their wives to work outside the home, which black women did in much higher proportions than white women. Most immigrant men came to America ahead of their families, and this created serious problems of desertion and marital estrangement. Husbands spent months and sometimes years adapting to America before the arrival of their wives, who suddenly seemed foreign to them. Japanese women crossed the Pacific as "picture brides," often to discover that their new husbands were much older than they expected.

All immigrants had to deal with the greater freedom enjoyed by women in America. Italians, for example, found this to be a nerve-racking challenge to their traditional way of life, which enshrined women in the home. On the other hand, Irish women and Eastern European Jewish women were accustomed to greater independence and thus adapted more easily to the ideal of modern womanhood. Because Jews and Irish Catholics came to America with the intention of settling down, unlike most immigrants who initially planned on repatriating, the women in these groups immediately played an important role as Americanizing agents. It was their responsibility to set up new homes as quickly as possible, which meant incorporating American goods and styles even as they maintained ethnic customs.

It is important to remember that in the families of all immigrants and black migrants, women faced the unique pressure of having to buttress husbands who were challenged by the rigors of work in a strange industrial world and by the loss of patriarchal authority over their Americanizing children. As mothers they were expected to transmit the culture of their native regions, but they also had to adapt home life to meet American standards (or Northern ones, for Southern blacks). Women living on Indian reservations west of the Mississippi, the domain of the once "Wild West," faced a unique type of culture shock, because their husbands and fathers were often traumatized by the loss of the physical mobility and independence they had formerly enjoyed.

In the years 1901–1929, ethnic minorities entered into American culture and politics more conspicuously than ever before. Given the universality of ethnic prejudice, it was probably inevitable that the emergence of such a wide variety of peoples provoked antagonisms. Southern whites tried to subordinate blacks with comprehensive laws of racial segregation and rituals of intimidation. Northern whites kept blacks at a distance with restrictive housing arrangements and by limiting their ability to advance in the workplace. Natives tried to control the number of newcomers by lobbying for federal laws to restrict immigration. Christians objected to the increase of Jews, Protestants to the increase of Catholics. Immigrants competed with one another, as well as with native whites and blacks, for control of jobs and neighborhoods. Despite these formidable antagonisms and tensions, "ethnic Americans" in this era established the cultural, political, and intellectual foundation for a cosmopolitan pluralist nation.

## THE STRENGTH OF THE AMERICAN ECONOMY

Sandwiched neatly between the depression of the 1890s and the Great Depression of the 1930s, the 1901–1929 period was prosperous, except for short recessions in 1907–1908, 1913–1914 and 1921–1922. Prosperity attracted immigrants and also offered new opportunities to migrating groups within the nation's borders, such as the hundreds of thousands of Southern blacks who steadily moved north. Real wages of urban laborers remained much higher than in other countries, and much higher in the North and West than in the American South. By crossing the border into the United States, Mexicans could earn ten times what they received for field work at home. The leap in wages was comparable for immigrants from other lands. Letters from America back to the Old Country typically boasted of the finery enjoyed in the New World, and periodic visits from well-dressed emigrants proved to be a powerful advertisement of American wealth to those who had not yet come to "the Golden Land." "All of Ayn Arab rushed to America," a Syrian immigrant recalled, "It was like a gold rush."

In the hands of immigrants, American wealth had enormous impact on the home countries. Whether they intended to repatriate or settle in the United States, newcomers mailed millions of dollars a year to relatives back home. The comparative wealth of Americans turned immigrant communities into treasuries for humanitarian and political aid abroad. Immigrant leaders stressed the monetary obligations of the Americanized to their poorer and politically oppressed countrymen in the Old World. Furthermore, they emphasized the basic compatibility between loyalty

to America and loyalty to the homeland. In the words of Ignace Paderewski, who personified the Polish national movement in America during World War I: "The Poles in America do not need any Americanization. . . . Be therefore the best Americans, but also help the Polish community." In 1912, after the outbreak of war between Turkey and Greece, hundreds of Greeks paraded in Los Angeles with Greek and American flags and with placards praising both American and Greek democracy: "Hail Sweet Land of Liberty." Greek immigrants not only contributed money for the war in the Balkans but tens of thousands left to fight, and then returned to the United States, believing that America, too, preserved the republican legacy of ancient Greece. The Irish and the Jews, who adjusted to American life fairly quickly, similarly equated Irish and Jewish nationalism with American ideals of freedom. Without the funds and encouragement of Irish and Jewish Americans, the struggles for an independent Ireland and a Jewish state in Palestine would have been far more difficult.

## ECONOMIC AND POLITICAL CAUSES OF IMMIGRATION AND BLACK MIGRATION

In addition to the attractiveness of the American economy, poor conditions abroad stimulated people to leave their homelands. Since the 1840s population explosions throughout Europe had given rise to a steady stream of emigrants, and overcrowding got worse as country folk with dwindling chances to live by the land moved to cities in search of a living as industrial laborers. Some kept to farm work by becoming seasonal migrants, crossing borders both within Europe and across the Atlantic in the off-season and returning to their native lands when planting time came again. Beyond the demographic problems that afflicted Europe, political oppression and chaos caused millions to seek a better fate elsewhere. The anti-Semitism of Tsarist Russia produced an exodus of more than 2 million Jews, most of whom came to the United States. Millions of Poles, Lithuanians, and other East Europeans also fled the Tsarist regime that had absorbed their countries in the eighteenth and nineteenth centuries. The Bolshevik Revolution of 1917 ended Tsarist oppression, and World War I reestablished the sovereignty of Poland and the Baltic states, but the Bolsheviks and the war created another set of human problems that hundreds of thousands sought to solve by coming to America in the early 1920s. Squirming under British rule, the Irish continued to emigrate in large numbers until they achieved a measure of sovereignty in 1921 with the creation of an independent state in southern Ireland. Mexicans suffered from the political chaos of their own government after the Revolution of 1910, which sparked an unprecedented flight north of the border into the American Southwest and California.

Within the boundaries of the United States, the Southern black population suffered afflictions that paralleled those of the Jews and the Irish abroad. Throughout this period, but especially after 1915, when war production cre-

ated a great demand for labor in Northern factories, several hundred thousand black Americans fled the South hoping, very much as immigrants hoped, to find a "promised land" of new opportunities.

## RACE AND THE LAW: DEGREES OF FREEDOM

The most important and disturbing legal development in the United States during this period was racial segregation. Between 1890 and 1914 every Southern state established laws that prohibited Negroes from attending the same schools; sitting in the same seats on trains, streetcars, and buses; and enjoying the same public services (from theaters to water fountains) as their white neighbors. This system of racial segregation, nicknamed "Jim Crow," created a degrading caste system. Laws determined who was "white" and who was "colored" based on bizarre ratios of white to black "blood" (often one thirty-second, meaning that one Negro great-great-grandparent marked a person as "black"). These dangerously absurd legal conceptions of race anticipated the notorious anti-Jewish laws of Nazi Germany.

Their purpose was somewhat different, however. Whereas Nazi law aimed at removing Jews from German society, American segregation law aimed at fixing Negroes in an inferior position as servants to whites. Jim Crow reminded Southerners every day in every social situation that "white" people were more moral, more refined, and more intelligent than "black" people. Black Americans understood the absurdity of this social system, but they could not protest for two reasons: terrorism and injustice. To violate the rules of racial deference (e.g., failing to step off the sidewalk when a white person approached, or looking defiantly at a white person) would invite swift punishment and possibly murder by an armed mob of angry whites, who usually attacked Negroes at night, burning their homes and assaulting and sometimes murdering men, women, and children. Second, Southern juries included only whites, which corrupted the entire justice system. Juries rarely convicted whites on the testimony of blacks, even in cases of cold-blooded murder. How was it possible for states like South Carolina, Georgia, Alabama, and Mississippi, with large black populations, to implement such a system? By eliminating the black vote. In this period, states passed laws with peculiar clauses designed to disqualify black voters.

## RACE AND HEALTH: LIFE EXPECTANCY AND INFANT MORTALITY

The rural South was the poorest region in the country, and racial discrimination made southern blacks poorer yet. At the turn of the century life expectancy at birth was 48 for white males and 51 for white females, compared with 32 for black males and 35 for black females. A white male who, in 1900, had already survived to age 20 could expect on average to reach 62, and a white female, 64; the corresponding figures for black men and women were 55 and 57. Life expectancy improved significantly for all Americans in the next three decades, but the racial gap persisted, with whites living about 10–12 years longer than blacks. White men and women born around 1930 could expect on average to live to 59 and 63; black men and women, to 48 and 50. Whites who reached the age of 20 by 1930 would live on average to the ages of 66 (men) and 69 (women); the corresponding figures for blacks were 56 and 57. Probably because so many black Americans moved North after 1915, their rate of infant mortality dropped more quickly than that of whites. Still, it remained 60 percent higher. By 1930 around sixty of every one thousand white infants died at birth, compared with one hundred of every one thousand babies classified as nonwhite.

## CITIZENSHIP AND NATURALIZATION

Just as artificial but legalized distinctions of race framed the lives of black Americans, so did they affect aliens. Laws of American citizenship remained complicated and discriminatory throughout the 1901–1929 period. Two provisions were clear: (1) the Fourteenth Amendment to the Constitution (1868) guaranteed citizenship to everyone born in the United States (with the exception of certain Native Americans affiliated with tribes, to be discussed later), (2) after 1870 federal law made whites and people of African descent eligible for citizenship.

This legal code stigmatized Asians,

making them the only group ineligible for citizenship until Congress reformed U.S. naturalization law in the 1940s and 1950s. (Local courts did naturalize a few thousand Asians despite the federal ban.) The odd stigma attached to Asians was highlighted by the 1923 Supreme Court decision in *Thind v. United States,* in which the plaintiff was a high-caste Hindu from northernmost India, and thus of Aryan descent. Frankly denying the biological and cultural subtleties of race, the Court argued that white meant whatever white people thought it meant: "the words of familiar speech, which were used by the original framers of the law, were intended to include only the type of man whom they knew as white."

Although Latin Americans were often viewed as nonwhite, the federal government granted them eligibility for citizenship. Immigrants from Western Asia, most of them Arabs and Jews from Syria and Palestine, or Armenians, generally attained citizenship. For a brief period (roughly 1910–1915) several contradictory rulings confused their situation, but the courts ended up classifying them as members of "the Semitic branch of the Caucasian race" and therefore eligible to become naturalized citizens.

As important as citizenship was for full civil and political equality, many immigrants disregarded or delayed the process of naturalization. With the conspicuous exception of the Jews and Irish, for whom America was a final haven from religious persecution, most newcomers intended to return to their native lands. Therefore, they initially had no intention of becoming U.S. citizens. By 1930 roughly 60 percent of white immigrants

were naturalized citizens. According to the U.S. Census from that year, one of every two Italians, and one of every two Poles remained an alien. Mexicans had an extremely low rate of naturalization; in 1930 only 24 percent (about one in four) were citizens. Immigrants from the Balkans and Iberia, who had high rates of repatriation, also balked at citizenship. World War I accelerated the rate of naturalization, as immigrants felt tremendous pressure to show their loyalty to the nation and to conform to the credo of 100 percent Americanism that dominated the wartime and postwar era. In the period 1907–1911, immigrants filed an average of 41,000 petitions for naturalization per year, whereas in the 1920s the annual average climbed to 188,430! The upsurge in citizenship after World War I meant millions of new voters who, as we shall see, changed the course of American politics.

The several hundred thousand members of the Native American tribes, the American Indians, endured a very complex and costly ordeal of citizenship. In the period between 1887 and 1934, federal Indian policy aimed to break up tribal lands and turn Indians into individualist citizen-farmers by assigning a standard homesteader's plot of land (160 acres) and full citizenship to the head of each household. This policy had dubious results. The tribes that cooperated with the government's plan lost 60 million of their 138 million acres of land to Congress (this was the "surplus" left over after the distribution of family allotments). Those Indians who became citizens by federal law sometimes found that individual states did not grant them voting rights, and tribes that voted against the individual-allotment plan stagnated on poverty-stricken reservations with virtually no legal rights. In 1924 Congress granted citizenship to all Indians born in the United States, but, like African Americans, they remained in many respects second-class citizens.

## IMMIGRATION RESTRICTION

The most dramatic break in the history of American immigration occurred in the 1920s. After the Chinese Exclusion Act of 1882, Congress had begun to restrict and monitor immigrants, but after 1900 a campaign developed to close the country's borders to a whole range of nationalities. Anti-Asian sentiment in California, born out of a desire to ban Chinese laborers, spread virulently to the Japanese. In 1907–1908 public pressure led President Roosevelt and the State Department to conclude the Gentleman's Agreement with Japan, whereby Japan agreed to limit the emigration of its workers, especially to the American mainland. (Despite the new limits, well over one hundred thousand Japanese immigrants arrived in the next twenty years, many settling in Hawai'i.) Not satisfied with the sizable reduction of Japanese immigrants, Californians lobbied fiercely until the state government in Sacramento—in 1913 and again in 1920—produced laws prohibiting aliens from purchasing and leasing land. Confronted with an immigrant group, the Japanese, that admirably fulfilled the American work ethic and succeeded as

farmers, Americans struck a devil's bargain. Logically, they should have lobbied for citizenship for these newcomers who helped build the rural economy of California. Instead they sought the opposite: total exclusion of the Japanese and all Asians. This movement in California merged with a national campaign directed against the great multitude of poor immigrants—most of them Catholic and Jewish—from Italy, Poland, Russia, Rumania, and Austria-Hungary. In 1921 and 1924 the restrictionists in Congress passed laws that drastically reduced the annual quotas of these targeted European groups and banned further immigration from Asia. Fueled by a nativist desire to restore America's "racial balance" and prevent the dilution of the so-called Nordic elements, these laws ended the national custom of welcoming European immigrants.

The two large immigrant groups not affected by the new law were the Canadians and the Mexicans, who continued to augment the American Catholic population. In the 1920s nearly a million Canadians, around a third of whom were French-speaking Catholics, and nearly five hundred thousand Mexicans emigrated to the Northeastern and Southwestern regions of the United States.

## ETHNIC SELF-DEFENSE

In response to discriminatory laws and acts, a number of ethnic minorities created legal defense organizations that became a vital part of the American civil rights tradition. The first important associations were the American Jewish Committee (1906), the National Association for the Advancement of Colored People (NAACP, 1909–1910), and the Anti-Defamation League (1913). A number of well-established Jewish leaders formed the American Jewish Committee after an awful wave of anti-Jewish massacres in Tsarist Russia. The Committee organized public rallies and petitioned the U.S. government to make formal diplomatic protests against Russia's anti-Semitic policies. The Jewish fraternal organization B'nai B'rith formed the Anti-Defamation League (ADL) during the Leo Frank affair, in which a Jew was unfairly convicted of murder and later lynched by a bigoted mob in Marietta, Georgia. The ADL aimed to expose and combat racial and religious prejudice in America.

African Americans supported the National Association for the Advancement of Colored People, a biracial organization set up to protest and attack the Jim Crow system. The NAACP published a dynamic monthly, The Crisis, under the editorship of W. E. B. DuBois. An impressive thinker and writer, DuBois used this publication to lambaste lynching, segregation, and the hypocrisy of such customs within an allegedly free society. In addition to vocalizing the deep discontents of African Americans, the NAACP successfully attacked discriminatory laws in the courts. Participating in Supreme Court cases of the 1910s and 1920s, it helped overturn the use of "grandfather clauses" that disfranchised black voters in the South (Guinn v. United States, 1915), defeated a law enforcing racial segregation in the Louisville housing market (Buchanan v. Warley, 1917), and secured federal intervention against mob-dominated state trials (Moore v. Dempsey, 1923). The timeliness of the NAACP was proved by the fact that more than four hundred branches of the organization appeared in the first decade of its existence.

Other organizations followed these forerunners. In 1914, the Society of Syrian National Defense organized in Charleston, South Carolina, in response to a court's denial of citizenship to a Syrian immigrant. Its protest produced a successful legal appeal (Dow v. United States), authorizing citizenship for Arabs from Western Asia. In the 1920s Mexican Americans, their numbers enlarged by hundreds of thousand of immigrants and their confidence boosted by participation in the war effort, formed a number of political associations that merged into LULAC, the League of United Latin American Citizens (1929). Like other such organizations, LULAC maintained two mutually supportive goals: 1) the integration of Mexicans into American society through citizenship and voting, and 2) the defense of both the dignity and legal rights of Mexican Americans through protest of degrading stereotypes and discrimination in the use of public services and in the selection of juries. The 1920s also witnessed the first effective defense against the government's disreputable Indian policy. In 1923 the American Indian Defense Association, organized by a (non-Indian) reformer, John Collier, rallied enough humanitarian interest to stop the reckless exploitation of Indian lands and promote a new, more humane policy in the 1930s.

## THE RISE OF ETHNIC COMMUNITIES AND "GHETTOS"

The new ethnic self-defense organizations were but one of many products of the ethnic communities that sprang up across America. Immigrants and black migrants from the South clustered in distinct regions of the country and neighborhoods of major cities. In the 1901–1929 period, more than 80 percent of America's foreign-born lived in the states of the Northeast and Midwest. Nearly three-fourths of the Irish immigrants concentrated in New England and the Middle Atlantic states. New England also housed roughly two-thirds of the French Canadians. More than one-third of the Germans settled in the eastern part of the Midwest (Ohio, Indiana, Illinois, and Missouri), and almost half of the Norwegians resided in the western part (Minnesota, Wisconsin, Iowa, and the Dakotas). The vast majority of the Jews concentrated in the middle Atlantic region and especially in New York City, where they comprised 28 percent of the population by 1915. Most Italians also gravitated to the New York-New Jersey-Pennsylvania area, and a third of them settled in the state of New York. Pennsylvania, Ohio, and Illinois became home to a large percentage of Polish and Slavic newcomers. Asians and Mexicans congregated in the West. Nearly half of the Chinese and more than three-fourths of the Japanese immigrants lived in California; nearly all Mexicans (88 percent) lived in Texas, New Mexico, Arizona, and California.

The new concentrations of immigrants altered the human geography of American cities. In 1910, 41 percent of the residents of New York City were foreign-born; in Chicago, 36 percent; Boston, 36 percent; Cleveland, 35 percent; Detroit, 34 percent; San Francisco, 34 percent; Providence, 34 percent; Newark, 32 percent; Seattle, 28 percent; Philadelphia, 25 percent. In the smaller Massachusetts city of Fall River, roughly four of every ten residents were French Canadians; in Milwaukee more than half of the city's population was of German ancestry. One of the most colorful demographic events of the early twentieth century was the appearance of ethnic neighborhoods in cities like these. The "Frenchvilles" or "Little Canadas" of Massachusetts, New Hampshire, Maine, and Rhode Island; the "Polonias" (Polish colonies) of Chicago and Buffalo; the "Little Italys" in cities throughout the Northeast; the Puerto Rican *colonias* of East and South Harlem and Brooklyn; the great Japantown of Los Angeles; and San Francisco's Chinatown stamped these places with a variety of languages, with the smells of ethnic markets and restaurants, and with the spectacle of public celebrations, honoring occasions such as the Chinese New Year and Catholic Saints Days. The Lower East Side of New York City, the densest urban neighborhood in the world, housed hundreds of thousands of Yiddish-speaking Jews; New York City was known as the New Jerusalem. The barrio of East Los Angeles had enough Mexican residents (more than ninety thousand in 1930) to rival cities in Mexico itself. On the upper part of Manhattan, Harlem emerged as the nation's most populous and distinctive Afro-American neighborhood. In the 1920s it became a kind of cultural capital, a gathering place for the rising stars of American jazz and blues, as well as the writers—Alain Locke, James Weldon Johnson, Langston Hughes, Zora Neale Hurston, to name a few—whose work earned the title "the Harlem Renaissance."

None of these areas were actually *ghettos*, a term that referred historically to parts of cities in Europe where Jews were literally locked in. Yet they harbored enough poverty and crime to seem like traps for neglected humanity. This was most true of black neighborhoods, Chinatowns, and Japantowns, where racial prejudice prevented easy exit into surrounding neighborhoods. Despite the problems of inner-city ethnic neighborhoods, they usually nourished a rich cultural life, generating exciting fusions of ethnic and American music, theater, literature, and art.

## RACE RIOTS

The convergence of different ethnic groups in American cities also produced serious conflicts between them. The teaching of native languages in schools, especially parochial schools, the nationality of priests and type of service in Catholic churches, and control over jobs, unions, and political positions all brought minorities into periodic power struggles. Immigrant memoirs are full of stories of "turf wars," in which gangs competed for control of the streets and youngsters ventured into "enemy" neighborhoods at their peril.

Without question, the most conspicuous and destructive form of conflict in the United States during this period was the "race riot." In addition to the gruesome practice of lynching, which ended the lives of more than one thousand black victims between 1900 and 1920, mob action against black Americans erupted frequently. Triggered by hysterical allegations or actual incidents of black-on-white crime, ugly crowds driven by deep fears of black power committed murders and burned buildings in Negro neighborhoods, In Statesboro, Georgia (1904), Springfield, Ohio (1904), Atlanta, Georgia (1906), Springfield, Illinois (1908), and East St. Louis, Illinois (1917), there were riots of varying severity, culminating in the "Red Summer" and Fall of 1919, when approximately twenty-five such outbreaks occurred. The worst such riot in American history took place in Chicago in July 1919. Sparked by the stoning of a black boy who had drifted into the "white" section of the beach on Lake Michigan, mobs of black and white men sprang up quickly and began a conflagration that lasted thirteen days. Fifteen whites and 23 blacks died in the conflict; 178 whites and 342 blacks sustained injuries. (Seventeen other murder victims were not racially identified.) Destruction of property left more than one thousand families, most of them black, homeless. Two years later Tulsa, Oklahoma, erupted, after an alleged assault upon a white woman by a black man.

Nine whites and twenty-one blacks died, hundreds were injured and large tracts of the city were burned out and reduced to rubble.

The causes of these bloody events varied in each case. Sometimes, as in the Chicago riot, masses of blacks collided with white immigrants in labor battles in the city's huge meat-packing industry. Labor unions, which typically excluded or discriminated against black workers, appealed to the immigrants to stand as one against the "bosses," while black laborers often worked as strikebreakers, believing that big employers such as Armour and Swift would give them a better deal than the unions had to offer. Labor conflicts and racial antagonisms formed a volatile mixture, easily ignited by the summer heat of a crowded industrial city.

In the South, riots served less as an outlet for tension between competing ethnic groups and more as a means of maintaining a racial caste system. The Atlanta riot of 1906, the worst in the South prior to World War I, followed a campaign in the press against the rising aspirations of Negro residents. In one of the great works of American documentary journalism, *Following the Color Line* (1908), reporter Ray Stannard Baker traced the arc of tension in Atlanta, a city with a large black population that enjoyed rising levels of prosperity and education.

> On the afternoon of the riot the newspapers in flaming headlines chronicled four assaults by Negroes on white women. I had a personal investigation made of each of those cases. Two of them may have been attempts at assaults, but two palpably were nothing more than fright on the part of both the white woman and the Negro, As an instance, in one case an elderly woman, Mrs. Martha Holcombe, going to close her blinds in the evening, saw a Negro on the sidewalk. In a terrible fright she screamed. The news was telephoned to the police station, but before the officials could respond. Mrs. Holcombe telephoned them not to come out. And yet this was one of the "assaults" chronicled in letters five inches high in a newspaper extra.

Baker discovered a white community intent on separating themselves from blacks, and a black community that deeply resented the Jim Crow regulations being implemented against them. "The underman will not keep his place," Baker reported. "He is restless, ambitious, he wants civil, political, and industrial equality."

Baker suggested an interesting parallel between Southern hysteria about potential racial equality and Northern reactions against immigrants: "Does democracy really include Negroes as well as white men? Does it include Russian Jews, Italians, Japanese? Does it include Rockefeller and the Slavonian street-sweeper?"

## THE NATIVIST REACTION OF THE 1920S

These questions acquired special importance in the 1920s, when American nativism reached full tide. World War I

THE CRITICAL PERIOD, 1901–1929 [425]

precipitated an anti-German hysteria of surprising proportions. The nation's largest white ethnic group, German Americans, suffered severe persecution during 1917 and 1918, as their neighbors mobbed, harassed, and ridiculed them. A 1918 federal law required all states receiving federal funds to guarantee that English be the primary language of instruction in both public and private schools. Under intense pressure to show their loyalty, German Americans drastically curtailed their distinctive cultural practices. American fears of political subversion spread from Germans to radicals in 1919, when the federal government deported hundreds of foreign-born socialists and anarchists. The restrictive immigration quotas of 1921 and 1924 were part of a larger reaction against foreign "elements" that allegedly weakened the native stock of America.

There was a soft and a hard side to the national perspective on immigrants in the 1920s. The soft side came from Americans who were neither xenophobic nor nativist but wanted to see immigrants assimilate into the larger society as quickly as possible. During World War I, nearly one million immigrants of nearly fifty nationalities served in the American army. This mobilization combined with a massive patriotic campaign to encourage the foreign-born to put their native lands in the backs of their minds and cultivate an uncomplicated loyalty to America and its values. Since 1917, then, the country had been vigorously espousing an ideal of *unhyphenated Americanism*. However, the line between Americanism and chauvinism was never a clear one. On the other side of

that line, the hard side of American public opinion included outright hostility toward ethnic minorities.

Revived in 1915, the Ku Klux Klan symbolized the ugly mood that waxed with the nation's isolationism and disillusionment after World War I. Unlike its predecessor of the 1860s, the new Klan combined anti-Negro racism with nativism and evangelical Protestantism. Branding Catholics and Jews as subversive foreign elements, terrorizing blacks who showed any signs of discontent with racial segregation, and punishing fellow white Protestants for adultery, gambling, drinking, and other licentious acts, the Ku Klux Klan enjoyed a brief period of social dominance in the early 1920s, especially in the Midwest and South. By the end of the decade scandal and internal conflicts weakened the Klan, state governments began to crack down on its vigilantism, and other Americans started to clash publicly with the white-robed bullies. In the summer of 1923, for example, a crowd of six thousand people, primarily Jews and Catholics, attacked and dispersed five hundred Klansmen who were meeting in the central New Jersey town of Perth Amboy. Despite the brevity of the Klan's terrorist reign, the notorious organization set an example of white supremacist militance for like-minded Americans in the decades after World War II.

The rough tactics of the Klan were complemented by the pseudoscientific racism of university professors and other members of the social elite. Relying on spurious theories of racial genetics, natural scientists, psychologists, and sociologists offered up evidence to support an idea that humankind broke down into several racially determined groups of varying intelligence. Nordics or Aryans, representing the Northern European, stood at the top of this hierarchy, Africans occupied the bottom tier, and everyone else fell somewhere in between. The founders and early advocates of intelligence testing, which became popular in the 1920s, subscribed to these genetic theories. Stanford psychologist Lewis Terman, who created the Stanford-Binet intelligence test; Harvard psychologist Robert Yerkes, who headed the U.S. Army's intelligence testing program during World War I; and Princeton psychologist Carl Brigham, author of the influential 1923 book *A Study of American Intelligence,* all added intellectual fuel to a nativist campaign whose most sensational books carried titles such as *The Passing of the Great Race* and *The Rising Tide of Color.* Elitist xenophobia hit Jews with particular force because Jews were entering prestigious colleges and universities in disproportionate numbers. To stem this academic tide, the nation's elite schools instituted quotas to minimize the number of Jewish students who were admitted. In some cases new psychological tests were used to support the claim that Jewish students were too intellectually intense and insufficiently balanced to mix in with the Ivy League set.

Although academic racism enjoyed a triumph in the passage of the highly restrictive immigration act of 1924, it faded away surprisingly quickly in the late 1920s and 1930s as a result of a powerful shift in American social science. Two of the most significant figures for that shift were professors at Colum-

bia University: the philosopher John Dewey and the anthropologist Franz Boas. The most influential American philosopher of the era, the Vermont-born Dewey delighted in the excitement and ethnic diversity of New York City. His distinctive, future-oriented philosophy of *pragmatism* made no room for old-fashioned views of racial heredity; instead it emphasized the idea that all human beings were capable of dynamic growth and *self-realization.* The anthropologist Franz Boas attacked racist theories directly. More than any other scholar, Boas changed the way Americans thought about race by replacing it with the concept of *culture.* A German Jew who immigrated to the United States in the 1880s, Boas assaulted the myth of a "pure" European or American race and the corollary claim that intermixture with immigrants and blacks would cause some sort of national degeneration. Although he had been producing studies on the subject since the early years of the century, Boas and an impressive group of scholars who had been his students finally achieved a position of intellectual dominance in the late 1920s and 1930s. Their research suggested that ethnic traits (including intelligence as measured by tests) were determined primarily by environmental factors and not by collective genetic differences. By the late 1930s *culture* was well on its way to replacing *race* as the primary way of describing ethnic differences.

Nevertheless, in day-to-day life, prejudices remained strong enough to make the 1920s a decade of egregious stereotypes of Jews and Italians. As a result of notorious gangsters like Al Capone and headlines about crime families in American cities, Italians acquired the reputation of being criminals by nature. In the summer of 1920 mobs brutally attacked Italians in the southern Illinois town of West Frankfurt, on the pretext of crimes attributed to a Sicilian criminal association. The famous murder case of Nicola Sacco and Bartolomeo Vanzetti, two Italian anarchists who were convicted in 1921 and executed over mass protests in 1927, mixed the associations of Italian criminality and foreign radicalism and so made a fair trial nearly impossible. In the early 1920s the famous automaker Henry Ford shocked the country by publishing a series of anti-Semitic articles on "The International Jew" in his newspaper *The Dearborn Independent*. Reflecting both age-old prejudices and newer stereotypes of Jews as rootless revolutionaries, Ford disseminated the *Protocols of the Elders of Zion*, a notorious piece of Russian propaganda claiming that a Jewish conspiracy was busily achieving world-wide domination. On a more prosaic level, Jews had to deal with the fact that many white-collar jobs were closed to them—job advertisements frequently stipulated that applicants be Christian.

One of the most interesting responses to the intolerance of the 1920s was that of black nationalist Marcus Garvey, a Jamaican immigrant who settled in Harlem. Deeply moved by the plight of black people in Africa, Europe, and the Americas, Garvey dedicated himself to the cause of a grand return to Africa. There his people, like the Zionists who were settling in Palestine, would establish their own government and possess

the dignity that went along with political independence. Garvey was a charismatic leader who appealed like no other to the masses of African Americans in northern cities. His Universal Negro Improvement Association included elaborate ranks, rituals, and regalia that generated feelings of pride among its thousands of members. With its belief in black superiority and racial separation, and its anti-Semitic and nativist undertones, Garvey's nationalism reflected some of the decadence of America's racial order. His Black Star Line, an ambitious shipping company that was designed to prove both that blacks could successfully operate their own businesses and that they would one day return to Africa, ultimately failed because of Garvey's dubious business practices, for which he was arrested and deported. A model for later expressions of black nationalism, Marcus Garvey tapped a deep current in the psyche of African Americans. Though he misjudged the desire of people to return to Africa, Garvey ingeniously stimulated the collective pride that helped sustain life in America.

## A NEW ETHNIC POLITICS

In light of the nativism of the 1920s, the unprecedented presidential candidacy of a Catholic, New York governor Al Smith, showed that politics would be a primary means of dealing with the insecurity felt by immigrants and their children. In that election many immigrants supported Smith (who wanted to repeal the Nineteenth Amendment) partly to oppose the Prohibitionists, who often linked immigrants with drunkenness and the corruption of American values.

The "new ethnicity" of American politics in this period had two primary elements, one symbolic and the other institutional. Symbolically, the rise of ethnic leaders to public importance and the celebration of ethnic holidays and occasions—such as the 1910 unveiling in Washington, D.C., of statues of Thaddeus Kosciusko and Casimir Pulaski, Polish heroes who served in the American Revolution—gave minorities a feeling of pride and acceptance. Institutionally, the influx of minorities into the Democratic Party radically altered the political system.

Another institutional component that must be mentioned, at least in passing, was the disproportionate involvement of immigrants in radical political parties and movements. Many ethnic mutual-aid societies were socialist in spirit, as was the nation's largest foreign-language newspaper, the Yiddish *Forverts* (Forward). Many prominent socialists and anarchists were immigrants (especially German, Jewish, and Italian), and after World War I the two most important black leaders, aside from Garvey, were both socialists—W. E. B. DuBois and A. Philip Randolph, who unionized Negro railway employees in the Brotherhood of Sleeping Car Porters. In the 1920s roughly 80 percent of the members of the American Communist Party were Jews and other East Europeans and Finns.

The new century started with a rush of political symbolism during the presidency of Theodore Roosevelt (1901–

1909). One month after taking office, upon the assassination of William McKinley by a foreign-born anarchist, Roosevelt invited Booker T. Washington to luncheon at the White House, the first such invitation ever extended to a black American. Grasping the symbolic implications of this event, Southern racists exploded in anger over what they considered the president's irresponsible approval of "social equality" between the races. Roosevelt's political prudence led him to avoid repeating this kind of public act, and he later alienated many black Americans when he rashly dismissed several companies of Negro soldiers after the Brownsville (Texas) riot of 1906. But he did rely on Booker T. Washington as a key broker of political appointments in the South. Furthermore, even though he displayed a prideful bias toward the Anglo-American heritage, Roosevelt believed that individuals should be judged according to merit rather than race or religion. Cognizant of the political symbolism of the act, he appointed the first Jewish and Catholic cabinet members in the nation's history. Unlike most Americans at the time, Roosevelt believed that Asians should not be excluded from citizenship (a belief he expressed privately). He condemned the ignorant prejudice of those who abused Asian Americans, and he had a much more respectful attitude toward the Japanese than most Americans did, even though he felt that anti-Japanese prejudice was so strong as to make it necessary to limit immigration from Japan. Well traveled, internationally minded, and highly inquisitive, Roosevelt was the first cosmopolitan president of the modern era.

In spite of his brusque patriotism and blunt roughrider persona, he inaugurated a new approach to ethnic minorities. He wanted to Americanize them as quickly as possible, but he recognized that they belonged to the body politic.

Of the presidents who came after Roosevelt in this period (Taft, Wilson, Harding, Coolidge, and Hoover), only Woodrow Wilson (1913–1920) had an important record vis-à-vis ethnic minorities, but one that was more ambiguous than Roosevelt's. The first Southerner to occupy the White House since the Civil War, Wilson originally displayed both nativist (anti-immigrant) and racist attitudes. In respect to race relations, he was culpable for allowing segregation into the federal government for the first time, in the departments of the Post Office and the Treasury, both of which were headed by Southern compatriots of his. In addition to importing the Southern caste system into the nation's capital, he accepted the invitation of Thomas Dixon, author of the viciously racist novel *The Clansman*, on which the famous film "Birth of a Nation" was based, to screen the movie in the White House. For Jews, however, the Wilson administration brought good tidings. Wilson succeeded in placing the eminent attorney Louis Brandeis on the Supreme Court, despite the opposition of anti-Semites both on and off the Court, and he supported the rising Zionist movement. Jews also appreciated Wilson's introduction of the Minorities Treaties at the Paris Peace Conference of 1919; these were designed to protect Europe's ethnic minorities from state-sponsored persecution. The Irish, however, rejected Wilson for his pro-British position; they helped thwart his campaign for the League of Nations and the Democratic Party's bid for the presidency in 1920. In sum, race, religion, and ethnicity played an important symbolic and practical role in national politics after 1900.

Accordingly, minorities began to deploy political strategies to affect both the policies and the symbolism that emanated from their government. The most important tactic was "getting out the vote" for candidates who supported various ethnic causes, especially in heavily immigrant cities such as New York, Chicago, Detroit, Cleveland, Boston, Philadelphia, Milwaukee, Buffalo, Pittsburgh, Baltimore, and Providence. Once sufficient numbers of immigrants became citizens and voters, political campaigns in American cities responded like barometers. St. Patrick's Day had long been an occasion for pro-Irish politicking, and in the early 1900s Italians lobbied successfully for Columbus Day. In these and other more local celebrations of ethnic heritage, politicians worked overtime amid the parades, extolling the virtues and achievements of immigrant Americans and suggesting how they might vote on the issues of the day.

Irish Americans were especially driven, as one of their leading historians explains, by an "addiction to and love of politics." By the 1890s they pioneered a distinctive style of urban politics, based on familiarity with the ethnic customs of city residents. Both takers of graft and givers of charity, ward politicians such as Big Tim Sullivan in New York City and Bathhouse John Coughlin of Chicago knew a smattering of foreign phrases, attended religious ceremonies different from their own, and gave their constituents a feeling of being protected and cared for in an impersonal and intimidating urban world. The diary of one day in the life of an Irish American boss, George Washington Plunkitt, included the following activities:

> 2 A.M. *Wakened by a boy with message from bartender to bail him out of jail.* . . . 6 A.M. Fire engines, up and off to the scene to see my election district captains tending the burnt-out tenants. Got names for new homes. 8:30 to police court. Six drunken constituents on hand. Got four released by a timely word to the judge. Paid the other's [sic] fines. 11 to 3 P.M. *Found jobs for four constituents.* 3 P.M. an Italian funeral, sat conspicuously up front. 4 P.M. *A Jewish funeral—up front again, in the synagogue.* . . . 8 P.M. Church fair. Bought ice cream for the girls; took fathers for a little something around the corner. . . . 10:30 a Jewish wedding. Had sent handsome present to bride. Midnight—to bed.

Generations of city politicians followed the Irish model, which combined an authoritarian and a cosmopolitan approach to the political order; inclusiveness, not exclusiveness, spelled victory at the polls.

To be sure, Irish domination of city politics generated conflicts with other ethnic groups, a striking example of which was the Italian challenge to Chicago potentate John Powers in the 1921 election for alderman. Three months after the election ended with a victory for Boss Powers, his opponent, Anthony D'Andrea, an alleged crime boss, was killed by a shotgun blast. We should also note the rise of a very different kind of politician from immigrant America, personified by Fiorello La Guardia, whose father was Italian and whose mother was Jewish. A reformer who rebelled against machine politics and championed the underprivileged (who were exploited by the same ward politicians who helped them), La Guardia enjoyed one of the most brilliant careers in the history of American urban politics, serving with remarkable effect as Congressman (1917–1919, 1923–1933), President of the Board of Aldermen (1919–1921) and Mayor of New York City (1933–1945).

Like immigrants, black Americans entered a new world of urban politics after the Great Migration from the South and produced their own bosses and reformers. But they faced unique conditions as well. In cities and states with significant black populations, political parties often pandered to the "whiteness" of European immigrants. For example, in Baltimore in 1905 and 1909, politicians tried unsuccessfully to pass a law that would disfranchise Maryland's Negro residents. They lobbied for the immigrant vote by emphasizing the racial differences between immigrants and Negroes. The city's foreign-born population appeared to accept this racial categorization whether or not they voted for the legislation. The vast majority of newcomers did not live in the South and did not usually vote on such explicitly racist proposals. But even in the North and West,

European immigrants quickly recognized that they had moved into a society divided along a color line. When that line appeared in elections they saw little benefit in siding with blacks and substantial rewards in identifying with the white majority.

Black Americans joined in the new urban politics despite the ever-present problem of racism, which made political power all the more vital to their future. While immigrants steadily gained political strength in the years before World War I, black residents of Northern cities had to deal with a *decline* in their position. As long as they had been a small percentage of a city's population, black Americans in the Northern states, despite racial prejudice, often lived in integrated neighborhoods and participated in municipal politics and society. Yet once their numbers swelled with thousands of Southern migrants, they faced two new realities: residential ghettos and more frequent discrimination in public places. In response to these unfortunate realities, black urban leaders developed a social and political philosophy of black self-sufficiency by promoting black businesses and politicians, so that the ghettoized population might gain economic and political power. Politicians built "little black Tammany Halls" that were part of a city's larger political machine but relied on the black vote and handled the problems of the black community. No different from their counterparts in immigrant neighborhoods, these machines benefited from the naiveté of poor, uneducated constituents and received a substantial amount of money from saloons, prostitution, and gambling rackets, all of which demoralized hard-working residents of the inner city. And yet, despite these blotchy trademarks of city politics, black Americans found their first nucleus of political power in the metropoles of the North. In Cleveland, for example, the black population increased from nine thousand to thirty-five thousand between 1910 and 1920 (an increase of nearly 300 percent compared to a 38 percent increase of the white population). Cleveland had its classic black "boss," a man named Thomas Fleming, but it also saw a new kind of political figure emerge in the late 1920s. As a result of dissatisfaction with the status quo in the black community, voters elected two new leaders, E. J. Gregg and Clayborne George, to join Fleming on the Cleveland City Council. Gregg and George refused to cozy up to a political party as Fleming had done with the Republicans. Instead, they held out until both political parties showed "a new respect for the Negro vote" by delivering valuable political appointments to black Clevelanders. On this political foundation Cleveland would elect the first black mayor of a major American city several decades later.

The new northern black electorate also made its presence felt in national politics during the 1920s. Traditionally partisans of the "party of Lincoln," Negro voters began to break ranks with the Republicans in 1924, when both the Democratic and the Progressive Party candidates for the presidency declared that race should not be a factor in American governance. The trend continued in 1928 when the Republican Party, in an effort to secure the Southern vote, refused to seat Negro delegates at their national convention. By 1932 the black vote swung to the Democratic Party and was not disappointed, as the Roosevelt administration gave a new prominence and dignity to African American leaders.

Nineteen twenty-eight was a turning point for another reason, too. For the first time since 1901 a Negro, Oscar de Priest of Chicago, won election to Congress. Like so many black Americans in this era, de Priest started life in the South (Alabama) and moved North. He arrived in Chicago in 1899 and instantly took to politics. Working his way up the Republican hierarchy, he became the first black alderman in Chicago. When he was sent to Washington as Representative of the First Illinois Congressional District, he leaped another hurdle, for no Negro from a Northern state had ever sat in the U.S. Congress. Echoing what happened over the Booker T. Washington invitation to the White House in 1901, white Southerners flew into a rage when Mr. and Mrs. De Priest attended a tea for the families of Congressmen. (In Birmingham, Alabama, the Ku Klux Klan burned him in effigy.) On the other hand, an Afro-American newspaper spoke for millions when it said De Priest's election gave his people "new hope, new courage, and new inspiration."

In the presidential campaign of 1928, racial and ethno-religious issues loomed larger than at any time since the Civil War. The Democratic Party's unprecedented nomination of a Catholic, Al Smith of New York City, evoked strong anti-Catholic prejudices. Yet paradoxically, the large contingent of southern Protestants who disliked Smith's Irish Catholicism had to abandon the one political party—the Democrats—that fought for white supremacy in the South. In New York State, where Smith was governor, he had been building a coalition of immigrant and black supporters, and this new political mix would quickly become the national norm of a new, more urban Democratic Party. In 1900 the Democratic Party spoke for rural people, especially in the South. Yet throughout the 1920s, when millions of foreigners emerged as naturalized voters, the party appealed strongly to them. And as we have seen, urban black voters also began to leave the Republicans. By the election of 1932 the new coalition of urbanized ethnic minorities had remade the Northern wing of the Democratic Party in their own image. For the remainder of the century the Republicans lost the cosmopolitan flavor that Theodore Roosevelt had given them. His distant cousin Franklin, the Democratic nominee for president in 1932, inherited that legacy.

## BEGINNINGS OF A COSMOPOLITAN CULTURE

If ethnic minorities reoriented politics in this period, they transformed culture. Since the rise of vaudeville in the 1870s, American popular entertainment offered an excellent medium for immigrant and ethnic talent. Many of the icons of popular culture were foreign-born or had clear ethnic roots. Prominent examples include movie stars and sex symbols Rudolph Valentino (Italian) and Mary

Pickford (Canadian), magician Harry Houdini (Jewish), comedians Charlie Chaplin (English) and the Marx Brothers (Jewish), singer Al Jolson (Jewish), musician and singer Louis Armstrong (African American) and popular wit Will Rogers (Cherokee American).

American music developed from the dynamic interplay of native and immigrant and white and black talent. Some of this interplay grew out of pathetically racialized styles such as black minstrelsy, which thrived on white performers wearing blackface makeup ("blacking up"), grossly mimicking Negro servile gestures, and acting out with an emotionalism that was considered inappropriate in normal life. Around the turn of the century, however, the emotional excitement and spontaneity associated with African American music and dance started to appear in revolutionary new forms that reshaped Western music.

The blues-and-jazz revolution dates to the years before World War I. Although music styles rarely result from the genius of a single person, historians have found it convenient to recognize W. C. (William Christopher) Handy as the "father of the blues," because he was the first to publish and promote the music. In 1909, Handy wrote "Memphis Blues" as a campaign song for a mayoral candidate. The tune caught on like wildfire among whites and blacks, making Handy's band the top band in that city. In 1912 Handy wrote the classic "St. Louis Blues." A few years later the Alabama-born musician moved to New York City, where he became the primary popularizer of the blues and an influential creator of other popular songs. Handy's business partner,

Harry Pace, went on his own to start the first Afro-American recording company; his first huge success came with the 1921 recordings of "Down Home Blues" and "Oh, Daddy" by Ethel Waters, who rose to stardom on Broadway and in Hollywood. As Handy's and Pace's careers illustrate, the rising music industry created an important new avenue of financial and artistic success for African Americans.

Further illustration may be found in the story of the discovery of Louis Armstrong in the 1920s. Fletcher Henderson, an accomplished musician who worked as an arranger for Harry Pace's record company, heard Armstrong play in New Orleans. Struck by the young trumpet player's virtuosity and stage presence, Henderson brought Armstrong to New York City to join his band at New York City's most prestigious dance hall, the Roseland Ballroom. That moment marked a turning point in the history of American music, for Armstrong turned out to be a musical pioneer, who popularized the solo and many of the nuances of singing and playing that defined the new music of jazz. Although a big-band music called *jazz* appeared before 1917, it was after World War I that "the Jazz Age" truly arrived, heralded by Louis Armstrong, blues singer Bessie Smith, and bandleader Duke Ellington. Radio, a new medium launched in the 1920s, brought these and other stars into living rooms across the country, and sales of phonograph records soared at the same time.

The formative role of African Americans in American popular music was matched by that of Jewish songwriters.

During this era many of the nation's best-loved songs came out of Tin Pan Alley, the area in downtown Manhattan where a number of talented Jews, led by Russian-born Irving Berlin, busily worked at writing catchy melodies and lyrics. Such favorites as "White Christmas" and "God Bless America" flowed from Berlin's pen. The other towering figure to come out of Tin Pan Alley and a Russian Jewish background, George Gershwin, electrified the Broadway stage in the 1920s and created a powerful new fusion of jazz and symphonic music when he composed his brilliant *Rhapsody in Blue* in 1924.

Jewish immigrants also played an unusual role in the development of the American movie industry. After breaking a monopoly of early film companies that stultified the business, Jewish entrepreneurs founded the great Hollywood studios—Metro-Goldwyn-Meyer (MGM), Paramount, Universal, Columbia, and Warner Brothers. Although most movies did not focus on immigrant themes, it was more than a coincidence that the first successful "talking" picture, *The Jazz Singer* (1927), told the story of an immigrant cantor's son torn between the Jewish religious tradition of his father and the lure of stardom in American show business. The movie featured Al Jolson, who had made this very transition—from the world of his father, an immigrant cantor, to American stardom.

Even though most entertainment was simply entertainment, the huge presence of immigrants and minorities in American show business made for interesting challenges to social conventions that ex-cluded them. In his silent pictures Charlie Chaplin portrayed the downtrodden but persevering "little guy," who might easily represent the ordinary immigrant, and who did so explicitly in the 1917 movie *The Immigrants*. Where Chaplin created poignant characterizations, the Marx Brothers introduced a distinctive kind of raucous comedy that shattered the snobbish pretensions of American patricians who disdained Jews and other outsiders. The groundbreaking musical and film *Show Boat* (based on Edna Ferber's 1926 novel) was authored, adapted, and produced by Jews, and it gracefully intertwined an indictment of racism and a conventional love story. Similarly, Louis Armstrong's stirring rendition of "Black and Blue" poignantly described the pain of racial prejudice.

More sentimental ethnic elements permeated American popular culture as well. The 1908 play *The Melting Pot*, by British Jewish writer Israel Zangwill, created one of the most enduring metaphors for America as a society of immigrants, *a melting pot* in which ethnic and religious differences disappear and a new American people emerges. The story is about two Russian immigrants, a Jew and a Christian, who fall in love despite severe family conflicts; it ends with their marriage and closes at the Statue of Liberty, with the lovers feeling sure that the varied races and nationalities in America will ultimately unite and create a new Republic of Man. *Abie's Irish Rose*, one of the longest-running plays of the 1920s, tells of another unlikely union, this time between a Jewish boy and an Irish girl. After predictable conflicts between the fathers, Solomon and Patrick, and bemused observation by their respective rabbi and priest, the couple weds in a Christian ceremony and has twins. This makes everyone happy, for the Jewish grandfather wanted a grandson and the Irish one a granddaughter! What made the sentimentality of these two popular plays particularly interesting was the fact that Jews had an extremely low rate of intermarriage. The dramas therefore reflected not a predominant fact but rather a grand vision of human compatibility and harmony across ethnic lines.

With the rise of radio in the 1920s a new genre of entertainment was born—the situation comedy—and some of the most popular early sitcoms focused on racial and ethnic themes. The groundbreaking show Amos 'n' Andy, launched in 1926 as Sam 'n' Henry but renamed in 1928, enjoyed unparalleled success and lasted through the 1950s. Played by two white entertainers, the characters Amos and Andy formed the nucleus of a daily story about African Americans from the South trying to make a life in New York City. Andy was unscrupulous, but Amos was sincere and portrayed with real humanity, despite the stereotyped buffoonery that marked most of the male characters on the show. African Americans split in their reactions to the show; some protested that it perpetuated degrading characterizations, while others appreciated the show as comedy, the only comedy featuring African American characters at all. Had African Americans possessed any real control over the content of radio shows, Amos 'n' Andy would

have been a very different production, more akin to The Goldbergs. Launched in 1929, this sitcom about a New York Jewish family achieved almost as much success as Amos 'n' Andy, and without purveying objectionable stereotypes.

## CONCEPTIONS OF RACE, ETHNICITY, AND AMERICAN IDENTITY

Virtually every ethnic minority in America experienced the dilemma of "dual identity." On the one hand, there was tremendous pressure to conform to the ways of the American majority, particularly during and after World War I, which brought nationalism to a fevered pitch. Yet inherited traditions and customs did not simply fall away like an old skin. Members of ethnic groups felt compelled to support the larger aims of their people. In The Souls of Black Folk (1903) W. E. B. Du Bois eloquently described the psychological condition of dual identity as it applied to African Americans:

> It is a peculiar sensation, this double-consciousness, this sense of always looking at one's self through the eyes of others, of measuring one's soul by the tape of a world that looks on in amused contempt and pity. One ever feels his twoness—an American, a Negro; two souls, two thoughts, two unreconciled strivings; two warring ideals in one dark body, whose dogged strength alone keeps it from being torn asunder. The history of the

American Negro is the history of this strife—this longing to attain self-conscious manhood, to merge his double self into a better and truer self. In this merging he wishes neither of the older selves to be lost. He would not Africanize America, for America has too much to teach the world and Africa. He would not bleach his Negro soul in a flood of white Americanism, for he knows that Negro blood has a message for the world. He simply wishes to make it possible for a man to be both a Negro and an American, without being cursed and spit upon by his fellows, without having the doors of Opportunity closed roughly in his face.

The dilemma of dual identity affected every group in a distinctive way. Each one had its "assimilationists" and "traditionalists." the former promoted Americanization at the expense of many traditional customs, and the latter, though not necessarily rejecting Americanization, insisted that many ethnic customs be preserved. Yet within the general framework of new ways versus old, there were many nuances. Mexicans, for example, retained a very strong tie to Mexico, which was just over the border and easy to return to. As a result, and because of historic grievances dating to the Mexican American War, most Mexican Americans considered themselves "essentially Mexican." Nevertheless, they could not help but change many of their ways, as other immigrants did. The most settled Mexican Americans looked down on the new arrivals, whose for-

eignness, they thought, jeopardized their reputation among Americans. In turn, the newer immigrants disdained the condescension of Americanized Mexicans and criticized them for losing Mexican culture.

Most European immigrants, once they decided to settle in the United States, did not endure the intense ambivalence felt by Mexican Americans. Still, they oscillated between feelings of gratitude for the freedoms they enjoyed and feelings of nostalgia for their homelands. As the characters in Abraham Cahan's stories of Jewish immigrants were wont to say in moments of frustration, "a pox on Columbus." Such evocations did not imply distrust of America—the Jews, in particular, saw America as a kind of beloved homeland—but rather a sense of being caught between two worlds. In 1915 Horace Kallen, an American Jewish thinker, developed the concept of "cultural pluralism" as a resolution of the two-worlds problem. According to Kallen's theory, Americanization did not require ethnic minorities to reject their ethnic customs. Rather, those ethnic differences might enrich American society.

Indian voices sounded a poignant note in the problem of reconciling new and old, American and ethnic identities. A landmark event in the history of American Indian relations was the publication of Geronimo's autobiography in 1906. Although living as a prisoner of war from 1886, when the U.S. Army captured him, until his death in 1909, the Apache leader attained fame in the early years of the century. Once he ceased to be a military threat, Americans converted him into a celebrity. Geronimo toured regional expositions, appeared as a guest of honor at Fourth of July celebrations in Oklahoma (where he lived), and rode in Theodore Roosevelt's inaugural parade in 1905 at the President's invitation. Having secured the president's permission to publish his autobiography while he remained technically a prisoner of war, Geronimo gave a fairly candid critique of the U.S. government's treatment of his people. A pragmatic leader, Geronimo counseled the Apaches to adapt to American ways for their own benefit, but he also retained a proud attachment to the tribal homeland. "I think that my people are now capable of living in accordance with the laws of the United States," the old warrior stated, "and we would, of course, like to have the liberty to return to that land which is ours by divine right."

Will Rogers, of mixed Cherokee and white background, brought the Indian predicament into public view once he rose to become America's favorite humorist in the 1920s. "The Navajo Indians held a conference and decided that they could get along without the services of about twenty-five white office holders that had been appointed to help look after them. The Indians said they were doing it to save the white man money. Who said the Indians didn't have any humor?" This barb typified Rogers's wit, which reflected the irony of living simultaneously as a celebrity and a descendant of a tribe that had been tragically herded into Oklahoma two generations before

his birth there. He was the first such public figure to remind Americans that even the "most native" among them were not quite as native as they liked to think. "My ancestors didn't come on the Mayflower," Rogers mused, "but they met the boat." Mapping out a new approach to the question of who belonged in America, Du Bois, Kallen, and Rogers pointed toward a more self-aware and cosmopolitan country than the one into which they had been born.

## BIBLIOGRAPHIC ESSAY

The following bibliography is restricted to books that treat the 1901–1929 period in some detail. In listing studies of specific immigrant groups, I emphasize books that make extensive use of primary sources, especially foreign-language sources such as immigrant newspapers, correspondence, and memoirs.

An excellent visual starting point is Peter C. Marzio, ed., *A Nation of Nations: The People Who Came to America as Seen Through Objects and Documents Exhibited at the Smithsonian Institution* (New York: Harper and Row, 1976).

On the critical legal and constitutional questions of race and immigration, see the entries on "Race and Racism," "Native Americans," and "Alienage and Naturalization" in Kermit L. Hall, ed., *The Oxford Companion to the Supreme Court of the United States* (New York: Oxford University Press, 1992).

Valuable interpretations of ethnicity as a factor in this era of American history are offered by Philip Gleason, *Speaking of Diver-*

*sity: Language and Ethnicity in Twentieth-Century America* (Baltimore: Johns Hopkins University Press, 1992); Werner Sollors, *Beyond Ethnicity: Consent and Descent in American Culture* (New York: Oxford University Press, 1986); Arthur Mann, *The One and the Many: Reflections on the American Identity* (Chicago: University of Chicago Press, 1979); and John Higham, *Send These to Me: Immigrants in Urban America* (Baltimore: Johns Hopkins University Press, 1975).

Reliable historical surveys of immigration, ethnicity, race and religious minorities include: Leonard Dinnerstein and David M. Reimers, *Ethnic Americans: A History of Immigration* (New York: Columbia University Press, 1999; orig. 1975); Alan M. Kraut, *The Huddled Masses: The Immigrant in American Society, 1880–1921.* (Arlington Heights, Ill.: Harlan Davidson, 2001); Thomas J. Archdeacon, *Becoming American: An Ethnic History* (New York: Free Press, 1983); Roger Daniels, Coming to America: *A History of Immigration and Ethnicity in American Life* (New York: HarperCollins, 1990); John E. Bodnar, *The Transplanted: A History of Immigrants in Urban America* (Bloomington: Indiana University Press, 1985); and James Olson, *The Ethnic Dimension in American History* (New York: St. Martin's Press, 1999; orig. 1979). An older classic work, written in an epic rather than textbook mode, is Oscar Handlin, *The Uprooted* (Boston: Little, Brown, 1951). Another, older book that offers an interesting view of immigrant contributions is Carl Frederick Wittke, *We Who Built America* (Cleveland: Press of Western Reserve University, 1939).

Surveys on African Americans, Native Americans, and Asian Americans include the following: John Hope Franklin, *From Slavery*

*to Freedom: A History of African Americans* (New York: Knopf, 2000; orig. 1947); Jacqueline Jones, *Labor of Love, Labor of Sorrow: Black Women, Work, and the Family from Slavery to the Present* (New York: Basic Books, 1985); Rayford W. Logan, *The Betrayal of the Negro: From Rutherford B. Hayes to Woodrow Wilson* (New York: Collier, 1965); Leon F. Litwack, *Trouble in Mind: Black Southerners in the Age of Jim Crow* (New York: Knopf, 1998); Francis Paul Prucha, *The Great Father: The United States Government and the American Indians* (Lincoln: University of Nebraska Press, 1984); John R. Wunder, *"Retained by the People": A History of American Indians and the Bill of Rights* (New York: Oxford University Press, 1994); Sucheng Chan, *Asian Americans: An Interpretive History* (Boston: Twayne, 1991); and Ronald T. Takaki, *Strangers from a Different Shore: A History of Asian Americans* (Boston: Little, Brown, 1989).

Specialized studies on racism, nativism, and anti-Semitism include John Higham, *Strangers in the Land: Patterns of American Nativism, 1860–1925* (New Brunswick: Rutgers University Press, 1955); Barbara Miller Solomon, *Ancestors and Immigrants* (Boston: Northeastern University Press, 1956); David M. Chalmers, *Hooded Americanism: The First Century of the Ku Klux Klan, 1865–1965* (Garden City, N.Y.: Doubleday, 1965); Kenneth T. Jackson, *The Ku Klux Klan in the City, 1915–1930* (New York: Oxford University Press, 1967); Kathleen M. Blee, *Women of the Klan: Racism and Gender in the 1920s* (Berkeley: University of California Press, 1991); Nancy MacLean, *Behind the Mask of Chivalry: The Making of the Second Ku Klux Klan* (New York: Oxford University Press, 1994); Leonard Dinnerstein, *Anti-Semitism in America* (New York: Oxford University

Press, 1994); Allan M. Kraut, *Silent Travelers: Germs, Genes and the "Immigrant Menace"* (Baltimore: Johns Hopkins University Press, 1994); Frederick C. Luebke, *Bonds of Loyalty: German-Americans and World War I* (Dekalb: Northern Illinois University Press, 1974); Roger Daniels, *The Politics of Prejudice: The Anti-Japanese Movement in California and the Struggle for Japanese Exclusion* (Berkeley: University of California Press, 1962); Sucheng Chan, *Entry Denied: Exclusion and the Chinese Community in America, 1882–1943* (Philadelphia: Temple University Press, 1991); Matthew Frye Jacobson, *Whiteness of a Different Color: European Immigrants and the Alchemy of Race* (Cambridge: Harvard University Press, 1998); Ian F. Haney-Lopez, *White by Law: The Legal Construction of Race* (New York: New York University Press, 1996); Thomas F. Gossett, *Race: The History of an Idea in America* (Dallas: Southern Methodist University Press, 1964); Elazar Barkan, *The Retreat of Scientific Racism: Changing Concepts of Race in Britain and the United States Between the World Wars* (Cambridge: Cambridge University Press, 1992); Michael M. Sokal, ed., *Psychological Testing and American Society, 1890–1930* (New Brunswick, N.J.: Rutgers University Press, 1987); and George W. Stocking, Jr., *Race, Culture, and Evolution: Essays in the History of Anthropology* (Chicago: University of Chicago Press, 1968).

Studies of specific immigrant and ethnic groups include the following, listed in chronological order of publication:

On the Irish and Germans, William V. Shannon, *The American Irish* (New York: Macmillan, 1963); Lawrence J. McCaffrey, *The Irish Catholic Diaspora in America* (Washington, D.C.: Catholic University of America Press, 1997; orig. 1976); Kerby A. Miller,

*Emigrants and Exiles: Ireland and the Irish Exodus to North America* (New York: Oxford University Press, 1985); Timothy J. Meagher, ed., *From Paddy to Studs: Irish-American Communities in the Turn of the Century Era, 1880–1920* (New York: Greenwood Press, 1986); Phyllis Keller, *States of Belonging: German-American Intellectuals and the First World War* (Cambridge: Harvard University Press, 1979); and Frederick C. Luebke, *Germans in the New World* (Urbana: University of Illinois Press, 1990).

On East European Jews, Moses Rischin, *The Promised City: New York's Jews, 1870–1914* (Cambridge: Harvard University Press, 1962); Deborah Dash Moore, *At Home in America: Second Generation New York Jews* (New York: Columbia University Press, 1981); Andrew R. Heinze, *Adapting to Abundance: Jewish Immigrants, Mass Consumption and the Search for American Identity* (New York: Columbia University Press, 1990); Susan A. Glenn, *Daughters of the Shtetl: Life and Labor in the Immigrant Generation* (Ithaca: Cornell University Press, 1990); Ewa T. Morawska, *Insecure Prosperity: Small-Town Jews in Industrial America, 1890–1940* (Princeton: Princeton University Press, 1996); Daniel Soyer, *Jewish Immigrant Associations and American Identity in New York, 1880–1939* (Cambridge: Harvard University Press, 1997); and Arthur A. Goren, *The Politics and Public Culture of American Jews* (Bloomington: Indiana University Press, 1999).

On Italians, Virginia Yans-McLaughlin, *Family and Community: Italian Immigrants in Buffalo, 1880–1930* (Ithaca: Cornell University Press, 1977); John W. Briggs, *An Italian Passage: Immigrants to Three American Cities, 1890–1930* (New Haven: Yale University Press, 1978); Dino Cinel, *From Italy to San*

*Francisco: The Immigrant Experience* (Palo Alto: Stanford University Press, 1982); Humbert S. Nelli, *From Immigrants to Ethnics: The Italian Americans* (New York: Oxford University Press, 1983); Donna R. Gabaccia, *From Sicily to Elizabeth Street: Housing and Social Change among Italian Immigrants, 1880–1930* (Albany: State University of New York Press, 1984); Robert A. Orsi, *The Madonna of 115th Street: Faith and Community in Italian Harlem, 1880–1950* (New Haven: Yale University Press, 1985); and Donna R. Gabaccia, *Militants and Migrants: Rural Sicilians Become American Workers* (New Brunswick: Rutgers University Press, 1988).

On East Europeans, Peter Paul Jonitis, *The Acculturation of the Lithuanians of Chester, Pennsylvania* (New York: AMS Press, 1986; orig. 1951); Victor R. Greene, *The Slavic Community on Strike: Immigrant Labor in Pennsylvania Anthracite* (Notre Dame, Ind.: University of Notre Dame Press, 1968); Victor R. Greene, *For God and Country: The Rise of Polish and Lithuanian Ethnic Consciousness in America, 1860–1910* (Madison: State Historical Society of Wisconsin, 1975); Ewa T. Morawska, *For Bread with Butter: The Life-Worlds of East Central Europeans in Johnstown, Pennsylvania, 1890–1940* (New York: Cambridge University Press, 1985); M. Mark Stolarik, *Immigration and Urbanization: The Slovak Experience, 1870–1918* (New York: AMS Press, 1989); John J Bukowczyk, *And My Children Did Not Know Me: A History of the Polish Americans* (Bloomington: Indiana University Press, 1987); June Granatir Alexander, *The Immigrant Church and Community: Pittsburgh's Slovak Catholics and Lutherans, 1880–1915* (Pittsburgh: University of Pittsburgh Press, 1987); and Dominic A. Pacyga, *Polish Immigrants and Industrial Chicago: Workers on the South Side, 1880–1922* (Columbus: Ohio State University Press, 1992).

On Mexicans, Albert Camarillo, *Chicanos in a Changing Society: From Mexican Pueblos to American Barrios in Santa Barbara and Southern California, 1848–1930* (Cambridge: Harvard University Press, 1979); Ricardo Romo, *East Los Angeles: History of a Barrio* (Austin: University of Texas Press, 1983); George Sanchez, *Becoming Mexican American: Ethnicity, Culture, and Identity in Chicano Los Angeles, 1900–1945* (New York: Oxford University Press, 1993); Camille Guerin-Gonzales, *Mexican Workers and American Dreams* (New Brunswick: Rutgers University Press, 1994); David G. Gutiérrez, *Walls and Mirrors: Mexican Americans, Mexican Immigrants, and the Politics of Identity* (Berkeley: University of California Press, 1995); Juan R. Garcia, *Mexicans in the Midwest, 1900–1932* (Tucson: University of Arizona Press, 1996); and Douglas Monroy, *Rebirth: Mexican Los Angeles from the Great Migration to the Great Depression* (Berkeley: University of California Press, 1999).

On Japanese (see earlier periods for bibliography on the Chinese), John Modell, *The Economics and Politics of Racial Accommodation: The Japanese of Los Angeles, 1900–1942* (Urbana: University of Illinois Press, 1977); Eileen Sunada Sarasohn, *The Issei: Portrait of a Pioneer: An Oral History* (Palo Alto, Cal.: Pacific Books, 1983); Evelyn Nakano Glenn, *Issei, Nisei, War Bride: Three Generations of Japanese American Women in Domestic Service* (Philadelphia: Temple University Press, 1986); and Yuji Ichioka, *The Issei: The World of the First Generation Japanese Immigrants, 1885–1924* (Urbana: University of Illinois Press, 1988).

On Greeks, Armenians, Syrians, Filipinos, and Puerto Ricans, Theodore Saloutos, *The Greeks in the United States* (Cambridge: Harvard University Press, 1964); Robert Mirak, *Torn Between Two Lands: Armenians in America, 1890 to World War I* (Cambridge: Harvard University Press, 1983); Alixa Naff, *Becoming American: The Early Arab Immigrant Experience* (Carbondale: Southern Illinois University Press, 1985); Antonio J. A. Pico, *The Filipinos in America* (New York: Center for Migration Studies, 1986); and Virginia E. Sanchez Korrol, *From Colonia to Community: The History of Puerto Ricans in New York City* (Westport, Conn.: Greenwood Press, 1983).

Comparative studies of ethnic groups include Josef J. Barton, *Peasants and Strangers: Italians, Rumanians, and Slovaks in an American City, 1890–1950* (Cambridge: Harvard University Press, 1975); Thomas Kessner, *The Golden Door: Italian and Jewish Immigrant Mobility in New York City: 1880–1915* (New York: Oxford University Press, 1977); Caroline Golab, *Immigrant Destinations* (Philadelphia: Temple University Press, 1977); John Bodnar, *Lives of Their Own, Blacks, Italians, and Poles in Pittsburgh, 1900–1960* (Urbana: University of Illinois Press, 1983); Melvin G. Holli and Peter d' A. Jones, eds., *Ethnic Chicago* (Grand Rapids, Mich.: W. B. Eerdmans, 1984); Judith E. Smith, *Family Connections: A History of Italian and Jewish Immigrant Lives in Providence, Rhode Island, 1900–1940* (Albany: State University of New York Press, 1985); Gary R. Mormino and George E. Pozzetta, *The Immigrant World of Ybor City: Italians and Their Latin Neighbors in Tampa, 1885–1985* (Gainesville: University Press of Florida, 1987); and Hasia R. Diner, *Hungering for America: Italian, Irish, and Jewish Foodways in the Age of Migration*

(Cambridge: Harvard University Press, 2001).

Studies of immigrants within the contexts of religion, education, and labor include Randall Miller and Thomas Marzik, eds., *Immigrants and Religion in Urban America* (Philadelphia: Temple University Press, 1977); James Hennesey, S. J., *American Catholics: A History of the Roman Catholic Community in the United States* (New York: Oxford University Press, 1981); Jay P. Dolan, *The American Catholic Experience* (New York: Doubleday, 1992); Bernard J. Weiss, ed., *American Education and the European Immigrant, 1840–1940* (Urbana: University of Illinois Press, 1982); Paula S. Fass, *Outside In: Minorities and the Transformation of American Education* (New York: Oxford University Press, 1989); James R. Barrett, *Work and Community in the Jungle: Chicago's Packinghouse Workers, 1894–1922* (Urbana: University of Illinois Press, 1987); and Gary Gerstle, *Working-Class Americanism: The Politics of Labor in a Textile City, 1914–1960* (New York: Cambridge University Press, 1989).

On black migration from the South, immigration from the West Indies, labor, the formation of "ghettos," and the Harlem Renaissance, see Nicholas Lemann, *The Promised Land: The Great Black Migration and How It Changed America* (New York: Vintage, 1991); James R. Grossman, *Land of Hope: Chicago, Black Southerners and the Great Migration* (Chicago: University of Chicago Press, 1989); Florette Henri, *Black Migration: Movement North, 1900–1920* (Garden City, N.Y.: Anchor Press, 1975); Ira de Augustine Reid, *The Negro Immigrant* (New York: Columbia University Press, 1939); Eric Arneson, *Brotherhoods of Color: Black Railroad Workers and the Struggle for Equality* (Cambridge: Harvard

University Press, 2001); Kenneth L. Kusmer, *A Ghetto Takes Shape: Black Cleveland, 1870–1930* (Chicago: Illinois University Press, 1976); Allan H. Spear, *Black Chicago: The Making of a Negro Ghetto, 1890–1920* (Chicago: University of Chicago Press, 1967); Gilbert Osofsky, *Harlem, the Making of a Ghetto: Negro New York, 1890–1930* (New York: Harper and Row, 1966); Nathan Irvin Huggins, *Harlem Renaissance* (New York: Oxford University Press, 1971); and Jervis Anderson, *This Was Harlem: A Cultural Portrait, 1900–1950* (New York: Farrar Straus Giroux, 1982).

On aspects of cultural creativity, see Lawrence W. Levine, *Black Culture and Black Consciousness* (New York: Oxford University Press, 1977); Irving Howe, *World of Our Fathers* (New York: Harcourt Brace Jovanovich, 1976); Burton Peretti, *The Creation of Jazz: Music, Race, and Culture in Urban America* (Urbana: University of Illinois Press, 1992); James Lincoln Collier, *Jazz: The American Theme Song* (New York: Oxford University Press, 1993); James Lincoln Collier, *Louis Armstrong, an American Genius* (New York: Oxford University Press, 1993); Jeffrey Melnick, *A Right to Sing the Blues: African Americans, Jews, and American Popular Song* (Cambridge: Harvard University Press, 1999); Richard M. Ketchum, *Will Rogers* (New York: American Heritage, 1973); Kenneth Aaron Kanter, *The Jews on Tin Pan Alley* (New York: Ktav, 1982); Neal Gabler, *An Empire of Their Own: How the Jews Invented Hollywood* (New York: Crown, 1988); Melvin Patrick Ely, *The Adventures of Amos 'n' Andy: A Social History of an American Phenomenon* (New York: Free Press, 1991).

On major political figures and trends, see Victor R. Greene, *American Immigrant Leaders, 1800–1910: Marginality and Identity* (Baltimore: Johns Hopkins University Press, 1987); Angie Debo, *Geronimo: The Man, His Time, His Place* (Norman: University of Oklahoma Press, 1976); Ronald H. Bayor, *Fiorello La Guardia: Ethnicity and Reform* (Arlington Heights, Ill.: Harlan Davidson, 1993); Thomas Kessner, *Fiorello H. La Guardia and the Making of Modern New York* (New York: McGraw-Hill, 1989); Oscar Handlin, *Al Smith and His America* (1958); David Levering Lewis, *W. E. B. Du Bois* (New York: Henry Holt, 1993, 2000), 2 vols.; Judith Stein, *The World of Marcus Garvey* (Baton Rouge: Louisiana State University Press, 1986); Jervis Anderson, *A. Philip Randolph* (New York: Harcourt Brace Jovanovich, 1973); David Burner, *The Politics of Provincialism: The Democratic Party in Transition, 1918–1932* (New York: Knopf, 1967); James J. Connolly, *The Triumph of Ethnic Progressivism: Urban Political Culture in Boston, 1900–1925* (Cambridge: Harvard University Press, 1998); Gwendolyn Mink, *Old Labor and New Immigrants in American Political Development: Union, Party, and State, 1875–1920* (Ithaca: Cornell University Press, 1986); John M. Allswang, *A House for All Peoples: Ethnic Politics in Chicago, 1890–1936* (Lexington: University of Kentucky Press, 1971); Edward R. Kantowicz, *Polish-American Politics in Chicago, 1888–1940* (Chicago: University of Chicago Press, 1975); Paul Avrich, *Sacco and Vanzetti: The Anarchist Background* (Princeton: Princeton University Press, 1991).

There are no complete analyses of the complicated racial and ethnic politics of Theodore Roosevelt and Woodrow Wilson. Thomas G. Dyer, *Theodore Roosevelt and the Idea of Race* (Baton Rouge: Louisiana State University Press, 1980) approaches the subject but misses the complexity of Roosevelt's attitudes, as does the otherwise excellent comparative biography by John Milton Cooper, Jr., *The Warrior and the Priest: Woodrow Wilson and Theodore Roosevelt* (Cambridge: Cambridge University Press, 1983). The reader should consult the leading biographies of these presidents.

For a sample of the many illustrative primary sources relevant to the 1901–1929 period, see Hutchins Hapgood, *The Spirit of the Ghetto* (Cambridge: Harvard University Press, 1902); W. E. B. Du Bois, *The Souls of Black Folk* (Chicago: A. C. McClurg, 1903); Thomas Dixon, *The Clansman: An Historical Romance of the Ku Klux Klan* (New York: Doubleday, Page, 1905); S. M. Barrett, ed., *Geronimo's Story of His Life* (New York: Duffield, 1906); Upton Sinclair, *The Jungle* (New York: Doubleday, Page, 1906); Ray Stannard Baker, *Following the Color Line* (New York: Harper and Row, 1908); Israel Zangwill, *The Melting Pot* (New York: Macmillan, 1909); Emily Greene Balch, *Our Slavic Fellow Citizens* (New York: Charities Publication Committee, 1910); Margaret F. Byington, *Homestead: The Households of a Mill Town* (New York: Charities Publication Committee, 1910); United States Immigration Commission, Reports (1911); James Weldon Johnson, *The Autobiography of an Ex-Colored Man* (Boston: Sherman, French, 1912; Reissued by Dover Publications, 1995); Mary Antin, *The Promised Land* (Boston: Houghton Mifflin, 1912); Edward Alsworth Ross, *The Old World in the New* (New York: Century, 1914); Madison Grant, *The Passing of the Great Race* (New York: Scribner's, 1916); Abraham Cahan, *The Rise of David Levinsky* (New York: Harper and Brothers, 1917); William I. Thomas and Florian Znaniecki, *The Polish Peasant in Europe*

*and America*, 2 vols. (Chicago: University of Chicago Press, 1918–1920); Robert F. Foerster, *The Italian Emigration of Our Times* (Cambridge: Harvard University Press, 1919); Philip Davis, *Immigration and Americanization* (Boston: Ginn and Company, 1920); Anzia Yezierska, *Hungry Hearts* (Salem, Mass.: Ayer Company, 1920) and *Bread Givers* (Garden City, N.Y.: Doubleday, 1925); Robert E. Park and Herbert A. Miller, *Old World Traits Transplanted* (New York: Harper, 1921); Robert E. Park, *The Immigrant Press and Its Control* (New York: Harper, 1922); Chicago Commission on Race Relations, *The Negro in Chicago: A Study of Race Relations and a Race Riot* (Chicago: University of Chicago Press, 1922); Jean Toomer, *Cane* (New York: Boni and Liveright, 1923); Horace Kallen, *Culture and Democracy in the United States* (New York: Boni and Liveright, 1924); Edith Abbot, *Immigration: Select Documents and Case Records* (Chicago: University of Chicago Press, 1924); Alain Locke, *The New Negro* (New York: A. and C. Boni, 1925); Louis Wirth, *The Ghetto* (Chicago: University of Chicago Press, 1928); Emma Goldman, *Living My Life* (New York: Knopf, 1931); Manuel Gamio, *The Mexican Immigrant: His Life-Story* (Chicago: University of Chicago Press, 1931); Yamoto Ichihashi, *Japanese in the United States* (Palo Alto: Stanford University Press, 1932).

Several films provide unique insight into the racial and ethnic dynamics of the era: *Birth of a Nation* (1915), about the Ku Klux Klan as a redeemer of the nation; *The Immigrants* (1917), Charlie Chaplin's comic portrayal of a newcomer; *The Jazz Singer* (1927), about the painful conflict between ethno-religious tradition and American stardom, featuring Al Jolson; *Broken Blossom*

(1919), a poignant, groundbreaking film about the relationship between a white woman and a Chinese man. Although it falls outside the period covered in this chapter, we should note the 1936 version of *Show Boat*, featuring singer Paul Robeson, which dramatized the themes of racial mixture and prejudice in the 1926 novel by Edna Ferber.

# DOCUMENTS

## "The South and Mr. Roosevelt," 1901

*The following editorial from the* New York Times *expresses a Northern liberal point of view on the famous luncheon of Booker T. Washington and President Theodore Roosevelt at the White House in October 1901. Note the significance of the phrase* social equality, *which meant mixing of the races in social situations, or what a later generation of Americans would call* integration. *This phrase was a bugaboo in the South, where the vast majority of whites understood it to mean the subversion of the proper social order (i.e., white supremacy). According to prevailing ideas, if blacks and whites socialized together, sharing the same public facilities and recreations, they would inevitably have sexual relations. Interracial sex, especially between Negro men and Caucasian women, was the single greatest fear of white southerners, for it threatened the delicate structure of the racial caste system. Roosevelt had both southern and northern ancestors, he was aware of the South's preoccupation with racial mixing, and he believed that, as a group, whites were culturally superior to blacks. Yet he did not accept the classic racist belief in immutable genetic differences making one people inferior to another, and he staunchly upheld the American value of individual self-improvement and advancement that Booker T. Washington, born a slave, personified. As a result his luncheon with Washington brought out a complex of issues about race, politics, and individualism in American society.*

*Source:* "The South and Mr. Roosevelt," *New York Times* (November 1, 1901).

A certain number of Southern papers and Southern politicians continue to scold about the incident of Mr. Booker T. Washington at the table of Mr. Roosevelt. Though we could bray them in a mortar of advice, we suppose that they would hardly cease from their folly. But their sincere friends in the North—and we venture to count ourselves in that class—cannot but regret that they are making so curious a mistake in this matter.

Does it not occur to these harsh and often insulting critics of Mr. Roosevelt not only that they are mistreating one of the best friends of their section, but that they are abusing him for the exercise of precisely the quality that makes him so sincere and so helpful a friend? Do they not perceive that the manly impulse of independence and of fairness which prompted Mr. Roosevelt to take the action he took in regard to Mr. Washington is the same impulse that prompted him to insist on worthy Democrats for Southern offices of importance when worthy Republicans were not provided? They threaten him with loss of political support in the South. That was exactly the threat that was used to dissuade him from doing justice to the South. He disregarded it. He certainly will not pay much heed to it from them, and for the same reason, that his acts are not shaped with reference to that consideration. Do they really imagine that it would be better for the South, the white South, if you please, to have a President in Washington who did so shape his acts?

They talk about his trying to break down the social barrier that exists in the South against intercourse with negroes.

Is that barrier, then, so fragile that the example of one Northern gentleman, who is a white, sitting down with one Southern gentleman who is black, can go far toward undermining it? Clearly Mr. Roosevelt never had any intention of producing such momentous consequences. He undoubtedly gave no thought to it at all, and the Southern men who abuse him might understand this if they could get it into their heads that he acted not as President of the United States, but as Theodore Roosevelt. As President, Mr. Roosevelt has shown that he is a wise, honorable, and courageous defender of the essential rights of the South as an integral part of the Union. Really it would seem that appreciation of that fact should determine the attitude toward him of all sensible and self-respecting Southerners.

## "Immigration," from *Mr. Dooley,* 1902

*From the 1890s through the 1910s Mr. Dooley ranked as one of America's most well-known people. Martin Dooley was a fictional character created by Finley Peter Dunne (1867–1936), a newspaperman who emerged as one of the country's greatest satirists. Born into a middle-class Irish American family in Chicago, Dunne came of age at a special time in the history of Irish Americans. The Irish were no longer the newest of the nation's immigrants and they were attaining political power in the nation's cities, yet they remained a stigmatized ethnic and religious minority. Dunne's Mr. Dooley, a saloonkeeper with a heavy Irish accent and a somewhat dimwitted sidekick named Hennessy, raked his keen wit over every section of American society. He spared neither the unscrupulous Irish ward politician nor the wealthy businessman whose corruption was papered over with testimonials and philanthropies. Dunne's wit was reminiscent of that of his friend Mark Twain, yet it had definite roots in Irish America. "He was an Irishman," writes historian William Shannon, "at a time when the American Irish community was reaching a new level of self-consciousness and self-confidence. . . . Mr. Dooley's comments reflect both the experience of power at one level and the sharp insights of the ambitious but largely powerless outsiders at the higher level." In the following essay from 1902, Mr. Dooley skewers the pretentiousness of those Americans, both native and foreign-born, who indicted the moral character and intelligence of the "new" immigrants.*

Source: "Immigration," in *Mr. Dooley: Now and Forever*, selected, with commentary and introduction by Louis Filler (1902; Stamford, Ca.: Academic Press, 1954), pp. 172–77.

"Well, I see Congress has got to wurruk again," said Mr. Dooley.

"The Lord save us fr'm harm," said Mr. Hennessy.

"Yes, sir," said Mr. Dooley, "Congress has got to wurruk again, an' manny things that seems important to a Congressman'll be brought up befure thim. 'Tis sthrange that what's a big thing to a man in Wash'nton, Hinnissy, don't seem much account to me. Divvle a bit do I care whether they dig th' Nicaragoon Canal or cross th' Isthmus in a balloon; or whether th' Monroe docthrine is enfoorced or whether it ain't; or

whether th' thrusts is abolished as Teddy Rosenfelt wud like to have thim or encouraged to go on with their neefaryous but magnificent entherprises as th' Prisidint wud like; or whether th' water is poured into th' ditches to reclaim th' arid lands iv th' West or th' money f'r thim to fertilize th' arid pocket-books iv th' conthractors; or whether th' Injun is threated like a depindant an' miserable thribesman or like a free an' indepindant dog; or whether we restore th' merchant marine to th' ocean or whether we lave it to restore itsilf. None iv these here questions inthrests me, an' be me I mane you an' be you I mane ivrybody. What we want to know is, ar-re we goin' to have coal enough in th' hod whin th' cold snap comes; will th' plumbin' hold out, an' will th' job last.

"But they'se wan question that Congress is goin' to take up that you an' me are intherested in. As a pilgrim father that missed th' first boats, I must raise me claryon voice again' th' invasion iv this fair land be th' paupers an' arnychists iv effete Europe. Ye bet I must— because I'm here first. 'Twas diff'rent whin I was dashed high on th' stern an' rockbound coast. In thim days America was th' refuge iv th' oppressed iv all th' wurruld. They cud come over here an' do a good job iv oppressin' thimsilves. As I told ye I come a little late. Th' Rosenfelts an' th' Lodges bate me be at laste a boat lenth, an' be th' time I got here they was stern an' rockbound thimsilves. So I got a gloryous rayciption as soon as I was towed off th' rocks. Th' stars an' sthripes whispered a welcome in th' breeze an' a shovel was thrust into me hand an' I was pushed into a sthreet excyvatin' as though I'd been born here. Th' pilgrim father who bossed th' job was a fine ol' puritan be th' name iv Doherty, who come over in th' Mayflower about th' time iv th' potato rot in Wexford, an' he made me think they was a hole in th' breakwather iv th' haven iv refuge an' some iv th' wash iv th' seas iv opprission had got through. He was a stern an' rockbound la-ad himsilf, but I was a good hand at loose stones an' wan day—but I'll tell ye about that another time.

"Annyhow, I was rayceived with open arms that sometimes ended in a clinch. I was afraid I wasn't goin' to assimilate with th' airlyer pilgrim fathers an' th' instichoochions iv th' counthry, but I soon found that a long swing iv th' pick made me as good as another man an' it didn't require a gr-reat intellect, or sometimes anny at all, to vote th' dimmycrat ticket, an' befure I was here a month, I felt enough like a native born American to burn a witch. Wanst in a while a mob iv intilligint collajeens, whose grandfathers had bate me to th' dock, wud take a shy at me Pathrick's Day procission or burn down wan iv me churches, but they got tired iv that befure long; 'twas too much like wurruk.

"But as I tell ye, Hinnissy, 'tis diff'rent now. I don't know why 'tis diff'rent but 'tis diff'rent. 'Tis time we put our back again' th' open dure an' keep out th' savage horde. If that cousin iv ye'ers expects to cross, he'd betther tear f'r th' ship. In a few minyits th' gates 'll be down an' whin th' oppressed wurruld comes hikin' acrost to th' haven iv refuge, they'll do well to put a couplin' pin undher their hats, f'r th' Goddess iv Liberty 'll meet thim at th' dock with an axe in her hand. Congress is goin' to fix it. Me frind Shaughnessy says so. He was in yisterdah an' says he: ''Tis time we done something to make th' immigration laws sthronger,' says he. 'Thrue f'r ye, Miles Standish,' says I; 'but what wud ye do?' 'I'd keep out th' offscourin's iv Europe,' says he. 'Wud ye go back?' says I. 'Have ye'er joke,' says he. ''Tis not so seeryus as it was befure ye come,' says I. 'But what ar-re th' immygrants doin' that's roonous to us?' I says. 'Well,' says he, 'they're arnychists,' he says; 'they don't assymilate with th' counthry,' he says. 'Maybe th' counthry's digestion has gone wrong fr'm too much rich food,' says I; 'perhaps now if we'd lave off thryin' to digest Rockyfellar an' thry a simple diet like Schwartzmeister, we wudden't feel th' effects iv our vittels,' I says. 'Maybe if we'd season th' immygrants a little or cook thim thurly, they'd go down betther,' I says.

"'They're arnychists, like Parsons,' he says. 'He wud've been an immygrant if Texas hadn't been admitted to th' Union,' I says. 'Or Snolgosh,' he says. 'Has Mitchigan seceded?' I says. 'Or Gittoo,' he says. 'Who come fr'm th' effete monarchies iv Chicago, west iv Ashland Av'noo,' I says. 'Or what's-his-name, Wilkes Booth,' he says. 'I don't know what he was—maybe a Boolgharyen,' says I. 'Well, annyhow,' says he, 'they're th' scum iv th' earth.' 'They may he that,' says I; 'but we used to think they was th' cream iv civilization,' I says. 'They're off th' top annyhow. I wanst believed 'twas th' best men iv Europe come here, th' la-ads that was too sthrong and indepindant to be kicked around be a boorgomasther at home an' wanted to dig out f'r a place where they cud get a chanst to make their way to th' money. I see their sons fightin' into politics an' their daughters tachin' young American idee how to shoot too high in th' public school, an' I thought they was all right. But I see I was wrong. Thim boys out there towin' wan heavy foot afther th' other to th' rowlin' mills is all arnychists. There's warrants out f'r all names endin' in 'inski, an' I think I'll board up me windows, f'r,' I says, 'if immygrants is as dangerous to this counthry as ye an' I an' other pilgrim fathers believe they are, they'se enough iv thim sneaked in already to make us aborigines about as infloointial as the prohibition vote in th' Twinty-ninth Ward. They'll dash again' our stern an' rock-bound coast till they bust it,' says I.

"'But I ain't so much afraid as ye ar-re. I'm not afraid iv me father an' I'm not afraid iv mesilf. An' I'm not afraid iv Schwartzmeister's father or Hinnery Cabin Lodge's grandfather. We all come over th' same way, an' if me ancestors were not what Hogan calls rigicides, 'twas not because they were not ready an' willin', on'y a king niver come their way. I don't believe in killin' kings, mesilf. I niver wud've sawed th' block off that curly-headed potintate that I see in th' pitchers down town, but, be hivins, Presarved Codfish Shaughnessy, if we'd begun a few years ago shuttin' out folks that wudden't mind handin' a bomb to a king, they wudden't be enough Anti-Impeeryal S'ciety,' says I. 'But what wud ye do with th' offscourin' iv Europe?' says he. 'I'd scour thim some more,' says I.

"An' so th' meetin' iv th' Plymouth Rock Assocyation come to an end. But if ye wud like to get it together, Deacon Hinnissy, to discuss th' immygration question, I'll sind out a hurry call f'r Schwartzmeister an' Mulcahey an' Ignacio Sbarbaro an' Nels Larsen an' Petrus Gooldvink, an' we 'll gather tonight at Fanneilnoviski Hall at th' corner iv Sheridan an' Sigel sthreets. All th' pilgrim fathers is rayquested f'r to bring interpreters."

"Well," said Mr. Hennessy, "divvle th' bit I care, on'y I'm here first, an' I ought to have th' right to keep th' bus fr'm bein' overcrowded."

"Well," said Mr. Dooley, "as a pilgrim father on me gran' nephew's side, I don't know but ye're right. An' they'se wan sure way to keep thim out."

"What's that?" asked Mr. Hennessy.

"Teach thim all about our instichoochions befure they come," said Mr. Dooley.

## W. E. B. Du Bois, "Of Our Spiritual Strivings," 1903

*William Edward Burghardt Du Bois (1868–1963) was born in Great Barrington, Massachusetts. Unlike most African Americans, his ancestors had been free since the time of the American Revolution. Describing his own ethnicity as deriving from "a flood of Negro blood, a strain of French, a bit of Dutch, and thank God! no 'Anglo-Saxon,'" Du Bois was the only African American child in his elementary and secondary schools, and he mixed easily with his white peers. His sense of difference grew as he matured, and from this inner awareness would blossom one of the most eloquent articulations of the problem of dual identity in the history of American literature. The first student of African descent to receive a Ph.D. from Harvard (1895), Du Bois expressed a grand intellect through a number of classic works of sociology, history, and literature, the most important of which was* The Souls of Black Folk *(1903). An inspiration for countless African American writers, this book interweaves Du Bois's reflections on the political, cultural, historical, and psychological predicament of black Americans. The excerpt that follows is the book's first chapter, which contains a particularly moving paragraph on being "both a Negro and an American."*

*Source:* W. E. B. Du Bois, "Of Our Spiritual Strivings," *The Souls of Black Folk* (Chicago: A. C. McClurg and Co., 1903).

## OF OUR SPIRITUAL STRIVINGS

Between me and the other world there is ever an unasked question: unasked by some through feelings of delicacy; by others through the difficulty of rightly framing it. All, nevertheless, flutter round it. They approach me in a half-hesitant sort of way, eye me curiously or compassionately, and then, instead of saying directly, How does it feel to be a problem? they say, I know an excellent colored man in my town; or, I fought at Mechanicsville; or, Do not these Southern outrages make your blood boil? At these I smile, or am interested, or reduce the boiling to a simmer, as the occasion may require. To the real ques-

tion, How does it feel to be a problem? I answer seldom a word.

And yet, being a problem is a strange experience—peculiar even for one who has never been anything else, save perhaps in babyhood and in Europe. It is in the early days of rollicking boyhood that the revelation first bursts upon one, all in a day, as it were. I remember well when the shadow swept across me. I was a little thing, away up in the hills of New England, where the dark Housatonic winds between Hoosac and Taghkanic to the sea. In a wee wooden schoolhouse, something put it into the boys' and girls' heads to buy gorgeous visiting-cards—ten cents a package—and exchange. The exchange was merry, till one girl, a tall newcomer, refused my card—refused it peremptorily, with a glance. Then it dawned upon me with a certain suddenness that I was different from the others; or like, mayhap, in heart and life and longing, but shut out from their world by a vast veil. I had thereafter no desire to tear down that veil, to creep through; I held all beyond it in common contempt, and lived above it in a region of blue sky and great wandering shadows. That sky was bluest when I could beat my mates at examination-time, or beat them at a foot-race, or even beat their stringy heads. Alas, with the years all this fine contempt began to fade; for the words I longed for, and all their dazzling opportunities, were theirs, not mine. But they should not keep these prizes, I said; some, all, I would wrest from them. Just how I would do it I could never decide: by reading law, by healing the sick, by telling the wonderful tales that swam in my head—some way. With other black boys the strife was not so fiercely sunny: their youth shrunk into tasteless sycophancy, or into silent hatred of the pale world about them and mocking distrust of everything white; or wasted itself in a bitter cry, Why did God make me an outcast and a stranger in mine own house? The shades of the prison-house closed round about us all: walls strait and stubborn to the whitest, but relentlessly narrow, tall, and unscalable to sons of night who must plod darkly on in resignation, or beat unavailing palms against the stone, or steadily, half hopelessly, watch the streak of blue above.

After the Egyptian and Indian, the Greek and Roman, the Teuton and Mongolian, the Negro is a sort of seventh son, born with a veil, and gifted with second-sight in this American world—a world which yields him no true self-consciousness, but only lets him see himself through the revelation of the other world. It is a peculiar sensation, this double-consciousness, this sense of always looking at one's self through the eyes of others, of measuring one's soul by the tape of a world that looks on in amused contempt and pity. One ever feels his twoness—an American, a Negro; two souls, two thoughts, two unreconciled strivings; two warring ideals in one dark body, whose dogged strength alone keeps it from being torn asunder.

The history of the American Negro is the history of this strife—this longing to attain self-conscious manhood, to merge his double self into a better and truer self. In this merging he wishes neither of the older selves to be lost. He would not Africanize America, for America has too much to teach the world and Africa. He would not bleach his Negro soul in a flood of white Americanism, for he knows that Negro blood has a message for the world. He simply wishes to make it possible for a man to be both a Negro and an American, without being cursed and spit upon by his fellows, without having the doors of Opportunity closed roughly in his face.

This, then, is the end of his striving: to be a co-worker in the kingdom of culture, to escape both death and isolation, to husband and use his best powers and his latent genius. These powers of body and mind have in the past been strangely wasted, dispersed, or forgotten. The shadow of a mighty Negro past flits through the tale of Ethiopia the Shadowy and of Egypt the Sphinx. Through history, the powers of single black men flash here and there like falling stars, and die sometimes before the world has rightly gauged their brightness. Here in America, in the few days since Emancipation, the black man's turning hither and thither in hesitant and doubtful striving has often made his very strength to lose effectiveness, to seem like absence of power, like weakness. And yet it is not weakness—it is the contradiction of double aims. The double-aimed struggle of the black artisan—on the one hand to escape white contempt for a nation of mere hewers of wood and drawers of water, and on the other hand to plough and nail and dig for a poverty-stricken horde—could only result in making him a poor craftsman, for he had but half a heart in either cause. By the poverty and ignorance of his people, the Negro minister or doctor was tempted toward quackery and demagogy; and by the criticism of the other world, toward ideals that made him ashamed of his lowly tasks. The would-be black *savant* was confronted by the paradox that the knowledge his people needed was a twice-told tale to his white neighbors, while the knowledge which would teach the white world was Greek to his own flesh and blood. The innate love of harmony and beauty that set the ruder souls of his people a-dancing and a-singing raised but confusion and doubt in the soul of the black artist; for the beauty revealed to him was the soul-beauty of a race which his larger audience despised, and he could not articulate the message of another people. This waste of double aims, this seeking to satisfy two unreconciled ideals, has wrought sad havoc with the courage and faith and deeds of ten thousand thousand people—has sent them often wooing false gods and invoking false means of salvation, and at times has even seemed about to make them ashamed of themselves.

Away back in the days of bondage they thought to see in one divine event the end of all doubt and disappointment; few men ever worshipped Freedom with half such unquestioning faith as did the American Negro for two centuries. To him, so far as he thought and dreamed, slavery was indeed the sum of all villainies, the cause of all sorrow, the root of all prejudice; Emancipation was the key to a promised land of sweeter beauty than ever stretched before the eyes of wearied Israelites. In song and exhortation swelled one refrain—Liberty; in his tears and curses the God he implored had Freedom in his right hand. At last it came—suddenly, fearfully, like a dream. With one wild carnival of blood and passion came the message in his own plaintive cadences:—

"Shout, O children!
Shout, you're free!
For God has bought your liberty!"

Years have passed away since then—ten, twenty, forty; forty years of national life, forty years of renewal and development, and yet the swarthy spectre sits in its accustomed seat at the Nation's feast. In vain do we cry to this our vastest social problem:—

"Take any shape but that, and my firm
    nerves
Shall never tremble!"

The Nation has not yet found peace from its sins; the freedman has not yet found in freedom his promised land. Whatever of good may have come in these years of change, the shadow of a deep disappointment rests upon the Negro people—a disappointment all the more bitter because the unattained ideal was unbounded save by the simple ignorance of a lowly people.

The first decade was merely a prolongation of the vain search for freedom, the boon that seemed ever barely to elude their grasp—like a tantalizing will-o'-the-wisp, maddening and misleading the headless host. The holocaust of war, the terrors of the Ku-Klux Klan, the lies of carpet-baggers, the disorganization of industry, and the contradictory advice of friends and foes, left the bewildered serf with no new watchword beyond the old cry for freedom. As the time flew, however, he began to grasp a new idea. The ideal of liberty demanded for its attainment powerful means, and these the Fifteenth Amendment gave him. The ballot, which before he had looked upon as a visible sign of freedom, he now regarded as the chief means of gaining and perfecting the liberty with which war had partially endowed him. And why not? Had not votes made war and emancipated millions? Had not votes enfranchised the freedmen? Was anything impossible to a power that had done all this? A million black men started with renewed zeal to vote themselves into the kingdom. So the decade flew away, the revolution of 1876 came, and left the half-free serf weary, wondering, but still inspired. Slowly but steadily, in the following years, a new vision began gradually to replace the dream of political power—a powerful movement, the rise of another ideal to guide the unguided, another pillar of fire by night after a clouded day. It was the ideal of "book-learning"; the curiosity, born of compulsory ignorance, to know and test the power of the cabalistic letters of the white man, the longing to know. Here at last seemed to have been discovered the mountain path to Canaan; longer than the highway of Emancipation and law, steep and rugged, but straight, leading to heights high enough to overlook life.

Up the new path the advance guard toiled, slowly, heavily, doggedly; only those who have watched and guided the faltering feet, the misty minds, the dull understandings, of the dark pupils of these schools know how faithfully, how piteously, this people strove to learn. It was weary work. The cold statistician wrote down the inches of progress here and there, noted also where here and there a foot had slipped or some one had fallen. To the tired climbers, the horizon was ever dark, the mists were often cold, the Canaan was always dim and far away. If, however, the vistas disclosed as yet no goal, no resting-place, little but flattery and criticism, the journey at least gave leisure for reflection and self-examination; it changed the child of Emancipation to the youth with dawning self-consciousness, self-realization, self-respect. In those sombre forests of his striving his own soul rose before him, and he saw himself—darkly as through a veil; and yet he saw in himself some faint revelation of his power, of his mission. He began to have a dim feeling that, to attain his place in the world, he must be himself, and not another. For the first time he sought to analyze the burden he bore upon his back, that dead-weight of social degradation partially masked behind a half-named Negro problem. He felt his poverty; without a cent, without a home, without land, tools, or savings, he had entered into competition with rich, landed, skilled neighbors. To be a poor man is hard, but to be a poor race in a land of dollars is the very bottom of hardships. He felt the weight of his ignorance—not simply of letters, but of life, of business, of the humanities; the accumulated sloth and shirking and awkwardness of decades and centuries shackled his hands and feet. Nor was his burden all poverty and ignorance. The red stain of bastardy, which two centuries of systematic legal defilement of Negro women had stamped upon his race, meant not only the loss of ancient African chastity, but also the hereditary weight of a mass of corruption from white adulterers, threatening almost the obliteration of the Negro home.

A people thus handicapped ought not to be asked to race with the world, but rather allowed to give all its time and thought to its own social problems. But alas! while sociologists gleefully count his bastards and his prostitutes, the very soul of the toiling, sweating black man is darkened by the shadow of a vast despair. Men call the shadow prejudice, and learnedly explain it as the natural defence of culture against barbarism, learning against ignorance, purity against crime, the "higher" against the "lower" races. To which the Negro cries Amen! and swears that to so much of this strange prejudice as is founded on just homage to civilization, culture, righteousness, and progress, he humbly bows and meekly does obeisance. But before that nameless prejudice that leaps beyond all this he stands helpless, dismayed, and well-nigh speechless; before that personal disrespect and mockery, the ridicule and systematic humiliation, the distortion of fact and wanton license of fancy, the cynical ignoring of the better and the boisterous welcoming of the worse, the all-pervading desire to inculcate disdain for everything black, from Toussaint to the devil—before this there rises a sickening despair that would disarm and discourage any nation save that black host to whom "discouragement" is an unwritten word.

But the facing of so vast a prejudice could not but bring the inevitable self-questioning, self-disparagement, and lowering of ideals which ever accompany repression and breed in an atmosphere of contempt and hate. Whisperings and portents came borne upon the four winds: Lo! we, are diseased and dying, cried the dark hosts; we cannot write, our voting is vain; what need of education, since we must always cook and serve? And the Nation echoed and enforced this self-criticism, saying: Be content to be servants, and nothing more; what need of higher culture for half-men? Away with the black man's ballot, by force or fraud—and behold the suicide of a race! Nevertheless, out of the evil came something of good—the more careful adjustment of education to real life, the clearer perception of the Negroes' social responsibilities, and the sobering realization of the meaning of progress.

So dawned the time of *Sturm und Drang*: storm and stress to-day rocks our little boat on the mad waters of the world-sea; there is within and without the sound of conflict, the burning of body and rending of soul; inspiration strives with doubt, and faith with vain questionings. The bright ideals of the past—physical freedom, political power, the training of brains and the training of hands—all these in turn have waxed and waned, until even the last grows dim and overcast. Are they all wrong—all false? No, not that, but each alone was oversimple and incomplete—the dreams of a credulous race-childhood, or the fond imaginings of the other world which does not know and does not want to know our power. To be really true, all these ideals must be melted and welded into one. The training of the schools we need to-day more than ever—the training of deft hands, quick eyes and ears, and above all the broader, deeper, higher culture of gifted minds and pure hearts. The power of the ballot we need in sheer self-defence—else what shall save us from a second slavery? Freedom, too, the long-sought, we still seek—the freedom of life and limb, the freedom to work and think, the freedom to love and aspire. Work, culture, liberty—all these we need, not singly but together, not successively but together, each growing and aiding each, and all striving toward that vaster ideal that swims before the Negro people, the ideal of human brotherhood, gained through the unifying ideal of Race; the ideal of fostering and developing the traits and talents of the Negro, not in opposition to or contempt for other races, but rather in large conformity to the greater ideals of the American Republic, in order that some day on American soil two world-races may give each to each those charactristics both so sadly lack. We the darker ones come even now not altogether empty-handed: there are to-day no truer exponents of the pure human spirit of the Declaration of Independence than the American Negroes; there is no true American music but the wild sweet melodies of the Negro slave; the American fairy tales and folklore are Indian and African; and, all in all, we black men seem the sole oasis of simple faith and reverence in a dusty desert of dollars and smartness. Will America be poorer if she replace her brutal dyspeptic blundering with light-hearted but determined Negro humility? or her coarse and cruel wit with loving jovial good-humor? or her vulgar music with soul of the Sorrow Songs?

Merely a concrete test of the underlying principles of the great republic is the Negro Problem, and spiritual striving of the freedmen's sons is the travail of souls whose burden is almost beyond the measure of their strength, but who bear it in the name of an historic race, in the name of this the land of their fathers' fathers, and in the name of human opportunity.

And now what I have briefly sketched in large outline let me on coming pages tell again in many ways, with loving emphasis and deeper detail, that men may listen to the striving in the souls of black folk.

## Geronimo, *Geronimo: His Own Story*, 1906

*Born in the 1820s in the mountainous country of southwestern New Mexico and southeastern Arizona, Geronimo was a member of the Bedonkohe, a subgroup of the Apache tribe known as Chiricahuas. Fierce and mobile warriors who often raided settlements for cattle and guns, the Apaches had been at war with the Spanish and Mexicans since the seventeenth century. Geronimo lost his first wife and children to Mexican forces in the 1840s, an experience that left him with a permanent hatred of Mexico, of which he spoke freely in his autobiography. When the Southwest came under U.S. sovereignty in 1848, a new era of conflict began between Apaches and Americans. After years of pursuit the U.S. Army captured Geronimo in 1886, and he spent the*

remaining thirteen years of his life as a prisoner of war, living primarily in Oklahoma.
Despite his official status as a prisoner, Geronimo became a kind of celebrity. He was
invited to participate in Fourth of July parades, in expositions such as the 1904 World's
Fair in St. Louis, and in Theodore Roosevelt's
inaugural parade in 1905. A tourist trade
developed around him; he sold buttons off his
coat for a quarter each, and one visitor paid
him five dollars (the equivalent of several
days' wages) for a common feather from his
hat. With the help of a young relative who
acted as his translator, Geronimo dictated his
autobiography to reporter S. M. Barrett, who
published it in 1906. It is noteworthy that
President Roosevelt authorized the publication
of Geronimo's story, since the old warrior had
given a critical account of the U.S. Army and
its treatment of the Apaches. However, the
president would not allow him to return to
the Apache reservation in Arizona for fear
that Geronimo retained enough power to in-
cite a mass exodus.

Source: Geronimo: His Own Story, As Told to S. M.
Barrett (1906; reprint, Frederick Turner, ed.,
New York: Meridian/Penguin, 1996), pp. 1,
132–38, 139–146; 155–162, 167–170.

## PREFACE

The initial idea of the compilation of this
work was to give the reading public an
authentic record of the private life of the
Apache Indians, and to extend to Geronimo as a prisoner of war the courtesy
due any captive, i.e., the right to state
the causes which impelled him in his opposition to our civilization and laws.

If the Indians' cause has been properly
presented, the captives' defense clearly
stated, and the general store of information regarding vanishing types increased, I shall be satisfied.

I desire to acknowledge valuable sug-
gestions from Major Charles Taylor, Fort
Sill, Oklahoma; Dr. J. M. Greenwood,
Kansas City, Missouri; and President
David R. Boyd, of the University of
Oklahoma.

I especially desire in this connection
to say that without the kindly advice and
assistance of President Theodore Roosevelt this book could not have been
written.

Respectfully,
S. M. Barrett.
Lawton, Oklahoma.
August 14, 1906.

## DEDICATORY

Because he has given me permission to
tell my story; because he has read that
story and knows I try to speak the truth;
because I believe that he is fair-minded
and will cause my people to receive justice in the future; and because he is chief
of a great people, I dedicate this story of
my life to Theodore Roosevelt, President of the United States.

## THE FINAL STRUGGLE

We started with all our tribe to go with
General Crook back to the United
States, but I feared treachery and de-
cided to remain in Mexico. We were not
under any guard at this time. The United
States troops marched in front and the
Indians followed, and when we became
suspicious, we turned back. I do not

know how far the United States army went after myself, and some warriors turned back before we were missed, and I do not care.

I have suffered much from such unjust orders as those of General Crook. Such acts have caused much distress to my people. I think that General Crook's death was sent by the Almighty as a punishment for the many evil deeds he committed.

Soon General Miles was made commander of all the western posts, and troops trailed us continually. They were led by Captain Lawton, who had good scouts. The Mexican soldiers also became more active and more numerous. We had skirmishes almost every day, and so we finally decided to break up into small bands. With six men and four women I made for the range of mountains near Hot Springs, New Mexico. We passed many cattle ranches, but had no trouble with the cowboys. We killed cattle to eat whenever we were in need of food, but we frequently suffered greatly for water. At one time we had no water for two days and nights and our horses almost died from thirst. We ranged in the mountains of New Mexico for some time, then thinking that perhaps the troops had left Mexico, we returned. On our return through Old Mexico we attacked every Mexican found, even if for no other reason than to kill. We believed they had asked the United States troops to come down to Mexico to fight us.

South of Casa Grande, near a place called by the Indians Gosoda, there was a road leading out from the town. There was much freighting carried on by the Mexicans over this road. Where the road ran through a mountain pass we stayed in hiding, and whenever Mexican freighters passed we killed them, took what supplies we wanted, and destroyed the remainder. We were reckless of our lives, because we felt that every man's hand was against us. If we returned to the reservation we would be put in prison and killed; if we stayed in Mexico they would continue to send soldiers to fight us; so we gave no quarter to anyone and asked no favors.

After some time we left Gosoda and soon were reunited with our tribe in the Sierra de Antunez Mountains.

Contrary to our expectations the United States soldiers had not left the mountains in Mexico, and were soon trailing us and skirmishing with us almost every day. Four or five times they surprised our camp. One time they surprised us about nine o'clock in the morning, and captured all our horses (nineteen in number) and secured our store of dried meats. We also lost three Indians in this encounter. About the middle of the afternoon of the same day we attacked them from the rear as they were passing through a prairie—killed one soldier, but lost none ourselves. In this skirmish we recovered all our horses except three that belonged to me. The three horses that we did not recover were the best riding horses we had.

Soon after this we made a treaty with the Mexican troops. They told us that the United States troops were the real cause of these wars, and agreed not to fight any more with us provided we would return to the United States. This we agreed to do, and resumed our march, expecting to try to make a treaty with the United States soldiers and return to Arizona. There seemed to be no other course to pursue.

Soon after this scouts from Captain Lawton's troops told us that he wished to make a treaty with us; but I knew that General Miles was the chief of the American troops, and I decided to treat with him.

We continued to move our camp northward, and the American troops also moved northward, keeping at no great distance from us, but not attacking us.

I sent my brother Porico (White Horse) with Mr. George Wratton on to Fort Bowie to see General Miles, and to tell him that we wished to return to Arizona; but before these messengers returned I met two Indian scouts—Kayitah, a Chokonen Apache, and Marteen, a Nedni Apache. They were serving as scouts for Captain Lawton's troops. They told me that General Miles had come and had sent them to ask me to meet him. So I went to the camp of the United States troops to meet General Miles.

When I arrived at their camp I went directly to General Miles and told him how I had been wronged, and that I wanted to return to the United States with my people, as we wished to see our families, who had been captured and taken away from us.

General Miles said to me: "The President of the United States has sent me to speak to you. He has heard of your trouble with the white men, and says that if you will agree to a few words of treaty we need have no more trouble. Geronimo, if you will agree to a few words of treaty all will be satisfactorily arranged."

So General Miles told me how we could be brothers to each other. We raised our hands to heaven and said that the treaty was not to be broken. We took an oath not to do any wrong to each other or to scheme against each other.

Then he talked with me for a long time and told me what he would do for me in the future if I would agree to the treaty. I did not greatly believe General Miles, but because the President of the United States had sent me word I agreed to make the treaty, and to keep it. Then I asked General Miles what the treaty would be. General Miles said to me: "I will take you under Government protection; I will build you a house; I will fence you much land; I will give you cattle, horses, mules, and farming implements. You will be furnished with men to work the farm, for you yourself will not have to work. In the fall I will send you blankets and clothing so that you will not suffer from cold in the winter time.

"There is plenty of timber, water, and grass in the land to which I will send you. You will live with your tribe and with your family. If you agree to this treaty you shall see your family within five days."

I said to General Miles: "All the officers that have been in charge of the Indians have talked that way, and it sounds like a story to me; I hardly believe you."

He said: "This time it is the truth."

I said: "General Miles, I do not know the laws of the white man, nor of this new country where you are to send me, and I might break their laws."

He said: "While I live you will not be arrested."

Then I agreed to make the treaty. (Since I have been a prisoner of war I have been arrested and placed in the guardhouse twice for drinking whisky.)

We stood between his troopers and my warriors. We placed a large stone on the blanket before us. Our treaty was made by this stone, and it was to last until the stone should crumble to dust; so we made the treaty, and bound each other with an oath.

I do not believe that I have ever violated that treaty; but General Miles never fulfilled his promises.

When we had made the treaty General Miles said to me: "My brother, you have in your mind how you are going to kill men, and other thoughts of war; I want you to put that out of your mind, and change your thoughts to peace."

Then I agreed and gave up my arms. I said: "I will quit the warpath and live at peace hereafter."

Then General Miles swept a spot of ground clear with his hand, and said: "Your past deeds shall be wiped out like this and you will start a new life."

## A PRISONER OF WAR

When I had given up to the Government they put me on the Southern Pacific Railroad and took me to San Antonio, Texas, and held me to be tried by their laws.

In forty days they took me from there to Fort Pickens (Pensacola), Florida.

Here they put me to sawing up large logs. There were several other Apache warriors with me, and all of us had to work every day. For nearly two years we were kept at hard labor in this place and we did not see our families until May, 1887. This treatment was in direct violation of our treaty made at Skeleton Cañon.

After this we were sent with our families to Vermont, Alabama, where we stayed five years and worked for the Government. We had no property, and I looked in vain for General Miles to send me to that land of which he had spoken; I longed in vain for the implements, house, and stock that General Miles had promised me.

During this time one of my warriors, Fun, killed himself and his wife. Another one shot his wife and then shot himself. He fell dead, but the woman recovered and is still living.

We were not healthy in this place, for the climate disagreed with us. So many of our people died that I consented to let one of my wives go to the Mescalero Agency in New Mexico to live. This separation is according to our custom equivalent to what the white people call divorce, and so she married again soon after she got to Mescalero. She also kept our two small children, which she had a right to do. The children, Lenna and Robbie, are still living at Mescalero, New Mexico. Lenna is married. I kept one wife, but she is dead now and I have only our daughter Eva with me. Since my separation from Lenna's mother I have never had more than one wife at a time. Since the death of Eva's mother I married another woman (December, 1905) but we could not live happily and separated. She went home to her people—that is an Apache divorce.

Then, as now, Mr. George Wratton superintended the Indians. He has always had trouble with the Indians, because he has mistreated them. One day an Indian, while drunk, stabbed Mr. Wratton with a little knife. The officer in charge took the part of Mr. Wratton and the Indian was sent to prison.

When we first came to Fort Sill, Captain Scott was in charge, and he had houses built for us by the Government. We were also given, from the Government, cattle, hogs, turkeys and chickens. The Indians did not do much good with the hogs, because they did not understand how to care for them, and not many Indians even at the present time keep hogs. We did better with the turkeys and chickens, but with these we did not have as good luck as white men do. With the cattle we have done very well, indeed, and we like to raise them. We have a few horses also, and have had no bad luck with them.

In the matter of selling our stock and grain there has been much misunderstanding. The Indians understood that the cattle were to be sold and the money given to them, but instead part of the money is given to the Indians and part of it is placed in what the officers call the "Apache Fund." We have had five different officers in charge of the Indians here and they have all ruled very much alike—not consulting the Apaches or even explaining to them. It may be that the Government ordered the officers in charge to put this cattle money into an Apache fund, for once I complained and told Lieutenant Purington that I intended to report to the Government that he had taken some of my part of the cattle money and put it into the Apache Fund, he said he did not care if I did tell.

Several years ago the issue of clothing ceased. This, too, may have been by the order of the Government, but the Apaches do not understand it.

If there is an Apache Fund, it should some day be turned over to the Indians, or at least they should have an account of it, for it is their earnings.

When General Miles last visited Fort Sill I asked to be relieved from labor on account of my age. I also remembered what General Miles had promised me in the treaty and told him of it. He said I need not work any more except when I wished to, and since that time I have not been detailed to do any work. I have worked a great deal, however, since then, for, although I am old, I like to work and help my people as much as I am able.

## AT THE WORLD'S FAIR

When I was at first asked to attend the St. Louis World's Fair I did not wish to go. Later, when I was told that I would receive good attention and protection, and that the President of the United States said that it would be all right, I consented. I was kept by parties in charge of the Indian Department, who had obtained permission from the President. I stayed in this place for six months. I sold my photographs for twenty-five cents, and was allowed to keep ten cents of this for myself. I also wrote my name for ten, fifteen, or twenty-five cents, as the case might be, and kept all of that money. I often made as much as two dollars a day, and when I returned I had plenty of money—more than I had ever owned before.

Many people in St. Louis invited me to come to their homes, but my keeper always refused.

Every Sunday the President of the Fair sent for me to go to a wild west show. I took part in the roping contests before the audience. There were many other Indian tribes there, and strange people of whom I had never heard.

When people first came to the World's Fair they did nothing but parade up and down the streets. When they got tired of this they would visit the shows. There were many strange things in these shows. The Government sent guards with me when I went, and I was not allowed to go anywhere without them.

In one of the shows some strange men with red caps had some peculiar swords, and they seemed to want to fight. Finally their manager told them they might fight each other. They tried to hit each other over the head with these swords, and I expected both to be wounded or perhaps killed, but neither one was harmed. They would be hard people to kill in a hand-to-hand fight.

In another show there was a strange-looking negro. The manager tied his hands fast, then tied him to a chair. He was securely tied, for I looked myself, and I did not think it was possible for him to get away. Then the manager told him to get loose.

He twisted in his chair for a moment, and then stood up; the ropes were still tied but he was free. I do not understand how this was done. It was certainly a miraculous power, because no man could have released himself by his own efforts.

In another place a man was on a platform speaking to the audience; they set a basket by the side of the platform and covered it with red calico; then a woman came and got into the basket, and a man covered the basket again with the calico; then the man who was speaking to the audience took a long sword and ran it through the basket, each way, and then down through the cloth cover. I heard the sword cut through the woman's body, and the manager himself said she was dead; but when the cloth was lifted from the basket she stepped out, smiled, and walked off the stage. I would like to know how she was so quickly healed, and why the wounds did not kill her.

I have never considered bears very intelligent, except in their wild habits, but I had never before seen a white bear. In one of the shows a man had a white bear that was as intelligent as a man. He would do whatever he was told—carry a log on his shoulder, just as a man would; then, when he was told, would put it down again. He did many other things, and seemed to know exactly what his keeper said to him. I am sure that no grizzly bear could be trained to do these things.

One time the guards took me into a little house that had four windows. When we were seated the little house started to move along the ground. Then the guards called my attention to some curious things they had in their pockets. Finally they told me to look out, and when I did so I was scared, for our little house had gone high up in the air, and the people down in the Fair Grounds looked no larger than ants. The men laughed at me for being scared then they gave me a glass to look through (I often had such glasses which I took from dead officers after battles in Mexico and elsewhere), and I could see rivers, lakes and mountains. But I had never been so high in the air, and I tried to look into the sky. There were no stars, and I could not look at the sun through this glass because the brightness hurt my eyes. Finally I put the glass down, and as they were all laughing at me, I, too, began to laugh. Then they said, "Get out!" and when I looked we were on the street again. After we were safe on the land I watched many of these little houses going up and coming down, but I cannot understand how they travel. They are very curious little houses.

One day we went into another show, and as soon as we were in, it changed into night. It was real night, for I could feel the damp air; soon it began to thunder, and the lightnings flashed; it was real lightning, too, for it struck just above our heads. I dodged and wanted to run away, but I could not tell which way to go in order to get out. The guards motioned me to keep still, and so I stayed. In front of us were some strange little people who came out on the platform; then I looked up again and the clouds were all gone, and I could see the stars shining. The little people on the plat-

form did not seem in earnest about anything they did; so I only laughed at them. All the people around where we sat seemed to be laughing at me.

We went into another place and the manager took us into a little room that was made like a cage; then everything around us seemed to be moving; soon the air looked blue, then there were black clouds moving with the wind. Pretty soon it was clear outside; then we saw a few thin white clouds; then the clouds grew thicker, and it rained and hailed with thunder and lightning. Then the thunder retreated and a rainbow appeared in the distance; then it became dark, the moon rose and thousands of stars came out. Soon the sun came up, and we got out of the little room. This was a good show, but it was so strange and unnatural that I was glad to be on the streets again.

We went into one place where they made glassware. I had always thought that these things were made by hand, but they are not. The man had a curious little instrument, and whenever he would blow through this into a little blaze the glass would take any shape he wanted it to. I am not sure, but I think that if I had this kind of an instrument I could make whatever I wished. There seems to be a charm about it. But I suppose it is very difficult to get these little instruments, or other people would have them. The people in this show were so anxious to buy the things the man made that they kept him so busy he could not sit down all day long. I bought many curious things in there and brought them home with me.

At the end of one of the streets some people were getting into a clumsy canoe, upon a kind of shelf, and sliding down into the water. They seemed to enjoy it, but it looked too fierce for me. If one of these canoes had gone out of its path the people would have been sure to get hurt or killed.

There were some little brown people at the Fair that United States troops captured recently on some islands far away from here.

They did not wear much clothing, and I think that they should not have been allowed to come to the Fair. But they themselves did not seem to know any better. They had some little brass plates, and they tried to play music with these, but I did not think it was music— it was only a rattle. However, they danced to this noise and seemed to think they were giving a fine show.

I do not know how true the report was, but I heard that the President sent them to the Fair so that they could learn some manners, and when they went home teach their people how to dress and how to behave.

I am glad I went to the Fair. I saw many interesting things and learned much of the white people. They are a very kind and peaceful people. During all the time I was at the Fair no one tried to harm me in any way. Had this been among the Mexicans I am sure I should have been compelled to defend myself often.

## HOPES FOR THE FUTURE

I am thankful that the President of the United States has given me permission to tell my story. I hope that he and those in authority under him will read my story and judge whether my people have been rightly treated.

There is a great question between the Apaches and the Government. For twenty years we have been held prisoners of war under a treaty which was made with General Miles, on the part of the United States Government, and myself as the representative of the Apaches. That treaty has not at all times been properly observed by the Government, although at the present time it is being more nearly fulfilled on their part than heretofore. In the treaty with General Miles we agreed to go to a place outside of Arizona and learn to live as the white people do. I think that my people are now capable of living in accordance with the laws of the United States, and we would, of course, like to have the liberty to return to that land which is ours by divine right. We are reduced in numbers, and having learned how to cultivate the soil would not require so much ground as was formerly necessary. We do not ask all of the land which the Almighty gave us in the beginning, but that we may have sufficient lands there to cultivate. What we do not need we are glad for the white men to cultivate.

We are now held on Comanche and Kiowa lands, which are not suited to our needs—these lands and this climate are suited to the Indians who originally inhabited this country, of course, but our people are decreasing in numbers here, and will continue to decrease unless they are allowed to return to their native land. Such a result is inevitable.

There is no climate or soil which, to

my mind, is equal to that of Arizona. We could have plenty of good cultivating land, plenty of grass, plenty of timber and plenty of minerals in that land which the Almighty created for the Apaches. It is my land, my home, my fathers' land, to which I now ask to be allowed to return. I want to spend my last days there, and be buried among those mountains. If this could be I might die in peace, feeling that my people, placed in their native homes, would increase in numbers, rather than diminish as at present, and that our name would not become extinct.

I know that if my people were placed in that mountainous region lying around the headwaters of the Gila River they would live in peace and act according to the will of the President. They would be prosperous and happy in tilling the soil and learning the civilization of the white men, whom they now respect. Could I but see this accomplished, I think I could forget all the wrongs that I have ever received, and die a contented and happy old man. But we can do nothing in this matter ourselves—we must wait until those in authority choose to act. If this cannot be done during my lifetime—if I must die in bondage—I hope that the remnant of the Apache tribe may, when I am gone, be granted the one privilege which they request—to return to Arizona.

## Leonard Covello, *The Heart Is the Teacher*, 1958

*Educator Leonard Covello (1887–1982) was the first Italian American high school principal in New York City. Covello spent most of his career at the Benjamin Franklin High School in East Harlem, located in a predominantly Puerto Rican and Italian neighborhood. He helped make Benjamin Franklin High one of the first public schools in the nation to focus on the distinctive needs of immigrant children rather than follow the predominant model of simple Americanization. In its sensitivity to the demands of a multiethnic urban environment, Covello's 1958 memoir* The Heart Is the Teacher *became a classic in the history of American public education. In the excerpt that follows, Covello reminisces about his family's arrival in the United States and about some of the emotional struggles that came with children's entrance into American schools at the turn of the century.*

*Source:* Leonard Covello, *The Heart Is the Teacher* (New York: McGraw-Hill, 1958), pp. 19–27.

In the autumn of 1896, we arrived in America.

As a boy of nine, the arduous trip in an old freighter did not matter very much to me or to my younger brothers. A child adapts to everything. It was the older people who suffered, those uprooted human beings who faced the shores of an unknown land with quaking hearts.

My mother had never been further from Avigliano than the chapel just a few kilometers outside the town, where we went on the feast days of *La Madonna del Carmine*. Suddenly she was forced to make a long and painful trip from Avigliano to Naples, through interminable mountain tunnels where choking black smoke and soot poured into the railroad carriages. Then twenty days across four thousand miles of ocean to New York.

When the sea threatened to engulf us, she did not scream and carry on like the rest, but held us close with fear and torment locked in her breast—voiceless, inarticulate. And when finally we saw the towering buildings and rode the screeching elevated train and saw the long, unending streets of a metropolis that could easily swallow a thousand Aviglianese towns, she accepted it all with the mute resignation of *"La volonta di Dio,"* while her heart longed for familiar scenes and the faces of loved ones and the security of a life she had forever left behind.

We spent two days at Ellis Island before my father was aware of our arrival. Two days and two nights we waited at this dreary place which for the immigrant was the entrance to America. Two days and two nights we waited, eating the food that was given us, sleeping on hard benches, while my mother hardly closed her eyes for fear of losing us in the confusion. Once during a physical examination men and boys were separated for a short time from the women. My mother was frantic as the guard led me and my two younger brothers away. When we ran back to her, she clutched us convulsively. Still in her eyes there was the disbelieving look of a mother who never expected to see her children again.

But her nightmare finally came to an end. We were on a small ferry boat crossing the lower bay of New York, going away from Ellis Island. My mother was standing at the railing with my father, and both of them happy—my father taller, more imposing than I remembered him, but still with his heavy mustache and short-cropped hair in the style of Umberto I. He held my younger brother by the hand and every once in a while glanced at me affectionately. The sunlight shone upon the water and upon the skyline of the city directly in front of us. I was standing with my brother Raffaele and a girl several years older than I who had accompanied my father to Ellis Island. She was dressed differently from the women of Avigliano, and her voice was pleasant and warm, and she could switch from our Italian dialect to English as she chose.

"You will like America," she chattered in Italian. "There are so many things to see. So many things to do. You will make many new friends. You will go to school. You will learn and maybe become somebody very important. Would you like that?"

My brother nodded vigorously. I was older. I only smiled. The girl now addressed herself to me. "Wouldn't you like that?"

I shrugged.

"Yes or no?" she teased.

"*Si.*"

"Oh, but no! You must say it in English. Y–E–S, yes. Say it after me. Yes."

"Y–ess."

"Good! Bravo!" the girl laughed. "It is your first word in English and you will never forget it."

"Why?" I asked.

"Because I told you, foolish one! Because I told you, you will never forget the word and you will never forget me."

It was true. Mary Accurso was her name. It might have been possible for me to forget how I learned to say "yes" in English. But Mary Accurso—never.

Our first home in America was a tenement flat near the East River at 112th Street on the site of what is now Jefferson Park. The sunlight and fresh air of our mountain home in Lucania were replaced by four walls and people over and under and on all sides of us, until it seemed that humanity from all corners of the world had congregated in this section of New York City known as East Harlem.

The cobbled streets. The endless, monotonous rows of tenement buildings that shut out the sky. The traffic of wagons and carts and carriages and the clopping of horses' hoofs which struck sparks in the night. The smell of the river at ebb tide. The moaning of fog horns. The clanging of bells and the screeching of sirens as a fire broke out somewhere in the neighborhood. Dank hallways. Long flights of wooden stairs and the toilet in the hall. And the water, which to my mother was one of the great wonders of America—water with just the twist of a handle, and only a few paces from the kitchen. It took her a long time to get used to this luxury. Water and a few other conveniences were the compensations the New World had to offer.

"With the Aviglianese you are always safe," my father would say. "They are your countrymen, *paesani*. They will always stand by you."

The idea of family and clan was carried from Avigliano in southern Italy to East Harlem. From the River to First Avenue, 112th Street was the Avigli-anese Colony in New York City and closest to us were the Accurso and Salvatore families. My father had lived with the Accursos during the six years he was trying to save enough for a little place to live and the money for *l'umbarco*. In fact, it was Carmela, wife of his friend Vito Accurso and mother of the girl who met us at the boat, who saved his money for him, until the needed amount had accumulated. It was Carmela Accurso who made ready the tenement flat and arranged the welcoming party with relatives and friends to greet us upon our arrival. During this celebration my mother sat dazed, unable to realize that at last the torment of the trip was over and that here was America. It was Mrs. Accurso who put her arm comfortingly about my mother's shoulder and led her away from the party and into the hall and showed her the water faucet. "Courage! You will get used to it here. See! Isn't it wonderful how the water comes out?"

Through her tears my mother managed a smile.

In all of her years in America, my mother never saw the inside of a school. My father went only once, and that was when he took me and my two younger brothers to *La Soupa Scuola* (the "Soup School"), as it was called among the immigrants of my generation. We headed along Second Avenue in the direction of 115th Street, my father walking in front, holding the hands of my two brothers, while I followed along with a boy of my own age, Vito Salvatore, whose family had arrived from Avigliano seven years before.

My long European trousers had been

replaced by the short knickers of the time, and I wore black ribbed stockings and new American shoes. To all outward appearances I was an American, except that I did not speak a word of English.

Vito kept chanting what sounded like gibberish to me, all the while casting sidelong glances in my direction as though nursing some delightful secret.

"Mrs. Cutter cut the butter ten times in the gutter!"

"What the devil are you singing—an American song?" I asked in the dialect of our people.

"You'll meet the devil all right." And again, in English, "Mrs. Cutter cut the butter ten times in the gutter! Only this devil wears skirts and carries a stick this long. Wham, and she lets you have it across the back! This, my dear Narduccio, is your new head teacher."

Was it possible? A woman teacher! "In Avigliano we were taught by men," I bragged to my friend. "There was Maestro Mecca. Strong? When he cracked your hand with his ruler it went numb for a week. And you are trying to scare me with your woman teacher . . ."

I spoke with pride. Already "yesterday" was taking on a new meaning. I was lonely. I missed the mountains. I missed my friends at the shoemaker shop and my uncles and the life I had always known. In the face of a strange and uncertain future, Avigliano now loomed in a new and nostalgic light. Even unpleasant remembrances had a fascination of their own. Who had felt the blows of Don Salvatore Mecca could stand anything.

The Soup School was a three-story wooden building hemmed in by two five-story tenements at 116th Street and Second Avenue. When Vito pointed it out I experienced a shock. It appeared huge and impressive. I was ashamed to let him know that in Avigliano our school consisted of only one room, poorly lighted and poorly heated, with benches that hadn't been changed in fifty years. However, at this moment something really wonderful happened to take my thoughts from the poverty of our life in Avigliano.

Before entering the school, my father led us into a little store close at hand. There was a counter covered by glass and in it all manner and kinds of sweets such as we had never seen before. "Candi!" my father told us, grinning. "This is what is called candi in America."

"C-a-n-d-y!" know-it-all Vito repeated in my ear.

We were even allowed to select the kind we wanted. I remember how I selected some little round cream-filled chocolates which tasted like nothing I had every eaten before. It was unheard-of to eat sweets on a school day, even though this was a special occasion. Anyway, the only candy I knew was confetti, the sugar-coated almond confection which we had only on feast days or from the pocket of my uncle the priest on some very special occasion, and for which we kissed his hand in return. But today my father was especially happy. He ate a piece of candy too. The picture of us there on the street outside the Soup School eating candy and having a good time will never fade.

The Soup School got its name from the fact that at noontime a bowl of soup was served to us with some white, soft bread that made better spitballs than eating in comparison with the substantial and solid homemade bread to which I was accustomed. The school itself was organized and maintained by the Female Guardian Society of America. Later on I found out that this Society was sponsored by wealthy people concerned about the immigrants and their children. How much this organization accomplished among immigrants in New York City would be difficult to estimate. But this I do know, that among the immigrants of my generation and even later *La Soupa Scuola* is still vivid in our boyhood memories.

Why we went to the Soup School instead of the regular elementary public school I have not the faintest idea, except that possibly the first Aviglianese to arrive in New York sent his child there and everyone else followed suit—and also possibly because in those days a bowl of soup was a bowl of soup.

Once at the Soup School I remember the teacher gave each child a bag of oatmeal to take home. This food was supposed to make you big and strong. You ate it for breakfast. My father examined the stuff, tested it with his fingers. To him it was the kind of bran that was fed to pigs in Avigliano.

"What kind of a school is this?" he shouted. "They give us the food of animals to eat and send it home to us with our children! What are we coming to next?"

By the standards I had come to know and understand in Avigliano, the Soup School was not an unpleasant experience. I had been reared in a strict code of behavior, and this same strictness was the outstanding characteristic of the first of my American schools. Nor can I say, as I had indicated to Vito, that a blow from Mrs. Cutter ever had the lustiness of my old teacher, Don Salvatore Mecca. But what punishment lacked in power, it gained by the exacting personality of our principal.

Middle-aged, stockily built, gray hair parted in the middle, Mrs. Cutter lived up to everything my cousin Vito had said about her and much more. Attached to an immaculate white waist by a black ribbon, her prince nez fell from her nose and dangled in moments of anger. She moved about the corridors and classrooms of the Soup School ever alert and ready to strike at any infringement of school regulations.

I was sitting in class trying to memorize and pronounce words written on the blackboard—words which had absolutely no meaning to me. It seldom seemed to occur to our teachers that explanations were necessary.

"B-U-T-T-E-R–butter–butter," I singsonged with the rest of the class, learning as always by rote, learning things which often I didn't understand but which had a way of sticking in my mind.

Softly the door opened and Mrs. Cutter entered the classroom. For a large and heavy-set woman she moved quickly, without making any noise. We were not supposed to notice or even pretend we had seen her as she slowly made her way between the desks and straight-backed benches. 'B-U-T-T-E-R," I intoned. She was behind me now. I could feel her presence hovering over me. I did not dare take my eyes from the blackboard. I had done nothing and could conceive of no possible reason for an attack, but with Mrs. Cutter this held no significance. She carried a short bamboo switch. On her finger she wore a heavy gold wedding ring. For an instant I thought she was going to pass me by and then suddenly her clenched fist with the ring came down on my head.

I had been trained to show no emotion in the face of punishment, but this was too much. However, before I had time to react to the indignity of this assault, an amazing thing happened. Realizing that she had hurt me unjustly, Mrs. Cutter's whole manner changed. A look of concern came into her eyes. She took hold of my arm, uttering conciliatory words which I did not understand. Later Vito explained to me that she was saying, "I'm sorry. I didn't mean it. Sit down now and be a good boy!"

Every day before receiving our bowl of soup we recited the Lord's Prayer. I had no inkling of what the words meant. I knew only that I was expected to bow my head. I looked around to see what was going on. Swift and simple, the teacher's blackboard pointer brought the idea home to me. I never batted an eyelash after that.

I learned arithmetic and penmanship and spelling—every misspelled word written ten times or more, traced painfully and carefully in my blankbook. I do not know how many times I wrote "I must not talk." In this same way I learned how to read in English, learned geography and grammar, the states of the Union and all the capital cities—and memory gems—choice bits of poetry and sayings. Most learning was done in unison. You recited to the teacher standing at attention. Chorus work. Repetition. Repetition until the things you learned beat in your brain even at night when you were falling asleep.

I think of the modern child with his complexes and his need for "self-expression"! He will never know the forceful and vitalizing influence of a Soup School or a Mrs. Cutter.

I vividly remember the assembly periods. A long narrow room with large windows at either end, long rows of hard benches without backs, and the high platform at one end with a piano, a large table, several chairs, and the American flag. There were no pictures of any kind on the walls.

Silence! Silence! Silence! This was the characteristic feature of our existence at the Soup School. You never made an unnecessary noise or said an unnecessary word. Outside in the hall we lined up by size, girls in one line and boys in another, without uttering a sound. Eyes front and at attention. Lord help you if you broke the rule of silence. I can still see a distant relative of mine, a girl named Miluzza, who could never stop talking, standing in a corner behind Mrs. Cutter throughout an entire assembly with a spring-type clothespin fastened to her lower lip as punishment. Uncowed, defiant—Miluzza with that clothespin dangling from her lip . . .

The piano struck up a march and from the hall we paraded into assembly—eyes straight ahead in military style. Mrs. Cutter was there on the platform, dominating the scene, her eyes penetrating every corner of the assembly hall. It was always the same. We stood at attention as the Bible was read and at attention as the flag was waved back and forth, and we sang the same song. I didn't know what the words meant but I sang it loudly with all the rest, in my own way, "Tree Cheers for de Red Whatzam Blu!"

But best of all was another song that we used to sing at these assemblies. It was a particular favorite of Mrs. Cutter's, and we sang it with great gusto, "Honest boys who never tread the streets." This was in the days when we not only trod the streets but practically lived in them.

Three or four years after we had established ourselves in our first home in America, word got around that the city was going to tear down several blocks of tenements to make way for a park. The park took a long time in coming. Demolition was slow and many families stayed on until the wrecking crews were almost at their doors.

The buildings had been condemned and turned over to the city, and together with Vito and my other companions, I played in a neighborhood of rubble and debris and abandoned buildings. We stole lead from the primitive plumbing to sell to the junk man. We stole bricks and chipped off the old mortar and sold them again. And in order to do this, we had to scour around the area for old baby-carriage wheels to make carts in which to carry off the stuff that we stole.

My father worked as general handyman in a German tavern or cafe on 22nd Street. Downstairs there were bowling alleys, and during the winter he was kept pretty busy setting up pins along with his other work, but in summer business slackened and he was often without work for weeks at a time. When he did work he made seven or eight dollars a week and extra tips. But work or no work, money in our house was scarce. My mother kept saying, "What are we going to do?" and my father would always answer, "What can I do?" If there is no work there is no work. You'll have to do the best you can."

It was a curious fatalistic attitude among our people in America that while they deplored their economic stuation they seldom tried hard to do anything about it. Generations of hardship were behind them. Life was such. "*La volonta di Dio!*" For them the pattern could never change, though it might, perhaps, for their children.

Our kitchen table was covered by an oilcloth with a picture of Christopher Columbus first setting foot on American soil. It was the familiar scene of Columbus grasping the flag of Spain, surrounded by his men, with Indians crowding around. More than once my father glared at this oilcloth and poured a malediction on Columbus and his great discovery.

One day I came home from the Soup School with a report card for my father to sign. It was during one of these particularly bleak periods. I remember that my friend Vito Salvatore happened to be there, and Mary Accurso had stopped in for a moment to see my mother. With a weary expression my father glanced over the marks on the report card and was about to sign it. However, he paused with the pen in his hand.

"What is this?" he said. "Leonard Covello! What happened to the *i* in Coviello?"

My mother paused in her mending. Vito and I just looked at each other.

"Well?" my father insisted.

"Maybe the teacher just forgot to put it in," Mary suggested. "It can happen." She was going to high school now and spoke with an air of authority, and people always listened to her. This time, however, my father didn't even hear her.

"From Leonardo to Leonard I can follow," he said, "a perfectly natural process. In America anything can happen and does happen. But you don't change a family name. A name is a name. What happened to the *i*?"

"Mrs. Cutter took it out," I explained. "Every time she pronounced Coviello it came out Covello. So she took out the *i*. That way it's easier for everybody."

My father thumped Columbus on the head with his fist. "And what has this Mrs. Cutter got to do with my name?"

"What difference does it make?" I said. "It's more American. The *i* doesn't help anything." It was one of the very few times that I dared oppose my father. But even at that age I was beginning to feel that anything that made a name less foreign was an improvement.

Vito came to my rescue. "My name is Victor–Vic. That's what everybody calls me now."

"Vica. Stricka. Nicka. You crazy in the head!" my father yelled at him.

For a moment my father sat there, bitter rebellion building in him. Then with a shrug of resignation, he signed the report card and shoved it over to me. My mother now suddenly entered the argument. "How is it possible to do this to a name? Why did you sign the card? Narduccio, you will have to tell your teacher that a name cannot be changed just like that. . . ."

"Mamma, you don't understand."

"What is there to understand? A person's life and his honor is in his name. He never changes it. A name is not a shirt or a piece of underwear."

My father got up from the table, lighted the twisted stump of a Toscano cigar and moved out of the argument. "Honor!" he muttered to himself.

"You must explain this to your teacher," my mother insisted. "It was a mistake. She will know. She will not let it happen again. You will see."

"It was no mistake. On purpose. The *i* is out and Mrs. Cutter made it Covello. You just don't understand!"

"Will you stop saying that!" my mother insisted. "I don't understand. I don't understand. What is there to understand? Now that you have become Americanized you understand everything and I understand nothing."

With her in this mood I dared make no answer. Mary went over and put her hand on my mother's shoulder. I beckoned to Vito and together we walked out of the flat and downstairs into the street.

"She just doesn't understand," I kept saying.

"I'm gonna take the *e* off the end of my name and make it just Salvator," Vito said. "After all, we're not in Italy now."

Vito and I were standing dejectedly

under the gas light on the corner, watching the lamplighter moving from post to post along the cobblestone street and then disappearing around the corner on First Avenue. Somehow or other the joy of childhood had seeped out of our lives. We were only boys, but a sadness that we could not explain pressed down upon us. Mary came and joined us. She had a book under her arm. She stood there for a moment, while her dark eyes surveyed us questioningly.

"But they don't understand!" I insisted.

Mary smiled. "Maybe some day, you will realize that *you* are the one who does not understand."

# George Kennan, "The Japanese in the San Francisco Public Schools," 1907

*George Kennan (1845–1924) was one of America's preeminent journalists from the 1880s to the 1920s. The country's first expert reporter on Russia, Kennan also turned his hand to other subjects of international and domestic interest, including the imbroglio between America and Japan that resulted from an attempt to segregate Japanese schoolchildren in San Francisco in 1906. In the article that follows, Kennan gives an excellent description of what happened in California and why. Like President Roosevelt, who was drawn into an unwanted predicament with Japan as a result of this local controversy, Kennan expressed dismay at the illiberalism and intolerance of Californians, many of whom were themselves of immigrant background, toward their Japanese neighbors.*

*Source:* George Kennan, "The Japanese in the San Francisco Public Schools," *The Outlook* 86 (June 1907): 246–252.

Soon after the almost complete destruction of San Francisco by earthquake and fire, in April, 1906, the Government of Japan telegraphed to the Government of the United States assurances of its sympathy and condolence, and a little later forwarded to the San Francisco Relief Committee and the American National Red Cross the sum of 492,000 yen ($246,000 gold) to be used in relieving the sufferings of the homeless people in the stricken city. Judged by American standards of wealth and charity, the amount thus sent was not so great as to be especially noteworthy but it exceeded the contributions of all the other foreign peoples of the earth put together, and, in view of the fact that it came from a comparatively poor nation, struggling to meet its financial obligations at the close of a great war, it was not only a generous gift, but a striking evidence of friendliness and good will.

A few weeks after the receipt of this money, and while the San Francisco Relief Committee was drawing checks against the fund of which it formed a part, Professor Omori, an eminent Japanese scientist—a man who enjoyed in his own country a reputation corresponding to that which the late Professor Langley had in ours—was stoned by hoodlums in the streets of the very city to which Japan had extended a friendly hand of sympathy and help and on the 8th of July his face was slapped by a labor union man in the California town of Eureka. In May Professor Nakamura, a member of Professor Omori's party, was personally assaulted by hoodlums in Golden Gate Park, San Francisco, and on the 8th of June he was covered with dust and ashes thrown at him by boys in the burnt district, where he was making scientific observations. In the months that immediately followed, attacks were made upon Japanese in many parts of San Francisco, and, in one case at least, upon Japanese Christians who were going peaceably to church. So far as I have been able to ascertain, such cases of violence were exceptional and sporadic, rather than general; but if American Christians had been assaulted, and if Alexander Graham Bell and Simon Newcomb had been stoned, slapped, and covered with dust and ashes by Oriental hoodlums in the streets of Sendai, just after we had sent a generous contribution for the relief of sufferers from famine in northern Japan, we should have been surprised, to say the least, and should have regarded the violence as an extraordinary return for American sympathy and help.

On the 11th of last October, less than six months after the San Francisco Relief Committee had accepted with thanks the Japanese contribution of $246,000, the San Francisco Board of Education adopted a resolution directing the principals of all the primary and grammar schools of the city to exclude Japanese pupils, and to segregate them in a so-called "Oriental School," established, originally, for the Chinese, under the provisions of a law enacted thirty-four years ago.

At first sight there would seem to be a certain strangeness and incongruity in this sequence of events. The Japanese send to the San Franciscans $246,000 as a token of helpful friendliness and sympathy, and the San Franciscans reciprocate by stoning eminent Japanese scientists in the streets, by attacking Japanese Christians who are on their way to a Sunday church service, and by excluding Japanese scholars from primary and grammar schools which they have attended for years and which are open to Italians, Germans, Scandinavians, Russians, Poles, Armenians, Mexicans, Greeks, Jews, and representatives of nearly all the nationalities of the Old World. What are the reasons for this intolerant hatred of the Japanese, which not only effaces remembrance of courtesy and kindness, but seems, in some of its manifestations, to overstep the bounds of decency and law? It must be a very strong feeling, and it must rest upon elemental facts and emotions of human nature. It is my purpose, in this article, to give the results of such study as I have been able to make of the Japanese school question on the Pacific Coast.

As the exclusion of Japanese children from the white public schools brought about the clash between the Federal authorities and the San Francisco Board of Education, I shall take up that subject first. It is, in itself, a comparatively trivial episode, but in it are involved all the factors of the Japanese problem, and it may properly serve, therefore, as an introduction to the larger and more important questions of economic competition and race antipathy.

The law under which the San Francisco Board of Education acted, when it barred the Japanese out of primary and grammar schools attended by whites, was enacted March 12, 1872, and was aimed exclusively at the Chinese. There was no Japanese immigration at that time, and the words "separate schools for children of Mongolian or Chinese descent" were evidently intended to apply only to immigrants from the Asiatic mainland. The "segregation" school established under the provisions of this law was situated in the heart of Chinatown, and was officially known, for many years, as the "Chinese School." When Japanese immigrants in considerable numbers began to arrive in San Francisco, their children were not "segregated" in the Chinese School, but were admitted, without question or objection, to the schools attended by whites; and, so far as I have been able to ascertain, it was not until 1901, when the labor unions obtained control of the city government, that any concerted action was taken against the Japanese, in the schools or out of them. After that time there slowly grew up a feeling of hostility to the Japanese, based partly upon their alleged untrustworthiness, partly on a fear of economic competition, and partly upon a feeling of race antipathy; and the Board of Education began to receive letters from the parents of white scholars, complaining of the enforced association of their children with the children of Japanese immigrants in the public schools. The Board, which was the creation of a labor union administration, sympathized, apparently, with these complaints, but was unable to take action upon them, owing to the fact that the Chinese School was already full, and

there was no money available for a second school of segregation.

In the early part of 1905 the Board made an effort to secure an appropriation for the opening and maintenance of a distinctively Japanese school, but, on account, apparently, of the indifference of the municipal administration, which was busily engaged in grafting, this effort had no result. It attracted the attention, however, of the Japanese Consul, and in March, 1905, that officer, learning that the chief objection to Japanese scholars in the primary and grammar schools was their advanced age, suggested to the Japanese newspapers of the city that they advise the voluntary withdrawal of the older pupils. The papers acted upon this suggestion, and most of the older pupils did withdraw. I refer to this incident only as a proof that the Japanese were amenable to reason, and were willing to act in a friendly way on a complaint that seemed to be well founded.

On the 7th of May, 1905, a number of trades union leaders founded the "Japanese and Corean Exclusion League," and this organization, by means of its meetings and its literature, soon increased the feeling of hostility to the Japanese, not only in San Francisco, but to some extent in the State. The earthquake and fire of April 18 destroyed the Chinese quarter of San Francisco, and drove so many of its residents to Oakland and Alameda that, when the Chinese School was reopened, there was room in it not only for all the Chinese scholars who presented themselves, but also for the Japanese, who at that time were distributed among twenty-three other schools. The Board of Education thereupon changed the name of the Chinese School, called it the "Oriental School," and attempted to segregate in it the Japanese scholars of the city, who for years had been attending primary and grammar schools on terms of perfect equality with children of American and European descent. When this discrimination against Japanese led to an international complication and forced the Federal Government to interfere, the Board of Education attempted to justify its action by pleading, first, that the provisions of the State law of 1872 were mandatory and gave the Board no discretion; and, second, that an overwhelming majority of the so-called Japanese "school-boys" were grown men, who ought not to be allowed to sit beside young children, and especially young girls, in primary schools. In the public and private discussion of the subject that immediately followed, the Board of Education, the California delegation in Congress, the San Francisco newspapers, the Exclusion League, and trade union leaders without exception, laid most stress upon the age of Japanese "boys" in the primary schools. Nobody attempted to ascertain the facts, but all declared, without inquiry or investigation, that the association of Japanese men with school-girls of tender years in the intimacy of school life was an intolerable evil which could no longer be endured. President Altmann, of the Board of Education, said: "We do not care to have our little children mixing with adult Japanese." (*San Francisco Chronicle,* December 7.) Senator Perkins declared that there were "not forty Japanese children of school age in San Francisco."

(*San Francisco Examiner,* December 7.) Representative Hayes said: "Most of the Japanese pupils are youths from fifteen to twenty-five. It is nothing more than right and just to prohibit their attending school with young children." (*San Francisco Chronicle,* December 4.) The *San Francisco Call* said (December 4): "It is deemed inexpedient that adults should associate with little children in the intimate relations of school life." According to the San Francisco Newsletter (December 8): "A city ordinance eliminating all children, of whatever race or color, from the primary schools, when over sixteen, would eliminate ninety-five per cent. of the Japanese." Alfred Roncovieri, Superintendent of Schools, declared that "these so-called Japanese children are, ninety-five per cent. of them, young men. We object to an adult Japanese sitting beside a twelve-year-old girl. If this be prejudice, we are the most prejudiced people in the world." (*San Francisco Examiner,* December 5.) Misled by these confident assertions, the usually accurate and well-informed correspondent of a prominent New York journal said: "It will be news to most Easterners that almost none of the Japanese school-boys are boys. Practically without exception, they are full grown men, between the ages of twenty and thirty. Yet Japan expects them to be allowed to sit side by side, day after day, with American boys, and, more extraordinary yet, girls of tender years." (*New York Sun,* December 13.)

Persons and newspapers hostile to the Japanese, however, did not base their opposition to the presence of the latter in white schools solely upon age. Without investigation or inquiry, they began to attribute to "adult" Japanese "school-boys" a low moral standard and corrupting influence. The Berkeley Gazette, for example, asked: "Is there a power lodged anywhere in the universe that may oblige our young children to associate with men, in or out of school, who are not up to our standard of morals?" It might pertinently be asked, perhaps, whether the standard of morals referred to is that of the municipal administration which has excluded the Japanese from the white schools, and whether the record of graft, frauds, assaults, hold-ups, burglaries, rapes, and murders, which has recently given San Francisco unenviable fame, could have been paralleled in Japan at any period of its history.

Taking practically the same view of "adults" in primary schools that is taken by the Berkeley Gazette, the conservative Sacramento Union said: "We will not consent that our little ones shall suffer infection, in mind, in morals, or in manners, to please anybody." The idea that an American boy might deteriorate mentally, or lose his good manners, as a result of associating with Japanese of any age, strikes an American who has lived in Japan as somewhat ludicrous; but I do not wish to be hypercritical.

Adopting, apparently, the view of the California papers with regard to the character of Japanese scholars, the Chicago Inter-Ocean inquired: "How would people in the East like to have their little daughters forced to associate in school with grown men, whose morals may be doubtful and whose moral ideas are certainly not American ?" The *San Francisco Call* said: "We regard the public schools as part of the home, and we are not willing that our children should meet Asiatics in intimate association. This is 'race prejudice,' and we stand by it. If the Japanese want to fight about trifles, they can be accommodated." The *Call* does not say who is going to accommodate them—the United States or the State of California; but the latter is by no means lacking in self-confidence. P. H. McCarthy, President of the San Francisco Building Trades Council, declared, at a mass-meeting of the Exclusion League, that "the States west of the Rockies could whip Japan at a moment's notice." He had perhaps forgotten, in the heat of oratorical excitement, the boasts of Russia in January, 1904.

Now, what conclusion would a disinterested and dispassionate reader draw from the statements, interviews, editorials, and speeches above set forth? Would he not be forced to believe that Japanese scholars swarm in the primary and grammar schools of San Francisco; that they are all males; that ninety-five per cent. of them are full-grown men; that they sit in the class-rooms beside "twelve-year-old girls" and "children of tender years;" that their ethical standard is low, and that their influence, generally, is demoralizing and corrupting? I do not see myself what other conclusion he could draw, when the President of the Board of Education, the Superintendent of Schools, the San Francisco newspapers, the Exclusion League, and the California delegation in Congress are all in substantial agreement as to the alleged facts. Now what are the real facts?

I talked with the Superintendent of Schools and every member of the Board of Education; I interviewed the Japanese Consul; I obtained and compared statistics from the Board of Education on one side and from the Japanese Association on the other, and availed myself, generally, of every source of information open to me. I found that the situation when the Japanese were excluded from the primary and grammar schools was as follows:

The total number of pupils in the San Francisco public schools was 28,736 (December 8, 1906). Judging from their names, they comprised representatives of almost every nationality in Europe. The Superintendent of Schools, Mr. Roncovieri, was an Italian, and the President of the Board of Education, Mr. Altmann, was a Jew—a representative of a race that is still excluded from schools, wholly or partially, in one of the greatest Empires of the Old World. Of the 28,736 school-children in San Francisco on the 8th of last December, there were, in primary and grammar schools, just 93 Japanese, or a little more than one to a school building. Of these 93 Japanese nearly one-third were born in the United States, and 28 were girls. Of the 65 boys 34 were under fifteen years of age. Of the 31 who were over fifteen only two had reached the age of twenty, and the average age of the remainder was 17.2. Twenty-five of them were in grammar schools, so that the number "sitting beside children of tender age" in primary schools was six, as follows:

Dudley Stone Primary 3
Grant Primary 1
Henry Durant Primary 1
Laguna Honda Primary 1
Total 6

Six Japanese over fifteen years of age, attending primary schools, in a total school population of 28,736, would not seem to constitute a very serious menace to American morality, even if they were all depraved, and even if it were not possible to seat them at a distance from infant girls; but *are* Japanese schoolboys depraved, or morally objectionable in any way? In an interview with a reporter of the San Francisco Chronicle, Mr. Altmann, President of the Board of Education, admitted that "nothing can be said against the general character and deportment of Japanese scholars." (*San Francisco Chronicle,* December 9.) In reply to a direct and comprehensive question on the subject Mr. Alfred Roncovieri, Superintendent of Schools, said to me personally: "No complaint of bad conduct, on the part of a Japanese scholar, has ever come to my knowledge." In a private letter now in my possession, one of the oldest and most experienced teachers in the San Francisco public schools says: "The statement that the influence of the Japanese in our schools has a tendency toward immorality is false and absolutely without foundation. From all I have ever heard in conferences with other school men, as well as from my own continuous and careful observation, there has never been the slightest cause for a shadow of suspicion affecting the conduct of one of these Japanese pupils. On the contrary, I have found that they have furnished examples of industry, patience, unobtrusiveness, obedience, and honesty in their work, which have greatly helped many efficient teachers to create the proper moral atmosphere for their class-rooms. Japanese and American children have always been on good terms in my class-rooms, and in others concerning which I was informed. They work side by side without interference or friction, and often a Japanese student would be a great favorite among his American classmates. In all my years of experience there has never come to me, orally or in writing, from the parents whose children have attended my school, one hint of complaint or dissatisfaction concerning the instruction of their children in the same school or in the same rooms with Japanese; nor has there ever been complaint or protest from teachers with regard to this co-education."

Mr. E. C. Moore, Superintendent of Schools in Los Angeles, says, in another private letter: "Replying to your inquiry as to the status of Japanese pupils in the schools of Los Angeles, I beg to say that during all the time I have been in the office of Superintendent of Schools here I have not heard a single word of protest against them. They are given every opportunity to attend school that American boys and girls have. We find them quiet and industrious in their school work, and such good students that our principals and teachers believe them to have a most helpful influence upon the other pupils with whom they associate. As a California school man, I bitterly regret the action of the San Francisco school authorities. It was wholly unnecessary, in my view, and is, I am glad to say, not

representative of public opinion in California."

Judging from my own observation of Japanese school-boys in Japan, I should say that the more American school-boys associate with them, the better for the latter's morals and manners. I once asked an Englishman, of mature years, who was teaching in a middle-class school in Kyoto, why there was so little misconduct in Japanese class-rooms. "I have been through dozens of schools," I said, "of all grades, and have listened to recitations in hundreds of class-rooms; but I have never seen any inattention, whispering, throwing of spit-balls, making of faces, or disorder of any sort. What is the reason?" He looked at me searchingly for a moment, as if to take my measure, and then replied quietly: "The Japanese are born civilized."

"Do you mean to suggest that we Westerners are not born civilized?" I demanded.

"Exactly that," he replied. "We, Englishmen and Americans, are born barbarians. Most of us become civilized, but we elevate ourselves, in youth, by effort and struggle. Japanese boys inherit the results of centuries of civilized training, and they have better control of themselves and are far more amenable to discipline than our boys are. At least that's my explanation of the fact that you have noticed."

When the English teacher made this reply to me, in January, 1906, I little thought that, before the end of the year, I should hear the exclusion of Japanese scholars from the San Francisco schools defended on the ground that they were likely to "infect the minds, morals, and manners" of American children. I should have said that the infection was far more likely to proceed in the opposite direction.

In scholarship the Japanese pupils have everywhere taken high rank. In a letter written on the 29th of December, 1906, to the Electrical Workers' Union of Oakland, the Secretary of the San Francisco Board of Education said: "You are doubtless aware that Japanese pupils, coming to this city partly educated, have been able so successfully to compete with our white children as to win from the latter the class medals that were intended for the children of our taxpayers." In other words, the Japanese, coming to America with an imperfect knowledge of the English language, or with no knowledge of it at all, have been so studious and diligent as to carry off most of the honors; and this is urged as a reason for their exclusion!

Although the ninety-three Japanese scholars in San Francisco were distributed among twenty-three schools, forty-two of them, or nearly one-half, were in two schools, viz., the Redding Primary and the Pacific Heights Grammar. In the former their average age was 9.6 years and in the latter 16.5. Most of the grammar school Japanese were probably older than the majority of their associates; but as the Board of Education could not give me age statistics of the latter in detail, I am unable to say how much older. The difference may have amounted to two or three years at the time of graduation. If, however, this difference was undesirable, and if there was objection to the six Japanese who were more than fifteen years old in the primary schools, the Board of Education had two simple and perfectly effective remedies: viz., first, the opening of a separate school for pupils of all nationalities who were advanced in age and backward in scholarship; and, second, the establishment of an undiscriminating age limit for all scholars in primary and grammar schools. Neither of these remedies would have raised a question of race or nationality, and neither would have given offense. Non-discriminating restriction, however, would not have met the approval of parents who objected to the association of their children with Japanese of any age (if there really were any such parents), nor would it have satisfied the Exclusion League and the labor union leaders, who feared the economic competition of Japanese adults, and who saw in the school question an excellent opportunity to excite feeling against the Japanese as a race, by appealing to the love of parents for their children, and by drawing imaginary pictures of immoral Japanese men "sitting beside twelve-year-old girls." There may possibly be schools, in some part of the world, where teachers allow "men," moral or immoral, to sit beside twelve-year-old girls; but in my tolerably varied experience I have never happened to come across such a school in Europe, Asia, or America. Everywhere and always I have found boys and girls at separate desks or in separate seats. The cry of "Asiatic men sitting beside immature American girls," however, was well calculated to fire the heart of the populace in California, and even to wake up the indifferent East. Tens of thousands of parents in San Francisco, and perhaps hundreds of thousands on the Pacific Coast, were deceived and excited by this unfair presentation of the case, and the Board of Education and the San Francisco newspapers are largely responsible for the state of feeling thus brought about. They declare, with much vehemence, that the President was chiefly to blame for the excitement over the school question, because he "meddled" with a matter that was none of his business; but it seems to me, upon a fair judgment of the case, that a far more potent cause of excitement was the reckless—not to say dishonest—method of dealing with the question which was adopted by the Board of Education, the Exclusion League, and the San Francisco press; the failure to investigate, the suppression of some facts and the exaggeration of others, and, above all, the constant holding up of imaginary pictures of full-grown Japanese men sitting beside American children, and especially "girls of tender years."

The San Francisco papers say: "It is a strange but instructive fact that in the miles and miles of editorials that we have seen in the Eastern papers, not one of the writers has taken the slightest pains to ascertain the facts." But can these journals seriously affirm that *they* have taken any pains to ascertain the facts? I read them carefully for several months, and if I had not had other sources of information, I might have supposed that there were hundreds, if not thousands, of Japanese in the public schools of San Francisco; that most of them were grown men; that there were great numbers of these "adults" sitting beside infant

children in the primary schools; and that their morals were doubtful, if not certainly bad. Up to the present time, no paper in San Francisco, so far as I am aware, has ever obtained and published detailed statistics of Japanese scholars in the primary and grammar schools, with the number in each grade, the average and maximum age in each grade, the age by grades as compared with that of American scholars, the number and distribution of adults, and the reports of teachers with regard to the character and deportment of Japanese pupils in general. All of this information might have been obtained, and it would have seemed the most natural thing in the world to get it and publish it, so that the people of the city, the State, and the United States might have a few definite and specific facts upon which to base a reasonable judgment. Such, however, is not the course of procedure in a community dominated by labor unions, when the subject in hand relates to an Asiatic race. It would be impossible to make an effective labor union weapon out of the school question if it were once admitted that Japanese scholars are studious, diligent, and moral, and that, in a school population of 28,736, only six Japanese boys above the age of fifteen are enrolled in the primary grade.

## Theodore Roosevelt to Philander Knox, February 8, 1909

*The anti-Japanese agitation in California, which came to a head in the 1906 San Francisco public school controversy, placed President Theodore Roosevelt in a difficult politi-*

*cal and diplomatic position. Angry at the San Franciscans for the hysterical intolerance of their effort to remove and segregate the small number of Japanese students in the public schools, and aware that their action would create an international incident with Japan, the president prevailed upon them to revoke the plan. In order to achieve this goal, however, Roosevelt had to negotiate the "Gentlemen's Agreement" with Japan (completed in 1908), by which Japan agreed to stop the emigration of Japanese laborers to the mainland United States. The following excerpts from a letter of Roosevelt's to the incoming Secretary of State Philander Knox illustrate the subtlety of Roosevelt's understanding of the Japanese American situation. The president was astute about the strategic importance of Japan, realistic about the prejudices of many Americans toward the Japanese, yet respectful toward both Japan and the Japanese. (Because Roosevelt respected power, his attitude toward China, then a weak nation, was much less charitable.)*

*Source:* Theodore Roosevelt, Letter to Philander Knox, February 8, 1909 (Papers of Theodore Roosevelt, Manuscript Division, Library of Congress), from Mortimer J. Adler, ed., *The Annals of America, vol. 13, 1905–1913, The Progressive Era* (Chicago: Encyclopedia Britannica, 1968), pp. 173–176.

*My Dear Senator Knox:*
You are soon to become secretary of state under Mr. Taft. At the outset both he and you will be overwhelmed with every kind of work; but there is one matter of foreign policy of such great and permanent importance that I wish to lay it before the President-to-be and yourself. I speak of the relations of the United States and Japan.

It is utterly impossible to foretell as regards either foreign or domestic policy what particular questions may appear as at the moment of most engrossing interest. It may be that there will be no ripple of trouble between Japan and the United States during your term of service. It may very well be that you will have acute trouble about Cuba, or with Venezuela or in Central America, or with some European power; but it is not likely that grave international complications—that is, complications which can possibly lead to serious war—can come from any such troubles. If we have to interfere again in Cuba, or take Possession of the island, it will be exasperating, and we may in consequence have to repeat our Philippine experiences by putting down an annoying but unimportant guerrilla outbreak. But this would represent merely annoyance. The same would be true of anything in Central America or Venezuela.

I do not believe that Germany has any designs that would bring her in conflict with the Monroe Doctrine. The last seven years have tended steadily toward a better understanding of Germany on our part, and a more thorough understanding on the part of Germany that she must not expect colonial expansion in South America. As for England, I cannot imagine serious trouble with her. The settlement of the Alaskan boundary removed the one grave danger. The treaties now before the Senate are excellent, and all we have to fear is some annoying, but hardly grave, friction in the event of the failure of the Senate to ratify them.

But with Japan the case is different. She is a most formidable military power. Her people have peculiar fighting capacity. They are very proud, very warlike, very sensitive, and are influenced by two contradictory feelings; namely, a great self-confidence, both ferocious and conceited, due to their victory over the mighty empire of Russia; and a great touchiness because they would like to be considered as on a full equality with, as one of the brotherhood of, Occidental nations, and have been bitterly humiliated to find that even their allies, the English, and their friends, the Americans, won't admit them to association and citizenship, as they admit the least advanced or most decadent European peoples. Moreover, Japan's population is increasing rapidly and demands an outlet; and the Japanese laborers, small farmers, and petty traders would, if permitted, flock by the hundred thousand into the United States, Canada, and Australia.

Now for our side. The events of the last three years have forced me to the clear understanding that our people will not permit the Japanese to come in large numbers among them; will not accept them as citizens; will not tolerate their presence as large bodies of permanent settlers. This is just as true in Australia and Colombia as in our Rocky Mountain and Pacific states; but at present the problem is more acute with us because the desire of the Japanese to come here has grown. The opposition to the presence of the Japanese, I have reluctantly come to feel, is entirely warranted, and not only must be. but ought to be, heeded by the national government in the interest of our people and our civilization; and this in spite of the fact that many of the manifestations of the opposition are unwise and improper to the highest degree.

To permit the Japanese to come in large numbers into this country would be to cause a race problem and invite and insure a race contest. It is necessary to keep them out. But it is almost equally necessary that we should both show all possible courtesy and consideration in carrying out this necessarily disagreeable policy of exclusion, and that we should be thoroughly armed, so as to prevent the Japanese from feeling safe in attacking us. Unfortunately, great masses of our people show a foolish indifference to arming, and at the same time a foolish willingness to be offensive to the Japanese.

Labor unions pass violent resolutions against the Japanese and almost at the same moment protest against strengthening our military resources on land or sea. Big corporations seek to introduce Japanese coolies so as to get cheap labor, and thereby invite agitation which they are powerless to quell. The peace societies, and senators and congressmen like Burton of Ohio, Perkins of California, Perkins of New York, Tawney of Minnesota, McCall of Massachusetts, and Bartholdt of Missouri blatantly or furtively oppose the Navy and hamper its upbuilding, while doing nothing whatever to prevent insult to Japan. The California legislature is threatening to pass the most offensive kind of legislation aimed at the Japanese, and yet it reelects a wretched creature like Perkins to the Senate although he has opposed, with his usual feeble timidity and so far as he dared, the upbuilding of the Navy, following Hale's lead.

We are therefore faced by the fact that our people will not tolerate, and ought not to tolerate, the presence among them of large bodies of Japanese; and that so long as they are here in large bodies there is always chance either of violence on the part of mobs or of indiscreet and improper action by the legislative bodies of the Western states under demagogic influence. Furthermore, in Hawaii the Japanese already many times outnumber the whites, and have shown on more than one recent occasion a spirit both truculent and insolent.

In Hawaii the trouble is primarily due to the shortsighted greed of the sugar planters and of the great employers generally, who showed themselves incapable of thinking of the future of their children and anxious only to make fortunes from estates tilled by coolie labor. Accordingly, they imported, first masses of Chinese laborers and, then masses of Japanese laborers. Throughout my term as President, I have so far as possible conducted our policy against this desire of the sugar planters, against the theory of turning Hawaii into an island of coolie tilled plantations, and in favor of making so far as possible the abode of small settler.

With this purpose, I have done everything I could to encourage the immigration of southern Europeans to the islands, and have endeavored so far as I could in the absence of legislation to restrict the entrance of Asiatic coolies. So far as possible our aim should be to diminish the number of Japanese in the islands without any regard to the fortunes of the sugar planters, and to bring in Europeans, no matter of what ancestry, in order that the islands may be filled with a white population of our general civilization and culture.

As regards the mainland, our policy should have three sides and should be shaped, not to meet the exigencies of this year or next but to meet what may occur for the next few decades. Japan is poor and is therefore reluctant to go to war. Moreover, Japan is vitally interested in China and on the Asiatic mainland and her wiser statesmen will, if possible, prevent her getting entangled in a war with us, because whatever its result it would hamper and possibly ruin Japan when she came to deal again with affairs in China. But with so proud and sensitive a people neither lack of money nor possible future complications will prevent a war if once they get sufficiently hurt and angry; and there is always danger of a mob outbreak there just as there is danger of a mob outbreak here.

Our task therefore is on the one hand to meet the demands which our own people make and which cannot permanently be resisted, and on the other to treat Japan so courteously that she will not be offended more than is necessary; and at the same time to prepare our fleet in such shape that she will feel very cautious about attacking us. Disturbances like those going on at present are certain to occur unless the Japanese immigration, so far as it is an immigration, for settlement, stops. For the last six months under our agreement with Japan it has been stopped to the extent that more Japanese have left the country than have come into it. But the Japanese should be made clearly to understand that this process must continue and if there is relaxation it will be impossible to prevent our people from enacting drastic exclusion laws; and that in such case all of us would favor such drastic legislation.

Hand in hand with insistence on the stopping of Japanese immigration should go insistence as regards our own people that they be courteous and considerate, that they treat the Japanese who are here well; and above all that they go on with the building of the Navy, keep it at the highest point of efficiency, securing not merely battleships but an ample supply of colliers and other auxiliary vessels of every kind. Much of the necessary expense would be met by closing the useless Navy yards. By the way, the fighting Navy should not be divided; it should be kept either in the Pacific or in the Atlantic, merely a squadron being left in the other ocean, and this in such shape that, in the event of war, it could avoid attack and at once join the main body of fighting ships.

All this is so obvious that it ought not to be necessary to dwell upon it. But our people are shortsighted and have short memories—I suppose all peoples are shortsighted and have short memories. The minute we arrange matters so that for the moment everything is smooth and pleasant, the more foolish peace societies, led by men like ex-Secretary of State Foster and ex-Secretary of the Navy Long, clamor for a stoppage in the building up of the Navy. On the other hand, at the very moment when we are actually keeping out the Japanese and reducing the number of Japanese here, demagogues and agitators like those who have recently appeared in the California and Nevada legislatures work for the passage of laws which are humiliating and irritating to the Japanese and yet of no avail so far as keeping out immigrants is concerned; for this can be done effectively only by the national government.

The defenselessness of the coast, the fact that we have no army to hold or reconquer the Philippines and Hawaii, the fact that we have not enough battleships nor enough auxiliaries in the Navy—all these facts are ignored and forgotten. On the other hand, the Japanese, if we do not keep pressure upon them, will let up in their effort to control the emigration from Japan to this country; and they must be continually reminded that unless they themselves stop it, in the end this country is certain to stop it, and ought to stop it, no matter what the consequences may be.

There is no more important continuing feature of our foreign policy than this in reference to our dealing with Japan; the whole question of our dealings with the Orient is certain to grow in importance. I do not believe that there will be war, but there is always the chance that war will come; and if it did come, the calamity would be very great. And while I believe we would win, there is at least a chance of disaster. We should therefore do everything in our power to guard against the possibility of war by preventing the occurrence of conditions which would invite war and by keeping our Navy so strong that war may not come or that we may be successful if it does come.

Sincerely yours,
Theodore Roosevelt

[*Handwritten*] P.S. I enclose a copy of my telegram to the speaker of the California Lower House; this was really meant almost as much for Japan as for California, and sets forth, seemingly as incidental, what our future policy must be.

[*Handwritten*] If possible, the Japanese should be shown, what is the truth, that our keeping them out means not that they are inferior to us—in some ways they are superior—but that they are *different*; so different that, whatever the future may hold, at present the two races ought not to come together in masses.

## Letters to *Forverts* (*Jewish Daily-Forward*), 1909

*The Yiddish newspaper* Forverts, *known in English as the* Jewish Daily Forward, *was founded in New York City in 1897. Under the editorship of Abraham Cahan, one of the premier immigrant writers in the U.S., the* Forward *became America's most popular foreign-language newspaper. By the 1920s it had more than a quarter of a million readers. Both in his fictional works and in his handling of the* Forward, *Cahan showed a great sensitivity to the details of Jewish immigrant life in New York City. In order to allow the masses of Yiddish readers to express themselves through the press, Cahan created the "Bintel Brief" ("bundle of letters") in 1906. In this popular daily column, immigrants asked for*

*advice about a great variety of personal problems. Their letters, and the* Forward's *replies, provide a unique view into the struggles and hopes of Eastern European Jews, one of the largest groups of immigrants to America in the early twentieth century. The letters that follow were written to the* Forward *in 1909.*

*Source:* Forverts *(Jewish Daily Forward), excerpted from Isaac Metzker, ed.,* A Bintel Brief: Sixty Years of Letters from the Lower East Side to the Jewish Daily Forward *(Garden City, N.Y.: Doubleday, 1971), pp. 86–101.*

1909

*Dear Editor,*

Please print my letter and give me an answer. You might possibly save my life with it. I have no peace, neither day nor night, and I am afraid I will go mad because of my dreams.

I came to America three years ago from a small town in Lithuania, and I was twenty years old at that time. Besides me, my parents had five more unmarried daughters. My father was a Hebrew teacher. We used to help out by plucking chickens, making cigarettes, washing clothes for people, and we lived in poverty. The house was like a Gehenna. There was always yelling, cursing, and even beating of each other. It was bitter for me till a cousin of mine took pity on me. He sent a steamship ticket and money. He wrote that I should come to America and he would marry me.

I didn't know him, because he was a little boy when he left our town, but my delight knew no bounds. When I came to him, I found he was a sick man, and a few weeks later he died.

Then I began to work on ladies' waists. The "pleasant" life of a girl in the dreary shop must certainly be familiar to you. I toiled, and like all shopgirls, I hoped and waited for deliverance through a good match.

*Landsleit* and matchmakers were busy. I met plenty of prospective bridegrooms, but though I was attractive and well built, no one grabbed me. Thus a year passed. Then I met a woman who told me she was a match-maker and had many suitors "in stock." I spilled out all my heartaches to her. First she talked me out of marrying a work-worn operator with whom I would have to live in poverty, then she told me that pretty girls could wallow in pleasure if they made the right friends. She made such a connection for me. But I had not imagined what that meant.

What I lived through afterwards is impossible for me to describe. The woman handed me over to bandits, and when I wanted to run away from them they locked me in a room without windows and beat me savagely.

Time passed and I got used to the horrible life. Later I even had an opportunity to escape, because they used to send me out on the streets, but life had become meaningless for me anyway, and nothing mattered any more. I lived this way for six months, degraded and dejected, until I got sick and they drove me out of that house.

I appealed for admission into several hospitals, but they didn't want to take me in. I had no money, because the rogues had taken everything from me. I tried to appeal to *landsleit* for help, but since they already knew all about me,

they chased me away. I had decided to throw myself into the river, but wandering around on the streets, I met a richly dressed man who was quite drunk. I took over six hundred dollars from him and spent the money on doctors, who cured me.

Then I got a job as a maid for fine people who knew nothing about my past, and I have been working for them for quite a while. I am devoted and diligent, they like me, and everything is fine.

A short time ago the woman of the house died, but I continued to work there. In time, her husband proposed that I marry him. The children, who are not yet grown up, also want me to be their "mother." I know it would be good for them and for me to remain there. The man is honest and good; but my heart won't allow me to deceive him and conceal my past. What shall I do now?

*Miserable*

## ANSWER:

Such letters from victims of "white slavery" come to our attention quite often, but we do not publish them. We are disgusted by this plague on society, and dislike bringing it to the attention of our readers. But as we read this letter we felt we dare not discard it, because it can serve as a warning for other girls. They must, in their dreary lives, attempt to withstand these temptations and guard themselves from going astray.

This letter writer, who comes to us with her bitter and earnest tears, asking advice, has sufficient reason to fear that if the man finds out about her past he will send her away. But it is hard to conceal something that many people know. Such a thing cannot be kept secret forever. When the man finds out about it from someone else, he would feel that she had betrayed him and it would be worse.

Therefore, "Honesty is the best policy." She should tell him the truth, and whatever will be, will be.

1909

*Worthy Editor,*

I find myself in such a situation that I need your advice. I am one of the immigrant shopgirls, twenty years old, and I earn a decent living.

A short time ago I became acquainted with a young man who goes to a preparatory school and wants to become a doctor. He came to my house many times to visit, but as time went on I began to fall in love with him. He also declared his love for me, and that's when my trouble began.

Six months ago I received a letter from my parents, in which they propose a match for me with one of our relatives who is also in America. He does not live in New York. I don't know the boy, but we correspond and have sent each other photographs. We liked each other from the pictures, and I know that he is a businessman and makes a decent living. But my heart draws me to the other boy.

Honorable Editor, tell me what to do. My friends have tried to talk me out of tying myself down to work for seven years to help my friend through his studies. I would be twenty-seven years old then and I will have lost the bloom of youth af-

ter seven years of toil in the shop. That is why I worry about my future.

How shall I solve this problem? Shall I refuse him and try to forget him? Whatever you advise me, I will do.

*Your constant reader,*

*A. B.*

### ANSWER:

After years of study many such young students often fall out of love and leave the girls who have helped them. A graduate doctor doesn't want to marry a toil-worn old maid. She has worked her fingers to the bone and exhausted herself to help him become "Sir Doctor." All that can be said to him when he leaves her is "You should be ashamed of yourself, Sir Doctor." But one cannot generalize and say that all young men who complete their education act this way. It may be possible that the letter writer's friend is different. However, it is hard to judge, and therefore difficult to advise the writer how to act. She must make her own decision in this matter.

1909

*Dear Mr. Editor,*

I was born in a small town in Russia, and until I was sixteen I studied in *Talmud Torahs* and *yeshivas*, but when I came to America I changed quickly. I was influenced by the progressive newspapers, the literature, I developed spiritually and became a freethinker. I meet with freethinking, progressive people, I feel comfortable in their company and agree with their convictions.

But the nature of my feelings is remarkable. Listen to me: Every year when the month of *Elul* rolls around, when the time of *Rosh Hashanah* and *Yom Kippur* approaches, my heart grows heavy and sad. A melancholy descends on me, a longing gnaws at my breast. At that time I cannot rest, I wander about through the streets, lost in thought, depressed.

When I go past a synagogue during these days and hear a cantor chanting the melodies of the prayers, I become very gloomy and my depression is so great that I cannot endure it. My memory goes back to my happy childhood years. I see clearly before me the small town, the fields, the little pond and the woods around it. I recall my childhood friends and our sweet childlike faith. My heart is constricted, and I begin to run like a madman till the tears stream from my eyes and then I become calmer.

These emotions and these moods have become stronger over the years and I decided to go to the synagogue. I went not in order to pray to God but to heal and refresh my aching soul with the cantor's sweet melodies, and this had an unusually good effect on me.

Sitting in the synagogue among *landsleit* and listening to the good cantor, I forgot my unhappy weekday life, the dirty shop, my boss, the bloodsucker, and my pale, sick wife and my children. All of my America with its hurry-up life was forgotten.

I am a member of a Progressive Society, and since I am known there as an outspoken freethinker, they began to criticize me for going to the synagogue.

The members do not want to hear of my personal emotions and they won't understand that there are people whose natures are such that memories of their childhood are sometimes stronger than their convictions.

And where can one hide on *Yom Kippur?* There are many of us, like me. They don't go to work, so it would be good if there could be a meeting hall where they could gather to hear a concert, a lecture, or something else.

What is your opinion of this? Awaiting your answer, I remain,

Your reader,
S. R.

## ANSWER:

No one can tell another what to do with himself on *Yom Kippur*. If one is drawn to the synagogue, that is his choice. Naturally, a genuinely sincere freethinker is not drawn to the synagogue. The writer of this letter is full of memories of his childhood days at home, and therefore the cantor's melodies influence him so strongly. Who among us isn't moved by a religious melody remembered from his youth? This, however, has no bearing on loyalty to one's convictions. On *Yom Kippur*, a freethinker can spend his time in a library or with friends. On this day he should not flaunt himself in the eyes of the religious people. There is no sense in arousing their feelings. Every man has a right to live according to his beliefs. The pious man has as much right to his religion as the freethinker to his atheism. To parade one's acts that insult the religious feeling of the pious, especially on *Yom Kippur*, the day they hold most holy, is simply inhuman.

1909

*Dear Editor,*

As a reader of the *Forward*, I am writing to you about a matter that will interest other people too. But first I will tell you a little about myself.

I am twenty-seven years of age, have been in the country ten years, and am still single. I have worked here at various trades, but never very long at one job. I enjoy traveling and seeing what's going on in the country. Now I've decided it's time to marry and settle down.

I came to North Dakota, where most people make their living from farming. But there are no Jews in this area. I started to work on a farm and I learned farming. I like this kind of life, and after working a year and a half I rented a farm for myself.

My capital was small, but Gentile neighbors helped me. I went into debt for thirteen hundred dollars, but by the end of the summer I had paid back almost all of my debts. I wrote to a friend of mine about joining me. He and his wife came and we work together. We carry on an independent life, have none of the problems of city life because we always have our own potatoes, butter, cheese, milk, chickens, a good home and are content.

This winter I went to Chicago and stayed a few weeks with friends. Most of my friends called me an idiot and told me they could not understand how a young, capable fellow like me became a farmer and leads such a lonely life.

Of all the girls I knew, who would have gladly married me before, not one was interested in going back to the farm with me. But this didn't discourage me. I returned to the farm and I'm now preparing for the spring season.

However, I want to ask you, did my friends have the right to call me "idiot"? Is there any logic in their argument? Please answer me.

*Thank you,*
*The Jewish Farmer*

## ANSWER:

There is certainly nothing to be ashamed of in living in the lap of Nature. Many people dream of becoming farmers. The cities are full of many diseases that are unheard of on farms. Tuberculosis, for instance, is a disease of the big cities. People in urban areas grow old and gray at forty, but most of the farmers are healthy and strong and live to be eighty and ninety.

Generally, it is a matter of choice. Debates between country people and city people about which have the better life are nothing new.

1909

*Dear Editor,*

I come from a small town in Russia. I was brought up by decent parents and got a good education. I am now twenty years old and am a customer-peddler in a Southern city. Since my customers here are colored people, I became acquainted with a young Negro girl, twenty-two years of age, who buys merchandise from me. She is light-skinned and a fine girl. She is a teacher, a graduate of a Negro college, and I think she is an honorable person.

I fell in love with the girl but I couldn't go around with her openly because I am white and she is colored. However, whenever I delivered her order, I visited with her for a while.

In time she went away to another city to teach, and I corresponded with her. When she came home for Christmas, I told her I loved her and I intended to marry her and take her North to live. But she refused me and gave me no reason. Perhaps it was because I am a white man.

I spoke about my love for her to my friends, who are supposedly decent people, and they wanted to spit in my face! They told me openly that if not for my good character they would have nothing to do with me because of "criminal" behavior. To them it appeared that I was about to commit a crime.

Therefore I would like to hear your answer as to whether I should be condemned for falling in love with a Negro woman and wanting to marry her. And if you can, explain to me also her reason for refusing me.

Respectfully,
Z. B.

**ANSWER:**

It is unthinkable to regard the writer's actions as criminal. But the fact is that in the South the whites have such a deep hatred for the Negroes that when a white man falls in love with a Negro woman it is considered a crime. Many of the Southerners, however, are hypocrites in this respect, because when the Negroes were their slaves, some of the black women bore their children.

Concerning the question as to why the Negro girl refused him and didn't want to marry him: either she does not love him, or this reflects the justly deserved distrust of the Negroes for the whites in the South.

1909

*Dear Editor,*

We, the undersigned, appeal to you to use your worthy newspaper to help save a family from going under.

This is about a family from Yekaterinaslav, Russia, who suffered greatly from the pogroms. The father and a child were murdered, the mother was crippled, a twenty-year-old boy had his head split open, and a sixteen-year-old boy had his arm broken.

The survivors of the family, the mother and three children, came to America, and lived in New Britain, Connecticut. Here the mother was forced to place one child in a Catholic orphanage and give the other two to good people. The older boy, whose head had been split by the hoodlums, had a recurrence of the effects of the blow and was taken into a government hospital in New York for a cure. Then the authorities decided that he has to be sent back to Russia— to the city where his father and brother had been murdered. His crippled mother intends to go with him, but she is desolate because she has to leave the other children behind.

What will become of this unfortunate's children who remain alone in

New Britain? What will happen to the child in the Catholic orphanage? We appeal to all Yekaterinaslaver societies and individuals to help save this family. The boy has been in the country over two years and something must be done to stop his being sent back. If this can't be done, it must at least be made possible for the mother and son to leave the country with a little money for the first piece of bread, because they don't have a red cent.

The boy is in the Staten Island Hospital and will be sent away any day now. *Landsleit* and friends, do your duty to this family that is so alone [here the name of the woman is given].

> With friendly regards,
> Your Readers from
> New Britain, Connecticut.

## ANSWER:

In this answer it is stated that a reporter from the *Forward* visited the family and verified that the condition was even worse than was described in the letter.

In the answer, the Jews and Jewish organizations are scolded for neglecting these victims of the pogrom for so long, and for not seeing to it that the child was at least placed in a Jewish orphanage. Attention is also called to all those active in Jewish organizations and to the Hebrew Immigrant Aid Society. They can still influence the authorities to keep the young man from being sent back. The Jewish welfare organization and the family's *landsleit* are ordered to act immediately on this case to help the unfortunates.

1909

*Worthy Editor,*

I often spend time with a group of forty people, thirty men and ten women. Among them are religious and non-religious people, and we do not pass the time in idle discussions.

Recently we read a report in a newspaper about the movement to give women the right to vote, and for the past few weeks we have been carrying on a debate about it. I am one of the group that is in favor of giving women full rights, but most of the others are against it. The opposed argue that it would be very bad to let the women get to the ballot box, because that would destroy their family life. The woman would then no longer be the housewife, the mother to her children, the wife to her husband—in a word, everything would be destroyed.

A woman must not mix in politics, they say. She was created to be dependent on man, obey him, love him, supply all his comforts and be a mother to his children. The question arises: Must the woman then be considered a slave, and the man the master? Isn't it obvious, then, that women in many cases show themselves to be cleverer than men? These same people who recently celebrated the hundredth birthday of Abraham Lincoln, for having freed the Negro slaves, now talk with a satirical grin about women's freedom. Just as the opponents of the Socialist movement point out that Socialism will be harmful, so those who argue against voting rights for women say that this will destroy family life.

This is not so, because a woman is a human being just like a man. The capabilities that women have already shown confirm this. Plenty of facts can be cited from the past. And if women are recognized as human beings, they must also be granted all the rights of human beings. I think that if women are considered human beings with all their rights, then family life would be better and richer.

*With Socialistic regards,*
*L. V.*

ANSWER:

The arguments against the opponents of women's rights are very good ones. The fact is that many intelligent women are already taking part in various activities and they still remain excellent homemakers.

Justice can reign among people only when they all have equal rights. If one has more power than the other, it leads to injustice. Those men who are opposed to giving women the same rights they possess are acting from tyrannical instincts because they actually want to rule the women.

### Theodora Kroeber, "Outside the Slaughter House," 1961

*In August of 1911 a wild man appeared out of the northern California wilderness and entered the town of Oroville. He spoke a language no one knew, and he was suffering from terrible hunger, fatigue, and fright. Notified of this strange event, two anthropologists from*

*the University of California at Berkeley, Alfred Kroeber and T. T. Waterman, came for the man and took him into their care. He was called Ishi, and he had somehow survived to middle age without any contact with the civilization that had grown up in Northern California after the Gold Rush of 1849. Kroeber and Waterman took Ishi to the new Museum of Anthropology in San Francisco, where they made a simple home for him as they learned his language, developed bonds of trust and friendship with him, and helped him adapt to their world. The newness of both the museum and the department of anthropology at the University of California reflected a rising public interest both in antiquities and in the native peoples and cultures of North America. Thousands of visitors came to watch Ishi practice his traditional techniques of bow and arrow making and to gain some fleeting sense of what life was like in California before the arrival of the Europeans. His story, part of which is excerpted below, is uniquely haunting, for it brought Americans face to face with the sole survivor of a culture that had been destroyed in the march of their civilization. Although Ishi was restored to bodily health and treated with great kindness by his new friends from Berkeley, the loss of his entire family, clan, and world was fatally traumatic—Ishi died in 1916.*

Source: "Outside the Slaughter House," Theodora Kroeber, *Ishi: In Two Worlds, A Biography of the Last Wild Indian in North America* (Berkeley and Los Angeles: University of California Press, 1961), pp. 3–10.

The story of Ishi begins for us early in the morning of the twenty-ninth day of

August in the year 1911 and in the corral of a slaughter house. It begins with the sharp barking of dogs which roused the sleeping butchers. In the dawn light they saw a man at bay, crouching against the corral fence—Ishi.

They called off the dogs. Then, in some considerable excitement, they telephoned the sheriff in Oroville two or three miles away to say that they were holding a wild man and would he please come and take him off their hands. Sheriff and deputies arrived shortly, approaching the corral with guns at the ready. The wild man made no move to resist capture, quietly allowing himself to be handcuffed.

The sheriff, J. B. Webber, saw that the man was an Indian, and that he was at the limit of exhaustion and fear. He could learn nothing further, since his prisoner understood no English. Not knowing what to do with him, he motioned the Indian into the wagon with himself and his deputies, drove him to the county jail in Oroville, and locked him up in the cell for the insane. There, Sheriff Webber reasoned, while he tried to discover something more about his captive he could at least protect him from the excited curiosity of the townspeople and the outsiders who were already pouring in from miles around to see the wild man.

The wild man was emaciated to starvation, his hair was burned off close to his head, he was naked except for a ragged scrap of ancient covered-wagon canvas which he wore around his shoulders like a poncho. He was a man of middle height, the long bones, painfully apparent, were straight, strong, and not heavy, the skin color somewhat paler in tone than the full copper characteristic of most Indians. The black eyes were wary and guarded now, but were set wide in a broad face, the mouth was generous and agreeably molded. For the rest, the Indian's extreme fatigue and fright heightened a sensitiveness which was always there, while it masked the usual mobility and expressiveness of the features.

It should be said that the sheriff's action in locking Ishi up was neither stupid nor brutal given the circumstances. Until sheriff Webber took the unwonted measure of keeping them out by force people filled the jail to gaze through the bars of his cell at the captive. Later, Ishi spoke with some diffidence of this, his first contact with white men. He said that he was put up in a fine house where he was kindly treated and well fed by a big chief. That he would eat nothing and drink nothing during his first days of captivity Ishi did not say. Such was the case; nor did he allow himself to sleep at first. Quite possibly it was a time of such strain and terror that he suppressed all memory of it. Or he may have felt that it was unkind to recall his suspicions which proved in the event groundless, for Ishi expected in those first days to be put to death. He knew of white men only that they were the murderers of his own people. It was natural that he should expect, once in their power, to be shot or hanged or killed by poisoning.

Meanwhile, local Indians and half-breeds as well as Mexicans and Spaniards tried to talk to the prisoner in Maidu,

Wintu, and Spanish. Ishi listened patiently but uncomprehendingly, and when he spoke it was in a tongue which meant no more to the Indians there than to the whites.

The story of the capture of a wild Indian became headline news in the local valley papers, and reached the San Francisco dailies in forms more or less lurid and elaborated. The story in the *San Francisco Call* was accompanied by a picture, the first of many to come later. In another newspaper story, a Maidu Indian, Conway by name, "issued a statement" that he had conversed with the wild man. Conway's moment of publicity was brief since the wild man understood nothing of what he said.

These accounts were read by Professors Kroeber and Waterman, anthropologists at the University of California, who were at once alerted to the human drama behind the event and to its possible importance, the more particularly because it recalled to them an earlier episode on San Nicolas Island, one of the Channel Islands of the Pacific Ocean some seventy miles offshore from Santa Barbara.

In 1835, the padres of Mission Santa Barbara transferred the San Nicolas Indians to the mainland. A few minutes after the boat, which was carrying the Indians, had put off from the island, it was found that one baby had been left behind. It is not easy to land a boat on San Nicolas; the captain decided against returning for the baby; the baby's mother jumped overboard, and was last seen swimming toward the island. Halfhearted efforts made to find her in subsequent weeks were unsuccessful: it was believed that she had drowned in the rough surf. In 1853, eighteen years later, seal hunters in the Channel waters reported seeing a woman on San Nicolas, and a boatload of men from Santa Barbara went in search of her. They found her, a last survivor of her tribe. Her baby, as well as all her people who had been removed to the Mission, had died. She lived only a few months after her "rescue" and died without anyone having been able to communicate with her, leaving to posterity this skeletal outline of her grim story, and four words which someone remembered from her lost language and recorded as she said them. It so happens that these four words identify her language as having been Shoshonean, related to Indian languages of the Los Angeles area, not to those of Santa Barbara.

Another reason for the anthropologists' particular interest in the wild man was that three years earlier, in 1908, some surveyors working a few miles north of Oroville had surprised and routed a little band of Indians. After hearing of this incident, Waterman with two guides had spent several weeks in an unsuccessful search for the Indians: the wild man of Oroville might well be one of them.

On August 31, 1911, Kroeber sent the following telegram: "Sheriff Butte County. Newspapers report capture wild Indian speaking language other tribes totally unable understand. Please confirm or deny by collect telegram and if story correct hold Indian till arrival Professor State University who will take charge and be responsible for him. Matter important account aboriginal history."

The sheriff's office must have confirmed the report promptly: Waterman took the train to Oroville the same day. That he and Kroeber correctly "guessed" Ishi's tribe and language was no *tour de force* of intuition. The guess was based on field work with Indians all up and down California; they knew that Oroville was adjacent to country which formerly belonged to the Yana Indians; presumably the strange Indian would be a Yana. He might even be from the southernmost tribe of Yana, believed to be extinct. If this were true, neither they nor anyone so far as they knew could speak his language. But if he were a Northern or Central Yana, there were files of expertly recorded vocabularies for those dialects from two old Yanas, Batwi, called Sam, and Chidaimiya, called Betty Brown.

With a copy of Batwi's and Chidaimiya's vocabularies in his pocket, Waterman arrived in Oroville where he identified himself to Sheriff Webber and was taken to visit the wild man. Waterman found a weary, badgered Indian sitting in his cell, wearing the butcher's apron he had been given at the slaughter house, courteously making what answer he could in his own language to a barrage of questions thrown at him in English, Spanish, and assorted Indian from a miscellaneous set of visitors.

Waterman sat down beside Ishi, and with his phonetically transcribed list of Northern and Central Yana words before him, began to read from it, repeating each word, pronouncing it as well as he

knew how. Ishi was attentive but unresponding until, discouragingly far down the list, Waterman said *siwini* which means yellow pine, at the same time tapping the pine framework of the cot on which they sat. Recognition lighted up the Indian's face. Waterman said the magic word again; Ishi repeated it after him, correcting his pronunciation, and for the next moments the two of them banged at the wood of the cot, telling each other over and over, *siwini, siwini!*

With the difficult first sound recognition achieved, others followed. Ishi was indeed one of the lost tribe, a Yahi; in other words, he was from the southernmost Yana. Waterman was learning that the unknown Yahi dialect differed considerably but not to the point of unintelligibility from the two northern ones of his list. Together he and Ishi tried out more and more words and phrases: they were beginning to communicate. After a while Ishi ventured to ask Waterman, *I ne ma Yahi?* "Are you an Indian?" Waterman answered that he was. The hunted look left Ishi's eyes—here was a friend. He knew as well as did his friend that Waterman was not an Indian. The question was a tentative and subtle way of reassuring and being reassured, not an easy thing to do when the meaningful shared sounds are few. Between meetings with Ishi, Waterman wrote to Kroeber from Oroville:

This man [Ishi] is undoubtedly wild. He has pieces of deer thong in place of ornaments in the lobes of his ears and a wooden plug in the septum of his nose. He recognizes most of my Yana words and a fair proportion of his own seem to be identical [with mine]. Some of his, however, are either quite different or else my pronunciation of them is very bad, because he doesn't respond to them except by pointing to his ears and asking to have them repeated. "No!" *k'u'i*—it is not—is one. "Yes!" *ähä*, pleases him immensely. I think I get a few endings that don't occur in Northern Yana on nouns, for example. Phonetically, he has some of the prettiest cracked consonants I ever heard in my life. He will be a splendid informant, especially for phonetics, for he speaks very clearly. I have not communicated with him successfully enough to get his story, but what can I expect? He has a yarn to tell about his woman, who had a baby on her back and seems to have been drowned, except that he is so *cheerful* about it.

Waterman misunderstood. In the excitement and relief of having someone to talk to, Ishi poured out confidences and recollections which Waterman could by no means comprehend even with the aid of an elaborate pantomime. Ishi's seeming pleasure was not in the recollected event, but was rather a near hysteria induced by human interchange of speech and feelings too long denied.

Waterman's letters continue:

We had a lot of conversation this morning about deer hunting and making acorn soup, but I got as far as my list of words would take me. If I am not mistaken, he's full of religion—bathing at sunrise, putting out pinches of tobacco where the lightning strikes, etc. I'll try rattlesnake on him when I go back after lunch. It was a picnic to see him open his eyes when he heard Yana from me. And he looked over my shoulder at the paper in a most mystified way. He knew at once where I got my inspiration. . . . We showed him some arrows last night, and we could hardly get them away from him. He showed us how he flaked the points, singed the edges of the feathering, and put on the sinew wrappings.

Even before Waterman had established a thin line of communication with Ishi, the sheriff had become convinced that his prisoner was neither insane nor dangerous. There were no charges against him; he did not properly belong in jail. The question was, what in place of the shelter of the jail was there for him? Waterman offered to take him to San Francisco. Phones and telegraph wires were kept busy for the next forty-eight hours between Oroville and San Francisco, where the University's Museum of Anthropology then was, and between the museum and Washington, D.C.

While these negotiations were going forward, the sheriff, at Waterman's suggestion, sent a deputy to Redding to find and bring back with him the old man, Batwi, to act as interpreter-companion to Ishi. Batwi came, and although he patronized Ishi outrageously, he was for the present a help. He and Ishi could communicate in Yana, not without some difficulty, but quite fully. Meanwhile, the Indian Bureau in Washington telegraphed permission for Ishi to go to the

University's museum whose staff was to be responsible for him at least until there was opportunity for fuller investigation. The sheriff of Butte County was greatly relieved; he at once made out a receipt of release from the jail to the University. This remarkable document seems not to have survived the years of moving and storing in odd corners which has been the fate of the museum files and specimens.

In any case, Waterman, Batwi, and Ishi, with the release and government permission, left Oroville on Labor Day, September 4, arriving in San Francisco somewhat before midnight. There remained to Ishi four years and seven months of life, years which were to pass within the shelter of the museum walls at the Affiliated Colleges, or in the hospital next door when he was sick.

Ishi was the last wild Indian in North America, a man of Stone Age culture subjected for the first time when he was past middle age to twentieth-century culture. He was content that it should be so, participating as fully as he could in the new life. Before examining more closely those astounding few years and what one Stone Age man contributed in so short a time to our understanding of man as such, let us go back to the years of childhood, young manhood, and middle age—almost a whole lifetime. These were years spent by him without experience or understanding of a way of life other than that of a tiny fugitive band of fewer than a dozen souls at most, opposing their ancient Yahi skills and beliefs to an unknown but hostile outside world.

There came the time—months, perhaps two or three years before August, 1911—when Ishi was the only one remaining of the little band, violence from without, old age and illness from within, having brought death to the others.

Ishi's arrival at the slaughter house was the culmination of unprecedented behavior on his part. A few days earlier, without hope, indifferent whether he lived or died, he had started on an aimless trek in a more or less southerly direction which took him into country he did not know. Exhaustion was added to grief and loneliness. He lay down in the corral because he could go no farther. He was then about forty miles from home, a man without living kin or friends, a man who had probably never been beyond the borders of his own tribal territory.

Our task is to piece together all that is known of Ishi's life before that day: from his own account of it; from what was learned of it on a camping trip with him in his own home country; and from the miscellany of rumor and fact and speculation as reported by surveyors, ranchers, rangers, and other white residents of Butte and Tehama counties. It is an episodic story, incomplete, and loosely strung across lacunae of time, ignorance, and events too painful for Ishi to relive in memory.

That Ishi should have crossed the boundaries of his homeland, and continued on into the unknown, means to be sure that he had also reached and crossed certain physical and psychic limits. But to begin to understand how profoundly disturbed he must have been, we must know how aberrant such behavior was, not for Ishi the man merely, but for Ishi the Yahi. His life becomes more of a piece if we step back from it, as from the detail of a face or feature in a painting, to focus briefly on the whole of the canvas, bringing its background and pattern into perspective. To understand Ishi's values and behavior and belief, and his way of life, we must know in a broad and general way something of his heritage: the land and people of Indian California.

## Horace M. Kallen, "Democracy Versus the Melting-Pot," 1915

*Horace Kallen (1882–1974) was an important social philosopher, born in Germany and educated at Harvard, where he helped establish the Menorah Society, an organization of Jewish students whose goal was to sustain their distinctive identity while participating in the life of the university. Under the influence of his teachers, especially philosopher William James and literature professor Barrett Wendell, Kallen began to realize that the highest expression of Americanness did not require the suppression of ethnic distinctiveness. On the contrary, as he argued in his famous 1915 essay "Democracy* Versus *the Melting-Pot," the notion of melting down ethnic traits into a single hybrid American character was an illusion. Kallen saw that immigrants tended to preserve many of their traditional values even as they adopted American customs. Reasoning that immigrants could change their outward way of life but could not change their grandfathers, Kallen developed the idea of cultural pluralism. Unlike*

*Israel Zangwill's metaphor of America as a melting pot, a pluralistic nation would allow men and women to sustain their ethnic sensibilities while they joined the larger society, which was unified by the English language and the political values of democracy. In the following excerpt, Kallen is responding to the eminent sociologist Edward A. Ross, who had published a book alleging that immigrants weakened the character of American society.*

*Source:* Horace M. Kallen, "Democracy Versus the Melting-Pot," *Culture and Democracy in the United States* (New York: Boni and Liveright, 1924), originally published in *The Nation* (February 18 and 25, 1915).

To-day the descendants of the colonists appear to be reformulating a Declaration of Independence. Again, as in 1776, Americans of British ancestry apprehend that certain possessions of theirs, which may be lumped under the word "Americanism" are in jeopardy. The danger comes, once more, from a force across the water, but the force is this time regarded not as superior, but as inferior. The relationships of 1776 are, consequently, reversed. To conserve the inalienable rights of the colonists of 1776, it was necessary to declare all men equal; to conserve the inalienable rights of their descendants in the 20th century, it becomes necessary to declare all men unequal. In 1776 all men were as good as their betters; in 1920 men are permanently worse than their betters. "A nation may reason," writes one nervous professor, in embattled defense, " 'Why burden ourselves with the rearing of children? Let them perish unborn in the womb of time. The immigrants will keep up the population.' A people that has no more respect for its ancestors and no more pride of race than this deserves the extinction that surely awaits it."

Respect for ancestors, pride of race! Time was when these would have been repudiated as the enemies of democracy, the antithesis of the fundamentals of the North American Republic, with its consciously proclaimed belief that "a man's a man for a' that." And now they are being invoked in defense of democracy, against the "melting-pot," by a sociological protagonist of the "democratic idea." How knowingly purposeful their invocation is cannot be said. But that its assumptions have unconsciously colored much of the social and political thinking of the United States from the days of the Cincinnati on, seems to me unquestionable, and it seems even more unquestionable that this apparently sudden and explicit conscious expression of them is the effect of an actual felt menace. This professor, in a word, is no voice crying in a wilderness. He simply utters aloud, and in his own peculiar manner, what is thought and spoken wherever Americans of British ancestry congregate feelingly. . . .

All immigrants and their offspring are by the way of undergoing "Americanization" if they remain in one place in the country long enough—say six or seven years. The general notion of "Americanization" appears to signify the adoption of the American variety of English speech, American clothes and manners, the American attitude in politics. "Americanization" signifies, in short, the disappearance of the external differences upon which so much race-prejudice often feeds. It appears to imply the fusion of the various bloods, and a transmutation by "the miracle of assimilation" of Jews, Slavs, Poles, Frenchmen, Germans, Hindus, Scandinavians and so on into beings similar in background, tradition, outlook and spirit to the descendants of the British colonists, the "Anglo-Saxon" stock. Broadly speaking, these elements of Americanism are somewhat external, the effect of environment; largely internal, the effect of heredity, social and personal. . . .

In these days of ready-made garments, factory-made furniture, refrigerating plants, "boiler-plate," movies and radio, it is almost impossible that the mass of the inhabitants of the United States should wear other than uniform clothes, use other than uniform furniture, utensils or eat anything but the same sorts of food, read anything but the same syndicated hokum, see anything but the same standardized romances and hear anything but the same broadcasted barbarisms. In these days of rapid transit and industrial mobility it must seem impossible that any stratification of population should be permanent. Hardly anybody seems to have been born where he lives, or to live where he has been born. The teetering of demand and supply in industry and commerce keep large masses of population constantly mobile: so that many people no longer can be said to have homes. This mobility reënforces the need of the immigrant to learn English—for a *lingua franca* intelligible everywhere becomes indispensable. And ideals that are felt to belong with the language tend to become "standardized," widespread, uniform, through the devices of the telegraph and the telephone, the syndication of "literature," the cheap newspaper and the cheap novel, the vaudeville circuit, the phonograph, the player piano, the movie, and the star-system and the radio. Even more significantly, mobility leads to the propinquity of the different stocks, thus promoting intermarriage and pointing to the coming of a new "American race"—a blend of at least all the European stocks (for some doubt is expressed even by the white population of the South as to whether negroes—of whom more than a third are already of mixed blood—should also constitute an element in this blend) into a newer and better being whose qualities and ideals shall be the qualities and ideals of the contemporary American of British ancestry. Apart from the unintentional impulsion of the conditions I have just enumerated toward this end, there exists in addition an instrument especially devised for this purpose. The instrument is called the public school. With it there may be reckoned to some extent the state institutions of higher education—normal schools and universities. That the end has been and is being attained, we have outstanding among many others the biographical testimony of such significant personalities as Jacob Riis and Edward Steiner and Mary Antin—a Dane and two Jews, intermarried, "assimilated" even in religion, and more excessively, self-consciously flatteringly American than the Americans. And another Jew, Mr. Israel Zangwill, of London, England, profitably promulgates this end as a principle and an aspiration, to the admiring approval of American audiences, under the device, "the melting-pot."

All is not, however, fact, because it is hope; nor is the biography of an individual, particularly of a literary individual, the history of a group. The Riises and Steiners and Antins together with Edward Bok and their numerous other recent imitators mostly female and Jewish, protest too much; they are too self-conscious and self-centered, their "Americanization" appears too much like an achievement, a *tour de force*, too little like a growth. . . .

At his core, no human being, even in a "state of nature," is a mere mathematical unit of action like the "economic man." Behind him in time and tremendously in him in quality, are his ancestors; around him in space are his relatives and kin, carrying in common with him the inherited organic set from a remoter common ancestry. In all these he lives and moves and has his being. They constitute his, literally, *natio*, the inwardness of his nativity, and in Europe every inch of his non-human environment wears the effects of their action upon it and breathes their spirit. The America he comes to, beside Europe, is Nature virgin and inviolate: it does not guide him with ancestral blazings: externally he is cut off from the past. Not so internally: whatever else he changes, he cannot change his grandfather. Moreover, he comes rarely alone; he comes companioned with his fellow nationals; and he comes to no strangers, but to kin and friends who have gone before. If he is able to excel, he soon achieves a local habitation. There he encounters the native American to whom he is merely a Dutchman, a Mick, a frog, a wop, a dago, a hunky, or a sheeny and no more; and he encounters these others who are unlike him, dealing with him as a lower and outlandish creature. Then, be he even the rudest and most primeval peasant, heretofore totally unconscious of his nationality, of his categorical difference from many men and similarity to some, he must inevitably become conscious of it. Thus, in the industrial and congested towns of the United States, where there are real and large contacts between immigrant nationalities, the first effect appears to be an intensification of spiritual dissimilarities, always to the disadvantage of the dissimilarities.

The second generation, consequently, devotes itself feverishly to the attainment of similarity. The social tradition of its parents is lost by attrition or thrown off for advantage. The merest externals of the new one are acquired— via the street and the public school. But as the public school imparts it, or as the social settlement imparts it, it is not really a *life*; it is an abstraction, an arrangement of words. America is a word: as a historic fact, or as a democratic ideal of life, it is not realized at all. . . .

He remains still the Slav, Jew, the German or the Irish citizen of the American state. Again, in the mass, neither he nor his children nor his children's children lose their ethnic individuality. True, there is intermarriage, often much of it. But on the whole and in the mass, marriage is determined by sexual selection and by propinquity, and the larger the homogeneous communities in any city, the less likely are mixed marriages to take place. Although the gross number of such marriages is considerably above what it was fifty years ago, the relative proportion in terms of variant units of population tends, I think, to be significantly less. As the stratification of the towns echoes and stresses the stratification of the country as a whole, the likelihood of a new "American" race is remote enough, and the fear of it unnecessary. But equally remote also is the possibility of a universalization of the inward bases of the old American life. Only the externals succeed in passing over. . . .

More and more public emphasis has been placed upon the unity of the English and American stock—the common interests of the "Anglo-Saxon" nations, and "Anglo-Saxon" civilization, the unity of the political, literary and social tradition. If all this is not ethnic nationality returned to consciousness, what is it?

Next in general estimation come the Germans and the Irish with the Jews a close third, although the position of the last involves some abnormalities. Then come the Slavs and Italians and other central and south Europeans, finally the Asiatics. The Germans, as Mr. Ross points out, have largely a monopoly of brewing and baking and cabinet-making. The Irish shine in no particular industries unless it be those carried on by municipalities and public-service corporations. The Jews mass in the garment-making industries, tobacco manufacture and in the "learned professions." The Scandinavians appear to be on the same level as the Jews in the general estimation, and going up. They are farmers, mostly, and outdoor men. The Slavs are miners, metalworkers and packers. The Italians tend to fall with the negroes into the "pick and shovel brigade." Such a country-wide and urban industrial and social stratification is no more likely than the geographical and sectional stratification to facilitate the coming of "the American race!" And as American political and "reforming" action is directed upon symptoms rather than upon fundamental causes, the stratification, as the country moves toward the inevitable equilibrium between wealth and population, will tend to grow more rigid rather than less. Thus far the pressure of immigration alone has kept the strata from hardening. Eliminate that and there may be set in motion the formation of a caste system based on ethnic diversity and mitigated to only a negligible degree by economic differences. . . .

Immigrants appear to pass through four phases in the course of being automatically Americanized. In the first phase they exhibit economic eagerness, the greedy hunger of the unfed. Since external differences are a handicap in the economic struggle, they "assimilate," seeking thus to facilitate the attainment of economic independence. Once the proletarian level of such independence is reached, the process of assimilation slows down and tends to come to a stop. The immigrant group is still a national group, modified, sometimes improved, by environmental influences, but otherwise a solidary spiritual unit, which is seeking to find its way out on its own social level. This search brings to light permanent group distinctions and the immigrant, like the Anglo-Saxon American, is thrown back upon himself and his ancestry. Then a process of dissimilation begins. The arts, life and ideals of the nationality become central and paramount; ethnic and national differences change in status from disadvantages to distinctions. All the while the immigrant has been uttering his life in the English language and behaving like an American in matters economic and political, and continues to do so. The institutions of the Republic have become the liberating cause and the background for the rise of the cultural consciousness and social autonomy of the immigrant Irishman, German, Scandinavian, Jew, Pole or Bohemian. On the whole, the automatic processes of Americanization have not repressed nationality. These processes have liberated nationality, and more or less gratified it.

Hence, what troubles Mr. Ross and so many other American citizens of British stock is not really inequality; what troubles them is *difference*. Only things that are *alike* in fact and not abstractly, and only men that are alike in origin and in feeling and not abstractly, can possess the equality which maintains that inward unanimity of sentiment and outlook which make a homogeneous national culture. The writers of the American Declaration of Independence and of the Constitution of the United States were not confronted by the practical fact of ethnic dissimilarity among the whites of the country. Their descendants are confronted by it. Its existence, acceptance and development are some of the inevitable consequences of the democratic principle on which the American theory of government is based, and the result at the present writing is to many worthies very unpleasant. Democratism and the federal principle have worked together with economic greed and ethnic snobbishness to people the land with all the nationalities of Europe, and to convert the early American nationality into the present American *nation*. For in effect the United States are in the process of becoming a federal state not merely as a union of geographical and administrative unities, but also as a coöperation of cultural diversities, as a federation or commonwealth of national cultures. . . .

What do Americans *will* to make of the United States—a unison, singing the old British theme "America," the America of the New England School? or a harmony, in which that theme shall be dominant, perhaps, among others, but one among many, not the only one? . . .

Biologically, life does not unify; biologically life diversifies; and it is sheer ignorance to apply social analogies to biological processes. In any event, we know what the qualities and capacities of existing types are; we know how by education to do something toward the conversion of what is evil in them and the conservation of what is good. "The American race" is a totally unknown thing; to presume that it will be better because (if we like to persist in the illusion that it is coming) it will be later, is no different from imagining that contemporary Poland is better than ancient Greece. There is nothing more to be said to the pious stupidity that identifies recency with goodness. The unison to be achieved cannot be a unison of ethnic types. It must be, if it is to be at all, a unison of social and historic interests, established by the complete cutting-off of

the ancestral memories of the American populations, the enforced, exclusive use of the English language and English and American history in the schools and in the daily life.

The attainment of the other alternative, a harmony, also requires concerted public action. But the action would do no violence to the ideals of American fundamental law and the spirit of American institutions nor to the qualities of men. It would seek simply to eliminate the waste and the stupidity of the social organization, by way of freeing and strengthening the strong forces actually in operation. Taking for its point of departure the existing ethnic and cultural groups it would seek to provide conditions under which each might attain the cultural perfection that is *proper to its kind*. The provision of such conditions has been said to be the primary intent of American fundamental law and the function of American institutions. And all of the various nationalities which compose the American nation must be taught first of all this fact, which used perhaps to be, to patriotic minds, the outstanding ideal content of "Americanism"—that democracy means self-realization through self-control, self-discipline, and that one is impossible without the other.

What is inalienable in the life of mankind is its intrinsic positive quality—its psycho-physical inheritance. Men may change their clothes, their politics, their wives, their religions, their philosophies, to a greater or lesser extent: they cannot change their grandfathers. Jews or Poles or Anglo-Saxons, in order to cease being Jews or Poles or Anglo-Saxons, would have to cease to be, while they could cease to be citizens or church members or carpenters or lawyers without ceasing to be. The selfhood which is inalienable in them, and for the realization of which they require "inalienable" liberty is ancestrally determined, and the happiness which they pursue has its form implied in ancestral endowment. This is what, actually, democracy in operation assumes. . . . And as intelligence and wisdom prevail over "politics" and special interests, as the steady and continuous pressure of the "inalienable" qualities and purposes of human groups more and more dominate the confusion of their common life, the outlines of a possible great and truly democratic commonwealth become discernible. Its form would be that of the federal republic; its substance a democracy of nationalities, coöperating voluntarily and autonomously through common institutions in the enterprise of self-realization through the perfection of men according to their kind. The common language of the commonwealth, the language of its great tradition, would be English, but each nationality would have for its emotional and involuntary life its own peculiar dialect or speech, its own individual and inevitable esthetic and intellectual forms. The political and economic life of the commonwealth is a single unit and serves as the foundation and background for the realization of the distinctive individuality of each *natio* that composes it and of the pooling of these in a harmony above them all. Thus "American civilization" may come to mean the perfection of the coöperative harmonies of "European civilization"—the waste, the squalor and the distress of Europe being eliminated—a multiplicity in a unity, an orchestration of mankind. As in an orchestra every type of instrument has its specific *timbre* and *tonality*, founded in its substance and form; as every type has its appropriate theme and melody in the whole symphony, so in society, each ethnic group may be the natural instrument, its temper and culture may be its theme and melody and the harmony and dissonances and discords of them all may make the symphony of civilization. With this difference: a musical symphony is written before it is played; in the symphony of civilization the playing is the writing, so that there is nothing so fixed and inevitable about its progressions as in music, so that within the limits set by nature and luck they may vary at will, and the range and variety of the harmonies may become wider and richer and more beautiful—or the reverse.

But the question is, do the dominant classes in America want such a society? The alternative is actually before them. Can they choose wisely? Or will vanity blind them and fear constrain, turning the promise of freedom into the fact of tyranny, and once more vindicating the ancient habit of men and aborting the hope of the world?

## Wartime Memos to Hugo Munsterberg, 1914–1916

*Hugo Munsterberg (1863–1916) was probably the most conspicuous German in America when World War I broke out. A professor of psychology at Harvard University, Munsterberg had been one of the most well-known psychol-*

ogists in the United States since the 1890s. A highly assimilated German Jew, Munsterberg identified intensely with Germany and devoted much of his public life to fostering a closer relationship between America and Germany. He wrote books and essays explaining American culture to Germans and vice versa, and when the war erupted he redoubled his efforts to maintain Germany's image and stem the rising tide of anti-German sentiment in the United States. Munsterberg never took American citizenship, he maintained close relations with important figures in the German government, and his outspoken defense of Germany after 1914 left him vulnerable to charges of being a spy. Below is a sample of the many notes he received during the last two years of his life. Two illustrate the new American hostility to Germans. The third note reflects the mixed feelings of a German immigrant who had been in America for many years. This man refers to Munsterberg's offer to resign his post at Harvard (Harvard declined the offer) after a colleague had accused him of unpatriotic conduct unbecoming a professor at an American school. He refers also to Munsterberg's 1914 book The War and America.

Source: The Hugo Munsterberg Papers, Boston Public Library, Special Collections.

## MEMO 1

[English]
Munsterberg
    Damn You Have Less Talk and Get Out of This Country.
    We Don't Want You Here.
    You German People Are Nothing But a Damn Lot of Schemers. Get Out—

## MEMO 2

[English and German]
With a Russian's compliments to the dirty fellow of a dirty people.

## MEMO 3

[Translation from German]
As the son of a German scholar who at one time stood on close terms with the Prussian royal family, let me take the liberty to express my most respectful congratulations on your dignified resignation. I do so as an American citizen of German origin. I've been in this country thirty-three years, and my wife is American, but now I am a reborn German who better understands his duty as a citizen of the United States after reading *The War and America*.

                        X. Y. Z., Minnesota

[Als er Sohn eines Deutschen Gelehrten, der einst als Professor in nahen Beziehungen zu der Preussischen Koenigsfamilie gestanden hat, nehme ich mir die Freiheit, Ihnen meinen hochachtenden Glueckwunsch auszuzprechen zu Ihrer wuerdevollen Resignation. Dasselbe tue ich als Amerikanischer Buerger deutscher Abkunft. Ich bin Dreiunddreisig Jabre in diesem Lande, meine Frau ist Amerikanerin, aber jetzt bin ich ein neu geborner Deutscher, der seine Pflicht als Buerger der Vereinigten Staaten heute besser wie je versteht, nachdem er "The War and America" gelesen hat. X. Y. Z., Minnesota]

## W. E. B. Du Bois, "Close Ranks," July 1918; "Returning Soldiers," May 1919

*Among his other accomplishments, William Edward Burghardt Du Bois (see notes to* The Souls of Black Folk *in this chapter) served as the founding editor of* The Crisis, *the journal of the National Association for the Advancement of Colored People (NAACP). When the United States entered World War I in 1917, black Americans faced a problem. Should they enlist in their country's service and fight for freedom in Europe when they were themselves denied freedom at home? In a famous editorial, "Close Ranks," Du Bois answered in the affirmative. Military service exerted a powerful effect on these soldiers, giving them a glimpse of a world in Europe without the deadening hand of Jim Crow, giving them guns and a feeling of both pride and power denied them at home, and giving them a potent sense of entitlement—after risking their lives to preserve freedom, surely they would now receive it. The second editorial below, "Returning Soldiers," reflects this complex of feelings. "Under similar circumstances, we would fight again," Du Bois intoned. "But by the God of Heaven, we are cowards and jackasses if now that that war is over, we do not marshal every ounce of our brain and brawn to fight a sterner, longer, more unbending battle against the forces of hell in our own land." As the tone of this essay suggests, the war produced in its wake the "New Negro" of the Harlem Renaissance, in which men and women asserted their ethnic pride in bolder and more creative ways than ever before.*

Source: *W. E. B. Du Bois, "Close Ranks,"* The Crisis *(July 1918); "Returning Soldiers,"* The Crisis *(May 1919).*

## CLOSE RANKS

This is the crisis of the world. For all the long years to come men will point to the year 1918 as the great Day of Decision, the day when the world decided whether it would submit to military despotism and an endless armed peace—if peace it could be called—or whether they would put down the menace of German militarism and inaugurate the United States of the World.

We of the colored race have no ordinary interest in the outcome. That which the German power represents to-day spells death to the aspirations of Negroes and all darker races for equality, freedom and democracy. Let us not hesitate. Let us, while this war lasts, forget our special grievances and close our ranks shoulder to shoulder with our white fellow citizens and the allied nations that are fighting for democracy. We make no ordinary sacrifice, but we make it gladly and willingly, with our eyes lifted to the hills.

## RETURNING SOLDIERS

We are returning from war! The Crisis and tens of thousands of black men were drafted into a great struggle. For bleeding France and what she means and has meant and will mean to us and humanity and against the threat of German race arrogance, we fought gladly and to the last drop of blood; for America and her highest ideals, we fought in far-off hope: for the dominant southern oligarchy entrenched in Washington, we fought in bitter resignation. For the America that represents and gloats in lynching, disfranchisement, caste, brutality and devilish insult—for this, in the hateful upturning and mixing of things, we were forced by vindictive fate to fight, also.

But today we return! We return from the slavery of uniform which the world's madness demanded us to don to the freedom of civil garb. We stand again to look America squarely in the face and call a spade a spade. We sing: This country of ours, despite all its better souls have done and dreamed, is yet a shameful land.

It *lynches*.

And lynching is barbarism of a degree of contemptible nastiness unparalleled in human history. Yet for fifty years we have lynched two Negroes a week, and we have kept this up right through the war.

It *disfranchises* its own citizens.

Disfranchisement is the deliberate theft and robbery of the only protection of poor against rich and black against white. The land that disfranchises its citizens and calls itself a democracy lies and knows it lies.

It encourages *ignorance*.

It has never really tried to educate the Negro. A dominant minority does not want Negroes educated. It wants servants, dogs, whores and monkeys. And when this land allows a reactionary group by its stolen political power to force as many black folk into these categories as it possibly can, it cries in contemptible hypocrisy: "They threaten us with degeneracy; they cannot be educated."

It *steals* from us.

It organizes industry to cheat us. It cheats us out of our land; it cheats us out of our labor. It confiscates our savings. It reduces our wages. It raises our rent. It steals our profit. It taxes us without representation. It keeps us consistently and universally poor, and then feeds us on charity and derides our poverty.

It *insults* us.

It has organized a nation-wide and latterly a world-wide propaganda of deliberate and continuous insult and defamation of black blood wherever found. It decrees that it shall not be possible in travel nor residence, work nor play, education nor instruction for a black man to exist without tacit or open acknowledgement of his inferiority to the dirtiest white dog. And it looks upon any attempt to question or even discuss this dogma as arrogance, unwarranted assumption and treason.

This is the country to which we Soldiers of Democracy return. This is the fatherland for which we fought! But it is *our* fatherland. It was right for us to fight. The faults of *our* country are *our* faults. Under similar circumstances, we would fight again. But by the God of Heaven, we are cowards and jackasses if now that that war is over, we do not marshal every ounce of our brain and brawn to fight a sterner, longer, more unbending battle against the forces of hell in our own land.

We *return*.

We *return from fighting*.

We *return fighting*.

Make way for Democracy! We saved it in France, and by the Great Jehovah, we will save it in the United States of America, or know the reason why.

## Marcus Garvey, "National Anthem of Universal Negro Improvement Association and African Communities League," 1918

*The postwar mood for which historian John Higham coined the phrase "The Tribal Twenties" produced a galvanic new form of black nationalism under the leadership of Marcus Garvey (1887–1940), a Jamaican immigrant who settled in Harlem. Garvey envisioned an epic return of black Americans to Africa, a unification of all people of African descent, and the rejection of white colonialist powers in Africa. He responded dramatically to the massive disappointment that attended the failure of America to secure the rights and freedom of its black citizens after they had joined the war that President Wilson called the war to "make the world safe for democracy." At his peak in the early 1920s, Garvey commanded a following of hundreds of thousands and perhaps well over a million men and women. The following song, which was renamed in 1920 the "Universal Ethiopian Anthem," expresses the yearning for a world without racial subjection and for the redemption of Africa.*

*Source:* Marcus Garvey, "National Anthem of Universal Negro Improvement Association and African Communities' League" (1918) in Robert A. Hill, ed., *The Marcus Garvey and UNIA Papers* (Berkeley: University of California Press, 1983), 1:280.

### NATIONAL ANTHEM OF UNIVERSAL NEGRO IMPROVEMENT ASSOCIATION AND AFRICAN COMMUNITIES' LEAGUE—TO BE SUNG ON ALL OCCASIONS.

Ethiopia, thou land of our fathers,
Thou land where the gods loved to be:

REFRAIN

As storm cloud at night sudden gathers,
Our armies come rushing to thee.
Shall we in the fight be victorious
    When swords are thrust outward to
    glean?
For us will the vic'try be glorious
    When led by the red, black and green?

CHORUS

    Advance, advance to victory!
    Let Africa be free!
    Advance to meet the foe
    With the might
    Of the red, the black, the green.
Shall aliens continue to spoil us?
Shall despots continue their greed?

REFRAIN

Will nations in mock'ry revile us?
Then our keen swords intercede!
And tremblings shall fall on the nations,
    As eyes of mankind hath not seen,
Defeat shall meet their preparations,
    And vic'try the red, black and green.
And when the great battle is ended,
The swords and the spears be laid down:

REFRAIN

The land which their might had defended,
Shall once more become as our own.
And peace and prosperity bless us,
Our standard shall float far above us:

With warfare nor sorrow between us;
The red, and the black, and the green.

## Willa Cather, *My Ántonia*, 1918

*When she was eleven years old, Willa Cather (1873–1947) took a job delivering mail to the farmers around Red Cloud, Nebraska. Her family had moved to Red Cloud from Virginia in the early 1880s, just about a decade after the town was founded. Her mail route gave the youngster first-hand encounters with immigrants from Central and Northern Europe—Germans, Austrians, Bohemians, Scandinavians—who formed part of the titanic human wave that swept across the Great Plains after 1865. Mixing her own experiences of moving to and from Nebraska with her observations of the foreign-born families there, especially the tenacious hard-working "hired girls" like Ántonia Shimerda, Cather created an enduring novel,* My Ántonia *(1918), and one of the great immigrant characters in American literature. Part of a literary movement away from drawing-room stories of the urban middle and upper classes, Cather replicated the burdens of daily life on the frontier and offered realistic depictions of immigrants and the particular kind of loneliness and alienation they experienced an ocean and half-a-continent away from their homelands. The following selections from* My Ántonia *(the accent falls on the first syllable of her name) show the narrator, a boy named Jim Burden, getting acquainted with his grandparent's new neighbors, the Shimerdas.*

Source: *Willa Cather,* My Ántonia *(Boston: Houghton Mifflin, 1918), chapters 3–5, 10, 12, 13 (part).*

### 3

On Sunday morning Otto Fuchs was to drive us over to make the acquaintance of our new Bohemian neighbours. We were taking them some provisions, as they had come to live on a wild place where there was no garden or chicken-house, and very little broken land. Fuchs brought up a sack of potatoes and a piece of cured pork from the cellar, and grandmother packed some loaves of Saturday's bread, a jar of butter, and several pumpkin pies in the straw of the wagon-box. We clambered up to the front seat and jolted off past the little pond and along the road that climbed to the big cornfield.

I could hardly wait to see what lay beyond that cornfield; but there was only red grass like ours, and nothing else, though from the high wagon-seat one could look off a long way. The road ran about like a wild thing, avoiding the deep draws, crossing them where they were wide and shallow. And all along it, wherever it looped or ran, the sunflowers grew; some of them were as big as little trees, with great rough leaves and many branches which bore dozens of blossoms. They made a gold ribbon across the prairie. Occasionally one of the horses would tear off with his teeth a plant full of blossoms, and walk along munching it, the flowers nodding in time to his bites as he ate down toward them.

The Bohemian family, grandmother told me as we drove along, had bought the homestead of a fellow countryman, Peter Krajiek, and had paid him more than it was worth. Their agreement with him was made before they left the old country, through a cousin of his, who was also a relative of Mrs. Shimerda. The Shimerdas were the first Bohemian family to come to this part of the county. Krajiek was their only interpreter, and could tell them anything he chose. They could not speak enough English to ask for advice, or even to make their most pressing wants known. One son, Fuchs said, was well-grown, and strong enough to work the land; but the father was old and frail and knew nothing about farming. He was a weaver by trade; had been a skilled workman on tapestries and upholstery materials. He had brought his fiddle with him, which wouldn't be of much use here, though he used to pick up money by it at home.

"If they're nice people, I hate to think of them spending the winter in that cave of Krajiek's," said grandmother. "It's no better than a badger hole; no proper dugout at all. And I hear he's made them pay twenty dollars for his old cookstove that ain't worth ten."

"Yes'm," said Otto; "and he's sold 'em his oxen and his two bony old horses for the price of good workteams. I'd have interfered about the horses—the old man can understand some German—if I'd 'a' thought it would do any good. But Bohemians has a natural distrust of Austrians."

Grandmother looked interested. "Now, why is that, Otto?"

Fuchs wrinkled his brow and nose. "Well, ma'm, it's politics. It would take me a long while to explain."

The land was growing rougher; I was told that we were approaching Squaw Creek, which cut up the west half of the Shimerdas' place and made the land of little value for farming. Soon we could see the broken, grassy clay cliffs which indicated the windings of the stream, and the glittering tops of the cottonwoods and ash trees that grew down in the ravine. Some of the cottonwoods had already turned, and the yellow leaves and shining white bark made them look like the gold and silver trees in fairy tales.

As we approached the Shimerdas' dwelling, I could still see nothing but rough red hillocks, and draws with shelving banks and long roots hanging out where the earth had crumbled away. Presently, against one of those banks, I saw a sort of shed, thatched with the same wine-coloured grass that grew everywhere. Near it tilted a shattered windmill frame, that had no wheel. We drove up to this skeleton to tie our horses, and then I saw a door and window sunk deep in the draw-bank. The door stood open, and a woman and a girl of fourteen ran out and looked up at us hopefully. A little girl trailed along behind them. The woman had on her head the same embroidered shawl with silk fringes that she wore when she had alighted from the train at Black Hawk. She was not old, but she was certainly not young. Her face was alert and lively, with a sharp chin and shrewd little eyes. She shook grandmother's hand energetically.

"Very glad, very glad!" she ejaculated. Immediately she pointed to the bank out of which she had emerged and said, "House no good, house no good!"

Grandmother nodded consolingly. "You'll get fixed up comfortable after while, Mrs. Shimerda; make good house."

My grandmother always spoke in a very loud tone to foreigners, as if they were deaf. She made Mrs. Shimerda understand the friendly intention of our visit, and the Bohemian woman handled the loaves of bread and even smelled them, and examined the pies with lively curiosity, exclaiming, "Much good, much thank!"—and again she wrung grandmother's hand.

The oldest son, Ambroźh—they called it Ambrosch—came out of the cave and stood beside his mother. He was nineteen years old, short and broad-backed, with a close-cropped, flat head, and a wide, flat face. His hazel eyes were little and shrewd, like his mother's, but more sly and suspicious; they fairly snapped at the food. The family had been living on corncakes and sorghum molasses for three days.

The little girl was pretty, but Ántonia—they accented the name thus, strongly, when they spoke to her—was still prettier. I remembered what the conductor had said about her eyes. They were big and warm and full of light, like the sun shining on brown pools in the wood. Her skin was brown, too, and in her cheeks she had a glow of rich, dark colour. Her brown hair was curly and wild-looking. The little sister, whom they called Yulka (Julka), was fair, and seemed mild and obedient. While I stood awkwardly confronting the two girls, Krajiek came up from the barn to see what was going on. With him was another Shimerda son. Even from a distance one could see that there was something strange about this boy. As he approached us, he began to make uncouth noises, and held up his hands to show us his fingers, which were webbed to the first knuckle, like a duck's foot. When he saw me draw back, he began to crow delightedly, "Hoo, hoo-hoo, hoo-hoo!" like a rooster. His mother scowled and said sternly, "Marek!" then spoke rapidly to Krajiek in Bohemian.

"She wants me to tell you he won't hurt nobody, Mrs. Burden. He was born like that. The others are smart. Ambrosch, he make good farmer." He struck Ambrosch on the back, and the boy smiled knowingly.

At that moment the father came out of the hole in the bank. He wore no hat, and his thick, iron-grey hair was brushed straight back from his forehead. It was so long that it bushed out behind his ears, and made him look like the old portraits I remembered in Virginia. He was tall and slender, and his thin shoulders stooped. He looked at us understandingly, then took grandmother's hand and bent over it. I noticed how white and well-shaped his own hands were. They looked calm, somehow, and skilled. His eyes were melancholy, and were set back deep under his brow. His face was ruggedly formed, but it looked like ashes—like something from which all the warmth and light had died out. Everything about this old man was in keeping with his dignified manner. He was neatly dressed. Under his coat he wore a knitted grey vest, and, instead of a collar, a silk scarf of a dark bronze-green, carefully crossed and held together by a red coral pin. While Krajiek was translating for Mr. Shimerda, Ántonia came up to me and held out her hand coaxingly. In a moment we were running up the steep drawside together, Yulka trotting after us.

When we reached the level and could see the gold tree-tops, I pointed toward them, and Ántonia laughed and squeezed my hand as if to tell me how glad she was I had come. We raced off toward Squaw Creek and did not stop until the ground itself stopped—fell away before us so abruptly that the next step would have been out into the tree-tops. We stood panting on the edge of the ravine, looking down at the trees and bushes that grew below us. The wind was so strong that I had to hold my hat on, and the girls' skirts were blown out before them. Ántonia seemed to like it; she held her little sister by the hand and chattered away in that language which seemed to me spoken so much more rapidly than mine. She looked at me, her eyes fairly blazing with things she could not say.

"Name? What name?" she asked, touching me on the shoulder. I told her my name, and she repeated it after me and made Yulka say it. She pointed into the gold cottonwood tree behind whose top we stood and said again, "What name?"

We sat down and made a nest in the long red grass. Yulka curled up like a baby rabbit and played with a grasshopper. Ántonia pointed up to the sky and questioned me with her glance. I gave her the word, but she was not satisfied and pointed to my eyes. I told her, and she repeated the word, making it sound like "ice." She pointed up to the sky, then to my eyes, then back to the sky, with

movements so quick and impulsive that she distracted me, and I had no idea what she wanted. She got up on her knees and wrung her hands. She pointed to her own eyes and shook her head, then to mine and to the sky, nodding violently.

"Oh," I exclaimed, "blue; blue sky."

She clapped her hands and murmured, "Blue sky, blue eyes," as if it amused her. While we snuggled down there out of the wind, she learned a score of words. She was quick, and very eager. We were so deep in the grass that we could see nothing but the blue sky over us and the gold tree in front of us. It was wonderfully pleasant. After Ántonia had said the new words over and over, she wanted to give me a little chased silver ring she wore on her middle finger. When she coaxed and insisted, I repulsed her quite sternly. I didn't want her ring, and I felt there was something reckless and extravagant about her wishing to give it away to a boy she had never seen before. No wonder Krajiek got the better of these people, if this was how they behaved.

While we were disputing about the ring, I heard a mournful voice calling, "Án-tonia, Án-tonia!" She sprang up like a hare. "*Tatinek! Tatinek!*" she shouted, and we ran to meet the old man who was coming toward us. Ántonia reached him first, took his hand and kissed it. When I came up, he touched my shoulder and looked searchingly down into my face for several seconds. I became somewhat embarrassed, for I was used to being taken for granted by my elders.

We went with Mr. Shimerda back to the dugout, where grandmother was waiting for me. Before I got into the wagon, he took a book out of his pocket, opened it, and showed me a page with two alphabets, one English and the other Bohemian. He placed this book in my grandmother's hands, looked at her entreatingly, and said, with an earnestness which I shall never forget, "Te-e-ach, te-e-ach my Án-tonia!"

4

On the afternoon of that same Sunday I took my first long ride on my pony, under Otto's direction. After that Dude and I went twice a week to the post-office, six miles east of us, and I saved the men a good deal of time by riding on errands to our neighbours. When we had to borrow anything, or to send about word that there would be preaching at the sod schoolhouse, I was always the messenger. Formerly Fuchs attended to such things after working hours.

All the years that have passed have not dimmed my memory of that first glorious autumn. The new country lay open before me: there were no fences in those days, and I could choose my own way over the grass uplands, trusting the pony to get me home again. Sometimes I followed the sunflower-bordered roads. Fuchs told me that the sunflowers were introduced into that country by the Mormons; that at the time of the persecution, when they left Missouri and struck out into the wilderness to find a place where they could worship God in their own way, the members of the first exploring party, crossing the plains to Utah, scattered sunflower seed as they

went. The next summer, when the long trains of wagons came through with all the women and children, they had the sunflower trail to follow. I believe that botanists do not confirm Fuchs's story, but insist that the sunflower was native to those plains. Nevertheless, that legend has stuck in my mind, and sunflower-bordered roads always seem to me the roads to freedom.

I used to love to drift along the pale-yellow cornfields, looking for the damp spots one sometimes found at their edges, where the smartweed soon turned a rich copper colour and the narrow brown leaves hung curled like cocoons about the swollen joints of the stem. Sometimes I went south to visit our German neighbours and to admire their catalpa grove, or to see the big elm tree that grew up out of a deep crack in the earth and had a hawk's nest in its branches. Trees were so rare in that country, and they had to make such a hard fight to grow, that we used to feel anxious about them, and visit them as if they were persons. It must have been the scarcity of detail in that tawny landscape that made detail so precious.

Sometimes I rode north to the big prairie-dog town to watch the brown earth-owls fly home in the late afternoon and go down to their nests underground with the dogs. Ántonia Shimerda liked to go with me, and we used to wonder a great deal about these birds of subterranean habit. We had to be on our guard there, for rattlesnakes were always lurking about. They came to pick up an easy living among the dogs and owls, which were quite defenceless against them; took possession of their comfortable houses and ate the eggs and puppies. We felt sorry for the owls. It was always mournful to see them come flying home at sunset and disappear under the earth. But, after all, we felt, winged things who would live like that must be rather degraded creatures. The dog-town was a long way from any pond or creek. Otto Fuchs said he had seen populous dog-towns in the desert where there was no surface water for fifty miles; he insisted that some of the holes must go down to water—nearly two hundred feet, hereabouts. Ántonia said she didn't believe it; that the dogs probably lapped up the dew in the early morning, like the rabbits.

Ántonia had opinions about everything, and she was soon able to make them known. Almost every day she came running across the prairie to have her reading lesson with me. Mrs. Shimerda grumbled, but realized it was important that one member of the family should learn English. When the lesson was over, we used to go up to the watermelon patch behind the garden. I split the melons with an old corn-knife, and we lifted out the hearts and ate them with the juice trickling through our fingers. The white Christmas melons we did not touch, but we watched them with curiosity. They were to be picked late, when the hard frosts had set in, and put away for winter use. After weeks on the ocean, the Shimerdas were famished for fruit. The two girls would wander for miles along the edge of the corn-fields, hunting for ground-cherries.

Ántonia loved to help grandmother in the kitchen and to learn about cooking and housekeeping. She would stand beside her, watching her every movement. We were willing to believe that Mrs. Shimerda was a good housewife in her own country, but she managed poorly under new conditions: the conditions were bad enough, certainly!

I remember how horrified we were at the sour, ashy-grey bread she gave her family to eat. She mixed her dough, we discovered, in an old tin peck-measure that Krajiek had used about the barn. When she took the paste out to bake it, she left smears of dough sticking to the sides of the measure, put the measure on the shelf behind the stove, and let this residue ferment. The next time she made bread, she scraped this sour stuff down into the fresh dough to serve as yeast.

During those first months the Shimerdas never went to town. Krajiek encouraged them in the belief that in Black Hawk they would somehow be mysteriously separated from their money. They hated Krajiek, but they clung to him because he was the only human being with whom they could talk or from whom they could get information. He slept with the old man and the two boys in the dugout barn, along with the oxen. They kept him in their hole and fed him for the same reason that the prairie-dogs and the brown owls house the rattle-snakes—because they did not know how to get rid of him.

5

We knew that things were hard for our Bohemian neighbours, but the two girls were lighthearted and never complained. They were always ready to forget their troubles at home, and to run away with me over the prairie, scaring rabbits or starting up flocks of quail.

I remember Ántonia's excitement when she came into our kitchen one afternoon and announced: "My papa find friends up north, with Russian mans. Last night he take me for see, and I can understand very much talk. Nice mans, Mrs. Burden. One is fat and all the time laugh. Everybody laugh. The first time I see my papa laugh in this kawn-tree. Oh, very nice!"

I asked her if she meant the two Russians who lived up by the big dog-town. I had often been tempted to go to see them when I was riding in that direction, but one of them was a wild-looking fellow and I was a little afraid of him. Russia seemed to me more remote than any other country—farther away than China, almost as far as the North Pole. Of all the strange, uprooted people among the first settlers, those two men were the strangest and the most aloof. Their last names were unpronounceable, so they were called Pavel and Peter. They went about making signs to people, and until the Shimerdas came they had no friends. Krajiek could understand them a little, but he had cheated them in a trade, so they avoided him. Pavel, the tall one, was said to be an anarchist; since he had no means of imparting his opinions, probably his wild gesticulations and his generally excited and rebellious manner gave rise to this supposition. He must once have been a very strong man, but now his great frame, with big, knotty joints, had a wasted

look, and the skin was drawn tight over his high cheekbones. His breathing was hoarse, and he always had a cough.

Peter, his companion, was a very different sort of fellow; short, bow-legged, and as fat as butter. He always seemed pleased when he met people on the road, smiled and took off his cap to everyone, men as well as women. At a distance, on his wagon, he looked like an old man; his hair and beard were of such a pale flaxen colour that they seemed white in the sun. They were as thick and curly as carded wool. His rosy face, with its snub nose, set in this fleece, was like a melon among its leaves. He was usually called "Curly Peter," or "Rooshian Peter."

The two Russians made good farmhands, and in summer they worked out together. I had heard our neighbours laughing when they told how Peter always had to go home at night to milk his cow. Other bachelor homesteaders used canned milk, to save trouble. Sometimes Peter came to church at the sod schoolhouse. It was there I first saw him, sitting on a low bench by the door, his plush cap in his hands, his bare feet tucked apologetically under the seat.

After Mr. Shimerda discovered the Russians, he went to see them almost every evening, and sometimes took Ántonia with him. She said they came from a part of Russia where the language was not very different from Bohemian, and if I wanted to go to their place, she could talk to them for me. One afternoon, before the heavy frosts began, we rode up there together on my pony.

The Russians had a neat log house built on a grassy slope, with a windlass well beside the door. As we rode up the draw, we skirted a big melon patch, and a garden where squashes and yellow cucumbers lay about on the sod. We found Peter out behind his kitchen, bending over a washtub. He was working so hard that he did not hear us coming. His whole body moved up and down as he rubbed, and he was a funny sight from the rear, with his shaggy head and bandy legs. When he straightened himself up to greet us, drops of perspiration were rolling from his thick nose down onto his curly beard. Peter dried his hands and seemed glad to leave his washing. He took us down to see his chickens, and his cow that was grazing on the hillside. He told Ántonia that in his country only rich people had cows, but here any man could have one who would take care of her. The milk was good for Pavel, who was often sick, and he could make butter by beating sour cream with a wooden spoon. Peter was very fond of his cow. He patted her flanks and talked to her in Russian while he pulled up her lariat pin and set it in a new place.

After he had shown us his garden, Peter trundled a load of watermelons up the hill in his wheelbarrow. Pavel was not at home. He was off somewhere helping to dig a well. The house I thought very comfortable for two men who were "batching." Besides the kitchen, there was a living-room, with a wide double bed built against the wall, properly made up with blue gingham sheets and pillows. There was a little storeroom, too, with a window, where they kept guns and saddles and tools, and old coats and boots. That day the floor was covered with garden things, drying for winter; corn and beans and fat yellow cucumbers. There were no screens or window-blinds in the house, and all the doors and windows stood wide open, letting in flies and sunshine alike.

Peter put the melons in a row on the oilcloth-covered table and stood over them, brandishing a butcher knife. Before the blade got fairly into them, they split of their own ripeness, with a delicious sound. He gave us knives, but no plates, and the top of the table was soon swimming with juice and seeds. I had never seen anyone eat so many melons as Peter ate. He assured us that they were good for one—better than medicine; in his country people lived on them at this time of year. He was very hospitable and jolly. Once, while he was looking at Ántonia, he sighed and told us that if he had stayed at home in Russia perhaps by this time he would have had a pretty daughter of his own to cook and keep house for him. He said he had left his country because of a "great trouble."

When we got up to go, Peter looked about in perplexity for something that would entertain us. He ran into the storeroom and brought out a gaudily painted harmonica, sat down on a bench, and spreading his fat legs apart began to play like a whole band. The tunes were either very lively or very doleful, and he sang words to some of them.

Before we left, Peter put ripe cucumbers into a sack for Mrs. Shimerda and gave us a lard-pail full of milk to cook them in. I had never heard of cooking cucumbers, but Ántonia assured me they were very good. We had to walk the pony all the way home to keep from spilling the milk.

## 10

For several weeks after my sleigh-ride, we heard nothing from the Shimerdas. My sore throat kept me indoors, and grandmother had a cold which made the housework heavy for her. When Sunday came she was glad to have a day of rest. One night at supper Fuchs told us he had seen Mr. Shimerda out hunting.

"He's made himself a rabbit-skin cap, Jim, and a rabbit-skin collar that he buttons on outside his coat. They ain't got but one overcoat among 'em over there, and they take turns wearing it. They seem awful scared of cold, and stick in that hole in the bank like badgers."

"All but the crazy boy," Jake put in. "He never wears the coat. Krajiek says he's turrible strong and can stand anything. I guess rabbits must be getting scarce in this locality. Ambrosch come along by the cornfield yesterday where I was at work and showed me three prairie dogs he'd shot. He asked me if they was good to eat. I spit and made a face and took on, to scare him, but he just looked like he was smarter'n me and put 'em back in his sack and walked off."

Grandmother looked up in alarm and spoke to grandfather. "Josiah, you don't suppose Krajiek would let them poor creatures eat prairie dogs, do you?"

"You had better go over and see our neighbours tomorrow, Emmaline," he replied gravely.

Fuchs put in a cheerful word and said prairie dogs were clean beasts and ought to be good for food, but their family connections were against them. I asked what he meant, and he grinned and said they belonged to the rat family.

When I went downstairs in the morning, I found grandmother and Jake packing a hamper basket in the kitchen.

"Now, Jake," grandmother was saying, "if you can find that old rooster that got his comb froze, just give his neck a twist, and we'll take him along. There's no good reason why Mrs. Shimerda couldn't have got hens from her neighbours last fall and had a hen-house going by now. I reckon she was confused and didn't know where to begin. I've come strange to a new country myself, but I never forgot hens are a good thing to have, no matter what you don't have."

"Just as you say, ma'm," said Jake, "but I hate to think of Krajiek getting a leg of that old rooster." He tramped out through the long cellar and dropped the heavy door behind him.

After breakfast grandmother and Jake and I bundled ourselves up and climbed into the cold front wagon-seat. As we approached the Shimerdas', we heard the frosty whine of the pump and saw Ántonia, her head tied up and her cotton dress blown about her, throwing all her weight on the pump-handle as it went up and down. She heard our wagon, looked back over her shoulder, and, catching up her pail of water, started at a run for the hole in the bank.

Jake helped grandmother to the ground, saying he would bring the provisions after he had blanketed his horses. We went slowly up the icy path toward the door sunk in the drawside. Blue puffs of smoke came from the stovepipe that stuck out through the grass and snow, but the wind whisked them roughly away.

Mrs. Shimerda opened the door before we knocked and seized grandmother's hand. She did not say "How do!" as usual, but at once began to cry, talking very fast in her own language, pointing to her feet which were tied up in rags, and looking about accusingly at everyone.

The old man was sitting on a stump behind the stove, crouching over as if he were trying to hide from us. Yulka was on the floor at his feet, her kitten in her lap. She peeped out at me and smiled, but, glancing up at her mother, hid again. Ántonia was washing pans and dishes in a dark corner. The crazy boy lay under the only window, stretched on a gunny-sack stuffed with straw. As soon as we entered, he threw a grain-sack over the crack at the bottom of the door. The air in the cave was stifling, and it was very dark, too. A lighted lantern, hung over the stove, threw out a feeble yellow glimmer.

Mrs. Shimerda snatched off the covers of two barrels behind the door, and made us look into them. In one there were some potatoes that had been frozen and were rotting, in the other was a little pile of flour. Grandmother murmured something in embarrassment, but the Bohemian woman laughed scornfully, a kind of whinny-laugh, and, catching up an empty coffeepot from the shelf, shook it at us with a look positively vindictive.

Grandmother went on talking in her polite Virginia way, not admitting their stark need or her own remissness, until Jake arrived with the hamper, as if in direct answer to Mrs. Shimerda's re-

proaches. Then the poor woman broke down. She dropped on the floor beside her crazy son, hid her face on her knees, and sat crying bitterly. Grandmother paid no heed to her, but called Ántonia to come and help empty the basket. Tony left her corner reluctantly. I had never seen her crushed like this before.

"You not mind my poor *mamenka*, Mrs. Burden. She is so sad," she whispered, as she wiped her wet hands on her skirt and took the things grandmother handed her.

The crazy boy, seeing the food, began to make soft, gurgling noises and stroked his stomach. Jake came in again, this time with a sack of potatoes. Grandmother looked about in perplexity.

"Haven't you got any sort of cave or cellar outside, Ántonia? This is no place to keep vegetables. How did your potatoes get frozen?"

"We get from Mr. Bushy, at the postoffice—what he throw out. We got no potatoes, Mrs. Burden," Tony admitted mournfully.

When Jake went out, Marek crawled along the floor and stuffed up the doorcrack again. Then, quietly as a shadow, Mr. Shimerda came out from behind the stove. He stood brushing his hand over his smooth grey hair, as if he were trying to clear away a fog about his head. He was clean and neat as usual, with his green neckcloth and his coral pin. He took grandmother's arm and led her behind the stove, to the back of the room. In the rear wall was another little cave; a round hole, not much bigger than an oil barrel, scooped out in the black earth. When I got up on one of the stools and peered into it, I saw some quilts and a pile of straw. The old man held the lantern. "Yulka," he said in a low, despairing voice, "Yulka; my Ántonia!"

Grandmother drew back. "You mean they sleep in there—your girls?" He bowed his head.

Tony slipped under his arm. "It is very cold on the floor, and this is warm like the badger hole. I like for sleep there," she insisted eagerly. "My *mamenka* have nice bed, with pillows from our own geese in Bohemie. See, Jim?" She pointed to the narrow bunk which Krajiek had built against the wall for himself before the Shimerdas came.

Grandmother sighed. "Sure enough, where *would* you sleep, dear! I don't doubt you're warm there. You'll have a better house after while, Ántonia, and then you will forget these hard times."

Mr. Shimerda made grandmother sit down on the only chair and pointed his wife to a stool beside her. Standing before them with his hand on Ántonia's shoulder, he talked in a low tone, and his daughter translated. He wanted us to know that they were not beggars in the old country; he made good wages, and his family were respected there. He left Bohemia with more than a thousand dollars in savings, after their passage money was paid. He had in some way lost on exchange in New York, and the railway fare to Nebraska was more than they had expected. By the time they paid Krajiek for the land, and bought his horses and oxen and some old farm machinery, they had very little money left. He wished grandmother to know, however, that he still had some money. If they could get through until spring came, they would buy a cow and chickens and plant a garden, and would then do very well. Ambrosch and Ántonia were both old enough to work in the fields, and they were willing to work. But the snow and the bitter weather had disheartened them all.

Ántonia explained that her father meant to build a new house for them in the spring; he and Ambrosch had already split the logs for it, but the logs were all buried in the snow, along the creek where they had been felled.

While grandmother encouraged and gave them advice, I sat down on the floor with Yulka and let her show me her kitten. Marek slid cautiously toward us and began to exhibit his webbed fingers. I knew he wanted to make his queer noises for me—to bark like a dog or whinny like a horse—but he did not dare in the presence of his elders. Marek was always trying to be agreeable, poor fellow, as if he had it on his mind that he must make up for his deficiencies.

Mrs. Shimerda grew more calm and reasonable before our visit was over, and, while Ántonia translated, put in a word now and then on her own account. The woman had a quick ear, and caught up phrases whenever she heard English spoken. As we rose to go, she opened her wooden chest and brought out a bag made of bed-ticking, about as long as a flour sack and half as wide, stuffed full of something. At sight of it, the crazy boy began to smack his lips. When Mrs. Shimerda opened the bag and stirred the contents with her hand, it gave out a salty, earthy smell, very pungent, even among the other odours of that cave. She measured a teacup full, tied it up in a bit of sacking, and presented it ceremoniously to grandmother.

"For cook," she announced. "Little now; be very much when cook," spreading out her hands as if to indicate that the pint would swell to a gallon. "Very good. You no have in this country. All things for eat better in my country."

"Maybe so, Mrs. Shimerda," grandmother said dryly. "I can't say but I prefer our bread to yours, myself."

Ántonia undertook to explain. "This very good, Mrs. Burden"—she clasped her hands as if she could not express how good—"it make very much when you cook, like what my mama say. Cook with rabbit, cook with chicken, in the gravy—oh, so good!"

All the way home grandmother and Jake talked about how easily good Christian people could forget they were their brothers' keepers.

"I will say, Jake, some of our brothers and sisters are hard to keep. Where's a body to begin, with these people? They're wanting in everything, and most of all in horse-sense. Nobody can give 'em that, I guess. Jimmy, here, is about as able to take over a homestead as they are. Do you reckon that boy Ambrosch has any real push in him?"

"He's a worker, all right, ma'm, and he's got some ketch-on about him; but he's a mean one. Folks can be mean enough to get on in this world; and then, ag'in, they can be too mean."

That night, while grandmother was getting supper, we opened the package Mrs. Shimerda had given her. It was full of little brown chips that looked like the shavings of some root. They were as light as feathers, and the most noticeable thing about them was their penetrating, earthy odour. We could not determine whether they were animal or vegetable.

"They might be dried meat from some queer beast, Jim. They ain't dried fish, and they never grew on stalk or vine. I'm afraid of 'em. Anyhow, I shouldn't want to eat anything that had been shut up for months with old clothes and goose pillows."

She threw the package into the stove, but I bit off a corner of one of the chips I held in my hand, and chewed it tentatively. I never forgot the strange taste; though it was many years before I knew that those little brown shavings, which the Shimerdas had brought so far and treasured so jealously, were dried mushrooms. They had been gathered, probably, in some deep Bohemian forest. . . .

11

During the week before Christmas, Jake was the most important person of our household, for he was to go to town and do all our Christmas shopping. But on the twenty-first of December, the snow began to fall. The flakes came down so thickly that from the sitting-room windows I could not see beyond the windmill—its frame looked dim and grey, unsubstantial like a shadow. The snow did not stop falling all day, or during the night that followed. The cold was not severe, but the storm was quiet and resistless. The men could not go farther than the barns and corral. They sat about the house most of the day as if it were Sunday; greasing their boots, mending their suspenders, plaiting whiplashes.

On the morning of the twenty-second, grandfather announced at breakfast that it would be impossible to go to Black Hawk for Christmas purchases. Jake was sure he could get through on horseback, and bring home our things in saddle-bags; but grandfather told him the roads would be obliterated, and a newcomer in the country would be lost ten times over. Anyway, he would never allow one of his horses to be put to such a strain.

We decided to have a country Christmas, without any help from town. I had wanted to get some picture books for Yulka and Ántonia; even Yulka was able to read a little now. Grandmother took me into the ice-cold storeroom, where she had some bolts of gingham and sheeting. She cut squares of cotton cloth and we sewed them together into a book. We bound it between pasteboards, which I covered with brilliant calico, representing scenes from a circus. For two days I sat at the dining-room table, pasting this book full of pictures for Yulka. We had files of those good old family magazines which used to publish coloured lithographs of popular paintings, and I was allowed to use some of these. I took "Napoleon Announcing the Divorce to Josephine" for my frontispiece. On the white pages I grouped Sunday-School cards and advertising cards which I had brought from my "old country." Fuchs got out the old candle-moulds and made tallow candles. Grandmother hunted up her fancy cake-cutters and baked gingerbread men and roosters, which we decorated with burnt sugar and red cinnamon drops.

On the day before Christmas, Jake packed the things we were sending to the Shimerdas in his saddle-bags and set off on grandfather's grey gelding. When he mounted his horse at the door, I saw that he had a hatchet slung to his belt, and he gave grandmother a meaning look which told me he was planning a surprise for me. That afternoon I watched long and eagerly from the sitting-room window. At last I saw a dark spot moving on the west hill, beside the half-buried cornfield, where the sky was taking on a coppery flush from the sun that did not quite break through. I put on my cap and ran out to meet Jake. When I got to the pond, I could see that he was bringing in a little cedar tree across his pommel. He used to help my father cut Christmas trees for me in Virginia, and he had not forgotten how much I liked them.

By the time we had placed the cold, fresh-smelling little tree in a corner of the sitting-room, it was already Christmas Eve. After supper we all gathered there, and even grandfather, reading his paper by the table, looked up with friendly interest now and then. The cedar was about five feet high and very shapely. We hung it with the gingerbread animals, strings of popcorn, and bits of candle which Fuchs had fitted into pasteboard sockets. Its real splendours, however, came from the most unlikely place in the world—from Otto's cowboy trunk. I had never seen anything in that trunk but old boots and spurs and pistols, and a fascinating mixture of yellow leather thongs, cartridges, and shoemaker's wax. From under the lining he now produced a collection of brilliantly coloured paper figures, several inches high and stiff enough to stand alone.

They had been sent to him year after year, by his old mother in Austria. There was a bleeding heart, in tufts of paper lace; there were the three kings, gorgeously apparelled, and the ox and the ass and the shepherds; there was the Baby in the manger, and a group of angels, singing; there were camels and leopards, held by the black slaves of the three kings. Our tree became the talking tree of the fairy tale legends and stories nestled like birds in its branches. Grandmother said it reminded her of the Tree of Knowledge. We put sheets of cotton wool under it for a snow-field, and Jake's pocket-mirror for a frozen lake.

I can see them now, exactly as they looked, working about the table in the lamplight: Jake with his heavy features, so rudely moulded that his face seemed, somehow, unfinished; Otto with his half-ear and the savage scar that made his upper lip curl so ferociously under his twisted moustache. As I remember them, what unprotected faces they were; their very roughness and violence made them defenceless. These boys had no practised manner behind which they could retreat and hold people at a distance. They had only their hard fists to batter at the world with. Otto was already one of those drifting, case-hardened labourers who never marry or have children of their own. Yet he was so fond of children!

12

On Christmas morning, when I got down to the kitchen, the men were just coming in from their morning chores—the horses and pigs always had their breakfast before we did. Jake and Otto shouted "Merry Christmas!" to me, and winked at each other when they saw the waffle-irons on the stove. Grandfather came down, wearing a white shirt and his Sunday coat. Morning prayers were longer than usual. He read the chapters from Saint Matthew about the birth of Christ, and as we listened, it all seemed like something that had happened lately, and near at hand. In his prayer he thanked the Lord for the first Christmas, and for all that it had meant to the world ever since. He gave thanks for our food and comfort, and prayed for the poor and destitute in great cities, where the struggle for life was harder than it was here with us. Grandfather's prayers were often very interesting. He had the gift of simple and moving expression. Because he talked so little, his words had a peculiar force; they were not worn dull from constant use. His prayers reflected what he was thinking about at the time, and it was chiefly through them that we got to know his feelings and his views about things.

After we sat down to our waffles and sausage, Jake told us how pleased the Shimerdas had been with their presents; even Ambrosch was friendly and went to the creek with him to cut the Christmas tree. It was a soft grey day outside, with heavy clouds working across the sky, and occasional squalls of snow. There were always odd jobs to be done about the barn on holidays, and the men were busy until afternoon. Then Jake and I played dominoes, while Otto wrote a long letter home to his mother.

He always wrote to her on Christmas Day, he said, no matter where he was, and no matter how long it had been since his last letter. All afternoon he sat in the dining-room. He would write for a while, then sit idle, his clenched fist lying on the table, his eyes following the pattern of the oilcloth. He spoke and wrote his own language so seldom that it came to him awkwardly. His effort to remember entirely absorbed him.

At about four o'clock a visitor appeared: Mr. Shimerda, wearing his rabbit-skin cap and collar, and new mittens his wife had knitted. He had come to thank us for the presents, and for all grandmother's kindness to his family. Jake and Otto joined us from the basement and we sat about the stove, enjoying the deepening grey of the winter afternoon and the atmosphere of comfort and security in my grandfather's house. This feeling seemed completely to take possession of Mr. Shimerda. I suppose, in the crowded clutter of their cave, the old man had come to believe that peace and order had vanished from the earth, or existed only in the old world he had left so far behind. He sat still and passive, his head resting against the back of the wooden rocking-chair, his hands relaxed upon the arms. His face had a look of weariness and pleasure, like that of sick people when they feel relief from pain. Grandmother insisted on his drinking a glass of Virginia apple-brandy after his long walk in the cold, and when a faint flush came up in his cheeks, his features might have been cut out of a shell, they were so transparent. He said almost nothing, and smiled rarely; but as he

rested there we all had a sense of his utter content.

As it grew dark, I asked whether I might light the Christmas tree before the lamp was brought. When the candle-ends sent up their conical yellow flames, all the coloured figures from Austria stood out clear and full of meaning against the green boughs. Mr. Shimerda rose, crossed himself, and quietly knelt down before the tree, his head sunk forward. His long body formed a letter "S." I saw grandmother look apprehensively at grandfather. He was rather narrow in religious matters, and sometimes spoke out and hurt people's feelings. There had been nothing strange about the tree before, but now, with some one kneeling before it—images, candles . . . Grandfather merely put his finger–tips to his brow and bowed his venerable head, thus Protestantizing the atmosphere.

We persuaded our guest to stay for supper with us. He needed little urging. As we sat down to the table, it occurred to me that he liked to look at us, and that our faces were open books to him. When his deep-seeing eyes rested on me, I felt as if he were looking far ahead into the future for me, down the road I would have to travel.

At nine o'clock Mr. Shimerda lighted one of our lanterns and put on his overcoat and fur collar. He stood in the little entry hall, the lantern and his fur cap under his arm, shaking hands with us. When he took grandmother's hand, he bent over it as he always did, and said slowly, "Good wo-man!" He made the sign of the cross over me, put on his cap and went off in the dark. As we turned back to the sitting-room, grandfather looked at me searchingly "The prayers of all good people are good," he said quietly.

## 13

The week following Christmas brought in a thaw, and by New Year's Day all the world about us was a broth of grey slush, and the guttered slope between the windmill and the barn was running black water. The soft black earth stood out in patches along the roadsides. I resumed all my chores, carried in the cobs and wood and water, and spent the afternoons at the barn, watching Jake shell corn with a hand-sheller.

One morning, during this interval of fine weather, Ántonia and her mother rode over on one of their shaggy old horses to pay us a visit. It was the first time Mrs. Shimerda had been to our house, and she ran about examining our carpets and curtains and furniture, all the while commenting upon them to her daughter in an envious, complaining tone. In the kitchen she caught up an iron pot that stood on the back of the stove and said: "You got many, Shimerdas no got." I thought it weak-minded of grandmother to give the pot to her.

After dinner, when she was helping to wash the dishes she said, tossing her head: "You got many things for cook. If I got all things like you, I make much better."

She was a conceited, boastful old thing. and even misfortune could not humble her. I was so annoyed that I felt coldly even toward Ántonia and listened unsympathetically when she told me her father was not well.

"My papa sad for the old country. He not look good. He never make music any more. At home he play violin all the time; for weddings and for dance. Here never. When I beg him for play, he shake his head no. Some days he take his violin out of his box and make with his fingers on the strings, like this, but never he make the music. He don't like this kawn-tree."

"People who don't like this country ought to stay at home," I said severely. "We don't make them come here."

"He not want to come, nev-er!" she burst out. "My *mamenka* make him come. All time she say: 'America big country; much money, much land for my boys, much husband for my girls.' My papa, he cry for leave his old friends what make music with him. He love very much the man what play the long horn like this"—she indicated a slide trombone. "They go to school together and are friends from boys. But my mama, she want Ambrosch for be rich, with many cattle."

"Your mama," I said angrily, "wants other people's things."

"Your grandfather is rich," she retorted fiercely. "Why he not help my papa? Ambrosch be rich, too, after while, and he pay back. He is very smart boy. For Ambrosch my mama come here."

Ambrosch was considered the important person in the family. Mrs. Shimerda and Ántonia always deferred to him, though he was often surly with them and contemptuous toward his father. Ambrosch and his mother had everything their own way. Though Ántonia loved her father more than she did anyone else, she stood in awe of her elder brother.

After I watched Ántonia and her mother go over the hill on their miserable horse, carrying our iron pot with them, I turned to grandmother, who had taken up her darning, and said I hoped that snooping old woman wouldn't come to see us any more.

Grandmother chuckled and drove her bright needle across a hole in Otto's sock. "She's not old, Jim, though I expect she seems old to you. No, I wouldn't mourn if she never came again. But, you see, a body never knows what traits poverty might bring out in 'em. It makes a woman grasping to see her children want for things. Now read me a chapter in *The Prince of the House of David.* Let's forget the Bohemians."

## W. I. Thomas and Florian Znaniecki, *The Polish Peasant in Europe and America*, 1927

*The Polish Peasant in Europe and America remains a landmark in the study of immigrants to the United States. Authored principally by William I. Thomas (1863–1947), a sociologist at the University of Chicago, this five-volume work synthesized a large number of letters between emigrants, usually young men, and their relatives back in Poland. Moreover, Thomas interpreted these correspondences, producing the first large-scale analysis of the experience of immigration to the U.S. With a steady emphasis on the im-*

*portance of the ethnic group to the destiny of the individual, he examined the dynamics of immigrant life in the cities. He appraised the demoralization that resulted from the cutting of familial and communal ties, and he placed the resulting problems of crime, juvenile delinquency, and sexual promiscuity in this larger sociological context. The Polish Peasant formed one of the cornerstones of the eminent Chicago school of sociology, which provided the first sophisticated studies of immigrants in urban America. The surest sign of the caliber of this scholarship is that it continues to be read by students of immigration today. The following selection is a complete chapter from the book, focusing on the letters of one family, the Kozłowskis. The family's complicated internal relationships give an idea of the kinds of personal difficulties immigrants experienced as they navigated emotionally between the old world and the new.*

Source: William I. Thomas and Florian Znaniecki, *The Polish Peasant in Europe and America* (1927; reprint New York: Dover, 1958, 2 vols.), 1:527–555.

The Kozłowskis are a poor family in the province of Lomza. At his death the father left a small farm of two morgs—possibly inherited from his mother. The widow, Franciszka, remained on the farm with the youngest boy, Franek. One daughter (stepdaughter?) of Franciszka married a shoemaker of the same village. The position of a village shoemaker is rather bad, and this explains the apparent cupidity of the daughter. The other children had gone to America. Meanwhile there had remained undivided a farm left by Franciszka's late husband's father, and the trouble begins with the division of this land. In the division six morgs of land are added to the small farm of Franciszka. She has no right to sell these 6 morgs, but at the same time she wishes to get as much profit from the situation as possible, and, on the other hand, she is really not in a position to take care of the whole farm until Franek grows up. The shoemaker's wife has a right to part of the value of the whole farm and she claims her share, but Franciszka wants to pay her only a sum corresponding to her part of the original farm of two morgs, and wishes to drive a sharp bargain even then. Her first plan is to sell the farm, conceal as much money as possible for herself, and go to America to be supported there by her children. But the children are unwilling to give her power of attorney; they seem rightly to distrust her. Then, as the opportunity to marry presents itself, she changes her plans, sells whatever can be sold without legal authority, gets money from her children to join them in America, invents pretexts for not going, gets married, and tries to keep the whole farm for her youngest son, while getting in addition as much money as possible from the sale of the forest and stock. She succeeds perfectly, and is evidently too clever for her children. They not only get no money from her, but she succeeds in getting some from them. Ultimately she conciliates even her most dangerous antagonists, the shoemaker and his wife.

All this shows no lack of maternal feeling. On the contrary, she shows that feeling on the occasion of her daughter's death. But she has a powerful personality, and she has probably been independent for a long time; she has governed her environment, and she does not wish to fall into the position of an old, helpless, and moneyless mother, supported by her children. And as having some money herself is the only way of keeping her independence, she endeavors by all means to get it. As a woman, she has not the same tradition of familial solidarity as men; she is not the head of the family, the rightful manager of the common property; there are no rights and responsibilities of leadership to set limits to her egotism. The family-group as a distinct whole does not exist for her; she means to deal always only with individuals and opposes to them her own individuality. In so far the case is different from that of the old Wróblewski, who shows a much more far-going moral degeneration, since he is the head of a family and nevertheless breaks off all relations with his sons.

The influence of Franciszka's personality upon her environment is very well shown by the circumstance that everybody who comes into immediate touch with her finally does whatever she wishes. Her youngest son is under her absolute control; her *kuma*, Maryanna Szczepańska, is dominated; her second husband manifests a real devotion to her; even the stepdaughter and the shoemaker are subjugated, though not without protest. Her brothers and children in America are, of course, less under her power, but even they cannot quite avoid her influence. The letters give us a good idea of the means by which the social environment may be controlled through merely psychological influences, without any socially acknowledged right to control—one of the practical problems of the peasant woman and solved by many of them in the same way as by Kozłowska.

The fundamental device is, of course, the appeal to sentiment. Kozłowska uses it artistically. In order to appreciate this we must remember the peasants' tendency to schematize people and things. Every person belongs to a certain determined social type and is presumed to have the attitudes of this type; every person has a determined position, and from this position conclusions about his behavior may be drawn. The surest way to provoke a desired sentimental reaction in the environment is therefore to assume and to keep consistently a character corresponding to the sentiment it is desired to provoke. Thus, for example, a noble, a priest, a teacher, an official, a newspaper man, an agitator, wishing to win the attachment of the peasants, must each act in a different way. There are also reactions which only a person in a determined position can arouse. For instance, envy is most easily awakened in peasants by a peasant. A priest or a noble will hardly succeed in provoking pity, etc.

Now, Kozłowska has a determined character and she tries to arouse only such feelings as are habitual with regard to a person of this character. She is a widow and therefore presumed to be helpless. The supposition of helplessness has a stronger basis, because she is old and formally poor, i.e., she has little which is rightfully her own. Further, she is a mother and grandmother, and supposed to have the feelings of love, longing for her absent children, grief for a child's death, anxiety for her grandchildren when they become orphans, etc. The type of favorable reaction which she can easily provoke in her environment is thus predetermined; it is pity for her helplessness and sympathy for her maternal feelings. And, indeed, she plays continually those two chords. And she does it with just the intensity required by the social milieu to which she belongs. In a more cultivated milieu, more accustomed to restrain the feelings, her behavior would appear highly unnatural, distasteful, and hysterical. Perhaps she is in fact a little hysterical, but certainly her behavior is adapted to her social sphere—one accustomed to a display of feelings. She has nothing to lose and much to win by exaggeration; therefore she exaggerates her helplessness as well as her motherly love, her poverty and her (certainly unreal) bad health, her grief and her gratitude.

Of course, her actions are not in accordance with her assumed character; but she knows like a master how to present them in a suitable light. The gradual selling of the forest is given as the result of her poverty and inability to farm. When she wants the farm sold, she appeals to her oldest son as her "guardian" and pretends to acknowledge his authority. When she marries, she pretends that she was forced to it by her helplessness. Her anger against "the shoemaker's wife" is justified by her motherly indignation, because of the invectives and curses which the stepdaughter hurls against her children. And the hardest blow to her is the—just or unjust—allegation of immoral conduct, which tends to wreck completely her assumed character.

But she knows also how to use other weapons. She appeals to religious feelings—by using in a clever way the name of God, by sending religious tokens, by exploiting the magical fear of a mother's curse, by presenting other people's duties toward her in a religious form, etc. Expressions of indignation and pride alternate with appeals to pity and strengthen each other by contrast.

The second typical means of control is the use of the feelings aroused, instead of rational arguments. In asking for anything or in explaining her conduct Kozłowska does not rely upon the strength of her arguments. On the contrary, she seems to avoid intentionally the real issue and instead creates around the problem an atmosphere of sentiment favorable to her. It is hardly a fully conscious, rationally motivated policy, any more than is her ability to provoke the desired feelings; both are certainly naïve. Her use of sentiment instead of argument is also largely due to her insufficient training in argumentation. Most of her arguments, are, in fact, rather weak, and in this respect she is also a type. The essential features of her argumentation are almost universal, not only among women, but also among men of the peasant class, and this is precisely the argumentation which is most efficient with peasants. In order to demonstrate something rationally, we must not only be able to develop a logically perfect chain of reasoning, but must also have an opponent able to follow this reasoning to

acknowledge its binding character; and first of all, we must have identical premises. But a peasant opponent is not trained to follow a line of reasoning, is not accustomed to accept a thing as true solely because it has been demonstrated to him. And even if he admits a premise explicitly, he has always some other implicit premises which he keeps intentionally unexpressed and which invalidate in his mind his opponent's conclusion. So it is a difficult task to get the peasant to accept your argument. But if, with regard to a given problem, you succeed in arousing a set of feelings favorable to your view, the work is done, for the peasant will *himself invent* arguments which will persuade him. This is the mechanism used consciously by all those who want to influence the peasant, and they imitate it from the half-conscious procedure of the peasants themselves, of which Kozłowska gives a good example.

The third means which the old woman uses to obtain what she wants is to be as exacting as possible. She not only does not give her children what is due to them, but she continually demands moneys from them, and not only from them but even from her brothers, who have no obligation whatever toward her. She simply reverses the situation, making demands which the others might naturally make. It can be understood then that under these conditions her son-in-law, instead of claiming his wife's dowry, would be satisfied if she sent him back his own money, or her son would be satisfied if she let him alone. The principle is the same as in bargaining, which is a general characteristic of the peasant as well as of the Jew. In their dealings with the manor-owners the peasants' claims are sometimes impudent. They do not expect those claims to be granted, but they hope to get at least something. In many cases the source of this unlimited exacting is found in a curious psychological identification of wish and right. Thus, the peasants' wish to get the land of the nobility gives rise to a half-determined, sometimes even fully determined and rationally justified, conception that they have the right to this land. In Kozłowska's case certainly there is much of this attitude. We find it also in most family quarrels about property, and in many lawsuits.

Among the other personalities in this series the most interesting is perhaps the *kuma* (Marysia's godmother), Maryanna Szczepańska. She is notable because of the nature of her friendship with Franciszka. This kind of old women's friendship is very frequent. It is based upon a community of interests and attitudes. The women seek in each other a help against their respective families and comfort in domestic troubles, and, being of the same generation and the same social group, they agree perfectly with each other, particularly as there are no practical problems to divide them. The necessity of such a friendship is felt mostly in older age by women who do not know how to adapt themselves to the young generation, and who begin to feel solitary in their own families. Of course if there is a close and harmonious relation between husband and wife such a friendship has less occasion to arise, and indeed we do not find it in most of our series. In their relation the old women manifest much mutual adulation, and this shows that their friendship has still another function; it is their only way of getting social recognition of the kind and degree they desire. It seems to be a tacit pact between them always to praise, never to blame each other. They behave in the same way when speaking about each other, and Maryanna's letters are good examples of this behavior.

Old men, like old bulls, do not care much for society. Their social standing is more assured, their instinct of domination finds place enough in the family, their familial attitude does not allow them to initiate strangers into their home affairs, and they do not need any help against their families. After their retirement the situation changes, and then we find them sometimes associated in friendship with retired neighbors of the same age. The usual consequence of retirement, however, is to strengthen the bonds between husband and wife.

THE FAMILY KOZŁOWSKI

Franciszka Kozłowska, a widow

Antoni (Antoś, her son, living in America

Franek (Franciszek), her son, living with her

Józef Plata, her second husband

Marysia (Mania) Baranowska, Zosia Bieniewska, Julcia Brzostowicz, her daughters, living with their husbands in America

"The shoemaker's wife," her daughter or stepdaughter

Antoni Hermanowicz, "the shoemaker"

Wincenty, Antòni, Franciszka's brothers (or brothers-in-law)

Maryanna Szczepańska, Franciszka's
*kuma*

*Letters 226–245 are mainly from Franciszka
Kozłowska in Poland, to Members of her fam-
ily in America; 237–238, from Maryanna
Szczepańska; 230, 239–241, from Franek;
242–243, from Józef Plata; 244–245, from
Antoni Hermanowicz.*

## 226

### DANIŁOWO, MARCH 15, 1906

[To Marysia and Jan Baranowski] In the
first words of my letter I speak to you
with these godly words, "Praised be Jesus Christus," and I hope that you will
answer me "In centuries of centuries,
Amen." . . .

I inform you, dear children, about my
grief. Were it not for my soul for which
I am anxious lest I lose it in eternity, I
should have drowned myself, and you
would have nobody to write to any
more. Dear children, I write to you and
I don't s these letters from crying. I am
only glad from your letter that you intend to take me to America. There perhaps I should still live some years more.
But, dear daughter and son-in-law, make
some plan about all this.

Dear daughter and son-in-law, the
worst is the forest, for I could find some
farmer for [renting] the field, but the
worst is about the forest. People would
cut it down [steal the wood in my ab-
sence]. Dear children, you said in your
first letter that you would take me, so
take me indeed, I beg you heartily.

Dear children, I describe to you my

grief. On the same day when I received
that letter from you, I received also a
notification from the bailiff that the shoemaker's wife wants it [the farm] sold at
auction, and the auction will be on
March 21. Now, dear children, when we
were at the court, I asked them: "How
much do you want to be paid off." She
said 60, and he [her husband] said 70.
She said that she wanted not only [the
inheritance] after her father, but also after her grandfather. I offered her 50. But
now I will give her nothing at all. Let
her go by [the way of] lawsuits, I will
give her nothing at all. Now, dear children, I inform you that she writes letters
to America, and particularly to Antoni.
Moreover, through acquaintances she
sends messages against me. And now
Antos has not written to me for more
than 3 months [as a result of this slan-
dering]. And perhaps, dear daughter and
son-in-law, dear children, perhaps they
[Antos and wife] don't know that you
wish to take me to America, and they
don't know. But, dear daughter and son-
in-law, don't be angry with me for the
thing which I shall mention. Dear children, I could not get to America for my
money. Why, and I should not go without my son who is with me. Dear daughter and son-in-law, perhaps you will send
me a ship-ticket. Dear children, sign, all
of you, that you want me to come. For
perhaps you want me to come, dear
daughter and son-in-law, and perhaps
those [the son and daughter-in-law]
don't want me to come at all. Dear
daughter, I ask you whether you received
that letter in which were the scapularies
and the veil of God's Mother? You say,
dear daughter and son-in-law, that I was

angry with you. No, I was not angry at all, I was very much satisfied, only I waited for your answer. Dear children, you are so dear to me, that I kiss these photographs of you upon the wall. . . .

*Franciszka Kozłowska*

## 227

### NOVEMBER 4, 1906

*My dear Children:*

. . . And now I inform you that I am healthy, but scarcely, from all this thinking which I have upon my mind. . . . I received your letter and 3 photographs; I gave one to Szczepańska and I have two left. I inform you that I am very much satisfied, dear daughter and son-in-law, may our Lord God bless you, and God's Mother. May she help you in your work and in everything. . . . Now I write, your mother, to all of you, my children, in general. First to you, dear son, and to my daughter-in-law, and to the Bieniewskis and to the Brzostowiczs and to the Baranowskis, and I wish you every good, whatever you want for yourselves, my dear children.

Now I inform you about this land, that to these 2 morgs were added during the new division, 2 morgs of field and 1 morgs of forest to each. . . . So there are now 6 morgs of field and 2 of forest, 8 morgs together. Now I inform you, dear children, on what spots we received this addition. [Describes in detail.] You, Antoś, and you, Marysia, you know where it is and in what position.

Now, my dear children, it would be the best if we sold it, for I have nothing from it except trouble. I don't sow the land, only [strange] people do, for I rented it, for I cannot manage it myself. Even if I wanted to sow myself, you know that there is no barn and there is no place to put the crops. I keep the forest, but again people steal. A man could guard it more easily, while it, a woman, what can I do? I have only trouble. So it would be the best, my dear children, to sell it, for all this is wasted for the land they pay [the rent]; but in the forest whatever anybody snatches is his own, and when I need money, I also sell some tree, and so all this is wasted. If you don't do as I advise you, dear children, after a few years it will be much cheaper [worth less]. Now they would give money, for they want to buy it, as it is in good order, the forest and the field. For the 2 morgs of forest they would give now 400 roubles, and for the 6 morgs of land they would give perhaps 300. And perhaps they would give more.

My dear children, consult one another and write me, how I shall do. But it would be the best, my dear son Antoś, if it were your head, for you are my guardian. Arrange it so that we may sell it and that you may take me and Franek to America, for I don't wish to farm here. I have the land, but I have no barn, nowhere to put [the crops], and you know that there is no place [near the house] to build it. So it would be the best to sell the field, if you don't wish to be upon it [to settle here], and if I must only grieve [have trouble] alone, I can sell it myself, only send me, all you children, an authorization, and let your uncles send me also an authorization, for they belong to the same farm [they have a right to a part of it]. Then I shall sell it and come to you, and we shall live together, and you will get sooner something of it, for now the value is greater as long as the forest is entire and nothing is missing. . . . I beg you, dear son, if you allow me to sell it, do it at once. . . . I beg you, dear son, do it for me, and you all, my dear children, and you, my dear brothers, do it for me, for I would see you once more, as long as we are still alive. [Greetings.]

Franciszka Kozłowska

*Dear daughter Marysia and son-in-law:*
Why are there in the [wedding-] photograph neither the Bieniewskis, nor the Brzostowiczs, nor my brothers, nor my sister-in-law, only strange people? This astonishes me much. What does it mean?

## 228

MARCH 4, 1907

*Dear Son:*
. . . You are obstinately bent against me and I am against you. I would not write to you, hut I must. I write you only: consult among yourselves [and decide] as you want to. The shoemaker's wife made an inventory [of the farm, for auction]. We stood before the court, and she quarreled with me, tooth against tooth, and moreover she cursed you for neither taking her man to America nor paying her off. Our guardians asked her how much she wanted to be paid off. Then this old beggar, this carcass [her husband] wanted 70 roubles, and she asked 60. I will give her 50, and the guardians also tell her to take 50 and no

more. But, dear son, I would rather give her nothing. What do you advise? I was everywhere [for advice], and I thought of either renting the field or selling the forest [to pay her]. But, dear son, I wish I had never lived until this new division and addition, since I am a hinderance to all of you and you are angry with me and you don't write me for half a year. Were it not for this affair I would rather have died [*zdechła*, used here vulgarly like the English "rotted," is properly used only of animals = German *krepiren*] and would not have written. Now, dear son, come rather to an understanding among yourselves, take it, sell it and make peace with this shoemaker's wife. Let her not call God's vengeance upon you and grieve me. And now after all this she intends to have an auction, for her part of the inheritance from your grandfather and your father. You left me here for sorrow only. Dear children, don't believe anybody, when the shoemaker's wife slanders me to people. Why, you get it [had words] also from her, dear son, into your eyes, and behind your eyes [proverbial, to your face and behind your back]. And you get still more from her. She says: "Much did he care for his mother! And when he came to Warsaw, he let his nails grow a *sążeń* long [6 feet] pretending to be a gentleman."

Dear son, I thank you for writing to me so often! But don't think, dear son, that I write it from my whole heart [that I am grieved]. I say it simply because you write once in a year. If I had known that you would guard me so! May our Lord God and your children care for you as much as you do for me! If you had not gone into the world you would have known better what a mother is, while now in return for my education [of you] you are ashamed of me. But Mańka did the same. She accidentally wrote one letter, that we might know only that she got married. Dear son, please say to Mańka about this letter that she rejoiced me awfully, that I don't know what to do in the country, and she gave me precisely such advice as the letters she writes [no letters, no advice]. To the shoemaker's wife she can well send bows and write, but when her godmother sends her a gift—she sent her scapularies and a veil of God's Mother— she did not even thank her. Dear son, and all my dear children together, I tell you sincerely I won't write you any more letters since you are so turned to stone against me. Since you are so little curious to learn what is going on here with us I won't inform you. I bless you all with the holy cross [old habit in bidding farewell].

Dear son, you said to Franek, "If you manage well I will send you some assistance." And now you don't even send a naked letter [without a stamp]. But if this shoemaker's wife sells our land at auction then our assistance is over. Dear son, we keep two pigs for ourselves, but there can be no cow from them [probably alluding to some promise to send money for a cow], the less so if the shoemaker's wife drags us about courts, as she is now doing. Dear son, I ask you, and do you answer me. Do you agree to pay her 50 roubles, as I wish, or not? Perhaps you will send us some money for this payment? For if we sell these pigs, we can have perhaps enough to buy a cow, I beg you, dear son, for a speedy answer. I salute you all, yourself and your wife and my grandchildren.

[Franciszka]

## 229

JUNE 2, 1907

*Dear Children:*
I inform you that I am not very healthy, for even an iron man would have no longer any health, I thank you heartily for this letter, dear children, which you sent me. And then, dear children, I received also the letter from Zosia. Dear children, I beg you all together, answer me, what is this "dirt" which I have on me? Answer me, who wrote that letter so that this "dirt" may not grieve me longer. Dear children, I have enough of my own trouble. Dear children, I can never in the world bear these troubles, for, dear children, in the week when I wrote this letter I went to Czerwin, and I hardly got there, for my feet were covered with blisters. And I went in vain, for not all of our guardians were there; 3 were and 3, not. Now I shall have to go again, and when winter comes and it is necessary to creep upon the snow, surely I shall die. And since the shoemaker's wife made the inventory, the guardians won't allow me to sell this property, for Franek is a minor.

And now, dear children, could you arrange so: Send me such a decision that I can rent [the farm] for some years. Now people are afraid to pay money down for some years, lest it be lost, I should be glad, dear children, to step away from her [the shoemaker's wife's] eyes. [*Ślepie*, in the original, is properly used only for the eyes of animals.] Let her not cause me any more grief. If I went to you perhaps God would guard me for a year or two, while thus, dear children, when these troubles fill my head I have [peace] neither day nor night. There is no work from me at all, and soon I shall go away from [lose] my reason, and I shall no longer understand any of your writing. O God my dear, God my dear, why do you keep me in this world? Dear children, I beg you, take me to you, I want to have one hour of relief at least and not have to listen to this [calling of] vengeance against you, dear son, and against Zosia. Moreover, she [the daughter] persuades some dogs like herself to write dirt against me. What dirt do they write against me? Perhaps she writes against me about this [man]? I who can hardly walk with my pains, and she writes dirt about me! For this land I should have more than one purchaser, but when I learned that the guardians won't let it be sold, I have no more strength to bear all this. Oh, nothing can be done, my dear children, evidently she must kill me with trouble in this country!

Dear brother, you ask me in your letter about money. I did not see any money and probably I am to see none. When you sent me some, I saw it, but now when you don't send, I see none.

I greet you also, my dear children. It is true that I received at last a letter from you, but I will remember it until my death—what [sorrow] you gave me about that dirt.

I have nothing more to write to you, dear children and brother. Remain with God. May God help you.

*[Franciszka]*

I salute my sister-in-law and my brother. Sister-in-law, why should we be angry with each other and what for? I have not seen you, sister-in-law, with my very eyes, and I shall die without seeing you. Well, my dear, let us kiss each other, at least by letter, at least through this paper; let us give hands to each other. I thank you so much, sister-in-law, for not forgetting me yet, and that you both remembered me. Dear brother, I thank you for this, for your knowing that I am your sister. Remember, dear, how you cared for me and I cared for you.

*[Franciszka]*

Dear children, I don't want to make you any trouble about taking me [sending me a ship-ticket]. I should prefer if you sent me a few roubles [in cash], but I should find my way more easily if you take me [if you send me a ticket].

## 230

[JUNE 2 1907]

*Dear Brother and Sisters:*

Have pity and take at least our mother, let her have at least a few easier hours. Dear brother and sisters and brothers-in-law, I beg you, if you want to see your mother before she dies, take her to you. Have pity, for, dear brother and sisters, you have written already 4 letters, thanks to God, and in each of them you say that you will take us to America. So mother waits for this letter like the mercy of God. When the letter comes, mother kisses it from joy and wets it with tears, but when she opens it [she is deceived].

[Franek]

## 231

[JUNE 12 1907]

*Dear Son Antoni:*

Answer me how I shall manage, for my son-in-law Baranowski sent me a letter saying that he is sending me a ship-ticket for myself and for my son, and wishes to take us to America. And you, dear son, come to an understanding yourself with the others, whether all of you know about it or not, for I am not just as I stand, but I have land and forest, and I don't know how to manage. It is true that my son-in-law is good. But you, my son, you are my guardian, and answer me, how I shall have it there [what conditions]. For, my dear son, there is a marriage opportunity for me, with Józef Plata, who is a very good man. So answer me, my son, as soon as possible, whether I may live in our country, for I don't need to wander about the world in my old years, only my [youngest] son wants us to go. Dear son, answer me as soon as possible, for I am awaiting this letter with my journey and with my wedding. . . . Dear son, reflect all of you only once, but well, for my son-in-law tells me to rent the land and the forest. . . . I cannot sell it myself, a fa-

ther can, but not I. I have nothing more to write, only I wish you health, happiness, and good success. . . . Dear son, when you receive this letter, don't show it to my daughter Mania, and don't tell her anything, for my son-in-law wishes to take me secretly to America [to surprise his wife].

*Franciszka Kozłowska*

## 232

SEPTEMBER 11 [1907]

. . . *Dear Son:*

. . . You advised me to go hut now I am not going. I have married that Plata who had Ewa Pieńkos as wife, from the same village I came from. What could I do in this misery? When I received the ship-tickets I did at once what you ordered me to do. I rented the land for 3 years, I sold the cow which I had and the forest which was left after father's death, while yours [inherited from the grandfather] is still there, I have wasted all the living which I had [store of grain, potatoes, etc.] and I have bought everything for the journey. And now living is expensive, and I spent some money on living, and I had to dress myself and Franek a little before going to you . . . and I bought 2 shawls for 13 roubles and 15 pounds of feathers for 12 roubles. [Went twice to the doctor, then to Libawa, and was sent back.] This journey cost us much, for everywhere money had to be paid, and I wasted everything. I have not written to you for I fell sick from grief and I waited until our Lord God changed [restored] me. But now I am somewhat better and I describe this to you. Her-manowiczowa [the "shoemaker's wife"] moved to me, to my lodging and I live with Plata. He built a new house, and Franek is with me. How good he [the husband] is to me, thanks to God! May he be always as good! For when I am sick, he at least cares well for me, and it is well now. I had decided to go to America, but when these Baranowskis managed it so badly, I changed my mind, for now I have no land, and therefore I had to marry. Inform the Baranowskis how I did, and let them send their ad-dress, then I shall send them the ship-tickets back. Don't be angry with me for having done so, for I have wasted every-thing through this. And in the office [in Libawa] they said that these are tickets for a working-ship [steerage?]. And you can know what this journey has cost me. From Warsaw to Libawa alone 42 rou-bles. . . .

[Franciszka]

[Postscript]

And I inform you that we went [started] to America all three, the shoe-maker went with us for money, for he borrowed it. When we returned he gave this money back at once, for he bor-rowed it from the priest and wished to go along with us.

I inform you also that when I in-tended to go to America I went to Go-worowo to a doctor. He poured some-thing into my eyes and almost burned my eyes. I went twice to Warsaw, and there the doctor said that I could have been blinded. You say that I did not wish to go. But I went twice to Ostrołęka to the [district-] chief for passports, and I

paid once one rouble, then two. So much trouble and cost I had.

. . . Now I inform you, my dear chil-dren, daughter and son-in-law, that I re-ceived your letter and we answer you at once and we inform you that we are in good health [wishes]. Now you write to me, son-in-law; and you are angry with me. But nothing can be done. I am not guilty at all in this matter, my dear son-in-law, for I was already on the way, in the last station, in Libawa, and from Li-bawa we were sent back. Now, my dear children, would I have caused such a cost for you without wishing to go to you? Why, our Lord God would punish me severely for it. And as to this, dear chil-dren, that I got married, don't persuade [reproach] this to me, for I got married only when I came back from my journey. If the ship-tickets had been good, I should be in America already, with you, for I wanted continuously [sic] to go to you. But since it happened so, nothing can be done, my dear son-in-law. You have made expenses for yourself, and I also, my dear children, have made ex-penses for myself, and I got totally ru-ined, for I wanted to go to you within an hour [immediately]. I had a cow; I wasted it. I had some small crops in the field; I wasted them also, for I prepared myself to go, and you don't believe me and are angry with me. As to my getting married, dear children, it was from this misery, when we had been sent back home, for I had wasted everything, so how could I live? And this year all living is expensive here, grain and potatoes are expensive, and so in putting things to-gether it is easier for me to live.

And as to my not having answered

you and sent you the tickets back, it was because I had not your address, and I was afraid to send them to these other children, for perhaps they would not have given them back to you. Now as soon as I received your letter, I sent you at once the ship-tickets, and these signs [checks] of these agents from Warsaw, to whom you wrote to care for us, I sent them to you for controlling. Dear children, how much trouble and weeping I had in that Libawa, God forbid! It is impossible to understand these Germans [sic!]. Were it not for an interpreter who explains everything in Polish I should not have got these ship-tickets back, for they threw them away at once and I could not find them. They wanted red ones, and these were black, and therefore they sent us back and we have all so much expense.

And now I inform you, dear children, about these 60 roubles. I have them not, for I have spent them. I inform you that from Warsaw to Libawa the railway cost us 21 roubles and 21 roubles back. Now I bought you, Marysia, 2 shawls, I gave 13 roubles, and 15 pounds of feathers, I gave 12 roubles, and all this is lying here. Now, dear children, I don't know what I shall do with all this myself, for I have my own shawl and I don't want yours. Write me, dear daughter; perhaps I can send you these shawls by somebody. As to the rest, dear children, forgive me. When I have more money, I will send you at least one half. As to my daughter and your wife, don't be angry, my son-in-law, that you did not take any fortune with her. If you want to come here, sell her part and take it, for it belongs to her. It is as if she had it in her pocket. . . .

Now I send you a greeting from myself, your mother, and from Franek, and from your father, my husband. Dear children, I did not marry a young man, only a man in the same age as I am, and he is good for me, and he does not hinder you at all, for he won't waste your fortune; he has enough of his own to live. In another letter I will write you still more about my journey, for it is too much writing at once.

*Your truly loving mother,*
*Franciszka Kozłowska*

## 234

DECEMBER 24, 1908

*Dear Son-in-law:*
I inform you that we received your letter on December 21, for which we thank you heartily. But instead of being comforted, I was grieved, and I should even prefer if you had not answered me so soon, for I should think her still alive. Why did you send me, dear children, such a letter, at once about money and about my dear dead daughter? Probably you intend to push me alive into the tomb through such writing as you write to me! You write, son-in-law, and you trouble me about sending you at least 100 roubles back. But I thank God that I have anything to put into my pot, for I have wasted everything through your fault. I rented the land, and I live now as I can, poor orphan, upon this world of God. And now, dear children, do you

think that I grieve only about your money? Oh no, my children, I grieve because my beloved daughter is dead and the orphans are left. How do they live there, my dear little grandchildren? And I grieve, because Franek will have to go to the army, and you all scattered about the world, away from me, poor orphan. And you cause me still more grief by this bit of paper, asking me to give you this money back. I know that you wasted money on me, but I wasted also everything which I owned upon this journey to you. But I don't deny what you sent me. Only, if you want to have this money, come back to our country, as other people do; you have your parts, sell them and you will have your money. But evidently you want to bury me alive into this holy earth, that I may not live any more upon this earth with my beloved daughter [sic!]. But why should you, dear son-in-law, persuade me that it is time for me to go into this holy earth? When I shall go to my tomb, you won't even know it. So, my dear son-in-law, don't make me grieve any more, for you made me grieve enough in a single letter.

Dear son-in-law B., I beg you, if it is very hard for you to be there with these children, I beg you, if it is possible, send me one child, so I can educate it. I beg you, dear son-in-law, do as you think the best. And I beg you, dear son-in-law Franu . . . [pet name], if you could send it, write me in a letter whether you will send it or not, my dear son-in-law!

Dear son-in-law [Janek] and daughter, although you are angry with me about this money, I beg you still, care for these orphans, for you see that they have no mother now. And if it is possible, I beg you, dear daughter, send me one child. I would keep it as long as my eyes shine upon this world. I beg you for it, my dear daughter. Reflect how you should act with regard to my words. May God grant us to live until this. Amen.

[Franciszka]

## 235

### APRIL 18, 1909

And now, dear children, we answer you "In centuries of centuries, Amen." And now we inform you that we received your letter on Good Friday, for which we thank you heartily, for not forgetting us [Health and wishes.] I am healthy, by the grace of God, only this death of Zosia torments me and gives me no peace. How is she buried there, and why was I not there when she was dying? But, dear daughter and son-in-law, try that at least these orphans get on well, that they don't suffer hunger, for you see that they cannot have a mother any more, only you are their guardians. Care for them, and God and Mother Mary will care for you.

And I ask you, my dear children, how do you live without your sister and my dear daughter, for I think continually about her, day and night. I gave money for recording her, and if God helps me I will give also for a holy mass for repose of her soul. And I pray for her to God and to our Mother Mary, that God may take her to himself. Pray you also to God for her soul, and God will forgive her certainly.

And now, dear daughter, you mention these feathers, asking me to send them to you. You see, it is so, dear daughter. These feathers which I had bought began to be eaten by mites, so I sold a part of them, but if somebody happens to go to America, I will buy some and send them to you. But if nobody goes, then nothing can be done, and don't be angry with me, dear daughter and son-in-law, for I am not guilty at all. It is true that it costs you a few roubles, but I have also lost everything which I had. So don't be angry with me, my dear children, for if I cannot reward you, I will pray to God for your health and success, and God will help you in your work. . . .

[Franciszka]

And I greet you, dear brother Wincenty. I cannot give you my hand in this [help you], for I have nothing myself, but you, children, do your best and nourish your uncle as you can. Dear brother, can you not help yourself in any way? Come to an understanding with our brother and make some plan, so that it may be well.

You see, dear brother, when you were in good condition, you did not want to know anything about your wife and children, and now you remember them!

## 236

### FEBRUARY 9, 1913

I received your letter, my dear children [Baranowskis], for which I thank you heartily, for I waited for it with longing. My dear children, you say that I am angry with you. Oh no, my dear children, I am not angry with you. You say that I did not answer your letter. It is true, my dearest children, that I did not answer you, but why? You see, it is true that you wished to take me to you, and I was glad because of your wish, but I don't know whether that ticket was bad or those guides. And so you sent me money and I sold everything, or rather wasted everything [sold too cheap] and went. And when I was returned, was it my fault? I wasted your money, and very little of mine was left. When I returned home, I found a desert house. What could I begin then, poor orphan? Should I have called to you, my dear children, and related to you my trouble? But my voice could not have reached you, for you are in a far country, and I was left, an orphan, among waste and troubles, and I had slowly to provide myself once more with the outfit which I had wasted. You were angry with me, dear children, as if I did so intentionally in order to take the money without coming to you. Oh my children, our Lord God is above us, He sees and hears everything. Should I lie?' Should I have renounced you and not [wanted] to go to you and not [wanted] to see you? Why, you know that I am left now alone, I have none of you, my dearest children, with me, I am left alone, an orphan, and I can see none of you alive, only I look continually upon these dead photographs. But you, dear daughter, surely you forgot me in truth, since you let a year pass without writing to me, and you forgot when I asked you for the photograph of that orphan after [left by] Zosia. You sent one to the shoemaker's wife and you did not even mention me. I asked the shoemaker's wife for this photograph, but she did not wish to give it to me. . . . Well, and now, dear daughter, you remembered that you have still a mother somewhere in the world, and you write, curious how I live here and how I succeed!. . . .

And now, dear daughter and son-in-law, please don't be angry about that which I shall ask for, and send me a photograph of these orphans; let me see them once more at least.

Now I send an image and a toy for my granddaughter. . . .

*[Franciszka]*

## 237

[NOVEMBER 4, 1906]

I write to you both, my dear goddaughter, I, your godmother Szczepańska, and I wish you every good and whatever you want from our Lord God, the best. I thank you for not forgetting about me, so I send you a gift. These are those scapularies from Częstochowa, and in this one scapulary with the cross there is sewed up a [part of the] veil of God's Mother of Częstochowa. This is important. I send you a blessing for your whole life. May God bless you, and God's Mother. And my daughter Helcia is very glad that you don't forget her. . . .

*Szczepańska*

## 238

[DECEMBER 28, 1908]

And now I, dear daughter, greet you, I, your godmother, greet you, Mania! Dear daughter, I write you about this: Why did you cause such costs for your mother that she might go to you, to America! Going to this America, your mother sold the forest and rented the land, and all the money which she had was wasted in journeying. She went twice to Ostrołęka; no little money was spent; twice to Warsaw on account of her eyes. Then at last they went to Libawa and there they remained for some time, and the rest of their money was spent on their living, for the ship-tickets were bad, and they had to return home. Your mother had sold everything, she had sold even her best petticoat for this journey, and when she came back, if Pl[ata] had not married her, I don't know how she would live, for she had not a grosz left. Now, you wrote that Zosia is no longer alive, and I am also sad, and what do you think about your own mother? And you make her grieve still more about this money. You have no idea what a sad Christmas your mother had this year, for she is grieved because of the death of her beloved daughter. And this field which your mother rented is still sown by strange people, until the years are ended [the renting-term], and your mother, as you know, is fed by Pl[ata] until [the end of] this time. And now, dear daughter Mania, don't be offended at my writing it to you, but your mother is almost senseless, and she continually cries and complains, what a bad fortune befell her upon this world.

> I, who love you, my daughter,
>> *Maryanna Szczepańska*

*Dear [god]daughter,*
I have learned to know your mother now. If she could take her heart out, she would give it to you, but she cannot take it out and what will she do with her misery? And now I bid you all goodbye. May God grant it. Amen.

## 239

OCTOBER 24, 1907

Dear Sister and Brother-in-law: I send you holy images. . . . Dear sister and brother-in-law, you don't believe us that we wanted to go to America; but . . . I, your brother, will draw my lot [be called to military service] in two years after next spring, so . . . I should be glad to see all of you at once. . . . Dear brother-in-law, I am very much grieved that you say that you will tear all the hair from your head [from despair]. Dear brother-in-law, it is not the fault of my sister. . . .

> *Franek Kozłowski*

## 240

[APRIL 18, 1909]

And now I, Franciszèk [Franek], thank you, dear brother-in-law and sister, for at least not forgetting me, for my brother dear [irony] does not write me

a single word. He is angry with me, I don't know what for. Although we ought to love each other, for we are only two and I must go to the army instead of him, he does not care for me. Such a good brother, loving his brother! It is bitter and hard for me to remember such a brother! What is my fault toward him? O God, be merciful to us, your sinners!

And now, dear brother-in-law and sister, I go to Prussia, so please write me a letter there. I will send you my address. I was in Częstochowa, but I did not expect that a letter from you, dear sister, would come, or else I should have brought a greater token. Now I send you only scapularies of Mary the Virgin, already consecrated, ready to be put around the neck. . . .

> *[Franek]*

## 241

JUNE 11, 1911

*Dear Sister and Brother-in-law:*
[Complains about military service.] May never any good man serve in the army, for here everybody must be a slave and is not free, as at home. And now I ask you, my dear sister Mania and brother-in-law, how do you succeed in that America, whether well or poorly. Write me please, dear sister, how are these orphans kept after Zosia['s death], . . . for I am very curious [interested]. And answer me, whether our brother-in-law B. married [a second time] or not. [Describes military life.]

And now, dear Mania and brother-in-law, I beg you write a letter to our sorrowful dear mother, and don't be angry with mother, for she is without guilt toward you, and sinful before God alone. Dear Mania and brother-in-law, you are probably angry since the time when you wanted to take her to America. But old mother then wanted to go to you as to God (without comparing it), and she rejoiced that in her old years she was to see her children. But what could she do when she was unable to go to you? And now, dear sister Mania and brother-in-law, you are angry with your sorrowful and grieved mother, while perhaps you won't see her any more unless in the next world. And with this anger you will go into the next world, and so we shall look upon one another—and what will God say to this? How shall we justify ourselves? Dear sister and brother-in-law, mother writes to me always and says that she has no letter from you, and she always weeps in her letter, so it is not pleasant for me either, for she is my mother and yours. . . . If you saw our mother, you would never recognize her, how she is now without children, for always something new happens [some new trouble].

Franek Kozłowski

## 242

### [JULY 12, 1907]

I, Józef Pl[ata], wish to take your dear mother for my wife. Answer as soon as possible whether you will take her or whether you tell her to marry me. I would give my life for her. I have noth-

ing more to write, only I send a low bow to you all, to the whole family.

Your well-wishing<br>Józef Pl[ata]

### [APRIL 18, 1909]

And now I, your father, salute you, together with your mother and my son, and we wish you every good, whatever you want for yourself from God. We greet [bless] also those little orphans. May God keep them in His holiest guardianship. And [if] perhaps anything in this letter displeases you, then please forgive, for your mother was terribly grieved. . . .

[Józef Plata]

## 244

### MARCH 27, 1912

*Dear Brother-in-law and dear Sister:*
It is very painful for me that I cannot see my family, and don't even receive a bit of paper that I might at least by letter speak with you. But God reward you even for this bit of paper which you send to mother, even this rejoices me. I should like to see my family there in America, but as I have no money I can do nothing, and there is nobody to help me. If you put together $10 each you could take me to you. I don't want the wrong of anybody, and would give it back with thanks, if only God grants me health. For when you sent the ship-ticket for mother and for Franek, I told mother as a joke: "Take me with you to America, it will be more pleasant to go together."

I had then much running to do and many expenses to bear, for I had to go 3 times to Ostrołęka to take an application for a passport, and twice to Warsaw. At last we three went and I had a ship-ticket, bought from the agent in Warsaw for money, and we went to Libawa. In the office in Libawa they refused to accept these tickets which you sent, and besides my ticket they wanted 21 roubles for a passport. I begged mother to lend me this money since I had had already so many expenses. But she refused to help me; she said, "I cannot." Then I said, "Send Franek instead of me, he will take these tickets with him and will settle the matter by words, and they [in America] won't lose so much." But mother answered, "I am not going and neither of you is going either," and I had to come back. As to this, what mother said, that "The shoemaker drags me about courts," I did not intend lawsuits as other people do, but I had to have a guardianship established, i.e., a family council. For mother received 2 morgs of forest, and wasted it half in vain. What was worth 5 roubles, she sold for 2, while now she must almost buy fuel herself. When I went once to the forest and said, "Why do you waste this timber?" they abused me, she and her son, and denied that there was anything to which I had any right. So I was obliged to have a guardianship established, because Franek was a minor and mother took rather too much liberty. And excuse me, don't be angry with me, dear sister and brother-in-law, for I tell the truth always into one's eyes, not behind one's eyes. For so many years since you have been in America I have never had even a small

sheet from you, except now this address, for which may God reward you. I should not go to America, except for my children. My daughter Mania can marry. She is 20 years old. My son Włeadzio is 16 years old, Zygmunt 6 years, Genia 4 years, and I am very sad that I cannot help them, for in our country there is no work and the expenses are big. What I earn is only enough for living, and when we have to pay the rent we must go hungry. If you could draw me to you I don't know how I could reward you. [I should be so grateful.]

*Antoni Herm[anowicz]*

## 245

### MAY 29, 1912

*Dear Sister and Brother-in-law:*

. . . As to the ship-ticket which I mentioned, I did not count on you alone, brother-in-law. For there are three of you. I don't count B., for he is like a strange man. I am not acquainted with you, so I did not look [to you alone]. I beg your pardon politely for importuning you. For I believe everything you wrote about Antoni, as if I were there myself. You tell me to borrow 140 roubles, but it is not so easy, for here people lend only to a man who has something to look upon [some property]. Meanwhile, I live only from these five fingers; I have nothing but what I earn. Even so our beloved [= "loving," ironical] mother, whenever she sees anything new of clothes upon us, wonders whence we get money for it. Instead of being glad that we manage to dress ourselves as we can, she is angry with us. How can I expect strange people to help us, when our own mother begrudges us a piece of bread? If I had wanted absolutely to be in America, I should have gone about 6 years ago when I went to Libawa with Franek and with mother. Then I had all my documents, and I begged mother to help me a little, but she did not want to. I said, "Then send Franek instead of me." But mother said, "I don't go and you shall not go either." And so mothers act toward their own children! Because she ruined herself, she wanted to ruin her children. But she returned to her own house, while I returned like the farmer whose buildings are all burned and who is left without a roof above his head. The few roubles which I had, I lost them for mother's sake, and later I was obliged to earn and economize again. And excuse me for writing this, for I tell the truth. As I believe you, so do you believe me, please. And now mother is angry for your not having sent money for Franek when he was going to the army. . . . Antośase [her son] sent her 10 roubles, and now Antoni [her brother] sent also 10 roubles, but all this is not enough for them. . . .

Antoni Herm—

## The Chicago Commission on Race Relations, *The Negro in Chicago: A Study of Race Relations and a Race Riot*, 1922

*The Chicago riot of 1919 was one of the most violent racial conflicts of the century, and the official report on that riot is an extraordinarily informative document of race relations*

*in a large industrial city. Chicago was a major destination for both southern blacks and European immigrants. Prior to the outbreak of World War I, African Americans held comparatively few jobs in Chicago's manufacturing sector; they concentrated instead in personal and domestic service. But wartime demand for labor, which stimulated the massive black migration from the South, created a new situation. Between 1915 and 1920, sixty-three industrial firms reported an increase in the number of black employees of more than 1,000 percent, from roughly one thousand to well over ten thousand. Unionization battles in the city's enormous meatpacking industry, and in other businesses, brought black and white (often immigrant) workers into sudden conflict with each other. This was one of several pressure points in wartime and postwar Chicago, along with schools and public recreational sites, that gave way to produce the violence of 1919. The following excerpt from the conclusions of the Chicago Commission report paints a fairly precise portrait of relations between the races in neighborhoods, schools, parks, beaches, stores, and workplaces. It also furnishes valuable evidence about attitudes and prejudices at work in urban America after the black migration to the North.*

*Source:* The Chicago Commission on Race Relations, *The Negro in Chicago: A Study of Race Relations and a Race Riot* (Chicago: University of Chicago Press, 1922), pp. 613–639.

## IV. RACIAL CONTACTS

The problems arising out of various occasions, both voluntary and enforced, for race association in Chicago, have, for convenience, been included in this report under the general classification of "racial contacts." Attention is given to contacts in the public schools, in public recreation places, on transportation lines, and in other relations exclusive of industry and housing which require special treatment. Negroes in Illinois are legally entitled to all the rights and privileges of other citizens. Actually, however, their participation in public benefits in practically every field is limited by some circumvention of the law.

## 1. Contacts in Public Schools

The public schools furnish one of the most important points of contact between the white and Negro races because of the daily association of thousands of Negro and white children at an impressionable age. The Chicago Board of Education makes no distinction between the races and keeps no separate records. Certain schools, therefore, with white American, Negro, and white foreign-born preponderances, were selected for special study.

### Physical Equipment of Schools

Twenty-two schools located in and near areas of Negro residence were selected and visited. Of these only five, or 23 per cent, have been built since 1900, and four of these five schools are in regions where the Negro population is smallest. The ten schools serving the largest percentage of Negroes were built, one in 1856, one in 1867, seven between 1880 and 1889, and only one after 1890. Of the 235 schools attended almost wholly by whites, 133, or 56 per cent, were

built after 1899. The old buildings will not accommodate modern equipment and cannot be enlarged. The absence of modern buildings is in part due to the old residence areas in which Negroes must live. The gymnasiums in fifteen of these twenty-two schools of predominant Negro attendance are poorly equipped, and in the other seven schools there are none. Playground space is about the same in all the schools, and there was no exceptional overcrowding in schools attended largely by Negroes except in one case where by the "shift" system a double attendance was made possible. In the schools of mixed attendance one instance was conspicuous: Fuller School—a branch of Felsenthal which is well equipped, and under the same principal, who is an advocate of segregation—is in a neighborhood where the percentage of Negroes is the same as that around Felsenthal, but it has no playground, is run down, and neglected. Yet it has 90 per cent Negroes, while Felsenthal has 38 per cent. Unmanageable white children are sent to Fuller.

### Retardation

The question of retardation of Negro children is of serious concern in race relations, since this fact is urged by advocates of separate schools as an unnecessary handicap for white children and a reason for segregation. Twenty-four schools were selected, with the aid of the Board of Education: six attended mainly by Negroes, six mainly by white Americans, and twelve mainly by children of immigrants. Of a total of 34,593 children there were 18,230, or 53 per cent, retarded—the same percentage as in the entire city; 10,250, or 30 per cent, normal; and 5,910, or 17 per cent, accelerated. In the schools attended mainly by white Americans, 49 per cent were retarded; in those attended mainly by children of immigrants 49 per cent; and in those attended mainly by Negroes 74 per cent. The percentage of retardation in schools attended mainly by Negroes ranges from 57 to 80 per cent; in schools attended mainly by children of immigrants from 32 to 71 per cent; and in schools attended mainly by white Americans from 40 to 62 per cent.

Predominating causes of this retardation of Negro children, according to the Board of Education's classification, are: "late entrance to school," "family difficulties," "fathers or mothers working," "lack of education in parents." The majority of retarded Negro children are southerners, and their retardation can be readily understood when the gross inadequacies of southern schools for Negroes are considered.

Among the whites, late entrance, inability to speak English, ill health, backwardness, and low mentality are the various causes. It is interesting to note that while it is often maintained that Negroes are mentally weak and incapable, classification of retardation figures according to causes does not bear out that theory. Negro children retarded from "late entrance" have made excellent records in attaining a normal rating, some completing three grades in a year.

One hundred and sixteen Negro children were picked at random for an intensive inquiry by the Commission into causes of retardation. Of these, 101 had been in school before coming to Chicago; and of the 101 children, eighty had lived in the South and had gone to southern schools; those born and educated in the North showed no greater rate of retardation than the whites. For much of the retardation the school facilities for Negroes in the South appear to be responsible. In Mississippi, for example, only eighty days' schooling is required in counties that do not absolutely reject the compulsory-education law. Other causes found were inadequate care and instruction at home due to the ignorance of parents, mothers working out, poor parental discipline, and the physical condition of homes.

*Contact Problems*

A wide variety of opinions was found among principals and teachers concerning the relations of white and Negro children. Several principals were distinctly antagonistic to Negroes, and in their schools the race relations of the pupils were not cordial. The most important factor in determining the attitude of teachers as well as of pupils was the attitude of principals. Kindergarten teachers found a natural, pleasant relationship existing between the young white and Negro children. As children grew older they became more race conscious, and in the high schools friction frequently arose from race groupings in class and social organizations. Negro teachers are assigned to schools attended by both Negroes and immigrants, and apparently have no difficulties with pupils or parents. Difficulties and bad feeling have been provoked by the disposition of certain white teachers to adapt their instruction in accordance with their assumptions concerning Negroes' mental and emotional characteristics, putting stress on singing and handicraft instead of on basic studies in arithmetic and grammar.

## 2. Recreation

In its investigation of recreation places, the Commission listed 127 parks, playgrounds, recreation centers, and beaches under the supervision of the Municipal Bureau of Parks, Playgrounds, and Bathing Beaches, and of the South Park, West Park, and Lincoln Park commissions. Of these, thirty-seven are in or near Negro areas. Though this figure represents a fairly adequate distribution, it is not an accurate picture. Twenty-three of these places are playgrounds attached to schools, fourteen being in, and nine near, Negro areas; and only thirteen have more than 10 per cent use by Negroes. Three bathing-beaches are within, and two near, Negro areas, while only one has more than 10 per cent use by Negroes. There are seven recreation centers near Negro areas, none within, and only one with more than 10 per cent use by Negroes. Armour Square, for example, is a recreation center bordering on the area of the largest Negro population; but the hostility of whites, especially gangs of hoodlums, attacks on Negro children, and the indifferent attitude of the director render attendance by Negroes extremely hazardous. Of a daily attendance of 1,500, less than 1 per cent are Negroes, despite the fact that over 50 per cent of the immediately surrounding population is Negro. Natural barriers of distance, unofficial discrimination of officials, and the hostility of neighborhood groups are largely responsible for the lack of participation.

The beaches have presented the most difficult problems of race control. The riot of 1919 began at the Twenty-ninth Street Beach, and since the riot numerous smaller clashes have occurred there. At Thirty-eighth Street, also on the edge of the largest area of Negro residence, Negroes are entirely excluded, the policeman on duty and the attendant in charge assisting in this exclusion to prevent clashes. In neighborhoods with a small Negro population, attendance at the recreation places is always much below the percentage of Negroes to the total population in such neighborhoods, this being due to the hostility shown by whites, especially of the hoodlum element, and also to the reluctance of Negroes to go where they feel unwelcome.

### Contacts

Most difficulties in parks and playgrounds have not been caused by the behavior of Negroes there. Such complaints against Negroes as have come from these contacts have concerned groups of rough or domineering children at the playgrounds rather than adults. Two playgrounds on the South Side make such complaints.

### Race Relations of the Children

Lack of racial antagonism was reported at a large number of playgrounds. Apparatus was used by both groups without friction. Negro and white children mingled freely in their games and in the swimming-pools, and both Negroes and whites played on baseball and athletic teams. The occasional playground fights usually lack any element of racial antipathy. "There might be personal misunderstandings and disagreements between a white and a black just the same as between two whites," said the director of Union Park, "but I wouldn't lay it to race prejudice. They work together and play together and seem to harmonize in most instances." When this director came to Union Park a year ago he found a tendency among Negroes and whites to separate into race groups, but steps were taken to bring them together in games of various kinds, and toward the end of the season the director felt that they "harmonized better and worked together more cordially than they did before." When the Commission's investigator visited Union Park Playground he saw small children of both races playing together on the same pieces of apparatus—a Negro child on one end of a teeter ladder and a white child on the other. Occasionally there is a disturbance, usually starting from a dispute over the apparatus; but on the whole the children play together peacefully.

*Voluntary Racial Grouping*

Voluntary racial grouping appears to be more characteristic of the large parks and beaches which adults frequent than of the playgrounds, which are used mainly by children. One instance of voluntary grouping among children was found at Copernicus Playground. The playing space is in the shape of an "L,"

one end intended for boys and the other for girls, but by common consent the children divide along race lines rather than sex.

In the general use of Lincoln and Washington parks the Negroes and whites stay in separate groups. There has never been any difficulty, according to the Lincoln Park representative, arising from the fact that Negroes have taken possession of a spot desired by whites for a picnic or other amusement. No part of either park is especially set aside for the use of one race, and groups of both Negroes and whites are seen everywhere in the parks, but they do not mingle.

Some directors attempt to regulate these contacts to avoid any mingling of groups. At the Municipal Pier, for example, an investigator learned that when Negro couples went on the dancing-pavilion floor the floor manager informed them that they were not dancing properly and took them to one side to acquaint them with the approved style of dancing; no matter how well they danced, they were to be prevented from going on the floor by the manager's judgment of their dancing. More recently, however, Negroes have reported that they have been able freely to use this dance floor.

Clashes in the various recreation places as early as 1913 were found to have been started mostly by gangs of white "roughs." On one occasion, for example, the secretary of boys' work of the Wabash Avenue department Y.M.C.A. (for Negroes) conducted a party of nineteen Negro boys to Armour Square. They had no difficulty in entering the park, but on leaving they were assailed by crowds of white boys. Some of them were tripped, trodden upon, and badly bruised. They took refuge in a neighboring saloon, where they remained for a half-hour, when a detachment of police scattered the white gang. On another occasion a group of boys from the same institution were driven from the lake at Thirty-first Street. In 1915 Father Bishop, of St. Thomas Episcopal Church, took a group of Negro boys to Armour Square to play basketball. The entire party, including Father Bishop, were beaten by white boys and their sweaters taken from them. In the same year an attempt was made by a Negro boys' club director to take seventy-five Negro boys through the Stock Yards. They had received tickets of admission to the stock show. In spite of the presence and efforts of four adult leaders, these boys were struck by sticks and other missiles while passing from one section of the show to another. Police assistance was required to get them from the pavilion to the street cars.

Gangs of white boys, sixteen and seventeen years of age, from the neighborhood of Fifty-ninth Street and Wentworth Avenue frequently interfered with Negro participants in baseball games in Washington Park, especially during the spring and summer of 1918 and 1919. They also annoyed Negro couples on the park benches. Where the Negro showed fight, minor clashes resulted. Park officials have not been able to restrain the ill feeling which these conflicts engender.

Clashes were noted in Ogden Park as early as 1914 and frequently since that time. A Negro playground director testified that he and other Negroes had been slugged while attending band concerts or attempting to use shower baths after a game in the park. At the boathouse in Washington Park, in the early summer of 1920, there were numerous clashes between Negroes and whites. In the following year, however, considerably fewer instances of friction were reported. Playground directors are of the opinion that friction is likely to occur where groups of Negro children for the first time come into parks theretofore exclusively used by whites. Adjustment is likely to follow after this period. In some cases, however, when the proportion of Negroes has grown larger than that of whites, a Negro director has been placed in charge of the park with the unofficial understanding that it should be turned over to Negroes.

The two causes of neighborhood antagonism back of the friction in the parks most commonly cited are the housing and sex problems. The playgrounds and parks usually share in a general way the sentiments of the mixed neighborhoods in or near which they are located.

One source of racial disorders is lack of co-operation between park and city policemen. The park police stop a fight between white and colored children and send them out of the park. When the fight is renewed outside the park they have no power to interfere. Spectators may then get into the fight, and serious clashes may be well under way before the city police can be summoned.

The most important remedies suggested to the Commission for the betterment of relations between Negroes and whites at the various places of recreation were: (1) additional facilities in Negro areas, particularly recreation centers which can be used by adults; (2) an awakened public opinion which will refuse to tolerate the hoodlum and will insist that the courts properly punish such offenders; (3) selection of directors for parks in neighborhoods where there is a critical situation who have a sympathetic understanding of the problem and will not tolerate actions by park police officers and other subordinate officials which tend to discourage Negro attendance; and (4) efforts by such directors to repress and remove any racial antagonism that may arise in the neighborhood about the park.

### 3. Contacts in Transportation

The study of contacts between whites and Negroes in street cars and other public conveyances was prompted by a usually unexplained emphasis on apparently trivial incidents connected with public conveyances, together with the observation that the greatest disturbances during the riot of 1919 commonly occurred along transportation lines and at transfer points.

Although many clashes and other instances of racial friction on the street cars were not serious enough to be reported to the newspapers or to be made the subject of complaint, information obtained by investigators for the Commission showed that the attitude of both Negroes and whites toward each other was being affected by contacts on the cars.

As affecting attitudes on race relations, transportation contacts, while im-

personal and temporary, are significant for several reasons. Many whites have no contact with Negroes except on the cars, and their personal impression of the entire Negro group may be determined by one or two observations of Negro passengers. Unlike contacts in the school, playground, and workshop, transportation contacts are not supervised, and if there is any dispute among passengers the settlement usually rests with themselves. Suspicion or prejudice on either side because of the difference in race accentuates any misunderstanding. And transportation contacts, at least on crowded cars, involve physical contact between Negroes and whites, which rarely occurs under other circumstances and sometimes leads to a display of racial feeling.

The Commission's investigators, white and Negro, men and women, made many trips for observation on the twelve lines carrying the heaviest volume of Negro traffic and therefore involving the greatest amount of contact. Counts of passengers, Negro and white, were made, behavior and habits were noted, and passengers and car crews were drawn into conversation. Officials of surface and elevated lines, starters, and station men were interviewed. Instances of friction which came to the attention of the Commission were noted and the circumstances studied.

Traffic counts made by the Chicago Traction and Subway Commission in 1916 showed 3,500,000 surface-railway and 500,000 elevated-railway passengers carried in a twenty-four-hour day. Negroes constitute 4 per cent of the city's population and probably about that percentage of the city's street-car traffic. Negro traffic, however, instead of being scattered over the city, is mainly concentrated upon twelve lines which traverse the Negro residential areas and connect those areas with the manufacturing districts where Negroes are employed. Because of this concentration the proportion of Negroes to whites on these twelve lines is much higher than 4 per cent, and on such lines as that on State Street, the principal business street of the South Side Negro residence area, it often happens that the majority of the passengers are Negroes.

There is no "Jim Crow" separation of races on street cars in Chicago. Contacts of Negroes and whites on the street cars did not provoke any considerable discussion before the period of migration of Negroes from the South, when occasional stories of clashes began to be circulated; and even then, such friction as developed did not come prominently to public attention. Only one incident involving a clash was reported in the newspapers. Even since the migration began, there have been very few complaints based upon racial friction. The Elevated Railroad Company, whose South Side line has the largest Negro traffic of any elevated line, replied to inquiries that, except during the riot of 1919, when a few cases of racial disorder were reported, there had been no complaints from motormen or trainmen since 1918, when a trainman was cut by a Negro. No complaints from white passengers had been received since the spring of 1917, when white office workers objected to riding with Stock Yards laborers, mainly Negroes, on the Stock Yards

spur of the elevated. White laborers in the Stock Yards mostly live within walking distance of their work, but Negroes found it necessary to use car lines running east to the main area of Negro residence. The Chicago Surface lines replied that complaints due to racial friction were negligible.

Many of the migrants are laborers who must use these lines going to and from work, and many of them are rough-mannered and entirely unfamiliar with standards of conduct in northern cities. Another serious factor is the recent entrance of Negroes into industry. Before the war the great majority of Negroes gainfully employed were engaged in some form of personal service which did not require use of transportation lines in their working clothes to and from the manufacturing centers. The migrants, many of them coming to a city like Chicago with no "Jim Crow" segregation, felt strange and uncertain as to how they should act. In fact, peculiarities of conduct on the part of these were noted by Negroes of longer residence in Chicago, and it has been remarked by whites and Negroes that they could tell a Negro migrant by his uneasy manner and often by his clothing. Conspicuous points of behavior of migrant Negroes before they became urbanized, which many whites noted and commented on were: "loud laughter and talking," "old and ill-smelling clothes," "roughness and his tendency to sit all over the car." These are easy to understand when one considers the background of the southern Negro. There are, on the other hand, exceptional cases where Negroes have walked miles rather than take a car, thus avoiding possible embarrassment. A Negro who has been in Chicago for a long time is not self-conscious about sitting near white persons. Negroes who get into trouble with whites about insisting on their right to a seat often belong to the class of suspicious and sensitive Negroes who fear that an attempt is being made to segregate them, and sometimes they are simply "greenhorns."

Soiled and ill-smelling clothing was found to be an objection applying to white as well as Negro laborers. These complaints came, for the most part, from clerical workers who objected to physical contact with persons who might "rub off." A difficulty involving this feature was adjusted by one packing company by dismissing its clerical workers and its laborers at different hours. A frequent source of misunderstanding has been a situation in which it appeared that Negroes had taken seats intended for white women. In several such cases thoroughly examined by the Commission's investigators the difficulties were found to have resulted from misunderstood actions.

Most of the difficulties in transportation contacts reported and generally complained of seem to have centered around the first blundering efforts of migrants to adjust themselves to northern city life. The efforts of agencies interested in assisting this adjustment, together with the Negro press and the intimate criticisms and suggestions for proper conduct of Chicago Negroes, have smoothed down many of the roughnesses of the migrants, and as a result friction from contacts in transportation seems to have lessened materially.

## 4. Crime and Vicious Environment

Many students of the race problem look upon public crime records as a register of the failure of Negroes to adjust themselves to the social fabric. Study of infractions of law by Negroes, of provocation to lawlessness, and of the history of their crimes would indeed reveal an interesting background of their present behavior in relation to whites, if such a study were possible from present records. The Commission carried its investigations into this field and found no means of determining how great a proportion of the city's crimes is committed by Negroes.

The prevailing impression that Negroes are by nature more criminal than whites and more prone to commit sex crimes has restricted their employment, increased unfair measures of restraint, and blackened the name of the entire Negro group. Two important facts were apparent from the Commission's study: (1) the danger inherent in the vicious environment in which Negroes are forced to live, and (2) the misrepresentative character of the statistics of Negro crime.

*Environment*
The limitations imposed on Negro residential areas have provided undue cause and occasion for crime. The entire population, good and bad, is thrown together, exposing children to the sight and temptation of vice and immorality. Ninety per cent of the Negro population has always lived near the city's former segregated vice districts, partly because white sentiment excluded them from other neigh-

borhoods, partly because rents in the neighborhood of vice were low enough to meet their meager economic resources, and partly because their weakness made their protests against the proximity of vice less effective than the protests of whites. When the vice districts were broken up and the inmates scattered, they entered the better neighborhoods of Negro residence and clandestinely plied their trade. In fact, according to the report of the Chicago Vice Commission in 1911, at one time prostitutes were promised immunity by the police if they confined themselves to a certain area in which Negroes predominated. The spread of the Negro population has always been accompanied by the spread of clandestine prostitution. The Vice Commission's report said:

> The history of the social evil in Chicago is intimately connected with the colored population. Invariably the large vice districts have been created within or near the settlements of colored people. In the past history of the city every time a new vice district was created downtown or on the South Side, the colored families were in the district moving in just ahead of the prostitutes. The situation along State Street from Sixteenth Street south is an illustration.

So whenever prostitutes, cadets, and thugs were located among white people and had to be moved for commercial or other reasons, they were driven to undesirable parts of the city, the so-called colored residential sections.

Most of the vicious resorts in the "Black Belt" are owned and operated by whites and are not interfered with by the authorities. Protests from Negroes have never succeeded in removing them. Opportunities for wholesome recreation in the Negro districts are limited, and commercial amusements, though probably no worse than in some other sections of the city, are of a distinctly inferior type and carelessly supervised. In such an infective environment it is not unnatural that many criminals should be developed.

But the study of crime statistics, aside from showing the unreliability of records due to careless methods of obtaining and presenting data, revealed that Negroes suffer gross injustice in the handling of criminal affairs. The general inaccuracy of criminal statistics is shown by the fact, for example, that the police reported 1,731 burglaries, or persons arrested for burglary, in 1919, while the Chicago Crime Commission reported 5,509 burglaries during the first eleven months of that year. The evidence at hand indicates that Negroes are debited with practically all their crimes, while others are not. It further appears, from the records and from the testimony of judges in the juvenile, municipal, circuit, superior, and criminal courts, of police officials, the state's attorney, and various experts on crime, probation, and parole, that Negroes are more commonly arrested, subjected to police identification, and convicted than white offenders; that on similar evidence they are generally held and convicted on more serious charges, and that they are given longer sentences. This bias, when reflected in the figures, serves to bolster by false figures the already existing belief that Negroes are more likely to be criminal than other racial groups.

## V. THE NEGRO IN CHICAGO INDUSTRIES

Out of Chicago's Negro population of approximately 110,000 in 1920, it is estimated that 70,000 were gainfully employed. The opportunity for engaging in industry in large numbers came to Negroes following the outbreak of the world-war. With the enormous demand from the belligerent countries for American goods, existing establishments were enlarged and new ones created. As an example of the increased demand for workers, one of the packing-plants in the Chicago Stock Yards increased its force during the war from 8,000 to 17,000. Immigration was almost wholly cut off. The labor shortage became acute after the entrance of the United States into the war in 1917. The migration of Negroes from the South during that period was mainly in response to this demand.

Prior to the beginning of the war in 1914, Negroes had been virtually limited to personal and domestic service in almost every city in the North. In 1910 more than 60 per cent of those gainfully employed were so engaged, 15 per cent in manufacturing, and 3 per cent in clerical occupations. The Commission's inquiries covered 136 establishments reporting five or more Negroes. In these were employed 118,098 whites and 21,987 Negroes—12,854 in manufacturing and 9,133 in non-manufacturing industries.

### 1. Increase in Negro Labor

Between 1915 and 1920 there was a remarkable increase in the number of Negroes employed in industries which before 1915 had either employed them in small numbers or not at all. In a total of sixty-two such plants there was an increase from 1,346 in 1915 to 10,587 in 1920, or more than 1,000 per cent. Labor shortage, or inability to obtain competent white workers, was the reason given in practically every instance for the large increase in Negro employees.

Frequent complaints have been made that large employers, particularly the packers, imported Negroes from the South and were thus responsible for the difficulties that followed. Definite effort was made to determine the facts, but the Commission found no basis for the statement.

### 2. Classification of Negro Workers

Absence of standards of classification for skilled, semi-skilled, and unskilled work invalidated the Commission's effort to classify Negro workers. In sixty-six industries with definite divisions in grades of work, it was found that out of 12,529 Negroes employed, 927 were skilled, 267 semi-skilled and 11,335 unskilled workers. In other returns, not capable of full classification, ten establishments reported 304 Negro molders; there were thirty-one Negro molders in 1910. Twelve factories reported 382 machine operators; in 1920 the census reports showed only twenty-eight.

Wages of Negroes in the branches of employment where they were permitted to work were generally the same as for white workers. There were instances, however, of discrimination in placing or keeping Negroes at work on processes in which they could not earn as much as in processes on which white men were engaged. Also there were instances of discrimination in piecework, the foremen invariably giving Negroes only the jobs yielding a low rate. For common labor the average wage was 45 and 50 cents an hour for an eight-, nine- and ten-hour day for men; $15 to $20 a week for women, and an average of $15 a week, with room and board, for domestics were the going wages.

### 3. Employers' Experience with Negro Labor

Whether or not the Negro will be able to hold the position in industry made possible for him by the war depends much on employers' attitude toward him as a worker. Common explanations given before this period as a reason for not employing Negroes more were that they were lazy, shiftless, irresponsible, and inefficient. Generalizations of this sort demonstrate their weakness in the fact that employers were not speaking from their own experiences. To reach a fair conclusion employers of Negroes in large numbers were interviewed by the Commission's investigators.

Employers drew a distinction between northern and southern Negroes; they thought that the latter had shortcomings when they first began work, but that this was due to former habits of work and familiarity with only simple industrial processes. Many of these southern workers were irregular at first in reporting for work and frequently drew their wages before pay day, thus confusing the bookkeeping. They were soon forced, however, to abandon these habits.

One question asked of all employers was: "Has your Negro labor proved satisfactory?" Of the 137 establishments employing five or more Negro workers, 118 reported that Negro labor had proved satisfactory; nineteen reported that Negro labor had not proved satisfactory. The 118 establishments reporting Negro workers as satisfactory employed 21,640 Negroes, while the nineteen reporting them as unsatisfactory employed 697. Comparing the efficiency of Negro and white workers, seventy-one employers interviewed (thirty-four manufacturers and thirty-seven non-manufacturers) considered the Negro equally efficient, twenty-two employers (thirteen manufacturers and nine non-manufacturers) considered the Negro less efficient. The seventy-one establishments included almost all the large establishments. A few gave the Negro a higher rating than the foreigners because of his knowledge of English.

Regarding reliability, ninety-two employers gave opinions. Sixty-three (thirty manufacturers and thirty-three non-manufacturers) believed that Negroes did not require more supervision than white workers, while twenty-nine (sixteen manufacturers and thirteen non-manufacturers) thought they required more supervision. Of the employers interviewed, fifty-seven expressed the opinion (twenty-three manufacturers and thirty-four non-manufacturers) that "absenteeism" among Negro workers was no greater than among whites, while thirty-six reported it was greater.

One plant employing 2,084 Negroes stated that the better living standards and ambitions had brought up the rating of Negro workers during the war period.

### 4. Labor Turnover

Of the thirty-two employers giving figures on relative labor turnover, twenty-four (eleven manufacturers and thirteen non-manufacturers) reported the Negro turnover to be the same as the white, and twenty-eight (eighteen manufacturers and ten non-manufacturers) believed the turnover to be greater. Closely connected with the labor turnover among Negroes is the question of "hope on the job," as one Negro expressed it. When Negroes are not allowed to advance to better positions in a given plant, or are discriminated against by foremen underrating their efficiency, the turnover in the plant is high.

### 5. Negro Women in Industry

Before the war Negro women were even more definitely restricted than Negro men in choice of occupations. Two-thirds of those gainfully employed were in two occupation groups: "servants" and laundresses, not in laundries, and domestic servants. Of the 137 establishments studied, forty-two had no Negro women employees, forty-five kept no separate records, and fifty reported a total of 3,407 Negro women workers. Although this study does not include all industries employing women, the total

given represents a large increase over the figure of 998 Negro women enumerated by the 1910 census as engaged in all industries in Chicago.

Many of the establishments in question had employed large numbers of Negro women as an experiment and had found them satisfactory. One mail-order house employed as many as 650 girls for clerical work. When the plant was investigated in 1920, there were 311 girls, 75 per cent of whom were high-school graduates, while 12 per cent had had two or more years in college. These employers said the girls felt that they were making history for the race and were, if anything, a little over-zealous. They were thought to be excitable and suspicious of the actions of the white girls.

Millinery establishments, manufacturers of clothing, lamp-shades, gas-mantles, paper-boxes, and cheese makers reported satisfactory experience with Negro women. Of twenty laundries employing Negro workers, satisfactory or unsatisfactory, four did not keep separate records. Twelve with 409 Negro Women reported their work satisfactory, and four with 134 Negro women reported it unsatisfactory. The chief complaint was unwillingness to work overtime or on Sundays. In both instances, however, employees interviewed complained that the hours were long (nine hours a day) and their treatment by the management harsh and inconsiderate.

Of 865 Negro employees interviewed, less than 1 per cent complained of disagreeable treatment by white workers and less than 50 per cent complained of conditions of work. Others expressed themselves as glad of the opportunity to earn good wages. Complaints against conditions of work were found in the iron and steel mills, Stock Yards, and dining-car and sleeping-car service.

## 6. Industries Excluding the Negro

Several important industries have not opened their doors to Negroes except as janitors and porters. Among these are the traction companies, elevated and surface, the State Street department stores, and the taxicab companies. Employers in these establishments express the belief that the public would object to Negroes.

Attention has been called to the waste involved in the limitations of Negroes in industry. Men with college training are forced to work as waiters and porters, and young-women college graduates are frequently forced to work as ushers in theaters and as ladies' maids. This condition helps to account for the ease with which 1,500 Negro girls with more than average schooling were recruited in less than two months for the mail-order houses.

## 7. Relations Between White and Negro Workers

Through working together friendliness between white and Negro workers has been increased, according to prevalent views. Information concerning relations was secured from all the 137 plants studied. Two reported that race friction was a disturbing factor in the plants. Minor instances of friction have occurred, but it appeared that as a rule the workers reflected the attitude of the management. The setting up of partitions separating the races developed an antagonistic sentiment, and in some instances this antagonism was removed when the partitions were taken down. Of 101 establishments visited eighteen, or 11 per cent, with 2,623 Negroes, maintained separate accommodations. This constituted a continuous source of dissatisfaction for Negro workers, who felt themselves "Jim Crowed." In the remaining 89 per cent, employing 19,714 Negroes among more than 100,000 whites, all accommodations were used in common by both races.

## 8. The Period of Industrial Depression

Following the war's inflation of industry a slump came in the winter of 1920–21. Common labor was reduced in all the large plants from 20 to 50 per cent. Negroes, mostly common laborers, suffered most from this reduction. At one period there were as many as 15,000 Negroes unemployed in Chicago. They were cared for during their enforced idleness by the Urban League and Negro churches and by popular contributions from working Negroes. The reduction of labor was usually carried out by employers with some system, and few instances of gross race discrimination were reported.

## 9. Organized Labor and Negro Workers

Clashing interests have manifested themselves conspicuously in the relations between union labor organizations and Negro workers, and this antagonism has been carried over into the relations of whites and Negroes generally. The efforts of union labor to promote its cause have built up a body of sentiment not easy to oppose by workers unsympathetic toward the labor movement. Circumstances have frequently made Negroes strike breakers, and thus centered upon them as a racial group all the bitterness of the unionist toward strike breakers as a class.

On the other hand, Negroes have often expressed themselves as having little faith in the union labor movement because the unions have manifested prejudices against permitting them to share equal benefits of membership; and again they have gained their first opportunity in a new industry frequently through the desire of a strike-bound employer to keep his plant running when his white employees have walked out.

From its beginning the American Federation of Labor has declared a uniform policy of non-racial discrimination, but this policy has not been carried out in practice by all its constituent or affiliated bodies. At several of its conventions resolutions have been passed embodying the official sentiment of the federation, but no means has yet been discovered to effect a uniform policy of fair dealing throughout all its affiliated bodies. Aside from those unions in which the membership privilege for Negroes is modified, eight of the 110 national or international unions affiliated with the American Federation of Labor explicitly bar the Negro by provisions in their constitutions or rituals. These unions are:

Brotherhood of Railway Clerks, Brotherhood of Railway Carmen of America, International Association of Machinists, American Association of Masters, Mates, and Pilots, Railway Mail Association, Order of Railroad Telegraphers, the Commercial Telegraphers' Union of America, and American Wire Weavers' Protective Association.

The general exclusion policy of the railway brotherhoods and several unions of the Railway Department of the American Federation of Labor has created a feeling of bitterness among Negroes, many of whom are employed in branches of the railway service. As a protest against this policy there has been formed the Railway Men's International Benevolent Industrial Association with seventeen locals in Chicago and a local membership of 1,200. Mr. Mays, president of this organization, stated that its purpose was merely to safeguard the ranks of Negro workers, and said that it was ready to merge itself into the general unions as soon as they were ready to accept them without discrimination and accord the same privileges as white railway workers.

The Commission obtained information from local unions in Chicago with a membership of 294,437, of whom 12,106 were Negroes. On the basis of policy toward the Negro, unions in Chicago may be divided into four classes or types:

A. Unions admitting Negroes to white locals
B. Unions admitting Negroes to separate or co-ordinate locals
C. Unions admitting Negroes to subordinate or auxiliary locals

D. Unions excluding Negroes from membership

Wherever and whenever Negroes are admitted on an equal basis and given a square deal, the feeling inside the union is nearly always harmonious. Examples of type A are the Amalgamated Meat Cutters and Butcher Workmen of the World, Hodcarriers, Flat Janitors, and Ladies' Garment Workers. In some of these organizations Negroes hold office.

Unions of type B give as reasons for organizing Negroes into separate locals, first, preference of Negro workers for locals of their own, and, second, unwillingness of white workers to admit Negroes to white locals. The Negro Musicians' Union belongs to this type and has the same wage scale as the white union. There appears to be little difficulty here because there is no conflict in contracts for work in the city. The painters, however, have had difficulties which have "hung fire" for more than a year; after being given a temporary charter they still were unable to work.

Unions of type C, admitting Negroes to subordinate locals, are few in number, apparently because Negroes strongly resent this form of affiliation. There is, however, one example of this type which permits Negro helpers in a certain trade to be organized as an auxiliary under the jurisdiction of the white local unions having jurisdiction over their district. By constitution it is provided that their minutes be submitted to the white locals and their grievances placed before the white locals. The constitution also provides that there shall be no transfer of colored helpers to any except Negro auxiliaries,

and that Negro helpers shall not be promoted to skilled trades or to helper apprentice, and shall not be admitted to shops where white helpers are employed. These Negro locals are represented by delegates selected by the white locals in their districts.

Unions of type D, excluding the Negro from membership, do so either in conformity with the laws of their national unions or in the exercise of local option. In addition to the eight internationals which exclude the Negro by constitutional provision, there are other locals which are known to reject Negro applicants. The Machinists' Union, for example, although complying in its constitution with the American Federation of Labor policy of no racial discrimination, still effectually bars the Negro by a provision in its secret ritual. With the Machinists' Union must be grouped such unions as the Amalgamated Sheet Metal Workers' International Alliance, the Electrical Workers, and the Plumbers and Steam Fitters.

Some Negro leaders, in view of these practices, have been strong in their advocacy of non-affiliation with union organizations, holding that the employers, after all, offer for Negroes the fairer terms, and that they have, in fact, given Negroes their first opportunity in industry. However, certain other Negroes have taken advantage of the rift between employers and labor unions to exploit Negro laborers. They have played upon racial sentiment to establish separate unions for Negroes, both in lines of work where they are admitted to the general unions and in lines of work where they are excluded. This type of leadership has been irresponsible and dangerous; it has made ridiculously generous promises, and has addressed its appeal to the less intelligent classes of Negro workers. Its literature has in turn provoked extreme bitterness among labor union members and officials, who have mistakenly accepted it as representative of the sentiment of all Negro workers.

Interviews with Negro workers outside of the unions reveal an attitude of indifference or suspicion which is attributed by both white and Negro labor leaders and union men to the following reasons: (1) the usual treatment of Negroes by white men, (2) traditional treatment of Negroes by white men, (3) influence of racial leaders who oppose unionism, (4) influence of employers' propaganda against unionism. Many of them, it was learned, have a distorted view of the purposes and principles of unionism, and many others, while sympathetic with the movement, object to the practices of the locals. An experience frequently referred to was the waiters' strike in 1911, when Negro union men walked out with white union men and were replaced by white girls, while the white union men returned to their jobs; since that time Negro waiters have been out of the more desirable hotel jobs.

The explanations by labor leaders of the practices of local unions are to the effect that while the general public race prejudice might be expected in organizations of white workingmen, the unions, as a group, are fairer to the Negro than other groups; that unions are blamed for conditions which are really due to general public opinion. They cite

as an example the fact that Negroes are not employed in Chicago as motormen or conductors on the surface or elevated lines because of public objection, and that they cannot be organized until they are in positions. Views were also expressed in condemnation of the exclusion policy of one local. These union officials believe that the unions will eventually be the most powerful agencies in the removal of race prejudice.

## VI. PUBLIC OPINION IN RACE RELATIONS

### A. Opinions of Whites and Negroes

The "Negro problem" is deeper and wider than the difficulties which center about the more specialized problems of Negro housing, Negro crime, and industrial relations involving Negroes. All such special studies conducted by the Commission left a baffling residuum of causes of racial discord, deep rooted in the psychology of the white and Negro groups in contact. The beliefs and attitudes, firmly fixed and accepted prejudices of the one race as to the other, grouped under the term "public opinion," thus became the subject of a novel but most interesting inquiry.

Public opinion with respect to the Negro forms a body of sentiment so definite and compact as to make it an excellent laboratory case for analysis and study; but the Commission's aim in investigating it was merely to make apparent and objective its place and importance in race relations; to indicate some of the ways in which it has developed;

how it expresses itself; how it affects both the white and Negro groups; how, in its present state, it is strengthened, weakened, polluted, or purified by deliberate agencies or even by its own action; and finally how it may be used to reduce, if not prevent, racial unfriendliness and misunderstanding.

Public opinion is regarded here as a phase of the social mind, but nevertheless as a definite reality. For purposes of examination, therefore, its study gives attention to that body of sentiments, beliefs, attitudes, and prejudices which, taken together, give to public opinion its content and meaning.

To present this subject intelligently, the following plan has been employed:

1. Beliefs and sophistications regarding Negroes, which exercise so great an influence in determining the conduct of white persons in relation to them, are described as they apply in the local environment, and in origin and background are traced suggestively to their responsible sources in literature and circumstance.

2. Types of sentiment which, in Chicago and similar northern communities, are variants of these basic beliefs are presented with a view to making them intelligible and classifying them according to resolvable factors of misunderstanding.

3. Since personal attitudes and beliefs are molded by traditions and heritages apart from the exclusive influence of literature, more significant material collected through intimate inquiry is presented objectively to describe the processes by which they appear to be created and grow. Replies to a searching questionnaire on attitudes and opinions are, in the instances quoted, the result of painstaking self-analysis.

4. The opinions and sentiments of Negroes on these same issues are described and illustrated with a view to making them understandable, and their interpretations of current white sentiment are explained as far as possible.

5. The report then turns to the agencies by which these opinions are made and perpetuated and the individual attitudes created. The chief of these are: (a) the press, (b) rumors, (c) myths, (d) propaganda. The conscious and unconscious abuse of these instruments of "opinion making" is pointed out and explained.

6. Finally, the study is intended to suggest means by which public opinion, where it is faulty, may correct itself and employ its own instruments in the creation of wholesome sentiments among Negroes with respect to whites, and among whites with respect to Negroes.

*1. Beliefs of Whites Concerning Negroes*
The conduct of individuals is largely determined by their attitudes toward a subject and their general beliefs concerning it. Definite beliefs concerning Negroes may be found in the North as well as in the South, varying with the individuals who hold them, according to degrees of contact with the Negro group and the individuals' traditional background. These may be divided according to their character and effect into two general classes: (a) primary beliefs or those fundamental

and firmly established convictions which have, all around, the deepest effect on the conduct of whites toward Negroes and are pretentiously supported by statistics, authorities, and scientific research; (b) secondary beliefs, or modifications and variants of important assumptions as to cardinal attributes.

A) PRIMARY BELIEFS

Among these primary beliefs are the following:

1. Mentality: That the mind of the Negro is distinctly and distinctively inferior to that of the white race. Some believe that this is due to backwardness in ascending the scale of civilization; some that the Negro belongs to a different species of the human family.
2. Morality: That Negroes are not yet capable of exercising social restraints common to white persons; that they are unmoral as well as immoral.
3. Criminality: That Negroes possess a constitutional character weakness, and a consequent predisposition to sexual crimes, petty stealing, and crimes of violence.
4. Physical unattractiveness: That physical laws prompt whites to avoid contact with Negroes.
5. Emotionality: That Negroes are highly emotional and for that reason are given to quick, uncalculated crimes of violence as easily as to noisy and emotional religious expressions.

B) SECONDARY BELIEFS

As continued repetition of any plausible statement without correction of its error eventually gives it credence, these secondary beliefs have rooted themselves deep in the public mind. Among other things it is believed that Negroes are: (1) lazy, (2) "happy-go-lucky," (3) boisterous, (4) bumptious, (5) over-assertive, (6) lacking in civic consciousness, (7) addicted to carrying razors, (8) fond of shooting craps, (9) flashy in dress and like gaudy, brilliant colors, especially red.

*2. Background of Prevailing Beliefs Concerning Negroes*

Soon after the first emergence of Negroes from slavery their illiteracy and general behavior in response to the novel experience of freedom created situations which appeared to justify judgments concerning their group traits. Scholars rationalized and tried to explain these apparent traits: If they were illiterate as a group they must be incapable of learning, and if they committed crimes, they must be fundamentally lacking in social restraints.

Dr. Jeffries Wyman, of Harvard, Professor A. H. Keene, author of *Man Past and Present*, Dr. J. C. Nott, author of *Types of Mankind*, and almost all the other anthropologists of that period, gave the stamp of scientific authority to the view that Negroes were of a different species and could never reach the level of the Caucasian. Even more recently mental tests were carried out on the same assumption and were made to prove it in some instances where the facts were unexpectedly contrary. Students of the race problem in the South continued to generalize about Negro character from selected specimens, other more popular writers and speakers, with their anecdotes, stories, and jokes, all of which went uncorrected, tended to strengthen this body of beliefs to a point where any difference of views was intolerable. Although the status of the Negro has changed, the beliefs remain the same, and have led to bitterness and resentment among Negroes, with consequent misunderstandings and friction.

In Chicago sentiments collected from a wide variety of sources and involving the views of several thousands of white persons indicate the persistence of these archaic beliefs and fears, so deep set and of such long standing that they are assumed by many persons to be instinctive.

To secure definite information upon the traditional background of beliefs concerning Negroes, fifteen white persons with no special interest in Negroes were selected at random from professions, business, and other vocations and submitted to a careful and searching inquiry. They were asked eighteen carefully prepared questions to draw out the raw material of their unqualified reactions on the question of the Negro and, as far as possible, the background in their early experience. They were asked for their opinions concerning Negroes, whether or not they believed that they possessed distinguishing traits of mentality and character; their attitudes were solicited by questions and propositions designed to provoke an expression of attitude. Questions were put regarding instances and experiences involving Negroes in their early experience; their first consciousness of racial differences; their first contacts; and information was sought on the definite sources of their knowledge or opinions concerning Negroes.

All the persons questioned had clearcut opinions and thought that Negroes possessed distinguishing traits ranging from "affectionate loyalty" to "mental and moral handicaps imposed by evolution." An abolitionist's son, for example, thought that "Negroes should desire segregation"; a man who had observed Negroes at Tuskegee and Lewis institutes would increase their education and meet the demands produced by education. One whose only contact had been with his "black mammy" thought that the Negroes were "affectionate and loyal, but lacking in racial pride, though evolutionarily handicapped, possessing the qualities of children." Another who had had an unfortunate experience with his Negro chauffeur thought that Negroes were characterized by "distinctly inferior mentality, deficient moral sense, shiftlessness, good-natured, and a happy disposition." They knew little about the activities of Negroes, their leaders, their papers, or their problems, and the sources on which they relied for their information, except in two instances, were undependable.

## 3. Negro Opinion

Negroes, although exposed to various forms of social contact, have been intellectually isolated from the white group. They have not participated fully and freely in community and cultural activities. The pressure of the white group in practically every ordinary experience has kept their attention and interest centered upon themselves, and they have become race conscious. Their thinking, therefore, on general questions, whether they involve race relations or not, is conditioned and largely controlled by the relation of these questions with group interests. The opinions of Negroes, therefore, on race relations are largely negative. White persons know very little about what Negroes are thinking, because they are not familiar with their experiences; they frequently do not accredit them with the sensibilities that they do possess; and are not acquainted with the processes of thought by which the opinions of Negroes are formed. Thus it is that many of the statements and expressions of feeling of Negroes are unintelligible to persons outside of their group. Similarly, many statements and expressions of feeling by white persons are unintelligible to Negroes. But in the understanding of white persons Negroes have the advantage, because they do read their papers, see them in the privacy of their homes, and are forced constantly to interpret their actions.

Among Negroes there may be found a group control as strong and binding as among white persons. One striking instance of the operation of this group control was the complete ostracism of a prominent Negro lawyer who was reported to have made a public statement contrary to the views and aspirations held by his group. When this Negro was reported in the press to have said, "This is a white man's country, and Negroes had better behave or they will get what rights they have taken away," he was first snubbed, then his life was threatened, and for several weeks he was forced to go about under police protection. He was seriously criticized and finally ostra-

cized. In less than a year he died. His friends declare that he was slanderously misquoted.

The sentiments of Negroes fall into somewhat the same classification as those of whites, but with one or two notable exceptions: there is (1) more discussion of race problems, more criticism of the conduct of leaders, more discussion of the practicability of programs of action; and (2) a great deal of literature and other expressions concerning the development of a defensive philosophy. In this latter are included various defensive policies, the stimulation of race pride, the explanation of behavior, and the struggle for status. There might also be included frequent evidences of the development of race consciousness. The emotional background, class consciousness, and the influences of group control are as evident in the sentiments of Negroes as of white persons.

A wide selection of views was obtained from Negroes and presented under the classifications in which they appeared naturally to fall. To get a more precise statement of views, a questionnaire was sent to Negroes representing a class intellectually able to subject themselves to self-analysis and to discuss various confusing angles of the race question. They were asked concerning interracial problems; whether or not race relations appear to be growing better or worse; whether the acquisition of wealth, or 100 per cent literacy, or unrestricted suffrage could affect race relations; they were asked questions concerning their adjustment to the present social system, their most pronounced mental complexes experienced in adjusting personal desires to the present social system; whether they were prejudiced against white persons; whether or not they were conscious of a feeling of race inferiority, or of a desire to compensate for a supposed inferiority. Concerning Negro problems they were asked whether or not there should be recognized leaders of Negroes; their criticisms of the policies of Negro leaders. Their racial philosophy was solicited. They were asked the distinction that they made between segregation and racial solidarity, and information was sought on the agencies responsible for their opinions. A most interesting array of views was secured, ranging from suspicion and abuse of the questions themselves to dispassionate analysis.

The war has produced a new type of sentiment. It not only brought disappointment and disillusionment for Negroes led into a new hope by the promises that accompanied the manifest efforts to stimulate patriotism, but actually gave to Negroes new experiences. Following the return of Negro soldiers from France, measures of restraint were increased, and from the usual lawlessness of the period of reconstruction they probably suffered more severely than others because they are to a much larger extent dependent upon law enforcement for security and comfort. Race riots, which are an expression of both loose machinery of community control and the development of a more determined resistance on the part of Negroes, grew more frequent in number and more serious in consequences. A new note was sounded in radical Negro literature, which appeared to carry a very popular appeal.

## B. Factors in the Making of Public Opinion

### 1. The White Press of Chicago

Aside from the agencies ordinarily responsible for providing the individual with his views, there are others equally as powerful in developing and influencing opinions. Most important of these is the press. For that portion of the public which depends upon the press for its contact with the Negro group and its information concerning it, this agency holds a controlling hand. Throughout the country it is pointed out, by both whites and Negroes, that the policies of many newspapers on racial matters have made relations more difficult, at times fostering new antagonisms and even precipitating riots by inflaming the white public against Negroes. A study was made of the three principal white daily newspapers of Chicago, covering a two-year period. Included in this study were 1,347 news items, 108 letters to the press, and ninety-six editorials on the Negro.

As an example of the type of publicity given to racial news concerning Negroes and the types of articles considered to have good news value, of the 1,338 articles published, 606, or nearly 50 per cent, dealt with riots, crime, and vice. Each of these articles specifically identified the persons involved as Negroes.

Constant identification of Negroes with certain definite crimes could have no other effect than to stamp the entire Negro group in the public mind as generally criminal. This in turn contributes to the already existing belief that Negroes as a group are more likely to be criminal than others, and thus they are arrested more readily than others. Publication of their names with race identification and with the crimes alleged against them keeps up a vicious circle. The unfortunate emphasis on sex offenses involving race, the subtle fanning of latent animosities by innuendo and suggestion, attaching the crime not only to the individual but to the race, direct a current of fear, intolerance, and ill will against the whole Negro group. An apt illustration, frequently cited by Negroes, is that if each time a crime was committed by a red-headed man, he was so described in telling of his crime, a popular fear and prejudice would soon develop against all red-headed men.

Crimes involving Negroes alone receive little attention. As with the Italians, as long as crimes are committed within the group, and this group is regarded as an isolated appendix of the community, they hold very little news value. When, however, a member of the isolated group comes into conflict with the community group, whether in industry, housing, or any relation, its representative significance is thus established, and the information becomes news. Publicity on housing, for example, stresses the conflict with other neighborhoods, the "invasion" of white districts, and plans for segregation. News items on politics involving Negroes get more space and prominence when they describe graft and corruption. In the list of articles studied are

included sixty-three articles particularly ridiculing the Negro group.

Incidents occurring during the activities of the Commission were checked up with reports of them appearing in the papers, and serious misrepresentations of the Negro group were revealed. One example was an article in the *Herald-Examiner* on January 4, 1920, with two-inch headlines across the entire first page: "Reds Plot Negro Revolt," "I.W.W. Bomb Plant Found on South Side." The article mentioned the alleged secret activities of Negroes and their plans to revolt against the government. The bomb plant and many of their secret plans were reported to have been discovered by the state's attorney. The article further said: "In Chicago it was learned that the headquarters for Negro revolutionary propaganda are centered in these four organizations: the Free Thought Society, Universal Negro Improvement Association, Negro Protective League, and the Soldiers and Sailors Club." The article and the reported "discoveries" of the state's attorney's office are evidence of the absurd ignorance frequently manifested by members of the white group concerning the activities of Negroes. Each of the organizations named was known to the Commission and visited by its representatives on numbers of occasions. All of their meetings are open to the public, though attended almost entirely by Negroes. The Universal Negro Improvement Association publishes all of its plans in its newspaper, the *Negro World*. Its slogan is "Back to Africa" and not "Down with the United States." The Free Thought Society mentioned is an organization designed to provide a medium of expression for persons who seek the "attainment of truth." Its discussions concern religion and philosophy, and it numbers among its members prominent Negro and white professional men. The Negro Protective League is an employment office and day nursery. The full name of the organization is the "Negro Equal Rights and Protective Association." The Soldiers and Sailors Club is a community house located on the South Side and a branch of the local War Camp Community Service. Eugene T. Lies, formerly of the United Charities, was its director. The occasion of the publicity in question was a convention of a national Negro Greek-letter fraternity, which held its meetings in the auditorium of the Soldiers and Sailors Club. This fraternity, like all others of its kind, excluded non-members and by so doing aroused the suspicion of the newspaper's informants. No correction appeared in the paper, and to date no further "discoveries" have been made.

Articles of this type illustrate the possible effect on the public mind of such misrepresentations of the Negro. One newspaper has abandoned its policy of identifying Negroes with reports of incidents, in recognition of the gross unfairness of the practice.

## 2. The Negro Press

The development of the Negro press was stimulated by several necessities important among which were:

a. The indifference of the white press to the Negro group; its emphasis on the unfortunately spectacular, and the consequent loss of items of interest about Negroes throughout the country.

b. The importance of developing the morale of the Negro group, creating a solidarity of interest and purpose for measures of defense, correcting the impressions created by general opinion, and centering the attention of Negroes upon themselves and their advancement.

Three of the most important local Negro weekly papers were studied. Their news items showed bias in reporting just the reverse of that which characterizes the reports of many white papers. They emphasize the Negro's view and may be said to provide a compensatory interpretation of the news. When, for example, the *Chicago Tribune* reports the approval in the Illinois Constitutional Convention of a civil-rights bill with the headline: "Miscegenation Is O.K.'d in New Constitution; Negroes Given All the Rights of Whites," the *Chicago Whip*, a Negro newspaper, headlines the same incident: "Morris Gets Civil Rights into Constitution; Victory for Race Won at Springfield."

The most important function exercised by the Negro press is its control of the Negro group and of their education in conduct. All of these papers give considerable space to such popular education.

## 3. Rumor

Rumor if unchecked, can do incalculable damage to race relations. Included under the term "rumor" are those unfounded tales, incorrectly deduced conclusions, partial statements of fact with significant content added by the narrator, all of which are given wide circulation and easy credence by the public. Other forms of rumor are tales of unheard-of brutality and of plots and plans which are either fabrications or partial statements of fact and serve only to stimulate resentment, fear, and a desire for retaliation. Of the rumors predicting riots, one example will illustrate: During the riot a white man was caught in the act of crawling beneath a house in which Negroes lived. In his pocket was found a bottle of kerosene. He confessed that his mission was arson and justified his act by repeating to the police the current rumor that it was known that Negroes had set fire to the houses of whites "back of the Yards."

A persistent tale circulated during and for a long time after the riot was to the effect that the bodies of hundreds of Negroes were taken from Bubbly Creek where they had been thrown after being killed by white rioters. The story was so frequently repeated that it was accepted and even repeated in Congress. It caused an intense feeling among Negroes. Investigation by the coroner, Police Department, and other agencies showed that no bodies had ever been thrown into Bubbly Creek or recovered from it.

A rumor given official sanction and carried into the files of the Department of Justice illustrates other possible dangers of this kind. This rumor concerned two prominent and highly accredited organizations for Negroes. Rumors connected them with "I.W.W. plots and plans to overthrow the government." These reports were founded upon scarcely anything more than suspicion due to lack of information and acquaintance with the Negro group. The National Urban League, for example, an organization of responsible Negroes and whites with branches in thirty-one cities, was reported to have asked William D. Haywood, head of the I.W.W., to speak at its convention in Detroit. This report grew out of the misreading of the name of William Hayward, a United States district attorney in New York, who is a member of the executive board and whose name appears on the stationery of the organization. The National Association for the Advancement of Colored People, also a reputable organization of whites and Negroes, was reported to be "planning to flood the colored districts with I.W.W. literature." This was entirely false, but the reports went to the Department of Justice headquarters secretly and could not be corrected by the persons most affected.

### 4. Myths

Group myths, like those about the American Indian, the Oriental, and the Jew, are very common. Usually they are the expression either of a wish or of fear, which sociologists call a negative wish. Mythical stories and anecdotes about Negroes, accepted by whites, are usually popular. Many of them may have had a reasonable origin, but as a matter of fact have long outgrown it. So long as they are uncorrected they hold and exercise a marked degree of control over personal conduct.

In the category of myths fall the popular beliefs of whites concerning the mentality of Negroes, and the more definite myth that the mind of the Negro child ceases to develop when he reaches the age of puberty. The sex myth is always in evidence. It involves the fear obsession of Negro men held by many white women, fear of miscegenation, the condonation of lynchings, repressive social restrictions, as well as attempts at legislative restraints. Negroes are by these myths shown to have a predilection for sex crimes. This sex myth has been stressed in almost every riot. It precipitated the Washington riot; it provoked the most brutal murder of the Chicago riot, and it was responsible for the brutality of the Omaha and Tulsa riots. Always resident in the background of popular consciousness, it shows the same head and features in almost every clash of races.

## 5. Propaganda

Conscious control of public opinion by propaganda has been used with tremendous effect by social, political, and religious organizations seeking popularity and support for their movements and reforms. Both Negroes and whites employed propaganda, sometimes openly, sometimes insidiously. Racial propaganda has probably a more powerful appeal than any other type because it is based upon the instinct of race and race differences, rivalry and jealousy. The most common forms of propaganda may be classified into the following types: (a) educational, (b) radical and revolutionary, (c) defensive, (d) malicious.

The activities and programs of the National Association for the Advancement of Colored People fall under the classification of educational propaganda; this propaganda is directed to the white public principally and is intended to change public opinion by providing a foundation of actual facts for the public's judgment.

The more striking examples of the radical and revolutionary propaganda are the appeals sent out by the Industrial Workers of the World to Negroes, carrying their doctrines and extending open arms to Negro workers and offering them what most other organizations refuse— the privilege of association and membership on the basis of brotherhood.

Defensive propaganda is more apparent within the Negro group and is usually designed for the purpose of combating aggression and injury to their purposes and aspirations from without. The appeals of this propaganda are directed first to Negroes as a means of cementing the group from within, and indirectly to the white group by way of impressing them with the strength of solidified opposition to insults. The Protective Circle of Chicago, organized to "oppose segregation, bombing, and defiance of the Constitution," admitted employing propaganda to accomplish its purpose.

Malicious propaganda is by far the most dangerous because it is founded upon race antagonism. In the appeal to the emotions facts are soon lost. Anti-Negro propaganda is not wholly new in the North, but when employed it has usually been done insidiously because "Negro-baiting is considered in bad taste." Recently, however, there have been conspicuous instances of open and organized efforts to influence the minds of whites against Negroes. Ignorance and suspicion, fear and prejudice, have been played upon deliberately. The stated purpose of the propaganda was to unite white property owners in opposition to the "invasion" of other residential areas by Negroes, but in the actual carrying out of the propaganda it was extended to all Negroes, and many methods were employed which could have no other effect than to arouse bitterness and antagonism leading to clashes. The *Property Owners' Journal*, the organ of an association of real estate men, became so violent in its preachments that the protest of whites forced its discontinuance. Appeals were made not only to the instinct of race but to the sex instincts and the protective instincts of white men. A pamphlet sent to the wives of prominent residents in that neighborhood, entitled *An Appeal of White Women to American Humanity*, recounted the "horrible conduct of French Colonials on the Rhine and the abuse of German white women," although there was little apparent connection between the conduct of Chicago Negroes and that of the black soldiers in the French Army of Occupation on the Rhine. This pamphlet, however, served to increase the fears of Negro men by white Women and to arouse the resentment and hatred of white men.

## Carl C. Brigham, *A Study of American Intelligence*, 1923

*Carl C. Brigham was a professor of psychology at Princeton University. His book* A Study of American Intelligence, *which appeared in*

*1923 at the height of the immigration restriction campaign, gave powerful support to that cause, offering "scientific" proof for the nativist theories of Madison Grant, whose book* The Passing of the Great Race *(1916) had alarmed Americans about the deleterious effect of immigrants and blacks on the nation's mental condition. Interpreting the intelligence tests that the U.S. Army had administered to American soldiers during World War I, Brigham concluded that these tests proved the Northern European (Nordic) race to be mentally superior to all others. Because a number of influential psychologists believed that intelligence was racially inherited, these tests were entangled from the start with racialist theories. In 1910 psychologists began testing immigrants at Ellis Island, and they promptly determined that a high percentage of newcomers were "morons" (the term for adults with a mental level of twelve or below) who would lower the national intelligence as they produced children. Brigham was determined to follow the same line of argument, even though the data suggested that environmental factors, such as the length of time an immigrant lived in America, strongly affected an individual's mental score. He also strained to discredit studies that showed Jewish immigrants testing as high as white Americans. In 1930 Brigham recanted his racialist interpretation, too late to undo its effect on American immigration policy.*

*Source:* Carl C. Brigham, *A Study of American Intelligence* (Princeton: Princeton University Press, 1923), pp. 182 (part), 205 (part)–210.

## SECTION X

### Comparison of Our Results with the Conclusions of Other Writers on the Subject

In a very definite way, the results which we obtain by interpreting the army data by means of the race hypothesis support Mr. Madison Grant's thesis of the superiority of the Nordic type: "The Nordics are, all over the world, a race of soldiers, sailors, adventurers, and explorers, but above all, of rulers, organizers, and aristocrats in sharp contrast to the essentially peasant and democratic character of the Alpines. The Nordic race is domineering, individualistic, self-reliant, and jealous of their personal freedom both in political and religious systems, and as a result they are usually Protestants. Chivalry and knighthood and their still surviving but greatly impaired counterparts are peculiarly Nordic traits, and feudalism, class distinctions, and race pride among Europeans are traceable for the most part to the north." "The pure Nordic peoples are characterized by a greater stability and steadiness than are mixed peoples such as the Irish, the ancient Gauls, and the Athenians, among all of whom the lack of these qualities was balanced by a correspondingly greater versatility." . . .

We may consider that the population of the United States is made up of four racial elements, the Nordic, Alpine, and Mediterranean races of Europe, and the negro. If these four types blend in the future into one general American type, then it is a foregone conclusion that this future blended American will be less intelligent than the present native born American, for the general results of the admixture of higher and lower orders of intelligence must inevitably be a mean between the two.

If we turn to the history of races, we find that as a general rule where two races have been in contact they have intermingled, and a cross between the two has resulted. Europe shows many examples of areas where the anthropological characteristics of one race shade over into those of another race where the two have intermixed, and, indeed, in countries such as France and Switzerland it is only in areas that are geographically or economically isolated that one finds types that are relatively pure. The Mongol-Tatar element in Russia is an integral part of the population. The Mediterranean race throughout the area of its contact with the negro has crossed with him. Some of the Berbers in Northern Africa show negroid characteristics, and in India the Mediterranean race has crossed with the Dravidians and Pre-Dravidian negroids. The population of Sardinia shows a number of negroid characteristics. Turn where we may, history gives us no great exception to the general rule that propinquity leads to opportunity and opportunity to intermixture.

In considering racial crosses, Professor Conklin states that "It is highly probable that while some of these hybrids may show all the bad qualities of both parents, others may show the good qualities of both and indeed in this respect resemble the children in any pure-bred family. But it is practically certain that the general or average results of the crossing of a superior and an inferior race are to strike a balance somewhere between the two. This is no contradiction of the principles of Mendelian inheritance but rather the application of these principles to a general population. The general effect of the hybridization of races can not fail to lead to a lowering of the qualities of the higher race and a raising of the qualities of the lower one."

And as to the possibility of a cross between races in the future, Professor Conklin writes: "Even if we are horrified by the thought, we cannot hide the fact that all present signs point to an intimate commingling of all existing human types within the next five or ten thousand years at most. Unless we can re-establish geographical isolation of races, we cannot prevent their interbreeding. By rigid laws excluding immigrants of other races, such as they have in New Zealand and Australia, it may be possible for a time to maintain the purity of the white race in certain countries, but with constantly increasing intercommunications between all lands and peoples such artificial barriers will probably prove as ineffectual in the long run as the Great Wall of China. The races of the world are not drawing apart but together, and it needs only the vision that will look ahead a few thousand years to see the blending of all racial currents into a common stream."

If we frankly recognize the fact that the crossing of races in juxtaposition has always occurred in the past, what evidence have we that such crosses have had untoward consequences? Our own data from the army tests indicate clearly the intellectual superiority of the Nordic race group. This superiority is confirmed by observation of this race in history. The Alpine race, according to our figures, which are supported by historical evidence, seems to be considerably below the Nordic type intellectually. However, our recruits from Germany, which represents a Nordic-Alpine cross, are about the same as those from Holland, Scotland, the United States, Denmark, and Canada, countries which have on the whole a greater proportion of Nordic blood than Germany. Again, the Nordic and Alpine mixture in Switzerland has given a stable people, who have evolved, in spite of linguistic differences, a very advanced form of government. The evidence indicates that the Nordic-Alpine cross, which occurred in Western Europe when the Nordics overwhelmed the Alpines to such an extent that the type was completely submerged and not re-discovered until recently, has not given unfortunate results.

This evidence, however, can not be carried over to indicate that a cross between the Nordic and the Alpine Slav would be desirable. The Alpines that our data sample come for the most part from an area peopled largely by a branch of the Alpine race which appeared late and radiated from the Carpathian Mountains. It is probably a different branch of the Alpine race from that which forms the primitive substratum of the present population of Western Europe. Our data on the Alpine Slav show that he is intellectually inferior to the Nordic, and every indication would point to a lowering of the average intelligence of the

Nordic if crossed with the Alpine Slav. There can be no objection to the intermixture of races of equal ability, provided the mingling proceeds equally from all sections of the distribution of ability. Our data, however, indicate that the Alpine Slav we have imported and to whom we give preference in our present immigration law is intellectually inferior to the Nordic type.

The Mediterranean race at its northern extension blends with the Alpine very considerably, and to a less extent with the Nordic. At the point of its furthermost western expansion in Europe it has crossed with the primitive types in Ireland. Throughout the area of its southern and eastern expansion it has crossed with negroid types. In this continent, the Mediterranean has crossed with the Amerind and the imported negro very extensively. In general, the Mediterranean race has crossed with primitive race types more completely and promiscuously than either the Alpine or the Nordic, and with most unfortunate results.

We must now frankly admit the undesirable results which would ensue from a cross between the Nordic in this country with the Alpine Slav, with the degenerated hybrid Mediterranean, or with the negro, or from the promiscuous intermingling of all four types. Granted the undesirable results of such an intermingling, is there any evidence showing that such a process is going on? Unfortunately the evidence is undeniable. The 1920 census shows that we have 7,000,000 native born whites of mixed parentage, a fact which indicates clearly the number of crosses between the native born stock and the European importations.

The evidence in regard to the white and negro cross is also indisputable. If we examine the figures showing the proportion of mulattoes to a thousand blacks for each twenty year period from 1850 to 1910, we find that in 1850 there were 126 mulattoes to a thousand blacks, 136 in 1870, 179 in 1890 and 264 in 1910. This intermixture of white and negro has been a natural result of the emancipation of the negro and the breaking down of social barriers against him, mostly in the North and West. In 1850, the free colored population showed 581 mulattoes to a thousand blacks as against 83 in the slave population. At each of the four censuses (1850, 1870, 1890 and 1910) the South, where the social barriers are more rigid than elsewhere, has returned the smallest proportion of mulattoes to a thousand blacks. The 1910 census showed 201 in the South, 266 in the North and 321 in the West, and the West has returned the highest proportion at each of the censuses except 1850.

We must face a possibility of racial admixture here that is infinitely worse than that faced by any European country today, for we are incorporating the negro into our racial stock, while all of Europe is comparatively free from this taint. It is true that the rate of increase of the negro in this country by ten year periods since 1800 has decreased rather steadily from about 30% to about 11%, but this declining rate has given a gross population increase from approximately 1,000,000 to approximately 10,000,000. It is also true that the negro now constitutes only about 10% of the total population, where he formerly constituted 18% or 19% (1790 to 1830), but part of this decrease in percentage of the total population is due to the great influx of immigrants, and we favor in our immigration law those countries 35% of whose representatives here are below the average negro. The declining rate of increase in the negro population from 1800 to 1910 would indicate a correspondingly lower rate to be expected in the future. From 1900 to 1920 the negro population increased 18.4%, while the native born white of native parents increased 42.6%, and the native born white of foreign parents increased 47.6%. It is impossible to predict at the present time that the rate of infiltration of white blood into the negro will be checked by the declining rate of increase in the negro blood itself. The essential point is that there are 10,000,000 negroes here now and that the proportion of mulattoes to a thousand blacks has increased with alarming rapidity since 1850.

According to all evidence available, then, American intelligence is declining, and will proceed with an accelerating rate as the racial admixture becomes more and more extensive. The decline of American intelligence will be more rapid than the decline of the intelligence of European national groups, owing to the presence here of the negro. These are the plain, if somewhat ugly, facts that our study shows. The deterioration of American intelligence is not inevitable, however, if public action can be aroused to prevent it. There is no reason why

legal steps should not be taken which would insure a continuously progressive upward evolution.

The steps that should be taken to preserve or increase our present intellectual capacity must of course be dictated by science and not by political expediency. Immigration should not only be restrictive but highly selective. And the revision of the immigration and naturalization laws will only afford a slight relief from our present difficulty. The really important steps are those looking toward the prevention of the continued propagation of defective strains in the present population. If all immigration were stopped now, the decline of American intelligence would still be inevitable. This is the problem which must be met, and our manner of meeting it will determine the future course of our national life.

## Franz Boas, "The Question of Racial Purity," 1924

*Franz Boas (1858–1942), one of the pioneers of anthropology, was born in Prussia into a well-educated and assimilated Jewish family. He emigrated to the United States in the 1880s and was a professor at Columbia University from 1899 until his death in 1942. In addition to his innovative scholarship in physical anthropology, linguistics, ethnology, and folklore, Boas claimed an important place within American popular thought. He was one of the first major thinkers in the United States to attack racialist theories that vaunted the superiority of the Nordic or Aryan race over all other peoples. By the 1920s his emphasis on the cultural rather than the genetic sources of human differences was well on the way to becoming a mainstream idea, pushing racist pseudoscience toward the fringes of American society. Since the 1910s Boas had spearheaded the intellectual battle against scholars who used hereditary theories to support the crusade for immigration restriction. Although he lost this battle, he would win the long-term academic war. In his 1924 essay "The Question of Racial Purity," excerpted below, Boas sets out his argument against the racialist position.*

Source: Franz Boas, "The Question of Racial Purity," *American Mercury* (October 1924): 163–69.

Seventy-one years ago Count Arthur de Gobineau published the first volume of his famous "Essay on the Inequality of the Races of Man." In it he tried to prove that the historical fate of a nation depends upon its racial constitution, that purity of race is the deciding element in the development of a people, and that only the Aryans are or can be the founders of a truly great civilization. He sought thereby to lay a solid foundation for the views of the importance of racial descent which had been expressed previously by Gustav Klemm in his "General History of Civilization" (1842–53) and by Karl Gustav Carus (1849). He was followed by the Americans, Josiah C. Nott and George R. Gliddon (1854), and since that time further attempts to prove the biological superiority of the white race, and more particularly of the blond Northwest European, have been made by many writers, among them Vacher de Lapouge,

Renan, Collignon, Stewart Houston Chamberlain, Wilser, Woltmann, Penka, Günther, Keith, and, in our own country, Madison Grant, Henry Fairfield Osborn, Charles Brigham and others. It is easily recognized that the majority of defenders of the superiority of this Northwest European type are swayed, not by scientific arguments but by prejudice, but it is equally true that the defenders of race equality who have risen to combat their views are no less influenced by a desire to defend the position of those races that have been designated inferior. . . .

The fundamental difficulty that besets us is that of differentiating between what is inherent in bodily structure, and what is acquired by the cultural medium in which each individual is set, or, to express it in biological terms, what is determined by hereditary and what by environmental causes. . . .

With our increasing knowledge of the laws of heredity and the exactness with which the distribution of traits in each generation of offspring can now be predicted, a strong incentive has been given to search for a definite distribution of mental traits in various races. If it is found that the individuals of a certain group behave in a manner that differentiates them from other groups, the inference readily presents itself that we are dealing with a phenomenon of heredity. However, this inference cannot be accepted without proof, because environmental cultural conditions may bring about a precisely similar result. To give an example: Among nations that, on account of their size and self-sufficiency, are not compelled to have frequent dealings with foreigners or to use foreign languages, the linguistic faculty seems to be at a low ebb, but it is highly developed in small nations that are compelled to use several languages. The United States on the one hand and Holland and Switzerland on the other are typical. But it would certainly be rash to argue that the lack of linguistic ability in the United States and its high development in Holland are due to hereditary causes. Often, however, the relation of cultural characteristics and external causes is less apparent. It seems, for instance, a justifiable question whether the mental reactions of the Negro in America are not conditioned by what psychologists like to call an inferiority complex. . . .

Investigators are too much inclined to consider as instinctive and hereditary every action that occurs without conscious reasoning. Thus, the particular kind of modesty that exists in our civilization is regarded as instinctive, but a study of the customs of different times and different cultural groups proves clearly that every particular form of modesty is almost entirely socially determined. While modesty itself may be instinctive, the particular form that we exhibit is acquired by the bringing up of each individual. It is automatic, not instinctive. In many cases close observation is required to prove that a reaction is automatic and not instinctive. The feeling engendered by the differences between races is of this character. There is no such thing as instinctive aversion between races; whatever race-aversion exists is automatic, not instinctive. An adult who has become completely ad-justed to this automatic reaction understands only with difficulty its acquired character, but its lack of universality in mankind and in members of the same race who live under different conditions is convincing proof of its non-instinctive character. Thus, in a scientific study of racial characteristics we must reject the assumption that mental traits are hereditary unless satisfactory proof of their biological foundation in the human organism is given.

A second argument that must be rejected is the one derived from cultural achievement. Claimants for the superiority of the white race point out its position in the modern world. From this they conclude that the white race is the only one that could or can ever achieve eminence, and that the fact is due to its hereditary qualities. In order to prove the weakness of this argument we need only consider the conclusions that a Maya Indian in the days when his civilization was at its height might have drawn from a comparison of his culture with conditions in Northwestern Europe. Lo, the poor Nordic! He was then an uncouth barbarian, without any arts or knowledge that could be compared with those of the Maya. Would not the Maya have been justified in calling him an inferior who would never achieve eminence? We must put aside all such faulty methods. . . .

We have the right to speak of the hereditary characteristics of family lines but not of the hereditary characteristics of nations or of races, because the latter vary within wide limits. Only if it is proved that the family lines constituting two races are through-out distinct can we speak of racial characteristics. For European local types such as the Northwest European or the Mediterranean such proof cannot be given. On the contrary, the variability of the types is so great that the forms in different European localities overlap–that is forms occurring in one area are not absolutely confined to that area. . . .

In a scientific investigation of the problem I should demand, therefore, as an indispensable part of the inquiry a determination of the adjustability of the individual to different demands, and of the adaptability of different individuals to the same demands.

It seems to me that the psychological tests which enjoy such a vogue at the present time fail in this respect. The mass of individuals subjected to the tests are not equally adjusted; therefore, before accepting the results of the tests as criteria of hereditary intelligence, as is done by many psychologists, we ought to insist that each individual be given an opportunity for adjustment. On the other hand, the reactions of the same individual under different environmental conditions should be studied in much greater detail than is ordinarily done. This is one of the reasons why the results obtained by Brigham in his study of the intelligence of immigrants in the United States are entirely unconvincing. When he finds that immigrants who came here twenty, fifteen, ten and five years ago do not respond equally well to his tests, the most recent arrivals showing the lowest records, we have to consider that they are not equally adjusted. The differences in the reactions do not prove anything in regard to their hereditary intelligence, as we are asked to believe. . . .

The claim made for the superiority of pure races has never been substantiated. As I have pointed out, the purity of any given racial type is a debatable question, and the claim that only extreme types are pure is founded on a misconception. Ethnological evidence is certainly not in favor of the assumption that mixed races are in any way culturally incapable. We may point out here again that Central Italy, a region which for very long periods has been a meeting ground of different races, has been one of the most powerful centres in the development of civilization. It is equally true that the people who have been historically most important in the development of Africa are found in the region where the North African tribes and the people of the Sahara come into close contact, and have intermingled. A general review of cultural forms the world over does not indicate that there is any correlation between the achievements of races and their supposed racial purity. . . .

Our knowledge of the reactions of men living in diverse cultural forms and the study of the cultural forms themselves lead us to infer that hereditary characteristics are irrelevant as compared to social conditions, and that anatomical form does not determine the cultural history of a people. It is particularly worth remarking that the current unfavorable opinion of the Negro is based largely on complete ignorance of African native conditions, and of Negro achievements in the industries and arts and in political organization, and that likewise the glorification of our own race is founded exclusively on a consideration of the cultural opportunities given to the few and on the complete neglect of the cultural primitiveness of the great mass of individuals, which finds expression intellectually in the uncritical acceptance of traditional attitudes and emotionally in the ease with which they succumb to the power of fashionable passions. We may say with certainty that the local types of a single race like the European are each so variable that fixed hereditary differences in mental characteristics between the types as a whole are most unlikely. We may say, furthermore, that cultural anthropology makes the existence of fundamental racial differences very improbable.

## Gong Lum v. Rice, 1927

*The last major Supreme Court decision in favor of segregated schooling,* Gong Lum v. Rice *(1927), arose from a Mississippi case in which a Chinese American man, Gong Lum, sued for the right to enroll his daughter Martha in the white public high school in their district. As in other Southern states, the Mississippi constitution provided that "separate schools shall be maintained for children of the white and colored races." Gong Lum argued that Martha was of pure Chinese ancestry and did not belong to the "colored races." Therefore, as no separate school existed for Asians, she should be allowed to attend the school set up for whites. The school authorities rejected Gong Lum's attempt to register Martha. The U.S. Supreme Court upheld the state's right to assign students to schools in whatever manner it chose, as long as each child had access to a public education.*

*Source: Gong Lum v. Rice* (1927), Findlaw Internet site http://caselaw.lp.findlaw.com/scripts/getcasepl?navby=case&court=US&vol=275&page=78

U.S. Supreme Court
GONG LUM v. RICE, 275 U.S. 78(1927)
275 U.S. 78
GONG LUM et al.
v.
RICE et al.
No. 29.
Submitted Oct. 12, 1927.
Decided Nov. 21, 1927.

Mr. James N. Flowers, of Jackson, Miss., for plaintiffs in error. [275 U.S. 78, 79] Messrs. Rush H. Knox, of Jackson, Miss., and E. C. Sharp, of Corinth, Miss., for defendants in error.

Mr. Chief Justice TAFT delivered the opinion of the Court.

This was a petition for mandamus filed in the state circuit court of Mississippi for the First judicial district of Bolivar county.

Gong Lum is a resident of Mississippi, resides in the Rosedale consolidated high school district, and is the father of Martha Lum. He is engaged in the mercantile business. Neither he nor she was connected with the consular service, or any other service, of the government of China, or any other government, at the time of her birth. [275 U.S. 78, 80] She was nine years old when the petition was filed, having been born January 21, 1915, and she sued by her next friend, Chew How, who is a nativeborn citizen of the United States and the state of Mississippi. The petition alleged that she was of good moral character, between the ages of 5 and 21 years, and that, as she was such a citizen and an educable child, it became her father's duty under the law to send her to school; that she desired to attend the Rosedale consolidated high school; that at the opening of the school she appeared as a pupil, but at the noon recess she was notified by the superintendent that she would not be allowed to return to the school; that an order had been issued by the board of trustees, who are made defendants, excluding her from attending the school solely on the ground that she was of Chinese descent, and not a member of the white or Caucasian race, and that their order had been made in pursuance to instructions from the state superintendent of education of Mississippi, who is also made a defendant.

The petitioners further show that there is no school maintained in the district for the education of children of Chinese descent, and none established in Bolivar county where she could attend.

The Constitution of Mississippi (Const. 1890, 201, 206) requires that there shall be a county common school fund, made up of poll taxes from the various counties, to be retained in the counties where the same is collected, and a state common school fund to be taken from the general fund in the state treasury, which together shall be sufficient to maintain a common school for a term of four months in each scholastic year, but that any county or separate school district may levy an additional tax to maintain schools for a longer time than a term of four months, and that the said common school fund shall be distributed among the several counties and separate school districts in proportion to the number of educable children in each, to be collected [275 U.S. 78, 81] from the data in the office of the state superintendent of education in the manner prescribed by law; that the Legislature encourage by all suitable means the promotion of intellectual, scientific, moral, and agricultural improvement, by the establishment of a uniform system of free public schools by taxation or otherwise, for all children between the ages of 5 and 21 years, and as soon as practicable, establish schools of higher grade.

The petition alleged that, in obedience to this mandate of the Constitution, the Legislature has provided for the establishment and for the payment of the expenses of the Rosedale consolidated high school, and that the plaintiff Gong Lum, the petitioner's father, is a taxpayer and helps to support and maintain the school; that Martha Lum is an educable child, is entitled to attend the school as a pupil, and that this is the only school conducted in the district available for her as a pupil; that the right to attend it is a valuable right; that she is not a member of the colored race, nor is she of mixed blood, but that she is pure Chinese; that she is by the action of the board of trustees and the state superintendent discriminated against directly, and denied her right to be a member of the Rosedale school; that the school authorities have no discretion under the law as to her admission as a pupil in the school, but that they continue without authority of law to deny her the right to attend it as a pupil. For these reasons the writ of mandamus is prayed for against the defendants, commanding them and each of them to desist from discriminating against her on account of her race or ancestry, and to give her the same rights and privileges that other educable children between the ages of 5 and 21 are granted in the Rosedale consolidated high school.

The petition was demurred to by the defendants on the ground, among others, that the bill showed on its face that plaintiff is a member of the Mongolian or yellow race, and [275 U.S. 78, 82] therefore not entitled to attend the schools provided by law in the state of Mississippi for children of the white or Caucasian race.

The trial court overruled the demurrer and ordered that a writ of mandamus issue to the defendants as prayed in the petition.

The defendants then appealed to the Supreme Court of Mississippi, which heard the case. Rice v. Gong Lum, 139 Miss. 760, 104 So. 105. In its opinion, it directed its attention to the proper construction of section 207 of the state Constitution of 1890, which provides:

"Separate schools shall be maintained for children of the white and colored races."

The court held that this provision of the Constitution divided the educable children into those of the pure white or Caucasian race, on the one hand, and the brown, yellow, and black races, on the other, and therefore that Martha Lum, of the Mongolian or yellow race, could not insist on being classed with the whites under this constitutional division. The court said:

"The Legislature is not compelled to provide separate schools for each of the colored races, and unless and until it does provide such schools, and provide for segregation of the other races, such races are entitled to have the benefit of the colored public schools. Under our statutes a colored public school exists in every county and in some convenient district, in which every colored child is entitled to obtain an education. These schools are within the reach of all the children of the state, and the plaintiff does not show by her petition that she applied for admission to such schools. On the contrary, the petitioner takes the position that, because there are no separate public schools for Mongolians, she is entitled to enter the white public schools in preference to the colored public schools. A consolidated school in this state is simply a common school conducted as other common schools are conducted; [275 U.S. 78, 83] the only distinction being that two or more school districts have been consolidated into one school. Such consolidation is entirely discretionary with the county school board, having reference to the condition existing in the particular territory. Where a school district has an unusual amount of territory, with an unusual valuation of property therein, it may levy additional taxes. But the other common schools under similar statutes have the same power.

"If the plaintiff desires, she may attend the colored public schools of her district, or, if she does not so desire, she may go to a private school. The compulsory school law of this state does not require the attendance at a public school, and a parent under the decisions of the Supreme Court of the United States has a right to educate his child in a private school if he so desires. But plaintiff is not entitled to attend a white public school."

As we have seen, the plaintiffs aver that the Rosedale consolidated high school is the only school conducted in that district available for Martha Lum as a pupil. They also aver that there is no school maintained in the district of Bolivar county for the education of Chinese children, and none in the county. How are these averments to be reconciled with the statement of the state Supreme Court that colored schools are maintained in every county by virtue of the Constitution? This seems to be explained, in the language of the state Supreme Court, as follows:

"By statute it is provided that all the territory of each county of the state shall be divided into school districts separately for the white and colored races; that is to say, the whole territory is to be divided into white school districts, and then a new division of the county for colored school districts. In other words, the statutory scheme is to make the districts, outside of the separate school districts, districts for the particular race, white or colored, so that the territorial limits of the school districts need [275 U.S. 78, 84] not be the same, but the territory embraced in a school district for the colored race may not be the same territory embraced in the school district for the white race, and vice versa, which system of creating the common school districts for the two races, white and colored, do not require schools for each race as such to be maintained in each district; but each child, no matter from what territory, is assigned to some school district, the school buildings being separately located and separately controlled, but each having the same curriculum, and each having the same number of months of school term, if the attendance is maintained for the said statutory period, which school district of the common or public schools has certain privileges, among which is to maintain a public school by local taxation for a longer period of time than the said term of four months under named conditions which apply alike to the common schools for the white and colored races."

We must assume, then, that there are school districts for colored children in Bolivar county, but that no colored school is within the limits of the Rosedale consolidated high school district. This is not inconsistent with there being at a place outside of that district and in a different district, a colored school which the plaintiff Martha Lum may conveniently attend. If so, she is not denied, under the existing school system, the right to attend and enjoy the privileges of a common school education in a colored school. If it were otherwise, the petition should have contained an allegation showing it. Had the petition alleged specifically that there was no colored school in Martha Lum's neighborhood to which she could conveniently go, a different question would have been presented, and this, without regard to the state Supreme Court's construction of the state Constitution as limiting the white schools provided for the education of children of the white or Caucasian race. But we do not find the petition to present such a situation.

[275 U.S. 78, 85] The case then reduces itself to the question whether a state can be said to afford to a child of Chinese ancestry, born in this country and a citizen of the United States, the equal protection of the laws, by giving her the opportunity for a common school education in a school which receives only colored children of the brown, yellow or black races.

The right and power of the state to regulate the method of providing for the education of its youth at public expense is clear. In Cumming v. Richmond County Board of Education, 175 U.S. 528, 545 , 20 S. Ct. 197, 201, persons of color sued the board of education to enjoin it from maintaining a high school for white children without providing a similar school for colored children, which had existed and had been discontinued. Mr. Justice Harlan, in delivering the opinion of the court, said:

"Under the circumstances disclosed, we cannot say that this action of the state court was, within the meaning of the Fourteenth Amendment, a denial by the state to the plaintiffs and to those associated with them of the equal protection of the laws, or of any privileges belonging to them as citizens of the United States. We may add that, while all admit that the benefits and burdens of public taxation must be shared by citizens without discrimination against any class on account of their race, the education of the people in schools maintained by state taxation is a matter belonging to the respective states, and any interference on the part of federal authority with the management of such schools cannot be justified, except in the case of a clear and

unmistakable disregard of rights secured by the supreme law of the land."

The question here is whether a Chinese citizen of the United States is denied equal protection of the laws when he is classed among the colored races and furnished facilities for education equal to that offered to all, whether white, brown, yellow, or black. Were this a new question, [275 U.S. 78, 86] it would call for very full argument and consideration; but we think that it is the same question which has been many times decided to be within the constitutional power of the state Legislature to settle, without intervention of the federal courts under the federal Constitution. Roberts v. City of Boston, 5 Cush. (Mass.) 198, 206, 208, 209; State ex rel. Garnes v. McCann, 21 Ohio St. 198, 210; People ex rel. King v. Gallagher, 93 N. Y. 438, 45 Am. Rep. 232; People ex rel. Cisco v. School Board, 161 N. Y. 598, 56 N. E. 81, 48 L. R. A. 113; Ward v. Flood, 48 Cal. 36, 17 Am. Rep. 405; Wysinger v. Crookshank, 82 Cal. 588, 590, 23 P. 54; Reynolds v. Board of Education 66 Kan. 672, 72 P. 274; McMillan v. School Committee, 107 N. C. 609, 12 S. E. 330, 10 L. R. A. 823; Cory v. Carter, 48 Ind. 327, 17 Am. Rep. 738; Lehew v. Brummell, 103 Mo. 546, 15 S. W. 765, 11 L. R. A. 828, 23 Am. St. Rep. 895; Dameron v. Bayless, 14 Ariz. 180, 126 P. 273; State ex rel. Stoutmeyer v. Duffy, 7 Nev. 342, 348, 355, 8 Am. Rep. 713; Bertonneau v. Board, 3 Woods, 177, 3 Fed. Cas. 294, No. 1,361; United States v. Buntin (C. C.) 10 F. 730, 735; Wong Him v. Callahan (C. C.) 119 F. 381.

In Plessy v. Ferguson, 163 U.S. 537,

544, 545 S., 16 S. Ct. 1138, 1140, in upholding the validity under the Fourteenth Amendment of a statute of Louisiana requiring the separation of the white and colored races in railway coaches, a more difficult question than this, this court, speaking of permitted race separation, said:

"The most common instance of this is connected with the establishment of separate schools for white and colored children, which has been held to be a valid exercise of the legislative power even by courts of states where the political rights of the colored race have been longest and most earnestly enforced."

The case of Roberts v. City of Boston, supra, in which Chief Justice Shaw, of the Supreme Judicial Court of Massachusetts, announced the opinion of that court upholding the separation of colored and white schools under [275 U.S. 78, 87] a state constitutional injunction of equal protection, the same as the Fourteenth Amendment, was then referred to, and this court continued:

"Similar laws have been enacted by Congress under its general power of legislation over the District of Columbia (Rev. Stat. D.C. 281, 282, 283, 310, 319), as well as by the Legislatures of many of the states, and have been generally, if not uniformly, sustained by the courts' citing many of the cases above named."

Most of the cases cited arose, it is true, over the establishment of separate schools as between white pupils and black pupils; but we cannot think that the question is any different, or that any different result can be reached, assuming the cases above cited to be rightly decided, where the issue is as between white pupils and the pupils of the yellow races. The decision is within the discretion of the state in regulating its public schools, and does not conflict with the Fourteenth Amendment.

The judgment of the Supreme Court of Mississippi is affirmed.

## The Mexican Immigrant, 1926–1927

*Manuel Gamio (1883–1960), an important Mexican archaeologist and anthropologist, produced one of the most valuable studies of immigrant life in the United States in the early twentieth century. Based on interviews Gamio and his researchers conducted in 1926–1927,* The Mexican Immigrant: His Life-Story *contains more than seventy first-person accounts of Mexicans living in the United States. Some of the people surveyed had been living in America for a few years and some for decades. As a result* The Mexican Immigrant *presents an excellent series of snapshots of Mexican American life, particularly in the West and Southwest, from around 1900 through the 1920s. It is important to remember that these interviews took place during the "jazz age," when Americans and especially the younger generation were caught up in new and provocative forms of music, fashion, and demeanor. The public behavior of American women, in particular, was much more assertive than had been the case prior to World War I, and it contrasted sharply with the more conservative protocol for women in Mexico. The excerpts below illustrate the complexity of attitudes about the way of life on both sides of the border. (The interviews were translated from Spanish, and the personal names were changed.)*

*Source:* Mario Gamio, *The Mexican Immigrant: His Life-Story, Autobiographic Documents Collected by Manuel Gamio* (1931; reprint, New York: Arno Press, 1969).

## JESUS GARZA

This man is a native of Aguascalientes, *mestizo*, markedly Indian; twenty-four years of age.

"I have been in this country for three years and a half, for even though I went to Aguascalientes to see my parents about a year and a half ago I didn't stay more than a month. It had been my purpose to stay at home and work there but I found everything changed and dull, in other words different from this country, and now I like it better here and if I were to go back to Mexico it is only to visit a while and then return.

"Since I was very small I had the idea of going out to know the world, to go about a lot in every direction. As I had heard a lot about the United States it was my dream to come here. My father, however, wouldn't let me leave home because I was too small. He was very strict. I reached the third grade in school. I was in a school where my father was teacher but when the revolution came and months went by without their paying him and there was a lot of trouble, my father resigned. He then started a store but I went on in a school where an uncle of mine, a brother of my father's, was a professor. This uncle, however, didn't take much interest in my learning so I

quit school and studied at home and helped my father in the store. My father was very strict. He would hardly let us go out on the street. I had two brothers and two sisters. My mother died last year. I was here at that time, and although I would have liked to have gone back, I couldn't because I only had $24.00 saved in the bank. I had just got back to Phoenix and that money wouldn't have been enough to even get to El Paso. Well, as I was telling you, when I was about twenty I decided to leave home and come here. I waited one day until my father went out and then I took money out of the strong box, gold coins especially. I took out enough to take me to San Antonio and took the train for Nuevo Laredo. I crossed the border there. I had no trouble, although it was the first time I had come. I paid my $8.00, passed my examination, then changed my Mexican coins for American money and went to San Antonio, Texas. When I arrived there I looked for work but couldn't find any so that I went to the agency of *renganches* and contracted to work. They said that it was to go and work on the *traque*. I didn't know what that was but I contracted to work because my money was giving out. I only had three dollars left. I gave one to the *renganchista*, and he then took me with a lot of Mexicans to a railroad camp. I worked all day, but as I wasn't used to such a heavy kind of work I thought of leaving. I could hardly finish out working that first day, I thought that I was going to die because the work was so hard. At night I asked the boys slyly where Dallas, Texas, was or some other large city and they told me down the tracks and said that if I wanted to go I should catch a freight train and go as a tramp. But I didn't let them suspect anything but told them I was only fooling. I also asked them how one could get there on foot and they said by following the tracks but that one should be careful and cross the bridges in a hurry so that a train wouldn't overtake one. In that part of Texas there are many bridges. On the next day, without their noticing it, I left on foot, and went down the tracks. I left at about seven in the morning and reached the outskirts of Dallas at about six in the evening. It was already getting dark and I only had a dollar with me as I hadn't even gotten my day's pay. On reaching the outskirts of Dallas I saw a man who seemed to me to be a negro and at the same time a Mexican and I thought of speaking to him. As I didn't know English I said to myself, if he is a negro he isn't going to pay any attention to me. Finally I spoke to him in Spanish and it turned out that he was Mexican, although to tell the truth he looked like a negro. I told him how I had come and he said that I could spend the night there in his house. He gave me something to eat and a mattress on which to sleep. On the next day the same man took me to the house of an old man who rented rooms. This old man received me very kindly into his home and gave me a room. When I told him that I didn't have either money or a job he said that I shouldn't worry. I could pay him when I had some. I was there about a month without working and the man and his wife, both of them quite old, took as good care of me as though I was paying them. They gave me food, my room, and even cleaned my clothes. They have some children now grown up. Finally I managed to get work laying pipes and I was working for two weeks earning $2.50 a day. Then they laid me off because they said that I wasn't strong enough for that hard work. I returned to be without work and then a Mexican advised me to look for work in the hotels and restaurants because that fitted me, but I couldn't find that, because it is necessary to speak English for those jobs. Then I got a job with an electric company. I thought that it was some office work or some decent job of engineering but it turned out that they wanted me to go down into a well with a pick to make it deeper. I think that it was 20 meters deep and I also had to wheel stones. This work was so hard that I could hardly finish the day, for at about four o'clock in the afternoon the foreman wanted me to lift a rock so big that I couldn't even move it much less lift it. He then said that if I couldn't do that it was better that I quit so that I asked for my time, and they gave me $2.50. I kept on looking for work and in about three days I found one in a restaurant as "vegetable-man" (peeling vegetables). I stayed there about two months and on account of a Mexican who went to tell the manager that I couldn't do that work they fired me. Then I went to another restaurant and hotel and there they gave me a job as dish-washer. I was then learning a little English. When they needed a new "vegetable-man" I told the foreman that I could do that work and he gave it to me with an increase in pay. I think that they paid me $45.00 a month and my food. That boss was an American but very good and he told me that he was going to teach me how to do everything so that when anyone was missing I could take their place. He taught me to be a cook and to do all the work of the kitchen, bake, etc. He even increased my pay until I was getting $75.00 a month and my food. By that time I stopped living at the house of the old man of whom I have told you. That was because I don't like to live at the edges of the town. In the outskirts there are no police nor authorities and one can be assaulted and even killed and no one will notice it. But I have remained very thankful to that old man and I told him that I would always be his friend and would go to visit him. I paid the old man there $4.00 a month but then I found a good friend with whom I took in the *pueblo* a room for which we paid between the two of us $15.00 a month, $7.50 each. I worked ten hours a day and he did also. My pal was a Mexican and we cared for each other more than brothers. When one didn't have money the other did and we helped each other in everything. We went on a vacation to San Antonio, Texas, once. I like that city because it is pretty and there are many Mexicans. But wages are very low there and work is very scarce. Once I told my friend that we should go to Mexico but he said not, because he was in love with a girl here who was his sweet-heart. I then told the boss to give me my time. The boss asked me why I wanted to go and if I wanted permission to go he would let me go for two weeks or a month. I then told him that I was going to Mexico to see my people. He answered that if I was going I should know

that I always had my job there anytime that I should come back. I then went to Aguascalientes taking a lot of clothes with me and a little money. I went to my home and my parents were very happy. But I found everything different, very dull, and very changed. I no longer wished to stay there but to return to Dallas. Then without my people knowing it I left again leaving all of my clothes for I only brought what I had on and a little money. I came to Ciudad Juarez and from there I went to El Paso without any trouble. There I sent a telegram to my boss in Dallas. He answered saying that my job was ready for me there. I was all ready to go to Dallas when some friends told me that Los Angeles was very pretty, that one could earn a lot of money there and a lot of other things, so that I took the train to Los Angeles. But as I came on the train I got sick and I decided to stay in Phoenix for I was afraid of getting sicker. As soon as I was well I began to look for work. Earlier I didn't mind being without work for weeks but now I did. I soon found work at a sanatarium of this city, there in the out-skirts. They paid me $65.00 a month and my board and room but I worked more than 10 hours for as soon as a patient came I had to give him water and food and had a lot of trouble. Once a patient got hard-boiled because I was late with the food. It wasn't my fault for the cook was late. I told him so and he said 'shut up, Mexican.' I then called him a 'son of a viche' and he said that he was going to ask to have me fired. I told him all right and then went to the doctor and asked him to give me my time. Then I told him what had happened and he told me not to answer the patients, not to pay any attention to them for they were like children or crazy people and said that the reason why we Mexicans don't get ahead is because we can't get used to staying in one place. I told him to give me my time and that was all, for I wasn't used to have anyone shout at me. He gave me my time but he told me that when I wanted to come back he would give me work. Then I came here to the town and got a job again as a 'vegetable-man' but when the boss saw that I knew how to cook and everything he raised my pay to $75.00 and put me as a cook together with the other cooks who are Americans or Greeks. I am the only Mexican there is in this hotel. The only thing is that here we don't have a day off for as there is little business they have few cooks and they can't substitute very easily. Only once in a while when I ask for rest do they give it to me and put a boy in my place. I began working ten hours but lately they have made it eleven. I don't mind that so much for the boss likes me a lot. I have more privileges than the others. When he goes out I take charge of the safe and a great many people have told me, and I don't tell you to flatter myself, that the boss says that I am the best worker he has had there. Besides he gives me tips, one or two dollars a week so that I can go to the movies or wherever I may want. I am waiting until June or July to go to Los Angeles for that is the time when they say there is the most work there. I want to go back to Aguascalientes but only to visit and then come back. I have two wool suits in which to go out on the streets and two pairs of

shoes, my felt hat for the winter and I buy a straw one in the summer. I also have trousers and shirts to work in the kitchen with. All told I live very happily here. I don't lack anything and I am free. I write very often to my family, especially to a sister of mine who is the one who cares for me most. I send her money once in a while and I also have my savings in the bank for it is better to be foresighted. I would also like to quit being a cook and enter the theatre for I think I could work as an artist singing and dancing. That is my ambition, to be an artist.

"I have learned a little English on account of all that I have heard and because I have happened to always work with Americans and hearing and speaking English all day but I have never gone to school. I would like to take a course by correspondence but I have never done it out of laziness. A short time ago I received a letter from a friend of mine in Dallas telling me that he had married and that I should go there to live with him and he would get me a girl so that I wouldn't be alone. I am not thinking of getting married now, but if I ever marry it will be with a Mexican even though she be born in the United States. I don't think that an American can care for one like one of one's own blood, nevertheless to have a good time I like the Americans because they are cleaner. I have been with American prostitutes and nothing has ever happened to me but the other day I went to a Mexican and I got sick with gonnorea and other social diseases and had to go to the doctor. I won't go back to the Mexicans, it is better for me to go to the Americans.

"I am Catholic and although I almost never go to Mass or pray, I do keep Holy Thursday and Friday ever year for I am accustomed to do that. At home I was very Catholic but that was on account of my parents.

"I haven't learned to cook Mexican style. I only cook American style and I have gotten used to eating American food. Only when I am hungry for it do I go to eat Mexican style in some restaurant in this city. In one of those restaurants I have my sweet-heart, her mother is the proprietor, my sweetheart is the waitress but she is very pretty. She is from here in Arizona but she is Mexican." . . .

## CARLOS IBÁÑEZ

Sr. Carlos Ibáñez, native of San Francisco, Zacatecas, says that he has lived in this country for more than twenty-five consecutive years. Ibáñez is *mestizo*, markedly Indian.

"I came to this country more than twenty-five years ago. My object, like that of all those who come here, was to seek a fortune; I wanted to work hard in order to see if I could get something together for old age. But although I have had good opportunities I haven't been able to do what I wanted for various reasons, but very especially on account of my weakness for women. In Zacatecas, at the time when I left there, I worked as a peon in San Francisco and scarcely earned my food and a few cents daily. It was so little that I don't even remember how much it was. For that reason I decided to leave in search of fortune and I came to California. After living here for a while I went to work in the beet fields, in the railroad tracks, and at other jobs from one place to another until finally I came back to this city [Los Angeles] because here it isn't as hot nor as cold as in other places. At times I have had work and at other times I haven't. When I have had work I have saved a little of my wages in order to meet the situations when I have been without work. I haven't wanted to get married because the truth is I don't like the system of the women here. They are very unrestrained. They are the ones who control their husband and I nor any other Mexican won't stand for that. We are rebels and our blood is very hot, and in this country a man who opposes his wife loses her and even his wages if he isn't careful, for the laws and the authorities are on the side of the woman. Now the Mexican women who come here also take advantage of the laws and want to be like the American women. That is why I have thought it better not to marry; and if I do get married some day it will be in Mexico.

"I have never had any trouble in any of the jobs I have had since I have been in the United States. No one has shown prejudice against me. I have been treated like the other Americans. I have rather to complain against the 'Raza' who get very bad as soon as they get to this country, very egotistical and don't want to give the others a chance. That is why they say that 'the wedge in order to tighten must be of the same wood.' Here in this country the Mexican has the place which he earns for himself. It is plain that if one doesn't try to get a good job and is subservient the others will do with one as they please. I have never had anything bad happen to me. I have lived in peace with everyone.

"I would rather cut my throat before changing my Mexican nationality. I prefer to lose with Mexico than to win with the United States. My country is before everything else and although it has been many years since I have gone back I am only waiting until conditions get better, until there is absolute peace before I go back. I haven't lost hope of spending my last days in my own country.

"I am a Catholic, for that is the religion which my fathers taught me, but I hardly ever go to Mass or pray because I have forgotten. I used to pray before going to bed, but little by little I kept forgetting. I don't believe in witches or in the evil eye and other such things. I don't even know if there are that kind of people here in California. Perhaps there are among the Mexicans but it is very rare, while over there in Zacatecas, in my town there were many and there are many witches almost all over Mexico.

"I have learned a little English especially at my work. I do anything and work hard when there is work. It is certain that I live better here than in Mexico, but I wouldn't change my citizenship on that account for anything in the world.

"I like music to dance with and especially the American music because one can dance very well with the jazz music. I know almost all the Mexican dance halls in this city and I go to all of them to have a good time.

"I eat Mexican style, American, Italian and every style. Sometimes I go to Mexican restaurants, other times I go to one of the American ones and so on. I eat when I am hungry and it doesn't make any difference to me what it is. Of course I like the Mexican food best, tamales and frijoles, enchiladas and other dishes. But as I have said food doesn't make any difference to me, it is the same to me whether it is of one style or another for it all ends up in the stomach and gets mixed up there.

"I like everything about this country, the business, the movies, driving around, the work too, because one can make good money. The only thing that I don't like, as I have said before, is the way the women carry on, so that they are the ones who boss the men and I think that he who lets himself be bossed by a woman isn't a man." . . .

## SRA. PONCE

Sra. Ponce is originally from a humble class. Her outward appearance and speech have not altered. Her house has a typical appearance, with pictures of the heroes Hidalgo and Juarez, a Virgin of Guadalupe, a Mexican flag, typical multicolored advertisements and gourds from Michoacan on the walls.

"I came to the United States fourteen years ago. We first came to San Antonio and were there four days. It is a very Mexican city, for they even sell tamales in the parks as they do in Mexico. My husband established a small restaurant and he also worked as a painter. But he was not like those of this country who only do one thing, whether it be painting pictures, walls or signs. My husband was like the painters of Mexico who do all of them. That was why he didn't want to work here as a painter and preferred to give his time to our restaurant.

"I am Catholic. I don't go to confession, but I go when I can to the church near here, which is French, on Saturdays. I no longer feel about those things as I did in Mexico. I am from Puebla, and there the people prayed in the morning to give thanks for breakfast, at noon for dinner and at night for supper, and they often beat themselves on the breast. Since something happened to me in Mexico I haven't gone to confession myself. Just imagine, I was about nineteen when I was married and my husband was sixty-six. I respected him but I didn't love him. His two former wives had died. My husband didn't know what was the matter with me and he gave me a card so that I would go to a priest and confess myself. I went to confession and told the priest that I didn't love my husband. The poor fool went and told my husband the next day and he got angry. We then came to the United States. That is why I no longer go to confession. My husband was very jealous and didn't want me to go out on the street, so that in the fourteen years that I was here I only went out twice, until a short time ago, when he died at an age of more than eighty. He was very strong and the Porto-Rican doctor who was taking care of him and who had known him since we had come here, would tell him jokingly that since he had had three children by me at his advanced age he was going to exhibit him in a park as a curiosity. He thought that a great joke. I always remember my Mexico but I haven't

wanted to go back, although the Consul offered to help me. I want my children to finish their education here and after that if they want to take me to Mexico, I will go. The children are in school and they talk English and Spanish, for they hear me and the other Mexicans and others who speak Spanish, but they speak it incorrectly. I speak very little English. I can only make myself understood enough to buy things. I import Mexican products from San Antonio and El Paso.

"The *mole* which I make is not as hot as it would be made in Mexico because my customers wouldn't like it. But there are many Mexicans who ask for very hot sauce. I make the *tortillas* by hand, out of corn.

"I have a son by a former marriage who is a musician. Although I expect to stay here you see that I have sarapes and the Virgin of Guadalupe. The children are Protestant now." . . .


## ANASTACIO TORRES

He is white, a native of Leon, Guanajuato.

"I was about seventeen years old, in 1911, when I came to the United States with my brother-in-law. I had worked until then as a clerk in a small store in my home town and also knew something about farm work. My brother-in-law managed to get me across the border without much trouble. We crossed the border at Ciudad Juarez and when we got to El Paso, Texas, we signed ourselves up for work in Kansas. We first went to work on the railroad and they paid us there $1.35 for nine hours of work a day. As that work was very hard I got a job in a packing house where I began by earning $1.25 a day for eight hours work but I got to earning as much as $2.00 when the foreman saw that I was intelligent and that I was very careful about my work. They almost always paid me a cent or two more an hour than my companions and as I was intelligent they didn't give me the hardest jobs.

"I was educated in a Catholic school and if it hadn't been that my mother was poor, I might perhaps have been a doctor or a lawyer, for I was one of the most advanced in the school. I even learned how to help to say mass although that has hardly helped me in any way in this country. I keep on being Catholic although I don't go to church very often. I was married to a girl from La Piedad, Michoacan, in Kansas City. She died there after we had been married about a year, leaving our little son. While working in the packing plant I broke my leg and then I wanted to collect damages but I wasn't able to. I was thinking of going to ask the Mexican Consul there to help me but some countrymen told me not to go to that Consul because he didn't help anybody. At about that time the time of the Great War came and they gave me a war registry questionnaire. They wanted me to go to the war with the American army but I told them that I wasn't an American. They then asked me why I lived in this country and they kept on trying to persuade me. I told them that I had a son and finally, so that they wouldn't keep on bothering me, I went to California where a brother of mine was. I worked for a long time in California and then I did register for the

draft, but at the same time declaring that I was a Mexican citizen and that I wasn't willing to change my citizenship. I was in the Imperial Valley, in Calipatria. I worked there first as a laborer with some Japanese. As they are very good and intelligent they showed me how to run all the agricultural implements, a thing which I learned easily with my intelligence. About the end of 1918 I went to Ciudad Juarez for my sister and her children. My father also came with her. Then we went to Calipatria and the whole family of us engaged in cotton picking. They paid very well at that time. They paid us $2.00 or $1.75 for every 100 pounds of cotton which we picked and as all of the family picked we managed to make a good amount every day. When the cotton crop of 1919 was finished we went to Los Angeles and then I got a job as a laborer with a paper manufacturing company. They paid me $3.40 a day for eight hours work. I was at that work for some time and then returned to the Imperial Valley for lemon picking. They paid me $3.00 a day for eight hours work. I became acquainted with a young lady in the Valley from San Francisco del Rincon, Guanajuato, and was married to her. This was my second marriage. In 1921 a Japanese friend for whom I was working as a laborer told me to keep the farm, for he was going to go soon. The owner of the land who was an American furnished the land, the water and the seeds, and we went on halves on the other expenses. Half of the crop was his and half mine. The first planting that I made was of 13 acres of lettuce. I also planted squash and tomatoes. We did very well on those for the crops turned out first class. I don't have anything to say against the Japanese for they have been very good people to me. They showed me how to use a plow, the cultivator, the disc and the planting machines and they have been my best bosses. Neither can I complain of the Americans, for in Kansas City when I was working in the packing plant, as well as in Los Angeles and wherever I have been and have worked with them they have treated me well.

"Afterwards, encouraged by the first good crop that I got, I rented forty acres of land at $30 a year for each acre. I had to furnish the water and the seed and this time things went bad for me. The crop wasn't any good, the seed was lost and I had to go and look for work elsewhere. I went from one place to another working in different ways. At times I earned $2.00 a day and at others as much as $4.00. Recently I had a job as a gardener in Beverly Hills. I was very well there, for they paid me $4.00 a day for taking care of the garden. I also had a little piece of land on which I could plant vegetables, which also brought in something. But one day they told me that as I wasn't an American citizen they were going to take away my job and put an American in my place. Then I went back to cultivating some land with an American. I planted forty acres again on halves. The crops turned out well, but the American took the products to a packing house which went bankrupt, so my partner and I were left without anything.

"I believe in God, but I have my doubts, for I was convinced in the Catholic school that all those beliefs are use-

less. They exploit the poor man anyway and steal his work."

He has had four children by his second wife, so that he has five children in all. He has baptized all of them according to what he says. He says that his wife is and isn't a Catholic, for she doesn't go to church very often nor does she have any saints in the house. Referring to his first days in school he says:

"I might perhaps have been a lawyer or a doctor if my parents had even sent me to a government school. But the school where I was was Catholic and they had us praying all day. As I was the most advanced in the class, for I had learned to read in less than a year, the parish priest taught me how to say Mass. I was getting big then and saw that they didn't do anything but pray in the school so I once asked the teacher to show me something about numbers so that I could keep accounts. I was then given some multiplication, which was foolish, for I couldn't even add. I then told the teacher that perhaps he himself couldn't do that multiplication and for that reason I stopped going to school.

"I don't have anything against the *pochos*, but the truth is that although they are Mexicans, for they are of our own blood because their parents were Mexicans, they pretend that they are Americans. They only want to talk in English and they speak Spanish very poorly. That is why I don't like them." . . .

## SOLEDAD SANDOVAL

I have lived in El Paso for nine years. "I am a native of Parral, Chihuahua. My family was one of the most well-to-do there. My parents had several pieces of property and mining interests and had a certain amount of money. I was in a secondary school, when the revolution of 1911 began. In spite of the revolution at first everything in our town went on well, in peace. There was work for everyone and business prospered. Then the famous Pancho Villa began his campaign, beginning by going to Parral. As he knew that people with money were living there he began to impose forced loans. Villa visited the city often with the sole purpose of securing loans and more loans until finally tired of these abuses many of the men of Parral, among them the men of our family, decided to join a federal army to fight Villa. They went to Ciudad Juarez and stayed there for some time, and then on account of the same revolution they had to go to El Paso, Texas. Finding themselves there alone they decided to send for their families and we, four sisters, came with our mother.

"We established ourselves in El Paso. I first studied English a little and then worked. I was employed by a Mexican newspaper which was published in this city and then on account of my work I got to be manager of that publication.

"I had a sweetheart in Mexico City. He was an aviator. He came here to El Paso and we were married in 1920. As soon as we were married we went to Mexico City to live with the parents of my husband.

"I ought to first say that I had a real desire to know the capital of our country and in general all of the interior. I was Popularity Queen several times in Ciudad Juarez and I liked to dance a lot. I have enjoyed myself a lot but I have never been able to accustom myself to the flapperism of this side [of the Border], like many girls of the middle and poor classes of Mexico who no sooner get here than they immediately turn flappers. Many of them say bad things about our country and don't want to speak Spanish.

"I was very happy in Mexico with my husband, enjoying all kinds of comforts and well being and the love of the parents of my husband who loved me as much as they did him, when my husband decided to make an acrobatic trip across the Republic. But a terrible accident occurred in which my husband was killed. He was making acrobatic maneuvers in the plane which they were piloting when something went wrong with the apparatus, and my husband was killed. I kept on living for some time with my parents-in-law who loved me more and more each day, but no longer finding any reason for living in Mexico I came to the home of my parents.

"I live with my family like a young unmarried lady, as if I was a child, and to tell the truth I feel that I lack something, and that is the love of my husband. It seems to me an irony of fate that I was left a widow two years after marrying and in my youth.

"In order to overcome my heart-aches somewhat, I decided to work and I am now working with a newspaper in this city. I translate from English the most important notices for the paper. At times I myself take charge of the type setting, also see to it that the paper circulates widely. I don't really have any definite work but I do everything that I can so that the publication will grow in strength and importance.

"As I was educated in Catholicism I am Catholic but I am tolerant not fanatic. What is more, as a result of my reading and general studies I believe only in an all powerful Being, God. I wouldn't attempt to define it, but I know that there is something superior to us which rules the destiny of mankind and of the universe.

"I pray every night. It doesn't matter that I have gone to some festival or that I have danced, I pray the evening rosary, a litany and other prayers before going to bed. I pray for my husband, not because I believe that his soul is suffering but for a certain spiritual feeling which draws me near to him and our happy past; that is the only reason why I pray.

"I don't believe in the sanctity or in the purity of the priests, or that they are invested with super-human powers. To me they are men like all the rest. That is why I don't pay any attention to their preachings.

"I make confession once in a while, but not because I have committed sins— I don't believe that I have any—but to talk with an intelligent man such as the priest to whom I make confession. When I go to him in the confessional the priest doesn't know me. If he asks me of what sins I wish to accuse myself I say "Father, I haven't killed, or robbed, or spoken ill of my neighbor, and I accuse myself of all the other sins for I am a woman, or rather, a human being." Then I talk for a long time with the priest, if he lets me, always trying to keep him from knowing me. I unbosom all my troubles to him and tell all that which I can't tell my parents nor my friends, so that I talk in a shrine where everything that I say stays. After one of those confessions I am happy, as if I had been freed from a load.

"When I was married I didn't confess myself for I then had a husband to whom I could tell all that spiritually tortured me or that bothered me in some way.

"In regards to my life in this country I ought to say that I haven't gone out of El Paso. Even though I have wished to visit other cities it is very hard for me to do so, for if I went alone I would meet the opposition of my parents and my family on the one hand and on the other, one is always rather weak to struggle for one's living alone. I also believe that woman was made for the home and for nothing more than that.

"I can't adapt myself to certain customs of this country. To tell the truth I am even opposed to its tendencies of dominion and of power. It wouldn't bother me much to attack it hard." . . .

## ELISA SILVA

Elisa Silva is from Mazatlan, Sinaloa, she is white, she has lived in the United States for three years with her family.

"I am twenty-three years old. I was married in Mazatlan when I was seventeen. My husband was an employee of a business house in the port but he treated me very badly and even my own mother advised me to get a divorce. A short time after I was divorced my father died. Then my mother, my two sisters and I decided to come to the United States.

As we had been told that there were good opportunities for earning money in Los Angeles, working as extras in the movies and in other ways, we sold our belongings and with the little which our father had left us we came to this place, entering first at Nogales, Arizona. From the time we entered I noticed a change in everything, in customs, and so forth, but I believed that I would soon become acclimated and be able to adjust myself to these customs. When we got to Los Angeles we rented a furnished apartment and there my mother took charge of fixing everything up for us. My sisters and I decided to look for work at once. One of my sisters, the oldest, who knew how to sew well, found work at once in the house of a Mexican woman doing sewing. My mother then decided that my youngest sister had better go to school and that I should also work in order to help out with the household expenses and with the education of my sister. As I didn't even know how to sew or anything and as I don't know English I found it hard to find work, much as I looked. As we had to earn something, a girl friend of mine, also a Mexican, from Sonora, advised me to go to a dance-hall. After consulting with my mother and my sisters I decided to come and work here every night dancing. My work consists of dancing as much as I can with everyone who comes. At the beginning I didn't like this work because I had to dance with anyone, but I have finally gotten used to it and now I don't care, because I do it in order to earn my living. Generally I manage to make from $20.00 to $30.00 a week, for we get half of what is charged for each dance. Each dance is worth ten cents so that if I dance, for example, fifty dances in a night I earn $2.50. Since the dances are short, ten cents being charged for just going around the ball-room, one can dance as many as a hundred. It all depends on how many men come who want to dance. Besides there are some who will give you a present of a dollar or two. This work is what suits me best for I don't need to know any English here. It is true that at times I get a desire to look for another job, because I get very tired. One has to come at 7.30 in the evening and one goes at 12.30, and sometimes at 1 in the morning. One leaves almost dead on Saturdays because many Mexican people come from the nearby towns and they dance and dance with one all night. In Mexico this work might perhaps not be considered respectable, but I don't lose anything here by doing it. It is true that some men at times make propositions to me which are insulting, but everything is fixed by just telling them no. If they insist one can have them taken out of the hall by the police. One man whom I liked a lot here in the hail deceived me once. He was a Mexican. But since that time it hasn't happened to me again. My mother takes a lot of care of me so that I won't make any bad steps. My sisters do the same.

"Of the customs of this country I only like the ones about work. The others aren't anything compared to those of Mexico. There the people are kinder than they are here, less ambitious about money. I shall never really like living this way, besides since I don't know English and believe that it won't be so easy for me to learn it, I don't believe I will ever be able to adjust myself to this country. I don't have time to study English, nor do I like it.

"Life, to be sure, is easier here because one can buy so many things on credit and cheaper than in Mexico. But I don't know what it is that I don't like. My youngest sister, who is in a business college learning English, says that she likes this city a lot and the United States as a whole and that if we go to Mazatlan she will stay here working. She is thinking of learning typewriting and stenography, both in English and in Spanish, so as to work in some American business, which will pay her well.

"I don't suffer in the matter of food, for my mother cooks at home as if we were in Mexico. There are some dishes which are different but we generally eat Mexican style and rice and beans are almost never lacking from our table.

"I am a Catholic, but I almost never go to church. Sometimes before coming to the dance hall I go to church, even if it only be to pray a little. I think that I have only confessed myself some four times in my life. My mother is very Catholic. She, and my younger sister also, go to mass every Sunday. At home we have a large image of the heart of Jesus and my sisters pray to it at night.

"I don't think of remarrying because I am disillusioned about men, but perhaps if some day I should find one who would really care for me I would love him a lot. If I do marry some day it would be with a Mexican. The Ameri-cans are very dull and very stupid. They let the women boss them. I would rather marry an American than a *pocho,* however." . . .

## SRA. ANTONIA VILLAMIL DE ARTHUR

This woman is a native of a little town near Zamora, Michoacan. She has lived in Arizona for more than thirteen years. She is married to an American.

"My mother was married very young. She must have been about twelve years old. This was due to the fact that her step-mother abused her a good deal. Three years after she was married, that is when she was about fifteen years old, I was born. My father died when I was four years of age so that I can say I never got to know him. My mother had several pieces of property in Zamora, which my father had left her, but we did not remain there but went about to different parts of the state until we settled permanently in Morelia. I finished growing up there and went to school there. I had some aunts there and some other relatives. I was left an orphan there, for my mother died when I was about fifteen. She left me some money with which I established a little store and this enabled me to live comfortably without worrying or working very much. Shortly after reaching the age of fifteen I was married. After six or seven years of married life I was left a widow with one child. My husband when he died left me several properties, among which were two little houses which I still retain and which shall some day be my son's. He is already quite grown up and is in Los Angeles now. It has been about fifteen years since I have seen him. I lived in Morelia until 1910. When the revolution began I went to Monterrey, Nuevo Leon. There I lived with a family who were friends of mine. This family afterwards came to Texas, first to San Antonio and afterwards to other places, until we got to El Paso. We were only sight-seeing and I had left my son in the care of a sister of mine. In El Paso I became acquainted with Arthur who is now my husband. At that time I returned to Morelia. Arthur went there too, and we were married. Then we came right back to Phoenix. Here he continued for a time his work on the railroad, but later he became a cook in a restaurant. He knows how to cook very well. Then he left this work and we established a fruit and drink stand. We remained a number of years with this business for we made money at it. Then we started a grocery store and engaged in some other business but just lately we bought this hotel. [They have bought the furnishings, the business rights, etc., but not the building.] The two of us take care of it. In the morning we clean all the rooms, make the beds, and do all the work that there is to do in a hotel. My husband takes charge of cooking the food for the two of us, I make the purchases and he cooks. At times he cooks Mexican food but almost always, as it is so warm here, we prefer to eat vegetables for they are more healthful. Sometimes we go to the movies at night. I go mostly because my husband doesn't like the movies and the films hurt his eyes. When I don't have

anything to do I read some Spanish novels because often months and months go by when I don't speak the language. Only Americans come to the hotel and they all speak English. It is true that my husband speaks Spanish. If he hadn't spoken it I wouldn't have married him but he no longer likes to talk it and it seems as though he was forgetting it. I hardly ever read any Mexican newspapers. We only get the morning daily in English. Once in a while some fellow countryman comes here to the hotel, as you have, and then I take real pleasure in speaking the language. We have a phonograph with several Mexican pieces, 'La Golondrina,' 'Entrada a los Toros,' 'Perjura' and others which are very pretty so that even the Americans like to hear them a lot. Since I have been in this country so long I have learned to speak English a little, to read it and to understand it. I understand it better than I can speak it but I have to speak it anyway in order to wait on those who come to the hotel. I used to know how to sing a lot in Spanish but I am forgetting that for I hardly even have time to sing. I am now reading a novel *El Suplicio de una Madre* which I like a lot. My husband doesn't know that I have two pieces of property in Zamora because I haven't told him. As he is a foreigner one can't help but be a little suspicious of him. Anyway, as my first husband left me that property I am going to leave it to my son because they really belong to him. An aunt is now taking care of them. She rents them and keeps the rent, for I have told her to do so. What is bad is that the little houses are hardly taken any care of and they are going to pieces. Anyway I am going to give them to my son when he is a little bit older. It has been many years, about fourteen, since I have seen my son because I haven't seen him since I was married. He grew up gradually and I know that he learned the mechanic's or carpenter's trade in some way. He came with some friends to the United States. It seems to me that he has been in Chicago and other large cities of this country but now he is in Los Angeles, for he has written me from there. I have hopes of seeing him soon for he has said that he is coming to see me. I wish that he would come with all my heart. I have no reason to complain of my husband, only he is blunt once in a while and very serious, as all Americans are. [By what the interviewer has seen, Mr. Arthur treats his wife with rudeness and the latter suffers this with patience as is the custom with Spanish-American women.] I live very happily with him, although at times we have our misunderstandings, for the truth is one can't ever make one's self understood as one can with a Mexican. I like everything that there is in this country, the ease with which one can go around alone, can go to the movies, and so on. I think that it would be hard for me to go back to the customs of Mexico. Some six or seven years ago I went to visit in Morelia. My uncle found me very much changed. I remember that one night we went alone to the movies and we were going home in the darkness when a man frightened us. I was quite shocked and always lived in fear, for nothing but shots and revolutions were talked about. My aunt said that 'they must be cowards in the United States for they get scared at nothing' and

that I had made myself like the Americans 'in all my ways.' The truth is that I felt very queer there, for even to go to the toilet I asked to be accompanied. The toilets there are almost always outside and far from the house, and the same is true of the bath. There are many inconveniences. Here I have gotten used to going out alone and to not being afraid of anyone. But here it is very different. Men respect women and the police always watch everything. Almost always when I go to the movies at night my husband leaves me at the door of the theatre and waits there for me at the time when he figures the show is over. The last time he didn't come to meet me so I went alone to the corner to wait for the streetcar, for we were then living rather far away. A man went by and stopping very slowly asked me if I wanted a ride. I acted as though I hadn't even seen him. In a moment a policeman came up and asked if I knew the man in the automobile and I told him that I didn't. He then asked me if he had said anything to me and I said that he had invited me for a ride. He then went to arrest him but the man in the automobile had gone out of sight. On Sunday mornings I go to the Church to Mass, for I am Catholic and I like to carry out the orders of the Holy Mother Church. The only thing that I hardly ever do is to confess. My husband doesn't even like me to do that. I always pray at night before going to bed. I think that every good Christian ought to do that. In Mexico I was more Catholic than here but there is more religion there, more churches and, above all, fewer things to do. I get very tired here from working all day and at night I read and go to bed at about twelve, after saying my prayers. I get up at 5 in the morning, pray, and then lie down a little while longer until six or seven to begin work again. That is my life and the way I do. The people who live in the hotel are the only friends I have here."

## Fats Waller, "Black and Blue," 1929

*The great trumpet player and singer Louis Armstrong (1901–1972) immortalized the Fats Waller song (words by Andy Razaf) "Black and Blue," which he recorded in 1929. It is impossible to understand the impact of the song without hearing Armstrong sing it, but the words below will convey at least a sense of its pathos and irony. In one respect "Black and Blue" was a signature tune for Armstrong, who had a unique ability to reject racial prejudice through performances that captivated both white and black audiences.*

*Source:* "Black and Blue" (recorded by Louis Armstrong, 1929; written by Fats Waller).

Cold empty bed
Springs hard as lead
Feel like old Ned
Wished I was dead,
What did I do
To be so black and blue?

Even the mouse
Ran from the house
They laugh at you
And scorn you too
What did I do
To be so black and blue?

I'm white inside
That don't help my case
Cause I can't hide
what is in my face

How would it end?
Ain't got a friend
My only sin
Is in my skin
What did I do
To be so black and blue?

# CHAPTER 7
# CHANGING RACIAL MEANINGS: RACE AND ETHNICITY IN THE UNITED STATES, 1930–1964

## THOMAS A. GUGLIELMO AND EARL LEWIS

IN THE EARLY 1940S, AS NAZI theories on Jewish inferiority received greater attention and censure worldwide, a small controversy was fast developing around the U.S. government's own racial categorization of Jews. It became clear at this time that some immigration officers were instructing Jews wishing to naturalize to fill in "Hebrew"—and not "white," as some applicants wished—in response to the race question on naturalization forms. Such directives rankled some members of American Jewish organizations like the Anti-Defamation League of B'nai B'rith and individuals like Arthur Hays Sulzberger, publisher of the New York Times. Formal letters of protest to leading government officials followed, setting off confusion within the federal government. Immigration and Naturalization Services (INS) Chief Earl G. Harrison commissioned a report specifically on whether the "Hebrews" are a race, while the Secretary of Labor, Frances Perkins, was forced to admit that such questions were extremely difficult to answer, since most scientists "don't agree what a race is, nor what races there are."

In time, and no doubt in part as a result of the pressure of the protesters and the vehement anti-Nazi context of the moment, the federal government revised its forms eliminating "Hebrew" (among many other groups) as an acceptable answer on the race question. As far as naturalization forms were concerned, racial identification for a wide range of people was greatly simplified. Instead of over fifty races—from Finn to Flemish, South Italian to Syrian—the government whittled its list down to six: White, African or African descent, Filipino, Indian, Eskimo, and Aleutian. Those groups who had been excluded from naturalization for years—namely most Asian groups—were not included on the list. In making these revisions, INS officials noted that "scientific opinion with regard to race has changed," and therefore their racial classifications had to comport better with "contemporary opinion."

This example speaks to the malleability of race; the ways in which power and politics—rather than biology or genetics—define race; the transformation of and resulting confusion with the race concept during the interwar and war years; and the ways in which race powerfully shaped people's opportunities, as in the case of naturalization rights and Asians.

This essay explores these issues and more. The first part of the essay examines the changing scientific meaning of race. The second and longer section of the essay addresses how the social and political meanings of race in people's everyday lives changed over time, in part as a result of shifts in race science. We explore how Americans encountered race and the nation's racial structure, with some Americans attempting to dis-

mantle that structure to gain greater equality and others attempting to shore it up to protect their own privileges. Finally, we will discuss the wartime emergence of "ethnicity" as a new social scientific category as a result of changing conceptions of race.

We argue that between 1930 and 1965 both the scientific and sociopolitical meaning of race changed dramatically. The race concept, in these years, came to mean a much more specific set of human groupings and lost virtually all of its scientific legitimacy as a natural, unchanging biological essence. Similarly, and in part as a result of these paradigmatic shifts in race science, the social and political meaning of race—that is, its power to shape people's everyday lives and opportunities—underwent important changes. In 1930, race meant that African Americans, Asian Americans, Latino/Latina Americans, and Native Americans were often restricted by legal or other means from many if not all of the following resources—a quality home, a quality education, a quality job, union membership, citizenship rights, the ability to marry exogamously, the right to be tried by a jury of one's peers, and the right to own land. At this time, race also meant that certain European groups, while generally accepted as white and therefore greatly privileged relative to nonwhite groups or the "colored races" mentioned above, still faced their share of racial discrimination and prejudice. This was particularly the case for the races of Southern and Eastern Europe, whose immigration to the United States had recently been drastically reduced by the federal government on racial grounds. Together these in-equalities—along with a set of ideologies (i.e., "racisms") that both explained and helped constitute them—made up the racial structure of the United States in 1930.

By 1965 this structure had changed dramatically. All racial divisions among Europeans had disappeared, leaving groups such as Italians, Poles, and Jews—now considered "ethnic groups" rather than races—facing no societal dis-advantage whatsoever on account of their race (i.e., their whiteness). Indeed, an Irish Catholic, John F. Kennedy, be-came president of the United States in 1961. As for the "colored races," they had, by 1965, through an increasingly powerful set of social movements, forced the federal government to abolish virtually all legal barriers to racial equality (e.g., Jim Crow segregation, disfranchisement, immigration exclu-sion, naturalization restrictions, restric-tive covenants, and alien land laws). By the mid-1960s racial discrimination still pervaded the United States, of course, but the American racial structure—in large part because of vigilant activism from below—had been profoundly and forever transformed.

## THE CHANGING SCIENTIFIC MEANING OF RACE

The scientific meaning of race under-went several critical changes in the in-terwar years. First, there was what his-torian Elazar Barkan has called the "retreat of scientific racism." Although social scientists such as Franz Boas and

Robert Park had for years been raising serious questions about the validity of the race concept, it was really in the 1930s and 1940s that a significant and powerful group of scientists, responding in part to the rise of Nazi racialism abroad, consciously rejected essentialist understandings of race. They argued in-stead that culture, and not some natural essence, was the most significant deter-minant of human behavior and capabili-ties. Exemplifying this shift were schol-arly works such as Ruth Benedict's Race: Science and Politics (1940), Ashley Mon-tagu's Race: Man's Most Dangerous Myth (1942), and especially Gunnar Myrdal's landmark An American Dilemma (1944), all of which gained a wide, popular au-dience during the war years. This shift in scientific race thinking culminated in the early 1950s with the publication of the United Nations Educational, Scientific, and Cultural Organization's (UNESCO) The Race Concept. A series of statements written by leading scientists from all over the world, it simply re-stated, reinforced, and lent great legiti-macy to the fact that unity much more than difference characterized humanity; that no evidence suggested that race was connected in any way to intelligence, psychology, culture, or character; and that "pure" races did not exist.

Second, the Depression and war years witnessed not only the "culturalization" of race, but its simplification as well. For much of the early twentieth century, race was used to describe the widest va-riety of human groupings, from large populations like whites, Negroes, Latins, and Anglo-Saxons to very small groups like the Manx and Moravians, Syrians and Serbians. In the interwar and war years, as a result of immigration restriction, African American migration from the South to the North and West, and the rise of Nazism abroad, scientists and other intellectuals became less interested in delineating the racial divisions of Europeans and more concerned with the "major branches of mankind." These branches varied, depending on the scientist, yet they almost always included at least the "big three": Caucasian, Mongoloid, and Negroid. An example of the simplification of race on the government's naturalization forms opened this chapter. But there were numerous other examples, particularly in the realm of science, where even UNESCO's work conceded that there were only three great races—the ones mentioned above. Certainly this shift was not instantaneous; nor was it necessarily always reflected at the popular level or present uniformly across the country. For instance, in wartime Los Angeles, the idea that Mexicans were a distinct race "became even more clearly defined and firmly entrenched." Still, when talking broadly about America's scientific and intellectual community, this shift was real.

Indeed, compelling proof of this fact is the wartime emergence of "ethnicity" as a new social scientific concept. A review of major academic journals in a wide range of disciplines—economics, history, anthropology, sociology, political science, and literature—reveals that only in the postwar years did "ethnicity" and "ethnic" become common scholarly terms or categories of analysis. This was so because of the changing meaning of race in these years. As the race concept was simplified to exclude peoples like Magyars and Montenegrins from its purview, something new was needed to refer to such groupings. *Ethnic* fast became the category of choice. Other possible options like *nationality* were no doubt ruled out because Magyars and Montenegrins, for example, did not fit neatly into any one nation.

These scientific changes had a complicated set of meanings that made it hard to predict how they would affect everyday social relations. On the one hand, these new scientific ideas certainly aided the cause of groups denied equal rights on the basis of scientifically discredited race thinking. It also, of course, made it more difficult for segregationists, racialists, and exclusionists to continue to rely upon the word of science to support their racial projects. On the other hand, the new simplification of race, as historian Matthew Jacobson has argued, did tend to consolidate many Greeks and Germans, Moravians, and Magyars into the white or Caucasian category and, in so doing, encouraged these groups to think of themselves as such. Moreover, "as scientists asserted over and over that 'Aryans,' 'Jews,' 'Italians,' 'Nordics,' and the like were not races, their myriad assertions themselves all buttressed an edifice founded upon three grand divisions of humankind—'Caucasian,' 'Mongoloid,' and 'Negroid'—whose differences by implication were racial." In the end, the political and social ramifications of the shift in race thinking were unclear. Therefore, it is only through social history that we can discern what the changing meaning of race meant to various people in their daily lives—when they sought to buy a house, enter a restaurant, join a union, get a job, immigrate to the United States, marry a partner, and so forth.

## THE CHANGING SOCIAL AND POLITICAL MEANING OF RACE

### The Great Depression

The stock market crash of October 1929 and the ensuing decade-long Great Depression brought incalculable loss and despair to millions of Americans. In the industrial North and Midwest, unemployment and eviction rates soared, while employers drastically reduced the hours and wages of those few people lucky enough to work. Southern and western ports, meanwhile, faced a dip in exports and a rapid increase in unemployment. In rural America conditions were just as bleak. With farm incomes declining by 60 percent between 1929 and 1932, one third of all farmers lost their land in these years. All the while, state and local relief systems, to say nothing of private charities, were wholly unequipped to deal with the magnitude of the Depression.

But Depression-era deprivation cannot be explained by or appreciated fully through economic statistics alone. Race mattered a great deal. How else could one explain the fact that African Americans, for example, suffered the sting of the Depression so much more severely than many other groups? For example,

in one survey of 106 cities, the Urban League reported "with a few notable exceptions . . . the proportion of Negroes unemployed was from 30 to 60 percent greater than for whites." In certain sections of Chicago, for example, African Americans' jobless rate had climbed as high as 85 percent. As a result, while making up less than 8 percent of the city's population, African Americans comprised over 30 percent of those on relief. And relief rarely amounted to much. The federal government's New Deal was often more like a raw deal for many African Americans: the Civilian Conservation Corp lodged them in segregated camps; the National Recovery Administration ignored job discrimination and pay disparities; the Tennessee Valley Authority excluded them almost entirely; and the Agricultural Adjustment Administration greatly favored white farmers. As writer Langston Hughes poignantly put it in his "Ballad of Roosevelt" (1934):

the pot's still empty,
And the cupboard's still bare,
And you can't build a
bungalow
Out o' air—
Mr. Roosevelt, listen!
What's the matter here?

These facts are a smaller part of a much larger story, however: the inequities of the U.S. racial structure, which varied some from one region to the next, but in which African Americans were always located close to if not on the bottom. In the South, African Americans were denied the right to vote, made subject to an extensive system of Jim Crow segregation, often lynched with impunity, and forced to comply with a range of racial etiquette rules that reinforced subordination daily. And things were not always radically better in the North and West, where restrictive covenants, real estate practices, financial institutions, neighborhood violence, and "improvement" organizations all worked to segregate African Americans residentially; where many unions barred them from membership and employers refused to hire them for high-paying, skilled jobs; and where, as in the South, equal access to public accommodations was rarely the rule.

African Americans were not the only group poorly positioned in this structure. Ethnic Mexicans, too, (all people of Mexican origin, citizens and noncitizens alike), throughout the Southwest, suffered from widespread segregation in schools, public accommodations, and neighborhoods; they were often excluded from serving on juries; and they were given the most menial jobs at the worst pay. The Depression era, moreover, brought a state-sponsored repatriation program, which sent hundreds of thousands of ethnic Mexicans (many American citizens among them) "back home" to Mexico, often involuntarily.

For Asians and Asian Americans things were no better. On the West Coast, for instance, widespread job discrimination forced groups like Japanese Americans and Chinese Americans to find work in their own ethnic enclaves; alien land laws robbed them of their right to own property; and antimiscegenation laws (which also targeted Af-

rican Americans and Native Americans in many states) prevented them from marrying any partner they wished. In addition, by the 1930s immigration and naturalization laws excluded all Asians from immigrating to the United States and deemed all immigrants making it to the U.S. prior to these laws ineligible for citizenship. As for Native Americans, their racial status had long made them exceedingly vulnerable to white aggression, landgrabs, and treaty violations. Indeed, by the time of the crash, and in large part because of the Dawes Act of 1887 (which instituted a new program of land allotment without any say from Native Americans), Indians were becoming increasingly a landless and destitute people. Virtually half of Native Americans who lived on reservations and who were subject to allotments had lost their land, while a slightly larger percentage earned on average less than $200 a year.

Even certain European groups suffered from racial discrimination. The racialist theories behind the Immigration Act of 1924 still circulated freely around the United States and continued to cause problems for some Europeans. Jews, for instance, continued to face restrictive covenants in certain cities, a rising Depression-era anti-Semitism reflected in the popularity of Father Coughlin and grassroots organizations like William Pelley's Silver Shirts and the Christian Front, and discrimination in college admissions at elite universities like Harvard. Other European groups encountered similar discrimination. In one extensive study of Italians in New Haven conducted in 1938, sociologist Irvin Child found that "there is . . . a widespread prejudice against Italians which makes it difficult for people of Italian descent to obtain the better jobs in the community." Similarly, in Chicago, for well into the 1930s Italians met with some degree of resistance from other European immigrants and some native-born whites when moving into certain neighborhoods. In his classic and highly influential text, *One Hundred Years of Land Values in Chicago* (1933), Homer Hoyt reproduced a list made by a West Side realtor that ranked "races and nationalities with respect to their beneficial effect upon land values." Southern Italians were eighth on this list of ten groups, just above African Americans and Mexican Americans.

Still, it must be stressed that all Europeans—even the putatively inferior groups—were largely accepted as whites from the moment they arrived in the United States by "the widest variety of people and institutions—naturalization laws and courts, the U.S. census, race science, newspapers, unions, employers, neighbors, realtors, settlement houses, politicians and political parties, and so forth." Generally speaking, this acceptance meant most concretely that all immigrants from Europe could become citizens of the United States, vote with no problems, join virtually any union once they became citizens, and move to virtually any neighborhood without any serious or organized resistance. This acceptance varied somewhat by religion and region most notably. Regardless, for certain groups their racialness as Italians, Poles, or Greeks mattered when it came to rights and resources; but their color status as whites mattered infinitely more.

As Matthew Jacobson has aptly put it, whiteness was the key that opened the Golden Door.

The U.S. racial structure, then, just as surely conferred advantage as disadvantage. Whoever was accepted as white in this system received access to better jobs, better housing, more powerful unions, better incomes, citizenship, and voting rights. And these privileges often transcended class and gender lines, such that, as Dana Frank has recently shown, "white working-class women entered a labor market in which they were below white men, but they were above women of color and—in many but not all cases—above men of color." For women who worked at home, privileges were just as numerous and striking. Residential segregation meant not only better housing but also better amenities, like electricity and running water, which made housework and child care incomparably easier. Moreover, white women of all class backgrounds, often because of the superior wages of their husbands, were much more likely than nonwhite women to hire domestic servants. Predictably, these servants were almost always women of the "colored races." Taken together, whiteness conferred great privilege on all who could lay claim to it—irrespective of one's gender, class, or *European* race.

Because of these great inequities, groups disadvantaged by the U.S. racial structure fought hard to make sense of it, restructure it, reform it, or eliminate it. This was particularly true during the Depression years, when many Americans lost faith in an economic system that was collapsing all around them and a political system that, at least initially, could do little about it. Efforts to change the U.S. racial structure were undertaken by a wide array of groups, in the name of a diverse range of ideologies, political projects, and social identities. African Americans all across the country, for instance, joined a range of groups and movements like the Communist Party, the Urban League, the CIO, and the NAACP. During this period blacks turned to the federal courts for protection, began the slow shift to the Democratic Party, organized to vote, and took part in massive studies to expose the underbelly of racism and discrimination as a blight on democracy. Away from the glare of the media they told stories and encouraged their children to fight for a better tomorrow. Through activism, they fought for better relief provisions, better jobs, better housing, anticolonialism in Ethiopia and antifascism in Spain, and antilynching and anti-poll tax legislation here in the United States.

Meanwhile, many ethnic Mexicans, deeply troubled by repatriation and a Depression era rise in anti-Mexican hysteria, responded in a variety of ways. Some Mexican Americans joined new organizations such as LULAC, which stressed assimilation as the solution to Mexican American problems in the United States. Others joined and built *mutualistas,* unions, and important umbrella organizations like Confederacion de Uniones Obreras Mexicanas. They encouraged cultural preservation and blamed Americans, not unassimilated immigrants, for the plight of la raza (the people).

Battles for greater racial justice in the 1930s did not always unfold within strict racial boundaries, however. Indeed, as Michael Denning has argued, much of the activism outlined above was part of a larger whole—"the Popular Front . . . the insurgent social movement forged from the labor militancy of the fledgling CIO, the anti-fascist solidarity with Spain, Ethiopia, China, and the refugees from Hitler, and the political struggles on the left wing of the New Deal." And African Americans, Mexican Americans, Asian Americans, and various European groups all became centrally involved in this movement as artists, writers, musicians, and workers. Many of these groups, as well, through their activism in the movement, attempted to restructure the U.S. racial order in whichever way they could—through poetry, plays, marches, union drives, strikes, and movements for the unemployed.

Naturally, all of this activism against the racial structure attracted its share of resistance—particularly during the Depression years when competition over scarce resources only increased. A great example of this comes from within the Popular Front itself or, more specifically, the CIO unions. Many white CIO workers, their "culture of unity" notwithstanding, never fully accepted the official union line of racial equality, whether this was in the workplace, in the union hall, or in social events like picnics and bowling. Instead, while many racial groups insisted on using their unions to work for greater social justice, many white workers—some of whom were of Southern- and Eastern-European origin—fought to maintain the racial status quo through the 1930s and well into the '40s. Speaking about Memphis's CIO unions, Michael Honey has argued that there was "a stormy and continuing confrontation . . . over the meaning of trade unionism—with blacks wanting to use the union to batter down segregation and whites wanting it to keep segregation in place." And, of course, resistance occurred in other places as well: in scores of AFL unions and railroad brotherhoods that excluded various non-Europeans from membership; in boardrooms, where corporate leaders devised and enforced racially stratified pay scales and job structures, and in workplace cafeterias and bathrooms; in homes where parents taught their children the importance and location of the color line; in neighborhoods and public accommodations where color boundaries were fiercely defended; through radio shows, movies, and other forms of popular entertainment that reinforced the place of whites and nonwhites daily; and—in the South—through lynchings and southern Democrats' tight control over Congress, among many other means.

The state, during the Depression, largely sided with those groups fighting to maintain—not undermine—the racial structure. Of course, this was not always the case. FDR hired a significant number of second-tier African American bureaucrats to his cabinet; protected the labor movement that proved so beneficial to many "colored races"; and made real progress with regard to Native Americans by appointing John Collier as Commissioner of Indian Affairs and by ending the disastrous allotment program. Moreover, some members of FDR's cabinet like Harry Hopkins and Harold Ickes, not to mention his wife

Eleanor, fought hard (if ultimately in vain) to ensure equal access to relief for all groups; and, particularly in the case of the latter, spoke out vigorously and frequently against racial injustice.

Still, larger problems remained. We have already discussed New Deal shortcomings when it came to African Americans' relief. In addition, FDR, in large part because he did not wish to alienate the powerful southern Democrats in Congress, did little to disturb the racial status quo of the South (i.e., its deep racial inequality). He refused to pass anti-poll tax or antilynching legislation, and his New Deal programs largely strengthened the hand of Black Belt planters, "the bulwark of the solid, segregationist South." Ethnic Mexicans too were often excluded from receiving relief because of rampant discrimination at the local level and were, as noted, victims of state-sponsored forced repatriation. Moreover, at the height of anti-Mexican hysteria, the state did not help matters when it reclassified Mexicans as nonwhite for the first time on the U.S. census in 1930. Finally, regarding Asian groups, the state continued to refuse them naturalization rights or immigration quotas of any kind. And for some Asians things only got worse during the 1930s. With passage of the Tydings-McDuffie Act in 1934, for example, the state reclassified Filipinos as aliens, making them no longer eligible for New Deal relief benefits and setting their annual immigration quota at a paltry fifty. For all of these groups, crucial reforms like the Social Security and Wagner Acts were disappointments. The former excluded domestic, agricultural, and common laborers—many of whom were African American, Latino, and Filipino; the latter did not protect the organizing rights of these same workers.

For some groups, however, the New Deal was nothing less than transformative. For Southern and Eastern Europeans, programs created and legislation enacted during the Depression—the Home Owners Loan Corporation, Federal Housing Administration loans, the Social Security Act, and the Wagner Act—provided them with enormous advantages over non-European groups in the housing and labor markets and when it came to state insurance benefits. It was these programs more than anything else that transformed so many working-class racially suspect "new" European immigrants into respectable middle-class "white ethnic" suburbanites. This transition really occurred during World War II and beyond; but its origins lay in New Deal programs created during the Depression.

And this point is really the theme of the era. For the "colored races" as well, little changed in the U.S. racial structure in these Depression years. However, just as the seeds for future transformations were sown for Southern and Eastern Europeans in these years, so too was this the case for groups like Mexican Americans and African Americans, who were beginning to join unions, civil rights groups, and other Popular Front organizations. Through expanded involvement in a broad array of organizations and institutions, many members of the "colored races" were building foundations for future social movements that ultimately transformed the U.S. racial structure.

## World War II

The pace of change to America's racial order increased significantly during the war years. Massive wartime production created millions of new, better-paying industrial jobs for women and men, while union strength was on the rise; organized labor added 7 million new members during World War II. Perhaps more important, however, was how the war was represented and understood. In battling totalitarianism and Nazism abroad, American propaganda machines worked overtime to portray the U.S. nation as antithetical to its enemies. This meant that if totalitarianism demanded conformity, mocked freedom, and preached racial hatred, then Americans were pleasantly plural and instinctively democratic. Popular films and novels during the war never tired of celebrating American racial diversity. As John Hersey wrote in the preface to his best-selling novel, A Bell for Adano (1944), "America is an international country. . . . No other country has such a fund of men . . . who understand the ways and have listened to their parents sing the folk songs and have tasted the wine of the land on their palate of their memories. This is a lucky thing for America."

And yet despite these lofty ideals, the rise in wartime job opportunities and paeans to pluralism did not magically transform the U.S. racial structure. As in the past, if real change were to occur on this front, "colored races" would have to demand it. And this is precisely what happened, as activism by African Americans and Mexican Americans came of age. Using wartime democratic propaganda for their own purposes and building on Depression-era activism, these groups turned Roosevelt's war for "four freedoms" into what W. E. B. Du Bois called "the War for Racial Equality." The result was a restructuring of the racial order by the 1960s.

Asian Americans, Native Americans, African Americans, Mexican Americans, and some European Americans all shared some similar strategies of democratizing the U.S. racial structure at this time. Large numbers of men and women of all groups, for instance, served in the armed forces, invested in war bonds, participated in scrap metal drives, and worked in war production plants, all of which can be seen, at least in part, as an attempt to prove to their compatriots that they too were patriotic Americans deserving of equal rights. Native Americans provide a particularly striking example of these efforts. So many Native Americans served in the armed forces during the war (twenty-five thousand total, including eight hundred women) that the *Saturday Evening Post* remarked, "we would not need the Selective Service if all volunteered like Indians."

But battles in the "War for Racial Equality" certainly occurred on other fronts as well. African Americans were active from the start, in part because the gap between wartime democratic rhetoric and their everyday experiences was so intolerably enormous. For example, while booming wartime production brought higher-paying jobs to so many Americans in the early years of the war, many of these industries barred African Americans outright. In 1940 African Americans comprised only "0.2 percent of workers in aircraft production." In addition, they had to serve in segregated military units and received only the most menial positions in the Armed Forces, while the Red Cross segregated their blood.

In response to these injustices, African Americans took action in a variety of ways. Labor leader A. Philip Randolph organized the March on Washington Movement, which ultimately forced FDR to sign Executive Order 8802. This established the Fair Employment Practices Commission (FEPC), which sought to eliminate racial discrimination in government defense jobs. African American newspaper editors launched a "Double V" campaign to push for victory over the Axis abroad and over racial discrimination at home. Meanwhile, old civil rights groups swelled in size—the NAACP increased its membership ninefold—and new organizations like the Congress Of Racial Equality (CORE) were born; African American workers continued to battle within a growing and strengthening labor movement, becoming active leaders in CIO (and some AFL) locals and internationals across the country; African American social scientists at institutions like Howard University conducted groundbreaking research into the meaning of race and the nature of race relations in the United States; activists, public officials, intellectuals, and artists worked to harness the national mass medium of radio to fight racial segregation and discrimination. Finally, and perhaps most important, 2 million African Americans from the South moved northward and westward in the 1940s to find, if not a promised land, at least a place with greater possibilities for freedom. There they voted, exchanged favors with bosses of urban political machines, built new community-based institutions, transported and transformed elements of a rural folk culture such as the blues into new expressions, and struggled against other forms of discrimination and racial hostility. Capturing this moment of promise, Margaret Walker wrote in her poem "For My People" (1942): "For my people . . . trying to fashion a world that will hold all the people, all the faces, all the adams and eves and their countless generations; Let a new earth rise. Let another world be born. . . . Let the martial songs be written, let the dirges disappear. Let a race of men now rise and take control."

For Mexican Americans, too, the war years produced an upsurge in political activism aimed at restructuring the U.S. racial order. Their history in Los Angeles is instructive. As historian Edward Escobar has argued, ongoing police harassment of Mexican Americans, coupled with the outbreak of the "Zoot Suit" Riot in 1943 (in which hundreds of "Anglo" servicemen attacked and viciously beat scores of Mexican American youth), forever transformed Mexican Americans' "narrow political focus into . . . community-wide activism." Of course, this new activism had its roots in the civil rights and labor politics of the previous decade. Still, it was during the war years that

Mexican Americans (particularly members of the second generation), mobilizing around the activities of community institutions like mutual aid societies, newspapers, and volunteer groups, built a new and assertive civil rights movement. As Escobar writes, "Mexican Americans [in Los Angeles] emerged from the wartime experience with a confidence and sophistication that exemplified a new political identity and a new political style. Simply put, they would no longer be ignored."

For groups like Japanese Americans, however, battling against racial injustice became even more challenging during the war years. Shortly after the bombing of Pearl Harbor and the U.S. declaration of war on Japan, anti-Japanese American feeling, always strong on the West Coast, reached a fever pitch among local and state politicians, farming interests, the press, labor unions, and everyday people. The *Los Angeles Times* noted, for instance, that "A viper is nonetheless a viper wherever the egg is hatched—so a Japanese American, born of Japanese parents—grows up to be a Japanese, not an American." Operating within this context of growing race hysteria, FDR ordered the internment in February 1942 of more than 110,000 Japanese and Japanese Americans living on the West Coast. General Dewitt, who oversaw the whole operation, justified it by stating that even among second- and third-generation Nisei "the racial strains are undiluted" and "racial affinities are not severed by migration."

Japanese Americans responded to the pains of war and internment in a variety of ways. Some sued the federal government all the way to the United States Supreme Court for violating their constitutional rights, with none gaining the relief desired. Others turned to traditional community institutions such as Christian churches and Buddhist temples, which "acted as racial-ethnic centers of protest" during the incarceration period. A few newspaper men and women, who avoided internment, continued publishing Japanese-American papers and in some cases fearlessly critiqued the government's treatment of Japanese Americans, encouraging the latter to use their rights to resist state oppression. Incensed by their treatment, and refusing to see themselves as other than loyal Americans, some organized protest movements in concentration camps to resist enlistment into the military until the government upheld Japanese Americans' civil rights. At the same time, some thirty-three thousand Japanese Americans joined the armed forces and pinned their hopes for future racial justice on their continued demonstration of patriotism and loyalty to America.

That attempts to restructure the racial order pervaded wartime America is perhaps best exemplified by the fierce resistance such attempts elicited. Pop culture's picture of pleasant pluralism notwithstanding, home-front America seethed with racial tensions. The Department of Labor reported that between July 1943 and October 1944, seventy-one race-related strikes had occurred throughout the country involving over sixty thousand female and male workers. Two impulses caused these strikes: either African Amer-

icans, sometimes with help from integrated unions, were demanding greater racial equality in the workplace or whites were demanding less.

Neighborhoods were another critical battle site. Due to restrictive covenants, discriminatory lending and real estate practices, and grassroots neighborhood resistance, African American communities in the urban North, South, and West were already severely crowded prior to the war. Thus, when war finally broke out, and larger and larger numbers of African Americans poured into these communities, a crisis fast developed. In Chicago, the Metropolitan Housing Council reported in 1943 that "[t]he Negro district, prevented from expanding by restrictions on all sides, housing an already overlarge population in 1940, and housing that population in deteriorated, inadequate, indecent accommodations, is today bursting at the seams. . . . An explosive situation exists." The MHC proved prophetic as full-scale race riots and/or disturbances plagued scores of cities and towns across America. The worst of these occurred in Detroit in June 1943, where battles between African Americans and whites swept through the city uncontrolled for three days, leading to hundreds of injuries and thirty-four deaths. In the end, six thousand national troops were required to quell the violence.

White riot and strike protagonists were sometimes of "new" European immigrant origin—that is, Poles, Italians, Hungarians, Russians, and Jews, among others. Their involvement speaks to another wartime transformation: the increasing salience among these groups of a white racial identity. Though much more research needs to be done on the subject, it appears that it was during the war years that Southern and Eastern Europeans began to mobilize most consciously and more frequently than ever before as whites. Why exactly this was the case—particularly when these groups were accepted as "white on arrival" in the United States—is an important and complicated question on which we can only speculate now. And certainly a compelling answer would vary some from one group to the next. It would seem, however, that for all Southern and Eastern Europeans the salience of a white racial identity had something to do with the simplification of racial discourse, which also simplified and limited Europeans' racial identity options; the northward and westward migration of "colored" groups, particularly African Americans, creating numerous housing and workplace battles around which a white identity could be both mobilized and constructed; and the increased feeling among immigrants and their second-generation children of belonging to America, which, as Arnold Hirsch has aptly noted, "seemed organically linked" to a sense of whiteness.

And indeed it was during the war years that many Southern and Eastern Europeans felt most American. To be sure, discrimination and prejudice still persisted. Fearing an anti-Semitic backlash, FDR refused in the late 1930s and early 1940s to alter immigration quotas to allow for the entry of thousands of European Jews wishing to escape Nazi terror. Indeed, at the height of the Ho-

locaust, 40 percent of Americans, according to one opinion poll, still believed Jews had too much power. Meanwhile, employers across the country—particularly during the early years of the war when intense labor shortages were still rare—attempted to restrict their hiring to "Nordics only."

Still, a transformation in the general treatment of European Americans was well underway. Only twenty years prior they were widely condemned as biologically inferior and unassimilable. Now they were seen as the very definition of a democratic America. If African Americans, Latinos, Native Americans, and Asian Americans were sometimes featured as members of America's exalted melting pot, it was really the European groups who appeared over and over as indispensable to it. As one character in Sinclair Lewis's best-selling novel *Cass Timberlane* (1945) remarks, "the new America is not made up of British stock and Irish and Scotch, but of the Italians and Poles and Icelanders and Finns and Hungarians and Slovaks." And to appreciate this fact was to "speak the American language." Similarly, one *Time* article, in describing a U.S. army raid in France, noted that the names of the GIs "sounded like the roster of an All-American eleven. . . . There were Edward Czeklauski of Brooklyn, George Pucilowski of Detroit, Theodore Hakenstod of Providence, Zane Gemill of St. Clair, Pa., Frank Christensen of Racine, Wi., Abraham Dreiscus of Kansas City. There were the older, but not better, American names like Ray and Thacker, Walsh and Eaton and Tyler. The war . . . was getting Americanized." Indeed, the concept of Americanization had come a long way since the days of Anglo-conformity in the World War I era. By World War II, Americanization seemed more like ethnicization, the process by which ethnics did not become more American, but rather Americans became more ethnic (i.e., *European* ethnic).

And *ethnic* is the right word here. These groups had become so accepted at this time that the differences between them and "Old" Americans ceased to be considered racial at all. It was for this reason that, as we saw at the outset of this essay, ethnicity emerged as a critical social scientific concept. When racial lines no longer separated a Magyar from a Moravian, ethnicity appeared as a term to describe their differences.

When war finally came to an end in Europe, in May 1945, and in the Pacific several months later, some important changes had certainly occurred to the U.S. racial structure. Foremost, there was a change in expectations across the board. As one Mexican American put it in 1942, "This war . . . has shown those 'across the tracks' that we all share the same problems. It has shown them what the Mexican Americans will do, what responsibility he will take, and what leadership qualities he will demonstrate. After this struggle, the status of the Mexican Americans will be different." Returning veterans joined with others in their communities to fight for basic civil rights in the next two decades. Among whites the war highlighted the underlying tension implicit in creating a truly democratic country. For those ethnics who identified more and more as white, they proved as hardened as southern whites in their opposition to close interactions with "colored" groups. Thus, while the war created greater opportunity for social and geographic mobility for all groups, it also placed the nation on a collision course with its existing racial order.

### The Cold War and Early 1960s Activism

If World War II marked a turning point in the efforts of certain racial groups to demand equal rights, then the postwar era marked a new chapter in the nation's long history with race. Many nonwhites did not waste much time in seeking to affect change. Japanese Americans, for instance, fresh out of wartime concentration camps, got right to work to eliminate racial restrictions against them on the West Coast. Japanese Americans such as Kajiro and Kohide Oyama and organizations such as the Japanese American Citizens League fought alien land laws in the courts and through public initiatives, and scored major victories. In 1948, in *Oyama v. California,* the U.S. Supreme Court declared that such laws were unconstitutional; eight years later, California voters passed Proposition 13, banning these laws forever.

But not all Asian Americans were as successful at pushing for equal rights. Chinese Americans had to concentrate more on protecting the rights they already had. The rise of Cold War anticommunism, the fall of China in 1949, and the outbreak of the Korean War a year later all contributed to a growing suspicion of Chinese Americans in the United States. In 1950, Congress passed the Internal Security Act, which permitted the federal government to intern Communists during times of national emergency. In the mid-1950s the government instituted the "Confession Program," which allowed undocumented Chinese immigrants to report themselves, and everyone else they knew to be in the United States illegally, to the INS; in exchange the INS granted these immigrants citizenship so long as they were innocent of any involvement in subversive activities. Scores of Chinese immigrants came forward—ten thousand in San Francisco alone—and gained citizenship in the process. However, through this program the federal government increased its surveillance of Chinese American communities, using information they received through "confessions" to find and deport Chinese immigrants suspected of communist activities or sympathies.

As for Mexican Americans in the 1950s, in response to state repression—especially the so-called Operation Wetback of 1954, in which the federal government swept through ethnic Mexican communities, apprehended undocumented immigrants, and deported more than 1 million of them—a "new, broader-based civil rights movement" among Mexican Americans emerged. At the heart of this movement was a wide range of organizations, from the GI Forum and LULAC in Texas to El Congreso, the Community Service Organization (CSO), and the Los Angeles Committee for the Protection of the Foreign Born in California. In 1949 in Los Angeles, the CSO registered fifteen thousand voters to help elect Edward Roybal to the Los Angeles City Council;

while five years later, thanks in part to LULAC's legal strategy and organizing, the Supreme Court, for the first time, extended fourteenth-amendment protection to Mexican Americans in the landmark *Hernandez v. Texas* decision.

The most powerful and influential of postwar movements, however, came from African Americans. And despite a real lack of historiographical attention, this movement may have begun in the North, "partly due to the greater access to the ballot and freedom to organize without violent retaliation." In New York, for instance, as historian Martha Biondi has recently shown, "in the first decade after the war . . . [African Americans] fought for better jobs, an end to police brutality, new housing, Black representation in government, and college education for their children. Their battles . . . pushed New York City and state to pass landmark anti-discrimination laws in employment, housing, public accommodations, and education, that inspired similar laws in dozens of other states, and became models for national legislation." And African Americans were active in the West too. In 1958, blacks in Oklahoma launched a six-year campaign to end segregation in restaurants, while African Americans in Denver staged a sit-in at the Governor's office to protest racial discrimination.

And yet this movement, for all its success, ran into massive resistance on a wide range of levels. First, the rising Cold War climate of anticommunism, as Mary Dudziak argues, did offer activists added leverage in their fight for equal rights, as the U.S. government became ever more committed to polishing its global image. Still, this climate also severely restricted the boundaries of acceptable antiracist protest. In addition, many African American activists lost their most committed allies in labor unions and civil rights organizations because of anticommunist purges. Second, resistance came in the urban North and parts of the urban West, from African Americans' white neighbors and coworkers. Through neighborhood improvement organizations, local politics, wildcat strikes, union activism, and violence, they resisted the integration of "their" workplaces and neighborhoods with everything in their power. Indeed, in Chicago, "between 1945 and 1950, some 485 racial 'incidents' were reported to the Chicago Commission on Human Relations" many of which were major disturbances in which thousands of white women, men, and children destroyed property and assaulted African Americans. The formerly "inferior races" of Southern and Eastern Europe were big actors in these dramas.

Finally, the most powerful force for resistance was the federal government, particularly in the realm of housing. The federal government, of course, was central to the Cold War purges, but they opposed African Americans in other, more insidious ways as well. As historian Arnold Hirsch has argued, "With the emergence of federal supports for the private housing industry, public housing, slum clearance, and urban renewal . . . government took an active hand, not merely in reinforcing prevailing patterns of segregation, but also in giving them a permanence never seen before. The implication of government in the second

ghetto was so deep, so pervasive, that it virtually constituted a new form of de jure segregation." The most disastrous of government programs was no doubt its FHA loan program, which because of its highly discriminatory appraisal methods, channeled billions of dollars in home loans away from African American and other "colored" neighborhoods and toward white suburbia. As historian Kenneth Jackson has shown, "the main beneficiary of the $119 billion in FHA mortgage insurance issued in the first four decades of FHA operation was [white] suburbia." Thus, the government in these years was intimately involved not just in making the second ghetto but in making the first all-white, multiethnic, middle-class suburb, as well. In the end, this suffocating housing discrimination, coupled with equally powerful obstacles in the labor market (deindustrialization, discrimination, etc.), went a long way in explaining the outbreak of African American revolts in hundreds of cities and towns across the country between 1965 and 1968.

Meanwhile, in the South, things developed a bit differently. In the immediate postwar years, African Americans, often led by returning World War II veterans, stepped up their drive to restructure the racial order in the South and had some success. In cities such as Winston-Salem, Greensboro, and Atlanta thousands of African Americans registered to vote for the first time, leading to the election in Winston-Salem of the first black alderman in 1947, and to the creation of black political machines in all three of these cities. Most impressively, "as a result of these efforts, the number of Negroes registered to vote in the south increased from 2 percent in 1940 to 12 percent in 1947." As historian C. Vann Woodward noted, "For the first time since the beginning of the century Negroes reappeared in elective and appointive office, largely in the upper South, on school boards, city councils, and other minor posts." Complementing these activities at the national level was the NAACP's ongoing legal strategy that continued to pay off in important ways. The Supreme Court outlawed segregation in interstate travel in 1946; segregation at state-funded graduate and law schools in 1950; and in 1954, in its landmark *Brown v. Board of Education,* reversed the Plessy decision of 1896, declaring that "in the field of public education the doctrine of 'separate but equal' has no place."

In these battles, however, the executive branch was decidedly less helpful. President Truman had his moments of rhetorical flourish when it came to African American civil rights; he also spoke out in favor of a permanent FEPC, desegregated the military, and created a Committee on Civil Rights which, after an extensive report on race in the United States, called for, among other things, the establishment of a civil rights division of the Justice Department and the passage of antilynching and anti–poll tax legislation. Still, when it came to following through on these recommendations or on his more inspired civil rights addresses, Truman did very little.

But if Truman, thanks in part to the power of Southern Democrats, was ineffective, Eisenhower was worse. When the Supreme Court handed down its momentous Brown decision and he was asked to comment, Eisenhower equivocated publicly and denounced it privately. Furthermore, when brutal anti-African American violence spread throughout the South, the President refused to do anything in word or deed about it. His sending troops into Little Rock, Arkansas, was too little too late, and his Civil Rights Act of 1957 was, according to one Southern segregationist, "in the main . . . a victory for the South."

Eisenhower's inaction sent a clear message to the white segregationist South—resist Brown if you wish; and this message was well received and very quickly acted upon. Throughout the region individuals and institutions organized a massive resistance against integration of any kind: the Southern white press vehemently and vocally denounced the Supreme Court decision; grass-roots resistance movements, like the White Citizens' Council, which claimed a membership of half a million people in the mid-1950s, emerged throughout the South; state legislatures passed scores of new prosegregation legislation; and 101 of the South's congressmen signed a manifesto in 1955 that, in the words of Anthony Lewis, made "defiance of the Supreme Court and the Constitution socially acceptable . . . [and gave] resistance to the law the approval of the Southern Establishment." The result of these varied efforts were staggering. By 1955, in eight southern states no school integration had taken place at all.

These events, taken together, taught many African Americans a lesson they had in fact learned many times before:

that if progress were to be made, they would have to rely on their own actions and their own pressure from below. We have already seen that this activism had been steadily rising for several decades. It reached a new mass direct-action phase in the late 1950s and early 1960s with the Montgomery Bus Boycott of 1955–1956 and especially the sit-in movement that spread throughout the South in the early 1960s.

Beginning in Greensboro, North Carolina, black college students used the power of their wallets and purses to draw attention to the ugliness of segregation. Students borrowed a chapter from the annals of American labor, which had mounted effective sit-down strikes during the 1930s. At North Carolina A&T, Fisk, and other campuses, disciplined corps of black students descended on local restaurants and lunch counters, quietly but defiantly demanding to be served. On many occasions they encountered hostile whites, determined to see the black youth obey the laws and practices of segregation. These students used these gatherings to galvanize adults and remind all that segregation could be attacked if blacks organized.

And so organize they did—in well-established civil rights groups such as the NAACP, the Urban League, and the National Colored Women's Association—and in newer ones like the Congress for Racial Equality (CORE), the Student Nonviolent Coordinating Committee (SNCC), and the Southern Christian Leadership Conference (SCLC). It should be pointed out, however, that despite popular emphasis upon the role of organizations like SCLC and leaders like Martin Luther King, this was first and foremost a movement of African American "local people." As historian David Garrow has noted:

> What the carefully scrutinized historical record shows is that the actual human catalysts of the movement, the people who really gave direction to the movement's organizing work, the individuals whose records reflect the greatest substantive accomplishments, were not administrators or spokespersons, and were not those whom most scholarship on the movement identifies as the 'leaders.' Instead, in any list, long or short, of the activists who had the greatest personal impact upon the course of the southern movement, the vast majority of names will be ones that are unfamiliar to most readers.

And it was these unfamiliar African Americans who, despite massive and violent resistance and a long apathetic federal government, built a movement that secured major civil rights legislation in 1964 and 1965: the Civil Rights Act of 1964 ended de jure segregation for good and the Voting Rights Act of 1965 finally returned the franchise to southern African Americans. Also coming out of this movement, if less directly, was the equally momentous Immigration Act of 1965. This abolished all racial quotas and excised all references to race in U.S. immigration policy and law. This would lead to new immigration waves from Latin America and Asia that would, like African American migration from the South several decades earlier, forever alter the demography, racial politics, and racial structure of the United States.

## BIBLIOGRAPHIC ESSAY

The history of race and ethnicity in the United States between the Great Depression and the passage of the Civil Rights Act of 1964 is characterized by profound and transformative changes in social relations and in the ideologies used to understand and shape these relations. For a general overview of these changes, read Ronald Takaki, *A Different Mirror: A History of Multicultural America* (Boston: Little, Brown, 1993) and Gary Gerstle, *American Crucible: Race and Nation in the Twentieth Century* (Princeton: Princeton University Press, 2000).

By the late 1930s the harsh realities of racist thinking as social policy found full form in Nazi Germany. At about the same time, new scholarship critical of scientific racism emerged. Eventually this scholarship served to undermine the logic of racism and segregation in the United States. See, for example, Gunnar Myrdal, *An American Dilemma: The Negro Problem and Modern Democracy* (New York: Harper, 1944); Ashley Montagu, *Race: Man's Most Dangerous Myth* (New York: Columbia University Press, 1942); Ruth Benedict, *Race: Science and Politics* (New York: Viking, 1943); UNESCO, *The Race Concept: Results on an Inquiry* (Paris: UNESCO, 1952); and Elazar Barkan, *The Retreat of Scientific Racism: Changing Concepts of Race in Britain and the United States Between the Wars* (Cambridge: Cambridge University Press, 1992).

For other work on race/ethnicity in the ideological and cultural realm during the prewar and/or postwar eras, see Lee D. Baker, *From Savage to Negro: Anthropology and the Construction of Race, 1896–1954* (Berkeley: University of California Press, 1998); Michael Denning, *The Cultural Front: The Laboring of American Culture in the Twentieth Century* (New York: Verso, 1997); and Elizabeth Grace Hale, *Making Whiteness: The Culture of Segregation in the South, 1890–1940* (New York: Pantheon, 1998).

For work on the racialization of various European immigrant groups, see Eric Arnesen, "Whiteness and the Historians' Imagination," *International Labor and Working-Class History* 60 (Fall 2001): 3–32; James R. Barrett and David R. Roediger, "In-between Peoples: Race, Nationality, and the 'New Immigrant' Working Class," *Journal of American Ethnic History*, 16 (spring 1997): 3–44; Thomas A. Guglielmo, *White on Arrival: Italians, Race, Color, and Power in Chicago, 1890–1945* (New York: Oxford University Press, 2003); Matthew Frye Jacobson, *Whiteness of a Different Color: European Immigrants and the Alchemy of Race* (Cambridge: Harvard University Press, 1998); and George Lipsitz, "The Possessive Investment in Whiteness: Racialized Social Democracy and the 'White' Problem in American Studies," *American Quarterly*, 47 (September 1997): 369–387.

For other important work on European groups and race/ethnic issues in these years, see Ronald H. Bayor, *Neighbors in Conflict: The Irish, Germans, Jews, and Italians of New York City, 1929–1941* (Baltimore: Johns Hopkins University Press, 1978); Lizabeth Cohen, *Making a New Deal: Industrial Workers in Chicago, 1919–1939* (New York: Cambridge University Press, 1990); and Gary Gerstle, *Working-Class Americanism: The Politics of Labor in a Textile City, 1914–1960* (New York: Cambridge University Press, 1989).

Materials in the files of the Immigration and Naturalization Services, Record Group 85, National Archives I, underscore the federal government's own role in reclassifying European immigrant communities in ethnic rather than racial terms.

Members of the "colored races" played pivotal roles in restructuring the U.S. racial order. There is a voluminous literature on these histories up to and through World War II. On African Americans, see St. Clair Drake and Horace Cayton, *Black Metropolis: A Study of Negro Life in a Northern City* (New York: Harcourt, Brace, 1945); Robin D. G. Kelley, *Hammer and Hoe: Alabama Communists During the Depression* (Chapel Hill: University of North Carolina Press, 1990); Earl Lewis, *In Their Own Interests: Race, Class, and Power in Twentieth-Century Norfolk, Virginia* (Berkeley: University of California Press, 1991); Ronald H. Bayor, *Race and the Shaping of Twentieth-Century Atlanta* (Chapel Hill: University of North Carolina Press, 1996); and Barbara Dianne Savage, *Broadcasting Freedom: Radio, War, and the Politics of Race, 1938–1948* (Chapel Hill: University of North Carolina Press, 1999).

On Mexican Americans, see Edward J. Escobar, *Race, Police, and the Making of a Political Identity: Mexican Americans and the Los Angeles Police Department, 1900–1945* (Berkeley: University of California Press, 1999); Neil Foley, *The White Scourge: Mexicans, Blacks, and Poor Whites in Texas Cotton Culture* (Berkeley: University of California Press, 1997); Vicki Ruiz, *From Out of the Shadows: Mexican Women in Twentieth-Century America* (New York: Oxford University Press, 1998); and George J. Sanchez, *Becoming Mexican American: Ethnicity, Culture, and Identity in Chicano Los Angeles, 1900–1945* (New York: Oxford University Press, 1993).

On Native Americans, see Jere Bishop Franco, *Crossing the Pond: The Native American Effort in World War II* (Denton: University of North Texas Press, 1999); and Peter Iverson, *We Are Still Here: American Indians in the Twentieth Century* (Wheeling, Ill.: Harlan Davidson, 1998). On Asian Americans, see Sucheng Chan, *Asian Americans: An Interpretive History* (Boston: Twayne, 1990); Alice Yang Murray, ed., *What Did the Internment of Japanese Americans Mean?* (Boston: Bedford, 2000); Ronald Takaki, *Strangers from a Different Shore* (Boston: Back Bay Books, 1989); David Yoo, *Growing up Nisei: Race, Generation, and Culture among Japanese Americans of California, 1924–1949* (Urbana: University of Illinois Press, 2000); Nayan Shah, *Contagious Divides: Epidemics and Race in San Francisco's Chinatown* (Berkeley: University of California Press, 2001); and Judy Yung, *Unbound Feet: A Social History of Chinese Women in San Francisco* (Berkeley: University of California Press, 1995).

The literature on the postwar struggles of these same groups and on the resistance they faced is also large. On the urban North and African Americans, see Arnold R. Hirsch, *Making the Second Ghetto: Race and Housing in Chicago, 1940–1960,* 2nd ed. (Chicago: University of Chicago Press, 1998); Martha Biondi, *To Stand and Fight: Black Radicals and the Struggle for Negro Rights in New York City, 1945–1955* (Cambridge: Harvard University Press, 2003); and Thomas J. Sugrue, *The Origins of the Urban Crisis: Race and Inequality in Postwar Detroit* (Princeton: Princeton University Press, 1996).

On the West and its more complicated set of race/ethnic groups, see David G. Gutiérrez, *Walls and Mirrors: Mexican Americans, Mexican Immigrants, and the Politics of Ethnicity*

(Berkeley: University of California Press, 1995); Peggy Pascoe, "Race, Gender, and the Privileges of Property: On the Significance of Miscegenation Law in the U.S. West," in Valerie J. Matsumoto and Blake Allmendinger, eds., *Over the Edge: Remapping the American West* (Berkeley: University of California Press, 1999), pp. 215–230; Chris Friday, "'In Due Time': Narratives of Race and Place in the Western United States," in Paul Wong, ed., *Race, Ethnicity, and Nationality in the United States: Toward the Twenty-First Century* (Boulder: Westview Press, 1999); and the works previously cited by Ruiz, Chan, Takaki, and Iverson.

The literature on the southern freedom struggle is, of course, enormous. For a sample of excellent works, see Taylor Branch, *Parting the Waters: America in the King Years* (New York: Simon and Schuster, 1988); Clayborne Carson, *In Struggle: SNCC and the Black Awakening of the 1960s* (Cambridge: Harvard University Press, 1981); Mary L. Dudziak, *Cold War Civil Rights: Race and the Image of American Democracy* (Princeton: Princeton University Press, 2000); Charles Payne, *I've Got the Light of Freedom: The Organizing Tradition and the Mississippi Freedom Struggle* (Berkeley: University of California Press, 1995); Belinda Robnett, *How Long? How Long?: African-American Women in the Struggle for Civil Rights* (New York: Oxford University Press, 1998); and Harvard Sitkoff, *The Struggle for Black Equality, 1954–1992* (New York: Hill and Wang, 1993).

For the role of the state in the struggles over the U.S. racial order during the prewar and postwar eras, see especially Desmond King, *Making Americans: Immigration, Race, and the Origins of the Diverse Democracy* (Cambridge: Harvard University Press, 2000); Daniel Kryder, *Divided Arsenal: Race and the American State during World War II* (Cambridge: Cambridge University Press, 2000); Harvard Sitkoff, *A New Deal for Blacks* (New York: Oxford University Press, 1978); and Patricia Sullivan, *Days of Hope: Race and Democracy in the New Deal Era* (Chapel Hill: University of North Carolina Press, 1996).

On organized labor, in addition to the many works already cited, see Michael K. Honey, *Southern Labor and Black Civil Rights: Organizing Memphis Workers* (Urbana: University of Illinois Press, 1993); Bruce Nelson, *Divided We Stand: American Workers and the Struggle for Black Equality* (Princeton: Princeton University Press, 2001); and Bruce Nelson, "Class, Race and Democracy in the CIO: The 'New' Labor History Meets the 'Wages of Whiteness'," *International Review of Social History* 41 (1996): 351–374.

On gender and the U.S. racial order, see especially Dana Frank, "White Working-Class Women and the Race Question," *International Labor and Working-Class History,* 54 (Fall 1998): 80–102; Ruth Feldstein, *Motherhood in Black and White: Race and Sex in American Liberalism, 1930–1965* (Ithaca: Cornell University Press, 2000); and Gwendolyn Mink, *The Wages of Motherhood* (Ithaca: Cornell University Press, 1995).

# DOCUMENTS

## Frances Perkins to Mr. Arthur Krock, April 22, 1940

*In this letter to Arthur Krock of the* New York Times, *Secretary of Labor Frances Perkins attempted to explain the federal government's racial classification schemes on its nat-*

*uralization forms. This document illustrates the increased wartime confusion about racial categories and the willingness on the part of some to rethink "what race is" and "what races there are."*

*Source:* Frances Perkins to Mr. Arthur Krock, April 22, 1940 (RG 85, Entry no. 26, Box 1041, File 44/5 part 2, NARA I).

DEPARTMENT OF LABOR
OFFICE OF THE SECRETARY
WASHINGTON
APRIL 22, 1940
MR. ARTHUR KROCK
WASHINGTON BUREAU
THE NEW YORK TIMES
ALBEE BUILDING
WASHINGTON, D.C.

*My dear Mr. Krock:*

Thanks very much for your letter of April 5, enclosing one from Arthur Sulzberger, in which he inquires about the questions, on the form for application for naturalization, which have to do with race.

You have, of course, hit upon one of those items which, when inquired into, lead to almost historical research in order to find the reason back of the inquiry. I have done a very interesting piece of research on the subject and shall be glad to give you roughly some of my discoveries in this field.

As you probably know, under the law with regard to naturalization of foreign-born persons in America, there is a clause which reads: "The provisions of this title (Naturalization) shall apply to aliens being free white persons and to aliens of African nativity and to persons of African descent." (Sec. 2169, U. S. Revised Statutes). I am told on inquiry of the Naturalization Service that it is because of this that they in 1906 decided to ask Question No. 5 on the Application for Declaration to Become a Citizen in the Statement of Facts, and to refer the applicant to the list of races on page 4. I am enclosing a copy of this application for your edification. I am sure you will be startled as I was to see how long and complicated a list it is, when the only people who are excluded from citizenship are really Chinese, Japanese, Malayans, East Indians, etc.

It has occurred to me, as I am sure it will to you, that the simple questions, "Are you a member of the white race? Are you of African birth or descent? Are you a Filipino, and if so, have you served in the Navy of the United States?," would be sufficient to give us all the information we need in order to pass upon the eligibility of an individual for citizenship. However, the Act of May 25, 1932 (47 Stat. 106) requires the Commissioner of Immigration and Naturalization to compile statistics to show race and nationality of persons seeking citizenship. Upon that direction rests the further continuance of the questions with regard to race.

I fully agree with you that no modern anthropologist or ethnologist believes that any of these questions are clearly and conclusively answerable. Most of these scholars, as a matter of fact, don't agree as to what a race is, nor what races there are. My geography, and perhaps yours, taught me when I was a child that there were five races of man—the white, black, yellow, brown and red—and I personally have found that as convenient a general classification as anything else. I am told, however, by the Immigration Service, that the list which appears on the back of our application blank and which also appears on the blank for the manifest of alien passengers for the United States, required to be filled in by all commanding officers of ships bringing immigrants to the United States, was compiled in 1899 by the Immigration Service under the direction of the Smithsonian Institute, but that the determination of races or peoples to be included in the list has always been one entirely of administrative decision. There always has been a diversity and there is a growing diversity in the views of scientists as to what these racial classifications really represent, some writers having reduced the basic races to three, while the Dictionary of Races or Peoples (Volume 5, Reports of the Immigration Commission of 1910) contains descriptions of more than 600 races. Some changes have been made in this list since 1899 and the following races have been added: Albanian, Estonian, Filipino, Latvian and Nanx. Each of these five was added because people of the countries or "races" which they represent came forward and demanded to be classified as a special race rather than being classified under the nationality or sovereignty which they acknowledge. What each of these apparently represent is a group that feels itself the inheritor of a special culture, wishing to maintain that culture within a sovereignty which they must admit, but for which they sometimes have little sympathy.

Mexican, I understand, was in the original list which was adopted in 1899, but it was eliminated rather recently because of objection on the part of the Mexican Government. The original list also contained North Italian and South Italian, upon complaint of the Italian government.

The use of this list by the master of a ship bringing immigrants to this country is based upon the requirement of the Immigration Act of 1917 (8 U. S. Code 148) which requires the transportation line to furnish descriptive lists or manifests to include the nationality, country of birth and race of such aliens. The Immigration Act of 1907 referred only to nationality and race, but the Immigration Service had made a practice of classifying the races of arriving aliens beginning with 1899.

This is the historical picture of the way this complicated classification crept into our forms.

The question as to whether the Hebrews are a race, culture, or merely those who practice a particular religion, is one which has been raised, I gather, from time to time and the report of the Immigration Commission of 1910 appears to be the authority for the description that the words "Hebrew," "Jewish" or "Israelite" equals a "people that originally spoke the Hebrew language, primarily of Semitic origin." Semitic, in my memory, was never classified as a race, but rather as one of the larger divisions of the human family which included a great many others than those who spoke the Hebrew language originally.

I really don't know what authority there is for regarding "Hebrew, Jewish or Israelite" as a race and I recognize, as does Mr. Sulzberger and as you do, the fact that this may be a source of considerable confusion to us.

I am glad you raised this question with me. I think we have over-complicated rather than simplified our problem by the list which we have prepared, both for the manifest and for the declaration of intention. I know there is no scholarly justification for such classifications as the Welsh race, or the Scotch race, the Bohemian race, the Estonian race, etc, and I doubt very much that this complication gives us in the United States any clue to the composition of our population. I am told by the Immigration Service that the figures in this classification are made use of primarily by students of anthropology and sociology and that, so far as they know, they have no other use.

We are taking this whole matter under consideration. The forms need revision from time to time on account of changes in the law or the procedure, and we shall take this up for discussion and possible simplification.

*Sincerely yours,*
*(Frances Perkins)*

### Ashley Montagu, *Man's Most Dangerous Myth: The Fallacy of Race*, 1942

*The following is from the preface to anthropologist Ashley Montagu's book* Man's Most Dangerous Myth, *published during World War II. It nicely points to the "retreat of scientific racism," which began in the 1930s in response to Nazi racialism. This challenge to the scientific underpinnings of racism received*

*ever-increasing popular and scholarly approval during and after the war years.*

Source: *Ashley Montagu, Man's Most Dangerous Myth: The Fallacy of Race, 4th ed. (1942; reprint, Cleveland: The World Publishing Co., 1964).*

In our time the problem of *race* has assumed an alarmingly exaggerated importance. Alarming, because racial dogmas have been made the basis for an inhumanly brutal political philosophy which has resulted in the death or social disfranchisement of millions of innocent human beings; exaggerated, because when the nature of contemporary "race" theory is scientifically analyzed and understood it ceases to be of any significance for social or any other kind of action. It has been well said that there is no domain where the sciences, philosophy, and politics blend to so great an extent and in their contact have so much importance to the man of the present day and of the future as in modern "race" theory. Few problems in our time more pressingly require solution than this. It is highly desirable, therefore, that the facts about "race," as science has come to know them, should be widely disseminated and clearly understood. To this end the present volume has been written.

This book is not, however, a textbook or a treatise on "race." It purports to be an examination of a contemporary aspect of "race" theory, and seeks only to clarify the reader's thinking upon an important subject about which clear thinking is generally avoided. It would be quite beyond the powers of a single person to say all that there is to be said upon the subject. As Aldous Huxley has put it, "The problem of race is as much a problem for historians and psychologists as for geneticists. Anything like a definite and authoritative solution of it must be cooperative. Also, to carry conviction, it should be official and international. The race theory claims to be scientific. It is, surely then, the business of science, as organized in the universities and learned societies of the civilized world, to investigate this claim."

It is as a contribution towards such an end from a scientist, who is a student both of human culture and human biology, that the present volume is offered.

It may appear to some that I have been a little hard on the physical anthropologists. I can only plead that as a physical anthropologist myself I believe it is high time that the traditional conception of "race" held by my professional brethren be dealt with frankly. Friends can afford to be frank, let enemies be cautious.

This book then is designed to expose the most dangerous myth of our age, the myth of "race," by demonstrating the falsities of which it is compounded. In the pursuit of this design it is difficult to avoid the appearance of "special pleading." By showing that the many differences which are alleged to exist between "races" do not in fact exist or that those which do exist are of no significance from the standpoint of social action, the cumulative effect upon some readers may be that the author's thesis is that there are no genuine differences between the various groups of mankind.

The fact is that there are numerous differences between ethnic groups, and even regional segments of such groups, in many bodily traits. These differences are real enough, and they are of the greatest interest to the student of variation. Their classification and analysis belong in a treatise of a nature more technical than this. Suffice it here to say that such variations prove that man is an extremely variable creature, constantly in process of undergoing change, and that these changes can be studied in the minutest detail in every living population. I have, in my own small way, demonstrated such variations in the teeth, in insignificant muscles, and in various structures of the skull, and I have shown how in the same nation local differences in the frequencies of such characters have appeared. All these are very real differences, and their meaning is of the greatest significance to the student of the evolution of man. To discuss these matters in this book would have been of some interest to the reader, and would certainly have served to give our discussion a better balanced appearance. And although to do so might have resulted in a more convincing demonstration of the truth that such variations are of moment alone to the theoretical biologist but are of no significance whatever in the practical universe of human relations, contemplation of the consequent increase in the size of this book acted as a sufficient deterrent.

Differences are not denied where they exist. What is denied is that they are biologically either great or significant enough to justify men in making them the pretext for social discrimination of any kind. If this is "special pleading," then this viewpoint is what the evidence set out in the following pages specially pleads with the reader to examine critically.

In the past the tendency has been strong to overstress the differences, as if stressing the differences were an argument against the likenesses. Looking back now upon the history of the nineteenth century it seems fairly clear that this drive to find differences in the "races" of mankind grew out of the general social climate of the day. A natural stratification of the races mirrored the social stratification of the classes, and in the light of the doctrine of "the survival of the fittest" justified the exploitation and oppression of both. Differences were therefore maximized and exaggerated. They still are in the service of much the same motives.

But the facts make it abundantly clear that these differences constitute the proof of the fundamental unity of all mankind. The very nature of the variations provides the completest evidence of that truth, of the basic likeness in difference. It is therefore as unnecessary to minimize as it is falsely to maximize the significance of these differences. All that should be required is to state the case against those who have endeavored to magnify the differences. This I have done, and somehow the decline in size of the differences seems automatically to have followed, while many other differences alleged to exist completely disappear in the light of the facts. If we can learn to understand the nature of the insignificant differences which remain, we shall then be happier in their presence,

and find them in every way as acceptable as we do those which exist within our own immediate group.

Since this book first left the press the world has been horrified by the calculated murder of millions of Jews and Poles by the Nazis. This represented the practical realization of the doctrine of "racism" which had been so viciously enthroned as a political doctrine in the Nazi *Weltanschauung*. That doctrine, from beginning to end, was an absurdity; but absurdities have never wanted for believers, and, as Voltaire remarked, "as long as people believe in absurdities they will continue to commit atrocities."

We, in the United States, have every hope of eradicating the contagion of "racism" from our own body politic; but hope alone will not suffice. We must act, and in order to do so intelligently we must know what this disease is and how it may best be dealt with. At a time when "race" riots and the Negro revolt have awakened many Americans to the seriousness of the problem of "race" on their own hearths, when discrimination against colored and "minority" groups in the armed forces and in industry has shocked many Americans into an awareness of their own guilt, it is incumbent upon every decent American to acquaint himself with the facts relating to the "race" problem, so that he may be prepared to deal with it in an intelligent, efficient, and humane manner.

It is even yet not widely enough realized that from its earliest beginnings the doctrine of the racists has had as its object the overthrow of democracy. This should become clear to anyone who reads the account which is given in the following pages of the rise and development of that doctrine.

## Declaration of Intention (to Naturalize) for Joseph Imburgia, Chicago, Ilinois, July 25, 1939

*When immigrants came to the United States and wished to become American citizens, they first had to file a Declaration of Intention with the Immigration and Naturalization Service. This form—and its awkward and overlapping categories of race, color, complexion, and nationality—illustrates well one government institution's social categories. The document also shows that European immigrants—even those with "dark" complexions and an "Italian (South)" racial background—were still categorized as "white."*

*Source:* Declaration of Intention (to Naturalize) for Joseph Imburgia, Chicago, Ilinois, July 25, 1939 (RG 21 US District Court, Chicago, Ilinois, Naturalization Cases, Volumes 1023–1024, Petition No. 252206, NARA, Great Lakes Branch).

I, Joseph Imburgia, now residing at 1114 Vernon Park Place, occupation Unemployed, aged 30 years, do declare on oath that my personal description is Sex Male, color White, Complexion Dark, color of eyes Brown color of hair Black, height 5 feet 9 inches; weight 170 pounds; visible distinctive marks none[;] race Italian (South); nationality Italian. I was born in Palermo, Italy, on March 28, 1909. I am married. The name of my wife is Mildred; we were married on April 8, 1929, at Joliet, Illinois; she was born at Voglia, Italy, on November 5, 1904, entered the United States at New York, N.Y., on unknown date, for permanent residence therein, and now resides with me. I have 3 children, and the name, date and place of birth, and place of residence of each of said children are as follows: Rose Mary—Feb. 20, 1930; Anthony—Jun. 5, 1931; Augusto—Jan. 15, 35: all born in Chicago and reside with me. I have not heretofore made a declaration of intention: . . . my last foreign residence was Italy. I emigrated to the United States of America from Naples, Italy; my lawful entry for permanent residence in the United States was at New York, N.Y. under the name of Imburgia, Giuseppe, on Sept. 28, 1912 on the vessel Mendoza.

I will, before being admitted to citizenship, renounce forever all allegiance and fidelity to any foreign prince, potentate, state, or sovereignty, and particularly, by name, to the prince, potentate, state, or sovereignty of which I may be at the time of admission a citizen or subject; I am not an anarchist; I am not a polygamist nor a believer in the practice of polygamy; and it is my intention in good faith to become a citizen of the United States of America and to reside permanently therein; and I certify that the photograph affixed to the duplicate and triplicate hereof is a likeness of me.

I swear (affirm) that the statements I have made and the intentions I have expressed in this declaration of intention subscribed by me are true to the best of my knowledge and belief: So help me God.

Subscribed and sworn to before me in the form of oath shown above in the office of the Clerk of said Court, at Chicago, Illinois this 25th day of July, anno Domini, 1939. Certification No 183391 from the Commissioner of Immigration and Naturalization showing the lawful entry of the declarant for permanent residence on the date stated above, has been received by me. The photograph affixed to the duplicate and triplicate hereof is a likeness of the declarant.

*Hoyt King*
*Clerk of the U.S. DISTRICT Court.*

## Helen Jackson Lee, *Nigger in the Window*, 1978

*Lee's penetrating comments about color divisions in the black community capture the insidious dimensions of racism.*

Source: Helen Jackson Lee, *Nigger in the Window* (Garden City, N.Y.: Doubleday and Company, 1978).

I was beginning to learn the high value Negroes placed on skin color, and I knew that our race comprised many skin colors, ranging from alabaster to deepest ebony. I sensed early that the color of my skin would have a great influence on how people would treat me, even my own kinfolks.

With his uncanny way of knowing human weaknesses, Brother teased me about my color, saying, "You're adopted. Mama found you on a dump!"

This sent me running to Mama for reassurance. "Silly goose!" she said, "go

ask the neighbors on Third Street. They'll tell you how I hollered with pain giving you birth that hot day in July."

Still I was uneasy. I constantly asked, "Mama, do you love me? Truly love me?" Time and time again Mama told me she loved me. "I love all my children equally," she vowed. Yet through the years the doubts remained. It was the color of my skin. Like a small stitch in the side, it was always there to bother me. Somehow I never could quite believe that Mama loved me, the little light-brown child, quite as much as she did her two fair-skinned children.

When I was eight, Mama took me out of the Catholic school which I had entered at the age of four, and sent me to the model school at Hartshorn College. The "better class of Negroes," it seemed, were now enrolling their daughters there for instruction, some of which was by senior doing their practice teaching. The college had been established by northern philanthropists after the Civil War. Mama had been a boarding student at Hartshorn. I was a day student.

I didn't like the model school. My schoolmates—daughters of ministers, physicians, undertakers, insurance men, and mail carriers—seemed wild to me. I missed the discipline of the Catholic school. These new girls threw spitballs across the room, talked back to the teachers, and did pretty much as they pleased. We were all clean and well-dressed, but sometimes I wished I could be back playing with some of the children with the scuffed shoes and torn dresses and tasting some of the cold pork chops and biscuits they brought in greasy brown paper bags. I used to beg Mama to fix my lunch in a bag instead of making me come home at lunch to eat at the table with a knife and fork from a plate and wipe my mouth on a linen napkin.

I got my first taste of snobbery at Hartshorn. At ten, my first cousin, Ella, was full of airs. She was better-looking than I, with keen features and skin like velvet gold, long smooth brown hair, and a pert nose with a snobbish tilt. Ella's father and Daddy were half-brothers, but you would never know they were kin. Uncle Bob was taller, with hazel eyes, fair skin, and dark-brown hair not quite as straight as Daddy's. I thought both were handsome.

I envied and disliked Ella at the same time. She was such a goody-goody in front of grownups, always polite, using good English, smoothing her dress. She looked down on me and tried to make me look cheap every chance she got. One day she whispered, "You've got the wrong name. My name is the right one. I'm legitimate, you're not."

Ella's remarks filled me with anxiety, especially that word *legitimate*. What did she mean? I could hardly wait for school to end so I could run home and tell Mama.

Mama put her arms around me while I sobbed out my story.

"Dry your tears, honey," she said, "and let me tell you the truth about both of your names. You have just as much right to being a Jackson as Ella has to being a Johnson. Ella's grandmother Mis' Georgia and your grandmother Mis' Eliza lived in houses side by side on Cedar Street. They both had several children, some of them by a well-to-do white man named Johnson. Ella's grand-mother just took the white man's name for herself and children, while your grandmother went by the name of Robert Jackson, whom she married. Mis' Eliza died giving birth to your daddy."

Mama hesitated a moment, then spoke. "I don't like to use the word, but there were bastards in both families."

I laughed out loud. I couldn't help but wonder what "Miss Priss" would say to that bit of family history.

"Your Uncle Bob's mother was really something," Mama went on with the story. "Old Man Johnson—that's what colored people called him-died in Mis' Georgia's bed. She got some of her boys to hitch up the wagon, put the old man's body in it, and take him back up to Westhampton—outside of Richmond, mostly country—where he lived when he wasn't on Cedar Street. When the boys got to the house they jumped out of the wagon, went around to the back door, and knocked. When the white man's wife came to the door, they pointed to the wagon and said, 'Here's your husband, lady. He's dead. Mama said you can have him now.' The white lady was mad as a hornet. She refused to accept her husband's body, so the boys just took him out of the wagon and dumped him on the ground and hauled themselves back to Richmond."

I rolled with laughter at the boldness of those boys. It never occurred to me that the white woman might have felt humiliated. Mama grew serious. "Don't ever tell Ella what I just told you. No colored person should try to make another colored person ashamed of his family background."

Gradually I learned a lot of things

about my race and how slavery had affected black families: that they were separated and sold to different plantations; that the white man routinely used the black woman to satisfy his lust; that in the South, especially in Virginia, there were a lot of white and black folks who were blood kin.

The story about my father aroused my curiosity, and as I advanced in school I read everything I could about the days of slavery and the days of reconstruction following the Civil War. I became an avid reader of Ellen Glasgow, who wrote novels about miscegenation in her native state, Virginia. The famed author had an office in the building where Daddy worked. I caught a glimpse of her once as she entered the elevator. She was a little, dried-up woman.

"What's she like?" I asked Daddy.

"I don't know. She only speaks to me when she wants some service. And she tips me one dollar a year, at Christmas," he added matter-of-factly.

I wanted badly to meet Ellen Glasgow and talk with her because I dreamed of being a writer too. Perhaps she could help me. But when I asked Daddy to introduce me to her, he put his foot down and said it was "a foolish idea." I was disappointed. Years later I realized Daddy was trying to protect me from what he felt would be the insulting treatment common among white women in their dealings with black girls or women who dared to approach them on any basis other than servant and mistress.

Daddy was becoming more prosperous, not just from his job at the bank, but by branching out with a sideline. The insurance company that he, his half-brothers, and some other black men ran, was flourishing. In the early 1900s beneficial societies and insurance companies sprang up and were supported wholeheartedly by the black masses. They took in millions of dollars and the officers of these companies were considered some of the elite of Negro society. The black men who ran the companies considered it a matter of pride to keep their wives out of white folks' kitchens and made it a matter of faith never to let their daughters go into service. Thus I grew up in an era when the so-called good-living black families shielded their daughters from the harshness of the white world. It was an unreal existence because at the same time we young black women were being kept away from daily contact with white people, it seemed to me that everything we learned at home, church, and school was based on the white man's scale of values. It was drummed into our heads that white people do things this way or that way; we should try to imitate white folks' ways. To misbehave was "acting like a nigger." This struggle to please my elders while trying to show some independence of thought and action caused a great deal of conflict in my mind. Deep in my heart I didn't mind being a nigger at all, because by acting like one I felt I was being courageous and defying the fate that made me black.

After Clay Street we moved about ten miles southeast of Richmond to Seven Pines, where the Old Confederate Cemetery was located. It was an exciting time for me, living in a new yellow-and-white frame bungalow and sharing a bedroom with my little sister.

We had gaslight in the city, but when

darkness came to Seven Pines oil lamps were lit, which gave an air of coziness to the house. There was plenty of yard space for us to play in, with a lot of apple, cherry, peach, and damson trees. Back of the house to the side Daddy built a summerhouse, where we sat during hot days drinking lemonade, reading, or listening to Mama tell stories.

Mama told many tales about her childhood in New Kent County, Virginia, where she was born July 4, 1878. She was next to the youngest of eight children. There were six brothers: Randolph, Tom, Willie, Eddie, Christopher, and Clarence, who years later was the valet of Daddy Browning and testified in the famous Peaches Browning court case. Eugenia, Mama's sister, was the oldest child. Her father was William Henry Brisby, born to a Negro man named Roger Lewis and Miranda Brisby, an Indian. My great-grandfather Lewis owned land in New Kent as early as 1827. Following Indian custom, Grandpa Brisby carried his mother's family name rather than his father's.

"My father used to take me back to the Pamunkey Indian reservation," Mama said. "I rode in a wagon with him and when we came to West Point where the train crossed the wooden bridge, we left the wagon hitched to a team of horses on the New Kent side and walked the rest of the way."

When Mama was twelve years old she found her mother dead in bed. Nobody ever told her how she died, but people began to whisper about "the black bottle." When people talked about the black bottle, Mama explained, it meant somebody had been poisoned. Soon after her

mother died, her father married a young, full-blooded Indian girl named Victoria. "I felt my father betrayed me," Mama told us, "although I never hated Miss Vic."

Shortly after we moved to Seven Pines, Grandpa Brisby and Miss Vic came from New Kent to live with us, because at eighty-four he was "touched in the head" and she couldn't handle him by herself. Miss Vic was a tall, thin, straight-backed woman who suffered from chronic bronchitis and was constantly hacking. She took over the cooking, fixed delicious meals, but refused to eat with us. Instead, she stood at the door between the kitchen and dining room staring at me while we ate. Mama told us it was Miss Vic's Indian blood that made her standoffish. The only sign of affection she ever displayed was toward my little sister, whom she held in her arms and prayed over and over: "God bless her gizzard, God bless her gall, God bless . . ."

## NAACP on Black Schoolteachers' Fight for Equal Pay, c. 1940

*From the late 1930s through the 1940s the NAACP successfully fought for equal pay for black schoolteachers, the majority of whom were women. In cities and towns, north and south, black teachers had to fight against their own impulse and urgings from community leaders to simply go along with the current inequitable situation.*

*Source:* NAACP Papers, box 1-D-91, Manuscript Division, Library of Congress.

# PETITION

To the School Board of the City of Norfolk, Virginia

The petition of Aline Elizabeth Black respectfully shows:

1. That she is a teacher in the Booker T. Washington High School located in Norfolk, Virginia, a public high school maintained and operated by the School Board of the City of Norfolk.

2. That your petitioner is a Negro, a graduate of the Booker T. Washington High School in Norfolk, holds a B. S. degree from Virginia State College, holds a M. S. degree from the University of Pennsylvania, and at present, is working toward a Doctor's of Philosophy degree at New York University. She holds a Collegiate professional teaching certificate which expires in 1946.

3. That your petitioner and other teachers and principals in the City of Norfolk are paid pursuant to salary schedule adopted and enforced by the School Board of the City of Norfolk.

4. That your petitioner and other teachers and principals in the City of Norfolk are paid pursuant to a salary schedule adopted and enforced by the School Board of the City of Norfolk.

5. That the aforementioned salary schedule provides for a maximum salary for female white high school teacher, of $1900, and a maximum salary for female Negro teachers of $1105; the said salary schedule provides a minimum salary for female white high school teachers of $970

and the minimum salary for female Negro high school teachers of $699. (The figures in this paragraph are quoted from the Annual Report of the Superintendent of Public Instruction of Virginia 1936–37.)

6. That said schedule provides a higher salary for white teachers and principals than for Negro teachers and principals with similar qualifications and experience in performing essentially the same duties; the said differentials are based solely on the ground of race or color.

7. That pursuant to said schedule petitioner is paid less salary than white female high school teachers with similar qualifications in experience and performing essentially the same duties.

8. That petitioner and others of her race acting as teachers and principals in the public schools of Norfolk are paid less salary than white teachers and principals with similar qualifications and experience; and performing essentially the same duties as the aforementioned.

9. That the School Board of the City of Norfolk in enforcing the said schedule has by means of the unjust discrimination mentioned above, according to the Annual Report of the Superintendent of Public Instruction of Virginia, 1936–37, paid white female high school teachers an average annual salary of $1627 and at the same time has paid Negro female high school teachers and average annual salary of $950 despite the fact that Negro teachers in the high schools of Norfolk perform substan-

tially the same qualifications and experience.

10. The School Board of the City of Norfolk in adopting and enforcing the salary schedule of teachers referred to above, and in Administering the said schedule, and in paying teachers salaries thereunder as mentioned above, has discriminated unjustly against the petitioner and others of her race similarly employed in the School System of the City or Norfolk solely because of their race or color in violation of the Constitution and laws of the State of Virginia; and has denied the petitioner and others of her race similarly employed in the School System of the City of Norfolk the equal protection of the laws guaranteed by the fourteenth amendment to the Constitution of the United States.

Wherefore:

Your petitioner prays:

1. That the School Board of the City of Norfolk adopt and enforce a new salary schedule equal as to all teachers and principals with the same qualifications and experience without any distinction being made as to race or color of teachers or schools.

2. That the petitioner and others of her race similarly employed in the School System of the City of Norfolk be paid salaries equal to that paid white teachers with the same qualifications and experience.

*Petitioner*

*Thurgood Marshall*

*J. Thomas Hewin, Jr.*
*Charles H. Houton*
*Leon A. Ransom*
*Counsel for Petitioner*

## George Streator to W. E. B Du Bois, April 18, 1935

*In the letter Streator, of the Amalgamated Clothing Workers of America, criticizes black leaders and businessmen who oppose unionization. He asks pointedly about racial loyalties and group improvement.*

Source: W. E. B. Du Bois Papers, Microfilm Edition, Reel 44–113 Off ProQuest Information and Learning, 300 N. Zeeb Road, Ann Arbor, Michigan, 48106.

APRIL 18, 1935

*Dear Dr Du Bois:*

Leaving here tomorrow, so address me at New York.

I do not think I am wholly wrong in criticizing your Washington address. As I recall, both you and Johnson said in whole or in part:

1. This is no time for philosophy, but for action. After Johnson's speech, your saying that dovetailed, and the crowd who are afraid interpreted it to mean, "Somehow, we can muddle through." Coming from one who had fought for thirty years a theoretical battle against inequality, it seemed to be a rejection of thought in favor of "action." I saw in it a recession to what Chas Johnson

has gradually made putrid as "Objective scholarship." After all, what did your experience in Texas teach, if not that the contradictions of the operations of capitalism make for that poverty you described? Then what was your remedy? As far as I could understand, you had none except a derision of the very socialism you have preached all your life. It ought to be pointed out also, that your attitude towards violence is a purely liberal attitude. If the mild program you are preaching, that is, a mild, social democratic program, were attempted in Atlanta, or in Texas, you would get as many Negroes killed aimlessly, as Ghandi has had killed in India to satisfy a childish passion for acting, and a not entirely non-Freudian love of flagellation.

2. Then, too your attitude towards organized labor is a product of battling craft unionism and its multiple discriminations with words and letters. Your information on the present day labor problem, its possible trends, your information on Southern white labor are on the whole poor. And there is no place for you to learn these things accept from the "youngsters" you are tending to bawl out, these days.

3. Your economic thought is too much determined by the notion that the establishment of a Negro bourgeoisie is an essential first step to an ultimate solution. What if the larger white bourgeoisie is crumbling? I went to Hampton the other day. A young Negro teacher of economies was talking about the great field for Negroes in building and operating filling stations. Does he know that there is already 1 to every 87 motor vehicles in the country? He does not. He simply has an injection of race pride.

I am not saying here that the capitalist world in [sic] crumbling. I am saying that the monopolies are congealing. If white filling stations owners can't make a living, how will the Negro entrepreneurs make a go of it? They can't. Why quibble on that point.

Consumer organizations? The British associations flourished under a rising capitalism. Most of the social services and inner-economic organizations you are proposing were adopted by the English system through the Trade Unions, which are the only effective group to put them in operation. And yet, your cooperation program would be based on the sympathetic interest of Negroes in themselves. And this is a flimsy interest. I always will recall that the liberals at the NAACP were willing for me to work ninety hours a week for $100 a month. Or that few of the Negro collges have a wage scale; that a top few of the "head men" get the only salary benefits; that the Norfolk Journal and Guide, which is typical of Negro business, pays the family a salary, but experienced and efficient men with wives and children of their own get $15 a week. There is no such thing as a Negro LOVING his race in the matter of capital investment and profit.

And don't forget that the leaders of the English system—the Macdonalds, etc., were the first to sacrifice their interests to keep the system going. I mean, were the first to sacrifice the English laboring masses.

I was particularly chagrined at your complete turning to the notion that a minority group can save itself. If so, why does not the majority group of Chinese save themselves from the minority Japs? Or the minority English? Am I contradicting my self? I am merely trying to learn to say what I know and feel deeply: that no one group can pull apart from world economy, no matter how spiritual and how resolved.

I heard that you were invited to the NC Teachers. And I have a couple of letters from Bennett teachers who were equally hurt over your complete acceptance of the leadership of the stinking Negro middle class.

Of course, so far as local issues are concerned, you have a swell opportunity to urge political action on the matter of teachers' salaries. There is no need to call that communism. The wages have a mean of $56. But if in pointing out the failure of political democracy you destroy all germs of mass action, you have done them an injury.

Having successfully accomplished my task of breaking the ranks of the company union and of signing up Negro workers in the same union with the white workers, and of doing this in face of a stupid opposition from the Negro upper "clawses." I am going home for a little rest, returning here later in the summer.

*Cheerio. George Streator*

## Ella Earls Cotton, *A Spark for My People,* 1954

*The significance of racial difference was learned early in the South. Research conducted by social scientists working with the NAACP in the* Brown v. Board of Education, Topeka, Kansas *(1954) case underscored the depths of that learning. Cotton knew it firsthand, as both a teacher and citizen of the South.*

Source: Ella Earls Cotton, *A Spark for My People* (New York: Exposition Press, 1954).

As already indicated, the professors of the little college and the small group of people living around it were of the highest class of educated and cultured white people. And the society of the section was composed of the college personnel and the outlying planters. Grandmother knew most of the families of the professors at the college. One day a beautiful woman, wife of one of those professors, came to see Grandmother and brought me the most beautiful doll I'd ever seen. When Grandfather came that night, Grandmother told him that the lady wanted me to stay with her. The inducement had completely captivated me and I was all ready to go until he looked down sadly into my eyes and said, "You don't want to be anyone's 'sarvant,' do you? They would put you in the basement to sleep. Would you want to sleep in anyone's basement?" It had never mattered to me before where I slept. But his high spirit and personal pride was transmitted to me in that first instance. And so, I know that he would not have allowed Grandmother to go out and work by the day for anyone, if she had wanted to go. And Grandmother herself, having been raised in her white family in which she considered herself a member, had never nor would ever have worked with a group of women who considered themselves only as servants rather than as helpers until such time as they too might become independent by working and saving.

There was one special capacity in which she was available. And to my knowledge she was the only one, white or colored, in that class. Whenever any of the professors' wives had babies, she was called in to look after the mother and baby for that month of confinement. In that capacity she was as happy to be with them as they were to have her, for they were "quality" people. She was always given a nice room nearby and was treated most kindly. She was good at that special care a woman needs who has just gone through the ordeal of motherhood. While she had no aptitude for practical nursing, she was a skilled dietician and an artist in the cooking of delicacies. She was also skilled in the care of the newly born babies, their bathing, dressing, feeding and the care of the dainty wear such mothers prepared for the coming babies.

Although they paid her well and heaped gifts upon her, I think what she prized most was the association with the class of people she had been accustomed to all of her life. And when they would bring their babies, which she called "her babies," to see her, as they often did, she would show her affection for them by biting them and the babies would cry, which would always alarm me for fear that the mothers would get angry at her. And the mothers didn't enjoy it, but they understood her kind of affection. And as soon as another baby came, again they would come for her.

The connected story of my grandmother is due to the fact that she was both proud and loquacious and told it often. And in her way she consistently followed her bent according to her lights, which in no way dimmed her good qualities that lay beneath a surface superficiality. Grandfather loved her dearly and petted and pampered her in every way. No doubt her little superficial airs of refinement appealed to him, as did her more sterling qualities as a wife. Anyway, in the home they were unusually affectionate toward each other even in their old age.

Whoever went without, it would not be Grandmother. Somehow from some place he would buy her the nicest clothes he possibly could, so that she was the best-dressed woman in the community even though the oldest. Those nice clothes she kept in her "chest" until some big meeting warranted her wearing them, which was seldom. She was quite small and had dainty feet, which my mother also inherited from her. And Grandfather loved to buy the fine high-laced shoes of those days for her. As scarce as money was, I recall one time that he bought her two pairs of those fine shoes. I might have remembered it so well because the weather was getting cold and I was expecting a pair of school shoes any day. I had my own Sunday shoes, but then they were for Sunday's use only, and unfit for the rough-and-tumble of the playground. While I never felt any sense of neglect, the early frosts would sometime catch my bare feet for a few days.

In the intimacy of us three, there was nothing expected of me but silence, and plenty of that. So, standing around and sizing things up as a child will, I got the impression that Grandmother was not fazed in the least because Grandfather could read and she could not. But her caste ideas of herself were sufficient to excuse her illiteracy and more. But she respected him and looked up to him. Like the hand and the glove, they fitted each other. When he would go off for any length of time and return, I would be completely mystified at the metamorphosis that would come over Grandmother. There would be such a diffusion from their affection for each other that its glow would extend over to me in their ignoring or excusing any misbehavior in me.

Sitting quietly, Grandfather absorbed it all in benign complacency. No outsiders, no fanfare, but the natural outflow of two old people who must have loved each other so fiercely in youth that the fires of their love continued to burn in their old age.

I, a child, latent in body and mind, looked unconscious of the whys or wherefores, but in complete absorption in the two people most intimate in my life. I was impressed by that love between them, all the more beautiful because it had survived the test of the years. As I developed in mind and body and matured to that stage of life where I, too, began to consider taking the most important step of my life in marriage,

from my subconsciousness, all unerringly, the directive for my step and life came to the fore in the example those two old people had set me.

The precept for me was great because they had lived it before my eyes. In that precept was the fact that love is the greatest force of life. If you have it, nothing else matters.

With no effort their lives proved to me that love does not necessarily cease after youth, or die because of old age. And so, involuntarily and without conscious resolution, I found such a foundation upon which to build a marriage of unusual happiness for myself and family after those who had set me the example were no more.

Grandmother's often repeated words, "You have to keep a tight line on a child," were no doubt a misunderstanding of Solomon's, "Train up a child in the way he should go." As I grew older she would occasionally slacken the "line" and some of the frigidness of her austerity would melt a little in some expansive mood in which I would find favor. Such rigid discipline applied only to my early childhood. After she graduated me from that period, no child had a dearer grandmother than I had. And often she would align me with her side of the family. In my darkness of complexion and cast of features, she would often say, I was a throwback, or in her words a "spitting image" of her Indian father. Much later in life I found this favor to be further assumed when I went out to Oklahoma on land business and it was suggested that if I had a good (?) lawyer, I would have no trouble in taking up the 360 acres of land, the allotment of an Indian or his heirs, on my resemblance. My younger daughter, fair from her father, had somewhat the same cast of features as I. All Indians are not swarthy. Some are brown-haired, as my daughter was, and some are even red-haired. My daughter, pursuing her degree in Cincinnati University, stopped to help me carry on the school to the end of the session when her father passed away. We were both badly broken up, and to divert our grief we went to the World's Fair in Chicago in 1933. There were Indians of every tribe gathered there from all over the United States. As the aborigines of America, they had a major part on the program—a whole afternoon, in fact— to give a replica of their ceremonies, dances and other rituals. For such rites all the Indians were dressed in vivid, strong colors of mixed red, yellow, orange and blue. Different tribes had different symbols. But the regalia in general was spectacular and brilliant, indeed, with beaded embroidery, feathers, necklaces of teeth and other ornamental decorations. The different tribes were indicated by the way the men's hair was shaved or cut, and by the pattern of their astounding headdresses. The women wore their hair in the traditional two plaits. Their ornamentation for it was a beaded band around the forehead.

By the hundreds they sat apart in their own section waiting to perform their parts in the ceremonies. It was at this juncture that my daughter and I decided to try out our Indian resemblance, by marching resolutely over to the section reserved for the Indians. They looked up, moved over, and we plumped down among them. They handed us programs and explained what certain ceremonies meant, etc. And they were most kind to us in what seemed to be a natural way. They may have known all the time that we were not pure Indians, but they accepted us. And from Indians that was quite enough, as they hardly make any pretense of what they do not feel. Anyway, as I looked around, I thought of my great-grandfather. And I was glad that his people had accepted us in friendship on the basis of our resemblance to him. And I am as glad to be a part of all other humanity.

## Chinese ILGWU Activity in 1930s California

*Chinese women, like a number of other workers, used the passage of the Wagner Act to press for better working conditions. A number used the act to form a union of the International Ladies Garment Workers Union to strike and fight for better conditions.*

Source: Judy Yung, ed., *Unbound Voices: A Documentary History of Chinese Women in San Francisco* (Berkeley: University of California Press, 1999).

JUDY YUNG: Why were all the officers of Local 341 [Chinese Ladies' Garment Workers' Union] Chinese men when the women members outnumbered the men?

SUE KO LEE: The men were not as afraid as the women at that time. (I didn't say all the men were not as afraid.) They were [the] decision makers. [Women] didn't want to assume the responsibility.

(I won't want to assume the responsibility at that time either.) They had families and they just [went] out and work to earn a little extra money.

JY: Even though the men were the officers and leaders, did the women participate just as actively in the strike as the men?

SL: (nods)

JY: Did they have a say in the decision making?

SL: Oh, sure.

JY: Did the women speak up during the meetings?

SL: Not too much, but they understood the issues. They [just] weren't use to speaking up and taking the leadership role.

*I appreciated her honesty and I was grateful to have found someone willing to talk to me about the strike. So you can imagine my delight when, without my prompting, Sue Ko Lee produced her scrapbook of the news clippings, newsletters, bulletins, and photographs she had kept in connection with the strike and her work with the ILGWU. With her permission, I have included a selection of these news articles and bulletins following her interview.*

*Sue Ko Lee was born in Honolulu, Hawaii, on March 9, 1910, and grew up in Watsonville, California, the eldest of ten children. At eighteen, she married Lee Jew Hing, who had immigrated to the United States in 1921 and was working as a bookkeeper at National Dollar Stores. They made their home in San Francisco Chinatown, where they had two sons. Soon after their marriage Sue Ko Lee found a job at the National Dollar Stores, and before long she was embroiled in a strike that would irrevocably change her life.*

## "WE WEREN'T BAD OFF"

Did you know almost everyone had to work for Joe Shoong's Dollar Stores? Because you couldn't get out of Chinatown and work anywhere else. You either worked in a laundry, restaurant, or your own barbershop. Women got into [it] because there were no other opportunities for them [except] pick shrimp at home. There weren't too many employers. All my family worked for Joe Shoong . . . all my brothers, my sister Mary, even my brother-in-law. It was [also] a matter of family connections. My husband got his job because his uncle was working for Joe Shoong.

In those days, as long as there was a machine empty, anyone could get a job since they didn't pay union wages and it was piece rate. There were no controls until Roosevelt came in. We come in and go as we liked. There was no set time. They opened until nine at night. I didn't see any sweatshop conditions there. The National Dollar Stores was clean and a good-size factory because they made all the things that were sold in their [retail] stores, simple things like flannel nightgowns, cotton housedresses, aprons, satin bloomers, all women's clothing. The factory was well lit. It was not in the basement but above ground with windows that opened on one side. Only the cutting room and rest rooms were downstairs.

I started learning on the most difficult machine—the over-lock with three needles. It worked over the seams that were trimmed off on the inside of the garment. I learned all the special machines. My husband had a steady job and was making $125 a month [as a bookkeeper]. I was averaging 25 cents an hour or something like that. I wasn't a very fast worker or a slow worker, just an average worker. And I couldn't work full time because my children came in 1927 and 1929. At $125 a month and with rent at $35 a month, we weren't bad off. We never had to live in places with community kitchens and all. [Did you make enough money to take care of expenses?] Yes, and enough for him [her husband] to send money home to his family [in China]. They never forget that, no matter how hard things got.

## "WAGES WAS THE MAIN THING"

I wasn't in the beginning of it [the strike]. I was working there, but I wasn't involved until later. You see, they [the union] came to organize us. The white shops were already organized, and the white shops were clamoring that the contractors were sending work out to the Chinese workers and that was a thorn [in their side]. So they had to organize the Chinese to counteract that [underbidding of Chinatown shops]. They tried and tried but they couldn't break the [racial] barrier until Jennie Matyas came. She was talking to people there, and that's the time I became aware of it. They had to get enough signatures from the workers for the local before they could present it to the employer to have a union.

[Did you sign up?] I must have, although I can't remember now. You see,

in each shop, they get the cutters first because if they don't cut, you don't have any work. We had a group meeting to talk about it.

[Was there a dispute over wages?] Yes, wages was the main thing. The depression was over and the hour wage laws were in effect and we weren't getting the thirty-three-and-a-third cents an hour. They were cheating on us. The hours were not kept legally. What they did was say what you earned was [based on] how many hours you worked to make the thirty-three-and-a-third cents. And there was already a home work rule, but they were [still] sending a lot of home work out. (My husband knew because he kept the records of that.) I think that was the incentive for the workers to join the union of their own will. The employer[s] definitely said they didn't want a union.

*After the majority of the workers voted for a union shop, establishing the Chinese LGWU under the ILGWU, National Dollar Stores sold the Chinatown factory to Golden Gate Manufacturing, a new company formed by two former managers of the National Dollar Stores. Seeing this move as a subterfuge to freeze them out and break up the union, the Chinese LGWU voted to call a strike and began picketing the National Dollar Stores factory and its three retail stores in San Francisco. Their demands were recognition of a union shop, $20 wages for a thirty-five-hour workweek, and a guarantee that National Dollar Stores would buy all its manufactured goods from Golden Gate and that Golden Gate would provide work for a minimum of eleven months of the year to its workers.*

## "WE WERE DETERMINED TO CLOSE THEM DOWN"

[How were you able to keep the strike going for fifteen weeks?] We organized our shifts, and the ones on the picket line were all together. We never mentioned anything about why we are doing this. What is there? Maybe they won't reopen the shop for us? There was no other recourse. There was nothing else. We were determined to close them down if necessary.

We all did it with the Chinese leadership and advice from the top because we didn't know anything. They had to tell us what to do. The men were not as afraid as the women at that time. (I didn't say all the men were not as afraid.) They were [the] decision makers. My husband was the vice-president and wrote all the bulletins that went out in Chinese. [Women] had families and they just [went] out to work to earn a little extra money. They didn't want to assume the responsibility. (I won't want to assume the responsibility at that time either.) They [women] weren't used to speaking up and taking the leadership role but they understood the issues. When you see a woman like this (*points to a picture showing an older Chinese immigrant woman picket*) on the picket line, isn't that something? They stuck in there too.

[Who was running the strike?] We all worked on the [picketing] schedules and all, but the legal stuff, they [ILGWU] had to do it for us. Everything had to be okayed by the officers of the [international] union because they might be liable and they were footing the bill.

[With] the support of the white people, the union people, we closed the downtown [retail] store. I don't know what we felt then. Certainly, Jennie Matyas made a difference.

[Can you tell me why Jennie Matyas was so effective with the Chinese?] She's not Chinese, but she's a woman. She's very dedicated and very honest and sincere. (Now you read about the corruption in the unions. I don't think you could corrupt her.) She really wanted to help us. I think it was also the large company [National Dollar Stores] that people did not like. I remember we were on the picket line and here came Mrs. Shoong and she said, "*Ni di sui tong yan* [these awful Chinese]!" So she's not Chinese, right?!

[Did you get any support from the Chinese Six Companies?] Of course not! They were against us. We had the whole Chinese community against us. They didn't do anything, but they didn't show us any support because we were all called troublemakers. It was unheard of! [But] we knew the union was behind us. The union would come by with donuts and coffee in the morning. Then we went back to the union hall for meetings. [What were some of the difficulties during the strike?] Survival. We got the strike benefit—five dollars a week, but that won't pay your rent. Thirteen weeks, that's three and a half months. If we got any help, it was borrowing from our relatives. I don't know how we managed. But when you're young, you don't think about these things.

[At any time was there any disagreement between the union and the workers?] Not until the time of the contract agreement. Jennie was trying to get them to accept it, and some of the militant workers were against it. It just wasn't good enough for them. And I said, at least that's something to begin with. And that's when she [Jennie Matyas] noticed me. It may not be what you wanted, but you take the best there is. At least you got something for one year. And maybe something better would come out of it. If you take longer, people are not going to stand around here. They can't afford to.

*The contract called for a closed union shop; a 5 percent raise (to $14 per week except for apprentices); a forty-hour workweek, with time and a half for overtime; a paid holiday for Labor Day; enforcement of health, fire, and sanitary conditions; guaranteed half-day of work whenever workers were called in; a shop steward authorized to collect dues and deal with grievances; the right to a hearing before an arbitration committee in the case of a dispute over the contract or a questionable discharge; a price committee to step in whenever piece rates did not yield the minimum wages for 75 percent of the factory workers; and an agreement that National Dollar Stores continue contracting work to the Golden Gate Company. The vote was close: thirty-one for the agreement, twenty-seven against. Workers went back to work a few days later. But when the contract expired one year later, the Golden Gate Manufacturing Company conveniently went out of business.*

## "THE BEST THING THAT EVER HAPPENED"

They closed the factory while we were picketing. Then because we picketed the downtown stores, they sold it [the factory] to Golden Gate and disengaged themselves from the main store. The contract said they had to stay open a year, so they stayed open a year and then closed it.

[What happened to everyone after the factory closed?] A lot of them went to work for white shops because the union found them jobs. You don't know how hard Jennie Matyas worked to get us into the white shops downtown. I heard this later: Edna was a presser. She didn't have any parents and she and her sister lived alone. So Jennie tried to place her, to get her into a white shop. The employer was willing, but the workers rebelled. They didn't want any Chinese because of the reputation that the Chinese will work for nothing and cut the wages down. Finally she got Edna in and she proved her worth. And after that, the door opened and employers began asking for Chinese workers. That's how the Chinese workers got out of Chinatown to work elsewhere. And that's the turning point for workers in Chinatown. Because of the garment workers' strike in Chinatown, everything changed. Later, the restaurant workers had shorter hours, days off. In my opinion, the strike was the best thing that ever happened. It changed our lives. We overcame bigotry, didn't we? The war came and that helped because there was a labor shortage. But even if it hadn't come, we would have still broken the barrier. Otherwise, we would have still been stuck in Chinatown working among our own race.

I know it was a turning point in my life. My husband went to work in a downtown shop [as a cutter] in clothes and suits. I worked the machines for a while in the little shops, and then Koret took over and that's how I got into quality control. I had a tape measure around my neck to make sure the button holes were spaced out [correctly]. (Koret had very good standards for their workmanship.)

[What was the main difference between working in Chinatown and in a white shop downtown?] You made more money and had set hours. You didn't jump in and out of the shop. You worked eight to five and there was holiday and vacation pay. It was still piecework, but the price had to come up so that you made your minimum. It's controlled that way. So the faster ones can make more, but at least the slowest ones made the minimum. During the trial period they paid to make up the difference in order for you to make the minimum, but after the trial period, if you can't keep up, they have a right to let you go. But in Chinatown, they just cut your hours on the records. I remember there was a fire in one of the little shops I was working for, and because they had insurance I was paid for staying home. If it was a Chinese shop, you would get nothing. Then through the union bargaining, we got health insurance and death benefits.

[Did they mistreat you in any way?] No, I won't let them. We had no problems getting along with the people in the shops. There was no discrimination. Where I worked I was respected. I'll just cite you a few instances. I was working on the floor at Koret during the Second World War. A co-worker told me another woman working the floor got a raise. You go ask for a raise," he said. On

another occasion, I was on the floor trying something on the machine, tucking. I didn't like that job, but I was willing to try any machine. Most people won't because if they went slow, it would lower their average. So this lady came to me and said, "Why didn't you tell me you can work on that machine?" I said (*smiling smugly,*) "You never asked me."

Later in the 1950s, I stopped working at Koret and went to work for the union [Local 101 of the ILGWU]. It started with the strike. I was working in the shop and was drawn into it. They needed someone with language skills, so I was appointed the business agent. That's when I became a delegate to the convention. [Was there any racial discrimination in ILGWU?] No. I was secretary of a *white* union. There were Blacks in there too, and we all got along. After the war [ILGWU was successful in getting other shops in Chinatown to unionize] because they worked through the manufacturers. If you send your work out and you're a union shop, you have to send it to a union [factory]. That's how they organized them. Otherwise, they would never be able to organize them and they won't strike. At least they [Chinatown workers] gained something. They never had death benefits and health insurance before. Now they have.

In a way the Chinatown shops are good for the people who cannot get out of Chinatown transportation-wise or know their way around. But the contractors are so greedy. You know the manufacturers pay them the price and overhead on top of the piece rate but they don't pass that on to the workers. Just like in real estate, they hurt their own people. And here these employees feel sorry for their employers. They give them the sad story, "You run through this at this price or we don't get any work." I know for a fact that the manufacturers pay them the same rate as they pay downtown and pay them for the overhead. But they're not happy with the overhead; they have to cheat the workers. That's what gets me disgusted! That's why I got out of it. I could have just gone along with it and take my pay. I would have been rich by now. But I can't take that out of the dues of the people. I'm not that kind of person.

I thought maybe I could help Chinatown, but I couldn't do it. (sighs) It's frustrating. They [Chinese workers] don't want to do anything for themselves. They want you to hand them the benefits, and still they won't fight for them. It's not like the Black people, [who are] more aggressive. Your mother is at the age where she can't understand it, but those younger ones, they should know better. I tried to explain to them, but they just don't want to change. So I said what's the use of me hanging around? I can't do anything. So that's why I quit the union in the 1960s and went to work for the state in the employment service.

*Source:* Sue Ko Lee, interview with author, October 26, 1989, El Cerrito, California.

*Sue Ko Lee died of cancer on May 15, 1996. The last time I saw her was on October 28, 1995, at the book party for* Unbound Feet. *Proudly sitting on stage at the Chinese culture Center in San Francisco Chinatown, she was one of seven outstanding women being honored that day.*

## FROM SUE KO LEE'S SCRAPBOOK

*In a light-brown-covered scrapbook Sue Ko Lee had carefully arranged and preserved an array of English- and Chinese-language newspaper clippings, mimeographed pages from union publications, handwritten Chinese bulletins, and photographs—all documenting the 1938 strike and her ILGWU activities. From them we get a detailed account of an intraethnic class struggle and the tactics employed by both sides—the Chinese garment workers and their employer, millionaire Joe Shoong. At stake were the reputation of Joe Shoong, on the one hand, and the rights of Chinatown workers to unionize and demand better working conditions, on the other. Both sides vied for the support and approval of the Chinese community, appealing to its sense of righteousness and to Chinese nationalist solidarity.*

*As the following excerpts from bulletins, news clippings, and newsletters show, Joe Shoong went to great lengths to fight the union, demanding an election of the workers, changing the ownership and name of the National Dollar Stores factory getting a court injunction against the pickets, suing the union, and finally closing down the factory when the contract expired. In the National Dollar Stores' "Statement to the Public" of March 2, 1938, Joe Shoong tried to come across as the benevolent employer, upstanding citizen, loyal Chinese nationalist, and victim of union tactics. In response, the Chinese local provided a reasoned point-by-point rebuttal that was published simultaneously in the Young China newspaper, arguing that the workers were victims of Joe Shoong's mistreatment and unscrupulous tactics. Over and over again, the Chinese LGWU issued bulletins that explained the union's position to the Chinatown community.*

These were often couched in leftist political rhetoric—labeling Joe Shoong a capitalist, arguing that the worker's welfare is the nation's welfare, and calling on workers to fight to the end to raise their living standards. The union even went so far as to join forces with leftist organizations such as the Chinese Workers Mutual Aid Association.

The excerpts from union publications show that throughout the strike the Chinese garment workers were determined to win. In the spirit of union solidarity, they kept fellow union members apprised of the situation, continued to bolster the membership's morale, and constantly expressed appreciation for all that the ILGWU was doing for them. They apparently really felt that "the ILGWU is behind us; we shall not be moved." Even after the strike was over and victory won, they remained stalwart members of the labor movement and avid supporters of Chinese nationalist causes. In the September 21 1938, bulletin printed below, they expressly made the connection between U.S.-China foreign relations and interethnic workers' solidarity, urging all of Chinatown not to cross the picket lines at department stores downtown "for the sake of national reputation and of promoting friendship between Chinese and American workers." Later, the Chinese local also contributed to the strike fund of other unions, campaigned against antilabor legislation, participated in the protest against U.S. shipment of war materials to Japan, and supported the boycott of non-union-made lisle stockings, which women wore in order to boycott Japanese silk products. Unfortunately, Chinese women's involvement in the labor movement proved short-lived as the movement dissipated with the coming of war, the end of the depression, and the repression of the left following World War II.

## A LETTER TO THE PUBLIC REGARDING THE STRIKE

*Dear Fellow Countrymen:*

Why are we striking and picketing? We are striking for better wages from the factory owner so that we can support our livelihood. This is not something that we want. However, since last October, because of inflation, we have had difficulty making ends meet. That is why we mobilized our fellow workers to fight for equality and decent wages. It has been three months since we formed our union. During these three months, we have tried repeatedly through peaceful methods to negotiate with the owner, but he has consistently used the oppressive tactics of the capitalist to stall for time. He forced us to have an election in the presence of his representatives to rectify the formation of the union. Supervised by the National Labor Relations Board and with a full quorum of workers, the election was carried out and our union received due recognition. Subsequently, his legal representatives signed an agreement with our union lawyer, but he continued to use all kinds of stalling tactics to defuse our unity. Then on top of that, he tried to turn the situation around by changing the name of the factory. His goal is to break our ricebowl. Therefore, we have no choice but to set up a picket line to fight for fair treatment.

*February 26, 1938*
*All the workers of the National Dollar*
*Stores factory*

Source: Handwritten Chinese bulletin. Translator: Ellen Yeung.

## A STATEMENT TO THE PUBLIC REGARDING THE DAMAGES DONE TO BUSINESS BY THE CHINESE LGWU STRIKE AGAINST NATIONAL DOLLAR STORES

Beginning February 26, the Chinese Ladies' Garment Workers' Union has been sending its members to picket our stores on Market Street, Mason Street, and Fillmore Street as well as our warehouse. The damage this is doing to our business, however, is not as significant as the impact it has on the whole overseas Chinese community. Our company had on February 8 sold the factory located at Washington and Kearny to the Golden Gate Manufacturing Company. That company had received State government approval to establish itself as a business and had also published a notice in the newspaper to raise capital by soliciting shareholders. Not only is their name different from ours, but their organization is different. They have absolutely no relationship with us. As for the negotiations going on between labor and capital, when the factory changed hands the Golden Gate Manufacturing Company agreed to continue the negotiations with the union. And instead of pursuing the matter with them, the union turned around and picketed our company. The union is in error for not being able to tell the difference. Moreover it is a great pity that they are hurting a Chinese business. Our company has always extended cooperation and excellent treatment to the workers. We have always adhered to government regulations regarding work hours and wages and have never op-pressed anyone or reduced anyone's wages. Therefore these workers of the Golden Gate Manufacturing Company are totally out of line in picketing us and distributing flyers in the name of the workers of a non-existing National Dollar Stores factory in order to confuse the public. In this time of national disaster, when unity among ourselves is crucial, it is really sad to think that such an unfortunate incident has happened. Because we are concerned that our countrymen may not know the truth, we are providing a brief explanation so that you may understand that we are the innocent victim in this dispute.

National Dollar Stores
March 2, 1938

Source: Young China newspaper, March 5, 1938, p. 4. Translator: Ellen Yeung.

## ANOTHER LETTER TO THE PUBLIC FROM LOCAL 341, THE CHINESE LADIES' GARMENT WORKERS' UNION

Yesterday we read the ridiculous statement from the National Dollar Stores. It is not even worth a response from intelligent people, but because we are concerned that our countrymen may not know the truth, we are providing a brief explanation of the oppression suffered by members of this union.

According to National Dollar Stores, "Beginning February 26, the Chinese Ladies Garment Workers Union (LGWU) has been sending its members to picket. . . ." Our sending members to picket National Dollar Stores was not really something that we wanted to do, but because of the low wages, the inflation, and the downward spiral of living standards, we had no choice but to raise the issue of a wage increase with the owner of National Dollar Stores. Instead of responding, the owner evicted four union members from the factory. After the attorney and the officers of the union took up the matter, the owner reinstated the four workers to their original jobs and recognized the Chinese LGWU.

At first he agreed to open negotiations with the union regarding wages and working hours. Then he reneged on his words and refused to recognize us, demanding instead that the workers vote in an election supervised by the National Labor Relations Board. The majority voted for a union, so finally the representative and the legal counsel for National Dollar Stores signed a document recognizing the union and agreeing to start negotiations over wages, working hours, and other issues. In the latter part of January, National Dollar Stores scheduled a meeting with our union representative at the Palace Hotel, at which time our union representative presented their company representative with a copy of the contract. Representatives and legal counsels from both sides also met on January 28 at the union attorney's office to sign a document stating that the National Dollar Stores factory was now a union shop, meaning that it cannot hire non-union workers. In the midst of negotiations, National Dollar Stores resorted to trickery, suddenly changing the name of the factory. They refused any further negotiations with the union but continued the talks about wages and

working hours under the name of the Golden Gate Manufacturing Company. Meanwhile, Golden Gate Manufacturing Company refused to provide any satisfactory responses and instead stalled for time. Work at the factory became unsteady. That was why union members were forced to strike.

National Dollar Stores said that they have "always extended cooperation and excellent treatment to the workers . . . have never oppressed anyone or reduced anyone's wages . . ." When workers ask for a wage increase from the employer and the latter evicts them, is that not oppression? Where in this case is the excellent treatment? When the National Recovery Administration (NRA) codes were in effect, weekly wages were at least $18, $19. After the NRA codes expired, wages were slashed to $13.30, a reduction of $5.60. How can the employer, claim not to have reduced wages? All this constitutes oppressive treatment of workers by the employer.

National Dollar Stores also said, "In this time of national disaster . . ." If the owner of National Dollar Stores is really interested in China's welfare, he should negotiate with the workers in good faith and allow workers to make a decent living so that they can afford to buy Chinese war bonds. We can barely survive on $13.30 a week, let alone contribute to the war effort. If the owner of National Dollar Stores is someone who is understanding, then he should negotiate with the union and raise the wages of the workers. Then not only will the workers benefit, but China will as well. We trust that wise people in the community will be able to judge for themselves as to who is right and who is wrong in this present dispute.

*March 5, 1938*

*Source: Young China* newspaper, March 5, 1938, p. 4. Translator: Ellen Yeung.

## TO THE MEMBERSHIP OF OUR ILGWU

The Chinese article on the opposite page is a letter written by our Chinese strikers to our membership. The underneath is a translation of it by Alice Dong, a striker.

APRIL 30, 1938

*Dear brothers and sisters,*

We, the members of the Chinese Ladies' Garment Workers' Union, Local 341, send our greetings to you all, and wish to bring to your attention the existence of our strike, now more than nine weeks old.

Ever since the end of last year, after we were granted our charter, we tried our utmost in every way to get an agreement from our employer, the National $ Stores Ltd., to assure us higher wages and better working conditions. In reply to our demands, our employers asked for time to consider the terms. Meanwhile, pending negotiations, the name of the factory in which we were working was changed from the National $ Stores Ltd., to the Golden Gate Mfg. Co., and our employer claimed the factory was sold.

When we heard of the sale of the factory we believed at the time, and still do believe now, that such a sale is only a means used by our employers to break our unionization and to avoid further responsibilities toward us. The strike was called February 26, and we started immediately to picket the factory and the three National $ Stores in San Francisco.

We continued to picket peacefully for three weeks until the firm obtained a temporary restraining order against us. This prevented us from picketing the stores. The hearing on the temporary injunction was held on April 12, '38. We did not as yet get our decision, but we sincerely hope that when it comes it will be in our favor so that we shall again be able to picket the stores, as we now picket the factory.

We appreciate deeply the help and the assistance that all the officers of the San Francisco locals, and Miss Jennie Matyas, our organizer, are giving us in our strike. We take this opportunity to thank them all and individually.

We also thank our headquarters, the ILGWU, in New York City, for all the support extended to us: moral support, economic support, legal support, and financial support. Every week a relief sum is handed to each of us to take care of arising needs. Legal advice is given readily whenever troubles or complications happen. With such supports behind us, we know we cannot fail. We will fight our fight to the end, and hope to raise the living conditions not only for ourselves but for the other workers in Chinatown as well.

Words cannot express our gratitude. All we say and sing forever is:

"The ILGWU is behind us
We shall not be moved."

We thank you all for the nice Easter party given to us and to our children, also.

*Strikers of Chinese Ladies' Garment*
*Workers' Union*
*Local No. 341*

Source: *Union Bulletin,* May 1938.

## ILGWU LOCAL #341, CHINESE LADIES' GARMENT WORKERS' UNION BULLETIN

*Dear Fellow Workers and Union*
*Members:*
Our request to the owner for a wage increase, reduction in work hours, and improved treatment not only failed to get the owner's sympathy and consent, but instead caused him to reveal his vileness and treachery. First he pretended to recognize the union and negotiate a contract in good faith. Then he changed the name of the factory in an effort to avoid further negotiations with the union. Then under the new name he tried to draw up a contract with the clause stipulating that "National Dollar Stores and the new company are not responsible." He would open the factory only one or two days a week, thus using economic pressure to intimidate the workers. Fortunately, our workers stood together and maintained a united front.

On February 26, the head of our local chapter mobilized all workers to begin picketing the National Dollar Stores factory and its three retail stores in San Francisco. That was two months ago. Then in the middle of March, while we were picketing, the owner obtained a temporary injunction from the court which stopped our picketing at the retail stores, but not at the factory. We are now waiting for the judge's final decision. We hope that the judge, who should be like a father to us, will base his judgment on law and justice, allowing us to resume picketing in front of the three retail stores so that we can continue our long-term struggle for justice from National Dollar Stores.

During our struggle, we have been lucky to have the backing of our New York headquarters, including material and moral support as well as financial, promotional and legal assistance. Dear workers, we must struggle on. No matter what happens, we must fight to the end, so that the support from our New York headquarters will not be in vain. We also hope that you members in all the other local chapters will help to publicize our situation in your areas and continue to give us your moral support.

*Happy May First*
*[International Workers Day].*
*Chinese Ladies' Garment Workers' Union,*
*Local # 341*
*May 1, 1938*

## NOTICE REGARDING THE STRIKE BY EMPLOYEES AT THE EMPORIUM

The Japanese invasion of China has brought about a national unity of such magnitude as has never been seen before. While the common people in China are sacrificing for their country, we overseas Chinese, besides giving financial assistance, should try actively to lobby through diplomatic channels for support for China. Our intense efforts have gained us the sympathy of all kinds of American workers and have generated a lot of moral and material support. However, we have not attained our goal of stopping the loading and unloading of Japanese goods and the shipment of weapons and ammunitions to Japan. In order to succeed, we need to work harder from now on to strengthen the bond between Chinese and American workers.

Recently, because of economic strife, workers at the Emporium, Woolworth, and a dozen other stores went on strike and began picketing the stores. Since we are not directly involved, we do not have a stake in which side is right or wrong. However, as long as the dispute is going on, we Chinese should not cross the picket line and enter any of the stores to shop so as not to give American workers a bad impression of us. Our Chinese community does not lack wise people who understand the implication of all this. However, there is always that small minority, who, for the sake of saving pennies, would cross a picket line to patronize a store. For the sake of national reputation and of promoting friendship between Chinese and American workers, we publish this notice hoping to call everyone's attention to the present situation.

*Chinese Workers Mutual Aid Association*

*Chinese LGWU*

*September 21, 1938*

## THE CHINESE LOCAL EXTENDS GREETINGS

The following is a translation of the Chinese Greeting on the opposite page, which besides being in our Bulletin, was distributed among a thousand Chinese workers in Chinatown. The Chinese, as well as the English translation, was written by the Chinese members, themselves.

We greet the New Year with new hopes. A year has passed since our local was organized. In the last year we won our first strike for union recognition, and better wages. Our strike lasted 105 days. We owed our success to the solidarity and determination of our members to fight "to the end" to raise our living standard.

We are grateful to our International for the fullest moral and financial support which it gave us so generously. We are grateful to the S.F. Joint Board and their officers for their generous help, also.

We are also grateful to Local 1100 for the full support they gave us in our strike. We shall never forget it.

We enjoyed the privilege of a union shop for over half a year, and we wish the rest of the Chinese garment workers were with us. With the beginning of the new year, we hope that they will realize, as we have realized, that a union will help them win better living conditions in all Chinatown.

We greet everyone of our friends in the ILGWU, and wish you all a happy and prosperous new year.

*Chinese Ladies' Garment Workers' Union*

*Local No. 341, ILGWU*

*Source: Union Bulletin, January 1939.*

# Mexican American Workers Join the CIO, 1939

*Americans of a variety of race and ethnic backgrounds used organized labor to improve conditions at work and in their home lives. In Chicago, Mexican Americans joined these efforts.*

*Source:* Interview with Jesse Perez by Betty Burke, June 21, 1939, Chicago, at http://lcweb2.loc.gov/ammem/ndlpedu/features/timeline/depwwii/unions/jperez.html.

The bosses in the yards never treat Mexican worker same as rest. For 'sample, they been treatin' me, well, ever since I start wearin' the button they start to pick an' 'scriminates. I was first to wear CIO button. . . .

I can butcher, but they won't give me job. They fired me on account of CIO union one time. I started organize the boys on the gang. I was acting as steward for CIO union. We had so much speed up and I was advisin' the boys to cut the speed and so when I start tellin' the boys we have a union for them they all join up. Almos' all join right away. So we talk all the time what the union goin' to do for us, goin' raise wages, stop speed-up, an' the bosses watch an' they know it's a union [comin'?].

So every day they start sayin' we behin' in the work. They start speedin' up the boys more an' more every day.

The boys ask me, what you gonna do? Can't keep on speed-up like this. We made stoppage. Tol' bosses we workin' too fast, can't keep up. The whole gang, thirteen men, they all stop. Bosses come

an' say, we ain't standin' for nothin' like this. So 4 days later they fire the whole gang, except 2. So we took the case in the labor board and they call the boys for witness. Labor board say we got to get jobs back. Boss got to promise to put us back as soon as they can. That time was slack, but now all work who was fired. All got work.

Now the bosses try to provoke strike before CIO get ready, before the men know what to do. Foremen always try to get in argument about work, to make the boys mad so they quit work. We know what they do, we don't talk back, got to watch out they don't play trick like that.

# Tydings–McDuffie Act, 1934

*This act reclassified Filipino immigrants to the United States as aliens and set their annual immigration quota at fifty. Although Filipinos were not excluded entirely from immigrating to the United States, as other Asian immigrants were, their miniscule quota demonstrates that the United States hardly welcomed them in large numbers.*

*Source:* Tydings-McDuffie Act, 1934 (73rd Congress, Sess. II, Ch. 84, March 24, 1934), from http://www.chanrobles.com/tydings mcduffieac.htm.

## IMMIGRATION AFTER INDEPENDENCE

Sec. 14. Upon the final and complete withdrawal of American sovereignty over the Philippine Islands the immigration laws of the United States (including all the provisions thereof relating to persons ineligible to citizenship) shall apply to persons who were born in the Philippine Islands to the same extent as in the case of other foreign countries.

# Wheeler-Howard Act, June 18, 1934

*With the appointment of John Collier to head the Bureau of Indian Affairs in 1933, federal policy toward Native Americans changed dramatically. The hallmark of this new policy was the Indian Reorganization Act. Passed by Congress in 1934, this act ended the disastrous allotment program and allowed for much greater Indian autonomy (among many other things).*

*Source:* Wheeler-Howard Act (Indian Reorganization Act), June 18, 1934, from http://www.warmsprings.com/history/treaty/wh_act.htm.

An Act to conserve and develop Indian lands and resources; to extend to Indians the right to form business and other organizations; to establish a credit system for Indians; to grant certain rights of home rule to Indians; to provide for vocational education for Indians; and for other purposes.

BE IT ENACTED *by the Senate and House of Representatives of the United States of America in Congress assembled,* That hereafter no land of any Indian reservation, created or set apart by treaty or agreement with the Indians, Act of Congress, Executive order, purchase, or otherwise, shall be allotted in severalty to any Indian.

*Sec. 2.* The existing periods of trust placed upon any Indian lands and any restriction on alienation thereof are hereby extended and continued until otherwise directed by Congress.

*Sec. 3.* The Secretary of the Interior, if he shall find it to be in the public interest, is hereby authorized to restore to tribal ownership the remaining surplus lands of any Indian reservation heretofore opened, or authorized to be opened, to sale, or any other form of disposal by Presidential proclamation, or by any of the public land laws of the United States; Provided, however, That valid rights or claims of any persons to any lands so withdrawn existing on the date of the withdrawal shall not be affected by this Act: Provided further, That this section shall not apply to lands within any reclamation project heretofore authorized in any Indian reservation: *Provided further,* That this section shall not apply to lands within any reclamation project heretofore authorized in any Indian reservation: *Provided further* That the order of the Department of the interior signed, dated, and approved by Honorable Ray Lyman Wilbur, as Secretary of the Interior, on October 28, 1932, temporarily withdrawing lands of the Papago Indian Reservation in Arizona from all forms of mineral entry or claim under the public land mining laws is hereby revoked and rescinded, and the lands of the said Papago Indian Reservation are hereby restored to exploration and location, under the existing mining laws of the United States, in accordance with the express terms and provisions declared and set forth in the Executive orders establishing said Papago Indian Reservation: *Provided further,* That the damages shall be paid to the Papago Tribe for loss of any improvements of any land located for mining in such a sum as may be determined by the Secretary of the Interior but not exceed the cost of said improvements: *Provided further,* That a yearly rental not to exceed five cents per acre shall be paid to the Papago Indian Tribe: *Provided further,* That in the event that any person or persons, partnership, corporation, or association, desires a mineral patent, according to the mining laws of the United States, he or they shall first deposit in the treasury of the United States to the credit of the Papago Tribe the sum of $1.00 per acre in lieu of annual rental, as hereinbefore provided, to compensate for the loss or occupancy of the lands withdrawn by the requirements of mining operations: *Provided further,* That patentee shall also pay into the Treasury of the United States to the credit of the Papago Tribe damages for the loss of improvements not heretofore said in such a sum as may be determined by the Secretary of the Interior, but not to exceed the cost thereof; the payment of $1.00 per acre for surface use to be refunded to patentee in the event that the patent is not required.

Nothing herein contained shall restrict the granting or use of permits for easements or rights-of-way; or ingress or egress over the lands for all proper and lawful purposes; and nothing contained therein, except as expressly provided, shall be construed as authority by the Secretary of the Interior, or any other person, to issue or promulgate a rule or regulation in conflict with the Executive

order of February 1, 1917, creating the Papago Indian Reservation in Arizona or the Act of February 21, 1931 (46 Stat. 1202).

*Sec. 4.* Except as herein provided, no sale, devise, gift, exchange or other transfer of restricted Indian lands or of shares in the assets of any Indian tribe or corporation organized hereunder, shall be made or approved; *Provided however,* That such lands or interests may, with the approval of the Secretary of the Interior, be sold, devised, or otherwise transferred to the Indian tribe in which the lands or shares are located or from which the shares were derived or to a successor corporation; and in all instances such lands or interests shall descend or be devised, in accordance with the then existing laws of the State, or Federal laws where applicable, in which said lands are located or in which the subject matter of the corporation is located, to any member of such tribe or of such corporation or any heirs of such member: *Provided further,* That the Secretary of the Interior may authorize voluntary exchanges of lands of equal value and the voluntary exchange of shares of equal value whenever such exchange, in his judgement, is expedient and beneficial for or compatible with the proper consolidation of Indian lands and for the benefit of cooperative organizations.

*Sec. 5.* The Secretary of the Interior is hereby authorized, in his discretion, to acquire through purchase, relinquishment, gift, exchange, or assignment, any interest in lands, water rights or surface rights to lands, within or without existing reservations, including trust or otherwise restricted allotments whether the allottee be living or deceased, for the purpose of providing lands for Indians.

For the acquisition of such lands, interests in lands, water rights, and surface rights, and for expenses incident to such acquisition, there is hereby authorized to be appropriated, out of any funds in the Treasury not otherwise appropriated, a sum not to exceed $2,000,000 in any one fiscal year: *Provided.* That no part of such funds shall be used to acquire additional land outside of the exterior boundaries of Navajo Indian Reservation for the Navajo Indians in Arizona and New Mexico, in the event that the proposed Navajo boundary extension measures how pending in congress and embodied in the bills (S. 2531 and H.R. 8927) to define the exterior boundaries of the Navajo Indian Reservation in Arizona, and for other purposes, and the bills (S. 2531 and H.R. 8982) to define the exterior boundaries of the Navajo Indian Reservation in New Mexico and for other purposes, or similar legislation, become law.

The unexpended balances of any appropriations made pursuant to this section shall remain available until expended.

Title to any lands or rights acquired pursuant to this Act shall be taken in the name of the United States in trust for the Indian tribe or individual Indian for which the land is acquired, and such lands or rights shall be exempt from State and local taxation.

*Sec. 6.* The Secretary of the Interior is directed to make rules and regulations for the operation and management of Indian forestry units on the principle of sustained-yield management, to restrict the number of livestock grazed on Indian range units to the estimated carrying capacity of such ranges, and to promulgate such other rules and regulations as may be necessary to protect the range from deterioration, to prevent soil erosion, to assure full utilization of the range, and like purposes.

*Sec. 7.* The Secretary of the Interior is hereby authorized to proclaim new Indian reservations on lands acquired pursuant to any authority conferred by this Act, or to add such lands to existing reservations: *Provided,* That lands added to existing reservations shall be designated for the exclusive use of Indians entitled by enrollment or by tribal membership to residence at such reservations shall be designated for the exclusive use of Indians entitled by enrollment or by tribal membership to residence at such reservations.

*Sec. 8.* Nothing contained in this Act shall be construed to relate to Indian holdings of allotments or homesteads upon the public domain outside of the geographic boundaries of any Indian reservation now existing or established hereafter.

*Sec. 9.* There is hereby authorized to be appropriated, out of any funds in the Treasury not otherwise appropriated, such sums as may be necessary, but not to exceed $250,000 in any fiscal year, to be expended at the order of the Secretary of the Interior, in defraying the expenses of organizing Indian chartered corporations or other organizations created under this Act.

*Sec. 10.* There is hereby authorized to be appropriated, out of any funds in the Treasury not otherwise appropriated, the sum of $10,000,000 to be established as a revolving fund from which the Secretary of the Interior, under such rules and regulations as he may prescribe, may make loans to Indian chartered corporations for the purpose of promoting the economic development of such tribes and of their members, and may defray the expenses of administering such loans. Repayment of amounts loaned under this authorization shall be credited to the revolving fund and shall be available for the purposes for which the fund is established. A report shall be made annually to Congress of transactions under this authorization.

*Sec. 11.* There is hereby authorized to be appropriated, out of any funds in the United States Treasury not otherwise appropriated, a sum not to exceed $250,000 annually, together with any unexpended balances of previous appropriations made pursuant to this section, for loans to Indians for the payment of tuition and other expenses in recognized vocational and trade schools: *Provided,* That not more than $50,000 of such sum shall be available for loans to Indian students in high schools and colleges. Such loans shall be reimbursable under rules established by the Commissioner of Indian Affairs.

*Sec. 12.* The Secretary of the Interior is directed to establish standards of health, age, character, experience, knowledge, and ability for Indians who maybe appointed, without regard to civil-service laws, to the various positions maintained, now or hereafter, by the Indian office, in the administrations functions or services affecting any Indian tribe. Such qualified Indians shall here-

after have the preference to appointment to vacancies in any such positions.

*Sec. 13.* The provisions of this Act shall not apply to any of the Territories, colonies, or insular possessions of the United States, except that sections 9, 10, 11, 12, and 16 shall apply to the Territory of Alaska: *Provided,* That Sections 2, 4, 7, 16, 17, and 18 of this Act shall not apply to the following named Indian tribes, together with members of other tribes affiliated with such named located in the State of Oklahoma, as follows: Cheyenne, Arapaho, Apache, Comanche, Kiowa, Caddo, Delaware, Wichita, Osage, Kaw, Otoe, Tonkawa, Pawnee, Ponca, Shawnee, Ottawa, Quapaw, Seneca, Wyandotte, Iowa, Sac and Fox, Kickapoo, Pottawatomi, Cherokee, Chickasaw, Choctaw, Creek, and Seminole. Section 4 of this Act shall not apply to the indians of the Klamath Reservation in Oregon.

*Sec. 14.* The Secretary of the Interior is hereby directed to continue the allowance of the articles enumerated in section 17 of the Act of March 2, 1889 (25 Stat.L. 891), or their commuted cash value under the Act of June 10, 1886 (29 Stat.L. 334), to all Sioux Indians who would be eligible, but for the provisions of this Act, to receive allotments of lands in severalty under section 19 of the Act of May 29, 1908 (25 (35) Stat.L. 451), or under any prior Act, and who have the prescribed status of the head of a family or single person over the age of eighteen years, and his approval shall be final and conclusive, claims therefor to be paid as formerly from the permanent appropriation made by said section 17 and carried on the books of the Treasury for this purpose. No person shall receive in his own right more than one allowance of the benefits, and application must be made and approved during the lifetime of the allotee or the right shall lapse. Such benefits shall continue to be paid upon such reservation until such time as the lands available therein for allotment at the time of the passage of this Act would have been exhausted by the award to each person receiving such benefits of an allotment of eighty acres of such land.

*Sec. 15.* Nothing in this Act shall be construed to impair or prejudice any claim or suit of any Indian tribe against the United States. It is hereby declared to be the intent of Congress that no expenditures for the benefit of Indians made out of appropriations authorized by this Act shall be considered as offsets in any suit brought to recover upon any claim of such Indians against the United States.

*Sec. 16.* Any Indian tribe, or tribes, residing on the same reservation, shall have the right to organize for its common welfare, and may adopt an appropriate constitution and bylaws, which shall become effective when ratified by a majority vote of the adult members of the tribe, or of the adult Indians residing on such reservation, as the case may be, at a special election authorized by the Secretary of the Interior under such rules and regulations as he may prescribe. Such constitution and bylaws when ratified as aforesaid and approved by the Secretary of the Interior shall be revocable by an election open to the same

voters and conducted in the same manner as hereinabove provided. Amendments to the constitution and bylaws may be ratified and approved by the Secretary in the same manner as the original constitution and bylaws.

In addition to all powers vested in any Indian tribe or tribal council by existing law, the constitution adopted by said tribe shall also vest in such tribe or its tribal council the following rights and powers: To employ legal counsel, the choice of counsel and fixing of fees to be subject to the approval of the Secretary of the Interior; to prevent the sale, disposition, lease, or encumbrance of tribal lands, interests in lands, or other tribal assets without the consent of the tribe; and to negotiate with the Federal, State, and local Governments. The Secretary of the Interior shall advise such tribe or its tribal council of all appropriation estimates or Federal projects for the benefit of the tribe prior to the submission of such estimates to the Bureau of the Budget and the Congress.

*Sec. 17.* The Secretary of the Interior may, upon petition by at least one-third of the adult Indians, issue a charter of incorporation to such tribe: *Provided,* That such charter shall not become operative until ratified at a special election by a majority vote of the adult Indians living on the reservation. Such charter may convey to the incorporated tribe the power to purchase, take by gift, or bequest, or otherwise, own, hold, manage, operate, and dispose of property of every description, real and personal, including the power to purchase restricted Indian lands and to issue in exchange therefor interests in corporate property, and such further powers as may be incidental to the conduct of corporate business, not inconsistent with law, but no authority shall be granted to sell, mortgage, or lease for a period exceeding ten years any of the land included in the limits of the reservation. Any charter so issued shall not be revoked or surrendered except by Act of Congress.

Sec. 18. This Act shall not apply to any reservation wherein a majority of the adult Indians, voting at a special election duly called by the Secretary of the Interior, shall vote against it application. It shall be the duty of the Secretary of the Interior, within one year after the passage and approval of this Act, to call such an election, which election shall be held by secret ballot upon thirty days' notice.

Sec. 19. The term "Indian" as used in this Act shall include all persons of Indian descent who are members of any recognized Indian tribe now under Federal jurisdiction, and all person who are descendants of such members who were, on June 1, 1934, residing within the present boundaries of any reservation, and shall further include all other persons of one-half or more Indian blood. For the purposes of this Act, Eskimos and other aboriginal peoples of Alaska shall be considered Indians. The term "tribe" wherever used in this Act shall be construed to refer to any Indian tribe, organized band, pueblo, or the Indians residing on one reservation. The words "adult Indians" wherever used in this Act shall be construed to refer to Indians who have attained the age of twenty-one years.

Approved, June 18, 1934.

## Zoot Suit Riot, 1943

*Dress and attire served as metaphor for change in wartime America. In 1943 anti-Mexican sentiment among military personnel erupted into a race riot that pitted men in uniform against a youthful contingent of Mexican-American males wearing zoot suits.*

*Source:* Al Waxman in *Eastside Journal,* as quoted in Carey McWilliams, *North From Mexico* (New York: Greenwood Press, 1968).

## "WE'RE LOOKING FOR ZOOT-SUITS TO BURN": MEXICAN AMERICANS AND THE ZOOT SUIT RIOTS

At Twelfth and Central I came upon a scene that will long live in my memory. Police were swinging clubs and servicemen were fighting with civilians. Wholesale arrests were being made by the officers.

Four boys came out of a pool hall. They were wearing the zoot-suits that have become the symbol of a fighting flag. Police ordered them into arrest cars. One refused. He asked: "Why am I being arrested?" The police officer answered with three swift blows of the night-stick across the boy's head and he went down. As he sprawled, he was kicked in the face. Police had difficulty loading his body into the vehicle because he was one-legged and wore a wooden limb. Maybe the officer didn't know he was attacking a cripple.

At the next corner a Mexican mother cried out, "Don't take my boy, he did nothing. He's only fifteen years old.

Don't take him." She was struck across the jaw with a night-stick and almost dropped the two and a half year old baby that was clinging in her arms. . . .

Rushing back to the east side to make sure that things were quiet here, I came upon a band of servicemen making a systematic tour of East First Street. They had just come out of a cocktail bar where four men were nursing bruises. Three autos loaded with Los Angeles policemen were on the scene but the soldiers were not molested. Farther down the street the men stopped a streetcar, forcing the motorman to open the door and proceeded to inspect the clothing of the male passengers. "We're looking for zoot-suits to burn," they shouted. Again the police did not interfere. . . . Half a block away . . . I pleaded with the men of the local police substation to put a stop to these activities. "It is a matter for the military police," they said.

## Japanese American Protests Internment, July 26, 1943

*The story of Japanese-American internment is often told as if internees did not protest their treatment as questionable Americans. Across the country, men, women, and children proclaimed their loyalty to the United States and their opposition to being singled out for removal.*

*Source:* Morris E. Opler, "Interview with . . . an Older Nisei," Manzanar Community Analysis Report No. 36, July 26, 1943, RG 210, National Archives, from http://historymatters. gmu.edu/d/5152/

## "EVACUATION WAS A MISTAKE": ANGER AT BEING INTERNED

If this country doesn't want me they can throw me out. What do they know about loyalty? I'm as loyal as anyone in this country. Maybe I'm as loyal as President Roosevelt. What business did they have asking me a question like that?

I was born in Hawaii. I worked most of my life on the West Coast. I have never been to Japan. We would have done anything to show our loyalty. All we wanted to do was to be left alone on the coast. . . . My wife and I lost $10,000 in that evacuation. She had a beauty parlor and had to give that up. I had a good position worked up as a gardener, and was taken away from that. We had a little home and that's gone now. . . .

What kind of Americanism do you call that? That's not democracy. That's not the American way, taking everything away from people. . . . Where are the Germans? Where are the Italians? Do they ask them questions about loyalty? . . .

Nobody had to ask us about our loyalty when we lived on the coast. You didn't find us on relief. . . . We were first when there was any civic drive. We were first with the money for the Red Cross and the Community Chest or whatever it was. Why didn't that kind of loyalty count? Now they're trying to push us to the East. Its always "further inland, further inland." I say, "To hell with it!" Either they let me go to the coast and prove my loyalty there or they can do what they want with me. If they don't want me in this country, they can throw me out. . . .

Evacuation was a mistake, there was no need for it. The government knows this, Why don't they have enough courage to come out and say so, so that these people won't be pushed around? . . .

I've tried to cooperate. Last year I went out on furlough and worked on the best fields in Idaho. There was a contract which said that we would be brought back here at the end of the work. Instead we just sat there. . . . We had to spend our own money. The farmers won't do anything for you. They treat you all right while you're working hard for them but as soon as your time is up, you can starve. . . . When I got back to [Camp] Manzanar, nearly all my money that I had earned was gone. . . .

## Restrictive Covenant, Pittsfield Township, Michigan, November 27, 1941

*As larger numbers of African Americans moved to the North and West during and after World War I, white realtors and homeowners became increasingly sophisticated at keeping their neighborhoods "lily-white." Toward this end, one of the most effective tools used was the restrictive covenant, an agreement between the seller and buyer not to rent or sell property to a particular group of people. These agreements excluded a wide variety of people—besides African Americans, Asian Americans, Latino/a Americans, Jews, Poles, Italians, and so forth. Throughout the urban North, however, as this document indicates, African Americans were these covenants' primary targets.*

*Source:* In Thomas Guglielmo's possession.

## AMERICAN TITLE CO.

## *AGREEMENT*

Louis O. Andrews & wife

to

Ivan Norman Cuthbert, et al

Register's Office Washtenaw County ss. Received for record the 27th. day of November A.D. 1941 at 8:30 o'clock A.M., and recorded to Liber 354 of Deeds on page 476.

Katherine W. Shsu Register of Deeds

Nilen Mager Clerk

## MODIFICATION OF BUILDING AND USE RESTRICTIONS DARLINGTON AND DARLINGTON NO. ONE SUBDIVISIONS PITTSFIELD TOWNSHIP, WASHTENAW COUNTY, MICHIGAN

THIS AGREEMENT made and entered into this 7th day of November, A.D. 1941, by and between Louis Andrews and Belle N. Andrews, his wife, of the City of Ann Arbor, Michigan, parties of the first part, and the undersigned lot owners in Darlington Subdivision and Darlington Subdivision Number One, parties of the second part.

WITNESSETH: . . .

NOW, THEREFORE, in consideration of the execution of this agreement by each of the other parties hereto and in consideration of the mutual benefits to be obtained by each of the signers hereof, it is agreed between the undersigned persons, each for himself or herself as follows: . . .

10. No lot in said Subdivisions shall be used or occupied by persons not of the Caucasian race except as guests or servants domiciled with an owner or tenant. . . .

12. Anything in this indenture to the contrary notwithstanding, all of the restrictions, conditions and covenants herein contained shall run with the land and continue until January 1, 1965 and thereafter the said covenants may be annulled, waived, changed or modified by the assent, evidenced by appropriate agreement entitled to record, of the owners of two-thirds of the assessed value of the property in this Subdivision, but otherwise shall continue of full force and effect.

13. Invalidation of any one of said restrictions or any part thereof by judgment or court order shall in no wise affect any or the other provisions, which shall remain in full force and effect.

## Memorandum from Elmer Henderson to Will Maslow, December 20, 1944

*Dozens of hate-strikes (targeting African Americans almost exclusively) erupted all across the United States during World War II. This document, from a wartime federal agency, describes one such strike occurring on the South Side of Chicago in December 1944. It illuminates especially well the various and (sometimes) competing roles the federal government, management, union leaders, union rank and file, local politicians, and African American workers played in these conflicts.*

*Source:* Civilian Records Unit (Archives II), RG 228, Entry no. 31, Box 404, Folder "Strike data," NARA.

DATE *December 20, 1944*

TO: Will Maslow, Director of Field Operations

FROM: *Elmer W. Henderson,* Regional Director, Region *VI*

RE: *Final* Report on Work Stoppages Involving Racial Factors (Intermediate or Final)

Report by *Henderson* Investigation by *Henderson-Gibson*

1. Employer involved *Pullman-Standard Car Mfg. Co., Shipbuilding Division*
2. Address of plant or plants involved *Calumet Shipyard, 130th & Stoney Island, Chicago, Illinois, United Steel Workers, CIO.*
3. Union involved *Local 2928*
4. Race of Strikers *White*
5. Date strike began *12/5/44*
6. Date strike ended *12/13/44*
7. Was strike authorized or "wildcat" *"Wildcat"*
8. Type of Union security *Maintenance of Membership*
9. Number of workers idle *at peak 1,100*
10. Number of man-days lost —
11. By whom and when was FEPC called in *Was not called in.*
12. Were there active complaints on file with FEPC before strike *Yes (but not in department in which strike occurred.)*
13. Incident which precipitated strike *Barney Morgan, a Negro, was appointed a leader over a mixed group of seven workers in the pipe-fitters' department.*
14. *Background (Include information on*

company policy toward minority groups before walkout; causes of strike underlying precipitating incident; factors or groups obstructing non-discriminatory policy). *The Pullman-Standard Car Mfg. Company in both its aircraft and shipbuilding divisions has had one of the better records in the Chicago area in the employment and upgrading of minorities. The November ES-270 report for the shipyard and the car shops shows 949 non-whites out of a total employment of 6,764.*

15. *Events during strike* (Include settlement efforts of interested agencies, and describe FEPC's participation). *See attached report. During the first several days of the strike there were rumors of possible racial clashes but no incident of this nature did occur.*

16. *Settlement of strike.* (Explain particularly disposition of precipitating factors, commitments made, and any revisions in company or union policy.) *See attached report. After one week, the strikers voted to return to work. None of their demands were met by the company and the Negro leader was never removed from his job. The company and the union adhered strictly to their positions and no alteration of policy was made.*

17. *General Comments* See attached report. *A great deal of credit should go to the Negro workers of this yard who in the face of the most provocative circumstances did not lose their heads or attempt retaliation against the strikers. This indicates a maturity that is well worth recognition.*

(Attach extra sheet if necessary)

## THE PULLMAN CAR MANUFACTURING COMPANY, SHIPBUILDING DIVISION STRIKE, DECEMBER 5–13, 1944

### Chronology

*December 5*

We first learned of the strike by a call from H. V. Sherman, Assistant to the Works Manager of the Company to Examiner Gibson around 3 P.M. Mr. Sherman seems to be about the highest authority in industrial relations in this company. We volunteered to get in touch with the local CIO leaders in an effort to get the men back to work. We tried to reach the proper officials of the United Steel Workers that afternoon but were unsuccessful. At first only 175 men stopped work.

*December 6*

The work stoppage spread but the men did not leave the yard. We reached George Mischeau, Sub-District Director of USW-CIO who stated categorically that the union did not support the strike and promised to try to get the men back to work.

Examiner Gibson talked to Lt. Commander H. L. Nunn, Director of Industrial Relations for the Ninth Naval District who had already sent Lt. C. P. Tiedje out to the plant. Commander Nunn was not acquainted with all of the details and was awaiting word from Lt. Tiedje. He promised to keep in close touch with us.

Mr. Gibson conferred with Mr. Sherman who declared management would stand fast on the appointment of the colored leader. He then called Commissioner Vincent, head of the United States Conciliation Service who had already sent a representative to the plant and was awaiting a report.

Howard Gould, Industrial Secretary of the Chicago Urban League called and said he would urge the CIO leaders to show more vigor in getting the men back to work. In a later conversation we agreed that Gould would call George Weaver in Washington and urge him to get Philip Murray to act. Gould did call.

Justin McCarthy, Labor Editor of the Chicago Sun called and gave us all of his information on the situation and asked for a statement. I did not desire to be quoted at that time. He promised to give me all of the information he could get. Richard Durham of the Chicago Defender also called for information and a statement.

We called Harry Walker, Acting Executive Director of the Mayor's Committee on Race Relations, to get the Committee alert to the situation and to see that Lt. Barnes, Chief of the Labor Detail of the Chicago Police Department had a sufficient number of men on the spot, that he make them aware of the delicacy of the situation and the need for careful handling. (This was probably one of our best moves as the subsequent support we received from Lt. Barnes and the police was excellent).

*December 7*
The situation developed into a real strike with the men leaving the plant and urging others to do likewise. The peak of 1,100 was reached out of a total day shift personnel of 2,400.

On Thursday we made periodic checks with management on the status of the strike. Management remained firm in the face of the strikers' demands that the Negro be removed.

We checked with McCarthy who had spent some time around the plant. He said the strike was spreading. We checked with Gould who planned to go out to the plant and called Ira Latimer, Executive Secretary of the Chicago Civil Liberties Committee to appeal to the strikers for racial tolerance and urge them to return to work.

We called Harry Walker to get the Mayor to make a statement and personnelly urge the strikers back to work. Walker called to say that Acting Chairman Peabody of the Mayor's Committee had talked to the Mayor and had urged him to call in the disputants which the Mayor had agreed to do. I then requested Walker to check with Police Lt. Barnes. He did and found that many of the strikers gathered around the gate of the plant that same morning to discourage other workers from going in. Lt. Barnes promised to break this up Friday morning.

We checked with Commander Nunn who informed me that the strikers were calling a mass meeting for the morning on 115th Street in a hall over a tavern. He also informed me that the original striking group was approximately one-half CIO members and one-half non-CIO including AFL and UMW-District 50 members and sympathizers. We called Latimer to attend the meeting and Walker to inform Lt. Barnes.

Sherman called later to say the strike was spreading and to confirm that the strikers had called a mass meeting for the following morning. He said he would not attend.

We decided that Examiner Schultz should attend the mass meeting as an observer.

Chairman Ross called from Washington to say he had been informed of the strike by Admiral Crisp of the Navy Department who appeared to believe that the strike was caused by the demotion of a white leader solely for the purpose of putting on a colored man. He suggested that both men might serve as leaders of the gang until the trouble blew over. I checked later with Commander Nunn who said the Admiral must have mis-interpreted his report.

We conferred with Commissioner Murray of the Conciliation Service who seemed a little hazy on the matter and was a little piqued at the company for its lack of cooperation with his office. Commissioner Murray felt that regardless of the merits of the issue the cause of the strike should be removed (meaning Morgan, the colored leader).

Later in the evening I conferred with Edward L. Doty, a Negro employee of the company and vice president of the union who gave me more background on the racial friction which had developed in the plant. He felt that the management had deliberately provoked the strikers and was definitely playing Negro against white worker to break up the union.

*December 8*

In the morning Miss Schultz went out to the mass meeting but was unable to gain admittance. The strikers would only allow workers with badges to enter.

Mr. Gibson conferred with Commissioner Vincent who informed him that the strike was not yet settled and that the company did not wish to deal further with the Conciliation Service.

Mr. Gibson called Mr. Sherman who informed him that the situation remained about the same. The strikers were having a meeting but he did not know what was being considered. He reiterated the company's position that it would stand firm on its action.

We called Commander Nunn and reached Lt. Tiedje. He also said the meeting was being held but no Navy man was in attendance. It was his hope that the Mayor or some outside organization could be induced to call a meeting of all the parties and exhort the strikers to do the just and patriotic thing and return to work.

McCarthy of the Sun gave me a summary of what occurred at the mass meeting as follows:

"Mr. Germano, Director of the District Office of the United Steel Workers of America, CIO, said that he had laid the cards on the table and that he told these men that they had no grievance, that their complaint was not just, that the union would not represent them, and, in other words, that none of them had any right to tell the management who could be put on the supervisory jobs. He said that the CIO union etc. was all against racial discrimination and these men were putting this on a racial basis and so had better go back to work.

"Mr. Germano was booed off the platform by all of these some 500 men. They held their meeting in a combination meeting room and tavern and had beer ever so often. It gave me a bad feeling because there was a lot of southern element there and their kind of talk was that way also—like—nothing like this would have happened down there. . . . sort of hill-billy stuff.

"I just stood around and listened. I got the impression that the leaders of this thing are slightly screwey where the southern element is concerned. The leaders sometimes are fairly sensible but are giving the southern element a chance to brew among the men here. Since at involved race, the few southern men got into the thing right away.

"The plant had a man there but they do not want it known. He is a plain-clothes man.

"The men in the meeting decided by vote, and they claimed it was unanimous, that they would not go back to work until the Navy "took over or until the Negro was demoted. The Navy apparently has no intention of doing this or does the company. So Germano said the men could stay out till hell freezes over. He has tried to get them back for three days and is now rather angry about it. As far as he is concerned, it is the end for these men. Mr. Sherman said the same thing. They were here and appeared on the platform as officials of the union and told the men what they thought, but the men would not go back to work. A lot of men, of course, are not union men.

"The meeting was badly organized with no good leadership. Everyone wanted to be boss. More people were busy keeping the newspaper men out than were sitting in the meeting.

"The policemen were kept out at first but the men finally let them in. The policemen said all they wanted to do was to keep order and made them take all the beer bottles out so that no one would get hit over the head with them. There was no flare-up of temper but there was a general overall feeling of emotion about the whole business.

"I think, however, that from what I have seen, the whole thing is pretty well broken up. Two hundred dribbled back to the plant this morning. I got this from Lt. Barnes and Mr. Quinn, the company public relations man. From their two estimates, about 200 went back to the plant.

"These men do not have any company support or the majority of the workers so they cannot win. The men made up a small amount of the workers . . . 500 out of 2500 . . . and only about 150 who are really in earnest. These 150 were the sort of a mob that will join anything to raise hell for a couple of days."

We then called Robert Lasch of the Editorial Staff of the Sun and asked for an editorial. He agreed and promised one for Sunday.

*December 9*
Examiner Gibson called Rozinski in the company's industrial relations department who informed him that all but 400 of the strikers had returned to work that morning and he felt that the strike would be completely broken by Monday. Actually, he said, many of the 400 still out would have returned that day but their

jobs were dependent upon those of the others who were out. He commended the loyalty of the colored workers during the crisis.

John Moresy, president of the local union called to inform me that the company was not wholly virtuous in this affair. He said that there was an aggressive pressure group among Negroes and an anti-Negro pressure group among the whites although most of the workers were tolerant and race relations in general had been good. He believed the company had no consistent policy but merely tried to meet the demands of the pressure groups no matter how contradictory they may have been. He cited other instances of gross discrimination against Negroes in the yard which the union had been trying unsuccessfully to correct for months.

*December 10*
The Chicago Sun printed an editorial on the subject. Copy attached.

*December 11*
The company was unable to state the status of the strike due to a heavy snowstorm in Chicago and a high rate of absences that day.

*December 12*
The strikers voted to return to work as their effort had been fruitless.

*December 13*
The strikers returned to work for the morning shift.

## Jackie Robinson to President Dwight Eisenhower, 1958

*Heralded as the first African American to break Major League baseball's color bar in 1947, Robinson went on to a successful business career. In this 1958 letter he challenges the president's call to black leaders to remain patient about civil rights.*

*Source:* Jackie Robinson, letter, Records of the United States Information Agency, RG 306 (306-PS-50–4730), *Still Pictures Branch*, National Archives at College Park, MD).

CHOCK FULL O' NUTS
425 LEXINGTON AVENUE
NEW YORK 17, N.Y.
MAY 13, 1958
THE PRESIDENT
THE WHITE HOUSE
WASHINGTON. D.C.

My dear Mr. President;
I was sitting in the audience at the Summit Meeting of Negro Leaders yesterday when you said we must have patience. On hearing you say this, I felt like standing up and saying, "Oh no! Not again."

I respectfully remind you sir, that we have been the most patient of all people. When you said we must have self-respect, I wondered how we could have self-respect and remain patient considering the treatment accorded us through the years.

17 million Negroes cannot do as you suggest and wait for the hearts of men to change. We want to enjoy now the rights that we feel we are entitled to as

Americans. This we cannot do unless we pursue aggressively goals which all other Americans achieved over 150 years ago.

As the chief executive of our nation, I respectfully suggest that you unwittingly crush the spirit of freedom in Negroes by constantly urging forbearance and give hope to those pro-segregation leaders like Governor Faubus who would take from us even those freedoms we now enjoy. Your own experience with Governor Faubus is proof enough that forbearance and not eventual integration is the goal the pro-segregation leaders seek.

In my view, an unequivocal statement backed up by action such as you demonstrated you could take last fall in dealing with Governor Faubus if it became necessary, would let it be known that America is determined to provide—in the near future—for Negroes—the freedoms we are entitled to under the constitution.

*Respectfully yours,*
*Jackie Robinson*

# CHAPTER 8
# RACIAL AND ETHNIC RELATIONS IN AMERICA, 1965–2000

## TIMOTHY J. MEAGHER

ON MARCH 21, 1965, MARTIN Luther King, Jr. led a march across the Pettus Bridge in Selma, Alabama, on the road to Montgomery, the state's capitol. The march capped a brutal battle between police and black protesters, including a vicious assault on marchers on this very bridge by local and state police just weeks before. As with other demonstrations of the era, most notably in Birmingham, Alabama, in 1963, the whole world was watching this confrontation on television. Black protesters may thus have been bloodied, but ultimately, they, not the police, the city of Selma, nor the state of Alabama would triumph. On August 6, 1965, President Lyndon B. Johnson would sign the Voting Rights Act of 1965, the second major piece of civil rights legislation passed in little over a year. Solid majorities in Congress for this new civil rights act and rapidly rising support for the civil rights movement suggested that race relations in the United States had reached an historic pass.

Over the next thirty-five years, from the march across the Pettus Bridge to our own time, racial and ethnic relations, boundaries, and identities in the United States were entirely transformed. A new configuration of ethnic and racial relations, a new structure of thinking about ethnicity and race—a new discourse—emerged. Before the 1960s, white privilege and power had kept African, Asian, and Latino Americans out of the arena of real political and economic competition. African Americans were still disfranchised in their heartland of the American South and only slowly and painfully beginning to move up economic and political hierarchies in northern cities. Native Americans were a forgotten people, most wasting away in desultory and desperate poverty on reservations or in the poorest neighborhoods of western cities. Asian Americans were a tiny minority, only 0.5 percent of the population as late as 1960, because restrictive immigration laws had choked off their entry into the United States. Latinos, made up largely of a Mexican American lumpen proletariat in the Southwest and impoverished Puerto Ricans in eastern cities, were, if anything, even more marginalized than African or Asian Americans.

Only whites competed among each other for important economic and political stakes or cultural recognition. Divisions among whites were still important—economically, socially, and politically—as late as the early 1960s. Ethnic divisions appeared to have collapsed into a religious "triple melting pot" of Protestant, Catholic, and Jew by the 1950s, but the boundaries separating those religious groups still seemed durable, and religious group identities still seemed charged at the end of that decade. Widely acclaimed studies of ethnic and racial relations in the early 1960s by Gerhard Lenski on Detroit and Daniel Patrick Moynihan and Nathan Glazer on New York predicted, as Moynihan and Glazer stated, "Religion [as well as race] seem to define the major groups into which American society is evolving as the specifically national aspect of ethnicity declines."

In the period after 1965 a new kind of ethnic and racial relations would emerge. Not only ethnic but even religious divisions among whites would weaken, as boundaries separating Catholics, Protestants, and even Jews grew porous. This process had origins long before 1965 and by the millennium even yet would remain incomplete. Nevertheless, the merging of white ethnic and religious groups—by any measure, residential integration, the diversification of the economic elite, or intermarriage—accelerated rapidly after 1965. At the same time, African, Native, Asian, and Latino Americans entered into arenas of political and economic competition and struggles for cultural recognition with a heretofore unknown power and confidence. Together these groups remade understanding of American racial and ethnic relations. In the case of Native, Asian, and Latino Americans, this was quite literally true, for all of them not only began to assert claims for equality and recognition with a new vigor, they also began to invent pantribal Indian or panethnic Asian or Latino American identities that had hardly existed before. As dynamic as those groups were, however, it was African Americans who took the lead in asserting minority claims most aggressively and consistently, and African Americans who were most responsible for the new configuration. By the 1980s, all of these groups had invented a new conception, a new language of American social and ethnic relations, a language of "minorities" and "multiculturalism" that set African, Asian, Latino, and Native Americans apart against an undifferentiated white America. How much that conception has fit the realities of racial and ethnic boundaries, identities, and relations, and whether it, too, will soon dissolve into a new configuration is difficult to judge or predict at this time, the beginning of a new millennium.

The civil rights movement that reached its peak in 1965 had been dedicated to eliminating Jim Crow—the state impositions of racial inferiority and discrimination that existed throughout much of the South. Buoyed by the discrediting of scientific racism that followed the defeat of the Nazis, by the American government's sensitivity to third-world nations during the Cold War, by the Democratic Party's recognition of black voters in northern cities, and by the decisions of an activist Supreme Court, the civil rights movement waged a steady, heroic, and successful "war" of nonviolent protest against Jim Crow from the mid-fifties to the midsixties. The Civil Rights Acts of 1964 and 1965 broke forever state-enforced Jim Crow in the South, and made deliberate, transparent state racism forever impossible.

Yet even as King and his followers crossed the Pettus Bridge in triumph, African Americans were already rethinking the place they sought in American life and how they expected to get there.

Though the mainstream civil rights organizations, the NAACP, and King's own Southern Christian Leadership Conference, remained committed to the goal of integration and tactics of nonviolent protest and legal challenge, new voices and new leaders emerged to question both, even as the movement was reaching its zenith. The most articulate new leader was a former Nation of Islam minister named Malcolm X, a man of stunning rhetorical gifts and charisma, who became a powerful influence on young black activists. Disturbed by its corruption, Malcolm X had left the Nation of Islam in 1964, but he carried with him its emphases on black solidarity, suspicion of whites, and openness to violent resistance. In the year between his departure from the Black Muslims and his assassination in 1965, Malcom X attempted to broaden and deepen that ideology with a critique of capitalism and identification with other colonized peoples.

Malcolm X's powerful personality, sharp rhetoric, and dramatic murder has made him a legendary figure for young blacks to this day, but he had a profound impact in his own time. In the early 1960s, while still a member of the Black Muslims, Malcolm X's influence spread through chapters of the Congress of Racial Equality (CORE) throughout the North. In 1965, he also had a powerful impact on Student Nonviolent Coordinating Committee (SNCC) activists when he delivered an electrifying speech to SNCC workers on the eve of the Selma protests. In 1963, CORE's members ousted James Farmer in favor of Floyd McKissick, and in 1965, Stokely

Carmichael took over SNCC. Both new leaders were militants and sympathetic to appeals to black solidarity. Carmichael quickly became the spokesman for a new vision of Black goals and strategies. In June of 1966, in a Greenwood, Mississippi, schoolyard Carmichael talked not of integration or nonviolence but "Black Power." The next year Carmichael wrote a book with the political scientist Charles Hamilton that defined Black Power as "a call for black people in the country to unite, to recognize their heritage, to build a sense of community . . . to define their own goals, to lead their own organizations, and to support those organizations." Yet, as Manning Marable notes, meanings of Black Power quickly came to vary across a wide political spectrum. Some on the left understood Black Power as a clarion call to a political and economic revolution and perhaps even the creation of a separate black state. Yet black Republicans—with Richard Nixon's blessing—also seized on the phrase to suggest that Black Power could best be translated as Black Capitalism. If left and right sometimes stretched the meaning of Black Power beyond recognition, the phrase was not hollow. Its emergence marked a major turning point in racial and ethnic relations in the United States. Tamar Jacoby contends that by the spring of 1967, less than a year after Carmichael's Black Power speech in Mississippi, the protest movements of the early 1960s seemed a "distant memory." Jacoby asserts: "Activists' clothes, their talk, their image, their very body language had changed completely. The word 'Negro' was virtually

dead, so was the phrase 'civil rights' and the idea of a multiracial crusade."

Jacoby exaggerates, but it was clear that African American understandings of their place in America were changing, and not just at the elite level of activists and intellectuals, but also below, among young African Americans living in northern cities. Beginning in Harlem in 1964 and rising to a crescendo in Detroit and Newark in 1967, African American ghettoes in cities across the United States erupted in riots. The eruption in Los Angeles of the Watts ghetto in 1965 cost thirty-four lives and forty million dollars in property damage. In Detroit forty-three people died, almost two thousand were injured, and fires ravaged fourteen square miles. Even the nation's Capital was not spared. In April of 1968, Washington's black ghettoes exploded. Martin Luther King's assassination touched off the Washington conflagration, but many of the other riots erupted after confrontations between blacks and white police officers. In Harlem in 1964, for example, residents rioted after a white police officer shot a fifteen-year-old black youth while trying to stop a fight. In Detroit, too, the spark came after police raided an after-hours nightclub in a black neighborhood. In all, the race riots from 1964 to 1972 resulted in more than 250 deaths, 10,000 serious injuries, and 60,000 arrests.

The riots suggested that the new militancy summed up in the phrase Black Power had deep and broad roots in the African American community. This new militancy was not all-pervasive among African Americans; indeed, polling data right up until King's death suggested broader support for him and his integrationist goals among blacks than for the newer Black Power advocates. Nevertheless, there was a palpable shift in sentiment even among those who continued to pay homage to King.

In large part, this was because of the very success of the civil rights movement. Julian Bond has described Black Power as "a natural extension of the civil rights movement . . . from the courtroom to the streets . . . [to the] ballot box to the meat of politics, the organization of votes into self interest units." In practical terms, the Voting Rights Act had finally guaranteed blacks political rights and permitted them to compete for political power anywhere in the United States. Black Power was the new slogan of that competition. In a less tangible but meaningful way, the civil rights movement and its successes had also aroused African Americans everywhere, helped them to shed fears born of years of savage repression, and raised their expectations of equality. Yet the civil rights movement, having accomplished those goals, could not move into the next phase. Civil rights protest tactics worked effectively in the South to provoke third parties, sympathetic whites in the North, and the federal government to put pressure on the southern states. There was strong white support in the North for the crusade to sweep away state legislated discrimination. Yet when the movement turned to the North itself, to cities like Chicago, it foundered among the rising expectations of black ghetto dwellers and the ambivalence or outright hostility of many northern whites. A change in tactics and attitude, a new militancy, had been brewing among members of northern CORE chapters, particularly in San Francisco and Brooklyn, long before the movement's final great southern victory after Selma.

Whatever the reasons, the changes in black strategies and attitudes summed up in Black Power had clearly been made, and they manifested themselves quickly in African American life. Instead of protest politics and the quest for rights, electoral politics and the drive for political office, substantive legislation and patronage began to dominate the black community. The results were impressive. Between March of 1969 and May of 1975, the number of black elected officials tripled from a little less than one thousand to nearly three thousand. In the South, the number of black office holders rose from less than one hundred in 1965 to one thousand in 1975. This was clearly the result of the Voting Rights Act, as the number of blacks registered to vote skyrocketed. In Mississippi it grew from 6.7 percent before 1965 to 59.8 percent of age-eligible blacks by 1969. Many of the newly elected, particularly in the South, won only minor posts—councilmen or school committeemen in small towns or cities. Yet almost every major city in the country would elect an African American mayor between 1965 and 1990, beginning with Carl Stokes in Cleveland and Kenneth Gibson in Newark, and ultimately including Coleman Young of Detroit, Maynard Jackson of Atlanta,

Harold Washington of Chicago, Tom Bradley of Los Angeles, Wilson Goode of Philadelphia, David Dinkins of New York, and Kurt Schmoke of Baltimore. The number of black congressmen also rose from three in 1961 to thirteen in 1971 and to thirty-nine in 1993.

Black Power was not just a commitment to political mobilization; it was also a call for cultural revival and recognition. The two were not unrelated; black pride and solidarity undergirded the push for political power. In 1972, Imamu Baraka, the poet; Richard Hatcher, Mayor of Gary, Indiana; and Charles Diggs, a congressman from Detroit, presided over a black political convention in Gary that drew more than twelve thousand participants who made that link explicit. Yet Black Power's cultural program was, in many ways, far more successful than even the new Black politics. Beginning in the late 1960s Black Power advocates launched an attack on accepted American ideals of assimilation and Anglo-American cultural supremacy. As Stokely Carmichael's and Charles V. Hamilton's *Black Power* flatly stated, "we reject the goal of assimilation into middle class America." Native, Asian, and Latino American activists, and even some white ethnic leaders, would take up this rhetorical assault on Anglo-American culture and it would have critically important consequences for American racial and ethnic relations.

Yet of course it had revolutionary consequences for the black community too. It prompted changes in African American life, from new hairstyles and clothes to new holidays—Kwan-zaa—to changes in names—personal names drawn from Islamic or African sources—and changes in the name of the race, substituting black or African American for Negro. Manufacturers, sensitive to this new market of racially conscious Blacks, made their own adjustments, producing everything from Black GI Joe and Barbie dolls to African-theme greeting cards. The most important, visible, and often controversial impact of the Black Power cultural revival was on the curricula of colleges and school systems. Before the late 1960s, the historian John Blassingame estimated, only five graduate history programs in the United States offered African American history courses and all of these were historically black colleges. By the middle 1970s, one observer estimated, there were Black Studies programs or courses in hundreds of colleges and universities across the country. These programs were often born in controversy; strikes and protests took place at schools as diverse as San Francisco State and Cornell University, and these schools would remain embattled throughout the 1970s and 1980s. By the latter decade, the numbers of Black Studies programs had begun to decline, but Black Studies and its offshoot, Afrocentric curricula, remained popular not only among many black college and university students and professors, but in the school departments of predominantly black cities like Detroit and Atlanta. Moreover, even most blacks who rejected what they perceived as the militant Afrocentrism of scholars like Molefi Asante remained fiercely committed to black pride and cultural recognition.

Black Power may not have worked a political revolution, but it had worked a cultural one.

The black revolution that began in the 1960s reverberated far beyond the African American community. Native, Latino, and Asian Americans, inspired by the black example, also began to assert themselves and helped African Americans transform American ideas about race and ethnicity. Yet they did more as well. They "made" new panethnic groups that had never existed before— Native, Latino, and Asian American peoples, out of existing constituent tribal or national groups. With blacks, then, they worked to try to forge a new multicultural nation defined by the four major minorities set against a white majority. Once boasting millions of people in tribes stretching across a North America that they had once ruled alone, the census counted but 523,391 Native Americans in the United States in 1960. The intent of Federal policy in the twentieth century was to encourage Indian assimilation; however, it also unwittingly laid the groundwork for the panethnic Indian identity that emerged in the 1960s. Federally funded Indian boarding schools may have tried to suppress Indian cultures among their charges, but because they drew students from a variety of tribes they also acted as little intra-Indian "melting pots." Policies aimed at terminating tribes and encouraging exodus from the reservation had the same effect. As Indians from all tribes gathered in the cities, they found each other there, discovered common grievances, and forged common organizations and institutions.

Between 1952 and 1972, the federal government helped to relocate an estimated hundred thousand Indians to cities where they joined thousands more who had migrated to urban areas on their own.

As it would for other minorities (Latinos and Asian Americans), the black-led civil rights crusade and its successor, the Black Power movement, sparked a Native American movement that would transform the meaning of being Indian in America. Indian activism had little direct connection with either the black-led civil rights movement or later Black Power organizations, but both clearly inspired and helped shaped the new Native American protest. As Joanne Nagel states, "Red Power borrowed from civil rights organizational forms, rhetoric, and tactics but modified them to meet the specific needs and symbolic purposes of Indian grievances, targets, and locations." Political stirrings were noticeable in the Indian community as early as 1961, when representatives from sixty tribes met at the University of Chicago to organize and lay out a common political strategy. The National Indian Youth Council (NIYC), formed out of that meeting, became a kind of nursery for later activists. In the mid-1960s, several tribes sponsored "fish-ins" to assert their claims to special treaty rights in disputed waters and territories. In 1966, Indians from several tribes gathered to protest and ultimately disrupt a meeting between the Secretary of the Interior, Stewart Udall, and the staff of the Bureau of Indian Affairs in Santa Fe, New Mexico. That same year, it appears, Vine

Deloria, Jr., used the phrase Red Power for the first time in a speech he made to the National Congress of American Indians.

It was, however, the occupation of Alcatraz Island in the middle of San Francisco Bay by scores of Indians on November 20, 1969, that sparked a new Red Power movement into life. The Alcatraz protesters pointed to a clause in an 1868 treaty between the Federal government and the Sioux to justify their occupation. That clause allowed Indians to claim unused federal property (in this case, the abandoned prison) on land that once had been tribal property but had been ceded to Federal authorities. The occupiers demanded that the island be remade into a center for Native American studies, an Indian Center for Ecology, and a training school. They stayed on the island for nineteen months, held news conferences, convened powwows and even launched occasional bow and arrow assaults on passing boats. The protest did not end until June 11, 1971, when Federal marshals removed the last fifteen remaining activists from the island. Alcatraz was a turning point in American Indian history, a decisive act giving birth to a Red Power movement. Indian activists like Deloria, Frances Wise, and George Horsecapture all agreed that Alcatraz "was a master stroke of Indian activism," and "a major turning point." Another veteran of Indian protest later told Joanne Nagel, "it started with Alcatraz; we got back our worth, our pride, our dignity, our humanity." Alcatraz not only sparked the Red Power movement to life; it embodied the movement's new panethnic identity.

The activists who took over the island were largely urban Indians. They included Sioux, Navajo, Cherokee, Mohawks, Yakimas, and Omahas. As significantly, they self-consciously celebrated a new panethnic identity, calling themselves the "Indians of All Tribes," who stated in their initial press release, "We the native Americans re-claim the land known as Alcatraz island in the name of all American Indians."

Alcatraz touched off nearly a decade of Red Power protests across the country. Most were, like Alcatraz, "supratribal," drawing on, and enacted in behalf of, a wide and various range of Native American peoples. Many were coordinated, or at least inspired, by a new Indian organization, the American Indian Movement (AIM), founded in Minneapolis in 1968 to fight for Indian civil rights and made up largely of urban Indians of diverse tribes. In 1970 and 1971, Indians occupied Fort Lawton and Fort Lewis, in Washington State, and Ellis Island, the old immigration depot in New York harbor, and tried to "invade" the Bureau of Indian Affairs in Washington, D.C. In 1972 caravans of Indians crossed the country in a well-publicized descent on the BIA's offices. After 1972, protests took on a more violent tone and turned from civil rights to treaty rights issues. From February to May of 1973, activists took over the village of Wounded Knee, the site of the last great conflict in the Indian wars on the Pine Ridge reservation in South Dakota. Two Indians were killed and many more Indians and whites wounded in that protest as gun battles broke out between activists and federal officials. The last major protest event in the decade was the "Longest Walk," another march on Washington in 1978.

By the time the Red Power protest movement had fizzled out in the late 1970s it had helped make Indians a far more powerful force in American politics than at any time in their twentieth-century history. The Indian population was too small to produce the kinds of gains in elected or appointed officials that marked African Americans' rising political power. Yet Indians' political clout was evident in the favorable legislation they wrung from Congress in the 1970s: the Self-Determination Act of 1975, the Health Care Improvement Act of 1976, and the Indian Child Welfare Act of 1978. Federal spending on Native Americans also skyrocketed, rising 22 percent a year from the 1960s until the late 1970s. Money for urban Indians alone rose from $8.5 million to $95.6 million over the same period. The Red Power protesters helped this cause by stoking Native American solidarity and making Indian issues more visible. They may also have acted as a radical foil that more moderate, conventional organizations, like the National Congress of American Indians and the National Tribal Chairman's Association, used to their advantage in negotiating with Congress and federal administrators. However they won their gains, Red Power produced tangible results.

Like Black Power, perhaps even more so, Red Power was as much a cultural clarion call as a battle cry for political struggle. Red Power's call for a renewal of Indian pride was electric. One Native American remembered that this new spirit of Indian pride swept his reservation like a "tornado" in the late 1960s and early 1970s. Yet, as with Black Power, Red Power was not just in the air; it worked a revolution in Indian culture, spawning new institutions and organizations dedicated to a revival of Native American culture. Over the last thirty years tribes across the United States, for example, have set up their own museums to interpret their cultures and traditions to their own people and visitors alike. In 1998, there were over one hundred and fifty such museums listed in the Smithsonian Institution's Tribal Museum Directory, and they meet regularly in a museum association known as the "Keepers of the Treasures." As that name suggests, Native Americans have been as concerned with regaining control of their culture as with educating their own people and others about it. Native Americans have thus sought to retrieve sacred objects and ancestral remains from white-run institutions that had collected them for study and display. In 1990, Native Americans helped push through the Native American Graves Protection and Repatriation Act to ensure such retrievals. In addition to museums, Indians have established their own radio shows, language classes, and tribal colleges. Today thirty-three tribal colleges, scattered from Michigan to California and Washington State to New Mexico, are members of the American Indian Higher Education Consortium. At the same time a number of major colleges and universities, including Arizona, California at Berkeley, Nebraska, Dartmouth, and Montana, have established Native American studies programs and many more offer courses in Native American history or literature.

These efforts did not merely revive specific tribal cultures and loyalties, however; Red Power political and cultural movements began to define a new people, a pantribal Indian people. In this way Red Power differed significantly from Black Power, which built on an existing race-wide consciousness of kind. Red Power emerged out of the Indian communities of the cities where tribal distinctions had blurred and intertribal marriage was common. From the beginning, organizations like AIM or NIYC pushed agendas that "emphasized the rights of all tribes and all Indians." In part such pantribalism was simply a pragmatic recognition of how Indians could operate most effectively within the American political system. Leaders understood they could make a more powerful impact on the Federal government as a broad national Indian people than as local tribes. Deloria has argued, "Pan-Indianism . . . accepted the definition of Indians as an American minority group and sought to make the group an identifiable constituency with recognizable influence, a group to whom successful white politicians owed favors. Thus today, we often talk about the Indian vote . . . we hardly ever . . . speak of the tribal vote." Yet through the Red Power movement, Pan-Indianism has become more than a political strategy; it has become a racial identity, emotionally felt and marked by distinctive "Indian" cultural customs. These included some rituals originally rooted in the cultures of specific tribes, like the sweat lodge, that eventually came to transcend their tribal

origins and became "one of the things [all] Indians did." "By the 1970s," Deloria suggests, "it was possible to find wholly new kinds of behavior generally accepted as Indian." Indeed, as early as 1973, a survey of Arapahoe and Shoshone high school students in Wyoming found that almost all of them identified themselves "supratribally" as well as tribally—as Native Americans or American Indians as well as Shoshone or Arapahoe. The results of the political and cultural mobilization of Native Americans were nothing short of revolutionary. Indians, pounded into passivity and hounded towards extinction in the 1950s, became confident, aggressive, and often successful political players by the 1970s. As important, buoyed by political protest, they regained pride in their heritage and helped black Americans challenge older American conceptions of assimilation. The revival of Indian pride had a remarkable effect on the Indian population. Dwindling down through the first part of the twentieth century, the Native American population began to grow after 1930, initially slowly, but by the 1960s and 1970s very rapidly. Indeed, between 1960 and 1990, the Indian population grew from a little over 500,000 to nearly 1.9 million. Natural increase did not account for this sky-rocketing growth; it involved nothing less than the "deassimilation" of hundreds of thousands of Americans; once ashamed of or indifferent to their native roots, they were now eager to re-claim their native past.

Latinos had lived within the continental boundaries of the United States before Anglo- or African Americans, but it was not until the twentieth century that migration from Mexico, Puerto Rico, Cuba, and other Latin American countries began to make Latinos a formidable force. Integration into world markets provoked economic dislocations throughout much of Latin America and many of the same countries suffered from the disruptions of war and revolution. Meanwhile, American economic growth accelerated, and improved communications raised awareness of the contrast between North America's apparent promise and Latin America's plight. By the 1970s and 1980s the urgency to migrate grew so strong that thousands crossed the southern border of the United States surreptitiously, and millions settled into a permanent illegal status after such secret crossings or after their visas for temporary stays ran out. Migration from Latin America to the United States, legal and illegal, thus boomed in the late twentieth century. Migrants from Mexico numbered less than fifty thousand in the 1910s, increased significantly in the 1920s, but fell back during the depression when some Mexican immigrants were even forced to return home. In the 1950s Mexican migration began to pick up again, rapidly accelerating by the 1970s. In the 1950s, about 250,000 Mexicans came to the United States, but by the 1970s the number increased to 650,000, and by the 1980s to over 1.5 million. Puerto Rican migration first reached significant size in the 1940s, and by 1950 there were about 300,000 first- and second-generation Puerto Ricans in the United States. By 1970, because of migration and natural increase, that population had quadrupled to almost 1.4 million and by 1980 had risen to over 2 million. Cubans had nineteenth-century roots in Florida, but the vast majority of today's Cuban Americans or their parents or grandparents came to the United States after Fidel Castro took over Cuba in 1959. From that year to 1990 an estimated eight hundred thousand Cubans fled to the United States. Finally, civil war and economic depression sent Salvadorans and Guatemalans to the United States in the 1970s and 1980s. In 1986, 138,000 Salvadorans, 51,000 Guatemalans and 15,000 Nicaraguans applied for amnesty under the terms of the new immigration law that went into effect that year. By 1990 there were an estimated 22 million Latinos in the United States and the number was rising so quickly that some experts predicted that there would be well over 40 million by 2010.

Like African Americans, Latinos lived on the margins of American economic, political, and cultural life until the 1960s, and, as with African Americans, a revolution in Latino life in the United States began in that decade. Mexican and Puerto Rican struggles for civil rights extended back into the early twentieth century, but the successes of the black-led civil rights movement inspired and energized Latinos as never before. Cesar Chavez and his United Farmworkers Union were among the most successful of the new organizations. Engaging in its first strike in 1965 and winning its first contract battles in 1966, Chavez's UFW was more like a social movement than a union. Learning from King and the black civil rights movements, the UFW did not launch a single strike but a series of continuous strikes blending into a single struggle on behalf of Mexican American farm workers. Chavez also pledged the UFW to nonviolence, a major break from Mexican traditions, and deliberately cultivated the sympathies of a broader public, reaching it through television and tying it to the movement through boycotts and volunteerism. Employing the same tactics as King's SCLC, the UFW's strikes began to blend into a broader civil rights struggle. The UFW would have a checkered subsequent history, but, as Geoffrey Fox has said, "from this period [the late 1960s and afterward] in part, because of Cesar Chavez's strategic discoveries, and in larger part because of the structural changes that had made the movement possible, the history of Mexican American political consciousness ceases to be a separate story from that of other protesting groups in the United States."

In the turbulence of the 1960s, trends of growing group assertion and solidarity in the Latino community paralleled the rise of Black Power among African Americans. As in the black community the new militancy appealed first to younger activists. In 1969, the National Chicano Youth Liberation Conference met for the first time in Denver and endorsed the idea of a national Chicano political party. Shortly thereafter, students in San Antonio founded La Rada Agnate (the United People) to contest local elections. The conference also heard the Chicano poet Aurita proclaim the Spiritual Plan of Aztlan, a vague claim to the American Southwest as the original homeland of the Mexica, Aztec, and other ancient Mexican peoples. In Los Angeles another group, the Brown Berets, emerged out of a church youth group, seeking to pull young Mexican Americans together into a coherent political force. Halfway across the country in Chicago, Illinois, a Puerto Rican gang called the Young Lords began to move from fights over street turf to community organizing. Jose Jiminez, their leader, had been impressed by black protest and inspired by Malcolm X while serving time in jail. By 1969, the Young Lords had established branches in New York and later Philadelphia. Like SNCC or CORE, these organizations led the shift to a more militant Latino politics in the late 1960s and early 1970s, a politics of group solidarity, pride, and self-assertion—"Brown Power."

Yet just as importantly, they saw themselves as members of more than just their own national groups—Mexicans or Puerto Ricans, for example. There were, of course, the black models that they saw as allies in their liberation struggle. Yet they also began to see the even closer links that potentially bound Puerto Ricans and Mexican Americans as Latinos—speakers of the same Spanish language. A riot in the Puerto Rican neighborhood of Chicago, provoked by conflicts with the police, eventually sparked the creation of a Spanish language community organization that served both the city's large Puerto Rican and Mexican American communities. In 1969, Jiminez and the Young Lords moved further afield, traveling to Los Angeles to link up with the leaders of the National Chicano Youth Liberation Conference and the Brown Berets. These were only small groups of young people, but they were pulling out of the radical rhetoric and ideology of the era and using a language of solidarity and liberation to forge a new panethnic identity for the Latino community in the United States. Geoffrey Fox suggests that "it was in the name of solidarity that various Chicano, Puerto Rican, and other Latino groups began exploring the alliances that would become key to building a wider Hispanic identity."

As in the African American community, Latino political mobilization followed quickly upon the emergence of group consciousness. Several groups emerged in the 1970s to encourage Latino voter registration—including, for example, the Southwest Voter Registration and Education Project (1974) and the National Puerto Rican Coalition (1977). The success of such groups is hard to measure. On the one hand, the percentage of Latinos of voting age registered to vote did not increase between 1972 and 1988. Indeed, it fell from a little over 44 percent to 35 percent in that time. Nevertheless, the absolute number of Latinos registered and participating in the election process rose significantly, simply because the volume of Latino migration to the country was so huge. These numbers and a new Latino self-confidence paid off in an increase in elected officials and significant political appointments. By 1993, there were 196 Hispanic mayors in the United States and more than fourteen hundred municipal officials. The latter figure represented a gain of 45 percent from 1983. Progress was, however, most clearly visible at the Federal level. The number of Latino congressmen rose from three

in 1961 to seventeen in 1993. Many of the gains came in the 1980s and 1990s when Latinos picked up eleven seats. As early as 1979, Latino politicians of all backgrounds had created their own organization: the National Association of Latino Elected and Appointed Officials. This increasing electoral strength in turn prompted an accompanying surge in federal appointments. While President Johnson appointed only three Latinos to the federal bench, President Carter selected nine Latino justices.

Again, as for Blacks and Native Americans, Latino or Hispanic Power, or its constituent elements—"Brown," Chicano or "Borriqueno" (Puerto Rican) Power, was as much a cultural movement as a political one. Latinos, like African Americans, challenged prevailing notions of assimilation, attempted to construct or preserve the integrity of group culture, and demanded recognition and respect for their cultural difference. Also as with African Americans, this effort created and drew strength from Hispanic or Latino ethnic studies programs in universities around the United States. In 1984, one survey estimated that 23 percent of higher education institutions in America offered courses in Hispanic studies and 6 percent permitted undergraduates to major in Hispanic or Latino Studies. Frank Bonilla, founder and longtime director of one such Latino Studies Center at the City University of New York, contended that such programs were necessary to rectify the distortions and demeaning stereotypes of standard accounts of Latinos, to help create a Latino intelligentsia, and to maintain a Latino "perspective" in the study of American life and community. In some universities, particularly in California, such programs were Chicano Studies, in the northeast, Puerto Rican Studies, and in the Southeast, at Florida International University, for example, Cuban Studies. Yet some programs broadened to encompass the cultures of a variety of nationalities within the broad framework of Latino Studies.

As with African Americans, Indians, and Latino Americans, a new Asian American solidarity and self-confidence emerged in the critical years of the late 1960s and early 1970s. The Asian American "movement" of that era differed from the other three in a number of ways. The battlegrounds for Asian Americans were more likely to be campuses than neighborhood streets, for example. The initial major battles were the Third World Strikes, at San Francisco State College in the fall and winter of 1968 and 1969 and the University of California at Berkeley in the winter of 1969. William We suggests, "probably more than any other single event, the Third World Strike at San Francisco State symbolized the potential of Asian American activism." The critical organizations in these early battles, the Intercollegiate Chinese for Social Action, the Asian American Political Alliance in California, and Asian Americans for Action on the East Coast drew heavily from college students. This did not mean that the movement had no links to local Chinatowns and other Asian American communities, or that students were not interested in making those links. Indeed, in 1970, members of the AAA estab-

lished the Asian American Community Center in New York's Chinatown and began work to preserve the neighborhood. Still, the initiative in the Asian American movement came largely from the campuses. Another important difference was the importance of the antiwar movement in provoking the new Asian American consciousness. In part, this reflected the movement's campus roots, but it also reflected the special significance of a war in Asia and its racial consequences for Asian people in the United States. Nevertheless, as We notes, "Although the antiwar movement politicized a generation of Asian Americans, the Black Power movement moved them toward the goals of racial equality, social justice, and political empowerment." At the "Asian American Experience in America—Yellow Identity Conference" held in Berkeley in 1969, Isao Fujimoto talked about the need "to shatter the myth of assimilation and to prove how the racist, colonialist majority exploited the minorities."

If the Asian American movement was inspired by Black Power, however, it undertook the same kind of effort as the Latino movement did to raise the consciousness of Asian Americans from various groups and simultaneously knit them together into a single panethnic entity, The names of student organizations suggested this deliberate attempt to forge a new group. Indeed, the Asian American Political Alliance may have been the first organization in American history to use the term Asian American. The choice of the name suggested both the rejection of the western "Oriental," as blacks had rejected Negro, and the recognition, as

Yuji Ichioka argued, that "If we rallied behind the Asian American banner . . . we could extend our influence."

While young Chinese, Japanese, and Filipino Americans caught the spirit of a new "Yellow Power," dramatic changes in immigration to America promised to make that rallying cry more than an empty slogan. Asian immigrants had been all but excluded from the continental United States since the turn of the century. Grudging acknowledgment of Cold War constraints allowed a small trickle of Chinese and other immigrants to enter the United States in the 1950s. In 1965 Congress completely overhauled the immigration laws. Inspired by the civil rights movement, the historic new law did away with the old noxious racist quotas that favored northwestern Europeans. Nevertheless, few believed that the new law would produce any significant changes in the origins of immigrants. While signing the bill, President Johnson remarked, "The bill we sign today is not a revolutionary bill," and Congressman Emmanuel Celler argued that abolition of nationality quotas would not end continued European dominance among the immigrants. Yet taking advantage of the new law's opportunities for educational, occupational, and family reunification exemptions, immigrants poured into the United States from Asia. In the 1970s, millions of Laotian, Cambodian, and Vietnamese refugees fleeing the debacle in Indochina added to this already surging immigrant tide from Asia. The number of Asian Americans thus rose more than 140 percent in the 1970s and more than 100 percent in the 1980s.

These numbers gave the Asian American community more political heft than they had ever enjoyed before. That heft, and the new sense of political consciousness among the Asian American leadership, translated into some important political gains for Asian Americans. By 1992, for example, there were nine Asian American congressmen. Asian Americans also won local offices in Monterey Park, Gardena, Cerritos, and Torrance, California, in the 1980s as well as the governorship of Washington in 1996. Hawai'i is the heartland of Asian American politics, however. In 1990, the Governor, Lieutenant Governor, and fifty-four state legislators were Asian Americans—largely Japanese Americans—in Hawai'i. Despite recent gains, the Asian American population has not increased enough to give the group the kind of voting power that African or Latino Americans can boast of in many states. Furthermore, Asian Americans, particularly the new immigrants, have been, if anything, even less likely to register to vote than members of the other two groups. A survey of California voters in 1990 found that only 39 percent of Asian Americans were registered to vote, compared to 65 percent for whites, 58 percent for blacks and 42 percent for Latinos. On the other hand, Asian American politicians have some advantages the other groups do not. If they cannot tap as many votes, such politicians can and have tapped the rich financial resources of upwardly mobile Asian Americans. Asian Americans, as Yen Le Espiritu points out, have been more likely to donate money to campaigns than other groups, and Asian

American politicians have parlayed those resources into success even when they have run in overwhelmingly non-Asian states or districts.

Ethnic Studies have played an important role for the Asian American movement, perhaps an even more important role than in the African American or Latino American movements. Indeed, the demand for Asian American Studies was the principal goal of the Movement's first major battles, the San Francisco State and California-Berkeley strikes. Students also staged a three-day takeover of a hall at the City University of New York in 1971 to force the establishment of Asian American Studies Programs. William We suggests that the initial willingness of colleges and universities to set up Asian American studies programs lasted only until about 1973, and many Asian American programs disappeared in the late 1970s and 1980s. Yet, he points out, there was a noticeable revival in the 1980s, producing new programs at M.I.T. and new courses and programs at a number of other East Coast colleges. The dramatic increase in Asian American student enrollments fueled this resurgence of interest in schools all across the nation. Like Latino and Black Studies professors, Asian American Studies scholars have sought to "raise the ethnic consciousness and self awareness of Asian American students" and to challenge perceived assimilationist or monocultural biases in the teaching of what America has been or should be. Such efforts, as for many Latino programs, have also helped shape a panethnic Asian American entity by linking together the experiences of Chinese, Korean, Japa-

nese, or other groups by, as one Asian American writer has contended, demonstrating "how Amerika screwed [all of] us."

The late 1960s and early 1970s were a watershed for African, Native, Latino, and Asian Americans. The small radical organizations proclaiming Black, Red, Brown, or Yellow Power foreshadowed broader political mobilization and cultural revivals among blacks, Latinos, and Asian Americans. Politically, the highpoint of this multicultural coalition probably came with Jesse Jackson's campaigns for the Democratic presidential nomination in 1984 and 1988, but through the 1980s and into the 1990s, representatives of all three groups continued to battle for cultural recognition by urging adoption of new course requirements or curriculum changes. Most of these efforts met stiff opposition from many whites, however, and in these and other battles over busing, immigration reform, or affirmative action, or through polarizing events like the O. J. Simpson Trial or the Los Angeles race riots, the boundaries between these groups and the white majority became hotly contested battlegrounds.

Such fights helped sharpen the identities and raise the consciousness of many minorities, but they also helped define a new "whiteness" in America. For while Asian, Latino, and African Americans were mobilizing over the last thirty-five years, whites were changing, too. In part they changed because of an internal transformation and in part as reaction to the newly self-conscious minorities, particularly African Americans. Because of these internal changes and external influences, ethnic and religious identities took on entirely new meanings among white Americans.

The initial response of many white Americans to the tumult of the late 1960s was to join in the celebration of ethnic roots, the assertion of ethnic group solidarity, and the challenge to old assimilationist ideals. The emergence of neighborhood activists like Barbara Mikulski in Baltimore or Stephen Adubato in Newark, the creation of organizations like Geno Baroni's Center for Urban Ethnic Affairs and a sudden flurry of books and articles by writers like Michael Novak or Richard Gambino seemed to herald a "white ethnic revival." Ironically, this revival represented both a resistance to the new challenge of black and minority power and an appropriation of Black Power rhetoric and ideas of ethnic assertion and pride. Most observers believe that the white ethnic revival was but a temporary interlude. Joshua Fishman suggests that by the late 1970s the ethnic boom seemed to have subsided considerably.

While the ethnic revival flashed and then sputtered, a more long-lasting and fundamental revolution appeared to be remaking the meaning of whiteness in America. Over the course of the period from the 1960s to the 1980s, white ethnic neighborhoods would all but disappear in American inner cities and, though "ghosts" of such ethnic residential clusters reappeared in some suburbs during this period, they too proved transient. Perhaps more important, intermarriage rates among white groups skyrocketed. These were not just rates for marriages across ethnic boundaries,

which had been steadily rising among most nineteenth- and early twentieth-century European migrant groups since the 1930s and 1940s; these were rates also for marriage across religious boundaries, which had remained low through the 1950s. The "triple melting pot" of Americanizing Protestants, Catholics, and Jews had fully emerged out of the old ethnic identities only in the 1950s, but by the 1960s and 1970s even it seemed to be fading away. While European Americans might still call themselves Irish, Italian, or Russian, and certainly Catholic or Jewish after the 1960s, those identities, even the religious ones, were increasingly freely chosen, not socially or politically determined. The social boundaries separating these groups were now lightly defended and porous.

There were both long- and short-term causes for these dramatic changes. The long-term causes lay in the rising social mobility of white ethnic groups. There is evidence that the older groups, like Irish and German Americans, achieved occupational and educational parity with white native-stock Americans sometime in the early twentieth century, and some newer groups, like Jewish Americans, had even surpassed native-stock Americans by the 1940s. The rise of unions, World War II prosperity, and the GI Bill significantly accelerated upward mobility for white ethnic Americans from the 1930s through the 1950s. By the 1950s and 1960s, Catholics and Jews were cashing in on this occupational progress and moving out of cities to the suburbs in increasing numbers—again, abetted by federal help from FHA and other programs. Such white ethnics had also achieved significant political power, as vital parts of the Democratic Party's New Deal coalition, as well as cultural power, as Jewish studio owners and the Catholic Church (through the Legion of Decency) consolidated their influence over America's film industry.

Yet it was the tumultuous events and movements of the 1960s that catalyzed these long-term trends and all but collapsed the already weakening boundaries separating white ethnics and religious groups. Kennedy's election and martyrdom and the Second Vatican Council's ecumenism, for example, undermined the old mutual enmity between Catholics and Protestants that had been a premise of political and social organization in the urban North since the nineteenth century.

One of the most remarkable and yet often overlooked trends of the last thirty-five years, reflecting these collapsing boundaries, has been the decline of the "Protestant Establishment." This does not mean that an economic elite, much less an elite class, has disappeared in America. Indeed, on the contrary, there is substantial evidence that the richest Americans have become richer and more powerful over the last twenty years as they added significantly to their proportion of the nation's wealth. That elite also remains overwhelmingly white, despite some minor inroads from Asians, Blacks, and Latinos. Yet that elite is by no means still exclusively Protestant. Not only Catholics, but Jews have moved into the corporate elite and have began to fill up the preparatory schools and men's eating clubs that make up its

organizational subcommunity. G. William Domhoff, long-time analyst of American elites, suggests that Catholics had penetrated the elite as early as the 1960s and Jews, he noted in 1998, "are [now] not merely 'the most middle class' and the most affluent white immigrant group. They have become full-blooded members of the power elite . . . " Moreover, though much of the elite organizational subculture—the men's eating clubs, preparatory schools, and country clubs—endures or even thrives, there is little or no recognition of the public authority of a social elite now in the United States. Indeed, as David Brooks has recently suggested, members of the new elite themselves do not believe in the social authority of elites.

The elite has changed in America for several reasons. One has been the changing nature of the economy—the rise in recent decades of sectors like computers or communications open to new entrepreneurs and the stagnation of the old, corporate-dominated heavy industries. But the civil rights and antiwar movements set the process in motion in the 1960s. Both encouraged what would become a broadly pervasive skepticism about authority in American culture. The civil rights movement also made it difficult to justify open racial or ethnic exclusion or prejudice at any level for any group, helping Catholic and Jewish Americans into the upper reaches of economy and society.

If, ironically, civil rights helped undermine the legitimacy of ethnic discrimination among upper-class whites, the Black Power, Latino, and Asian American movements also helped prompt racial solidarity among working-class and lower middle-class whites. The new challenge—African, Latino, and Asian Americans fighting for equality in arenas of politics and society that had once been closed to them—encouraged whites to forget ethnic differences and band together to resist perceived threats to jobs, neighborhoods, or simply status. This had been going on for a long time. White resistance to African American competition in employment and housing ignited violence in Chicago, Detroit, and other city neighborhoods in the 1950s. Yet it surfaced more broadly in the 1960s and 1970s, driving groups like lower middle-class Jews and working-class Italians together, in the embrace of a vaguely defined whiteness, in embattled neighborhoods like Canarsie in New York. In the new racial competition of the 1970s and 1980s, white simply made more sense, seemed a more rational and functional identity to Irish or Italian or Polish ethnics as conflicts between whites and racial others eclipsed older ethnic rivalries.

And yet, if the older white ethnic identities ceased to be "rational" or functional, seemed no longer to mean much in contests for power and resources, or even to reflect social realities in terms of group institutional infrastructure and endogamy, they nonetheless did not die. Indeed, white ethnic identities have never thrived as much in American public life as they have in the last thirty years. The politics and protests of the white ethnic revival might have petered out by the middle to late 1970s, but the cultural production of the revival continues to this day. As Marilyn Halter has documented, celebration of racial and ethnic pride has become big business, spawning products from key chains, ethnic cookbooks, and greeting cards to homeland tours and hosts of ethnic festivals. She points out that much of the new ethnic marketing is directed at the multicultural minorities, but a substantial amount of the new ethnic trade targets white ethnic groups like the Jews and Irish. Genealogy, once the preserve of the old Protestant elite, has become a hobby for hundreds of thousands of more common folk. The web site of the National Genealogical Society, for example, lists Irish, Jewish, Italian, Canadian, Belgian, and Norwegian American genealogical societies or resources as well as links to traditional genealogical groups such as the Daughters of the American Revolution. Like black, Asian, and Latino studies, white ethnic studies programs sprouted up in universities and colleges. As early as 1973, 135 colleges and universities offered courses in the history or culture of one or more of the white ethnic American groups. Irish Studies, for example, has emerged as an academic discipline only within the last forty years. All the major Irish Studies programs at Boston College, Catholic University, the College of St. Thomas, New York University, and Notre Dame have been founded in the last forty years, as has the American Conference for Irish Studies, the national academic organization devoted to the encouragement of scholarship and teaching in Irish Studies. As Lawrence McCaffrey, one of the founders of the Conference, suggested recently, "In American colleges and universities, Irish Studies enjoys a prestige unimaginable forty five years ago."

Perhaps the most striking evidence of this ethnic cultural revival, however, has been the explosion of white ethnic images in American television and movies. Images of Italian Americans, for example, have become far more numerous and prominent in the movies than ever before. Films featuring Italian Americans since the 1960s have included The Godfather and its two sequels; *Rocky* and its four sequels; *First Blood,* featuring the character "John Rambo," and its two sequels; *Mean Streets; Raging Bull; Goodfellas; Moonstruck;* and *Saturday Night Fever.* All of these films were spectacular financial successes, or critically acclaimed, or both. Five of the films—*Rocky, The Godfather, Saturday Night Fever, Rambo: First Blood,* and *Rocky IV*—were ranked among the top fifty money-making films of all time at one time or another in the 1980s. In 1988, *Moonstruck* finished ninth among the top-grossing films of the year; *Rambo III* was thirteenth. In 1990 The *Godfather Part III, Rocky V,* and *Goodfellas* were all among the top fifty grossing films.

Some of the profits from these movies were as unexpected as they were huge. *Rocky* was made on a shoestring, $1 million, but grossed more than $56 million at the box office. A year later *Saturday Night Fever,* made quickly and cheaply to cash in on the disco-dancing craze, earned over $70 million. Since 1972, three films about Italian Americans—*The Godfather, The Godfather Part II,* and *Rocky*—have won Academy Awards for best picture. Little wonder, then, that Richard Alba has pointed out that Italian Americans have become"Hollywood's favorite ethnic group" in the last thirty years.

Italian Americans were not the only ethnics to enjoy a new prominence in American movies and television. Depictions of Jews, for example, had been surprisingly rare in the movies before the 1960s. Indeed, Lester Friedman notes that the number of films about Jews actually fell to an all-time low in the 1950s. Before the tumult of the 1960s, Jewish studio owners and producers worried about the public's response to Jewish characters, but in the postassimilation age, Jews and other ethnics became much more marketable. In the 1960s, Friedman points out, more films were made about Jews than in any other decade in the history of motion pictures.

In many cases, the new depictions of ethnics still traded on older stereotypes—Italian gangsters and Irish cops, for example. Yet most depictions were more complex than they had been before. Friedman suggests that the new wave of films about Jews presented "an unparalleled range of Jewish characters," and even many of the Italian American criminal characters featured on screen seemed to provoke public fascination, even sympathy, in the new era. Mary Waters reports from her surveys in the 1980s that people of mixed ancestry, with English or German as well as Italian forefathers, for example, invariably identified as Italian. They saw, she said, "Italian as a good ancestry to have . . . because they [Italians] have good food and a warm family life."

If white ethnics seemed more visible, more celebrated after the 1960s than ever before, most social scientists nonetheless dismiss the new interest in white ethnic identities as little more than a consumer fad. Joanne Nagel argues that symbolic white ethnic identities hardly have the same meaning for white ethnics as the "mandatory ethnicity" imposed on African, Asian, or Latino Americans. Mary Waters agrees, contending that for white ethnics "ethnicity is not something that influences their lives unless they want it to" and that it "cannot be the same as an identity that results from and is nurtured by societal exclusion and rejection." Marilyn Halter and Joshua Fishman take the new white ethnic identifications more seriously but agree that such allegiances do not mean the same as they once did, when they represented real political and economic interests and identifications were forged in competition for power and resources. Halter locates the new ethnic identifications in "a search for recognizable or familiar points of reference in a cold, impersonal, and fragmented world . . . a longing to feel included."

Such explanations may underestimate the importance of white ethnic identities and overlook the critical, if new, ways in which white ethnic identities serve their members' interests. To claim loyalty to their specific ethnic group may not have helped or hindered the upward mobility of Irish Americans or Italian Americans after the 1960s, for example. Yet understanding themselves as part of a broad tradition of nineteenth- and twentieth-century European immigrants may, in fact, have been very useful to third- or fourth-generation Irish or Italians in the late twentieth century. Matthew Jacobson uses the term *Ellis Island Whiteness* to define such people's identities. Ellis Island whites are not just people from a specific European nation but all the people who share a story of immigrant flight from Europe to America in the nineteenth and twentieth centuries. It does not matter whether it is an Irish story or an Italian or Jewish one, only that it is part of the same great epic of nineteenth- and twentieth-century European immigration to America. In the thirty years since the 1960s, Ellis Island Whiteness, grounded in this heroic story, has served the interests of such people well. As Jacobson suggests, their story of immigration, discrimination, and ultimate success has provided them a rhetorical weapon to help fend off African American or other minority claims for power or resources. First, it absolves white ethnics from responsibility for the establishment of America's oppressive racial regime because they arrived long after that regime was instituted through slavery. More important, this myth of a white ethnic triumph over poverty and against prejudice also offers a rebuttal to black or other minority demands for special government redress for sufferings of discrimination. Ellis Island Whiteness, however, also helped white ethnics make successful claims for full acceptance on their own terms to places in the highest ranks of American society. In the 1950s, ambitious white ethnics believed that they had to hide their backgrounds and conform to the cultural dictates of a Protestant establishment if they wished to gain acceptance by the WASP elite;

such tensions were a commonplace, for example, for the Irish American characters in the writer John O'Hara's novels. If white ethnics had continued to hold that belief in the 1960s and after, the old Protestant Establishment might not have collapsed so swiftly. Yet in the 1970s and 1980s, white ethnics no longer thought such conformity necessary. They now claimed a heritage as good as any other, and a series of national commemorations from the nation's Bicentennial in 1976 through the Centennial of the Statue of Liberty in 1986 confirmed their claim by establishing the Ellis Island epic as one of the foundational stories of the nation. The renovation of Ellis Island in the early 1990s and its elevation to the status of a national icon, rivaling or even surpassing Plymouth Rock or Jamestown in popularity, capped this rise of Ellis Island Whiteness. In Jacobson's terms, Ellis Island Whiteness had routed Mayflower Whiteness.

The emergence of these new multicultural and white ethnic identities provoked several issues, which became important points of conflict between whites and minorities, especially African Americans, over the course of the 1970s and 1980s. Such issues did not erupt outside of the political process but were enmeshed in it. The two major political parties tried to capitalize on these issues throughout the era in order to gain political advantage. Generally, the Republicans played upon them to try to pry whites from both North and South out of the Democratic Party and make the GOP the nation's majority party. In this effort they had some success—at least

initially—rolling up big election victories behind Richard Nixon and Ronald Reagan. Political competition over these issues, however, did more than disrupt the partisan balance, it helped exacerbate ethnic tensions, sharpen group identities, and charge boundaries.

The first such issue was school busing—busing children from one neighborhood to another in order to racially integrate local schools. The Supreme Court decisions at the end of the 1960s and the beginning of the 1970s helped shift the battlegrounds of school integration from self-consciously legislated school segregation in the South to the segregation of schools in the North, reflecting residential segregation that school departments permitted or even encouraged. Court-ordered desegregation in Detroit, and particularly in Boston, encountered fierce, often violent, resistance from whites in the early and mid-1970s. Busing controversies, however, extended beyond a few cities to become critical issues in national politics as George Wallace and later Richard Nixon took up opposition to it. Nationally, polls found that three quarters of whites surveyed opposed busing throughout the 1970s.

While the struggle over busing rose to a climax in the 1970s, a new conflict over immigration began brewing in that decade. Few of the older anti-immigration groups like the Daughters of the American Revolution played a critical role in the new anti-immigration fights, and there seemed to be less interest in overturning the 1965 immigration reform law's repeal of the older racist quotas, than on enforcing the restrictions of that and subsequent laws more rigorously. In particular, the movement sought to limit, and perhaps even roll back, the tide of illegal or undocumented aliens who had come to the United States in such great numbers since the mid-1960s. Opponents of illegal immigrants lodged a wide range of grievances against them, but one of the most popular was the suggestion that illegal immigrants were costing taxpayers in welfare, public schooling, and public supported health services. As early as 1975, the state of Texas tried to bar undocumented children from attending local schools. More seriously, in 1994, California voters passed a referendum, Proposition 187, to deny public services to illegal aliens. Courts overturned such laws, but the size of the majority for the California referendum, 59 percent to 41 percent, suggested the power of anti-immigrant feelings in the state at that time. Most legislative efforts to restrict or roll back illegal immigration focused not on the existence of public services for illegal immigrants but on employment of them. Again, as early as 1971, states like California passed laws to punish employers who hired illegals. Throughout the seventies and eighties Congress considered several bills that would have sanctioned employers but passed none of them. Sentiment, however, was strong enough to push the legislation through one or the other of the chambers throughout that period. From 1982 to 1985, congressional efforts focused on the Simpson-Mazzoli Bill, named after Republican Senator Alan Simpson and Democratic Congressman Romano Mazzoli. A version of this bill,

a compromise mix of employer sanctions with amnesty for illegals who were longtime residents of the nation, passed as the Immigration Reform and Control Act of 1986.

Though most critics of illegal immigration were not overtly racist or opposed to immigration per se, the campaign against illegal immigrants exacerbated ethnic tensions. As David Reimers notes, the new nativism's focus on illegals may have funneled a broader disquiet with increasing immigration onto the most vulnerable target. Given that illegal immigrants were overwhelmingly (though by no means exclusively) Latino or Asian, the conflicts over them fed and fed off racial and ethnic tensions. Moreover, some of the more vociferous critics of immigration, like the political commentator and presidential candidate Patrick Buchanan, trod very close to the old racism when they openly questioned the ability of newer immigrants to assimilate into American society.

Struggles over affirmative action began as early as the 1960s and have lasted to the present. The phrase affirmative action may have appeared first in an executive order issued by John F. Kennedy in 1961, but the first meaningful argument in behalf of the concept came in Lyndon Johnson's famous speech at Howard University in 1965. "It is not enough," Johnson said, "just to open the gates of opportunity . . . we seek . . . not just equality as a right and theory, but equality as a fact and result." Johnson later issued an executive order of his own, Order no. 11246, authorizing new federal agencies and empowering old ones to create minority hiring requirements for the government and for businesses with government contracts. Ironically, however, it was the Nixon administration's Philadelphia Plan, requiring Philadelphia construction firms under federal contract to meet specific goals for minority hiring, that became the most important first step in implementing the executive order. By 1971, the Supreme Court had agreed to the basic factor underlying the affirmative action concept: that statistics reflecting disproportionately few minority employees may prove discrimination even when overt evidence of discrimination could not be found.

By then, however, affirmative action had also become controversial. Though the Nixon Administration had introduced the Philadelphia Plan in 1969, within a few years President Nixon began to court the growing ranks of affirmative action's opponents. White workers and students claiming reverse discrimination continued to bring suits against governments, businesses, or universities in the courts, despite the Supreme Court's earlier decision. The most celebrated case was Alan Bakke's claim against the University of California at Davis Medical School. Bakke argued that he was a stronger applicant than some of the minority students accepted by the School. While the court agreed with Bakke in this instance it did not overturn affirmative action programs in general as a means of overcoming discrimination against minorities. Nevertheless, affirmative action has remained controversial. Ronald Reagan attacked it in his first press conference, and his administration led an open assault on Ex-

ecutive Order 11246. More recently, conservatives in California placed the issue of affirmative action on the state ballot in 1996 and won their battle, thereby preventing the state or its agencies from employing affirmative action policies.

A host of other issues, incidents, and events have emerged or erupted over the last thirty years that have marked off and reinforced the racial and ethnic boundaries of the new multicultural era. The educational curriculum has been one particularly hotly contested battleground. Probably the most broadly divisive question in cultural contests over education has been the issue of the primacy of the English language. In the face of extensive immigration, several older-stock white organizations have sought to reaffirm the nation's commitment to English as the nation's official language. Some states have responded to the pressure by passing resolutions confirming the official status of English. Most battles over language have centered on the practical issues of languages in schools and, in particular, bilingual education programs. Californians, taking advantage of their easy referendum process, voted to dismantle those programs in 1998, but the issue has been controversial throughout the Southwest, particularly in metropolitan areas with large immigrant populations. Less long-lasting, but indicative of the cultural tensions emerging over school curricula, was the controversy over Ebonics, "Black English" or "African American Vernacular English" as linguists describe it. That controversy erupted when the Oakland School Board encouraged its teachers to begin with an understanding of the African American vernacular to teach students standard English. Critics saw it as a kind of African American bilingual program—or worse, as an indulgence of improper English.

Beyond the fights over language, there were also struggles over history standards and new social studies curricula, such as the proposed New York State Social Studies curriculum in 1991. These conflicts ran all the way up the educational hierarchy and across the country, provoking battles at California-Berkeley and San Francisco State, Cornell, and California State-Northridge over courses and academic programs from the 1960s through the 1990s.

Many of these battles in the culture wars took place in rarefied academic circles and may have seemed distant to ordinary Americans, but there was plentiful evidence of more pervasive ethnic and racial polarization. Small riots broke out periodically in cities across the country from the seventies to the nineties, and turf fights in white or minority neighborhoods were common. Lynching also continued: as late as 1980, twelve lynchings of blacks by white mobs or vigilantes were reported in Mississippi alone.

In the 1990s race seemed as important as it had ever been in the United States. Three incidents in that decade underlined and reinforced the stubborn persistence of racial and ethnic animosity. In 1992 Los Angeles policemen arrested an African American man, Rodney King, for a driving violation. A videotape of the arrest showed that some of the officers mauled King while apprehending him, but a jury in the largely white and conservative Simi Valley suburb of Los Angeles found them not guilty of police brutality. On April 29, 1992, shortly after the verdict became known publicly, minority neighborhoods in Los Angeles exploded in angry violence over the verdict. When the violence subsided, fifty-eight people were dead, more than thirteen thousand were arrested, and more than one thousand buildings were destroyed. About two years after the King riot, Nicole Brown Simpson, former wife of O. J. Simpson, and her friend Ronald Goldman were found dead at Nicole Simpson's home in a Los Angeles suburb. O. J. Simpson, a legendary football player and television and film personality, was charged with the crime. Combining sex, celebrity, and violence, the trial drew unprecedented attention. The case, however, was no mere media ballyhoo; it had serious racial overtones and became both a stark reflection of the depth of racial division and an aggravation of that animosity. Polls revealed not only public interest among both blacks and whites but almost diametrically opposed opinions between the races about Simpson's guilt. The Simpson case raised once again the persistent issue of white police prejudice in the testimony of policeman Mark Fuhrman, who led the investigation of Simpson. More important, the case's alleged black male violence against a white woman told a story that lay at the heart of the oldest and darkest fears of white Americans' racial imagination. In the midst of Simpson's trial, Lewis Farrakhan, former Nation of Islam minister outspoken in his condemnations of whites (particularly Jews), called for a million black men to march on Washington on October 16, 1995, in order to "recommit and renew our determination to do God's will and seek justice, freedom, and empowerment for our people." A million men did not come, but hundreds of thousands did. Here again, opinion surveys revealed a sharp racial split: blacks applauded the Million Man March, but whites, suspicious of Farrakhan's militant and racially hostile rhetoric, were skeptical.

As recently as the mid-1990s, then, racial division seemed as intractable as it had ever been in America. Indeed, shortly after the Rodney King riot in Los Angeles, a *Time* magazine reporter lamented, "It had not exactly been unknown that race relations were worsening. . . . But not until last week did many whites and blacks realize how deep an abyss had been opening at their feet." American discussions of race had become so bitter and charged that the Clinton administration launched not one but two initiatives to encourage racial understanding: the National Endowment for the Humanities' National Conversation on American Pluralism and Identity and the President's Committee on Race.

But what was the real state of American ethnic and racial relations at the end of the millennium? The language of a multicultural America, composed of an undifferentiated white (if shrinking) majority and African, Asian, and Latino American minorities, has become commonplace in talking about race and ethnicity in America. But does it adequately describe the reality of America's racial and ethnic identities, boundaries, and cultures?

For African Americans, it appears that racial identities remain central and racial boundaries remain charged. African Americans still lag economically behind whites. Indeed, after some success in closing the income gap with whites over a roughly thirty-year period from World War II to the early 1970s, black progress seemed to slow through the 1970s and much of the 1980s. Some scholars suggest that it may even have halted or slipped backward. Andrew Hacker points out, for example, that median white family income rose by nearly 9 percent between 1970 and 1990, but black median income grew but 2 percent. Similarly, average black male earnings relative to whites rose from a ratio of $450 to $1,000 in 1939 to one of $654 to $1,000 in 1969, but, from 1969 to 1989, it rose to only $716 to $1,000.

As Hacker and others note, however, such statistics can mask more complicated economic changes in the black community. African American middle classes expanded significantly in the 1970s and 1980s, but the ranks of impoverished blacks did not decline substantially. The persistent economic difficulties of unskilled black workers—complicated by an economy that offered fewer blue-collar opportunities and by problems of drugs, violence, and family rupture—remained an important source of division between blacks and whites in America. African Americans had an interest in maintaining or expanding welfare programs as well as government-funded programs aimed at alleviating poverty. Many whites, particularly working-class whites, who had once backed New Deal welfare programs, now came to see government programs as black programs.

Yet even the black and white middle classes did not necessarily share the same interest. Scholars, like the general public, disagree over the efficacy of affirmative action programs, but it is true that a disproportionate number of African Americans, and middle-class African Americans in particular, have found jobs in local, state, or federal governments. As Hacker points out, African Americans held 20 percent of the jobs in the Postal Service and made up the same proportion of the Armed Services, about double their percentage of the total population. Police officer was one of the fastest growing occupations for blacks between 1970 and 1990, rising by almost 300 percent. Even higher up the economic scale, the government is an important employer for African Americans; one third of all black lawyers and almost one third of all black scientists worked for the government in 1990. This means that the black middle class has a heavy stake in maintaining or expanding governments and insuring—through affirmative action, strict antidiscrimination, or old-fashioned political patronage—that such governments hire African Americans.

This distinct black economic interest undergirds a distinct black politics. African Americans have made up a powerful and visible voting bloc in the American electorate for the entire thirty-five-year period from 1965 to the present. Black support for the Democratic Party, begun with Franklin Roosevelt's New Deal and confirmed by Johnson's civil rights legislation, has rarely fallen below two-thirds in presidential elections, and even many congressional elections, in the last three decades. Most African Americans clearly believe that such solidarity is critical to defend and advance their interests, whether in electing sympathetic white Democrats to the presidency or their own as congressmen or mayors. Such political solidarity, however, also continues to sustain the group, reinforce identity, and charge its boundaries.

It is difficult to tell how long such identities and boundaries will endure, for there have been some noticeable trends in recent years that appear to have undermined black solidarity. The rising tide of immigration from the Caribbean and more recently Africa, for example, has brought thousands of African or African-descent people to the United States. By 1990 there were nearly one and a half million foreign-born blacks in the United States, and they constituted nearly a quarter of the black population in New York. Such immigrants bring their own perspectives on race and race identity to the United States. As Mary Waters has reported, many West Indian black immigrants have tried to distance themselves from American blacks, viewing American blacks as lazy and obsessed with racial slights. These West Indians believed that they enjoyed higher status in America as members of their own immigrant peoples than as members of a black racial group and thus insisted on identification with their Caribbean homelands rather than with Black America. As black immigration increases, it appears to open a potential fissure in Black racial solidarity in America. There are also trends toward racial integration that may be sapping black solidarity. There is some evidence, for example, that the economic boom at the end of the 1990s began to pull members of all races in, even the poorest blacks and minorities of urban ghettoes, and promised to recast African American conceptions of the economic interests of their race. There has also been a rising trend in intermarriage across the black and white boundary. As late as the 1950s, southern states officially banned such marriages altogether. The 1960s swept away such laws, and the sexual revolution of the decade and its emphasis on individual sexual and romantic fulfillment not only helped reinforce civil rights but inspired tolerance in opening up romantic and sexual relations across racial lines. Thus the number of black-white marriages has tripled since 1970. African Americans have also begun to break into the government elite and become national heroes—Martin Luther King, for example, and popular culture icons such as Michael Jordan.

Still race, at least as defined in black and white terms, continues to matter in America, and it is likely to matter for a long time. Black immigrants, for example, may insist on their separate ethnic identities, but, as Waters points out, the "overwhelming pressure" of the broader culture appears to force a significant proportion of their children to merge into an African American melting pot, identify as African Americans, and take up African American culture. Waters found that only a minority of the American-born children of black immigrants identified with their parents' ethnic group,

and most of them were the children of successful middle-class immigrant parents. A larger proportion of the children of black immigrants found that the structure of race relations and white perceptions in the United States lumped them with native black Americans, and they accepted that racial designation. They thus rejected their parents' ethnicity along with their disdain for African American culture. These second-generation blacks eagerly took up black youth culture from "Black English" to rap and hip-hop music.

Moreover, there have been clear limits to the extent of black social integration even over the last ten years. Black residential segregation has dropped only slightly over the last decade, despite the economic boom. As professor John Yinger told the New York Times in the summer of 2001, "One of the surprising things about black-white segregation over the years is that it has been, and remains, so much higher than other kinds." Similarly, for all the powerful and pervasive influence of the civil rights and sexual revolutions, marriages between blacks and whites still account for less than 10 percent of all marriages among black males.

Certain trends among whites have also suggested that the boundary between blacks and whites could remain tense for many years. Particularly striking has been the weakening of alliances that once crossed the racial border. Union decline has sapped the strength of class coalitions across racial boundaries. Yet racial tension and conflict may not be as much a result as a cause of the decline of class feeling and union strength. As Bruce Nelson has recently argued, over the last thirty years, white workers have often strongly resisted black challenges to seniority systems or to white monopolies of skilled positions. Thomas Edsall and others have also charted dramatic shifts of white blue-collar workers from Democrats to conservative Republicans over a whole range of social issues, but particularly over race, in the 1980s. More recently, scholars such as Thomas Sugrue, Nelson, and others, cite evidence of white worker resistance to African American integration of jobs and neighborhoods back to the earliest years of the civil rights era, in the 1940s and 1950s, casting doubt on how viable working-class alliances across racial lines have ever been. Whatever the potential for working-class alliances across racial lines may have been in the past, the possibility of such cross-race, class coalitions has seemed more distant in recent years.

Not only did working class alliances across racial lines break down in the new era of race relations, but cooperation between blacks and their longtime white allies, American Jews, also seemed to founder. The apparent demise of alliances between blacks and Jews has seemed a particularly telling example of the new hardening of racial boundaries. Jews had played a prominent role in supporting black civil rights back into the early twentieth century. Jews had helped found the NAACP and the Urban League and over time had played an increasingly important role in sustaining both organizations. From that time through the great civil rights struggles of the 1960s, Jews played an unusually significant role in black struggles. Such efforts reflected an historic Jewish commitment to protecting minority rights, a commitment rising both out of the values of Jewish culture and the practical consideration of Jewish vulnerability as a small non-Christian minority in a largely Christian and sometimes anti-Semitic American society.

Yet even as Jews and blacks fought together in civil rights struggles, strains appeared in their relationship. In the 1950s and 1960s, blacks and Latinos crowding into clothing manufacturing, for example, bridled at the Jewish monopoly of union leadership in these trades and the failure of those leaders to work aggressively for the new minority workers' needs for better pay and working conditions. The turning point in black-Jewish relations, however, came in 1968, in the Brooklyn neighborhood of Ocean Hill-Brownsville. In an experiment aimed at improving the education of poor African American children, the city, drawing on Ford Foundation funding, sought to increase local input and control of the schools in that black neighborhood. The experiment turned into a two-year war pitting black activists against the schoolteachers and their union, the United Federation of Teachers. Many of the teachers and the union's leadership were Jewish, and the battle dissolved into a bitter wrangle of charges and countercharges of racism and anti-Semitism. Ocean Hill-Brownsville was the first broadly visible revelation of the new strains in black-Jewish relations, but in succeeding years there would be many more. Some Jewish organizations would line up against black ones over legal challenges to racial affirmative action plans, such as the DeFunis case in 1974 and the

Bakke case in 1978. These cases were, Cheryl Greenberg notes, "the first time black and Jewish organizations had publicly and formally positioned themselves on opposite sides of a civil rights question." Meanwhile, some popular black leaders, most notably the Nation of Islam minister, Lewis Farrakhan, spoke openly and heatedly of alleged longtime Jewish exploitation of blacks extending as far back as the slave trade. Black and Jewish leaders also clashed over foreign policy, most notably over Israel and its treatment of Palestinian Arabs.

The growing divisions between blacks and Jews appeared to grow out of increasing divergences of perceived interests. Jews had, by and large, been successful in American life and became even more so after the 1960s as the old Protestant elite collapsed and new industries emerged. Despite suffering discrimination and stereotyping, Jews, Cheryl Greenberg suggests, understood their success as vindication of America's potential to work best as a race-blind meritocracy, rewarding individuals, not groups. Trying to win power or success through assertion of group solidarity and group claims, such as affirmative action allotments, Jews believed, only threatened to set a dangerous precedent that could easily be exploited to establish the privileges of some groups over others. Such notions clashed with many African Americans' sense of how the United States had worked—or better, had not worked—for them in the past, as well as their conviction that they had to assert group claims to expect any measurable change in their people's status.

Clashes of black and Jewish interests

did not take place only over affirmative action. Everyday encounters between Jewish teachers or social workers and black students or clients exacerbated the conflicts too. There were also conflicts over neighborhood turf. Jews, as Gerald Gamm and others have noted, were more likely to move quickly out of racially changing neighborhoods than Catholic ethnics, who more often dug in and resisted the influx of new minorities. Still, particularly in the outer borough neighborhoods of New York City, where many lower middle- and working-class Jews had settled, movement out of old neighborhoods was not easy, and clashes over territory provoked mutual hostility between blacks and Jews. "Physical closeness to blacks," Jonathan Rieder argued in his book on the New York neighborhood of Canarsie, "widened the chasm" between Jews and Italians on one side and African Americans on the other.

Yet blacks and Jews clashed not just because of conflicting interests, but also because of changing understandings of what constituted a minority in American life. As Greenberg suggests, the new multiculturalism set in motion by Black Power "putting race first as it does, removes Jews from the outsider community that they helped to legitimize. Instead, Jews have become Euro-Americans with their cultures and contributions subsumed under that broad heading (and their victimization by other Europeans thereby effaced). Now outsiders are racial minorities, African Americans, Asian Americans, native Americans and Hispanics." This is not simply a rhetorical redefinition. Jews' easy upward mobility into the highest ranks of the American elite made Jews look "settled and safe," in short, no different from other whites, to blacks and many other minorities. Indeed, some African Americans and other minorities have seen Jewish opposition to affirmative action and other minority causes as evidence of a Jewish retreat from their civil rights traditions and identification with their new white-skin privilege.

Yet as Greenberg contends, "most Jews do not see themselves privileged as simply white people . . . instead they view themselves as outsiders . . . an insecure minority with a separate culture and a set of beliefs and values." And, as important, they are a people with a history of suffering oppression. Jewish American remembrances of the Holocaust, the Nazi slaughter of over six million European Jews, would have occurred whatever the state of their relations with other minorities or whatever the changes in their own status. Yet the pattern of the remembering, particularly its timing—emerging in the late 1960s and early 1970s—suggests that it must have been influenced by the cultural and social strains and by the confusion that Jewish people were trying to work through as they moved from the outside to the inside. It suggests the dilemma of American Jews in the late twentieth century: on the one hand, a people reminded of their vulnerabilities by the recent horrors visited on their European cousins; on the other hand, a people enjoying the greatest economic and social success in their American history as many of them moved into the highest ranks of the American economy.

Such invocations of the Holocaust, like the Ellis Island narratives, could be dismissed as mere rhetorical strategies for masking Jewish and white ethnics' new white privilege, not unlike the privilege that whites have long enjoyed in the South. Indeed, roiling protests over busing in the North, resistance to affirmative action there, the flight of millions of northern white ethnics from the Democratic party to George Wallace, Richard Nixon, and Ronald Reagan—even the sudden popularity of country-western music above the Mason Dixon line—convinced observers as diverse as social scientists Nathan Glazer and Daniel Moynihan, historian Michael Denning, and journalist Peter Applebone that the United States was being "southernized" in the late twentieth century. It appeared that diverse ethnic and religious groups in the North had collapsed into a single white people confronting African Americans and other minorities, i.e., a southern, bipolar pattern of group identity had spread across the nation.

Yet it is not clear that this "southernization" has yet happened or even will happen. In recent years, as states in the South turned increasingly to the Republican Party, states in the northeast, particularly New England, have pivoted in turn in the opposite direction to the Democrats. This has happened for many reasons, but one may be that the charged racial battles of the seventies and eighties—the fights over busing, for example, now seem old and dormant. With the end of the big black migrations, and with declining crime rates, slashed welfare rolls, and rising prosperity, racial relations in the North have quieted. The absence of racial controversies may simply have allowed other issues that divide northern whites from southern, both cultural and economic, to emerge. Still, one wonders whether the Ellis Island whites, who make up such vast proportions of the white populations in northeastern states, have forged a pluralist political culture different from what exists in the South. Most historians of race relations in the North would be skeptical of an assertion that relations between whites and blacks there have been anything but bipolar, or that whites have ever treated blacks as just another ethnic group. But is there a liberal flip side to Ellis Island whiteness traditions? Is there still a lingering sense of being outsiders, perhaps, or a wariness of political and cultural hegemonies that helps make those northeastern states where Ellis Island whites are numerous approach ethnic and racial diversity differently from the way it is approached in the South? Though Jews have achieved great success and have quarreled with blacks in recent decades, they remain among the most, if not the most, liberal voters in the nation on almost all issues, including minority rights. Even Catholics, who were and remain more conservative than Jews on a host of issues, nonetheless remain more liberal and more Democratic than American Protestants, and far more so than evangelical Protestants. It is too early to tell entirely, but in the Northeast, and perhaps the other parts of the United States, white people may still be a different shade of white than white people in other parts of the nation, most notably the South.

Blacks and whites, however, do not necessarily define the new America.

Growing populations of Latinos, Asians, and even Native Americans and, as important, the rising self-consciousness of all these new groups has assured that. Yet, at the close of the century, it is still not clear what the future of each of these groups in America will be. Will the new panethnic identities endure and grow stronger or are they too weak to override the diverse national allegiances of their peoples? Furthermore, what will the relationships of these minorities be to whites and blacks—working with African Americans to remake America into a multicultural nation or seeking assimilation into white culture and admission into white privilege?

There is substantial evidence, for example, to suggest that Native Americans will continue to be a vital group. Despite urbanization, many Native Americans remain on reservations, where they provide a core group of strong identifiers and sustain the tribal museums, colleges, and other organizations that are at the heart of the Indian organizational infrastructure. Economic interests help bolster a separate Indian identity as well. Most Native Americans on reservations are still poor in comparison to whites and, as with blacks, this helps to nourish their sense of difference. And like African Americans, Native Americans depend heavily on the federal government to alleviate this poverty. Some reservations have recently increased their wealth by opening gambling casinos, but these too depend on tribal identification and solidarity. There are, then, many reasons why Native Americans will remain a distinct, bounded people.

Nevertheless, Native American ethnicity is complicated in the late twentieth century. The upsurge of Red Power and pantribal identity did not eliminate tribes. Indeed, tribes are the foundation of Native American ethnicity; they are the only legally sanctioned Indian communities as well as the original touchstones of Indian ethnicity for all Native Americans. Tribal identities probably could not have melted into broader Indian identities, given the communal, political, and economic roles that they play. Tribal allegiances thus persist as a potential source of division among Native Americans. Another source of division that has emerged more recently is the conflict between urban and reservation Indians. During some of the Red Power protests, older Native Americans on reservations sometimes resented urban activists who claimed to speak for them even though, as some reservation residents believed, these activists knew little about their problems.

There is, however, a broader, more fundamental problem looming for American Indian identity and solidarity in the future. The dramatic rise in the Indian population recorded by censuses since 1960 speaks to that problem, for the census figures include hundreds of thousands of people who decided to declare themselves Indians who had not identified themselves in that way in the past. Who is or can be an Indian then? Is it a matter of self-identification, and if so, is being an Indian an identity lightly worn, an ethnic option not forced by circumstance but chosen as a lifestyle? This kind of Indian identification seems more akin to white ethnic symbolic allegiances than to African or even Asian or Latino American racial identities. It appears to have all of the same attractions—a legendary past, romantic homelands, traditional rituals, and evocative values. Indeed, it may offer more than that, for Native Americans are also eligible for affirmative action programs.

Indian leaders are aware and wary of the sudden popularity of Indian identification. They have assailed New Age writers claiming Indian roots like Jamake Hightower, author of *The Primal Mind*. The Association of American Indian and Alaska Native Professors issued a statement in 1993 attacking "ethnic fraud" and the Indian "wannabies," who claim authority to speak as Indians as well as take jobs and apply for grants as Indians. Most such Indian leaders demand that all people claiming to be Indians establish their membership in a tribe through proof of ancestry. Yet the fact that in the last twenty years only half to two-thirds of Native Americans did so suggests the complications of Indian identity and solidarity that have emerged from 1965 to the birth of the twenty-first century. It reveals the variable meanings of being Indian and the varying porousness of the boundaries of those different Indian ethnicities: from a hard core of oppressed tribal people on reservations; to new Indian migrants exploring pantribal identities in cities; to people who had long been integrated into white society and opt for Indian status because it satisfies needs for belonging and tradition.

What does the future hold for the migrant peoples in the multicultural configuration, Asian and Latino Americans? More specifically, what will become of their newly minted panethnic identities? There has been a significant amount of cultural production among both Asian Americans and Latino Americans over the last thirty years. Among Asian Americans, for example, there has been a remarkable burgeoning of ethnic literature written by authors like David Louie, Frank Chin, and Maxine Hong Kingston. Museums in New York, Seattle, and Los Angeles and scholars in Asian American Studies programs have also worked hard to recover and fashion a new Asian American history. Latino American literature, movies, and art have also flourished during the last forty years, suggesting a cultural base for the broader panethnic identity. More important in providing common ground to disparate Latino nationalities is, of course, the Spanish language itself. In this case, Latino ethnicity profits not just from the work of a few cultural activists but from an explosion of profit-driven media outlets seeking to capitalize on the growing Spanish language market here in the United States as well as the even bigger one lying on its doorstep in neighboring countries to the south. As Geoffrey Fox notes, "No other minority now or in the history of the United States has had as extensive an apparatus for maintaining its language." There are, for example, two national Spanish language television networks: Univision, first broadcasting as Spanish International Network in 1969, and Telemundo, which began in 1986. With Spanish-speaking migrants continuing to pour into the country and the prospect of producing programming for huge markets south of the border, neither the Spanish language media behemoth nor the visibility it gives to the language is likely to die soon.

What is difficult to determine is whether such cultural production helps individual Asian and Latino Americans mark off a distinct identity from whites while at the same time finding common ground with members of other nationalities in their panethnic group. There is evidence that American-born members of both groups are more sympathetic to such panethnic identities and cultures than immigrants are. But it is not clear how vital such culture is to the everyday life of members of the new American-born generations or how critical it is to their self-identification. Survey data suggests, for example, that although the vast majority of second- and later-generation Latinos use English, not Spanish, in everyday life, a substantial proportion know and honor Spanish as the ancestral language.

Even if new American-born generations are sympathetic to panethnic identities, conflicts among nationalities within the two groups are not likely to disappear soon. Immigrants tend to hold such national loyalties dear, and now (and probably for a long time in the foreseeable future) they make up substantial proportions of both the Latino and Asian American groups. Moreover, even for later generations, the differences among the various national groups, reinforced by enduring class and regional differences, simply seem too strong to become irrelevant soon.

Among both Latinos and Asians, members of each group's nationalities have entered the country with very different backgrounds, for very different reasons, and at very different times—with very different subsequent histories. Some Asian American groups, such as Japanese and Korean Americans, carry long traditions of mutual enmity with them to the United States. Similarly, among Latino Americans, Cubans understand themselves to be political exiles from Communism and thus have a history and historical memory very different from those of Mexicans or Puerto Ricans.

Class and regional distinctions reinforce these national differences and exacerbate internal conflict. Among both Latinos and Asians, members of some groups either enter America better equipped than others or have been here long enough to learn the necessary skills that enable them to reap the benefits of the American economy. Japanese and, to a lesser extent, Chinese Americans have generally been very successful at moving up the American economic ladder. Vietnamese and Filipinos have come later than the Japanese and, in most cases, with less education than the Chinese, and thus struggle to move up. Among Latinos, many of the initial Cuban exiles were well educated and middle-class, setting them apart from the mass of their fellow Latinos. Regional divisions also fracture the panethnic groups, particularly Latinos. The three biggest constituent elements—Mexican, Puerto Rican, and Cuban Americans—all have their own regional heartlands, the Southwest, the Northeast, and south Florida respectively, and mix only in certain limited contexts, such as in Chicago or New York.

National loyalties reinforced by class and regional differences inevitably complicate Asian American or Latino American panethnic organizational efforts. Among Latinos, the two largest groups—Puerto Ricans and Mexicans—have worked together in the same pan-Latino organizations or crusades, but they continue to eye each other warily. Some Puerto Ricans, Fox suggests, "fear that any Hispanic agenda that gets worked out will necessarily be a Mexican American agenda in which the Puerto Ricans' particular concerns will be lost." In 1994, several Puerto Rican organizations, miffed at Chicano indifference to the advancement of a Puerto Rican candidate for the Supreme Court, banded together in an ad hoc coalition, "Boricua First," and issued a statement complaining that "our issues . . . get diluted within a larger Hispanic or Latino agenda." Moreover, neither shares the rabid anti-Communism that dominates the third most powerful Latino group, Cuban Americans. Asian American panethnic efforts suffer from some of the same internal conflicts. Japanese and Chinese Americans dominated the early Asian American movements and resulting pan-Asian organizations, but the dramatic influx of Filipinos and Vietnamese since 1965 has altered the numerical balance of power and raised new issues within the Asian American group. Conflicts between Japanese and Chinese American leaders and Filipino or Vietnamese staff or clients have chronically troubled Asian American social service organizations, for example. Yen Le Espiritu recounts the lament of Filipino community advocates about an Asian American welfare agency in California:

"The funding is dominated by the Chinese and Japanese. The director is Japanese and the next person is Chinese. They hire Filipinos, but only for the lower jobs or community workers way down the organizational ladder."

What interests, then, hold these groups together? What Geoffrey Fox asked about Latino Americans could apply equally to the disparate groups of Asian Americans: "Is there an issue important to all Hispanics, rural and urban Mexican Americans, inner city Puerto Ricans, Dade County Cubans, and all the many other Hispanic populations equally? And more important to them than the non-Hispanics? How many such issues are there where they all have common interest?"

Issues that are critical to African Americans, such as affirmative action and government action in behalf of workers and the poor, although subject to debate, remain important to Latino Americans, primarily because the great majority of Latino immigrants remain near the bottom of the American economic hierarchy. Immigration restriction and enforcement laws and Spanish language issues are also critical to many Latino Americans. Nevertheless, Latino Americans have not rallied around a clear cluster of interests into a solid voting bloc. While black support for the Democratic Party ran from two-thirds to four-fifths or more in the 1980s and 1990s, Latino support for the Democrats has never been nearly as large. In the presidential elections of the eighties, the Latino Democratic vote ranged from 55 percent to 66 percent. Moreover, Latinos have displayed little consistency in

individual races. In 1986 Latinos voted two to one for a Republican Senatorial candidate in Florida, a little less than two to one for a Democratic candidate for Senate in New York, and 57 percent to 43 percent for a Democratic Senate hopeful in Colorado.

Asian American political preferences and allegiances have, if anything, been even more variable. Many Asian Americans have little interest in the perpetuation of affirmative action programs, at least in colleges and graduate schools. While some wish to maintain solidarity with African and Latino Americans against what they perceive as continuing racism in America, others believe that open admissions at universities will favor Asian American students. Few other issues bind all other Asian Americans together. They have thus displayed few consistent partisan preferences over the last thirty years. Outside of Hawai'i, Yen Le Espiritu concluded in 1992, "as a group, Asian Americans have not aligned themselves with either the Republicans or the Democrats." She points to evidence that Asian Americans split almost evenly between the Democrats and Republicans in the 1984 elections. The *Los Angeles Times* found the same ambivalence among Southern California's Chinese Americans in the 1990s.

What such numbers suggest is not just a question about the internal coherence and solidarity of each group, but a question about the larger group's solidarity as part of an alliance of multicultural others opposed to a white majority. Jesse Jackson's campaign in 1984, the Rainbow Coalition, posited such an alliance of racial and other outsiders. Yet in the fiery passions of Los Angeles, exploding after the Rodney King verdict, the differences and latent hostilities among these multicultural partners became all the more evident as Latinos and Koreans fought openly with African Americans. At a fundamental level, the viability of a multicultural coalition lies ultimately in a shared sense of exclusion, understanding that the boundary between all these groups on one side and whites on the other remains so charged and impassable that it renders tensions among the minorities themselves insignificant.

Such groups have certainly shared that sense of exclusion in the past, but do they still do so in the present, and will they in the future? One answer may be found in evidence of interracial dating and marriage. Rates have risen dramatically since the 1960s and have increased enormously in just the last two decades. In 1980, a Gallup survey found that just 17 percent of the nation's teenagers had dated someone of another race; by 1997, 57 percent had done so. Yet the changing rates also reveal that some racial and ethnic boundaries remain more important than others. Asian-white and Latino-white rates of dating and intermarriage far exceed black-white proportions.

In 1997, ABC Television broadcast a new version of Hammerstein's musical "Cinderella." In 1957, when the show first opened on Broadway, white actors and actresses played all the leading roles. In the new television version, Brandy, a young African American singer, played Cinderella; Roberta Peters, a white actress, was her stepmother; one stepsister was white and one black; the Prince, Paolo Montalban was Filipino American, but his father, played by Victor Garber, was white and his mother, played by Whoopi Goldberg, was black. In one sense this new version of Cinderella seemed a natural embodiment of the multicultural revolution that began in the 1960s. "In the truest form of the word, it is truly a rainbow," Montalban contended. Yet in another sense, the show suggested an America where race and ethnicity were irrelevant, even invisible—where a young black heroine might have a white stepmother and black and white stepsisters and, more remarkably, a young hero would be Asian, with a white father and a black mother. Brandy inadvertently acknowledged as much when she suggested that "when you watch the movie, you forget that everyone is a different race."

Whether this version of Cinderella captures a real present or prefigures a probable future is difficult to tell. Given the evidence of weak political solidarity and the porous boundaries revealed in the dating and marriage data for some Asian and even Latino Americans, race seems likely to decline in significance over the next half century. If the long run of economic growth of the late 1990s returns and opens up sufficient opportunity for all races, softens racial competition, and tempers ethnic rhetoric, then, for the best-educated, upwardly mobile, and longest resident Asian and even Latino Americans, race may indeed become irrelevant. Yet for African Americans, as the political, economic, and intermarriage evidence suggests, race is likely to remain critical into the foreseeable future and the new version of Cinderella still a fantasy.

## ANNOTATED BIBLIOGRAPHY

Brooks, David. Bobos in Paradise: *The New Upper Class and How They Got There.* New York: Simon and Schuster, 2000.
Brooks's book is a wry and skeptical discussion of the emergence of the new American elite in the post1960s era that is itself disdainful of the pretensions to authority displayed by elites.

Daniels, Roger. *Coming to America: A History of Immigration and Ethnicity in American Life.* New York: Harper Collins, 1990.
Daniels's history is a comprehensive, basic survey of immigration to the United States that is very useful as an overview or as an introduction to the subject. It is arranged chronologically by immigration era and then by group within each era.

Edsall, Thomas Byrne. *The Impact of Race, Rights, and Taxes on American Politics.* New York: Norton, 1991.
The Edsall book is a brilliant analysis of how linkages forged over racial, welfare, and taxation issues broke up the old Democratic majority coalition in American politics and helped to lure many blue-collar workers, "Reagan Democrats," into the Republican Party.

Fishman, Joshua, et al. *The Rise and Fall of the Ethnic Revival: Perspectives on Language and Ethnicity.* New York: Mouton, 1985.
Several authors, including Fishman himself, analyze the impact and durability of the ethnic revival. Fishman's essay traces the shift in the meaning of ethnic identity for white ethnics.

Fox, Geoffrey. *Hispanic Nation: Culture, Politics, and the Constructing of Identity.* Seacaucus, N.J.: Carol, 1996.
Fox's very readable study traces the origins of Latino or Hispanic panethnicity from the "Brown Power" radicals of the 1960s through the creation of the Spanish-language and television-media empires in the 1980s and 1990s. In doing this, however, Fox also points out the persistence of internal rivalries and regional differences that still divide the group as well as the effects of American popular culture on language retention of new generations of Hispanics that threaten its future.

Glazer, Nathan, and Daniel Patrick Moynihan. *Beyond the Melting Pot: The Negroes, Puerto Ricans, Jews, Italians, and Irish of New York City.* Cambridge: M.I.T. Press, 1970.
This classic of American ethnic studies wisely detected the surprising durability of white ethnic loyalties in New York City during the 1960s, after most social scientists had declared them long dead. Like many observers of the period, however, they overestimated the potential persistence of religious divisions in American life.

Goldfield, David. *Black, White, and Southern: Race Relations and Southern Culture, 1940 to the Present.* Baton Rouge: Louisiana State University Press, 1990.
Goldfield's work is a careful, well-documented and sober recounting of modern racial politics in the South through the civil rights revolution and its aftermath. While acknowledging the revolutionary impact of the civil rights movement, Goldfield also recounts persisting inequalities and conflicts.

Greenberg, Cheryl. "Pluralism and Its Discontents: The Case of Blacks and Jews," in David Biale, Michael Galchinsky, and Susan Heschel, eds. *Insider/Outsider: American Jews and Multiculturalism.* Berkeley: University of California Press, 1998.
Greenberg's short essay thoughtfully an-

alyzes recent relations between Jewish and African Americans and the causes of their growing mutual suspicions.

Hacker, Andrew. *Two Nations, Black and White, Separate, Hostile, Unequal.* New York: Scribner's, 1992.

Though many have hailed African American progress since the civil rights revolution, Hacker was far less sanguine in the early 1990s, pointing to a wide range of persistent inequalities and enduring sources of tensions.

Halter, Marilyn. *Shopping for Identity: The Marketing of Ethnicity.* New York: Schocken, 2000.

Halter's book documents the emergence of ethnic marketing in American industries, from greeting cards to tourism. This marketing, she argues, is directed not only at the "multicultural" racial groups like African and Latino Americans but at white ethnics like Jewish and Irish Americans.

Jacoby, Tamar. *Someone Else's House: America's Unfinished Struggle for Integration.* New York: Basic Books, 1998.

Jacoby's book is an exhaustive look at racial politics over the last third of the twentieth century. She decries the emergence of Black Power ideologies and the abandonment of integrationist goals among blacks. The book discusses points of contention, including local control of schools, busing, affirmative action, and Afrocentric curricula, both nationally and in three cities—New York, Detroit, and Atlanta.

Krickus, Richard. *Pursuing the American Dream: White Ethnics and the New Populism.* Bloomington: Indiana University Press, 1976.

This is a contemporary account of the "white ethnic revival" of the 1970s that provides a comprehensive survey of the revival's organizations and leaders across the country.

Le Espiritu, Yen. *Asian American Pan-Ethnicity: Bridging Institutions and Identities.* Philadelphia: Temple University Press, 1992.

This is a sophisticated examination of the recent emergence of an Asian American panethnic identity among Chinese, Japanese, Filipino, and other ethnic groups descended from immigrants from Asia. It focuses on the evolution of this new group identity through electoral politics, funding of social service agencies, census category definitions, and responses to anti-Asian violence.

Marable, Manning. *Race, Reform and Rebellion: The Second Reconstruction in Black America, 1945–1982.* Jackson: University of Mississippi Press, 1984.

In this chronological overview of American racial politics, Marable recognizes the gains of the "Second Reconstruction," but he is critical of white and black leaders for their failure to understand that the central issue was "not the narrow battle for integration or political rights but the effort to achieve economic democracy."

Nagel, Joanne. *American Indian Ethnic Revival: Red Power and the Resurgence of Identity and Culture.* New York: Oxford University Press, 1996.

This sociological study explores the revival of Native American ethnicity through the "Red Power" political movement and the creation of a number of new cultural movements and institutions. Nagel is also concerned with the evolution of a panethnic Indian identity and its relation to tribal identities.

Nelson, Bruce. *Divided We Stand: American Workers and the Struggle for Black Equality.*

Princeton: Princeton University Press, 2000.

This book investigates the "intersection of class and race" in twentieth-century American society through a study of white and black longshoremen and steelworkers. Building on previous studies of "whiteness," Nelson argues powerfully for the need to consider "the role of the worker's own agency in building and defending the ramparts of racially based inequality."

Reimers, David. *Still the Golden Door: The Third World Comes to America.* New York: Columbia University Press, 1992.

This is a smart, well-researched, and rich examination of the shift, during the second half of the twentieth century, from Europe as the principal source of American immigration to Latin America, Asia, and Africa. In addition to his thorough treatment of the groups themselves, he examines the making of immigration legislation since World War II.

Rieder, Jonathan. *Canarsie: The Jews and Italians of Brooklyn Against Liberalism.* Cambridge: Harvard University Press, 1985.

This is an exceptionally rich investigation of racial tensions in an outer borough New York neighborhood that carefully and thoroughly explores the attitudes of white Italian and Jewish ethnics towards blacks in the post civil rights era.

Smith, Carolyn, ed. *The 88 Vote—ABC News.* New York: Capital Cities/ABC, 1988.

A compendium of the results of ABC exit poll surveys, not only from the 1988 election but from several elections in the 1980s that break down votes by ethnic identity as well as other demographic categories.

Waters, Mary. "Optional Ethnicities: For Whites Only?" in Silvia Pedraza and Ruben G. Rumbaut, eds. *Origins and Destinies: Immigration, Race, and Ethnicity in America.* Belmont, Cal.: Wadsworth, 1996.

Well known for work on optional ethnicities, Waters reminds us here that white racial attitudes restrict how much Mexican Americans and even African immigrants can invent or choose their group identities.

Wei, William. *The Asian American Movement.* Philadelphia: Temple University Press, 1993.

This is a rich and insightful survey of the emergence of the Asian American protest movement. It takes the reader from early campus battles at San Francisco State and the University of California at Berkeley to the creation of Asian American social-service programs, cultural organizations, and Asian studies programs, as well as a rising Asian American presence in electoral politics. Wei's study analyzes Asian Americans' new energy and organizational proliferation and their simultaneous efforts to forge a panethnic Asian American identity.

Zweigenhaft, Richard, and G. William Domhoff. *Diversity in the Power Elite: Have Women and Minorities Reached the Top?* New Haven: Yale University Press, 1998.

This is Domhoff's most recent analysis of the American elite in a series stretching back to the 1960s. Using a variety of methods to identify elite members, he chronicles the emergence of Jews among the elite, noting the continued underrepresentation of minorities such as Latinos and blacks.

# DOCUMENTS

## Malcolm X, Speech, 1964

*Malcolm X gave this speech to the Militant Labor Forum on April 8, 1964, shortly after he had left Elijah Muhammad's Nation of Islam. The speech offers the broad outlines of Malcolm X's new vision for African American political strategies; the disdain for civil rights protest and integration; the appeal to black pride and celebration of black nationalism; links between the black cause in the United States and the causes of the Third World; and support for peaceful revolution by ballot if possible but violent revolution if necessary.*

*Source:* Malcolm X, *"The Black Revolution," Two Speeches by Malcolm X* (New York: Merit, 1965), taken from Thomas R. Frazier, ed., *Afro-American History*, 2d ed. (Belmont, Cal.: Wadsworth Publishing, 1988), pp. 383–396.

Friends and enemies, tonight I hope that we can have a little fireside chat with as few sparks as possible being tossed around. Especially because of the very explosive condition that the world is in today. Sometimes, when a person's house is on fire and someone comes in yelling fire, instead of the person who is awakened by the yell being thankful, he makes the mistake of charging the one who awakened him with having set the fire. I hope that this little conversation tonight about the black revolution won't cause many of you to accuse us of igniting it when you find it at your doorstep.

I'm still a Muslim, that is, my religion is still Islam. I still believe that there is no god but Allah and that Mohammad is the apostle of Allah. That just happens to be my personal religion. But in the capacity which I am functioning in today, I have no intention of mixing my religion with the problems of 22,000,000 black people in this country. Just as it's possible for a great man whom I greatly respect, Ben Bella, to be a Muslim and still be a nationalist, and another one whom I greatly respect, Gamal Nasser to be a Muslim and still be a nationalist, and Sukarno of Indonesia to be a Muslim and still be a nationalist, it was nationalism which enabled them to gain freedom for their people.

I'm still a Muslim but I'm also a nationalist, meaning that my political philosophy is black nationalism, my economic philosophy is black nationalism, my social philosophy is black nationalism. And when I say that this philosophy is black nationalism, to me this means that the political philosophy of black nationalism is that which is designed to encourage our people, the black people, to gain complete control over the politics and the politicians of our own community.

Our economic philosophy is that we should gain economic control over the economy of our own community, the businesses and the other things which create employment so that we can provide jobs for our own people instead of having to picket and boycott and beg someone else for a job.

And, in short, our social philosophy means that we feel that it is time to get together among our own kind and eliminate the evils that are destroying the moral fiber of our society, like drug addiction, drunkenness, adultery that leads to an abundance of bastard children, welfare problems. We believe that we should lift the level or the standard of our own society to a higher level wherein we will be satisfied and then not inclined toward pushing ourselves into other societies where we are not wanted.

All of that aside, tonight we are dealing with the black revolution. During recent years there has been much talk about a population explosion and whenever they are speaking of the population explosion, in my opinion they are referring primarily to the people in Asia or in Africa—the black, brown, red, and yellow people. It is seen by people of the West that as soon as the standard of living is raised in Africa and Asia, automatically the people begin to reproduce abundantly. And there has been a great deal of fear engendered by this in the minds of the people of the West, who happen to be, on this earth, a very small minority.

In fact, in most of the thinking and planning of whites in the West today it's easy to see the fear in their minds, conscious minds and subconscious minds, that the masses of dark people in the West, in the East rather, who already outnumber them, will continue to increase and multiply and grow until they eventually overrun the people of the West like a human sea, a human tide, a human flood. And the fear of this can be seen in the minds, in the actions, of most of the people here in the West in practically everything that they do. It governs political views and it governs their economic views and it governs most

of their attitudes toward the present society.

## REASON FOR FILIBUSTER

I was listening to Dirksen, the Senator from Illinois, in Washington, D.C., filibustering the civil-rights bill and one thing that he kept stressing over and over and over was that if this bill is passed it will change the social structure of America. Well, I know what he's getting at, and I think that most other people today, and especially our people, know what is meant when these whites who filibuster these bills, and express fears of changes in the social structure, our people are beginning to realize what they mean.

Just as we can see that all over the world one of the main problems facing the West is race, likewise here in America today, most of your Negro leaders as well as the whites agree that 1964 itself appears to be one of the most explosive years yet in the history of America on the racial front, on the racial scene. Not only is this racial explosion probably to take place in America, but all of the ingredients for this racial explosion in America to blossom into a world-wide racial explosion present themselves right here in front of us. America's racial powder keg, in short, can actually fuse or ignite a world-wide powder keg.

And whites in this country who are still complacent when they see the possibilities of racial strife getting out of hand and you are complacent simply because you think you outnumber the racial minority in this country, what you have to bear in mind is wherein you might outnumber us in this country, you don't out-number us all over the earth.

And any kind of racial explosion that takes place in this country today, in 1964, is not a racial explosion that can be confined to the shores of America. It is a racial explosion that can ignite the racial powder keg that exists all over the planet that we call earth. Now I think that nobody would disagree that the dark masses of Africa and Asia and Latin America are already seething with bitterness, animosity, hostility, unrest, and impatience with the racial intolerance that they themselves have experienced at the hands of the white West.

And just as they themselves have the ingredients of hostility toward the West in general here we also have 22,000,000 African-Americans, black, brown, red, and yellow people in this country who are also seething with bitterness and impatience and hostility and animosity at the racial intolerance not only of the white West but of white America in particular.

## BLACK NATIONALIST PARTY

And by the hundreds of thousands today we find our own people have become impatient turning away from your white nationalism, which you call democracy, toward the militant uncompromising policy of black nationalism. I point out right here that as soon as we announced we were going to start a black nationalist party in this country we received mail from coast to coast, especially from young people at the college level, the university level, who expressed com-plete sympathy and support and a desire to take an active part in any kind of po-litical action based on black nationalism, designed to correct or eliminate, immediately evils that our people have suffered here for 400 years.

The black nationalists to many of you may represent only a minority in the community. And therefore you might have a tendency to classify them as something insignificant. But just as the fuse is the smallest part or the smallest piece in the powder keg it is yet that little fuse, that ignites the entire powder keg. The black nationalists to you may represent a small minority in the so-called Negro community. But they just happen to be composed of the type of ingredient necessary to fuse or ignite the entire black community. And this is one thing that whites—whether you call yourselves liberals or conservatives or racists or whatever else you might choose to be—one thing that you have to realize is, where the black community is concerned, although there the large majority you come in contact with may impress you as being moderate and patient and loving and long suffering and all that kind of stuff, the minority who you consider to be Muslims or nationalists happen to be made of the type of ingredient that can easily spark the black community This should be understood. Because to me a powder keg is nothing without a fuse.

1964 will be America's hottest year; her hottest year yet; a year of much racial violence and much racial bloodshed. But it won't be blood that's going to flow only on one side. The new generation of black people that have grown up in this country during recent years are already forming the opinion, and it's a just opinion, that if there is to be bleeding, it should be reciprocal—bleeding on both sides.

It should also be understood that the racial sparks that are ignited here in America today could easily turn into a flaming fire abroad which only means it could engulf all the people of this earth into a giant race war. You cannot confine it to one little neighborhood, or one little community, or one little country. What happens to a black man in America today happens to the black man in Africa. What happens to a black man in America and Africa happens to the black man in Asia and to the man down in Latin America. What happens to one of us today happens to all of us. And when this is realized I think that the whites— who are intelligent even if they aren't moral or aren't just or aren't impressed by legalities—those who are intelligent will realize that when they touch this one, they are touching all of them; and this in itself will have a tendency to be a checking factor.

The seriousness of this situation must be faced up to. I Was in Cleveland last night, Cleveland, Ohio. In fact I was there Friday, Saturday and yesterday. Last Friday the warning was given that this is a year of bloodshed, that the black man has ceased to turn the other cheek, that he has ceased to be non-violent, that he has ceased to feel that he must be confined to all these restraints that are put upon him by white society in struggling for what white society says he was supposed to have had a hundred years ago.

So today, when the black man starts reaching out for what America says are his rights, the black man feels that he is within his rights—when he becomes the victim of brutality by those who are depriving him of his rights—to do whatever is necessary to protect himself. And an example of this was taking place last night at this same time in Cleveland, where the police were putting water hoses on our people there and also throwing tear gas at them and they met a hail of stones, a hail of rocks, a hail of bricks. Couple weeks ago in Jacksonville, Florida, a young teenage Negro was throwing Molotov cocktails.

Well Negroes didn't do this ten years ago. But what you should learn from this is that they are waking up. It was stones yesterday, Molotov cocktails today; it will be hand grenades tomorrow and whatever else is available the next day. The seriousness of this situation must be faced up to. You should not feel that I am inciting someone to violence. I'm only warning of a powder-keg situation. You can take it or leave it. If you take the warning perhaps you can still save yourself. But if you ignore it or ridicule it, well death is already at your doorstep. There are 22,000,000 African-Americans who are ready to fight for independence right here. When I say fight for independence right here, I don't mean any non-violent fight, or turn-the-other-cheek fight. Those days are gone. Those days are over.

If George Washington didn't get independence for this country non-violently, and if Patrick Henry didn't come up with a non-violent statement, and you taught me to look upon them as patriots and heroes; then it's time for you to realize that I have studied your books well.

## POWER OF MINORITY

Our people, 22,000,000 African-Americans, are fed up with America's hypocritical democracy and today we care nothing about the odds that are against us. Every time a black man gets ready to defend himself some Uncle Tom tries to tell us, how can you win? That's Tom talking. Don't listen to him. This is the first thing we hear: the odds are against you. You're dealing with black people who don't care anything about odds. We care nothing about odds.

Again I go right back to the people who founded and secured the independence of this country from the colonial power of England. When George Washington and the others got ready to declare or come up with the Declaration of Independence, they didn't care anything about the odds of the British Empire. They were fed up with taxation without representation. And you've got 22,000,000 black people in this country today, 1964 who are fed up with taxation without representation, and will do the same thing. Who are ready, willing and justified to do the same thing today to bring about independence for our people that your forefathers did to bring about independence for your people.

And I say your people because I certainly couldn't include myself among those for whom independence was fought in 1776. How in the world can a Negro talk about the Declaration of In-

dependence when he is still singing "We Shall Overcome." Our people are increasingly developing the opinion that we just have nothing to lose but the chains of segregation and the chains of second-class citizenship.

## STRUGGLES WILL MERGE

So 1964 will see the Negro revolt evolve and merge into the world-wide black revolution that has been taking place on this earth since 1945. The so-called revolt will become a real black revolution. Now the black revolution has been taking place in Africa and Asia and in Latin America. Now when I say black, I mean non-white. Black, brown, red or yellow. Our brothers and sisters in Asia, who were colonized by the Europeans, our brothers and sisters in Africa, who were colonized by the Europeans, and in Latin America, the peasants, who were colonized by the Europeans, have been involved in a struggle since 1945 to get the colonialists, or the colonizing powers, the Europeans, off their land, out of their country.

This is a real revolution. Revolution is always based on land. Revolution is never based on begging somebody for an integrated cup of coffee. Revolutions are never fought by turning the other cheek. Revolutions are never based upon love your enemy; and pray for those who spitefully use you. And revolutions are never waged singing, "We Shall Overcome." Revolutions are based upon bloodshed. Revolutions are never compromising. Revolutions are never based upon negotiations. Revolutions are never based upon any kind of tokenism whatsoever. Revolutions are never even based upon that which is begging a corrupt society or a corrupt system to accept us into it. Revolutions overturn systems, and there is no system on this earth which has proven itself more corrupt, more criminal than this system, that in 1964 still colonizes 22,000,000 African-Americans, still enslaves 22,000,000 Afro-Americans.

There is no system more corrupt than a system that represents itself as the example of freedom, the example of democracy and can go all over this earth telling other people how to straighten out their house, and you have citizens of this country who have to use bullets if they want to cast a ballot. The greatest weapon the colonial powers have used in the past against our people has always been divide and conquer.

America is a colonial power. She has colonized 22,000,000 Afro-Americans by depriving us of first-class citizenship, by depriving us of civil rights, actually by depriving us of human rights. She has not only deprived us of the right to be a citizen, she has deprived us of the right to be human beings, the right to be recognized and respected as men and women. And in this country, the black can be 50 years old and he is still a "boy."

I grew up with white people. I was integrated before they even invented the word and I have never met white people yet—if you are around them long enough—who won't refer to you as a "boy" or a "gal," no matter how old you are or what school you came out of, no matter what your intellectual or professional level is. In this society we remain "boys."

## AMERICA'S STRATEGY

So America's strategy is the same strategy as that which was used in the past by the colonial powers: divide and conquer. She plays one Negro leader against the other. She plays one Negro organization against the other. She makes us think we have different objectives, different goals. As soon as one Negro says something, she runs to this Negro and asks him what do you think about what he said. Why anybody can see through that today—except some of the Negro leaders.

All of our people have the same goals. The same objective. That objective is freedom, justice, equality. All of us want recognition and respect as human beings. We don't want to be integrationists. Nor do we want to be separationists. We want to be human beings. Integration is only a method that is used by some groups to obtain freedom, justice, equality and respect as human beings. Separation is only a method that is used by other groups to obtain freedom, justice, equality or human dignity.

So our people have made the mistake of confusing the methods with the objectives. As long as we agree on objectives, we should never fall out with each other just because we believe in different methods or tactics or strategy to reach a common objective.

We have to keep in mind at all times that we are not fighting for integration, nor are we fighting for separation. We are fighting for recognition as human beings. We are fighting for the right to live as free humans in this society. In fact, we are actually fighting for rights that are even greater than civil rights and that is human rights.

We are fighting for human rights in 1964. This is a shame. The civil-rights struggle has failed to produce concrete results because it has kept us barking up the wrong tree. It has made us put the cart ahead of the horse. We must have human rights before we can secure civil rights. We must be respected as humans before we can be recognized as citizens.

Among the so-called Negroes in this country, as a rule the civil-rights groups, those who believe in civil rights, they spend most of their time trying to prove they are Americans. Their thinking is usually domestic, confined to the boundaries of America, and they always look upon themselves as a minority. When they look upon themselves upon the American stage, the American stage is a white stage. So a black man standing on that stage in America automatically is in the minority. He is the underdog, and in his struggle he always uses an approach that is a begging, hat-in-hand, compromising approach.

Whereas the other segment or section in America, known as the nationalist, black nationalists, are more interested in human rights than they are in civil rights. And they place more stress on human rights than they do on civil rights. The difference between the thinking and the scope of the Negroes who are involved in the human-rights struggle and those who are involved in the civil-rights struggle—those so-called Negroes involved in the human-rights struggle don't look upon themselves as Americans.

They look upon themselves as a part of dark mankind. They see the whole struggle not within the confines of the American stage, but they look upon the struggle on the world stage. And, in the world context, they see that the dark man outnumbers the white man. On the world stage the white man is just a microscopic minority.

So in this country you find two different types of Afro-Americans, the type who looks upon himself as a minority and you as the majority, because his scope is limited to the American scene; and then you have the type who looks upon himself as part of the majority and you as part of a microscopic minority. And this one uses a different approach in trying to struggle for his rights. He doesn't beg. He doesn't thank you for what he give him, because you are only giving him what he should have had a hundred years ago. He doesn't think you are doing him any favors.

## NO PROGRESS

He doesn't see any progress that he has made since the Civil War. He sees not one iota of progress because, number one, if the Civil War had freed him, he wouldn't need civil-rights legislation today. If the Emancipation Proclamation, issued by that great shining liberal called Lincoln, had freed him, he wouldn't be singing "We Shall Overcome" today. If the amendments to the Constitution had solved his problem, still his problem wouldn't be here today. And even if the Supreme Court desegregation decision of 1954 was genuinely and sincerely designed to solve his problem, his problem wouldn't be with us today.

So this kind of black man is thinking, he can see where every maneuver that America has made—supposedly to solve this problem—has been nothing but political trickery and treachery of the worst order. So today he doesn't have any confidence in these so-called liberals: Now I know that you—all that have come in here tonight don't call yourselves liberals. Because that's a nasty name today. It represents hypocrisy. So these two different types of black people exist in the so-called Negro community and they are beginning to wake up and their awakening is producing a very dangerous situation.

So you have whites in the community who express sincerity when they say they want to help. Well how can they help? How can a white person help the black man solve his problem? Number one: you can't solve it for him. You can help him solve it, but you can't solve it for him today. One of the best ways that you can solve it—or to help him solve it—is to let the so-called Negro, who has been involved in the civil-rights struggle, see that the civil-rights struggle must be expanded beyond the level of civil rights to human rights. Once it is expanded beyond the level of civil rights to the level of human rights, it opens the door for all of our brothers and sisters in Africa and Asia, who have their independence, to come to our rescue.

## CRIMINAL SITUATION

Why, when you go to Washington, D.C., expecting those crooks down

there to pass some kind—and that's what they are—to pass some kind of civil-rights legislation to correct a very criminal situation, what you are doing is encouraging the black man, who is the victim, to take his case into the court that's controlled by the criminal that made him the victim. It will never be solved in that way. Just like running from the wolf to the fox. The civil-rights struggle involves the black man taking his case to the white man's court. But when he fights it at the human-rights level, it is a different situation. It opens the door to take Uncle Sam to the world court. The black man doesn't have to go to court to be free. Uncle Sam should be taken to court and made to tell why the black man is not free in a so-called free society. Uncle Sam should be taken into the United Nations and charged with violating the UN charter on human rights.

You can forget civil rights. How are you going to get civil rights with men like Eastland and men like Dirksen and men like Johnson? It has to be taken out of their hands and taken into the hands of those whose power and authority exceed theirs. Washington has become too corrupt. Uncle Sam's conscience—Uncle Sam has become bankrupt when it comes to a conscience—it is impossible for Uncle Sam to solve the problem of 22,000,000 black people in this country. It is absolutely impossible to do if in Uncle Sam's courts—whether it is the Supreme Court or any other kind of court that comes under Uncle Sam's jurisdiction.

The only alternative that the black man has in America today is to take it out of Senator Dirksen's and Senator

Eastland's and President Johnson's jurisdiction and take it downtown on the East River and place it before that body of men who represent international law and let them know that the human rights of black people are being violated in the county that professes to be the moral leader of the free world.

Any time you have a filibuster in America, in the Senate, in 1964 over the rights of 22,000,000 black people, over the citizenship of 22,000,000 black people or that will effect the freedom and justice and equality of 22,000,000 black people, it's time for that government itself to be taken before a world court. How can you condemn South Africa? There are only 11,000,000 of our people in South Africa, there are 22,000,000 of them here. And we are receiving an injustice which is just as criminal as that which is being done to the black people of South Africa.

So today those whites who profess to be liberals—and as far as I am concerned it's just lip profession—you understand why our people don't have civil rights. You're white. You can go and hang out with another white liberal and see how hypocritical they are. While a lot of you sitting right here, know that you've seen whites up in a Negro's face with flowery words and as soon as that Negro walks away you listen to how your white friend talks. We have black people who can pass as white. We know how you talk.

We can see that it is nothing but a governmental conspiracy to continue to deprive the black people in this country of their rights. And the only way we will get these rights restored is by taking it out of Uncle Sam's hands. Take him to

court and charge him with genocide, the mass murder of millions of black people in this country—political murder, economic murder, social murder, mental murder. This is the crime that this government has committed and, if you yourself don't do something about it in time, you are going to open the doors for something to be done about it from outside forces.

I read in the paper yesterday where one of the Supreme Court Justices, Goldberg, was crying about the violation of human rights of 3,000,000 Jews in the Soviet Union. Imagine this. I haven't got anything against Jews, but that's their problem. How in the world are you going to cry about problems on the other side of the world when you haven't got the problems straightened out here? How can the plight of 3,000,000 Jews in Russia be qualified to be taken to the United Nations by a man who is a Justice in this Supreme Court, and is supposed to be a liberal, supposed to be a friend of black people and hasn't opened up his mouth one time about taking the plight of black people down here to the United Nations?

## POLITICALLY MATURE

Our people are becoming more politically mature. Their eyes are coming open. They are beginning to see the trend in all of the American politics today. They notice that every time there is an election it is so close among whites that they have to count the votes over again. This happened in Massachusetts when they were running for governor, this happened in Rhode Island, it happened in Minnesota, and many other places, and it happened in the election between Kennedy and Nixon. Things are so close that any minority that has a bloc vote can swing it either way.

And I think that most students of political science agree that it was the 80 percent support that Kennedy got from the black man in this country that enabled him to sit in the White House. Sat down there four years and the Negro was still in the doghouse. The same ones that we put in the White House have continued to keep us in the doghouse. The Negro can see that he holds the balance of power in this country politically.

It is he who puts in office the one who gets in office. Yet when the Negro helps that person get in office the Negro gets nothing in return. All he gets is a few appointments. A few handpicked Uncle Tom handkerchief-head Negroes are given big jobs in Washington, D.C. And then those Negroes come back and try and make us think that that administration is going to lead us to the promised land of integration. And the only ones whose problems have been solved have been those handpicked Negroes. A few big Negroes got jobs who didn't even need the jobs. They already were working. But the masses of black people are still unemployed.

The present administration, the Democratic administration, has been there for four years. Yet no meaningful legislation has been passed by them that proposes to benefit black people in this country, despite the fact that in the House they have 267 Democrats and only 177 are Republicans. They control two thirds of the House. In the Senate there are 67 Democrats and only 33 Republicans. The Democrats control two thirds of the government and it is the Negroes who put them in a position to control the government. Yet they give the Negroes nothing in return but a few handouts in the form of appointments that are only used as window-dressing to make it appear that the problem is being solved.

## TRICKERY AND TREACHERY

No, something is wrong. And when these black people wake up and find out for real the trickery and the treachery that has been heaped upon us you are going to have revolution. And when I say revolution I don't mean that stuff they were talking about last year about "We Shall Overcome." The Democrats get Negro support, yet the Negroes get nothing in return. The Negroes put the Democrats first, yet the Democrats put the Negroes last. And the alibi that the Democrats use—they blame the Dixiecrats.

A Dixiecrat is nothing but a Democrat in disguise. You show me a Dixiecrat and I'll show you a Democrat. And chances are, you show me a Democrat and I'll show you a Dixiecrat. Because Dixie in reality means all that territory south of the Canadian border. There are 16 Senatorial committees that run this government. Of the 16 Senatorial committees that run the government, ten of them are controlled by chairmen that are from the South. Of the 20 Congressional committees that help run the government, 12 of them are controlled by Southern segregationists.

Think of this: ten of the Senatorial committees are in the hands of the Dixiecrats, 12 of the 20 Congressional committees are in the hands of the Dixiecrats. These committees control the government. And you're going to tell us that the South lost the Civil War? The South controls the government. And they control it because they have seniority. And they have seniority because in the states that they come from, they deny Negroes the right to vote.

If Negroes could vote south of the— yes, if Negroes could vote South of the Canadian border—south South, if Negroes could vote in the southern part of the South, Ellender wouldn't be the head of the Agricultural and Forestry Committee, Richard Russell wouldn't be head of the Armed Services Committee, Robertson of Virginia wouldn't be head of the Banking and Currency Committee. Imagine that, all of the banking and currency of the government is in the hands of a cracker.

In fact, when you see how many of these committee men are from the South you can see that we have nothing but a cracker government in Washington, D.C. And their head is a cracker President. I said a cracker President. Texas is just as much a cracker state as Mississippi—and even more so. In Texas they lynch you with a Texas accent and in Mississippi they lynch you with a Mississippi accent.

And the first thing this man did when he came in office was invite all the big Negroes down for coffee. James Farmer was one of the first ones—the head of CORE. I have nothing against him. He's all right—Farmer, that is. But could that same President have invited James Farmer to Texas for coffee? And if James Farmer went to Texas, could he have taken his white wife with him to have coffee with the President? Any time you have a man who can't straighten out Texas, how can he straighten out the country. No, you're barking up the wrong tree.

If Negroes in the South could vote, the Dixiecrats would lose power. When the Dixiecrats lost power, the Democrats would lose power. A Dixiecrat lost is a Democrat lost. Therefore the two of them have to conspire with each other to stay in power. The Northern Dixiecrat puts all the blame on the Southern Dixiecrat. It's a con game, a giant political con game. The job of the Northern Democrat is to make the Negro think that he is our friend. He is always smiling and wagging his tail and telling us how much he can do for us if we vote for him. But, at the same time he's out in front telling us what he's going to do, behind the door he's in cahoots with the Southern Democrat setting up the machinery to make sure he'll never have to keep his promise.

This is the conspiracy that our people have faced in this country for the past 100 years. And today you have a new generation of black people who have come on the scene who have become disenchanted with the entire system, who have become disillusioned over the system and who are ready now and willing to do something about it. So in my conclusion in speaking about the black revolution, America today is at a time or in a day or at an hour where she is the first country on this earth that can actually have a bloodless revolution. In the past revolutions have been bloody. Historically you just don't have a peaceful revolution. Revolutions are bloody, revolutions are violent, revolutions cause bloodshed and death follows in their paths. America is the only country in history in a position to bring about a revolution without violence and bloodshed. But America is not morally equipped to do so.

Why is America in a position to bring about a bloodless revolution? Because the Negro in this country holds the balance of power and if the Negro in this country were given what the Constitution says he is supposed to have, the added power of the Negro in this country would sweep all of the racists and the segregationists out of office. It would change the entire political structure of the country. It would wipe out the Southern segregationism that now controls America's foreign policy, as well as America's domestic policy.

And the only way without bloodshed that this can be brought about is that the black man has to be given full use of the ballot in every one of the 50 states. But if the black man doesn't get the ballot, then you are going to be faced with another man who forgets the ballot and starts using the bullet.

Revolutions are fought to get control of land, to remove the absentee landlord and gain control of the land and the institutions that flow from that land. The black man has been in a very low condition because he has had no control

whatsoever over any land. He has been a beggar economically, a beggar politically, a beggar socially, a beggar even when it comes to trying to get some education. So that in the past the type of mentality that was developed in this colonial system among our people, today is being overcome. And as the young ones come up they know what they want. And as they listen to your beautiful preaching about democracy and all those other flowery words, they know what they're supposed to have.

So you have a people today who not only know what they want, but also know what they are supposed to have. And they themselves are clearing another generation that is coming up that not only will know what it wants and know what it should have, but also will be ready and willing to do whatever is necessary to see that what they should have materializes immediately. Thank you.

## Stokely Carmichael and Charles V. Hamilton, *Black Power*, 1967

Black Power *was probably the fundamental text of the newly conceived multicultural nation and one of the most significant documents in American race relations in the late twentieth century. Carmichael and Hamilton stress, in particular, black self-reliance and solidarity and reject assimilation and dependence on whites, even white liberals. These major themes of* Black Power *will be taken up by Indian, Asian American, and Latino American activists in the 1960s and 1970s and set the agenda for the new multiculturalism for a generation.*

Source: Stokely Carmichael and Charles V. Hamilton, *Black Power* (New York: Vintage Books, 1967).

Today, the American educational system continues to reinforce the entrenched values of the society through the use of words. Few people in this country question that this is "the land of the free and the home of the brave." They have had these words drummed into them from childhood. Few people question that this is the "Great Society" or that this country is fighting "Communist aggression" around the world. We mouth these things over and over, and they become truisms not to be questioned. In a similar way, black people have been saddled with epithets.

"Integration" is another current example of a word which has been defined according to the way white Americans see it. To many of them, it means black men wanting to marry white daughters; it means "race mixing"—implying bed or dance partners. To black people, it has meant a way to improve their lives—economically and politically. But the predominant white definition has stuck in the minds of too many people.

Black people must redefine themselves, and only *they* can do that. Throughout this country, vast segments of the black communities are beginning to recognize the need to assert their own definitions, to reclaim their history, their culture; to create their own sense of

community and togetherness. There is a growing resentment of the word "Negro," for example, because this term is the invention of our oppressor; it is *his* image of us that he describes. Many blacks are now calling themselves African-Americans, Afro-Americans or black people because that is our image of ourselves. When we begin to define our own image, the stereotypes—that is, lies—that our oppressor has developed will begin in the white community and end there. The black community will have a positive image of itself that *it* has created. This means we will no longer call ourselves lazy, apathetic, dumb, good-timers, shiftless, etc. Those are words used by white America to define us. If we accept these adjectives, as some of us have in the past, then we see ourselves only in a negative way, precisely the way white America wants us to see ourselves. Our incentive is broken and our will to fight is surrendered. From now on we shall view ourselves as African-Americans and as black people who are in fact energetic, determined, intelligent, beautiful and peace loving.

There is a terminology and ethos peculiar to the black community of which black people are beginning to be no longer ashamed. Black communities are the only large segments of this society where people refer to each other as brother—soul-brother, soul-sister. Some people may look upon this as *ersatz,* as make-believe, but it is not that. It is real. It is a growing sense of community. It is a growing realization that black Americans have a common bond not only among themselves, but with their African brothers. In *Black*

*Man's Burden,* John O. Killens described his trip to ten African countries as follows:

> Everywhere I went people called me brother. . . . "Welcome, American brother." It was a good feeling for me, to be in Africa. To walk in a land for the first time in your entire life knowing within yourself that your color would not be held against you. No black man ever knows this in America [p. 160].

More and more black Americans are developing this feeling. They are becoming aware that they have a history which pre-dates their forced introduction to this country. African-American history means a long history beginning on the continent of Africa, a history not taught in the standard textbooks of this country. It is absolutely essential that black people know this history, that they know their roots, that they develop an awareness of their cultural heritage. Too long have they been kept in submission by being told that they had no culture, no manifest heritage, before they landed on the slave auction blocks in this country. If black people are to know themselves as a vibrant, valiant people, they must know their roots. And they will soon learn that the Hollywood image of man-eating cannibals waiting for, and waiting on, the Great White Hunter is a lie.

With redefinition will come a clearer notion of the role black Americans can play in this world. This role will emerge clearly out of the unique, common experiences of Afro-Asians. Killens concludes:

I believe furthermore that the American Negro can be the bridge between the West and Africa-Asia. We black Americans can serve as a bridge to mutual understanding. The one thing we black Americans have in common with the other colored peoples of the world is that we have all felt the cruel and ruthless heel of white supremacy. We have all been "niggerized" on one level or another. And all of us are determined to "deniggerize" the earth. To rid the world of "niggers" is the Black Mans's Burden, human reconstruction is the grand objective [p. 176].

Only when black people fully develop this sense of community, of themselves, can they begin to deal effectively with the problems of racism in *this* country. This is what we mean by a new consciousness; this is the vital first step.

The next step is what we shall call the process of political modernization—a process which must take place if the society is to be rid of racism. "Political modernization" includes many things, but we mean by it three major concepts: (1) questioning old values and institutions of the society; (2) searching for new and different forms of political structure to solve political and economic problems; and (3) broadening the base of political participation to include more people in the decision-making process. These notions (we shall take up each in turn) are central to our thinking throughout this book and to contemporary American history as a whole. As David Apter wrote in *The Politics of Mod-*

ernization, ". . . the struggle to modernize is what has given meaning to our beliefs. . . . So compelling a force has it become that we are forced to ask new questions of our own institutions. Each country, whether modernized or modernizing, stands in both judgment and fear of the results. Our own society is no exception" (p. 2).

The values of this society support a racist system; we find it incongruous to ask black people to adopt and support most of those values. We also reject the assumption that the basic institutions of this society must be preserved. The goal of black people must *not* be to assimilate into middle-class America, for that class—as a whole—is without a viable conscience as regards humanity. The values of the middle class permit the perpetuation of the ravages of the black community. The values of that class are based on material aggrandizement, not the expansion of humanity. The values of that class ultimately support cloistered little closed societies tucked away neatly in tree-lined suburbia. The values of that class do *not* lead to the creation of an open society. That class *mouths* its preference for a free, competitive society, while at the same time forcefully and even viciously denying to black people as a group the opportunity to compete.

We are not unmindful of other descriptions of the social utility of the middle class. Banfield and Wilson, in *City Politics*, concluded:

The departure of the middle class from the central city is important in other ways. . . . The middle class supplies a social and political leavening in the life of a city. Middle-class people demand good schools and integrity in government. They support churches, lodges, parent-teacher associations, scout troops, better-housing committees, art galleries, and operas. It is the middle class, in short, that asserts a conception of the public interest. Now its activity is increasingly concentrated in the suburbs [p. 14].

But this same middle class manifests a sense of superior group position in regard to race. This class wants "good government" *for themselves;* it wants good schools *for its children.* At the same time, many of its members sneak into the black community by day, exploit it, and take the money home to their middle-class communities at night to support their operas and art galleries and comfortable homes. When not actually robbing, they will fight off the handful of more affluent black people who seek to move in; when they approve or even seek token integration, it applies only to black people like themselves—as "white" as possible. *This class is the backbone of institutional racism in this country.*

Thus we reject the goal of assimilation into middle-class America because the values of that class are in themselves anti-humanist and because that class as a social force perpetuates racism. We must face the fact that, in the past, what we have called the movement has not really questioned the middle-class values and institutions of this country. If anything, it has accepted those values and institutions without fully realizing their racist nature. Reorientation means an emphasis on the dignity of man, not on the sanctity of property. It means the creation of a society where human misery and poverty are repugnant to that society, not an indication of laziness or lack of initiative. The creation of new values means the establishment of a society based, as Killens expresses it in *Black Man's Burden,* on "free people," not "free enterprise." (p. 167). To do this means to modernize—*indeed, to civilize*—this country.

Supporting the old values are old political and economic structures; these must also be "modernized." We should at this point distinguish between "structures" and "system." By system, we have in mind the entire American complex of basic institutions, values, beliefs, etc. By structures, we mean the specific institutions (political parties, interest groups, bureaucratic administrations) which exist to conduct the business of that system. Obviously, the first is broader than the second. Also, the second assumes the legitimacy of the first. Our view is that, given the illegitimacy of the system, we cannot then proceed to transform that system with existing structures.

The two major political parties in this country have become non viable entities for the legitimate representation of the real needs of masses—especially blacks—in this country. Walter Lippmann raised the same point in his syndicated column of December 8, 1966. He pointed out that the party system in the United States developed before our society became as technologically complex as it is now. He says that the ways in which men live and define themselves are changing radically. Old ideological is-

sues, once the subject of passionate controversy, Lippmann argues, are of little interest today. He asks whether the great urban complexes—which are rapidly becoming the centers of black population in the U.S.—can be run with the same systems and ideas that derive from a time when America was a country of small villages and farms. While not addressing himself directly to the question of race, Lippmann raises a major question about our political institutions; and the crisis of race in America may be its major symptom.

Black people have seen the city planning commissions, the urban renewal commissions, the boards of education and the police departments fail to speak to their needs in a meaningful way. We must devise new structures, new institutions to replace those forms or to make them responsive. There is nothing sacred or inevitable about old institutions; the focus must be on people, not forms. . . .

The adoption of the concept of Black Power is one of the most legitimate and healthy developments in American politics and race relations in our time. The concept of Black Power speaks to all the needs mentioned in this chapter. It is a call for black people in this country to unite, to recognize their heritage, to build a sense of community. It is a call for black people to begin to define their own goals, to lead their own organizations and to support those organizations. It is a call to reject the racist institutions and values of the society.

The concept of Black Power rests on a fundamental premise: *Before a group can enter the open society, it must first close ranks.* By this we mean that group solidarity is necessary before a group can operate effectively from a bargaining position of strength in a pluralistic society. Traditionally, each new ethnic group in this society has found the route to social and political viability through the organization of its own institutions with which to represent its needs within the larger society. Studies in voting behavior specifically, and political behavior generally, have made it clear that politically the American pot has not melted. Italians vote for Rubino over O'Brien; Irish for Murphy over Goldberg, etc. This phenomenon may seem distasteful to some, but it has been and remains today a central fact of the American political system. There are other examples of ways in which groups in the society have remembered their roots and used this effectively in the political arena. Theodore Sorensen describes the politics of foreign aid during the Kennedy Administration in his book *Kennedy:*

> No powerful constituencies or interest groups backed foreign aid. The Marshall Plan at least had appealed to Americans who traced their roots to the Western European nations aided. But there were few voters who identified with India, Colombia or Tanganyika [p. 351].

The extent to which black Americans can and do "trace their roots" to Africa, to that extent will they be able to be more effective on the political scene.

A white reporter set forth this point in other terms when he made the following observation about white Mississippi's manipulation of the anti-poverty program:

> The war on poverty has been predicated on the notion that there is such a thing as a community which can be defined geographically and mobilized for a collective effort to help the poor. This theory has no relationship to reality in the deep South. In every Mississippi county there are two communities. Despite all the pious platitudes of the moderates on both side, these two communities habitually see their interests in terms of conflict rather than cooperation. Only when the Negro community can muster enough political, economic and professional strength to compete on somewhat equal terms, will Negroes believe in the possibility of true cooperation and whites accept its necessity. En route to integration, the Negro community needs to develop a greater independence—a chance to run its own affairs and not cave in whenever "the man" barks—or so it seems to me, and to most of the knowledgeable people with whom I talked in Mississippi. To OEO, this judgment may sound like black nationalism . . . [Jencks, *New Republic,* April 16, 1966].

The point is obvious: black people must lead and run their own organizations. Only black people can convey the revolutionary idea—and it is a revolutionary idea—that black people are able to do things themselves. Only they can help create in the community an aroused and continuing black consciousness that will provide the basis for political strength. In the past, white allies have often furthered white supremacy without the whites involved realizing it, or even wanting to do so. Black people must come together and do things for themselves. They must achieve self-identity and self-determination in order to have their daily needs met.

Black Power means, for example, that in Lowndes County, Alabama, a black sheriff can end police brutality. A black tax assessor and tax collector and county board of revenue can lay, collect, and channel tax monies for the building of better roads and schools serving black people. In such areas as Lowndes, where black people have a majority, they will attempt to use power to exercise control. This is what they seek: control. When black people lack a majority, Black Power means proper representation and sharing of control. It means the creation of power bases, of strength, from which black people can press to change local or nation-wide patterns of oppression—instead of from weakness.

It does not mean *merely* putting black faces into office. Black visibility is not Black Power. Most of the black politicians around the country today are not examples of Black Power. The power must be that of a community, and emanate from there. The black politicians must start from there. The black politicians must stop being representatives of "downtown" machines, whatever the cost might be in terms of lost patronage and holiday handouts.

Black Power recognizes—it must recognize—the ethnic basis of American politics as well as the power oriented nature of American politics. Black Power therefore calls for black people to consolidate behind their own, so that they can bargain from a position of strength. But while we endorse the *procedure* of group solidarity and identity for the purpose of attaining certain goals in the body politic, this does not mean that black people should strive for the same kind of rewards (i.e., end results) obtained by the white society. The ultimate values and goals are not domination or exploitation of other groups, but rather an effective share in the total power of the society.

Nevertheless, some observers have labeled those who advocate Black Power as racists; they have said that the call for self-identification and self-determination is "racism in reverse" or "black supremacy." This is a deliberate and absurd lie. There is no analogy—by any stretch of definition or imagination—between the advocates of Black Power and white racists. Racism is not merely exclusion on the basis of race but exclusion for the purpose of subjugating or maintaining subjugation. The goal of the racists is to keep black people on the bottom, arbitrarily and dictatorially, as they have done in this country for over three hundred years. The goal of black self-determination and black self-identity—Black Power—is full participation in the decision-making processes affecting the lives of black people, and recognition of the virtues in themselves as black people. The black people of this country have not lynched whites, bombed their churches, murdered their children and manipulated laws and institutions to maintain oppression. White racists have. Congressional laws, one after the other, have not been necessary to stop black people from oppressing others and denying others the full enjoyment of their rights. White racists have made such laws necessary. The goal of Black Power is positive and functional to a free and viable society. No white racist can make this claim. . . .

One of the tragedies of the struggle against racism is that up to this point there has been no national organization which could speak to the growing militancy of young black people in the urban ghettos and the black-belt South. There has been only a "civil rights" movement, whose tone of voice was adapted to an audience of middle-class whites. It served as a sort of buffer zone between that audience and angry young blacks. It claimed to speak for the needs of a community, but it did not speak in the tone of that community. None of its so-called leaders could go into a rioting community and be listened to. In a sense, the blame must be shared—along with the mass media—by those leaders for what happened in Watts, Harlem, Chicago, Cleveland and other places. Each time the black people in those cities saw Dr. Martin Luther King get slapped they become angry. When they saw little black girls bombed to death in *a church* and civil rights workers ambushed and murdered, they were steaming mad. We had nothing to offer that they could see, except to go out and be beaten again. We helped to build their frustration.

We had only the old language of love and suffering. And in most places—that is, from the liberals and middle class we

got back the old language of patience and progress. The civil rights leaders were saying to the country: "Look, you guys are supposed to be nice guys, and we are only going to do what we are supposed to do. Why do you beat us up? Why don't you give us what we ask? Why don't you straighten yourselves out?" For the masses of black people, this language resulted in virtually nothing. In fact, their objective day-to-day condition worsened. The unemployment rate among black people increased while that among whites declined. Housing conditions in the black communities deteriorated. Schools in the black ghettos continued to plod along on outmoded techniques, inadequate curricula, and with all too many tired and indifferent teachers. Meanwhile, the President picked up the refrain of "We Shall Overcome" while the Congress passed civil rights law after civil rights law, only to have them effectively nullified by deliberately weak enforcement. "Progress is being made," we were told.

Such language, along with admonitions to remain nonviolent and fear the white backlash, convinced some that that course was the *only* course to follow. It misled some into believing that a black minority could bow its head and get whipped into a meaningful position of power. The very notion is absurd. The white society devised the language, adopted the rules and had the black community narcotized into believing that that language and those rules were, in fact, relevant. The black community was told time and again how *other* immigrants finally won *acceptance:* that is, by following the Protestant Ethic of Work and

Achievement. They worked hard; therefore, they achieved. We were not told that it was by building Irish Power, Italian Power, Polish Power or Jewish Power that these groups got themselves together and operated from positions of strength. We were not told that "the American dream" wasn't designed for black people. That while today, to whites, the dream may *seem* to include black people, it cannot do so by the very nature of this nation's political and economic system, which imposes institutional racism on the black masses if not upon every individual black. A notable comment on that "dream" was made by Dr. Percy Julian, the black scientist and director of the Julian Research Institute in Chicago, a man for whom the dream seems to have come true. While not subscribing to "black power" as he understood it, Dr. Julian clearly understood the basis for it: "The false concept of basic Negro inferiority is one of the curses that still lingers. It is a problem created by the white man. Our children just no longer are going to accept the patience we were taught by our generation. We were taught a pretty little lie—excel and the whole world lies open before you. I *obeyed the injunction and found it to be wishful thinking.*" (Authors' italics)

A key phrase in our buffer-zone days was non-violence. For years it has been thought that black people would not literally fight for their lives. Why this has been so is not entirely clear; neither the larger society nor black people are noted for passivity. The notion apparently stems from the years of marches and demonstrations and sit-ins where black people did not strike back and the violence always came from white mobs. There are many who still sincerely believe in that approach. From our viewpoint, rampaging white mobs and white night-riders must be made to understand that their days of free head-whipping are over. Black people should and must fight back. Nothing more quickly repels someone bent on destroying you than the unequivocal message: "O.K., fool, make your move, and run the same risk I run—of dying."

When the concept of Black Power is set forth, many people immediately conjure up notions of violence. The country's reaction to the Deacons for Defense and Justice, which originated in Louisiana, is instructive. Here is a group which realized that the "law" and law enforcement agencies would not protect people, so they had to do it themselves. If a nation fails to protect its citizens, then that nation cannot condemn those who take up the task themselves. The Deacons and all other blacks who resort to self-defense represent a simple answer to a simple question: what man would not defend his family and home from attack?

But this frightened some white people, because they knew that black people would now fight back. They knew that this was precisely what *they* would have long since done if *they* were subjected to the injustices and oppression heaped on blacks. Those of us who advocate Black Power are quit clear in our own minds that a "non-violent" approach to civil rights is an approach black people cannot afford and a luxury white people do not deserve. It is crystal clear to us—and it must become so with the white society—*that there can be no social order without social justice.* White people must be made to understand that they must stop messing with black people, or the blacks *will* fight back!

Next, we must deal with the term "integration." According to its advocates, social justice will be accomplished by "integrating the Negro into the mainstream institutions of the society from which he has been traditionally excluded." This concept is based on the assumption that there is nothing of value in the black community and that little of value could be created among black people. The thing to do is siphon off the "acceptable" black people into the surrounding middle-class white community.

The goals of integrationists are middle-class goals, articulated primarily by a small group of Negroes with middle-class aspirations or status. Their kind of integration has meant that a few blacks "make it," leaving the black community, sapping it of leadership potential and know-how. As we noted in Chapter I, those token Negroes—absorbed into a white mass—are of no value to the remaining black masses. They become meaningless showpieces for a conscience-soothed white society. Such people will state that they would prefer to be treated "only as individuals, not as Negroes"; that they "are not and should not be preoccupied with race." This is a totally unrealistic position. In the first place, black people have not suffered as individuals but as members of a group; therefore, their liberation lies in group action. This is why SNCC—and the concept of Black Power affirms that helping *individual* black people to solve

their problems on an *individual* basis does little to alleviate the mass of black people. Secondly, while color blindness *may* be a sound goal ultimately, we must realize that race is an overwhelming fact of life in this historical period. There is no black man in this country who can live "simply as a man." His blackness is an ever present fact of this racist society, whether he recognizes it or not. It is unlikely that this or the next generation will witness the time when race will no longer be relevant in the conduct of public affairs and in public policy decision-making. To realize this and to attempt to deal with it does not make one a racist or overly preoccupied with race; it puts one in the forefront of a significant *struggle*. If there is no intense struggle today, there will be no meaningful results tomorrow.

"Integration" as a goal today speaks to the problem of blackness not only in an unrealistic way but also in a despicable way. It is based on complete acceptance of the fact that in order to have a decent house or education, black people must move into a white neighborhood or send their children to a white school. This reinforces, among both black and white, the idea that "white" is automatically superior and "black" is by definition inferior. For this reason, "integration" is a subterfuge for the maintenance of white supremacy. It allows the nation to focus on a handful of Southern black children who get into white schools at a great price, and to ignore the ninety-four percent who are left in unimproved all black schools. Such situations will not change until black people become equal in a way that means something, and integration ceases to be a one-way street. Then integration does not mean draining skills and energies from the black ghetto into white neighborhoods. To sprinkle black children among white pupils in outlying schools is at best a stop-gap measure. The goal is not to take black children out of the black community and expose them to white middle-class values; the goal is to build and strengthen the black community.

"Integration" also means that black people must give up their identity, deny their heritage. We recall the conclusion of Killian and Grigg: "At the present time, integration as a solution to the race problem demands that the Negro foreswear his identity as a Negro." The fact is that integration, as traditionally articulated, would abolish the black community. The fact is that what must be abolished is not the black community, but the dependent colonial status that has been inflicted upon it.

The racial and cultural personality of the black community must be preserved and that community must win its freedom while preserving its cultural integrity. Integrity includes a pride—in the sense of self-acceptance, not chauvinism—in being black, in the historical attainments and contributions of black people. No person can be healthy, complete and mature if he must deny a part of himself; this is what "integration" has required thus far. This is the essential difference between integration as it is currently practiced and the concept of Black Power.

The idea of cultural integrity is so obvious that it seems almost simple-minded to spell things out at this length. Yet millions of Americans resist such

truths when they are applied to black people. Again, that resistance is a comment on the fundamental racism in the society. Irish Catholics took care of their own first without a lot of apology for doing so, without any dubious language from timid leadership about guarding against "backlash." Everyone understood it to be a perfectly legitimate procedure. Of course, there would be "backlash." Organization begets counterorganization, but this was no reason to defer.

The so-called white backlash against black people is something else: the embedded traditions of institutional racism being brought into the open and calling forth overt manifestations of individual racism. In the summer of 1966, when the protest marches into Cicero, Illinois, began, the black people knew they were not allowed to live in Cicero and the white people knew it. When blacks began to demand the right to live in homes in that town, the whites simply reminded them of the status quo. Some people called this "backlash." It was, in fact, racism defending itself. In the black community, this is called "White folks showing their color." It is ludicrous to blame black people for what is simply an overt manifestation of white racism. Dr. Martin Luther King stated clearly that the protest marches were not the cause of the racism but merely exposed a long-term cancerous condition in the society.

We come now to the rhetoric of coalition as part of the traditional approach to ending racism: the concept of the civil rights movement as a kind of liaison between the powerful white community and a dependent black community. "Coalition" involves the whole question of how one approaches politics and political alliances. It is so basic to an understanding of Black Power that we will devote an entire chapter to the subject.

## Native American Graves and Repatriation Act, 1990

*The Native American Graves and Repatriation Act, passed in 1990, was part of a broad effort by Native Americans to overturn older notions of them as primitive others and assert claims for respect and control of their heritage. It required museums, which collected Native American human remains in an earlier era for research and display, to return those remains and/or sacred artifacts used in burials of the bodies to tribal descendants.*

*Source:* http://www4.law.cornell.edu/uscode/25/ch32.htm#pc32

## SEC. 4. ILLEGAL TRAFFICKING

*(a) ILLEGAL TRAFFICKING.* Chapter 53 of title 18, United States Code, is amended by adding at the end thereof the following new section: *SEC. 1170. ILLEGAL TRAFFICKING IN NATIVE AMERICAN HUMAN REMAINS AND CULTURAL ITEMS*

"(a) Whoever knowingly sells, purchases, uses for profit, or transports for sale or profit, the human remains of a Native American without the right of possession to those remains as provided in the Native American Graves Protection and Repatriation Act shall be fined in accordance with this title, or impris-

oned not more than 12 months, or both, and in the case of a second or subsequent violation, be fined in accordance with this title, or imprisoned not more than 5 years, or both.

"(b) Whoever knowingly sells, purchases, uses for profit, or transports for sale or profit any Native American cultural items obtained in violation of the Native American Graves Protection and Repatriation Act shall be fined in accordance with this title, imprisoned not more than one year, or both, and in the case of a second or subsequent violation, be fined in accordance with this title, imprisoned not more than 5 years, or both."

(b) TABLE OF CONTENTS. The table of contents for chapter 53 of title 18, United States Code, is amended by adding at the end thereof the following new item:

"1170. Illegal Trafficking in Native American Human Remains and Cultural Items."

## SEC. 5. INVENTORY FOR HUMAN REMAINS AND ASSOCIATED FUNERARY OBJECTS

(a) *IN GENERAL.* Each Federal agency and each museum which has possession or control over holdings or collections of Native American human remains and associated funerary objects shall compile an inventory of such items and, to the extent possible based on information possessed by such museum or federal agency, identify the geographical and cultural affiliation of such item.

*(b) REQUIREMENTS.* (1) The inventories and identifications required under subsection (a) shall be

(A) completed in consultation with tribal government and Native Hawaiian organization officials and traditional religious leaders;

(B) completed by not later than the date that is 5 years after the date of enactment of this Act, and

(C) made available both during the time they are being conducted and afterward to a review committee established under section 8.

(2) Upon request by an Indian tribe or Native Hawaiian organization which receives or should have received notice, a museum or federal agency shall supply additional available documentation to supplement the information required by subsection (a) of this section. The term "documentation" means a summary of existing museum or Federal agency records, including inventories or catalogues, relevant studies, or other pertinent data for the limited purpose of determining the geographical origin, cultural affiliation, and basic facts surrounding acquisition and accession of Native American human remains and associated funerary objects subject to this section. Such term does not mean, and this Act shall not be construed to be an authorization for, the initiation of new scientific studies of such remains and associated funerary objects or other means of acquiring or preserving additional scientific information from such remains and objects.

*(c) EXTENSION OF TIME FOR INVENTORY.* Any museum which has made a good faith effort to carry out an inventory and identification under this section, but which has been unable to complete the process, may appeal to the Secretary for an extension of the time requirements set forth in subsection (b)(1)(B). The Secretary may extend such time requirements for any such museum upon a finding of good faith effort. An indication of good faith shall include the development of a plan to carry out the inventory and identification process.

*(d) NOTIFICATION.* (1) If the cultural affiliation of any particular Native American human remains or associated funerary objects is determined pursuant to this section, the Federal agency or museum concerned shall, not later than 6 months after the completion of the inventory, notify the affected Indian tribes or Native Hawaiian organizations.

(2) The notice required by paragraph (1) shall include information

(A) which identifies each Native American human remains or associated funerary objects and the circumstances surrounding its acquisition;

(B) which lists the human remains or associated funerary objects that are clearly identifiable as to tribal origin; and

(C) which lists the Native American human remains and associated funerary objects that are not clearly identifiable as being culturally affiliated with that Indian tribe or Native Hawaiian organization, but which, given the totality of circumstances surrounding acquisition of the remains or objects, are determined by a reasonable belief to be remains or objects culturally affiliated with the Indian tribe or Native Hawaiian organization.

(3) A copy of each notice provided

under paragraph (1) shall be sent to the Secretary who shall publish each notice in the Federal Register.

*(e) INVENTORY.* For the purposes of this section, the term "inventory" means a simple itemized list that summarizes the information called for by this section.

## SEC. 6. SUMMARY FOR UNASSOCIATED FUNERARY OBJECTS, SACRED OBJECTS, AND CULTURAL PATRIMONY

*(a) IN GENERAL.* Each Federal agency or museum which has possession or control over holdings or collections of Native American unassociated funerary objects, sacred objects, or objects of cultural patrimony shall provide a written summary of such objects based upon available information held by such agency or museum. The summary shall describe the scope of the collection, kinds of objects included, reference to geographical location, means and period of acquisition and cultural affiliation, where readily ascertainable.

*(b) REQUIREMENTS.* (1) The summary required under subsection (a) shall be

(A) in lieu of an object-by-object inventory;

(B) followed by consultation with tribal government and Native Hawaiian organization officials and traditional religious leaders; and

(C) completed by not later than the date that is 3 years after the date of enactment of this Act.

(2) Upon request, Indian tribes and

Native Hawaiian organizations shall have access to records, catalogues, relevant studies or other pertinent data for the limited purposes of determining the geographic origin, cultural affiliation, and basic facts surrounding acquisition and accession of Native American objects subject to this section. Such information shall be provided in a reasonable manner to be agreed upon by all parties.

## SEC. 7. REPATRIATION

*(a) REPATRIATION OF NATIVE AMERICAN HUMAN REMAINS AND OBJECTS POSSESSED OR CONTROLLED BY FEDERAL AGENCIES AND MUSEUMS.* (1) If, pursuant to section 5, the cultural affiliation of Native American human remains and associated funerary objects with a particular Indian tribe or Native Hawaiian organization is established, then the Federal agency or museum, upon the request of a known lineal descendant of the Native American or of the tribe or organization and pursuant to subsections (b) and (e) of this section, shall expeditiously return such remains and associated funerary objects.

(2) If, pursuant to section 6, the cultural affiliation with a particular Indian tribe or Native Hawaiian organization is shown with respect to unassociated funerary objects, sacred objects or objects of cultural patrimony, then the Federal agency or museum, upon the request of the Indian tribe or Native Hawaiian organization and pursuant to subsections (b), (c) and (e) of this section, shall expeditiously return such objects.

(3) The return of cultural items cov-

ered by this Act shall be in consultation with the requesting lineal descendant or tribe or organization to determine the place and manner of delivery of such items.

(4) Where cultural affiliation of Native American human remains and funerary objects has not been established in an inventory prepared pursuant to section 5 or where Native American human remains and funerary objects are not included upon any such inventory, then, upon request and pursuant to subsections (b) and (e) and, in the case of unassociated funerary objects, subsection (c), such Native American human remains and funerary objects shall be expeditiously returned where the requesting Indian tribe or Native Hawaiian organization can show cultural affiliation by a preponderance of the evidence based upon geographical, kinship, biological, archaeological, anthropological, linguistic, folkloric, oral traditional, historical, or other relevant information or expert opinion.

(5) Upon request and pursuant to subsections (b), (c) and (e), sacred objects and objects of cultural patrimony shall be expeditiously returned where

(A) the requesting party is the direct lineal descendant of an individual who owned the sacred object;

(B) the requesting Indian tribe or Native Hawaiian organization can show that the object was owned or controlled by the tribe or organization; or

(C) the requesting Indian tribe or Native Hawaiian organization can show that the sacred object was owned or controlled by a member thereof, provided that in the case where a sacred object

was owned by a member thereof, there are no identifiable lineal descendants of said member or the lineal descendants, upon notice, have failed to make a claim for the object under this Act.

*(b) SCIENTIFIC STUDY.* If the lineal descendant, Indian tribe, or Native Hawaiian organization requests the return of culturally affiliated Native American cultural items, the Federal agency or museum shall expeditiously return such items unless such items are indispensable for completion of a specific scientific study, the outcome of which would be of major benefit to the United States. Such items shall be returned by no later than 90 days after the date on which the scientific study is completed.

*(c) STANDARD OF REPATRIATION.* If a known lineal descendant or an Indian tribe or Native Hawaiian organization requests the return of Native American unassociated funerary objects, sacred objects or objects of cultural patrimony pursuant to this Act and presents evidence which, if standing alone before the introduction of evidence to the contrary, would support a finding that the Federal agency or museum did not have the right of possession, then such agency or museum shall return such objects unless it can overcome such inference and prove that it has a right of possession to the objects.

*(d) SHARING OF INFORMATION BY FEDERAL AGENCIES AND MUSEUMS.* Any Federal agency or museum shall share what information it does possess regarding the object in question with the known lineal descendant, Indian tribe, or Native Hawaiian organization to assist in making a claim under this section.

*(e) COMPETING CLAIMS.* Where there are multiple requests for repatriation of any cultural item and, after complying with the requirements of this Act, the Federal agency or museum cannot clearly determine which requesting party is the most appropriate claimant, the agency or museum may retain such item until the requesting parties agree upon its disposition or the dispute is otherwise resolved pursuant to the provisions of this Act or by a court of competent jurisdiction.

*(f) MUSEUM OBLIGATION.* Any museum which repatriates any item in good faith pursuant to this Act shall not be liable for claims by an aggrieved party or for claims of breach of fiduciary duty, public trust, or violations of state law that are inconsistent with the provisions of this Act.

# Huey Newton, Interview, 1968, and Black Panther Party Platform, 1966

*The Black Panther Party for Self Defense emerged in Oakland in 1966. The Panthers were probably the best known of the most militant and radical wing of the new black politics. They drew up their platform, reprinted below, in October of 1966.*

*Source:* Huey Newton, "Huey Newton Speaks from Jail," *Motive* 29 (October 1968): 8–16; The Black Panther Party, "Platform and Program of the Black Panther Party," October 1966, in Thomas Frazier, ed., *Afro-American History,* 2d ed. (Belmont, Cal.: Wadsworth Publishing, 1988).

## HUEY NEWTON INTERVIEW

QUESTION: The question of nationalism is a vital one in the black movement today. Some have made a distinction between cultural nationalism and revolutionary nationalism. Would you comment on the differences and give us your views?

HUEY P. NEWTON: Revolutionary nationalism first is dependent upon a people's revolution with the end goal being the people in power. Therefore, to be a revolutionary nationalist you would by necessity have to be a socialist. If you are a reactionary nationalist your end goal is the oppression of the people.

Cultural nationalism, or pork chop nationalism, as I sometimes call it, is basically a problem of having the wrong political perspective. It seems to be a reaction instead of a response to political oppression. The cultural nationalists are concerned with returning to the old African culture and thereby regaining their identity and freedom. In other words, they feel that the African culture automatically will bring political freedom.

The Black Panther Party, which is a revolutionary group of black people, realizes that we have to have an identity. We have to realize our black heritage in order to give us strength to move on and progress. But as far as returning to the old African culture, it's unnecessary and not advantageous in many respects. We believe that culture itself will not liberate us. We're going to need some stronger stuff.

A good example of revolutionary nationalism was the revolution in Algeria when Ben Bella took over. The French were kicked out, but it was a people's revolution because the people ended up in power. The leaders that took over were not interested in the profit motive where they could exploit the people and keep them in a state of slavery. They nationalized the industry and plowed the would-be profits into the community. That's what socialism is all about in a nutshell. The people's representatives are in office strictly on the leave of the people. The wealth of the country is controlled by the people and they are considered whenever modifications in the industries are made.

The Black Panther Party is a revolutionary Nationalist group and we see a major contradiction between capitalism in this country and our interests. We realize that this country became very rich upon slavery and that slavery is capitalism in the extreme. We have two evils to fight, capitalism and racism. We must destroy both racism and capitalism.

QUESTION: Directly related to the question of nationalism is the question of unity within the black community. There has been some question about this since the Black Panther Party has run candidates against other black candidates in recent California elections. What is your position on this matter?

HUEY: A very peculiar thing has happened. Historically, you have what Malcolm X calls the field nigger and the house nigger. The house nigger had some privileges. He got the worn-out clothes of the master and he didn't have to work as hard as the field black. He came to respect the master to such an extent that he identified with the master, because he

got a few of the leftovers that the field blacks did not get. And through this identity with him, he saw the slavemaster's interest as being his interest. Sometimes he would even protect the slavemaster more than the slavemaster would protect himself. Malcolm makes the point that if the master's house happened to catch on fire, the house Negro would work harder than the master to put the fire out and save the master's house, while the field black was praying that the house burned down. The house black identified with the master so much that, when the master would get sick, the house Negro would say, "Master, we's sick!"

Members of the Black Panther Party are the field blacks; we're hoping the master dies if he gets sick. The black bourgeoisie seem to be acting in the role of the house Negro. They are pro-administration. They would like a few concessions made, but as far as the overall setup, they have more material goods, a little more advantage, a few more privileges than the black have-nots, the lower class, and so they identify with the power structure and they see their interest as the power structure's interest. In fact, it's against their interest.

The Black Panther Party was forced to draw a line of demarcation. We are for all of those who are for the promotion of the interests of the black have-nots, which represents about 98 percent of blacks here in America. We're not controlled by the white mother country radicals nor are we controlled by the black bourgeoisie. We have a mind of our own and if the black bourgeoisie cannot align itself with our complete program, then the black bourgeoisie sets itself up as our enemy.

QUESTION: The Black Panther Party has had considerable contact with white radicals since its earliest days. What do you see as the role of these white radicals?

HUEY: The white mother country radical is the offspring of the children of the beast that has plundered the world exploiting all people, concentrating on the people of color. These are children of the beast that seem now to be redeemed because they realize that their former heroes, who were slavemasters and murderers, put forth ideas that were only façades to hide the treachery they inflicted upon the world. They are turning their backs on their fathers.

The white mother country radical, in resisting the system, becomes a somewhat abstract thing because he's not oppressed as much as black people are. As a matter of fact, his oppression is somewhat abstract simply because he doesn't have to live in a reality of oppression.

Black people in America, and colored people throughout the world suffer not only from exploitation, but they suffer from racism. Black people here in America, in the black colony, are oppressed because we're black and we're exploited. The whites are rebels, many of them from the middle class and as far as any overt oppression this is not the case. Therefore, I call their rejection of the system a somewhat abstract thing. They're looking for new heroes. They're looking to wash away the hypocrisy that their fathers have presented to the world. In doing this they see the people who are really fighting for freedom. They see the people

who are really standing for justice and equality and peace throughout the world. They are the people of Vietnam, the people of Latin America, the people of Asia, the people of Africa, and the black people in the black colony here in America.

This presents something of a problem in many ways to the black revolutionary, especially to the cultural nationalist. The cultural nationalist doesn't understand the white revolutionaries because he can't see why anyone white would turn on the system. He thinks that maybe this is some more hypocrisy being planted by white people.

I personally think that there are many young white revolutionaries who are sincere in attempting to realign themselves with mankind, and to make a reality out of the high moral standards that their fathers and forefathers only expressed. In pressing for new heroes, the young white revolutionaries found these heroes in the black colony at home and in the colonies throughout the world.

The young white revolutionaries raised the cry for the troops to withdraw from Vietnam, to keep hands off Latin America, to withdraw from the Dominican Republic and also to withdraw from the black community or the black colony. So we have a situation in which the young white revolutionaries are attempting to identify with the oppressed people of the colonies against the exploiter.

The problem arises, then, in what part they can play. How can they aid the colony? How can they aid the Black Panther Party or any other black revolutionary group? They can aid the black revolutionaries first, by simply turning away from the establishment, and secondly, by choosing their friends. For instance, they have a choice between whether they will be a friend of Lyndon Baines Johnson or a friend of Fidel Castro. A friend of mine or a friend of Johnson's. These are direct opposites. After they make this choice, then the white revolutionaries have a duty and a responsibility to act.

The imperialistic or capitalistic system occupies areas. It occupies Vietnam now. It occupies areas by sending soldiers there, by sending policemen there. The policemen or soldiers are only a gun in the establishment's hand, making the racist secure in his racism, the establishment secure in its exploitation. The first problem, it seems, is to remove the gun from the establishment's hand. Until lately, the white radical has seen no reason to come into conflict with the policeman in his own community. I said "until recently," because there is friction now in the mother country between the young revolutionaries and the police; because now the white revolutionaries are attempting to put some of their ideas into action, and there's the rub. We say that it should be a permanent thing.

Black people are being oppressed in the colony by white policemen, by white racists. We are saying they must withdraw.

As far as I'm concerned, the only reasonable conclusion would be to first realize the enemy, realize the plan, and then when something happens in the black colony—when we're attacked and ambushed in the black colony—then the white revolutionary students and intellectuals and all the other whites who support the colony should respond by defending us, by attacking the enemy in their community.

The Black Panther Party is an all black party, because we feel, as Malcolm X felt, that there can be no black-white unity until there first is black unity. We have a problem in the black colony that is particular to the colony, but we're willing to accept aid from the mother country as long as the mother country radicals realize that we have, as Eldridge Cleaver says in *Soul on Ice,* a mind of our own. We've regained our mind that was taken away from us and we will decide the political, as well as the practical, stand that we'll take. We'll make the theory and we'll carry out the practice. It's the duty of the white revolutionary to aid us in this.

QUESTION: You have spoken a lot about dealing with the protectors of the system, the armed forces. Would you like to elaborate on why you place so much emphasis on this?

HUEY: The reason that I feel so strongly is simply because without this protection from the army, the police and the military, the institutions could not go on in their racism and exploitation. For instance, as the Vietnamese are driving the American imperialist troops out of Vietnam, it automatically stops the racist imperialist institutions of America from oppressing that particular country. The country cannot implement its racist program without guns. The guns are the military and the police. If the military were disarmed in Vietnam, then the Vietnamese would be victorious.

We are in the same situation here in

America. Whenever we attack the system, the first thing the administrators do is to send out their strong-arm men. If it's a rent strike, because of the indecent housing we have, they will send out the police to throw the furniture out the window. They don't come themselves. They send their protectors. To deal with the corrupt exploiter, we are going to have to deal with his protector, which is the police who take orders from him. This is a must.

QUESTION: Would you like to be more specific on the conditions which must exist before an alliance or coalition can be formed with the predominantly white groups? Would you comment specifically on your alliance with the California Peace and Freedom Party?

HUEY: We have an alliance with the Peace and Freedom Party because it has supported our program in full, and this is the criterion for a coalition with the black revolutionary group. If it had not supported our program in full, then we would not have seen any reason to make an alliance with them, because we are the reality of the oppression. They are not. They are only oppressed in an abstract way; we are oppressed in the real way. We are the real slaves! So it's a problem that we suffer from more than anyone else and it's our problem of liberation. Therefore we should decide what measures and what tools and what programs to use to become liberated. Many of the young white revolutionaries realize this and I see no reason not to have a coalition with them.

QUESTION: Other black groups seem to feel that from past experience it is impossible for them to work with whites and impossible for them to form alliances. What do you see as the reasons for this and do you think that the history of the Black Panther makes this less of a problem?

HUEY: There was a somewhat unhealthy relationship in the past with the white liberals supporting the black people who were trying to gain their freedom. I think that a good example of this would be the relationship that SNCC had with its white liberals. I call them white liberals because they differ strictly from the white radicals. The relationship was that the whites controlled SNCC for a very long time. From the very start of SNCC until recently, whites were the mind of SNCC. They controlled the program of SNCC with money and they controlled the ideology, or the stands SNCC would take. The blacks in SNCC were completely controlled program-wise; they couldn't do any more than the white liberals wanted them to do, which wasn't very much. So the white liberals were not working for self-determination for the black community. They were interested in a few concessions from the power structure. They undermined SNCC's program.

Stokely Carmichael came along, and realizing this, started Malcolm X's program of Black Power. Whites were afraid when Stokely said that black people have a mind of their own and that SNCC would seek self-determination for the black community. The white liberals withdrew their support, leaving the organization financially bankrupt. The blacks who were in the organization,

Stokely and H. Rap Brown, were left angry and bewildered with the white liberals who had been aiding them under the guise of being sincere.

As a result, the leadership of SNCC turned away from the white liberal, which was good. I don't think they distinguished between the white liberal and the white revolutionary; because the revolutionary is white also, and they are very much afraid to have any contact with white people—even to the point of denying that the white revolutionaries could help by supporting programs of SNCC in the mother country. Not by making programs, not by being a member of the organization, but simply by resisting.

I think that one of SNCC's great problems is that they were controlled by the traditional administrator: the omnipotent administrator, the white person. He was the mind of SNCC. SNCC regained its mind, but I believe that it lost its political perspective. I think that this was a reaction rather than a response. The Black Panther Party has NEVER been controlled by white people. We have always had an integration of mind and body. We have never been controlled by whites and therefore we don't fear the white mother country radicals. Our alliance is one of organized black groups with organized white groups. As soon as the organized white groups do not do the things that would benefit us in our struggle for liberation, that will be the point of our departure. So we don't suffer in the hang-up of a skin color. We don't hate white people; we hate the oppressor.

QUESTION: You indicate that there is a psychological process that has historically existed in white-black relations in the U.S. that must change in the course of revolutionary struggle. Would you like to comment on this?

HUEY: Yes. The historical relationship between black and white here in America has been the relationship between the slave and the master; the master being the mind and the slave the body. The slave would carry out the orders that the mind demanded him to carry out. By doing this, the master took the manhood from the slave because he stripped him of a mind. In the process, the slave-master stripped himself of a body. As Eldridge Cleaver puts it, the slave-master became the omnipotent administrator and the slave became the super-masculine menial. This puts the omnipotent administrator into the controlling position or the front office and the super-masculine menial into the field.

The whole relationship developed so that the omnipotent administrator and the super-masculine menial became opposites. The slave being a very strong body doing all the practical things, all of the work becomes very masculine. The omnipotent administrator in the process of removing himself from all body functions realizes later that he has emasculated himself. And this is very disturbing to him. So the slave lost his mind and the slave-master his body.

This caused the slave-master to become very envious of the slave because he pictured the slave as being more of a man, being superior sexually, because the penis is part of the body. The omnipotent administrator laid down a decree when he realized that in his plan to enslave the black man, he had emasculated himself. He attempted to bind the penis of the slave. He attempted to show that his penis could reach further than the super-masculine menial's penis. He said "I, the omnipotent administrator, can have access to the black woman." The super-masculine menial then had a psychological attraction to the white female (the ultra-feminine freak) for the simple reason that it was forbidden fruit. The omnipotent administrator decreed that this kind of contact would be punished by death.

At the same time, in order to reinforce his sexual desire, to confirm, to assert his manhood, he would go into the slave quarters and have sexual relations with the black women (the self-reliant Amazon), not to be satisfied but simply to confirm his manhood. If he could only satisfy the self-reliant Amazon then he would be sure that he was a man. Because he didn't have a body, he didn't have a penis, but psychologically wanted to castrate the black man. The slave was constantly seeking unity within himself: a mind and a body. He always wanted to be able to decide, to gain respect from his woman, because women want one who can control.

I give this outline to fit into a framework of what is happening now. The white power structure today in America defines itself as the mind. They want to control the world. They go off and plunder the world. They are the policemen of the world exercising control especially over people of color.

The white man cannot gain his man-hood, cannot unite with the body, because the body is black. The body is symbolic of slavery and strength. It's a biological thing as he views it. The slave is in a much better situation because his not being a full man has always been viewed psychologically. And it's always easier to make a psychological transition than a biological one. If he can only recapture his mind, then he will lose all fear and will be free to determine his destiny. This is what is happening today with the rebellion of the world's oppressed people against the controller. They are regaining their mind and they're saying that we have a mind of our own. They're saying that we want freedom to determine the destiny of our people, thereby uniting the mind with their bodies. They are taking the mind back from the omnipotent administrator, the controller, the exploiter.

QUESTION: You have mentioned that the guerilla was the perfect man and this kind of formulation seems to fit directly with the guerilla as a political man. Would you comment on this?

HUEY: The guerilla is a very unique man. This is in contrast to Marxist-Leninist orthodox theories where the party controls the military. The guerilla is not only the warrior, the military fighter; he is also the military commander as well as the political theoretician. Regis Debray says "poor the pen without the guns, poor the gun without the pen." The pen being just an extension of the mind, a tool to write down concepts, ideas. The gun is only an extension of the body, the extension of our fanged teeth that we lost through evolution. It's the weapon, it's the claws that we lost, it's the body. The guerilla is the military commander and the political theoretician all in one.

What we have to do as a vanguard of the revolution is to correct this through activity. The large majority of black people are either illiterate or semi-literate. They don't read. They need activity to follow. This is true of any colonized people. The same thing happened in Cuba where it was necessary for twelve men with the leadership of Che and Fidel to take to the hills and then attack the corrupt administration, to attack the army who were the protectors of the exploiters in Cuba. They would have leafleted the community and they could have written books, but the people would not respond. They had to act and the people could see and hear about it and therefore become educated on how to respond to oppression.

In this country black revolutionaries have to set an example. We can't do the same things that were done in Cuba because Cuba is Cuba and the U.S. is the U.S. Cuba had many terrains to protect the guerilla. This country is mainly urban. We have to work out new solutions to offset the power of the country's technology and communication. We do have solutions to these problems and they will be put into effect. I wouldn't want to go into the ways and means of this, but we will educate through action. We have to engage in action to make the people want to read our literature. They are not attracted to all the writing in this country; there's too much writing. Many books make one weary.

QUESTION: Kennedy before his death, and to a lesser extent Rockefeller and Lindsay and other establishment liberals, have been talking about making reforms to give black people a greater share of the pie and thus stop any developing revolutionary movement. Would you comment on this?

HUEY: I would say this: If a Kennedy or a Lindsay or anyone else can give decent housing to all of our people; if they can give full employment to our people with a high standard; if they can give full control to the black people to determine the destiny of their community, if they can give fair trials in the court system by turning the structure over to the community; if they can end their exploitation of people throughout the world; if they can do all these things, they will have solved the problems. But I don't believe under this present system, under capitalism, that they will be able to solve these problems.

I don't think black people should be fooled by their come-ons because everyone who gets in office promises the same thing. They promise full employment and decent housing; the Great Society, the New Frontier. All of these names, but no real benefits. No effects are felt in the black community, and black people are tired of being deceived and duped. The people must have full control of the means of production. Small black businesses cannot compete with General Motors. That's just out of the question. General Motors robbed us and worked us for nothing for a couple hundred years and took our money and set up factories and became fat and rich and then talks about giving us some of the crumbs. We want full control. We're not interested in anyone promising that the private owners are going to all of a sudden become human beings and give these things to our community. It hasn't ever happened and, based on empirical evidence, we don't expect them to become Buddhists overnight.

QUESTION: The Panthers' organizing efforts have been very open. Would you like to comment about the question of an underground political organization versus an open organization at this point in the struggle?

HUEY: Some of the black nationalist groups feel that they have to be underground because they'll be attacked, but we don't feel that you can romanticize being underground. They say we're romantic because we're trying to live revolutionary lives, and we are not taking precautions. But we say that the only way we would go underground is if we're driven underground. All real revolutionary movements are driven underground.

This is a pre-revolutionary period and we feel it is very necessary to educate the people while we can. So we're very open about this education. We have been attacked and we will be attacked even more in the future, but we're not going to go underground until we get ready to go underground because we have a mind of our own. We're not going to let anyone force us to do anything. We're going to go underground after we educate all of the black people and not before that time. Then it won't really be necessary for us to go underground because you can see black anywhere. We will just have the stuff to protect ourselves and the strategy to offset the great power that the strong-arm men of the establishment have and are planning to use against us.

QUESTION: Do you see the possibility of organizing a white Panther Party in opposition to the establishment, possibly among poor and working whites?

HUEY: As I said before, Black Power is people's power and as far as organizing white people we give white people the privilege of having a mind and we want them to get a body. They can organize themselves. We can tell them what they should do, but their responsibility, if they're going to claim to be white revolutionaries or white mother country radicals, is to arm themselves and support the colonies around the world in their just struggle against imperialism. Anything more than that they will have to do on their own.

QUESTION: What do you mean by Black Power?

HUEY: Black Power is really people's power. The Black Panther Program, Panther Power as we call it, will implement this people's power. We have respect for all of humanity and we realize that the people should rule and determine their destiny. Wipe out the controller. To have Black Power doesn't humble or subjugate anyone to slavery or oppression. Black Power is giving power to people who have not had power to determine their destiny. We advocate and we aid any people who are struggling to determine their destiny. This is regardless of color. The Vietnamese say Vietnam should be able to determine its own destiny. Power of the Vietnamese people. We also chant power of the Vietnamese people. The Latins are talking about Latin America for the Latin Americans. Cuba, si and Yanqui, no. It's not that they don't want the Yankees to have any power; they just don't want them to have power over them. They can have power over themselves. We in the black colony in America want to be able to have power over our destiny, and that's black power.

QUESTION: How would you characterize the mood of black people in America today? Are they disenchanted, wanting a larger slice of the pie, or alienated, not wanting to integrate into Babylon? What do you think it will take for them to become alienated and revolutionary?

HUEY: I was going to say disillusioned, but I don't think that we were ever under the illusion that we had freedom in this country. This society definitely is a decadent one and we realize it. Black people cannot gain their freedom under the present system, the system that is carrying out its plans to institutionalize racism. Your question is what will have to be done to stimulate them to revolution. I think it's already being done. It's a matter of time now for us to educate them to a program and show them the way to liberation. The Black Panther Party is the beacon light to show black people the way to liberation.

You notice the insurrections that have been going on throughout the country; in Watts, in Newark, in Detroit. They were all responses of the people demanding that they have freedom to determine their destiny, rejecting exploitation. The Black Panther Party does not think that the traditional riots, or insurrections, that have taken place are the answer. It is true that they have been against the Establishment, they have been against authority and oppression within their community; but they have been unorganized. However, black people have learned from each of these insurrections.

They learned from Watts. I'm sure that the people in Detroit were educated by what happened in Watts. Perhaps this was wrong education. It sort of missed the mark. It wasn't quite the correct activity, but the people were educated through the activity. The people of Detroit followed the example of the people in Watts, only they added a little scrutiny to it. The people in Detroit learned that the way to put a hurt on the administration is to make Molotov cocktails and to go into the streets in mass numbers. So this was a matter of learning. The slogan went up, "burn, baby, burn." People were educated through the activity and it spread throughout the country. The people were educated on how to resist, but perhaps incorrectly.

## THE PLATFORM

1. *We want freedom. We want power to determine the destiny of our Black Community.*

We believe that black people will not be free until we are able to determine our destiny.

2. *We want full employment for our people.*

We believe that the federal government is responsible and obligated to give every man employment or a guaranteed income. We believe that if the white American businessmen will not give full employment, then the means of production should be taken from the businessmen and placed in the community so that the people of the community can organize and employ all of its people and give a high standard of living.

3. *We want an end to the robbery by the white man of our Black Community.*

We believe that this racist government has robbed us and now we are demanding the overdue debt of forty acres and two mules. Forty acres and two mules was promised 100 years ago as restitution for slave labor and mass murder of black people. We will accept the payment in currency which will be distributed to our many communities. The Germans are now aiding the Jews in Israel for the genocide of the Jewish people. The Germans murdered six million Jews. The American racist has taken part in the slaughter of over fifty million black people; therefore, we feel that this is a modest demand that we make.

4. *We want decent housing, fit for shelter of human beings.*

We believe that if the white landlords will not give decent housing to our black community, then the housing and the land should be made into cooperatives so that our community, with government aid, can build and make decent housing for its people.

5. *We want education for our people that exposes the true nature of this decadent American society. We want education that teaches us our true history and our role in the present-day society.*

We believe in an educational system that will give to our people a knowledge of self. If a man does not have knowledge of himself and his position in society and the world, then he has little chance to relate to anything else.

6. *We want all black men to be exempt from military service.*

We believe that black people should not be forced to fight in the military service to defend a racist government that does not protect us. We will not fight and kill other people of color in the world who, like black people, are being victimized by the white racist government of America. We will protect ourselves from the force and violence of the racist police and the racist military, by whatever means necessary.

7. *We want an immediate end to POLICE BRUTALITY and MURDER of black people.*

We believe we can end police brutality in our black community by organizing black self-defense groups that are dedicated to defending our black community from racist police oppression and brutality. The Second Amendment to the Constitution of the United States gives a right to bear arms. We therefore believe that all black people should arm themselves for self-defense.

8. *We want freedom for all black men held in federal, state, county and city prisons and jails.*

We believe that all black people should be released from the many jails and prisons because they have not received a fair and impartial trial.

9. *We want all black people when brought to trial to be tried in court by a jury of their peer group or people from their black communities, as defined by the Constitution of the United States.*

We believe that the courts should follow the United States Constitution so that black people will receive fair trials. The 14th Amendment of the U.S. Constitution gives a man a right to be tried by his peer group. A peer is a person from a similar economic, social, religious, geographical, environmental, historical and racial background. To do this the court will be forced to select a jury from the black community from which the black defendant came. We have been, and are being tried by all-white juries that have no understanding of the "average reasoning man" of the black community.

10. *We want land, bread, housing, education, clothing, justice and peace. And as our major political objective, a United Nations-supervised plebiscite to be held throughout the black colony in which only black colonial subjects will be allowed to participate, for the purpose of determining the will of black people as to their national destiny.*

When, in the course of human events, it becomes necessary for one people to dissolve the political bands which have connected them with another, and to assume, among the powers of the earth, the separate and equal station to which the laws of nature and nature's God entitle them, a decent respect to the opinions of mankind requires that they should declare the causes which impel them to the separation.

We hold these truths to be self-evident, that all men are created equal; that they are endowed by their Creator with certain unalienable rights; that among these are life, liberty, and the pursuit of happiness. *That, to secure these rights, governments are instituted among men, deriving their just powers from the consent of the governed; . . .*

So when we turn to a Black Agenda for the Seventies, we move in the truth of history, in the reality of the moment. We move recognizing that no one else is going to represent our interests but ourselves. *The society we seek cannot come unless Black people organize to advance its coming.* We lift up a Black Agenda recognizing that white America moves towards the abyss created by its own racist arrogance, misplaced priorities, rampant materialism, and ethical bankruptcy. Therefore, we are certain that the Agenda we now press for in Gary is not only for the future of Black humanity, but is probably the only way the rest of America can save itself from the harvest of its criminal past.

So, Brothers and Sisters of our developing Black nation, we now stand at Gary as people whose time has come. From every corner of Black America, from all liberation movements of the Third World, from the graves of our fathers and the coming world of our children, we are faced with a challenge and a call: Though the moment is perilous we must not despair. We must seize the time, for the time is ours.

We begin here and now in Gary. We begin with an independent Black political movement, an independent Black Political Agenda, an independent Black spirit. Nothing less will do. We must build for our people. We must build for our world. We stand on the edge of history. We cannot turn back.

## National Black Political Agenda, 1972

*On March 11 and 12, 1972, more than three thousand African American political and cul-*

*tural leaders met at a National Black Political Convention in Gary, Indiana, cochaired by Congressman Charles C. Diggs of Detroit, Mayor Richard Hatcher of Gary, and the poet Imamu Baraka. The convention's "National Black Political Agenda" is excerpted here. Addressed to black people, it reflects well the new spirit of Black Power, with its emphasis on black self-determination and self-reliance.*

*Source:* Claybourne Carson et al., *The Eyes on the Prize Civil Rights Reader* (New York: Penguin, 1991), pp. 493–499.

## INTRODUCTION

The Black Agenda is addressed primarily to Black people in America. It rises naturally out of the bloody decades and centuries of our people's struggle on these shores. It flows from the most recent surgings of our own cultural and political consciousness. It is our attempt to define some of the essential changes which must take place in this land as we and our children move to self-determination and true independence.

The Black Agenda assumes that no truly basic change for our benefit takes place in Black or white America unless we Black people organize to initiate that change. It assumes that we must have some essential agreement on overall goals, even though we may differ on many specific strategies.

Therefore, this is an initial statement of goals and directions for our own generation, some first definitions of crucial issues around which Black people must organize and move in 1972 and beyond. Anyone who claims to be serious about

the survival and liberation of Black people must be serious about the implementation of the Black Agenda.

## WHAT TIME IS IT?

We come to Gary in an hour of great crisis and tremendous promise for Black America. While the white nation hovers on the brink of chaos, while its politicians offer no hope of real change, we stand on the edge of history and are faced with an amazing and frightening choice: We may choose in 1972 to slip back into the decadent white politics of American life, or we may press forward, moving relentlessly from Gary to the creation of our own Black life. The choice is large, but the time is very short.

Let there be no mistake. We come to Gary in a time of unrelieved crisis for our people. From every rural community in Alabama to the high-rise compounds of Chicago, we bring to this Convention the agonies of the masses of our people. From the sprawling Black cities of Watts and Nairobi in the West to the decay of Harlem and Roxbury in the East, the testimony we bear is the same. We are the witnesses to social disaster.

Our cities are crime-haunted dying grounds. Huge sectors of our youth— and countless others—face permanent unemployment. Those of us who work find our paychecks able to purchase less and less. Neither the courts nor the prisons contribute to anything resembling justice or reformation. The schools are unable—or unwilling—to educate our children for the real world of our struggles. Meanwhile, the officially approved epidemic of drugs threatens to wipe out the minds and strength of our best young warriors.

Economic, cultural, and spiritual depression stalk Black America, and the price for survival often appears to be more than we are able to pay. On every side, in every area of our lives, the American institutions in which we have placed our trust are unable to cope with the crises they have created by their single-minded dedication to profits for some and white supremacy above all.

## BEYOND THESE SHORES

And beyond these shores there is more of the same. For while we are pressed down under all the dying weight of a bloated, inwardly decaying white civilization, many of our brothers in Africa and the rest of the Third World have fallen prey to the same powers of exploitation and deceit. Wherever America faces the unorganized, politically powerless forces of the non-white world, its goal is domination by any means necessary—as if to hide from itself the crumbling of its own systems of life and work.

But Americans cannot hide. They can run to China and the moon and to the edges of consciousness, but they cannot hide. The crises we face as Black people are the crises of the entire society. They go deep, to the very bones and marrow, to the essential nature of America's economic, political, and cultural systems. They are the natural end-product of a society built on the twin foundations of white racism and white capitalism.

So, let it be clear to us now: The desperation of our people, the agonies of our cities, the desolation of our countryside, the pollution of the air and the water—these things will not be significantly affected by new faces in the old places in Washington, D.C. This is the truth we must face here in Gary if we are to join our people everywhere in the movement forward toward liberation.

## WHITE REALITIES, BLACK CHOICE

A Black political convention, indeed all truly Black politics must begin from this truth: *The American system does not work for the masses of our people, and it cannot be made to work without radical fundamental change.* (Indeed, this system does not really work in favor of the humanity of anyone in America.)

In light of such realities, we come to Gary and are confronted with a choice. Will we believe the truth that history presses into our face—or will we, too, try to hide? Will the small favors some of us have received blind us to the larger sufferings of our people, or open our eyes to the testimony of our history in America?

For more than a century we have followed the path of political dependence on white men and their systems. From the Liberty Party in the decades before the Civil War to the Republican Party of Abraham Lincoln, we trusted in white men and white politics as our deliverers. Sixty years ago, W. E. B. Du Bois said he would give the Democrats their "last chance" to prove their sincere commitment to equality for Black people—and he was given white riots and official segregation in peace and in war.

Nevertheless, some twenty years later we became Democrats in the name of Franklin Roosevelt, then supported his successor Harry Truman, and even tried a "non-partisan" Republican General of the Army named Eisenhower. We were wooed like many others by the superficial liberalism of John F. Kennedy and the make-believe populism of Lyndon Johnson. Let there be no more of that.

## BOTH PARTIES HAVE BETRAYED US

Here at Gary, let us never forget that while the times and the names and the parties have continually changed, one truth has faced us insistently, never changing: Both parties have betrayed us whenever their interests conflicted with ours (which was most of the time), and whenever our forces were unorganized and dependent, quiescent and compliant. Nor should this be surprising, for by now we must know that the American political system, like all other white institutions in America, was designed to operate for the benefit of the white race: It was never meant to do anything else.

That is the truth that we must face at Gary. If white "liberalism" could have solved our problems, then Lincoln and Roosevelt and Kennedy would have done so. But they did not solve ours nor the rest of the nation's. If America's problems could have been solved by forceful, politically skilled and aggressive

individuals, then Lyndon Johnson would have retained the presidency. If the true "American Way" of unbridled monopoly capitalism, combined with a ruthless military imperialism could do it, then Nixon would not be running around the world, or making speeches comparing his nation's decadence to that of Greece and Rome.

If we have never faced it before, let us face it at Gary: The profound crisis of Black people and the disaster of America are not simply caused by men nor will they be solved by men alone. These crises are the crises of basically flawed economics and politics, and of cultural degradation. None of the Democratic candidates and none of the Republican candidates—regardless of their vague promises to us or to their white constituencies—can solve our problems or the problems of this country without radically changing the systems by which it operates.

## THE POLITICS OF SOCIAL TRANSFORMATION

So, we come to Gary confronted with a choice. But it is not the old convention question of which candidate shall we support, the pointless question of who is to preside over a decaying and unsalvageable system. No, if we come to Gary out of the realities of the Black communities of this land, then the only real choice for us is whether or not we will live by the truth we know, whether we will move to organize independently, move to struggle for fundamental transformation, for the creation of new directions, towards a concern for the life and the meaning of Man. Social transformation or social destruction, those are our only real choices.

If we have come to Gary on behalf of our people in America, in the rest of this hemisphere, and in the Homeland—if we have come for our own best ambitions—then a new Black Politics must come to birth. If we are serious, the Black Politics of Gary must accept major responsibility for creating both the atmosphere and the program for fundamental, far-ranging change in America. Such responsibility is ours because it is our people who are most deeply hurt and ravaged by the present systems of society. That responsibility for leading the change is ours because we live in a society where few other men really believe in the responsibility of a truly humane society for anyone anywhere.

## WE ARE THE VANGUARD

The challenge is thrown to us here in Gary. It is the challenge to consolidate and organize our own Black role as the vanguard in the struggle for a new society. To accept that challenge is to move independent Black politics. There can be no equivocation on that issue. History leaves us no other choice. White politics has not and cannot bring the changes we need.

We come to Gary and are faced with a challenge. The challenge is to transform ourselves from favor-seeking vassals and loud-talking, "militant" pawns, and to take up the role that the organized masses of our people have attempted to

play ever since we came to these shores: That of harbingers of true justice and humanity, leaders in the struggle for liberation.

A major part of the challenge we must accept is that of redefining the functions and operations of all levels of American government, for the existing governing structures—from Washington to the smallest county—are obsolescent. That is part of the reason why nothing works and why corruption rages throughout public life. For white politics seeks not to serve but to dominate and manipulate.

We will have joined the true movement of history if at Gary we grasp the opportunity to press Man forward as the first consideration of politics. Here at Gary we are faithful to the best hopes of our fathers and our people if we move for nothing less than a politics which places community before individualism, love before sexual exploitation, a living environment before profits, peace before war, justice before unjust "order," and morality before expediency.

This is the society we need, but we delude ourselves here at Gary if we think that change can be achieved without organizing the power, the determined national Black power, which is necessary to insist upon such change, to create such change, to seize change.

## TOWARDS A BLACK AGENDA

So when we turn to a Black Agenda for the seventies, we move in the truth of history, in the reality of the moment. We move recognizing that no one else is going to represent our interests but ourselves. *The society we seek cannot come unless Black people organize to advance its coming.* We lift up a Black Agenda recognizing that white America moves towards the abyss created by its own racist arrogance, misplaced priorities, rampant materialism, and ethical bankruptcy. Therefore, we are certain that the Agenda we now press for in Gary is not only for the future of Black humanity, but is probably the only way the rest of America can save itself from the harvest of its criminal past.

So, Brothers and Sisters of our developing Black nation, we now stand at Gary as people whose time has come. From every corner of Black America, from all liberation movements of the Third World, from the graves of our fathers and the coming world of our children, we are faced with a challenge and a call: Though the moment is perilous we must not despair. We must seize the time, for the time is ours.

We begin here and now in Gary. We begin with an independent Black political movement, an independent Black Political Agenda, an independent Black spirit. Nothing less will do. We must build for our people. We must build for our world. We stand on the edge of history. We cannot turn back.

To those who say that such an Agenda is "visionary," "utopian," and "impossible," we say that the keepers of conventional white politics have always viewed our situation and our real needs as beyond the realm of their wildest imaginations. At every critical moment of our struggle

in America we have had to press relentlessly against the limits of the "realistic" to create new realities for the life of our people.

This is our challenge at Gary and beyond, for a new Black politics demands new vision, new hope and new definitions of the possible. Our time has come. These things are necessary. All things are possible.

## Molefi Kete Asante, *The Afrocentric Idea,* 1987

*Molefi Asante of Temple University was one of the leading exponents of Afrocentrism. Afrocentrism emerged out of black power's cultural challenge to the primacy of Anglo American culture and sparked a number of controversies in colleges and school systems in the 1980s and 1990s. This selection from Asante's book* The Afrocentric Idea *reflects Afrocentrism's rejection of the alleged objectivity of white scholarship, the reorientation of perspective to place Africa at the center of history and Europe on the periphery, and the horrors that slavery visited on African Americans.*

Source: Molefi Asante, *The Afrocentric Idea* (Philadelphia: Temple University Press, 1987), pp. 3, 58, 126–127, 159.

## DANCING BETWEEN CIRCLES AND LINES

What has fascinated me is the manner in which most of my colleagues have written theory and engaged in the social sciences in relationship to African people.

They have often assumed that their "objectivity," a kind of collective subjectivity of European culture, should be the measure by which the world marches. I have seldom fallen in step, insisting (gently) that there are other ways in which to experience phenomena, rather than viewing them from a Eurocentric vantage point.

My work has increasingly constituted a radical critique of the Eurocentric ideology that masquerades as a universal view in the fields of intercultural communication, rhetoric, philosophy, linguistics, psychology, education, anthropology, and history. Yet the critique is radical only in the sense that it suggests a turnabout, an alternative perspective on phenomena. It is about taking the globe and turning it over so that we see all the possibilities of a world where Africa, for example, is subject and not object. Such a posture is necessary and rewarding for Africans and Europeans. The inability to "see" from several angles is perhaps the one common fallacy in provincial scholarship. Those who have delighted us most and advanced thought most significantly have been thinkers who explored different views and brought new perspectives. . . .

## AFRICAN FOUNDATIONS OF NOMMO

Any interpretation of African culture must begin at once to dispense with the notion that, in all things, Europe is teacher and Africa is pupil. This is the central point of my argument. To raise the question of an imperialism of the intellectual tradition is to ask a most meaningful question as we pursue African rhetoric, because Western theorists have too often tended to generalize from a Eurocentric base. What I seek to demonstrate in this section is the existence of an African concept of communication rooted in traditional African philosophies. Later, I will expand this by referring to a close description and examination of Akan culture, particularly as that culture exemplifies the use of words in the organization of society. . . .

## CHOOSING FREEDOM

The Europeanization of human consciousness masquerades as a universal will. Even in our reach for Afrocentric possibilities in analysis and interpretation we often find ourselves having to unmask experience in order to see more clearly the transformations of our history.

Nat Turner and Henry Highland Garnet represent two powerful symbols in African American history. They stand against the tide of Europeanization in their discourse, even though the representational language of their discourse was American English. Yet the individual sense of community responsibility was in both their cases a striking motif of Afrocentricity.

In the old spiritual, "Good Lord, I done done, Good Lord, I done done, I done done what you told me to do," are all the complexities of the messianic idiom in the history of black discourse. As Shango, Anokye, Sundiata, and Tarharka receded into the past, Africans, enslaved in America, found in certain Judeo-Christian tenets the heroics of Moses, the mission of Jesus, and the heady wine of rebellion. Garnet gathered the cloak to himself, but he was not the first or the last to try the delicate messianic maneuver.

The messianic idiom is the most prevalent motif in radical black discourse. In fact, in traditional black politics, such as Jesse Jackson's case, one sees its continuation. Such a formula, all-encompassing in its focus, is nothing more than the transformation of the idea of mission into a radical individualistic posture. The messiah is mission-oriented and feels a moral or supra-rational need to stand as the deliverer of the people. Our tenure in the United States is replete with acts of individual courage and valor where the *one* attempts to make a sacrifice for the *whole*. Few of these acts ever resulted in major victories, but their frequent happening is fact enough to demonstrate the internal thrust for group and even, in some cases, national salvation. To have a mission in the sense of messianism implies deliverance as an objective. No other historical motif is so present in radical black discourse, probably because so much of it is clothed in religious symbolism.

Yet messianism has no tradition in Africa; it became for the African in America, enslaved and abused, the one tenet of an apocalyptic-Judaic-Platonic heritage that immediately made sense. Domination by whites assured the individual transformations that would give meaning to the dynamics of liberation discourse even if they dressed up and went to church. The enormous eman-cipatory possibilities were present because someone dared to risk life to make them so. In this sense, the position I have staked out recognizes the inherent problems of a Eurocentric perspective when one treats the question of black protest discourse. Inasmuch as the protest discourse is engaged in a liberation project from extreme Eurocentric practice, it becomes impossible for a Eurocentric critique to reveal the many intricacies of the protest discourse. The reason for this is that the discourse pits itself against the universe of the critiquing ideology.

Radical spokespersons have indicated their sense of mission in the dynamism of their rhetorical style; their force of speech has given substance to the search for *something better*. . . .

## THE SEARCH FOR AN AFROCENTRIC METHOD

Throughout this book, I have been arguing that all analysis is culturally centered and flows from ideological assumptions; this is the fundamental revelation of modern intellectual history. An Afrocentric method is concerned with establishing a world view about the writing and speaking of oppressed people. Current literary theories—phenomenology, hermeneutics, and structuralism, for example—cannot be applied, whole cloth, to African themes and subjects. Based as they are on Eurocentric philosophy, they fail to come to terms with fundamental cultural differences. Consequently, some authors have mistaken European agitation, manifested as a rhetorical reaction to social, religious, and political repression, with African protest discourse that seeks the removal of oppression. Repression presumes that the persecuted have certain rights; oppression is the denial of these rights and humanity.

The principal crisis with which the Afrocentric writer or speaker is concerned remains the political/cultural crisis with all of its attendant parts, economic and social. Indeed, the same themes spring to life in the revolutionary work of African American musicians, artists, and choreographers who challenge assumptions about the universality of Eurocentric concepts. We are on a pilgrimage to regain freedom; this is the predominant myth of our life.

## Vine Deloria Jr., "This Country Was a Lot Better Off When the Indians Were Running It," March 1970

*Vine Deloria Jr. was executive director of the National Congress of American Indians, professor of Native American Studies, and author of ten books, including* Custer Died for Your Sins; We Talk, You Listen; Behind the Trail of Broken Treaties; An Indian Declaration of Independence *and* The Nations Within; *and* The Past and Future of American Indian Sovereignty. *He is credited with inventing the term "Red Power." The article below appeared in the* New York Times Magazine *in March of 1970 about four months after Indian protestors took over Alcatraz Island and is a personal account of the history leading up to the birth of the Red Power movement.*

*Source:* New York Times Magazine, *March 8, 1970.*

On Nov. 9, 1969, a contingent of American Indians, led by Adam Nordwall, a Chippewa from Minnesota, and Richard Oakes, a Mohawk from New York, landed on Alcatraz Island in San Francisco Bay and claimed the 13-acre rock "by right of discovery." The island had been abandoned six and a half years ago, and although there had been various suggestions concerning its disposal nothing had been done to make use of the land. Since there are Federal treaties giving some tribes the right to abandoned Federal property within a tribe's original territory, the Indians of the Bay area felt that they could lay claim to the island.

For nearly a year the United Bay Area Council of American Indians, a confederation of urban Indian organizations, had been talking about submitting a bid for the island to use it as a West Coast Indian cultural center and vocational training headquarters. Then, on Nov. 1, the San Francisco American Indian Center burned down. The center had served an estimated 30,000 Indians in the immediate area and was the focus of activities of the urban Indian community. It became a matter of urgency after that and, as Adam Nordwall said, "it was GO." Another landing, on Nov. 20, by nearly 100 Indians in a swift midnight raid secured the island.

The new inhabitants have made "the Rock" a focal point symbolic of Indian people. Under extreme difficulty they have worked to begin repairing sanitary facilities and buildings. The population has been largely transient, many people have stopped by, looked the situation over for a few days, then gone home, unwilling to put in the tedious work necessary to make the island support a viable community.

The Alcatraz news stories are somewhat shocking to non-Indians. It is difficult for most Americans to comprehend that there still exists a living community of nearly one million Indians in this country. For many people, Indians have become a species of movie actor periodically dispatched to the Happy Hunting Grounds by John Wayne on the "Late, Late Show." Yet there are some 315 Indian tribal groups in 26 states still functioning as quasi-sovereign nations under treaty status; they range from the mammoth Navajo tribe of some 132,000 with 16 million acres of land to tiny Mission Creek of California with 15 people and a tiny parcel of property. There are over half a million Indians in the cities alone, with the largest concentrations in San Francisco, Los Angeles, Minneapolis and Chicago.

The take-over of Alcatraz is to many Indian people a demonstration of pride in being Indian and a dignified, yet humorous protest against current conditions existing on the reservations and in the cities. It is this special pride and dignity, the determination to judge life according to one's own values, and the unconquerable conviction that the tribes will not die that has always characterized Indian people as I have known them.

I was born in Martin, a border town on the Pine Ridge Indian Reservation in South Dakota, in the midst of the Depression. My father was an Indian missionary who served 18 chapels on the eastern half of the reservation. In 1934, when I was 1, the Indian Reorganization Act was passed, allowing Indian tribes full rights of self-government for the first time since the late eighteen-sixties. Ever since those days, when the Sioux had agreed to forsake the life of the hunter for that of the farmer, they had been systematically deprived of any voice in decisions affecting their lives and property. Tribal ceremonies and religious practices were forbidden. The reservation was fully controlled by men in Washington, most of whom had never visited a reservation and felt no urge to do so.

The first years on the reservations were extremely hard for the Sioux. Kept confined behind fences they were almost wholly dependent upon Government rations for their food supply. Many died of hunger and malnutrition. Game was scarce and few were allowed to have weapons for fear of another Indian war. In some years there was practically no food available. Other years rations were withheld until the men agreed to farm the tiny pieces of land each family had been given. In desperation many families were forced to eat stray dogs and cats to keep alive.

By World War I, however, many of the Sioux families had developed prosperous ranches. Then the Government stepped in, sold the Indians' cattle for wartime needs, and after the war leased the grazing land to whites, creating wealthy white ranchers and destitute Indian landlords.

With the passage of the Indian Reorganization Act, native ceremonies and practices were given full recognition by

Federal authorities. My earliest memories are of trips along dusty roads to Kyle, a small settlement in the heart of the reservation, to attend the dances. Ancient men, veterans of battles even then considered footnotes to the settlement of the West, brought their costumes out of hiding and walked about the grounds gathering the honors they had earned half a century before. They danced as if the intervening 50 years had been a lost weekend from which they had fully recovered. I remember best Dewey Beard, then in his late 80's and a survivor of the Little Big Horn. Even at that late date Dewey was hesitant to speak of the battle for fear of reprisal. There was no doubt, as one watched the people's expressions, that the Sioux had survived their greatest ordeal and were ready to face whatever the future might bring.

In those days the reservation was isolated and unsettled. Dirt roads held the few mail routes together. One could easily get lost in the wild back country as roads turned into cowpaths without so much as a backward glance. Remote settlements such as Buzzard Basin and Cuny Table were nearly inaccessible. In the spring every bridge on the reservation would be washed out with the first rain and would remain out until late summer. But few people cared. Most of the reservation people, traveling by team and wagon, merely forded the creeks and continued their journey, almost contemptuous of the need for roads and bridges.

The most memorable event of my early childhood was visiting Wounded Knee where 200 Sioux, including women and children, were slaughtered in 1890 by troopers of the Seventh Cavalry in what is believed to have been a delayed act of vengeance for Custer's defeat. The people were simply lined up and shot down much as was allegedly done, according to newspaper reports, at Songmy. The wounded were left to die in a three-day Dakota blizzard, and when the soldiers returned to the scene after the storm some were still alive and were saved. The massacre was vividly etched in the minds of many of the older reservation people, but it was difficult to find anyone who wanted to talk about it.

Many times, over the years, my father would point out survivors of the massacre, and people on the reservation always went out of their way to help them. For a long time there was a bill in Congress to pay indemnities to the survivors, but the War Department always insisted that it had been a "battle" to stamp out the Ghost Dance religion among the Sioux. This does not, however, explain bayoneted Indian women and children found miles from the scene of the incident.

Strangely enough, the Depression was good for Indian reservations, particularly for the people at Pine Ridge. Since their lands had been leased to non-Indians by the Bureau of Indian Affairs, they had only a small rent check and the contempt of those who leased their lands to show for their ownership. But the Federal programs devised to solve the national economic crisis were also made available to Indian people, and there was work available for the first time in the history of the reservations.

The Civilian Conservation Corps set up a camp on the reservation and many Indians were hired under the program. In the canyons north of Allen, S.D., a beautiful buffalo pasture was built by the C.C.C., and the whole area was transformed into a recreation wonderland. Indians would come from miles around to see the buffalo and leave with a strange look in their eyes. Many times I stood silently watching while old men talked to the buffalo about the old days. They would conclude by singing a song before respectfully departing, their eyes filled with tears and their minds occupied with the memories of other times and places. It was difficult to determine who was the captive—the buffalo fenced in or the Indian fenced out.

While the rest of America suffered from the temporary deprivation of its luxuries, Indian people had a period of prosperity, as it were. Paychecks were regular. Small cattle herds were started, cars were purchased, new clothes and necessities became available. To a people who had struggled along on $50 cash income per year, the C.C.C. was the greatest program ever to come along. The Sioux had climbed from absolute deprivation to mere poverty, and this was the best time the reservation ever had.

World War II ended this temporary prosperity. The C.C.C. camps were closed; reservation programs were cut to the bone and social services became virtually nonexistent; "Victory gardens" were suddenly the style, and people began to be aware that a great war was being waged overseas.

The war dispersed the reservation people as nothing ever had. Every day, it seemed, we would be bidding farewell to families as they headed west to work in the defense plants on the Coast.

A great number of Sioux people went west and many of the Sioux on Alcatraz today are their children and relatives. There may now be as many Sioux in California as there are on the reservations in South Dakota because of the great wartime migration.

Those who stayed on the reservation had the war brought directly to their doorstep when they were notified that their sons had to go across the seas and fight. Busloads of Sioux boys left the reservation for parts unknown. In many cases even the trip to nearby Martin was a new experience for them, let alone training in Texas, California or Colorado. There were always going-away ceremonies conducted by the older people who admonished the boys to uphold the old tribal traditions and not to fear death. It was not death they feared but living with an unknown people in a distant place.

I was always disappointed with the Government's way of handling Indian servicemen. Indians were simply lost in the shuffle of 3 million men in uniform. Many boys came home on furlough and feared to return. They were not cowards in any sense of the word but the loneliness and boredom of stateside duty was crushing their spirits. They spent months without seeing another Indian. If the Government had recruited all-Indian outfits it would have easily solved this problem and also had the best fighting units in the world at its disposal. I often wonder what an all-Sioux or Apache company, painted and singing its songs, would have done to the morale of élite German panzer units.

After the war Indian veterans straggled back to the reservations and tried to pick up their lives. It was very difficult for them to resume a life of poverty after having seen the affluent outside world. Some spent a few days with the old folks and then left again for the big cities. Over the years they have emerged as leaders of the urban Indian movement. Many of their children are the nationalists of today who are adamant about keeping the reservations they have visited only on vacations. Other veterans stayed on the reservations and entered tribal politics.

The reservations radically changed after the war. During the Depression there were about five telephones in Martin. If there was a call for you, the man at the hardware store had to come down to your house and get you to answer it. A couple of years after the war a complete dial system was installed that extended to most of the smaller communities on the reservation. Families that had been hundreds of miles from any form of communication were now only minutes away from a telephone.

Roads were built connecting the major communities of the Pine Ridge country. No longer did it take hours to go from one place to another. With these kinds of roads everyone had to have a car. The team and wagon vanished, except for those families who lived at various "camps" in inaccessible canyons pretty much as their ancestors had. (Today, even they have adopted the automobile for traveling long distances in search of work.)

I left the reservation in 1951 when my family moved to Iowa. I went back only once for an extended stay, in the summer of 1955, while on a furlough, and after that I visited only occasionally during summer vacations. In the meantime, I attended college, served a hitch in the Marines, and went to the seminary. After I graduated from the seminary, I took a job with the United Scholarship Service, a private organization devoted to the college and secondary-school education of American Indian and Mexican students. I had spent my last two years of high school in an Eastern preparatory school and so was probably the only Indian my age who knew what an independent Eastern school was like. As the program developed, we soon had some 30 students placed in Eastern schools.

I insisted that all the students who entered the program be able to qualify for scholarships as students and not simply as Indians. I was pretty sure we could beat the white man at his own educational game, which seemed to me the only way to gain his respect. I was soon to find that this was a dangerous attitude to have. The very people who were supporting the program—non-Indians in the national church establishments—accused me of trying to form a colonialist "élite" by insisting that only kids with strong test scores and academic patterns be sent east to school. They wanted to continue the ancient pattern of soft-hearted paternalism toward Indians. I didn't feel we should cry our way into the schools; that sympathy would destroy the students we were trying to help.

In 1964, while attending the annual convention of the National Congress of American Indians, I was elected its executive director. I learned more about life in the N.C.A.I. in three years than I had in the previous 30. Every conceivable problem that could occur in an Indian society was suddenly thrust at me from 315 different directions. I discovered that I was one of the people who were supposed to solve the problems. The only trouble was that Indian people locally and on the national level were being played off one against the other by clever whites who had either ego or income at stake. While there were many feasible solutions, few could be tried without whites with vested interests working night and day to destroy the unity we were seeking on a national basis.

In the mid-nineteen-sixties, the whole generation that had grown up after World War II and had left the reservations during the fifties to get an education was returning to Indian life as "educated Indians." But we soon knew better. Tribal societies had existed for centuries without going outside themselves for education and information. Yet many of us thought that we would be able to improve the traditional tribal methods. We were wrong.

For three years we ran around the conference circuit attending numerous meetings called to "solve" the Indian problems. We listened to and spoke with anthropologists, historians, sociologists, psychologists, economists, educators and missionaries. We worked with many Government agencies and with every conceivable doctrine, idea and program ever created. At the end of this happy round of consultations the reservation people were still plodding along on their own time schedule, doing the things they considered important. They continued to solve their problems their way in spite of the advice given them by "Indian experts."

By 1967 there was a radical change in thinking on the part of many of us. Conferences were proving unproductive. Where non-Indians had been pushed out to make room for Indian people, they had wormed their way back into power and again controlled the major programs serving Indians. The poverty programs, reservation and university technical assistance groups were dominated by whites who had pushed Indian administrators aside.

Reservation people, meanwhile, were making steady progress in spite of the numerous setbacks suffered by the national Indian community. So, in large part, younger Indian leaders who had been playing the national conference field began working at the local level to build community movements from the ground up. By consolidating local organizations into power groups they felt that they would be in a better position to influence national thinking.

Robert Hunter, director of the Nevada Intertribal Council, had already begun to build a strong state organization of tribes and communities. In South Dakota, Gerald One Feather, Frank La-Pointe and Ray Briggs formed the American Indian Leadership Conference, which quickly welded the educated young Sioux in that state into a strong regional organization active in nearly every phase of Sioux life. Gerald is now running for the prestigious post of Chairman of the Oglala Sioux, the largest Sioux tribe, numbering some 15,000 members. Ernie Stevens, an Oneida from Wisconsin and Lee Cook, a Chippewa from Minnesota, developed a strong program for economic and community development in Arizona. Just recently Ernie has moved into the post of director of the California Intertribal Council, a statewide organization representing some 130,000 California Indians in cities and on the scattered reservations of that state.

By the fall of 1967, it was apparent that the national Indian scene was collapsing in favor of strong regional organizations, although the major national organizations such as the National Congress of American Indians and the National Indian Youth Council continued to grow. There was yet another factor emerging on the Indian scene: the old-timers of the Depression days had educated a group of younger Indians in the old ways and these people were now becoming a major force in Indian life. Led by Thomas Banyaca of the Hopi, Mad Bear Anderson of the Tuscaroras, Clifton Hill of the Creeks, and Rolling Thunder of the Shoshones, the traditional Indians were forcing the whole Indian community to rethink its understanding of Indian life.

The message of the traditionalists is simple. They demand a return to basic Indian philosophy, establishment of ancient methods of government by open council instead of elected officials, a revival of Indian religions and replacement of white laws with Indian customs; in short, a complete return to the ways of the old people. In an age dominated by tribalizing communications media, their message makes a great deal of sense.

But in some areas their thinking is opposed to that of the National Congress of American Indians, which represents officially elected tribal governments organized under the Indian Reorganization Act as Federal corporations. The contemporary problem is therefore one of defining the meaning of "tribe." Is it a traditionally organized band of Indians following customs with medicine men and chiefs dominating the policies of the tribe, or is it a modern corporate structure attempting to compromise at least in part with modern white culture?

The problem has been complicated by private foundations' and Government agencies' funding of Indian programs. In general this process, although it has brought a great amount of money into Indian country, has been one of cooptation. Government agencies must justify their appropriation requests every year and can only take chances on spectacular programs that will serve as showcases of progress. They are not willing to invest the capital funds necessary to build viable self-supporting communities on the reservations because these programs do not have an immediate publicity potential. Thus, the Government agencies are forever committed to conducting conferences to discover that one "key" to Indian life that will give them the edge over their rival agencies in the annual appropriations derby.

Churches and foundations have

merely purchased an Indian leader or program that conforms with their ideas of what Indian people should be doing. The large foundations have bought up the well-dressed, handsome "new image" Indian who is comfortable in the big cities but virtually helpless at an Indian meeting. Churches have given money to Indians who have been willing to copy black militant activist tactics, and the more violent and insulting the Indian can be, the more the churches seem to love it. They are wallowing in self-guilt and piety over the lot of the poor, yet funding demagogues of their own choosing to speak for the poor.

I did not run for re-election as executive director of the N.C.A.I. in the fall of 1967, but entered law school at the University of Colorado instead. It was apparent to me that the Indian revolution was well under way and that someone had better get a legal education so that we could have our own legal program for defense of Indian treaty rights. Thanks to a Ford Foundation program, nearly 50 Indians are now in law school, assuring the Indian community of legal talent in the years ahead. Within four years I foresee another radical shift in Indian leadership patterns as the growing local movements are affected by the new Indian lawyers.

There is an increasing scent of victory in the air in Indian country these days. The mood is comparable to the old days of the Depression when the men began to dance once again. As the Indian movement gathers momentum and individual Indians cast their lot with the tribe, it will become apparent that not only will Indians survive the electronic world of Marshall McLuhan, they will thrive in it. At the present time everyone is watching how mainstream America will handle the issues of pollution, poverty, crime and racism when it does not fundamentally understand the issues. Knowing the importance of tribal survival, Indian people are speaking more and more of sovereignty, of the great political technique of the open council, and of the need for gaining the community's consensus on all programs before putting them into effect.

One can watch this same issue emerge in white society as the "Woodstock Nation," the "Blackstone Nation" and the block organizations are developed. This is a full tribalizing process involving a nontribal people, and it is apparent that some people are frightened by it. But it is the kind of social phenomenon upon which Indians feast.

In 1965 I had a long conversation with an old Papago. I was trying to get the tribe to pay its dues to the National Congress of American Indians and I had asked him to speak to the tribal council for me. He said that he would but that the Papagos didn't really need the N.C.A.I. They were like, he told me, the old mountain in the distance. The Spanish had come and dominated them for 300 years and then left. The Mexicans had come and ruled them for a century, but they also left. "The Americans," he said, "have been here only about 80 years. They, too, will vanish but the Papagos and the mountain will always be here."

This attitude and understanding of life is what American society is searching for.

I wish the Government would give Alcatraz to the Indians now occupying it. They want to create five centers on the Island. One center would be for a North American studies program; another would be a spiritual and medical center where Indian religions and medicines would be used and studied. A third center would concentrate on ecological studies based on an Indian view of nature—that man should live *with* the land and not simply *on* it. A job-training center and a museum would also be founded on the island. Certain of these programs would obviously require federal assistance.

Some people may object to this approach, yet Health, Education and Welfare gave out $10-million last year to non-Indians to study Indians. Not one single dollar went to an Indian scholar or researcher to present the point of view of Indian people. And the studies done by non-Indians added nothing to what was already known about Indians.

Indian people have managed to maintain a viable and cohesive social order in spite of everything the non-Indian society has thrown at them in an effort to break the tribal structure. At the same time, non-Indian society has created a monstrosity of a culture, where people starve while the granaries are filled and the sun can never break through the smog.

By making Alcatraz an experimental Indian center operated and planned by Indian people, we would be given a chance to see what we could do toward developing answers to modern social problems. Ancient tribalism can be incorporated with modern technology in an urban setting. Perhaps we would not succeed in the effort, but the Government is spending billions every year and still the situation is rapidly growing worse. It just seems to a lot of Indians that this continent was a lot better off when we were running it.

## "We Must Hold On to the Old Ways," December 16, 1969

*On November 20, 1969, scores of Native Americans took over a former federal prison on Alcatraz Island in the middle of the San Francisco Bay. Many Indian activists would later recall this as the first big battle of the new Red Power movement, and it had an electric effect on Indians across the nation. The protestors issued the statement below on December 16, 1969. Note its emphasis on the need to preserve Indian culture and pan tribal unity, a pan ethnic Indian identity, just then emerging.*

Source: Alvin M. Josephy Jr., *Red Power* (New York: McGraw-Hill, 1970), pp. 199–201.

ALCATRAZ ISLAND
DECEMBER 16, 1969

*Dear Brothers and Sisters:*
This is a call for a delegation from each Indian nation, tribe or band from throughout the United States, Canada, and Mexico to meet together on Alcatraz Island in San Francisco Bay, on December 23, 1969, for a meeting to be tentatively called the Confederation of American Indian Nations (CAIN).

On November 20, 1969, 78 Indian people, under the name "Indians of all Tribes," moved onto Alcatraz Island, a former Federal Prison. We began cleaning up the Island and are still in the process of organizing, setting up classes and trying to instill the old Indian ways into our young.

We moved onto Alcatraz Island because we feel that Indian people need a Cultural Center of their own. For several decades, Indian people have not had enough control of training their young people. And without a cultural center of their own, we are afraid that the old Indian ways may be lost. We believe that the only way to keep them alive is for Indian people to do it themselves.

While it was a small group which moved onto the island, we want all Indian people to join with us. More Indian people from throughout the country are coming to the island every day. We are issuing this call in an attempt to unify all our Indian Brothers behind a common cause.

We realize that there are more problems in Indian communities besides having our culture taken away. We have water problems, land problems, "social" problems, job opportunity problems, and many others.

And as Vice President Agnew said at the annual convention of the National Congress of American Indians in October of this year, now is the time for Indian leadership.

We realize too that we are not getting anywhere fast by working alone as individual tribes. If we can gather together as brothers and come to a common agreement, we feel that we can be much more effective, doing things for ourselves, instead of having someone else doing it, telling us what is good for us.

So we must start somewhere. We feel that if we are going to succeed, we must hold on to the old ways. *This is the first and most important reason we went to Alcatraz Island.*

We feel that the only reason Indian people have been able to hold on and survive through decades of persecution and cultural deprivation is that the Indian way of life is and has been strong enough to hold the people together.

We hope to reinforce the traditional Indian way of life by building a Cultural Center on Alcatraz Island. We hope to build a college, a religious and spiritual center, a museum, a center of ecology, and a training school.

We hope to have the Cultural Center controlled by Indians, with the delegates from each Indian nation and urban center present for the first meeting on December 23, and at future meetings of the governing body.

We are inviting all our brothers to join with us on December 23, if not in person, then in spirit.

We are still raising funds for Alcatraz. The "Alcatraz Relief Fund" is established with the Bank of California, Mission Branch, 3060 16th Street, San Francisco, California 94103, and we are asking that donations of money go to the bank directly.

Many Indian Centers and tribal groups from throughout the country have supported the people on Alcatraz by conducting benefits, funded drives, and so forth. We are deeply appreciative of all the help we have received, and hope that all Indian people and people of good will, will join us in this effort.

We are also asking for formal resolutions of support from each organized

Indian tribe and urban center. We can have great power at the bargaining table if we can get the support and help of all Indian people.

We have made no attempts at starting a hard and fast formal organization. We have elected spokesmen because someone has had to be a spokesman. We feel that all Indian people should be present or represented at the outset of a formal national Indian organization.

We have also elected a Central Council to help organize the day-to-day operation of the Island. This organization is not a governing body, but an operational one.

We hope to see you on December 23rd.

*Indians of All Tribes*
*Alcatraz Island*

## El Plan Espiritual de Aztlan, 1969

*The Chicano poet Alurista proclaimed "El Plan de Espiritual de Aztlan" at the National Chicano Youth Liberation Conference in Denver, Colorado, in 1969. It was the emotional highlight of that meeting and later appeared in many literary journals and anthologies. Like calls for Black and Yellow Power, the "Plan" invokes Chicano solidarity, self-determination, and cultural revival. It also suggests Mexican American claims to the southwestern United States as the ancestral home of the Aztec people. This suggestion inspired "Brown Power" advocates but alarmed some Anglo Americans in the southwest, who feared a Mexican American uprising to take back that territory.*

*Source:* Antonio Camejo, ed., *Documents of Chicano Struggle* (New York: Pathfinder Press, 1971).

In the spirit of a new people that is conscious not only of its proud historical heritage but also of the brutal "gringo" invasion of our territories, *we,* the Chicano inhabitants and civilizers of the northern land of Aztlan from whence came our forefathers, reclaiming the land of their birth and consecrating the determination of our people of the sun, *declare* that the call of our blood is our power, our responsibility, and our inevitable destiny.

We are free and sovereign to determine those tasks which are justly called for by our house, our land, the sweat of our brows, and by our hearts. Aztlan belongs to those who plant the seeds, water the fields, and gather the crops and not to the foreign Europeans. We do not recognize capricious frontiers on the bronze continent.

Brotherhood unites us, and love for our brothers makes us a people whose time has come and who struggles against the foreigner "gabacho" who exploits our riches and destroys our culture. With our heart in our hands and our hands in the soil, we declare the independence of our mestizo nation. We are a bronze people with a bronze culture. Before the world, before all of North America, before all our brothers in the bronze continent, we are a nation, we are a union of free pueblos, we are *Aztlan.*

*For La Raza to do. Fuera de La Raza nada.*

## PROGRAM

El Plan Espiritual de Aztlan sets the theme that the Chicanos (La Raza de Bronze) must use their nationalism as the key or common denominator for mass mobilization and organization. Once we are committed to the idea and philosophy of El Plan de Aztlan, we can only conclude that social, economic, cultural, and political independence is the only road to total liberation from oppression, exploitation, and racism. Our struggle then must be for the control of our barrios, campos, pueblos, lands, our economy, our culture, and our political life. El Plan commits all levels of Chicano society—the barrio, the campo, the ranchero, the writer, the teacher, the worker, the professional—to La Causa.

## NATIONALISM

Nationalism as the key to organization transcends all religious, political, class, and economic factions or boundaries. Nationalism is the common denominator that all members of La Raza can agree upon.

### ORGANIZATIONAL GOALS

1. UNITY in the thinking of our people concerning the barrios, the pueblo, the campo, the land, the poor, the middle class, the professional-all committed to the liberation of La Raza.
2. ECONOMY: economic control of our lives and our communities can only come about by driving the exploiter out of our communities, our pueblos, and our lands and by controlling and developing our own talents, sweat, and resources. Cultural background and values which ignore materialism and embrace humanism will contribute to the act of cooperative buying and the distribution of resources and production to sustain an economic base for healthy growth and development. Lands rightfully ours will be fought for and defended. Land and realty ownership will be acquired by the community for the people's welfare. Economic ties of responsibility must be secured by nationalism and the Chicano defense units.
3. EDUCATION must be relative to our people, i.e., history, culture, bilingual education, contributions, etc. Community control of our schools, our teachers, our administrators, our counselors, and our programs.
4. INSTITUTIONS shall serve our people by providing the service necessary for a full life and their welfare on the basis of restitution, not handouts or beggar's crumbs. Restitution for past economic slavery, political exploitation, ethnic and cultural psychological destruction and denial of civil and human rights. Institutions in our community which do not serve the people have no place in the community. The institutions belong to the people.
5. SELF-DEFENSE of the community must rely on the combined strength of the people. The front line defense will come from the barrios, the campos, the pueblos, and the ranchitos. Their involvement as protectors of their people will be given respect and

dignity. They in turn offer their responsibility and their lives for their people. Those who place themselves in the front ranks for their people do so out of love and carnalismo. Those institutions which are fattened by our brothers to provide employment and political pork barrels for the gringo will do so only as acts of liberation and for La Causa. For the very young there will no longer be acts of juvenile delinquency, but revolutionary acts.

6. CULTURAL values of our people strengthen our identity and the moral backbone of the movement. Our culture unites and educates the family of La Raza towards liberation with one heart and one mind. We must insure that our writers, poets, musicians, and artists produce literature and art that is appealing to our people and relates to our revolutionary culture. Our cultural values of life, family, and home will serve as a powerful weapon to defeat the gringo dollar value system and encourage the process of love and brotherhood.

7. POLITICAL LIBERATION can only come through indepen-dent action on our part, since the two-party system is the same animal with two heads that feed from the same trough. Where we are a majority, we will control; where we are a minority, we will represent a pressure group; nationally, we will represent one party: La Familia de La Raza!

ACTION

1. Awareness and distribution of El Plan Espiritual de Aztlan. Presented at every meeting, demonstration, confrontation, courthouse, institution, administration, church, school, tree, building, car, and every place of human existence.

2. September 16, on the birthdate of Mexican Independence, a national walk-out by all Chicanos of all colleges and schools to be sustained until the complete revision of the educational system: its policy makers, administration, its curriculum, and its personnel to meet the needs of our community.

3. Self-defense against the occupying forces of the oppressors at every school, every available man, woman, and child.

4. Community nationalization and organization of all Chicanos: El Plan Espiritual de Aztlan.

5. Economic program to drive the exploiter out of our community and a welding together of our people's combined resources to control their own production through cooperative effort.

6. Creation of an independent local regional, and national political party.

A nation autonomous and free—culturally, socially, economically, and politically—will make its own decisions on the usage of our lands, the taxation of our goods, the utilization of our bodies for war, the determination of justice (reward and punishment), and the profit of our sweat.

El Plan de Aztlan is the plan of liberation!

## La Raza Unida Party, "Preamble," 1969

*At the same National Chicano Youth Liberation Conference Meeting in Denver in 1969 where Alurista proclaimed El Plan Espiritual de Aztlan, Rodolfo Gonzales and Jose Angel Guitterez decided to create a national Mexican American political party, La Raza Unida, The United People. The party won some early local victories but was discredited after it received help from the Republicans in fights with the Democratic party in 1972 and faded out of existence by 1973. This preamble to the party's first platform lays out its response to racism, its rejection of the Republican and Democratic parties, and its commitment to Latino solidarity and self-determination.*

*Source:* Antonio Camejo, ed., *Documents of Chicano Struggle* (New York: Pathfinder Press, 1971).

### PREAMBLE

I. When we begin to illuminate and examine the so-called "dark chapters" in the history of this nation, the most affluent and powerful nation in the world, we see that the history of La Raza is to be found therein, and that from the beginning, the United States used the labor of our people to build not only the Southwest but this entire country and to amass fortunes for the Anglo exploiters of our people.

We examine further. We see that our lands were stolen from us. We see that the only payment was in poverty, starvation, disease, racist mockeries made of our language and culture and race. This was the payment for the labor which our people put into the building of this country, for the lands that were unjustly stolen from us. This country has seen fit to use and brutalize our people and to attempt at the same time to trick us into thinking that it bears no responsibility for our oppression and that its greatest desire is to help us. The two political parties in this country, and particularly the Democratic Party, have been the primary tools of our oppression.

Because we see through the trickery of the Democratic and Republican politicians and see that these two political parties have completely failed us in their promises and understand that in reality they have been working for the benefit of the wealthy Anglos by furthering and perpetuating the oppression of our people.

Because our people are still starving, are still being miseducated, are being increasingly brutalized by police authority;

Because poverty and death from curable diseases are still rampant among our people;

Because our people are not given the benefit of the justice that is due them as citizens of this land and therefore fill the jails in outrageous numbers;

Because the denial of education and job opportunities to our women has placed them in an even more oppressed situation than the men of La Raza;

And because this total, racist oppression of our people is an integral part of an economic system which uses as its political arm the two-party system, two parties working for the same wealthy few, two parties between which there is no significant difference in our eyes;

Given that these factors of oppression form the common denominator that unites us, THEREFORE, WE THE PEOPLE OF LA RAZA, have decided to reject the existing political parties of our oppressors and take it upon ourselves to form LA RAZA UNIDA PARTY, which will serve as a unifying force in our struggle for self-determination.

We understand that our real liberation and freedom will only come about through independent political action on our part. Independent political action, of which electoral activity is but one aspect, means involving La Raza Unida Party at all levels of struggle in actions which will serve to involve and educate our people. We recognize that self-determination can only come about through the full and total participation of La Raza in the struggle.

Because of the cultural genocide committed against our indigenous population by an outside invader and in full recognition of the daily oppression, humiliation, degradation, psychological and spiritual assassination, economic exploitation and the continuing misery of our people in violation of their basic constitutional and human rights, we consider it not only our right but our obligation to struggle for our full and complete liberation by any means necessary.

These oppressive conditions that form the common denominator that unites us give rise to a spiritual cohesiveness, a collective consciousness, that forms the basis of RAZA NATIONALISM.

We further specify that although the protection of our culture and the continuing maintenance of it will be a necessary part of our struggle, we recognize that our culture alone cannot produce our freedom and that only an organized and protracted struggle, confronting our oppressors at every level and involving the greatest number of our people, can bring about our goal of complete self-determination and total freedom.

II. La Raza Unida Party will not support any candidate of the Democratic or Republican Party or any individual who supports these parties.

III. Membership: Any person of La Raza registered in La Raza Unida Party and/or who works actively to support the program and activities of the party will be considered a member with the right to participate in all decision-making processes of the party on the basis of one person, one vote.

By "La Raza" we mean those people who are descendants of or come from Mexico, Central America, South America, and the Antilles.

## Asian American Political Alliance, 1969

*The Asian American Political Alliance (AAPA) was one of the early protest organizations of the Asian American movement. It was, for example, represented in the Third World Liberation Front coalition of minorities that carried out the strike at San Francisco State in 1968 and 1969. Like many of the other early Asian American protest groups, the AAPA was interested in working with Asian American communities as well as college students. As historian William Wei notes, however, it was unique in that "its main interest was in the then novel idea of creating a pan-Asian identity." Indeed, the AAPA was one of the first organizations in the country to call itself Asian American.*

Source: Amy Tachiki, Eddie Wong, and Franklin Odo, with Buck Wong, eds., *Roots: An Asian American Reader* (Los Angeles: UCLA Asian American Studies Center, 1971).

## UNDERSTANDING AAPA

We Asian Americans believe that we must develop an American Society which is just, humane, equal, and gives the people the right to control their own livesbefore we can begin to end the oppression and inequality that exists in this nation.

We Asian Americans realize that America was always and still is a White Racist Society. Asian Americans have been continuously exploited and oppressed by the racist majority and have survived only through hard work and resourcefulness, but their souls have not survived.

We Asian Americans refuse to cooperate with the White Racism in this society which exploits us as well as other Third World people, and affirm the right of Self-Determination.

We Asian Americans support all oppressed peoples and their struggles for Liberation and believe that Third World People must have complete control over the political, economic, and educational institutions within their communities.

We Asian Americans oppose the imperialistic policies being pursued by the American Government.

## AAPA PERSPECTIVES

The Asian American Political Alliance is people. It is a people's alliance to effect social and political changes. We believe that the American society is historically racist and one which has systematically employed social discrimination and economic imperialism, both domestically and internationally, exploiting all non-white people in the process of building up their affluent society.

They did so at the expense of all of us. Uncontrolled capitalism has pushed all of the non-white people into a social position so that only manual jobs with subhuman pay are open to them. Consequently, we have been psychologically so conditioned by the blue-eye-blond-hair standard that many of us have lost our perspective. We can only survive if "we know our place"—shut up and accept what we are given. We resent this kind of domination and we are determined to change it.

The goal of AAPA is political education and advancement of the movement among Asian people, so that they may make all decisions that affect their own lives, in a society that never asks people to do so. AAPA is not an isolated group, and should never profess to be such. Its only legitimacy and value is in the effects it has on many people, not just a small group of people. In the same vein, AAPA is not meant to isolate Asians from other people; it is unhealthy as well as unwise to do such a thing. AAPA must constantly expand and grow, and reach out to other people and groups. At the same time, AAPA must meet the needs of its own members and deal with its own problems.

In the past political organizations have tended to subject themselves to rigid, traditional levels of structure in which a few make the decisions, present them to the body, and the body can vote either "yes" or "no." This hierarchistic organization, however, is only a manifestation of the elite control, primidal structure mentality in which you are not capable of making your own decisions, an idea drilled into you from the foundations of this society.

AAPA is only what the people make it. We have adopted a structure which better fits the needs and goals of our alliance, not a structure to which we have to adjust ourselves. Furthermore, there is no membership in AAPA in the strict sense of the word. There are workers who for common interests join together with one or more people to intensify the effectiveness of an action.

Since May, 1968, AAPA has grown from a small group of students and community workers to a powerhouse for Asian thought and action. AAPA is now a member of the Third World Liberation Front, Asian Association, and Asian Coalition. Some past activities of Berkeley AAPA include: Free Huey Rallies at the Oakland Courthouse, Chinatown Forums, McCarran Act lobbies, MASC Boycott, Third World Liberation Front Strike, development of Asian Studies, and liaison with and development of other AAPA's throughout the state.

AAPA is only a transition for developing our own social identity, a multiplication of efforts. In fact, AAPA itself is not the important link but the ideas generated into action from it—that we

Asian Americans are no longer going to kowtow to white America in order to gain an ounce of respect; that we must begin to build our own society alongside our black, brown and red brothers as well as those whites willing to effect fundamental social, economic, political changes; that we have the right for determining our own lives and asserting our yellow identity as a positive force in a new life based on human relationships and cooperation.

## Amy Uyematsu, "The Emergence of Yellow Power in America," 1969

*Amy Uyematsu wrote this analysis of the Yellow Power movement in the underground Asian American newspaper, Gidra, in October of 1969, and it was later reprinted in Roots: An Asian American Reader, edited by Amy Tachiki, Eddie Wong, Franklin Odo, and Buck Wong, a collection often used in early Asian American Studies courses. It was one of the most important early assertions and discussions of "Yellow Power," decrying "token acceptance" by white America, the psychological empowerment found in racial pride, and the explicit links between Black Power and Yellow Power—"a direct outgrowth of the Black Power movement."*

Source: Amy Tachiki, Eddie Wong, and Franklin Odo, with Buck Wong, eds., *Roots: An Asian American Reader* (Los Angeles: UCLA Asian American Studies Center, 1971).

Asian Americans can no longer afford to watch the black-and-white struggle from the sidelines. They have their own cause to fight, since they are also victims—with less visible scars—of the white institutionalized Racism. A yellow movement has been set into motion by the black power movement. Addressing itself to the unique problems of Asian Americans, this "yellow power" movement is relevant to the black power movement in that both are part of the Third World struggle to liberate all colored people.

## PART 1: MISTAKEN IDENTITY

The yellow power movement has been motivated largely by the problem of self-identity in Asian Americans. The psychological focus of this movement is vital, for Asian Americans suffer the critical mental crises of having "integrated" into American Society—"No person can be healthy, complete, and mature if he must deny a part of himself; This is what 'integration' has required so far" (Stokely Carmichael & Charles V. Hamilton).

The Asian Americans' current position in America is not viewed as a social problem. Having achieved middle-class incomes while presenting no real threat in numbers to the white majority, the main body of Asian Americans (namely, the Japanese and the Chinese) have received the token acceptance of white America.

Precisely because Asian Americans have become economically secure, do they face serious identity problems. Fully committed to a system that subordinates them on the basis of non-whiteness, Asian Americans still try to gain complete acceptance by denying their yellowness. They have become white in every respect but color.

However, the subtle but prevailing racial prejudice that "yellows" experience restricts them to the margins of the white world. Asian Americans have assumed white identities, that is, the values and attitudes of the majority of Americans. Now they are beginning to realize that this nation is a "White democracy" and that yellow people have a mistaken identity.

Within the past two years, the "yellow power" movement has developed as a direct outgrowth of the "black power" movement. The "black power" movement caused many Asian Americans to question themselves. "Yellow power" is just now at the stage of "an articulated mood rather than a program—disillusionment and alienation from white America and independence, race pride, and self-respect." Yellow consciousness is the immediate goal of concerned Asian Americans.

In the process of Americanization, Asians have tried to transform themselves into white men—both mentally and physically. Mentally, they have adjusted to the white man's culture by giving up their own languages, customs, histories, and cultural values. They have adopted the "American way of life" only to discover that this is not enough.

Next, they have rejected their physical heritages, resulting in extreme self-hatred. Yellow people share with the blacks the desire to look white. Just as blacks wish to be light-complected with thin lips and unkinky hair, "yellows" want to be tall with long legs and large eyes. The self-hatred is also evident in the yellow male's obsession with unobtainable white women, and in the yellow female's attempt to gain male approval by aping white beauty standards. Yellow females have their own "conking" techniques—they use "peroxide, foam rubber, and scotch tape to give them light hair, large breasts and double-lidded eyes."

The "Black is Beautiful" cry among black Americans has instilled a new awareness in Asian Americans to be proud of their physical and cultural heritages. Yellow power advocates self-acceptance as the first step toward strengthening personalities of Asian Americans.

Since the yellow power movement is thus far made up of students and young adults, it is working for Asian-American ethnic studies centers on college campuses such as Cal and U.C.L.A. The re-establishment of ethnic identity through education is being pursued in classes like U.C.L.A.'s "Orientals in America." As one student in the course relates:

> I want to take this course for a 20–20 realization, and not a passive glance in the ill-reflecting mirror; the image I see is W.A.S.P., but the yellow skin is not lily white . . . I want to find out what my voluntarily or subconsciously suppressed Oriental self is like; also what the thousands of other (suppressed?) Oriental selves are like in a much larger mind and body—America . . . I want to establish my ethnic identity not merely for the sake of such roots, but for the inherent value that such a background merits.

The problem of self-identity in Asian Americans also requires the removal of stereo types. The yellow people in America seem to be silent citizens. They are stereotyped as being passive, accommodating, and unemotional. Unfortunately, this description is fairly accurate, for Asian Americans have accepted these stereotypes and are becoming true to them.

The "silent" Asian Americans have rationalized their behavior in terms of cultural values which they have maintained from the old country. For example, the Japanese use the term "enryo" to denote hesitation in action or expression. A young Buddhist minister, Reverend Mas Kodani of the Los Angeles Senshin Buddhist Temple, has illustrated the difference between Japanese "enryo" and Japanese-American "enryo": in Japan, if a teacher or lecturer asks, "Are there any questions?," several members of the class or audience respond; but in the United States the same question is followed by a deathly silence.

Reverend Kodani has also commented on the freedom of expression between family members that is absent in Asian Americans. As an American-born student in Japan, he was surprised at the display of open affection in Japanese families. This cultural characteristic is not shown in Japanese-American families, who react with embarrassment and guilt toward open feelings of love and hate.

This uneasiness in admitting and expressing natural human feelings has been a factor in the negligible number of Asian Americans in the theater, drama, and literary arts. Not discounting the race prejudice and competition in these fields, yellow Americans cannot express themselves honestly, or in the words of Chinese-American actor James Hong they cannot feel "from the gut level."

The silent, passive image of Asian Americans is understood not in terms of their cultural backgrounds, but by the fact that they are scared. The earliest Asians in America were Chinese immigrants who began settling in large numbers on the West Coast from 1850 through 1880. They were subjected to extreme white racism, ranging from economic subordination, to the denial of rights of naturalization, to physical violence. During the height of anti-Chinese mob action of the 1880's, whites were "stoning the Chinese in the streets, cutting off their queues, wrecking their shops and laundries." The worst outbreak took place in Rock Springs, Wyoming, in 1885, when twenty-eight Chinese residents were murdered. Perhaps, surviving Asians learned to live in silence, for even if "the victims of such attacks tried to go to court to win protection, they could not hope to get a hearing. The phrase 'not a Chinaman's chance' had a grim and bitter reality."

Racist treatment of "yellows" still existed during World War II, with the unjustifiable internment of 110,000 Japanese into detention camps. When Japanese Americans were ordered to leave their homes and possessions behind within short notice, they co-operated with resignation and not even voiced opposition. According to Frank Chumann, onetime president of the Japanese American Citizens League, they "used the principle of shikataganai—realistic resignation—and evacuated without protest."

Today the Asian Americans are still scared. Their passive behavior serves to keep national attention on the black people. By being as inconspicuous as possible, they keep pressure off of themselves at the expense of the blacks. Asian Americans have formed an uneasy alliance with white Americans to keep the blacks down. They close their eyes to the latent white racism toward them which has never changed.

Frightened "yellows" allow the white public to use the "silent Oriental" stereotype against the black protest. The presence of twenty million blacks in America poses an actual physical threat to the white system. Fearful whites tell militant blacks that the acceptable criterion for behavior is exemplified in the quiet, passive Asian American.

The yellow power movement envisages a new role for Asian Americans:

"It is a rejection of the passive Oriental stereotype and symbolizes the birth of a new Asian—one who will recognize and deal with injustices. The shout of Yellow Power, symbolic of our new direction, is reverberating in the quiet corridors of the Asian community."

As expressed in the black power writings, yellow power also says that "When we begin to define our own image, the stereotypes—that is, lies—that our oppressor has developed will begin in the white community and end there."

Another obstacle to the creation of

yellow consciousness is the well-incorporated white racist attitudes which are present in Asian Americans They take much false pride in their own economic progress and feel that blacks could succeed similarly if they only followed the Protestant ethic of hard work and education. Many Asians support S. I. Hayakawa, the so-called spokesman of yellow people, when he advises the black man to imitate the Nisei: "Go to school and get high grades, save one dollar out of every ten you earn to capitalize your business." But the fact is that the white power structure allowed Asian Americans to succeed through their own efforts while the same institutions persist in denying these opportunities to black Americans.

Certain basic changes in American society made it possible for many Asian Americans to improve their economic condition after the war. In the first place, black people became the target group of West Coast discrimination. During and after World War II, a huge influx of blacks migrated into the West, taking racist agitation away from the yellows and onto the blacks. From 1940 to 1950, there was a gain of 85.2 percent in the black population of the West and North; from 1950 to 1960, a gain of 71.6 percent; and from 1960 to 1966, a gain of 80.4 percent.

The other basic change in society was the shifting economic picture. In a largely agricultural and rural West, Asian Americans were able to find employment. First- and second-generation Japanese and Filipinos were hired as farm laborers and gardeners, while Chinese were employed in laundries and restau-

rants. In marked contrast is the highly technological and urban society which today faces unemployed black people. "The Negro migrant, unlike the immigrant, found little opportunity in the city; he had arrived too late, and the unskilled labor he had to offer was no longer needed." Moreover, blacks today are kept out of a shrinking labor market, which is also closing opportunities for white job-seekers.

Asian Americans are perpetuating white racism in the United States as they allow white America to hold up the "successful" Oriental image before other minority groups as the model to emulate. White America justifies the blacks' position by showing that other non-whites—yellow people—have been able to "adapt" to the system. The truth underlying both the yellows' history and that of the blacks has been distorted. In addition, the claim that black citizens must "prove their rights to equality" is fundamentally racist.

Unfortunately, the yellow power movement is fighting a well-developed racism in Asian Americans who project their own frustrated attempts to gain white acceptance onto the black people. They nurse their own feelings of inferiority and insecurity by holding themselves as superior to the blacks.

Since they feel they are in a relatively secure economic and social position, most Asian Americans overlook the subtle but damaging racism that confronts them. They do not want to upset their present ego systems by honest self-appraisal. They would rather fool themselves than admit that they have prostituted themselves to white society.

## PART 2: THE RELEVANCE OF POWER FOR ASIANS IN AMERICA

The emerging movement among Asian Americans can be described as "yellow power" because it is seeking freedom from racial oppression through the power of a consolidated yellow people. As derived from the black power ideology, yellow power implies that Asian Americans must control the decision-making processes affecting their lives.

One basic premise of both black power and yellow power is that ethnic political power must be used to improve the economic and social conditions of blacks and yellows. In considering the relevance of power for Asian Americans, two common assumptions will be challenged: first, that the Asian Americans are completely powerless in the United States; and second, the assumption that Asian Americans have already obtained "economic" equality.

While the black power movement can conceivably bargain from a position of strength, yellow power has no such potential to draw from. A united black people would comprise over ten percent of the total American electorate; this is a significant enough proportion of the voting population to make it possible for blacks to be a controlling force in the power structure. In contrast, the political power of yellows would have little effect on state and national contests. The combined populations of Chinese, Japanese and Filipinos in the United States in 1960 was only 887,834—not even one-half percent of the total population.

However, Asian Americans are not completely weaponless, in the local political arena. For instance, in California, the combined strength of Chinese, Japanese, and Filipinos in 1960 was two percent of the state population. Their possible political significance lies in the fact that there are heavy concentrations of these groups in San Francisco and Los Angeles. In the San Francisco-Oakland metropolitan area, 55% of the Chinese, 16% of the Japanese, and 33% of the Filipinos live. On an even more local level, Japanese and Chinese in the Crenshaw area of Los Angeles form about one-third of the total residents; and Japanese in the city of Gardena own forty percent of that city' s property.

In city and county government, a solid yellow voting bloc could make a difference. As has been demonstrated by the Irish, Italians, Jews, and Poles, the remarkable fact of ethnic political power is it's ability to "control a higher proportion of political control and influence than their actual percentage in the population warrants."

Even under the assumption that yellow political power could be significant, how will it improve the present economic situation of Asian Americans? Most yellow people have attained middle-class incomes and feel that they have no legitimate complaint against the existing capitalist structure.

The middle-class attainment of Asian Americans has also made certain blacks unsympathetic to the yellow power movement. In the words of one B.S.U. member, it looks like Asian Americans "just want more of the money pie." It is difficult for some blacks to relate to the yellow man's problems next to his own total victimization.

Although it is true that some Asian minorities lead all other colored groups in America in terms of economic progress, it is a fallacy that Asian Americans enjoy full economic opportunity. If the Protestant ethic is truly a formula for economic success, then why don't Japanese and Chinese who work harder and have more education than whites earn just as much? Statistics on unemployment, educational attainment, and median annual income reveal an inconsistency in this "success" formula when it applies to non-whites.

In 1960, unemployment rates for Japanese and Chinese males were lower than those for white males in California:

2.6 percent for Japanese
4.9 percent for Chinese
5.5 percent for whites

In the same year, percentage rates for Japanese and Chinese males who had completed high school or college were higher than those for white males:

HIGH SCHOOL
34.3 percent for Japanese
24.4 percent for Chinese

COLLEGE (4 YEARS OR
MORE)
13.3 percent for Chinese
11.9 percent for Japanese
10.7 percent for whites

Despite these figures, the median annual income of Japanese and Chinese was considerably lower than the median annual income of whites. Chinese men in California earned $3,803; Japanese men earned $4,388; and white men earned $5,109.

The explanation for this discrepancy lies in the continuing racial discrimination toward yellows in upper-wage level and high-status positions. White America praises the success of Japanese and Chinese for being highest among all other colored groups. Japanese and Chinese should feel fortunate that they are accepted more than any other non-white ethnic group, but they should not step out of place and compare themselves with whites. In essence, the American capitalistic dream was never meant to include non-whites.

The myth of Asian American success is most obvious in the economic and social position of Filipino Americans. In 1960, the 65,459 Filipino residents of California earned a median annual income of $2,925, as compared to $3,553 for blacks and $5,109 for whites. Over half of the total Filipino male working force was employed in farm labor and service work; over half of all Filipino males received less than 8.7 years of school education. Indeed, Filipinos are a forgotten minority in America. Like blacks, they have many legitimate complaints against American society.

A further example of the false economic and social picture of Asian Americans exists in the ghetto communities of Little Tokyo in Los Angeles and Chinatown in San Francisco. In the former, elderly Japanese live in rundown hotels in social and cultural isolation. And in the latter, Chinese families suffer the poor living conditions of a community that has the second highest tuberculosis rate in the nation.

Thus, the use of yellow political power is valid, for Asian Americans do have definite economic and social problems which must be improved. By organizing around these needs, Asian Americans can make the yellow power movement a viable political force in their lives.

## Reparations for Japanese-American Internees, April 20, 1988

*With the rise of Asian American group consciousness and "Yellow Power" challenges to the dominant culture, Asian Americans pointed to previous racist treatment by American governments that excluded or punished them. No recent incident in Asian American history seemed such an egregious and blatant violation of America's professed ideals as the wholesale internment of Japanese Americans in World War II. This internment not only violated the constitution but continued even as Japanese American soldiers fought for the United States in Europe. After intense lobbying by the Japanese American community, Congress created a commission to investigate the incident in 1980, and in 1983 the commission issued a report recommending an award of $20,000 to each surviving internee. In 1988 Congress voted reparations to Japanese Americans as a "symbolic gesture" of apology. Not all Congressmen agreed, however, as the following excerpt from the Congressional debate reveals.*

Source: Reparations for Japanese-American Internees, April 20, 1988, Historic Documents

of 1988 (Washington, D.C.: Congressional Quarterly, Inc., 1989).

After an intense and at times emotional debate, the Senate April 20, 1988, approved by a 69–27 vote a measure providing for apologies and reparations to be made to 60,000 Japanese-Americans who were interned in U.S. relocation camps during World War II. The Japanese-Americans had been forcibly removed from their homes on the West Coast and placed in inland camps early in 1942 in response to Japan's attack on U.S. naval and military bases in Hawaii December 7, 1941, which triggered America's entry into the war.

The legislation provided for the payment of $20,000 to each of the survivors from among 120,000 Japanese-Americans held during the war and also for about 900 Aleuts who were evacuated from Alaska's Pribilof Islands after the 1942 Japanese seizure of two islands in the Aleutian chain some two thousand miles away. The House had passed a similar measure September 17, 1987. After both chambers approved a conference report, President Ronald Reagan signed the measure into law on August 10, 1988, to "right a grave wrong."

The law sets up a trust fund of ultimately $1.25 billion to pay the reparations over a period of ten years. The first payments are due to go to former internees who are now elderly. All who receive the payments must agree to drop any legal claims resulting from their internment. Although the legislation provides money, it was widely viewed as a mainly symbolic move to redress what many Americans regarded as a woeful injustice. In Senate debate, Pete Wilson, R-Calif., called the wartime internment of the Japanese-Americans "one of the great travesties of our history." President Reagan said at the White House ceremony: "Yes, the nation was then at war struggling for its survival. And it's not for us today to pass judgment upon those who made mistakes in that great struggle. Yet we must recognize that the internment of Japanese-Americans was just that, a mistake."

## BACKGROUND

Most of the internees were U.S. citizens; the others held the status of resident aliens. Once taken from their homes, they were sent to assembly centers and eventually to the relocation camps, as was required by an executive order President Franklin D. Roosevelt issued February 19, 1942. Through another executive order, issued about a month later, Roosevelt authorized the creation of a War Relocation Authority to administer the operation.

So sudden was the evacuation that many of the Japanese-Americans were forced to sell or lease their homes or businesses at substantial losses. Even though Japanese-Americans living in Hawaii were never detained, the internment in the continental United States continued through the war. Wilson told the Senate that "having made that mistake, we persisted in it for four long years." There was never any evidence of disloyalty to the United States on the part of the Japanese-Americans.

## WEST COAST FEARS

The evacuation of the Japanese-Americans took place during a time of great unease on the West coast. The bombing of Pearl Harbor was followed quickly by Japanese military victories in the Pacific, creating fear that the U.S. mainland was in danger of attack. Ted Stevens, R-Alaska, recalled during Senate debate that as a young boy living in Los Angeles he heard antiaircraft guns "shooting at the moon, literally," because someone had falsely reported a Japanese attack. Many West Coast residents and military officials feared that the Japanese-Americans might communicate with Japanese ships offshore and assist in an invasion.

At relocation centers in six western states and Arkansas, the Japanese-Americans were jammed into tar-papered barracks in bleak surroundings. There was little regard for privacy. Sen. Alan Simpson, R-Wyo., remembered Heart Mountain Relocation Center— with 15,000 people the third largest community in his home state—as a place enclosed by barbed wire and guard towers. Among its occupants, he discovered to his surprise, were Boy Scouts working on merit badges just as he was.

## COMMISSION REPORT

Generally, the legislation implemented recommendations made by the Commission on Wartime Relocation and Internment of Civilians in its reports of February 24 and June 16, 1983. The nine-member, nonpartisan commission had been established by Congress in 1980. The commission estimated that the interned Japanese-Americans lost income and property worth up to $2 billion in terms of the dollar value in 1983. The panel proposed that each surviving internee be awarded a payment of $20,000, together with official apologies. (Report on Internment of Japanese-Americans, Historic Documents of 1983, p. 211)

The commission found that President Roosevelt was advised to intern the Japanese-Americans by Army Lt. Gen. John L. DeWitt, commander of West Coast defense, and Secretary of War Henry L. Stimson. Without cabinet discussion, Roosevelt issued his order. For a brief time Milton Eisenhower, a brother of President Dwight D. Eisenhower and many years later president of Johns Hopkins University, headed the War Relocation Authority. He took the job reluctantly and in later years described the internment as "an inhuman mistake."

Earl Warren, the attorney general of California and later the chief justice of the United States, backed the detainment when it occurred. When he was appointed to the Supreme Court, Warren said that he "deeply regretted the removal and my own testimony [to a congressional committee] advocating it. . . ."

## CONGRESSIONAL ACTION

Barney Frank, D-Mass., the chief sponsor of the reparations measure in the House, told his colleagues that the payments to the internees were not intended as compensation but as a "symbolic gesture." He also said, "We have an obligation to act as people in charge of the government today." Two Japanese-American members of the House who had themselves been interned, Norman Y. Mineta and Robert T. Matsui, both California Democrats, pushed hard for passage of the measure. The House passed the bill 343–141.

In the Senate, the measure's principal advocate was Spark M. Matsunaga, D-Hawaii. Matsunaga had persuaded authorities to let him join the U.S. Army during World War II. With other Japanese-American volunteers, he served in a special regiment that engaged in bitter fighting in the Italian campaign. He was wounded twice. His fellow senator from Hawaii, Daniel K. Inouye, served in the same unit and lost his right arm in combat. "A stigma has haunted Japanese-Americans for forty-five years," Matsunega told his Senate colleagues. He urged their support of the legislation to remove the cloud "over their heads."

Sen. Jesse Helms, R-N.C., an opponent of the legislation, said he "could not buy this business of kicking our government around at a time when horrible destruction had occurred at Pearl Harbor, unprovoked. . . . It is all very well on Monday morning to replay the game of Saturday. But the president . . . had a responsibility to protect this country as best he could based on the information available to him." Senator Simpson said that while the internment was "the gravest of injustices," giving money to the victims was not the proper way to make an apology.

Writing in the *New York Times* August 11, 1988, Kathleen Bishop said that leaders of organizations that had pushed for the legislation reacted to its enactment "with a collective sigh of relief." Bishop quoted Ben Takeshita, a spokesman for the Japanese American Citizens League, as saying that while the payments could not "begin" to compensate a person for "lost freedom, property, livelihood or for the stigma of disloyalty," it showed that the government's apology was "sincere."

*Following are* Congressional Record *excerpts from Senate debate April 20, 1988, on reparations for interned Japanese-Americans:*

MR. [DANIEL K.] INOUYE [D-HAWAII]. . . . The measure before us is the source of much anguish and much controversy. Because of the commitment and dedication of Senator [Spark M.] Matsunaga [D-Hawaii], he has been able to convince 72 of his colleagues to join him in this endeavor.

Many fellow Americans, including my colleague from Nevada, have asked: "Why should Japanese-Americans be compensated?" During times of war, especially in times of fear, all people suffer. That is a very common argument made against this measure.

[W]hile it is true that all people of this Nation suffer during wartime, the Japanese-American internment experience is unprecedented in the history of American civil rights deprivation. I think we should recall, even if painful, that Americans of Japanese ancestry were de-

termined by our Government to be security risks without any formal allegations or charges of disloyalty or espionage. They were arbitrarily branded disloyal solely on the grounds of racial ancestry.

No similar mass internment was deemed necessary for Americans of German or Italian ancestries, and I think we should recall and remind ourselves that in World War II, the Japanese were not our only enemies.

These Japanese-Americans who were interned could not confront their accusers or bring their case before a court. These are basic rights of all Americans. They were incarcerated, forced to live in public communities with no privacy, and stripped of their freedom to move about as others could.

Japanese-Americans wishing to fight for this country were initially declared ineligible. However, once allowed to volunteer, they volunteered in great numbers. In fact, proportionately and percentagewise, more Japanese-Americans put on the uniform of this country during World War II, more were wounded and more were killed, even if they were restricted to serving in ethnically-restricted military units.

The individual payments acknowledge the unjust deprivation of liberty, the infliction of mental and physical suffering, and the stigma of being branded disloyal, losses not compensable under the Japanese Evacuation Claims Act of 1948. . . .

The Presidentially appointed Commission on Wartime Relocation and Internment of Civilians found no documented acts of espionage, sabotage, or fifth column activity by any, Mr. President, by any identifiable American citizen of Japanese ancestry or resident Japanese aliens on the west coast.

This was supposed to have been the rationale for this mass evacuation and mass incarceration, that these Americans were not to be trusted, that these Americans were agents of an enemy country, that these Americans would spy and carry out espionage, and this Presidentially appointed Commission, which incidentally was made up of leading citizens throughout this land—and only one member of that Commission was of Japanese ancestry—declared that there were no acts of espionage whatsoever. And sadly, the Commission in its 1983 report concluded that internment was motivated by racial prejudice, war hysteria, and a failure of political leadership. . . .

[T]he goal of S. 1009 is to benefit all citizens of our Nation by educating our citizens to preclude this event from occurring again to any other ethnic or religious group or any person suspected of being less than a loyal citizen. This bill reinforces the strength of our Constitution by reaffirming our commitment to upholding the constitutional rights of all our citizens. So, respectfully, I strongly urge its passage and in so doing once again commend and congratulate my distinguished colleague from Hawaii. . . .

MR. MATSUNAGA. I congratulate the senior Senator from Hawaii for his excellent statement. Coming from one who served in the 442d Regimental Combat Team, the most highly decorated military unit in the entire history of the United States, and having been highly decorated

with the second highest award, the Distinguished Service Cross, and having sacrificed an arm in that war, I believe what the senior Senator from Hawaii has to say should be taken most seriously. . . .

MR. [TED] STEVENS [R-ALASKA]. . . . As recounted yesterday what happened when the United States military removed 900 American citizens—Aleuts, who lived on the Aleutian chain and the Pribilof Islands—from their homes and took them to abandoned canneries and gold mining camps in southeastern Alaska.

Not many people understand the distances in our State. Attu and Kiska, which the Japanese invaded, are the most western islands in the Aleutian chain. The military saw fit to remove all Aleuts from all of the islands. Alaskans believed they did that because they wanted to occupy the islands and just did not want any local people in their way.

The Pribilof Islands were over 1,000 miles from the two islands the Japanese had taken. The Japanese never attempted to move further up along the Aleutian chain. They made an invasion of those two islands and fortified them. But there was really no necessity to remove these people. . . . Let us assume that the Japanese came to Baltimore. The action of the United States military removing the Aleuts would be like going to Chicago and then going west from Chicago about 1,000 miles and taking everyone between Chicago and Denver and moving them out of harm's way.

The record is clear that in terms of this internment—and it was an internment—was for the convenience of the

Government. And these people, because they were of native descent, were taken and interned. They were kept for 2 to 3 years in those camps. In those days, Alaska was a territory, under wartime conditions, and it was not possible to travel.

I related yesterday how one of my friends, Flore Lekanoff, was taken from one of those camps in southeastern Alaska back to the Pribilof Islands to hunt for seals for the military. He was never paid for that. He was never recognized as being in the service of the Government. None of these people were treated as though they were in the service of the Government. They were literally just shoved aside. . . .

They have waited a long, long time. Most of them never recovered financially, particularly the people I represent in the Aleutian chain. Many are still destitute. This settlement is the final act to close this chapter of history and try to make restitution for that period of hysteria.

The people who made those decisions were good Americans. They were defending the country. They made mistakes. . . .

MR. [DANIEL J.] EVANS [D-WASH.] . . . As a Senator from the State of Washington, I have a special interest in this legislation. The first group of Japanese citizens to be removed from their homes under President Roosevelt's Executive Order were from Bainbridge Island, WA. They were the first of nearly 13,000 Japanese-Americans from the State of Washington to be funneled into assembly centers and eventually into relocation facilities.

Victims of Executive Order 9066 were given very short notice that they would be sent to relocation facilities. Most were granted just a few days to abandon their homes and belongings. As a result they were forced to sell or lease their property and businesses at prices reflecting only a fraction of their worth. Substantial economic losses were incurred. Once they arrived at the relocation centers they found a quality of life which was atrocious. They were overcrowded and families suffered from an acute lack of privacy with no borders or walls to separate them from others.

Opponents of this legislation choose to ignore raw, racial prejudice woven in what was supposed to be legitimate national security justification for internment. The evacuees, however, were guilty of no crime other than the apparent crime of being of Japanese ancestry. Japanese-Americans left their homes in an atmosphere of racial prejudice and returned to the same.

What is perhaps most alarming about the Japanese internment is that it took place in the United States of America. This is the same country which has prided itself on freedom, justice, and the preservation and protection of individual rights.

Thirty-four years after the last citizens were released from captivity, Congress established the Commission on the Wartime Relocation and Internment of Japanese-American Citizens to assess the decision to intern and relocate Japanese-Americans. Two years after its inception, the Commission issued certain factual findings and subsequent recommendations. I have cosponsored legislation to implement these recommendations throughout my tenure in the U.S. Senate.

The $20,000 compensation that would be allotted to each victim, and the educational fund established by this legislation are a modest attempt to redress wrongs against loyal Americans. Although we cannot restore completely what already has been lost, the legislation would serve as a symbol to all that the United States can come to terms with its own tragic mistake. . . .

MR. [JESSE A.] HELMS [R-N.V.]. . . . Nobody is, in retrospect, proud of the relocation of the Japanese-Americans during World War II, but as I said earlier, we lived in a time of terror in this country immediately after the attack on Pearl Harbor. Nobody knew what was coming next. . . . We had just been attacked by a totalitarian regime which had enjoyed a virtually unbroken string of military successes, both before and immediately after the Government of Japan attacked the United States of America. . . .

I think it is only fair to look back to that time, and recall the fact that our intelligence community told the then President of the United States, Franklin Delano Roosevelt, that there was great risk. Now we can see that it was a mistake.

I have no vision problem with respect to that. We will have 20–20 vision by hindsight, and I am perfectly willing for this Senate and this Congress to declare that this kind of thing must never happen again.

But the Senate has just voted to give the priority emphasis to money, $1.3 bil-

lion. So I think we ought to look at our priorities. . . .

[T]he U.S. Government, contrary to suggestions otherwise, has not ignored the suffering that occurred as a result of the relocation and internment during the war. The Government has officially recognized that much unjustified personal hardship was, in fact, caused. Previous Congresses, Presidents and Attorneys General have taken steps to acknowledge and compensate Japanese-Americans for the injuries they suffered.

For example, in 1948, Congress enacted the American Japanese Claims Act, which authorized compensation for "any claim" for damages to or loss of real or personal property "as a reasonable consequence of the evacuation or exclusion of" persons of Japanese ancestry as a result of governmental action during World War II.

I might add that this act of 1948 was subsequently amended to liberalize its compensation provisions.

Under the amended act, the Justice Department received claims seeking approximately $147 million. Ultimately, 26,568 settlements were achieved. . . . True enough, the American Japanese Claims Act did not include every item of damage that was or could have been suggested. It did, however, address the hardships visited upon persons of Japanese ancestry in a comprehensive, considered manner taking into account individual needs and losses, and this effort to correct injustice to individuals was in keeping with our Nation's best tradition of individual rather than collective response, and it was far more contemporaneous with the injuries to the claimants than would be any payments at this late date. . . .

MR. [ALAN K.] SIMPSON [R-WYO.]. It has been a very interesting debate for me. I have been paying attention to it on the monitor. It has made me recall some most interesting and memorable parts of my own life because I was a young boy in Cody, WY, in 1941 when the war started. I was 10 then.

Two years later, at the age of 12, somewhere between the years of 12 and 13, the third largest community in Wyoming was constructed between the communities of Powell and Cody, WY, a city of 15,000 people which really literally went up overnight. And the name of it, of course, was Heart Mountain War Relocation Center, known to the people of the area simply as the "Jap Camp," a term which may be hard for us to believe now but that is what it was referred to then; swiftly built by those who had not been dratted into the war, or older men in their 40's who were not able to be taken into the war effort.

And so came into being Heart Mountain, WY, War Relocation Center. There was barbed wire around it. There were guard towers at the edges of it. It was a very imposing area. . . . I remember one night very distinctly when the scoutmaster—I was a Boy Scout, a rather nominal one, but I enjoyed the activities of the group. And he said, "We are going to go out to the War Relocation Center and have a scout meeting." I said, "Well, I mean, are there any of them out there?" He said, "Yes, yes, these are American citizens, you see." And that put a new

twist on it because we thought of them as something else—as aliens; we thought of them as spies; we thought of them as people who were behind wire because they were trying to do in our country.

So I shall not forget going to the Boy Scout meeting and meeting Boy Scouts from California, most of them, I recall, same merit badges, same scout sashes, same clothing.

And why not? Some of them were second- or third-generation American citizens. . . . I also remember those other nights we would go into the compound—which it was in every sense, with searchlights and with wire—visiting with some of the older people. There were very few young men there from the ages of 17 through 28, because many of them were in the armed services of the United States. But I do remember visiting with the older people and there were many of them there.

The younger and the older were there. Those were the principal inhabitants. I remember a woman, a very old woman to me at that age, said, "Do you have grandparents?"

I said, "Yes, I do."

She said, "Where do they live?"

I said, "In Cody, down the road there."

She said, "Well, what kind of a house do they have?"

I thought, well, that is interesting to ask. I described it.

"What do they do?"

And then I remember she showed me pictures of her family.

She said, "This is my son. He is in Italy now fighting for this country, the United States of America."

Then we would go downtown in Cody, WY, and there would be a sign on the restaurant that said, "No Japs allowed here." And then you would go down to another place of business, it might be a sign that said, "My son was killed at Iwo Jima. How do you think I feel?"

And the trustees would come into town. They were remarkable people. Usually the best and the brightest. Maybe those who had been involved in agriculture and whose lands had been taken from them—confiscated.

So I really had a lot of trouble sorting that all out at the age of 13. I maybe have some of the same kind of trouble sorting it all out at the age of 56. But let me just say that I preserve it as a very formative part of my life. . . . There is no question about it being the gravest of injustices. And it may be hardly a repayable one. How do you ever really repay these people for the wages, the property, the opportunity, the education, the part of their lives lost during this period? And this taxpayer expenditure is a troubling part of the bill for me.

I have trouble with the money. An apology may be long overdue and may be so appropriate. But, coupled with money, it takes away some of the sincerity of the apology, somehow. If you did that with a friend, a lovely friend, and you said: I am sorry for what I did. I know that was very harmful to you and hurtful. But I am sorry and I apologize and I want to give you some money.

I think that somehow is unbecoming. It may not be to some. It is a troubling aspect of it to me. . . . So we will conclude this, and I think probably we will revisit this issue again, not with this situation but in other populations of our country, and we best know indeed, that will likely take place.

There is not one of us here today with what we have been through with our civil rights activities in 1964 and Selma that probably thinks: "How could this have ever occurred?" And yet at the time it occurred, it seemed at that time of our lives to be the most important step that could be taken.

That decision was made by people with much greater wisdom than I had at the age of 13 in Cody, WY.

Hopefully, we will conclude this debate shortly and move on to other issues of the day because this is an old and sad and very painful thing that we have reopened here in this debate. The sooner we close that wound and suture it with love and understanding and affection, we will be better off. And suturing it with money does not seem like the best way to conclude the issue.

## Jesse Jackson, Speech to Democratic Convention, 1984

*In the early 1980s Jesse Jackson emerged as the leader of a national multicultural alliance that he dubbed the "Rainbow Coalition." In 1984 he launched the first major campaign by an African American for president in the Democratic primaries. That campaign won him the opportunity to make this major address to the Democratic Convention in San*

*Francisco that year. In it he invokes the rainbow, as well as the quilt, as a metaphor for the nation and explicitly lists African, Native, Latino, and Asian Americans in a litany of the new multicultural nation.*

*Source:* http://www.wakeamerica.com/index .html

Tonight we come together bound by our faith in a mighty God, with genuine respect and love for our country, and inheriting the legacy of a great party, the Democratic Party, which is the best hope for redirecting our nation on a more humane, just and peaceful course.

This is not a perfect party. We are not a perfect people. Yet, we are called to a perfect mission: our mission to feed the hungry; to clothe the naked; to house the homeless; to teach the illiterate; to provide jobs for the jobless; and to choose the human race over the nuclear race. (Applause)

We are gathered here this week to nominate a candidate and adopt a platform which will expand, unify, direct and inspire our Party and the Nation to fulfill this mission.

My constituency is the desperate, the damned, the disinherited, the disrespected, and the despised. They are restless and seek relief. They've voted in record numbers. They have invested faith, hope and trust that they have in us. The Democratic Party must send them a signal that we care. I pledge my best to not let them down.

There is the call of conscience, redemption, expansion, healing and unity. Leadership must heed the call of con-

science, redemption, expansion, healing and unity, for they are the key to achieving our mission. Time is neutral and does not change things. With courage and initiative, leaders can change things.

No generation can choose the age or circumstance in which it is born, but through leadership it can choose to make the age in which it is born, an age of enlightenment, an age of jobs and peace and justice. (Applause)

Only leadership—that intangible combination of gifts, the discipline, information, circumstance, courage, timing, will and divine inspiration—can lead us out of the crisis in which we find ourselves. The leadership can mitigate the misery of our nation. Leadership can part the waters and lead our nation in the direction of the Promised Land. Leadership can lift the boats stuck at the bottom.

I've had the rare opportunity to watch seven men, and then two, pour out their souls, offer their service and heal—and heed the call of duty to direct the course of our Nation. There is a proper season for everything. There is a time to sow, a time to reap. There is a time to compete, and a time to cooperate.

I ask for your vote on the first ballot as a vote for a new direction for this Party and this Nation. (Applause) A vote of conviction, a vote of conscience. (Applause)

But I will be proud to support the nominee of this convention for the Presidency of the United States of America. (Applause) Thank you.

I have watched the leadership of our party develop and grow. My respect for both Mr. Mondale and Mr. Hart is great.

I have watched them struggle with the crosswinds and crossfires of being public servants, and I believe they will both continue to try to serve us faithfully.

I am elated by the knowledge that for the first time in our history a woman, Geraldine Ferraro, will be recommended to share our ticket. (Applause)

Throughout this campaign, I've tried to offer leadership to the Democratic Party and the Nation. If in my high moments, I have done some good, offered some service, shed some light, healed some wounds, rekindled some hope, or stirred someone from apathy and indifference, or in any way along the way helped somebody, then this campaign has not been in vain. (Applause)

For friends who loved and cared for me, and for a God who spared me, and for a family who understood, I am eternally grateful.

If, in my low moments, in word, deed or attitude, through some error of temper, taste or tone, I have caused anyone discomfort, created pain or revived someone's fears, that was not my truest self. If there were occasions when my grape turned into a raisin and my joy bell lost its resonance, please forgive me. Charge it to my head and not to my heart. My head—so limited in its finitude; my heart, which is boundless in its love for the human family. I am not a perfect servant. I am a public servant doing my best against the odds. As I develop and serve, be patient. God is not finished with me yet.

This campaign has taught me much; that leaders must be tough enough to fight, tender enough to cry, human enough to make mistakes, humble enough to admit them, strong enough to absorb the pain and resilient enough to bounce back and keep on moving. (Applause)

For leaders, the pain is often intense. But you must smile through your tears and keep moving with the faith that there is a brighter side somewhere.

I went to see Hubert Humphrey three days before he died. He had just called Richard Nixon from his dying bed, and many people wondered why. I asked him. He said, "Jesse, from this vantage point, with the sun setting in my life, all of the speeches, the political conventions, the crowds and the great fights are behind me now. At a time like this you are forced to deal with your irreducible essence, forced to grapple with that which is really important to you. And what I have concluded about life," Hubert Humphrey said, "When all is said and done, we must forgive each other, and redeem each other, and move on."

Our party is emerging from one of its most hard fought battles for the Democratic Party's presidential nomination in our history. But our healthy competition should make us better, not bitter. (Applause)

We must use the insight, wisdom, and experience of the late Hubert Humphrey as a balm for the wounds in our Party, this Nation and the world. We must forgive each other, redeem each other, regroup and move on.

Our flag is red, white and blue, but our nation is a rainbow—red, yellow, brown, black and white—and we're all precious in God's sight.

America is not like a blanket—one piece of unbroken cloth, the same color, the same texture, the same size. America is more like a quilt—many patches, many pieces, many colors, many sizes, all woven and held together by a common thread. The white, the Hispanic, the black, the Arab, the Jew, the woman, the native American, the small farmer, the businessperson, the environmentalist, the peace activist, the young, the old, the lesbian, the gay and the disabled make up the American quilt. (Applause)

Even in our fractured state, all of us count and all of us fit somewhere. We have proven that we can survive without each other. But we have not proven that we can win and progress without each other. We must come together. (Applause)

From Fannie Lou Hamer in Atlantic City in 1964 to the Rainbow Coalition in San Francisco today; from the Atlantic to the Pacific, we have experienced pain but progress as we ended American apartheid laws, we got public accommodation, we secured voting rights, we obtained open housing, as young people got the right to vote. We lost Malcolm, Martin, Medgar, Bobby, John and Viola. The team that got us here must be expanded, not abandoned. (Applause) Twenty years ago, tears welled up in our eyes as the bodies of Schwerner, Goodman and Chaney were dredged from the depths of a river in Mississippi. Twenty years later, our communities, black and Jewish, are in anguish, anger and pain. Feelings have been hurt on both sides.

There is a crisis in communications. Confusion is in the air. But we cannot afford to lose our way. We may agree to agree; or agree to disagree on issues; we must bring back civility to these tensions.

We are co-partners in a long and rich religious history—the Judeo-Christian traditions. Many blacks and Jews have a shared passion for social justice at home and peace abroad. We must seek a revival of the spirit, inspired by a new vision and new possibilities. We must return to higher ground. (Applause)

We are bound by Moses and Jesus, but also connected with Islam and Mohammed. These three great religions, Judaism, Christianity and Islam, were all born in the revered and holy city of Jerusalem.

We are bound by Dr. Martin Luther King Jr. and Rabbi Abraham Heschel, crying out from their graves for us to reach common ground. We are bound by shared blood and shared sacrifices. We are much too intelligent; much too bound by our Judeo-Christian heritage; much too victimized by racism, sexism, militarism and anti-Semitism; much too threatened as historical scapegoats to go on divided one from another. We must turn from finger pointing to clasped hands. We must share our burdens and our joys with each other once again. We must turn to each other and not on each other and choose higher ground. (Applause)

Twenty years later, we cannot be satisfied by just restoring the old coalition. Old wine skins must make room for new wine. We must heal and expand. The Rainbow Coalition is making room for Arab Americans. They, too, know the pain and hurt of racial and religious rejection. They must not continue to be made pariahs. The Rainbow Coalition is making room for Hispanic Americans who this very night are living under the threat of the Simpson-Mazzoli bill. (Applause) And farm workers from Ohio who are fighting the Campbell Soup Company with a boycott to achieve legitimate workers' rights. (Applause)

The Rainbow is making room for the Native American, the most exploited people of all, a people with the greatest moral claim amongst us. We support them as they seek the restoration of their ancient land and claim amongst us. We support them as they seek the restoration of land and water rights, as they seek to preserve their ancestral homelands and the beauty of a land that was once all theirs. They can never receive a fair share for all they have given us. They must finally have a fair chance to develop their great resources and to preserve their people and their culture.

The Rainbow Coalition includes Asian Americans, now being killed in our streets, scapegoats for the failures of corporate, industrial and economic policies.

The Rainbow is making room for the young Americans. Twenty years ago, our young people were dying in a war for which they could not even vote. Twenty years later, young America has the power to stop a war in Central America and the responsibility to vote in great numbers. (Applause) Young America must be politically active in 1984. The choice is war or peace. We must make room for young America.

The Rainbow includes disabled veterans. The color scheme fits in the Rainbow. The disabled have their handicap revealed and their genius concealed; while the able-bodied have their genius revealed and their disability concealed. But ultimately, we must judge people by their values and their contribution. Don't leave anybody out. I would rather have Roosevelt in a wheelchair than Reagan on a horse. (Applause)

The Rainbow includes for small farmers. They have suffered tremendously under the Reagan regime. They will either receive 90 percent parity or 100 percent charity. We must address their concerns and make room for them.

The Rainbow includes lesbians and gays. No American citizen ought to be denied equal protection from the law.

We must be unusually committed and caring as we expand our family to include new members. All of us must be tolerant and understanding as the fears and anxieties of the rejected and of the party leadership express themselves in so many different ways. Too often what we call hate—as if it were some deeply rooted in philosophy or strategy—it is simply ignorance, anxiety, paranoia, fear and insecurity. (Applause)

To be strong leaders, we must be long-suffering as we seek to right the wrongs of our Party and our Nation. We must expand our Party, heal our Party and unify our Party. That is our mission in 1984. (Applause)

We are often reminded that we live in a great nation—and we do. But it can be greater still. The Rainbow is mandating a new definition of greatness. We must not measure greatness from the mansion down, but from the manger up.

Jesus said that we should not be judged by the bark we wear but by the fruit that we bear. Jesus said that we must measure greatness by how we treat the least of these.

President Reagan says the nation is in recovery. Those 90,000 corporations that made a profit last year but paid no Federal taxes are recovering. The 37,000 military contractors who have benefited from Reagan's more than doubling of the military budget in peacetime surely they are recovering.

The big corporations and rich individuals who received the bulk of a three-year, multibillion tax cut from Mr. Reagan are recovering. But no such recovery is under way for the least of these. Rising tides don't lift all boats, particularly those stuck at the bottom.

For the boats stuck at the bottom there's a misery index. This Administration has made life more miserable for the poor. Its attitude has been contemptuous. Its policies and programs have been cruel and unfair to working people. They must be held accountable in November for increasing infant mortality among the poor. In Detroit (Applause)—in Detroit, one of the great cities in the western world, babies are dying at the same rate as Honduras, the most underdeveloped Nation in out hemisphere. This Administration must be held accountable for policies that have contributed to the growing poverty in America. There are now 34 million people in poverty, 15 percent of our Nation. Twenty-three million are White, 11 million Black, Hispanic, Asian and others. By the end of this year, there will be 41 million people in poverty. We cannot stand idly by. We must fight for change now. (Applause)

Under this regime, we look at Social Security. The 1981 budget cuts included nine permanent Social Security benefit cuts totaling $20 billion over five years.

Small businesses have suffered on the Reagan tax cuts. Only 18 percent of total business tax cuts went to them, 82 percent to big businesses.

Health care under Mr. Reagan has already been sharply cut. Education under Mr. Reagan has been cut 25 percent. Under Mr. Reagan there are now 9.7 million female head families. They represent 16 percent of all families. Half of all of them are poor. Seventy percent of all poor children live in a house headed by a woman, where there is no man.

Under Mr. Reagan, the Administration has cleaned up only six of 546 priority toxic waste dumps.

Farmers' real net income was only about half its level in 1979.

Many say that the race in November will be decided in the South. President Reagan is depending on the conservative South to return him to office. But the South, I tell you, is unnaturally conservative. The South is the poorest region in our nation and, therefore, the least to conserve. In his appeal to the South, Mr. Reagan is trying to substitute flags and prayer cloths for food, and clothing, and education, health care and housing. (Applause)

Mr. Reagan will ask us to pray, and I believe in prayer. I have come to this way by power of prayer. But then, we must watch false prophecy. He cuts energy assistance to the poor, cuts breakfast programs from children, cuts lunch programs from children, cuts job training from children, and then says to an empty table, "Let us pray." (Applause) Apparently he is not familiar with the structure of prayer. You thank the Lord for the food that you are about to receive, not the food that just left. (Laughter and applause) I think that we should pray, but don't pray for the food that left. Pray for the man that took the food—to leave.

We need a change. We need a change in November. (Applause)

Under Mr. Reagan, the misery index has risen for the poor. The danger index has risen for everybody. Under this administration, we have lost the lives of our boys in Central America and Honduras, in Grenada, in Lebanon, in a nuclear standoff in Europe. Under this Administration, one-third of our children believe they will die in a nuclear war. The danger index is increasing in this world.

All the talk about the defense against Russia; the Russian submarines are closer, and their missiles more accurate. We live in a world tonight more miserable and a world more dangerous. While Reaganomics and Reaganism is talked about often, so often we miss the real meaning. Reaganism is a spirit, and Reaganomics represents the real economic facts of life.

In 1980, Mr. George Bush, a man with reasonable access to Mr. Reagan, did an analysis of Mr. Reagan's economic plan. Mr. George Bush concluded that Reagan's plan was "voodoo economics." He was right. (Applause)

Third-party candidate John Anderson said "a combination of military spending, tax cuts and a balanced budget by 1984

would be accomplished with blue smoke and mirrors." They were both right.

Mr. Reagan talks about a dynamic recovery. There's some measure of recovery. Three and a half years later, unemployment has inched just below where it was when he took office in 1981. There are still 8.1 million people officially unemployed, 11 million working only part-time. Inflation has come down, but let's analyze for a moment who has paid the price for this superficial economic recovery.

Mr. Reagan curbed inflation by cutting consumer demand. He cut consumer demand with conscious and callous fiscal and monetary policies. He used the Federal budget to deliberately induce unemployment and curb social spending. He then weighed and supported tight monetary policies of the Federal Reserve Board to deliberately drive up interest rates, again to curb consumer demand created through borrowing. Unemployment reached 10.7 percent. We experienced skyrocketing interest rates. Our dollar inflated abroad. There were record bank failures; record farm foreclosures; record business bankruptcies; record budget deficits; record trade deficits.

Mr. Reagan brought inflation down by destabilizing our economy and disrupting family life. He promised—he promised in 1980 a balanced budget. But instead we now have a record toward a billion dollar budget deficit. Under Mr. Reagan, the cumulative budget deficit for his four years is more than the sum total of deficits from George Washington through Jimmy Carter combined.

I tell you, we need a change. (Applause)

How is he paying for these short-term jobs? Reagan's economic recovery is being financed by deficit spending—$200 billion a year. Military spending, a major cause of this deficit, is projected, over the next five years, to be nearly $2 trillion, and will cost about $40,000 for every taxpaying family.

When the Government borrows $200 billion annually to finance the deficit, this encourages the private sector to make its money off of interest rates as opposed to development and economic growth.

Even money abroad, we don't have enough money domestically to finance the debt, so we are now borrowing money abroad, from foreign banks, governments and financial institutions: $40 billion in 1983; $70–80 billion in 1984 (40 percent of our total); and over $100 billion (50 percent of our total) in 1985. By 1989, it is projected that 50 percent of all individual income taxes will be going just to pay for interest on the debt.

The United States used to be the largest exporter of capital, but under Mr. Reagan we will quite likely become the largest debtor nation.

About two weeks ago, on July 4th, we celebrated our Declaration of Independence, yet every day supply-side economics is making our Nation more economically dependent and less economically free. Five to six percent of our Gross National Product is now being eaten up with President Reagan's budget deficits. To depend on foreign military powers to protect our national security would be foolish, making us dependent and less secure, yet Reaganomics has us increasingly dependent on foreign economic sources. This consumer-led but deficit-financed recovery is unbalanced and artificial. We have a challenge as Democrats to point a way out. Democracy guarantees opportunity, not success. Democracy guarantees the right to participate, not a license for either a majority to dominate. The victory for the Rainbow Coalition in the Platform debates today was not whether we won or lost, but that we raised the right issues.

We could afford to lose the vote; issues are non-negotiable. We could not afford to avoid raising the right questions. Our self-respect and our moral integrity were at stake. Our heads are perhaps bloody, but not bowed. Our back is straight. We can go home and face our people. Our vision is clear. (Applause)

When we think, on this journey from slaveship to championship, that we have gone from the planks of the Boardwalk in Atlantic City in 1964 to fighting to help write the planks in the platform in San Francisco in 1984 there is a deep and abiding sense of joy in our souls in spite of the tears in our eyes. Though there are missing planks, there is a solid foundation upon which to build. Our party can win, but we must provide hope, which will inspire people to struggle and achieve; provide a plan that shows a way out of our dilemma and then lead the way.

In 1984, my heart is made to feel glad because I know there is a way out—justice. The requirement for rebuilding America is justice. The linchpin of progressive politics in our nation will not come from the North, they in fact will come from the South.

That is why I argue over and over again. We look from Virginia around to Texas, there's only one black Congressperson out of 115. Nineteen years later, we're locked out the Congress, the Senate and the Governor's mansion.

What does this large black vote mean? Why do I fight to win second primaries and fight gerrymandering and annexation and at-large elections? Why do we fight over that? Because I tell you, you cannot hold someone in the ditch unless you linger there with them. (Applause) Unless you linger there. (Applause)

If you want a change in this nation, you enforce that voting rights act. We'll get 12 to 20 Black, Hispanics, female and progressive congresspersons from the South. We can save the cotton, but we have got to fight the boll weevils. We have got to make a judgment. We have got to make a judgment.

It is not enough to hope that ERA will pass. How can we pass ERA? If Blacks vote in great numbers, progressive Whites win. It is the only way progressive Whites win. If Blacks vote in great numbers, Hispanics win. When Blacks, Hispanics and progressive Whites vote, women win. When women win, children win. When women and children win, workers win. We must all come together. We must come together. (Spontaneous demonstration) Thank you.

I tell you, in all our joy and excitement, we must not save the world and lose our souls. We should never short-circuit enforcing the Voting Rights Act at every level. When one of us rises, all of us will rise. Justice is the way out. Peace is the way out. We should not act as if nuclear weaponry is negotiable and debatable.

In this world in which we live, we dropped the bomb on Japan and felt guilty, but in 1984 other folks have also got bombs. This time, if we drop the bomb, six minutes later we, too, will be destroyed. It is not about dropping the bomb on somebody. It is about dropping the bomb on everybody. We must choose to develop minds over guided missiles, and then think it out and not fight it out. It is time for a change. (Applause)

Our foreign policy must be characterized by mutual respect, not by gunboat diplomacy, big stick diplomacy and threats. Our Nation at its best feeds the hungry. Our Nation at its worst, at its worst, will mine the harbors of Nicaragua; at its worst will try to overthrow their government, at its worst will cut aid to American education and increase the aid to El Salvador; at its worst, our Nation will have partnership with South Africa. That is a moral disgrace. It is a moral disgrace. It is a moral disgrace. (Applause)

We look at Africa. We cannot just focus on Apartheid in Southern Africa. We must fight for trade with Africa, and not just aid to Africa. We cannot stand idly by and say we will not relate to Nicaragua unless they have elections there, and then embrace military regimes in Africa overthrowing democratic governments in Nigeria and Liberia and Ghana. We must fight for democracy all around the world, and play the game by one set of rules.

Peace in this world. Our present formula for peace in the Middle East is inadequate. It will not work. There are 22 nations in the Middle East. Our nation must be able to talk and act and influence all of them. We must build upon Camp David, and measure human rights by one yard stick. In that region we have too many interests and too few friends.

There is one way out, jobs. Put America back to work.

When I was a child growing up in Greenville, South Carolina, the Reverend Sample used to preach ever so often a sermon relating to Jesus and he said, "If I be lifted up, I will draw all men unto me." I didn't quite understand what he meant as a child growing up, but I understand a little better now. If you raise up truth, it is magnetic. It has a way of drawing people.

With all this confusion in this Convention, the bright lights and parties and big fun, we must raise up the single proposition: If we lift up a program to feed the hungry, they will come running; if we lift up a program to start a war no more, our youth will come running; if we lift up a program to put America back to work, and an alternative to welfare and despair, they will come running.

If we cut that military budget without cutting our defense, and use that money to rebuild bridges and put steel workers back to work, and use that money and provide jobs for our cities, and use that money to build schools and pay teachers and educate our children, and build hospitals, and train doctors and train nurses, the whole nation will come running to us. (Applause)

As I leave you now, we vote in this convention and get ready to go back across this nation in a couple of days, in this campaign I tried to be faithful to my promise. I lived in old barrios, ghettos and in reservations and housing projects.

I have a message for our youth. I challenge them to put hope in their brains and not dope in their veins. (Applause) I told them that like Jesus, I, too, was born in the slum, and just because you're born in a slum does not mean the slum is born in you and you can rise above it if your mind is made up. (Applause) I told them in every slum there are two sides. When I see a broken window that's the slummy side. Train some youth to become a glazier; that is the sunny side. When I see a missing brick, that is the slummy side. Let that child in a union and become a brick mason and build; that is the sunny side. When I see a missing door, that is the slummy side. Train some youth to become a carpenter, that is the sunny side. When I see the vulgar words and hieroglyphics of destitution on the walls, that is the slummy side. Train some youth to be a painter and artist, that is the sunny side. We leave this place looking for the sunny side because there's a brighter side somewhere. I am more convinced than ever that we can win. We will vault up the rough side of the mountain. We can win. I just want young America to do me one favor, just one favor.

Exercise the right to dream. You must face reality, that which is. But then dream of a reality that ought to be, that must be. Live beyond the pain of reality with the dream of a bright tomorrow. Use hope and imagination as weapons of survival and progress. Use love to motivate you and obligate you to serve the human family.

Young America, dream. Choose the human race over the nuclear race. Bury the weapons and don't burn the people. Dream—dream of a new value system. Teachers who teach for life and not just for a living; teach because they can't help it. Dream of lawyers more concerned about justice than a judgeship. Dream of doctors more concerned about public health than personal wealth. (Applause) Dream of preachers and priests who will prophesy and not just profiteer. Preach and dream! Our time has come. Our time has come.

Suffering breeds character. Character breeds faith, and in the end faith will not disappoint. Our time has come. Our faith, hope and dreams have prevailed. Our time has come. Weeping has endured for nights but that joy cometh in the morning.

Our time has come. No grave can hold our body down. Our time has come. No lie can live forever. Our time has come. We must leave the racial battle ground and come to the economic common ground and moral higher ground. America, our time has come. We come from disgrace to amazing grace. Our time has come. Give me your tired, give me your poor, your huddled masses who yearn to breathe free and come November, there will be a change because our time has come.

Thank you and God bless you.

## Kerner Commission Report, 1968

*President Johnson established the National Advisory Commission on Civil Disorders—often called the Kerner Commission, after its chairman Governor Otto Kerner of Illinois—in 1967 to investigate the rash of riots that erupted in American cities in the mid 1960s. Its report issued the next year was notable for its condemnation of white racism as a root cause of the riots: "white society," the report said, "is deeply implicated in the ghetto."*

Source: Report of the National Advisory Commission on Civil Disorders, March 1, 1968 (Washington, D.C. 1968), taken from Thomas Frazier, ed., *The Many Sides of America* (New York: Harcourt Brace, 1996).

## REPORT OF THE NATIONAL ADVISORY COMMISSION ON CIVIL DISORDERS

The summer of 1967 again brought racial disorders to American cities, and with them shock, fear and bewilderment to the nation.

The worst came during a two-week period in July, first in Newark and then in Detroit. Each set off a chain reaction in neighboring communities.

On July 28, 1967, the President of the United States established this Commission and directed us to answer three basic questions:

What happened?

Why did it happen?

What can be done to prevent it from happening again?

To respond to these questions, we have undertaken a broad range of studies and investigations. We have visited the riot cities; we have heard many witnesses; we have sought the counsel of experts across the country.

This is our basic conclusion: Our nation is moving toward two societies, one black, one white—separate and unequal.

Reaction to last summer's disorders has quickened the movement and deepened the division. Discrimination and segregation have long permeated much of American life; they now threaten the future of every American.

This deepening racial division is not inevitable. The movement apart can be reversed. Choice is still possible. Our principal task is to define that choice and to press for a national resolution.

To pursue our present course will involve the continuing polarization of the American community and, ultimately, the destruction of basic democratic values.

The alternative is not blind repression or capitulation to lawlessness. It is the realization of common opportunities for all within a single society.

This alternative will require a commitment to national action—compassionate, massive and sustained, backed by the resources of the most powerful and the richest nation on this earth. From every American it will require new attitudes, new understanding, and, above all, new will.

The vital needs of the nation must be met; hard choices must be made, and, if necessary, new taxes enacted.

Violence cannot build a better society. Disruption and disorder nourish repression, not justice. They strike at the freedom of every citizen. The community cannot—it will not—tolerate coercion and mob rule.

Violence and destruction must be ended—in the streets of the ghetto and in the lives of people.

Segregation and poverty have created in the racial ghetto a destructive environment totally unknown to most white Americans.

What white Americans have never fully understood—but what the Negro can never forget—is that white society is deeply implicated in the ghetto. White institutions created it, white institutions maintain it, and white society condones it.

It is time now to turn with all the purpose at our command to the major unfinished business of this nation. It is time to adopt strategies for action that will produce quick and visible progress. It is time to make good the promises of American democracy to all citizens—urban and rural, white and black, Spanish-surname, American Indian, and every minority group.

Our recommendations embrace three basic principles:

To mount programs on a scale equal to the dimension of the problems;

To aim these programs for high impact in the immediate future in order to close the gap between promise and performance;

To undertake new initiatives and experiments that can change the system of failure and frustration that now dominates the ghetto and weakens our society.

These programs will require unprecedented levels of funding and performance, but they neither probe deeper nor demand more than the problems which called them forth. There can be no higher priority for national action and no higher claim on the nation's conscience.

We issue this Report now, four months before the date called for by the President. Much remains that can be learned. Continued study is essential.

As Commissioners we have worked together with a sense of the greatest urgency and have sought to compose whatever differences exist among us. Some differences remain. But the gravity of the problem and the pressing need for action are too clear to allow further delay in the issuance of this Report.

In addressing the question, "Why did it happen?" we shift our focus from the local to the national scene, from the particular events of the summer of 1967 to the factors within the society at large that created a mood of violence among many urban Negroes.

These factors are complex and interacting; they vary significantly in their effect from city to city and from year to year; and the consequences of one disorder, generating new grievances and new demands, become the causes of the next. Thus was created the "thicket of tension, conflicting evidence and extreme opinions" cited by the President.

Despite these complexities, certain fundamental matters are clear. Of these, the most fundamental is the racial attitude and behavior of white Americans toward black Americans.

Race prejudice has shaped our history decisively; it now threatens to affect our future.

White racism is essentially responsible for the explosive mixture which has been accumulating in our cities since the end of World War II. Among the ingredients of this mixture are:

> *Pervasive discrimination and segregation* in employment, education and housing, which have resulted in the continuing exclusion of great numbers of Negroes from the benefits of economic progress.
>
> *Black in-migration and white exodus,* which have produced the massive and growing concentrations of impoverished Negroes in our major cities, creating a growing crisis of deteriorating facilities and services and unmet human-needs.
>
> *The black ghettos* where segregation and poverty converge on the young to destroy opportunity and enforce failure. Crime, drug addiction, dependency on welfare, and bitterness and resentment against society in general and white society in particular are the result.

At the same time, most whites and some Negroes outside the ghetto have prospered to a degree unparalleled in the history of civilization. Through television and other media, this affluence has been flaunted before the eyes of the Negro poor and the jobless ghetto youth.

Yet these facts alone cannot be said to have caused the disorders. Recently, other powerful ingredients have begun to catalyze the mixture:

> *Frustrated hopes* are the residue of the unfulfilled expectations aroused by the great judicial and legislative victories of the Civil Rights

Movement and the dramatic struggle for equal rights in the South.

*A climate that tends toward approval and encouragement of violence* as a form of protest has been created by white terrorism directed against nonviolent protest; by the open defiance of law and federal authority by state and local officials resisting desegregation; and by some protest groups engaging in civil disobedience who turn their backs on nonviolence, go beyond the constitutionally protected rights of petition and free assembly, and resort to violence to attempt to compel alteration of laws and policies with which they disagree.

*The frustrations of powerlessness* have led some Negroes to the conviction that there is no effective alternative to violence as a means of achieving redress of grievances, and of "moving the system." These frustrations are reflected in alienation and hostility toward the institutions of law and government and the white society which controls them, and in the reach toward racial consciousness and solidarity reflected in the slogan "Black Power."

*A new mood* has sprung up among Negroes, particularly among the young, in which self-esteem and enhanced racial pride are replacing apathy and submission to "the system."

*The police are not merely a "spark" factor.* To some Negroes police have come to symbolize white power, white racism and white repression. And the fact is that many police do reflect and express these white attitudes. The atmosphere of hostility and cynicism is reinforced by a widespread belief among Negroes in the existence of police brutality and in a "double standard" of justice and protection—one for Negroes and one for whites.

To this point, we have attempted to identify the prime components of the "explosive mixture." In the chapters that follow we seek to analyze them in the perspective of history. Their meaning, however, is clear:

In the summer of 1967, we have seen in our cities a chain reaction of racial violence. If we are heedless, none of us shall escape the consequences.

The future of our cities is neither something which will just happen nor something which will be imposed upon us by an inevitable destiny. That future will be shaped to an important degree by choices we make now.

We have attempted to set forth the major choices because we believe it is vital for Americans to understand the consequences of our present failure to choose—and then to have to choose wisely.

Three critical conclusions emerge from this analysis:

1. The nation is rapidly moving toward two increasingly separate Americas.

Within two decades, this division could be so deep that it would be almost impossible to unite:

a white society principally located in suburbs, in smaller central cities, and in the peripheral parts of large central cities; and

a Negro society largely concentrated within large central cities.

The Negro society will be permanently relegated to its current status, possibly even if we expend great amounts of money and effort in trying to "gild" the ghetto.

2. In the long run, continuation and expansion of such a permanent division threatens us with two perils.

The first is the danger of sustained violence in our cities. The timing, scale, nature, and repercussions of such violence cannot be foreseen. But if it occurred, it would further destroy our ability to achieve the basic American promises of liberty, justice, and equality.

The second is the danger of a conclusive repudiation of the traditional American ideals of individual dignity, freedom, and equality of opportunity. We will not be able to espouse these ideals meaningfully to the rest of the world, to ourselves, to our children. They may still recite the Pledge of Allegiance and say "one nation . . . indivisible." But they will be learning cynicism, not patriotism.

3. We cannot escape responsibility for choosing the future of our metropolitan areas and the human relations which develop within them. It is a responsibility so critical that even an unconscious choice to continue present policies has the gravest implications.

That we have delayed in choosing or, by delaying, may be making the wrong choice, does not sentence us either to separatism or despair. But we must choose. We will choose. Indeed, we are now choosing.

## Jews and Blacks, Ocean-Hill Brownsville School Controversy, 1969

*Jews and blacks were longtime allies in the Civil Rights movement, but in the 1960s they began to drift apart. No incident was more critical in this breakup than the 1968 struggle between black community leaders and Jewish teachers over control of the public schools in the Ocean Hill-Brownsville neighborhood of New York City. In the following selection Nat Hentoff, a Jewish American writer for the* New Yorker *and the* Village Voice, *interviews Julius Lester, an African American radio host, in the midst of the struggle. Lester had aired a controversial poem written by an African American child during the crisis.*

Source: Nat Hentoff, "Blacks and Jews": An Interview with Julius Lester, Evergreen Review 13, no. 65 (1969): 21–21, 25, 71–76, taken from Maurianne Adams and John Bracey, eds., Strangers and Neighbors (Boston: University of Massachusetts Press, 1999).

Leslie Campbell is a teacher in Ocean Hill-Brownsville, a focal point in the struggle for community control of schools in New York City between the black community and the predominantly white United Federation of Teachers (headed by Albert Shanker). Last December, on Julius Lester's WBAI-FM program, Campbell read a poem by a fifteen-year-old student of his. Titled "Anti-Semitism," and "dedicated to albert shanker," the poem begins: "Hey, jew boy with that yamaka on your head / You pale faced Jew boy, I wish you were dead." The last two lines are: "I hated you jew boy cause your hang up was the Torah / And my only hang up was my color."

The tumultuous aftermath of the reading was the filing of a complaint to the FCC by the United Federation of Teachers and demands that the station's license be revoked or suspended by the New York Board of Rabbis, the Workmen's Circle, and the Jewish Defense League, among other groups.

QUESTION: By now, that poem has become an issue not only in New York, but nationally as well. You said you expected some degree of reaction at the time, but was the extent and durability of the hostile response surprising to you?

ANSWER: Yes, very surprising, because the reaction came three weeks after the poem was read on the air. I felt, at the time, that it was simply being used as a device to get at Les Campbell, who has been under attack for some months now. And then, secondly, it was interesting that Shanker's complaint to the FCC about WBAI was made the day after the courts ruled that the principals should go back into Ocean Hill-Brownsville. I felt it was a politically inspired move. Why wait three weeks? In terms of the reaction of people who heard the program— yes, they were disturbed; they were upset. They talked about it on the air, on the show, but I didn't start receiving hate mail until after *The New York Times* came out with their story.

Q: And was there much hate mail?

A: Oh, tons. Quite a bit. And you know, threats and this type of thing.

Q: Getting back to the poem itself, I'm not asking you to speak for Les Campbell, but speaking for yourself, having seen the poem, if you had been her teacher, wouldn't you then have tried to communicate with the student and explore with her the stereotypical reactions manifested in her poem? It was, after all, clearly anti-Semitic and indiscriminately made all Jews the enemy.

A: One thing people don't understand is that when you're working with blacks, there is a time when people are ready to hear certain things, and that time is not now for some things. Let's put it this way: You start where the people are and try to move from there. So, OK, you involve yourself in things which you yourself disagree with. But if there's going to be any change of attitude, then it's not going to come by preaching moralistic sermons; that's just like what white people have always done. And so, when I saw the poem—yeah, there were things wrong in terms of intellectual content. However, I'm not concerned with that. I'm concerned with the basic emotion that's there, and if all the facts are wrong, it's totally irrelevant to that basic emotional content. So it's redundant and ridiculous of me to point out that Jews have suffered for more than fifteen years; the girl who wrote the poem doesn't care. And it wouldn't change what she was feeling.

Q: And that not all Jewish teachers are the kind of teachers she's talking about?

A: Right.

Q : But if this kind of feeling is allowed to grow unchallenged, won't the result be that the girl will grow up rigidly prejudiced—just as most whites, if not all, have had racism embedded in them? You say that you have to move from where the people are, but do you withhold all comment of your own?

A : I think that you have to consider the genesis of the poem. To my mind, the poem is an act of self-defense, because of the racism which was involved in the teacher's strike. The black community was attacked head-on, and specifically in Ocean Hill-Brownsville, where this girl is a student. And so, as far as I'm concerned, she is defending herself with the only weapon at her command. She is hurt, and therefore she is going to hurt back as much as she can.

I think one of the difficulties is that people are equating the poem with traditional anti-Semitism, which is rooted in God knows what—Christ-killers and what have you. That has no relationship to the black community. The black community does not fall within that. I mean, even at thirty years of age, I don't know that a person is a Jew from looking at him, or by his name, or anything like that. Now that's true of most black people, I think.

Q : Richard Wright, in *Black Boy,* said "All of us black people who lived in the neighborhood hated Jews, not because they've exploited us, but because we have been taught at home and in Sunday School the Jews were 'Christ-killers.'" That's not analogous to your experience?

A : No. I was twenty years old before I began to have any consciousness that there was anything other than black people and white people, that there were subcategories of white people, and that Jews were one of them. It came about through Exodus, and then, from that I went to a synagogue. Yes, I was aware in terms of the Bible, and in terms of spirituals— Moses, this kind of thing. It meant nothing, except later I became conscious that Einstein was a Jew, that Jews had an intellectual tradition, and being an intellectual of sorts, I could respect that. So what feelings I had were, shall we say, kindred.

Q : You came initially from the South, and I wonder whether you think that the hostility toward the Jew in some black urban communities comes from the fact that a preponderance of the merchants in these black areas are Jewish?

A : Yes, but growing up in Nashville, they were white people. They weren't Jews. There were crackers and there were niggers. So I came to New York in '61, and I found out—well, Jesus, there are Irish, and there are Polish, Germans, and all these other things. Each one acts differently. But I was conscious of white people, and that was all.

Q : And you don't think this identification with the Jew as merchant and then as white is as widespread as many sociologists claim?

A : Perhaps in the North it is. In terms of Harlem, yes. I would say it is.

Q : I asked because someone pointed out in an analysis that in some areas the Negro would frequently refer to his "Jew landlord," even though his name might be O'Reilly, Kowalski, or Santangelo. And,

I suppose, again that comes out of the preponderance of Jewish merchants and landlords in those areas.

A : Right, yes.

Q : In another program on WBAI, and this is something you've commented on, there was a remark by a black student from N.Y.U.: "As far as I'm concerned, more power to Hitler. He didn't make enough lampshades out of them." Well, that's the kind of thing that, to a Jew listening in, even if he's totally out of the religion, out of any kind of Jewish communal feeling, immediately conjures up the very real, quite recent past. And he would ask, "How come you didn't say anything about that at the time?"

A : The reason I didn't say anything about it at the time was that I recognized he was speaking symbolically, and that he was speaking from a feeling of how can I most effectively hurt these people. It should be obvious that black people don't have the capabilities to carry out any pogrom against Jews, and then, I don't even think black people have the desire to carry out any pogrom against Jews. I took his statement totally on the symbolic level.

Q : Because he was so angry, particularly in the context of the recent teachers' strike and the various reactions after that to Les Campbell, this was the kind of thing he would say—to hurt?

A : Yes, right. And, OK, if you want to isolate it from that, yes, like it's a horrible statement; it's a horrible thing that happened. But, once again, emotionally, black people have no connection with what happened in Germany and in Eastern Europe. We were too busy fighting for our own survival.

Q : Some social scientists would say, "OK, it was symbolic. It was perhaps defensive." But it's out of symbolism, out of this use of rhetoric, that the climate in the past in places you've mentioned eventually led to political anti-Semitic movements and actual pogroms and concentration camps.

A : What really gets me angry, see, is that, for crying out loud, for six months we had a George Wallace going around the country who created an atmosphere that did provoke unwarranted attacks upon black people, that did create a whole climate in the country of which the UFT thing is a part. And where were these so-called friends, be they either Jews or Anglo-Saxons, when this was happening? A few of them were interested, a few of them were protesting, but they were all saying, "Oh, if Wallace ever did get elected, America would never wipe out black people"—the same thing that was said in Germany. If white people started a pogrom against Jews, then OK, Jews would be in trouble, because whites have the power to carry it out. But black people have no thought of carrying out any sort of pogrom against Jews.

Q : During the UFT strike, which closed down the schools and was, in reality, an attempt to destroy the Ocean Hill-Brownsville Experimental District and community control of the schools, there was a large amount of racist, anti-black invective on UFT picket lines, which was barely reported, and against which I don't think there was much of a record of protest by any group, certainly by none of the groups clamoring now. And after the strike, there was a teacher at

Franklin K. Lane High School, who is as yet unidentified, who was quoted in the *New York Post* as saying, "Well, we're not going to live in fear. I think that if the black people don't get into line, then we'll have to either annihilate them or neutralize them. That's not as harsh as it sounds. It has happened in other societies. It may be the only way of dealing with this." So what I'd ask you, and I suppose it's in a sense a rhetorical question, how does one expect—let's say the girl in Les Campbell's class, the student at N.Y.U., to exist under this kind of state of siege, as they see it, and not react emotionally?

A : I react emotionally to that, you know. Because that is a reality as far as I'm concerned; the teacher at Franklin K. Lane is not joking. This country is capable of annihilating black people.

But how else is one to react to that? I didn't see Mayor Lindsay going around to a Baptist church, putting on the choir robes to explain to the black congregation that he wasn't going to allow that in the city. You know, like I was not even interested in Ocean Hill-Brownsville, the school fight—nothing. Until one day I was looking at TV, and all of a sudden, I hear Shanker talking about mob action and extremists.

Q : Vigilantes, Nazis.

A : Right. That to me means one thing! He's so hung up on niggers! They wouldn't be accusing us of anti-Semitism if we had the finesse of George Wallace and Shanker. Like, the guy who made that statement that Hitler should have made more lampshades could have got on there and said the same thing in Shanker's way. But he's

the cat off the block; he said it direct from the gut. And why be dishonest about it? But you say that Shanker said he is for decentralization of the schools and all that. And so people take this and they don't hear what I'm hearing the man say. Hell, we were talking about decentralization and education and Shanker starts yelling anti-Semitism. Rhody McCoy was talking politics; Shanker started talking race.

Q : Then what is your explanation for so many Jews having reacted so emotionally and so vehemently to the poem and to the statement by the N.Y.U. student? In other words, why were you so surprised at this reaction?

A : Well, I guess because my knowledge of the Jewish community as such is nonexistent. I know quite a few individuals who are Jews. I expected some reaction, yes. But it was just ignorance on my part as to how deep the fear is inside the Jewish community. But that's not saying I would've done differently in this situation.

I think there's another aspect to it. For the past five or ten years in this country, Jews have sort of been "in"—the Jewish novel, *How to Be a Jewish Mother.* For the first time in world history, a country exists where Jews are "in"—*Fiddler on the Roof,* and what have you. And they were feeling good with this, and all of a sudden comes this attack from the left—or from the right, depending on where you sit—which, of course, feeds back again into what I guess is an insecurity.

Then there's the whole Israel thing. I've been thinking about the progression in terms of this whole issue of black anti-Semitism. The first column I wrote for the *Guardian,* in the fall of 1967 I think, dealt with Israel and the Mideast War and the whole thing. In that column, I said it was necessary for Jews to look upon Israel politically, at what its political role was. And, of course, the reaction I got was the same that came this time—that there's another black-Jewish division here, that naturally the Jewish attitude toward Israel was going to be very personal, very emotional, and a very moral one. And because six million Jews were killed during World War II, it sort of seems that a Jew can do no wrong, that the State of Israel can do no wrong. And I think Jews in this country have that sort of attitude. Nobody mentions the ten million who died in Stalingrad alone in World War II; there were twenty million in Russia that got wiped out, which explains a lot to me about Russia's present international position. What about these people who are just forgotten? Hell, fifteen million died in the camps. It would seem to me that Jews are falsifying history to let nine million people be forgotten.

Then the other things is that the cat in the corner would say, "OK, six million Jews got it. I didn't do it. Don't tell me about it."

Q : Which, to a Jew, I think, would be the attitude of the non-Jewish population at large. I think the essential thing to keep in mind is that those Jews who still have any kind of concept of themselves as Jews are aware of the fact that it's been a long, tough pull for an awfully long time. The fact that any Jew survived is quite remarkable. Israel to them is not only the

last place, but the only place, where anybody can go if he's Jewish. It's also a radical change in Jews' attitude toward themselves. To use a term from the new movement, "It's one place where Jews don't play victims anymore."

A : Right, OK. Then why is it that they can understand Israel and can't let us have Ocean Hill-Brownsville? That's the same thing; they should understand that better than anybody in this country. But the reason is that they have the power now, and they don't want to relinquish their power to the black people. So therefore we fight.

Q : In an article in *Commentary,* "The Black Revolution & the Jewish Question," Earl Raab, executive director of the Jewish Community Relations Council in San Francisco, says the black movement "is developing an anti-Semitic ideology. On one coast, there's talk about how the 'Jewish establishment' is depressing the education of black students. On the other coast, a black magazine publishes a poem calling, poetically of course, for the crucifying of rabbis. 'Jew Pig' has become a common variant of the standard expressivist metaphor. On this level, there are daily signals." Do you think he is taking these "signals" out of proportion in building this case?

A : I would think so. There's a certain expression which comes from what the press would describe as militant black intellectuals. There's another expression which I think comes from black people in the community. I think he is taking it out of proportion. In a ghetto situation, the people are not adverse to the idea of sharing power. They're not at the point of, say, where Kenya is in terms of kicking out Asians. I haven't heard of any Jewish merchants being firebombed out of the ghettos since this has happened— any sort of campaign directed against them. I think the danger is that, because of the Jewish reaction to what's been going on, the blacks will move to an absolute position, which, of course, is very dangerous because then you're pitting one power against another power, and that's a war.

Q : You mean that the reaction is of such vehemence, like the demand that you be fired and WBAI be shut down, that that in itself will create anti-Semitism?

A : I don't know if you can call what blacks feel anti-Semitism. It's more of an anti-racism racism, that act of self-defense, and to call it anti-Semitism is to fail to understand it.

You see, the thing which has hurt me most in this is where has the New Left been? Where has the radical movement been? OK, you know, they say we want to be relevant in the black struggle. We want to speak to the white community. Here is opportunity busting down the door. Here it is, if you're a white who understands anything about the black framework. But what happens is that so many young kids in SDS, whose background is Jewish, hate that background so much and want to get so far away from it that they refuse to relate to where they've come from.

Q : Whereas they could have been of some help in moving around in Jewish communities, putting all this in perspective?

A : As far as black radicals go, I'm a conservative because I have a theoretical belief

in coalition, and if it's possible for me to say to a cat who don't want to hear white people, "Hey man, listen, ten thousand white folks were out there on the line yesterday doing this, that, and the others," he might change his mind. But then he looks out there and sees, like I do, a hostile mass, and the rest silent. Hey, well, you know, fuck it!

Q : All during the teachers' strike, and all during this furor about the poem, about WBAI, I don't know of any attempt, organized, anyway, where white radicals, or people who call themselves white radicals, went into their home communities or into communities in which they can easily move, to try to explain what was going on.

A : I know of no attempt. I know of only two groups which have done anything, and that was Youth Against War and Fascism, and Coalition For An Anti-Imperialist Movement. And then it was very gratifying to me that both groups came up and counter-picketed the night others were out picketing me at the station.

I did a column on the Arab-Israeli thing and one on the school strike, both saying the same thing—that I felt the Jewish community should examine itself, and reexamine a lot of the things that it had formerly thought. One of my instincts in terms of the poem, and it was very conscious at the time—like the Zen monk who used to slap the student in the face—OK, let's try it and see what happens. But that's not my role, really. It's the responsibility of young Jews who have been in the radical movement to be the Zen monks, not me. But maybe I'm wrong.

At any rate, I think all of this has caused some self-examination inside the Jewish community and some discussions by the Jewish community, but I cannot really speak to the Jewish community; I don't know the Jewish community.

Q : Leonard Fein, Associate Director of the MIT-Harvard Joint Center for Urban Studies, said in *Time:* "Jews, in a perverse kind of way, need anti-Semites. Jews in this country are in fairly serious trouble spiritually and ideologically, and it is very comforting to come once again to an old and familiar problem. By confronting others, you can avoid the much more challenging confrontation with yourself." A big problem, as people always say at meetings of Jewish organizations, is that the young people are falling away from Judaism, and I would add that it is doubtful that they'll come back on a program of anti-anti-Semitism. As Rabbi Arthur Hertzberg puts it, "Negatives won't work to create a Jewish identity for our young people. The only thing that will work is a set of affirmatives that forms them as a people."

A : There seems to me to be a schizophrenia in the Jewish community. I get many letters and take many phone calls on the air and people say, "I'm white and I'm Jewish," which means that, like, when it's convenient I can be white, and then, when I'm attacked, I'm Jewish. They got to deal with that.

Q : That's a "schizophrenia" that's almost endemic to the American Jewish experience. The lower-class Jew, whose parents came from Eastern Europe, has always felt himself an outsider. I can't imagine any such Jewish kid in school pledging allegiance to the flag who really thought that it was his flag entirely. That feeling of vulnerability intensifies in time of stress.

A : I find it interesting that every other group, including blacks, will say they are Italian-American, German-American, Afro-American—except Jews. I think one of the things which is happening now, if it can be allowed to happen, is that the relationships between the Jewish community and the black community are being reordered. It's been a very patronizing relationship; the Jews haven't realized that. OK, Shanker marches in Selma. Be serious. I mean who cares, for crying out loud! The relationship has not been defined by black people. And so you go around the country, and you talk and talk and talk, or you write and write and write—I just reread *The Fire Next Time*—it is fantastically contemporary, just as valid now as it was in '62. Bestseller and all that—it didn't do no good; nobody listened to it. So it takes a poem by a fifteen-year-old girl, that kick in the stomach, that Zen slap, to finally make people really take what you say seriously. Like Baldwin says in *The Fire Next Time*—is there going to be any hope, will it mean that white people, and I include Jews, are going to have to look at themselves differently, are going to have to change themselves. You know, I didn't know that Shanker was a Jew until he accused me of being an anti-Semite; I'm talking about me, as a black person. Then I figured that he was a Jew. All right, when he's going to accuse me of being something which I'm not—then my only defense is, all right, I'll go ahead and be it, goddammit!

Q: But in your own case, being an intellectual, isn't there a tension between intellect and emotion at that point?

A: Well, I think it's a question of being an intellectual who is divorced by twenty leagues from the masses of people or being divorced by five leagues. You're never going to be totally with them. And my reaction is just as a human being— I'm not much of an intellectual, you know—I had this experience: I did a TV interview in Cleveland. I really hated the producer and the moderator of the show. I really hated them. I hated them as people. They thought I hated them as whites. There was no way I could let them know that I hated them as people, because of who they were. And this is the same thing! They were the kind of liberals whose basic attitude was, "Yes, you can come here and say what you want to say, but I'm not going to listen, and it's not going to change my mind. I'm going to be nice and courteous the entire time, and you're just not going to reach me." If Shanker accuses me of being an anti-Semite, then I cannot prove that I'm not anti-Semitic. It would be futile for me to stand up and say, "Oh no, but I'm not; don't accuse me of that." Then I'm fighting the battle on his territory as he defines it, and that becomes a problem. The problem is one of the relationship of power. But Jews think it's a question of morality.

Q: But does that necessarily mean, as you said earlier, that if he's going to call you one, you're going to be one? I mean, if you're not an anti-Semite, why let him make you into one?

A: Let's put it this way: If it's very clear that he is brutalizing me for his own ends,

then I'm going to retaliate, and I will retaliate in the way that will most hurt him. I don't think I have any other choice. I don't want to be called an anti-Semite for it. And that can be better understood if you understand that black people are a colonized people. You have, you know, two groups—the colonized and the colonizers. And the Jewish community is in the position of being on the side of the colonizer.

Q: This reminds me of your line on the radio the other night, which was not covered by the press, that "We are America's Jews, the Jews think we are the Germans."

A: Right. And the Jews are in the position of being Germans.

Q: Yet there is this thesis, that black people, if and when they are anti-Semitic, feel themselves, at least in that way, to be part of the majority. And there is a corollary to that, from historian Joseph Boskin, that selecting the Jew as a scapegoat fills an important psychic need for the black. To bait the Jew is to claim superiority to the Jew and to identify with the white community that still contains considerable elements of anti-Semitism.

A: You see, once again, he's hooking into traditional concepts of anti-Semitism. Jews are not being used as a scapegoat for the problems of black people. Jews happen to be in a position of power. Blacks want power, thus Jews and blacks are in conflict. There is no scapegoat involved; they are directly involved in the life and the control of the black community. We are not reaching outside. It's not that the schools are filled with Irish and we are looking over to Scarsdale or someplace, and it's the fault of the Jews.

They are right there in the community. So no scapegoat; they are the ones. They are not the only ones. Every black person I've had on my show has pointed that out, and Les pointed it out, and the three guys from N.Y.U. pointed it out—they are not what's called "the enemy"; but if you are a colonized people, then you are not going to break down the colonizer into categories of lesser or greater magnitude of enemy. The enemy is the enemy, and you deal with him as you come to him, and right now we are dealing with him on the level of schools, and there he is.

Q : In Ocean Hill-Brownsville, where there is at least some degree of community control, twenty-two of the Jewish teachers, led by Chuck Isaac, said at a press conference the other day they didn't feel any anti-Semitism there, and specifically not from Les Campbell.

A : What really ticks me is the fact that I didn't know until I went out to do some interviews at Ocean Hill-Brownsville that over 50 per cent of the new teachers they had hired were Jewish. And then you find out the thing which you pointed out in your column, about passing out a leaflet to the kids explaining what Rosh Hashana was, and all of this. I've sat in Les' Black History class twice. I've been amazed that Les never once used the word white. He used a variety of words, slave trader, slave owner; he never once used the word white. Whereas, in my class, you know, I'm much harder than Les is in terms of talking about white people. I spent quite a bit of time talking to the Jewish teachers who were there, the young kids. My feeling was I wish the school had all black teachers, but there aren't enough blacks available who could do the job these white kids are doing. They are pulling really fantastic poetry out of these kids, doing what seemed to me to be good things; I had no objection to it. If the time comes when the black community can take over the school completely and do the same job, then I want blacks to do it, but in the meantime, I mean like, wow, these whites were really filling a role. And these were young kids who had been politically active, politically involved, and were very aware and were working hard. There are some beautiful kids out there.

Q : Now there comes the inevitable question. You say, if at such time the black community can staff the schools by itself, with all black teachers—does that mean you are opting for separatism?

A : Let me put it this way. At the present point in my own life, and at the present point in American history, I don't see any other alternative. We are separate, you know. Great Neck, L. I., is going to bus in some black kids to add some color. That's a Jewish community and it's separate. It would be much better to institutionalize that as much as possible and to take care of business, rather than to keep trying to deal with a bunch of people who don't understand, who won't understand.

Q : So you would probably say that the function of the white Jewish teachers who are now in Ocean Hill-Brownsville and doing well would be to perhaps address their educational and spiritual skills to white kids if and when the time comes when black teachers will fully staff the Ocean Hill-Brownsville schools?

A : They are the only ones who can do it, and they could do a fantastic job. That's where it needs to happen. White kids need to study black history as much as black kids do. And you know, if a white cat's running it down to white kids, white teachers who understand the black frame of reference, that black reality, that's the only way the change is going to happen. But the thing that it comes down to is that young whites don't like white people, and blacks happen to like black people, so they want to be with us. I come back to what I said before: Where has the New Left been when we needed them? Like, I'll speak to white high school students now; I will not speak to white college students anymore.

Q : Why?

A : Because you speak and you speak and you speak, you write books, they read books, and all that, and they understand, you know. Still, when you need them, they aren't there. There is a need which exists in the black community which I can fill. There is a need in the white community which they can fill. I mean, why hasn't SDS been able to run into a synagogue as quick as they ran into N.Y.U. to keep James Reston of *The Times* from speaking?

Q : You've mentioned SDS going into N.Y.U. to stop Reston from speaking; they also shouted down the South Vietnamese ambassador to the U.N. It seems to me that this, in its way, is very similar to people trying to suppress you and WBAI. So that if I am, and I am, for Les Campbell having absolute freedom to say whatever he wants to say anywhere, I have to add that applying "discriminative tolerance," as Herbert Marcuse would put it, anywhere, really injures anyone's right to free speech and thereby seriously

limits the possibility of bringing real social and political change.

A : I've had very mixed reactions, you know, having been picketed and having that strange experience of being escorted through a police line by a cop.

Q : How did that feel?

A : It felt very normal—the people were going to kill me if they could have gotten me, but I could understand that. I felt that the cop was doing what he should be doing, helping black people. But my feeling toward the people who were picketing me was that they had a right to do that. I thought first of going to the station early, at four o'clock; they wouldn't be there until seven—and just staying inside the station. And then I said, no, they have a right. They hate me so much, they should at least have a chance to see me and really scream and yell and do whatever else. I even felt, which is my own personal whatever you want to call it, that they had a right to beat me if they could have gotten me. I wouldn't willingly have given myself to them. But I understood how they felt because if I could have gotten my hands on Dean Rusk I would have felt that I had the right to beat him. OK now, you know, there is the position that the oppressed can do no wrong. And the oppressor can do no right. On a humanistic basis, I would have to agree with you. On a revolutionary basis, I don't think that the ambassador from South Vietnam should be allowed to speak.

Q : But this is like the cliché about being slightly pregnant. Once you start limiting that right to speak—even for what you consider the best revolutionary reasons—you start precedents that other people can use against you.

A : Who am I to say who can speak and who can't speak? If I don't feel this cat has a right to say who can speak and who can't speak, then he feels that naturally I don't have the right to limit him. So to reach a compromise everybody speaks, and I support that. I have to support that, I really do, despite the fact that there are a lot of people I don't want to speak to and whom I would like to punch in the mouth once they start speaking. OK, let them talk. So that makes me an Uncle Tom revolutionary, I guess.

But there's another dimension here. One of my black listeners wrote me and said that freedom of speech is OK as long as it is white people's. I have really resented all the people who ask me, why I didn't say something to disclaim the remark the guy made—you know, about Hitler and the lampshades. There's the assumption that I was the Establishment's representative on the air. He made a flat statement. I was shocked by the statement. I would not have said it. However, knowing damn well that the black community does not have honest access to the air, I was not going to put him down. He had a perfect right to say that, you know. And that is my role in the media—to give the black community access to speak as they see fit. I'm not going to set the standards. But white folks and I guess Jews, too, expected me to be their representative, and that's what shook them up— that they had a black man at a microphone who was not going to be their representative.

Q : Probably for the first time in your life you've had this kind of instant fame, if fame is the word, in which you have become a stereotyped, faceless person to all those people who are demanding all kinds of things done to you, or because of you. How does that feel?

A : On the one hand, it makes me feel like I'm a sitting duck, because *The New York Times* can sit there and shoot at me, day after day after day, and I can't do a damn thing. I know that my listeners, however many I have, do not have the same reaction. I've been thinking a lot about Alger Hiss who is now synonymous with traitor, and will be through time immemorial—like Benedict Arnold—and Alger Hiss is probably a very beautiful cat. It doesn't matter. On the other hand, I'm glad that my listeners know me as an individual and I think they relate to me like that, not as a black individual. I'm very, very patient on the air with people, I am a person who happens to be black whom they can talk to. I won't cuss them out and all that—that's my personality, I don't cuss out people, because it takes too much energy. And also I really believe in people. I believe if you take people where they are, and don't put them down, they will move from point A to point B. It's a political decision I made a couple of years ago to be that way. So to them, my listeners, I became an individual. But I'm not. For most of my life, I was a nigger. So you write a couple of books and you're on the radio and suddenly you're an individual. I was in no danger of being under any illusion about being an individual, and this only helps remind me that when I say something white folk don't like, I'm still a nigger, you know, ain't nothing changed. They will view me as they seek to view me, not as I define myself. They won't come to me and find out. I don't want my listeners or anybody to ever forget that any differences between me and the young brother on the block with a 38 in his belt are only superficial.

Q: Did *The New York Times* ever contact you to find out what you thought?

A: Never, never. The story broke in the early Thursday morning edition of the *Times. The New York Post* called me at 3 A.M. and asked me my reaction, and they printed it. New York's Channel 2 (WCBS) has interviewed me twice, even though they only used ten or fifteen seconds once, but *The New York Times* never contacted me about any of it. They published a few sentences from the WBAI statement on it. They, more than any other news media in New York, I hold responsible for this problem, and I'm really very, very bitter about the way they have handled it. I mean, they don't realize it, not that it matters, but they have set the black community up for the most dire of consequences—given the hatred of blacks which exists and which I think Jews have been surprised to feel in themselves. What if Nixon makes any moves against the black community in toto? You see, I will never forget the Times editorial on the death of Malcolm X. They said he who lives by the sword shall die by the sword, and good riddance. That is exactly what they said. If anything is being created in the city, it's an anti-black hysteria which I have not even seen in the South. This is the second time it's happened since I've been here. The first time was in 1964—when the attempt was made to close the World's Fair on the first day, and was followed by the whole

"Blood Brothers" myth and the Harlem Six case. I thought I was back down South. I really feel that the reaction of even sedate middle-class black people I've been in contact with has been one of "I have no choice but to go out in the streets and start shooting people:" No, they don't even give us the benefit of the doubt that maybe we have a thought-out position. They hear the dog bark and so they react and they say that is what the dog is barking about.

Q: And the Jews who are now so fearful seem unable to recognize the fear that black people feel?

A: Yeah, right. I can sit down and be interviewed, talk on the radio, write and all this, but whites have to communicate with that fifteen-year-old kid on the block with the 38 in his belt; he ain't going to talk to them like I do. If he sees 100,000 white people on the street marching on City Hall, marching against *The New York Times,* that will communicate to him, but don't tell him about no good white folks or no good Jews, because he is not an individual. They are not going to ask him, did you major in English or did you shine your shoes this morning—they are going to shoot him.

Q: Do you think it is going to get worse?

A: Hey, it is election year. 1969 in New York City is going to be so bad. You know, I would not be surprised if Mayor Lindsay takes a trip to Israel before the election. And if Mayor Lindsay has totally written off the black community, he is running scared and whoever the Democrats put up—you already have hints that they are going to use the school thing, they are going to use the law and order thing, they are going to use. . . .

Q : The first candidate is James Scheuer, the Congressman from the Bronx, who has a good voting record in Congress, but is so far running in part on a law and order program.

A : Right. And I think that this election is going to so further divide this city and exacerbate what now exists—and what now exists is thousands of tons of TNT—that, you know, I feel like we are sitting in this damn canoe going down the Colorado Rapids and there ain't nothin' nobody can do because they never believe what black people say anyway. We screamed racism for 400 years. It was not believed until the Kerner Commission comes out and says, hey, there's racism. Now all the white folks say, "Yeah, there's racism in America, that's right!" We've been saying it all along. So that once again, we're asking, where are those people who understand, why aren't they saying something?

### Michael Novak, *The Rise of the Unmeltable Ethnics*, 1971

*Michael Novak is the grandson of Slovak immigrants. Educated in theology at Harvard and the Gregorian University in Rome, he has published books in philosophy and theology ranging from* The Catholic Ethic and the Spirit of Capitalism *to* The Joy of Sports *and taught at Harvard, Syracuse, Notre Dame, and Stanford. He is currently the George Frederick Jewett Scholar in Religion, Philosophy, and Public Policy at the American Enterprise Institute. He wrote* The Rise of the Unmeltable Ethnics *in 1971 as a kind of manifesto for the white ethnic revival.*

*Source:* Michael Novak, *The Rise of the Unmeltable Ethnics* (New York: Macmillan, 1973), pp. 61–78.

## THE PRICE OF BEING AMERICANIZED

My grandparents, I am sure, never guessed what it would cost them and their children to become "Americanized."

In their eyes, no doubt, almost everything was gain. From the oppression experienced by Slovaks at the hands of the Austro-Hungarian empire, the gain was liberty; from relative poverty, opportunity; from an old world, new hope. (There is a town in Pennsylvania, two hundred miles from where they now lie buried, called "New Hope.")

They were injured, to be sure, by nativist American prejudices against foreigners, by a white Anglo-Saxon Protestant culture, and even by an Irish church. (Any Catholic church not otherwise specified by nationality they experienced and described as "the Irish church.")

What price is exacted by America when into its maw it sucks other cultures of the world and processes them? What do people have to lose before they can qualify as true Americans?

For one thing, a lot of blue stars—and silver and gold ones—must hang in the window. You proved you loved America by dying for it in its wars. The Poles, Italians, Greeks, and Slavs whose acronym Msgr. Geno Baroni has made to stand for all the non-English-speaking ethnic groups—pride themselves on "fighting for America." When my father saw my youngest brother in officer's uniform, it was one of the proudest days of his life . . . even though it (sickeningly) meant Vietnam.

I don't have other figures at hand. But when the Poles were only four percent of the population (in 1917–19) they accounted for twelve percent of the nation's casualties in World War I. "The Fighting Irish" won their epithet by dying in droves in the Civil War.

There is, then, a blood test. "Die for us and we'll give you a chance."

One is also expected to give up one's native language. My parents decided never to teach us Slovak. They hoped that thereby we would gain a generation in the process of becoming full Americans.

They kept up a few traditions: Christmas Eve holy bread, candlelight, mushroom soup, fish, and poppyseed. My mother baked *kolacky*. *Pirohi*, however, more or less died with my grandmother, who used to work all day making huge, steaming pots of potato dumplings and prune dumplings for her grandchildren. No other foods shall ever taste so sweet.

My parents, so far as I know, were the first Slovaks in our town to move outside the neighborhoods traditional for our kind of people and move into the "American" suburbs. There were not, I recall, very many other Catholics in the rather large, and good, public school I attended from grades two until six. I remember Mrs. S., the fifth-grade teacher, spelling "Pope Pius" with an "o" in the middle, and myself with gently firm righteousness (even then) correcting her.

What has happened to my people since they came to this land nearly a century ago? Where are they now, that long-awaited fully Americanized third generation? Are we living the dream our grandparents dreamed when on creaking decks they stood silent, afraid, hopeful at the sight of the Statue of Liberty? Will we ever find that secret relief, that door, that hidden entrance? Did our grandparents choose for us, and our posterity, what they should have chosen?

Now the dice lie cold in our own uncertain hands.

## CONFESSIONS OF A WHITE ETHNIC

Three is no other way but autobiography by which to cure oneself of too much objectivity. It is a cure many in America might profitably indulge.

A discussion of ethnicity incites emotion. The stereotypes are not so old that they no longer injure.

While working on this book during the past year, I discovered many things about myself: my relation to my parents; my discomfort (intellectual and emotional) with a dominant conception of intellectual and professional life; my suspicion of both liberal and radical politics; my appreciation for certain kinds of writing; my unhappiness with the sterility of political debate, no less between President Nixon and his opposition than between the various epigones of the Left.

Friends of mine and critics sometimes complain that they do not know where

I am, or where I am coming from. My standpoint is not fairly described (whose is?) as radical, or liberal, or conservative. So I have been trying to trace its roots.

No available public standpoint works for me. I have had to go in search of my own. A search through memory and instinct by way of history has helped. Awareness of ethnicity is not some golden thread that, taken in one's fingers and given a sudden pull, establishes the pattern of the tapestry. It is, however, an additional light for the understanding.

To understand a person's attitudes or perceptions, it is helpful to know his history. Not in order to "explain" him—for history and ethnicity "explain" nothing—but in order to estimate, against a concrete context, the weight one should assign some of his emphases. We depend on others for most of the picture of the arena in which we act. The task is to learn to see it as they see it, in order to know how to interpret what they say.

Nothing, of course, is so painful as to have one's views discounted according to some ethnic or religious stereotype. "Jews are always complaining." "A WASP *would* think so!" "You're from Mississippi, aren't you?" "New York intellectuals . . ." "That's a surprising view from a Catholic!" The knowing put-down is intolerable.

Perhaps that is why even so courageous a writer as Norman Mailer has rather steadfastly avoided Jewish materials. He tried to embrace the melting pot. When he dramatizes an encounter, central to his work, between a stud and a Jewish maid, the stud is named Sergius O'Shaugnessy but given a sensibility of felt Jewishness thinly pasted over Irish. The Jewish force in Mailer is almost always hiding behind projection into Irishmen, Poles, Anglo-Saxon Texans. Mailer may want his mother's Irishness to win, but it doesn't—hardly ever. The celebrated writer's block may here have one of its sources. Meanwhile, his journalism benefits by Jewish self-dramatization. One who stands outside the usual political conflicts between WASPS, ethnics, and blacks has a fascinating alternative to the WASP style of objectivity. He gives us dramas of self and dramas of history. Sheer talent, sheer craftsmanship, divert us from the guarded core.

So the risks of letting one's own secrets out of the bag are rather real. Yet there is no other way.

### 1. Neither WASP nor Jew nor Black

Growing up in America has been an assault upon my sense of worthiness. It has also been a kind of liberation and delight.

There must be countless women in America who have known for years that something is peculiarly unfair, yet who only recently have found it possible, because of Women's Liberation, to give tongue to their pain. In recent months I have experienced a similar inner thaw, a gradual relaxation, a willingness to think about feelings heretofore shepherded out of sight.

I am born of PIGS—those Poles, Italians, Greeks, and Slavs, those non-English-speaking immigrants numbered so heavily among the workingmen of this nation. Not particularly liberal or radical; born into a history not white Anglo-Saxon and not Jewish; born outside what, in America, is considered the intellectual mainstream—and thus privy to neither power nor status nor intellectual voice.

Those Poles of Buffalo and Milwaukee—so notoriously taciturn, sullen, nearly speechless. Who has ever understood them? It is not that Poles do not feel emotion—what is their history if not dark passion, romanticism, betrayal, courage, blood? But where in America is there anywhere a language for voicing what a Christian Pole in this nation feels? He has no Polish culture left him, no Polish tongue. Yet Polish feelings do not go easily into the idiom of happy America, the America of the Anglo-Saxons and yes, in the arts, the Jews. (The Jews have long been a culture of the word, accustomed to exile, skilled in scholarship and in reflection. The Christian Poles are largely of peasant origin, free men for hardly more than a hundred years.) Of what shall the young man of Lackawanna think on his way to work in the mills, departing his relatively dreary home and street? What roots does he have? What language of the heart is available to him?

The PIGS are not silent willingly. The silence burns like hidden coals in the chest.

All four of my grandparents, unknown to one another, arrived in America from the same county in Slovakia. My grandfather had a small farm in Pennsylvania; his wife died in a wagon accident. Meanwhile, Johanna, fifteen, arrived on Ellis Island, dizzy from witnessing births and deaths and illnesses aboard the crowded ship. She had a sign around her neck lettered PASSAIC.

There an aunt told her of a man who had lost his wife in Pennsylvania. She went. They were married. She inherited his three children.

Each year for five years Grandma had a child of her own. She was among the lucky; only one died. When she was twenty-two and the mother of seven (my father was the last), her husband died. "Grandma Novak," as I came to know her many years later, resumed the work she had begun in Slovakia at the town home of a man known to my father only as "the Professor"; she housecleaned and she laundered.

I heard this story only weeks ago. Strange that I had not asked insistently before. Odd that I should have such shallow knowledge of my roots. Amazing to me that I do not know what my family suffered, endured, learned, and hoped these last six or seven generations. It is as if there were no project in which we all have been involved, as if history in some way began with my father and with me.

The estrangement I have come to feel derives not only from lack of family history. Early in life, I was made to feel a slight uneasiness when I said my name.

Later "Kim" helped. So did Robert. And "Mister Novak" on TV. The name must be one of the most Anglo-Saxon of the Slavic names. Nevertheless, when I was very young, the "American" kids still made something out of names unlike their own, and their earnest, ambitious mothers thought long thoughts when I introduced myself.

Under challenge in grammar school concerning my nationality, I had been instructed by my father to announce proudly: "American." When my family moved from the Slovak ghetto of Johnstown to the WASP suburb on the hill, my mother impressed upon us how well we must be dressed, and show good manners, and behave—people think of us as "different" and we mustn't give them any cause. "Whatever you do, marry a Slovak girl," was other advice to a similar end: "They cook. They clean. They take good care of you. For your own good." I was taught to be proud of being Slovak, but to recognize that others wouldn't know what it meant, or care.

When I had at last pierced the deception—that most movie stars and many other professionals had abandoned their European names in order to feed American fantasies—I felt only a little sadness. One of my uncles, for business reasons and rather late in life, changed his name, too, to a simple German variant—not long, either, after World War II.

Nowhere in my schooling do I recall any attempt to put me in touch with my own history. The strategy was clearly to make an American of me. English literature, American literature, and even the history books, as I recall them, were peopled mainly by Anglo-Saxons from Boston (where most historians seemed to live). Not even my native Pennsylvania, let alone my Slovak forebears, counted for very many paragraphs. (We did have something called "Pennsylvania History" somewhere; I seem to remember its puffs for industry. It could have been written by a Mellon.) I don't remember feeling envy or regret: a feeling, perhaps, of unimportance, of re-

moteness, of not having heft enough to count.

The fact that I was born a Catholic also complicated life. What is a Catholic but what everybody else is in reaction against? Protestants reformed "the whore of Babylon." Others were "enlightened" from it, and Jews had reason to help Catholicism and the social structure it was rooted in fall apart. The history books and the whole of education hummed in upon that point (for during crucial years I attended a public school): to be modern is decidedly not to be medieval; to be reasonable is not to be dogmatic; to be free is clearly not to live under ecclesiastical authority; to be scientific is not to attend ancient rituals, cherish irrational symbols, indulge in mythic practices. It is hard to grow up Catholic in America without becoming defensive, perhaps a little paranoid, feeling forced to divide the world between "us" and "them."

English Catholics have little of the sense of inferiority in which many other Catholic groups tend to share—Irish Catholics, Polish Catholics, Lithuanians, Germans, Italians, Lebanese, and others. Daniel Callahan (*The Mind of the Catholic Layman, Generation of the Third Eye*) and Garry Wills ("Memories of a Catholic Boyhood," in *Esquire*) both identify, in part, with the more secure Catholicism of an Anglo-Catholic parent. The French around New Orleans have a social ease different from the French Catholics of Massachusetts. Still, as Catholics, especially vis-à-vis the national liberal culture, nearly all have felt a certain involuntary defensiveness. Granted our diverse ethnic circumstances, we share a certain communion of memories.

We had a special language all our own, our own pronunciation for words we shared in common with others (Augústine, contémplative), sights and sounds and smells in which few others participated (incense at Benediction of the Most Blessed Sacrament, Forty Hours, wakes, and altar bells at the silent consecration of the Host); and we had our own politics and slant on world affairs. Since earliest childhood, I have known about a "power elite" that runs America: the boys from the Ivy League in the State Department as opposed to the Catholic boys in Hoover's FBI who (as Daniel Moynihan once put it), keep watch on them. And on a whole host of issues, my people have been, though largely Democratic, conservative: on censorship, on communism, on abortion, on religious schools, etc. "Harvard" and "Yale" long meant "them" to us.

The language of Spiro Agnew, the language of George Wallace, excepting its idiom, awakens childhood memories in me: of men arguing in the barbershop, of my uncle drinking so much beer he threatened to lay his dick upon the porch rail and wash the whole damn street with steaming piss—while cursing the niggers in the mill below, and the Yankees in the mill above—millstones he felt pressing him. Other relatives were duly shocked, but everybody loved Uncle George; he said what he thought.

We did not feel this country belonged to us. We felt fierce pride in it, more loyalty than anyone could know. But we felt blocked at every turn. There were

not many intellectuals among us, not even very many professional men. Laborers mostly. Small businessmen, agents for corporations perhaps. Content with a little, yes, modest in expectation, and content. But somehow feeling cheated. For a thousand years the Slovaks survived Hungarian hegemony and our strategy here remained the same: endurance and steady work. Slowly, one day, we would overcome.

A special word is required about a complicated symbol: sex. To this day my mother finds it hard to spell the word intact, preferring to write "s——." Not that much was made of sex in our environment. And that's the point: silence. Demonstrative affection, emotive dances, an exuberance Anglo-Saxons seldom seem to share; but on the realities of sex, discretion. Reverence, perhaps; seriousness, surely. On intimacies, it was as though our tongues had been stolen, as though in peasant life for a thousand years—as in the novels of Tolstoi, Sholokhov, and even Kosinski—the context had been otherwise. Passion, certainly; romance, yes; family and children, certainly; but sex rather a minor if explosive part of life.

Imagine, then, the conflict in the generation of my brothers, sister, and myself. (The reviewer for the *New York Times* reviews on the same day two new novels of fantasy—one a pornographic fantasy to end all such fantasies [he writes], the other in some comic way representing the redemption wrought by Jesus Christ. In language and verve, the books are rated evenly. In theme, the reviewer notes his embarrassment in even reporting a religious fantasy, but no embarrassment at all about preposterous pornography.) Suddenly, what for a thousand years was minor becomes an all-absorbing investigation. Some view it as a drama of "liberation" when the ruling classes (subscribers to the *New Yorker,* I suppose) move progressively, generation by generation since Sigmund Freud, toward concentration upon genital stimulation, and latterly toward consciousness-raising sessions in Clit. Lib. But it is rather a different drama when we stumble suddenly upon mores staggering any expectation our grandparents ever cherished. Fear of becoming "sexual objects" is an ancient fear that appears in many shapes. The emotional reaction of Maria Wyeth in Joan Didion's *Play It as It Lays* is exactly what the ancient morality would have predicted.

Yet more significant in the ethnic experience in America is the intellectual world one meets: the definition of values, ideas, and purposes emanating from universities, books, magazines, radio, and television. One hears one's own voice echoed back neither by spokesmen of "middle America" (so complacent, smug, nativist, and Protestant), nor by the "intellectuals." Almost unavoidably, perhaps, education in America leads the student who entrusts his soul to it in a direction which, lacking a better word, we might call liberal: respect for individual conscience, a sense of social responsibility, trust in the free exchange of ideas and procedures of dissent, a certain confidence in the ability of men to "reason together" and adjudicate their differences, a frank recognition of the vitality of the unconscious, a willingness to pro-

tect workers and the poor against the vast economic power of industrial corporations, and the like.

On the other hand, the liberal imagination has appeared to be astonishingly universalist and relentlessly missionary. Perhaps the metaphor "enlightenment" offers a key. One is *initiated into light*. Liberal education tends to separate children from their parents, from their roots, from their history, in the cause of a universal and superior religion. One is taught regarding the unenlightened (even if they be one's uncles George and Peter, one's parents, one's brothers, perhaps) what can only be called a modern equivalent of *odium theologicum*. Richard Hofstadter described anti-intellectualism in America (more accurately, in nativist America rather than in ethnic America), but I have yet to encounter a comparable treatment of anti-unenlightenment among our educated classes.

In particular, I have regretted and keenly felt the absence of that sympathy for PIGS which simple human feeling might have prodded intelligence to muster, that same sympathy which the educated find so easy to conjure up for black culture, Chicano culture, Indian culture, and other cultures of the poor. In such cases one finds the universalist pretensions of liberal culture suspended; some groups, at least, are entitled to be both different and respected. Why do the educated classes find it so difficult to want to understand the man who drives a beer truck, or the fellow with a helmet working on a site across the street with plumbers and electricians, while their sensitivities race easily to Mississippi or even Bedford-Stuyvesant?

There are deep secrets here, no doubt, unvoiced fantasies and scarcely admitted historical resentments. Few persons in describing "middle Americans" "the silent majority," or Scammon and Wattenberg's "typical American voter" distinguish clearly enough between the nativist American and the ethnic American. The first is likely to be Protestant, the second Catholic. Both may be, in various ways, conservative, loyalist, and unenlightened. Each has his own agonies, fears, betrayed expectations. Neither is ready, quite, to become an ally of the other. Neither has the same history behind him here. Neither has the same hopes. Neither lives out the same psychic voyage, shares the same symbols, has the same sense of reality. The rhetoric and metaphors proper to each differ from those of the other.

There is overlap, of course. But country music is not a polka; a successful politician in a Chicago ward needs a very different "common touch" from the one needed by the county clerk in Normal. The urban experience of immigration lacks that mellifluous, optimistic, biblical vision of the good America which springs naturally to the lips of politicians from the Bible Belt. The nativist tends to believe with Richard Nixon that he "knows America, and the American heart is good." The ethnic tends to believe that every American who preceded him has an angle, and that he, by God, will some day find one, too. (Often, ethnics complain that by working hard, obeying the law, trusting their political leaders, and relying upon the American dream, they now have only their own naiveté to blame for rising no higher than they have.)

It goes without saying that the intellectuals do not love "middle America," and that for all the good, warm discovery of America that preoccupied them during the 1950s no strong tide of respect accumulated in their hearts for the Yahoos, Babbitts, Agnews, and Nixons of the land. Willie Morris in *North Toward Home* writes poignantly of the chill, parochial outreach of the liberal sensibility, its failure to engage the humanity of the modest, ordinary little man west of the Hudson. The Intellectual's Map of the United States is succinct: "Two coasts connected by United Airlines."

Unfortunately, it seems, the ethnics erred in attempting to Americanize themselves before clearing the project with the educated classes. They learned to wave the flag and to send their sons to war. They learned to support their President—an easy task, after all, for those accustomed to obeying authority. And where would they have been if Franklin Roosevelt had not sided with them against established interests? They knew a little about communism—the radicals among them in one way, and by far the larger number of conservatives in another. To this day not a few exchange letters with cousins and uncles who did not leave for America when they might have, whose lot is demonstrably harder than their own and less than free.

Finally, the ethnics do not like, or trust, or even understand the intellectuals. It is not easy to feel uncomplicated affection for those who call you "pig," "fascist," "racist." One had not yet grown accustomed to not hearing "hunkie," "Polack," "spic," "mick," "dago," and the rest. A worker in Chicago told reporter

Lois Wille in a vividly home-centered outburst:

The liberals always have despised us. We've got these mostly little jobs, and we drink beer and, my God, we bowl and watch television and we don't read. It's goddamn vicious snobbery. We're sick of all these phoney integrated TV commercials with these upper-class Negroes. We know they're phoney.

The only time a Pole is mentioned it's to make fun of him. He's Ignatz Dumbrowski, 274 pounds and 5-foot-4, and he got his education by writing into a firm on a matchbook cover. But what will we do about it? Nothing, because we're the new invisible man, the new whipping boy, and we still think the measure of a man's what he does and how he takes care of his children and what he's doing in his own home, not what he thinks about Vietnam.

At no little sacrifice, one had apologized for foods that smelled too strong for Anglo-Saxon noses; moderated the wide swings of Slavic and Italian emotion; learned decorum; given oneself to education, American style; tried to learn tolerance and assimilation. Each generation criticized the earlier for its authoritarian and European and old-fashioned ways. "Up-to-date" was a moral lever. And now when the process nears completion, when a generation appears that speaks without accent and goes to college, still you are considered "pigs," "fascists," and "racists."

Racists? Our ancestors owned no slaves. Most of us ceased being serfs only in the last two hundred years—the Russians in 1861. Italians, Lithuanians, Slovaks, Poles are not, in principle, against "community control," or even against ghettoes of our own.

Whereas the Anglo-Saxon model appears to be a system of atomic individuals and high mobility, our model has tended to stress communities of our own, attachment to family and relatives, stability, and roots. Ethnics tend to have a fierce sense of attachment to their homes, having been homeowners for less than three generations: a home is almost fulfillment enough for one man's life. Some groups save arduously in a passion to *own;* others rent. We have most ambivalent feelings about suburban assimilation and mobility. The melting pot is a kind of homogenized soup, and its mores only partly appeal to ethnics: to some, yes, and to others, no.

It must be said that ethnics think they are better people than the blacks. Smarter, tougher, harder working, stronger in their families. But maybe many are not sure. Maybe many are uneasy. Emotions here are delicate; one can understand the immensely more difficult circumstances under which the blacks have suffered; and one is not unaware of peculiar forms of fear, envy, and suspicion across color lines. How much of this we learned in America by being made conscious of our olive skin, brawny backs, accents, names, and cultural quirks is not plain to us. Racism is not our invention; we did not bring it with us; we had prejudices enough and would gladly have been spared new ones. Especially regarding people who suffer more than we.

When television commentators and professors say "humanism" or "progress," it seems to ethnics like moral pressure to abandon their own traditions, their faith, their associations, in order to reap higher rewards in the culture of the national corporations. Ethnic neighborhoods usually do not like interviewers, consultants, government agents, organizers, sociologists. Usually they resent the media. Almost all spokesmen they meet from the world of intellect have disdain for them. It shows. Do museums, along the "Black art" and "Indian art," have "Italo-American" exhibitions or "Lithuanian-American" days? Dvorak wrote the *New World Symphony* in a tiny community of Bohemian craftsmen in Iowa. All over the nation in print studios and metal foundries when the craftsmen immigrants from Europe die, their crafts will die with them. Who here supports such skills?

### 2. A Cumulative Political Awakening

Such a tide of resentment begins to overwhelm the descendant of "the new immigration" when he begins to voice repressed feelings about America that at first his throat clogs with despair. Dare he let resentment out? Shouldn't he keep calm? Can he somehow, out of anything available, put together categories and words, and shoot them aloft, slim silver missiles of despair? The incoming planes are endless. The illusions of Americans are vast.

Allies are foes; foes are friends. A language for ethnic divergence does not exist. Prejudices are deep in social structures and institutions; deep, too, in moralities and philosophies; not shallow in families and close relationships. American politics is going crazy because of a fundamental ignorance. Intellectuals, too, are blind.

The battle is partly in one's own soul. On the one hand American, enlightened, educated; on the other, stubbornly resistant, in love with values too dear to jettison, at home neither in the ethnic community nor in any intellectual group, neither with theorists nor with practical politicians, convinced of a certain rightness in one's soul and yet not confident that others will see, can see, the subtle links in a different way of life. It is the insecurity of certainty: the sense that something of value is not likely to he understood. The planes keep droning on and on.

A Slovak proverb: When trees are blown across the road in front of you, you know a tornado's coming.

It is impossible to define people out of existence, or to define their existence for them. Sooner or later, being free, they will explode in rage.

If you are a descendant of southern and eastern Europeans, everyone else *has* defined your existence. A pattern of "Americanization" is laid out. You are catechized, cajoled, and condescended to by guardians of good Anglo-Protestant attitudes. You are chided by Jewish libertarians. Has ever a culture been so moralistic?

The entire experience of becoming American is summarized in the experience of being made to feel guilty.

For southern and eastern Europeans,

there is one constant in their experience of America—abated and relieved for perhaps the decade of the fifties only. They are constantly told to gear up for some new morality. Even in being invited to give a speech on ethnic problems (as the token ethnic), one is told chummily by the national organizer: "As far as I'm concerned, the white ethnics are simply a barrier to social progress." Catching himself, he is generous: "Though I suppose they have their problems, too."

The *old* rule by which ethnics were to measure themselves was the WASP ethic. The *new* rule is getting "with it." The latter is based on new technologies and future shock. The latter could not have existed without the family life and social organization of the former. Parent and child are now at war. In the middle—once again—are southern and eastern Europeans. We are becoming almost Jewish in our anticipation of disaster. When anything goes wrong, or dirty work needs doing, we're *it*.

I never intended to think this way. I never intended to begin writing—ye gods!—as an *ethnic*. I never intended to dig up old memories.

What began to prod me were political events. The anomaly in American publishing and television of William F. Buckley, Jr., had long troubled me: a Catholic who was making a much-needed criticism of American "enlightenment," but from a curiously Anglo-Saxon and conservative point of view. I hoped he was not a dotted line which a larger Catholic movement would fill in.

By the time of the Goldwater campaign of 1964 and the Wallace campaign of 1966, I was alarmed by the cleavage between the old WASP and the new technological consciousness. Catholics might be driven to choose, and might choose the older ways. Worse still, I began to be irritated by the controlled, but felt, anti-Catholic bias among journalists and intellectuals. Despite myself, I disliked the general American desire to believe that ethnic groups do not exist, or if they do, should not. I had nothing to do with ethnic groups myself, and no intention of linking myself to them. I was neither ashamed of them nor hostile to them; it simply seemed to me important, even from their point of view, for me to live the fullest life and to do the best work I could.

But then interpretations of the Wallace vote among Catholics in Wisconsin and Maryland seemed to me grossly false and unfair. I wasn't about to *identify* with the pro-Wallace voters. But I felt increasingly uncomfortable with the condescension and disdain heaped upon them. So I found myself beginning to say "we," rather than "they," when I spoke of ethnics. It is not an entirely comfortable "we," for many ethnics have not been to college, or travelled, or shared the experiences I've had. I wasn't sure I wanted to defend them, or whether I was entitled to do so after too many years of separation from them. I couldn't be sure whether in the next decade the ethnics or the intellectuals would first abandon the path of community, diversity, integrity, and justice. Despite their internal diversity, intellectuals are by and large as capable of minority rule and a relatively narrow ideology as any other group. Meanwhile, the despair and frustration of ethnic groups might become so great that they will think only of their own survival and welfare, and close their hearts to everybody else. American life sometimes hardens. It has not yet hardened, but the present decade is (as usual) crucial.

Which group offers a better chance for social progress—the intellectuals or the ethnics? The sixties have convinced me. The intellectuals cannot do it alone. Arrogance is their principal defect, an arrogance whose lash everybody else in America has felt. A Boston policeman gave Robert Coles the picture:

> I think the college crowd, the left-wing college crowd, is trying to destroy this country, step by step. They're always looking for trouble. They're never happy, except when everyone pays attention to them—and let me tell you, the ordinary people of this country, the average working-man, he's sick and tired of those students, so full of themselves, and their teachers who all think they're the most important people in the human race.

Then a gas station attendant gave Coles some advice to pass along to Daniel Berrigan in jail:

> And tell him he's wasting his time, because this country is run by the big industrialists, and the politicians who do what they're told to do, and the big-mouthed professors (they're all so

swellheaded) who are always whispering advice to people—as if they know how the world works! That's what I say: tell the poor father to mind his own business and get out of prison and speak honestly to his flock, but stay away from politics and things like that—or else he'll start sounding like a crook himself. All politicians learn to sugarcoat the truth; they just don't talk straight from the shoulder. I guess they look down on the ordinary American workingman. I guess they don't trust us. I guess they figure they can con us, all the time con us.

## 3. The Flag, That Flag

From 1870 until 1941 ethnics were told they were not worthy of America. They are cynical about authority, but they believed the dream.

The flag to ethnic Americans is not a symbol of bureaucracy or system (of which the middle classes know far more than they). It is a symbol of spiritual and moral value. It was held beyond their grasp for generations. The flag invoked asceticism, struggle, a long climb up a bitterly contested mountain. Blood flowed until it was implanted on the peak. Iwo Jima was another Calvary.

To ethnics, America is almost a religion. The flag alone proves that they are not stupid, cloddish, dull, but capable of the greatest act men can make: to die for others. The flag is not a patriotic symbol only. It is the symbol of poor and wretched people who now have jobs and homes and liberties. It is a symbol of transcendence. Many millions proved that they were men, not PIGS, by expressing a willingness to die beneath those colors. When that flag flaps, their dignity is celebrated.

Those who attack the flag attack the chief symbol of transcendence, human dignity, and acceptance available to millions of human beings.

"I AM AN AMERICAN!" How many humiliations were endured until one could say those words and not be laughed at by nativists.

Where has the dream led, in reality? 'While a young Italian lawyer was working with a civil rights team in Mississippi, his home city was running an expressway through the traditional homes of his family. While a young Pole was in Vietnam, his brother was laid off from work. His parents became so furious at being stereotyped as racists they are wondering why they ever came to America.

The new experiences awaken memories that are too painful. A white nativist woman in a coal town in Pennsylvania establishes the historical perspective:

Why, I would just as soon live alongside a nigger family as some of these foreigners. I think that the niggers are whiter than the foreigners are because at least they speak your own language . . . [Foreigners] might be plotting to kill you and you wouldn't even know it. . . .They remind me of these old-time people back in the Bible. The women would have a shawl of some kind on their head. . . . They had a different look from us . . . couldn't talk our language.

Our parents "began to go out of their way in order to act American. You see, they could not stand shame, and shame was one of the means used to get them to come over and change their habits." In those dark days the flag, at least, meant pride. It was not *their* flag. It was *ours*.

## Monsignor Geno Baroni, 1975, and Gerard Muench, 1975, The White Ethnic Revival

*Monsignor Geno Baroni was one of the most important leaders of the white ethnic revival of the 1960s and 1970s. In 1971 he received a grant from the Ford Foundation to establish the Center for Urban Ethnic Affairs. Throughout his career he was a staunch advocate of poor and working-class Italian, Polish, Irish, and other white ethnic Americans. Here he testifies before the Bicentennial Committee of the United States Catholic Conference in Newark, New Jersey, in December of 1975. He provides an overview of his career and a good summary of his understanding of the white ethnic revival, an understanding of it as both a reassertion of ancestral cultures and a defense of concrete interests such as jobs and neighborhoods.*

*Mr. Muench, a Ukrainian American, also testified before the Bicentennial Committee of the United States Catholic Conference in December of 1975. His short speech candidly reveals many of the class and racial resentments felt by working-class whites in the late 1960s and early 1970s.*

Source: National Conference of Catholic Bishops, Bicentennial Committee, "Ethnicity and

Race," 1975 (3211 4th Street, N.E., Washington, D.C. 20017).

MSGR. BARONI: Thank you very much Cardinal Dearden. I want to thank all of you for the opportunity of being here to share my experiences and views in this important discussion and dialogue.

Some of the people of St. Lucy's know I've been here many times for their great feast. More often, I have been to Newark on a regular basis since 1971, and have been involved in the development of the North Ward Educational and Cultural Center headed by Mr. Steve Adubato.

I would be remiss if I didn't mention here some of those who got me involved in all of this. I have to mention my father, an immigrant coal miner, and my mother, still living in western Pennsylvania. My father is suffering from black lung. He was a union organizer. It was he who taught me his favorite songs, "Sixteen Tons." "You load 16 tons, and what do you get? Another day older and deeper in debt."

It was he who taught me first and best about social justice, and it was my mother who taught me the theology: "There, but for the grace of God, go I."

I'd also like to mention people like Cardinal O'Boyle of Washington, who helped me get involved in the urban arena of race and ethnicity at both the national and the local level. I'd like to discuss some part of this very important and complex question in this context:

What is the role of an urban church in urban society that's rapidly changing?

How do we face the difficult challenge of the persistence of ethnicity and race in spite of the old fashioned and long-standing melting pot mentality in which we've all been raised? How do we develop a new concept or a new framework to deal with cultural pluralism and parish neighborhood development? What is the future of urban ethnicity in our independent cultural society? How can we—if we can—an institution of faith, a believing institution, help to create a new urban social policy that could provide liberty and justice for all?

One challenge facing the church and society in the bicentennial era is to develop an urban policy that legitimizes ethnic, racial and cultural pluralism and includes the revitalization of the parish neighborhood as an essential building block for renewing cities.

If we are to provide increased liberty and justice for all, we must turn to the cities. It is no coincidence that we are here in Newark to begin this sixth Bicentennial hearing sponsored by the National Conference of Catholic Bishops on the theme of liberty and justice for all. Mayor Gibson, whom I know very well, is famous for saying in 1971: "Wherever cities are going, Newark is going to get there first." Someone else also said, and this explains Mayor Gibson's statement, that cities like Newark are fast becoming "black, brown and broke." These ideas conjure up fantasies of a new American type of apartheid—of abandoned cities surrounded by hostile suburbs.

Newark is a symbol because Newark exemplifies the dynamics of deterioration of northern urban cities, especially when one looks at the uncertain relationship between the growing black and Hispanic populations and the whites remaining in the cities. New York City is another symbol of American cities because of its financial bankruptcy and the threatened breakdown of its human services to meet human needs.

If we are to use these Bicentennial hearings to listen, to share experiences and to dialogue, then we might begin to ask: What is the role of the church, if any, in the development of some new, more humane urban social policy?

A theologian (Harvey Cox) once suggested that the decline of the relevance of the major faiths was creating a secular city, indicating that the churches have no role in the urban malaise. Is this so? Allow me to begin to answer this question from a personal perspective.

I was an inner-city priest and social activist in the '60s. Like so many others, I felt overwhelmed by the loneliness and overcrowding, the bad housing, the fear, the violence of life, and all the forces that were at work stifling development of human life and spawning misery in that marvelous achievement of man that is called the city. (Lewis Mumford)

Lorraine Hainesbury was more than prophetic in the early 1960s when she said: "What happens to a dream deferred? Does it dry up like a raisin in the sun or does it explode?" They exploded in cities like Detroit, Newark, Watts and 57 other centers of urban life. A year later the Kerner Commission revealed that we had indeed become a "divided society," that there was an "inevitable group conflict between the rising expectations of minority groups and the fears of the white middle class in America." Years before Gunnar Myrdal, in a classic work, had described race as the "American dilemma."

But there is another dimension to this dilemma which hasn't yet been written, although Oscar Handlin suggested it when he wrote about the experience of the immigrants in *The Uprooted*.

We all know the inscription that welcomes the immigrants at the base of the Statue of Liberty: "Give me your tired, your poor, your huddled masses yearning to be free." We were "aliens" and we became naturalized, "Americanized," only to discover by the 1970s that like Pogo, who said, "I have met the enemy and he is us."

I had high hopes in the early 1960s when I was working in a parish in the inner-city of Washington, D.C. I had high hopes because I was Catholic coordinator of the civil rights march of 1963.

The church matched, project for project, federal poverty program efforts. But by 1967–68, when some of my own diocesan programs began to fall apart and when our urban centers exploded, I began to seriously re-evaluate the challenge of American's urban crisis.

I began to try to react to many of my friends who called my family hard-hats, racists, dumb-dumbs, pigs. I began to react to some of my liberal friends both in and out of the church by saying, "All right, if we whites are part of the problem, then we had best be part of the solution."

Year after year the United States Catholic Conference had issued statements about race relations that culminated in the urban crisis document of

1968, "The Racial Crisis," which established the Urban Task Force. By chance circumstance and coincidence I had become, in the middle '60s, director of urban affairs for the Archdiocese of Washington, D.C. In 1969, I became program director of the Urban Task Force of the United States Catholic Conference.

One major accomplishment of the Urban Task Force was the development of the Campaign for Human Development, another great example of the Church's involvement. This was part of the Church's response. This indeed was a new step. It provided seed money to local grassroot organizations to begin programs of self-help and self-determination.

More importantly, the Campaign for Human Development was to be an education program, an instrument to raise the consciousness of American Catholics and to help form a public moral will that would generate a greater public response to the hellish cycle of poverty, because we knew even in the '60s that Galbraith had said, "Oh, yes, we're an affluent society." But many of us knew that if we were an affluent society, that was wrong because in our midst were many people living without hope, some because of poverty, some because of race, and some because of both.

By 1970, as part of my interest in the growing polarization between white, black and brown urban groups, I began to follow my own hunches that the traditional black-white human relations projects were insufficient to deal with the polarization, to deal with alienation. I began to look at 75–80 American cities to determine who the whites were who

lived next to the growing black and Hispanic urban communities.

I found those people who lived between the ghetto and the suburb, those people who were very heavily first, second and third generation Catholics, particularly of eastern and southern European background. They had refused, and our research since then has indicated that many of them did not want to and still do not want to leave the city, their communities, their neighborhoods. North Ward Newark, for instance, has over 300 social clubs, in its own area, something that could not be duplicated in terms of our suburban sprawl.

But neither my training nor my education prepared me to understand and appreciate the ethnic factor in urban society. Once I did, I planned a small workshop, the first Catholic-sponsored conference on the ethnic factor in urban society. My friends from the Washington Post thought I should have talked to the food editor. But most of my social activist and liberal friends, both in and out of the Church, were skeptical, sometimes hostile and more than cynical in their attitudes and comments at that workshop.

But I became convinced in going from city to city, neighborhood to neighborhood, that we could not understand the urban crisis unless we understood the ethnic and class factor in urban American life.

During 1970, Msgr. Higgins of the United States Catholic Conference, who was very supportive and encouraging, and I jointly prepared a Labor Day Statement which was one of the first Catholic documents to raise the question of the ethnic and class factor in terms of the urban crisis. This statement declared that we should not ignore the legitimate concerns of the white working class people who had remained in our cities.

Just prior to that, Dr. James Coleman, author of the famous Coleman Report, claimed that integration in our cities has failed because we have ignored some of the real concerns of the white working class. Statements such as these had been supportive of my initial hunch.

In 1971, with the assistance of the Ford Foundation, I established an independent, non-profit corporation with the blessing and approval of Cardinal O'Boyle. With some presumption on my part, I called that organization the National Center for Urban Ethnic Affairs. This center has since developed projects and research and development programs in 42 cities at a cost of more than $5 million.

These programs were designed to sensitize the public and private institutions to the ethnic factor in our urban society, and to seek out what little research and knowledge was available on first, second and third generation heavily ethnic, heavily Catholic people, who for some reason had remained in the middle of our cities, of a troubled urban America.

Since then we have done an extensive study with the Department of Commerce of 18 metropolitan areas to analyze who is left in the neighborhood. This study shows that white ethnic groups who share the cities with black and brown communities seem to be caught in the middle on every social, educational and economic scale.

We have also done studies of the major Fortune 500 corporations to determine the Polish, Italian, black and Latin representation on the boards of directors and the staffs of these corporations. While these groups make up 40 percent of the total population in the study area, they make up less than three percent of the top personnel of these corporations.

We have also become involved with the disinvestment practices that are destroying changing neighborhoods in most of our major urban areas. Banks and financial institutions take local savings out of a community—that is called disinvestment—and then "redline" this same community by failing to reinvest loans for repairs and home mortgages to low income and working class people in "changing neighborhoods."

I believe that no single issue has been more destructive of neighborhoods than the disinvestment and redlining practices of these financial institutions. They not only exacerbate tensions between racial and ethnic groups, but they destroy the viability and stability of older communities, making them unable to deal adequately with rapid social change.

This issue has now become a focus for national legislation. It has been outlined in the recent U.S. bishops' statement on housing. We need to develop a programmatic effort for and in almost every major city and parish neighborhood to fight disinvestment and to develop reinvestment strategies for urban neighborhoods.

Other programs within our own experience at the Center include: Firstly, work with the U.S. Civil Service Commission in training city officials to understand the role of racial and ethnic neighborhoods in the strengthening of cities. It is our contention that neighborhoods are the building blocks of the city, not the downtown renaissance, not the downtown malls, but the neighborhoods. If the neighborhoods are allowed to die, then cities also die with these neighborhoods. Then we are no longer able to meet and serve the changing needs of the community.

Secondly, with other government agencies, we have begun to develop a national project in terms of neighborhood revitalization for commercial and economic development at the neighborhood level. We believe there is an important role for the parish in the revitalization of our cities and neighborhoods.

Thirdly, at the same time we have worked with public officials in and out of government to develop the intercultural dimension of ethnic studies to a point that truly respects and reflects the diversity of our children and our nation. I believe very strongly that fear and polarization are by-products of the monocultural melting pot mentality of both the public and private school system. Because we have ignored cultural, racial, ethnic and class diversity, we have trained and educated a whole nation of people who are unable to deal with ethnic and racial diversity and second culture experience in their own neighborhoods and local parishes. We have grown up in a sense to become interculturally incompetent from both a personal and an professional perspective.

During the 1960s, many dioceses and parishes followed and supported the secular policies and programs developed by the government—urban renewal, model cities, housing, poverty programs, and civil rights. While the Church played an important role in developing urban programs, most of our Catholic urban activists seemed to step out of their own Catholic labor tradition, a tradition of our own working class. We seemed in the '60s to step out of that tradition and background of the '20s, '30s and '40s, and ignore the labor union movement and what it had done for poor people, blacks, whites and browns. Many seemed to ignore the legitimate needs of the lower middle class, heavily Catholic population that makes up such a large part of our urban society.

Following the secular model once more, we found ourselves, even in the Church, guilty of either catering to our people's fears from the right or scapegoating our people's concerns from the left. In a sense we ignored or neglected, for the most part, the essential ministry to our own people's alienation. We did this even though we knew that, for the most part, working class people were indeed more supportive of minimum wage legislation, more supportive of health care, more supportive of housing and educational programs than our more affluent bankers, lawyers, doctors and businessmen and their national lobbying organizations.

I was reminded of this recently when I was in Detroit and called my mother on a Sunday. She was 82 years old the other day, and she asked what was this Third World. I said, "What do you mean, Mom?"

She said, "Am I allowed to eat grapes? Am I allowed to eat lettuce?"

I said, "What do you mean?"

She said, "One of your friends was here, the one that was here last year and said don't eat grapes."

I said, "Yes."

"Remember the last year or year before he said we're not allowed to eat lettuce?"

I said, "Yes."

"He was here this Sunday saying I'm responsible for the Third World."

I said, "What are you talking about?" I said, "What do you mean?"

She said, "I know you have trouble with limbo and purgatory and all those things, but," she says, "I don't know anything about the Third World." She said, "I just believe in heaven and hell."

In a sense, I believe that somehow, in some way, we should not cater to our people's fears.

In a sense the politics of innovation of the '60s was defined very much in terms of class and race. Coming out of a Vietnam war and into an economic recession in a time of rapid social change, America was exacerbated by economic, social, cultural and increasing political alienation. We found ourselves in a constant battle of values and in conflict with the first-changing American culture.

As Bruno Bettleheim put it in a sensitive paper on the problem of the generation, "Whenever the older generation has lost its bearings the younger generation is lost with it." This reminds us of Simone Weil's warnings that uprooted people tend to uproot others.

And perhaps it reminds me, too, of the seminary where I go once in a while, that the major subject with kids these days seems to be death and dying. That kind of bothers me because I think that we should be talking about celebrating life as well as being concerned in such a

major way with death and dying. Does that mean our young people are on the battlelines with a conflict of culture?

Where do we go from here? The Department of Housing and Urban Development admits that there is no national urban policy. Many in Washington are now calling for national economic planning because we have none. We are in a tough situation.

Take employment. You have five people looking for three jobs. If those five people were white, you'd have trouble. If those five people looking for three jobs are black, brown or white, men or women, you'd have trouble.

Housing is the same way. In the next ten years we expect to build perhaps only 18 million units of housing, but we'll have 28 million families looking for and competing for those 18 million units. Twenty-eight families looking at 18 units. That's going to exacerbate whatever we mean by black, white, or brown, ethnic and cultural differences.

Basically, our urban policies have destroyed neighborhoods where the real social action takes place between people of different ethnic, racial and cultural classes.

As we enter this bicentennial era, America—and this includes American Indians, Hispanics, blacks, and the children of affluence who have formed the counter-culture—is beginning to ask: "Who am I and who are we as Americans?" And I believe that we as American Catholics will also he asking: "Who am I and who are we as American Catholics?" We desperately need a new ideal for ourselves and a new idea of ourselves. We do not have a national sense of purpose.

We do not have a national sense of identity. We do not have a national sense of commitment. And we hardly have a national sense of patriotism.

The Church has an important role and can provide an important model to help America legitimize her own cultural, racial and ethnic diversity as she looks for a new idea and a new vision by which to define herself. The Church can do this by courageously following the lead of the 1919 statement by the American bishops, "Program of Social Reconstruction," and developing a new pastoral urban social policy which responds to America's intercultural pluralism.

Intercultural pluralism must be a dimension of this new urban social policy. A new social policy must be intercultural to the extent that it includes the genius of American ethnic, racial and cultural experience. It must encourage ideas, programs, and projects that enhance cultural differentiation, and ideas, programs and projects that cultivate the interplay of possibilities that would be valuable to all Americans from each ethnic, racial or cultural group.

In going away from the melting pot, this redefinition means America must see itself as the most ethnical, racially, culturally, regional lifestyle, pluralistic country.

In the words of Rene Dubos, a very famous anthropologist: "Although the persistence of human diversity has many drawbacks, it also has beneficial consequences. It creates social tensions which lead to a strenuous quest for attitudes and laws designed to give equal rights to all citizens—irrespective of religion and race, of ethnicity, of culture, of age and sex. Human diversity makes tolerance more than a virtue; it makes tolerance a requirement for survival."

I would like to make the following five suggestions for the development of a new intercultural, pastoral urban social policy that might come out of the bicentennial hearings. At least it ought to be part of the discussion.

One, we must begin to develop our own American theology of pluralism based upon our own Catholic experience as individuals and collectively as an American Church, including rights and cultures and ethnicity and race. We can no longer import German or Dutch or even Third World liberation theology. Later on, perhaps, when we understand and analyze our own American experience, we can dialogue with the diversity and pluralism of the universal Church.

Secondly, we need to review and understand what has happened to us as we moved from being aliens to being naturalized, to being "Americanized." American Catholic young people will be facing new challenges and new cultural conflicts as they strive to find out what it means to be third and fourth and fifth generation. What does it mean to be Catholic? What does it mean to be Catholic in America?

We need to understand, as Cardinal Dearden said earlier, the importance of our heritage, our identity, our values, and our faith. We know very little about the persistence of the ethnic factor in our own multi-ethnic families and society. We must take this opportunity to go beyond ethnic chauvinism, get to know "our own story," and share our experience with one another. We must respect our cultural diversity and then, together, not separately, find our unity.

As a young student who got involved in a counter-culture said to me, "I want to be somebody." He said, "I'd rather be German bread, Greek bread, or brown bread, or whatever, but not this tasteless, odorless, Americanized Wonder Bread which is a symbol of American life." He said, "This blandness reminds us of the emptiness of American society."

Our young people, the so-called flower children, were looking not for more cars, not for bigger houses, not for swimming pools. Symbolically, be it Patty Hearst, or be it anyone else, these children of the counter-culture, the children of the best and brightest, these children rebelled against materialism. They rebelled and began to look for values. They began to look for flour for the soul. So, our own American Catholic children will be next in the '80s in terms of struggling to decide what it means to be Catholic and what it means to be American.

Thirdly, in a sense the future of Catholicism and its healthiness in this country means the development of an intercultural ministry that goes beyond the melting pot to a legitimate cultural diversity. We must find out how to minister to the most ethnically, racially, culturally, and regionally diverse country in the world. We must not just add a bilingual of bicultural program of this group or that group. We must develop an intercultural ministry that includes the personal and professional competency that helps us to deal with second culture and multi-cultural experiences.

I believe this is perhaps what Archbishop Jadot was alluding to when he suggested, at the first of these bicentennial hearings, that "we must respect cultural traditions, cultural values, local values, practical ways of life. But this entails more than a passive respect. What we must provide is support, upbuilding and help." This, the apostolic delegate indicated, is a requirement of "cultural justice." This idea brings me to my next point.

Four, we need a new sense of cultural justice that not only affects and demands respect for the background of the American Indians, blacks, Chicanos, but also of European ethnics, and would foster equality in the transmission of their children and cultural values as a matter of giving them what is due them.

What I am talking about is not just a passing benefit, but a right of each individual, as Vatican Council II clearly states: "Energetic effort must also be expended to make everyone conscious of his right to culture and of the duty he has to develop himself culturally and to assist others." (Pastoral Constitution on the Church in the Modern World)

The Council also warns against cultural discrimination. I believe instead of fighting the first amendment Church and State battle for Catholic schools, we ought to take a new tactic. We ought to say our schools are valuable and important in a cultural democracy, that it is our right to transmit our values and culture and story to our children, that it is a cultural right in a cultural democracy, not in a mono-cultural, homogeneous kind of nation that has given us negative sensitivities on the question of abortions or schools. The United States Supreme Court would have to deal with us. We're one fourth of the people. It would have to deal with us in an intercultural way.

We must in our schools create models of intercultural education. What is a good school? A good school should be a place that our people know it so well, and not the tragedy of the situation that happened in Boston and other places. A good school might be creating a new kind of image that perhaps children, rich and poor, black and white, might share their cultural heritage, and we might not be wiped out in developing a homogenous melting pot kind of Miss America, Miss Virginia Slims, Marlboro Man, empty type of person.

We need to develop an intercultural program that would lead the public sector as well into a new area of understanding and appreciation between ethnically, racially and culturally diverse people because we already live in a world that is an intercultural village.

Fifthly, what is most important is that we reexamine the role of the parish in neighborhood revitalization. We need to reaffirm that the parish has a key role in the future of the neighborhood. To rebuild the parish neighborhoods is to rebuild and revitalize the city.

Pope Paul VI said, "There is an urgent need to remake, at the level of the street, of the neighborhood or of the great agglomerative dwellings of the social fabric whereby man may be able to develop the needs of his or her personality. Centers of special interest and of culture must be created or developed at the community and parish levels with different forms of associations, recreation centers, and spir-

itual and community gatherings where the individual can escape from isolation and form a new fraternal relationship."

"To build up the city, the place where men and their expanded communities exist, to create new modes of neighborliness and responsibility for this collective future, which is foreseen as difficult, is the task in which Christians must share." ("A Call to Action," May 1971)

I claim that this task can best and most effectively be done through the parish, as a catalyst. The parish has an important liturgical and sacramental focus, but as a pastoral institution, it must also have a clearly visible social focus. If the neighborhood dies, the parish dies. Again and again, I repeat this: The parish will die. And if more and more parishes and more and more neighborhoods die, our cities will continue to die. You will find it even more difficult as we enter a new era of American apartheid.

The parish must revitalize the neighborhood not only around the altar where we are one in the unity of the eucharist, but the parish must develop a new sense of community development. The parish must become a catalyst for revitalizing neighborhoods in order to help them with rapid social change, racial and cultural change.

The parish and the neighborhood are partners to the family, and are the size and scope necessary for creating a sense of community that can be the real building block of the cities. Cities are so large and so complicated by themselves, but by developing a new sense of parish-neighborhood revitalization we may begin to provide healthy neighborhoods which can be the nucleus for rebuilding our cities. Otherwise, no one will be able to escape to the distant suburbs or rural areas and not be affected by the creeping cancer of urban decay.

In developing whatever might come of this bicentennial hearing by way of some future pastoral and social policy program, I think we have to have all the courage and daring of our own Catholic past. We need, of course, to take strength from the great social statements of Popes Leo XIII, John XXIII, and Paul VI, but also people like Cardinal Gibbons and Bishop Haas, P. Murray, John Ryan, Cesar Chavez, and many, many others.

Particularly, I look at that landmark of the U.S. Catholic bishops that I hope the bicentennial hearings will equal— that you will put together somehow in the Detroit Conference next year a document—that statement of 1919, John Ryan's great document, "Program for Social Reconstruction."

Now is the time for a similar vision. Now is the time for the American Catholic Church to rediscover its own identity and offer itself as a model for American cultural diversity. Then we can believe that justice is a constituent part of our gospel message. Then we can celebrate together what it really means to be American and Catholic. Then we can celebrate together the variants of our common humanity as we struggle for the twin goals of economic justice and for a cultural democracy in our efforts to provide liberty and justice for all. Thank you very much.

BISHOP MCNICHOLAS: Monsignor, I have two brief questions: Number one, the vast majority of Catholics who live in the suburbs are removed from the eth-

nicity and the ethnic background by several generations, and even more by their custom of living. They really are Americanized. What are the values in the Church preaching ethnicity and the statements you made to this group that make up a large part of our dioceses?

The second one, and I ask this from my own ignorance, have you personally, or the National Center for Urban Affairs, taken a position on the question of busing for racial integration?

MSGR. BARONI: Both are very difficult questions but important ones, I'm sure.

The question of assimilation, of course, is a very real one, it's true. Look what happened to the counter-culture children of the 1960s who came to Washington in what I call their Brooks Brothers jeans, sensitive about war and peace. They were very upset at having two cars and two swimming pools. In a sense, they had everything materially, but they were looking for values; they were looking for a way of life, and that's a religious question.

I just happen to believe that a sense of story in our own tradition and the tradition of others related to a faith which sometimes asks, "Why are we eating this meal tonight?"

There has to be a sense of identity. My father's most important concern was that we would certainly be Americans; but he always wanted to make sure we knew who we were. He'd always ask, "What is your name? What's your identity?" I think that it's not a sense of romantics, a sense of going back to something in the past, but it's knowing who our parents and grandparents were.

I have a hunch, Bishop, that if you give

up your identity with your group, you'll also give up the values and faith of that group.

I was at Harvard last year in the Kennedy School of Government, in the graduate school, in the Institute of Politics, and I was often asked why I was still a Catholic, suggesting that I should probably be past that. I just cannot see giving up my identity.

Abramson, at the University of Connecticut, says there are a lot of standards about who are the best Catholics, but when it comes down to it, he talks particularly about the Spanish-Americans. To the degree that they are sensitive to being Spanish, that's the degree they'll always be strongly Catholic. That's Abramson's thesis.

I'm saying somehow we have to put that together in terms of our own story.

Now the question of busing is much more complicated and much more difficult. But somehow, in some way, I believe this is going to be a big Catholic issue, not only in Boston but in northern cities. Somehow, some say, I think there is a great hypocrisy in that question. My thesis would be to put the PhDs on the first bus, the MAs on the second bus, and then I think working class people would follow.

That may sound facetious, but there is a lot of economic segregation.

I remember Gonzaga never had a white child living within 16 miles of it, but people walked three miles to get to Gonzaga. Sometimes people took their father's car to Gonzaga, and the father took the bus to work.

We valued education, but it is whose kids you go to school with that counts.

I think the burden is unfairly upon

poor blacks and working class whites. And unless we deal with the hypocrisy of the better educated intellectual community, who must share the burden of busing, then I don't think we can ask our people to do any more than the people with the best education.

We have two real issues here: rapid social change, and who's going to shape and who's going to share the burden of that change.

I think our people will be fair and I think our people will follow because they've been taught very well about what's a good school. It's a good school where the doctors go, the lawyers go. I don't think we can ask our people to share lousy schools, be they black, or be they white, by themselves.

MR. FINN: Msgr. Baroni, since my question may seem hostile, I should suggest that my intent is sympathetic. As a parent of immigrants and a native of Gary, Indiana, which is one of the cities that has been torn by the strife, I've learned a lot from what you've said.

I would like you to answer why, if we have a culture which is so homogeneous, that we would describe as America, it would necessarily be as bland as Wonder Bread? Why could we not have a culture in which one could say I am Catholic and American, rather than I am Catholic and Italian-American, Catholic and Irish-American, Catholic and Spanish-American?

I'm asking you what that intercultural dimension, to use your term, is, that would be different from a homogenized culture which might be rich and profound and distinct as others, say European cultures, are.

MSGR. BARONI: One of the best pastors I had, Msgr. O'Leary, was the chancellor in the Sacred Heart parish, my first parish. I believed in being all-American. As he described the parish, he would say, "The German people are great; they give money to the Church. The Irish are great; they give money to the priest. The Italians are great, but they sing in the choir."

We have done studies ourselves to show that there is a difference between different groups, even in the fourth and fifth generation, in alcohol, in drugs.

My father wants to go to the hospital to die. Other groups want to go to the hospital because they have all the equipment there.

So, we don't need health care even in the fourth and fifth generations. There are nuances that are always in the heads of how people describe themselves. But our studies about children from third, fourth generations from Polish, Italian and Irish backgrounds in terms of drugs are very different from others.

My point, though, is, of course, that even in one family there are mixed ethnics; you know, Irish-Italian, and that's a new type of ethnicity. You know, ethnicity will never go away. Take the Welsh in England, the Scotch in Ireland, the Belgians in the Basques.

We're not the European kind of ethnic. We share an American culture, a fantastic American culture. But, you know, there is a difference. The Irish, I think, send their kids mostly to Catholic schools. I went two weeks to Catholic school to make my First Communion, and I came home with a note my name should be changed to Kevin. My father said, "There is no way. He doesn't look like Kevin."

Then we had a bishop named Gilfoyle who wanted us to take the pledge at twelve. Again, my father had a problem. We drink wine with our first glass of water. My father also kept asking, what was the sermon today, and how many times the sermon was about sex and drinking and Communism. He said, "Sex and drinking? That's not my problem. That's the American Catholic Church."

Consider the bankruptcy of our culture. Take novels. Now, who writes the novels? Which groups came in when the Kennedy Center was being done up for the performing arts, theater, dance, opera? Jewish and black groups. Because they had an identity. What I'm saying is we have to do our own *Portnoy's Complaint*.

BISHOP HEAD: You made reference to disinvestment and redlining, and we are all very interested that the redlining bill goes through and is signed. You made reference to redlining and disinvestment as the cause, one of the major causes, of deterioration.

Would you not rather say that they are the causes for the perpetuation of deterioration of neighborhoods rather than the causes of it?

MSGR. BARONI: Well, perhaps both. There are some studies now. The center was involved in developing legislation with Senator Proxmire on that bill.

Disclosure is not going to be the only answer. In the North Ward, some people asked should we decide to stay to try to work together, live together. We decided to stay.

There are counter incentives both in

the public and private sectors. As the neighborhood goes from the decaying Central Ward, from a deteriorated neighborhood to a declining neighborhood, this cancer keeps spreading.

I'm saying there can be cancer on the toe and there can be cancer on the arm. We have to deal with it wherever our parishes are, in these changing or older neighborhoods, or else we will die. Let me put it this way: Somebody decides I need new shingles and a new roof. They go down to the savings and loan and they say: "We live on Collingwood in Murray Hill." And they are told, "That's a changing neighborhood. We don't make loans anymore, even of your own money." So, you decide, "I'm going to move out." But the person next to you says: "If you stay, I'm going to stay." You create a psychology. You have to reinvest in the community.

When Jones' Drug Store closes up and Smith's Market closes up, even though your house may be perfectly beautiful six blocks away, you say, "Oh, the neighborhood is going. I've got to leave."

We're seeing this with HUD. HUD is now the tenth largest city in the country in terms of the houses they own in cities like Detroit and other places.

So that there are a lot of factors here, but let's look at the counter incentives that make a neighborhood psychologically say something is wrong. How do you turn that around and reinvest and deal with those senses of security, self-sufficiency, that are desperately needed in creating the community?

There is so much community in these neighborhoods. We need to revitalize

them as part of a healthy nucleus. We have got to see what we can do in the suburbs and see what we can do in other central wards.

I do believe the question of disinvestment is not only money, it's a psychological kind of thing. We have buildings that could help meet the needs of new people, but if you don't have a healthy neighborhood, it can't deal with the needs either of the older people or the new people and we end up like the South Bronx, large sections of inner cities without governments. And that's dangerous and that's disasterous.

CARDINAL DEARDEN: Thank you, Msgr. Baroni.

CARDINAL DEARDEN: We'll return now with the series of briefer presentations such as we had in this afternoon's session. The first presentation is that of Gerard Muench.

MR. MUENCH: I'm a member of St. John the Baptist Church of the Ukrainian rite here in Newark. I've been working with young people all my adult life, both as a teacher in the Archdiocese of Newark and as a counselor. For the last 15 years I've been counseling the children of the Ukrainian community here in Newark.

I would like to address the committee this evening on the problems of the white ethnic youth in the city. These are the youth who are made to feel like second-class citizens because they speak a foreign language in their homes. These are the youth who are made fun of when they must pronounce their last names. These are the youth who are thought of as being different.

Look at the youth today. The upper

middle-class youth are having an identity problem. They don't know their background. They have no real cultural ties. So they don't know where to look. They turn to the superficial culture of long hair and rock music, or even more tragically, to the drug culture. The black and Puerto Rican youth often feel they are not a part of society, and so they drop out.

The one group of youth not having these problems is the ethnic youths. They know who they are and what their culture is. They also know their value system.

Who are these white ethnic youths? They're the children of the non-English speaking immigrants. A large part make up the blue-collar class in this country, but the greater part are Catholic and they live in their own ghettos.

But let us look at some of the problems these young people do have. They look around to see the student radicals, and many of the radical clergy for what they really are. They see these phonies in their poor boy outfits as rich kids playing in the gutter, making fun of the values of ethnic groups. These values of education, ownership and cleanliness are sacred to the ethnics, and they feel hurt and angry.

Another of their values is respect. They see ridicule on all sides. Imagine how they feel when they see adults going to communion with their hands in their pockets! As for family life, it's made fun of on all sides.

Remember also that the ethnics are usually found at the edge of the black ghetto. They're used by the suburbanites as a buffer against the blacks. They're accused of being racists. But, remember,

racism is not their invention. They found it here. Why should they pay the price for America's guilt? Their ancestors owned no slaves. Many ceased being serfs themselves only in the last 100 years.

These young people also resent the moral pressure to abandon their own traditions and language in order to reap the higher rewards of the culture of quantity, replacement and mobility.

The church in this country has put much of this pressure on our youth. It's been closing their national churches. It has even made fun of many national religious customs. The church in America has never tried to solve the problem of preserving diversity. What has the church done for the ethnic youth? It has taken away their national customs and replaced them with guitar music and prayer meetings.

Why doesn't the church let them keep their native customs? Why can't you bishops encourage the different national devotions?

Especially hurt by this attitude of the Latin church are those youths who happen to be members of the Eastern churches. I have worked with youth in our parish for 15 years, and never once were we invited by a Latin-rite church to share our ideas with them. We have been invited by Protestants and Othodox youths. The CYO can take on numerous causes, but never once did I hear them ask for liberty and justice for the Ukrainian Church.

What have you bishops for these ethnic youths? Are you not their fathers, also?

To sum up my thoughts, I think basically I have been saying this: Perhaps you have not been fair to the youth of our ethnic groups. You have pampered the children of the rich; you have consoled the children of the poor; but you have made fun of the ethnic youth.

How has this group paid back the church? They're the youth who are entering the religious orders. They are the youth who are refilling the seminaries. They are the youth who work days so they can attend college at night. These are the youth who can't afford a Catholic college. The scholarships go to the "needy." These are the youth who look forward to having a family and owning a house.

What I ask is that you help these youth keep their culture, their heritage. I ask you to help them to get scholarships to Catholic schools and colleges. I ask you to accept them for what they are, your children. I ask you to stop playing politics—to stop pushing these youths aside for the rich liberals. I ask you to give liberty and justice to the ethnic youth.

CARDINAL DEARDEN: Do any of the panelists have questions?

BISHOP DOUGHERTY: You seem to fault bishops exclusively.

MR. MUENCH: No.

BISHOP DOUGHERTY: So, the question is do you fault the bishops exclusively?

MR. MUENCH: No. I'm sorry if that was the impression. I think I fault the whole Christian community.

CARDINAL DEARDEN: Since there are no further questions from the panel, we have one from the floor.

FATHER MARTIN: I am Father Martin,

O. S. E. of Holy Faith Monastery, Clifton, N.J.

I wish to throw in this correction. I immigrated to this country as a seven-year-old boy from Italy. From Assisi, Italy we immigrated to Trenton. I attended St. Joseph's School. We moved to Philadelphia, attended St. Rita's School. We came to Newark. I was taught in Philadelphia by St. Francis, in Trenton by the Sopina Sisters. When we came to Newark, I attended Mt. Carmel School by the same sisters, the Sopina Sisters. Then the school was demolished.

In every school I attended, we had both languages. Italian one hour in the afternoon. When the school was demolished those who lived on this side of the Pennsylvania Railroad had to go to St. John's on Mulbern Street, and those who were living on the other side of the railroad went to St. James.

CARDINAL DEARDEN: Father, do you have a question?

FATHER MARTIN: What I'm trying to correct is that I got a scholarship. You say there were no scholarships. I got a scholarship for half tuition at St. Benedict's. I'm a graduate of St. Benedict's.

When I was a freshman at St. Benedict's, Bishop Mugavero, who is here present, was a senior. I went to Seton Hall. I didn't pay a penny. I got the scholarship. There were many, many scholarships given.

CARDINAL DEARDEN: Do you want to comment on that?

MR. MUENCH: I think the point has been made clearly enough. I realize there have been some scholarships.

CARDINAL DEARDEN: Thank you.

## Lee Iacocca, Remarks to the Ethnic Heritage Council of the Pacific Northwest, 1984

*Lee Iacocca, the child of Italian immigrants, was something of a business* wunderkind *in the 1960s and 1970s, serving first as president of Ford Motor Company and then as president and chair of the board at Chrysler. In the early 1980s President Reagan appointed him chairman of the Statue of Liberty—Ellis Island Commission. The commission was charged with the renovation of the statue and restoration of the Ellis Island immigrant reception facility, which had fallen into ruin. In this speech to the Ethnic Heritage Council of the Pacific Northwest in Seattle in 1984, Iacocca invokes the heroic epic of nineteenth- and twentieth-century immigration to America, implies that it is a foundational myth akin to the pilgrims or the founding fathers, and hails Ellis Island and the statue as the principal shrine of this myth.*

Source: Matthew Seeger, ed., "I Gotta Tell You" (Detroit: Wayne University Press, 1994), pp. 316–323.

## SEATTLE, WASHINGTON, OCTOBER 20, 1984

Thank you. Good evening ladies and gentleman.

It's always a real pleasure to come to the great Pacific Northwest. Thank you for inviting me. Originally, I was going to say "Washington." But I'm so tired of going to the other Washington, I couldn't muster the strength to say it.

I first want to thank all of you for your support of the Statue of Liberty-Ellis Island project.

I also want to congratulate you on forming this Ethnic Heritage Council four years ago. I think it's important for all of us to hold on to our own heritage . . . whatever it is. But we ought to share it, too. And learn more about other people's heritage. You're helping each other do that.

We started doing that in Detroit a few years ago. During the summer we have a series of ethnic festivals on the riverfront. One week the Germans take over, the next the Polish, and then the Italians, and the Greeks, and so on. And everybody's welcome. You get a sense of diversity and unity at the same time, and I guess that's what America is all about.

I know that's true of this group. You're coming together tonight to pay tribute to a most important symbol of our unity as a nation—the Statue of Liberty. And yet the diversity is just as evident. When I was invited, they sent me some background material on your organization. It had the names of board members and committee heads. There's a Filipino named Koslosky . . . a Norwegian named Morrison . . . and a Japanese named Sanchez. And then there's Carin Jacroux. That sounds awfully *French* to me, but she says she's *German,* she works at the *Austrian* Consulate, and she's here representing an *Italian* club!

Now, come on. That's carrying things a little too far! Maybe she just likes going to lots of parties. If she lived in Detroit, she'd have to spend the whole summer camped out at the ethnic festivals on the riverfront!

Well, it's fun to dress up in the old costumes . . . to dance to the old music . . . to eat the food and listen to stories about the old country. That's important, and I hope we never lose it.

But when a bunch of us got together a couple of years ago to do something about the Statue of Liberty and Ellis Island, the mood was pretty serious. The Statue looks the same from a distance, but inside her bones are breaking apart. Pieces have actually fallen off and washed up in New Jersey.

Ellis Island is only a half a mile away, and it's a mess. It's been shut down for thirty years now. I don't know how many of you have been there, but to me the place is haunted with 17 million ghosts. That's how many people came through there between 1892 and 1954. Every time I walk into the Great Hall, I feel like I'm in church.

When President Reagan asked me to be chairman of a committee to restore both the Statue and Ellis Island, I was honored. Believe me, I had my hands full at Chrysler, and I wasn't looking for any hobbies. But this is something I had to do. It's a labor of love for me.

Both my parents came through Ellis Island . . . my dad twice. The first time was in 1902. He was twelve years old and scared to death. The second time was in 1921, after he'd returned to Italy to bring back a bride . . . my mother.

So, my roots run deep—and my attachment is great—as I'm sure it is with so many of you in this room.

Well, the restoration is a big job. The statue—for those of you who haven't been in it—is basically a copper skin about as thick as a half-dollar, connected to a structural framework by iron straps. When you put iron next to copper and add a little moisture, you have a battery.

That causes galvanic corrosion. The copper skin is in pretty good shape, but the iron straps have just about been eaten away. We're replacing two thousand of them, this time with an alloy that won't react with the copper.

We also have to strengthen the right arm . . . the one that holds the torch. It was damaged during World War I when a munitions plant blew up a few miles away in New Jersey. If the plant was sabotaged—as many people believe—then she was one of the casualties of that war.

The torch itself has been removed, and it will have to be replaced. The new one will be identical, of course, and the old one will be displayed somewhere— I don't know where yet—maybe it will move around the country. By the way, you Huskie fans will be able to see it on New Year's Day in the Rose Bowl Parade.

Ellis Island is an empty shell now. But in two years the Great Hall will be rehabilitated and some of the first exhibits will be in place. By 1992, when the project is completed, Ellis Island will be not just a museum but a living monument to the whole immigration experience in America. You'll enjoy visiting it. It will freeze a moment in time. You'll see it as they saw it. You'll experience their music and literature, and their food and arts and crafts. It will be sort of an ethnic Williamsburg—but not commercial.

Coincidentally, 1992 will be the five hundredth anniversary of Christopher Columbus's first voyage to the New World. That will be a big day for *all* Americans, but especially for Italians, because he was Italian. And I guess for the Spanish, too, because they put up all the dough. See, cooperation started early in this country.

The whole project—the statue and Ellis Island—will cost about $230 million. That sounds like a lot, but it's only a buck for each American . . . the price of a pack of cigarettes. None of that will come from public funds. All of it will be from private individuals, groups like yours, and companies, big and small. We're already over a $120 million in cash and pledges.

Your participation out here has been tremendous. You just saw me get a check for a quarter of a million from the employees at Boeing.

I want to thank all the employees at Boeing for that.

And you may not know this, but the biggest single corporate sponsor in the country is the Chateau St. Michelle winery here in Washington . . . and get this—they've already pledged five million bucks! So my thanks to all the people at St. Michelle.

We're looking for a million and a half from people in Washington, not counting corporate contributions. And a million from Oregon.

So far, we've got about 50 million committed from companies around the country, and a little more than that from individuals and groups—the grass roots effort!

We've got almost 2 million bucks from school kids sending us their nickels and dimes. I opened my mail last Monday and there was a letter from a kid. He said: "Dear Mr. Iacocca, here's my allowance for this week." And there were two $1 bills attached. He said, "Spend it wisely!"

The kids are fantastic. You know, kids are always raising money for something . . . a new school bus, football uniforms, a class trip. But this project has really caught on. They're washing cars, and having bake sales. You name it.

But that's the magic—and the fun of it. Everybody is getting into the act. Right here in Seattle, the Bellevue Terrace Nursing Center is sponsoring Wheel-a-thons, and they've raised thousands of dollars.

One guy rode a motorized surfboard over three thousand miles to raise money.

How about this—we even got $2,000 from the Hell's Angels! Leather jackets, motorcycles, and all—would you believe underneath those guys are patriots?

And when people send in money, they always seem to write a letter. I wish you could read them. People who are immigrants say, "America has been good to me, and I just want to pay a little of it back." The second-generation people say, "Here's something for my mom and dad . . . for all they went through for me." And you can almost see the tear-stains on the letters.

One day a guy came into my office and gave me a million dollars. Right out of the blue. He told me about how his family had come here poor, like everybody else. And obviously they did well . . . they got rich. And the man felt a big debt to this country. All he asked was that I never reveal his name. So, if anybody here has a million—I promise to keep you anonymous, too.

Maybe the most touching letter of all came from a man in Poland. He sent some silver certificates worth about $2 for the Statue, and asked for a picture of what he called "This beautiful symbol."

And what a beautiful symbol she is! To us, and to the rest of the world.

I think it's important to remember that we didn't build her. It wasn't our idea. A hundred years ago, French schoolkids collected pennies to build Miss Liberty, just like our kids are doing today. The idea began right after the Civil War. Some people in France were as thankful as we were that this country . . . this experiment in liberty . . . had held together through its darkest hours. They were thankful because in this American experiment they saw an example for the rest of the world. It was an example of hope, and they built the statue as a symbol of that hope.

The greatest gift, as Robert Burns said, is to see ourselves as others see us. It took the French to provide us with this "beautiful symbol." But I wonder if any of us here tonight can see what the Statue of Liberty stands for quite as clearly as that man in Poland. It seems freedom means more if you don't have it. If you do, you just take it for granted.

Americans a hundred years ago didn't really appreciate the importance of that symbol. After the French sent the statue over, our government refused to put up the money for a base to put it on. Some people started a fund drive, but it didn't work . . . until Joseph Pulitzer got involved. He was an immigrant from Hungary, and he owned a newspaper in New York. He made the Statue a major cause. He especially went after the silk stocking crowd in New York, and embarrassed them into contributing.

So even from the beginning, Americans didn't really appreciate what they had . . . what the Lady in the Harbor stood for.

To really understand, you may have to look through somebody else's eyes. Think back with me for a minute what it must have meant to my parents, or yours, or your grandparents . . . to all those 17 million people who came during the big immigration wave.

First, they left their families and their homes. Most knew they'd never get back to see them again. What makes people do that? Courage . . . desperation . . . determination to be free . . . wanting to give their kids a decent life? All of those, I guess. But what a wrenching thing it must have been!

And then seventeen or eighteen days on the ocean . . . down below in steerage . . . where almost everybody was seasick. My mother got typhoid fever. They had two to three crowded, smelly weeks to think about what they'd left, and wonder if just half the stories about America were really true.

None of them remembered that boat ride very fondly. But they remembered the day they got to New York. They all came up on deck, dressed up in their best clothes because this was the biggest day of their lives. They stood on the deck with just those clothes on their back, and maybe a suitcase with a rope around it. And the first thing they saw was the Statue of Liberty.

It was shiny then, because the copper hadn't turned green yet. And they could see it gleaming in the harbor from miles out.

I don't care how sick they were, or

how scared, or how lonely, the sight of the Lady saying "welcome" made the whole thing worth it. They never forgot that . . . or what happened next.

If the statue was a symbol of hope, Ellis Island was the reality. They called it "The Island of Tears," and for good reason.

They were herded off the boat into this gigantic building . . . thousands in a single day. It looked like a cathedral, but inside it was a cattle barn. Everybody was jammed in long lines, hanging onto each other, and to the kids, and to the suitcase with the rope around it.

The sheer numbers meant nothing was personal. There were quick medical exams, and some of them were humiliating. They had tags hung around their necks, and they didn't know what they meant. An immigration agent asked them thirty questions in two minutes . . . in a language they didn't understand.

Twenty percent of them were detained on the island for medical or legal reasons, sometimes for days, sometimes for weeks. One in fifty was put back on the boat for Europe. For them the dream was over!

Ellis Island, was reality, all right . . . an almost brutal counterpoint to that hope they were feeling just a few hours before. Earlier this year, a man wrote a letter to the *New York Times*. He called Ellis Island a "charnal house" and said we shouldn't try to restore it we should tear it down. He said it was a symbol "best forgotten."

Well, he's wrong. We need that symbol as much as we do the statue. Because that's where the story really began.

That's where they were really introduced to America. They took a ferry across to the Battery and—guess what—they found the streets were *not* paved with gold. They were on their own. The adventure was over. Now they had to go to work. Now they had to build something—with brains, and strong backs, and sheer guts.

They went to work in factories, and in the mines, and on the railroad . . . generally at the lowest jobs those always went to the new arrivals. But in just a couple of decades they built an Industrial America that was the wonder of the world!

They also built homes and neighborhoods and churches. Their kids went to college, fought in our wars, and became leaders in their communities.

So both the statue and Ellis Island are important symbols, One of the shining hope for freedom and a better life. And one of the sacrifice, and the suffering, and the plain hard work that turned that hope into reality.

We need them both.

Almost half of the people in America today are direct descendants of those 17 million whose first glimpses of America were those two symbols.

But they are equally important to *every* American, whether his forebears came three hundred years ago to find religious freedom;

Whether they came from Ireland during the potato famine;

Or from Germany and Eastern Europe to escape their endless wars;

Or from Scandinavia to farm the prairies, or to cut the timber here in the Northwest;

Or from China and Japan to *this* coast . . . or north from Mexico . . . or south from Canada.

The Statue of Liberty stands for the same thing for all of us . . . even those whose ancestors were brought here in chains . . . as slaves. Maybe she is especially important for them.

And the process goes on and on, doesn't it? Let me say again how much I appreciate this beautiful painting that was given to me tonight. Ms. Houng and thousands of other Vietnamese who've risked so much to get here are telling us that everything Miss Liberty has stood for is still alive today. And I think we need them to remind us.

We've let some of our symbols decay, but now we're repairing them. But in the last twenty years or so, we've seen America jerked in a dozen confusing directions, so that some believe that even the basic values behind those symbols are decaying as well.

We've seen our leaders shot down . . . our cities burn in racial violence . . . a president thrown out in disgrace . . . and a war that forced us—painfully—to confront our own limitations.

We've also seen the economic order in the world change. And for the first time in our memory, we are no longer clearly in command of it.

Our own economic base is changing, too. Our heavy industry is shrinking. The jobs that for so long were filled by the newest Americans are moving out of America to the Far East and the Third World.

Some people are even beginning to say that America can't compete anymore—that we can't cut the mustard.

Well, I've spent a lot of time on the Statue of Liberty and Ellis Island. And other people are working *full*-time on it. Millions of people have sent in money. This thing has caught on because these symbols still stand for something beautiful.

We aren't spending $230 million just so the Statue won't fall into the harbor and become a hazard to navigation. We aren't fixing up Ellis Island so people will have a nice place to go on Sunday afternoon. We're doing it because we want to remember, and to honor, and to save the basic values that made America great.

Values like hard work, dignified by decent pay. Like the courage to risk everything and start over. Like the wisdom to adapt to change. And maybe most of all—self-confidence. To believe in ourselves. Nothing is more important than that.

The symbols mean nothing if the values aren't there.

I've heard it said—and so have you— that our kids will be the first generation of Americans that will have to settle for less than their parents had.

I pray to God our kids don't believe that. But I can see how they might. Look at the size of the public debt we're saddling them with. We're paying our way today by mortgaging their futures. Our parents didn't do that to us. And they'd be ashamed of *us* for doing it to *our* kids.

And look at all the whining they're starting to hear about how America can't compete anymore. That's what everybody told us at Chrysler five years ago, remember? How many of you remember the *Wall Street Journal* telling Chrysler to quit fighting—and to "die with dignity"?

Well, we didn't see a hell of a lot of dignity in six hundred thousand people losing their jobs. So we did what we had to do—including a lot of painful things. We practically had to start over. But we survived. We got out of debt. We got rid of the government as our business partner. This year we made a billion and a half dollars just in the first six months. And I just approved a five-year business plan that'll mean investing over $10 billion in technology and jobs right here in America.

Hell, if we could do it, anybody can. Because we had less going for us than just about anybody, believe me.

The country is going through some big changes today. I don't know what to call it . . . "the information age" . . . "the hightech era" . . . "the postindustrial society." And people are scared. They wonder if there'll be a place for them.

Well, hell, what are they scared about? There was a revolution going on eighty years ago, too, when those millions of people were being pushed through the chutes at Ellis Island. It was called the industrial revolution. They came out of the sulphur pits in Sicily and the coal mines in Silesia, and then jumped right into the middle of it. And they didn't even speak the language!

So what's so tough about today? And why can't our kids look forward to— even *more* than we have, not *less?*

We make a mistake if we think the Statue of Liberty is just a *historical* monument. We're missing the boat if we think she stands for the *past.* She has *never*

stood for the past. Every immigrant, every returning GI and doughboy who sailed by her, was *escaping* the past and entering the *future.*

She may be almost one hundred years old, but the values she stands for—better *not* be as weathered as she is. And I don't think they are. Maybe when we get her polished up, more people will see that.

We're not just preserving a statue here, we're preserving all that she stands for.

And if that's not worth remembering, and honoring, and saving . . . if that's not worth passing on to our kids . . . then let me ask you, ladies and gentlemen—what the hell is?

Thank you.

## Mario Cuomo, "Abraham Lincoln and Our 'Unfinished Work,' " February 12, 1986

*Mario Cuomo is the American-born son of Italian immigrants. He served three terms as governor of New York from 1983 to 1995 and after his famous keynote address at the Democratic Convention in 1984 was frequently touted as a possible presidential candidate. In the 1980s he was perhaps the best known and most articulate white ethnic liberal Democrat in the country. In this selection from a speech on Lincoln, he weaves his own family's immigrant story together with Lincoln's vision in order to argue for liberal values.*

Source: Mario Cuomo, *More Than Words* (New York: St. Martin's Press, 1993), pp. 86–89.

What a great gift Lincoln is! In this speech I use him to inspire us and to remind us that we are still in the process of perfecting the Union, still a "Tale of Two Cities," still struggling to complete America "the unfinished work." Lincoln serves, too, as a strong witness against the Reagan assault on government as a pernicious force. Lincoln's own view was a balanced one using government to do things which he believed the private sector was not doing adequately, such as making "land improvements." Today that would mean investing in our infrastructure.

Something else was at work in the 1980s that was troublesome and could benefit from Lincoln's soaring intellect and penetrating rhetoric. There was a harshness growing, a loss of civility. Lincoln, who stretched his sinewy arms around his young nation and kept it from division and fragmentation with his strength and compassion, is still a powerful voice against the destructive force of racial, ethnic, and religious discrimination. I had in mind especially some new unpleasantness involving Italian-Americans that had been in the news just before the time of this address, and I talked about it specifically in the speech.

*It is for us, the living, rather, to be dedicated here*
*to the unfinished work . . . that this nation,*
*under God, shall have a new birth of*
*freedom—and that government of the people,*
*by the people, for the people, shall not perish*
*from the earth.*

Gettysburg Address (Everett Copy)
November 19, 1863

It is an intimidating thing to stand here tonight to talk about the greatest intellect, the greatest leader perhaps the greatest soul, America has ever produced.

To follow such legendary orators as William Jennings Bryan and Adlai Stevenson.

Only a struggling student myself, to face as imposing an audience as the Lincoln scholars: Tough-minded. Demanding. Harsh critics. Highly intelligent.

And to face so many Republicans: Tough-minded. Demanding, harsh critics.

And I certainly wasn't encouraged after I learned that when another New York governor, Franklin D. Roosevelt, announced his intention to come here to speak on Lincoln, a local political stalwart threatened him with an injunction.

To be honest with you, I feel a little like the Illinois man from one Lincoln story. When he was confronted by a local citizens' committee with the prospect of being tarred and feathered and run out of town on a rail, he announced, "If it weren't for the honor of the thing, I'd just as soon it happened to someone else."

I should tell you one more thing before I go on with my remarks. It would be foolish to deny that there has been some speculation surrounding this event about ambitions for the presidency. Let me be candid. I don't know anyone who wouldn't regard it as the highest possible political privilege to be president. And governors are, perhaps, better prepared than most to be president.

Governors like Teddy Roosevelt and FDR and even governors from places like Georgia and California. Particularly governors of great industrial states with good records. That's because governors do more than make speeches. They have to make budgets and run things—and that's what presidents do.

So, the truth is, despite what might be said about planning to run again for governor, the speculation about the presidency is plausible.

I wouldn't be a bit surprised—if the election goes well this year for him—if early next year you heard a declaration of interest from a reelected governor of a large state—Jim Thompson of Illinois.

Good Luck, Jim!

But seriously, this is an event beyond the scope of partisan politics.

When Lincoln gave his one and only speech in my capital, Albany, New York, he told the Democratic governor, "You have invited and received me without distinction of party."

Let me second that sentiment, and thank you for inviting and receiving me in the same spirit.

To be here in Springfield, instead of at the memorial in Washington, to celebrate this "high holy day" of Lincoln remembrance gives us a special advantage.

In Washington, Lincoln towers far above us, presiding magisterially, in a marble temple.

His stony composure, the hugeness of him there, gives him and his whole life a grandeur that places him so far above and beyond us that it's difficult to remember the reality of him.

We have lifted Lincoln to the very pinnacle of our national memory. En-

larged him to gargantuan proportions in white stone recreations.

We have chiseled his face on the side of a mountain, making him appear as a voice in the heavens.

There is a danger when we enshrine our heroes, when we lift them onto pedestals and lay wreaths at their feet. We can, by the very process of elevating them, strain the sense of connection between them and the palpable, fleshy, sometimes mean concerns of our own lives.

I have come to remember Lincoln as he was. The flesh-and-blood man. Haunted by mortality in his waking and his dreaming life. The boy who had been uprooted from one frontier to another across Kentucky and Indiana and Illinois, by a father restless with his own dreams.

To remember some of Lincoln's own words—which taken altogether, are the best words America has ever produced

To remember the words that he spoke ten days after his lyrical, wrenching farewell to Springfield on his way to his inauguration as our sixteenth president.

"Back in my childhood," he said then, "the earliest days of my being able to read, I got hold of a small book . . . Weems's *Life of Washington.*

"I remember all the accounts there given of the battlefields and struggles for the liberties of the country and the great hardships of that time fixed themselves on . . . my memory.

"I recollect thinking then, boy even though I was, that there must have been something *more* than *common* that those men struggled for.

"I am exceedingly anxious that the thing which they struggled for, that something even more than national independence; that something that held out a promise to all the people of the world for all time to come, . . . shall be perpetuated in accordance with the original idea for which the struggle was made . . ."

Here was Lincoln, just before his inauguration, reminding us of the source of his strength and eventual greatness. His compelling need to understand the meaning of things and to commit to a course that was directed by reason, supported by principle, designed to achieve the greatest good. He was a man of ideas, grand and soaring ones. And he was cursed by the realization that they were achievable ideas as well, so that he could not escape the obligation of pursuing them, despite the peril and the pain that pursuit would inevitably bring.

Even as a boy he grasped the great idea that would sustain him—and provoke him—for the rest of his days. The idea that took hold of his heart and his mind. The idea that he tells us about again and again throughout his life. It became the thread of purpose that tied the boy to the man to the legend—the great idea, the dream, the achievable dream, of equality, of opportunity . . . for all.

"The original idea for which the struggle was made . . ." The proposition that all men are created equal. That they are endowed by their Creator with certain unalienable rights. That among these are life, liberty, and the pursuit of happiness.

Even by Lincoln's time, for many the words had been heard often enough so that they became commonplace, part of

the intellectual and historical landscape, losing their dimension, their significance, their profoundness.

But not for Lincoln.

He pondered them. Troubled over their significance. Wrestled with their possibilities.

"We did not learn quickly or easily that all men are created equal," one Lincoln scholar has observed.

No. We did not learn those words quickly or easily. We are still struggling with them in fact.

As Lincoln did. For a whole lifetime. From the time he read Weems's little book, until the day he was martyred, he thought and planned and prayed to make the words of the Declaration a way of life.

Equality and opportunity, for *all*. But truly, for *all*.

Lincoln came to believe that the great promise of the founding fathers was one that had only begun to be realized with the founding fathers themselves. He understood that from the beginning it was a promise that would have to be fulfilled in degrees. Its embrace would have to be widened over the years, step by step, sometimes painfully, until finally it included everyone.

That was his dream. That was his vision. That was his mission.

With it, he defined, for himself and for us, the soul of our unique experiment in government: the belief that the promise of the Declaration of Independence—the promise of equality and opportunity—cannot be considered kept until it includes everyone.

For him, that was the unifying principle of our democracy. Without it, we had no nation worth fighting for. With it, we had no limit to the good we might achieve.

He spent the rest of his life trying to give the principle meaning. He consumed himself doing it.

He reaffirmed Jefferson's preference for the human interest and the human right. "The principles of Jefferson," he said, "are the definitions and axioms of free society."

But Lincoln extended those instincts to new expressions of equality.

Always, he searched for ways to bring within the embrace of the new freedom, the new opportunity, *all* who had become Americans.

Deeply, reverently, grateful for the opportunity afforded *him,* he was pained by the idea that it should be denied others. Or limited.

He believed that the human right was more than the right to exist, to live free from oppression.

He believed it included the right to achieve, to thrive. So he reached out for the "penniless beginner."

He thought it the American promise that every "poor man" should be given his chance.

He saw what others would or could not see: the immensity of the fundamental ideas of freedom and self-determination that made his young nation such a radically new adventure in government.

But he was not intimidated by that immensity. He was willing to *use* the ideas as well as to admire them. To mold them so as to apply them to new circumstances. To wield them as instruments of justice and not just echoes of it.

Some said government should do no more than protect its people from insurrection and foreign invasion and spend the rest of its time dispassionately observing the way its people played out the cards that fate had dealt them.

He scorned that view. He called it a "do nothing" abdication of responsibility.

"The legitimate object of government," he said, "is to do for the people what needs to be done, but which they cannot, by individual effort, do at all, or do so well, for themselves. There are many such things . . ." he said.

So he offered the "poor" *more* than feedom and the encouragement of his own good example: He offered them government. Government that would work aggressively to help them find the chance they might not have found alone. He did it by fighting for bridges, railroad construction, and other such projects that others decried as excessive government.

He gave help for education, help for agriculture, land for the rural family struggling for a start.

And always at the heart of his struggle and his yearning was the passion to make room for the outsider; the insistence upon a commitment to respect the idea of equality by fighting for inclusion.

Early in his career, he spoke out for women's suffrage.

His contempt for the "do-nothings" was equaled by his disdain for the "Know-Nothings."

America beckoned foreigners, but many Americans—organized around the crude selfishness of the nativist movement—rejected them. The nativists sought to create two classes of people, the old-stock Americans and the intruders from other places, keeping the intruders forever strangers in a strange land.

Lincoln shamed them with his understanding and his strength. "I am not a Know-Nothing," he said. "How could I be? How can anyone who abhors the oppression of Negroes be in favor of degrading classes of white people? . . . As a nation we began by declaring 'all men are created equal.'

"We now practically read it: 'All men are created equal except Negroes.' When the Know-Nothings get control, it will read 'All men are created equal except Negroes, and Catholics and Foreigners.' "

Then he added: "When it comes to this I shall prefer emigrating to some country where they make no pretense of loving liberty—to Russia for instance, where despotism can be taken pure, and without the base alloy of hypocrisy."

Had Lincoln not existed, or had he been less than he was and the battle to keep the nation together had been lost, it would have meant the end of the American experiment. Secession would have bred secession, reducing us into smaller and smaller fragments until finally we were just the broken pieces of the dream.

Lincoln saved us from that.

But winning the great war for unity did not preserve us from the need to fight further battles in the struggle to balance our diversity with our harmony, to keep the pieces of the mosaic intact, even while making room for new pieces.

That work is today, as it was in 1863, still an unfinished work . . . still a cause that requires "a full measure of devotion."

For more than 100 years, the fight to include has continued:

- In the struggle to free working people from the oppression of a ruthless economic system that saw women and children worked to death and men born to poverty live in poverty and die in poverty, in spite of working all the time.
- In the continuing fight for civil rights, making Lincoln's promise real.
- In the effort to keep the farmer alive.
- In the ongoing resistance to preserve religious freedom from the arrogance of the Know-Nothing and the zealotry of those who would make their religion the state's religion.
- In the crusade to make women equal, legally and practically.

Many battles have been won. The embrace of our unity has been gradually but inexorably expanded.

But Lincoln's work is not yet done.

A century after Lincoln preached his answer of equality and mutual respect, some discrimination—of class or race or sex or ethnicity—as a bar to full participation in America still remains.

Unpleasant reminders of less enlightened times linger. Sometimes they are heard in whispers. At other times they are loud enough to capture the attention of the American people.

I have had my own encounter with this question, and I have spoken of it.

Like millions of others, I am privileged to be a first-generation American.

My mother and father came to this country more than sixty years ago with nothing but their hopes. Without education, skills, or wealth.

Through the opportunity given them here to lift themselves through hard work, they were able to raise a family. My mother has lived to see her youngest child become chief executive of one of the greatest states in the greatest nation in the only world we know.

Like millions of other children of immigrants, I know the strength that immigrants can bring. I know the richness of a society that allows us a whole new culture without requiring us to surrender the one our parents were born to. I know the miraculous power of this place that helps people rise up from poverty to security, and even affluence, in the course of a single lifetime. With generations of other children of the immigrants, I know about equality and opportunity and unity in a special way.

And I know how, from time to time, all this beauty can be challenged by the misguided children of the Know-Nothings, by the shortsighted and the unkind, by contempt that masks itself as humor, by all the casual or conscious bigotry that must keep the American people vigilant.

We heard such voices again recently saying things like: "Italians are not politically popular."

"Catholics will have a problem."

"He has an *ethnic* problem."

An ethnic problem.

We hear the word again. "Wop."

"We oftentimes refer to people of Italian descent as Wops,' " said one public figure, unabashedly.

Now, given the unbroken string of opportunity and good fortune provided me by this great country, I might simply have ignored these references. I could easily have let the words pass as inconsequential, especially remembering Lincoln, himself the object of scorn and ridicule But the words took on significance because they were heard beyond my home or my block or even my state. Because they were heard by others who remembered times of their own when words stung and menaced *them* and *their* people.

And because they raised a question about our system of fundamental American values that Lincoln helped construct and died for. Is it true? Are there really so many who have never heard Lincoln's voice, or the sweet sound of reason and fairness? So many who do not understand the beauty and power of this place, that they could take of the tint of your skin or the sex you were born to or the vowels of your name an impediment to progress in this, the land of opportunity?

I believed the answer would be clear. So I asked for it by disputing the voices of division. By saying, "It is not so. It is the voice of ignorance, and I challenge you to show me otherwise."

In no time at all the answer has come back from the American people. Everyone saying the same things:

"Of course it's wrong to judge a person by the place where his forebears came from. Of course that would violate all that we stand for, fairness and common sense. It shouldn't *even* have been brought up. It shouldn't *even* have been a cause for discussion."

I agree. It should not have been. But it was. And the discussion is now concluded, with the answer I was sure of and the answer I am proud of as an American. The answer Lincoln would have given: "You will rise or fall on your merits as a person and the quality of your work. All else is distraction."

Lincoln believed, with every fiber of his being, that this place, America, could offer a dream to all mankind, different than any other in the annals of history.

More generous, more compassionate, more inclusive.

No one knew better than Lincoln our sturdiness, the ability of most of us to make it on our own given the chance. But at the same time, no one knew better the idea of family, the idea that unless we helped one another, there were some who would never make it.

One person climbs the ladder of personal ambition, reaches his dream, and then turns . . . and pulls the ladder up.

Another reaches the place he has sought, turns, and reaches down for the person behind him.

With Lincoln, it was that process of turning and reaching down, that commitment to keep lifting people up the ladder, which defined the American character, stamping us forever with a mission that reached even beyond our borders to embrace the world.

Lincoln's belief in America, in the American people, was broader, deeper, more daring than any other person's of his age—and, perhaps, ours, too.

And *this* is the near-unbelievable greatness of the man—that with that belief, he not only led us, he *created* us.

His personal mythology became our national mythology.

It is as if Homer not only chronicled the siege of Troy, but conducted the siege as well.

As if Shakespeare set his play writing aside to lead the English against the Armada.

Because Lincoln embodied his age in his actions and in his words.

Words, even and measured, hurrying across three decades, calling us to our destiny.

Words he prayed, and troubled over—more than a million words in his speeches and writings.

Words that chronicled the search for his own identity as he searched for a nation's identity.

Words that were, by turns, as chilling as the night sky and as assuring as home.

Words his reason sharpened into steel, and his heart softened into an embrace.

Words filled with all the longings of his soul and of his century.

Words wrung from his private struggle, spun to capture the struggle of a nation.

Words out of his own pain to heal that struggle.

Words of retribution, but never of revenge.

Words that judged, but never condemned.

Words that pleaded, cajoled for the one belief—that the promise *must* be kept, that the dream *must* endure and grow, until it embraces everyone.

Words ringing down into the present.

All the hope and the pain of that epic caught, somehow, by his cadences: The tearing away, the binding together, the leaving behind, the reaching beyond.

As individuals, as a people, we are still reaching up, for a better job, a better education, a better society, even for the stars, just as Lincoln did.

But because of Lincoln, we do it in a way that is unique to this world.

What other people on earth have ever claimed a quality of character that resided not in a way of speaking, dressing, dancing, praying, but in an idea?

What other people on earth have ever refused to set the definitions of their identity by anything other than that idea?

No, we have not learned quickly or easily that the dream of America endures only so long as we keep faith with the struggle to include. But Lincoln, through his words and his works, has etched that message forever into our consciousness.

Lincoln showed us, for all time, what unites us.

He taught us that we cannot rest until the promise of equality and opportunity embraces every region, every race, every religion, every nationality . . . and every class. Until it includes, "the penniless beginner" and the "poor man seeking his chance."

In his time, Lincoln saw that as long as one in every seven Americans was enslaved, our identity as a people was hostage to that enslavement.

He faced that injustice. He fought it. He gave his life to see it righted.

Time and again since then, we have had to face challenges that threatened to divide us.

And time and again, we have conquered them.

We reached out—hesitantly at times, sometimes only after great struggle—but always we reached out, to include impoverished immigrants, the farmer and the factory worker, women, the disabled.

To all those whose only assets were their great expectations, America found ways to meet those expectations, and to create new ones.

Generations of hardworking people moved into the middle class and beyond.

We created a society as open and free as any on earth. And we did it Lincoln's way—by founding that society on a belief in the boundless enterprise of the American people.

Always, we have extended the promise. Moving toward the light, toward our declared purpose as a people: "to form a more perfect Union," to overcome all that divides us, because we believe the ancient wisdom that Lincoln believed— "a house divided against itself cannot stand."

Step by step, our embrace grows wider.

The old bigotries seem to be dying. The old stereotypes and hatreds that denied so many their full share of an America they helped build have gradually given way to acceptance, fairness, and civility.

But still, great challenges remain.

Suddenly, ominously, a new one has emerged.

In Lincoln's time, one of every seven Americans was a slave.

Today, for all our affluence and might, despite what every day is described as our continuing economic recovery, nearly one in every seven Americans lives in poverty, not in chains—because Lincoln saved us from that—but trapped in a cycle of despair that is its own enslavement.

Today, while so many of us do so well, one of every two minority children is born poor, many of them to be oppressed for a lifetime by inadequate education and the suffocating influence of broken families and social disorientation.

Our identity as a people is hostage to the grim facts of more than 33 million Americans for whom equality and opportunity is not yet an attainable reality, but only an illusion.

Some people look at these statistics and the suffering people behind them, and deny them, pretending instead we are all one great "shining city on a hill."

Lincoln told us for a lifetime—and for all time to come—that there can be no shining city when one in seven of us is denied the promise of the Declaration.

He tells us today that we are justly proud of all that we have accomplished, but that for all our progress, for all our achievement, or all that so properly makes us proud, we have no right to rest, content.

Nor justification for turning from the effort, out of fear or lack of confidence.

We have met greater challenges with fewer resources. We have faced greater perils with fewer friends. It would be a desecration of our belief and an act of ingratitude for the good fortune we have had to end the struggle for inclusion because it is over for some of us.

So, this evening, we come to pay you

our respects, Mr. Lincoln. Not just by recalling your words and revering your memory, which we do humbly and with great pleasure.

This evening, we offer you more, Mr. President. We offer you what you have asked for, a continuing commitment to live your truth, to go forward painful step by painful step, enlarging the greatness of this nation with patient confidence in the ultimate justice of the people.

Because—as you have we told us, Mr. President—there is no better or equal hope in the world.

Thank you.

## Michael McDonald, *All Souls: A Family Story from Southie,* Boston and Busing, 1999

*Nowhere was the opposition to busing for racial integration fiercer and more persistent than in Boston, where white ethnics, particularly Irish Americans in the South Boston neighborhood, violently resisted African American integration of the local schools. This is an excerpt from Michael McDonald's recent memoir about growing up in South Boston,* All Souls: A Family Story from Southie, *which vividly recounts the neighborhood's resistance to busing.*

Source: Michael McDonald, *All Souls: A Family Story from Southie* (Boston: Beacon Press, 1999).

Ma's tunes on the accordion started to be all about the busing. She played them at rallies, sit-ins, and fundraisers for the struggle, all over Southie. The songs sounded like a lot of the Irish rebel songs we grew up with. They had the same tunes, but the words had changed: "So come on Southie, head on high / They'll never take our pride. . . ." The Black and Tans, the murderous regiments who'd wreaked havoc on Ireland on behalf of the English Crown, became the TPF (Tactical Police Force), the special force that was turning our town into a police state. The Queen of England was gone from Ma's songs too, her place taken by Judge Garrity, the federal judge who'd mandated busing, "the law of the land": "Judge Garrity and traitors too / We've just begun to fight." Garrity had an Irish name, which made it all the worse, as the Irish hated nothing more than a traitor. That's why we hated Ted Kennedy; he'd sided with the busing too, and was seen as the biggest traitor of all, being from the most important Irish family in America.

The English themselves weren't completely absent from our struggle, though. They ran the *Boston Globe* and were behind the whole thing. My friends and I started stealing stacks of the *Globe* left outside supermarkets in the early mornings. We could sell them for a dime to people on their way to work, who'd have been paying a quarter if it weren't for us. That's when I found out the *Globe* was the enemy. We tried to sell it in Southie, but too many people said they wouldn't read that liberal piece of trash if it was free, that it was to blame for the busing, with all its attacks on South Boston. I heard a few people say it was a communist paper. "Not only are they

communists, they're the rich English, keeping up their hate for the Irish and Southie," Coley told me. He showed me the names of the *Globe's* owners and editors: "Winship, Taylor. All WASPs," he said, "White Anglo Saxon Protestants, forever gettin' back at the Irish for chasing them out of Boston."

Boy, was I confused now that the English were involved. We'd always hated the English for what they did to the Irish. But whatever that was, listening to Ma's Irish songs, I'd thought it was in the past and across a great big ocean. Now it was right here in Southie. I was glad to be doing my part anyway, stealing the *Boston Globe* and making a couple bucks on their loss. The rich English liberal communist bastards!

That September, Ma let us skip the first week of school. The whole neighborhood was boycotting school. City Councilor Louise Day Hicks and her bodyguard with the bullhorn, Jimmy Kelly, were telling people to keep their kids home. It was supposed to be just the high school kids boycotting, but we all wanted to show our loyalty to the neighborhood. I was meant to be starting the third grade at St. Augustine's School. Ma had enrolled Kevin and Kathy in the sixth and seventh grades there as well. Frankie was going to Southie High, and Mary and Joe were being sent to mostly black Roxbury, so they really had something to boycott. But on the first day, Kevin and Kathy begged Ma not to send them. "C'mon Ma, please?" I piped in. It was still warm outside and we wanted to join the crowds that were just then lining the streets to watch the busloads of black kids come into Southie. The excitement built as police helicopters hovered just above our third-floor windows, police in riot gear stood guard on the rooftops of Old Colony, and the national news camped out on every corner. Ma said okay, and we ran up to Darius Court, along the busing route, where in simpler times we'd watched the neighborhood St. Paddy's Day parade.

The whole neighborhood was out. Even the mothers from the stoop made it to Darius Court, nightgowns and all. Mrs. Coyne, up on the rooftop in her housedress, got arrested before the buses even started rolling through the neighborhood. Everyone knew she was a little soft, and I thought the excitement that day must have been a bit much for her. She ran up to the roof and called the police "nigger lovers" and "traders," and started dancing and singing James Brown songs. "Say it loud, I'm black and I'm proud!" She nearly fell off the roof before one cop grabbed her from behind and restrained her. Everyone was laughing at that one: big fat Mrs. Coyne rolling around on the rooftop kicking and screaming, with a cop in full riot gear on top of her. Little disturbances like that broke out here and there, but most people were too intent on seeing the buses roll to do anything that might get them carted away.

I looked up the road and saw a squadron of police motorcycles speeding down Dorchester Street, right along the curb, as if they would run over anyone who wasn't on the sidewalk. The buses were coming. Police sirens wailed as hundreds of cops on motorcycles aimed at the crowds of mothers and kids, to clear the way for the law of the land. "Bacon . . . I smell bacon!" a few people yelled, sniffing at the cops. I knew that meant the cops were pigs. As the motorcycles came closer I fought to get back onto the sidewalk, but it was too crowded. I ran further into the road to avoid one motorcycle, when two more came at me from the middle of the street. I had to run across to the other side of the road, where the crowd quickly cleared a space for me on the sidewalk. All the adults welcomed me, patting me on the shoulder. "Are you all right?" "Those pricks would even kill a kid." "Pigs!" someone else shouted. I thought I'd lost Kevin and Kathy, but just then I saw them sitting on top of a mailbox up the street for a good view of the buses. They waved to me, laughing because they'd seen me almost get run over.

The road was cleared, and the buses rolled slowly. We saw a line of yellow buses like there was no end to them. I couldn't see any black faces though, and I was looking for them. Some people around me started to cry when they finally got a glimpse of the buses through the crowd. One woman made the sign of the cross and a few others copied her. "I never thought I'd see the day come," said an old woman next to me. She lived downstairs from us, but I had never seen her leave her apartment before. I'd always thought she was crippled or something, sitting there in her window every day, waiting for Bobby, the delivery man who came daily with a package from

J. J.'s Liquors. She was trembling now, and so was everyone else. I could feel it myself. It was a feeling of loss, of being beaten down, of humiliation. In minutes, though, it had turned to anger, rage, and hate, just like in those Irish rebel songs I'd heard all my life. Like "The Ballad of James Connolly": "God's curse on you England / You cruel hearted monster / Your deeds they would shame all the devils in Hell." Except we'd changed it to "God's curse on you Garrity."

Smash! A burst of flying glass and all that rage exploded. We'd all been waiting for it, and so had the police in riot gear. It felt like a gunshot, but it was a brick. It went right through a bus window. Then all hell broke loose. I saw a milk crate fly from the other side of the street right for my face. More bricks, sticks, and bottles smashed against the buses, as police pulled out their billy clubs and charged with their riot shields in a line formation through the crowds. Teenagers were chased into the project and beaten to the cement wherever they were caught.

I raced away about a block from the fray, to a spot where everyone was chanting "Here We Go Southie, Here We Go," like a battle cry. That's when I realized we were at war. I started chanting too, at first just moving my lips because I didn't know if a kid's voice would ruin the strong chant. But then I belted it out, just as a few other kids I didn't know joined the chorus. The kids in the crowd all looked at each other as if we were family. *This is great,* I thought. I'd never had such an easy time as this, making friends in Southie. The buses kept passing by, speeding now, and all I could see in the windows were black hands with their middle fingers up at us, still no faces though.

The buses got through the crowd surrounded by the police motorcycles. I saw Frankie running up toward Southie High along with everyone else. "What are you doing out here!" he yelled. "Get your ass home!" He said there was another riot with the cops up at the high school, and off he ran with the others. Not far behind were Kevin and his friends. He shouted the same thing at me: "Get your ass home!" I just wanted to find Ma now and make sure she wasn't beaten or arrested or anything, so I ran home. The project was empty—everyone had followed the buses up the St. Paddy's parade route. Ma wasn't home, but the TV was on, with live coverage of the riots at Southie High. Every channel I turned to showed the same thing. I kept flipping the dial, looking for my family, and catching glimpses of what seemed to be all the people I knew hurling stones or being beaten by the police, or both. *This is big,* I thought. It was scary and thrilling at the same rime, and I remembered the day we'd moved into this neighborhood, when Ma said it looked just like Belfast, and that we were in the best place in the world. I kept changing the channels, looking for my family, and I didn't know anymore whether I was scared or thrilled, or if there was any difference between the two anyhow.

The buses kept rolling, and the hate kept building. It was a losing battle, but we returned to Darius Court every day after school to see if the rage would explode again. Sometimes it did and sometimes it didn't. But the bus route became a meeting place for the neighborhood. Some of my neighbors carried big signs with Resist or Never or my favorite, Hell No We Won't Go. There was always someone in the crowd keeping everyone laughing with wisecracks aimed at the stiff-looking state troopers who lined the bus route, facing the crowds to form a barrier. They never moved or showed any expression. We all wanted to get them to react to something. But we wanted a reaction somewhere between the stiff inhuman stance and the beatings. When my friends and I tried to get through to them by asking questions about their horses and could we pet them, they told us to screw. And it wasn't long before some kids started trying to break the horses' legs with hockey sticks when riots broke out. One day the staties got distracted by a burning effigy of Judge Garrity that came flying off a rooftop in the project. That's when I saw Kevin make his way out of Darius Court to throw a rock at the buses. A trooper chased him, but Kevin was too fast. His photo did end up in the *Boston Globe* the next day, though, his scrawny shirtless body whipping a rock with all his might. It looked like the pictures we'd always seen of kids in war-torn countries throwing petrol bombs at some powerful enemy. But Kevin's rock hit a yellow bus with black kids in it.

I threw a rock once. I had to. You were a pussy if you didn't. I didn't have a good aim, though, and it landed on the street before it even made it to the bus. I stared at my rock and was partly re-

lieved. I didn't really want it to smash a bus window. I only wanted the others to see me throwing it. On that day there were so many rocks flying that you didn't know whose rock landed where, but everyone claimed the ones that did the most damage. Even though I missed, a cop came out of nowhere and treated me just like they treated the kids with good aim. He took me by the neck and threw me to the dirt. I sat there for a few minutes to make sure that everyone had seen that one. I was only eight, but I was part of it all, part of something bigger than I'd ever imagined, part of something that was on the national news every night.

Every day I felt the pride of rebellion. The helicopters above my bedroom window woke me each morning for school, and my friends and I would plan to pass by the TPF on the corners so we could walk around them and give them hateful looks. Ma and the nuns at St. Augustine's told me it was wrong to hate the blacks for any of this. But I had to hate someone, and the police were always fracturing some poor neighbor's skull or taking teenagers over to the beach at night to beat them senseless, so I hated them with all my might. SWAT teams had been called into the neighborhood. I'd always liked the television show "S.W.A.T.," but they were the enemy now. We gave the SWAT sharpshooters standing guard over us on the rooftops the finger; then we'd run. Evenings we had to be off the streets early or else the cops would try to run us down with their motorbikes. No more hanging our on corners in Old Colony. A line of motorbikes straight across the street and sidewalks would appear out of nowhere and force everyone to disappear into hallways and tunnels. One time I had to jump into a bush because they were coming from both ends of the street. I was all cut up, and I really hated them then.

It felt good, the hate I had for the authorities. My whole family hated them, especially Frankie, Kathy, and Kevin, who got the most involved in the riots. I would've loved to throw Molotov cocktails myself, along with some of the adults, but I was only a kid and the cops would probably catch me and beat me at the beach. So I just fantasized about killing them all. They were the enemy, the giant oppressor, like Goliath. And the people of South Boston were like David. Except that David won in the end, and we knew we were going to lose this one. But that made us even more like the Irish, who were always fighting in the songs even if they had to lose and die a glorious death.

One Friday in early October we took part in what Louise Day Hicks called National Boycott Day. Everyone boycotted school again. We'd all heard about the kids who'd gone to school during boycotts and who were threatened over the phone with getting their things cut off. Kevin told Ma we'd better not risk castration, and we got to stay home and watch the rally and march down Broadway. The rally was a good one. When the thousands of people sang the national anthem, with their right hands over their chests, I cried. It was as if we were singing about an America that we wanted but didn't have, especially the part about the land of the free. Louise Day Hicks really squealed that part out from the bandstand microphone, and we all knew what she was getting at.

When the rally was over, the crowds marched to Judge Garrity's home in the Boston suburb of Wellesley. We weren't allowed to go because Ma thought people would surely be arrested. I wanted to go because I'd heard that where the Judge lived everyone was rich and white and I wanted to see what they looked like. But I couldn't, so I just watched the march on its way down Broadway.

The signs at the marches were starting to change. Instead of Restore Our Alienated Rights and Welcome To Moscow America, more and more now I saw Bus The Niggers Back To Africa, and one even said KKK. I was confused about that one. The people in my neighborhood were always going on about being Irish, with shamrocks painted on the brick walls and tattooed to their arms. And I had always heard stories from Grandpa about a time when the Ku Klux Klan burned Irish Catholics out of their homes in America. I thought someone should beat up the guy with the KKK sign, but no one seemed to mind that much. I told my friend Danny about the Ku Klux Klan burning out the Irish families, and that the guy with the KKK sign was in the wrong town. He laughed. He said he'd never heard that one before. "Shut up," he said. "They just hate the niggers. What, d'ya wanna be a nigger?" *Jesus no,* I thought to myself.

With National Boycott Day, everything got more scary. In the afternoon, after all the speeches, chants, and the tearful national anthem, crowds gathered at Darius Court once again to taunt the police and to throw rocks at the buses. The TPF chased one man into the Rabbit Inn tavern across the street, and a crowd of people at the bar protected him from the cops. Everyone knew the Rabbit Inn was no place to mess with. That's where the Mullen gang hung out—the toughest bar in Southie. The next night, after dark, we were all called out of our apartments in Old Colony. The mothers on the stoop were yelling up to windows that the TPF was beating people at the Rabbit Inn to get back at them for the night before. Ma wasn't home, so I ran to Darius Court with all of the neighbors, some of them carrying baseball bats, hockey sticks, and big rocks. When I got there, the dark streets were packed with mobs rushing the police. I saw Kevin running through a maze of people carrying a boulder with both hands. He was excited and told me that the TPF had beat the shit out of everyone at the Rabbit Inn, with their police badges covered. Just then I saw people covered in blood being taken from the bar into the converging ambulances.

The mothers in Old Colony showed their Southie loyalty that night. They went up against the entire police force that was filling the streets. I kept getting knocked around by bigger people running in all directions. Someone said the TPF had split open an eleven-year-old's head. I pushed through the crowd to get a look at the kid, and was relieved to see through all the blood that he wasn't Kevin. I wondered if I'd better get

home, in case people started getting killed. As the sirens screeched, I saw the blue lights flashing onto the face of Kristin O'Malley, a four-year-old from my building sitting on her big brother's shoulders and smiling at all the excitement. I figured if she could stay our then so could I.

Someone propped up his stereo speakers in a project window, blasting a favorite at the time: "Fight the Power" by the Isley Brothers. We always did that in Old Colony, blare our speakers out of our windows for the whole neighborhood to hear. It was obvious this guy was doing it for good background music to the crashes and thumps of battle.

Everyone sang along to "Fight the Power." The teenagers in Southie still listened only to black music. The sad Irish songs were for the older people, and I never heard anyone listening to rock and roll in Old Colony. One time an outsider walked through Old Colony wearing a dungaree vest with a big red tongue and the rolling stones printed on the back. He was from the suburbs and was visiting his cousins in Old Colony. He got a bottle thrown at his head and was called a pussy. Rock and roll was for rich suburban people with long hair and dirty clothes. Mary had a similar tongue painted on her bedroom wall, but that was for Rufus and Chaka Khan; it was okay to like them. Of course no one called it black music—we couldn't see what color anyone was from the radio— but I knew the Isley Brothers were black because I'd seen them on "Soul Train." But that didn't bother anyone in the crowd; what mattered was that the Isley

Brothers were singing about everything we were watching in our streets right now, the battle between us and the law: "And when I rolled with the punches I got knocked on the ground / By all this bullshit goin' down."

The mob started pushing and swaying toward the cop cars, blocking them from going down the street. Mrs. Coyne was out there again, and was the first to put a bat through a police windshield. Then everyone surrounded the cops and smashed all of their windows. I started to see things fly through the air: pipes, bricks, bats, and even a hubcap.

Just then I saw my mother pushing through the crowd, yelling at me to run home. "They're beating kids!" she screamed. She kept getting knocked from side to side. She grabbed me by the collar and said she couldn't find Kevin and Kathy; she had a crying voice on her. I didn't want to go home without her, but she made me, while she went looking through the crowds, dodging everything flying through the air. Later on Ma dragged Kevin and Kathy home and gave into us for running up to Darius Court to join the riot. Frankie was still up there, Ma couldn't find him, and we were mad that the three of us couldn't do everything that the older kids could. Ma couldn't yell at us for long; Kevin drowned her out by blasting the television news reports. And soon we were all glued to the set once again, watching for those we knew in the crowd getting dragged into paddy wagons at Darius Court.

## Immigration Reform and Control Act, and Statement of President Ronald Reagan, 1986

*Efforts to pass national legislation addressing employment of illegal immigrants occurred regularly through the late 1970s and early 1980s. Bills even passed either the House or Senate those years only to fail in the other chamber. Finally, Congress worked out a compromise in the Simpsom-Mazzolli Bill in 1986, which, in an attempt to stem or roll back the tide of illegals, mandated fines for employers who knowingly hired illegal immigrants. In return, the law provided amnesty for immigrants who had been in the country since 1982 and, in an attempt to satisfy the large farmers of the southwest, created a program to supply them with temporary migrant labor.*

*Source:* "Reagan's Statement on Signing Immigration Bill, November 6, 1986," Historic Documents of 1986 (Washington, D.C.: Congressional Quarterly, Inc., 1987), pp. 966–969.

Congress had been trying for five years to enact legislation overhauling the nation's immigration laws. During this time bills were approved three times in the Senate and twice in the House, and conference committees were set up to try to iron out differences. Yet Congress was unable to agree upon a new immigration law until October 17, 1986, when the Senate, by a 63–24 vote, approved a compromise measure that had been passed by the House two days earlier. President Ronald Reagan signed the bill, known as the Immigration Reform and Control Act of 1986, on November 6.

The new law was designed primarily to staunch the flow of illegal aliens into the United States. The statute, which went into effect on the day Reagan signed the bill, for the first time made it a federal violation for employers knowingly to hire foreigners who were in the country illegally. Such employers faced fines of $250 to $10,000 per illegal alien—and in flagrant cases, six-month jail terms—although the penalties would not become effective until May 1988. These sanctions marked what the New York Times characterized as a "major change in American immigration policy," because under previous laws, while it was illegal to enter the country without proper papers and illegal to work here, it was not a violation of the law for an employer to hire so-called "undocumented workers." The law also beefed up criminal penalties for smuggling aliens into the United States. Under the law a violator could be imprisoned for up to five years per smuggled alien and fined in accordance with fines specified in the federal criminal code.

## AMNESTY PROVISIONS

The immigration law also set up a mechanism for giving legal status, or amnesty, to perhaps millions of illegal aliens who could prove they had resided continuously in the United States since January 2, 1982. There was also a provision barring newly legalized aliens from most forms of federal public assistance, such as food stamps and welfare payments,

for five years. Exceptions were made for emergency medical care, aid to aged, blind, or disabled, for serious injury, or assistance that would be in the interest of the public health.

While the amnesty program was created upon enactment, the law mandated that the attorney general must establish regulations for it. Aliens who believed they were eligible would be able to apply during a twelve-month period scheduled to start May 5, 1987, six months after the law took effect. From November 6 to May 5 illegal aliens apprehended by government authorities would not be deported if they appeared to have a reasonable chance of gaining legal status.

## OTHER PROVISIONS

Another major provision was the creation of a new program designed to assure that western farm owners, who historically relied on an illegal work force, would have an adequate supply of labor to harvest crops. The program provides temporary resident status for up to 350,000 foreigners who could prove that they had worked at least ninety days in American agriculture between May 1985 and May 1986. The bill also appropriated $1 billion per year for four years after enactment to reimburse states for the public assistance, health, and education costs resulting from legalized aliens.

The law also contained antidiscrimination language designed to ease fears by Hispanics that employers, worried about possible penalties, would refuse to hire anyone who either looked or sounded

foreign. The new law's antidiscrimination measures, among other things, included a provision—sponsored by Representative Barney Frank, D-Mass., but
opposed by the bill's chief sponsor in the
Senate, Alan K. Simpson, R-Wyo., and
the Reagan administration—that set up
an Office of Special Counsel in the
Justice Department to investigate and
prosecute any charges of discrimination
stemming from unlawful immigration-
related employment practices. Another
provision barred employers from discriminating against legal resident aliens
simply because they were not full-
fledged citizens of the United States.

## THE SIGNING STATEMENT

The immigration law, which generated
impassioned debate during its long legislative history, continued to be a source of
controversy after its passage by Congress.
When Reagan signed the bill into law, he
also issued a detailed, four-page statement, giving his reservations about some
sections of the bill and containing his interpretation of the controversial antidiscrimination provisions. The president's
statement called into question the wording of the provision that prohibited employers from discriminating against legal
aliens. The president said that to bring a
successful suit under this section an alien
would have to prove that an employer
acted with "discriminatory intent."

Members of Congress, Hispanic
groups, and civil rights advocates took
strong exception to the president's statement, maintaining that he interpreted
the provision too narrowly. Frank, for

example, called the president's interpretation "intellectually dishonest, mean-
spirited," and incorrect. "A pattern or
practice of discriminatory activity,"
Frank said, "would violate the law even
if you cannot prove an intent to
discriminate."

## EFFECTS OF THE NEW LAW

Ramifications of the law were felt within
weeks after it was enacted. Immigration
officials reported that arrests of illegal
aliens along the U.S.-Mexican border
dropped sharply. "The word our agents
have now is that the alien smugglers are
confused. They're not really sure what
this new law includes," said Jerry Hicks,
deputy chief patrol agent for the border
patrol in McAllen, Texas. "They're afraid
there's a lack of a market now for
aliens."

Hispanic groups and immigration
lawyers reported that employers in
Texas and other western states had begun laying off many workers within days
after the immigration bill was passed,
even though the law would not prosecute employers for hiring illegal aliens
prior to November 6. There also were
reports of extreme uneasiness among
Hispanic employers, who traditionally
have hired many illegal aliens. "Employers are petrified," said Macario Ramirez,
the head of a sixty-four-store Hispanic
shopping center in Houston. "They say,
'who am I going to hire?' They are
caught in a dilemma. It is complex to
have to screen people, but they need
people to work."

Immigration experts said that big

questions remained unanswered. It was not clear, for example, exactly how many illegal aliens would respond to the amnesty offer. Nor was it certain whether the Immigration and Naturalization Service would have enough personnel to monitor the amnesty program or to force employers to comply with the law. If the INS could enforce it adequately, the immigration law might be effective in stopping illegal immigrants. The experts believed that success in stemming illegal immigration ultimately would depend on employers voluntarily helping immigration officials enforce the new law's provisions. "If people believe in this . . . it may work," said immigration expert Michael S. Teitelbaum of the Alfred P. Sloan Foundation. "But if they view it like the sale of drugs on the streets in New York City, with the profits high, the police on the take, and a revolving door in the courts, they will just breed cynicism, and they will fail."

*Following is President Ronald Reagan's statement on signing the Immigration Reform and Control Act of 1986, November 6, 1986:*

The Immigration Reform and Control Act of 1986 is the most comprehensive reform of our immigration laws since 1952. In the past 35 years our nation has been increasingly affected by illegal immigration. This legislation takes a major step toward meeting this challenge to our sovereignty. At the same time, it preserves and enhances the Nation's heritage of legal immigration. I am pleased to sign the bill into law.

In 1981 this administration asked the Congress to pass a comprehensive legislative package, including employer sanctions, other measures to increase enforcement of the immigration laws, and legalization. The act provides these three essential components. The employer sanctions program is the keystone and major element. It will remove the incentive for illegal immigration by eliminating the job opportunities which draw illegal aliens here.

We have consistently supported a legalization program which is both generous to the alien and fair to the countless thousands of people throughout the world who seek legally to come to America. The legalization provisions in this act will go far to improve the lives of a class of individuals who now must hide in the shadows, without access to many of the benefits of a free and open society. Very soon many of these men and women will be able to step into the sunlight and, ultimately, if they choose, they may become Americans.

Section 102(a) of the bill adds section 274B to the Immigration and Nationality Act. This new section relates to certain kinds of discrimination in connection with employment in the United States. Section 274B(a) provides that it is an "unfair immigration-related employment practice" to "discriminate against" any individual in hiring, recruitment or referral for a fee, or discharging from employment "because of" such individual's national origin or—if such individual is a United States citizen or an alien who is a lawful permanent resident, refugee admitted under INA section 296, or asylee granted asylum under section 208, and who has taken certain steps evidencing an intent to become a United States citizen—because of such individual's citizenship status. Employers of fewer than four employees are expressly exempted from coverage. Discrimination against an "unauthorized alien," as defined in section 274A(h)(3), is also not covered. Other exceptions include cases of discrimination because of national origin that are covered by title VII of the Civil Rights Act of 1964, discrimination based on citizenship status when lawfully required under government authority, and discrimination in favor of a United States citizen over an alien if the citizen is at least "equally qualified."

The major purpose of section 274B is to reduce the possibility that employer sanctions will result in increased national origin and alienage discrimination and to provide a remedy if employer sanctions enforcement does have this result. Accordingly, subsection (k) provides that the section will not apply to any discrimination that takes place after a repeal of employer sanctions if this should occur. In the light of this major purpose, the Special Counsel should exercise the discretion provided under subsection (d)(1) so as to limit the investigations conducted on his own initiative to cases involving discrimination apparently caused by an employer's fear of liability under the employer sanctions program.

I understand section 274B to require a "discriminatory intent" standard of proof: The party bringing the action must show that in the decisionmaking process the defendant's action was motivated by one of the prohibited criteria. Thus, it would be improper to use the "disparate impact" theory of recovery, which was developed under paragraph (2) of section 793(a) of title VII, in a line

of Supreme Court cases over the last 15 years. This paragraph of title VII does not have a counterpart in section 274B. Section 274B tracks only the language of paragraph (1) of section 703(a), the basis of the "disparate treatment" (discriminatory intent) theory of recovery under title VII. Moreover, paragraph (d)(2) refers to "knowing and intentional discrimination" and "a pattern or practice of discriminatory activity." The meaning of the former phrase is self-evident, while the latter is taken from the Supreme Court's disparate treatment jurisprudence and thus includes the requirement of a discriminatory intent.

Thus, a facially neutral employee selection practice that is employed without discriminatory intent will be permissible under the provisions of section 274B. For example, the section does not preclude a requirement of English language skill or a minimum score on an aptitude test even if the employer cannot show a "manifest relationship" to the job in question or that the requirement is a "bone fide occupational qualification reasonably necessary to the normal operation of that particular business or enterprise," so long as the practice is not a guise used to discriminate on account of national origin or citizenship status. Indeed, unless the plaintiff presents evidence that the employer has intentionally discriminated on proscribed grounds, the employer need not offer *any* explanation for his employee selection procedures.

Section 274B(c) provides that the President shall appoint, with the advice and consent of the Senate, a Special Counsel for Immigration-Related Unfair

Employment Practices within the Justice Department, to serve for a term of 4 years. I understand this subsection to provide that the Special Counsel shall serve at the pleasure and with the policy guidance of the President, but for no longer than for a 4-year term (subject to reappointment by the President with the advice and consent of the Senate).

In accordance with the provisions of section 174B(h) and (j)(4), a requirement to pay attorneys fees may be imposed against non-prevailing parties—including alleged victims or persons who file on their behalf as well as employers—if claims or defenses are made that do not have a reasonable foundation in both law and fact. The same standard for the imposing of attorneys fees applies to all nonprevailing parties. It is therefore expected that prevailing defendants would recover attorneys fees in all cases for which this standard is satisfied, not merely in cases where the claim of the victim or person filing on their behalf is found to be vexatious or frivolous.

The provisions of new INA section 245A(a)(4)(B) and (b)(1)(C)(ii), added by section 201(a) of the bill, state that no alien would qualify for the lawful temporary or the permanent residence status provided in that section if he or she has been convicted of *any* felony or three or more misdemeanors committed in the United States.

New INA section 245A(d)(2) states that no alien would qualify for the lawful temporary or permanent residence status provided in that section if "likely to become [a] public charge [ ]." This disqualification could be waived by the Attorney General under certain circumstances. A likelihood that an applicant would become a public change would exist, for example, if the applicant had failed to demonstrate either a history of employment in the United States of a kind that would provide sufficient means without public cash assistance for the support of the alien and his likely dependents who are not United States citizens or the possession of independent means sufficient by itself for such support for an indefinite period.

New INA section 245A(a)(3) requires that an applicant for legalization establish that he has been "continuously physically present in the United States since the date of the enactment" but states that "brief, casual, and innocent absences from the United States" will not be considered a break in the continuous physical presence. To the extent that the INS has made available a procedure by which aliens can obtain permission to depart and reenter the United States after a brief, casual, and innocent absence by establishing a *prima facie* case of eligibility for adjustment of status under this section, I understand section 245A(a)(3) to require that an authorized departure and illegal reentry will constitute a break in "continuous physical presence."

New INA section 210(d), added by section 302(a) of the bill, provides that an alien who is "apprehended" before or during the application period for adjustment of status for certain "special agricultural workers," may not under certain circumstances related to the establishment of a nonfrivolous case of eligibility for such adjustment of status be excluded or deported. I understand this subsection not to authorize any alien to apply for admission to or to be admitted to the United States in order to apply for adjustment of status under this section. Aliens outside the United States may apply for adjustment of status under this section at an appropriate consular office outside the United States pursuant to the procedures established by the Attorney General, in cooperation with the Secretary of State, as provided in section 210(b)(1)(B).

Section 304 of the bill establishes the Commission on Agricultural Workers, half of whose 12 members are appointed by the executive branch and half by the legislative branch. This hybrid Commission is not consistent with constitutional separation of powers. However, the Commission's role will be entirely advisory.

Section 304(g) provides that upon request of the Commission's Chairman, the head of "any department or agency of the United States" must supply "information necessary to enable it to carry out [the] section." Although I expect that the executive branch will cooperate closely with the Commission, its access to executive branch information will be limited in accordance with established principles of law, including the constitutional separation of powers.

Section 601 establishes a Commission for the Study of International Migration and Cooperative Economic Development, all of whose members are appointed by the legislative branch. Section 601(d)(1) states that the access to executive branch information required under section 304(g) must be provided to this Commission also. Accordingly,

the comments of the preceding paragraph are appropriate here as well.

New INA section 274A(a)(5) provides that a person or entity shall be deemed in compliance with the employment verification system in the case of an individual who is referred for employment by a State employment agency if that person or entity retains documentation of such referral certifying that the agency complied with the verification system with respect to the individual referred. I understand this provision not to mandate State employment agencies to issue referral documents certifying compliance with the verification system or to impose any additional affirmative duty or obligation on the offices or personnel of such agencies.

Distance has not discouraged illegal immigration to the United States from all around the globe. The problem of illegal immigration should not, therefore, be seen as a problem between the United States and its neighbors. Our objective is only to establish a reasonable, fair, orderly, and secure system of immigration into this country and not to discriminate in any way against particular nations or people.

The act I am signing today is the product of one of the longest and most difficult legislative undertakings of recent memory. It has truly been a bipartisan effort, with this administration and the allies of immigration reform in the Congress, of both parties, working together to accomplish these critically important reforms.

Future generations of Americans will be thankful for our efforts to humanely regain control of our borders and thereby preserve the value of one of the most sacred possessions of our people: American citizenship.

## Patrick J. Buchanan, "West's Doors Closing?" June 7, 1993

*Patrick Buchanan was an advisor to Presidents Nixon and Reagan, a newspaper reporter and columnist, and a television commentator. He also ran for president in the Republican primaries in 1992 and 1996 and as the Reform Party candidate in 2000. An Irish Catholic, he set himself as a conservative populist spokesman for working-class white ethnics. He was a strong opponent of abortion, gay rights, and free trade. He also strongly backed immigration restriction and crackdowns on illegal immigrants. In this speech in June of 1993, he outlines his position on immigration.*

*Source:* http://www.buchanan.org/ooo-p-articles.html Internet Brigade Web site, 47671 Whirlpool Square, Potomac Falls, Va. 20165, Linda Muller, webmaster.

> *The great American Melting Pot is not melting, as once it did. . . .*

If our prime minister believes that 50 years hence "spinsters will still be cycling to Communion on Sunday morning," he had best think again. Rather, "the muezzin will be calling Allah's faithful to the High Street mosque" for Friday prayers.

Thus did the grandson of Winston Churchill, a week ago, call for a halt to the "relentless flow of immigrants" into Great Britain.

A volley of protest followed. "The *Times* of London . . . chastised him for . . . a 'tasteless outburst,' " reports the *New York Times,* "[A] leading Labor Party politician described his remarks as 'putrid and racist.' Michael Howard, the Home Secretary, archly denounced what he described as 'any intervention which could have the effect of damaging race relations . . .' Downing Street said Prime Minister John Major agreed with Mr. Howard."

But, on this issue, Mr. Churchill speaks for Europe and its growing concern over the swelling tide of immigration from the East and the Third World, and the impact on the fate and future of the West.

For Mr. Churchill's remark came just days before France's interior minister called for "zero immigration," and only days after Germany voted to amend its asylum law. Mr. Churchill spoke the same weekend a neo-Nazi teenager was charged with arson-murder in that firebombing in Solingen that took the lives of five Turkish girls and women. The riots triggered by that atrocity left Solingen's town center gutted. All over Europe the doors to the East and South are being shut.

Before condemning Germany for restricting asylum-seekers, we ought to remember: Germany is smaller than Oregon and Washington combined, yet is home to almost 80 million people, among them 1.8 million Turks Still, 167,000 new immigrants arrived in the first four months of this year. (How would Oregon and Washington react to 500,000 immigrants this year?) Moreover, Germany has accepted more Bosnian refugees than all other nations combined.

To their credit, the Germans have coddled neither the neo-Nazi skin-heads, nor the Turkish and leftist vandals—as some Americans did after our L.A. riots that made Solingen look like a panty raid.

But Germany today could be America tomorrow, if we do not address the twin issues of immigration and assimilation.

Consider the change in our own country in four decades. In 1950, America was a land of 150 million, 90 percent of European stock. Today the US population is 250 million—about 75 percent white, 12 percent black, 9 percent Hispanic, and the balance largely Asian-American.

By 2050, according to the Census Bureau, whites may be near a minority in an America of 81 million Hispanics, 62 million blacks and 41 million Asians. By the middle of the next century, the United States will have become a veritable Brazil of North America.

If the future character of America is not to be decided by our own paralysis, Americans must stop being intimidated by charges of "racist" "nativist," and "zenophobe"—and we must begin to address the hard issues of race, culture and national unity.

Already, California faces yearly fiscal crises due to the soaring cost of services for illegal aliens, perhaps a million of whom walk into the United States every year from Mexico.

And the great American Melting Pot is not melting, as once it did. After decades of heroic effort to integrate blacks more fully into American society, our failures remain as conspicuous as our successes. Racial tension is rising. In the L.A. riots, not only were whites the victims of attempted lynchings, Koreatown was pillaged by blacks and Hispanics. Many of the latter were illegal, as four in 10 felonies in San Diego County are the work of illegals.

While white-on-black crime has become relatively rare (white criminals choose black victims only 2 percent of the time), black criminals now choose white victims, in rapes and muggings, 50 percent of the time.

And demands are growing that our heritage of individual rights be superseded by a new system of racial entitlements. Quotas are routine in government and private business. On college campuses, there are new demands for all-black dorms and all-black cultural centers; blacks, whites, Hispanics and Asians tend to congregate, more and more, only with each other.

Supporters of open immigration contend that Hispanic, Asian and Arab immigrants often bring with them the same strong family ties, respect for authority, and work ethic Americans have always cherished and celebrated.

Undeniably true. But it is equally true that many Third World immigrants are living off public services, and many are going into crime. It is also true that America's generous asylum laws are being abused. The man who allegedly murdered the CIA workers in McLean, the men arrested for the World Trade Center bombing, were supposedly fleeing persecution abroad.

America needs to take what some have called a "time out" on immigration: a closing of our southern frontier to invading illegals, by troops if necessary, a toughening of our asylum laws, a cutback on legal immigration to spouses and minor children of those already here.

Looking back down the 20th century, we see that all the great multinational empires have fallen apart. Now, the multinational states—Canada, Czechoslovakia, India, Russia, Yugoslavia, South Africa, Ethiopia—are breaking apart. Are we immune to all this?

After a quarter-century of wide open immigration, we need at least a decade to assimilate the tens of millions who have come in. Else, Russia's fate in the '90s may be America's in the new century.

## Amendment to the Constitution on Affirmative Action, and Statement of Martin Kilson, 1983

*Affirmative action had become a very controversial issue by the late 1970s and early 1980s. Orrin Hatch, a Republican senator from Utah, offered the constitutional amendment below outlawing affirmative action. Martin Kilson, an African American professor from Harvard, testified at hearings on the amendment chaired by Hatch.*

Source: Thomas Frazier, ed., *The Many Sides of America: 1945 to the Present* (New York: Harcourt Brace, 1996); original in Hearings Before the Subcommittee on the Constitution of

the Committee of the Judiciary, U.S. Senate, 1983.

## JOINT RESOLUTION

### Proposing an Amendment to the Constitution of the United States Relating to Affirmative Action

Resolved by the Senate and House of Representatives of the United States of America in Congress assembled, (two-thirds of each House concurring therein), That the following article is proposed as an amendment to the Constitution of the United States, which shall be valid to all intents and purposes as part of the Constitution if ratified by the legislatures of three-fourths of the several States:

## ARTICLE—

*Section 1.* Neither the United States nor any State shall make or enforce any law which makes distinctions on account of race, color, or national origin.

*Section 2.* All laws of the United States or any State which prohibit discrimination on account of race, color, or national origin by private individuals or enterprises shall not be construed to permit the establishment or maintenance by such private individuals or enterprises of any program or policy that makes distinctions on account of race, color, or national origin.

*Section 3.* Neither the United States nor any State shall establish or maintain, or require or permit any private individual or enterprise within the scope of section 2 to establish or maintain, goals, quotas, timetables, ratios, or numerical objectives which make distinctions on account of race, color, or national origin.

*Section 4.* Neither the United States nor any State shall make any law which prohibits any person in the absence of intent to discriminate on account of race, color, or national origin, to take actions, otherwise lawful, which have a disproportionate impact or effect upon individuals on the basis of race, color, or national origin.

*Section 5.* All limitations in this article upon laws, regulations, orders, programs, or actions which make distinctions on account of race, color, or national origin shall encompass laws, regulations, orders, programs, or actions which either make express distinctions on account of such race, color, or national origin or which are intended to result in distinctions on such account.

*Section 6.* No order or decree shall be issued by any court of the United States or of any State that makes distinctions on account of race, color, or national origin (except to the extent that such order or decree is necessary to remedy the enforcement of a law by the United States or any State, or the establishment or maintenance of a program or policy by a private individual or enterprise, that is in violation of this article).

*Section 7.* The Congress and the States shall have power to enforce this article by appropriate legislation.

## STATEMENT OF MARTIN KILSON, PROFESSOR OF GOVERNMENT, HARVARD UNIVERSITY

MR. KILSON. Thank you Senator Hatch. I am very pleased to be here.

Let me say straight off by way of introduction—and which I do not say here in the text which I have called "Affirmative Action Is Fair and Reasonable," a copy of which I have already given to the staff and which I will present in a moment as swiftly as I can—in my text I do not say what I want to say here: First, that my remarks are based upon a distinction among those who have been critics of affirmative action.

I distinguish between the bad critics— whom I often like to call also the loudmouth critics—and the good, sympathetic critics. Perhaps the most eloquent, fervent, and brilliant exponent is this great gentleman, Dr. Morris Abram, to my right.

I walk, in my thinking about affirmative action, a tightrope of sympathy toward the good critics—Dr. Morris Abram, a long-standing defender of equal opportunity, who put his career, his life, and his status on the line in behalf of it— on the one hand—and skepticism toward his passionate and rigorous opposition to quotas and preferential treatment as the most operative mode of affirmative action. It is not an easy tightrope to walk— that tightrope of respect for a colorblind approach to equality, on the one hand, and my own belief that a colorblind democracy can in fact be true to its longrun values of equality while at the same time use public policy to aid, in a racially skewed manner, Afro-Americans to gain parity of opportunity for social mobility with white Americans. This is, perforce, a process that will be rather messy, not always true to principles of colorblind democracy, but nevertheless it is a process that the history of racism dictates. After all the critics of affirmative action—either good or bad ones—can hardly claim that our system has never adopted other public policies whose application produced conflict between competing ideals.

I defend affirmative action as equal opportunity. I am much less in defense of it as quotas and preferential treatment, and I will get around to that.

There are several familiar criticisms from the critics of affirmative action—as I have just mentioned the good critics and the bad. Let me state them, and then I will address them.

First, that skewing of opportunity for occupational and social mobility in favor of blacks, women, and other groups identified under affirmative action guidelines in legislation is unprecedented and thus unfair—it is argued—for no other group or sectors in American political history and life have been affirmatively assisted through public policy. That is one argument.

Second, helping Afro-Americans to gain occupational parity with whites after a century of massive discrimination against Afro-Americans violates the new status of equality before the law that was created by the civil rights legislation in the 1960's.

A third criticism is that those citizens who are asked to sustain restitution to Afro-Americans by way of affirmative action practices—for example, Alan Bakke—did not, themselves, commit injuries or oppressive acts against Afro-Americans in the past.

A fourth criticism is that merit, obviously so fundamental to efficiency and fairness in our modern society, will be made a shambles by affirmative action practices.

I should like to comment on these several criticisms.

First, it is not correct, I think, to argue that affirmative action practices are without precedent in American politics—as many bad critics do—and, therefore, that white groups were never affirmatively assisted through public policy.

Politics in American cities, counties, and States have involved the control of extensive social resources and benefits—patronage, if you will—which, by means fair and foul, have been skewed for long periods of time in behalf of specific ethnic and interest groups.

For a century or more, this has amounted, I suggest, to a form of de facto affirmative action, though never labeled such—affirmative action, that is, for Irish Americans, for Anglo Protestants in the South and elsewhere, for Italian, Slavic, and other white ethnic groups—a point the bad critics have always failed to recognize.

The same skewing of resources and opportunity for occupational and social mobility through politics and public policy has favored other types of white interest groups—groups like veterans or producer groups like tobacco farmers, cotton farmers; dairy farmers, and other such groups.

In San Francisco, for example, between 1879 and 1900, Irish Americans, a controlling force in the city's politics, received 30 percent of all white-collar public jobs, and by 1900 the public sector in San Francisco employed 10 percent of all Irish white-collar workers. And I could give you so many more examples of such.

This, I dare say, is and was and has been a form of affirmative action. So, too, was the skewing in favor of whites of some 10 million housing units provided by the FHA between 1935 and 1955, a skewing that was mandated by FHA guidelines, guidelines that explicitly excluded Afro-Americans as housing recipients and a skewing the political practices of city and State governments helped to carry out.

This affirmative action for whites in the past has meant in this particular case that barely 1 percent of FHA-provided housing went to Afro-Americans between 1935 and 1955. The brilliant analysis of this process—anyone who is interested—can be found in the work of Dr. Abram's namesake, the great Charles Abram, the major FHA Administrator in those years.

A similar form of affirmative action for white groups was apparent in the admissions practices of America's great State university systems from their very founding in the late 19th century down to the 1960's—nearly a four-generation period when white preferential treatment for admission to public colleges was based upon nearly total exclusion of Afro-Americans.

Thus, in these and in many, many other areas that one could mention, social mobility was linked to public policy between the late 19th century and the 1960's. It is not an exaggeration, sir, to say that, while not called affirmative action, something rather like it applied to whites and, by contrast, what we can call affirmative discrimination applied to Afro-Americans.

Curiously enough, the affirmative action policies for Afro-Americans since 1970 have been labeled by critics of these policies—the bad critics—as a form of affirmative discrimination against whites. My colleague at Harvard University, Nathan Glazer, perhaps was the first to use the term "affirmative discrimination" in his widely-read book by that title.

The argument is twofold. First, it is claimed that the new status of equality before the law provided by civil rights legislation of the 1960's—that great epic—is adequate for the typical Afro-American to start the occupational and social race for parity of mobility with white Americans. Second, in this affirmative discrimination argument, it is claimed that reinforcing Afro-Americans' equality before the law with policies which aid them or compensate them in gaining occupational and educational positions is unprecedented and unduly discriminatory toward white Americans— in short, a denial of equality before the law since the 1960's.

In regard to the first aspect of the affirmative discrimination claim, I think it is based on a rather shallow understanding of the awful legacy of institutional constraint and psychic trauma visited upon Afro-Americans by racist practices including the white supremacy ideological orientations and the shameful violence that sustained the worst racist practices for nearly a century.

Conservative and other critics of affirmative action fail, I suggest, to grasp that the century-old assault of racism on Afro-Americans' chances for equal opportunity was too complex to be corrected merely by the final mandating in the 1960's of a colorblind Federal Government and Constitution. . . .

In regard to the issue of who should sustain the costs of restitution or the element of restitution that is associated with affirmative action, my Harvard colleague, a conservative, Prof. James Q. Wilson in my own department of political science—or, as we like to call it at Harvard 'of government'—offers the following comment in the *Washington Post,* March 4: "Affirmative action is often thought of as a form of restitution, but those who pay—for example, Alan Bakke—are not those responsible for the earlier evil."

I suggest that this perspective is entirely wrong. No serious observer would apply this formulation to, say, indemnities imposed on the German State for expropriating property and destroying careers and lives of millions of Jews during World War II. Nor would a serious observer of these kinds of problems apply this formulation to a court's damages on a chemical corporation for contaminating the drinking water or the housing sites of an American community.

Successor politicians to the German States and—yes—their citizens too, while not having themselves harmed the Jews, are liable in international and civil law to acknowledge restitution, and the same is true for the new executives and stockholders of the polluting firms, while not themselves the polluters.

Thus, I submit that affirmative action policies, if enacted by our Government and courts after finding massive violations of Afro-American rights in the past, are as valid as the indemnities on the German State or damages on a polluting corporation.

It is, of course, the task of our politicians—a difficult task—and of our leaders in private institutions, in finance, industry, education, and the like, to carry out the compensatory features if they are associated with affirmative action, and they have the clearly difficult task of trying to do this in a judicious manner, in a manner beneficial to Afro-Americans but not destructive of whites' interest.

It is here, of course, where the issue of merit looms large. There are two sides, at least, to the merit issue. First is the matter of quality and efficiency. Second is the matter of goals and quotas, so brilliantly spoken to just a moment ago by Dr. Abram.

With regard to the matter of the quality of personnel-selected for all kinds of jobs with the aid of affirmative action policies, practices, or guidelines, I myself do not think there is any intrinsic reason why merit has to be destroyed under affirmative action any more, say, than it had to be destroyed during a century of patronage-driven politics controlled in cities by white ethnics or controlled in southern counties and States by white Protestants.

It happens that American pragmatism—one of our really great gifts to the world—has allowed us to interpret meritocratic criteria broadly rather than rigidly.

Thus, meritocratic criteria are, in

practice, more relative then they are absolute. Any WASP in early 20th century Boston could tell you that the training of professional occupations in American universities varies greatly at the time in regard to merit criteria as between, say, the elite Harvard Law School and the elite MIT, on the one hand, and the professional and technical schools by the hundreds founded in early 20th century Boston and elsewhere for students from ethnic and lower strata families like New England School of Law, on the other hand.

In fact, the New England School of Law—originally Portia Law School—did not require bachelor's degree training—an undergraduate degree—as a condition for picking up some skills regarding the law. I think that remained so until about 1953.

Here, then—and this is my point— was a redefinition of existing meritocratic criteria as defined by upper class WASP institutions in order to open up new opportunity, new paths for social mobility for, say, Irish Americans, Italians, no status or redneck Protestants, Greeks, and others.

Yet, college-trained Afro-Americans —I submit here today—while accepting the validity of affirmative action practices and programs, surely have a vested interest in protecting the proper use of merit.

Simple-minded dismissal of merit by some elements in black leadership is a disservice to all blacks. Therefore, I agree with Dr. Abram. I oppose changing the rules in favor of blacks who take the entry civil service examinations. This is a

transparent effort to deny what I call the proper use of meritocratic criteria.

The matter of goals and quotas is, of course, a difficult feature of affirmative action practices, and rightly so. Groups like American Jews who have had quotas used against them naturally resist a public policy that employs quotas or some variant thereof in allocating jobs and college slots.

Quotas employed in a rigid manner are not, I think, necessary to affirmative action. Yet, some kind of numerical yardstick—let us say some generalized notion of goals—is somewhat necessary for affirmative action. Sensitive administrators, when carefully watched by vigilant officials and interest groups, can, I think, walk this delicate tightrope between what I call rigid quotas and preferential treatment, on the one hand, and some generalized notion of goals, on the other.

Interestingly enough, Senator Hatch, quotas and preferential treatment as a form of affirmative action, suggesting, as they do, in fact, too much rigidity in basing these decisions on gender or race, are rejected in a 1977 Gallup poll and in more recent polls, by the way—and I just picked up the data closest to me when I was preparing this last week—by blacks and whites—rejected by 55 percent of blacks and 84 percent of whites as a form for executing affirmative action and equal opportunity.

Yet—it is important to note—over two-thirds of whites and blacks support the practice of affirmative action as a form of equal opportunity in jobs and education without rigid quotas being employed.

Furthermore, the most recent survey on these matters by Sindlinger poll—which actually exists about two towns away from where I grew up in the eastern central part of Pennsylvania; it operates out of Valley Forge—in 1980, asked white folks whether minorities—mainly blacks—and women aided in training and jobs by affirmative action policies: "affected your own attitude toward minority and women doctors and lawyers?"

To this query, 20 percent of white adults said yes, but 75 percent no.

When asked another query: "Whether qualifications of a black lawyer or woman doctor are likely to be worth as much as those of other doctors and lawyers"—and the presumption is that these are persons whose mobility into these professions was assisted by affirmative action policies—17 percent of whites said no, but 67 percent said yes.

Finally, when asked by Sindlinger Poll: "If you would yourself avoid dealing with a black doctor or a woman lawyer," 11 percent said yes, but 84 percent said no.

Mr. Chairman, very much to their credit, most white Americans, despite clear uneasiness with aspects of affirmative action, are behaving quite decently and maturely toward it and its outcomes. Blacks have white allies on this issue among both Democrats and Republicans, and I hope some of those allies sit on this committee today.

Further reasons for being sanguine about white allies are found in another set of recent survey data, relating less to the issue of quotas in affirmative action than to the overall activity of the Federal Government in specifically aiding greater social mobility for Afro-Americans. A Roper poll in February 1980 found 33 percent of voters responding "gone too far" but 67 percent saying "about right" or "not far enough," 43 percent the former, 24 percent later when asked: "What about blacks and job opportunities—do you think that we in this country have gone too far, not far enough, or have done about the right amount in making job opportunities for blacks?" While an overwhelming proportion of liberal respondents, 76 percent, said "about right" or "not far enough," 41 percent and 35 percent respectively, a rather sizable proportion of conservative respondents, 61 percent also replied "about right" or "not far enough," 41 percent and 20 percent respectively. Only 24 percent of liberals said "gone too far," but, interestingly enough, only 39 percent of conservatives felt this way. And all polls since Reagan's election have about two-thirds of voters, liberal and conservative, favoring expenditures on CETA programs. For example, a recent *New York Times*/CBS poll, May 3, 1981, found 16 percent of liberals favoring cutbacks in CETA funds and only 32 percent of conservatives backing cutbacks.

Thus if the current Congress, and especially the Senate with its new Republican majority, has the will to sustain affirmative action programs, there is rather strong support for this policy among voters. On the other hand, if the militant conservatives in Congress wish to apply to affirmative action their ideological preference to reduce drastically Government's role in American life, they might well get away with it without fear of voter reaction at the ballot box. For though a clear majority of voters favors the current status of affirmative action—save their opposition to quotas—it is doubtful that the intensity of this support is great enough to threaten Congressmen who vote to weaken affirmative action.

Thus, like the "First Reconstruction" a century ago, the future of what might be called the "Third Reconstruction" [the "Second Reconstruction" being President Johnson's civil rights and Great Society policies] depends upon those elusive ingredients of successful leadership in American politics—namely, moral fiber and political courage. It is hoped that these leadership attributes are not wanting as Congress considers the future of affirmative action in this and coming sessions—that, indeed, the pathetic failure of moral fiber and political courage that allowed Congress to wreck the "First Reconstruction" a century ago will not repeat itself in the 1980's.

Thank you.

## The Bakke Case, 1978

Regents of the Univ. of California v. Bakke, *argued before the Supreme Court in 1978, was one of the most important of several court cases over the last thirty years addressing the issue of affirmative action. When Alan Bakke applied to the University of California at Davis Medical School, there were very few spots available in the first-year class for the thousands of applicants. Most of those spots were filled through the normal admissions process, but a small number were set aside for minority students. Bakke, a white* *male, was rejected twice and filed suit against the university, accusing it of reverse discrimination. Excerpts from the Court's decision follow. The Court ruled in favor of Bakke in this instance but did not prevent schools from taking race into account in admissions processes.*

*Source:* Thomas Frazier, ed., *The Many Sides of America: 1945 to the Present* (New York: Harcourt Brace, 1996), p. 649.

*Mr. Justice Powell announced the judgment of the Court.*

The state certainly has a legitimate and substantial interest in ameliorating, or eliminating where feasible, the disabling effects of identified discrimination. The line of school desegregation cases, commencing with Brown, attests to the importance of this state goal and the commitment of the judiciary to affirm all lawful means towards its attainment. In the schools cases, the states were required by the courts to redress the wrongs worked by specific instances of racial discrimination. That goal was far more focused than the remedying of "societal discrimination," an amorphous concept of injury that may be ageless in its reach into the past.

Hence, the purpose of helping certain groups whom the faculty of the Davis Medical School perceived as victims of "societal discrimination" does not justify a classification that imposes disadvantages on persons like respondent, who bear no responsibility for whatever harm the beneficiaries of the special admissions program are thought to have suffered. To hold otherwise would be to convert a remedy heretofore reserved for violations of legal rights into a privilege that all institutions throughout the nation could grant at their pleasure to whatever groups are perceived as victims of societal discrimination. That is a step we have never approved.

*Mr. Justice Powell concluded.*

In summary, it is evident that the Davis special admission program involves the use of an explicit racial classification never before countenanced by this Court. It tells applicants who are not Negro, Asian, or "Chicano" that they are totally excluded from a specific percentage of the seats in an entering class. No matter how strong their qualifications, quantitative and extracurricular including their own potential for contribution to ethnic diversity, they are never afforded the chance to compete with applicants from the preferred groups for the special admissions seats. At the same time, the preferred applicants have the opportunity to compete for every seat in the class.

The fatal flaw in petitioner's preferential program is its disregard for individual rights as guaranteed by the Fourteenth Amendment. Such rights are not absolute. But when a state's distribution of benefits or imposition of burdens hinges on the color of a person's skin or ancestry, that individual is entitled to a demonstration that the challenged classification is necessary to promote a substantial state interest. Petitioner has failed to carry this burden. For this rea-

son, that portion of the California court's judgment holding petitioner's special admissions program invalid under the Fourteenth Amendment must be affirmed.

In enjoining petitioner from ever considering the race of an applicant, however, the courts below failed to recognize that the state has a substantial interest that legitimately may be served by a properly devised admissions program involving the competitive consideration of race and ethnic origin. For this reason, so much of the California court's judgment as enjoins the petitioner from any consideration of race must be reversed.

## President Lyndon Johnson, Commencement Address at Howard University, "To Fulfill These Rights," June 4, 1965

*Lyndon Baines Johnson gave this speech at the commencement of Howard University in June of 1965. The speech came as the Voting Rights Act was making its way through Congress. Johnson would sign that bill on August 6, 1965. This speech, however, foreshadowed the great issues that would dominate the future of American race relations, most notably affirmative action. In a frequently quoted passage, Johnson suggests, "You do not take a person who for years has been hobbled by chains and liberate him, bring him up to the starting line of a race and then say, 'You are free to compete. . . .'"*

*Source:* http://www.lbjlib.utexas.edu/johnson/archives.hom/speeches/hom/650604.html.

Dr. Nabrit, my fellow Americans:

I am delighted at the chance to speak at this important and this historic institution. Howard has long been an outstanding center for the education of Negro Americans. Its students are of every race and color and they come from many countries of the world. It is truly a working example of democratic excellence.

Our earth is the home of revolution. In every corner of every continent men charged with hope contend with ancient ways in the pursuit of justice. They reach for the newest of weapons to realize the oldest of dreams, that each may walk in freedom and pride, stretching his talents, enjoying the fruits of the earth.

Our enemies may occasionally seize the day of change, but it is the banner of our revolution they take. And our own future is linked to this process of swift and turbulent change in many lands in the world. But nothing in any country touches us more profoundly, and nothing is more freighted with meaning for our own destiny than the revolution of the Negro American.

In far too many ways American Negroes have been another nation: deprived of freedom, crippled by hatred, the doors of opportunity closed to hope.

In our time change has come to this Nation, too. The American Negro, acting with impressive restraint, has peacefully protested and marched, entered the courtrooms and the seats of government, demanding a justice that has long been denied. The voice of the Negro was the call to action. But it is a tribute to America that, once aroused, the courts and the Congress, the President and most of the people, have been the allies of progress.

## LEGAL PROTECTION FOR HUMAN RIGHTS

Thus we have seen the high court of the country declare that discrimination based on race was repugnant to the Constitution, and therefore void. We have seen in 1957, and 1960, and again in 1964, the first civil rights legislation in this Nation in almost an entire century.

As majority leader of the United States Senate, I helped to guide two of these bills through the Senate. And, as your President, I was proud to sign the third. And now very soon we will have the fourth—a new law guaranteeing every American the right to vote.

No act of my entire administration will give me greater satisfaction than the day when my signature makes this bill, too, the law of this land.

The voting rights bill will be the latest, and among the most important, in a long series of victories. But this victory—as Winston Churchill said of another triumph for freedom—"is not the end. It is not even the beginning of the end. But it is, perhaps, the end of the beginning."

That beginning is freedom; and the barriers to that freedom are tumbling down. Freedom is the right to share, share fully and equally, in American society—to vote, to hold a job, to enter a public place, to go to school. It is the right to be treated in every part of our national life as a person equal in dignity and promise to all others.

## FREEDOM IS NOT ENOUGH

But freedom is not enough. You do not wipe away the scars of centuries by saying: Now you are free to go where you want, and do as you desire, and choose the leaders you please.

You do not take a person who, for years, has been hobbled by chains and liberate him, bring him up to the starting line of a race and then say, "you are free to compete with all the others," and still justly believe that you have been completely fair.

Thus it is not enough just to open the gates of opportunity. All our citizens must have the ability to walk through those gates.

This is the next and the more profound stage of the battle for civil rights. We seek not just freedom but opportunity. We seek not just legal equity but human ability, not just equality as a right and a theory but equality as a fact and equality as a result.

For the task is to give 20 million Negroes the same chance as every other American to learn and grow, to work and share in society, to develop their abilities—physical, mental and spiritual, and to pursue their individual happiness.

To this end equal opportunity is essential, but not enough, not enough. Men and women of all races are born with the same range of abilities. But ability is not just the product of birth. Ability is stretched or stunted by the family that you live with, and the neighborhood you live in—by the school you go to and the poverty or the richness of your surroundings. It is the product of a hundred unseen forces playing upon the little infant, the child, and finally the man.

## PROGRESS FOR SOME

This graduating class at Howard University is witness to the indomitable determination of the Negro American to win his way in American life.

The number of Negroes in schools of higher learning has almost doubled in 15 years. The number of nonwhite professional workers has more than doubled in 10 years. The median income of Negro college women tonight exceeds that of white college women. And there are also the enormous accomplishments of distinguished individual Negroes—many of them graduates of this institution, and one of them the first lady ambassador in the history of the United States.

These are proud and impressive achievements. But they tell only the story of a growing middle class minority, steadily narrowing the gap between them and their white counterparts.

## A WIDENING GULF

But for the great majority of Negro Americans—the poor, the unemployed, the uprooted, and the dispossessed—there is a much grimmer story. They still, as we meet here tonight, are another nation. Despite the court orders and the laws, despite the legislative victories and the speeches, for them the walls are rising and the gulf is widening.

Here are some of the facts of this American failure.

Thirty-five years ago the rate of unemployment for Negroes and whites was about the same. Tonight the Negro rate is twice as high.

In 1948 the 8 percent unemployment rate for Negro teenage boys was actually less than that of whites. By last year that rate had grown to 23 percent, as against 13 percent for whites unemployed.

Between 1949 and 1959, the income of Negro men relative to white men declined in every section of this country. From 1952 to 1963 the median income of Negro families compared to white actually dropped from 57 percent to 53 percent.

In the years 1955 through 1957, 22 percent of experienced Negro workers were out of work at some time during the year. In 1961 through 1963 that proportion had soared to 29 percent.

Since 1947 the number of white families living in poverty has decreased 27 percent while the number of poorer nonwhite families decreased only 3 percent.

The infant mortality of nonwhites in 1940 was 70 percent greater than whites. Twenty-two years later it was 90 percent greater.

Moreover, the isolation of Negro from white communities is increasing, rather than decreasing as Negroes crowd into the central cities and become a city within a city.

Of course Negro Americans as well as white Americans have shared in our rising national abundance. But the harsh fact of the matter is that in the battle for true equality too many—far too many—are losing ground every day.

## THE CAUSES OF INEQUALITY

We are not completely sure why this is. We know the causes are complex and subtle. But we do know the two broad basic reasons. And we do know that we have to act.

First, Negroes are trapped—as many whites are trapped—in inherited, gateless poverty. They lack training and skills. They are shut in, in slums, without decent medical care. Private and public poverty combine to cripple their capacities.

We are trying to attack these evils through our poverty program, through our education program, through our medical care and our other health programs, and a dozen more of the Great Society programs that are aimed at the root causes of this poverty.

We will increase, and we will accelerate, and we will broaden this attack in years to come until this most enduring of foes finally yields to our unyielding will.

But there is a second cause—much more difficult to explain, more deeply grounded, more desperate in its force. It is the devastating heritage of long years of slavery; and a century of oppression, hatred, and injustice.

## SPECIAL NATURE OF NEGRO POVERTY

For Negro poverty is not white poverty. Many of its causes and many of its cures are the same. But there are differences—deep, corrosive, obstinate differences—radiating painful roots into the community, and into the family, and the nature of the individual.

These differences are not racial differences. They are solely and simply the consequence of ancient brutality, past injustice, and present prejudice. They are anguishing to observe. For the Negro they are a constant reminder of oppression. For the white they are a constant reminder of guilt. But they must be faced and they must be dealt with and they must be overcome, if we are ever to reach the time when the only difference between Negroes and whites is the color of their skin.

Nor can we find a complete answer in the experience of other American minorities. They made a valiant and a largely successful effort to emerge from poverty and prejudice.

The Negro, like these others, will have to rely mostly upon his own efforts. But he just can not do it alone. For they did not have the heritage of centuries to overcome, and they did not have a cultural tradition which had been twisted and battered by endless years of hatred and hopelessness, nor were they excluded—these others—because of race or color—a feeling whose dark intensity is matched by no other prejudice in our society.

Nor can these differences be understood as isolated infirmities. They are a seamless web. They cause each other. They result from each other. They reinforce each other.

Much of the Negro community is buried under a blanket of history and circumstance. It is not a lasting solution to lift just one corner of that blanket. We must stand on all sides and we must raise the entire cover if we are to liberate our fellow citizens.

## THE ROOTS OF INJUSTICE

One of the differences is the increased concentration of Negroes in our cities. More than 73 percent of all Negroes live in urban areas compared with less than 70 percent of the whites. Most of these Negroes live in slums. Most of these Negroes live together—a separated people.

Men are shaped by their world. When it is a world of decay, ringed by an invisible wall, when escape is arduous and uncertain, and the saving pressures of a more hopeful society are unknown, it can cripple the youth and it can desolate the men.

There is also the burden that a dark skin can add to the search for a productive place in our society. Unemployment strikes most swiftly and broadly at the Negro, and this burden erodes hope. Blighted hope breeds despair. Despair brings indifferences to the learning which offers a way out. And despair, coupled with indifferences, is often the source of destructive rebellion against the fabric of society.

There is also the lacerating hurt of early collision with white hatred or prejudice, distaste or condescension. Other groups have felt similar intolerance. But success and achievement could wipe it away. They do not change the color of a man's skin. I have seen this uncomprehending pain in the eyes of the little, young Mexican-American schoolchildren that I taught many years ago. But it can be overcome. But, for many, the wounds are always open.

## FAMILY BREAKDOWN

Perhaps most important—its influence radiating to every part of life—is the breakdown of the Negro family structure. For this, most of all, white America must accept responsibility. It flows from centuries of oppression and persecution of the Negro man. It flows from the long years of degradation and discrimination, which have attacked his dignity and assaulted his ability to produce for his family.

This, too, is not pleasant to look upon. But it must be faced by those whose serious intent is to improve the life of all Americans.

Only a minority—less than half—of all Negro children reach the age of 18 having lived all their lives with both of their parents. At this moment, tonight, little less than two-thirds are at home with both of their parents. Probably a majority of all Negro children receive federally-aided public assistance sometime during their childhood.

The family is the cornerstone of our society. More than any other force it shapes the attitude, the hopes, the ambitions, and the values of the child. And when the family collapses it is the children that are usually damaged. When it happens on a massive scale the community itself is crippled.

So, unless we work to strengthen the family, to create conditions under which most parents will stay together—all the rest: schools, and playgrounds, and public assistance, and private concern, will never be enough to cut completely the circle of despair and deprivation.

## TO FULFILL THESE RIGHTS

There is no single easy answer to all of these problems.

Jobs are part of the answer. They bring the income which permits a man to provide for his family.

Decent homes in decent surroundings and a chance to learn—an equal chance to learn—are part of the answer.

Welfare and social programs better designed to hold families together are part of the answer.

Care for the sick is part of the answer.

An understanding heart by all Americans is another big part of the answer.

And to all of these fronts—and a dozen more—I will dedicate the expanding efforts of the Johnson administration.

But there are other answers that are still to be found. Nor do we fully understand even all of the problems. Therefore, I want to announce tonight that this fall I intend to call a White House conference of scholars, and experts, and outstanding Negro leaders—men of both races—and officials of Government at every level.

This White House conference's theme and title will be "To Fulfill These Rights."

Its object will be to help the American Negro fulfill the rights which, after the long time of injustice, he is finally about to secure.

To move beyond opportunity to achievement.

To shatter forever not only the barriers of law and public practice, but the walls which bound the condition of many by the color of his skin.

To dissolve, as best we can, the antique enmities of the heart which diminish the holder, divide the great democracy, and do wrong—great wrong—to the children of God.

And I pledge you tonight that this will be a chief goal of my administration, and of my program next year, and in the years to come. And I hope, and I pray, and I believe, it will be a part of the program of all America.

## WHAT IS JUSTICE

For what is justice?

It is to fulfill the fair expectations of man.

Thus, American justice is a very special thing. For, from the first, this has been a land of towering expectations. It was to be a nation where each man could be ruled by the common consent of all—enshrined in law, given life by institutions, guided by men themselves subject to its rule. And all—all of every station and origin—would be touched equally in obligation and in liberty.

Beyond the law lay the land. It was a rich land, glowing with more abundant promise than man had ever seen. Here, unlike any place yet known, all were to share the harvest.

And beyond this was the dignity of man. Each could become whatever his qualities of mind and spirit would permit—to strive, to seek, and, if he could, to find his happiness.

This is American justice. We have pursued it faithfully to the edge of our imperfections, and we have failed to find it for the American Negro.

So, it is the glorious opportunity of this generation to end the one huge wrong of the American Nation and, in so doing, to find America for ourselves, with the same immense thrill of discovery which gripped those who first began to realize that here, at last, was a home for freedom.

All it will take is for all of us to understand what this country is and what this country must become.

The Scripture promises: "I shall light a candle of understanding in thine heart, which shall not be put out."

Together, and with millions more, we can light that candle of understanding in the heart of all America.

And, once lit, it will never again go out.

*Note:* The President spoke at 6:35 P.M. on the Main Quadrangle in front of the library at Howard University in Washington, after being awarded an honorary degree of doctor of laws. His opening words referred to Dr. James M. Nabrit, Jr., President of the University. During his remarks he referred to Mrs. Patricia Harris, U.S. Ambassador to Luxembourg and former associate professor of law at Howard University.

The Voting Rights Act of 1965 was approved by the President on August 6, 1965.

## "One Nation, Many People: A Declaration of Cultural Independence," 1991

*In the 1980s and early 1990s a number of battles broke out over American history and social studies curricula in universities and public school systems. In 1991 a special committee for the New York Commissioner of Education issued a report, "One Nation, Many People: A Declaration of Cultural Independence," urging a revision of social science curricula in the New York public schools to emphasize cultural diversity. As the preamble of the report states "previous ideals of assimilation have been put into question and are now slowly being set aside." This report provoked substantial controversy as critics decried what they sensed was the report's indifference or even hostility to an American common culture.*

Source: Historic Documents of 1991 (Washington, D.C.: Congressional Quarterly, Inc., 1992).

### PREAMBLE

The United States is a microcosm of humanity today. No other country in the world is peopled by a greater variety of races, nationalities, and ethnic groups. But although the United States has been a great asylum for diverse peoples, it has not always been a great refuge for diverse cultures. The country has opened its doors to a multitude of nationalities, but often their cultures have not been encouraged to survive or, at best, have been kept marginal to the mainstream.

Since the 1960s, however, a profound reorientation of the self-image of Americans has been under way. Before this time the dominant model of the typical American had been conditioned primarily by the need to shape a unified nation out of a variety of contrasting and often conflicting European immigrant communities. But following the struggles for civil rights, the unprecedented increase in non-European immigration over the last two decades and the increasing recognition of our nation's indigenous heritage, there has been a fundamental change in the image of what a resident of the United States is.

With this change, which necessarily highlights the racial and ethnic pluralism of the nation, previous ideals of assimilation to an Anglo-American model have been put in question and are now slowly and sometimes painfully being set aside. Many people in the United States are no longer comfortable with the requirement, common in the past, that they shed their specific cultural differences in order to be considered American. Instead, while busily adapting to and shaping mainstream cultural ideals commonly identified as American, in recent decades many in the United States—from European and non-European backgrounds—have been encouraging a more tolerant, inclusive, and realistic vision of American identity than any that has existed in the past.

This identity, committed to the democratic principles of the nation and the nation-building in which all Americans are engaged, is progressively evolving from the past model toward a new model marked by respect for pluralism and awareness of the virtues of diversity.

This situation is a current reality, and a multicultural education, anchored to the shared principles of a liberal democracy, is today less an educational innovation than a national priority.

It is fitting for New York State, host to the Statue of Liberty, to inaugurate a curriculum that reflects the rich cultural diversity of the nation. The beacon of hope welcomes not just the "wretched and poor" individuals of the world, but also the dynamic and rich cultures all people bring with them.

Two centuries after this country's founders issued a Declaration of Independence, focused on the political independence from which societies distant from the United States have continued to draw inspiration, the time has come to *recognize cultural interdependence*. We propose that the principle of respect for diverse cultures is critical to our nation, and we affirm that a right to cultural diversity exists. We believe that the schoolroom is one of the places where this cultural *interdependence* must be reflected.

It is in this spirit that we have crafted this report, "One Nation, Many Peoples." We see the social studies as the primary avenue through which the school addresses our cultural diversity and interdependence. But the study of cultural diversity and interdependence is only one goal. It is through such studies that we seek to strengthen our national commitment and world citizenship, with the development of intellectual competence in our students as the foundation. We see the social studies as directed at the development of intellectual competence in learners, with the capacity to view the world and understand it from multiple perspectives as one of the main components of such competence. Multicultural knowledge in this conception of the social studies becomes a vehicle and not a goal. Multicultural content and experience become instruments by which we enable students to develop their intelligence and to function as human and humane persons.

## I. INTRODUCTION

### *Affirmation of Purpose*

This Committee affirms that multicultural education should be a source of strength and pride. Multicultural education is often viewed as divisive end even as destructive of the values and beliefs which hold us together as Americans. Certainly, contemporary trends toward separation and dissolution in such disparate countries as the Soviet Union, South Africa, Canada, Yugoslavia, Spain, and the United Kingdom remind us that different ethnic and racial groups have often had extraordinary difficulty remaining together in nation-states. But national unity does not require that we eliminate the very diversity that is the source of our uniqueness and, indeed, of our adaptability and viability among the nations of the world. *If the United States is to continue to prosper in the 21st century, then all of its citizens, whatever their race or ethnicity, must believe that they and their ancestors have shared in the building of the country and have a stake in its success.* Thus, multicultural education, far from being a source of dissolution, is necessary for the cultural health, social stability, and economic future of New York State and the nation.

The Committee believes that to achieve these ends, the teaching of social studies should emphasize the following:

*First,* beginning in the earliest grades social studies should be taught from a global perspective. The earth is humankind's common home. Migration is our common history. The earth's peoples, cultures, and material resources are our common wealth. Both humankind's pain and humankind's triumphs must be shared globally. The uniqueness of humankind is our *many ways of being human,* our remarkable range of cultural and physical diversity within a common biological unity.

*Second,* the social studies will very likely continue to serve nation-building purposes, among others, even as we encourage global perspectives. With efforts to respect and honor the diverse and pluralistic elements in our nation, special attention will need to be given to those values, characteristics, and traditions which we share in common. Commitment to the presentation of multiple perspectives in the social studies curriculum encourages attention to the traditional and dominant elements in our society, even as we introduce and examine minority elements which have been neglected or those which are emerging as a result of new scholarship and newly recognized voices.

*Third,* the curriculum must strive to be informed by the most up-to-date scholarship. It must be open to all relevant input, to new knowledge, to fresh perspectives. Human history is to be

seen as ongoing, often contradictory, and subject to reasonable differences based on contrasting perceptions and distinct viewpoints.

*Fourth,* students need to see themselves as active makers and changers of culture and society; they must he helped to develop the tools by which to judge, analyze, act, and evaluate.

*Fifth,* the program should be committed to the honoring and continuing examination of democratic values as an essential basis for social organization and nation-building. The application of democracy to social organization should be viewed as a continuing process which sometimes succeeds and sometimes fails, and thus requires constant effort.

*Sixth,* one of the central aims of the social studies is the development of the intellect; thus, the social studies should be taught not solely as information, but rather through the critical examination of ideas and events rooted in time and place and responding to social interests. The social studies should be seen not as some dreary schoolroom task of fact mastery to be tested and forgotten, but as one of the best curricular vehicles for telling the story of humanity in a way that motivates and inspires all of our children to continue the process of responsible nation-building in a world context. . . .

## Background: The Social Studies and the Changing Society

Recent debate concerning change in New York State's social studies curriculum often implies that the curriculum stands as a fixed and unchanging prescription for the classroom, its stability protecting the inculcation of basic values from shifting political and economic winds. Closer examination, however, reveals that the curriculum has grown and been transformed over time in response to societal change, as a few examples will show. . . .

Unlike literature and languages, the social studies and their parent disciplines of history and geography were not a major part of the mainstream of the school curriculum until the present century. In 1899, a Committee of Seven of the American Historical Association (founded in 1884) made a recommendation which led to the study of European and American history and government in schools, including those of New York State. Other subject-matter organizations, as they were formed, also began to press for inclusion in the school curriculum (the American Political Science Association and the American Sociological Association, for example, founded respectively in 1903 and 1905).

In the second decade of this century, the need to accommodate the surge of immigration led to the view that the schools should help students develop the attitudes and skills necessary for good citizenship. In 1916 a Committee on the Social Studies of the American Historical Association declared this to be the goal of schooling, bringing the term "social studies" into formal use. In 1951, responding to the mood of national insecurity reflected in McCarthyism, New York State dropped the term "social studies" in favor of "citizenship education," and the amount of American history in the secondary curriculum was greatly increased

("social studies" re-emerged in 1960). Between 1965 and the late 1980s, as international communication and commerce increased, the curriculum was enlarged to include more global studies, such as year-long courses in Asian and African Studies (grade 9) and European Studies (grade 10). Since 1987, these in turn have been replaced by a two-year global studies sequence.

Indeed, the processes of contest, debate, and transformation are integral parts of the rich history of education in the United States. That history has reflected the society of which it is a part, and societal changes over the past 30 years have brought with them rising interest in the study of diverse cultures in the United States and the world. In the universities, scholarly attention has turned to previously neglected groups (those that have historically been minorities in the United States and women) and topics (social history, ethnic and cultural studies). Such scholarship has brought to light much that had been omitted from U.S. and world history, as traditionally studied.

In the 1970s and early 1980s, elementary and secondary schools, like colleges and universities, were faced with the recognition that much of the experience, cultural values, and collective pasts of their students was not identified or represented in the curriculum. Corresponding to what James A. Banks has termed the "demographic imperative" of increasing numbers of minority students enrolled in public schools, parents, students and communities served by the schools became more forceful in demanding that their children learn about their own pasts. There was a new recognition that the teaching of social studies as a single officially sanctioned story was inaccurate as to the facts of conflict in American history, and further, that it was limiting for white students and students of color alike.

Much of the heat of debate concerning the importance of valuing cultural difference in the schools arises from divergent opinions on whether preparing students to become members of U.S. society necessarily means assimilation. While the goal of assimilation has historically been relatively explicit in American schooling, in recent years many thoughtful writers and educators have argued against assimilation when interpreted as erasure of distinctive cultural identities. *Education must respond to the joint imperatives of educating toward citizenship in a common polity while respecting and taking account of continuing distinctiveness.* Even more, as we have argued, the perspectives of a number of major groups in American society must he recognized and incorporated. Nor is assimilation essential to educate citizens who value this country's ideals and participate in its polity and economy. . . .

Over the past two decades, elementary, middle, and secondary schools and postsecondary institutions have seen efforts to restructure the curriculum in order to represent more adequately the diverse cultures of the student body and the world in which students must eventually function. Shifts in curriculum design in such states as California, Oregon, Iowa, Ohio and Florida reflect an increasing awareness that children and society are inadequately served when study

is limited to the intellectual monuments of Western civilization. Comprehensive study of multiple cultures is increasingly recognized as having critical relevance for students who will face a national economy and political structures that grow more globally interdependent and increasingly diverse. . . .

## II AND III. [OMITTED]
## IV. THE STATE SYLLABI

### The Syllabi in Relation to the Other Components of a Program

The current New York State Social Studies syllabi include a series of twelve publications: one booklet each for kindergarten and grades 1, 2, 3, 4, 5, 6, and 11; one for grades 7–8; one for 9–10; one for the first half of grade 12, and another for the second half. The publications vary in length from 73 to 202 pages. They are reviewed and updated periodically by committees of teachers and professors under the guidance of the Bureau of Social Studies Education. All of the current publications carry dates of revision between 1987 and 1989.

Statewide syllabi are not found in most other states, but in New York, with its long history of attempting to direct education from the top down, State syllabi are regarded as very important policy documents. And because such a large and influential state does officially adopt these documents, they acquire much more importance and visibility than do the locally and regionally developed curriculum outlines and syllabi elsewhere. It is vital, therefore, that the syllabi be accurate and comprehensive, and that they reflect up-to-date scholarship. The present syllabi were drawn up with participation of content specialists and practitioners, and the Committee recognizes the effort that was made to be comprehensive and to include subject matter about all parts of the world, about women, and about groups that have been minorities in the U.S. population. . . .

## Specific Findings and Illustrations with Regard to the Present New York State Syllabi and Social Studies Program

### Number One

*Finding: Need for multiple perspectives.* The Committee noted how frequently social studies slips into a "we-they" framework. All too often when communities are perceived as monolithic, it is common to teach from one perspective, usually that of the so-called dominant culture. For example, in the primary grades children examine neighborhoods and communities. Educators need to be aware that many of the typical features cited for study (such as banks, government buildings, department stores, and other major economic institutions) may not necessarily be present in inner-city or rural communities. Students need to be exposed to the strengths and potential of what does exist in their community, despite obstacles such as drugs and high visibility of crime. What does exist in the students' immediate real world should be used to help them become more aware of and sensitive to their civic responsibilities and possibilities in building their community. To take another in-

stance, the story of the early colonization in the eastern U.S. has too often been told from the perspective of the colonists, not the Native Americans already settled on the land. Or the story of the western United States is told as one of westward expansion, assuming the perspective of the migrating Easterners and disregarding the native men and women already there or the long-established Hispanic influence and settlements in the West.

*Related Finding: Unequal regard for the importance of national/regional boundaries and distinctions.* For example:

- In the syllabus for grades 9–10, all nations south of the United States are lumped together in the unit entitled "Latin America," tending to omit the information that a number of islands in the Caribbean and nations in Central and South America trace their traditions to non-Latin European nations, to Africa, India, and Indonesia, as well as to native roots. Attention is rarely paid to the complex and controversial relationship between Puerto Rico and the United States.

- The syllabus for grades 9/10 suggests: "Using pictures of Greek, Roman, and Oriental art and architecture, students could identify similarities." Does the term "Oriental" refer to Asians? If so, which Asians? The reference should be to specific Asian people, corresponding with the Greeks and Romans.

- Northern Africa often is implicitly or explicitly incorporated in the "Middle East" in the teaching of social studies at grade 6.

*Related Finding: A disregard for the under-standing and study of indigenous social, po-litical, economic, and technological struc-tures, and the precolonial histories of indigenous peoples.* For example, the treatment of the European colonization of Africa in the syllabi inadequately ad-dresses the great loss of lives and the eradication of many varieties of tradi-tional culture and knowledge. Similarly, the long and rich history of India before the British conquest is not properly treated. The K-6 syllabi, for example, focus on celebrations such as Thanksgiv-ing and Columbus Day without exam-ining other perspectives than those of Europeans, such as the perspectives of Native Americans.

*Related Finding: Effects are often seen as unidirectional (with the European partici-pants as the actors) rather than bi-directional.* For example, the syllabus for grades 9/10 recommends that teachers explore the effects of European rule on Africa with their students, but the effects that contact with Africa had on Eu-rope—or the dehumanizing effects on Europeans of their role as colonizers— are not mentioned. In the syllabus for grades 7/8, the connection between Toussaint L'Ouverture's defeat of Na-poleon in Haiti and the Louisiana Pur-chase is not made. In the grade 9/10 syllabus, the influence of Islam upon the religious, cultural, economic and politi-cal systems of lands extending from Spain to Sumatra is highlighted, but not the impact upon Islam of the peoples of these lands.

*Related Finding: Complex and large-scale issues are often simplified because they are* seen from a single, implicit perspective. For example, superficial discussions of the origins and eventual abolition of slavery in the Americas frequently omit the eco-nomic basis for the persistence of slavery as an institution. The syllabi for grades 7/8 and 11 do not adequately address the incarceration of Japanese Americans; nor do they discuss the deportation from the U.S. of thousands of people of Mex-ican origin in the 1920s, regardless of citizenship.

*Recommendation:* Social studies should be taught from multiple perspective, global in scope. Beyond the successes, the complexities and shortcomings of U.S. policy should be explored.

*Number Two*

*Finding: Language sensitivity.* Although specific terms fall into and out of cur-rency and the language of the syllabi may not be deliberately or intentionally sex-ist, racist, or prejudicial from the point of view of diversity and inclusiveness, the language used is often dated, narrow, and in some cases insensitive. For ex-ample, the syllabi refer to "slaves" or "the everyday life of a slave," as if being a slave were one's role or status, similar to that of gardener, cook, or carpenter. To refer, rather, to "enslaved persons" would call forth the essential humanity of those enslaved, helping students to understand from the beginning the true meaning of slavery (in contrast to the sentimental pictures of contented slaves, still found in some texts).

Many geographical terms are Western-derived, sometimes almost un-consciously. Terms like "the Far East" should be replaced by ones like "East Asia." Ideally, even the term "Middle East" should become "Southwest Asia and North Africa." To Native Americans, the Western Hemisphere is not "the New World." It was the newly arriving Europeans following Christopher Columbus who were new in the Western Hemisphere. Should the term "America" to mean only the United States be used sparingly and should the *hemispheric* meaning of the term be the usual usage?

Differential use of adjectives, the passive as opposed to the active voice, and other syntactic and semantic usages can betray unintended, unrecognized, but nonetheless real bias. For example, in the syllabus for grades 9/10, the African climate is described as essentially hostile to human migration ("There are few jungle environments in Africa and nearly 45% of the continent consists of desert or dry steppe . . ."), while that of Western Europe is described in the following terms: "Western Europe's environment exhibits great diversity in terms of physical geography and climate. Europeans have used technology to reshape their physical environment, Most of Western Europe has easy access to warm water ports. . . ." Why is desert seen as a hostile environment, but not freezing cold and snow?

Perhaps the most persistent and fundamental language problem in the teaching of social studies is the use of the terms "minority," "minorities," "minority persons" or "minority groups." Although commonly used, such terms nonetheless establish in the minds of all students inaccurate perceptions of the

world and, increasingly, of our own nation. If social studies are to be taught from a global perspective, many of the so-called "minorities" in America are more accurately described as part of the world's majorities, a profoundly important point for young Americans who will come to maturity in the next century.

*Recommendation:* The syllabi and all related support materials and locally developed curricula should be regularly reviewed to insure that the language used is accurate and reflects current scholarship. Classroom instruction must include sensitivity to and awareness of the changing legitimacy of terms, such as the shift in meaning of terms such as "third world," "Negro," and "Oriental."

*Number Three*
*Finding: A limited range of examples.* There is a tendency to use white male examples of achievement and to leave out examples of the contributions of women and of the many men and women of other than the traditional white groups. When women and people of color are mentioned, they are often marginalized as "other" groups "also" to be studied, implying that all the remaining content must not be about them. For example: the syllabus for grade 11 notes that "Inventions . . . in the 19th century were often the product of individual genius . . ., including that of lesser known, minority inventors," It recommends, under "Model Activities" on labor unionization: "Also examine the roles of women and racial/ethnic minorities at this time in labor history." Standard definitions of "achievement," too, omit the seemingly

ordinary lives of people of all groups—lives which, in aggregate, help us understand the human experience of a time and place. . . .

Early in its work the *Committee agreed that to reflect a multicultural perspective, the syllabi need not attempt to provide an encyclopedic list of every contribution by every person and group. Rather, as the emphasis shifts from an information-based to a conceptual curriculum, the syllabi should offer many appropriate examples of the experiences of many people and groups.* Further, the Committee believes that it can be particularly intriguing to students to examine with care what the elements are that hold together a nation or culture in spite of what are often great differences. This surely is one of the central questions to be considered in any course in American history.

*Recommendation:* The syllabi and other materials should provide teachers with several examples, drawn from different peoples, as appropriate to each topic. In this way, what begins to take shape in the mind of the student is an appreciation of the broader range of contributions of many people and groups to the building of our nation and the world.

*Number Four*
*Finding: The visual environment of the classroom and school is a major educational element.* Maps and pictures hang on classroom walls, silently sending messages all day, all year. Many of the maps used in social studies are out of date; they often portray areas only from one perspective, not unlike the famous *New Yorker* cover showing the rest of the nation as a minor

place west of the Hudson. For example, a map representing North America in 1700 might give the impression that nobody lived in the areas which were home to native peoples. Similarly, photographs on walls that show only white male inventors and heroes teach their own powerful, distorted lessons.

*Recommendation:* The visual environments of schools should reflect multicultural perspectives. . . .

## VI. REFLECTIONS ON THE WORK OF THE NYS SOCIAL STUDIES SYLLABUS REVIEW COMMITTEE

### Statement by Edmund W. Gordon and Francis Roberts, Cochairpersons

. . . As the Cochairpersons of this very challenging enterprise, we too have elected to identify a few of the currents which we have observed to flow throughout our deliberations. The Committee does not have a consensus position on these issues, but it seems that these concerns are important enough to be a part of the continuing discourse concerning the place of attention to cultural and other sources of human diversity in the social studies curriculum.

We are asked to consider how the social studies syllabi of the public schools of New York State should be modified, the better to ensure that our children understand and know about themselves, other people in their state and country, and the cultures and histories of the world in which they live. This very reasonable request and goal led us into discussions and debates concerning the nature of the canon as well as the knowledge which it enshrines. A high degree of importance attaches to the integrity of the canon, but problems arise when we consider the boundaries of the canon. Thus questions concerning the validity of various knowledge components constantly stood just beneath the surface of many of our discussions. Some of us were more comfortable with knowledge and sources that have been recognized and certified by the academy: Others repeatedly called attention to new knowledge, new sources and new voices and their claim to validity equal to that assigned to the traditional and the hegemonic. The tension between these two positions is not a new phenomenon. The history of human societies, our own nation included, is marked by debates and even wars over different conceptions of truth and views of reality. It is a measure of human progress that we have arrived at the stage of societal development that in democratic societies, these debates are verbal and written and not the subject of physical combat. However, they are nonetheless critical, in part, because in modern societies the changing conception of what it means to be an educated and intelligent person includes our capacity to entertain and understand phenomena from perspectives different from our own, on our way to arriving at wise judgments and the reconciliation of differences. Without falling into the futile debate concerning whose canon shall be taught we have elevated the question to include pedagog-

ical problems concerning how we enable learners to respect and deal with multiple perspectives, i.e., multiple ways of seeing things and using different sources of knowledge better to understand experiences and information. This is not to argue that all information is necessarily valid. Rather, we argue that all information deserves to be understood in the context within which it has been developed. This assertion is advanced, in part, because for much of our knowledge validity is difficult to establish independent of context.

This plea for tolerance and openness in the examination of ideas and perspectives came into conflict with another set of important purposes and values. One of the long-recognized functions of the social studies is to prepare students for citizenship in support of the continuing effort at nation-building. *We recognize that nation-building, especially in so diverse a populace, requires that we give attention, not so much to our differences as to our commonalities.* Some of us feel strongly that social studies should stress the nation's common values and traditional conceptions of our history. Others of us feel that those values and conceptions have become truncated as a result of the hegemonic ascendance of cultural elements, values and world views that tend to be associated with our European ancestry alone. Thus the insistence on the inclusion of broader perspectives and non-dominant knowledge sources. But the question arises as to whether we can conjointly serve both *pluribus* and *unum. . . .*

Some of us were shocked by the depth of feelings about diverse renditions of history. Some of us who are comfortable in the belief that the history that we know is valid were offended by the assertion that much of that history is incomplete or false. Some of us who feel that the standard histories have excluded or misrepresented important players found it difficult to assert our claims dispassionately. In the views represented by some of us, it appears that much of the dominant or traditional information available to us is viewed with doubt, skepticism and distrust because it does not fit comfortably with the experiences of some, while for others, it is simply counter-intuitive. Deciding what to teach under such existential circumstances confronts us with problems of monumental complexity. Even more problematic for the teaching and learning of history and the social studies is the ease with which information, ideology and belief become commingled in the minds of people whose interests are at stake—sometimes so much that these concepts, despite their differential order, come to be interchangeable one for the other. Although we were generally in agreement that histories tend to reflect the interests and perspectives of those who write them, there was a ubiquitous undercurrent of concern for the recognition of historical and other truth.

It may well be a limited understanding of the meaning of the word "truth" that will create the most difficulty as we seek to reconcile our search for 'truth' with our conception of education as being directed at the development of intellect and understanding. . . .

## ADDITIONAL COMMENTS

### Nathan Glazer

This report is not a document that stands by itself, without interpretation. Different members of the Committee, as well as different elements of the public, will read it differently, and selectively. Probably no member of the committee accepts every part and point in the report with equal commitment, and we differ in the way we see dangers in how the report will be read, and how we would like the broad direction it sets for the development of social studies in New York State developed in detail.

The report does reject two extremes in the treatment of ethnic and racial diversity in American social studies: One is the emphasis on forceful Americanization and assimilation that characterized much of American public education during the period of the great European immigration and for some time later. The other is the parceling out of American history into a different and incompatible story for each group, generally told by a few activists and militants speaking for the group. . . .

Within the broad spectrum that remains after the extremes have been rejected, the report points out a very general direction, rather than specifies the details of a syllabus or curriculum. It continues a debate, rather than concludes it.

Even within the bounds of this broad arena of development and debate, there is one major danger I see against which we must be alert, one to which the report offers some support. This is the danger of the hypostatization of race, ethnic groups, culture, people. (To hypostatize: "to make into, or regard as, a separate and distinct substance; . . . to assume a reality.") The various ethnic group, races, sub-cultures, the components of what we like to call with some exaggeration "the peoples of America," are not composed of a "distinct and separate substance." The groups we refer to when we speak of "multiculturism" are not monolithic and unchanging realities. Each is made up of different classes with different interests, each has been marked by differences created by the time of arrival of different waves under different circumstances, each has undergone various degrees of assimilation, acculturation, intermarriage, and each carries different attitudes to its past: European immigrants overwhelmingly see their assimilation to the United States, under the system of public education they experienced, as a good thing, even if their specific culture and language at the time played no role in the curriculum. Many of us recognize no identity other than American. When we speak of "multiculturism," we should be aware there are no fully distinct cultures in the United States, aside from American culture. We should not make of something labile, changeable, flexible and variable—the cultures people bring with them to the United States or develop as variants of our common American culture—something hard and definite and unchanging, something that establishes itself as a distinct and permanent element in American society and polity. That is not the way our society works, or should work. . . .

## A DISSENTING COMMENT

*Kenneth T. Jackson, Jacques Barzun Professor of History and the Social Sciences, Columbia University*

The purpose of this Committee is a good one. Certainly, we should celebrate the cultural diversity which has made the United States almost unique among the world's nations. Certainly, we should acknowledge that heterogeneity has made this land rich and creative. Certainly, we should give our students a varied and challenging multicultural education.

Just as certainly, we should celebrate the common culture that Americans share. Unfortunately, our report seems to disparage "Anglo" conformity. Leaving aside the debatable question of whether or not we in fact have conformity (from Broadway in New York to Broadway in Los Angeles we can easily find more diversity than exists anywhere else on earth) or whether earlier immigrant groups were "required" to "shed their specific cultural differences in order to be considered Americans," I would argue that it is politically and intellectually unwise for us to attack the traditions, customs, and values which attracted immigrants to these shores in the first place. The people of the United States will recognize, even if this Committee does not, that every viable nation has to have a common culture to survive in peace. As our own document indicates, one need look no further than Yugoslavia, the Soviet Union, or Canada to see the accuracy of this proposition. We might want to add India after the events of the past two weeks. The dominant American culture might have been German or French or Chinese or Algonquin or African, but for various historical reasons the English language and British political and legal traditions prevailed. Whether or not we would have been better off if Montcalm had defeated Wolfe on the Plains of Abraham is beside the point. . . .

A better strategy for this Committee would have been to argue in a positive rather than a negative way. Because we are made up of many peoples and cultures, because all these peoples and cultures have contributed to national greatness, and because the United States has typically done a better job of integrating newcomers into its social and political fabric (with racial prejudice being a glaring and persistent exception) than other places, its educational system should reflect that experience. We have been multicultural, we are multicultural, and we hope that we will always be multicultural. Moreover, the enemies of multiculturism are not teachers, textbooks, or curricular guides, but shopping centers, fast food outlets, and situation comedies, all of which threaten to turn us into an amorphous mass.

The report highlights the notion that all cultures are created equal. This may be true in the abstract, and I have no problem with the philosophical concept. But I cannot endorse a "Declaration of Cultural Independence," which is the subtitle of our Committee report. Within any single country, one culture must be accepted as the standard. Unfortunately, our document has virtually nothing to say about the things which hold us together. . . .

## A DISSENTING OPINION

### Arthur Schlesinger, Jr.

I agree with many of the practical recommendations in the report. It is unquestionably necessary to diversify the syllabus in order to meet the needs of a more diversified society. It is unquestionably necessary to provide for global education in an increasingly interdependent world. Our students should by all means be better acquainted with women's history, with the history of ethnic and racial minorities, with Latin American, Asian and African history. Debate, alternative interpretations, "multiple perspectives" are all essential to the educational enterprise. I welcome changes that would adapt the curriculum to these purposes. If that is what the report means by multicultural education, I am all for it.

But I fear that the report implies much more than this. The underlying philosophy of the report, as I read it, is that ethnicity is the defining experience for most Americans, that ethnic ties are permanent and indelible, that the division into ethnic groups establishes the basic structure of American society and that a main objective of public education should be the protection, strengthening, celebration and perpetuation of ethnic origins and identities. Implicit in the report is the classification of all Americans according to ethnic and racial criteria.

These propositions are assumed rather than argued in the report. They constitute an ethnic interpretation of American history that, like the economic interpretation, is valid up to a point but misleading and wrong when presented as the whole picture.

The ethnic interpretation, moreover, reverses the historic theory of America—which has been, not the preservation and sanctification of old cultures and' identities, but the creation of a *new* national culture and a *new* national identity. . . .

Of course students should learn more about the rich variety of peoples and cultures that have forged this new American identity. They also should understand the curse of racism—the great failure of the American experiment, the glaring contradiction of American ideals and the still-crippling disease of American society. But we should also be alert to the danger of a society divided into distinct and immutable ethnic and racial groups, each taught to cherish its own apartness from the rest.

While I favor curricular changes that make for more inclusive interpretations of past and present, I do not believe that we should magnify ethnic and racial themes at the expense of the unifying ideals that precariously hold our highly differentiated society together. The republic has survived and grown because it has maintained a balance between *pluribus* and *unum*. The report, it seems to me, is saturated with *pluribus* and neglectful of *unum*. . . .

Obviously the reason why the United States, for all its manifest failure to live up to its own ideals, is still the most successful large multi-ethnic nation is precisely because, instead of emphasizing and perpetuating ethnic separatism, it has assimilated immigrant cultures into a new *American* culture. . . .

If the ethnic subcultures had genuine vitality, they would be sufficiently instilled in children by family, church and community. It is surely not the office of the public school to promote ethnic separatism and heighten ethnic tensions.

Should public education move in this direction, it will only increase the fragmentation, resegregation and self-ghettoization of American life. The bonds of national cohesion in the republic are sufficiently fragile already. Public education should aim to strengthen those bonds, not to weaken them. . . .

What has held Americans together in the absence of a common ethnic origin has been the creation of a new American identity—a distinctive American culture based on a common language and common adherence to ideals of democracy and human rights, a culture to which many nationalities and races have made emphatic contributions in the past and will (one hopes) make emphatic contributions in the future. Our democratic ideals have been imperfectly realized, but the long labor to achieve them and to move the American experiment from exclusion to participation has been a central theme of American history. It should be a central theme of the New York social studies curriculum.

And it is important for students to understand where these democratic ideals come from. They come of course from Europe. Indeed, Europe is the *unique* source of these ideals—ideals that today empower people in every continent and to which today most of the world aspires. That is why it is so essential (in my view) to acquaint students with the western history and tradition that created our democratic ideals—and why it is so wrong to tell students of non-European origin that western ideals are not for them.

I regret the note of Europhobia that sometimes emerges in vulgar attacks on "Eurocentric" curriculums. Certainly Europe, like every other culture, has committed its share of crimes. But, unlike most cultures, it has also generated ideals that have opposed and exposed those crimes.

The report, however, plays up the crimes and plays down the ideals. Thus, when it talks about the European colonization of Africa and India, it deplores "the eradication of many varieties of traditional culture and knowledge." Like infanticide? slavery? polygamy? subjection of women? suttee? veil-wearing? foot-binding? clitorectemies? Nothing is said about the influence of European ideas of democracy, human rights, self-government, rule of law. . . .

I also am doubtful about the note occasionally sounded in the report that "students must be taught social criticism" and "see themselves as active makers and changers of culture and society" and "promote economic fairness and social justice" and "bring about change in their communities, the nation, and the world." I very much hope that, as citizens, students will do all these things, but I do not think it is the function of

the schools to teach students to become reformers any more than I ever thought it the function of the schools to teach them the beauty of private enterprise and the sanctity of the status quo. I will be satisfied if we can teach children to read, write and calculate. If students understand the nature of our western democratic tradition, they will move into social criticism of their own. But let us not politicize the curriculum on behalf either of the left or of the right. . . .

## Arthur Schlesinger, Jr., and Multiculturalism, 1992

*Arthur Schlesinger, Jr., has been an important historian, influential liberal intellectual, and advisor to presidents. In 1992 he wrote* The Disuniting of America: Reflections on a Multicultural Society, *a reaffirmation of assimilation to European American ideals and a critique of multiculturalism's emphasis on group identities.*

Source: Arthur Schlesinger, Jr., *The Disuniting of America* (New York: Norton, 1992), taken from Thomas R. Frazier, ed., *The Many Sides of America: 1945 to the Present* (New York: Harcourt Brace, 1996).

"The era that began with the dream of integration," Richard Rodriguez has observed, "ended up with scorn for assimilation." Instead of casting off the foreign skin, as John Quincy Adams had stipulated, never to resume it, the fashion is to resume the foreign skin as conspicuously as can be. The cult of ethnicity has reversed the movement of American history, producing a nation of minorities—

or at least of minority spokesmen—less interested in joining with the majority in common endeavor than in declaring their alienation from an oppressive, white, patriarchal, racist, sexist, classist society. The ethnic ideology inoculates the illusion that membership in one or another ethnic group is the basic American experience.

Most Americans, it is true, continue to see themselves primarily as individuals and only secondarily and trivially as adherents of a group. Nor is harm done when ethnic groups display pride in their historic past or in their contributions to the American present. But the division of society into fixed ethnicities nourishes a culture of victimization and a contagion of inflammable sensitivities. And when a vocal and visible minority pledges primary allegiance to their groups, whether ethnic, sexual, religious, or, in rare cases (communist, fascist), political, it presents a threat to the brittle bonds of national identity that hold this diverse and fractious society together.

A peculiarly ugly mood seems to have settled over the one arena where freedom of inquiry and expression should be most unconstrained and civility most respected—our colleges and universities. It is no fun running a university these days. Undergraduates can be wanton and cruel in their exclusion, their harassment, their heavy pranks, their wounding invective. Minority students, for the most understandable reasons, are often vulnerable and frightened. Racial cracks, slurs, insults, vilification pose difficult problems. Thus posters appear around the campus at the University of Michigan parodying the slogan of the United Ne-

gro College Fund: A Mind Is A Terrible Thing To Waste—Especially On A Nigger. Decent white students join the protest against white bullies and thugs.

Presidents and deans begin to ask themselves, which is more important—protecting free speech or preventing racial persecution? The Constitution, Justice Holmes said, embodies "the principle of free thought—not free thought for those who agree with us but freedom for the thought that we hate." But suppose the thought we hate undercuts the Constitution's ideal of equal justice under law? Does not the First Amendment protect equality as well as liberty? how to draw a bright line between speech and behavior?

One has a certain sympathy for besieged administrators who, trying to do their best to help minority students, adopt regulations to restrict racist and sexist speech. More than a hundred institutions, according to the American Civil Liberties Union, had done so by February 1991. My own decided preference is to stand by the First Amendment and to fight speech by speech, not by censorship. But then, I am not there on the firing line.

One can even understand why administrators, not sure what best to do for minorities and eager to keep things quiet, accept—even subsidize—separatist remedies urged by student militants. They might, however, ponder Kenneth Clark's comment: "The white liberal . . . who concedes black separatism so hastily and benevolently must look to his own reasons, not the least of them perhaps an exquisite relief." And it is sad, though instructive, that the administrations especially disposed to encourage

racial and ethnic enclaves—like Berkeley, Michigan, Oberlin, the University of
Massachusetts at Amherst—are, Dinesh
D'Souza (himself an Indian from India)
points out, the ones experiencing the
most racial tension. Troy Duster, a
Berkeley sociologist, finds a correlation
between group separatism and racial
hostility among students.

Moderates who would prefer fending
for themselves as individuals are bullied
into going along with their group.
Groups get committed to platforms and
to we-they syndromes. Faculty members
appease. A code of ideological orthodoxy emerges. The code's guiding principle is that nothing should be said that
might give offense to members of minority groups (and, apparently, that anything can be said that gives offense to
white males of European origin).

The Office of Student Affairs at Smith
College has put out a bulletin listing
types of oppression for people belatedly
"realizing that they are oppressed." Some
samples of the Smith litany of sins:

Ableism: Oppression of the differently
abled by the temporarily able.
Heterosexism: Oppression of those of
sexual orientation other than
heterosexual, such as gays, lesbians,
and bisexuals; this can take place by
not acknowledging their existence.
Lookism: The belief that appearance is
an indicator of a person's value; the
construction of a standard for
beauty/attractiveness; and
oppression through stereotypes and
generalizations of both those who
do not fit that standard and those
who do.

Can they be kidding up there in
Northampton?

The code imposes standards of what
is called, now rather derisively, "political
correctness." What began as a means of
controlling student incivility threatens to
become, formally or informally, a means
of controlling curricula and faculty too.
Clark University asks professors proposing courses to explain how "pluralistic
(minority, women, etc.) views and concerns are explored and integrated in this
course." A philosopher declined to sign,
doubting that the university would ask
professors to explain how "patriotic and
pro-family values are explored and
integrated."

Two distinguished American historians at Harvard, Bernard Bailyn and Stephan Thernstrom, offered a course in
population history called "The Peopling
of America." Articles appeared in *Harvard Crimson* criticizing the professors for
"racial insensitivity," and black students
eventually presented them with a bill of
particulars. Thernstrom, an advocate of
ethnic history, the editor of the *Harvard
Encyclopedia of American Ethnic Groups,*
was accused of racism. He had, it developed, used the terms "Indians" instead of "Native Americans." He had also
referred to "Oriental" religion—the ad-
jective was deemed "colonial and imperialistic." Bailyn had recommended
diaries of Southern planters without
recommending slave narratives. And so
on, for six single-spaced pages.

The episode reminds one of the right-
wing students who in Joe McCarthy days
used to haunt the classrooms of liberal
Harvard professors (like me) hoping to
catch whiffs of Marxism emanating from

the podium. Thernstrom decided to hell with it and gave up the course. A signal triumph for political correctness.

Those who stand up for what they believe invite smear campaigns. A favorite target these days is Diane Ravitch of Columbia's Teachers College, a first-class historian of American education, an enlightened advocate of school reform, and a steadfast champion of cultural pluralism. She is dedicated to reasoned and temperate argument and is perseveringly conciliatory rather than polemical in her approach. Perhaps the fact that she is a woman persuades ethnic chauvinists that they can bully her. Despite nasty efforts at intimidation, she continues to expose the perils of ethnocentrism with calm lucidity.

Ravitch's unpardonable offense seems to be her concern about *unum* as well as about *pluribus*—her belief that history should help us understand how bonds of cohesion make us a nation rather than an irascible collection of unaffiliated groups. For in the end, the cult of ethnicity defines the republic not as a polity of individuals but as a congeries of distinct and inviolable cultures. When a student sent a memorandum to the "diversity education committee" at the University of Pennsylvania mentioning her "deep regard for the individual," a college administrator returned the paper with the word *individual* underlined: "This is a *red flag* phrase today, which is considered by many to be *racist*. Arguments that champion the individual over the group ultimately privileges [sic] the 'individuals' belonging to the largest or dominant group."

The contemporary sanctification of

the group puts the old idea of a coherent society at stake. Multicultural zealots reject as hegemonic the notion of a shared commitment to common ideals. How far the discourse has come from Crevecoeur's "new race," from Toequeville's civic participation, from Emerson's "smelting pot," from Bryce's "amazing solvent," from Myrdal's "American Creed"!

Yet what has held the American people together in the absence of a common ethnic origin has been precisely a common adherence to ideals of democracy and human rights that, too often transgressed in practice, forever goad us to narrow the gap between practice and principle.

The American synthesis has an inevitable Anglo-Saxon coloration, but it is no longer an exercise in Anglo-Saxon domination. The republic embodies ideals that transcend ethnic, religious, and political lines. It is an experiment, reasonably successful for a while, in creating a common identity for people of diverse races, religions, languages, cultures. But the experiment can continue to succeed only so long as Americans continue to believe in the goal. If the republic now turns away from Washington's old goal of one people," what is its future?—disintegration of the national community, apartheid, Balkanization, tribalization?

"The one absolutely certain way of bringing this nation to ruin, of preventing all possibility of its continuing to be a nation at all," said Theodore Roosevelt, "would be to permit it to become a tangle of squabbling nationalities, an intricate knot of German-Americans, Irish-

Americans, English-Americans, French-Americans, Scandinavian-Americans, or Italian-Americans, each preserving its separate nationality." Three-quarters of a century later we must add a few more nationalities to T.R.'s brew. This only strengthens his point.

## Oakland, California, School Board and Ebonics, 1996

*In December of 1996 the School Board of the City of Oakland voted unanimously to pass the following resolution. The resolution recognizing Black English as a language was controversial, provoking criticism even by longtime multicultural advocate Jesse Jackson. The "ebonics" controversy was one of many debates over school curriculum that addressed the question of cultural resistance and assimilation.*

*Source: The Black Scholar 27, no. 1 (spring 1997): 4.*

WHEREAS, numerous validated scholarly studies demonstrate that African-American students as a part of their culture and history as African people possess and utilize a language described in various scholarly approaches as "Ebonics" (literally "Black sounds") or "Pan-African Communication Behavior" or "African Language Systems": and

WHEREAS, these studies have also demonstrated that African Language Systems are genetically based and not a dialect of English: and

WHEREAS, these studies demonstrate that such West and Niger-Congo African languages have been officially recognized and addressed in the mainstream public educational community as worthy of study; understanding or application of its principles, laws and structures for the benefit of African-American students both in terms of positive appreciation of the language and these students' acquisition and mastery of English language skills; and

WHEREAS, such recognition by scholars has given rise over the past fifteen years to legislation passed by the State of California recognizing the unique language stature of descendants of slaves, with such legislation being prejudicially and unconstitutionally vetoed repeatedly by various California state governors; and

WHEREAS, judicial cases in states other than California have recognized the unique language stature of African-American pupils, and such recognition by courts has resulted in court-mandated education programs which have substantially benefited African American children in the interest of vindicating their equal protection of the law rights under the Fourteenth Amendment to the United States Constitution: and

WHEREAS, the Federal Bilingual Education Act (20 U.S.C. 1402 et seq) mandates that local educational agencies build their capacities to establish, implement and sustain programs of instruction for children and youth of limited English proficiency: and

WHEREAS, the interests of the Oakland Unified School District in providing equal opportunities for all of its students dictate limited English proficient educational programs recognizing the English language acquisition and improvement skills of African-American students are as fundamental as is application of bilingual education principles for others whose primary languages are other than English: and

WHEREAS, the standardized tests and grade scores of African-American students in reading and language arts skills measuring their application of English skills are substantially below state and national norms and that such deficiencies will be remedied by application of a program featuring African Language Systems principles in instructing African-American children both in their primary language and in English: and

WHEREAS, standardized tests and grade scores will be remedied by application of a program with teachers and aides who are certified in the methodology of featuring African Language Systems principles in instructing African-American children both in their primary language and in English. The certified teachers of these students will be provided incentives including, but not limited to salary differentials.

NOW, THEREFORE, BE IT RESOLVED that the Board of Education officially recognizes the existence, and the cultural and historic bases of West and Niger-Congo African Language Systems, and each language as the predominantly primary language of African-American students:

and

BE IT FURTHER RESOLVED that the Board of Education hereby adopts the report recommendations and attached Policy Statement of the District's African-American Task Force on language stature of African-American speech; and

BE IT FURTHER RESOLVED that the Superintendent in conjunction with her staff shall immediately devise and implement the best possible academic program for imparting instruction to African-American students in their primary language for the combined purposes of maintaining the legitimacy and richness of such language whether it is known as "Ebonics." "African Language Systems," "Pan-African Communication Behaviors" or other description, and to facilitate their acquisition and mastery of English language skills; and

BE IT FURTHER RESOLVED that the Board of Education hereby commits to earmark District general and special funding as is reasonably necessary and appropriate to enable the Superintendent and her staff to accomplish the foregoing; and

BE IT FURTHER RESOLVED that the Superintendent and her staff shall utilize the input of the entire Oakland educational community as well as state and federal scholarly and educational input in devising such a program: and

BE IT FURTHER RESOLVED, that periodic reports on the progress of the creation and implementation of such an educational program shall be made to the Board at least once per month commencing at the Board meeting of December 18, 1996.

# California, Proposition 227, Bilingual Education, 1998

*In 1998 California voters passed Proposition 227 by a large majority. The proposition sought to end bilingual programs in California public schools. The California Secretary of State's publication of the proposition, arguments for and against it, and a legislative analyst's estimate of the fiscal impact are reprinted here.*

*Source:* http://primary98.ss.ca.gov/voter.guide/welcome

## Summary of Legislative Analyst's Estimate of Net State and Local Government Fiscal Impact:

- Impacts on individual school districts would depend on how schools, parents, and the state respond to the proposition's changes. These impacts could vary significantly by district.
- Requires state spending of $50 million per year for ten years to teach tutors of limited English proficient students. Total state spending on education, however, probably would not change.

## OFFICIAL TITLE AND SUMMARY PREPARED BY THE ATTORNEY GENERAL

### English Language in Public Schools: Initiative Statute

- Requires all public school instruction be conducted in English.
- Requirement may be waived if parents or guardian show that child already knows English, or has special needs, or would learn English faster through alternate instructional technique.
- Provides initial short-term placement, not normally exceeding one year, in intensive sheltered English immersion programs for children not fluent in English.
- Appropriates $50 million per year for ten years funding English instruction for individuals pledging to provide personal English tutoring to children in their community.
- Permits enforcement suits by parents and guardians.

## ARGUMENT IN FAVOR OF PROPOSITION 227

### Why Do We Need to Change California's Bilingual Education System?

- Begun with the best of intentions in the 1970s, bilingual education has failed in actual practice, but the politicians and administrators have refused to admit this failure.
- For most of California's non-English-speaking students, bilingual education actually means monolingual, SPANISH-ONLY education for the first 4 to 7 years of school.
- The current system fails to teach children to read and write English. Last year, only 6.7 percent of limited-English students in California learned enough English to be moved into mainstream classes.
- Latino immigrant children are the principal victims of bilingual education. They have the lowest test scores

and the highest dropout rates of any immigrant group.

- There are 140 languages spoken by California's schoolchildren. To teach each group of children in their own native language before teaching them English is educationally and fiscally impossible. Yet this impossibility is the goal of bilingual education.

## Common Sense About Learning English

- Learning a new language is easier the younger the age of the child.
- Learning a language is much easier if the child is immersed in that language.
- Immigrant children already know their native language; they need the public schools to teach them English.
- Children who leave school without knowing how to speak, read, and write English are injured for life economically and socially.

## What "English for the Children" Will Do

- Require children to be taught English as soon as they start school.
- Provide "sheltered English immersion" classes to help non-English speaking students learn English; research shows this is the most effective method.
- Allow parents to request a special waiver for children with individual educational needs who would benefit from another method.

## What "English for the Children" Won't Do

It will:

- NOT throw children who can't speak English into regular classes where they would have to "sink or swim."
- NOT cut special funding for children learning English.
- NOT violate any federal laws or court decisions.

## Who Supports the Initiative?

- Teachers worried by the undeniable failure of bilingual education and who have long wanted to implement a successful alternative—sheltered English immersion.
- Most Latino parents, according to public polls. They know that Spanish-only bilingual education is preventing their children from learning English by segregating them into an educational dead-end.
- Most Californians. They know that bilingual education has created an educational ghetto by isolating non-English speaking students and preventing them from becoming successful members of society.

## Who Opposes the Initiative?

- Individuals who profit from bilingual education. Bilingual teachers are paid up to $5,000 extra annually and the program provides jobs to thousands of bilingual coordinators and administrators.
- Schools and school districts which receive HUNDREDS OF MILLIONS of extra dollars for schoolchildren clas-

sified as not knowing English and who, therefore, have a financial incentive to avoid teaching English to children.

• Activist groups with special agendas and the politicians who support them.

*Alice Callaghan*
*Director, Las Familias del Pueblo*
*Ron Unz*
*Chairman, English for the Children*
*Fernando Vega*
*Past Redwood City School Board Member*

## REBUTTAL TO ARGUMENT IN FAVOR OF PROPOSITION 227

Several years ago, the 1970's law mandating bilingual education in California expired.

Since then local school districts—principals, parents and teachers—have been developing and using different programs to teach children English.

Many of the older bilingual education programs continue to have great success. In other communities some schools are succeeding with English immersion and others with dual language immersion programs. Teaching children English is the primary goal, no matter what teaching method they're using.

Proposition 227 outlaws all of these programs—even the best ones—and mandates a program that has never been tested anywhere in California! And if it doesn't work, we're stuck with it anyway.

Proposition 227 proposes

• A 180-day English only program with no second chance after that school year.

• Mixed-age classrooms with first through sixth graders all together, all day, for one year.

Proposition 227 funding comes from three wealthy men . . . one from New York, one from Florida, and one from California.

The New York man has given Newt Gingrich $310,000!

The Florida man who put up $45,000 for Proposition 227 is part of a fringe group which believes "government has no role in financing, operating, or defining schooling, or even compelling attendance."

These are not people who should dictate a single teaching method for California's schools.

If the law allows different methods, we can use what works. Vote NO on Proposition 227.

*John D'Amelio*
*President, California School Boards*
*Association*
*Mary Bergan*
*President California Federation of Teachers,*
*AFL-CIO*
*Jennifer J. Looney*
*President, Association of California School*
*Administrators*

## "Understanding the L.A. Riot," *Los Angeles Times*, 1992

*On April 29, 1992, a jury in a suburb of Los Angeles found white police officers not guilty of manhandling an African American man, Rodney King, despite a videotape of the incident that clearly suggested they had beaten him. That day the city of Los Angeles exploded in a riot, a riot that included Latinos as well as blacks and against Korean Americans as well as whites. The riot would leave fifty-eight people dead and one thousand buildings destroyed. Shortly after the riot and then six months later, the* Los Angeles Times *ran two series of interviews, titled "Understanding the Riot," with local and national figures. The interviews below are from those two series.*

*Source: Los Angeles Times, May 3 and 15, 1992; November 16 and 19, 1992*

## ROBERT SCHEER, "CECIL MURRAY: A VOICE OF REASON IN A TIME OF TROUBLES," MAY 3, 1992

In the first night of the riot, a building was burning a half-block away from Pastor Cecil L. (Chip) Murray's First AME Church, home of Los Angeles' oldest black congregation. The fire, he recalls, "was burning like Dante's inferno" threatening the 5,000 parishioners and community leaders gathered in response to Murray's call for peace and justice.

"We felt utterly helpless standing there, those 5,000 people at the church meeting," the 62-year-old pastor said, his booming baritone reduced to a sad whisper. "Soon the palm branches and the fronds would catch; it would leap across the street. We would be consumed."

Murray, 62, an ex-combat pilot and Claremont Ph.D., who has led his congregation for 15 years, does not easily accommodate the sense of feeling help-less. When told the firemen would only come if guaranteed protection, he organized a group of more than 100 men to stand between them and the rock-throwing rioters for over three hours. There was no blood shed.

All in a night's work for someone who believes, "The church exists to set the moral climate and moral program" for the community. But those are not the words of some commercialized and ever-safe television preacher. Murray has a long history in the trenches of his mid-City community, fighting to protect and educate a flock that extends far beyond his 7,500 parishioners. Some of them are famous—like Arsenio Hall, who, during the riots, had Murray close his show with a prayer for tolerance. But many of his followers are poor. These people are his main concern because, he explains, "It really takes an arrogant black person to fail to see that 'There, but for the grace of God, go I.'"

Murray is no pie-in-the-sky ameliorator of his people's discontents. His capacity for outrage over the death blows of racism are never muted; they have proved to be ever channeled and thoughtful. The night the jury in Simi Valley debated their verdict in the Rodney G. King case, Murray, in a terribly prescient sermon, warned "Be cool. . . . Even in anger be cool. And if you're gonna burn something down, don't burn down the house of the victims, brother! Burn down the Legislature! Burn down the courtroom. Burn it down by voting, brother!"

His words did not still the night following the verdict. And while he understood the rage boiling up—he did not condone it: "Under no circumstances will we pretend that the looting, the burning, the arson are excusable. They are totally inexcusable. And in the same breath that we say that, we must say this miscegenation of justice in the court system in Simi Valley was injurious to us all. It is inexcusable. And the system that condones it is inexcusable. So while we're handing out blame, guilt and default, let's make sure we are an equal-opportunity employer. The blame belongs to more than just the people burning." It is sad that, only after nights of death and destruction, men of power might finally pay serious attention to Murray's message and to the community that he so obviously loves.

QUESTION: Where are we this Sunday after days and nights of rioting?

ANSWER: By Sunday, the armed might of the state will have been demonstrated, and we will be at a different level, I tend to think, one of smoldering ashes and smoldering resentments.

Q: Do you see the violence and the fires as having an economic base?

A: I think everything in history is pulled by an economic engine: Our train of thought is pulled by an economic engine. To pretend that you can be poor and depressed and poor and racially discriminated against without an explosion sooner or later—that is Disneyland. There is no such existence.

Then, too, what's happened among our poor in this city and in America at large is we have a rising level of expectations. As long as they weren't exposed to something better, then you could keep

a slave with a plantation mentality. But then when the plantation-mentality slave sees Paree, how you going to keep him down on the farm? People need a way to live. Even our middle-income people need a way to live. Apparently, our lawmakers need a way to live, given the way they've cheated on their check-writing; and our billionaires who pay no taxes.

Q: So you're saying this was not just rage over a racist verdict?

A: People don't burn down a city over a singular unique event. They burn down a city over 200 years of events.

Q: But the mood in poorer urban communities seems to have become particularly desperate in the last few years.

A: I quite agree with you. For the vast one-third below the poverty line, things are worse than ever. You can't sustain yourself on $6,000 a year, $15,000 a year, $18,000 a year. Now someone will say, "Does that give me the right to go out and burn?" Of course not. And we're not talking about right—we're talking about reality. The people have been fed sour grapes and their teeth are set on edge.

Q: But after the riots of the '60s, there was the Kerner Commission and programs for change, including the War on Poverty. What went wrong?

A: We had 15 years of hope and then the reaction set in—Nixon, Reagan, Bush, trickle-down and benign neglect. If our leadership had set before us, courageously and with vision, a dream, we would have been floating by now as a country. But instead they pitted the haves against the have-nots. Imagine a President saying: Just treat them with benign neglect as one treats a recalcitrant puppy, one that you don't want to be around. And another saying, "Give it to the haves, and it'll trickle down to the have-nots"? What an absurd philosophy. And it could only be endorsed and condoned in a racist atmosphere, because racism blinds people. It did it in South Africa. It did it in the U.S. South. It did in south Los Angeles. Just blindness.

Q : It's hard to comprehend what it means to be a 17-year-old living a block from your church. What are the prospects? What are the conditions?

A : Isn't that the truth: Where do I go at 17, angry, alienated, too little space at home, little regularity, hypocrisy in the country, 60% unemployment rate, the chief cause of death in my age range is homicide, the second-leading cause is suicide. And so they'll tell you: "Might as well die, die of something. Gotta die some time— might as well go out young, make a beautiful corpse," All of that—which is just nihilism. It's death. And we can do better than that. If we despise our young, we will not survive.

Q : The way it's been reported in the media it's made to seem that only a few bad apples, only a few punks, gang members. But there seems to be a much wider range of rage out there.

A : And I believe it's universal. We saw it in Beijing. We saw it at the Berlin Wall. We saw it in South African apartheid. We see it in the United States. Nobody, in the late 1990s, is going to predominate over anybody else on a system of inequity. If the haves do not make room for the have-nots, then nobody will have. No one is going to be satisfied being spat upon or despised. However you do it:

economically, emotionally, morally, deprivation of history, deprivation of culture, flaunting yourself above someone else. Nobody's taking that any more; that day died.

Q : How do you answer those people who say, "Well, they had the opportunities, why didn't they use them; we just coddle them with welfare?"

A : Lincoln said, "I feel sorry for the man who can't feel the whip when it's on another man's back." And that's white America's fault and pain—it cannot feel the whip on another person's back. Right now the economy's bad, and the plant layoffs and the $50,000–$60,000-a-year jobs are gone, and white America's in a red-hot rage. Suppose they'd had that for two centuries? If the shoe had been on the other foot, and the situation had been reversed, this city would be smoldering ashes; white people would have burned it to the ground.

Q : But some things have changed since the Watts riots in terms of the black community. We have a black mayor, we have some . . .

A : We have some 800 black elected officials at high-level positions and another 800 at another. But one swallow does not make a spring. And that's the thing—it's a large degree of tokenism; the black bourgeoisie will make it anywhere. They are the best of black and the best of white. But it is totally unfair to ask a person to fight all the odds. If someone fights the odds and wins, you proclaim that person a champion; that's what medals are for. But you cannot ask the normal run-of-the-mill person to fight upstream like a salmon all of his life.

Q: Are you telling me that since Watts, despite the riots that came after, and the Kerner Commission and War on Poverty, it has still been that kind of uphill swim?

A: It has certainly been. Look at what's happening to affirmative action now. Twenty years of affirmative action and it's struck down, just as some gains were being made. The Civil Rights Act under attack. Every gain whittled, step-by-step-by-step, as if we're walking in reverse, and anybody who's saying anything else just doesn't know the facts. Economically, what are we allowed to own? Nothing. You try to produce, you run across red-lining, you run across insurance no-can-get, you run across bank loans no-can-get. We can own nothing. And you want to know why the rage?

Q: Why can't you own?

A: Because of the financial setup of our country. It isn't encouraged to advance money to blacks. It's by banks, the red-lining—and anybody who tells you there's not redlining is obviously an ingenue. Anybody knows that red-lining is going on, blacks have no access to capital.

Over the past year and half, we've been trying to rehab a number of properties that we still have not been able to get the money necessary to do that. Look at the clips in your own *L.A. Times* files on the study by the federal government, which showed that even the same income levels and credit histories, blacks get fewer loans than any other ethnic group.

Q: How do we pick up the pieces?

A: The problems are complex and our morals are no prayer books, but we're going by with scars and what we know, and the problem is primarily economic. The problem is in the head of a white person who is an orthodox economic conservative. If only they could begin to see the potential in blacks and to see blacks in the truer light.

Now we are set back a little bit more. Every picture on television that shows the people scene shows young black people looting—it's a part of the reality of what's happening. It must be seen. But there's nothing to offset that, because that's all they've ever seen of blacks.

The truth of the matter is: I know we have to be among the most law-abiding Americans. I know black people do obey the law because we live among each other. Our criminal class is hard-core criminal, but that's 3%, 4%, 5% of us. We need a new vision in the eyesight of white people. Then that will loosen up the purse strings and the means of earning a living.

Q: Where do we go from here?

A: Now, in rebuilding. What we're asking is an economic power base: using federal, state, county, city resources to create job training and jobs. That is obviously a must. It is a necessity to develop a Marshall Plan for Los Angeles. That's not rhetoric; it is a necessity.

Now that L.A. has become a prototype for the nation, we had better make this prototype succeed, because every time there's a flash point in L.A., there will be a flash point in Philadelphia, New York, Detroit and Miami.

We have a unique opportunity in that we do not have the unhealthiest climate of opinion and finances in the world. It's workable. And the book is still being written—it's not closed—so that our racist attitudes are not necessarily locked in. Out of this burning must obviously come a yearning for an agenda for the 21st Century, to unite the 146 nations that make up Los Angeles. We cannot afford the smallness of our differences.

Q : So what should people of good will, who say what you're saying makes sense and they want to get with the program, do?

A : Good, let us do something economically. Let the white power—which is magnificent once it gets to moving—it can put a Hubble telescope in space and look to the very beginnings of the universe; it can't find a way to open up 5,000–10,000 job openings in Los Angeles?

After the Nazis tried to kill us, we go and revive Germany—and also Japan. It can revive Korea, where our sons lie buried beneath the soil? But it can't do anything for the people here? Forty-six founders of Los Angeles, 42 of them were Native Americans and African-Americans. Pico Boulevard is named after the late territorial governor of this territory—he was black. So we are part and parcel of this community. Then, why aren't we allowed to take our righteous share?

Q : On Sunday, after people read this, what should they go and do on Monday? What should they be calling for?

A : White people of good intentions—use your ingenuity to enable economically the depressed communities of our city, whether they are black, Latino, Asian or white.

But if you want to be specific, if you want to help black people, help us find a way to redeem ourselves economically and dispel yourselves of the notion that blacks are lazy or have no work ethic. We have been working longer and harder and without compensation than any other ethnicity in America. We are willing to work, we are willing to walk through the door. But for goodness' sake, please unlock it.

## JEFFERSON MORLEY, "JACK KEMP, L.A.'S 'HOMEBOY' IN WASHINGTON HAS PLANS TO PUT OUR HOUSE IN ORDER," MAY 15, 1992

"I'm a homeboy," says Jack F. Kemp, the secretary of Housing and Urban Development, who has emerged as the Bush Administration's point man after the Los Angeles riots. Kemp, a former pro quarterback and congressmen, explains that he grew up in West L.A. and his father owned a trucking business on South Central Avenue. But among the patrician millionaires in the Bush Cabinet, Kemp's middle-class pedigree qualifies him as a man who came up from the streets.

For years, Kemp has been urging his fellow Republicans to appeal to black voters and to adopt innovative programs that address problems of urban poverty. The secretary's notable lack of success on both counts does not seem to have discouraged him. He speaks regularly to black groups—like the National Conference of Black Mayors—that rarely hear from Republicans seeking higher office. His style is earnest, irrepressible and slightly old-fashioned. He is one of the few politicians in America, black or white, who appear genuinely stirred by the memory of Abraham Lincoln—his office suite features two busts and an oil painting of the Great Emancipator.

His policy proposals, while based on Republican precepts of entrepreneurship and less government intervention, were not a priority on President George Bush's legislative agenda—at least not until the riots. Nor were they warmly received by Democratic mayors and congressmen, who believe that increased federal funding is essential for addressing urban problems. But now, when all other urban-policy proposals are blocked by the federal budget deficit and all-but-certain presidential veto, Kemp's ideas define the limits of post-riot political possibilities in Washington.

Born in Los Angeles in 1935, Kemp graduated from Occidental College in 1957. He is the author of two books, "An American Renaissance: Strategy for the 1980s" and "The American Idea: Ending the Limits to Growth." He and his wife, Joanne, have four children and live in Bethesda, Md. But he has well-known ambitions to reside at 1600 Pennsylvania Ave., come 1997. This moment, when his proposals are Bush's top priority, could make the difference.

QUESTION: Sections of Detroit and Washington that were destroyed in the riots of the 1960s are still in ruins. Why shouldn't we expect parts of South Los Angeles to be similarly devastated 25 years from now?

ANSWER: Well, they will be unless we do something new and radical. I'm a conservative Republican talking about radical change. . . . The only answer to poverty in my view is to build an incentive-based, market-oriented democratically initiated entrepreneurial system in the inner city. That means overhauling the welfare system and restoring the link between effort and reward. . . . Broader ownership both of business and of housing for low-income people. Greater educational opportunity, more school choice, more magnet schools. . . . That would be the beginning—along with infrastructure development—of an urban renaissance.

Q: There's been a lot of controversy about what worked in the past and what didn't. Where do you come down in that debate?

A: The Great Society primarily focused on the net of safety under which people should not be allowed to fall and lose their dignity, but to a certain extent the focus in the '60s and '70s and, unfortunately, in the '80s, was with the net and not with the ladder. The ladder was neglected. . . . The problem with the ladder is that there are no rungs at the bottom. The welfare system, as one woman said in Nickerson Gardens, is that it punishes us for trying. . . . In America today, in our welfare system, the reward for working on the bottom five or six rungs of the ladder is lower than it is for welfare. . . . I'm going to say something that I never thought I'd say, and I'm saying it increasingly: The people in the inner cities of America that I've met represent great talent and potential for this country.

Q: What can people outside of riot-torn areas do to help?

A: I'm not going to give Peter Ueberroth any gratuitous advice but I think he needs to make sure that in trying to help low-income people and inner-city residents, whether they are from Korea or Central

America or Mexico or if they're African-American . . . that he include them in whatever is designed to rebuild the inner city. The frustration that President Bush heard . . . that most of the solutions of the past never included the residents, the neighbors . . . particularly the young minority youths who didn't get access to the jobs and the job training. We are redesigning all of our HUD modernization (programs) for public housing to make sure that if you go out and spend millions of dollars in rehabbing Jordan Downs or Nickerson Gardens or La Strada Courts in East L.A., that you make sure it's the residents that get the jobs and the job training that go along with putting money into brick and mortar.

Q: The host of a local radio talk show here said that, in the wake of the Rodney King verdict, law firms, offices, factories should organize discussions of racism, and white racism in particular. Do you think this is a useful suggestion? Do you think white racism is a significant factor in what's gone wrong?

A: It is a good suggestion. It is important to begin in the Anglo community—as well as in the black community, and the Korean community—consciousness raising discussions about differences in culture. . . . Different needs, different attitudes, and different patterns of behavior. I am a great believer that at the bottom of all people's behavior is the dream that Dr. King talked about, the dream that Jaime Escalante calls ganas—desire, ambition. Everybody shares a universal dream to improve their lot in life. And if you can remind Anglo people as I try to do in my speeches to audiences that might not ever get a chance to go where I have been

going . . . there is a black rage over the fact that black unemployment rates are double or triple what the Anglo rate is. . . . John Jacob said in his speech on the state of black America that of the 14.1 million businesses in the United States less than 2% are black. . . . Probably 70% of white Americans own their own homes (while) somewhere between a third and 40% of blacks get a chance to own their own home. . . . One other (thing) that is important for white people to understand about the black experience: Just as you can't understand Israel or the Jewish experience without understanding the Holocaust, you cannot understand the black experience without understanding slavery . . . and the fact that they came out of the Emancipation Declaration and the war between the states with nothing but the shirts on their back. No credit. No capital. No property. No jobs. It's a wonder that they were able to create so many enterprises in the early 20th Century.

Q: How would you assess strengths and weaknesses of the Republican Administrations in the last 12 years, specifically on urban policy and civil-rights policy?

A: Republicans and particularly conservative Republicans were not there when blacks needed us in the 1950s and '60s in the first civil-rights revolution. They were nowhere to be found. . . .

When Rosa Parks sat down on a bus and refused to give up her seat to a white man in Montgomery, Ala., in December, 1955, I doubt very much whether there were many conservatives expressing moral outrage at the treatment of a black woman. . . .

From then on, the Republican Party,

with some notable exceptions, wrote off the black vote. Now that brings us up to today. There has been an increase in spending on cities' urban problems almost continuously since the '60s—albeit for different reasons. Yes, revenue sharing went down, but CDBG is still there, the $3-billion Community Development Block Grant. Urban Development Action Grants, which went to wealthy hotel developers, were killed, and housing construction programs—which were mightily flawed in my view—were killed. But spending for housing subsidies went way up . . . from $6 billion in 1980 to probably $16 or $17 billion by 1992. . . . Public housing construction was replaced with spending to give someone a voucher so that they could go out and seek where they want to live. . . .

We've gone from serving 3.5 million people/families with vouchers to serving 4.6 million people/families. I'm not saying it's the end-all and be-all of housing policy but it's . . . not getting discussed in this debate. Aid to cities and states and to people on social welfare (programs) has gone from maybe $30 billion in 1970 to $180 billion by 1993.

Q: Let's talk about two of your ideas, enterprise zones and home ownership. Can you bring those to Los Angeles?

A: Yes. We're doing it to a limited degree, and we've asked for more money than the Congress is willing to give us. The President asked for $1 billion in the HOPE (Home Ownership for People Everywhere) proposal which would give every resident in public housing a chance to homestead. This is the 130th anniversary of Lincoln's Homestead Act which gave poor people—particularly black

families—160 acres of land if they would fulfill two obligations: (a) occupy it and (b) improve it. Now it is fundamental to human nature that you don't have to tell people to improve that what they own. . . . And the failure to give people a chance to own undermines their respect for property of their own and for their neighbor's property.

You cannot bring stability to the inner city without expanding ownership opportunities. . . . I met with Mayor Eddie Vincent (of Inglewood) and Mayor Walter Tucker of Compton, two very progressive young black mayors, and they're absolutely enthusiastic about the HOPE proposal and the enterprise zone proposal. Not that it's a solution but that it's the beginning of finding some solutions. . . . The President asked me to look at getting some credit into some of these red-lined communities. They've been red-lined!. . . . The only way to make up for a de facto redline is to flood Watts and East L.A. and Compton and Inglewood and Lynwood and North Long Beach with credit and capital.

Q: It seems that a lot of people have lost sympathy with the black community because of the high crime rate of young black males. What do you say to those people?

A: It isn't enough to express rage. To understand the black experience is not to excuse or condone, but . . . when you've got unemployment among black males at 40% and 50% . . . you're going to have problems.

Q: You've described some of Gov. Clinton's comments on the riots as demagoguery.

A: Wait. I only said that it was demagoguery to blame the riots on Republicans and George Bush and Ronald Reagan, just as its similar demagoguery to say that the riot was caused by the War on Poverty or the Great Society.

Q : Is more racial integration a solution? You have opposed mandatory racial integration policies.

A : Everybody opposes mandatory racial integration. . . . You can't force people to live in harmony with each other. You certainly can encourage it. When people have access to capital and credit and ownership and jobs . . . integration is the result of the dynamics of a liberal society.

Q : Your party and the business community in general has an image problem—

A : I agree.

Q : —as not being compassionate, as not being involved. Who else is going to take leadership and say that there is an important social function for business prosperity? Who in the Congress? Who in the Republican Party? Who in the business community is going to come with you now to say, "We take these problems seriously?"

A : Irrespective of the lack of credibility or the image problem of the Republican Party, we can't do without Republicans, and I would say to conservative Republicans, do-nothingism will lead to putting more troops in L.A. Pat Buchanan said, just put them all in jail. I don't think there's jails enough to house the population if we don't find some answers to these social and economic problems that are at the heart of urban poverty. The President has to lead, as does the Congress. And both Republicans and Democrats have a lot to answer for in terms of the failure to address these problems

in the past. . . . Now is the time to get something through the Congress, and if we miss this opportunity it will be a moral stain on our nation and on both political parties.

## ROBERT SCHEER, "JESSE JACKSON: A COMMUNITY LEADER SPEAKING FOR THOSE WHO HAVE NO VOICE," MAY 15, 1992

The man does make his presence known. Jesse Jackson came to this stunned, riot-torn city when the fires were still burning and immediately plunged into a pastiche of meetings with groups of people who were not, at the moment, on speaking terms with each other. He talked with merchants in Koreatown, Episcopalians in Pasadena and elected officials downtown. His message was ecumenical and passionate.

It was also familiar, which bothered those in the media who tended to forget that the social problems intrinsic to the riot are also not exactly new—a dismal reality that his large audiences seemed to grasp readily. Like it or not—and there are plenty who don't—Jackson is that rare individual who can traverse the immensely complicated racial and religious terrain of this crazy quilt of a city "keeping hope alive."

He has been there. Perhaps more than any American, Jackson took up the cry from a fallen Martin Luther King Jr. that the country could not survive without solving the problems of urban racism and poverty. Over the past decade, when few cared to listen, Jackson made the journey from the Bronx through Chicago or Atlanta and on to Watts—preaching his anti-drug, pro-education message combined with a singularly successful effort to get young people of every color to register and vote. He is particularly proud that once again, this time in South Los Angeles, he carried his message of power through the ballot box. "I said, 'Would you have liked to be in the jury on the Rodney King case? Well, you can't be on a jury if you're not registered.'"

It ought not be necessary to add that in two national Democratic primaries the overwhelming majority of blacks—and a good number of others—said clearly that, on such matters, he speaks for a large, if underrepresented, constituency.

After seeing Jackson on a corner off Crenshaw a couple of weeks ago, talking to some tough-looking young people that the larger society had sought to discard, one wonders why the media finds it so difficult to accept that this man has a role to play. Jackson is, after all, a reverend who believes in getting the word out. He has been dealing with the task of securing jobs and education for inner-city youth at least since 1971, when he founded Operation PUSH. No one has been more prescient in warning of the tinderbox of ghetto America. And like it or not, people who do not listen to anyone else listen to Jackson. So listen.

QUESTION: Where do we go from here? How do you bring the Koreans and blacks and everybody else together?

ANSWER: Our first step, when we sit down, should be to think about it differently. So many people are trying to play Watts Part II and are missing very different urban dynamics. For example, South Central L.A. is now 55% black, 45% Hispanic. Of those arrested, 51% were Hispanics, 37% black, 12% white. That shows a very different profile than Watts. . . .

Q: So it's more complex. Where does that lead us?

A: In terms of remedy, it is time now for blacks and Jews and Hispanics and Asians to get into the real significance of multicultural education. You can't have people living that close together who have no operative appreciation of each other. . . . Multicultural education ceases to be a debatable theory. It becomes a necessity for surviving in the multicultural arrangement. We have to have an appreciation of how we each got here—the suffering of Jewish displaced persons and Japanese in American concentration camps. We have to stop viewing others as parasites. The fact is—all of us are hosts, and none of us are parasites.

Q: What about the current planning to bring L.A. back from the abyss?

A: What we now see is a reaction rather than a response. A reaction is, "We got to do something real, real fast." Now some things we must do real, real fast. But a response is more measured. That is, a plan with some time schedules. And the premise must be driven not by fear, but with a cause that's morally right, and necessary, and cost-effective. The problem 35 years ago has now become a condition. A condition is different than a problem because it's a more advanced stage. It means it takes more time, more understanding, more money, and more mercy because you've allowed the sore to become gangrene.

Q : There are all sorts of proposals to cure the sore. What's wrong with them?

A : The planning is always top down. Coming up with Ueberroth—nice guy. Come up with Webster—nice guy. We have not seen a black, male or female, or an Hispanic, male or female, put in a prominent position yet. Even now, they ain't got the point. I mean, they're still bringing in more white males, more Santa Clauses, to dole out. That does not address bridge-building. . . .

Q : Aside from the choice of personnel, what about the vision?

A : It has to be much bolder and recognize the analogy between the needs of urban America and what was done to get Europe and Japan back on their feet after World War II. It means the same kind of funding and training now being proposed for the former Soviet republics. It means that folks who live there will have priority on loans, debt forgiveness, jobs and training. It means that the new enterprise zone exists for the benefit of those who live there, not for somebody else's benefit. This is not to create an incentive for Americans wealthiest top 1%. You need to create an incentive for those locked out in the first place. . . . We obviously need a long-term urban plan. It is in our national interest to do so.

Q : Do you think you can get around this tremendous hostility in some parts of the black communities toward Koreans?

A : Well, I think walls of hostility can come down if leadership develops an under-standing and builds a constant level. We don't have the luxury not to build bridges because the absence of bridges are gulfs, and gulfs become traps. . . .

Q : What do you make of Jack Kemp's approach to rebuilding the ghetto?

A : What they are about is new rhetoric without touching the old reality. There was an urban crisis of abandonment before the Rodney King incident. It is like spontaneous combustion, where you discard material for a long period of time and then some spark ignites it. You have a generation of discarded people and the Rodney King situation set it ablaze. And essentially what Kemp and Bush want to do is change the furniture around when the foundation is in trouble.

Q : But you must concede that there is some truth to their claim that the Great Society programs failed to solve problems.

A : No, I don't concede that. The Great Society programs lifted a whole lot of people out of poverty: prenatal care and Head Start and day care worked. The joint venture with the churches worked, the programs to help seniors worked. It was lifting people out of poverty. The War on Poverty did not fail, it got diverted—it collapsed because resources were shifted to the war in Vietnam. You must remember the context: We had just had the end of apartheid, we had just gotten the right to vote, people were living in poverty.

Q : It clearly did not solve the problems of Watts and South Central Los Angeles.

A : It was stopped before it could. When you are putting water on a fire, you don't stop while the fire is still raging. What was missing was the economic self-determination dimension. It never went as far as a Marshall Plan for Europe and similar efforts for Japan. We had our priorities clear there. The Marshall Plan said here is a body of people who need help now—here is a formula for their development. . . . We knew it required time and there was a long-term plan to accomplish it.

Why, there are $1 trillion in public pension funds. Why can't we borrow from that to build affordable housing? . . . And use the trained people who live in the area to build the housing.

Q : C'mon—where is the support going to come for such programs? You have had a conservative tide with the Republicans and even the likely Democratic candidate is more conservative on these issues.

A : Change never comes about because of the vision of people in power in government. The vision for change has to come from outside the process. The vision for ending segregation and extending the right to vote didn't come from there. Lyndon Johnson told Martin Luther King it wouldn't happen . . . and King went out and organized it. . . .

Somewhere between Selma and Montgomery, when the people moved, we saw Lyndon Johnson saying one night, to our surprise and to our delight, "We shall overcome." That means the vision for the voting rights did not come from the White House. It was the people in motion. Last week, the people in motion were in L.A. and now people are discussing things like urban policy for the first time in a decade.

Q : How do you transform that into political muscle?

A : That's why I keep putting my focus on voter registration. Bring in new voters. There's also a message gap. We need to inspire new voters. Not with these little plans that are proposed for tinkering on the edges—little gift certificates like the flat tax or round tax. No, the nation needs perestroika—a substantial restructuring of our economy and its priorities. Riots in L.A., flooding because of infrastructure collapse in Chicago, 10 million unemployed, enormous debts rack up because of savings and loan and other looters. You need . . . a commitment to new plants, new ways of doing education and creating jobs. This is the time for big dreams and big things—we are at a critical moment.

Q : Sounds good, but most people do not share that optimism. We have indeed become cynical about the prospects for change and rebuilding.

A : Cynicism is a luxury and is something that people who have real needs can't afford. I can't afford to be cynical because it is hope that keeps the people alive. When your job is gone, and your electricity is turned off, and your loved ones are injured or dead, and your job is gone, and you are down to your irreducible essence, only hope stands between you and collapse. It can't collapse. That's why we have to keep hope alive. It's so fundamental to the human spirit. The very least that leaders can do, when they can't supply the material goods yet, is to sustain imagination and hope.

Q : One of the ironies in the current situation is that the hope comes only in the aftermath of the riots. Despite the terrible cost, the fact is that without the riot, we wouldn't even be having this discussion.

A : You are right about that. Man, what a terrible price to pay. How much wax is there in the President's ear, and how thick the blinders, if it takes 60 deaths and 2,000 injuries and enormous losses in business to get the attention of an indifferent President and a stagnant Congress for a minute? But what a price for a wake-up call.

Q : Do you think that wake-up call is going to work, or, six months from now, will it be back to business-as-usual?

A : I hope that we could see the window of opportunity L.A. presents us. If not, L.A. could be the salad, not the entree to this explosion. This could be the opening of the rebellion to the indifference and all this neglect. I mean, we cannot assume that the calling out the Guards and Marines in every city addresses the problems. . . . You have all those guns and drugs and crushed dreams.

Q : And other provocations?

A : Well, yes. Look at Daryl Gates personally arresting those kids and then he came back and had a press conference. It's being provocative as opposed to being mature. That's very immature, but it looks like a jaded mind.

Q : So, it is really all about the loss of the very jobs that attracted blacks and others north from the South.

A : There is a big problem of those jobs not existing now. When you lose those jobs in the defense industry, you need a national plan to retrain. The Japanese have got a $3-trillion plan to rebuild their roads, bridges, sewers. Putting their people back to work. And we've got a 10-year, $3-trillion plan to defend them while they do it. . . .

Rebuild the infrastructure. I was in Chicago, and they got some contractor to do a major part of a road reconstruction. And there were blacks, whites, Hispanic, men and women out there working 24 hours a day. It was a big boost to everybody. They were buying stuff and paying taxes. That way you work your way out of a recession as opposed to welfaring your way into despair.

## MILES CORWIN, "CARLOS VAQUERANO, REBUILD L.A. BOARD MEMBER; IMMIGRANTS ADVOCATE," NOVEMBER 16, 1992

Carlos Vaquerano is an advocate for Central American immigrants who works in the Pico-Union area, which suffered severe riot damage. A board member of Rebuild L.A. and community relations director of the Central American Refugee Center, Vaquerano, 31, says he fled El Salvador 13 years ago after three brothers, who were political activists, were killed by the U.S.-backed Salvadoran army.

Q : How would you assess race relations in Los Angeles today?

A : After the riots there's been a lot of tension. But there also have been some positive things. We never had any relations at all with the Asian community. But now we've been meeting and working with them. The same with the African-American community. This kind of dialogue never happened in the past. The riots created the opportunity for bringing communities together. And we've been taking advantage of that opportunity.

Q: How?

A: We've been trying to create bridges in a few ways. We recently started a program where youths from our community meet with youths from the black and Asian communities. We're having a conference called "Breaking the Boundaries of Color" to deal with some of these issues. We plan to have more of these events in future. I've been meeting with politicians and leaders from the other ethnic communities . . . and we've had a lot of people from the different communities talk to us. But these kinds of things aren't enough. Social and economic inequality is the real problem. That's what needs to be addressed.

Q: Why was there such extensive rioting in Pico-Union?

A: It's poverty and lack of jobs and economic injustice. Pico-Union has been an area neglected by the local government. Unfortunately, the riots had to happen for local government to pay attention to this area. . . . This community has been forgotten.

Q: Why has the area been neglected?

A: One reason is there are many undocumented immigrants here, and they don't vote. So people say, "Who cares about them." As a result, people here are very isolated. . . . They are even isolated from the established Latino community on the Eastside, who don't put enough attention into the problems of these new communities. But it's not the fault of the Latinos. It's the fault of the whole system.

Q: Has your community received a fair share of the rebuilding resources?

A: Most of the resources are going to South-Central. I believe the African-American community deserves the resources. But they're not the only ones. We Central Americans also suffered the consequences of the riots. About 250 Latinos lost small businesses and about 70 buildings were burned here. Many people lost their jobs. Many have not received any assistance yet. I don't think it's fair to focus just on South-Central. Pico-Union, whether people like it or not, has to be part of the rebuilding effort.

Q: Six months after the riots, how would you assess the rebuilding effort in Pico-Union?

A: I don't see many changes right now. I don't think we'll see a major change in the next six months. I think it is going to take some time. My concern is that in the beginning we created many expectations that everything was going to be changed in a few months. Little by little we're recognizing it's going to take longer.

Q: Are you optimistic about the long-term prospects for rebuilding?

A: It all depends on changes at the federal level. The problems in Pico-Union and other areas of Los Angeles are not isolated from the national problem. What Pico-Union is going through is part of the economic crisis in the United States. As long as there are no economic opportunities for poor communities there will be more problems in the future. . . .

If government and corporations don't take an interest in this community and devote resources to it, things will not change. If things don't change, we'll see more riots.

Q: Does our government have a responsibility for Central Americans who live in Pico-Union because of U.S. involvement in Central America?

A: Me and a lot of other people wouldn't be here if it wasn't for the war and if it wasn't for the U.S. backing governments in El Salvador and Guatemala. . . . We need more opportunities. First to those who are undocumented—to give them a permanent residence so they can stay here legally. We want to be a productive force in this country. We want to contribute to this nation too.

## STEPHANIE CHAVEZ, Q & A: ANGELA OH, PRESIDENT, LOS ANGELES KOREAN-AMERICAN BAR ASSN., NOVEMBER 19, 1992

A Los Angeles native, Angela Oh initially envisioned a career in public health, but after earning her bachelor's and master's degrees from UCLA, she opted to attend law school at UC Davis. A trial lawyer here for the past five years, Oh is president of the Los Angeles Korean-American Bar Assn. and served as co-counsel to the state Assembly Special Committee on the Los Angeles Crisis. She was interviewed by staff writer Stephanie Chavez shortly after the riots:

Q: Why do you think people are having so much difficulty getting along right now?

A: I think people do not understand each other in the most fundamental of ways. In times of plenty, people will find it in themselves to extend a certain amount of tolerance, to stop and think about something other than their immediate needs. But right now, everyone is so focused on immediate needs. . . . You can talk about rebuilding or building a new L.A., but if you don't have the human relations and community relations elements down, it's going to be meaningless.

Q: What in the rebuilding or recovery process should come first?

A: What comes first is the things that are the easiest to do—bringing in the business and the dollars, giving people jobs. Those are the things we can actually identify a strategy for and resources that just need to be tapped. . . .

People who have never talked to each other have to talk to each other—that's what coalition building is all about. . . . I don't think we are through yet; I think we are still in the middle of it. The waiting for the feds to prosecute the four officers who beat Rodney King, the liquor store situation in South-Central. We have so many flash points out there and nobody is turning in their guns. There is a lot of firepower out there.

Q: What needs to be done differently this time around?

A: There's nothing new about rebuilding devastated areas. What is new is that this rebuilding effort from its inception understands the need for community involvement. . . . Because of all the destruction and violence, they see how devastating it will be if we don't take this principle to heart. What is operating right now is a level of fear that we have never seen before on the part of all the established institutions and structures and people who have been in complicity with these established institutions for the past two decades.

Q: What are they afraid of?

A: It's rooted in racism and a fear of poverty. I believe that many people . . . see the homeless on the street, see the overwhelming problems facing our nation and our state, and in their minds they think, "There (but for) the grace of God go I." I really think that's why everyone is so concerned at this point.

Q : What issues do you think should be addressed in the upcoming mayoral campaigns?

A : We need to think about police-community relations. I don't know who the next mayor will be, but we cannot have a situation like we had in our recent history where the mayor is not working with the Police Department and vice versa. . . . For all the economic development that is going on, unless the community feels it is safe and has confidence in law enforcement, a lot of this economic development will be very difficult to achieve.

I know this is very unpopular, but we've got to find a way of raising revenue. I was sort of in disbelief when, after the uprising, we could not get a temporary 1/2-cent tax increase. Obviously it is going to take additional dollars to do the work that has to be done, and I don't think we can get there without thinking in terms of increasing our tax base to realistically address the huge problems that are confronting our city and our state.

Q : What needs to change about the way business is conducted, to make it more inclusive?

A : The human relations angle needs to be incorporated in every structural program that is introduced. I don't think there is a special class you can take; you learn those things in the context of working on other projects. Business doesn't get done at the conference table; business gets finished at the conference table and at places where poor people and women of color traditionally don't appear. . . . We're talking about business not going on as usual. . . . We're talking about trust as a fundamental operating concept. Trust is what makes the deals happen—you look at someone and say you know that this person's instincts are right, this person's energy level is right. That's how business gets done, that's how coalitions are formed, that's how people fall in love. It's one of the most important things that happens in life.

Now there is a risk, when you look for and include people who don't think just like you and don't look just like you and don't act just like you. It's a hard thing to do. . . . But I think we—and I mean communities of color and women—are ready to help make decisions and we're ready to take responsibility and we're ready to be accountable for our decisions. We will make mistakes, as we are entitled to do as human beings. Hopefully, they won't be big mistakes, but we are ready to try.

And that's what is going on right now. We are trying to communicate that in very clear terms—we want to be there when decisions are made and we want to give you some guidance. And I think the guidance we have to offer is different from the models that have been operating in the past. And it's going to require taking a few risks and that leap of faith that all important decisions in life require. . . . But it's going to take us a lot farther. I know in my gut that it is much more effective to work on a coalition basis than within the community alone. You will only get so far that way. And I think what has happened on a societal level is that the network that has been operating has reached its point. . . . It is now time to think in terms of broadening. And we ought to look for leaders who are open to that.

## Trial Transcript from the O. J. Simpson Trial, 1995

*In 1995 the nation was transfixed by the trial of O. J. Simpson, the former football and tele-vision and movie star, for the murder of his former wife Nicole and her friend Ronald Goldman. Polling data suggested that blacks and whites had completely different perspec-tives on the trial and opinions about Simpson's guilt: most blacks believed in his innocence, and many understood the trial as a plot by a racist Los Angeles police department; most whites were certain of his guilt. The alleged racism of one of the arresting officers, Mark Fuhrman, was an important subplot in the trial that helped stoke its racial divisiveness. In this section of the trial transcript, Johnny Cochrane, an African American lawyer on the Simpson defense team, gives his final summa-tion to the jury and invokes Fuhrman's racist reputation as a defense of Simpson.*

*Source:* http://simpson.walraven.org [private site maintained by Jack Walraven].

MR. COCHRAN: Witnesses willfully false in one material part, distrusted in others. These two form basically the cor-nerstone of the prosecution's case. Now, you know people talk all the time, well, you know, you are being conspiratorial and whatever. Gee, how would all these police officers set up O. J. Simpson?

Why would they do that? I will answer that question for you. They believed he was guilty. They wanted to win. They didn't want to lose another big case. That is why. They believed that he was guilty. These actions rose from what their belief was, but they can't make that—the pros-ecutors can't make that judgment. No-body but you can make that judgment. So when they take the law into their own hands, they become worse than the peo-ple who break the law, because they are the protectors of the law. Who then po-lices the police? You police the police. You police them by your verdict. You are the ones to send the message. Nobody else is going to do it in this society. They don't have the courage. Nobody has the courage. They have a bunch of people running around with no courage to do what is right, except individual citizens. You are the ones in war, you are the ones who are on the front line. These people set policies, these people talk all this stuff, you implement it. You are the peo-ple. You are what makes America so great, and don't you forget it. And so understand how this happened. It is part of a culture of getting away with things. It is part of what looking the other way. We determine the rules as we go along. Nobody is going to question us. We are the LAPD. And so you take these two twins of deception, and if as you can un-der this law wipe out their testimony, the prosecutors realize their case then is in serious trouble. From Riske to Bushey they came together in this case because they want to win. But it is not about them winning; it is about justice being done. They have other cases. This is this man's one life that is entrusted or will be soon, to you. So when we talked about this evidence being compromised, contaminated and corrupted, some people didn't believe that. Have we proved that? Have we proved that it was compromised, contaminated and corrupted? And yes, even something more sinister—I think you will believe we do, but there is something else about this man Fuhrman that I have to say before I am going to terminate this part of my opening argument and relinquish the floor to my learned colleague Mr. Barry Scheck, is something that Fuhrman said. And I'm going to ask Mr. Douglas and Mr. Harris to put up that Kathleen Bell letter. You know, it is one thing, and I dare say that most of you, when you heard Fuhrman said he hadn't used the "N" word, that you probably thought, well, he is lying, we know that is not true. That is just part of it. That is just want the prosecutors want to do, just talk about that part of it. That is not the part that bothers us on the defense. I live in America. I understand. I know about slights everyday of my life. But I want to tell you about what is troubling, what is frightening, what is chilling about that Kathleen Bell letter. Let's see if we can see part of it, and I think you will agree, so I want to put the focus back where it belongs on this letter and its application to this case. You will recall that god is good and he always brings you a way to see light when there is a lot of darkness around, and just through chance this lady had tried to reach Shapiro's office, couldn't reach it, and in July of 1994 she sent this fax to my office, and my good, loyal and wonderful staff got that letter to me early on. And this is one you just couldn't pass up.

You get a lot of letters but you couldn't pass this one up because she says some interesting things. And she wasn't a fan of O. J. Simpson. What does she say? "I'm writing to you in regards to a story I saw on the news last night. I thought it ridiculous that the Simpson Defense team would even suggest that there might be racial motivation involved in the trial against Mr. Simpson." Yes, there are a lot of people out there who thought that at that time, and you know, you can't fault people for being naive, but once they know, if they continue to be naive, then you can fault them. That is what it is and this is why this case is important. Don't ever say again in this county or in this country that you don't know things like this exist. Don't pretend to be naive any more. Don't turn your heads. Stand up, show some integrity.

"And so I then glanced up at the television. I was quite shocked to see that officer Fuhrman was a man that I had the misfortune of meeting. You may have received the message from your answering service last night that I called to say that Mr. Fuhrman may be more of a racist than you could even imagine." I doubt that, but at any rate, it was something that got my attention. "Between 1985 and 1986 I worked as a real estate agent in Redondo Beach for Century 21 Bob Maher Realty now out of business. At the time my office was located above a marine recruiting center off of pacific coast highway. On occasion I would stop in to say hello to the two marines working there. I saw Mr. Fuhrman there a couple of times. I remember him distinctly because of his height and build, you know, he is tall."

"While speaking to the men I learned that Mr. Fuhrman was a police officer in Westwood." Isn't that interesting? Just exactly the place where Laura McKinny met him. "And I don't know if he was telling the truth but he said that he had been in a special division of the marines. I don't know how this subject was raised but officer Fuhrman says that when he sees a Nigger, as he called it, driving with a white woman, he would pull them over. I asked what if he didn't have a reason and he said that he would find one. I looked at the two marines to see if they knew he was joking, but it became obvious to me that he was very serious." Now, let me just stop at this point. Let's back it up a minute, Mr. Harris. Pull it back down, please. If he sees an African American with a white woman he would stop them. If he didn't have a reason, he would find one or make up one. This man will lie to set you up. That is what he is saying there. He would do anything to set you up because of the hatred he has in his heart. A racist is somebody who has power over you, who can do something to you. People could have views but keep them to themselves, but when they have power over you, that is when racism becomes insidious. That is what we are talking about here. He has power. A police officer in the street, a patrol officer, is the single most powerful figure in the criminal justice system. He can take your life. Unlike the supreme court, you don't have to go through all these appeals. He can do it right there and justify it. And that is why, that is why this has to be routed out in the LAPD and every place. Make up a reason because he made a judgment. That is what happened

in this case. They made a judgment. Everything else after that is going to point toward O. J. Simpson. They didn't want to look at anybody else. Mr. Darden asked who did this crime? That is their job as the police. We have been hampered. They turned down our offers for help. But that is the prosecution's job. The judge says we don't have that job. The law says that. We would love to help do that. Who do you think wants to find these murderers more than Mr. Simpson? But that is not our job; it is their job. And when they don't talk to anybody else, when they rush to judgment in their obsession to win, that is why this became a problem. This man had the power to carry out his racist views and that is what is so troubling. Let's move on Making up a reason. That is troubling. That is frightening. That is chilling. But if that wasn't enough, if that wasn't enough, the thing that really gets you is she goes on to say: "Officer Fuhrman went on to say that he would like nothing more than to see all niggers gathered together and killed. He said something about burning them or bombing them. I was too shaken to remember the exact words he used. However, I do remember that what he said was probably the most horrible thing I had ever heard someone say. What frightened me even more was that he was a police officer sworn to uphold the law." And now we have it. There was another man, not too long ago in the world, who had those same views who wanted to burn people, who had racist views and ultimately had power over people in this country.

People didn't care. People said he was just crazy, he is just a half-baked painter.

They didn't do anything about it. This man, this scourge, became one of the worse people in the history of this world, Adolph Hitler, because people didn't care or didn't try to stop him. He had the power over his racism and his anti-religion. Nobody wanted to stop him, and it ended up in world war ii, the conduct of this man. And so Fuhrman, Fuhrman wants to take all black people now and burn them or bomb them. That is genocidal racism. Is that ethnic purity? What is that? What is that? We are paying this man's salary to espouse these views? Do you think he only told Kathleen Bell whom he just had met? Do you think he talked to his partners about it? Do you think commanders knew about it? Do you think everybody knew about it and turned their heads? Nobody did anything about it. Things happen for a reason in your life. Maybe this is one of the reasons we are all gathered together this day, one year and two days after we met. Maybe there is a reason for your purpose. Maybe this is why you were selected. There is something in your background, in your character that helps you understand this is wrong. Maybe you are the right people at the right time at the right place to say no more, we are not going to have this. This is wrong. What they've done to our client is wrong. This man, O. J. Simpson, is entitled to an acquittal. You cannot believe these people. You can't trust the message. You can't trust the messengers. It is frightening. It is quite, frankly frightening, and it is not enough for the Prosecutors now to stand up and say, oh, well, let's just back off. The point I was trying to make, they didn't understand that it is not just using the "N" word.

Forget that. We knew he was lying about that. Forget that. It is about the lengths to which he would go to get somebody black and also white if they are associated with black. That is pretty frightening. It is not just African Americans, it is white people who would associate or deign to go out with a black man or marry one. You are free in America to love whoever you want, so it infects all of us, doesn't it, this one rotten apple, and yet they cover for him. Yet they cover for him. And so how do we do it and what do we do with regard to this man? Well, we call some witnesses. And you recall these witnesses. And before I talk about these witnesses just briefly, and I'm going to conclude my remarks with regard to them, I indicated to you that by the nature of this case I'm going to pass the baton to Mr. Barry Scheck. You have been great from the standpoint of listening and watching, and I stayed longer than I planned to, but I hope you agree that some of these things were important. And I will get one more time to conclude with some concluding remarks after Mr. Scheck finishes. The good news is that Mr. Scheck and I will both hopefully finish today and turn it back over to Miss Clark, so in a day or so you are going to get this case. You don't have to hear lawyers talk to you any more. It will time to hear you talk, time to hear you speak out. And I will be happy. I will be able to relax tonight knowing that soon it will be in your hands. We are real comfortable about that, all of us, and you should know that, so please give Mr. Scheck the attention to which you've given me. And understand all parts of this case are very important and it all ties together because it is—all the evidence in this case went through that LAPD and that black hole over there, that cesspool of contamination and you listen into him about what he has to say in that regard. Mr. Darden said that in a textbook fashion we had impeached Mr. Fuhrman. We thank him for that. We take no pride in that, but that is what did happen. In addition to calling Kathleen Bell where you saw her—and she is not the kind of lady that—you know, in looking at her—you probably remember her. Unless you know it would be very interesting—you know he is lying about not knowing her, but this man used these words and these racial epithets so much he probably can't remember who he said it to you. He said it to whoever came in contact with him, on tape. Can you imagine the gall about that that you would have these racist views and yet would you put it on tape? Thank God he put it on tape. And so Kathleen Bell came in here and told you the same things in those letters. You saw her. You observed her. You know she told us the truth. They couldn't mess with her because now we had those tapes. And then there was Natalie Singer. Barely knew this man. He was dating her roommate. This man is an indiscriminate racist. He talks so bad that she didn't want him back in the house. What does he say to her in her presence? "The only good Nigger is a dead Nigger."

You probably all heard that expression sometime in your background somewhere or heard somebody say this. And that is tremendously offensive. He just says it in the presence of his partner's girlfriend, like they are going to go on a date. I mean, I hope that in homes throughout this country people aren't acting like this. This happened to come to light, but I would be pretty frightened if I felt that the majority of people in this country acted like this behind closed doors or whatever. Because what you do in the dark is going to come to the light. Remember that. That is what this case is about. It came to the light and just in time to get it to you. So you saw her on the stand. You saw her graphically. We will talk about that. Any doubt in anybody's mind she is telling you the truth? Any one of you think she is not telling you the truth? And then finally we had Roderic Hodge, and this series of witnesses. And Roderic Hodge, intelligent young man, understands something about his rights, too, because when—after this run-in with Fuhrman and his partner when he is in the back of the police car, Fuhrman turns around and says to him words that I want you to remember in this case, "I told you I'd get you, Nigger" that is what he tells Roderic Hodge. Why is that important? Because from 1985, when he went on that one call involving the Mercedes, that was this man's mindset vis-à-vis O. J. Simpson, I'm going to get that guy. And in 89 when he wrote that report, indelibly impressed on his mind, and in '94 he had his chance, still in west Los Angeles, he had his chance. So Hodge is important because you can espouse all these epithets and talk theoretically about your racism, but when it is directed toward a human being—and I said to him, "Mr. Hodge, tell this jury how that made you feel." He said, "It made me feel angry and upset and frustrated." It was dehumanizing in a free society. But this man, Fuhrman, does it with immunity and his partner sat there and heard it and didn't report it. There is something rotten about this kind of conduct, that it is going on too long, and so that is why he is important. But the capper was finding those tapes, something that you could hear. Lest there be any doubt in anybody's mind, Laura McKinny came in here, and I can imagine the frustration of the Prosecutors, they've had the glove demonstration, they have seen all these other things go wrong and now they got to face these tapes. And they didn't know how to handle her. Quite frankly, she was a reluctant witness. You know that. Mr. Darden asked her those questions where he became negative with her. She is very smart, not like some others who didn't know how to handle it. He says, "Why are we having this negative conversation? Why are you acting and treating me like this?" I didn't try to stop him about cover-ups and things. "Why are you asking me these questions? I am the one who is here under subpoena. Why are you treating me like this?" You know it is true because they have heard the tapes. Why are you messing with this lady? You obviously get so wrapped up with what you are doing, I guess. Why are they messing with this lady? We owe a debt of gratitude to this lady that ultimately and finally she came forward. And she tells us that this man over the time of these interviews uses the "N" word 42 times is what she says. And so-called Fuhrman tapes. And you of course had an opportunity to listen to this man and espouse this evil, this personification of evil. And so I'm going to ask Mr. Harris to play

exhibit 1368 one more time. It was a transcript. This was not on tape. The tape had been erased where he said, "We have no niggers where I grew up." These are two of 42, if you recall. Then this was his actual voice.

*(At 10:00 A.M., Defense exhibit 1368, a videotape, was played.)*

MR. COCHRAN: This is the word text for what he then says on the tape. Now, you heard that voice. No question whose voice that is. Mr. Darden concedes whose voice that is. They don't do anything. Talking about women. Doesn't like them any better than he likes African Americans. They don't go out and initiate contact with some six foot five inch Nigger who has been in prison pumping weights. This is how he sees this world. That is this man's cynical view of the world. This is this man who is out there protecting and serving. That is Mark Fuhrman. And he is paired in this case with Phil Vannatter. They are both beacons that you look at and look to as the messengers that you must look through and pass. They are both people who have shown that they lie, will lie, did lie on the stand under oath. And you know, one little parenthetical thing how these people all try to stick together from the standpoint of law enforcement. The FBI agent come in here and he talks about—when I bring out the facts he says that Vannatter says they are not there to save lives. On cross-examination, he says, well, I think he was being sarcastic, Vannatter was being sarcastic or maybe it was a joke. But you know, when I listened to that, I thought about that, I said, well, what is the joke? What is the sarcasm? Is the constitution this man's rights to be safe and secure in his home? Is that the joke? Is that the sarcasm? Sad state of affairs. That is the lead detective I'm talking about, these two twin devils of deception. You think about it and keep them in mind. Thank you for your attention during this first part of my argument. I hope that during this phase of it I have demonstrated to you that this really is a case about a rush to judgment, an obsession to win, at all costs, a willingness to distort, twist, theorize in any fashion to try to get you to vote guilty in this case where it is not warranted, that these metaphors about an ocean of evidence or a mountain of evidence is little more than a tiny, tiny stream, if at all, that points equally toward innocence, that any mountain has long ago been reduced to little more than a molehill under an avalanche of lies and complexity and conspiracy. This is what we've shown you. And so as great as America is, we have not yet reached the point where there is equality in rights or equality of opportunity. I started off talking to you a little bit about Frederick Douglas and what he said more than a hundred years ago, for there are still the Mark Fuhrmans in this world, in this country, who hate and are yet embraced by people in power. But you and I, fighting for freedom and ideals and for justice for all, must continue to fight to expose hate and genocidal racism and these tendencies. We then become the guardians of the constitution, as I told you yesterday, for if we as the People don't continue to hold a mirror up to the face of America and

say this is what you promised, this is what you delivered, if you don't speak out, if you don't stand up, if you don't do what's right, this kind of conduct will continue on forever and we will never have an ideal society, one that lives out the true meaning of the creed of the constitution or of life, liberty and justice for all. I'm going to take my seat, but I get one last time to address you, as I said before. This is a case about an innocent man wrongfully accused. You have seen him now for a year and two days. You observed him during good times and the bad times. Soon it will be your turn. You have the keys to his future. You have the evidence by which you can acquit this man. You have not only the patience, but the integrity and the courage to do the right thing. We believe you will do the right thing, and the right thing is to find this man not guilty on both of these charges. Thank you very, very much. I appreciate your attention. I think, your Honor, we may need a brief break . . .

## Million Man March, Louis Farrakhan's Statement and The Black Woman's Statement of Support, 1995

*On October 16, 1995, hundreds of thousands of African Americans gathered on the Washington Mall in front of the Capitol as part of the "Million Man March." The march's purpose was, the official packet declared, to mark a "Holy Day of Atonement and Reconciliation." Yet it was a polarizing event from its beginnings. Its organizer, Rev. Lewis*

*Farrakhan, minister of the Nation of Islam, had frequently condemned whites, especially Jews, during his career and was quoted by one news service assailing Jews as "bloodsuckers" only weeks before the march. Still, many black men saw the demonstration as an opportunity to recommit themselves to the needs of their families and their people as well as a chance to find solidarity and community in the face of white hostility. Blacks as diverse as Dick Gregory, the rap star Hammer, Stevie Wonder, and the poet Maya Angelou (one of the few women present) attended the demonstration, which was one of the largest in Washington's history.*

Source: "Million Man March, 'A Holy Day of Atonement and Reconciliation,'" National Organizing Committee Packet (145 Kennedy Street, N.W., Washington, D.C. 20011).

## Louis Farrakhan's Statement: The Vision for the Million Man March

### WHY A MILLION MAN MARCH?

There is an increasingly conservative and hostile climate growing in America towards the aspirations of Black people and people of color for justice. The "Contract with America," proposed by the Republicans and thus far agreed to by the Congress is turning back the hands of time, depriving the Black community of many of the gains made through the suffering and sacrifice of our fellow advocates of change during the '50s and '60s.

The recent Supreme Court decision on Affirmative Action has set the stage in the U.S. for closing the doors, thereby impeding the progress made in Black enrollment in, and graduation from, colleges and universities; and minimizing business opportunities and the hiring of Black Americans in the public and private sectors.

Each day, somewhere in this nation, the Black community witnesses and falls prey to an increased rate of crime and violence. Aspects of the "Crime Bill" suggest that Black males will be filling the jails of America and will spend the rest of their lives working for little or no pay in the new prison industrial coalition. The unfair use of the death penalty to punish the Black male is in fact a systematic genocidal tool being institutionalized to significantly decrease the Black population.

The proliferation of drugs and gun-related violence in the Black community, and the escalation of Black male fratricide has diminished the positive role and attributes of Black men, and instead has elevated ugly images of Black men as thieves, criminals, and savages projected through movies, music and other communications technologies throughout the world.

The epitome of these major challenges to the Black male and our community is this mounting force of hate being built against our people, particularly Black men. We, therefore, have deemed it necessary in this critical hour to call for one million disciplined, committed, and dedicated Black men, from all walks of life in America, to march in Washington, D.C.—showing the world a vastly different picture of the Black male.

## PURPOSE OF THE MILLION MAN MARCH

We recognize October 16th as "*A Holy Day of Atonement and Reconciliation.*" As the sons of proud people, we are coming together and moving forward to chart the course for our future as responsible heads of our families; to reclaim and build our neighborhoods; to unify our families; and to save our children who will lead us into the next millennium. We believe that it is only when we are at one or at peace with ourselves and our Creator that we are fortified with the ability and the capacity to successfully reconcile our differences with each other, and accelerate the upward mobility of the Black community.

We believe that as men, we must recognize and praise our brothers that work hard everyday to protect family values, unify and improve the quality of life for the Black man, woman and child. And yes—we as Black men must Atone, take responsibility—open the eyes, teach and embrace our brothers who need to achieve their unfulfilled potential. As strong and worthy Black men, nation builders, fathers, husbands, sons, leaders, we must appreciate and support the very essence and strength of the Black woman. We will not—we will not stand for the abuse or misuse of the Black woman by anyone. No, not anyone.

Our presence in Washington, D.C.— the capital of the United States—is a day set aside to reconcile our spiritual inner beings and to redirect our focus to developing our communities, strengthening our families, working to uphold and protect our civil and human rights, and empowering ourselves through the Spirit of God, more effective use of our dollars, and through the power of the vote.

We are asking all religious leaders of the various denominations of Christianity and the various Faith Traditions within the Black community to declare October 16, 1995, as a *Holy Day of Atonement and Reconciliation*—a day of fasting and prayer for those who are able. This will be the first time since the institution of slavery that Black people would have declared a *Holy Day* for our people.

We are asking all members of college, high school, and professional sports teams to observe the *Holy Day* and to not engage in sports activities. We are asking our musicians and entertainers not to perform on this day, as a show of solidarity. We are asking on this declared Holy Day that none of us go to work or school; none of us participate in shopping; and none of us engage in drinking alcohol, drugs, or any unclean or illegal act during the *Holy Day.* We must designate and recognize this day in accordance with the Word of our Creator.

We are asking the Black woman, particularly our mothers, to be with our children teaching them the value of home, self-esteem, family, and unity; and to work with us to ensure the success of the March and our mission to improve the quality of life for our people.

We take this historical moment to recognize the major contributions that the Black woman has made, and continues to make, toward the advancement of our people. Bonded under the guise of leadership and strength, we, as one people must come together to improve the quality of life for our children and for the Black family. For, the long and winding road that we must travel to define our future shall be determined by the depth of our unification.

We are asking that the church doors be opened and that all those who have differences within the congregation go to their house of worship to reconcile their differences. Parents, our children, and members of our community should come together by the end of the day at a religious temple of any denomination to pray for the success and well-being of the Black man, woman, and child, and our community.

We are asking all those who have not registered to vote to go to a house of worship on October 16th, to get registered. There are approximately eight million Black persons in the U.S. eligible to vote, but who remain unregistered. Our goal is to have a registrar in as many churches as possible. There will be teachers present to provide guidance, instructions, and information. The most critical election of this century will be held in 1996. This will be the last presidential election of the century. We are determined that never again shall any political party take the Black vote for granted.

We are asking that you join many of our leaders who have gathered together to develop a national agenda for our people, as a follow-up to the Million Man March. Religious, political, civic, and youth leaders will be called to come together to incorporate sound ideas and

recommendations; and to amend and finalize this national platform of action. We shall take this platform of action to various communities in America to hold town meetings to encourage the Black community's input and secure our people's approval and active support of this agenda. In turn, every presidential candidate will receive our platform of action and will be invited to address the Black community, based on our agenda. We shall emphasize in our actions and in the written word that the Black community shall not give our vote to anyone who is against, or is not willing to represent, the best interests of our people.

We believe that by the grace and goodness of our Creator, the success we envision for the Million Man March, and beyond October 16, 1995—our first declared Holy Day of Atonement and Reconciliation—will be captured in the annals of history as a landmark period in which Black people came together to effect the greatest promise of change for Black people in America, and throughout the world.

## MILLION MAN MARCH FACT SHEET

### What Is the Million Man March?

The Million Man March is a Holy Day of Atonement and Reconciliation for, and by, Black men in the United States of America, who will March in Washington, D.C., to convey to the world a vastly different picture of the Black male, and to publicly proclaim to the global community that the Black man is prepared and moving forward to unify our families and build our communities.

## What Is the Purpose of the Million Man March?

The purpose of the Million Man March is to enable and encourage Black men in the U.S. to take a greater responsibility and play a greater role in caring for, and uplifting the status of, the Black family. Heretofore, Black women have disproportionately carried the burden of caring for our families. The Million Man March is calling for at least one million Black men to pledge their commitment to the restoration of their roles as sustainers and providers for the Black family and community.

## What Is the Million Man March Guiding Principle?

"If my people, which are called by my name, shall humble themselves, and pray, and seek my face, and turn from their wicked ways; then will I hear from heaven, and will forgive their sin, and will heal their land." II Chronicles 7:14

## Where and When Will the Million Man March Take Place?

The Million Man March will be held on Monday, October 16, 1995, and will take place in Washington, D.C.

## What Are the Main Issues to Be Addressed?

There are three key issue areas that will be addressed:

1. *The Black Family and Community Development.* This includes self-responsibility, loving, nurturing, and caring for the Black family; and working to end self-destruction, Black-on-Black crime and the epidemic of drug and other substance abuse. Coming together and being at one with God, and with one another.

2. *Affirmative Action and Voting Rights Support.* We support affirmative action and are opposed to the dismantling of policies and regulations which uphold and protect our civil and human rights. We support Representative Cynthia McKinney and other policy-makers in the restoration of voting rights.

3. *Corporate America's Reinvestment in the Black Community.* We are asking Corporate America to reinvest in the Black Community. Economic viability is a sound and effective means to minimize the incidence of violence and crime, to provide business and employment opportunities, and to improve the quality of life in the Black Community. According to recent figures from the *Wall Street Journal,* the Black Community in America spends $433 billion annually in disposable income.

## The Black Woman's Statement of Support for the Million Man March

Recognizing the historical contributions that Black women have made, and continue to make, toward the advancement of Black people in America, we are proud to endorse and actively support the *Million Man March*. Joining our brothers in the development, planning, and implementation of this landmark event, we embrace their position that:

- October 16, 1995, must be established and recognized as a "*Holy Day of Atonement and Reconciliation.*"

- There is an increasingly conservative and hostile climate growing in America towards the aspirations of Black people and people of color for justice.

- The recent Supreme Court decision on Affirmative Action has set the stage in the U.S. for closing the doors, thereby impeding the progress made in Black enrollment in, and graduation from, colleges and universities; and minimizing business opportunities and the hiring of Black Americans in the public and private sectors.

- The proliferation of drugs and gun-related violence in the Black community, and the escalation of Black male fratricide has diminished the positive role and attributes of Black men, and instead has elevated ugly images of Black men as thieves, criminals, and savages—projected through movies, music and other communications technologies throughout the world.

- The time and the hour has come for the world to see a vastly different picture of Black men, and for Black men to convey to the world that they are the sons of a proud people who are coming together and moving forward with Black women, to chart the course of our future as responsible heads of our families; to reclaim and

build our neighborhoods; and to save our children.

- The Black man must recognize and unconditionally *Atone* for the absence, in too many cases, of the Black male as the head of the household, positive role model and builder of our community.

- The Black man must *Atone* for and establish positive solutions to the abuse and misuse of Black women and girls.

- Together, we must redirect our focus to developing our communities, strengthening our families, working to uphold and protect our civil and human rights, and empowering ourselves through the power of the vote.

- We encourage Corporate America to reinvest in the Black Community. We agree that economic viability is a sound and effective means to minimize the incidence of violence and crime, to provide business and employment opportunities, and to improve the quality of life in the Black Community.

- The most critical election of this century will be held in 1996. We agree, and are equally determined, that never again shall any political party take the Black vote for granted.

- We shall emphasize in our actions and in the written word that the Black community shall not give our vote to anyone who is against, or is not willing to represent, the best interests of our people.

- We believe the success envisioned for the Million Man March, and beyond October 16, 1995—the first Holy Day of Atonement and Reconciliation—will be captured in the annals of history as a landmark period in which Black people came together to effect the greatest promise of change for Black people in America, and throughout the world.

## Commission on Race, Town Meeting, 1997

*In 1997 President Clinton established a Commission on Race, chaired by the distinguished historian John Hope Franklin. The charge for the commission was to investigate the state of race relations in the United States and recommend means of improving them. The commission held hundreds of meetings, including a "town meeting" with President Clinton in Akron, Ohio, on December 3, 1997. Excerpts from that town meeting are reprinted here. In September of 1998, the commission submitted its report to President Clinton and ended its work.*

*Source:* Web site of Coming Together Project, P.O. Box 1543, Akron, Ohio 44309. http:// clinton4.nara.gov/initiatives/oneamerica/prac tices/pp_19980728.3185.html

MODERATOR   DAVID   LIEBERTH. Welcome to the Akron community. This is the first one of President Clinton's initiatives.

This dialogue has room for many stories, candid personal stories and different opinions. We begin with the dialogue where there are not right answers, the strength of this conversation will be in its diversity. Our audience in the hall can participate best by not recognizing individual opinions with applause, there is no simple point of view and one hat our participants seek to cheer. We do want to engage as many people on the stage as possible and I will ask you to join me at the end of our program in thanking all of our participants.

Ladies and gentlemen the President of the United States, accompanied by Dr. Marion Ruebel.

Today's gathering is a tremendous example about what is best in our country. People of varying races, creeds and backgrounds, led by the President of the United States, talking about a subject vital to the future success of our nation. The University of Akron is thrilled to host this important event.

As a university, we are committed to seeking knowledge and truth. And as any student will tell you, that isn't easy, it takes perseverance and courage.

Today we all come together as students seeking knowledge from one another and truth about our society.

We all are part of a process that with diligence and determination will help us identify our challenges and create solutions together. Through the hard work of the Akron community, our national recognized Coming Together Project, and our elective leaders, we begin to take the steps that make our region and our nation more vibrant and tolerant of those we live with. Thank you, Mr. President, for beginning your ambitious discussion of race in Akron. Thank you for coming and sharing the concerns and stories of people here. We're proud of the steps we've taken, we want to join you in leading our nation to a better understanding of what makes us united as a people, our celebration of diversity.

Ladies and gentlemen, the President of the United States.

PRESIDENT CLINTON: Thank you very much, thank you. Thank you. Thank you, thank you. Thank you very much, Dr. Ruebel, we're delighted to be here at the University of Akron. I want to thank my good friend Senator John Glenn and our Congressman, Tom Sawyer, Congressman Lou Stokes, and Sherrod Brown for being here. Thank you for making Akron so available and doing all you can to help us.

Thank the County Executive, Tim Davis, and all the people here in Akron, it's just wonderful helping us put this together. I thank the people who are behind me who agreed to be part of our panel today and kind of put themselves on the line on behalf of all the rest of you, and I hope on behalf of all Americans in launching this important dialogue.

There are 96 watch sites that have been set up around the country by our regional administrators, situation groups, and others who will be kind of doing what we're doing here in their own way as they watch us.

I'd also like to acknowledge the presence here today of members of our racial advisory board, John Hope Franklin, the chairman, Johnson Cook and Jeanne Winston, our Executive Director. Ladies and gentlemen, last June at the University of San Diego I challenged all Americans to join me for at least a year in addressing the enormous challenge of making one America out of all of our racial diversity in this country. At the time I did it a lot of people said, "Well, why is he doing this, we're not having any riots in cities, the economy is best it's been in a generation." And my answer

was "That's precisely why I'm doing it now."

Because what I have tried to do as your President is to get all of us to think about and work on things that are going to be critical to our future before the wheel runs off, because if we plan together and work together to make the most of our common future we can avoid some of the terrible things that have happened in other countries, and we can avoid repeating some of the darker chapters of our own history.

And by the way, we're getting knowledge that we still have some problems, and we need to get them out on the table and deal with them.

Now, to me this is a critical part of the larger challenge of preparing our country to live in the next century. It's not just a new century and new millennium, it's a whole new world out there the way we learn and work and relate to each other. All of you know—and I have done my best to pursue a vision that would create opportunity for everybody responsible and to maintain our country's leadership in the global theater, and for world peace and security and freedom, to give everybody a chance to be a part of the winner's circle in America.

But I know it can't be done unless we recognize the fact that we are rapidly becoming the most diverse and integrated democracy in the world. We have to deal with a lot of the older racial issues that have been with us from the beginning, from the time of Africans coming here on the slave ships between blacks and whites; from the time of our moving Indian tribes off the land of Native Americans; and white Americans from the time of the war with Mexico, between Americans and Mexican Americans, now, increasingly enriched and diversified by all the peoples that have come to America in the 20th century.

In the school district that's just across the river from my office in Washington, D.C. there are now students from over 180 national groups with over a hundred different native languages in one school district. We are becoming a very richly multiracial, multiethnic society at a time when in the last few years we've read of ethnic and racial hatred and problems and wars in Bosnia to the Middle East to Africa to Russia, India, you name it, and we're beating the odds so far with all of our problems. But I think it is very important that we understand that this is something that we have to keep dealing with honestly and openly. There are many people today with whom I have great sympathy who say, "Well, the President shouldn't be talking about race out of context. Most of the problems that minorities have today are problems of economic and educational opportunity that they share with people who aren't in that group, and what we really need is an affirmative opportunity agenda, more educational opportunities for everybody." I basically agree with that.

I agree with that, but you have only to look at the rest of the world and your own experience to know that in addition to that there is something unique about racial difference that affects the way people relate to each other, and every society in the world. It can be wonderful. It can be truly wonderful.

We ought not—I don't like it when people say we ought to tolerate our differences. I think we ought to respect and celebrate our differences. Tolerance is the wrong word. But we also have to struggle constantly to identify what unites us. That's more important than what's different about us, and that's why we're having these town hall meetings. Now let me say I want to now turn to the people who are here, and I want to ask all of you who won't be talking to carry on this conversation in your mind, and all of those at the other sites around the country, when this is over I want you to go out and do this all over again at work, or in any other groups that you're in, because what we're trying to do here is drop the pebble in the pond and have it ripple all across America, because I honestly believe that this is a good country, full of good people, there has never been a challenge we couldn't face.

And so I ask all of you to join me and to help us in that. I also would remind you if you don't speak frankly about what we believe, then when it's over we won't feel very good. I told our speakers you have to imagine that we're at a cafe downtown sitting around a table drinking coffee together. Forget that people are sitting around watching you and you're on television. Now, I don't say this in the way you think. It's very proper to say this, whatever you have to say, the more you think is most honest so that we can move forward together.

Again let me say that this dialogue to me is an important part of where we're going. Now we have responsibilities in Washington too. There is an economic responsibility, there is an education responsibility.

A few weeks ago I announced that we

were going to support scholarships for people who go out and teach, and education is the primary goal in deprived areas where we needed more teachers. Today we are releasing a proposal to create educational opportunities to award school districts and rural areas to undertake the kind of sweeping reform that Chicago has embraced in the last couple of years, closing failing schools, provided school lunches, holding teachers and parents responsible for providing opportunities for students who have learning problems, to learn independently, giving people high school diplomas that don't mean anything.

I think we should support that sort of thing. We will do that. We have a policy of responsibility, I think we should build on our economic efforts to create an affirmative economic opportunity, again, really across racial lines, and the same thing with education, the same thing with health care, the same thing with Family Medical Leave Law to help people balance and support a family. Yes, there is a public responsibility here.

But this country in the end rises and falls on the day-to-day activities of its ordinary citizens. Let me say that I thank the racial advisory board for the work they've done here. I said I see Governor Voinovich is here and four or five members of his Cabinet. I received a letter, and I see here—hello, I was told you weren't coming. That makes our Board members happy. That's good. So we're going to do our part, but I don't want anybody for a moment minimizing the importance of this sort of dialogue. The reason we came to Akron, as—as was said earlier, in part is because of this

Coming Together Project that you've done. I believe that we can find constructive ways for people to work together, learn together, talk together, be together. That's the best shot we've got to avoid some of the hard problems we see in the rest of the world, to avoid some of the difficult problems we've had in our own history, and to eliminate the problems we come here to face today.

Now, I think it's appropriate we begin the dialogue with young people because they have more time in front of them than behind them, and it's their lives that will be most affected by this incredible explosion of diversity in the global diversity than the rest of us, so let's begin. Our first student here is McHughson Chambers, and he has an interesting ethnic background himself. I'd like to ask him basically to begin by trying to level with us about what impact, if any, race has on his life, whether he believes it affects any of his relationships with other people and his future prospects in life. McHughson?

MCHUGHSON CHAMBERS: My name is McHughson Chambers and I'm an electrical engineering student here at the University of Akron. I'm bi-racial, and I think the only time race ever comes up in my mind is when I'm reminded of it by other people, just in terms of like experiences where I'm discriminated against or just treated differently because of what I look like.

Growing up, growing up in their early days, I didn't really have much experience with this, but later when I got to high school I transferred to a private high school, and I think that it seemed like every day that people would, you know, make some kind of comment or they would say something that would just keep the pressure on you and keep you tense and keep you stressed. That, I think, was unnecessary.

Different experiences I've had, like I've been to banks where I've given them a check to deposit for my mother and, you know, I mean, it was a pretty low sum of money and I've given it to them and they've put holds on them unnecessarily, and I've seen them talking to people, calling on the telephone, and just it really seems like sometimes people only realize half of who I am, and they only realize—they only think about what I look like, that—I mean just basically the stereotypical things other than I'm an educated person.

PRESIDENT CLINTON: Our second student, Jonathan Morgan. Jonathan, where are you? What do you think about what he said? Do you think there is still discrimination in—here at this school or in this community, here in the country, and do you think that most people want to live in an integrated society?

JONATHAN MORGAN: Yeah, I do honestly think that there is still discrimination in this country to a point. There are a lot of prejudiced people out there, the historical opinion, and my honest opinion about that is that those people are the older people, the older generations, 30's, 40's, 50's and up. I'm not saying all of them are.

PRESIDENT CLINTON: Maybe we need a panel on aging instead of racism. I apologize. That makes it worse, don't do that.

JONATHAN MORGAN: You're right. The main thing I'm getting at is, I mean,

I can look at Avery McHuhn and say he's my friend, he's a fellow student here at the University of Akron, and we have something in common, whereas maybe someone older just might have preconceived prejudices that just haven't been ironed out yet, and I think it has been ironed out in our generation.

PRESIDENT CLINTON: Do you think it's because of personal experience that you've had more direct personal experience with people from different age groups, or do you think it's because you grew up in a different time where the climate, legal, social, political climate was different?

JONATHAN MORGAN: I think it was because I grew up in a different time. We grew up watching television, the Cosby Show is my favorite show.

PRESIDENT CLINTON: Therefore if you work in a bank and a black person came in with a check you wouldn't hold it because you saw Bill Cosby. No, no, this is important.

JONATHAN MORGAN: Yeah, I don't think I would give him a hard time, but at the same time I have my own prejudices, whereas if I'm walking downtown on a street and I see a black man walking towards me that's not dressed as well I might be a little bit scared, so, I mean, at the same time I have those prejudices.

PRESIDENT CLINTON: Do you think that's because of television crime shows or because of personal experience?

JONATHAN MORGAN: It has nothing to do with personal experience. Just from the media, television shows and things that I've heard.

PRESIDENT CLINTON: Christine Ibarra, what do you think about that? Do you believe that attitudes are better among young people, do you think that there is still discrimination today? Is it worse for African-Americans than it is for other minority groups, is it different or what do you think?

CHRISTINE IBARRA: Yes, I do agree there is still a lot of discrimination, I do feel that it is in younger adults as well as older. But I do feel that that occurs simply because of how people were raised.

Getting back to what John said, yes, I feel that older people do tend to discriminate more and maybe base their stereotypes of people rather than getting to know them, and I feel that people our age do that as well until they do go out in the world and experience different people, and I know a lot of people who until they came to college, until they came to Akron, would have prejudices, did have prejudices, beliefs, until they came here and had classes with different minorities and they realized that we as people didn't fit so many stereotypes that they had thought that we would, that they got to know us as people and realized that minorities as well as, you know, white people could interact and be friends, and they could be wrong and that there are very many similarities between us all, we are all people and that's how I feel.

PRESIDENT CLINTON: So do you believe—let me ask you this, do you believe that having an integrated educational environment is the primary reason that young people have better attitudes, more open attitudes than older people, because they've been able to go to school with people of different races?

CHRISTINE IBARRA: I feel that that benefits them, but I feel it's by choice as well. Older people obviously interact with other minorities in every day life as well. It's just a matter of choice whether you're going to love and to accept—whether you're going to allow yourself to accept these people into your lives or whether you're not. I feel it's all choice.

PRESIDENT CLINTON: Let me ask you one other question, then I want to go on to the moderator so he can talk about the next group of folks.

There is a big difference even in college campuses between the racial composition of the student body and the daily lives of the students, at least in a lot of places that there are a lot of places where the student body is integrated, but social life is largely segregated.

Is that always a bad thing, is it—what—what about that, what about that here, and what do you think about that?

Its churches of worship are segregated on Sunday. Is that a bad thing or a good thing? What should be our—in other words, one of the things that I want to try to get America to think about is how do we define success here?

I don't personally think it's a bad thing that there is—that people in many ways like to be with other people of their own racial and ethnic group any more than their own religious group, but on the other hand it could become a bad thing if it goes too far, as we've seen in other countries, so how do you know whether the environment is working for you and for other people?

How much integration is enough, how much—what kind of segregation is acceptable if it's voluntary, how do you deal with all of that? Have you ever thought about it in that way? Go ahead.

TOWN HALL PARTICIPANT: Well, I basically think that, you know, once people come to, say, the university, most of the time it's a new place and I think that when people go to a new place they're going to stick—try and find people like them.

Now, in my case I grew up in a predominantly white area and went to white high schools and stuff like that, so I think that when I came to the university I sought the other side of my ethnic background, so I don't think—I do think that when people get together with people of their own ethnic background or religion I think it is good, but I think that—I think that you should also respect the other people and try and learn and be forced to learn about other people as well as yourself and your own background.

TOWN HALL PARTICIPANT: I believe that you can measure success just by equality. I think that certainly segregation is okay if people feel more comfortable with their own race, then that's fine, as long as you don't put down other races; and I think that's how you would be able to measure success. Whether you hang out with different races all the time or sometime or no—you know, no time at all, I think that that's okay as long as you can accept these other people and not feel that you're any more superior than anybody else.

And I feel Akron is very segregated. I think that there are certain parts of the campus where you know white people hang out here, and black people hang out here, in our Student Center as well as athletic events and—you know, as a Hispanic coming from a Mexican background, where does that put me? I'm nei-

ther one. So I just have friends of both, which I'm very fortunate, but that's kind of an awkward situation as well, and it's—you know, it seems students could come together more and integrate more, I think that would be better.

MR. LIEBERTH: Mr. President, we are joined today by three authors who you have invited, whose books on race are now the subject of national debate. David Shipler is a former reporter for the New York Times. His book on Arabs and Jews won the Pulitzer Prize. His book today is A Country of Strangers: Blacks and Whites in America.

Dr. Abigail Thernstrom, a senior Fellow at the Manhattan Institute, has co-authored America in Black and White: One Nation Indivisible with her husband Stephan, the Winthrop Professor of history at Harvard.

And Dr. Beverly Daniel Tatum, a psychologist, educator, and professor at Mount Holyoke College in South Hadley, Massachusetts. Her book Why Are All the Black Kids Sitting Together in the Cafeteria, and Other Conversations about Race.

PRESIDENT CLINTON: I'd like to just start very briefly by giving the authors a chance to comment on how—what they've heard from these students today, how it meshes with what they heard when they were preparing their books.

David, start with you.

MR. SHIPLER: It's very familiar. I spent about five years traveling around the country talking to people, adults, ordinary folks, blacks and whites, about their interactions with each other, but I feel we're in a different phase of race relations in this country than we used to be.

In some ways it's a more complicated phase. Bigotry for the most part is not as blatant and obvious and outrageous as it used to be, it's gone underground, it takes subtler forms, encrypted forms. Prejudice is a shape shifter, it's very agile in taking forms that seem acceptable on the surface. Just yesterday in Akron, for example, the Beacon Journal had a very interesting article discussing the reasons why blacks are underrepresented in honors courses in the public schools here, and one of the reasons seems to be that some guidance counselors discourage blacks from enrolling by saying to them "This is very difficult," you know, "Are you sure you can do the work?" And some black students absorb these images of themselves as less intelligent or less competent. The fewer blacks that are in the honors courses, the fewer blacks want to be. It becomes uncomfortable. There is some peer pressure against it. This image of blacks as less capable is a powerful one that still runs under the surface of America.

I met a white couple in California, for example, who adopted a bi-racial girl, and she was never—she was allowed to drift in high school. She drifted to the teachers, she looked black, her friends were mostly black. Their biological children who were white got lots of attention. When they fell behind, teachers were on the phone, sending notes home.

When the daughter who looked black fell behind there were no notes, no phone calls. It was as close to a laboratory experiment as you could get in the deference in attitudes and expectations. Now, the teachers were not wearing

white hoods, they were not standing in the schoolhouse door barring integration. It came from the mainstream of white America which still harbors many of these powerful assumptions.

I think for us as white Americans to understand some of this we have to reflect on the differences in experiences that we've had as opposed to those that blacks and other minorities have had. One of the things that I learned as I was working on A Country of Strangers is how little I understood, and perhaps how little I still understand about this.

Toward the end of my research I attended a workshop in Washington run by a facilitator named Lehman Roth. I asked a group of us—diverse group of blacks, Caucasians, one of the questions asked goes to what you said earlier. He asked, "I don't have to worry that a check or a credit card will be refused because of my race. If you—if you agree with that, stand."

The only people in the room who stood were whites. And he left us standing there looking at each other and at the others for a long time.

He said, "How many of you have been stopped by police officers because of your race?" And the black men stood, and a few black women. None of the whites. "How many of you expect the next President of the United States will be of my race or ethnic group," and again only we whites were able to stand.

And then he asked a very powerful question that I never thought to ask in all of my research. Have I considered not having children because of racism, and the young African-American woman sitting near me rose to her feet as gracefully as if she were at a funeral, and she looked down at me, and I looked up at her, and we realized we were looking at each other across an enormous chasm of different experiences.

I think in any dialogue of this kind the key is to listen, not just to talk, because we talk a lot, and we talk pretty well about race, but we don't listen about it. And I'm hoping if we listen to each other we can begin to diminish the size of that chasm, and perhaps even make this society of ours into less and less of a country of strangers. Let me just briefly first of all thank you very much . . .

PRESIDENT CLINTON: Thank you. First of all, the reason I wanted to do this, a lot of these things is—I believe that there are in any given community literally millions of instances like this where we're not ever fully aware of the motivations behind what we do, or where other people will perceive there may be a racial motivation where there isn't one which is also just as bad because you have the same bottom line result, which is drifting apart of people.

I don't think there is any legal policy answer to this. I think that, you know, this is something we really have to work our way through. Jonathan, I was proud of you for saying that if you were working and spotted Bill Cosby—all of your classmates—if you were walking down the street alone at night and you saw a black man coming at you, and you were better dressed, you would be scared. That's kind of gutsy for you to say that, but we have to get this out on the table. We need to get this.

Parenthetically, David, I had a group of African-American journalists in to see me a couple months ago. Every journalist, each with college degrees, every single man in the crowd had been stopped by a police officer for no apparent reason, every one, a hundred percent of them I asked. So these are things we have to get out there and discuss.

Abigail—

MS. THERNSTROM: Well, I said—

PRESIDENT CLINTON: She has a rosier view, and I hope she has the guts to say it here. Oh, come on.

MS. THERNSTROM: I definitely have the guts to say it. In fact, all sorts of reporters said to me before you came, said "You're going to fudge." I never fudge. Indeed I won't talk immediately about preferences, but one of the reasons I said I was invited here is I'm a dissenting voice on preferences. I don't like any racial preferences or racial classifications, the boxes we're all put in, and I hope we can return a little bit to that.

But let me say in response to these wonderful voices of the students, I think they reaffirm the picture of progress that we provide overwhelming evidence in our book America in Black and White. Black progress is indisputably here to stay, growth of the significant black middle class, increasing suburbanization, rising home ownership rates, and so forth, this is a train that left the station fifty years ago and there is no going into reverse.

I mean, just think in 1940 sixty percent of employed black women were domestic servants. Today sixty percent of black women are white collar workers and two percent are domestic help. As late as 1964, the year the great Civil Rights Act was passed, only 20 percent of whites had black neighbors. Today 61 percent of whites have black neighbors. I mean, despair in this country has become very fashionable, but the truth is ordinary Americans, black and white, are living together, they're working together, they're dining together, they're forming interracial friendships, they're dating members of the other race, and increasing—and in small but rapidly increasing numbers they are marrying across racial lines.

America is outgrowing its racial past and these students are the voice of—of that fact. I mean, there is a recent poll showing that nine out of ten black teenagers say racism is a negligible factor in their daily lives. The young have come of age, they understand the good news, they've come of age in a transformed nation.

There are absolutely wonderful other figures showing in terms of the percentage of blacks who say they have dated a white, it turns out to be 39 percent. The percentage of whites who say they have dated someone who is black, it turns out to be 24 percent.

Asked this year, teenagers were asked this year about dating, only 13 percent in this country said they would never date somebody of another race. And 83 percent of whites approve of interracial marriage. It is perfectly right that there are generational differences. They don't start, however, as young as 34. But when you see—when you see evidence of bigotry it is mostly the older people, and this is—this is a nation that's trans–that is being transformed.

Of course, real racial inequality still persists, and I think much of it is driven by an appalling and unacceptable racial gap in educational performance, and I love what you're doing in taking Chicago as a model and, you know, dedicating the federal government to this. I would go much further in terms of radical educational reform. Let me say just one last thing.

We also need—if we're going to move forward on the racial front we need to recapture our confidence in ourselves. In my lifetime America has undergone an unprecedented transformation, we have changed from a nation in which one region resembled South Africa under apartheid, to one in which Martin Luther King's racial equality has become, in his widow's words, deeply imbedded in the fabric of America. Dr. King and the entire civil rights movement understood our capacity for change. It's time to recapture their optimism, their faith in America. This is a good country as you just said. Thanks.

PRESIDENT CLINTON: Thank you. Let me just say I believe that it's a lot better. I grew up in the segregated south, so I have personal experience of what—how it's changed since I'm one of those older people Jonathan talked about. I've actually gotten kind of used to it now.

But to me that makes this effort all the more important because what—what I want the American people to do is have confidence. We know now we can make our economy work, we know we can make the crime rate go down, we know we can reduce the number of people on welfare and have people at work. We know things we didn't know a few years ago.

We know we can make progress on this whole complex of issues, but I think it's also important to point out that there is a lot of residue there, like what McHughson told, our little banker story, and that progress should give us energy for the work ahead, not put us into denial. That's the only thing I want to make sure we don't do.

Go ahead, what would you like to say about this?

MS. TATUM: Well, I would agree there has been progress, but there is still a lot of work to do. When I talk to my students at Mount Holyoke College on the psychology of racism my students talk in a very racially mixed context, they talk about their fears, their difficulties, even to engage in this kind of dialogue.

I think the opportunity to talk about these issues is really important. What I hear from my students, there are very few opportunities that they had in their pre-college experience, and even sometimes in their college context to talk honestly about these issues. There is a lot of fear about that.

You know, I think that there is fear on the part of white people to speak honestly about the things they've learned. I also want to applaud Jonathan's honesty about that. It's information which we've all gotten, not just what white people take in negative messages about people of color, but we all get misinformed about people different from ourselves or, as I like to say, we get misinformation on people like us as well.

In that context we internalize that information and act on it as we're hearing, but when we try to create spaces for people to talk about it it's very difficult.

Not only do I work with students, I work with public school educators in a professional development course which is specifically focused on helping educators feel more comfortable about racial issues, understanding how they're manifested in schools and how they can talk about them with their students because there is a lot of silence about these issues; and I think breaking the silence is something many people are afraid of doing, and yet we can't—as you pointed out, we can't really fix this problem or continue the improvement unless we're able to really engage in honest dialogue about that and get past the fear.

You know, I talked about the fact white people are fearful. Also I think people of color, black, Latino, Asian students, certainly in my classes, say, You know, part of my fear is I'll tell my story, I'll talk about being in the bank, you know, talk about feeling isolated on the campus where I am, and it's going to fall on deaf ears. You know, I'll open up wounds that will be hard to speak about and people will say, oh, it wasn't that bad or you're exaggerating or somehow that experience is going to be invalidated.

Of course, in that case the person speaking wonders was it worth the effort, did it really matter that I came and talked about this experience. If it hasn't been received in the way that moves people to take some action about it. So I think the point being made by David about listening is very important as well.

But we all have to be willing to take that leap of faith, I think to risk some discomfort because these conversations are not comfortable usually, and we should just anticipate that, and that sometimes we do say things that are offensive to others, not because we want to but because we've been breathing in that smog. You know, like I say, if you breathe in the smog occasionally you'll cough some up, and we're all smog breathers in that way, but it is possible for us to engage in this kind of honest dialogue if we're willing to take the risk to do it.

I think it's wonderful all of these people have gathered here for that purpose.

PRESIDENT CLINTON: Abigail?

MS. THERNSTROM: Let me say something on the optimism front. Those of us who are optimistic and against racial preferences, we're not naive, we do not think America has become color-blind, that we've solved our racial problems, that racism has disappeared. I mean, only fools believe that.

And yet I'm often accused of thinking that because—it is said well, you're against preferences, you must think this country has solved its problems. Of course, I don't think that. We have a long ways to go, nevertheless. If we go on the basis of optimism we'll get there, pessimism is incredibly self-destructive.

PRESIDENT CLINTON: I agree with that. If I could make one other point, then I'll call on David.

One reason I think all of this talking business is more important than ever before is that if you posit the fact—if you look at the growth in educational attainments and the growth of the middle class among African-Americans you can say "Well, things have gotten a lot better." And then if you identify with what the continuing problems are, like what

McHughson just said about—the examples David cited, you say these things require changes in human perception, human heart, you have to have more talking.

I think the thing that's more profound is when you look at the communities that have—there are several counties in America with people who have more than a hundred racial and ethnic groups now, they're all different in many ways. They have different perceptions and cultural patterns.

I know after the Los Angeles riots I walked the streets and I was stunned by the gulf between Korean grocers and African-American customers. I've been in cities where there are Arab-American merchants and Hispanic customers or African-American customers, all of these things proliferate. That's the kind of thing that you see eating other countries alive from the inside out, and that's why we have to begin to deal with this because a lot of you have to bring the insights you have from your own not only personal but historic experiences to bear on a whole different America.

It's a new thing out there where there is somebody from everyplace out there with a family and a community and a culture and a set of perceptions that they will bring to bear on all of their interactions.

Go ahead, David.

MR. SHIPLER: There are a lot of good people, as you said earlier, working on this. They don't get much publicity though. The press, as an old newspaper man, even though I'm no longer a newspaper man, I feel able to criticize the press on this, the press tends to go to the extremes and report the most strident voices, but I ran across a lot of people who were working quietly without publicity in their jobs, in their communities, to overcome racial problems, so I think that this dichotomy that some people have set up between optimism and pessimism is a false dichotomy. Optimism is too close to complacency, pessimism is too close to resignation, neither of the categories fits the racial situation now. Things are getting better, things have gotten better, things are getting worse at the same time.

# CONCLUSION

ALL HISTORIANS WOULD AGREE that America is a nation of nations. But what does that mean in terms of the issues that have moved and shaped us as a people? Contemporary concerns such as bilingualism, incorporation/assimilation, dual identity, ethnic politics, quotas and affirmative action, residential segregation, and the level of immigration itself resonate with a past that dealt with variations of these modern factors. American history is particularly complex because it is not the history of just one people but of many—some who strived to become one people and some who resisted. And as this book indicates, there was little in this history (from Indian Wars to Civil War and from expansionism to progressivism to Civil Rights) that American pluralism did not affect or by which it was not affected.

This book was conceived as a beginning, a place to start for those seeking knowledge of American history with a particular perspective. The chapter essays are designed to provide a concise overview of the various eras in this history, whereas the documents offer primary sources from the pertinent topics, organizations, individuals, and events that allow readers to look at the actual historical building blocks. Annotated bibliographies and bibliographic essays offer important works for further reading and research. Each author picks up common themes that are carried through the book, only increasing in complexity as new immigrants arrive and the nation becomes more diverse. Carol Berkin's essay immediately reveals conflicts with the Native Americans and between Europeans, which encompassed struggles over land and trade as well as culture. Cultural and power struggles are evident throughout American history. Yet there was a good deal of cooperation as well, which reveals another trend in American life. Survival for the colonist, as it would be for a later more diverse United States, also depended on working with and understanding the "others." The themes of cooperation and conflict, acceptance, exclusion, and subjugation (especially with the beginning of slavery) permeate U.S. history—whether it is English and Indians, Anglos and Mexicans, Irish and Yankees, blacks and Jews. Other than the institution of slavery and institutionalized racial segregation, the alliances formed or conflicts fought were temporary—shifting as circumstances changed.

The dominance of English culture, later termed *Anglo-conformity,* is raised early in the chapters. Graham Hodges contends that Anglicization did not immediately prevail, and certainly not in areas where the English were the smaller population. Other cultures and identities remained and flourished. Subsequent authors, particularly Andrew Heinze and Timothy Meagher, respectively, deal with the Americanization/Anglo-conformity of the early twentieth century and the mul-

ticulturalism of the late twentieth century, both of which were directly related to the colonial cultural struggles. Although English became and remains the dominant language, other languages vied for equality at various times and places (e.g., German and Spanish). Recent "English Only" organizations, which worked to make English the official language, reflect concerns over the effects of bilingualism and multicultural influence. Religion as well was a culturally identifying factor, and the colonies saw varied religious observances within their populations. In the mid to late twentieth century, Anglo-American cultural preeminence drew opposition from those who placed a new emphasis on multiculturalism and from the identity and interest-group politics of blacks, Asians, Latinos, and Native Americans. Whether there are benefits or liabilities for national unity in multiculturalism is still a hotly debated topic. Whatever the eventual outcome, it is clear that group recognition and assertion of rights and interests are significant factors in contemporary American life as they have been in the past.

Naturalization is also an issue that weaves through American history. Who was entitled to become a citizen? This concern was raised early and immediately became part of a nativist reaction to the foreign-born. Restrictionism, which was to reach an apogee in the 1920s, first appeared, as Marion Casey writes, in the 1790s. Discussions ensued about who would make a good American citizen and whether the country needed more immigrants. Arguments against immigration were similar to those raised many decades later. The Alien and Sedition Acts (1798) were directed at foreigners in regard to residency requirements for citizenship and at those, especially foreign-born, who disagreed with government policies. Suspicion of foreigners and efforts to limit dissent are evident also with the Espionage and Sedition Acts of 1917–1918 and with the immigration quota laws of the 1920s. But whether it is Harrison Gray Otis or Madison Grant or Pat Buchanan writing, the premise is the same: certain immigrants cannot become good Americans and will eventually undermine the nation. Catholics, the Irish, Germans, Jews, Italians, Asians, Mexicans and other Latinos, and most recently Arabs have all, at one time or another, been the target of nativist fears. One only need to remember the anti-German-American campaign during World War I or the incarceration of Japanese Americans during World War II to realize this. In the modern era, these fears have been accentuated by the 1965 Immigration Act, which had the effect of shifting the primary sources of immigration to other countries, and the September 11 tragedy. Euro-centric nativists now lashed out at those who were coming, once again, from the "wrong" countries. As China, Mexico, and Korea replaced Italy, Poland, and Germany, and migration from Muslim countries increased as well, a frenzy of criticism and discussion broke out over the new laws and over legal and illegal immigration, resulting in increased fears about America's racial/ethnic future.

As a sense of nation and peoplehood developed, nativism grew stronger and its reasoning more varied. Immigrants were radicals, who would bring foreign ideologies and political violence to our shores; they were disease carriers, who planted virulent strains in our midst; they would outbreed the "real" Americans and replace them with inferior races; they would lower wages for American workers. A number of the authors in the volume (Casey, Topp, Ngai, Heinze, and Meagher) pick up these themes and show their persistence in American life.

It is clear from these essays as well that race has had a significant place in U.S. history, especially as it related to African Americans. It is not just the subjugation of blacks through slavery and Jim Crow laws that reflects the obsession with race, but also the need for certain European immigrants to situate themselves quickly in the racial hierarchy by proclaiming their whiteness. Thomas Guglielmo and Earl Lewis speak particularly to this issue and note the "malleability of race; the ways in which power and politics—rather than biology or genetics—define race." A white classification opened the door to opportunity. It also led eventually, as Meagher and others relate, to a coalescence of European nationalities into a generalized white group, with various ethnic identities subsumed under the white label. At first considered not fully white, or at least less white than Anglo-Saxons, these "in-between peoples" eventually, as Ngai writes, "embraced whiteness as a strategy for economic and social advancement."

While white immigrants worked to clarify their racial classification, blacks, Asians, Indians, and Latinos developed various strategies for coping with America's Manifest-Destiny expansion into Native American and Mexican territory, the treatment of degraded minority workers such as blacks, Chinese, and Mexicans, and the wars and other strategies to eliminate "unacceptable" minorities through violence, draconian legislation, pervasive discrimination, segregation, social ostracism, and assimilation. The questioning of a group's "racial capacity for civilization," as Ngai states in relation to Indians in the 1890s, reflects the country's attitude toward disfavored minorities. Policies that were developed to subjugate blacks and Indians were used on other groups as well. A constant battle with America's exclusionary laws and discriminatory behavior affected land ownership, job opportunity, political recognition, and cultural preservation. This long struggle is noted in all the chapters, with the culmination in the civil rights movement and some attitude change chronicled in the Guglielmo-Lewis and Meagher chapters. But the modern period did not end the controversy over race; contention over busing, affirmative action, open housing, race riots; and income gaps continued.

Although the volume authors delineate some of the problems and conflicts immigration generated, they also provide a chronicle of immigration's importance to the growth and strength of the United States. Each group, whether vilified or immediately accepted, voluntary or involuntary, contributed to the nation. Whether it was blacks working as tenant farmers in the South, the Irish and Chinese building the transcontinental rail lines, or Mexicans in western agriculture, the nation prospered from their labor.

Culturally, the contributions of such figures as Irving Berlin, Louis Armstrong, and Will Rogers illustrate the benefits of a diverse population, as do political leaders like Fiorello LaGuardia and intellectual notables such as W. E. B. Du Bois. A group's contribution, however, was oftentimes not related to acceptance. An ambivalence existed, which is still evident in contemporary America. Some politicians, for example, rail against illegal immigrants, bemoan porous borders, and claim that the nation does not need more immigrants; yet they acknowledge not only the role of migrant Mexican farm workers and Chinese garment laborers in maintaining cheap prices for these American products but the unwillingness of many citizens to do this work.

This book's purpose has been to focus on the racial and ethnic aspects of U.S. history and thereby show how intertwined those factors were with the growth and shaping of the country. Although not intended as a fully comprehensive history revealing every detail of this connection, the volume shows clearly the salience of immigration, race, and ethnicity. It also shows that these issues still resonate, still stir controversy and debate.

The questions raised by this history are perennial ones and key issues are worth pointing out as suggestions for further research and discussion topics. Most important is the question, "Who is the American?" How has this person been defined in the country's history, and has that definition changed with time? We want to know how to define assimilation and if retention of old-world culture, including language, precludes becoming an American. Can immigrants have a dual identity? How have strong ethnic ties to the ancestral home affected U.S. foreign policy? What was the rationalization for excluding or subjugating others due to race, religion, ethnicity, and immigrant status, and has that changed over the last four centuries? The role of stereotypes is important in this regard, and their malleability over time requires investigation. We can see, for example, how transformations in Irish images from the nineteenth century to the twentieth illustrate changing portrayals.

Regional variations, as Michael Topp relates, must also be considered in assessing attitudes toward particular groups, and, as in the colonial period, the level of Anglicization or acculturation for these groups. How has American expansionism and the wars we have fought indicated the effect of racial and ethnic concerns?

While many questions remain, and the racial and ethnic configurations of the nation are still developing, the main point is that America has always been and remains a nation of nations.

# CONTRIBUTORS

**RONALD H. BAYOR** is Professor of History at Georgia Tech and founding and present editor of the *Journal of American Ethnic History*. His books include *Neighbors in Conflict: The Irish, Germans, Jews, and Italians of New York City, 1929–1941* (1978); *Fiorello LaGuardia: Ethnicity and Reform* (1993); *Race and the Shaping of Twentieth-Century Atlanta* (1996), winner of an Outstanding Book Award from the Gustavus Myers Center for the Study of Human Rights in North America. He is also the coeditor, with Timothy Meagher, of *The New York Irish* (1996), winner of the James S. Donnelly, Sr., Prize of the American Conference for Irish Studies for the best book in Irish or Irish American history and the social sciences (1997).

**CAROL BERKIN** is currently Professor of History at The City University of New York Graduate Center and Baruch College, where she teaches American colonial, early Republic, and women's history. Her books include *Jonathan Sewall: Odyssey of an American Loyalist*, which was nominated for the Pulitzer Prize; *First Generations: Women in Colonial America;* two edited volumes, *Women of America: A History* and *Women, War,* *and Revolution;* and a collection of primary documents, *Women's Voices/ Women's Lives: Documents in Early American History.* Her latest book is *A Brilliant Solution: Inventing the American Constitution* (2002).

**MARION R. CASEY** is Assistant Professor of History and Faculty Fellow in Irish American Studies at New York University. She is the author of *The Irish Image in American Popular Culture* (forthcoming, The John Hopkins University Press) and *The Irish American Experience: A History in Documents* (forthcoming, Columbia University Press); essays in *The New York Irish,* Ronald H. Bayor and Timothy J. Meagher, eds. (1996); as well as entries in *The Encyclopedia of New York City, The Encyclopedia of American Studies,* and *The Encyclopedia of Ireland.* She also has production credits on the documentary films *From Shore to Shore: Irish Traditional Music in New York* (1993) and *Emigrant Savings Bank, Since 1850, The Spirit of Thrift* (2000).

**THOMAS GUGLIELMO** is an Assistant Professor in the Department of American Studies at the University of Notre Dame. He is the author of *White On Arrival: Italians, Race, Color, and Power in Chicago, 1890–1945* (Oxford University Press, 2003).

**ANDREW R. HEINZE** is Professor of History and Director of the Swig Judaic Studies Program at the University of San Francisco. He is the author of *Adapting to Abundance: Jewish Immigrants, Mass Consumption, and the Search for American Identity* (1990), and his recent articles on ethnicity, immigration, and race have appeared in the *Journal of American History,* the *American Quarterly, Religion and American Culture,* and *American Jewish History.* He has recently completed a book called *Jews and the American Soul: How Jewish Thinkers Changed American Ideas of Human Nature in the 20th Century* (Princeton University Press, 2004).

**GRAHAM RUSSELL HODGES** is Professor of History at Colgate University. He is the author of numerous books and articles, including *New York City Cartmen, 1667–1850 (1986)* and *Root and Branch: African Americans in New York and East Jersey, 1613–1863* (1999).

**EARL LEWIS** is Professor of History and Afroamerican and African Studies, Vice Provost for Academic Affairs— Graduate Studies, and Dean of the Graduate School at the University of Michigan. He is the author, coauthor, and editor of five books and, with Robin D. G. Kelly, general editor of an eleven-volume history of African Americans for young adults. The author of many articles and reviews, he is, or has been, a member of several editorial boards and boards of directors, including The Council of Graduate Schools and the Graduate Record Exam, or GRE.

**TIMOTHY J. MEAGHER** is Curator of American Catholic History Collections and teaches Irish American and American immigration history at Catholic University. He was Director of the Center for Irish Studies at the University. Meagher has edited the collection of essays *From Paddy to Studs: Irish Amer-*

*ican Communities at the Turn of the Century,* and co-edited with Ronald H. Bayor the collection *The New York Irish.* The latter won the James S. Donnelly Sr. Prize for the best book in Irish or Irish American history and the social sciences offered by the American Conference for Irish Studies (1997). Meagher's book *Inventing Irish America: Generation, Class, and Ethnic Identity in a New England City, 1880 to 1928* was published in the spring of 2001. He is currently writing *A Guide to Irish American History* for Columbia University Press. He has also written several essays and articles on Irish American and American Catholic history.

**MAE M. NGAI** is Assistant Professor of U.S. History at the University of Chicago, where she teaches Asian American and comparative immigration history. She is author of "The Architecture of Race in American Immigration Law: A Re-examination of the Immigration Act of 1924," *Journal of American History* (June 1999); "Legacies of Exclusion: Illegal Chinese Immigration During the Cold War Years," *Journal of American Ethnic History* (Fall 1998); "The Strange Career of the Illegal Alien: Immigration Restriction and U.S. Deportation Policy, 1921–1965," *Law and History Review* (Spring 2003); and *Illegal Aliens and Alien Citizens: Immigration Restriction, Race, and Nation, 1924–1965* (Princeton University Press, forthcoming 2004).

**MICHAEL M. TOPP** is an Associate Professor of History at the University of Texas, El Paso. He is the author of *Those Without a Country: The Political Culture of Italian American Syndicalists* (2001) and of *"That Agony Is Our Triumph": A Documentary History of the Sacco-Vanzetti Trial* (forthcoming, Bedford/St. Martin's Press). He has also written several essays dealing with issues of race, gender, and transnationalism.

# INDEX

Kenneth T. Jackson, "A Dissenting Comment." Reprinted with the permission of the author.

John Jea, excerpt from "The Life, History, and Unparalleled Sufferings of John Jea, the African Preacher" as found in *Black Itinerants of the Gospel: The Narratives of John Jea and George White, Second Edition*, edited by Graham Russell Hodges. Reprinted with the permission of Dr. Hodges and Palgrave Publishers, Ltd.

Professor Martin Kilson, statement in Congress objecting to proposed amendment to the Constitution. Reprinted with the permission of the author.

Rudyard Kipling, "The White Man's Burden" from *McClure's Magazine,* XII, no. 4 (February 12, 1899): 290–291. Reprinted with the permission of A. P. Watt, Ltd. on behalf of The National Trust for Places of Historic Interest or Natural Beauty.

Theodora Kroeber, "Outside the Slaughter House" from *Ishi in Two Worlds: A Biography of the Last Wild Indian in North America* (Berkeley: University of California Press, 1961). Copyright © 1961 by The Regents of the University of California. Reprinted with permission.

Helen Jackson Lee, excerpt from *Nigger in the Window.* Copyright © 1978 by Helen Jackson Lee. Reprinted with the permission of Doubleday, a division of Random House, Inc.

Sue Ko Lee, "Sue Ko Lee and the 1938 National Dollar Store Strike" from *Unbound Voices: A Documentary History of Chinese Women in San Francisco*, edited by July Yung. Copyright © 1999 by Judy Yung. Reprinted with the permission of the University of California Press.

Little Bear, "The Sand Creek Massacre" from George E. Hyde, *Life of George Bent: Written from His Letters.* Copyright 1934 by the University of Oklahoma Press. Reprinted with the permission of the University of Oklahoma Press.

Michael Patrick MacDonald, excerpt from *All Souls: A Family Story from Southie.* Copyright © 1999 by Michael Patrick MacDonald. Reprinted with the permission of Beacon Press, Boston.

Million Man March Organizing Committee, "Million Man March Fact Sheet" and "The Black Woman's Statement of Support for the Million Man March" from National Organizing Committee, Million Man March packet Reprinted with permission.

Ashley Montagu, excerpt from "Preface" from *Man's Most Dangerous Myth: The Fallacy of Race, Fourth Edition.* Reprinted with the permission of AltaMira Press, a division of Rowman & Littlefield Publishers, Inc.

Jefferson Morley, "Jack Kemp; L.A.'s 'Homeboy' in Washington Has Plans to Put Our House in Order" from *Los Angeles Times* (May 15, 1992). Copyright © 1992 by Jefferson Morley. Reprinted with the permission of Sterling Lord Literistic, Inc.

NAACP, petition to the School Board of the City of Norfolk, Virginia. The Editor wishes to thank The National Association for the Advancement of Colored People for authorizing the use of this work.

Huey Newton, "Huey Newton Speaks from Jail" from *Motive* (October 1968). Reprinted with the permission of Frederika Newton and the Dr. Huey P. Newton Foundation.

Michael Novak, excerpt from *The Rise of the Unmeltable Ethnics* (New York: Macmillan, 1971). Copyright © 1971 by Michael Novak. Reprinted with the permission of Sterling Lord Literistic, Inc.

Old Lady Horse, "The Disappearance of the Buffalo" from Alice Marriot and Carol K. Rachlin, *American Indian Mythology.* Copyright © 1968 by Alice Marriot and Carol K. Rachlin. Reprinted with the permission of HarperCollins Publishers, Inc.